Ramsay's Catalogu

British Model Trains

Volume 1

Bachmann Class C 0-6-0 in SE&CR livery

**Warners Group Publications Plc.
The Maltings, West Street,
Bourne, Lincolnshire, PE10 9PH
Phone 01778 391027 Fax: 01778 425437**

Published by

Compiler & Editor: Pat Hammond

1st Edition Published 1998
2nd Edition Published 2000
3rd Edition Published 2002
4th Edition Published 2004
5th Edition Published 2006
6th Edition Published 2008
7th Edition Published 2011
8th Edition Published 2013

Copyright © Warners Group Publications plc.

The right of Patrick Hammond to be identified as the author of this edition of 'Ramsay's British Model Trains Catalogue' has been asserted in accordance with the Copyright, Designs and Patents Act 1988 Sections 77 and 78

ISBN 978-1-907292-66-8

The contents, design and layout of this book are fully protected by copyright. Permission is hereby granted for copyright material to be quoted by publishers in newspapers, magazines and collector society publications, also by dealers in advertising matter, price lists and circulars distributed free provided that acknowledgement of source given. This permission does not extend to any book catalogue or price list, album or any publication offered for sale unless prior permission has been obtained in writing in each instance from publishers of this catalogue.

Book compiled by Pat Hammond.
Published by Warners Group Publications plc.
Pictures by the author unless otherwise stated.

Front Cover Illustration:
Provided by Tony Wright

Contents

Introduction
Acknowledgments 5
Advertisers' index 672
Codes & explanations 8
Collectors' clubs 15
Determining value 11
Further reading 18
History of model manufacturing 12
History of model collecting 14
How to use this book 6
Scales and gauges 7
Welcome 4

0 Gauge
Ace Trains 21
Bachmann Brassworks 125
Bassett-Lowke 129
Bassett-Lowke by Corgi/Hornby 153
Bonds 157
Bowman 161
Dapol 163
Darstaed 255
Exley 261
Heljan 347
Hornby Series/Trains 349
Leeds (LMC) 397
Lima (British) 449
Milbro 479
MTH (British) 489
Novo 641
Red Rocket 641
Skytrex 633
Tri-ang Big Big 641

00/H0 Gauge
Airfix 33
Anbrico 40
Bachmann Branchline 47
British Trix 651
Dapol 163
Exley 267
Fleischmann (British) 273
GMR 33
Graham Farish 275
Heljan (British) 339

Hornby 517
Hornby Dublo 377
Hornby Railways 517
Jouef (British) 393
Kitmaster 395
Liliput UK 651
Lima H0 (British) 419
Lima 00 425
Mainline Railways 457
Marklin (British) 469
MasterModels 471
OO Works 491
Peco Wonderful Wagons 499
Playcraft 503
Replica Railways 509
Rivarossi (British) 515
Rovex 517
Thomas and Friends (Hornby) 517
Trackmaster 517
Tri-ang Hornby 517
Tri-ang Railways 517
Tri-ang Wrenn 673
Trix Trains 651
Trix Twin 651
ViTrains 671
Wrenn Railways 673

TT Gauge
Kitmaster 395
Peco Wonderful Wagons 499
Tri-ang 645

N Gauge
Arnold by Hornby 45
Dapol 229
Graham Farish 283
Graham Farish by Bachmann 297
Hornby Minitrix 485
Ixion 391
Lima (British) 418
Lone Star 451
Mathieson 477
Minitrix (British) 485
Peco 493
Union Mills 669
Wrenn Micromodels 673

Welcome

Welcome to the Eighth Edition of **Ramsay's British Model Trains Catalogue**. It contains over 3000 new entries and there has been much sorting out to make it easier to find what you are looking for. As a result, almost all current brands, as well as some no longer active ones, have had their tables renumbered. In the case of current brands, this is likely to happen with every new edition. This is so the models can be kept in the set order that runs throughout the book and new models can be slipped in where they belong.

Almost every chapter is arranged in the same set order, which, once learnt, enables the reader to quickly find their way around the book. However, some of the older chapters do not conform to this order and gradually they are being reorganised to bring them into line. In this edition, this particularly applies to Hornby 0 gauge. Another change throughout the book is that models that were announced but not subsequently made are now listed in grey lettering.

Those users of this reference book who have found the splitting of Lima H0 scale models between the H0 and 00 chapters confusing may be pleased to find that all continental models used in the British range are now together in the Lima H0 chapter, irrespective of the type of coupling fitted.

You will find that this edition is a lot more colourful, the purpose being to help you to find what you are looking for more quickly. As the book continues to grow in size, it is important to find new ways of guiding readers to their targets in the shortest possible time. I hope you find the added colour is useful.

Information about the prototype and further details of the basic model is gradually being added to the top of each table. This has been completed for most chapters and it is hoped to extend this before the next edition in two year's time.

In each edition of this book I repeatedly warn readers of the danger of taking the suggested values too seriously. They are only suggestions, based on known sale prices and on a lot of guesswork. But they rarely get updated, as I do not have a team of assistants to research this information for me. There is only me. Anyway, there are no such things as fixed values in this field, except for the recommended retail price (RRP) set by manufacturers. When newly announced models are added to the book, I quote the RRP (usually rounded down) in the second value column. In all other cases the value of a model is what you are prepared to pay for it or what you are prepared to sell it for. I do, however, listen to advice when it is given and usually make adjustments accordingly.

For those unfamiliar with the book and buying it for the first time, the editing policy of Ramsay's British Model Trains Catalogue has, as its three priorities, comprehensiveness, accuracy and fast access to information. It sets out to comprehensively list model railway equipment made for the British market but it cannot cover every make and brand as there are far too many of them.

I have tried to cover the main proprietary brands of the last 100 years, that are collected, and I have been adding further brands with each past edition of the guide. Main omissions at present are models larger than 0 gauge and smaller than N gauge, cheap tinplate toys such as Brimtoy, Mettoy and Chad Valley and there were some overseas who manufactured for Bassett-Lowke and Gamages, who also sold their British outline models direct to retailers. These manufacturers included Bing, Carette and Marklin. I hope to include all of these at some time, but I am waiting until comprehensive lists of their locomotives and rolling stock are available to use.

If there is a brand of collected ready-to-run models (not kits) produced for the British market that you would like to see added, please get in touch with me. I will need a comprehensive list of the models made by the company, with all the usual details such as catalogue numbers, running numbers, liveries and dates of introduction. I also need advice on market values of the things listed. Notice the word 'collected' as this is a collector's guide.

I failed to mention, in the last edition, the work done by Carette expert David Ramsey on sorting out the listing of Bassett-Lowke wagons made by Georges Carette and featured in a series of articles he wrote for *Train Collector* magazine.

I continue to be dependent on regular suppliers of information and, again, Mike Pincott is singled out for his regular supply of information on newly released 00 scale wagons. This time I am also particularly indebted to Brian Martin who has gone through all the N gauge listings with a fine-tooth comb and done much sorting out. In particular, N gauge enthusiasts should find a much better listing of Dapol models.

I am grateful to Mike, Brian and all the others whose contributions are vital to the comprehensiveness of this publication. This includes the manufacturers who are always helpful - especially Simon Kohler at Hornby and Dennis Lovett at Bachmann. Ramsay's British Model Trains Catalogue is not the result of one man, but a joint effort by collectors and the trade and the acknowledgements list on page 5 reads like a Who's Who of the collecting and model railway community.

Thanks also go to New Zealander Robbie McGavin who has once again donated several of his splendid computer works of art in which he sets our much loved model locomotives in real settings and brings them to life. Look out for Hornby's coasters which also carry Robbie's artwork.

As usual, the book contains question marks where knowledge is missing, or where I am not sure of the information given. I would welcome your help in reducing the number of these. If you can help, please email me at pe.hammond@btinternet.com or write to me at:

Ramsay's British Model Trains Catalogue,
PO Box 199,
Scarborough
YO11 3GT

It remains for me to thank all those who have helped to make the guide the comprehensive reference book it is today and to thank Warners for the work involved in publishing it. Enjoy it!

      Pat Hammond
      Scarborough
      June 2013

Acknowledgements

A work of this nature cannot be achieved by one man's efforts alone but depends upon many experts sharing their knowledge with us all. Special thanks go to Roy Chambers who wrote much of the original 0 gauge text, and to John Ingram who expanded it. The text and lists were (and still are) checked and expanded by a host of established experts whose important contribution to this book I am pleased to acknowledge. I should particularly like to mention:

Colin Albright - Graham Farish N gauge
Rolande Allen - prices
Richard Ashby - Bachmann and Dapol wagons
David Atkins - 00 locomotives
Peter Baker - Lima, Bachmann and Dapol
Peter Berry - Graham Farish 00
Derrick Barratt - Hornby 0 wagons
Mike Black - Graham Farish N
Bowman Circle Members - Bowman
Dave Bracken - Irish versions of models
Richard Bradford - Wrenn
Paul Brookes - MasterModels
Roy Chambers - Hornby 0, Bassett-Lowke, Leeds, Milbro, Exley, Bonds and Bowman
Tony Carder - N gauge.
Jim Clark - Bachmann
Alan Cliff - various pre-1940
Tony Colbeck - Anbrico
Peter Corley - Graham Farish 00 and Anbrico
Simon Culverhouse - Minitrix and other N gauge
George Dawson - Graham Farish N gauge
James Day - Playcraft
Martin Doubleday - Lone Star
Ian Dorrell - Lone Star
Terry Durrant formerly of Lacy Scott & Knight
John Entwistle - Modern Hornby locos
Merl Evans - Bachmann, Mainline and Airfix
Jeremy Everett - Airfix, Bachmann, Dapol, Mainline
Alan Farrow - Exley 00
Bob Field - Hornby Dublo
Robert Forsythe - various
Clive Gehle - Lone Star
Peter Gomm - Airfix, Mainline etc.
Patrick Gower - modern Hornby
Chris & Julie Graebe - Hornby 0 gauge
Maurice Gunter - Wrenn
Peter Gurd - Bowman, Dublo and Graham Farish 00
Henk Guijt - various N gauge
Martin Hale - Peco Wonderful Wagons
John Hammond - Skytrex
Don Haslow - 00 gauge
Jack Holmes - prices
Graham Hubbard - Bachmann Europe plc.
John Ingram - Bassett-Lowke, Leeds, Milbro, Bonds
Malcolm Inston - Wrenn prices
John Jarvis - Dapol wagons
Darryl Judkins - Dapol & Bachmann
John Keane - 00 gauge rolling stock
Stephen Knight - Kitmaster and Playcraft
Simon Kohler - Hornby Hobbies Ltd
Eric Large - Tri-ang TT
Brian Lee of George Kidner (Auctioneers)
Oliver Leetham - Dapol wagons
Bob Leggett - Playcraft, Hornby Railways
Allen Levy - Ace Trains
Mike Little - Bassett-Lowke
Martin Long – unlisted Dapol wagons
Dennis Lovett - N gauge and Bachmann products
Quentin Lucas - Exley 0
Robert Newson - Lone Star
Hugo Marsh - Christies & SAS Auctions
Brian Martin - N Gauge
Len Mills - Corgi Bassett-Lowke
Keith Moore - Tri-ang Hornby chassis variations
David O'Brien - Trix
Nigel Overington - various 00 gauge
David Peacock - Leeds Model Company
Daniel Pearson - Bachmann diesels
Tony Penn - Peco Wonderful Wagons
Mike Pincott - 00 wagon variations
Barry Potter - prices and photographs
Tony Pritchard – Dapol
David Ramsey – Bassett-Lowke by Carette
Ron Rayner - Hornby Dublo
Matthew Richter - Graham Farish N
Owen Roberts - Bowman and Peco
Paul Rouse - Tri-ang TT
Fleetwood Shaw - Bassett-Lowke
Des Sheppard - Bachmann & Dapol
George Smith of Dapol Ltd
Graham Smith-Thompson - Airfix, Mainline, Replica and Dapol
Nicholas Smith - Tri-ang TT
Nick Sparks - Hornby Dublo
Chris Thornburn - Trix rolling stock
Allan Trotter - BR standard coaches
Barry Turner - Bachmann coaches
John Turner - prices
Vectis Auctions - photographs and prices
Davina Vine - Dapol 00 wagons
Wallis & Wallis (Auctioneers)
Mike Wightman - Airfix
David Wild – Union Mills, Farish N and various 00
Chris Wright - N wagon variations
Martin Wrigley - prices
Martin Wykes - H0 models

Many others have also contributed information used in this book and considerable use was also made of the following books:

Hornby Dublo Trains by Michael Foster published by New Cavendish Books (ISBN 0904568180).
The Hornby 0 Gauge System by Chris & Julie Graebe, published by New Cavendish Books (ISBN 0904568350).
The History of Trix H0/00 Model Railways in Britain by Tony Matthewman, published by New Cavendish Books (ISBN 0904568768).
Let's Stick Together by Stephen Knight, published by Irwell Press (ISBN 1871608902).
The Story of Wrenn by Maurice Gunter, published by Irwell Press (ISBN 1903266424).
The Bassett-Lowke Story by Roland Fuller, published by New Cavendish Books (ISBN 0904568342)
Brilliantly Old Fashioned parts 1 & 2 by Allen Levy published by New Cavendish Books (ISBN 1904562078)
Tri-ang Railways (2nd Edition) (ISBN 1872727298)
Tri-ang Hornby (ISBN 1872727581)
Hornby Railways (ISBN 1904562000)
The above three by Pat Hammond and published by New Cavendish Books
Bachmann Branchline Pocket Guide by Pat Hammond and published by Warners Group Publications (ISBN 1907292170)
The Leeds Model Company 1912-2012 by David Peacock (ISBN 0956910509)

How to Use This Catalogue

The catalogue has been designed as a reference work and, as such, a high priority has been the ease with which models can be traced. Having said that, it helps if you have some idea as to what the model is.

The book is also principally a reference work for locomotives and rolling stock and, with a few exceptions, there is little likelihood that you will be able to use it to identify a lineside accessory.

Most models today have the manufacturer's name on them but this was not so in the case of minor manufacturers in days gone by. Nor is it always the case with non-proprietary models, for it is quite possible that your model was not originally bought readymade, but was either scratch built or made from a kit. Such models are not covered by the catalogue, although Kitmaster kits have been included because they are particularly collectable in their unmade state.

Hornby Dublo post-war LNER A4 Sir Nigel Gresley (SAS)

Determine the size
If you do not know the name of the manufacturer, a good starting point is to look at the size of the model. Railway models are governed in size by the gauge of the track they were made to run on. You can determine the gauge of the model by measuring the distance between the backs of the wheels and referring to the section on **Scales and Gauges**.

Having determined the gauge, turn to the **Contents** page where you will find listed all the makes of that gauge that have been included, together with the number of the page on which their listing starts. The contents list is not comprehensive and there is always a chance that the make of the model you are trying to identify has not yet been covered by the catalogue. You will notice that '00' and 'H0' scales are grouped together. This is because both 00 and H0 models use the same gauge track but 00 models are made to a scale of 4mm:1ft and H0 models to 3.5mm:1ft. The former are, therefore, slightly larger than the latter when you compare like subjects.

If, having found the right part of the catalogue, you are still not sure of the make, compare the model with pictures in that section.

Looking for the Number
Having found the section you want, it does help if you know the name of the prototype that has been modelled. This will allow you to find the correct table for that model and to search through it for the model variation that matches your own. If this is not the case, note the number on the side of the locomotive (or its tender) and check through the tables until you find it. This is particularly easy to do in the case of diesel and electric locomotives as these mostly have modern TOPS numbering and have been listed in numerical order.

With two of the largest product ranges (Hornby 0 gauge and Bassett-Lowke) 'loco search' tables have been provided.

All the known numbers carried by models in each of these groups have been listed in numerical order alongside the number of the table(s) in which they should be found. You will find that this is a very fast way of tracing your model.

Bassett-Lowke Esso tank wagon (Vectis)

Understanding the Tables
In almost all cases, all the models listed in each table are structurally the same and differ only in the livery they carry or in minor added detail. You will find that the table gives you the catalogue number (if known), the name and number the model carries, its basic colour and livery together with other distinguishing features, either the years it was available in shops or the year of release (in italics) and a range of prices you might expect to pay for one (see **Determining Value**).

Some of the information is in code form in order to save space. Where those codes are specific to that model the codes are shown under the title of the table but where the codes are common to many models of that make they may be listed in the introduction to the section. Codes commonly used throughout the catalogue will be found under **Codes and Explanations** in this front section of the catalogue.

The tables also contain information about limited and special editions (Ltd Edn and Sp Edn). Where known, this information includes the number made and, in the case of special editions, the shop or organisation that commissioned it (in brackets).

We hope that the above notes help you to find what you are looking for.

Exley O Gauge 6-wheel passenger brake (Lacy, Scott & Knight)

Scales and Gauges

'Scale' refers to the linear scale of the model, for example: 4mm to 1 foot (the OO scale measurement). Gauge referes to the distance between the running rails of the track, listed here are a few of the more common scales and gauges.

Gauge name	Scale	Gauge distance
'N' (British)	2mm to 1 foot	9mm
'OOO'	2mm to 1 foot	9.5mm
'TT' (British)	3mm to 1 foot	12mm
'H0'	3.5mm to 1 foot	16.5mm
'OO'	4mm to 1 foot	16.5mm
'EM'	4mm to 1 foot	18mm
'O' (British)	7mm to 1 foot	32mm
'No.1'	10mm to 1 foot	45.45mm
'No.2'	7/16inch to 1 foot	51mm
'No.3'	12/32", 1/2" or 14mm to 1 foot	63.5mm

The illustrations below are only approximately to scale to give some idea of the difference in size between the various gauges.

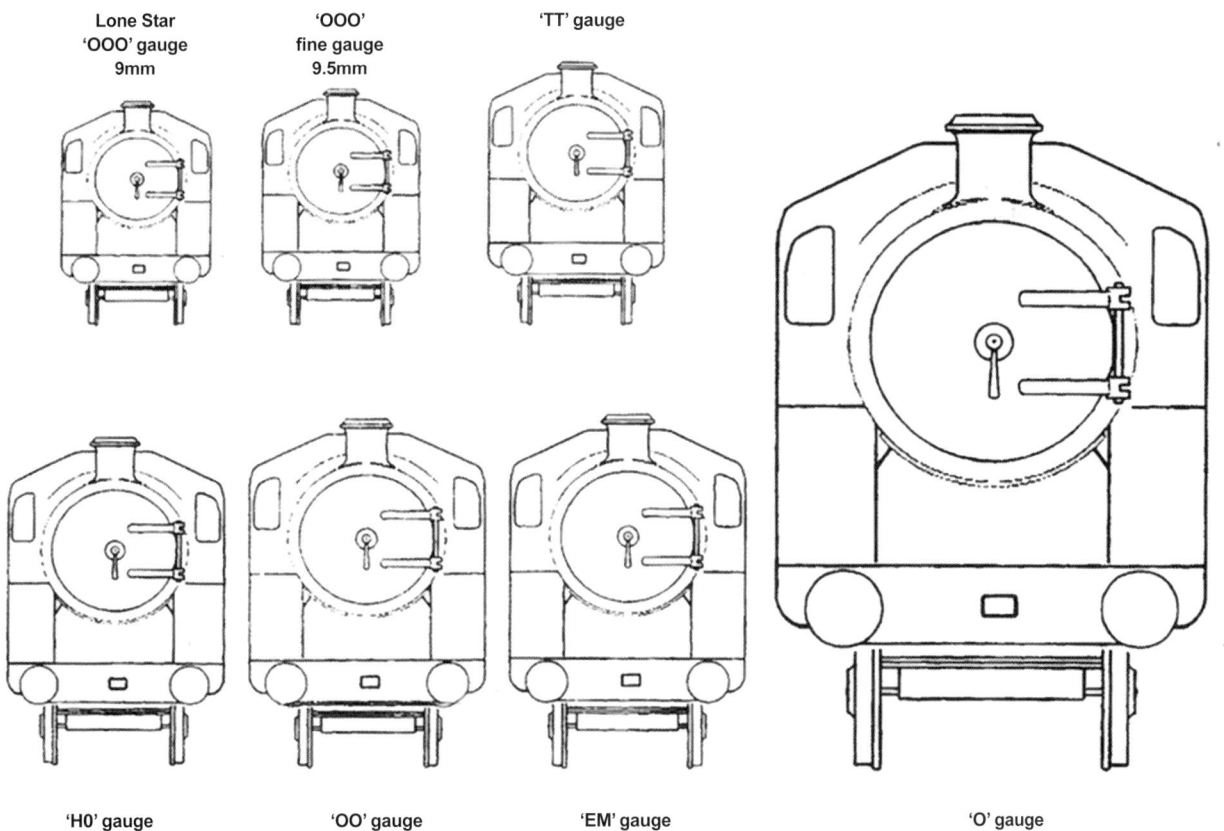

Lone Star 'OOO' gauge 9mm
'OOO' fine gauge 9.5mm
'TT' gauge
'H0' gauge
'OO' gauge
'EM' gauge
'O' gauge

8th Edition — Visit the BRM website at: www.model-railways-live.co.uk

Codes and Explanations

Abbreviations

While some sections in the catalogue have their own set of abbreviations, the following codes are common throughout the guide:

Ltd Edn (followed by the number made, if known) = Limited Edition. These are usually initiated by the manufacturer with the undertaking that the model in this form will not be repeated for a number of years. The term does not always mean that only a small number were produced. Indeed, some standard issues have been produced in smaller quantities than limited editions! The absence of a number indicates that we do not have that information.

Sp Edn (followed by the number made, if known) = Special Edition. These are models that have been commissioned by a shop or other interested party and therefore are usually available from only that source. They also have, in brackets, the name of the shop or organisation that commissioned the model. These are also limited editions and usually described as such on the accompanying certificate but to help users of this catalogue to distinguish between them we have adopted the alternative name - 'Special Edition'.

Ace Trains LNWR van (Ace Trains)

The following codes are used for decals carried by models:

BRa - 'BRITISH RAILWAYS'.
BRb - lion astride wheel.
BRc - lion holding wheel (in a roundel on multiple units and coaches and a few diesel hydraulics). This is also known as the 'ferret and dart board' logo!
BRd - lion in crown (briefly used on West Coast Main Line electric locomotives)
BRe - double arrow logo
BReLL - double arrow (large logo)

Other abbreviations used in the book include:
ECML = East Coast Main Line
Con = Construction
Dist = Distribution
I-C = Inter-City or InterCity
IC = *INTERCITY*

ICs = *INTERCITY* with swallow motif
LH = LoadHaul
LWB = Long wheelbase
Met = Metals
NSE = Network SouthEast
Rft = Railfreight
Reg Rlys = Regional Railways
RES = Rail Express Systems
S&T = Signal & Telegraph
Trans = Transrail
WCML = West Coast Main Line

The following are abbreviations used for railway companies:

Arriva TW = Arriva Trains Wales
Arriva TPE = Arriva Transpennine
BR = British Railways
Cen = Central Trains
CLR = Central London Railway
CR = Caledonian Railway
DRS = Direct Rail Services
DRS (compass) = DRS new livery incorporating a compass
EWS, EW&S = English Welsh & Scottish
FGBRf = First GB Railfreight
FGW = First Great Western (see also GWT)
FNW = First North Western
FScotRail, FSr = First ScotRail
GBRf = GB Railfreight
GCR = Great Central Railway
GER = Great Eastern Railway
GNER = Great Northern Eastern Railway
GNR = Great Northern Railway
GWR or **GW** = Great Western Railway
   shirt or **shirt button** = round logo
   () = a crest contained within the inscription
GWT = Great Western Trains (see also FGW)
HR = Highland Railway
LBSCR, LB&SCR = London Brighton & South Coast Railway
LM City = LondonMidland City
LMR = Longmoor Military Railway
LMS = London Midland & Scottish Railway
LNER = London & North Eastern Railway
LNWR, L&NWR = London & North Western Railway
LSWR, L&SWR = London & South Western Railway
LT = London Transport
LYR = Lancashire & Yorkshire Railway

Bachmann 3-plank wagon Easter Iron Mines

M&GN = Midland & Great Northern Railway
Met = Metropolitan Railway

Codes and Explanations

MML = Midland Mainline
MR = Midland Railway
MSLR = Mid Suffolk Light Railway
NBR = North British Railway
NE = London North Eastern Railway
NER = North Eastern Railway
NLR = North London Railway
NR = Northern Rail
S&D or **S&DJR** = Somerset & Dorset Joint Railway
SECR = South East & Chatham Railway
SER = South Eastern Railway
SR = Southern Railway
SWT = South West Trains
Thames TEx = Thames Trains Express
TPE = TransPennine Express
VT = Virgin Trains
WCR = West Coast Railways

CN = Canadian National, Canadien National
CP = Canadian Pacific
VR = Victorian Railways (Australia)
TA = TransAustralia
TR = Tri-ang Railways
TC = Transcontinental

Tonnage
Older wagons have their weight shown in Imperial tons (T) while more recent wagons have their weight given in Metric tonnes (t).

Colours and Liveries
While some experts on railway liveries may cringe at my use of the term 'red' or 'maroon' (shortened to 'mrn' or 'marn') instead of 'crimson lake' to describe the colour of LMS stock, this has been done so that the description is understood by the non-expert as well those knowledgeable in railway liveries. Likewise, early BR carmine and cream is listed as 'red+cream'. Distinguishing between red and maroon can be difficult especially when the model has not actually been seen.

'Teak' is the description used for LNER coaching stock which was unpainted light wood with a varnish finish. On some models the wood grain has been reproduced by a chemical process in the plastic, but in other cases a yellow-brown paint has been used instead. 'Dark brown and cream' (or just 'brown+cream') is used to describe the GWR coach livery otherwise known as 'chocolate and cream'. A similar colour scheme was used on Pullman cars.

Lima 20-wheel transporter GEC transformer (Rails of Sheffield)

GWR locomotives were usually finished in 'Brunswick' green which was darkish and described here simply as 'green' as the same shade became standard on British Railways (BR) locomotives used purely for passenger work. In contrast, LNER locomotives were generally 'Apple' or 'Doncaster' green which was a lot lighter and is sometimes described here as 'light green' (or lt.green). Southern Railway locomotives were usually green but the shade changed over the years and two shades commonly reproduced today on passenger stock are the early 'Olive' green and the later 'Malachite' which is a light slightly bluish green.

The use of the abbreviations '**l**.' or '**lt**.' as a prefix to the colour means that it is a 'light' shade while 'dark' may be referred to by '**d**.' or '**dk**.' prefixes, bright as '**bt**.' and pale as '**pl**.'

Weathering
More recently 'weathered' finishes have been popular and these are identified in the listing with a capital **'W'**, generally after the colour.

Running Numbers
These are the numbers carried on the side (and often the front) of locomotives and also by coaches and wagons. They are useful as a means of identifying a particular model and in a few cases 'loco search' tables have been provided to help you trace a model by its running number. The absence of a number may infer that the model did not carry one but in most cases it is because we did not know what it was. We would therefore welcome this information where it has been left out but please make sure that the number is original and has not been added after leaving the factory.

Hornby O gauge M3 type LMS tank engine (Vectis)

Italics
Dates are shown in italics in the tables, in order to make it easier to pick these out.

Motors
All locomotive models are electric powered unless otherwise stated. **c/w** = clockwork

Prices
NA = Not Applicable or Not Available
NPG = No Price Given
(see - **Determining Value - The Impossible Task**).

Detail
The absence of detail in the description of a model is not evidence that the detail is not carried by the model. Furthermore, a feature may be mentioned on one model but not on another that also carries it. Often information is provided only where it is felt that it may be helpful in distinguishing between like models.

Listing Order
The listing of models is not always done in the same way as, in each case, an order of listing has been chosen that best suits the subject and makes it easiest for you to find what you are

Codes and Explanations

looking for. The method of listing is sometimes explained at the start of each section.

Generally speaking, however, there has been a move towards a common system which lists locomotives in the order of tank engines, tender engines, diesels, electric locomotives, DMUs and EMUs. Coaches are listed with pre-nationalised stock first (GWR, LMS, LNER and SR) and then Mk1s, Mk2s, Mk3s and Mk4s. The wagons usually start with flat wagons and follow with timber open wagons, steel open wagons, hoppers, tankers, vans, brake vans and bogie wagons.

Dates

Different systems for dating models have been adopted depending on the level of information available. Wherever possible, the span of dates when a model was available have been given but, in some cases, models were produced in batches with hardly any carryover from year to year. This is particularly common today as manufacturers can sell more models by constantly changing their livery or the number they carry. In these cases a single date applies i.e. the year the batch was released.

In the case of earlier models, catalogues were the only source of information as no other records have survived.

Code 3 Models

A Code 3 model is one that has been finished outside the factory by a secondary 'manufacturer'. These are often retailers who buy a quantity of a certain model and re-release it in a modified form. To count as a Code 3, it has to have been produced in the modified form in quantity and to a common specification. This means that one off modifications do not count. Batches of 50 upwards are more usual. These often have a numbered certificate to authenticate them and to indicate how many of them were modified. These have their own niche market and are no longer listed in this guide.

Hornby OO 7-plank wagon - D.R. Llewellyn

'Not Made'

This means that the model did not reach full production. However, it can be confusing when examples of the model turn up. This is usually because, prior to production starting, a small batch of samples was made for individuals to comment on. This is commonly the case where the models are manufactured in the Far East. These samples often find their way on to the market where they can command a high price if the model did not go into full production. This is where it pays to know your subject so that you can recognise the genuine article when you see it.

Pre-Production Models

This is a similar situation except that the models rarely look like production models. They were hand made and hand painted and were produced prior to a decision being taken on whether the subject should be put into production.

With completely new models, the sample may have been built by a model maker using plasticard or may be assembled from a proprietary model kit. It may even have been scratch built using some parts from an existing model in the range. When it was proposed to release an existing model in a new livery, a production model will have been taken off the production line and resprayed and detailed in the new livery as a sample for approval.

Mastermodels street personnel with box

Pre-production samples (commonly referred to in the factory as 'prototypes' or 'visuals') were often finished on one side only and the writing and logos are often skilfully hand painted. Where two exist, one would have gone to the studio preparing the catalogue and the other retained in the factory for draughtsmen and engineers to refer to.

Once approved for production a 'proving' model was made. This was structurally identical to what the final production model would be and its component parts would be used in the preparation of the drawings for the toolmaker.

Pre-production models (prototypes, samples and proving models) sometimes come on the market but it is usually a problem proving that they are what someone claims them to be. While many collectors would like to buy them, uncertainty about authenticity can be a disincentive to do so.

This is really an area of collecting which requires a lot of experience in handling examples in order to recognise the genuine from the fake. Where the provenance is good, they can fetch a high price and four figure sums have been known to change hands - but this is not the norm. Where there is no provenance, they may be purchased quite cheaply but there is a risk you could burn your fingers. None of these are listed in this guide.

Trix Twin S.R 0-4-0 locomotive (Vectis)

Determining Value - The Impossible Task!

For Guidance Only
The first thing to remember about quoted prices is that they are **for guidance only**. Both at auction and on swapmeet stalls, prices vary enormously and who is to say what is the exact value of a given model. What is worth £200 to one collector may be worth only £150 (or even £100) to another buyer or seller.

Swapmeet Prices
On the whole, stall holders are very knowledgeable about what they sell but each tends to be a specialist. They sometimes find themselves with models that are outside their specialised area. If advice is not at hand they have to guess at the price to put on it. This can lead to bargains for knowledgeable buyers but can also cause frustration when the object is severely overpriced.

Remember, the price seen on a model at a swapmeet is not necessarily the price at which it sells. Most stall holders are prepared to haggle. So what is the true value of the model; the price at which he bought it in, the price he put on it or the price at which you finally buy it?

Putting an accurate value to individual models is impossible. All we can do is show comparisons and that is all this price guide sets out to do.

Auction Prices
There is, usually, a fair gap between what you pay for a model and what you would expect to get for it when selling it again. We have set out prices at what we think the models will fetch at auction, prior to the addition of the buyer's premium. Even at auction, prices vary erratically depending on who is bidding. As a result of this, we have had to deal with conflicting valuations from different auctions and, in each case, have tried to arrive at a compromise.

Auction prices can be used only for more valuable items as less valuable models are put together in groups to be sold as mixed lots. It is impossible to estimate how much of the hammer price applied to each item in the lot as some would have been more valuable than others.

eBay
Since this price guide was started, on-line auctions have grown in importance and amongst these eBay is by far the most used by model railway collectors. Here prices can be more erratic than anywhere else. This is a world-wide auction room and overseas bidders buying into a market they are unfamiliar with will sometimes take a model well over its perceived value. At other times an otherwise valuable model struggles to get anywhere near its 'normal' value. We have largely avoided using eBay prices for this reason.

Our Valuations
Our suggested values are presented in two columns to the right of each table. For reasonably recent releases, where mint boxed items may still be around, the right hand column gives a 'mint boxed' price and the left hand column an 'excellent unboxed' value. If the item was not released on its own, authentically boxed examples are unlikely to exist and so the right hand column carries an 'NA' for 'not available'. Likewise, where a price is given for a boxed set of models, or a train pack, there is an 'NA' in the left hand column.

With many of the older, obsolete, model ranges mint boxed examples are practically an impossibility and so the two columns are used to show the price range for examples in very nice condition. There are cases where there is doubt whether a model actually exists or, alternatively, no example of one having been sold can be found. In these cases the price columns are marked with an 'NPG' for 'no price given'. The guide contains about 30,000 listings and so it is not feasible to trace known prices on each one. A lot of it has to be guesswork.

Effect of Quality
Obviously, value falls as quality falls but not always by the same percentage. It depends how rare the model is and even what make it is. The lack of a box can reduce the value of a model by 40% or more. Generally the rarer the model, the more valuable the box. For poorer quality models the lack of a box has less impact on price.

The gulf between the price first class models are fetching and that paid for those of a lower standard is ever widening and in some ranges the prices of poorer quality models is going down. Models that have had detailing added after leaving the factory (except in the case of Code 3 models) are likely to be of lower value to collectors even though the detailing has improved the appearance of the model. The same applies to repainted models, although there are very early 0 gauge models for which a professional repaint is acceptable as few, if any, good unrestored examples exist in reasonable condition.

Fluctuating Prices
Prices can fluctuate from year to year and from decade to decade. With the sale of the G&R Wrenn in the early '90s, the price of Wrenn models quickly escalated but, more recently, fell to more modest levels. The publication of the Maurice Gunter book on Wrenn, once again pushed up the prices. The fairly recent end of Lima production saw the almost immediate increase in the demand for Lima models. Thus Lima prices rose before falling again.

At auction, the sale of a famous comprehensive collection can bring out top bidders with the result that average prices may rise on the day with rare and common items both selling at figures well above the norm.

High and Low Values
As already indicated, the price gap between rare and common (or poor quality) items is ever widening. This means that rare and top quality models are a much better investment than common or poor quality ones.

Train Packs
Nowadays, some manufacturers sell their models in train packs. These consist of a locomotive and some coaches or wagons but no track etc. As already indicated, the right hand column price is for the complete train pack. Multiple units (DEMUs, EMUs etc.) are sold as train packs and no price is given for individual parts of these as it is assumed that unboxed the units will be sold together. The price in the left hand column is therefore for the complete 2-car or 3-car unit without its packaging.

The History of Model Train Manufacture

In the Beginning
The first commercially built model railways were imported into Britain from Germany in 1902 and were made for Bassett-Lowke by the German companies, Bing, Carette and Marklin.

Up until the First World War, the most popular gauge was known as gauge 1 but after the war gauge 0 really came into its own.

The war was to have a dramatic effect on the model railway industry as post-war anti-German feeling made German imports unpopular and Bassett-Lowke Ltd were forced to manufacture more of their products themselves. It also created an opportunity for other British manufacturers to enter the fray.

The most successful of these was Meccano Ltd, a company that had been founded in 1908 to manufacture the Meccano engineering construction system. They introduced their toy trains in 1920 and these took the name of the Company's founder - Frank Hornby - and were sold as 'Hornby Trains'. Hornby, from the start, chose to manufacture in 0 gauge and early models constructed with Meccano nuts and bolts soon gave way to tinplate tab and slot construction. Some were direct copies of Bing models.

Other notable manufacturers of the inter-war period were the Leeds Model Company, Mills Brothers, Exley and Bond's - all of which are covered by this book. These principally manufactured their own ranges of 0 gauge models but also produced some gauge 1 equipment and Bond's and Exley branched into 00 scale in later years. All also provided bespoke services for those who wanted specific models built specially for them.

First 00 Scale System
As early as 1922, Bassett-Lowke introduced to Britain a tabletop railway made in Germany by Bing and considered to be 00 gauge - i.e. half the size of the popular 0 gauge. Within a very short time this was available as an electric system. The Bing company was to fall victim to the rise of Nazi power in Germany and trading became very difficult. Out of these difficulties came a more commercial small scale system known as Trix and this was introduced to Britain in 1936, again with the assistance of Bassett-Lowke.

Within a very short time it was being made by a satellite company of Bassett-Lowke at Northampton. Meccano Ltd could see the way the wind was blowing and quickly responded with their own 00 system which they called Hornby Dublo. This was launched in 1938 and, unlike the Trix Twin system, was initially available in clockwork form as well as electric.

Post World War 2
The Second World War brought to an end all commercial model railway production but post-war Britain saw major changes in both demand and response. It was soon clear that 0 gauge was no longer the leading scale and over the years production of it gradually declined.

The new principal gauge in Britain was 00 and it was to remain so to the present day.

Hornby Dublo returned after the war but while it was the market leader for a while, Meccano Ltd did not recognise the importance of expanding it fast to meet the growing demands from the public. The gap in demand was quickly filled by a new system called Tri-ang Railways which was made by Rovex Scale Models Ltd, a subsidiary of Lines Bros.

The New Contender
The Tri-ang system had several advantages that would play in its favour during the struggle for market domination that lay ahead. It was a two-rail system making the track look more realistic, it used plastic mouldings that could show much more detail, it was a lot cheaper while still being reliable and the range expanded quickly to offer the public plenty of choice when building a layout. Within a few years it had become the market leader.

The early post-war years saw many other companies trying to break into the model railway market. Principal amongst these was Graham Farish who marketed an 00 system with some very attractive models but which, initially, were not too reliable mechanically.

Trix in the meantime failed to respond quickly enough to the demand for realism and slowly faded. The business changed hands a few times and new investment resulted in some good models being produced. One of its problems became obvious in the late '50s and that was its adoption of the Continental HO scale instead of British 00. This meant that when some excellent models started to arrive they looked out of scale when mixed with those of other makes.

Meanwhile Tri-ang's onslaught was injuring Hornby Dublo and although Meccano Ltd made major improvements to their range, including a 2-rail system and use of plastic mouldings, its response came too late to save the company, which was being bombarded on other fronts at the same time.

Big Take-overs
In 1964 Meccano Ltd was taken over by Lines Bros. who renamed their own model railway system 'Tri-ang Hornby' and sold some of the Hornby Dublo tools to another of their subsidiaries - G&R Wrenn. For the next decade Tri-ang Hornby virtually had the market to itself. The only competition came from a Trix system, which limped along, and Playcraft which was made by Jouef in France and marketed in Britain by Mettoy Ltd. 1973 saw a bid by Lima to break into the British market but they made the mistake of using the smaller HO scale. Although by 1976 Lima had changed to 00 scale, their day had not yet dawned.

In 1971, the Lines Bros. Group fell apart. Profitable Rovex, the member of the group making Tri-ang Hornby, was sold to Dunbee Combex Marx (DCM) and Tri-ang Hornby was renamed Hornby Railways. G&R Wrenn became an independent company again and continued to manufacture Wrenn Railways for the next 20 years using mainly the former Hornby Dublo tools. The British part of Meccano Ltd (based in Liverpool), who no longer made trains, was sold to Airfix while Meccano France (based in the former Tri-ang factory in Calais) was acquired by General Mills who also owned Palitoy.

New Competition
Both Airfix and Palitoy separately judged that there was a place in the market for better quality model railways and decided to fill it. The Airfix and Mainline (Palitoy) systems were both launched in the mid '70s but it had taken them two years from announcing their intentions to supplying shops and this gave Rovex the breathing space they required to respond with their Hornby Railways system. By 1980 it was a four horse race with Hornby closely chased by Mainline and Airfix and Lima coming up on the outside. Meanwhile, trailing some way behind, was British Trix and Playcraft was now out of view.

This seems an appropriate point at which to stop and look at what else was happening.

Smaller Scales
Tri-ang had seen a need to experiment with yet smaller scales and in 1957 had launched their TT system. This never really caught on although it was well developed as a system and was supported by manufacturers of accessories. It had died in the mid '60s.

The even smaller scale of 000 or N gauge was tried by Lone Star as a push-along system in 1957 with an electric system following in 1960. Lines Bros. were invited to buy the system but turned it down and it died out in the 1970s. Lima had produced a more sophisticated N gauge system which they had offered to

History of Manufacture

Lines Bros. in the 1960s and they agreed to market it through their subsidiary, G&R Wrenn. This was sold as Wrenn Micromodels for many years.

Following the purchase of Rovex in 1971 by Dunbee Combex Marx they entered into an agreement with the German Trix company to import their Minitrix system (formerly made at Wrexham by Trix Trains) and sell it as Hornby Minitrix. New models were produced to Rovex's requirements, leaving Rovex free to concentrate on developing Hornby Railways. The arrangement was quite successful and lasted several years.

The only British company to really grasp the N gauge nettle was Graham Farish. Remember them? We last saw them in the 1950s with a nice but not too successful 00 system. This had limped along through the '60s with much shrinkage until they turned their attention to developing an N gauge system at the end of the '60s. In a virtual vacuum, but with a steadily growing demand for good N gauge models at reasonable prices, the Grafar N gauge system has expanded and now offers considerable choice to the N gauge modeller. Many small companies have developed to provide accessories, resprays etc. on the back of this system.

Before returning to 00 gauge it is worth mentioning that 0 gauge virtually petered out in the mid '60s as Hornby, Bassett-Lowke's and the Leeds Model Company's production ground to a halt. Despite this, in the mid-1960s, Tri-ang produced their toy-like Big Big trains, the tools for which were later sent to Russia, and Lima produced some acceptable models of British outline.

The Tools Merry-go-round

In 1980 DCM were in the receivers hands and the future of the Hornby Railway system was once again in question. The same year Airfix went bust and its railway system was taken over by Palitoy and its models absorbed into the Mainline system. By 1981, Hornby Hobbies (formerly Rovex) were an independent company again for the first time in 30 years. Ten glorious years of expansion followed. During the 1980s Lima firmly took hold of the modern image locomotive market bringing out models of many of the better known subjects. Then, in 1990, it all changed again!

In 1984, General Mills, who owned Palitoy, had given up toy production and the assets of their Mainline system, including the Airfix tools, were sold to another up and coming company called Dapol Ltd. They were by then producing their own new, high quality, models of locomotives. Dapol later also purchased the tools and intellectual assets of G&R Wrenn when George Wrenn retired in the early 1990s. However, Palitoy had not owned the tools for the manufacture of their Mainline models as these belonged to Kader of China who had made them. Kader were supplying some models to Godfrey Hayes for his Replica Railways range, Hayes having paid for completion and improvement of some of the Mainline tooling.

Enter the Dragon

Kader were interested in expanding their model railway manufacturing and in 1988 took control of the American model company, Bachmann. In 1989 they formed Bachmann Industries Europe Ltd to develop and market models in Europe through bases in Britain and Germany. The Bachmann Branchline range was launched in Britain in 1990, using the former Mainline tools. Building on these, Kader, by the late 1990s, were manufacturing models to a quality never before seen in Britain. This was the Blue Riband range.

Once again Hornby found their commanding place in the market threatened and had to respond. To allow them to expand their range fast, and quickly improve the quality of their models, they needed to buy ready to use new tooling. As we have seen, Dapol had produced some high quality models of their own but also owned the former Airfix tools they had bought from Palitoy along with a few Mainline tools not owned by Kader. Following a major fire which destroyed much of their stock, Dapol needed to raise money quickly and put up for sale some of their tools. In 1996 Hornby bought them and this gave them four years breathing space in which to develop their own new models. In the summer of 2000, the first of these arrived in the shops. with the promise that all new Hornby models would be to the new standard.

New Groupings

Graham Farish was taken over by Bachmann in 2000, who set about retooling its models to a far higher specification. Dapol, having extracted the wagon tooling they required to boost their own range, sold the remainder of G&R Wrenn to an independent company. Efforts at Dapol were now directed towards producing their own quality N gauge system which was launched in 2003.

By 2002 it had become clear that Lima were in difficulties and as they struggled to stay in business the Danish company, Heljan, made a bid for part of the British 00 diesel market. Hornby and Bachmann joined in to pick off Lima's diesel subjects and produce superior versions of them.

The Lima Group went into liquidation and most of its assets were bought by Hornby in 2004, along with the Lima, Rivarossi, Jouef and Arnold names. They also purchased the leading Spanish company, Electrotren. Lima's British models started to appear in the Hornby catalogue in 2006, most of them relegated to the newly established Hornby RailRoad budget range.

In 2007 Hornby bought Airfix and Humbrol and in 2008 added Corgi Classics to their collection of brands. With Corgi came Bassett-Lowke which brought together, under one roof, the names of the two great pre-war brands - Hornby and Bassett-Lowke.

New Faces, New Future

Today, the major 00 market in Britain is dominated by Hornby and Bachmann with Heljan and Dapol retaining a toehold, as well as relative newcomer ViTrains. The N gauge market is dominated by a much improved Graham Farish and Dapol but with Peco showing renewed interest. The 0 gauge market is dominated by Ace Trains, with recent additional competitors in Skytrex and Darstaed making themselves felt. Dapol and Heljan have also entered the 0 gauge market and the American MTH company has also dipped its toe in British 0 gauge water.

Hornby and Bachmann have everything manufactured in China, including their various continental brands. Other model manufacturers also make much of their products in the Far East or in Eastern Europe.

Hornby launched an 00 scale live steam system and satisfied that niche market before closing down production. They see their future as an international group and are marketing Electrotren, Lima, Rivarossi, Jouef and Arnold under their own names. Arnold in 2013 produced its first British outline N gauge model and a new name in N gauge wagons is Mathieson.

The future could be very interesting. While shops, clubs and magazines have been commissioning their own versions of models for sometime, a more recent development has been the commissioning of brand new subjects. In some cases the agreement has been a guaranteed purchase of stock in exchange for two years exclusive use of the tooling; in other cases the commissioning organisation pay for and own the tooling. This arrangement appears to be growing in popularity and is increasing the range of models available.

Despite the economic downturn, railway modelling appears to be holding its own. One new development in 2012 was Hornby's 'design clever' programme aimed at reducing the manufacturing cost of high quality models. In 2013 the future looks as exciting as ever.

***

This has been a simplified history of the principal manufacturers of ready-to-run models and toy trains and does not reflect the enormous contribution made to the industry by the scores of smaller firms that specialise in kits, materials and accessories. Without them it would be a far less interesting hobby.

The History of Collecting

The collecting of toy trains did not really get under way in Britain until the late 1960s when operators of Hornby 0 gauge were looking for additional stock. One way in which the exchange of models was effected was through the organisation of meetings by groups of enthusiasts and this lead to the invention of a new word in the English language - the Swapmeet.

Out of this growth in interest, the Hornby Railway Collectors Association was formed in 1969 and following a period of sometimes heated argument through the pages of the Association's magazine, membership was extended to Hornby Dublo collectors, some of whom had formed the Dublo Circle. The HRCA has steadily grown over the years and is by far the largest club of its kind in the UK. It has also spawned a number of satellite organisations abroad.

The mid 1970s saw a growing interest in collecting of other makes of toy trains and the formation, in 1975, of two more organisations. The first of these was the Tri-ang Hornby Collectors Club which survived for many years, chronicling the diversities of the range, before disbanding. The other new organisation was the Trix Twin Railway Collectors Association which has flourished and remains a well supported organisation producing its own spares, special models for members and an excellent magazine.

It was not until 1979 that collectors in Britain had an organisation that catered for 'any make, any gauge, any age'. This is the by-line of the Train Collectors Society which has stuck to its principles and not tried to set close restrictive limits to its member's interest. The result is a very friendly society that does not take itself, or its hobby, too seriously. In recent years the TCS has grown in size and many collectors have seen the value of dual membership (membership of a specialist club and membership of the TCS for the wider interest).

Other specialised clubs followed with the Kitmaster Collectors Club in 1980, the Bassett-Lowke Society in 1991, the Graham Farish Circle in 1994, the Lima Collectors Society in 1995, the Wrenn Railways Collectors Club in 1998 and the Tri-ang Society, with its fairly broad interest in the products of the Lines Bros. Group, in 1999. More recently we have seen an ACE Trains Owners Club formed.

Recent years have seen a growing recognition, by the manufacturers, of the expanding market for new models made specially for collectors. To this end, they produce collectors editions of their models. Some, like Bachmann, Hornby, Dapol and Wrenn have their own collectors clubs and Hornby established collectors centres that exclusively receive some of their limited editions.

Outside the scope of this book are those British clubs that cater for collectors of foreign makes. These include the Fleischmann Model Railway Club and the Lionel Collectors Club UK.

Computer enhanced Hornby OO Class B17 'Thorpe Hall' - 'A Windy Evening on Shed' by Robbie McGavin

Collectors' Clubs

Anyone interested in collecting railway models should consider joining one of the growing number of specialist collecting clubs. The following are relevant to the systems covered by this guide:

Train Collectors Society
This is a society with a broad interest in toy and model train collecting and has the motto 'Any Make, Any Gauge, Any Age'. Founded in 1978, the Society publishes a 52 page full colour quarterly magazine called *Train Collector* and has a spares and information service, digital magazine index, very active website and is developing an archive of digital images which currently holds over 50,000 pictures. It holds three major gatherings each year, but members also exhibit at other events.
Contact : Tony Stanford, tel: 01442 266658
Website : www.traincollectors.co.uk

Ace Trains Celebration Class 4-4-0 (Lacy, Scott & Knight)

ACE Trains Owners Club
The club was formed in 2007 for collectors of ACE Trains products. It publishes a newsletter four times a year and is independent of the company whose products it promotes.
Contact : webmaster@acetrainsownersclub.org.uk
Website : www.ACETrainsownersclub.org.uk

Bachmann Class D11 'Butler Henderson' (Bachmann)

Bachmann Collectors' Club
For a number of years the company sponsored an enthusiasts club called Bachmann Times which operated at arms-length. In 2000 the club was reformed in-house under the name: Bachmann Collectors' Club. Members receive a free wagon each year and a quarterly magazine updating them on development progress and with feature articles related to the models and real railways.
Contact : Bachmann Collectors Club, PO Box 7820, 13 Moat Way, Barwell, Leicestershire LE9 8EY.
Website : www.bachmann.co.uk

Bassett-Lowke Society
The Bassett-Lowke Society, founded in 1992, caters for those who collect and operate Bassett-Lowke models. It publishes a quarterly magazine called *Lowko News* and organises events to which members may take their stock to run. The Society is also sympathetic towards other pre-war 0 gauge brands such as Bonds, Leeds and Milbro.
Contact : Tracy Haydon-White, tel: 0121 5502775
E-mail : tracyhw@blueyonder.co.uk
Website : www.bassettlowkesociety.org.uk

Bassett-Lowke LMS 2-6-4 tank (Vectis)

Dapol Nthusiasts Club
This is a club for Dapol's N gauge customers. On joining you receive a number of promotional freebies and the opportunity of receiving a special club wagon each year. There is a newsletter and access to special releases.
Contact : Through the website
Website : www.dapol.co.uk (details in N gauge shop section)

Dapol N gauge Britannia (Tony Wright)

Hornby Collectors Club
This is a club supported by Hornby Hobbies plc for subscribing customers. The club was formed in 1997 and publishes a full colour bimonthly magazine called *The Collector*. Through the club, members have the opportunity to purchase special collectors editions of models produced by Hornby but also receive a free specially produced loco each year.
Contact : Sarah Woodhouse, Hornby Collectors Club, PO Box 25, Melton Mowbray, Leicestershire. Tel: 0871 248 6000
Website : www.hornby.com

Hornby N15 'Sir Meliagrace'

Hornby Railway Collectors' Association
The HRCA was founded in 1969 and caters for collectors of both Hornby 0 gauge and Hornby-Dublo. It is the largest of the clubs listed here and has overseas associate organisations.

Collectors' Clubs

The Association publishes 11 issues of its magazine, called *The Hornby Railway Collector*, each year and has a very well developed spares service.
Contact : John Harwood, tel: 01935-474830
Website : www.hrca.net

Hornby O gauge LMS No. 2 loco (Lacy, Scott & Knight)

Kitmaster Collectors Club
Enthusiasts of the Kitmaster kit range are well catered for by the Kitmaster Collectors Club which was founded in 1980. The club publishes a magazine called *Signal* twice a year and includes in the subjects covered the railway kits by Airfix and Dapol. The magazine is available on the club's website
Contact : Steve Knight
Email : steve@kitmaster.freeserve.co.uk
Website : www.rosebud-kitmaster.co.uk

Leeds Model Co. 0-6-0 tank (Dutch HRCA)

Leeds Stedman Trust
The Leeds Stedman Trust is an organisation run by David Peacock to help collectors and operators of LMC models to keep them running by supplying spare parts. It is not a club but you can be placed on a mailing list for the annual price list of parts.
Contact : David Peacock, email : dpeacock@btconnect.com
Website : www.leedsstedmantrust.org

Tri-ang original plunger 'Princess'

Tri-ang Society
The Tri-ang Society was formed in 1999 and caters for all Tri-ang products including Tri-ang Railways, Tri-ang Hornby, Tri-ang Railways TT, Big-Big Trains and Minic Motorway. The Society has a regular magazine called *The Tri-ang Telegraph* and arranges displays at various model shows and vintage events. It also organises two of its own events each year.
Contact : Miles Rowland, tel : 0161 976 5059
Website : www.tri-angsociety.co.uk

Trix 0-6-2 tank (LSL)

Trix Twin Railway Collectors' Association
The Trix Twin Railway Collectors Association (TTRCA) was founded in 1975 and caters for enthusiasts of Trix Twin, Trix Express, Trix Trains and the models of Liliput UK. It publishes a quarterly magazine called *Trix Twin Gazette* and offers a spares service to its members.
Contact : Brian Arnold, tel: 0116 271 5943
Website : www.ttrca.co.uk

Wrenn Collectors Club
The club was founded in 2007 and caters for the collectors of all products of G&R Wrenn Ltd. It publishes two half-colour newsletters each year and offers its members a discount on certain company items and the right to buy the annual wagon release.
Contact : Maurice Gunter, tel : 01707 35459
Website : www.gandr-wrenn.co.uk

Wrenn Railways Collectors Club
The club was founded in 1998 and caters for the collectors of all products of G&R Wrenn Ltd. It publishes a quarterly magazine called *The Wrenn Tracker* and organises gatherings for its members, contributing displays at various vintage events.
Contact : Barry Fentiman, tel : 01628 488455
Website : www.wrennrailways.co.uk

Wrenn Royal Scott Class 'The Royal Air Force' (Vectis)

Magazines
As indicated above, many of the collecting organisations publish magazines for their members and there is no better way of keeping in touch with developments and the history of specific makes than through these publications. Since the demise of *Model Railway Enthusiast/Model Railway Collector* there has been no national magazine specifically catering for the toy train and railway model collector but the Train Collectors Society's *Train Collector* tries to fill this gap. Besides this, *British Railway Modelling*, *Hornby Magazine* and *Model Rail* all carry occasional articles on model railway history.

Internet
Finally, there are Yahoo chat groups on the Internet with specialisms which marry with those of several of the clubs listed above. These are excellent sources of information, as too are a lot of private websites run by enthusiasts.

In addition, the free *Model Railway Express* magazine (MREmag) at www.mremag.com provides thrice weekly updates of news for collectors and modellers. It also has reviews of newly released models looked at from the collector's point of view.

TRAIN COLLECTOR

Britain's only comprehensive magazine for the collector of British and overseas brands of model trains.

If you collect trains of any make, gauge or age you should be reading **Train Collector**. It is available by subscription only. Articles from the last eight issues include:-

'Kirdon Power Units'
'Bonds O' Euston Road'
'British Diecast Trains'
'Tri-ang Canadian Train Sets'
'Steamcraft'
'Dating Hornby 0 Wagons'
'Hornby 0 Milk Tankers'
'Ratio Wooden Coach Kits'
'Playcraft Innovation'
'Bassett-Lowke at Steam'
'Chad Valley Trains'
'Trix Twin Train Sets'
'Bing's Black Prince'
'British H0'
'G Scale Outdoors'
'Marx Hong Kong'
'Hornby 0 PO Vans'
'Zenith Model Co.'
'Hachette'
'USA Floor Trains'
'Wagons Hornby Nearly Made'
'Australian Robilt Models'
'Lone Star Inspiration'
'Rowell'
'Shops I Remember'
'H&M Power Units'
'Marklin 0 Tinplate'
'Airfix Wagons'
'Zeppelin Railcars'
'Carette Gauge 1 Wagons'
'Tinplate Stations'
'Trix Plastic Coal Wagons'
'Italian Floor Trains'
'Wells Brimtoy Streamliners'
'The Hamblings Gnat'
'Trains & Slot Cars'
'Bassett-Lowke Wagons'
'Distler Electric Trains'
'Alresford 2013'
'Gem Coaches'
'The Hordern LMC Layout'
'Bachmann Vans'
'Exley 0 Catering Cars'
'Dyke & Ward'
'00 Grain Wagons'
'Astral Kits'
'Tinplate Signal Boxes'
'Sandy 2013'

access and keeps you up to date with train collectors events and auctions held during the year. To subscribe or seek further information, phone: 01442 266658 or go to the TCS website at: www.traincollectors.co.uk. where you can subscribe online.

Train Collector is published four times a year - December, March, June and September. It costs £23 per annum which also gives you full membership of the Train Collectors Society, access to a spares & repairs service, an index and back issues service, access to TCS events at members' rates, the opportunity to participate in the TCS Internet chat group, discounted museum

8th Edition

Further Reading

When toy train collecting was in its infancy, there was a dearth of information about manufacturers and model ranges with the result that any book, however simple, that included text or pictures about toy trains, was pounced on by knowledge hungry collectors.

Two such books were **'Older Locomotives (1900-42)'** [ISBN 172132088] by Peter Gomm and **'Recent Locomotives (1947-70)'** [ISBN 172132096] by Peter Randall. Both were published in 1970 by Thomas Nelson and Sons Ltd in their Troy Model Club Series for collectors and such was the demand for them that even libraries could not guarantee supplying you with a copy on loan.

While books on British manufacturers remained scarce, those on the international scene started to appear in the '70s. 1972 saw the release in Britain of the English language edition of Gustav Reder's **'Clockwork, Steam and Electric'** (ISBN 0711003718). This is a classic study of early toy train making and is a must for anyone with an international interest in the subject.

A better illustrated book with more of a British slant is **'A Century of Model Trains'** [ISBN 0517184370] by Allen Levy and published in 1974 by Crescent Books.

Another international book which is good for its mouth watering coloured photographs is Udo Becher's **'Early Tin Plate Model Railways'** [ISBN 0852426690] which was published by Argus Books in 1980.

A much more general history of toy manufacturing is the very detailed **'The Toy Collector'** [ISBN 0801578469] by Louis H Hertz and published in 1976 by Hawthorn Books Inc. of New York.

Books specifically for the British collector took a step forward with F.R.Gorham's compilation of extracts from Hornby catalogues published between 1927 and 1932. Titled **'Hornby Book of Trains'** [ISBN 0090288820X] it was released by the Oxford Publishing Co. in 1973. This idea of using extracts from old publications was adopted by The Cranbourne Press Ltd. for their booklets. These were made up from Meccano Magazine and Tri-ang catalogue pages and included **'Main Line Ending'** by Peter Randall (Hornby 0 Gauge), **'Hornby Dublo Trains 1938-1939'** by Ronald Truin and **'A Short History of Tri-ang Railways'** by Tony Stanford.

Little more was available for several years and then, suddenly, there was an explosion of publishing in the late '70s starting in 1977 with the excellent **'Collectors Guide to Model Railways'** [ISBN 0852425295] by James Joyce. This remains, today, one of the best broad-brush studies of the British model railway industry, despite the fact that it needs bringing up to date. It was published by Argus books as, too, was **'Toyshop Steam'** [ISBN 085242583X] by Basil Harley, which was released the following year.

That same year saw the release of the first volume of a series of books that was to set the benchmark for specialist books on individual subjects. I refer, of course, to The Hornby Companion Series by New Cavendish. Volume 1 **'The Products of Binns Road - A General Survey'** [ISBN 0904568067] by Peter Randall provided us with the first study of Meccano Ltd and, for the first time, included full colour reproductions of three catalogues. The series went on to cover individual toy ranges from this important company as well as their paperwork and publications. There were also compendia published for some of the volumes which provided check lists of products made.

Volume 2 of The Hornby Companion Series was devoted to Meccano super models but Volume 3 was the much awaited **'Hornby Dublo Trains 1938-1964'** [ISBN 0904568180] by Michael Foster. I distinctly remember the excitement with which I waited for my volume to arrive and then shutting myself away for a week to study it.

Volume 4 was Mike & Sue Richardson's famous treatise on Dinky Toys and this was followed by what I think is the best written book in the whole series. It is of course Volume 5 **'The Hornby O Gauge System'** [ISBN 0904568350] by Chris & Julie Graebe. A better researched and illustrated book would be hard to find. The series went to seven volumes plus five compendia and several of the books have run to second editions.

A magazine popular at the time among collectors was the **'History of Model & Miniature Railways'** which built up into two bound volumes. The close-up photography used for this series was to spawn a number of look-alike books, one of which was **'The World of Model Trains'** [ISBN 086124009X] edited by Patrick Whitehouse and Allen Levy and published by Bison Books in 1978.

A remarkable book of this period was the **'International Model Railways Guide'** [ISBN 3920877160] which was a German publication, written in three languages (German, French and English). This was, in effect, a large catalogue of model railway manufacturers around the world illustrating in colour many (but not all) of the models available at the time (1978-79). 1979 also saw the publication of **'Mechanical Toys'** [ISBN 0600363317] by Charles Bartholomew and published by Hamlyn, but this had only limited information about toy trains.

Of special interest to Tri-ang Hornby collectors was **'The Hornby Book of Trains 25 Year Edition'** [ISBN 095065860X] which was published in 1979. It was edited by S.W.Stevens-Stratten and chapters on everything from real trains to the manufacturing process at Margate were largely written by staff at the factory - much of it by Richard Lines. The book was followed in 1983 by **'The Art of Hornby'** [ISBN 071823037X], also written by Richard Lines, which looked at catalogue and leaflet designs by Meccano Ltd for their Hornby Series and Hornby Dublo as well as for Tri-ang Hornby and Hornby Railways.

An important reference series started in 1980 was **'Cade's Locomotive Guide'** [ISBN 0905377079] which was written by Dennis Lovett and Leslie Wood. This ran to three volumes [ISBN 0905377117] [ISBN 090537715X] and was re-released in a combined volume in 1988 [ISBN 0905377397]. The aim of the series was to provide background information about the real locomotives that are the subjects of models. After each account there were details and photographs of relevant models.

By now articles on model railway collecting were beginning to appear in the model railway press although these remained few and far between. One exception was a series by Peter Gomm called **'Tinplate Topics'** which was a regular feature in *Model Railway News* for several years and looked principally at Hornby 0 gauge. This was followed in 1984 by a series in *Model Railway Constructor* called **'Collector's Corner'** which became a regular feature and ran for several years.

Another attempt at a 'world catalogue' had come in 1983, this time in English, with the publication of **'The World Guide to Model Trains'** [ISBN 0722188242] which was compiled by Peter McHoy with the help of Chris Ellis and was published by Sphere Books Ltd.

A new major work appeared in 1984 when Roland Fuller's **'The Bassett-Lowke Story'** [ISBN 0904568342] reached the shops. This excellent book, published by New Cavendish Books, contained a considerable number of archive photographs and is a valuable reference work.

For quality coloured photographs, the series by Salamanda Books Ltd cannot be beaten. The volume called **'The Collector's All-Colour Guide to Toy Trains'** [ISBN 1855010259] (1985) was compiled by Ron McCrindell and contains excellent pictures of many rare items; most of which are in superb condition having been drawn from several famous collections.

Following this, in 1986, we had one of the best in depth studies of the subject in **'Toy Trains - A History'** by Pierce Carlson [ISBN

Further Reading

0575.3890X] - again with excellent illustrations but virtually restricted to pre WW2 developments.

As an aside, an interesting book published in 1992 was the autobiography of Ian Allan called **'Driven by Steam'** (ISBN 0711021155). Many a toy train collector spent his youth thumbing through the ABC locomotive books, recording locomotives he had seen. This book tells you how those little books came about.

Now for three New Cavendish books from the early 1990s. The first of these looked at the whole field of British toy manufacturers and, although railway content was small when compared with the rest, the detail provided is so good that it is a 'must' for any toy collector's library. This is **'British Tin Toys'** [ISBN 0904568865] by Marguerite Fawdry, which was published in 1990 and covers more than just tin toys!

The next is my own book **'Tri-ang Railways'** [ISBN 0904568571] which New Cavendish Books published in 1993. It is the first in a trilogy about the Rovex company better known today as Hornby plc. This first volume deals with the years from 1950 to 1965 when the product was known as Tri-ang Railways.

This was followed the next year by Tony Matthewman's beautiful volume **'The History of Trix H0/00 Model Railways in Britain'** [ISBN 0904568768]. For me the book comes a close second to Chris & Julie Graebe's Hornby 0 Gauge book for the excellence of its research and presentation. This, like **'Tri-ang Railways'** (and its sequels), was produced in landscape format to match the Hornby Companion Series.

A small book, also released in 1994, was the Shire Album Series No.255 **'Toy Trains'** [ISBN 0747800871] by David Salisbury. And another book published that year was **'Model Trains - The Collector's Guide'** [ISBN 1854227807] by Chris Ellis. Published by Magna Books, it contains an easy to follow history and some good photographs.

1996 brought with it Jeff Carpenter's **'Bings Table Railway'** [ISBN 1900897008], published by Diva Publishing, which provides not only a full account of the small Bing system but also the histories of many other miniature trains such as those by Karl Bub, Distler and Jep Mignon.

November 1993 had seen the launch of *Model Railway Enthusiast* which was a model railway magazine with some articles for collectors. In February 1998 content for collectors was raised to 50% of the magazine and in November 1999 to 100% when the magazine was renamed *Model Railway Collector*.

1998 saw the release of Donald Troost's first Lone Star guide which, by 2005, was in its 9th Edition and ran to three thick volumes. Independently published, it is the most detailed guide on the subject, to be found.

1998 saw the release of my second book **'Tri-ang Hornby'** [ISBN 1-872727-58-1], again by New Cavendish Books, and also the first edition of **'Ramsay's British Model Trains Catalogue'** [ISBN 0952835231], published by Swapmeet Publications.

In 1999, two useful books on kits were published. The first of these was Steven Knight's excellent study of Kitmaster kits in **'Let's Stick Together'** [ISBN 1871608902], published by Irwell Press (completely revised and expanded in 2012) and the second was Arthur Ward's **'Airfix Plastic Kits'** [ISBN 0004723279] published by Harper Collins.

It was also in 1999 that **'Wenman Joseph Bassett-Lowke'** [ISBN 1900622017] was published by Rail Romances, who at the same time released a video recording based on films taken by W.J.Bassett-Lowke, including footage inside the factory. The book had been written by his niece Janet Bassett-Lowke.

In 2000, the first of a series of planned volumes called **'A History of Locomotive Kits'** [ISBN 0953772004] by Robert Forsythe was published by Amlor Publishing. This covers kits by K's, Nu-Cast, Wills and South Eastern Finecast.

The second edition of **'Ramsay's Catalogue'** also appeared that year under new editorship. Another 2nd edition appeared in 2001 and this was **'Tri-ang Railways'** which had had a further 32 pages of information added.

2002 was a bumper year for new books. Harper Collins published Ian Harrison's **'Hornby - The Official Illustrated History'** [ISBN 000715173X] and **'Frank Hornby - News & Pictures'** was written and published by Jim Gamble [ISBN 095420610X]. The 3rd edition of Ramsay's Catalogue was released - now with comprehensive listing of locos and rolling stock covering some 25 brands produced for sale in Britain over the last 80 years.

The final two books for 2002 were principally aimed at the classic tinplate collector. Firstly there was the excellent **'Christie's Toy Railways'** by Hugo Marsh which covers history and development from the earliest times. This was published by Pavilion Books [ISBN 1862055254]. The second is the magnificent English edition of Paul Klein Schiphorst's **'The Golden Years of Tin Toy Trains'** published by New Cavendish Books [ISBN 187272759X]. This contains possibly the finest collection of images of early tinplate trains ever to be assembled.

We jump now to 2004 and the release Stan Buck's book **'E.W.Twining, Model Maker, Artist & Engineer'** (ISBN 1843061430), which gives us new insight into his relationship with Bassett-Lowke.

A foreign language book published in 2004 that was of special interest to British collectors was Clive Lamming's **'Jouef Marque Deposee'** (ISBN 2903651388) with its history and extensive listing of the Jouef model railway system, including coverage of the Playcraft range sold by Mettoy in Britain. As one might expect, the text is in French.

Also in 2004 the long awaited book on G&R Wrenn arrived. Called **'The Story of Wrenn - From Binns Road to Basildon'** it was written by Maurice Gunter and published by Irwell Press [ISBN 1903266424].

That year will also saw the publication of my third volume in the Story of Rovex Series and titled **'Hornby Railways'**. This was published by New Cavendish Books and covers the years 1972-1996 [ISBN 1904562000].

Also by this publisher and released in 2005 was Allen Levy's book **'Brilliantly Old Fashioned - The Story of ACE Gauge 0 Trains'** which provides much information about how ACE came into being and how the products have developed. This was followed in 2010 by **Part 2** which was a compilation of all printed material and published comment on the ACE Trains range.

In 2007 Barry Potter published his autobiography **'The Toy Job - A Lifetime of Toys and Trains'** (ISBN 9780955508608) which takes us behind the scenes of the auction and swapmeet business.

2009 saw the release of Paul Brookes' book **'The Illustrated Kemlows Story'** (ISBN 0956187901). This includes coloured illustrations of the entire range of Mastermodels and was published by Paul Brookes himself.

Also published in 2009 were two thick volumes containing the history of **'Bowman Steam Toys and Pond Yachts'** (ISBN 9780900443169 & ISBN 9780900443176).

2010 saw the publication of the book **'Bachmann Branchline Pocket Guide'** (ISBN 9781907292170) by myself. This provides an extensive listing and study of the Bachmann 00 Branchline range, as well as Brassworks and Underground Ernie.

In 2011 a useful book was published for collectors who like to have buildings on their layouts. This is Brian Salter's excellent volume on **'Building Toys'** (ISBN 9780747808152) in the Shire Library series. It covers Bayko, Lott's Bricks. Brickplayer, Arkitex and many other familiar makes.

Finally, 2011 saw the release of another important new comprehensive history. This is **'The Leeds Model Company 1912-2012'** (ISBN 0956910509) by David Peacock, which also includes a DVD containing two videos and over 100 excellent stills of the Leeds Stedman Trust Collection.

Thus, from a dearth of books in 1970, today we have quite a library to choose from and there is every indication that the choice will continue to grow as the cost of publishing 'short run' books falls.

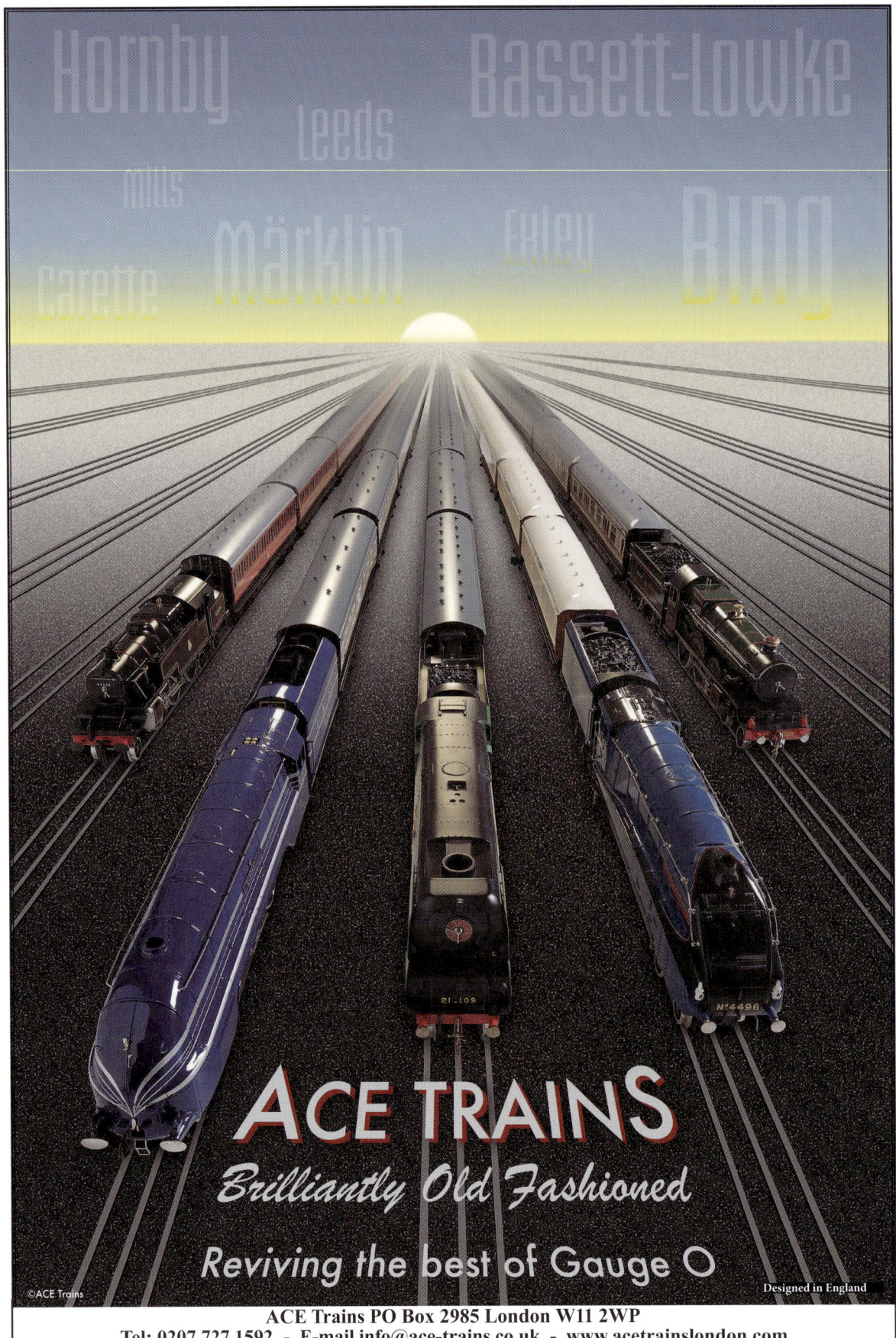

ACE Trains

HISTORY

ACE Trains originated from an arrangement to produce a limited run of electric Hornby replica 4-4-4 tank locomotives in Southern livery - the colour scheme most in demand with collectors. The parties to this arrangement were Ron Budd (the importer of Darstead Marklin style coaches) and Andries Grabowsky who acquired the Darstead business in the early 1990s.

This arrangement did not come to fruition and Allen Levy agreed to take on and expand the 4-4-4 project which was designated E/1. A company named Alchem Trains Ltd was formed in 1995 which commenced trading under the name ACE Trains.

The production and assembly of the 4-4-4T was initially concentrated in Taiwan and later at the Grabowsky family factory in Madras, India. Later still it moved to Bangkok. The 4-4-2 derivative of the E/1 followed. The locomotives were designed to run on all types of 3-rail tinplate standard track including that by Hornby, Marklin, Bing, JEP and MDF and also have an interchangeable rear coupling.

Freelance 4-4-2 tank engine [L1] (Ace)

The C/1 coach range, covering more railway systems than any former manufacturer, came on the market in 1999. The tin printing for this range was carried out by Cyril Luff in Wales who produced some of the last Hornby 0 gauge and Hornby Dublo tin printed sheets. A five-car Merseyside Express set became the last lithographed toy train product of the twentieth century. The Company introduced the first of a range of EMU units early in 2000.

A Class A4, with its cast alloy body, broke new ground in modern 0 gauge development and was followed by an A3 and a model of the GWR 'Castle' locomotive class.

Some impressive East Coast coach sets, incorporating articulated coaches, arrived in 2004 and 2005 and the first wagons, both petrol and milk tankers, fitted into the same time scale.

In 2005, ACE Trains adopted a practice, common between the wars, of initiating a generic 0-6-0 tender locomotive and changing its more prominent features such as cab, funnel, dome and tender to turn it into different classes of locomotive built by different railway companies.

There was also co-operation with Corgi (Bassett-Lowke), in respect of the 'Royal Scot' boxed set which was a train pack with a Bassett-Lowke loco and ACE coaches.

ACE Trains identified a gap in the market and have been successfully filling it. They have established a market not only in the UK but around the world and have agents in a number of countries.

A major change came when Len Mills, who had been the engineer behind the new Bassett-Lowke locomotives, left Corgi and started to work on the ACE Trains range. His influence can be seen in the beautiful GWR 'Castle' Class and LMS Stanier 2-6-4 tank locomotives, as well as the 'Schools' and Bulleid Pacific.

On May 11th, 2004, Alchem Trains Ltd had changed its name to The ACE Electric Train Co. Ltd and in 2008, Andries Grabowsky parted company with ACE Trains. Following the split, in 2009, production moved from Bangkok to China.

Further Reading

Allen Levy's book *Brilliantly Old Fashioned - The Story of ACE Gauge 0 Trains*, published in 2005, provides much information about how ACE came into being and how the products have developed. A second part, published in 2010, provides a collection of all printed material and press references concerning ACE Trains, as well as reproductions of correspondence.

LOCOMOTIVES

Motors - About 10 locos were supplied with 12V motors. 24v was standardised on all ACE Trains locomotives run on 6 - 20V and draw 0.7amp the distinction became academic.

Couplings - All couplings (on locos and coaches) are replaceable except the front hook on the LMS and Metropolitan EMUs and the front buffer couplings on the E/1 and E/2 locos. The Southern EMU units have replaceable couplings throughout but the coaches are without buffers as per the originals.

Cat No.	Company, Number, Colour, Date	£	£

Tank Locomotives

4-4-2T

L1.   Freelance 4-4-2T Engine (1997)

The E/2 series of locomotives was made in Taiwan. They are DC only and are fitted with a neutral switch allowing them to stand stationary on live track. They seem to have been based on an LNWR Whale 4-4-2T. Two cab styles were available for this short lived series. A German style 4-4-2T [E/2G] (after Marklin) with two domes was planned, but not put into production.

Cat No.	Company, Number, Colour, Date	£	£
E/2LB	22 LB&SCR brown gloss - 97	300	425
E/2LN	40 L&NWR black gloss - 97	300	400
E/2LM	6822 LMS maroon gloss - 97	200	270
E/2S	2001 Southern green gloss - 97	320	380
E/2BR	32085 BR black gloss - 97	250	320
E/2NZR	green NZR gloss Sp Edn (Railmaster Exports NZ) - 98	300	400

4-4-4T

L2.   Freelance 4-4-4T Engine (1996)

Made in Taiwan, this E/1 model was based on the 'No.2 Tank Engine' in the pre-war Hornby Series, which went out of production in 1929. The original models were available only with a clockwork mechanism but the E/1 locomotives by ACE Trains have 20v electric mechanisms with remote control in AC/DC. IS = in DC only with isolating switch.

Freelance 4-4-4 tank engine [L2] (Vectis)

Cat No.	Company, Number, Colour, Date	£	£
ECR/1	4-4-4 CR blue gloss or matt IS - 96	230	250
EMR/1	108 Metropolitan maroon gloss or matt - 96	200	220
EGW/1	7202 GWR green gloss or matt - 96	180	200
ELM/1	4-4-4 LMS maroon gloss or matt IS - 97	180	200
EMB/1	4-4-4 LMS black gloss or matt - 97	180	200
ELG/1	4-4-4 LNER green gloss or matt - 96	180	200
ELB/1	4-4-4 LNER black matt - 97	180	200
ESB/1	E492 SR black gloss or matt * IS - 96	250	300
ESG/1	B604 SR green gloss or matt * IS - 96	250	300
EET/1	2-2-2 ETAT black matt - 96	250	325
EPO/1	2-2-2 PO grey matt - 96	250	325
EPL/1	PLM red matt ** - 96	290	370
END/1	Nord brown matt - 96	250	294

ACE Trains

END/2	Nord green matt - *96*		250	325
EES/1	EST black matt - *96*		250	325
EES/2	EST brown matt - *96*		250	325
ENZ/1	NZR black matt - *96*		300	400

A total of 44 of the E/1 series in Southern livery were given a very large range of factory produced names at the request of customers (1996/97). These were gold transfers and were said to be in homage to the SR 'River' Class tanks. ** Some of the PLM version carried factory produced names on gold transfer nameplates.

0-6-0T

L3.   GWR Class 57xx 0-6-0PT (2013)
The model will be produced in association with ETS. The locomotive will have twin motors both incorporating a clutch mechanism. Correct GWR style and colour jewelled lamps will be provided.

E/21-A	**5764** Great Western gloss green - *?*		NPG	325
E/21-B	**7702** GWR (shirt button) gloss green - *?*		NPG	325
E/21-C	**5701** GWR gloss green - *?*		NPG	325
E/21-D	**5796** BRb plain black - *?*		NPG	325
E/21-E	**5775** BRc plain black - *?*		NPG	325
E/21-G	**L89** LT gloss red - *?*		NPG	325
E/21-H	**L91** LT gloss red - *?*		NPG	325

L4.   SR A1x Class 'Terrier' 0-6-0T (2013)
This model was still at the 'proposed' stage as we went to press.

SR 0-6-0 'Terrier' tank [L4] (Ace)

E/23	**70** *Poplar* LBSCR Stoudley livery - *?*		NPG	310
E/23	**82** *Boxhill* LBSCR Stoudley livery - *?*		NPG	310
E/23	**55** *Stepney* LBSCR Stoudley livery - *?*		NPG	310
E/23	**32635** *Brighton Works* LBSCR Stoudley livery - *?*		NPG	310

0-6-2T

L5.   LNER Class N2 0-6-2T (2011)
The centre drivers are flangeless on most models, in order to facilitate tight curves and there was an option of a smoke unit on 25 of the models. Fitted with a 2-rail/3-rail switch, the model was made by ETS with twin ETS motors fitted. Scottish versions of the locomotive did not have the prominent condensing pipes and so these are missing from the Scottish model. The locos have Jewelled lamps, 4 clear and 2 red as well as 4 white disks and destination boards for 'Kings +' and 'Hertford Nth'. The paint finishes are satin.

E/11A	**2674** LNER lined black - *11*		350	395
E/11B	**4744** LNER lined black - *11*		350	395
E/11C	**2587** LNER black Scottish non-condensing - *11*		350	395
E/11	**9522** LNER lined green - *11*		380	425
E/11H	**69506** BRc lined black - *11*		350	395
E/11D	**69529** BRa lined black - *11*		350	395
E/11E	**69538** BRb lined black - *11*		350	395
E/11G	**69569** BRc lined black (also shown as 69579 in some lists) - *11*		350	395

2-6-4T

L6.   LMS 2-6-4T Stanier 3-Cylinder Tank Engine (2009)
Made in China, these are of all metal construction and have all wheels flanged. They have sprung oval buffers, sprung bogies, jewelled lamps, removable code discs and are supplied with reversible destination boards. They have a 2-rail/3-rail switch, firebox glow, smoke generator and are 24V DC.

E/8	**2546** CR lined gloss blue 2-cylinder - *09*		400	495
E/8	**2524** LMS lined gloss black 3-cylinder - *09*		400	495
E/8	**2429** LMS lined gloss black 2-cylinder - *09*		400	495
E/8	**2526** LMS lined satin black 3-cylinder - *09*		400	495
E/8	**2546** LMS lined satin black 2-cylinder - *09*		400	495
E/8	**2465** LMS lined gloss maroon 2-cylinder - *09*		400	495
E/8	**42576** BRa lined gloss black 2-cylinder - *09*		400	495
E/8	**42510** BRa lined gloss black 3-cylinder - *09*		400	495
E/8	**42516** BRb lined gloss black 3-cylinder - *09*		400	495
E/8	**42608** BR lined gloss black 3-cylinder - *09*		400	495
E/8	**42534** BR lined satin black 3-cylinder - *09*		400	495
E/8	**42465** BR lined satin black 2-cylinder - *09*		400	495
E/8	**47546** BRc lined gloss green Ltd Edn - *09*		400	525

Stanier 3-cylinder 2-6-4 tank [L6] (Wallis & Wallis)

Tender Locomotives

4-4-0

L7.   Freelance 4-4-0 'Celebration' Class (2006)
Based on the 1920s Hornby 2711 and with Bassett-Lowke leanings, these are 24V DC electric. They have working front lights, an isolating switch are 3-rail only. They have an updated version of the E1 mechanism. These were made in Thailand using tooling from previous models. All are numbered 2006 with a GWR style number plate.

E/3	**2006** CR blue (also released in sets with 2 C/1 CR coaches) - *06*		180	200
E/3	**2006** LNWR black (also released in sets with 2 C/1 LNWR coaches) - *06*		180	200
E/3	**2006** *Prince William* LNWR black (also released in sets with 2 C/1 LNWR coaches) - *06*		180	200
E/3	**2006** NER green - *not made*		NA	NA
E/3	**2006** GCR black - *06*		155	170
E/3	**2006** *John H Kitchen* GCR black - *07*		180	200
E/3	**2006** *Butler Henderson* GCR black - *07*		180	200
E/3	**2006** LB&SCR brown - *06*		180	200
E/3	**2006** SECR green - *not made*		NA	NA
E/3	**2006** GWR green - *06*		170	190
E/3	**2006** GWR green with brass dome - *07*		170	190
E/3	**2006** LMS maroon - *06*		160	180
E/3	**2006** LMS black - *06*		160	180
E/3	**2024** LNER green - *06*		160	180
E/3	**2006** LNER green - *06*		160	180
E/3	**2006** LNER black - *06*		160	180
E/3	**2006** SR green - *06*		160	180
E/3	**2006** SR black - *06*		160	180
E/3	**2006** BR blue - *06*		160	180
E/3	**2006** *Prince William* BRb blue - *06*		160	180
E/3	**2006** BR black - *07*		160	180
E/3	**2006** P*rince William* BRb black (also released in sets with 2 C/1 BR coaches) - *07*		160	180
E/3	**62360** BR black - *?*		160	180
E/3	**2006** *Jay Beale* BRb black - *07*		200	249
E/3	**2006** EST black - *not made*		NA	NA
E/3	**2006** ETAT black - *not made*		NA	NA
E/3	**2006** Nord brown - *not made*		NA	NA
E/3	**2006** NSWGR green - *08*		200	249
E/3	**2006** NZR black - *08*		200	249
E/3	**2006** PLM green - *not made*		NA	NA
E/3	**2006** PO grey - *not made*		NA	NA
E/3	**2005** VR maroon - *08*		200	249

L8a.   GWR 'Bulldog' 4-4-0 (original deep frames) (2012)
These original 'Bulldogs' were produced in the ETS factory in Prague in The Czech Republic. They were followed by a straight framed versions, seen in the next table.

E/16-E	**3441** *Blackbird* Great Western plain green - *12*		400	495
E/16-E	**3449** *Nightingale* Great Western plain green - *12*		400	495

ACE Trains

E/16-E	3454 *Skylark* Great Western plain green - *12*		400	495
E/16-D	3441 *Blackbird* BRb black - *12*		400	495
E/16-D	3449 *Nightingale* BRb black - *12*		400	495
E/16-D	3454 *Skylark* BRb black - *12*		400	495

GWR 'Bulldog' Class 4-4-0 [L8a] (Ace)

L8b. GWR 'Bulldog' 4-4-0 (straight frames) (2013)

These later straight frame 'Bulldogs' were produced in the ETS factory in Prague in The Czech Republic.

E/16-G	3343 *Camelot* GWR lined green+Indian red - *13*	400	495
E/16-G	3349 *Lyonesse* GWR lined green+Indian red - *13*	400	495
E/16-G	3352 *Pendragon* GWR lined green+Indian red - *13*	400	495
E/16-H	3343 *Camelot* Great Western plain green - *13*	400	495
E/16-H	3349 *Lyonesse* Great Western plain green - *13*	400	495
E/16-H	3352 *Pendragon* Great Western plain green - *13*	400	495
E/16-K	3343 *Camelot* GWR (shirt button) green - *13*	400	495
E/16-K	3349 *Lyonesse* GWR (shirt button) green - *13*	400	495
E/16-K	3352 *Pendragon* GWR (shirt button) green - *13*	400	495

L9. SR 'Schools' Class 4-4-0 (2010)

Made in China, the model is fitted with a new 24V DC 4-coupled mechanism and has a 2-rail/3-rail switch. All locomotives come complete with six white code disks. Chimneys, as appropriate, are the Bulleid (le Maitre type) or the Maunsell original type. Both are supplied. The numbers given to *St. Trinnean's*, *Fettes* and *Gordonstoun* are the dates of their respective foundations. Models have their coloured areas in gloss and black areas in satin finish excluding black rims on coloured wheels. In addition to the official releases, you could order a loco with the name of any school of your own choice. The models for which there was a choice of names/numbers are shown as 'custom' in the table.

E/10A2	900 *Eton* SR olive green - *10*	NPG	545
E/10A1	E900 *Eton* SR olive green, no smoke deflectors - *10*	NPG	545
E/10E	926 *Repton* SR olive green - *10*	NPG	545
E/10L	custom SR olive green - *10*	NPG	545
E/10G	919 *Harrow* SR sage green - *10*	NPG	545
E/10H	908 *Westminster* SR wartime satin black - *10*	NPG	545
E/10P	custom SR wartime black - *10*	NPG	545
E/10C	935 *Sevenoaks* SR Malachite green - *10*	NPG	545
E/10M	custom SR malachite green - *10*	NOG	545
E/10D	30925 *Cheltenham* BRb gloss black - *10*	NPG	545
E/10R1	custom BRb lined gloss black - *10*	NPG	545
E/10R2	custom BRc lined gloss black - *10*	NPG	545
E/10	30928 *Stowe* BR green - *not made*	NA	NA
E/10B	30903 *Charterhouse* BRc gloss green - *10*	NPG	545
S/10S	custom BRc lined gloss green - *10*	NPG	545
E/10K2	1870 *St Fettes* CR blue ** - *10*	NPG	545
E/10K1	1933 *Gordonstoun* CR blue ** - *10*	NPG	545
E/10T	1885 *Roedean* navy blue *, female crew - *10*	NPG	545
E/10J	1922 *St Trinneans* pink, female crew *** - *10*	NPG	545

* Acknowledging the school's wartime link with HMS Vernon. ** Echoing Marklin's CR version of 1938. ***This has crossed Hockey Sticks suitably mounted on the loco.

0-6-0

L10. Cambrian Railways 0-6-0
This will be based on the LMS 4F (below) with modifications,

L11. CR McIntosh Class 812 0-6-0
Project abandoned for the time being.

L12. LMS Fowler Class 4F 0-6-0 (2013)
Made in China, the model is fitted with a mechanism similar to that used in the 2-6-4T E/8. They have a coal load in the tender, sprung buffers, detailed backhead and interchangeable couplings. They are fitted with 0-24V DC motors suitable for 2-rail and 3-rail operation.

E/5H	59 S&DJR lined gloss dark blue - *13*	275	325
E/5G	4328 LMS lined gloss maroon - *13*	275	325
E/5E	4422 LMS lined gloss black - *13*	275	325
E/5D	4454 LMS satin black - *13*	275	325
E/5C	44497 BRa satin black - *13*	275	325
E/5B	44252 BRb satin black - *13*	275	325
E/5A	44027 BRc gloss black - *13*	275	325

L13. NBR Holmes LNER Class J36 0-6-0
Project abandoned for the time being.

L14. GER/LNER J19 Class 0-6-0
This was advertised at the time of the SR Q Class 0-6-0 (below) and would have used the same basic parts. The tooling had been made at the time that the company split occurred and the models were produced by Darstaed the following year under the Vintage Trains label. Other 0-6-0 locomotives had been planned with common parts but, around 2007, with Len Mills joining the team at Ace Trains, the decision was taken not to proceed with generic locomotives but to concentrate on more accurate models.

E/5	8245 LNER green (number on tender) - *not made*	NA	NA
E/5	8141 LNER black - *not made*	NA	NA
E/5	64670 BR black - *not made*	NA	NA

SR Q Class 0-6-0 [L15] (Vectis)

L15. SR Q Class 0-6-0 (2006)
This was the first of the 0-6-0 range to be released and was made in Thailand. It has an ACE all axle geared chassis incorporating a helical gear drive and has a 24 volt DC motor with isolation switch and all axles driven. A 24volt AC version was available to order. The models are of diecast and sheet metal construction with three working front lights which have a sequence changer for route and load type. They have a coal load in the tender, sprung buffers, detailed backhead and interchangeable couplings.

E/5	541 SR black with Maunsell chimney - *06*	250	345
E/5	533 SR black with sunshine lettering - *07*	250	345
E/5	540 SR green with Maunsell chimney - *06*	250	345
E/5	30548 BRa black - *08*	250	345
E/5	30548 BRb black - *06*	250	345
E/5	30548 SAR black Ltd Edn 20 (Australia) - *08*	250	345
E/5	30548 NZR black Ltd Edn (New Zealand) - *08*	250	345

4-6-0

L16. GWR 'Castle' Class 4-6-0 (2008)
Models in the first series of 'Castles' were made in Thailand, while later ones, including those produced for Modelfair, were made in China. These are marked in the table below with a 'C'. Both 2-rail and 3-rail versions were planned. The models are 24V DC (AC to order), have a diecast body, twin motors driving all 3 axles through a gearbox, working front lights, firebox glow, detailed backhead, new wheel patterns and were available as single and double chimney (dc) versions. In order to simplify construction of the E/7 range, from mid March 2008, the single motor version fitted with the ACE/Mills motor was available at a lower price. All E/7 locos are supplied with either BR or GWR headboards with reporting numbers for the 'Cornish Riviera', 'Torbay Express', 'The Bristolian' or 'The Red Dragon'.

dc = double chimney.

Great Western - Green			
E/7	100 *100 A1 Lloyds* - *09?*	600	695

ACE Trains

E/7	111 *Viscount Churchill* - 09?	600	695
E/7	4016 *Knight of the Golden Fleece* - 09?	600	695
E/7	4073 *Caerphilly Castle* - 08	600	695
E/7	4079 *Pendennis Castle* - 08	600	695
E/7	4081 *Warwick Castle* - 08	600	695
E/7	4082 *Windsor Castle* - 08	600	695
E/7	4095 *Harlech Castle* - 09?	600	695
E/7	4096 *Highclere Castle* - 09?	600	695
E7/1	5000 *Launceston Castle* C Sp Edn 5 (Modelfair.com) - 08	670	695
E7/1	5001 *Llandovery Castle* C Sp Edn 5 (Modelfair.com) - 08	670	695
E/7	5002 *Ludlow Castle* - 08	600	695
E/7	5009 *Shrewsbury Castle* - 08	600	695
E/7	5011 *Tintagel Castle* - 08	600	695
E7/1	5013 *Abergavenny Castle* C Sp Edn 5 (Modelfair.com) - 08	670	695
E/7A	5018 *St.Mawes Castle* C - 08	600	695
E/7C	5069 *Isambard Kingdom Brunel* C - 08	600	695
E7/1	5070 *Sir Daniel Gooch* C Sp Edn 5 (Modelfair.com) - 08	670	695
E7/1	5071 *Spitfire* shirt button – 11?	400	425
E7/1	5072 *Hurricane* C Sp Edn 5 (Modelfair.com) - 08	670	695
E7/1	5079 *Lydander* shirt button – 11?	400	425
E7/1	5071 *Defiiant* shirt button – 11?	400	425
E/7	7007 *Great Western* – ?	600	695
E/7	7013 *Bristol Castle* - made?	NPG	NPG
E/7	7023 *Penrice Castle* - 09?	600	695
E/7J	7029 *Clun Castle* C - 08	600	695
E7/1	7029 *Great Western* C Sp Edn 5 (Modelfair.com) - 08	670	695
E/7M	custom - 11	NPG	425
E/7N	custom GWR (button) - 11	NPG	425

E/7G	7013 *Bristol Castle* BRb C - 08	600	695
E/7H	7013 *Bristol Castle* BRc dc C - 08	600	695
E/7K	7029 *Clun Castle* BRb C - 08	600	695
E/7L	7029 *Clun Castle* BRc dc C - 08	600	695
E7/1	7029 *Great Western* C Sp Edn 5 (Modelfair.com) - 08	670	695
E7/1	7037 *Swindon* - 08	600	695

BR Experimental 'Pea' Green *

E7/2	4091 *Dudley Castle* BRb C Sp Edn 50 (Modelfair) - 08	630	725
E7/2	5010 *Restormel Castle* BRb C Sp Edn 50 (Modelfair) - 08	630	725
E/7V	5010 *Avondale Castle* BRa C Sp Edn (Modelfair) - 08	630	725
E/7T	5023 *Brecon Castle* BRa C Sp Edn (Modelfair) - 08	600	695
E7/2W	7011 *Banbury Castle* BRa C Sp Edn 50 (Modelfair) - 08	630	725
E/7P	custom BRb - 11	NPG	NPG
E/7Q	custom BRc - 11	NPG	NPG
E/7R	custom BRc dc - 11	NPG	NPG

GWR (button) Wartime Plain Green **

E7/3X	5071 *Spitfire* C Sp Edn 24 (Modelfair) *** - 08	640	725
E7/3Y	5079 *Lysander* C Sp Edn 24 (Modelfair) *** - 08	640	725
E7/3Z	5080 *Defiant* C Sp Edn 24 (Modelfair) *** - 08	640	725

* In commemoration of the 60th Anniversary of Nationalisation of the railways. ** With plated over cab windows. *** with wartime blocked cab window.

L17. LMS 'Black 5' 4-6-0 (2013)

This model will be fitted with a 24V motor and is suitable for 2-rail and 3-rail DC (only) operation. Full Details and specification to be announced.

E19A	5294 LMS lined gloss black - 13	500	595
E19E	M4763 BRs experimental light green - 13	500	595
E19B	45158 *Glasgow Yeomanry* BRa lined gloss black - 13	500	595
E19C	45126 BRb lined gloss black - 13	500	595
E19D	45154 *Lanarkshire Yeomanry* BRc lined gloss black - 13	500	595

L18. LMS 'Jubilee' 4-6-0 (2013)

This model will be fitted with a 24V motor and is suitable for 2-rail and 3-rail DC (only) operation. Full Details and specification to be announced.

E18A	5552 *Silver Jubilee* LMS lined gloss black - 13	NPG	NPG
E18G	5573 *Newfoundland* LMS gloss maroon - 13	NPG	NPG
E18H	5692 *Leander* LMS gloss maroon - 13	NPG	NPG
E18J	5699 *Galatea* LMS gloss maroon - 13	NPG	NPG
E18K	5701 *Conquerer* LMS gloss maroon - 13	NPG	NPG
E18L	5712 *Victory* LMS gloss maroon - 13	NPG	NPG
E18G	45610 *Gold Coast* BRa gloss black - 13	NPG	NPG
E18B	45565 *Victoria* BR experimental light green - 13	NPG	NPG
E18D	45593 *Kolhapur* BRb gloss green - 13	NPG	NPG
E18E	45596 *Bahamas* BRc gloss green - 13	NPG	NPG

4-6-2

L19. LMS 'Duchess' 4-6-2 (2013)

This model is fitted with 0-24V motor suitable for 2-rail and 3-rail operation (DC only). Full Details and specification to be announced.

E12D	6231 *Duchess of Athol* LMS gloss maroon, no smoke deflectors - 13	NPG	NPG
E12E	6233 *Duchess of Sutherland* LMS gloss maroon - 13	NPG	NPG
E12J	6235 *City of Birmingham* LMS gloss lined black, semi - 13	NPG	NPG
E12P	6256 *Sir William Stanier* FRS LMS gloss lined black - 13	NPG	NPG
E12K	46241 *City of Edinburgh* BR gloss blue, semi - 13	NPG	NPG
E12L	46224 *King George Vi* BR gloss express blue, semi - 13	NPG	NPG
E12G	46232 *Duchess of Montrose* BRb gloss green - 13	NPG	NPG
E12H	46221 *Queen Elizabeth* BRc gloss green - 13	NPG	NPG
E12M	46245 *City of London* BRc gloss maroon - 13	NPG	NPG
E12N	6256 *Sir William Stanier* FRS BRc gloss maroon - 13	NPG	NPG

GWR 'Castle' Class 4-6-0 [L16] (Wallis & Wallis)

BRc Green

E/7	4073 *Caerphilly Castle* - 08	600	695
E/7	4079 *Pendennis Castle* - 08	600	695
E/7	4081 *Warwick Castle* - 08	600	695
E/7	4082 *Windsor Castle* - 08	600	695
E7/1	5000 *Launceston Castle* C Sp Edn 5 (Modelfair.com) - 08	670	695
E7/1	5001 *Llandovery Castle* C Sp Edn 5 (Modelfair.com) - 08	670	695
E/7	5002 *Ludlow Castle* - 08	600	695
E/7	5009 *Shrewsbury Castle* - 90?	600	695
E/7	5009 *Leonard Castle* Sp Edn - 90?	600	695
E/7	5011 *Tintagel Castle* - 08	600	695
E7/1	5013 *Abergavenny Castle* C Sp Edn 5 (Modelfair.com) - 08	670	695
E/7B	5018 *St.Mawes Castle* BRb C - 08	600	695
E/7	5029 *Nunney Castle* - 08	600	695
E7/1	5043 *Earl of Mount Edgecumbe* BR C – 11?	400	425
E/7S	5043 *Earl of Mount Edgecumbe* BRb dc Sp Edn (MAAT) – 08?	670	750
E/7D	5069 *Isambard Kingdom Brunel* BRb C - 08	600	695
E/7E	5069 *Isambard Kingdom Brunel* BRc dc C - 08	600	695
E7/1	5070 *Sir Daniel Gooch* C Sp Edn 5 (Modelfair.com) - 08	670	695
E7/1	5072 *Hurricane* C Sp Edn 5 (Modelfair.com) - 08	670	695

ACE Trains

LMS 'Coronation' Class [L20] (Ace)

LNER A3 Class [L21] (Tony Wright)

L20. LMS Streamlined 'Coronation' 4-6-2 (2013)
A range of liveries is planned. Fitted with 0-24V DC motor suitable for 2-rail and 3-rail, Full details and specification to be announced.

E12A	6220 *Coronation* LMS gloss blue - *13*	NPG	NPG
E12B	6229 *Duchess of Hamilton* LMS gloss maroon - *13*	NPG	NPG
E12C	6247 *City of Liverpool* LMSplain satin black - *13*	NPG	NPG

L21. LNER A1/A3 Class 4-6-2 (2006)
Based on the A4 chassis with disc wheeled tender, the A3 models were made in Thailand. The model is 3-rail with twin 12/24V DC motors (24AC to special order), each driving opposed spindles. Power is transferred to all 3 axles through a series of gears. Generally speaking, those locos in Doncaster green have a round dome and those in other liveries have a banjo dome. In 2006 a batch of one-off models was produced for Modelfair which they advertised for sale in September 2006. These unique models are marked M. sd = smoke deflectors. dc = double chimney

	LNER Doncaster Green		
E/6	2500 *Windsor Lad* - *06*	450	500
E/6	2502 *Hyperion* banjo dome M - *06*	700	750
E/6	2506 *Salmon Trout* banjo dome M - *06*	700	750
E/6	2508 *Brown Jack* banjo dome M - *06*	700	750
E/6	2545 *Diamond Jubilee* - *06*	450	500
E/6	2547 *Doncaster* - *06*	450	500
E/6	2550 *Blink Bonny* - not made	NA	NA
E/6	2563 *William Whitelaw* - *06*	450	500
E/6	2598 *Blenheim* - *06*	450	500
E/6	2743 *Felstead* - *06*	450	500
E/6	2744 *Grand Parade* - *06*	450	500
E/6	2745 *Captain Cuttle* - *06*	450	500
E/6	2748 *Colorado* banjo dome M - *06*	700	750
E/6	2749 *Flamingo* - *06*	450	500
E/6	2750 *Papyrus* - *06*	450	500
E/6	4427 *Flying Scotsman* - *06*	450	500
E/6	4427 *Flying Scotsman* banjo dome - *06*	450	500
E/6	4427 *Flying Scotsman* sd as preserved - *06*	450	500
E/6	4427 *Flying Scotsman* with 2 tenders (for USA) - *06*	850	900
E/6	4475 *Flying Fox* - *06*	450	500
	NE Wartime Black		
E/6	2500 *Windsor Lad* - *06*	450	500
E/6	2545 *Diamond Jubilee* - *06*	450	500
E/6	2550 *Blink Bonny* - *06*	450	500
E/6	2744 *Grand Parade* - *06*	450	500
E/6	2750 *Papyrus* - *06*	450	500
E/6	2752 *Spion Kop* - *06*	450	500
	Post-War LNER Green		
E/6	65 Knight of the Thistle - *06*	450	500
E/6	60037 *Hyperion* banjo dome - *06*	450	500
E/6	60041 *Salmon Trout* banjo dome - *06*	450	500
E/6	60043 *Brown Jack* banjo dome - *06*	450	500
E/6	60094 *Colorado* banjo dome - *06*	450	500
	BRb Express Blue		
E/6	5 4 57 *Anglo Thai* (assumed a one-off) - *06?*	700	750
E/6	60035 *Windsor Lad* - *06*	450	500
E/6	60037 *Hyperion* M - *06*	700	750
E/6	60038 *Firdaussi* - *06*	450	500
E/6	60046 *Diamond Jubilee* - *06*	450	500
E/6	60051 *Blink Bonny* - *06*	450	500
E/6	60053 *Sansovino* M - *06*	700	750
E/6	60061 *Pretty Polly* - *06*	450	500
E/6	60063 *Isinglass* - *06*	450	500
E/6	60066 *Merry Hampton* - *06*	450	500
E/6	60069 *Sceptre* M - *06*	700	750
E/6	60090 *Grand Parade* - *06*	450	500
E/6	60096 *Papyrus* - *06*	450	500
-	60100 *Spearmint* M - *06*	700	750
E/6	60103 *Flying Scotsman* - *06*	450	480
	Thompson Blue		
E/6	60084 *Trigo* - *06*	450	500
	BRb Brunswick Green		
E/6	60035 *Windsor Lad* dc - *06*	450	500
E/6	60038 *Firdaussi* dc M - *06*	700	750
E/6	60039 *Sandwich* sd M - *06*	700	750
E/6	60041 *Salmon Trout* - *06*	450	500
E/6	60046 *Diamond Jubilee* dc - *06*	450	500
E/6	60048 *Doncaster* - *06*	450	500
E/6	60049 *Galtee More* sd M - *06*	700	750
E/6	60050 *Persimmon* sd M - *06*	700	750
E/6	60051 *Blink Bonny* dc sd - *06*	450	500
E/6	60052 *Prince Palatine* - *06*	450	500
E/6	60055 *Woolwinder* - *06*	450	500
E/6	60058 *Blair Athol* - *06*	450	500
E/6	60060 *The Tetrarch* - *06*	450	500
E/6	60063 *Isinglass* dc M - *06*	700	750
E/6	60064 *Tagalie* - *06*	450	500
E/6	60068 *Sir Visto* - *06*	450	500
E/6	60070 *Gladiateur* - *06*	450	500
E/6	60072 *Sunstar* dc M - *06*	700	750
E/6	60073 *St Gatien* - *06*	450	500
E/6	60077 *White Knight* sd M - *06*	700	750
E/6	60078 *Knight Hawk* sd M - *06*	700	750
E/6	60079 *Bayardo* - *06*	450	500
E/6	60080 *Dick Turpin* - *06*	450	500
E/6	60083 *Sir Hugo* - *06*	450	500
E/6	60087 *Blenheim* - *06*	450	500
E/6	60088 *Book Law* sd M - *06*	700	750
E/6	60090 *Grand Parade* dc - *06*	450	500
E/6	60090 *Grand Parade* dc sd - *06*	450	500
E/6	60093 *Coronach* - *06*	450	500
E/6	60095 *Flamingo* - *06*	450	500
E/6	60096 *Papyrus* dc sd - *06*	450	500
E/6	60098 *Spion Cop* - *06*	450	500
E/6	60100 *Spearmint* - *06*	450	500
E/6	60101 *Cicero* BRb M - *06*	700	750
E/6	60103 *Flying Scotsman* dc sd - *06*	450	500
E/6	60104 *Solario* dc M - *06*	700	750
E/6	60105 *Victor Wild* - *06*	450	500
E/6	60106 *Flying Fox* - *06*	450	500
E/6	60107 *Royal Lancer* - *06*	450	500
E/6	60110 *Robert the Devil* - *06*	450	500
E/6	60111 *Enterprise* dc M - *06*	700	750

The locomotive is also available with blank nameplates and unnumbered.

ACE Trains

LNER Class A4 [L22] (Ace)

L22. LNER A4 4-6-2 (2003)

All of the A4 models were made in Thailand. Purchasers could choose their own names and numbers and all models were produced in 3-rail only. For the first three years the models were produced as AC/DC but, after that, as DC only. The loco body is pressure diecast and the tender is made from brass (corridor or non-corridor). The loco is fitted with matching twin 24v motors driving all 3 axles and with an isolating switch. The models have working headlights and firebox glow. Single and double chimney versions were available and the second batch had smaller lamps. By the start of 2005 the diecast body had been amended to improve lining band details on fully lined types such as BR and green LNER.

	LNER Silver Grey with Valances		
E/4	2509 *Silver Link* - 04	550	685
E/4	2510 *Quicksilver* - 04	550	685
E/4	2511 *Silver King* - 04	550	685
E/4	2512 *Silver Fox* - 04	550	685
	LNER Doncaster Green with Valances		
E/4	4463 *Sparrow Hawk* - 05	550	685
E/4	4467 *Wild Swan* - 05	550	685
E/4	4482 *Golden Eagle* - 05	550	685
E/4	4483 *Kingfisher* - 05	550	685
E/4	4484 *Falcon* - 05	550	685
E/4	4485 *Kestrel* - 05	550	685
E/4	4486 *Merlin* - 05	550	685
E/4	4487 *Sea Eagle* - 05	550	685
E/4	4489 *Woodcock* - 05	550	685
E/4	4494 *Osprey* - 05	600	700
E/4	7143 *Frank Hornby** Ltd Edn 4 - 05	800	900
E/4	7144 *WJ Bassett-Lowke** Ltd Edn 3 - 05	800	900
E/4	7145 *Stanley Beeson** Ltd Edn 2 - 05	800	900
E/4	7146 *RF Stedman** Ltd Edn 2 - 05	800	900
E/4	7147 *WHG Mills** Ltd Edn 1 - 05	800	900
E/4	7148 *Edward Exley** Ltd Edn 2 - 05	800	900
E/4	7149 *Gebruder Bing** Ltd Edn 2 - 05	800	900
E/4	7150 *Georges Carette** Ltd Edn 3 - 05	800	900
E/4	7151 *Gebruder Marklin** Ltd Edn 2 - 05	800	900
E/4	7152 *Joshua Lionel Cowen** Ltd Edn 3 - 05	800	900
E/4	7153 *J E Fournereau** Ltd Edn - 05	800	900
E/4	7154 *Henry Greenly** Ltd Edn - 05	800	900
E/4	7155 *Andries Grabowsky** Ltd Edn - 05	800	900
E/4	7156 *Count Giansanti Coluzzi** Ltd Edn 1 - 05	800	900
E/4	7157 *Marcel Darphin** Ltd Edn 1 - 05	800	900
E/4	7158 *Allen Levy** Ltd Edn - 05	800	900
E/4	7159 *Leonard W Mills** Ltd Edn - 05	800	900
E/4	7160 *Robert Marescot** Ltd Edn - 05	800	900
	LNER Garter Blue With Valances		
E/4	2512 *Silver Fox* - 03	550	685
E/4	4462 *Great Snipe* - 03	550	685
E/4	4464 *Bittern* - not made	NA	NA
E/4	4466 *Sir Ralph Wedgewood* - not made	NA	NA
E/4	4468 *Mallard* - 03	550	685
E/4	4482 *Golden Eagle* - 03	550	685
E/4	4483 *Kingfisher* - not made	NA	NA
E/4	4485 *Kestrel* - not made	NA	NA
E/4	4486 *Merlin* - not made	NA	NA
E/4	4488 *Union of South Africa* - not made	NA	NA
E/4	4489 *Woodcock* - not made	NA	NA
E/4	4489 *Dominion of Canada* - 03	550	685
E/4	4490 *Empire of India* - 03	550	685
E/4	4491 *Commonwealth of Australia* - not made	NA	NA
E/4	4492 *Dominion of New Zealand* - 03	550	685
E/4	4494 *Osprey* - 03	550	685
E/4	4495 *Golden Fleece* - 03	550	685
E/4	4496 *Golden Shuttle* - not made	NA	NA
E/4	4496 *Dwight D Eisenhower* - not made	NA	NA
E/4	4497 *Golden Plover* - 03	550	685
E/4	4498 *Sir Nigel Gresley* - 03	550	685
E/4	4901 *Capercaillie* - not made	NA	NA
E/4	4902 *Seagull* - not made	NA	NA
E/4	4903 *Peregrine* - not made	NA	NA
E/4	7160 *Terence Cuneo** Ltd Edn 10 - 03	800	900

LNER Class A4 in wartime black [L22] (Vectis)

	NE Black Without Valances		
E/4	2512 *Silver Fox* - 05	550	685
E/4	4468 *Mallard* - 05	550	685
E/4	4469 *Wild Swan* - 05	550	685
E/4	4467 *Sir Ralph Wedgewood* - 05	550	685
E/4	4493 *Woodcock* - 05	550	685
E/4	4494 *Andrew K McCosh* - 05	550	685
E/4	4498 *Sir Nigel Gresley* - 03	550	685
E/4	4901 *Capercailie* - 05	550	685
E/4	4901 *Sir Charles Newton* - 05	550	685
E/4	4903 *Peregrine* - 05	550	685
	LNER Garter Blue Without Valances		
E/4	6 *Sir Ralph Wedgewood* - not made	NA	NA
E/4	7 *Sir Nigel Gresley* - 03	550	685
E/4	8 *Dwight D Eisenhower* - not made	NA	NA
E/4	9 *Union of South Africa* - not made	NA	NA
E/4	10 *Dominion of Canada* - not made	NA	NA
E/4	11 *Empire of India* - not made	NA	NA0
E/4	12 *Commonwealth of Australia* - 03	550	685
E/4	13 *Dominion of New Zealand* - not made	NA	NA
E/4	14 *Silver Fox* - 03	550	685
E/4	19 *Bittern* - not made	NA	NA
E/4	22 *Mallard* - not made	NA	NA
E/4	23 *Golden Eagle* - not made	NA	NA
E/4	24 *Kingfisher* - not made	NA	NA
E/4	27 *Merlin* - not made	NA	NA
E/4	30 *Golden Fleece* - not made	NA	NA
E/4	4468 *Mallard* - 03	550	685
E/4	4469 *Sir Ralph Wedgwood* - 03	550	685
E/4	4483 *Kingfisher* - 03	550	685
E/4	4486 *Merlin* - 03	550	685
E/4	4489 *Dominion of Canada* - 03	550	685
E/4	4496 *Dwight D Eisenhower* - 03	550	685
E/4	? *Reg Saxton** Ltd Edn 1 - 05	800	900
	BRa Garter Blue		
E/4	60006 *Sir Ralph Wedgewood* - 03	550	685
E/4	60022 *Mallard* - 03	550	685
E/4	60024 *Kingfisher* - 03	550	685
E/4	60034 *Lord Farringdon* Ltd Edn 3 - 05	800	900
	BRa Thompson Blue (red lining)		
E/4	60024 *Kingfisher* - 03	550	685
E/4	60027 *Merlin* - 03	550	685
E/4	60028 *Walter K Whigham* - 03	550	685
E/4	60029 *Woodcock* - 03	550	685
	BRb Express Blue (white lining)		
E/4	60007 *Sir Nigel Gresley* Sp Edn (A4 Society) - 03	550	685
E/4	60010 *Dominion of Canada* - 03	550	685
E/4	60012 *Commonwealth of Australia* - 03	550	685
E/4	60020 *Guillemot* - 03	550	685
E/4	60022 *Mallard* - 03	550	685
E/4	60032 *Gannet* - 03	550	685

ACE Trains

BR A4 Class 'Bittern' with double tender [L22] (Vectis)

	BRb & BRc Brunswick green		
E/4	7160 *Terence Cuneo** Ltd Edn 1 (presented to Carol Cuneo) - *05?*	800	900
E/4	60003 *Andrew K McCosh* - *03*	550	685
E/4	60007 *Sir Nigel Gresley* BRb - *03*	550	685
E/4	60008 *Dwight D Eisenhower* BRb - *03*	550	685
E/4	60009 *Union of South Africa* - *03*	550	685
E/4	60010 *Dominion of Canada* - *03*	550	685
E/4	60011 *Empire of India* BRb - *03*	550	685
E/4	60012 *Commonwealth of Australia* - *03*	550	685
E/4	60013 *Dominion of New Zealand* - *03*	550	685
E/4	60016 *Silver King* - *04*	550	685
E/4	60017 *Silver Fox* - *03*	550	685
E/4	60019 *Sparrow Hawk* - *03*	550	685
E/4	60019 *Bittern* BRb - *03*	550	685
E/4	60019 *Bittern* BRc dc Sp Edn double tender - *05?*	1100	1300
E/4	60022 *Mallard* - *03*	550	685
E/4	60024 *Kingfisher* - *03*	550	685
E/4	60025 *Falcon* - *03*	550	685
E/4	60026 *Miles Beevor* - *03*	550	685
E/4	60027 *Merlin* - *03*	550	685
E/4	60029 *Woodcock* - *03*	550	685
E/4	60031 *Golden Plover* - *03*	550	685
E/4	60032 *Gannet* - *03*	550	685
E/4	60033 *Seagull* - *04*	550	685
E/4	60034 *Lord Farringdon* Ltd Edn 3 - *03*	800	900

* This was fictitious.

In association with John Shawe, a high pressure live steam version of the A4 has been developed which uses the A4 body. Marketed under the name ACE/Shawe, this was developed by The ACE Live Steam Locomotive Company Ltd. It had its inaugural run in 2007 running for over 35 minutes on one filling of spirit. It pulled 15 LNER 'teak' coaches.

SR 'Battle of Britain' Class [L23] (Ace)

L23. SR Class BB/WC 'Spamcan' Bulleid 4-6-2 (2009)

This is a 2-rail/3-rail model fitted with 24V DC motors and an isolating switch and all wheels are flanged. Most of the range were initially released with 'Golden Arrow' boards and flags as well as 'Devon Belle' boards and 4 white discs. But later these were sold with 'Atlantic Express' boards and discs, the other extras being sold separately.

	Lined Malachite Green		
E/9-B	21C108 *Padstow* SR - *09*	500	595
E/9-D	21C123 *Blackmoor* Vale SR - *09*	500	595
E/9-E	21C136 *Westward* Ho SR - *09*	500	595
E/9-K	21C165 *Hurricane* SR - *09*	500	595
E/9-M	21C167 *Tangmere* SR - *09*	500	595
E/9-R	21C167 *Leonard Cheshire* VC SR Sp Edn of 1 (Leonard Cheshire Homes) - *10*	1400	1500
E/9R	custom SR - *09*	550	635
E/9	34056 *Croydon* BRa - *made?*	NPG	NPG
E/9-P	34090 *Sir Eustace Missenden* BRb Sp Edn 1 - *09*	1200	1300
	Photographic Grey		
E/9-H	21C164 *(Fighter Command)* SR - *09*	500	595
	BR Gloss Lined Green		
E/9-A	34001 *Exeter* - *09*	500	595
E/9-C	34015 *Exmouth* - *09*	500	595
E/9-G	34051 *Winston Churchill* BRb - *09*	500	595
E/9-J	34064 *Fighter Command* - *09*	500	595
E/9-L	34066 *Spitfire* - *09*	500	595
E/9R	custom BR - *09*	550	635
E/9-S	34617 *Leonard Cheshire* VC SR Sp Edn of 1 (auctioned) - *10*	1400	1500

Metropolitan electric locomotive [L24] (Ace)

Electric Locomotive

L24 Metropolitan Vickers Bo-Bo Electric (2012)

This was developed with ETS. Both bogies are motorised with 2-axle drive on each. The model is fitted with 0-24V motor suitable for 2-rail and 3-rail operation in DC. It has a lithographed body casing, steel chassis and detailed roof. There are directional, cab and driving lights, clear and frosted window glazing on all windows and four integrated flasher units.

E/17-A	2 *Oliver Cromwell* Met brown - *12*	275	325
E/17-C	8 *Sherlock Holmes* Met brown - *12*	275	325
E/17-E	12 *Sarah Siddons* Met brown - *12*	275	325
E/17-J	15 *Wembley* 1924 Met brown - *12*	275	325
E/17-K	19 Met brown - *12*	275	325
E/17-L	18 *Michael Faraday* Met brown - *12*	275	325
E/17-?	13 *Dick Whittington* Met brown + Met bogie coaches, ex-150th Metropolitan Railway Anniversary set - *13*	NA	495
E/17-D	8 *Sherlock Holmes* LT red - *12*	275	325
E/17-G	12 *Sarah Siddons* LT red - *12*	275	325
E/17-H	14 LT wartime grey - *13*	275	325
E/17-M	18 *Michael Faraday* LT red - *12*	275	325
E/17-B	5 *John Hampton* - LT red - *12*	275	325

L25. Westinghouse Steeple Cab Bo-Bo (2013)
Under development.

Electric Multiple Units

L26. 3-Car & 4-Car EMUs (1999)

Made in India, all units comprise a powered motor coach (DC only) with 3rd class accommodation, a first class coach and a dummy 3rd class motor coach. All are tin printed and have punched out windows. Extra trailer cars for these sets were available.

C1E/LM	**LMS** maroon Broad Street - Richmond 3-car unit - *99*	250	295
C1	**LMS** maroon extra trailer car for above - *99*	55	65
C1E/Met	**Metropolitan** brown Baker Street - Harrow 4-car unit - *99*	250	295
C1	**Metropolitan** brown extra trailer car for above - *99*	55	65
C1E/S	**SR 1973** (1528/1664/1783) green 3-car unit V and L route boards carried, white roof - *00*	370	420
C1E/S	**SR 1973** (1528/1664/1783) green 3-car unit V and L route boards carried, grey roof - *00*	370	420
C1	**SR 1664** green extra car route boards - *00*	48	55
C/1G	3-car German Triebwagen set with pantograph - *03?*	450	495

8th Edition

ACE Trains

LMS 3-car EMU [L26] (Special Auction Services)

L27. 4CEP/BEP 2-Car EMU (2013)
Units comprise a powered motor coach and a dummy motor coach. They will be made in China and sold as a 2-car unit.

C/17	S61389 motor coach BR SR coach green	NPG	NPG
C/17	S61388 driving trailer BR SR coach green	NPG	NPG
C/17	above two as set BR SR coach green - 12	NPG	NPG

L28 Brighton Belle 5-BEL 5-Car EMU
This model was being made in China, including car interiors and working table lamps. However, in the light of the release of the Darstaed 'Brighton Belle', its future is in question.

	Pullman Chocolate & Cream		
C/17	No.88 Motor/Brake livery	NPG	NA
C/17	No.86 3rd Parlour Car	NPG	NA
C/17	No.89 Dummy Motor/Brake	NPG	NA
set 3051	above 3 cars for unit 3051	NA	NPG
C/17	Doris 1st class kitchen car for unit 3051	NPG	NPG
C/17	Hazel 1st class kitchen car for unit 3051	NPG	NPG
C/17	No.90 Motor/Brake livery	NPG	NA
C/17	No.87 3rd Parlour Car	NPG	NA
C/17	No.91 Dummy Motor/Brake	NPG	NA
set 3052	above 3 cars for unit 3052	NA	NPG
C/17	Audrey 1st class kitchen car for unit 3052	NPG	NPG
C/17	Vera 1st class kitchen car for unit 3052	NPG	NPG
C/17	No.92 Motor/Brake livery	NPG	NA
C/17	No.85 3rd Parlour Car	NPG	NA
C/17	No.93 Dummy Motor/Brake	NPG	NA
set 3053	above 3 cars for unit 3053	NA	NPG
C/17	Gwen 1st class kitchen car for unit 3053	NPG	NPG
C/17	Mona 1st class kitchen car for unit 3053	NPG	NPG

COACHES

Cat No.	Company, Number, Colour, Date	£	£

C1. Clemenson 6-Wheel Stock
These coaches are sold in sets of three made up of a composite 1st/3rd (or all 1st), a full 3rd and a brake 3rd. They have a working rear light and are suitable for 2-rail and 3-rail and 2ft curves. Clerestory roofs are available for separate sets of 3. An Ace interior kit is included with each set.. These were made in China.

C/24	LMS 1st/3rd maroon	50	NA
C/24	LMS all 3rd maroon	50	NA
C/24	LMS brake 3rd maroon	50	NA
Set 1	above 3 LMS coaches	NA	175
C/24	LNER 1st/3rd teak	50	NA
C/24	LNER all 3rd teak	50	NA
C/24	LNER brake 3rd teak	50	NA
Set 2	above 3 LNER coaches	NA	175
C/24	SR 1st/3rd green	45	NA
C/24	SR all 3rd green	45	NA
C/24	SR brake 3rd green	45	NA
Set 3	above 3 SR coaches	NA	160
C/24	GWR 1st/3rd brown+cream	50	NA
C/24	GWR all 3rd brown+cream	50	NA
C/24	GWR brake 3rd brown+cream	50	NA
Set 4	above 3 GWR coaches	NA	175
C/24	LNWR 1st/3rd very dark brown+white	45	NA
C/24	LNWR all 3rd very dark brown+white	45	NA
C/24	LNWR brake 3rd very dark brown+white	45	NA
Set 5	above 3 LNWR coaches	NA	160
C/24	LSWR 1st/3rd pink+very dark brown	45	NA
C/24	LSWR all 3rd pink+very dark brown	45	NA
C/24	LSWR brake 3rd pink+very dark brown	45	NA
Set 6	above 3 LSWR coaches	NA	160
C/24	CR 1st/3rd plum+white	45	NA
C/24	CR all 3rd plum+white	45	NA
C/24	CR brake 3rd plum+white	45	NA
Set 7	above 3 CR coaches	NA	160
C/24	Met all 1st teak	45	NA
C/24	Met all 3rd teak	45	NA
C/24	Met brake 3rd teak	45	NA
Set 8	above 3 Metropolitan coaches	NA	160
C/24	NZR all 1st maroon	50	NA
C/24	NZR all 3rd maroon	50	NA
C/24	NZR brake 3rd maroon	50	NA
Set 8	above 3 Metropolitan coaches	NA	175

Clemenson 6-wheel LMS all 3rd [C1] (Ace)

Tin printed and manufactured in India. Some coaches had clerestory roofs and the roofs could be bought separately to convert standard coaches in this range. A total of 11,000 units were made.

C/1	LNWR brown+white all 1st - 99	50	60
C/1	LNWR brown+white all 3rd - 99	50	60
C/1	LNWR brown+white brake 3rd - 99	50	60
C/1	above 3 LNWR coaches - 00	NA	180
C/1	Metropolitan brown all 1st - 99	80	100
C/1	Metropolitan brown all 3rd - 99	50	60
C/1	Metropolitan brown brake 3rd - 99	50	60
C/1	above 3 Metropolitan coaches - 00	NA	450
C/1	LBSCR brown+white all 1st - 99	50	60
C/1	LBSCR brown+white all 3rd - 99	50	60
C/1	LBSCR brown+white brake 3rd - 99	50	60
C/1	above 3 LBSC coaches - 00	NA	180
C/1	Caledonian plum+white all 1st - 99	50	60
C/1	Caledonian plum+white all 3rd - 99	50	60
C/1	Caledonian plum+white all brake 3rd - 99	50	60
C/1	above 3 Caledonian coaches - 00	NA	180
C/1	GWR dark brown+cream all 1st - 99	40	45
C/1	GWR dark brown+cream all 3rd - 99	40	45
C/1	GWR dark brown+cream brake 3rd - 99	40	45
C/1	above 3 GWR coaches - 99	NA	170
C/1CL	GWR dark brown+cream clerestory all 1st - 00	40	45
C/1CL	GWR dark brown+cream clerestory all 3rd - 00	40	45
C/1CL	GWR dark brown+cream clerestory brake 3rd - 00	40	45
C/1CL	above 3 GWR clerestory coaches - 00	NA	170
C/1	LMS maroon all 1st - 99	40	45
C/1	LMS maroon all 3rd - 99	40	45
C/1	LMS maroon all brake/3rd - 99	40	45
C/1	above 3 LMS coaches - 00	NA	130
C/1CL	LMS maroon clerestory all 1st - 01	45	55
C/1CL	LMS maroon clerestory all 3rd - 01	45	55
C/1CL	LMS maroon clerestory brake 3rd - 01	45	55
C/1CL	above 3 ex-MR clerestory coaches - 01	NA	150
C/1	HRCA maroon all 1st - 99	40	45
C/1	HRCA maroon all 3rd - 99	40	45
C/1	HRCA maroon all brake/3rd - 99	40	45
C/1	above 3 HRCA 30th Anniversary coaches - 99	NA	150
C/1	LNER 21397 light teak all 1st - 99	40	45
C/1	LNER 1948 light teak all 3rd - 99	40	45
C/1	LNER 21508 light teak brake 3rd - 99	40	45
C/1	above 3 LNER coaches - 00	NA	130

ACE Trains

C/1CL	LNER light teak clestory all 1st - 01	45	55
C/1CL	LNER light teak clestory all 3rd - 01	45	55
C/1CL	LNER light teak clestory brake 3rd - 01	45	55
C/1CL	above 3 ex-GER teak clerestory coaches - 01	NA	150
C/1	Southern green brake 3rd - 99	45	50
C/1	Southern green all 1st - 99	45	50
C/1	Southern green all 3rd - 99	45	50
C/1	above 3 Southern coaches - 00	NA	160
C/1	BR M43277 maroon composite - 99	45	50
C/1	BR M43279 maroon all 3rd - 99	45	50
C/1	BR M43278 maroon brake 3rd - 99	45	50
C/1	above 3 BR coaches - 00	NA	160
C/1NZ	NZR maroon all-2nd	65	NA
C/1NZ	NZR maroon all-1st	65	NA
C/1NZ	NZR maroon brake 2nd	65	NA
C/1NZ	above 3 NZR coaches Sp Edn (Railmaster Exports NZ) - 99	NA	200
C/1D	3 German Triebwagens - ?	NA	175
C/1F	Etat green clerestory sets of 3 - 99	NA	175
C/1F	Est maroon 1st class	55	NA
C/1F	Est green+orange-brown 2nd/3rd	55	NA
C/1F	Est orange-brown 3rd class	55	NA
C/1F	above 3 coaches	NA	175
C/1F	PO green 1st/2nd composite	55	NA
C/1F	PO green 1st/2nd composite	55	NA
C/1F	PO green brake 3rd	55	NA
C/1F	above 3 coaches - 99	NA	175
C/1F	Nord green 1st/2nd composite	55	NA
C/1F	Nord green 1st/2nd composite	55	NA
C/1F	Nord green 1st/2nd composite	55	NA
C/1F	above 3 coaches - 99	NA	175
C/1F	PLM postal car	55	NA
C/1F	PLM baggage car	55	NA
C/1F	PLM passenger car	55	NA
C/1F	PLM passenger car	55	NA
C/1F	PLM passenger car	55	NA
C/1F	above 5 coaches - 99	NA	300
C/1 Bge	French baggage car green - 99	45	55
C/1F	SNCF green 1st/2nd composite	55	NA
C/1F	SNCF green 1st/2nd composite	55	NA
C/1F	SNCF green 1st/2nd composite	55	NA
C/1F	above 3 coaches - 99	NA	175

GWR

GWR Hawksworth full brake [C3] (Ace)

C3. GWR Collett & Hawksworth Stock (2005)

These coaches use a new 40cm chassis. Made in Thailand, they are fitted with insulated wheels and a PCB board for light connection is fitted to one brake end.

	Brown + Cream		
C/12	GWR 1779 Hawksworth brake end	70	NA
C/12	GWR 7798 Hawksworth 1st/3rd	70	NA
C/12	GWR 8002 Hawksworth 1st	70	NA
Set A	above 3 GWR coaches - 05	NA	260
C/12	GWR 7381 Hawksworth brake composite	70	NA
C/12	GWR 831 Hawksworth 3rd	70	NA
C/12	GWR 1297 Collett open 3rd	70	NA
Set B	above 3 GWR coaches - 05	NA	260
C/12	GWR 9676 Collett buffet car - 05	70	85
C/12	GWR 295 Hawksworth full brake - 05	70	85

LMS

C4. Merseyside Express Sets (1999)

These coaches were made in India and have domed roofs and litho silver windows. They have Merseyside Express - London (Euston) and Liverpool (Lime Street) name boards in the printing design except where indicated.

	Maroon		
C/2	LMS 4195 composite	35	NA
C/2	LMS 4195 all 3rd	35	NA
C/2	LMS 4799 restaurant car	35	NA
C/2	LMS 4183 all 1st	35	NA
C/2	LMS 26133 brake 3rd	35	NA
Set A	above 5 coaches with name boards Ltd Edn 300 - 99	NA	180
C/2	LMS 4195 composite	35	40
C/2	LMS 4195 all 3rd	35	40
C/2	LMS 26133 brake 3rd	35	40
Set B	above 3 coaches no name boards Ltd Edn - 00	NA	120

LMS restaurant car [C4] (Special Auction Services)

C5. LMS 40cm Stanier Coaches
Proposed

	Maroon		
C/18	LMS 1935 all 3rd	NPG	NA
C/18	LMS 1083 all 1st	NPG	NA
C/18	LMS 5062 brake 1st	NPG	NA
Set A	above 3 coaches	NA	NPG
C/18	LMS 8953 all 3rd	NPG	NA
C/18	LMS 3953 composite	NPG	NA
C/18	LMS 5769 brake 3rd	NPG	NA
Set B	above 3 coaches	NA	NPG
C/18	LMS 30078 kitchen coach (35cm long)	NPG	NPG
C/18	LMS 125 dining coach	NPG	NPG

C6. LMS 'Coronation Scot' Coaches
Planned to be made in China. The brake ends will have working rear lights.

	Blue		
C/20	LMS 1071 corridor 1st	NPG	NA
C/20	LMS 8931 full 3rd	NPG	NA
C/20	LMS 5054 corridor brake 1st	NPG	NA
Set A	above 3 Maunsell coaches forming set 209	NA	NPG
C/20	LMS 7509 corridor 1st	NPG	NA
C/20	LMS 9029 full 3rd	NPG	NA
C/20	LMS 5814 corridor brake 3rd	NPG	NA
Set B	above 3 Maunsell coaches forming set 250	NA	NPG
C/20	LMS 3088 35cm dining car	NPG	NPG
C/20	LMS 3089 35cm dining car	NPG	NPG
C/20	LMS 8950 full 3rd	NPG	NA

C7. LMS Stanier Main Line Coach Kits (2000)

These Thailand made kits have lower roofs and cut-out windows. They come with a choice of the following destination boards: 'The Royal Scot', 'The Merseyside Express', 'The Mancunian' and 'The Yorkshireman' (16 boards). Apart from the unpainted roofs, all other parts were pre-coloured.

	Maroon		
AC/C3	LMS 4195 1st/3rd - 00	NA	35
AC/C3	LMS 4195 full 3rd - 00	NA	35
AC/C3	LMS 4183 full 1st - 00	NA	35
AC/C3	LMS 26133 3rd brake - 00	NA	35
AC/C3	LMS 4799 restaurant car - 00	NA	35

LNER

C8a. LNER Gresley Stock (printed windows) (2002)

The coaches, made in Thailand, are supplied with slots in the roof and coach roof boards to fit them carrying the name 'Flying Scotsman'. They had black printed windows. A run of only 50 of each were made and there was a rear working light on the brake end.

	Teak		
C/4	LNER 6461 brake 1st	70	NA
C/4	LNER 61639 all 3rd	70	NA

ACE Trains

C/4	**LNER** 1516 brake 3rd	70	NA
Set A	above 3 with rear light - 02	NA	245
C/4	**LNER** 689 teak all 1st brake	70	NA
C/4	**LNER** 1865 teak all 3rd	70	NA
C/4	**LNER** 62659 teak brake 3rd	70	NA
Set B	3 more coaches complimenting Set A - 02	NA	245
C/4	**LNER** 63291 1st/3rd composite - 02	70	85
C/4	**LNER** 650 3rd buffet car - 02	70	85

LNER Gresley buffet car [C8a] (Ace)

C8b. LNER Gresley Stock (clear windows) (2003)
The coaches, also made in Thailand, are supplied with slots in the roof and coach roof boards to fit them carrying the name 'Flying Scotsman'. They has cut-out glazed windows. The first batch made of Set A had no internal partitions (nip) but later ones did, or you could have them retrospectively fitted. There was a rear working light on the brake end.

	Teak		
C/4/T	**LNER** 6461 brake 1st nip	70	NA
C/4/T	**LNER** 61639 all 3rd nip	70	NA
C/4/T	**LNER** 1516 brake 3rd nip	70	NA
set A	above three teak coaches without partitions - 03	NA	260
C/4/T	**LNER** 6461 all 1st brake	70	NA
C/4/T	**LNER** 61639 all 3rd	70	NA
C/4/T	**LNER** 1516 brake 3rd	70	NA
set A	above three teak coaches with partitions - 03	NA	260
C/4/T	**LNER** 62659 brake 3rd	70	NA
C/4/T	**LNER** 1865 all 3rd open	70	NA
C/4/T	**LNER** 689 all 1st open	70	NA
set B	above three teak coaches - 03	NA	280
C/4/T	**LNER** 63291 corridor comp - 03	70	85
C/4/T	**LNER** 650 3rd buffet car - 03	70	85

C8c. LNER 1926 Articulated Gresley Cars (2002)
This 1926 stock was made in Thailand.

C/6	**LNER** 1204 + 1205 teak sleeping cars, boards (King's Cross - Edinburgh) - 02	170	200

C9. LNER East Coast Articulated Stock (2004)
These sets comprise articulated units with interior lighting and a rear light. They were made in Thailand.

	Coronation Sets		
C/7	**LNER** [C] + [B] blue+white, silver roof	150	NA
C/7	**LNER** [A] + [G] blue+white, silver roof	150	NA
C/7	**LNER** [D] + [H] blue+white, silver roof	150	NA
	above 6 coaches - 05	NA	495
LME1	**LNER** Beaver Tail blue+white, silver roof - 05 1938 Record Breaking Set	80	95
C/8	**LNER** 6-car Coronation set Ltd Edn 50 plus ACE/Wright Dynamometer car - 04	NA	575

	West Riding Limited Sets		
C/9	**LNER** 45801[A]+45802[B] blue+white, grey roof	150	NA
C/9	**LNER** 45811[C]+45812[D] blue+white, grey roof	150	NA
C/9	**LNER** 45831[G]+45832[H] blue+white, grey roof	150	NA
C/9	above 6 coaches Ltd Edn 50 - 05	NA	475
C/9	**LNER** Beaver Tail blue+white, grey roof - 05	80	95

	Tourist/Excursion Set		
C/10	**LNER** 32774+32775 articulated green+cream	150	NA
C/10	**LNER** 32772+32773 articulated green+cream	150	NA
C/10	**LNER** 31108 buffet car green+cream	80	95
C/10	**LNER** 31862 brake end green+cream	80	95
C/10	above 6 coaches - 05	NA	495

	Silver Jubilee Set		
C/11setA	**LNER** [A]+[B] silver - 05	NA	160
C/11setB	**LNER** [C]+[D] silver - 05	NA	160
C/11setC	**LNER** silver centre kitchen car - 05	70	80
C/11setD	**LNER** [E]+[F] silver - 05	NA	160
C/11	**LNER** Beaver Tail silver - 05	80	95

SR

LNER Silver Jubilee coach [C9] (Vectis)

C10a. SR Maunsell Pre-War Coaches
Proposed to be made in China. The brake ends will have working rear lights.

	Olive Green		
C/22	**SR** 7411 full 1st	NPG	NA
C/22	**SR** 1127 full 3rd	NPG	NA
C/22	**SR** 3722 brake 3rd	NPG	NA
Set A	above 3 Maunsell coaches forming set 209	NA	NPG
C/22	**SR** 7674 1st/3rd composite	NPG	NA
C/22	**SR** 1884 full 3rd	NPG	NA
C/22	**SR** 2785 brake 3rd	NPG	NA
Set B	above 3 Maunsell coaches forming set 250	NA	NPG
C/22	**SR** 7866 dining car	NPG	NPG
C/22	**SR** 1450 3rd open	NPG	NPG

C10b. SR Maunsell Post-War Coaches
Planned to be made in China. The brake ends will have working rear lights.

	Malachite Green		
C/23	**SR** 7229 full 1st	NPG	NA
C/23	**SR** 1123 full 3rd	NPG	NA
C/23	**SR** 3718 brake 3rd	NPG	NA
Set A	above 3 Maunsell coaches forming set 205	NA	NPG
C/23	**SR** 7216 1st/3rd composite	NPG	NA
C/23	**SR** 1199 full 3rd	NPG	NA
C/23	**SR** 2781 brake 3rd	NPG	NA
Set B	above 3 Maunsell coaches forming set 248	NA	NPG
C/23	**SR** 7869 dining car	NPG	NPG
C/23	**SR** 1445 3rd open	NPG	NPG

C11. SR/BR Bulleid Coaches (2011)
Planned to be made in China. The brake ends will have working rear lights.

	Malachite Green		
C/21	**BR** 7887 restaurant 3rd car	NPG	NA
C/21	**BR** 1457 full 3rd	NPG	NA
C/21	**BR** 4361 brake 3rd	NPG	NA
Set A	above 3 Bulleid coaches forming set 269 - 11	NA	NPG
C/21	**BR** 7683 restaurant 1st car	NPG	NA
C/21	**BR** 5746 1st/3rd composite	NPG	NA
C/21	**BR** 4362 brake 3rd	NPG	NA
Set B	above 3 Bulleid coaches forming set 269 - 11	NA	NPG

BR

C12a. BR Mk1 Coaches (2002)
Made in Thailand, these are 40cm tin-printed, as supplied with the Bassett-Lowke 'Royal Scot' train pack (set B). All sets had punched out windows and included internal compartments as appropriate. There were rear working lights on the brake end of Set A and 'The Elizabethan' name boards were included.

	Red + Cream		
C/5	**BR** E1303 full 1st	60	NA
C/5	**BR** E5029 full 3rd	60	NA
C/5	**BR** E35260 brake 3rd	60	NA
Set A	above 3 BR coaches - 02	NA	175
C/5	**BR** M15578 full 1st	60	NA
C/5	**BR** M24123 full 3rd	60	NA
C/5	**BR** M21089 brake 3rd	60	NA
Set B	above 3 BR coaches - 02	NA	175

Visit the BRM website at: www.model-railways-live.co.uk

8th Edition

ACE Trains

C/5	BR E302 restaurant car - *02*		60	75
C/5	BR E80675 full brake - *02*		60	75

BR restaurant car [C12a] (Ace)

C12b. BR Mk1 Coaches (2005)

Also made in Thailand, these tin-printed coaches use a new 40cm chassis with sprung Commonwealth bogies. They are fitted with insulated wheels and a PCB board for light connection is fitted to one brake end. They are supplied with appropriate destination boards

	Brown + Cream			
C/13	BR(WR) W24165 corridor 2nd		65	NA
C/13	BR(WR) W13065 corridor 1st		65	NA
C/13	BR(WR) W3095 open 1st		65	NA
Set A	above 3 coaches - *06*		NA	245
C/13	BR(WR) W34154 brake 2nd		65	NA
C/13	BR(WR) W15426 corridor composite		65	NA
C/13	BR(WR) W4917 open 2nd		65	NA
Set B	above 3 coaches - *06*		NA	140
C/13	BR(WR) W80723 full brake - *06*		65	80
C/13	BR(WR) W1728 buffet/restaurant - *06*		65	80
	Green			
C/13	BR(SR) S3068 open 1st		65	NA
C/13	BR(SR) S24169 corridor 2nd		65	NA
C/13	BR(SR) S13003 corridor 1st		65	NA
Set A	above 3 coaches - *05*		NA	245
C/13	BR(SR) S34156 brake 2nd		65	NA
C/13	BR(SR) S15032 corridor composite		65	NA
C/13	BR(SR) S4375 open 2nd		65	NA
Set B	above 3 coaches - *05*		NA	245
C/13	BR(SR) S81039 full brake - *05*		65	80
C/13	BR(SR) S1717 buffet/restaurant - *05*		65	80
	Maroon			
C/13	BR 3099 open 1st		65	NA
C/13	BR 24147 corridor 2nd		65	NA
C/13	BR 13089 corridor 1st		65	NA
Set A	above 3 coaches - *06*		NA	245
C/13	BR 34134 brake 2nd		65	NA
C/13	BR 15328 corridor composite		65	NA
C/13	BR 3754 open 2nd		65	NA
Set B	above 3 coaches - *06*		NA	245
C/13	BR 80567 full brake - *06*		65	80
C/13	BR 1712 buffet/restaurant - *06*		65	80

Pullman

C13. Mk1 Pullman Cars (2005)

Made in Thailand, the sets are available with both white and grey roofs.

	Dark Brown + Cream			
C/14	Pullman Eagle kitchen 1st		75	NA
C/14	Pullman Amethyst parlour 1st		75	NA
C/14	Pullman No.351 parlour 2nd		75	NA
Set A	above 3 Pullman cars - *05*		NA	275
C/14	Pullman Falcon kitchen 1st		75	NA
C/14	Pullman Emerald parlour 1st		75	NA
C/14	Pullman No.336 parlour 2nd		75	NA
Set B	above 3 Pullman cars - *05*		NA	275
C/14	Pullman Hadrian Bar, grey roof - *05*		75	90

Pullman Hadrian Bar [CB] (Vectis)

C14a. Pullman Cars 1930s Style

Planned, and were to be made in China, along with the 'Brighton Belle'. The brake ends were to have a working rear light and all the coaches would have had interiors with working table lamps.

	Dark Brown + Cream			
C/15	Pullman Iolanthe kitchen 1st		NPG	NA
C/15	Pullman Car No.66 parlour 3rd		NPG	NA
C/15	Pullman No.65 brake 3rd		NPG	NA
Set A	above 3 Pullman cars - ?		NA	NPG
C/15	Pullman No.68 kitchen 3rd		NPG	NA
C/15	Pullman Eunice parlour 1st		NPG	NA
C/15	Pullman No.62 brake 3rd		NPG	NA
Set B	above 3 Pullman cars - ?		NA	NPG
C/15	Pullman Fingall kitchen 1st - ?		NPG	NPG
C/15	Pullman No.73 parlour 3rd		NPG	NA
C/15	Pullman Fingall kitchen 1st		NPG	NA
C/15	Pullman Agatha parlour 1st		NPG	NA
Set C	above 3 Pullman cars - ?		NA	NPG
C/15	Pullman Lorraine parlour 1st - ?		NPG	NPG
C/15	Pullman Thelma kitchen 1st - ?		NPG	NPG

C14b. Golden Arrow Pullman Cars

These were to have been made in China, with interiors and working table lamps and working rear lights on the brake ends.

	Dark Brown + Cream			
C/19	Pullman Adrian kitchen 1st		NPG	NA
C/19	Pullman Zenobia kitchen 1st		NPG	NA
C/19	Pullman Niobe parlour 1st		NPG	NA
Set A	above 3 Pullman cars - ?		NA	NPG
C/19	Pullman Onyx kitchen 1st		NPG	NA
C/19	Pullman Montana brake 1st		NPG	NA
C/19	Pullman Tranon Bar		NPG	NA
Set B	above 3 Pullman cars - ?		NA	NPG

ACE/WRIGHT SERIES

This is a small series of ready-to-run special vehicles designed by Brian Wright using overlays and made in Britain. The models are made of lithographed heavily varnished card applied to ACE C/1, C/4, C/5 and C/6 coaches.

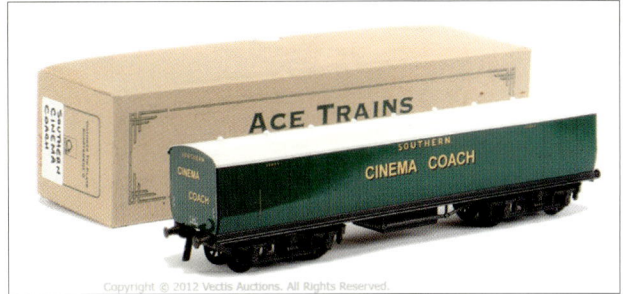

SR cinema coach [CA/WI] (Vectis)

Cat No.	Company, Number, Colour, Date	£	£
CA/W1.	**Various Stock**		
W1	LNWR ? travelling postal van - *05*	70	90
W1	GWR 1054 full brake with low roof - *03?*	70	80
W1	GWR ? full brake with clerestory roof - *03?*	80	90
W1	GWR 1259 Siphon G with pre-war lettering - *03?*	60	70
W1	GWR ? Ocean Mails coach - *05*	70	80
W1	LMS ? Stanier full brake c1930 - *03?*	60	70
W1	LMS ? maroon ex-MR mail van with clerestory roof - *03?*	90	150
W1	LMS ? scenery coach - *05*	60	70
W1	LMS 30233 Stanier postal van - *05*	70	90
W1	LNER 5219 teak full brake The Flying Scotsman - *04*	100	120
W1	LNER 23591 teak clerestory dynamometer car ex-set - *05*	75	NA
W1	LNER 45412 all 3rd + 45411 brake 3rd articulated pair teak - ?	80	100
W1	LNER beaver tail observation car blue+white - *07*	120	150
W1	SR 2464 parcel van c1930 with ribbed roof - *03?*	70	75
W1	SR 1308S cinema coach with 4-wheeled generator van - *05*	70	75

8th Edition

ACE Trains

WAGONS

Cat No.   Company, Number, Colour, Date   £   £

W1.   5-plank Open Wagon (2013)
These will have fully detailed chassis.

W2a.   Petrol/Spirit Tank Wagon (2004)
These are sold in sets of three and have interchangeable couplings. The bodies are lithographed in four colours and are fitted to a detailed chassis with brake gear. The tank has cross ties as well as end stays and the chassis has dropout side frames for lubricating axle boxes. The models were made in Thailand.

Cat No.	Description	£	£
G/1	'ACE Trains Oil' - 04	35	NA
Set 1	3 tanks (ACE + Esso yellow + Mobiloil) - 04	NA	120
G/1	'Esso' grey	35	NA
G/1	'Wakefield Castrol' green	35	NA
G/1	'Regent' silver	35	NA
Set 2	above 3 tanks - 04	NA	120
G/1	'Pratt's Spirit' brown	35	NA
G/1	'Pratt's Spirit' green	35	NA
G/1	'Pratt's High Test Sealed' orange	35	NA
Set 3	above 3 tanks - 04	NA	120
G/1	'Anglo American Oil Co.' brown	35	NA
G/1	'Colas' red	35	NA
G/1	'BP Motor Spirit' yellow	35	NA
Set 4	above 3 tanks - 04	NA	120
G/1	'Royal Daylight' grey	35	NA
G/1	'Redline-Gilco' dark blue	35	NA
G/1	'Shell Motor Spirit' red	35	NA
Set 5	above 3 tanks - 04	NA	120
G/1	'National Benzole Mixture' ochre	35	NA
G/1	'Pool' grey	35	NA
G/1	'Colas' blue	35	NA
Set 6	above 3 tanks - 04	NA	120
G/1	'Esso' yellow	35	NA
G/1	'BP Motor Spirit' grey	35	NA
G/1	'Power Ethyl' green	35	NA
Set 7	above 3 tanks - 07	NA	120
G/1	'BP British Petrol' green	35	NA
G/1	'Mobiloil' grey	35	NA
G/1	'Pool' Fuel Oil black	35	NA
Set 8	above 3 tanks - 07	NA	120

A selection of petrol tank wagons [W2a] and the brake van [W4] (Vectis)

W2b.   Milk Tank Wagon (2005)
These are also sold in sets of three and are the same as the petrol tanks, but without cross strapping and riveting. They also have a smaller filler cap with a valve on either side. Made in Thailand.

Cat No.	Description	£	£
G/1M	'United Dairies' white	35	NA
G/1M2	3 of above tank wagons - 05	NA	120
G/1M	'Express Dairy' white	35	NA
G/1M1	3 of above tank wagons - 05	NA	120
G/1M	'Nestles Milk' white	35	NA
G/1M3	3 of above tank wagons - 05	NA	120
G/1M	'Express Dairy' white	35	NA
G/1M	'United Dairies' white	35	NA
G/1M	'Nestles Milk' white	35	NA
G/1M4	set of above 3 tank wagons - 05	NA	120

W3.   12T Goods Van (2009)
These have fully detailed sprung chassis with sprung wheels and are sold in sets of three. They were made in China.

Cat No.	Description	£	£
G/2	'ACE Trains' dark blue	20	NA
G/2	LNER 13897 brown	20	NA
G/2	LNWR grey	20	NA
G/2-1	above 3 vans - 09	NA	99
G/2	SR 570027 brown yellow spot banana van	20	NA
G/2	BR B755414 brown XP	20	NA
G/2	SR 51298 cream meat van	20	NA
G/2-2	above 3 vans - 09	NA	99
G/2	SR 47375 dark brown	20	NA
G/2	CR blue	20	NA
G/2	GWR 134053 grey	20	NA
G/2-3	above 3 vans - 09	NA	99
G/2	GCR 727445 light grey	20	NA
G/2	ED 7271502 dark green Permanent way Dept.	20	NA
G/2	LMS 203975 dark brown	20	NA
G/2-4	above 3 vans - 09	NA	99
G/2	BR S50494 white Insulmeat - 09	20	NA
G/2-5	3 of the above vans - 09	NA	99
G/2	'Cadbury's' deep blue	25	NA
G/2	'Crawford's Biscuits' deep red	25	NA
G/2	'Fyffes Bananas' yellow	25	NA
G/2-6	above 3 vans - 10	NA	110
G/2	'Carr's Biscuits' blue	25	NA
G/2	'Palethorpes Royal Cambridge' dark brown	25	NA
G/2	'Colman's Mustard Traffic' yellow	25	NA
G/2-7	above 3 vans - 09	NA	110
G/2	LNWR ? red gunpowder van	25	NA
G/2	'Jacob & Co. Biscuits' dark brown	25	NA
G/2	'The True-Form Boot Co.' grey	25	NA
G/2-8	above 3 vans - 09	NA	110
G/2	'Seccotine' deep blue	25	NA
G/2	NE red gunpowder van.	25	NA
G/2	'Huntley & Palmer Biscuits' dark brown	25	NA
G/2-9	above 3 vans - 09	NA	110
G/2	BR E2327 maroon horse box	25	NA
G/2	'Ace Trains' black	25	NA
G/2	'Cadbury's Chocolate' purple	25	NA
G/2-10	above 3 vans - 12	NA	110
G/2	'Colman's Mustard Traffic' yellow	25	NA
G/2	'Colman's Mustard Traffic' yellow	25	NA
G/2	'Carr's Biscuits' blue	25	NA
G/2-11	above 3 vans - 12	NA	110
G/2	'The True-Form Boot Co.' blue-grey	25	NA
G/2	'Palethorpes Royal Cambridge' brown	25	NA
G/2	LNER 2327 horse box	25	NA
G/2-12	above 3 vans - 12	NA	110
G/2	SR Refrigerator Van pink-cream	25	NA
G/2-13	3 of the above van - 12	NA	110

Three of the vans [W3] (Ace)

W4.   Brake Van (2007)
The model, which was made in Thailand, has a fully detailed chassis, working rear and internal lighting. There are also 2-rail and 3-rail versions.

Cat No.	Description	£	£
G/4	brown - 07	35	47

Airfix GMR

HISTORY

Airfix are best remembered for their comprehensive range of plastic construction kits but in 1971, on the collapse of the Lines Group, they had bought Meccano Ltd who, incidentally, had been stripped of all connection with the model railway industry seven years earlier.

In the mid 1970s Airfix decided to extend their toy range by

> **Milestones**
> 1971 Airfix buy Meccano Ltd.
> 1975 Airfix announce the launch of a ready-to-run railway system.
> 1976 First samples seen at toy fairs.
> 1976 Class 31 and Doctor X set released for Christmas.
> 1977 Airfix draw up their production plan.
> 1979 GMR name adopted and wagon production starts in the UK.
> 1980 Airfix empire crumbles.
> 1981 Production ceases and Palitoy acquires the model railway tools.
> 1985 Tools acquired by Dapol.
> 1996 Tools pass to Hornby.

buying from the American Bachmann company a Wild West adventure train set. This was made by Kader in Hong Kong. To complement it, they decided to add an in-house concept - a Dr X mystery set which was made for them by Sanda Kan, also in Hong Kong, and based on British prototype models - a Class 31 diesel, 'Lowmac' machine wagons and an ex-GWR 'Toad' brake van. When test shots of these models arrived, it was realised that they were so well detailed that they would appeal to serious railway modellers. Thus, Airfix saw the potential in expanding the system with some additional models and Airfix Railways was born. The 61XX 2-6-2T, Intercity BSK and 12T van were intended to compliment the set items and test the market too.

GWR Class 14xx [L1]

So it was that in 1975 Airfix announced their intention of entering the ready-to-run model railway market. Unfortunately for them, the American backed Palitoy toy company had seen a gap in the British market for better quality 00 gauge railway models and decided to fill it.

In the early 1970s, the Hong Kong Trade Development Commission had been looking for business for local factories and this had resulted in the Hong Kong companies, Sanda Kan and Cheong Tak, producing models for Airfix. The Stanier coaches (corridor and non corridor) were made at Cheong Tak who also produced the 'Royal Scot', 4F and were working on the projected 'Compound' to be followed by a 'Crab', 'Black 5' or 8F. Most of the other models were made by Sanda Kan.

The first samples were displayed at the Harrogate and Brighton Toy Fairs in 1976 where they received a cool reception due to their poor quality. They had been cobbled together in a hurry and bore little resemblance to what was to follow.

Mechanically the locomotives were not exceptional but the mouldings were good and brought much praise. The first locomotive release was the Class 31 from the 'Doctor X' set, which arrived in time for Christmas 1976.

In 1977, Airfix drew up an overall programme that was to give a balanced range. There were to be 5 groups: Midland, Western, Southern, Eastern and BR. Each group was going to have an express passenger, mixed traffic, goods, large tank and small tank engines. In addition, the coaches for each group were to be gangwayed (express mainline) and 'suburban'.

The range of locomotives, coaches and wagons expanded in 1978. Other planned models were the N2, 'Dean Goods', 'Schools' and B1, but production delays, due to Hong Kong factories not adhering to Airfix's increasing design requirements, were now affecting future plans.

It was becoming more apparent that communication with Hong Kong and control of the finished product was not very good, whereas UK production, although more expensive, would deliver as good a product, on time, to Airfix's specifications, without masses of communication and without so many hidden costs. The company, therefore, produced some wagons themselves in the UK and the success of these proved this point and would have ultimately lead to the phasing out of overseas production.

This change happened in 1979 and, at the same time, the name of the product was altered to GMR which stood for Great Model Railways, to better separate the product line from the Airfix kits. The new branding was launched at the Toy Fair at Earls Court and the selling line was 'Precision made by Airfix'.

The GMR assembly line was to be at Charlton (South East London) and the 'Dean Goods' its first locomotive product - 5-plank and 7-pank wagons had been made there since 1978 and the Syphons since 1979. As the 'Dean Goods' was about to go into production in mid 1980, the Airfix empire was crumbling. Other parts of the company were being closed down, moved or sold off. £7M was spent in an attempt to save Meccano and when this failed Airfix went into receivership.

Airfix/GMR exhibited for the last time at the 1981 Toy Fairs but shortly after this they ceased production. The Airfix model railway interests were acquired by its rival - Palitoy - the makers of Mainline Railways. Many models were made by Palitoy from Airfix tooling and later by Dapol and today Hornby - each adding their improvements.

The moulds used in China had been owned by the Hong Kong factories. When Airfix ceased production, existing UK railway stock and UK tools (R-T-R wagons, 'Siphons' and the Dean Goods loco) went to Palitoy (Mainline) via Humbrol. Dapol were independently dealing with Sanda Kan, to use the Airfix tools owned by them. Dapol also acquired remaining Airfix stock held by Sanda Kan some of which was repackaged by them.

With the exception of the 4F, none of the Cheong Tak models were seen again. However, the 4F has ended up in the Hornby stable along with the Sanda Kan and Palitoy owned models. The 'Royal Scot' and Stanier coach moulds could still be sitting in store somewhere, but none of them would be of interest to Hornby today as they have produced their own high quality models of these subjects.

Airfix had started work on the Stanier all 3rd with Cheong Tak and the 12-wheel diner with Sanda Kan. Palitoy did consider them but passed on them. Replica had the all 3rd completed and released some of them, probably through Cheong Tak, while Dapol released the 12-wheel diner through Sanda Kan.

Ex-GWR Class 61xx [L3]

Further Reading

A detailed listing of the Airfix and Mainline model railway systems was produced by the late Charles Manship in the 1980s but it is no longer available. However, there has been a series of articles by Graham Smith-Thompson, in *Model Railway Enthusiast* magazine, profiling the Airfix and Mainline ranges and other systems that later

Airfix GMR

used the tools. There were six parts devoted specifically to Airfix published in the July-December issues in 1998. Later, a detailed history of the Airfix railway range by Pat Hammond was published in *British Railway Modelling*.

Collectors Club

The Airfix Collectors Club caters for collectors of any Airfix product including the model railway range and publishes a newsletter called *Constant Scale*. Further information about this organisation may be obtained from Jeremy Brook at 29 Elley Green, Neston, Nr. Corsham, Wiltshire SN13 9TX (brookjeremy@hotmail.com) or by visiting them at their website which is at http://pws.prserv.net/gbinet.dbjames/acc.htm

Dates - The dates used in the following tables are based on catalogues and price lists and factory records and should not be taken as evidence of availability.

Samples on the Market - Far East manufacturers sent samples to their customers for approval before proceeding with full production. These samples often ended up in collections and today they command a good price. Samples of models that did not reach the production stage are of greater interest to collectors.

LOCOMOTIVES

Listing - The locomotives are arranged in the order of size from smallest to largest, starting with tank engines and finishing with diesels.

LMS Class 4F [L6]

Cat No.	Company, Number, Colour, Date	£	£
L1.	**GWR Class 14xx 0-4-2T (1978)**		

The model is based on Collett's 1932 design of a small locomotive suitable for light branch lines. 95 were built, the last 20 without push-pull equipment. The last was withdrawn in 1965 and four have been preserved.

The model first appeared in the Airfix catalogue in 1978 and the tooling passed to Palitoy in 1981 and to Dapol in 1985. In 1996, Dapol sold the tools to Hornby who still make the model.

54152	**1466** GWR green - *78-81*	20	30
54153	**1466** BRb lined green - *78-81*	22	32
L2.	**LNER Class N2 Tank 0-6-2T (see Mainline)**		

This was a Gresley design of suburban tank introduced on the Great Northern Railway in 1920. A total of 107 were built and most of them worked out of Kings Cross and Moorgate. 40 of these were built without the condensing pipes for use in Scotland, but only one member of the class has been preserved.

The model was designed by Airfix and tooled in China, but the models arrived after Airfix had gone into receivership and they were sold by Palitoy. They are therefore shown here as not having been released by Airfix.

54154	**9522** LNER green - *	NA	NA
54155	**69531** BRb black - *	NA	NA
L3.	**GWR Class 61xx 'Prairie' Tank 2-6-2T (1977)**		

This was a Collett Prairie tank design of 1931 and 70 were built. They were the GWR's London suburban tank engines and were required to pull heavy suburban trains from Paddington at fairly high speeds. Like most suburban tank engines, they were displaced by DMUs and were moved on to parcel trains and empty stock duties.

On the demise of Airfix Products Ltd in 1981, the tooling passed to Palitoy and to Dapol in 1985. Finally the tooling was sold to Hornby, in 1996, who are still producing the model.

54150	**6110** Great Western green - *77-81*	18	30
54151	**6167** BRb lined black - *77-81*	20	32
L4.	**American 4-4-0s (1977)**		

These two models are straight from the Bachmann American range. They were used to launch the Airfix model railway range while work commenced on designing British outline models.

54170-5	**Jupiter** Central Pacific red + silver (CPRR) - *77-80*	20	30
54171-8	**119** Union Pacific RR red + black - *77-80*	20	30
L5.	**GWR Class 2301 'Dean Goods' 0-6-0 (see Mainline)**		

This was Dean's standard 0-6-0 goods locomotive of 1883. It also undertook light passenger duties. 62 saw service in France during the First World War and 108 were sent abroad during the Second World War. Only 54 of the class passed to British Railways and one has been preserved.

The moulds for the plastic parts of this model were made for Airfix by Heller in France and taken over by Palitoy who shipped them out to Sanda Kan in Hong Kong to make. They were sold by Palitoy in Mainline packaging. With the demise of the Mainline range, the tools passed first to Dapol and finally to Hornby who now make their own versions of the model.

54156	**2516** GWR green - *not released by Airfix*	NA	NA
54157	**2538** BRb black - *not released by Airfix*	NA	NA
L6.	**LMS Class 4F 0-6-0 (1978)**		

This was a Fowler Midland Railway design of 1911. The building of them carried on until 1942 and a total of 772 were produced. Some later ones were made for the S&DJR. Some briefly were oil burners in 1947-48 but converted back again and some were fitted with tender cabs for running tender first.

The model is based on later built ones and had tender drive. The tender was semi-permanently attached to the loco. The tools followed the same path as others following the closedown of Airfix in 1981.

54122	**4454** LMS black - *78-81*	25	30
54123	**44454** BRb (small) black - *78-80*	25	35
54122-6	**44423** BRb (small) black - *?*	NPG	NPG
54123	**44454** BRb (large) black - *80-81*	30	40

LMS 'Royal Scot' (rebuilt) [L7]

L7.	**LMS Class Rebuilt 'Royal Scot' 4-6-0 (1978)**		

Introduced by the LMS as express passenger locomotives in 1927, the 'Royal Scot' Class was designed by Sir Henry Fowler and was loosely based on the Southern Railway's 'Lord Nelson' Class. In 1943, work started on rebuilding the entire class with tapered boilers and a 'Jubilee' style cab. This process was not completed until 1955. The last was withdrawn in 1965 and two have been preserved.

The tooling for this model did not pass to Palitoy who already had a similar model in their range and the tooling was lost.

54120	**6103** *Royal Scots Fusilier* LMS black - *78-81*	25	40
54121	**46100** *Royal Scot* green BRb smoke deflectors, badly positioned decals on tender - *78-81*	25	40
L8.	**GWR Class 4073 'Castle' 4-6-0 (1979)**		

The 'Castles' were a post-Grouping design by Collett and were made between 1923 and 1950, to produce a class of 166 locomotives. The design was a development of Churchward's excellent 'Star' Class of 1907.

This was probably the best of the Airfix locomotives and passed through Palitoy to Dapol, who tooled up a flat-sided Hawksworth tender and also a Hawksworth 'County' Class version. In 1996 the tooling for both passed to Hornby.

54124	**4073** *Caerphilly Castle* Great ( ) Western green - *79-81*	40	60
54125	**4079** *Pendennis Castle* BRb green incorrectly numbered in cat - *79-81*	40	60

Powderham Castle and *Pembroke Castle* were Airfix models renamed and renumbered by Dapol but sold in original Airfix boxes. These will be found listed under Dapol.

L9.	**Class 31/4 Diesel A1A-A1A (1977)**		

263 members of the class were built between 1957 and 1962 and were intended for mixed traffic duties, originally on the Eastern Region. They were built at the Brush Electrical Engineering Company plant at Loughborough and 28 have been preserved.

This was another of the Airfix locomotives whose tooling did not end up with Hornby. It did however pass to Palitoy and Dapol, but Hornby decided not to buy it when it was offered to them.

54109-9	**D5531** green BRc box code C - *77-81*	15	30

Airfix GMR

Cat No.	Company, Number, Colour, Date	£	£
54100-6	**31401** BRe blue, box code IP02 - *77-81*	15	30

Might Have Beens

With Airfix in the hands of the receivers early in 1981, they left plans for new locomotives half finished. Some of these were in a fairly advanced stage of development while others were just a glint in the eye of the designer. They included the following with planned release dates, where known:

Preproduction model for a GWR Class 43xx

SR 'Schools' Class - 1982 *
LNER B1 Class Mayflower 1982
LMS 'Compound' - 1982 *
LT 1938 Stock Underground train *
GWR 43xx Class 'Mogul' *
SR 'Lord Nelson' Class - 1982
WD 2-8-0 - 1983
SR U Class 'Mogul' - 1983
LNER J69 tank - 1984
LMS 'Crab'' Mogul' - 1984
SR ex-LSWR Class O2 Adams tank
LMS 'Black 5'
LMS 8F

* pre-production mock-up exists.

The SR Class O2 Adams tank was to be produced as both a mainland and an Isle of Wight version. An extra chassis was envisaged and the body tool was to have inserts to allow an SR Class G6 0-6-0T to be made. The O2/G6 was to be the next UK produced loco after the 'Dean Goods'.

The underground train was to have been sold as a 4-car set, complete with a platform and accessories. It was to have been powered by a specially adapted Mabuchi motor and to this end a testing model was built. This was also to have a non-powered driving end and, in presentation packaging, it would have been aimed at the tourist market. This was going to be tied in with the double decker bus and Austin Taxi model kits.

COACHES

The marketing department had difficulty in getting the production manager to understand the market. He repeatedly rejected tooling for the 2nd class Mk2D coach on the grounds that sales had slowed drastically on the 1st class model. It was thought to be pure folly to do another so similar. He had to be persuaded, that it was needed. The result was the initial run of 7,000 2nd class models quickly sold out and another run of equal size had to be placed straight away.

A similar situation occurred with the 'B' coach. Airfix had large stocks of it in GWR livery, due to over ordering rather than lack of sales. The BR livery version was put off and when permission was finally given, the BR livery 'B' coach sold out immediately. More were to be ordered but factory capacity became a problem at that time.

The Airfix coaches, with very minor exceptions, were excellent scale models, moulded in plastic, assembled, spray painted and tampo printed with accurate detail. They helped to set a new standard in the ready-to-run market of the 1970s. They were the correct length, had flush fitting windows and proper interior detail. Errors did occur and these included the choice of bogies for the two Siphons and the colour of the LMS coaches which was much too dark. The latter was put down to the matt varnish used to finish them. A new batch, in the correct shade, was ordered but these were retained in the store until all the old stock had been cleared. By then, the company was in the liquidators hands and Palitoy inherited the new stock which they sold in the Mainline range.

With the take-over of Airfix railway assets by Palitoy in 1981, many of the Airfix coaches were absorbed into the Mainline range, mostly as new production runs. The tools were then sold on to Dapol in the mid '80s and to Hornby in the mid '90s both of whom produced their own models from them.

Cat No.	Company, Number, Colour, Date	£	£
C1.	**U.S. Passenger Cars (Bachmann) (1976)**		
These were in the 54051 Wild West set and were made by Bachmann who marketed their version of the set in America.			
(54051)	**CPRR** 3 red saloon car with a trapdoor in roof - *76-78*	10	15
(54051)	**CPRR** 5 red exploding baggage car - *76-78*	12	18
C2.	**GWR Suburban 'B Set' Coach (1977)**		
'B Set' coaches were brake ends which were built by the GWR in 1933 to run in two car sets. Each contained five 3rd class and one 1st class non-corridor compartments and a guards/luggage area at one end.			
On the demise of the company, the tooling passed to Palitoy and then Dapol before being bought by Hornby in 1996, who still made the model.			
54250	**GWR** 6869 dark brown+cream - *77-81*	10	16
54250	**GWR** 6895 dark brown+cream - *?*	10	16
54250	**GWR** (button) 6896 dark brown+cream - *?*	10	16
54250	**GWR** 4895 dark brown+cream - *78-80*	10	16
54257	**BR** W6894W maroon - *80*	12	22

GWR auto-trailer [C3]

Cat No.	Company, Number, Colour, Date	£	£
C3.	**GWR Auto-Trailer (1978)**		
Auto-trailers were used for push-pull operation on branch lines and many small batches were built by the GWR. They were eventually displaced by DMUs.			
The Airfix model arrived in 1978 but the tools passed to Palitoy in 1981, then Dapol and are now owned and used by Hornby and still in use.			
54255	**GWR** 187 dark brown+cream - *78-81*	8	14
54256	**BR** W187W maroon Didcot sign - *78-81*	8	14
C4.	**GWR Centenary Stock (1980)**		
Just 4 'Centenary' composite coaches and 6 brake 3rd coaches were built at Swindon in 1938. The composites carried 48 passengers in 7 compartments - four 1st class with 6 seats each and three 3rd class with 8 seats in each. The brake 3rd had 2 compartments and seating for 16 passengers. There was a guard's compartment and the rest of the coach was given over to luggage space.			
Palitoy took over the tooling in 1981 and it passed to Dapol in 1985, finally being bought by Hornby in 1996.			
54207	**GWR** 6659 dark brown+cream comp* - *80-81*	10	15
54209	**GWR** 4575 dark brown+cream brake 3rd* - *80-81*	10	15
54208	**BR** W6659W maroon composite** - *80-81*	12	18
54208	**BR** W6661W maroon composite** - *?*	12	18
54210	**BR** W4576W maroon brake 3rd** - *80-81*	12	18
* With 'Cornish Riviera Limited' coach boards (the pre-production sample models had 'Plymouth and Paddington Ocean Express'). ** With 'Paddington, Newport, Cardiff and Swansea' coach boards.			
C5.	**LMS Stanier Corridor Stock (1978)**		
These are LMS Period 3 coaches and were developed during Stanier's time as CME. It seems that the tooling passed to Palitoy and Dapol but was not bought by Hornby.			
54202	**LMS** 3935 maroon 1st/3rd 60' - *78-81*	10	16
54202	**LMS** 3935 maroon 1st/3rd 60' - *	NA	NA
54204	**LMS** 5542 maroon brake 3rd 57' - *78-81*	10	16
54204	**LMS** 5542 maroon brake 3rd 57' - *?*	NA	NA
54258	**LMS** 9072 maroon vestibule 3rd 57'** - *not made*	NA	NA
54203	**BR** M3935M red+cream 1st/3rd 60' - *78-81*	10	16
54205	**BR** M5542M red+cream brake 3rd 57' - *78-81*	10	16

Airfix GMR

54259   **BR** M9103M red+cream vestibule 2nd 57' * - *not made*   NA   NA

* These resulted from a colour correction ordered by Airfix but were kept in store until old stocks were used up. They were inherited by Palitoy who boxed and sold them. ** These were in the design stage at Airfix (scheduled for 1982) when they went into receivership and the models were later finished and sold by Replica Railways.

LMS corridor composite [C5]

C6. LMS 57' Non-Corridor Stock (1979)

This consisted of 2 coaches: a composite and a brake 3rd. It is likely that this tooling is still owned by Dapol as it would appear that these coaches are once again in the Dapol catalogue.

Cat No.	Description	£	£
54251	**LMS** 19195 maroon 1st/3rd - *79-81*	10	16
54253	**LMS** 15185 maroon brake 3rd - *79-81*	10	16
54253	**LMS** 25250 maroon brake 3rd - ?	12	20
54254	**LMS** 25250 maroon brake 3rd - ?	12	20
54252	**BR** M19195M maroon 1st/3rd - *79-81*	12	20
54254	**BR** M25250M maroon brake 3rd - *79-81*	12	20

C7. LMS 68' Dining Car (12 wheels)

The model was based on an LMS Period 2 coach.

These were in the design stage when Airfix went into receivership and Mainline took up the project. They were to have been released by Airfix in 1982. After Palitoy, the project next fell into the hands of Dapol who actually produced the first batch of models. Their tools, thought to have been damaged in a factory fire, were later sold to Hornby who modified them and have produced many versions of the model.

54260	**LMS** - maroon - *not made*	NA	NA
54261	**BR** M236M red+cream - *not made*	NA	NA

C8. BR Mk2d Stock (1977)

The models are thought to be based on Mk2D stock built by BR Derby Carriage and Wagon Works around 1970. The standard class vehicle has eight large windows, against seven on the first class coach.

Airfix released their first models in 1977 and the tooling passed to Palitoy in 1981. In 1985 the coaches passed to Dapol and then to Hornby in 1996 and are still in production.

	Inter-City blue + grey		
54201	**BR** E3170 FO 1st open - *77-81*	8	14
54200	**BR** E9479 BSO brake 2nd - *77-81*	8	14
54206	**BR** E5690 TSO 2nd Open - *80*	10	20

Might Have Beens

At the time of the demise of Airfix there were new coach models in the pipeline in various stages of development but not yet advertised. These included:

SR Bulleid Corridor Stock (3 types) - 1981
LNER Gresley Corridor Stock (3 types) - 1982
SR Birdcage Stock (2 types) - 1983
LMS Sleeper - 1983
LNER Gresley Non-Corridor Stock (2 types) - 1984

Quotes for the Bulleid coaches were obtained in the UK and they were to have been produced in two liveries. A pre-production sample was made up from a Phoenix kit and, finished in BR(SR) green, it was numbered S5806S.

Listing - Earliest styles of coaches are listed first and finishing with more modern British Railways designs.

WAGONS

The same standards of accuracy that had been applied to locomotives and coaches were also applied to the wagons Airfix produced. However, for the sake of economy, there was standardisation on chassis, wheels etc. 12 of the body types used no more than 4 chassis for a total of 48 models. Only spoked and solid wheels were used and, despite publicity photographs showing metal tyred and white rimmed wheels, neither type was used on production models.

Attention, however, was given to getting liveries reasonably accurate, although those on some of the vans were not authentic. These are interesting as some were re-liveried models, done in batches of 7,000 to use up surplus stocks of BR ventilated vans. Not all the liveries were fictitious. The 'English Eggs' one was seen on the LMS and the 'Lyons Tea' livery appeared on some railway containers.

Additionally, some wagons were deliberately done in very small quantities of incorrect colours to generate an interest in collecting them. It had been intended to do a batch 500 of each, but the factory manager misunderstood and did only about 20 of each model. These deliberate 'errors' are very rare and therefore command a high price.

Listing - The wagons are arranged in the order of: flats, open wagons, hoppers, tankers, vans, brake vans and bogie stock.

Cat No.	Company, Number, Colour, Date	£	£

W1. 'Lowmac' MS (1977)

This was a BR design which seems to have been influenced by the LNER 'Mac' machinery wagons.

Airfix released the model with 3 different loads: a crate, a container and a lorry trailer. In 1981, the tooling passed to Palitoy, who did not use it. It was acquired by Dapol in 1985 and finally passed to Hornby in 1996 who still manufacture the model from time to time.

54330	**BR** B904662 red-brown + crate - *77-81*	8	10
54333	**BR** B904662 red-brown 'Conflat' ISO + **'Sea Land'** container - *78-79*	10	16
54334	**BR** B904662 red-brown + **'NCL'** trailer - *78-79*	10	16
(54052)	**BR** B904662 red + **'NCL'** trailer with opening doors from 54052 'Dr. X' pack brown - *77*	14	NA

BR 'Conflat A' with BK container [W2]

W2. 'Conflat' with Container (1978)

The 'Conflat A' was a post-war Swindon design and the first 400 were built at Swindon and Wolverton. Over the next ten years, 200,000 of them were built, most of them during the BR era. There is little difference between the GWR and BR versions.

This was an attractive model and the tooling was acquired by Palitoy in 1981, who sent it to Kader in Hong Kong to be altered to take the AF container. It is thought that Dapol had already had duplicate tooling made of the Airfix wagon and subsequently received the former Airfix tools in 1985 for the 'Conflat' but not the container. The replica 'Conflat' and container went to Hornby who are still making versions of it.

54331	**GWR** 39005 dark grey + **GW** brown container BK - 1829 - *78-81*	7	10
54337	**LNER** 39324, 240749 grey + **'J Miles'** container* - *80-81*	8	12
54332	**BR** B735833, B735700 red brown + **BR** furniture container - *78-81*	8	12

* This was a non-authentic livery, although the Leeds-based company existed and had

Airfix GMR

asked for a promotional model for their customers. It is based on the livery of the company's vans.

W3.   5-plank Open Wagon (1978)
Samples based on both LMS and GWR designs were made and the production model was a compromise between the two.

54374	'Devizes Sand' 1 grey - 78-79	6	10
54375	'Spencer' 24 red - 78-81	6	10
54376	'Arnold' 156 brown - 78-81	6	10
54377	'Harts Hill' 2 brown - 78-79	6	10
54388	'Alloa' 1124 yellow - 80-81	6	10
54389	'ICI' L3110 grey - 80-81	6	10
54372	GWR 109458 dark grey - 78-81	6	9
54373	LMS 404104 grey - 78-81	6	9
54364	BR M407562 grey - 79-81	6	9
54365	BR M411459 red brown - 79-81	6	9

W4.   7-plank Open Wagon (1978)
This was a compromise design to allow a range of liveries. This involved stretching what would have been the body of a 9' wheelbase wagon to fit a 10' chassis and also stretching the artwork to match.

54380	'Gloucester Gas Light Company' 51 black - 78-79	6	10
54381	'Broadoak' 460 brown - 78-79	6	9
54381	'Broadoak' 460 grey Ltd Edn 20 - 78-79	35	45
54382	'Highley Mining' 425 brown - 78-79	6	9
54382	'Highley Mining' 425 grey Ltd Edn 20 - 78-79	35	45
54383	'Hales Fuels' 241 grey - 78-81	6	9
54383	'Hales Fuels' 241 brown Ltd Edn 20 - 78-79	35	45
54390	'Carlton' 4372 black - 80-81	6	10
54391	'Stalybridge' 15 brown - 80-81	6	10
54391	'Stalybridge' 15 grey Ltd Edn 20 - 80	35	45
54378	GWR 29017 dark grey - 78-81	6	10
54379	LMS 40781 grey - 79-81	6	9
54379	LMS 602604 grey - 79-81	6	9
54366	BR P130286 grey - 80-81	6	10

Rare limited edition 7-plank wagon [W4]

W5.   NE 20T 9-plank Mineral Wagon (1981)
The model was based on the first coal wagons built by the LNER around 1928. They had a 20 ton capacity and were constructed in wood. They were built with end and bottom doors and with twin drop-down doors in each side. It is still in production in China for Hornby.

54369	LNER 31273 grey - 81	7	10
54359	BR E30995, E10995 grey - 81	7	10

W6.   GWR 20T Steel Mineral Wagon (1979)
The model was based on a GWR design of the 1930s, many of which were built for locomotive coal transportation. BR continued to construct similar looking wagons after Nationalisation.

The tooling passed to Palitoy in 1981 and to Dapol in 1985. From the latter it passed to Hornby who still make the wagon.

?	'Avon Tyres'* black - not made	NA	NA
54370	GWR 83516 dark grey - 79-81	7	10
54371	BR P339371K grey - 79-81	7	8

* This livery was suggested to Airfix by Palitoy who supplied a picture of it. Airfix prepared the artwork ready for a release in 1981. The artwork was amongst the assets acquired by Palitoy on the demise of Airfix and they brought out the wagon themselves.

W7.   NE 21T Hopper Wagon (1980)
The model was based on an LNER 20 ton coal hopper wagon design of 1936 for use in the North East. At Nationalisation, the LNER handed over more than 8000 of them to BR, who continued to build more as their standard 21 ton hopper wagon. They were built by a number of different firms and later by BR Shildon Wagon Works, so there were detail differences. They all had two bottom doors for gravity unloading.

The Airfix tooling passed to Palitoy in 1981 and to Dapol in 1985. Hornby purchased the tooling in 1996 and still make the model.

54367	LNER 193258 grey - 80-81	7	10
54368	BR E289595K grey - 80-81	7	10

W8.   20T Tank Wagon (1979)
This was an authentic model of a 12' chassis tank wagon done from Railway Clearing House drawings but the liveries are not strictly authentic, belonging as they do to other styles of tanker. The tooling is still being used by Hornby.

54345	'Esso' 135 silver - 79-81	8	14
54346	'Shell BP' 3967 black - 79-81	8	12
54347	'Shell' 2373 buff - 79-81	8	14

W9.   BR 12T Planked Single Vent Van (1978)
The private owner versions were mainly re-sprayed and reprinted BR ventilated vans of which there was a large stock unsold. They were done in batches of about 7,000 at the Airfix factory in the UK. For the roofs, six specific greys were stocked, from light grey through very dark grey. Roofs were painted in batches of one spray gun full at a time and with each filling another shade of grey was used.

54302	'Lyon's Tea' 528163 blue - 78-79	8	14
54301	'English Eggs' 506150 dark blue - 78-81	9	16
54303	'Blue Circle' 520112 yellow - 78-79	10	16
54310	'Lyle's Golden Syrup' 547117 green - 80-81	8	14
54311	'Tizer' 561772 yellow - 80-81	8	14
54312	'Spratt's' 538422 white, name brown - 80-81	8	14
54312	'Spratt's' 538422 white, name in red Ltd Edn 20 - 80	35	45
54313	'Huntley & Palmer' 566327 green - 80-81	7	14
54314	'Persil' 547921 green - 80-81	8	14
54315	'Nestle's Milk' 531179 blue - 80-81	8	14
54300	BR B751707 red brown, brown roof - 76-80	6	10
54300	BR B751707 red brown, grey roof - 78?	6	10
54300	BR B760563 red brown, grey roof - 78?	6	10
54300	BR B751705 red brown, black roof - ?	6	10

Rare limited edition vent van with red lettering [W9]

W10.   SR 12T Ventilated Box Van (1979)
The Southern Railway box vans had a vari-curve roof and some were built for the GWR and LMS during the war. This model is based on the type with even width planking.

The tooling passed to Palitoy and Dapol before being bought by Hornby in 1996, who still make it.

54304	SR 44392 brown - 79-81	6	10
54305	BR S44437 grey - 79-81	6	10

W11.   GWR 20T Brake Van (1977)
Like so much on the GWR, the 'Toad' brake van changed very little in appearance over time. It had a verandah at only one end and no side duckets. The 'Toads' had mostly restricted use ('RU' painted on their sides) and generally carried the name of the yard to which they allocated.

This model had its own unique chassis and is still made by Hornby.

54363	GWR 114875 dark grey 'Swindon' - 78-81	8	12
54363	GWR 56616 dark grey 'Oxford' - 78-81	10	14
54360	BR 114926 grey - 77-83	8	12

Airfix GMR

GWR 'Toad' brakevan [W11]

W12. LMS 20T Brake Van (1977)
The body was typical of brake vans built at Derby in the 1930s. In 1981 the model, which had its own chassis, passed to Palitoy and they made a few of them in 1984. Today it is the LMS brake van in Hornby's range.

54361	**LMS** 730097 grey - *77-81*	8	12
54362	**BR** 114875 red-brown+yellow - *77-78*	8	12
54362	**BR** B950016 red-brown+yellow - *79-81*	8	12

W13. LNER/BR Standard 20T Brake Van
This model was still at the planning stage when Airfix Products Ltd went into receivership. It was later made by Bachmann in 2001 using the original Airfix drawings.

54386	**LNER** 182922 brown - *not made*	NA	NA
54387	**BR** brown+yellow - *not made*	NA	NA

W14. GWR 'Macaw H' Bogie Bolster Wagon (1981)
The 20 ton 'Macaw H' was smaller than the standard 'Macaw B' which was more widely used. It was built in the late 1930s and, when taken over by British Railways in 1948, the wagons were recoded as 'Bogie Bolster A'.

The model was released by Airfix in 1981 and immediately afterwards, Airfix went into receivership. The tooling passed to Palitoy and then to Dapol, Hornby buying the tooling in 1996. It is likely that most of the original Airfix stock was sold by Dapol.

54336	**GWR** 107364 dark grey box of 2 - *81*	NA	22
(54336)	as above single unboxed	8	NA
54335	**BR** W107364 grey box of 2 - *81*	NA	22
(54335)	as above single unboxed	8	NA

W15. GWR 'Siphon G' Bogie Milk Van (1980)
This is a GWR built van, with corridor connections, for transporting milk in churns. They were built in batches between 1913 and 1927.

As a cost cutting exercise, the two GWR 'Siphons' were fitted with bogies from the GWR 'Centenary' coaches. While authentic, examples on the railways with these bogies were rare. They should have been a 9' American type.

54306	**GWR** 1478 dark brown - *80-81*	10	14
54307	**BR** W1452 maroon - *80-81*	10	14

W16. GWR 'Siphon H' Bogie Milk Van (1980)
This is a GWR designed milk van with end doors and built in 1919. Besides being used for milk, they could be used as scenery vans or for the transportation of motor vehicles. Hornby still manufacture both 'Siphon' models

54308	**GWR** 1437 dark brown - *80-81*	10	14
54309	**BR** W1429 maroon - *80-81*	10	14

W17. US Freight Cars (Bachmann) (1977)
These were in the 54053 'Wild West Freight' train set and were made by Bachmann who marketed their version of the set in America.

54270	**Union Pacific** 556 red box car - *77-78*	4	NA
54271	**Union Pacific** yellow caboose - *77-78*	4	NA

Might Have Beens
The last display of new liveries was at the 1981 Toy Fair and included some which Airfix did not have time to produce. These included the 20T steel mineral wagon in the livery of 'Avon Tyres' and the 12T ventilated van finished as 'Meccano', 'Camp Coffee' and 'OXO'. There were also to be a 5-plank 'BAC', a 7-plank 'Perfection Soap' and a 'Conflat' with a 'Frasers' container. Some of these liveries were later taken up by Palitoy.

Also planned for 1982 was an LNER type brake van which was based on vehicle ESR 49028 from which the drawings had been prepared. This was to have been followed by a 9' chassis for more accurately scaled private owner wagons. The model would have been based on a Gloucester design and was due for release during 1981.

Other wagons being considered (with the year of their proposed introduction) were:

SR 25T brake van - 1982
LNER 9' wheelbase fruit van - 1982
GWR Cowans Sheldon 45T mobile crane and jib carrier - 1983
GWR 'Tube' wagon - 1983
GWR 'Ro-Rail' milk wagon - 1983
16T mineral wagon - 1983
'Plate' wagon - 1983

It was also planned to, each year, add further liveries to the 5-plank, 7-plank, tank wagon, container and mineral wagon ranges.

ACCESSORIES
There were very few accessories for the Airfix range but they included, in 1979, a series of card lineside structures which were both available separately and provided in the train sets. The models released that first year were a signal box (54650-6), tunnel (54651-9) and a station (54652-2).

Track was supplied by Peco while Airfix supplied both battery and mains power units. At the end Airfix launched their own version of Zero 1 which was called 'MTC' which stood for Multiple Train Controller

SETS
Airfix tried hard to sell their sets and produced a total of 19 before they went into liquidation. Retailers always wanted sets made up of boxed items so that they could break up sets that did not sell and offer the items individually. As the Airfix range is relatively small and so easy to build a complete collection of, there is a growing interest in Airfix train sets. This particularly applies to those of the pre GMR days. Of special interest are the adventure sets - 'Doctor X' and the two Wild West sets which can fetch as much as £80. Another interesting set is the Cornish Riviera without the gold beading on the splashers of the locomotive or with it applied as printed splasher labels. The latter were done in an emergency to cover a production mistake.

CotteeS
Auctions Limited
Est. 1907

Model Railway and Collectable Toy Sales

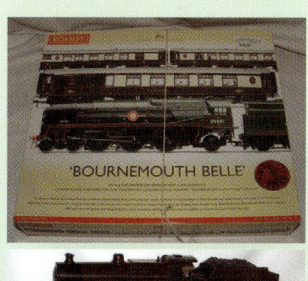

We are traditional auctioneers embracing on-line technology offering friendly expert advice and competitive commission rates. If you have single items or large collections speak to us first.
Collection arranged countrywide.

- On-line catalogues www.cottees.co.uk or £3.50 by post
- Live on-line bidding for these auctions at www.the-saleroom.com
- Commission and telephone bids welcome
- Visa, Switch and Mastercard accepted
- Cafe and parking on site

Viewing: Fridays prior to sales 10am - 5pm and morning of sales from 8.30am - 10am.

We hold these specialised sales every March, June, September and December.

Registered Office: The Market, East Street, Wareham, Dorset. BH20 4NR
Tel: 01929 552826   Fax: 01929 554916

Anbrico 00

HISTORY

The Anbrico name, associated with A.B.Colbeck, was first used in 1932 in connection with hand-built scale models, in particular 0 gauge railway items for use in the home market. As the years went by, the firm became known as Anbrico Scale Models and all types and sizes were made for sale in countries all over the World.

Anbrico was also producing for other firms in the model trade. Some of the largest models built were coaches in 1:12 scale for use in booking offices around the UK.

In later years, Anbrico Scale Models produced rolling stock for both 0 and 00 gauges but was concentrating more on coaches. After several years, the ranges covering all the various types of BR diesel multiple units and railbuses were introduced with a diesel locomotive series which was added a couple of years later.

Group of 8 Anbrico diesels (Paul Colbeck)

The family owned company was based in Pudsey, between Leeds and Bradford, and appropriately the first DMU modelled was that used on the Leeds-Bradford service via Pudsey. Anbrico even supplied the first six twin units to a model shop in Leeds six weeks prior to BR starting up the service.

The DMUs, railbuses and single unit parcels vans were hand-built to customer's orders in 00 and EM scale and the units contained either a destination box, a route number box or both (combined or separate). Any destination up to 14 letters in length, was included in the price as well as the route number. Appropriate regional stock numbers were also included, together with under-floor detail.

Single-link couplings were fitted as standard and each car was fitted out with full interior detail. The motor was well concealed and, on the railbuses, was slung beneath to give the car clear space within.

In 1960, a range of ready-to-run trams was produced in 00 which became popular with both customers in the UK and abroad and was available on either 00 or TT gauge chassis.

In 1968 the first range of 00 cast metal bus kits was introduced covering the popular British outline double and single decker buses and coaches. The range was intended to cover the lack of types available for use with model railways, but added interest was found from the enthusiasts who just enjoyed making models of buses and coaches.

An enthusiast group was just starting up at the time and Anbrico was contacted to see if they would be prepared to make some of the types they were interested in and which, by chance, fell in with the survey Anbrico had done earlier on the subject. Sometime later a series of cast metal tramcar kits was introduced in which provision was made for a small motor to be fitted for customers wishing to operate them on their layout.

Before kit production ceased, some 80 were available including some 00 railcar and railbus kits.

Production of parts ceased in September 1987 and the hand-built model section closed sometime later, after the completion of outstanding orders for models and patterns for firms in the model trade. The company had been producing models for 50 years and had 300 sales agents around the world. The factory was sold at the end of 1989 and has since been converted into a house.

All items connected with the scale model business were sold to private collectors when the old premises were emptied for conversion. The models from the showcases in the Pudsey showroom were added to the private collection of one of the business partners and were retained to illustrate the history of the firm since the original models made in 1932.

Class 26 (Paul Colbeck)

New Information - Since publication of the 7th Edition, I have had access to about 1000 coloured photographs taken by the Colbeck family of a major Anbrico collection. As a result it has been possible to add detail of specific models seen in photographs. It is assumed that the models seen were all to 00 scale but it is possible that some were 0 gauge.

Running Numbers - It should be noted that the running numbers may be hand-painted (little on the crude side), transfers (mainly on coaches) or heat printing (mainly on DMUs and EMUs). It is possible that the hand-painted numbers identify one-off models made for specific customers.

Prices - As Anbrico models rarely come up for sale at auction and collectors of the range are few and far between, it is very difficult to suggest realistic prices. Hopefully those shown can be modified as information comes in. The prices suggested here show a range of values for models in good condition.

LOCOMOTIVES

The models shown here are based on a list published in 1966/67. It is not known whether every item on the list was manufactured and sold but the prices quoted are what they are thought likely to sell for at auction if they did turn up. Also, there may have been subjects modelled earlier that were not available at the time of the list. So little information remains that it is difficult to give clear guidance.

Class 29 (Paul Colbeck)

Cat No.	Company, Number, Colour, Date	£	£
L1.	**Type 1 Diesels**		
-	D8000-8199 English Electric Bo-Bo	240	360
-	D8200-8243 BTH/Paxman Bo-Bo	240	360
-	D8500-8587 Clayton/Paxman Bo-Bo	240	360
L2.	**Type 2 Diesels**		
-	D5000-5299 BR/Sulzer Bo-Bo (**D5000** in BRc green seen)	240	360
-	D5300-5414 Birmingham RC&WCo Bo-Bo (**D5300** in BRc green seen)	240	360
-	D5900-5909 English Electric Bo-Bo	240	360

Anbrico 00

-	D6100-6157 North British Bo-Bo (6102 in **BRc** green seen)	240	360
-	D6300-6357 North British Bo-Bo	240	360

L3.	**Type 2/3 Diesels**		
-	D5500-5699 Brush A1A-A1A	240	360

L4.	**Type 3 Diesels**		
-	D6500-6597 Birmingham RC&WCo Bo-Bo (**6500** in BRc green seen)	240	360
-	D6700-6999 English Electric Co-Co	240	360
-	D7000-7400 Beyer-Peacock ('Hymek') B-B (**D7063** in BRc green seen)	240	360

Class 35 'Hymek' [L3] (Paul Colbeck)

L5.	**Type 4 Diesels**		
-	D1-139 BR/Sulzer 1Co-Co1	240	360
-	D200-399 English Electric 1Co-Co1	240	360
-	D400-449 English Electric Co-Co	240	360
-	D1000-1073 'Western' C-C	240	360
-	D1500-1999 Brush Co-Co (**D1859** in BRc 2-tone green seen)	240	360

L6.	**Type 5 Diesels**		
-	D9000-9021 English Electric 'Deltic' Co-Co	270	450

L7.	**4-Wheel Railbuses**		
-	**BRb** green un-numbered British United Traction	120	200
-	**BRc** W79978 green AC	120	200
-	**BR** Park Royal	120	200
-	**BR** Wickham	120	200
-	**BR** Bristol/Eastern Coach Works	120	200
-	**BRc** green E59960 Waggon und Maschinenbau	120	200
-	**BRc** green E79962 Waggon und Maschinenbau	120	200

AC railbus (Paul Colbeck)

L8.	**Single Unit Parcels Vans**		
-	**BRc** green un-numbered Cravens Limited 57'	160	220
-	**BRc** green M55988 Gloucester RC&W Co. 64' (Western & Midland)	160	220

L9.	**DMUs**		
These were first advertised in 1956.			
-	**GWR** No.11 brown+cream AEC Autocar	120	200
-	**BRc** green un-numbered Metropolitan-Cammell 57' 2-car	220	300
-	**BRb** green E56362+E51204 Metropolitan-Cammell 57' 2-car	220	300
-	**BRc** green M50325+M59056+M50328 Metropolitan-Cammell 57' 3-car	280	350
-	**BRc** green Metropolitan-Cammell 57' 4-car	320	400
-	**BRc** green un-numbered Cravens 57' 2-car	220	300
-	**BRc** green E50920 Cravens 57' 3-car	280	350
-	**BRc** Cravens 57' 4-car	320	400
-	**BRc** Gloucester RC&WCo. 57' 2-car	220	300
-	**BRc** W55023 green Gloucester RC&WCo. 64' single car	90	150
-	**BRc** W55017 green Gloucester RC&WCo. 64' single car	90	150
-	**BRc** Park Royal Vehicles Ltd 57' 2-car	220	300
-	**BRc** green un-numbered Birmingham RC&WCo 57' 2-car	220	300
-	**BRc** Birmingham RC&WCo 57' 3-car	280	350
-	**BRc** Birmingham RC&WCo 57' 4-car	320	400
-	**BRc** Birmingham RC&WCo Suburban 64' 3-car	280	350
-	**BRc** M79901 green Derby Lightweight single car	90	150
-	**BRc** E50601+E56192 green Derby original design 57' 2-car	220	300

BR 'Derby' DMU [L9] (Paul Colbeck)

-	**BRc** Derby original design 57' 4-car	320	400
-	**BRc** Derby new style 57' 2-car	220	300
-	**BRc** Derby new style 57' 3-car	280	350
-	**BRc** Derby new style 57' 4-car	320	400
-	**BRc** Derby new style 64' 2-car	220	300
-	**BRc** Derby Suburban 64' 3-car	280	350
-	**BRc** Derby Suburban 64' 4-car	320	400
-	**BRc** green E56170+E50415 Wickham 57' 2-car	220	300
-	**BRc** Pressed Steel Suburban 64' single car	90	150
-	**BRc** blue SC75604+SC61484+SC75569 'Blue Train' Class 303 Pressed Steel Suburban 64' 3-car	280	350
-	**BRc** green SC79094+SC79442(buffet)+SC79095 3-car Swindon Inter-City 64'	280	350
-	**BRc** green SC79096+SC79474+SC79097 3-car Swindon Inter-City 64'	280	350
-	**BRc** green W50715+W59269(buffet)+W50666) 3-car Swindon Cross Country 64'	280	350
-	**BRc** E50920+?+? green Gloucester RC&WCo. Cross Country 64' 3-car	280	350

L10.	**EMUs**		
-	**SR** 4619 green 4-SUB 4-car	280	350
-	**SR** 5062 green 4-EPB 4-car	280	350
-	**BRc** Unit 384 maroon S3212S+S6563S	120	200

LNER steam railcar (Paul Colbeck)

L11.	**Steam Railcar**		
-	**GWR** 18 brown+cream Swindon railcar	120	200
-	**LNER** 35 Nettle green+cream Sentinel railcar	280	350
-	**LNER** 2257 Defiance green+cream Sentinel railcar	280	350

COACHES

The list shown here is of models available from 1959.

BR coaches were offered in maroon, green or chocolate and cream with appropriate regional numbers. A small extra charge was made for rail blue and blue/grey livery.

In 1969, Anbrico Scale Models were also offering a range of 00

Anbrico 00

scale coach kits taken from their ready-to-run range. These, however, were withdrawn when other competing coach kits came on the market.

Cat No.	Company, Number, Colour, Date	£	£

C1. LNWR Stock
Dark Purple & White

		£	£
-	LNWR 315 full brake	70	100
-	LNWR 107 12-wheel 1st dining saloon	70	100
-	LNWR 5310 12-wheel dining saloon	70	100
-	LNWR 5917 12-wheel dining car	70	100
-	LNWR 12-wheel sleeper	60	90

West Coast Joint Stock all-3rd [C2] (Paul Colbeck)

C2. WCJS Stock
Dark Purple & White

		£	£
-	WCJS 506 all 3rd	80	120
-	WCJS 509 all 1st	80	120
-	WCJS 510 1st/3rd composite	80	120
-	WCJS 520 1st/3rd composite	80	120
-	WCJS 494 two compartment brake 3rd	80	120
-	WCJS 496 three compartment brake 3rd	80	120
-	WCJS 498 three compartment brake 3rd	80	120
-	WCJS 316 full brake	80	120
-	WCJS 317 full brake	80	120

C3a. Caledonian 8-wheel Stock
Dark Purple & White

		£	£
-	CR 3339 all 3rd	70	100
-	CR 6663? all 3rd	70	100
-	CR 917 1st/3rd composite	70	100
-	CR 7669 brake composite	70	100
-	CR 7389 brake composite	70	100

C3b. Caledonian 12-wheel Stock
Dark Purple & White

		£	£
-	CR 510 all 3rd	70	100
-	CR 917 1st/3rd composite	70	100
-	CR 351 brake 3rd	70	100

C4. Midland Stock

		£	£
-	MR Clerestory 54' corridor coach	60	90
-	MR Clerestory 12-wheel diner	60	90
-	MR Clerestory 12-wheel sleeper	60	90
-	MR 6-wheel 31' stock	60	90

SE&CR brake 3rd 'Birdcage' stock [C5] (Paul Colbeck)

C5. SE&CR Birdcage Stock

		£	£
-	SE&CR 1070 maroon all 3rd	80	100
-	SE&CR 5351 maroon 1st/3rd composite	80	100
-	SE&CR 5350 maroon 1st/2nd/3rd composite	80	100
-	SE&CR 2297 maroon brake 3rd	80	100
-	SE&CR 2298 maroon brake 3rd	80	100
-	SE&CR 2303 maroon brake 3rd	80	100
-	SE&CR 2303 maroon brake 3rd	80	100

C6. Pullman Stock
Dark Brown & Cream

		£	£
-	Pullman Car No.84 parlour 3rd	80	100
-	Pullman Belinda parlour 1st	80	100
-	Pullman Car No.77 brake 3rd	80	100

C7. GWR Clerestory Stock
Dark Brown & Cream

		£	£
-	GWR (shields) un-numbered brake 3rd	60	90
-	GWR 1701 brake 3rd	60	90

C8. GWR Dreadnought Stock
No details.

C9. GWR Top Light Stock
No details.

		£	£
-	GWR (shields) 3940? corridor 3rd	40	70

C10. GWR Bow-Ended Stock
Dark Brown & Cream

		£	£
-	GWR (button) 2507 corridor 3rd	40	70
-	GWR ? corridor 1st	40	70
-	GWR (button) 2695 corridor composite	50	80
-	GWR (button) 2698 corridor composite	50	80
-	GWR (button) 7276 corridor composite	50	80
-	GWR (shields) ? corridor brake/3rd	50	80

C11. GWR 'Suburban' Stock
Dark Brown & Cream

		£	£
-	GWR (button) 22 3rd	50	80
-	GWR (button) 1010 3rd	40	70
-	GWR ? 1st	40	70
-	GWR (shields) ? composite	40	70
-	GWR (shields) 2010 brake 3rd	40	70
-	GWR (button) 2017 brake 3rd	40	70
-	GWR (shields) 6061 B-set brake/composite	40	70
-	GWR (button) 2615 brake composite	50	80
-	GWR (button) 2617 brake composite	50	80
-	GWR (button) 2661 brake composite	50	80
-	GWR (button) 2665 brake composite	50	80
-	GWR (button) 170 50' full brake parcels van	40	70

WR corridor brake 3rd [C12] (Paul Colbeck)

C12. GWR General Stock
Dark Brown & Cream

		£	£
-	GWR (button) 751 corridor 3rd	40	70
-	GWR (button) 770 corridor 3rd	40	70
-	GWR (button) 771 corridor 3rd	40	70
-	GWR (button) 7000 corridor 3rd	40	70
-	GWR (button) 7010 corridor 3rd	40	70
-	GWR (button) 5017 corridor 1st	40	70
-	GWR (button) 8100 corridor 1st	40	70
-	GWR (button) 8111 corridor 1st	40	70
-	GWR (button) 8118 corridor 1st	40	70
-	GWR (button) 7280 corridor composite	40	70
-	GWR (button) 1627 corridor brake 3rd	40	70
-	GWR (button) 1630 corridor brake 3rd	40	70
-	GWR (button) 2125 corridor brake 3rd	40	70
-	GWR (button) 2010 corridor brake 3rd	40	70

Anbrico 00

-	**GWR** (button) 2110 corridor	40	70
-	**GWR** (button) 1175 full brake	40	70
-	**GWR** (button) 1177 full brake	40	70
-	**GWR** (button) 1170 Ocean Mails full brake	40	70
-	**GWR** (button) 1171 Ocean Mails full brake	40	70
-	**GWR** (button) 1173 Ocean Mails full brake	40	70
-	**GWR** ? unclassified restaurant car	50	80
-	**GWR** ? auto-train trailer coach 187-196 series	60	90
-	**GWR** (button) 22 auto-train trailer coach	60	90
-	**GWR** (shields) 188 auto-train trailer coach	60	90

C13. LMS 'Suburban' Stock
Maroon

-	**LMS** ?1470? suburban 3rd	40	70
-	**LMS** 10120 suburban 1st	40	70
-	**LMS** ? suburban composite	40	70
-	**LMS** 20789 suburban brake 3rd	40	70
-	**LMS** 24405 suburban brake 3rd	40	70
-	**LMS** 24405 push-pull brake 3rd	40	70
-	**LMS** 24407 push-pull brake 3rd	40	70
-	**BR** ? push-pull brake 3rd	40	70

C14. LMS Main Line Stock
Maroon

LMS 50ft engineer's inspection saloon [C14] (Paul Colbeck)

-	**LMS** 1567 corridor 3rd	40	70
-	**LMS** 1658 corridor 3rd	40	70
-	**LMS** 4890 corridor 3rd	40	70
-	**BR** M1807M corridor 3rd	40	70
-	**LMS** 2349 open 3rd	40	70
-	**LMS** 3490 open 3rd	40	70
-	**LMS** 6076 open 3rd	40	70
-	**LMS** 6078 open 3rd	40	70
-	**BR** M6077M open 3rd	40	70
-	**LMS** 1067 corridor 1st	40	70
-	**LMS** 1068 corridor 1st	40	70
-	**LMS** 1078 corridor 1st	40	70
-	**LMS** 1239 corridor 1st	40	70
-	**LMS** 1278 corridor 1st	40	70
-	**LMS** 6785 corridor 1st	40	70
-	**LMS** 1278 open 1st	40	70
-	**LMS** 7507 open 1st	40	70
-	**LMS** 7567 open 1st	40	70
-	**LMS** 4567 corridor composite	40	70
-	**LMS** 4590 corridor composite	40	70
-	**LMS** ? open composite	40	70
-	**LMS** 5123 corridor brake 3rd	40	70
-	**LMS** 5126 corridor brake 3rd	40	70
-	**LMS** 6010 corridor brake 3rd	40	70
-	**LMS** ? open brake 3rd	40	70
-	**LMS** 5056 corridor brake 1st	40	70
-	**LMS** 5067 corridor brake 1st	40	70
-	**LMS** 12378 full brake	40	70
-	**LMS** 30569 full brake	40	70
-	**BR** M107M parcels van	40	70
-	**LMS** 30154 6-wheel 'Stove'	70	90
-	**LMS** 412 maroon kitchen car	70	90
-	**LMS** 403 maroon kitchen car	70	90
-	**LMS** ? restaurant car 3rd	40	70
-	**LMS** 234 dining car 3rd 12-wheel	40	70
-	**LMS** 243 dining car 1st 12-wheel	40	70
-	**BR** M250M restaurant car 1st	40	70
-	**LMS** ? restaurant car unclassified	40	70
-	**LMS** ? restaurant car unclassified 12-wheel	40	70
-	**LMS** 589 maroon sleeping car 3rd	40	70
-	**LMS** ? sleeping car 1st	40	70
-	**LMS** ? sleeping car 1st/3rd	40	70
-	**LMS** 45023 engineer's inspection saloon	70	90
-	**LMS** 45024 engineer's inspection saloon	70	90
-	**LMS** 45123 engineer's inspection saloon	70	90

The Coronation Scot

-	**LMS** 6077 blue Corridor 1st	70	90

C15. LNER Articulated Stock
Teak Finish

-	**LNER** ? Triplet dining car set	160	240
-	**LNER** 86701/86702/86703/86704/86705 Quint set	220	300
-	**LNER** ? Quad set	280	260

LNER articulated caches [C15] (Paul Colbeck)

C16. LNER Clerestory Stock
No details.

C17. LNER Gresley Bow-Ended Stock
Teak Finish

-	**LNER** 42345 open 3rd	60	90
-	**LNER** 51290 open 3rd	60	90
-	**BR** E1717E open 3rd	60	90
-	**LNER** 1167 open 1st	60	90
-	**LNER** 1234 open composite	60	90
-	**LNER** 1278 open composite	60	90
-	**LNER** 5634 brake 3rd	60	90
-	**LNER** 5689 brake 3rd	60	90
-	**LNER** 4156 gangwayed full brake	60	90
-	**LNER** 4529 gangwayed full brake	60	90
-	**LNER** 678 1st restaurant car	60	90

C18. LNER Gresley General Stock
Teak Finish

-	**LNER** ? corridor 3rd	60	90
-	**LNER** 1134 corridor 1st	60	90
-	**LNER** 1167 corridor 1st	60	90
-	**LNER** 63280 corridor composite	60	90
-	**LNER** 63281 corridor composite	60	90
-	**LNER** 63489 corridor composite	60	90
-	**LNER** 62347 corridor brake 3rd	60	90
-	**LNER** 62547 corridor brake 3rd	60	90
	BR Maroon		
-	**BR** E1135E corridor 1st	60	90
-	**BR** E1261E corridor composite	60	90
-	**BR** E1262E corridor composite	60	90
-	**BR** E5071E corridor brake 3rd	60	90

C19. LNER Thompson Stock
These coaches have oval lavatory windows.
Teak Finish

-	**LNER** ? corridor 3rd	50	80
-	**LNER** ? corridor 1st	50	80
-	**LNER** ? corridor composite	50	80
-	**LNER** ? corridor brake 3rd	50	80
-	**LNER** ? restaurant car	50	80

C20. SR 59ft Bulleid Stock
SR Green

-	**SR** 101 corridor 3rd	50	80
-	**SR** 102 corridor 3rd	50	80
-	**SR** 110 corridor 3rd	50	80
-	**SR** 5710 corridor 3rd	50	80
-	**SR** 1710 corridor 1st	50	80

Anbrico 00

SR Bullied all-3rd [C20] (Paul Colbeck)

-	SR 1717 corridor 1st	50	80
-	SR 8071 corridor 1st	50	80
-	SR 5717 corridor composite	50	80
-	SR 2707 corridor brake 3rd	50	80
-	SR 6701 corridor brake 3rd	50	80
-	SR 6717 corridor brake 3rd	50	80

C21. BR Mk1 'Suburban' Stock

-	BR 57' composite	40	70
-	BR 64' composite	40	70
-	BR 57' brake/2nd	40	70
-	BR 64' brake/2nd	40	70
-	BR 57' 2nd class	40	70
-	BR 64' 2nd class	40	70
-	BR 57' lavatory composite	40	70
-	BR 57' lavatory open 2nd	40	70
-	BR 57' open 2nd	40	70
-	BR 64' open 2nd	40	70

C22 BR Mk1 64ft Corridor Stock

-	BR S24302 green corridor 2nd	40	70
-	BR E25857 maroon corridor 2nd	40	70
-	BR Sc3487 maroon open 2nd	40	70
-	BR E13117 maroon corridor 1st	40	70
-	BR ? corridor open 1st	40	70
-	BR ? corridor composite	40	70
-	BR Sc34725 maroon corridor brake 2nd	40	70
-	BR E35251 maroon corridor brake 2nd	40	70
-	BR ? corridor open brake 2nd	40	70
-	BR ? corridor brake 1st	40	70
-	BR ? corridor brake composite	40	70
-	BR M30962 maroon full brake	40	70
-	BR ? corridor sleeper 2nd	40	70
-	BR ? corridor sleeper 1st	40	70
-	BR ? corridor sleeper composite	40	70

BR Mk1 1st class corridor coach [C22] (Paul Colbeck)

C23. BR Mk1 Catering Stock

-	BR ? buffet/kitchen (KB)	40	70
-	BR ? buffet/kitchen (RKB)	40	70
-	BR ? kitchen car (RK)	40	70
-	BR ? open 2nd miniature buffet (RMB)	40	70
-	BR ? restaurant 1st (RF)	40	70
-	BR ? restaurant 1st (RFO)	40	70
-	BR ? restaurant 2nd (RSO)	40	70
-	BR ? restaurant unclassified (RU)	40	70

C24. BR Utility Stock

-	BR ? general utility van (GUV)	50	80

C25. US Passenger Stock

	New York Central Pullman passenger car	40	70
	New York Central passenger car	40	70
	New York Central catering car	40	70
	New York Central sleeping car	40	70
	New York Central mail car	40	70
	New York Central baggage car	40	70
	New York Central observation car	40	70
	Pullman aluminium bodied passenger car	40	70
	unmarked aluminium bodied passenger car	40	70

C25. South African Railways Stock

-	SAR 8817 maroon+cream passenger car	40	70

UK TOY & MODEL AUCTIONS LIMITED

Specialist Auctioneers of Toys and Models

THINKING OF SELLING YOUR COLLECTION?

TOYS & MODELS WANTED

FOR OUR FORTHCOMING AUCTIONS

We are able to give help if selling as part of an estate etc. Send your lists or contact

46 Wirral Gardens, Bebington, Wirral, Merseyside CH63 3BH
Telephone Barry Stockton 0151-334 3362
or Tony Oakes 01270 652773

www.uktoyauctions.com

MODEL RAILWAYS LIVE

Visit *British Railway Modelling's* website
www.model-railways-live.co.uk
for modelling news, reviews and products.

Arnold (British)
Hornby Arnold

HISTORY

Founded in 1906 by Karl Arnold in Nürnberg, K. Arnold & Co. began its life producing tin toys and related items. They produced an extensive line of model ships, doll house items and other toys. In 1935, K. Arnold & Co. appointed Max Ernst as their managing director. Ernst was to play an important roll in the future of Arnold.

During the war the Arnold factory was bombed and, after the war, the company moved to Upper Palatinate (Oberpfalz). The post-war operation of the company was under the control of Max Ernst and Ernst Arnold, son of Karl Arnold. The factory in Nürnberg was rebuilt and the Arnold Company continued to expand.

'Brighton Belle'

The development of Arnold Rapido lead to N scale becoming a commercial proposition. It was not the sole developer of commercial 2mm scale, but Arnold Rapido was the first and the Rapido coupling would be adopted as the international N gauge standard.

Max Ernst, who remained as Managing Director for over forty years until 1976, was largely responsible for the development and success of Arnold Rapido. Company founder, Karl Arnold, died in October, 1946, leaving his son and Max Ernst as principals in the company.

At the time of Max Ernst's retirement in 1976, Arnold employed 200 to 250 people, using three facilities in the Nürnberg area. It continued as a family business until 1995, when the company went into bankruptcy and was sold to Rivarossi of Italy. Rivarossi, in turn, also went bankrupt, leading to the sale of all assets to Hornby in Britain. Arnold became part of Hornby International and production moved to Sanda Kan in China.

Under Hornby, Arnold has continued to develop N gauge for its traditional markets but in 2012 with Hornby's co-operation, it was decided to test the British market. Now part of the Hornby organisation it had access to Hornby's on going research. A recently released new model in the Hornby 00 range was the 'Brighton Belle' classic 5-car EMU. It was decided that, with no similar model currently being made in 2mm scale, it would be a good subject to try. The model was announced at Nürnberg in 2013 and the news was received with great interest in Britain. The question everyone was asking was – "is this the first sign of Hornby entering the British N gauge market?"

In the past the company had turned down an invitation to buy Lone Star, has marketed Lima N gauge through its then G&R Wrenn subsidiary and worked with Trix on the design and marketing of Hornby Minitrix - but it has always steered clear of becoming directly involved with the manufacture of the models. Since 2004, however, it has owned four companies with experience in N gauge, two of which are currently actively involved in manufacturing high quality N gauge products.

LOCOMOTIVE

The model is accurate UK N scale – 1:148

Cat No.	Company, Number, Colour, Date	£	£
L1.	**5-BEL 'Brighton Belle' EMU (2013)**		

This is one of the most famous trains to operate on British tracks. It ran between London Victoria and Brighton and was the first all-electric Pullman service in the World. The service commenced in June 1934 and continued until April 1972, with only a period during the Second World War when it was suspended. There were three 5-Car units specifically built by Metropolitan Cammell. Now, under the patronage of the Transport Trust, a group is reconstituting and restoring a 5-BEL set to bring it back into service under private ownership.

The model has a high performance motor with flywheel, a 6-pin DCC decoder socket, illuminating table lamps and bogie design differences.
DMBPT = Driver Motor Brake Parlour Third.

Cat No.	Company, Number, Colour, Date	£	£
HN3000	**Pullman** 'Brighton Belle' (1934) ? (?+?) dark brown+cream 2-car pack (powered DMBPT + non-powered DMBPT) - *13*	NA	130
HN3001	**Pullman** 'Brighton Belle' (1969) ? (?+?) blue+grey 2-car trailer pack (powered DMBPT + non-powered DMBPT) - *13*	NA	130

COACHES

These consist of coach packs containing the three trailer cars for the 'Brighton Belle' EMU.

Cat No.	Company, Number, Colour, Date	£	£
C1.	**'Brighton Belle' Trailer Car Packs (2013)**		

TPFK = Trailer Pullman First Kitchen, TPT = Trailer Pullman Third.

Cat No.	Company, Number, Colour, Date	£	£
-	**Pullman** 'Brighton Belle' ? TPFK	NPG	NA
-	**Pullman** 'Brighton Belle' ? TPFK	NPG	NA
-	**Pullman** 'Brighton Belle' ? TPT	NPG	NA
HN3500	the above three (1934) dark brown+cream trailer cars - *13*	NA	80
-	**Pullman** 'Brighton Belle' ? TPFK	NPG	NA
-	**Pullman** 'Brighton Belle' ? TPFK	NPG	NA
-	**Pullman** 'Brighton Belle' ? TPT	NPG	NA
HN3500	the above three (1969) blue+grey trailer cars - *13*	NA	80

Hornby 'Britannia' Class - computer enhanced photograph by Robbie McGavin

Ixion Model Railways

WINNER O Gauge Steam Locomotive of the Year 2012

Now the best-selling 7mm finescale loco ever

Hudswell Clarke 0-6-0ST
RTR O Gauge 7mm scale, three liveries.

Features: Diecast chassis and 40:1 gearing for slow, smooth running; Finescale wheels; Will traverse 36" radius curves. DCC and sound ready; Moulded fire irons, bucket & oil bottles. Choice of etched brass builder's, name and number plates.

NEW FOR 2013

7mm GWR No.1 Fowler 0-4-0 DM

Features: Smooth-running diecast chassis, 40:1 gearing; Sprung buffers; Finescale wheels; Will traverse 36" radius curves. DCC and sound ready; Moulded wrenches, hammers, lamps & oil can. Plus etched brass builder's, name and number plates.

Available in the UK from:
AC Models, Eastleigh; Antics; Bournemouth Model Railway Centre; Dragon Models Wales; EDM Models; 53A Models, Hull; Hereford Model Centre; Locolines Ltd, Basildon, Essex; Mikron Models, Taunton; Peter Spares Model Railways, Middlesbrough; Roxey Mouldings, Surrey; Scograil, Ipswich; Tennents Trains, Halesowen; The Hobby Shop, Faversham; Tower Models, Blackpool; and www.7mm.co (online shop).

Ixion Model Railways Limited
Tel (UK): +44 (0) 7775 782086
Tel (Aust): +61 (0) 2 9626 9273
Web: www.ixionmodels.com
Email: info@ixionmodels.com

Bachmann Branchline

HISTORY

The name Bachmann came from a German emigrant to the USA who, in 1835, founded a company in Philadelphia. Amongst other things, the company made tinplate toys and, many years later, was one of the pioneers of plastic goods, including toy trains. Bachmann went on to become the largest distributor of toy trains and model railways in America.

Milestones
- 1835 Bachmann founded in Philadelphia.
- 1925 Ting Hsiung-chao buys a battery company in Shanghai.
- 1948 Ting founds Kader in Hong Kong.
- 1975 Kader start producing Mainline models for Palitoy.
- 1987 Kader buys Bachmann.
- 1989 Bachmann Industries Europe Ltd formed.
- 1990 Bachmann Branchlines launched in UK initially using former Mainline tools.
- 1993 Kader acquires Liliput.
- 1998 Bachmann Industries Europe Ltd introduce their Blue Riband range.
- 2000 Bachmann buy Graham Farish.
- 2005 Heritage range started in association with the NRM.
- 2006 Bachmann Europe plc take over UK distribution of Mahano
- 2009 The demise of Mehano and the end of the agency agreement.
- 2013 Bachmann take on responsibility for marketing EFE diecast models.

Meanwhile, in 1925, in China, a man named Ting Hsiung-chao bought a battery manufacturing company in Shanghai for US$500. During the civil war between the Nationalist and Communist factions in China he was imprisoned for political reasons by the Communists and was unable to tend to his business, which ultimately collapsed as a result. He was eventually forced to flee from Communist China, to re-establish what became a thriving business in North Point, Hong Kong.

His company, Kader, was founded in 1948 and went on to become the largest manufacturer of toys in the Far East. In the mid 1950s, the Company started manufacturing for Bachmann and by 1987, Kader had bought Bachmann outright.

Kader Industrial Co. Ltd, one of the Kader group of companies, is now based in Kowloon Bay, very near the old airport, Kai Tak.

One British company, for which it manufactured, was Palitoy, the owners of the Mainline Railways range which was prominent in the late 1970s and early 1980s. Palitoy had an arrangement whereby they required the manufacturers to produce their own tools for their products, with the tools remaining in the ownership of the manufacturing company. As a result of this, when Palitoy closed down and its model railway assets were acquired by Dapol, the latter did not acquire the Far East tools of Kader origin.

A1 class Tornado [L48] (Tony Wright)

By the late 1980s, Kader were looking at the European market. With their good collection of tools for making locomotives and rolling stock for the British market (former Mainline range), they decided to form a European company to develop the local potential. Thus, Bachmann Industries Europe Ltd was formed in June 1989 (although it

Bachmann 'Jubilee' Class 45587 Baroda - computer artwork by Robbie McGavin titled 'A Wet Night at Preston'.

Bachmann Branchline

had really started as early as May 1988) and the model railway press in Britain announced the newly launched Bachmann Branchline range in January 1990. Kader also acquired Liliput which is based in Altdorf, near Nuremberg, Germany. A new purpose built block has been added to the Zhong Tang factory complex, in Guang Dong Province, dedicated solely to the manufacture of model railways in various gauges for the UK, Continental Europe, China and US markets. This also included the Graham Farish N gauge range which Bachmann acquired in 2000. While Bachmann models are made at Zhong Tang, the parent company, Kader Industrial Co. Ltd, is still based in Kowloon Bay, Hong Kong.

It seems that the Bachmann Branchline models were not the first British outline subjects produced for Bachmann by Kader. Back in 1985 and 1986, in association with Bachmann in America, two train sets were produced using the former Mainline tooling. This was only two years after Mainline production had ended and Kader had been left holding the tools. The sets were sold under the Bachmann name - one in bright red called 'The Flying Scot' set and the other in royal blue called 'The Royal Scot' set. These contained a *Royal Scot* locomotive with a mix of Collett and LMS panelled stock passenger brake vans (four in each set). The extraordinary colour schemes and odd choice of coaches, were nothing compared to the hilarious inscription on the boxes. These were pure fantacy and showed a total lack of knowledge of British Railway history. The sets were almost certainly produced for the American market.

Although the former Mainline tools formed the basis of the Bachmann British range, the years since then have seen considerable improvements made to the models and, early on, the launch of many new models. This process continues with Bachmann setting a new standard for ready-to-run 00 scale models in the UK which rivals were forced to follow.

Blue Riband Models - With the ever increasing strive for higher quality in their models, in 1998, Bachmann launched their Blue Riband range. This badge is worn only by those models that Bachmann consider to be to the high standard they have set themselves to achieve and it is expected that all completely new models will fall into this category. The name comes from transatlantic shipping where the Blue Riband was awarded to the fastest liner to ply the route.

BR brake corridor composite [C12h] (Tony Wright)

FURTHER READING
A series of articles was written by Graham Smith-Thompson, in Model Railway Enthusiast and Model Railway Collector magazines, profiling the Airfix and Mainline ranges and other systems that later used the tools. The first part on Bachmann models was published before the magazine ceased publication in the summer of 2000 but subsequent parts were not published. The magazine of the Bachmann Collectors Club (see below) is developing into a useful source of information for further research.

COLLECTORS CLUB
For a number of years the company sponsored an enthusiasts club called Bachmann Times which operated at arms-length. In 2000 the club was reformed in-house under the name Bachmann Collectors Club (BCC) and members receive a quarterly magazine. Further information about this may be obtained by writing to the Club at Bachmann Europe plc, Moat Way, Barwell, Leicestershire LE9 8EY.

Bachmann frequently offer members limited edition models and these are marked in the tables below with 'BCC'.

Dates - It is difficult to date Bachmann Branchline models by their appearance in catalogues as some models have not been ready for distribution until one or two years after their catalogue launch. As near as possible, in the tables below, we have given the years in which we believe the models first appeared in the shops. Please bear in mind that these may sometimes be incorrect.

A single date has been given because Bachmann operated a batch production supply system. Generally there is only an initial batch of models which, when sold-out, is not repeated. Instead, the model is either dropped from the catalogue or replaced by a similar model renumbered and often improved in finish. Some models have been available in the shops for several years from the date of the initial production - the length of time being dependent on the popularity of the model.

Catalogue Numbers - Generally, the addition of a letter suffix to a catalogue number indicates a modification of some kind to the model. This could be a change of number or an alteration to the chassis. For general release models, the letters are taken from the start of the alphabet i.e. 'A', 'B', 'C' etc. but for commissioned models (specials ordered by shops or societies) lettering starts with 'Z' and works upwards from the bottom of the alphabet. (See also the note on 'Wagon Numbers' in the Wagons section, as this may also apply to locos and coaches).

More recently, some locomotive catalogue numbers have received a '**DC**' or '**DS**' suffix. DC indicates that the locomotive already carries a decoder chip and DS that it also fitted for 'sound'.

Buyers should be aware that box numbering errors have sometimes occurred and that boxes with a 'new' number suffix sometimes contain a model with the old number.

Boxes - wooden presentation cases (**wpc**) have been provided for a number of limited or special editions.

Weathering - Bachmann were one of the first to turn out models with a weathered finish (although Tri-ang had tried it in 1965). It started with wagons and spread to locomotive and eventually coach models. To save space, weathered models are coded in the text with a '**W**' after the colour

Heritage Range - From 2005, a number of models, based on subjects in the National Collection, were released by Bachmann in a new 'Heritage Range'.

LNER Class J72 0-6-0T in Apple Green [L9]

LOCOMOTIVES
Bachmann took the 'Spectrum' quality of their American range and applied it to the British models to give very superior performance far removed from the old Mainline standard. A skew armature replaceable Mabuchi can motor was fitted with an excellent gear drive and brass flywheel.

'DCC Ready' - (Catalogue No. suffix) - Since 2003, some locomotives

Bachmann Branchline

have been released ready to receive a DCC decoder ('DCC ready'). This means that they are fitted inside with a blanked-off socket ready to take a DCC decoder (chip).

'DCC8' or **'DCC21'** - This indicates the pins on the decoder that the fitted socket will take. The 21 pin decoders allow for a greater number of functions, including sound.

'DC Fitted' - From 2006 some locomotives were marketed with a DCC decoder already fitted. As mentioned above, these carry a 'DC' catalogue number suffix.

'DS' - From 2006, a selection of locomotives were equipped with DCC sound units and these carry a 'DS' catalogue number suffix.

Economy Sound - As we close for press, Bachmann have announced that they will be producing an economy series of sound-fitted locomotives. These will be:

35-600	Class 20 diesel	(RRP £143)
35-625	Class 37 diesel	(RRP £148.85)
35-650	45xx 2-6-2T	(RRP £143)
35-675	57xx Pannier Tank	(RRP £132)
35-700	BR 5MT 4-6-0	(RRP £181)

Bachmann's 2007 range of starter locos (Tony Wright)

Interestingly, the new sound system can be used on both DCC and DC analogue systems, giving 00 scale DC users a sound option. This uses a system developed with the American company Soundtraxx.

Cat No.	Company, Number, Colour, Date	£	£

Tank Engines

0-4-0T

L1.   Freelance 0-4-0ST (2004)

It was decided to produce some models and train sets aimed at the younger market and, in order to keep the retail price to a minimum, use was made of existing tooling. The first of these was the 0-4-0 saddle tank model which had originally been produced as Percy in the 'Thomas the Tank Engine & Friends' range in America, and for other overseas markets. However, after an initial two models, Bachmann were prevented from further use of the tooling for licencing reasons.

(30-040)DC	**31** *Greg* red, DCC chip fitted, ex-set - *04*	20	NA
30-905	**311** GWR (shirt-button) green - *05*	20	25

2-4-2T

L2.   L&Y Aspinall Radial Class 5 2-4-2T (2013)

This was a short bunker version of Aspinall's radial passenger tank of 1889 produced for the Lancashire & Yorkshire Railway. They passed to the LMS in 1923 and to British Railways in 1948.

At the time of writing, this model has not yet been released, but it is understood that it will have a highly detailed cab interior and a 6-pin DCC decoder socket fitted.

31-165	**10818** LMS black - *13*	NPG	80
31-166	**50636** BRb black - *13*	NPG	80
31-166	**50795** BRb black - *not made*	NA	NA
31-167DC	**50764** BRb black W, DCC chip fitted - *13*	NPG	80

0-6-0T

L3.   Freelance 0-6-0T (2004)

As with the 0-4-0 saddle tank described in L1 above, this model was originally produced for the American and overseas market in the 'Thomas the Tank Engine & Friends' series, in this case as Thomas himself. For the British market it has taken on other identities, but, for licencing reasons, Bachmann were prevented from further sales of it and it was withdrawn.

(30-005)DC	**4** *Billy* green ex-set, DCC chip fitted - *04*	20	NA
(30-040)DC	**49** *Stuart* blue ex-set, DCC chip fitted - *04*	20	NA
30-900	**2005** red - *05*	20	25

L4.   Freelance 0-6-0ST (2007)

This was a later addition to the freelance 'starter' range and makes use of the chassis produced for Thomas in the American series but with the addition of a different body. The new body allowed more space for a DCC 8-pin socket to be provided making the model 'DCC ready'.

(30-941)DC	**3** *Digby* red ex-set, DCC chip fitted - *07*	20	26
(30-007)	***Jack*** GER lined blue ex-'Jack The Saddle Tank' set - *11*	24	NA
30-920	**7** LNER green - *07*	20	26
30-921	**8** BRb lined black - *11*	25	30

0-6-0 saddle tank Jack [L4]

L5a.   GWR Class 57xx 0-6-0PT (ex-Mainline) (1991)

This was a Collett pannier tank design of 1929, but with a Churchward cab. A total of 863 locomotives were built between 1929 and 1950. The last was withdrawn in 1966. 13 had been sold to London Transport between 1957 and 1963 and the last of these worked on the London Transport network until 1971. 16 of the class have been preserved, including 6 of those sold to London Transport.

Although shown as solo models in the catalogue from 1993, these may not have had their debut until later. The plastic used for the first batch of loco bodies was found to be susceptible to damage from lubricating oil and so they were withdrawn. From 1996, these were given an improved chassis.

imp = improved chassis.

31-900	**7760** Great Western green - *93*	30	40
31-900A	**7702** GWR green imp - *96*	25	35
31-901A	**8700** GWR (button) green imp - *96*	25	35
31-903*	**L94** London Transport maroon imp Sp Edn 500 (LT Museum) - *99*	40	55
(30-200)	**L91** LT maroon ex-sets - *91*	80	NA
(30-201)	**L99** LT maroon ex-sets - *93*	30	NA
31-901	**5796** BRb black - *93*	30	40
31-902	**7754** BRb black - *93*	30	40
31-902A	**5775** BRc black imp - *96*	25	35

* Box unnumbered.

L5b.   GWR Class 57xx 0-6-0PT (2005)

The former Mainline model was replaced in 2005 by a retooled Class 57xx, with new bunker and a new cab with good interior detail. It was given circular water fillers and lamp brackets and made use of the chassis produced for the subclass 8750 (below).

From 2007, these well detailed models had 8-pin sockets fitted.

(30-075)	**5764** Great Western green ex-Local Freight set - *10*	50	NA
32-218	**8709** Great Western green - *13*	60	74
32-215	**5775** GWR green - *10*	45	58
32-210	**5786** GWR green - *05*	40	52
32-213DC	**7788** GWR green, DCC chip fitted - *07*	55	66
32-214	**5766** BRb black - *09*	45	56
32-219	**7717** BRb black W - *13*	65	80
32-211	**7739** BRb black - *05*	40	52
32-212	**5757** BRc black - *05*	40	52
32-216	**8732** BRc black - *11*	50	65
32-217	**L89** London Transport lined maroon - *11*	50	65
32-210Z	**L95** London Transport lined maroon Sp Edn 504 (Kernow Model Rail Centre) - *07*	50	60
(30-076)	**L97** London Transport maroon ex-Midnight Metropolitan set - *12*	60	NA
32-210Z	**L99** London Transport maroon Sp Edn 504		

Bachmann Branchline

	(Kernow MRC) - not made	NA	NA
32-210Z	L95 London Transport lined maroon Sp Edn 504 (Kernow Model Rail Centre) - 07	50	60
32-210Y	7754 NCB green W Sp Edn 512 (ModelZone) - 10	60	70
32-200K	3650 Stephenson Clarke blue W Sp Edn 504 (BCC) - 10	45	56

GWR Class 8750 0-6-0 Pannier tank [L5c]

L5c. GWR Class 8750 0-6-0PT (1999)

These are usually considered to be part of the Class 57xx and were introduced to the GWR in 1933 by Collett, as a heavier version. They had a modified cab, for better visibility by the crew, and better weather protection.

During 2007 the models became 'DCC ready' with 8-pin sockets fitted.

32-204	4612 Great Western green - 06	40	52
32-206	8751 Great Western green - 08	40	53
(32-010)	3705 GWR green ex-Coaler train set - 05	35	NA
32-200B	3715 GWR green - 03	35	45
32-200A	6752 GWR green blue spot - 01	35	45
32-208	6757 GWR green - 10	45	58
32-208A	9635 GWR green - 13	60	74
32-200	9643 GWR green - 99	35	45
32-209	3711 BRb black - 11	50	65
32-201	8763 BRb lined black - 99	35	45
32-205	9736 BRb black - 06	40	52
32-203	4666 BRc black W - 03	40	48
32-202	4672 BRc black - 99	35	45
32-203A	4680 BRc black W - 13	65	80
32-202A*	9735 BRc black - 02	40	48
32-202B	9753 BRc black - 04	40	48
32-200DC	9759 BRc black, DCC chip fitted - 06	52	64
32-207	9761 BRc black - 09	45	56

* Box found labelled '9735'.

L6. GWR Class 64xx 0-6-0PT (2013)

A total of 40 of the class were built between 1932 and 1950. The last was withdrawn in 1964 and three have been preserved.

Not yet released at the time of writing, it is understood that this highly detailed model will have an 8-pin DCC decoder socket fitted.

31-635	6407 GWR green - 13	64	77
31-636	6403 BRb black - 13	64	77
31-637	2005 BRc lined green - 13	64	77

L7. MR Class 1F 0-6-0T (2014)

The locomotives were built to an 1874 design between 1878 and 1879 for the Midland Railway. A large number were rebuilt from 1919 onwards with Belpaire fireboxes. The last was withdrawn in 1966 and one has been preserved.

Not yet released at the time of writing, this model will have a 6-pin DCC decoder socket fitted.

31-430	1725 LMS black - 14	65	80
31-431	41708 BRb black (as preserved) - 14	65	80
31-432	41661 BRc black - 14	65	80

L8. LMS Class 3F 'Jinty' 0-6-0T (2004)

The class was designed for the LMS by Henry Fowler, based on an earlier Johnson design. The 'Jinty' became the company's standard 0-6-0 tank shunting engine and 422 were built between 1924 and 1931, much of the work being contracted out. They were highly versatile engines and found themselves on both freight and passenger trains. Seven spent a period on the S&DJR and two went to Northern Ireland in 1944. Some survived to the last days of steam and 10 have been preserved.

Some of the models have bodies moulded with 'keyholes' in the bottom of the tank sides and some without. The 2006 pioneer 'DCC fitted' model was 'hard-wired', but, from 2011, a DCC decoder socket has been fitted.

Xkh = without 'keyhole' in the tank sides.

32-226W	16440 MR red Sp Edn 504 (Cheltenham Model Centre) (32-225W) - 05	45	56
32-225Y	18 NCC black Y Class Ltd Edn 250 - 05	40	55
32-225Z	19 NCC black Y Class Ltd Edn 250 - 05	40	55
32-225V	24 S&DJR dark blue Sp Edn 504 (Cheltenham Model Centre) - 05	40	55
32-233	23 S&DJR dark blue - 13	58	73
32-227	7524 LMS black - 04	40	48
32-227A	7309 LMS black - 09	45	56
32-226	47354 BRb black - 04	40	48
32-231	47394 BRb black - 11	52	64
32-321A	47314 BRb black -12	NPG	NPG
32-229	47279 BRb black (K&WVR) Xkh - 05	40	53
(30-016)	47310 BRb lined black Xkh ex-'Jinty Suburban' set - 06	40	NA
32-230	47483 BRb black - 09	45	56
32-225	47410 BRc black - 04	40	48
32-232	47500 BRc black - 11	50	64
32-225DC	47629 BRc black, DCC chip fitted - 06	48	62
32-225X	47357 BRc red Sp Edn 500 *- 05	65	90
32-228	47506 BRc black Xkh - not made	NA	NA
32-228	47266 BRc black Xkh - 05	40	53
32-225U	47472 BRc black W Sp Edn (Transport Models) - 06	45	61
32-225K	(47445) PO black+yellow Sp Edn 504 (BCC) - 11	45	58

* This was initially released at the 2005 Toyfair as a gift for retailers. It is understood that over 100 were distributed this way. The remainder were bought by Bachmann Club members on the basis of a draw.

Someset & Dorset Joint Railway 'Jinty' 0-6-0T [L8]

L9. LNER Class J72 0-6-0T (ex-Mainline) (1990)

This was Wilson Worsdell's 1898 design for the North Eastern Railway, for goods yard shunting. They were built over a long period of time, initially at Darlington and privately by Armstrong Whitworth & Co. The LNER built some at Doncaster and BR built a batch at Darlington between 1949 and 1951. The last was withdrawn in 1966 and one has been preserved.

The Bachmann model is similar to the last Mainline J72 but the drive was slightly redesigned with an improved open frame motor driving on the centre axle and leaving the cab clear. The wheelsets were also improved and the problem of axles splitting was resolved. The model has yet to be converted to take a DCC decoder socket.

* full length ejector pipe.

(30-060)	581 LNER green ex- Kader 60th Anniv. pack - 08	50	NA
31-050	8680 LNER green - 90	28	35
31-050A	8680 LNER green lined - 99	30	40
31-054	2313 LNER black lined * - 96	25	35
31-057	8693 LNER black unlined * - 98	30	40
31-052	68680 BRb black lined - 90	28	35
31-055	68680 BRb green lined * - 96	25	30
31-055A	68737 BRb black W * - 02	30	45
(30-100)	68745 BRb plain black Ross 'pop' valves ex-set - 94	50	NA
31-053	69012 BRc plain black - 90	27	35
31-056	69025 BRc plain black * - 96	27	35
31-058	68727 BRc black W - 05	32	45
31-059	69022 BRc plain black - 08	40	51
31-051	69023 BRc/NER light green - 90	25	35
31-056	68723 BRc/NER light green - 05	30	41

L10. LB&SCR Class E4 0-6-0T (2013)

This was a class of 75 locomotives built for the London Brighton & South Coast Railway between 1897 and 1903. Four were rebuilt as the E4X Class in 1911. The last of the class was withdrawn in 1963 and one locomotive has been preserved.

Bachmann Branchline

At the time of writing, this model has not yet been released but it is understood that a 6-pin DCC decoder socket will be fitted.

35-075	**579** LB&SCR brown - *13*	NPG	NPG
35-076	**473** SR green - *13*	NPG	NPG
35-077	**32556** BRb black - *13*	NPG	NPG
35-078	**32470** BRc black - *13*	NPG	NPG

L10a. SR Class USA 0-6-0T (2014)

93 of these were built in 1942-43 by Vulcan Works, Wilkes-Barre, PA in the USA for the US Army Transport Corps. A further 289 were built by other companies. After the war, 15 were bought by the Southern Railway in 1947 and all but one passed to BR. Several of them survived through to 1967 and 4 have been preserved.

This model was commissioned by Model Rail magazine.

-	**1959** WD grey - *14*	NPG	105
-	**69** SR black - *14*	NPG	105
-	**30069** BRb black - *14*	NPG	105
-	**30073** BRc lined green - *14*	NPG	105

0-6-2T

GWR Class 56xx 0-6-2T [L11] (Tony Wright)

L11. GWR Class 56xx 0-6-2T (2002)

Between 1924 and 1928, 200 of these Collett designed heavy freight tanks were built, mostly to work coal trains in the Welsh valleys. They were built at Swindon and gradually replaced older tank engines that had been absorbed by the GWR in 1923. In the Welsh Valleys they were also used on passenger trains and this led to some being given a lined Brunswick green livery in later years. The last was withdrawn from BR service in 1966 and 9 have been preserved.

Both tall and short safety valve covers have been modelled by Bachmann and, from 2005, this was shown as being 'DCC ready' with an 8-pin DCC decoder socket.

32-076	**6676** Great Western green - *02*	35	45
32-075C	**5623** GWR green - *not made*	NA	NA
32-075	**5667** GWR green - *02*	35	45
32-075A	**6600** GWR green - *03*	35	45
32-075B	**6606** GWR green - *05*	38	51
32-075C	**6623** GWR green - *10*	38	54
32-084	**6677** GWR green - *13*	NPG	NPG
32-082	**5639** BRc plain black W - *10*	40	57
32-081	**5660** BRb plain black W - *06*	40	53
32-079	**6624** BRb plain black - *03*	35	45
32-085	**6639** BRb plain black - *13*	NPG	NPG
32-076DC	**6671** BRc lined green, DCC chip fitted - *06*	50	63
32-077	**5658** BRc lined green - *02*	35	45
(30-055)DC	as above with ex-set, DCC chip fitted - *06*	45	NA
32-083	**6658** BRc lined green - *11*	50	66
(32-015)	**6622** BRc plain green ex-set - *06*	35	45
32-080	**5601** BRc plain green - *03*	35	45

2-6-2T

L12a. GWR Class 45xx 2-6-2T (2003)

This is a Churchward designed tank dating from 1906 and was a development of his earlier Class 44xx, which they closely resembled. The most noticeable difference was the larger driving wheels. They were built at Wolverhampton or Swindon and construction continued until 1929, bringing the total to 175. In 1953 15 were fitted for push-pull work in the Cardiff area and those in the Taunton area were fitted with an automatic staff changing apparatus. The last of the class was withdrawn in 1965 and 14 have been preserved.

The model has a heavy diecast chassis block, a metal chimney, alternative smokebox doors and a highly detailed cab interior. Models planned for 2013 have an 8-pin DCC decoder socket fitted.

32-127B	**4555** Great Western green - *13*	70	85
32-127	**4550** GWR green - *03*	40	50
32-127A	**4527** GWR green - *04*	40	54
32-129A	**4545** BRb lined black - *13*	70	85
32-129	**4557** BRb lined black - *07*	45	57
32-126	**4560** BRb plain black - *03*	40	50
32-128	**4573** BRb plain black W - *04*	45	56
32-125DC	**4507** BRc lined green, DCC chip fitted - *07*	50	69
32-125	**4566** BRc lined green - *03*	40	50
32-125A	**4569** BRc lined green - *04*	40	54
32-130	**4571** BRc lined green - *11*	60	75

Ex-GWR Class 45xx in BR lined green [L12a]

L12b. GWR Class 4575 2-6-2T (2004)

These were 45xx tanks built to the modified design of 1927. They had larger side tanks, giving an extra 300 gallons water capacity and sloping tank tops to improve driver visibility. These later locomotives all had the larger bunker to increase coal capacity.

Like the rest of the class (above), the model has a heavy diecast chassis block and highly detailed cab. It is fitted with sprung buffers and a metal chimney. Models planned for 2013 have an 8-pin DCC decoder socket fitted.

32-136	**5555** Great Western green - *04*	40	54
32-139	**5513** GWR green - *12*	65	80
32-135	**5531** GWR green - *04*	40	54
32-135A	**5565** GWR green - *08*	45	57
32-138	**5550** BRc green DCC8 - *10*	45	64
32-137	**5559** BRb plain black - *not made*	NA	NA
32-137	**5500** BRb plain black - *04*	40	54
32-140	**4585** BRb lined green - *12*	65	80
32-135Y	**5552** BRc lined green Ltd Edn 504 (Kernow Model Rail Centre) - *04*	45	65
32-135Z	**5553** BRc lined green Ltd Edn 1000 (BCC) - *04*	38	55
32-136Z	**L150** LT lined maroon Ltd Edn 504 (London Transport Museum)* - *13*	80	98

* The museum has leased and painted privately owned No.5521 in this livery for the LT150 celebrations in 2013.

L13. LMS Ivatt Class 2MT 2-6-2T (1995)

This was an Ivatt mixed traffic design of 1946 and was a tank version of his 6400 Class tender engines. Only 8 were built by the LMS before nationalisation, but BR continued building them until 1952. With modifications, it then became the standard 84xxx 2-6-2T Class. The class became a common sight on branch lines and 60 were fitted with push-pull equipment. The last was withdrawn in 1967. Of the 130 built, four have survived into preservation.

Models are now fitted with an 8-pin DCC decoder socket.
p-p = push-pull equipment.

31-453	**1206** LMS black - *95*	35	48
31-453A	**1202** LMS black - *98*	35	48
31-450	**41221** BRb black p-p - *95*	30	44
31-450B	**41281** BRb lined black p-p - *98*	30	44
31-450E	**41273** BRb fine lined black p-p - *02*	40	52
31-451	**41241** BRb lined black - *95*	35	45
31-451A	**41250** BRb lined black - *96*	35	45
31-451C	**41247** BRb lined black - *00*	40	50
31-451D	**41243** BRb lined black - *01*	40	52
31-454	**41286** BRb lined black - *02*	40	50
31-457	**41310** BRb lined black - *11*	NPG	70
31-440	**41243** BRb lined black - *12*	NPG	NPG
31-450A	**41272** BRc black p-p plaque as 7000th loco from Crewe - *96*	35	50
31-450C	**41224** BRc lined black p-p - *00*	40	52
31-450D	**41324** BRc fine lined black p-p - *02*	40	52
31-452	**41313** BRc lined black - *95*	30	44

Bachmann Branchline

31-452A	**41202** BRc lined black - *96*	35	44
31-452B	**41233** BRc lined black - *98*	35	44
31-452C	**41304** BRc fine lined black - *01*	35	52
31-455	**41212** BRc lined black - *05*	40	52
31-456	**41264** BRc lined black - *08*	47	61
31-441DC	**41291** BRc lined black, DCC chip fitted - *12*	NPG	NPG
31-450K	**41241** KWVR lined maroon + headboard Sp Edn 650 (BCC) - *08*	47	61

Ex-LNER Class V3 [L14]

L14. LNER Class V1 & V3 2-6-2T (1992)

The V1 large passenger tanks were built in the 1930s, initially for use on the widened Metropolitan lines, but were sent to Scotland. A later batch was deployed north of London but the final ten, built with higher pressure boilers as V3s, went to the North East. Gradually most of the V1s were rebuilt as V3s between 1942 and 1961. A total of 92 locomotives were built and withdrawls started in 1960, most going in the wholesale cull of 1962 and none was preserved.

Arriving in 1992, the models were the first new Bachmann locomotives, not to have come from tooling produced for Palitoy's Mainline range. The models originally had a split-chassis and were not fitted with DCC decoder sockets. Those released from 2013 will have an upgraded chassis to take an 8-pin DCC decoder socket.

hb = hopper bunker. csp = cranked steam pipes. West = Westinghouse pump

31-600	**7684** LNER green (V3) hb - *92*	32	48
31-608	**7684** LNER green hb (V3) - *99*	40	52
31-603	**466** LNER black (V1) hb csp - *92*	34	48
31-606	**448** LNER lined black hb (V1) - *97*	35	48
31-606A	**2911** LNER black csp (V1) - *00*	40	52
31-607	**67684** BRa lined light green hb (V3) - *97*	30	44
31-602	**67664** BRb black (V1) hb - *92*	32	48
31-605	**67610** BRb lined black (V1)* csp - *96*	35	48
31-609	**67673** BRb black West hb (V1)* - *99*	40	52
31-609A	**67669** BRb lined black West hb (V3) - *02*	45	57
31-610	**67645** BRb lined black csp (V1) - *02*	40	52
31-615	**67690** BRb lined black hb (V3) - *13*	NPG	90
31-601	**67601** BRc black (V1) csp - *92*	45	57
31-614	**67609** BRc black (V3) csp - *13*	NPG	90
31-613	**67628** BRc lined black csp (V3) - *11*	57	71
31-604	**67666** BRc black (V3) hb - *96*	35	48
31-611	**67635** BRc lined black W (V1) - *02*	45	57
31-612	**67682** BRc lined black W West hb - *06*	45	57
31-613	**67628** BRc lined black csp (V3) - *09*	50	63

* The box indicates that this was a V3.

L15. BR Class 3MT 2-6-2T (2009)

This was the Riddles larger mixed traffic 2-6-2T locomotive of 1952 which was designed and built at Swindon for light passenger work. 45 were built and all had gone by the end of 1967. None was preserved, but the Severn Valley Railway has a new one under construction.

The model features an opening smoke box door, highly detailed cab interior, different styles of lamp brackets and cab roofs with small or large opening air vents. Models are correctly fitted with either fluted or plain coupling rods and Western Region locomotives feature the extra handrail on the top of the boiler. The models also have an 8-pin DCC decoder socket fitted.

SR = BR(SR) allocation with extra lamp brackets for white discs.

31-979	**82001** BRb lined black - *12*	75	92
31-979A	**82001** BRb lined black W - *13*	NPG	NPG
31-977	**82016** BRb lined black SR - *09*	60	76
31-975A	**82020** BRb black - *10*	60	78
31-975	**82029** BRb lined black - *09*	60	76
31-978	**82019** BRc black - *10*	60	78
31-976	**82005** BRc lined green - *09*	60	76
31-976	**82005** BRc green - *10*	60	76
31-980	**82020** BRc plain green - *13*	NPG	NPG

Ex-LMS Class 3MT 2-6-2T [L15] (Tony Wright)

2-6-4T

L16. LMS Fairburn Class 4P 2-6-4T (2006)

Designed by Charles Fairburn during the Second World War, a total of 277 of these tank engines were constructed between 1945 and 1951 at the LMS Derby Works. After Nationalisation, a further 41 were made at the former Southern Railway works in Brighton. They were an 'improved' version of Stanier's 2-6-4 tank. The last Fairburn tank was withdrawn in 1965 and 2 have been preserved on the Lakeside & Haverthwaite Railway.

The model was launched before the model railway press in October 2006 at Haverthwaite. It has an 8-pin DCC decoder socket, heavy internal weights, glazed cab windows and detailed pipework.

32-875	**2691** LMS plain black - *06*	55	70
32-875DC	**42085** BRb lined black, DCC chip fitted - *11*	90	110
32-876	**42096** BRb lined black - *07*	55	70
32-878	**42691** BRb lined black - *08*	60	80
32-877	**42073** BRc lined black - *06*	55	70
32-879	**42267** BRc lined black W - *08*	55	83
32-875K	**2085** CR blue Ltd Edn 504 (BCC) - *06*	85	100

L17. BR Class 4MT Tank 2-6-4T (2001)

Riddles designed this mixed traffic locomotive which first made its appearance in 1951. A total of 155 locomotives were built between 1951 and 1957. They were used mainly for branch line and suburban passenger duties. The last was withdrawn in 1967 and 15 have been preserved.

The model has separately fitted water tanks and a very detailed cab interior. The original batch of these had a smokebox door that could be opened, but Bachmann subsequently released them with the door lightly glued in place. The 4MT tank models made from 2002 onwards were fitted with higher quality 3-pole motors and lower gearing. From 2005, the models were fitted with 8-pin DCC decoder sockets.

32-350	**80061** BRb lined black - *01*	45	58
32-350DC	**80009** BRb lined black DCC chip fitted - *06*	65	82
32-352	**80032** BRb lined black - *02*	50	64
32-355	**80136** BRb lined black - *03*	50	64
32-358	**80118** BRb lined black - *08*	60	78
32-359	**80053** BRb lined black - *10*	65	82
32-351	**80097** BRc lined black - *01*	45	60
32-351DC	**80140** BRc lined black, DCC chip fitted - *08*	70	92
32-353	**80135** BRc lined green - *02*	50	75
32-354	**80002** BRc lined black - *02*	50	64
32-354A	**80120** BRc lined black W - *03*	55	68
32-356	**80038** BRc lined black W - *04*	55	68
32-357	**80079** BRc lined black - *06*	55	70
32-360	**80121** BRc lined black - *13*	80	100

Tender Locos

4-4-0

GWR City of Truro [L18] (Tony Wright)

Visit the BRM website at: www.model-railways-live.co.uk — 8th Edition

Bachmann Branchline

L18. GWR 'City' Class 37xx 4-4-0 (2009)

Ten locomotives of the 'City' Class were built at Swindon in the Spring of 1903. A further ten were rebuilt from locomotives of the 'Atbara' Class between 1902 and 1909 to make a total of 20.

Following on from the success of the model of the prototype 'Deltic', produced exclusively for the NRM in 2007, Bachmann were asked to produce a second exclusive model – the GWR 4-4-0 3440 *City of Truro*. The agreement with the NRM was that the tooling could be used by Bachmann for other members of the class after a period of two years. The model, which has a 21-pin DCC decoder socket fitted, was voted best 00 steam locomotive model of 2009.

31-725	**3440** *City of Truro* GWR green with brown chassis Sp Edn (NRM) sold in special platinum box - *09*	90	180
31-725	as above but in a standard box GWR - *10*	90	145
31-725A	**3717** *City of Truro* GWR green with black chassis * Sp Edn (NRM) - *10*	90	150
31-726	**3433** *City of Bath* Great (garter)Western lined green with black chassis - *12*	100	123
31-727	**3439** *City of London* GWR (monogram), lined green with brown chassis - *12*	100	123

* The loco was repainted in 2010 in its 1912 livery, and given its earlier number, for the GWR 175th Anniversary celebrations.

L19. GWR 'Earl' Class 32xx ('Dukedog') 4-4-0 (2013)

Designed by C.B.Collett, the 'Earls' were a 1936-39 rebuild which used the chassis of locomotives from the 'Bulldog' Class and the boilers and cabs from the 'Duke' Class - thus the nickname 'Dukedog' applied to these locomotives. With their external frames, they looked very old fashoned for their time. The last was withdrawn in 1961 and one has been preserved on the Bluebell Railway.

At the time of writing, the model has not yet been released, but it is understood that it is to be a highly detailed model and fitted with a 21-pin DCC decoder socket. It has a heavy diecast alloy frame, prototypical outside frames and all new tender tooling.

31-087DC	**3203** GWR (button) green, DCC chip fitted - *not made*	NA	NA
31-087DC	**9003** GWR green, DCC chip fitted - *13*	NPG	140
31-086	**9017** *Earl Berkeley* BRb black as preserved - *13*	NPG	123
31-085	**9022** BRb black W - *13*	NPG	135

L20a. MR 'Midland Compound' 4-4-0 (2011)

On the Midland Railway, Samuel Johnson's first 'Compound' was introduced in 1902 and modified versions were produced by Richard Deeley in 1905. The 45 locos were originally classified as Class 4 but this was later changed to 4P, as their primary function was express and local passenger services. The model was produced exclusively for the National Railway Museum and is based on the locomotive in the National Collection.

31-930NRM	**1000** MR maroon - *11*	120	140
31-930	**1000** MR maroon Special Edition 500 (NRM) + plynth + 'platinum' box - *11*	120	170
(?)	**1000** LMS maroon Sp Edn 100 ex-train set (NRM Shildon) - *12*	120	NA

Midland Railway 'Compound' [L20a]

L20b. LMS 'Compound' 4-4-0 (2012)

The LMS adopted the Midland 'Compound' as a standard design and building of them continued from 1924 until 1932. A total of 195 were built and worked throughout the LMS system. Much of their work was later taken over by the 'Jubilee' and 'Black 5' classes. The LMS 'Compounds' had 7ft driving wheels as opposed to 6ft 9in ones on the 'Midland Compounds' and Bachmann have reflected this difference. Other differences include a flatter top to the dome, strengthened frame extension, exhaust ejector and a shortened chimney. Up until the Second World War, the locomotives were painted in Crimson Lake livery. The last 'Compound' was withdrawn in 1961.

Bachmann's LMS 'Compound' shares much with the model of the 'Midland Compound' (above). The models have metal frames and running plates for extra weight, adjustable tender coupling bars, 3-pole motors and are DCC ready with fitted 21-pin decoder sockets in the tenders. Provided separately are fire irons, cylinder drain cocks, bogie splash guards, dummy screw-link couplings and vents for the Fowler tender.

31-931	**1189** LMS black - *12*	110	132
31-932DC	**40934** BRb lined black, DCC chip fitted - *13*	125	150
31-933	**41157** BRc lined black - *13*	110	132

L21a. LNER Class D11/1 'Improved Director' 4-4-0 (2012)

The 'Director' Class was a late development in an extended line of 4-4-0 locomotives based on Thomas Parker's Class 11 design of 1895. The 11E 'Director' Class of the GCR emerged in 1913 and proved to be an excellent machine. Ten were built at Gorton Works in 1913 and were named after members of the GCR's management board. At the end of 1919 the first of the five 'Improved Directors' arrived from Gorton Works and these were classified as Class 11F. Six more followed in 1922. A year later, with the Great Central Railway absorbed into the new LNER, the 'Directors' become the LNER's Class D10 and the 'Improved Directors' the Class D11

The models have a heavy diecast running plate, detailed cab interior and detailed smokebox chamber with an opening door. They are fitted with 21-pin DCC decoder sockets.

31-145	**62660** *Butler Henderson* GCR Lined green Sp Edn (National Railway Museum) - *12*	110	130*
31-146	**62663** *Prince Albert* BRb lined black - *12*	90	117

* The Platinum edition in a silver coloured box was priced £170.

L21b. LNER Class D11/2 'Scottish Director' 4-4-0 (2012)

In need of new locomotives for the former North British Railway routes, 24 more D11 'Improved Directors' were ordered by the LNER and these are called the 'Scottish Directors'. Half the locomotives were built by Armstrong Whitworth and half by Kitson. They were coded D11/2 and were given names of characters in the novels of Sir Walter Scott. The locomotives had a slightly lower boiler height, suited to the tighter loading gauge adopted by the NBR. They were introduced in 1924 for passenger work.

The models have a heavy diecast running plate, detailed cab interior, an opening smokebox door with detailed smokebox chamber and the chimney, dome and cab are lower than on Bachmann's D11/1 model, as on the prototype. The models are fitted with 21-pin DCC decoder sockets.

31-137	**6399** *Allan-Bane* LNER lined light green - *13*	90	117
31-136K	**62683** *Hobbie Elliott* BRb lined light green Sp Edn 504 (BCC) - *12*	90	117
31-138	**62682** *Haystoun of Bucklaw* BRb lined black - *13*	90	117
31-135	**62690** *Lady of the Lake* BRb lined black - *12*	90	117
31-136DC	**62677** *Edie Ochiltree* BRc lined black, DCC chip fitted - *12*	110	136

Ex-LNER 'Scottish Director' 4-4-0 [L21b]

4-4-2

L21A. LBSCR 'Brighton Atlantic' 4-4-2 (2015)

As we went to press, Bachmann announces their intention to model a Class H2 'Brighton Atlantic'.

0-6-0

L22. GWR Class 2251 'Collett Goods' 0-6-0 (1998)

Following the Grouping of 1923, the GWR found itself with a number of lightly constructed lines. The existing Dean 0-6-0s were getting old and so a new class of light 0-6-0 tender engines was required. The building of 120 of Collett's standard 0-6-0 class started at Swindon in 1930 and continued in batches until 1948. They were initially used for pick-up goods trains but, in BR days, they were acknowledged as mixed traffic engines, finding themselves on both cross-country routes and branch lines and pulling passengers as well as freight.

The model has a copper capped chimney and, from 2007, has been fitted with an 8-pin DCC decoder socket.

ch = Churchward tender.

32-300	**3202** GWR green ch - *98*	35	50
32-310	**3217** GWR green ROD tender - *11*	55	68
32-304	**2294** GWR (button) green ch - *05*	45	57
32-301	**2260** BRb black - *98*	35	50
32-303	**2251** BRb green - *99*	35	50
32-305	**2217** BRb plain black W ch - *05*	45	59
32-306	**2253** BRb plain black W ch - *10*	45	60
32-311	**2259** BRb plain black ROD tender - *11*	55	68
32-300DC	**2244** BRc lined green ch, DCC chip fitted - *07*	55	70
32-302	**2277** BRc lined green - *98*	35	50
(30-052)	**3205** BRc lined green ex-'Western Rambler' set - *11*	45	NA

8th Edition

Bachmann Branchline

L23. MR Class M (LMS 3F) 0-6-0 (2011)

A total of 335 of the Midland Railway M Class were delivered between 1892 and 1902. They were produced by Sharp Stewart, Neilson, Kitson, Vulcan Foundry and Dubs. Like all 3F class locomotives, they underwent considerable rebuilding during their lifetime. During their working life they could be seen all over the former Midland Railway system, from Swansea to Sheffield and from Templecombe to Carnforth. The 3Fs enjoyed a long life, the last remaining in service until 1964. However, none of them was preserved.

The model is fitted with a 21-pin DCC decoder socket and the tender used with the model is the modified Johnson type with a capacity of 3250 gallons.

31-627	**3205** LMS plain black - *11*	60	79
31-627A	**3709** LMS plain black - *12*	70	83
31-626	**43186** BRb plain black - *not made*	NA	NA
31-626	**43762** BRb plain black - *11*	60	79
31-626A	**43257** BRb plain black - *12*	70	83
31-625	**43474** BRc plain black - *11*	60	79
31-628DC	**43620** BRc plain black W, DCC chip fitted - *12*	90	109
31-625Z	**43586** BRc plain black Sp Edn (Keighley & Worth Valley Railway) - *13*	60	75
31-625Z	**43586** BRc partly lined black, Sp Edn (Keighley & Worth Valley Railway) - *13*	70	85
31-625Z	**43586** BRc partly lined black, headboard, Sp Edn 512 (Keighley & Worth Valley Railway) - *12*	80	99

LMS Class 3F [L23]

L24. LMS Class 4F 0-6-0 (2013)

Designed by Sir Henry Fowler these locomotives were introduced in 1924 as a standard design for the LMS and as a variant of the Midland 4F. They were built for freight work and were occasionally used on branch passenger trains. The last was withdrawn in 1966 and three have been preserved.

The models have not been released at the time of writing but it is understood that they will come with a choice of Fowler or Johnson tenders and that all models are to be fitted with a 21-pin DCC decoder socket.

31-880	**58** SDJR dark blue - *13*	75	90
31-880K	**3851** LMS plain black Johnson/Deeley tender - *13*	75	90
31-881	**43875** BRb plain black Johnson/Deeley tender - *13*	75	90
31-882	**43924** BRc plain black Fowler tender - *13*	75	90

L25. GCR/LNER Class J11 'Pom-Pom' 0-6-0 (2014)

Designed by J.G.Robinson for the Great Central Railway, these were introduced in 1901 for freight and occasional passenger duties. They have a highly detailed cab, different buffers, safety valve and chimney options, three types of smokebox front and are the lower boiler variant. All models will be fitted with a 21-pin DCC decoder socket.

31-318	**5317** LNER plain black - *14*	NPG	NPG
31-319	**64311** BRb plain black - *14*	NPG	NPG
31-320DC	**64325** BRc plain black, DCC chip fitted - *14*	NPG	NPG

L26. LNER Class J39 0-6-0 (1994)

The Gresley standard 0-6-0 freight locomotive of 1926 replaced many of the 800 plus 0-6-0 locomotives that the LNER inherited in 1923 and which were approaching retirement age They were intended for freight services but were also used on passenger services. 289 of the class were built between 1926 and 1941 and they would have been seen with a wide variety of tenders, which had been handed down as older classes were replaced. This also included the Group Standard 4,200 gallon tenders with either straight sides or with the stepped top, both of which have been modelled by Bachmann. The last of the class was withdrawn in 1962 and none was preserved.

The model has a split-chassis and has not yet been converted to take a DCC decoder socket.

st = stepped tender. gst = group standard 4,200 gallon tender

31-850	**1974** LNER lined black - *94*	32	52
31-853	**1996** LNER black - *96*	35	52
31-855	**1856** LNER lined black - *00*	35	54
31-860	**1496** LNER black st - *99*	35	54
31-851	**64964** BRb black - *94*	32	48
31-851A	**64958** BRb black - *96*	35	52
31-854	**64960** BRb black W gst - *05*	40	54
31-861	**64838** BRb black st - *99*	35	48
31-855A	**64897** BRb black gst - *07*	45	59
31-865	**64838** BRc black st - *07*	45	59
31-852	**64967** BRc black - *94*	32	48
31-852A	**64970** BRc black - *96*	35	54
31-862	**64791** BRc black st - *99*	35	54
31-864	**64841** BRc black W st - *05*	40	56

South Eastern & Chatham Railway Class C [L27]

L27. SE&CR Class C 0-6-0 (2012)

The locomotives were designed by Henry Wainwright and built between 1900 and 1908 for freight services and occasional passenger duties on the newly formed South Eastern & Chatham Railway. The first 15 were built by Neilsons and the next 15 by Sharp, Stewart. The SE&CR built a further 70 at its Ashford works and the final 9 were built at Longbridge Works. The Southern Railway fitted steam heating equipment for passenger duties and 107 of the locomotives passed into BR ownership. Most had been scrapped by 1963 but three survived in service until 1966 as Ashford works shunters, one eventually being preserved on the Bluebell Railway.

The model has three types of smokebox and two chimney options as well as a highly detailed cab. All are fitted with 21-pin decoder sockets and sealed 3-pole motors.

31-460K	**689** SE&CR plain grey Sp Edn 504 (BCC) - *13*	75	84
31-460	**592** SE&CR lined green - *12*	70	85
31-463	**271** SE&CR plain green - *13*	NPG	NPG
31-461	**1256** SR black - *12*	70	85
31-464	**593** SR lined black - *13*	NPG	NPG
31-462	**31086** BRb plain black - *12*	70	85
31-465	**31579** BRc plain black - *13*	NPG	NPG

2-6-0

L28a. GWR Class 43xx 2-6-0 (ex-Mainline) (1996)

This was Churchward's mixed traffic design of 1911. 342 of these locomotives were built between 1911 and 1925, the final 20 as Class 93xx (see below). They were numbered in the 43xx, 53xx, 63xx and 73xx series. Members of the class undertook a wide range of duties and were found throughout the GWR network. Some even saw service in France during the First World War. In the 1930s, 80 were dismantled to build 'Granges' and 20 became 'Manors'. The Second World War brought the project to a close. The last was withdrawn from service in 1965 and one of the original class has been preserved.

The models have a split-chassis and have not yet been converted to take a DCC decoder socket. They have sprung buffers.

31-829	**4331** Great () Western lined green - *01*	40	54
31-830	**5321** Great Western green - *06*	48	60
31-825	**4318** GWR green - *96*	30	48
31-827	**5355** GWR (button) green - *96*	30	48
31-828	**5370** BRb lined black red nameplates - *01*	40	48
31-831	**4358** BRb lined green - *08*	50	63
31-826	**6384** BRc unlined green - *96*	30	48
31-827A	**4377** BRc lined green - *03*	40	50
31-2000/2	**5358** BRc lined ex-Cambrian Coast Express set - *01*	65	NA

L28b. GWR Class 93xx 2-6-0 (partly ex-Mainline) (1992)

Collett built a final batch of 20 of Churchward's 43xx Class mixed traffic Moguls in 1932. These had an improved cab with side windows and a longer roof to give greater protection to crew.

While not shown as an ex-Mainline model, it was in fact the Mainline Class 43xx with a bit of retooling to give it a Class 93xx cab (with windows) and a different (screw type) reversing gear. The models have split-chassis and are not fitted with DCC decoder sockets.

31-801	**9319** GWR green - *92*	35	48
31-802	**9308** BRb black - *92*	35	48
31-803	**7332** BRc green - *92*	35	48

LMS 'Crab' 2-6-0 [L29]

Bachmann Branchline

L29. LMS 'Crab' 2-6-0 (2003)

The 'Crab' Moguls were easily recognisable locos in train-spotting days due to their prominent and steeply angled cylinders, which gave them their nickname. They were the first LMS standard locomotive, being based on a planned Caledonian Railway design. Also called 'Horwich Moguls', they were built at Horwich and arrived in 1926 with a Fowler tender. Building continued until 1932 and the class finally totalled 425. They were a short but powerful design, with large boilers, and were used for both passenger and freight workings, including express work. The last was withdrawn in 1967 and 3 were preserved, including one in the National Collection.

An all new 3,500 gallon Fowler style tender was tooled up for this model and was made to be available in both riveted and welded versions. They have full representation of the very detailed valve gear. From 2004 the models have been fitted with an 8-pin DCC socket.

cr = coal rail on tender. rt = riveted tender.

32-181	13000 LMS maroon - 11	75	96
32-175	13098 LMS maroon - 03	50	65
32-178	2715 LMS lined black - 04	60	77
32-176	42765 BRb lined black cr - 03	50	65
32-179	42942 BRb lined black W cr, rt - 04	60	76
32-177	42789 BRc lined black cr, rt - 03	50	65
32-180	42919 BRc lined black cr, rt - 09	65	83

L30. LMS Stanier Mogul 2-6-0 (2013)

Stanier's Moguls date from 1933 and 40 were built at Crewe for lighter mixed traffic duties. They arrived in 1934 and were widely distributed within the LMS. Unlike the 'Crabs', these had the Stanier tapered boiler.

At the time of writing, the moidels have yet to be released, but it is understood that they will be fitted with 21-pin DCC decoder soickets.

31-690	2955 LMS Black - 13	NPG	119
31-691	42969 BRb lined black - 13	NPG	119
31-692	42968 BRc lined black - 13	NPG	119

L31. LMS Ivatt Class 2MT 2-6-0 (2007)

This was the Ivatt mixed traffic design of 1946 and 128 of the class were built between 1946 and 1952. Construction continued under British Railways and light axle loadings allowed them to be used on branch line passenger and freight duties. Their almost enclosed cabs made them ideal for working tender first. The last was withdrawn in 1967 and 7 have been preserved.

The model was launched before the model railway press at Preston Docks in July 2007. Each model is fitted with an 8-pin DCC decoder socket. They have a tender cab back and detailed pipework. To enable closer coupling of the loco and tender, an alternative drawbar is provided.

32-827	6404 LMS black - 07	58	72
32-830	6402 LMS black - 08	58	77
32-826	46440 BRb lined black - 07	58	72
32-826Z	46443 BRc lined black W Sp Edn 504 (The Signal Box) - 07	70	87
32-829	46426 BRc lined black - 08	58	77
32-825	46521 BRc lined green - 07	58	72
32-828	46520 BRc lined green - 08	58	77
32-828A	46526 BRc lined green W - 12	NPG	NPG
32-825K	46441 BRc maroon (livery in preservation) Sp Edn 504 (BCC) - 07	65	73
32-829A	46446 BRc lined black - 10	68	80

Ex-LMS Class 4MT [L32]

L32. LMS Ivatt Class 4MT 2-6-0 (2005)

This is the powerful Ivatt mixed traffic design of 1947 with the nicknames 'Flying Pig' and 'Mucky Duck'. They were the last class of locomotive to be designed by the LMS and this was the class on which the BR Standard 76xxx Class 4MT 2-6-0 were based. 162 were built at Horwich, Darlington and Doncaster between 1947 and 1952. Only three were released in LMS livery. The locomotives had an almost completely enclosed cab which made it easier for them to be driven tender first, as they did with some passenger services. The last was withdrawn in 1968 and one has been preserved.

The high running plate made them easy to maintain but difficult to model. The models are all fitted with 8-pin DCC sockets and some models have tablet catchers on the tender for single line working.

dc = double chimney. sc = single chimney. tc = tablet catcher.

32-575	3001 LMS black dc - 05	60	78
32-575K	43050 BR lined black Sp Edn (BCC) - *not made*	NA	NA
32-575K	43050 BR lined black W Sp Edn 1000 (BCC) - 05	60	77
32-577	43160 BRb lined black - 05	60	77
32-581	43018 BRb lined black dc - 11	90	116
32-578	43038 BRb lined black dc - 06	60	78
32-586DC	43154 BRb lined black sc tc, DCC chip fitted - 07	78	93
32-576	43047 BRc lined black - 05	60	77
32-579	43096 BRc lined black sc - 06	60	78
32-585	43106 BRc lined black sc tc - 07	65	82
32-580	43019 BRc lined black W* sc - 07	65	82

* Commemorating the last days of steam.

L33. LNER Gresley K3 2-6-0 (2004)

This was Gresley's 3-cylinder heavy freight and occasional passenger locomotive of 1924, which was based on the earlier GNR Class H4, but built to the LNER loading gauge. 183 were built between 1924 and 1937, most at Darlington and Doncaster. From 1931, construction was farmed out to independent manufacturers. They were widely used on express goods and passenger duties. The arrival of the V2s displaced some K3s from their normal work but until the great cull of 1962, which wiped out the class, they continued to pull the fish trains out of Grimsby. None survived into preservation.

The models are fitted with 8-pin DCC sockets.

gst = group standard 4200 gallon tender. st = stepped tender.

32-275	2934 LNER black gst - 05	65	74
32-279	1935 LNER green gst - 08	70	82
32-276	61932 BRb lined black gst - 04	65	74
32-277	61907 BRc lined black st - 05	65	74
32-277	61949 BRc lined black st - 04	65	74
32-278	61823 BRc lined black st - 08	70	86
32-275K	61811 BRc lined black W st Sp Edn 1,000 (BCC) - 04	65	77
32-280	61869 BRc lined black W - 11	80	100

Ex-SR Class N 2-6-0 [L34]

L34. SE&CR/SR Maunsell Class N 2-6-0 (1998)

Maunsell designed these 'Woolwich' mixed traffic locomotives for the SE&CR and the first took to the rails in 1917. Despite a number of teething problems, it proved to be a very successful design. To provide work for unemployed munitions workers at the end of the First World War, it was agreed that 100 of the locomotives should be built at Woolwich Arsenal. Some were sold as kits of parts and Ashford finished the job, rebuilding others. Eventually the Southern Railway had a class of 80 and, in addition, 27 were sold to work in Ireland. Smoke deflectors were a late addition to many of them and the last loco was withdrawn in 1966. One has been preserved.

Early tenders on this model tended to derail. On one batch of locos the metal footplates started to distort, due to impurities in the metal, and these were replaced by Bachmann. The models did not have DCC decoder sockets until 2011, when 6-pin ones were used. wpc - wooden presentation case. sst = slope sided tender. xsd = no smoke deflectors. From 2011, all new models introduced were 'DC ready' with a 6-pin socket.

32-150/1	810 SE&CR grey Ltd Edn 1000 - 98	50	NA
32-150/2	1863 SR green Ltd Edn 1000 - 98	50	NA
32-150	above two locos wpc* Kader 50th Anniversary - 98	NA	165
32-153	1824 SR olive green - 98	45	60
32-153A	1821 SR olive green - 99	30	52
32-160	1406 SR olive green xsd sst - 02	40	62
32-163	1404 SR olive green sst - 02	40	62
32-155	1854 SR malachite green - 00	35	58
32-150V	1860 SR black Sp Edn 512 6-pin (ModelZone) - 11	85	100
32-150Z	31874 *Brian Fisk* BRb black Sp Edn 500 (Beatties) wpc - 99	85	145
32-152	31813 BRb lined black - 98	35	45
32-156	31844 BRb lined black W - 02	40	55
32-161	31862 BRb lined black sst - 01	40	55
32-165DC	31869 BRb lined black W DCC chip fitted - 11	90	110
32-151	31860 BRc lined black - 98	35	45
32-151A	31816 BRc lined black - 99	35	45

Bachmann Branchline

32-154	31843 BRc lined black - 00		35	45
32-154A	31404 BRc lined black W DCC6 - 12		NPG	NPG
32-162	31401 BRc lined black sst - 01		40	55
32-164	31411 BRc lined black sst - not made ***		NA	NA
32-164	31406 BRc lined black sst - 08		62	76
32-150W	383 CIE grey+black Class K1 Sp Edn 640 (Murphy's Models) - 00		45	75
32-150X	376 (matt), 388 (gloss) CIE black Class K1 Sp Edn 640 (Murphy's Models) - 00		45	75
32-150Y	372, 385, 390** CIE green Class K1 Sp Edn 504 (Murphy's Models) - 99		50	75
(00651)	CIE green GSR Class K1 ex-set - 04		60	NA

* Price quoted is for the complete set in a case. ** 3 alternative numbers supplied as transfers. *** 31411 was a left-hand drive loco and so unsuitable, as the model is a right-hand drive one. It was replaced by 31406.

BR Class 4MT 2-6-0 [L35]

L35. BR Riddles Class 4MT 2-6-0 (2007)

This was Riddles' BR Standard mixed traffic design of 1952 and was based on Ivatt's 'Mucky Duck' LMS 4MT Mogul of 1947. The 115 locomotives were more attractive looking, having the aesthetically pleasing lines that are common to all of the BR Standard locomotives. This includes the standard cab and chimney. Designed at Doncaster, they were built there and at Horwich. The class were used on cross-country and secondary routes pulling both freight and passenger trains. Those allocated to the Southern Region had high capacity BR1B tenders, whereas elsewhere they were paired with BR2 and BR2A types. The last was withdrawn in 1967 and 4 were preserved.

The model was launched in October 2007, in front of the model railway press, on the East Lancashire Railway, where 76079 is based. The model is fitted with an 8-pin DCC socket.

32-953DC	76020 BRb lined blk BR2 tender, DCC chip fitted - 07	80	95
32-950	76053 BRb lined black BR1B tender - 07	65	80
32-952A	76079 BRb lined black BR2 tender - 09	70	86
32-954	76058 BRb lined black BR1B tender - 12	80	103
32-951	76069 BRc lined black BR1B tender - 07	65	80
32-952	76079 BRc lined black BR2 tender - 07	68	83
32-952Z	76114 BRc lined black ? tender Sp Edn 512 (British Railway Modelling) - 11	80	100
32-955	76109 BRc lined black BR2 tender - 12	80	103

2-6-2

L36. LNER Class V2 2-6-2 (1992)

This was Gresley's express passenger and freight locomotive of 1936. They were built at Doncaster or Darlington and totalled 184. They did sterling work throughout the Second World War with heavy freight and troop trains to pull, including 700 ton trains of 24 coaches! Three different tenders could be found paired with them and there was much tender swapping over the years. Some were given double chimneys. The last one was withdrawn in 1966 and Green Arrow, in the National Collection, is the only survivor.

The model has a glazed cab and several body variations affecting steam pipes, chimneys and type of tender. The model received a new chassis in 2012 and an 8-pin DCC decoder socket.

st = stepped tender. osp = outside steam pipes. wpc - wooden presentation case. dc = double chimney. spn = separate printed nameplates. gst = group standard 4200 gallon tender.

	Green Arrow		
31-550	4771 LNER light green Ltd Edn* 1000 wpc - 92	110	150
31-550A	4771 LNER light green as preserved, Heritage Collection - 08	70	90
31-550B	4771 LNER light green as preserved, Heritage Collection - 12	95	7
31-551	60800 BRb black - 92	50	65
31-559	60800 BRc green Ltd Edn 500 - 00	70	80
31-550	60800 BRc green dc ** - 04	65	80
31-550	60800 BRc green gst *** - 06	68	82
	Others		
31-555	4801 LNER light green - 92	45	64
31-558	4844 Coldstreamer LNER light green spn - 96	50	65
31-560	4806 The Green Howard LNER light green st - 99	65	80
31-556	3650 LNER unlined black - 92	45	64
31-553	60807 BRa black - 92	45	64
31-553A	60807 BRb black - 97	45	64
31-564	60860 Durham School BRb lined black - 12	95	117
31-557	60884 BRb green osp - 97	50	65
31-562	60834 BRb lined black W st - 04	50	65
31-552	60964 The Durham Light Infantry BRc green - 92	50	65
31-554	60903 BRc green dc - 92	45	64
31-561	60825 BRc green osp st - 99	65	80
31-565	60862 BRc green dc - 12	95	117
31-563	60865 BRc green osp st - 09	75	91

This was Bachmann's 2nd limited edition and the certificates were numbered between 1001 and 2000. ** This was incorrectly issued with a double chimney and so Bachmann supplied single chimney bodies, on request, as replacements.

LNER Class V2 [L36]

4-6-0

L37. GWR 'Manor' Class 4-6-0 (ex-Mainline) (1991)

Coming in 1938, Collett's 'Manor' Class was quite a late introduction for the GWR. The 30 locomotives were built at Swindon between 1938 and 1950 for mixed traffic duties, on cross-country routes and lightly constructed branch lines. They were a lighter version of a 'Grange'. The last was withdrawn in 1966 and 8 have been preserved.

The Mainline model arrived in 1980 and was reintroduced in the Bachmann Branchline range as early as 1991. It has sprung buffers and a heavy diecast chassis block, but has not yet been converted to DCC compatibility.

en = etched metal nameplates.

31-300	7802 Bradley Manor GWR green - 91	35	58
31-304	7800 Torquay Manor GWR (button) green - 96	35	64
31-305	7805 Broome Manor GWR green - 96	35	64
(30-021)	7811 Dunley Manor GWR (button) green ex-'Cambrian Coast Express' set - 06	70	NA
31-300Z	7816 Frilsham Manor BR green, black metalwork en Sp Edn 500 (Brunswick Railways Ltd) - 99	40	80
31-301	7820 Dinmore Manor BRb unlined green - 91	35	52
31-303	7829 Ramsbury Manor BRb lined black red plates - 91	35	58
31-303A	7829 Ramsbury Manor BRb lined black red plates modified chassis - 99	35	60
31-307	7813 Freshford Manor BRb black red plates modified chassis - 02	45	65
(30-061)	7819 Hinton Manor, BRb, black, red plates, modified chassis, ex-GWR 175 Severn Valley Sp Edn 500 (SVR) set in a wood presentation case** - 10	50	NA
31-302	7823 Hook Norton Manor BRc lined green - 91	35	65
31-306	7822 Foxcote Manor BRc lined green - 96	35	60
31-308	7825 Lechlade Manor BRc green - 06	50	68
31-2000	7828 Odney Manor BRc green Ltd Edn 1000 + 5358 Class 43XX + 6 Mk1 coaches 'Cambrian Coast Express' set wpc - 01	NA	140*
31-2000/1	7828 Odney Manor BRc green from above set - 01	70	NA

* Price shown is for complete 'Cambrian Coast Express' set (31-2000).
** The model was sold with 4930 Hagley Hall as a celebratory set.

Ex-GWR 'Hall' Class [L38a]

L38a. GWR Class 4900 'Hall' 4-6-0 (2005)

In 1924, Collett modified one of his successful 'Saint' Class locomotives (2925 St Martin) to create the first of the 'Hall' Class. Production started in 1928 when 80 of the new class were built and a further 178 were ordered. They were mixed traffic locomotives and sometimes found themselves on express services when larger locomotives were

Bachmann Branchline

unavailable. They were seen with various tenders including the small 3,500 gallon ones but most had the 'Castle' 4,000 gallon tenders. The last was withdrawn in 1966 and 10 have been preserved.

The models are fitted with 8-pin DCC decoder sockets and are available with either 4000 gallon Collett stepped tender (st) or Hawksworth flat-sided tender (Ht).

32-003	4936 *Kinlet Hall* Great()Western green st - *05*	55	76
32-003Z	4953 *Pitchford Hall* Great()Western green Sp Edn 750 (Buffers) - *07*	75	90
32-004	4970 *Sketty Hall* Great()Western green st - *09*	75	87
32-004	9614 *Langton Hall* Great()Western green st - *not made***	NA	NA
(30-061)	4930 *Hagley Hall,* GWR (button), green, ex-GWR 175 Severn Valley SP Edn 500 (SVR) set in a wood presentation case * - *10*	75	NA
32-005	4962 *Ragley Hall* BRb green st - *11*	NPG	100
32-002	5960 *Saint Edmund Hall* BRb lined black st - *05*	55	78
32-000DC	5927 *Guild Hall* BRc green Ht, DCC chip fitted - *07*	75	93
32-006	6922 *Burton Hall* BRc green Ht - *13*	90	109
32-001	6937 *Conyngham Hall* BRc green st - *05*	55	78

* The model was sold with 7819 *Hinton Manor* as a celebratory set.. **This was dropped in favour of *Sketty Hall*.

L38b. GWR 'Modified Hall' 4-6-0 (ex-Replica) (1996)

This was Hawksworth's version of Collett's 'Hall' and 71 were built from 1944 until 1949. They were paired with flat sided 4,000 gallon tenders designed by Hawksworth. Six 'Modified Halls' have been preserved.

This was a model which Palitoy had planned to make in its Mainline Railways range and work on the project had reached the test-shop stage at the time of the demise of the company. Godfrey Hayes of Replica Railways paid for the completion of the model's development. This included improvements to the work already done and a complete retooling of the tender. In 1990, Replica marketted three versions of the model - after which, Bachmann took it over. The model receive a rebuilt chassis in 2013 with an 8-pin DCC decoder socket.

st = stepped tender. Ht = Hawksworth flat sided tender. wpc = wooden presentation case

31-777	6962 *Soughton Hall* G()W green st - *96*	35	62
31-779	6960 *Raveningham Hall* G()W green, 9ct gold nameplates 9th Ltd Edn 2000 wpc - *97*	40	85
31-778	6969 *Wraysbury Hall* BRb green Ht - *96*	35	62
31-781	7903 *Foremarke Hall* BRb black st -*13*	90	109
31-775	6990 *Witherslack Hall* BRb black red plates - *96*	35	62
31-776	7915 *Mere Hall* BRc green st - *96*	35	62
31-780	6988 *Swithland Hall* BRc green Ht - *13*	90	109
(00639)	*Hogwarts Castle* red ex-US set - *01*	40	NA

Hawksworth's 'Modified Hall' Class [L38b]

L39. LMS 'Royal Scot' 4-6-0 (ex-Mainline) (1994)

This was Fowler's express passenger design of 1927 and 71 were built between 1927 and 1930. The first batch of 50 was built in Glasgow by the North British Locomotive Company in 1927 and the next batch at the LMS Derby Works in 1930. They were mainly used on express passenger services, until replaced by Stanier's Pacifics. Many members of the class carried old L&NWR locomotive names but, 25 of them were later renamed after regiments, like most of the rest of the class. From 1947, smoke deflectors were fitted and all of them were rebuilt with tapered boilers between 1943 and 1955. (see below).

The Mainline model was released in 1981. Bachmann models have a split-chassis and are not yet fitted with DCC decoder sockets.

Ft = Fowler 3500 gallon tender with coal rails. St = Stanier 4,000 gallon tender. xsd = no smoke deflectors. wpc = wooden presentation case. cre = coal rail extensions. crest = crest on cabsides and number on tender.

LMS Maroon			
31-275	6100 *Royal Scot* St brass bell special nameplates 4th Ltd Edn 1000 (3001>) wpc - *94*	75	125
31-275Z	6110 *Grenadier Guardsman* Ft xsd crest Sp Edn 500 (Beatties) wpc - *98*	75	120
31-277	6112 *Sherwood Forester* Ft xsd - *94*	40	64
31-279	6130 *The West Yorkshire Regiment* Ft cre angled deflectors - *96*	40	64
31-280Z	6131 *The Royal Warwickshire Regiment* St Sp Edn (Castle Trains) - *09*	70	85
31-280	6106 *Gordon Highlander* St - *98*	50	65
31-281	6155 *The Lancer* Ft - *02*	55	70
31-283	6119 *The Lancashire Fusilier* Ft - *06*	55	71
LMS Black			
31-276	6134 *The Cheshire Regiment* St curved top deflectors - *94*	40	60
BRb Green			
31-278	46148 *The Manchester Regiment* St - *95*	40	60
31-282	46151 *The Royal Horse Guardsman* W St - *02*	60	75
31-284	46165 *The Ranger (12th London Regt)* St - *08*	60	76

LMS 'Royal Scot' Class [L39]

L40a. LMS Rebuilt 'Royal Scot' 4-6-0 (ex-Mainline) (1985)

Stanier commenced rebuilding the whole of the 'Royal Scot' Class in 1943 and this process continued until 1955, when the last one received its No.2a tapered boiler. The first to be rebuilt had been the experimental locomotive 6399 *Fury* in 1935, as a one-off. Throughout the class the original single chimneys were replaced by double ones but, with the exception of *Fury*, the 'rebuilds' retained their Fowler cabs. *Fury* was given a 'Jubilee' cab. From 1947 smoke deflectors started to appear on members of the class. The last locomotive was withdrawn in 1965 and two have been preserved.

The original Mainline model was released as early as 1977, with a steam-sound version available by 1980. The Bachmann model has a split-chassis and no DCC decoder socket. xsd = no smoke deflectors. St = Stanier 4,000 gallon tender. wpc = wooden presentation case.

31-226	6133 *Green Howards* LMS black xsd - *97*	50	65
31-225	46102 *Black Watch* BRb green etched brass military crest - *96*	45	64
31-277Z	46159 *The Royal Air Force* ** BRc green Sp Edn 500 (Jennings Models) - *00*	65	80
31-228	46141 *The North Staffordshire Regiment* BRb green - *04*	50	65
31-275X	46169 *The Boy Scout* BRb green St - *01*	65	80
31-275W	46168 *The Girl Guide* BRc green St - *01*	65	80
31-275Y	Above 2 models Sp Edn 350 wpc (TMC) 'Mancunian' headboard - *99*	NA*	175
31-227	46162 *Queens Westminster Rifleman* BRc green - *97*	50	65
(30-020)	46100 *Royal Scot* BRb green St ex-'Royal Scot' set - *?*	50	65
(40-0190)	46100 *Flying Scot* bright red ex-US 'The Flying Scot' set - *86*	70	NA
(40-?)	46100 *Royal Scot* bright blue ex-US 'The Royal Scot' set - *85*	70	NA

* Price quoted is for the pair in the presentation box. ** Commemorating the 60th Anniversary of the Battle of Britain.

L40b. LMS Rebuilt 'Royal Scot' 4-6-0 (2007)

All-new tooling was planned for 2007 but it was discovered that Hornby were already working on a super-detailed model. Bachmann announced that, as the market could not support two brand new models of the same prototype, they would concentrate their efforts on the other LMS 4-6-0 locomotives already announced (the 'Jubilee' and original 'Patriot').

The xsd = no smoke deflectors. St = Stanier 4,000 gallon tender.

31-525	6166 *London Rifle Brigade* LMS black xsd st - *not made*	NA	NA
31-526	46115 *Scots Guardsman* BRb green St - *not made*	NA	NA
31-527DC	46148 *The Manchester Regiment* BRc green st, DCC chip fitted - *not made*	NA	NA

Ex-LMS 'Patriot' Class [L41a] (Bachmann)

Bachmann Branchline

L41a. LMS 'Patriot' 4-6-0 (2008)

Sometimes called 'Baby Scots', they were Fowler's mixed traffic loco of 1930 of which 52 were built. They were used in main line service alongside the 'Royal Scots'. All were built at either Derby or Crewe between 1930 and 1934 as replacements for the ageing L&NWR 'Claughtons', which were being retired. They were given a Fowler design of tender. In 1946, Ivatt started rebuilding the Patriots (see below).

The models have the Fowler tender and etched metal smoke deflectors. All are fitted with 8-pin DCC sockets, except where a sound chip is fitted and a 21-pin socket is provided.

31-212	5541 *Duke of Sutherland* LMS maroon - 08	85	102
31-210	45503 *The Royal Leicestershire Regiment* BRb green - 08	85	102
31-213DS	45504 *Royal Signals* BRc green, DCC sound chip fitted - 12	200	259
31-214	45538 *Giggleswick* BRb green - 13	NPG	NPG
31-211	45543 *Home Guard* BRc green - 08	85	102

L41b. LMS Rebuilt 'Patriot' 4-6-0 (ex-Mainline) (1991)

This was Ivatt's 1946 rebuild of Fowler's 'Patriot' Class. The rebuilt loco looked very much like a 'Rebuilt Royal Scot' but while the 'Scots' retained their Fowler cabs, the 'Patriots' were given 'Jubilee' cabs. The Fowler tender was also disposed of and a Stanier 4,000 gallon tender provided in its place. The last loco was withdrawn in 1965.

The Mainline model was released in 1980 and five versions were marketed. The tooling transferred to Bachmann and the model was a very early addition to the Branchline range. There are no DCC compatible examples.

xsd = no smoke deflectors.

31-202	5526 *Morecambe and Heysham* LMS blk xsd - 96	40	64
31-200	45528 BRa black - 91	38	64
31-203	45528 *R.E.M.E* BRb green - 01	50	68
31-201	45545 *Planet* BRc green - 91	45	60

L42a. LMS 'Jubilee' 4-6-0 (ex-Mainline) (1990)

Designed by Sir William Stanier for the LMS, 191 locomotives were built between 1934 and 1936. This was his Class 5 express passenger locomotive for all but the heaviest duties and they were named after countries and states within the British Empire, as well as former admirals and warships. Originally classified 5XP, the class was later reclassified 6P, the same as the 'Royal Scots'. The last was withdrawn in 1967 and 4 have been preserved.

The Mainline model was released in 1979 and some were available with steam and whistle sound. Later Bachmann models were fitted with sprung buffers. This version of the model had a split-chassis and was not fitted with DCC decoder sockets. It was replaced in 2007 with a completely retooled model which will be found in the next table.

sc = single chimney. dc = double chimney. en = etched nameplate. Ft = Fowler tender with coal rails. St = Stanier 4,000 gallon tender. wpc = wooden presentation case.

31-150A	5699 *Galatea* LMS maroon St Sp Edn 600 (Loco Marketing Services) red card presentation box - 96	100	150
31-154	5721 *Impregnable* LMS maroon St - 94	40	64
31-155	5699 *Galatea* LMS maroon Ft - 94	47	64
31-155A	5699 *Galatea* LMS maroon Ft - 00	35	64
31-157	5684 *Jutland* LMS maroon St ** - 00	45	70
31-150	5552 *Silver Jubilee* LMS black * 1st Ltd Edn 500 (numbered 501>) wpc - 90	250	330
31-159	5711 *Courageous* LMS black Ft ** - 03	45	65
31-152	45568 *Western Australia* black BRb (small) Ft - 90	45	66
31-158	45742 *Connaught* BRb green St ** - 00	45	65
31-150X	45682 *Trafalgar* BRb green St Ltd Edn 1,000 wpc - 05	55	96
31-150T	45670 *Howard of Effingham* BRb green St en - 01	45	75
31-150S	45679 *Armada* BRc green Ft en - 01	45	75
31-150Y	above 2 locos wpc Sp Edn 250 (TMC) - 00	NA	175
31-150V	45733 *Novelty* BRb green St en - 01	45	75
31-150U	45732 *Sanspareil* BRc green St en - 01	45	75
31-150Z	above 2 locos wpc Sp Edn 250 (TMC) 'The Rainham Trials' - 00	NA	175
31-151	45552 *Silver Jubilee* BRb green en St - 90	40	60
31-153	45596 *Bahamas* BRc green dc St - 90	48	68
31-156	45715 *Invincible* BRb green Ft - 97	40	62
31-156A	45715 *Invincible* BRb green Ft - 99	45	62
31-160	45697 *Achilles* BRc green W St - 05	55	73

* 1930s livery with chrome plated fittings. The chrome plating was applied before the black paint and the latter tends to peel off. ** Single and double chimneys supplied with the model.

Ex-LMS 'Jubilee' Class [L42b] (Tony Wright)

L42b. LMS 'Jubilee' 4-6-0 (2007)

This is the completely retooled model of Stanier's 1934 standard Class 5 express passenger locomotive. Features include an opening smokebox door and a fall plate. Models are fitted with an 8-pin DCC socket, unless fitted with a sound chip, in which case they have a 21-pin socket.

sc = single chimney. dc = double chimney. en = etched nameplate. Ft = Fowler tender with coal rails. St = Stanier 4,000 gallon tender (r = riveted, w = welded).

31-185	5563 *Australia* LMS maroon Ft - 07	80	95
31-175K	5593 *Kolhapur* LMS maroon Sp Edn 504 (BCC) - 08	80	95
31-187	5664 *Nelson* LMS maroon sc St - 13	NPG	NPG
31-175	45611 *Hong Kong* BRb green sc St(r) - 07	80	95
31-175Z	45637 *Windward Islands* BRb green St Sp Edn (ModelZone) - 07	80	105
31-175Y	45609 *Gilbert and Ellice Islands* BRb green Ft Sp Edn 500 (Rails) - 07	80	105
31-177DS	45593 *Kolhapur* BRb green, DCC sound chip fitted - 10	190	225
31-189	45606 *Falkland Islands* BRb green W sc St - 13	NPG	NPG
31-176DC	45562 *Alberta* BRc green sc St(w), DCC chip fitted - 07	85	106
31-188	45565 *Victoria* BRc green W St - 09	85	101
31-186	45587 *Baroda* BRc green sc Ft - 09	85	101
31-176Z	45596 *Bahamas* BRc green W dc St Sp Edn 504 (Hornby Magazine) - 09	90	115
31-178DC	45659 *Drake* BRc green St(r) sc, DCC chip fitted - 10	90	114

L43. LMS Rebuilt 'Jubilee' 4-6-0 (1991)

Only two 'Jubilees' were rebuilt with a larger boiler and double chimney and this was in 1942.

Each model has a Stanier tender, split-chassis and is not fitted with a DCC decoder socket.

xsd = no smoke deflectors.

31-250	45735 *Comet* BRa black xsd - 91	45	64
31-251	45736 *Phoenix* BRc green - 91	45	64

Ex-LNER Class B1 [L44]

L44. LNER Class B1 4-6-0 (ex-Replica) (1994)

Edward Thompson designed the B1 as a mixed traffic locomotive and they were built between 1942 and 1950. Some of the work was contracted out to the Vulcan Foundry and the North British Locomotive Co. The rest were built at Darlington, except for 10 at Gorton. 59 of the class received names - consisting of types of Antelope and directors of the LNER. The last of the class was withdrawn in 1967 and two have been preserved.

Palitoy were working on a model during their final days and a pre-production sample had been produced, with production planned for 1984. Replica Railways paid Kader to complete the tooling and about 8 versions of the model were produced for Replica, before Bachmann took over the tooling. From 2011 the model has had a new chassis and an 8-pin DCC decoder socket fitted.

31-7??	1000 *Springbok* LNER light green - see Replica Railways	NA	NA
31-706	1041 *Roedeer* LNER lined black - 98	45	62
31-7??	1059 LNER lined black - see Replica Railways	NA	NA
31-715	1123 LNER light green - 11	NPG	93
31-711	1189 *Sir William Gray* LNER green - 07	55	70
31-700	1264 LNER green - 95	30	56

Cat. No.	Details		Price	
31-705	**1306 Mayflower** LNER green 9ct gold nameplates wpc 8th Ltd Edn 2000 - *96*		60	85
31-707	**61002 Impala** BRa light green - *98*		45	62
31-712	**61000 Springbok** BRb lined black - *07*		55	70
31-701	**61241 Viscount Ridley** BRb black - *94*		40	62
31-714	**61250 A.Harold Bibby** BRb lined black - *11*		NPG	93
31-710	**61251 Oliver Bury** BRb lined black, electric lights - *not made*		NA	NA
31-701A	**61399** BRb black - *96*		35	55
31-708	**61003 Gazelle** BRc lined black - *03*		45	64
31-713	**61003 Gazelle** BRc lined black - *10*		55	73
31-709	**61008 Kudu** BRc black W - *05*		50	65
31-710	**61009 Hartebeeste** * BRc black Sp Edn 250 (Rails) wpc - *96*		75	95
31-703	**61010 Wildebeeste** BRc black - *96*		35	62
31-710A	**61018 Gnu** * BRc black Sp Edn 100 (Rails) wpc - *96*		95	110
31-716	**61180** BRc lined black W - *11*		80	100
31-702A	**61190** BRc black - *96*		40	58
31-700Z	**61247 Lord Burghley** BRc lined black W Sp Edn 500 (SMC) - *03*		55	95
31-710	**61251 Oliver Bury** BRc lined black, electric lights - *06*		55	67
31-702	**61354** BRc black - *94*		35	55

*61009 Hartebeeste and 61018 Gnu were finished by Fox for Rails of Sheffield and some may therefore consider these to be Code 3 models.

Ex-SR 'Lord Nelson' Class [L45]

L45. SR 'Lord Nelson' Class 4-6-0 (1992)

This was Maunsell's express passenger locomotive of 1926, in its final form, as rebuilt by Bulleid. 16 had been were built at Eastleigh with Belpaire fireboxes, but conversion to larger boilers was started by Bulleid in 1937. They also received redesigned cylinders and Lemaitre chimneys, which dramatically improved their steaming. The 'Lord Nelsons' remained the Southern Railway's principal express locomotive until the arrival of the Bulleid Pacifics in 1941. The last was withdrawn from service in 1962 and one was preserved.

Palitoy had started work on this model before it stopped production on the Mainline Railways range and Bachmann took over the project. The model went out of production for a while and slight tooling revisions were undertaken before it was re-released in 2006. The models have a split-chassis and are not fitted with a DCC decoder socket.

osc = original small chimney

31-404	**855 Robert Blake** SR olive green, osc - *96*		48	72
31-400	**850 Lord Nelson** SR malachite green 9ct gold nameplates 3rd Ltd Edn 1000 * wpc - *92*		90	120
31-401	**864 Sir Martin Frobisher** SR malachite green - *92*		40	72
31-407	**856 Lord St.Vincent** SR malachite - *98*		45	72
31-402	**30851 Sir Francis Drake** BRb green - *92*		45	72
31-405	**30852 Sir Walter Raleigh** BRb green - *96*		45	72
31-408	**30850 Lord Nelson'** BRb green** - *06*		65	82
31-409	**30865 Sir John Hawkins** BRb green - *08*		70	83
31-403	**30861 Lord Anson** BRc green - *92*		45	72
31-406	**30850 Lord Nelson** BRc green - *98*		50	75

* numbering of certificates start at 2001. ** Issued as Heritage Range model.

L46a. BR Standard Class 4 4-6-0 (ex-Mainline) (1990)

This was a Riddles mixed traffic locomotive design introduced in 1951. It was effectively a tender version of the Riddles 4MT 2-6-4 tank. Their intended use was mixed traffic duties off main lines. 80 were built by BR at Swindon between 1951 and 1957 and 19 were fitted with double chimneys. The first 65 built had BR2/2A 3,500 gallon tenders and the rest had 4,725 gallon BR1B tenders. The last was withdrawn in 1968 and 6 were preserved.

The model was originally designed by Palitoy for their Mainline Railways. Following the demise of Palitoy, an improved version was made for Replica Railways in 1990. It then became the first locomotive to be released in the new Branchline range. This original model had a split-chassis, sprung buffers and was not fitted with a DCC decoder socket. It was completely retooled for release in 2008 and those models are listed in the next table.

dc = double chimney.

31-100	**75014** BRb black BR2 tender - *96*		35	48
31-100A	**75059** BRb black BR2 tender - *98*		45	55
31-102	**75073** BRb black BR1B tender - *90*		35	48
31-102A	**75072** BRb black BR1B tender - *98*		45	55
31-108	**75063** BRb black W - *not made*		NA	NA
31-108	**75065** ** BRb black W BR1B tender - *02*		45	60
31-103	**75020** BRc black dc BR2 tender - *90*		36	48
31-105	**75078** BRc black dc BR1B tender - *90*		36	48
31-105A	**75075** BRc black dc BR1B tender - *98*		45	55
31-101	**75023** BRc green BR2 tender - *96*		35	48
31-104	**75069** BRc green dc BR1B tender - *90*		35	48
31-106	**75029** * BRc green dc BR2 tender - *90*		40	50
31-106A	**75003** BRc green dc BR2 tender - *98*		35	55
31-107	**75027** BRc green BR2 tender - *02*		40	55

*This was supplied with brass nameplates for *The Green Knight* which were made for Bachmann by Jackson Evans. ** The box carries the number '75063' and describes the tender as 'BR18' instead of 'BR1B'.

BR Standard Class 4 [L46b] (Tony Wright)

L46b. BR Standard Class 4 4-6-0 (2008)

This is the completely retooled model of 2008. It has much surface detail and, unless stated otherwise, it is fitted with an 8-pin DCC socket.

dc = double chimney. sc = single chimney. All models are fitted with an 8-pin DCC decoder socket.

31-117DC	**75074** BRb lined black BR1B tender sc, DCC chip fitted - *08*		85	105
(30-060)	**75001** BRc lined green ex-Kader 60th Anniv, pack - *08*		90	NA
31-115	**75027** BRc lined green W * BR2 tender sc - *08*		78	92
31-118	**75033** BRc lined black BR2 tender sc - *08*		78	92
31-119	**75035** BRc lined black BR2 tender sc - *13*		NPG	NPG
31-116	**75069** BRc lined green BR1B tender dc - *08*		78	92

* Commemorating the last days of steam.

L47. BR Standard Class 5 4-6-0 (2002)

This was another of Riddles' mixed traffic designs which also started to appear on the national network in 1951. They were designed at Doncaster, 172 were built there and at Derby between 1951 and 1957. They were a standard equivalent of the LMS 'Black Five'. They incorporated the final boiler design used by Ivatt on the LMS locos and had the standard Riddles cab and the same wheels, cylinders and valve gear used for the 'Clans'. 30 of the class were built with BR Caprotti valve gear. They were allocated to all the regions and six different tender types were used with them. Some allocated to the Southern Region adopted names from withdrawn 'King Arthur' Class locomotives. The last was withdrawn in 1968 and 5 have been preserved.

The model has optional etched nameplates, removable coal load, different tenders and varying whistle positions. They are fitted with higher quality 3-pole motors and have low gearing. Since 2005 the model has been fitted with an 8-pin DCC socket.

wp = without Westinghouse pump. sc = single chimney.

32-502	**73082 Camelot** BRb black BR1B - *02*		55	65
32-503	**73030** BRb lined black BR1 tender wp - *03*		70	88
31-503Z	**73050 City of Peterborough** BRb lined black BR1G tender Sp Edn 512 (British Railway Modelling) - *09*		75	95
32-509	**73109** BRb lined black BR1B tender - *12*		100	123
32-500	**73068** BRc green BR1C tender - *02*		55	65
32-501	**73158** BRc black BR1B tender - *02*		55	65
32-504	**73014** BRc lined green BR1 tender - *02*		70	88
32-505	**73069** BRc plain black W BR1C tender - *03*		70	88
32-506	**73110 The Red Knight** BRc lined black BR1F tender - *04*		70	88
32-507	**73050** BRc lined black W * sc - *08*		70	88
32-508	**73049** BRc lined green BR1 tender - *12*		100	123

* Commemorating the last days of steam.

Bachmann Branchline

4-6-2

'New build' Class A1 Tornado [L48]

Ex-LNER Class A2 [L49] (Tony Wright)

L48. LNER Peppercorn Class A1 4-6-2 (2001)

This later A1 express passenger Class, designed by AH Peppercorn was built at Doncaster between 1948 and 1949 and totalled 49 locomotives. They started to arrive in 1948, after Nationalisation of the railways, and, consequently, none appeared in full LNER livery. The class was a development of Thompson's 1945 rebuild of Great Northern (A1/1) and was originally unnamed. They later received names, including some dropped from the A4s when they were renamed. Others were of racehorses, LNER personnel and pre-Grouping railway companies that made up the LNER. The first 36 locomotives off the production line were painted in LNER lined Apple green but with 'British Railways' on the tender sides. The rest of the class were painted Express blue and carried the early BR insignia. In August 1951, Brunswick green had replaced Express blue and the whole class had been repainted by the Summer of 1953.

The model has a removable coal load and optional chimneys. From 2005 the models have been fitted with an 8-pin DCC decoder socket, except for those with a sound chip which have a 21-pin socket.

wpc = wooden presentation case.

32-550K	**60163 *(Tornado)*** works grey Sp Edn 504 (BCC), 'w w w.a1steam.com' on tender ** - *10*	250	300
32-554	**60114 *W.P.Allen*** BRa light green - *03*	70	90
32-550A	**60163 *Tornado*** BRa light green ** - *10*	110	140
32-553	**60161 *North British*** BRb blue - *03*	80	100
32-550C	**60163 *Tornado*** BRb blue - *13*	NPG	NPG
32-558	**60115 *Meg Merrilies*** BRb green - *09*	70	90
32-551DS	**60139 *Sea Eagle*** BRb green DCC sound chip fitted - *11*	200	254
32-552	**60147 *North Eastern*** BRb green - *02*	70	90
32-551	**60158 *Aberdonian*** BRc green - *01*	70	90
32-550B	**60163 *Tornado*** BRb green ** - *12*	120	150
32-555	**60130 *Kestrel*** BRc green - *03*	70	90
(30-090)	**60143 *Sir Walter Scott*** BRc green ex-Bachmann 15th Anniversary set - *04*	90	NA
32-557	**60144 *King's Courier*** BRc green - *07*	80	110
32-556	**60156 *Great Central*** BRc green - *05*	70	90
32-559	**60157 *Great Eastern*** BRc green - *10*	92	116
32-550	**60163 *Tornado*** BRc green wpc Sp Edn 1000 (A1 Steam Trust) - *03*	250	300

* The motif on the packaging gives the date as 2001 - possibly this was the intended year of release but it got delayed. ** The 2010 issue of Tornado has a different tender top to the production A1s as it has a greater water carrying capacity.

L49. LNER Peppercorn Class A2 4-6-2 (2010)

Here we have another Peppercorn designed express passenger locomotive, this time of 1948. The A2s were made up of rebuilt locomotives and 'new builds'. The class included 15 built from 1947 (A2s) by AH Peppercorn. Designed as express passenger locomotives, Peppercorn's 15 engines were based on Thompson's A2/2 but were almost 2 feet shorter. They started to arrive in 1947 and only two carried LNER livery. An order for a further 20 engines was cancelled. They were sometimes used for mixed traffic duties. The last of the class was withdrawn in 1966 and one, Blue Peter, survived into preservation.

The models listed here are based on the 15 Peppercorn A2s. These models are fitted with 21-pin sockets making them 'DCC ready'. They have etched smoke deflectors and nameplates, removable coal load, highly detailed cab interiors and optional chimneys.
wpc = wooden presentation case. sc = single chimney. dc = double chimney.

31-525	**525 *A.H.Peppercorn*** LNER light green sc - *10*	100	126
31-530	**526 *Sugar Palm*** LNER light green - *11*	115	139
31-527	**60528 *Tudor Minstrel*** BRa light green sc - *10*	100	126
31-527K	**60532 *Blue Peter*** BRa light green dc wpc Sp Edn 504 (BCC) (like the actual loco when surveyed, the model has a black nameplate on one side and a blue one on the other) - *10*	100	129
31-529	**60534 *Irish Elegance*** BRb green - *11*	115	139
31-526	**60537 *Bachelor's Button*** BRb green sc - *10*	100	126
20-2009	**60532 *Blue Peter*** BRc green dc wpc Ltd Edn - *10*	100	129
31-528	**60533 *Happy Knight*** BRc green - *11*	115	139

L50. LNER Class A4 4-6-2 (1995)

Designed by Sir Nigel Gresley, the A4s were introduced in 1935 and were largely based on the Gresley A3s. They were built in batches at Doncaster and the class eventually reached 35 in number. The first batch was built for the Silver Jubilee service and had the word 'silver' in their names. Most of the rest were initially given the names of birds but later extensive renaming took place to honour individuals and the five British Commonwealth dominions. While built as crack passenger express locomotives, in later years they were sometimes seen on freight trains. The last was withdrawn from service in 1966 and six of the class preserved.

The model is based on the former Trix/Liliput model mouldings, to which 112 minor modifications were made. It used a Bachmann split-chassis, but from 2011 the model had a new chassis and an 8-pin decoder socket.
dc = double chimney. sc = single chimney. ct = corridor tender. nct = non-corridor tender. v = valances fitted. xv = no valances. bm = blackened metalwork. wpc = wooden presentation case. swb = simulated wood finish box. en = etched nameplate. lcw = large chime whistle.

LNER Grey			
31-950X	**2509 *Silver Link*** Sp Edn 500 (Southampton MC) - *03*	60	100
31-952A	**2512 *Silver Fox*** v st - *98*	55	80
LNER Green			
31-956	**4482 *Golden Eagle*** v sc - *97*	55	70
LNER Blue			
31-959	**26 *Miles Beevor*** xv - *98*	55	70
31-952	**4468 *Mallard*** v dc**** - *05*	70	90
31-952B	**4468 *Mallard*** v dc nct DCC8 Heritage Collection - *12*	100	122
31-950	**4489 *Dominion of Canada*** v sc brass bell *** 5th Ltd Edn 2000 wpc - *95*	60	125
31-953B	**4496 *Dwight D Eisenhower*** sc ct bm Ltd Edn 500 US wpc - *97*	80	120
31-952	**4903 *Peregrine*** v dc st - *96*	50	70
LNER Black			
31-962Z	**4 *William Whitelaw*** NE Sp Edn 350 (Rails) swb - *99*	80	125
31-962X	**2510 *Quicksilver*** LNER Sp Edn 350 (Rails) swb - *99*	80	125
31-962Y	**4496 *Golden Shuttle*** LNER Sp Edn 350 (Rails) swb - *99*	80	125
BR Blue			
31-953A	**60008 *Dwight D Eisenhower*** BRb sc ct Ltd Edn 500 US wpc - *96*	80	135
31-954A	**60007 *Sir Nigel Gresley*** BRb W xv sc - *04*	75	90

Ex-LNER Class A4 [L50]

BR Express Blue			
31-954	**60007 *Sir Nigel Gresley*** BRb sc - *96*	75	94
31-954	**60007 *Sir Nigel Gresley*** BRb dc - *07*	75	94
31-954B	**60007 *Sir Nigel Gresley*** BRb dc - *12*	100	125
BR Green - Early Insignia			
31-953C	**60008 *Dwight D Eisenhower*** BRb sc en Ltd Edn 500 USA wpc - *99*	60	120
31-951A	**60009 *Union of South Africa*** BRb sc ct short run - *96*	55	90
31-950A	**60011 *Empire of India*** BRb en Sp Edn 500 (Rails) wpc - *99*	60	135
31-955	**60013 *Dominion of New Zealand*** BRb nct lcw sc - *96*	55	95
31-965	**60021 *Wild Swan*** BRb sc DCC8 - *11*	100	122

Bachmann Branchline

	BR Green - Late Insignia		
31-964	**60004** *William Whitelaw* BRc dc nct DCC8 - *12*	100	122
31-954A	**60007** *Sir Nigel Gresley* BRc dc en Ltd Edn 350, some swb - *00*	55	80
31-953	**60008** *Dwight D Eisenhower* BRc dc nct en Ltd Edn 250 US wpc - *95*	150	300
31-953	**60008** *Dwight D Eisenhower* BRc dc ct - *12*	100	125
31-966	**60008** *Dwight D Eisenhower* BRc dc - *13*	100	NPG
31-951	**60009** *Union of South Africa* BRc dc en and plaques - *95*	100	150
31-951Z	**60009** *Osprey* ** BRc Sp Edn (75069 Fund) 350 swb en - *98*	90	145
31-955	**60010** *Dominion of Canada* BRc dc optional front bell - *12*	100	125
31-967	**60010** *Dominion of Canada* BRc dc - *13*	100	NPG
31-955	**60013** *Dominion of New Zealand* BRc nct lcw sc - *96*	60	120
31-960A	**60015** *Quicksilver* BRc W dc - *03*	75	90
31-960	**60017** *Silver Fox* BRc + 6 BR maroon Thompson coaches, video & book Ltd Edn 1000 Elizabethan set * wpc - *96*	NA	275
(31-960)	**60017** *Silver Fox* BRc ex above set - *96*	85	NA
31-963	**60019** *Bittern* BRc dc nct - *09*	75	96
31-958	**60020** *Guillemot* BRc dc - *98*	55	70
31-957	**60033** *Seagull* BRc dc - *97*	55	70
	Loco Sets		
31-961/1	**4468** *Mallard* LNER blue v Ltd Edn 1000 - *98*	65	NA
31-961/2	**60022** *Mallard* BRc green dc Ltd Edn 1000 - *98*	65	NA
31-961	above 2 locos 60th anniversary release Ltd Edn 1000 wpc - *98*	NA	150
31-2001/1	**4491** *Commonwealth of Australia* LNER blue from set - *00*	70	NA
31-2001/2	**60012** *Commonwealth of Australia* BRb blue from set - *00*	70	NA
31-2001/3	**60012** *Commonwealth of Australia* BRc green dc from set - *00*	70	NA
31-2001	above 3 in Ltd Edn 1000 wpc - *00*	NA	245

* Price given is for the complete set. ** The models in the original batch had unacceptable body mouldings and were re-bodied. However, a few of the original models have survived. *** The model has sterling silver fittings. **** This was issued as Heritage Range model.

0-8-0

L51. LNWR Class G2A 0-8-0 (2008)

Webb designed this heavy freight locomotive of 1921. According to the catalogue, models released in 2008 were fitted with an 8-pin DCC decoder socker but from 2009 a 21-pin one replaced it. As modelled it has a Bowen-Cooke tender.
cbot = cab back on tender.

31-476	**9301** LMS black - *not made*	NA	NA
31-476	**9449** LMS black (G2) - *08*	70	86
31-478	**49287** BRb black - *09*	75	91
31-475*	**49395** BRb black, cbot - *08*	70	86
31-476DS	**49402** BRb black, cbot DCC sound - *not made***	NA	NA
31-476A	**49402** BRb black, cbot - *11*	75	94
31-475A	**49064** BRc black, cbot - *09*	75	91
31-477DC	**49094** BRc black DCC chip fitted - *not made*	NA	NA
31-479	**49094** BRc black W - *11*	85	105
31-477DC	**49361** BRc black, DCC chip fitted - *08*	80	98

* Issued as Heritage Range model and erroneously described as a G2a on the box when it is in fact a G2. ** A suitable sound recording was not available and so it was replaced by 31-476DC.

Ex-LMS Class G2A [L51]

2-8-0

L52. GWR Class 30xx 'ROD' 2-8-0 (2011)

For the Railway Operating Division (ROD) of the Royal Engineers, 521 locomotives were ordered to be built of a Great Central Railway Class 8K 2-8-0 design. They were delivered from 1917 until 1919 for use on the Western Front. After the war, some were loaned to British railway companies before being offered for sale. The GWR initially bought 20 in 1919 and a further 80 in 1925. They modified the locomotives by fitting new chimneys, top feed, dome etc. The last GWR version was withdrawn in 1958.

The model has a highly detailed cab, an adjustable drawbar and different styles of smokebox door. Haulage capacity is greatly aided by a substantial and heavy chassis and all are fitted with 21-pin DCC sockets.

31-129A	**3028** Great Western green - *13*	NPG	NPG
31-129	**3031** Great Western green - *11*	125	152
31-129	**3099** GWR green– *not made*	NA	NA
31-127	**3023** BRb plain black - *11*	125	152
31-128	**3036** BRb plain black W - *11*	130	160
31-128	**?** BRc plain black – *not made*	NA	NA

GWR Class 30xx [L52]

L53. S&DJR Class 7F 2-8-0 (2010)

The 7F 2-8-0 was produced by the Midland Railway at Derby for the Somerset & Dorset Joint Railway. Six locomotives were delivered in 1914 and a further five, with larger boilers, delivered in 1925. All were taken into LMS stock in 1928 and passed to British Railways in 1948.

All models feature the smaller boiler and S&D Fowler tender without water pick up apparatus. For 2012, a new Fowler/Deeley hybrid tender was provided. The model has an adjustable drawbar, S&DJR tablet catcher detail and a 21-pin DCC decoder socket. wpc = wooden presentation case.

31-2012	**88** S&DJR blue, 150th commemorative model in wpc. Fowler/Deeley tender -*13*	120	156
31-010	**53806**, BRb, black - *10*	55	70
31-012	**53808**, BRc, black, weathered - *not made*	NA	NA
31-011	**53809**, BRc, black - *10*	55	70
31-012	**53810** BRc, black W - *10*	55	70
31-013	**53808** BRc plain black. Fowler/Deeley tender - *12*	100	130

L54. GCR Class 8K/LNER O4 'ROD' 2-8-0 (2010)

In 1911, Robinson designed his Class 8K as a heavy freight locomotive for the Great Central Railway. 126 locos were built, some at Gorton and the rest by Kitson & Co. and the North British Locomotive Co. During the First World War, a further 521 were built for the Ministry of Munitions for the ROD between 1917 and 1919, the work being undertaken by a number of contractors. After the war, the GCR bought 3, the GWR 20 and the LNWR 30. Many of the rest were loaned out until the winding up of the ROD in 1921. They were then sold at bargain prices to get rid of them and the LNER bought 273, the GWR a further 80 and the LMS a further 75. The rest went to China (24) and Australia (13). The LNER locomotives, including those inherited from the GCR, became the Class O4. Some again served overseas in the Second World War and 329 eventually passed to BR in 1948. The last was withdrawn in1966 and one was preserved. Three of the batch sold to Australia have also survived.

The model has a highly detailed cab, an adjustable drawbar and different styles of smokebox door. Haulage capacity is greatly aided by a heavy chassis. All are fitted with 21-pin DCC sockets.

31-001Y	**1185** GCR lined black Sp Edn 500 (NRM) - *10*	110	140
31-005	**3547** LNER black - *11*	NPG	145
31-003	**3693** LNER black - *not made*	NA	NA
31-003	**3291** LNER black - *not made*	NA	NA
31-003	**6190** LNER black - *10*	100	125
31-004	**63598** BRb black W - *11*	NPG	152
31-002	**63635** BRb black - *10*	100	125
31-001Z	**63743** BRb black W Sp Edn 512 (Hattons) - *10*	120	145
32-001*	**63601** BRc black - *10*	100	125

* Issued as Heritage Range model.

War Department 2-8-0 locomotive [L55]

Bachmann Branchline

L55. WD 'Austerity' 2-8-0 (1999)

Riddles designed this heavy freight locomotive in 1943 for use in the Second World War. What was needed for the invasion of Europe was an austerity locomotive of equivalent power to an LMS 8F. 390 with 8-wheel tenders were built in the US and delivered to the Continent and 935 constructed at Vulcan Foundry and North British started to arrive in 1943. 733 of them passed to British Railways in 1948 (200 through the LNER who had bought them after the war). The rest were bought by the Railway Executive in 1948 and some were sold to China, Sweden and Holland. Two were retained by the MOD on the Longmoor Military Railway.

The models have a removable coal load and sprung buffers. The models are not fitted with DCC decoder sockets. When re-released in 2012 it was fitted with a 21-pin DCC decoder socket.

West = Westinghouse pump fitted.

32-255	78697 WD 21st Army Transport Group green *** - 00	75	95
32-255A	7199 WD WW2 Desert Sand - 02	80	100
32-250	400 *Sir Guy Williams* LMR blue Ltd Edn 2000 wpc - 99	60	85
32-250W	90733 *Remembrance - Lest We Forget* BRc black Sp Edn 500 (K&WVR) - 08	90	120
32-254	3085 LNER black West - 00	70	90
32-251	90274 **** BRb black - 99	70	90
32-253	90312 BRb black - 00	70	90
32-257	90015 BRb black W Ltd Edn - 00	70	85
32-257A	90732 Vulcan BRb black - 03	75	95
32-258	90423 BRb black - 06	80	105
32-261	90441 BRb plain black - 12	NPG	NPG
32-252	90445 BRc black W - 99	75	95
32-252	90445 BRc black - 99	75	95
32-252A	90201 BRc black W - 03	75	95
32-256	90566 BRc black - 00	70	90
32-259	90630 BRc black W - 06	85	111
32-260DC	90448 BRc plain black, DCC chip fitted - 12	125	147
32-250X	NS4479 NS green North British type Ltd Edn 500 (Tasco Nederland BV) - 03?	90	110
32-250Y*	NS4310 NS green Vucan Foundry type Ltd Edn 500 (Tasco Nederland BV) - 00	45	110
32-250Z	NS4329 NS green North British type Ltd Edn 500 (Tasco Nederland BV) - 00	80	100
32-250KCR	21 Kowloon Canton Railway green+red Sp Edn 1000 (K&CR) - 00	80	150

* The Dutch agent allocated his own number of 32.259 to this model. ** This was made as a Millennium model for sale in Hong Kong with only 200 being put on sale in the UK. *** Some were originally printed with the red and blue on the shields reversed. **** Box shows '90275'.

2-10-0

BR Standard Class 9F [L56]

L56. BR Class 9F 2-10-0 (2006)

The ultimate locomotive development by Riddles for his BR standard classes was the heavy freight 2-10-0 Class 9F. It benefited from experience gained with the WD 2-10-0s built during the war. The 9Fs later proved their versatility and pulled many a passenger train. 251 were built, mostly at Crewe. The rest were built at Swindon - including *Evening Star*, the last steam locomotive built by British Railways. Most later ones had a double chimney and 10 were fitted with Franco-Croti boilers. Some were fitted with dual Westinghouse pumps to operate doors on the Consett iron ore trains in the North East. The last was withdrawn in 1968 and nine of the class have been preserved.

The models are fitted with 8-pin DCC sockets and have etched smoke deflectors and various tenders.

dc = double chimney. sc = single chimney.

32-856	92002 BRb black sc BR1G tender - 08	100	129
32-854	92006 BRb black sc BR1G tender - 07	95	117
32-852	92116 BRb black BR1C tender - 06	90	112
32-853	92044 BRc black W sc BR1F tender - 07	100	125
32-857	92077 BRc black sc BR1C tender - 08	100	129
32-858DC	92185 BRc black W dc BR1F tender, DCC chip fitted - 08	100	123
32-851	92192 BRc black dc BR1F tender - 06	90	112
32-850K	92203 *Black Prince* BRc black Sp Edn 504 (BCC) - 06	90	112
32-850	92220 *Evening Star* BRc green BR1G tender * - 06	90	112
32-850A	92220 *Evening Star* BRc green BR1G tender DCC8 Heritage Collection - 10	110	135
32-859	92233 BRc plain black W, dc, BR1G Pines Express headboard - 13	120	145
32-850Z	92240 BRc black W BR1G tender Sp Edn 504 (ModelZone) - 06	100	125
32-855	92249 BRc black dc BR1B tender - 07	95	117

* Issued as Heritage Range model.

Diesels

L57. Freelance Diesel 0-6-0 (2006)

This model was developed for starter sets but was also available as a solo model

(30-041)DC	2 *Charlie* yellow+red ex-set - 07	18	NA
(30-006)	25 *Harry* blue with red wheels DC8 ex-set - 06	18	NA
30-915	95 *Rusty* green - 06	18	25
30-910	99 blue - 13	NPG	NPG

L58. Wickham Trolley Car (2013)

These were built between 1948 and 1990 and totalled over 600 in all. Many were exported and they ran on narrow gauge and broad gauge as well as standard gauge lines. They were used by engineers working on the railway and can travel at up to 30mph. Many are found on preserved lines.

The model was under development at the time of writing.

32-993	BR Engineers' yellow with wasp stripes - 13	NPG	46
32-991	BR maroon - 13	NPG	46
32-992	BR Engineers' yellow - 13	NPG	46

L59a. Class 03 0-6-0DS (ex-Mainline) (1991)

In all 230 were built at Doncaster and Swindon between 1957 and 1962. They were used on all regions, initially, but later activity was concentrated on the Eastern and London Midland Regions. Eight locomotives on the Western Region, were given cut down cabs for working between Burry Port and Cwmmawr.   The 03s were used for general shunting and pilot duties and, with a weight of just 30 tons, could be used on lines with severe weight limitations.

In 1997, the tooling was altered to produce the Class 04 and so no further Class 03 models could be made with those tools. For 2010, a new Class 03 model was tooled from scratch (see below). The models in this table have split-chassis and are not fitted with DCC decoder sockets.

ats = air tanks supplied.   xhs = no hazard stripes.   cx = conical exhaust.   cfc = cast flared chimney

31-350	D2000 BRc green xhs cx - 91	35	45
31-351	D2012 BRc green cx - 91	35	45
31-353	03197 BRe blue cfc ats - 91	35	45
31-352	03371 BRe blue cx ats - 91	35	45

BR Class 03 diesel shunter [L59b] (Tony Wright)

L59b. Class 03 0-6-0DS (2010)

The first locomotive was withdrawn from BR in 1968, although one example (03079) remained in use on the Isle of Wight until 1993. The locomotives became popular with heritage lines and 51 of them have been preserved. A number remain in industrial use in Belgium, Italy and the UK.

This new super-detailed model was planned for 2009 and was made from all new tooling. It arrived in 2010 and is fitted with a 6-pin decoder socket, because of limited space within the body.

Bachmann Branchline

ats = air tanks supplied. xhs = no hazard stripes. cx = conical exhaust. cfc = cast flared chimney.

Cat No	Description		
31-361A	**D2009** BRc green cx - *11*	50	62
31-360	**D2011** BRc green xhs cx - *10*	45	55
31-366	**D2016** BRc green xhs cx - *13*	NPG	NPG
31-364	**D2383** BRc green W cfc - *13*	NPG	NPG
31-361	**D2388** BRc green cfc - *10*	45	55
31-362A	**03045** BRe blue cfc - *11*	50	62
31-362	**03066** BRc green ats - *10*	45	55
31-360Y	**03160** BRe blue cfc Sp Edn 512 (*Rail Express Modeller* magazine) - *10*	45	55
31-363	**03162** BRe blue W cx - *11*	50	65
31-365	**03162** BRe blue W cfc - *13*	NPG	NPG
31-360X	**03371** BRe blue cx Sp Edn 512 (*Rail Express Modeller* magazine) - *10*	45	55
31-360Z	**03179** NSE blue+white+grey cut-down cab Sp Edn 750 (ModelZone) - *10*	50	60
31-360K	**03179** *Clive* WAGN white+grey cut-down cab Sp Edn 504 (BCC) - *10*	45	54

L60. Class 04 0-6-0DS (1997)

Drewry Car designed this loco in 1952 and it was ideal for dockyards and other confined spaces. 140 of these were built by Drewry (but subcontracted to Vulcan Foundry) and Robert Stephenson & Hawthorn between 1952 and 1962. The total number of the fleet was 142. They were used for shunting and pilot duties and on lines with severe weight limitations. The first four locomotives had fitted side skirts and 'cowcatchers' to enable them to operate on the Wisbech & Upwell Tramway and other former LNER lines with on-street running. The last 04 was withdrawn from the national network in 1972, many being sold on for industrial use and 18 going for preservation.

As mentioned above, this model was produced by adapting the former Mainline tools for the Class 03. It has sprung buffers, cab interior detail and conical exhaust. The models had split-chassis and were not fitted with DCC decoder sockets until 2013 when the newer Class 03 chassis started to be used with its 8-pin DCC decoder sockets fitted. xhs = no hazard stripes.

Cat No	Description		
31-339	**11217** BRb black W xhs - *05*	35	44
31-343	**11219** BRb black xhs - *13*	NPG	NPG
31-341	**11222** BRb black xhs - *07*	38	47
31-335	**11226** BRb black xhs - *97*	25	36
31-337A	**D2223** BRc green - *02*	30	40
31-337B	**D2228** BRc green - *02*	30	40
31-337B	**D2228** BRc green W - *04*	35	40
31-338	**D2254** BRe blue W - *05*	35	43
31-336A	**D2258** BRe blue - *02*	35	43
31-342	**D2264** BRc green xhs - *07*	38	47
31-340	**D2267** BRe blue W - *06*	35	43
31-337	**D2280** BRc green - *97*	30	35
31-338	**D2282** BRc green xhs - *99*	30	35
31-336B	**D2294** BRe blue - *04*	35	40
31-344	**D2332** *Lloyd* NCB yellow W xhs - *13*	NPG	NPG
31-336	**D2334** BRe blue - *97*	25	36

BR Class 04 diesel shunter [L60]

L61. Class 08/09 0-6-0DS (2000)

The standard BR diesel shunter, dating from 1952, was based on an LMS design of 1945. 894 were built between 1953 and 1962, for shunting and station pilot duties. For a specific function, they were the most standardised locomotives in Britain. The Class 09 shunters look the same but have up-rated engines. They were built between 1959 and 1962 and all were allocated to the Southern Region. As the fleet was reduced, due to shrinking freight traffic and pilot duties, many found their way into industry and, at the time of writing, at least 60 have found their way onto heritage lines.

The models have flywheel drive and 5-pole motors. From 2005 they were 'DCC ready', with 8-pin DCC sockets, and had an improved pickup design. The term 'no ladders' refers to the ladders originally fitted up either side of the radiator that were later removed as they interfered with forward vision from the cab. The absence of this comment in the table should not be taken as meaning that there are ladders present on the model.

Cat No	Description		
32-110	**13029** BRb black hinged door - *04*	35	46
32-114A	**13050** BRb black hinged door - *13*	NPG	NPG
32-114	**13238** BRb black hinged doors - *08*	40	56
32-100	**13365** BRc green - *00*	30	40
32-113	**D3032** BRc plain green hinged door - *05*	38	51
32-110Z	**D3052** BRb black W with wasp stripes Sp Edn (*Model Rail* magazine) - *11*	63	70
32-113Z	**D3232** BRc plain green W hinged door Sp Edn 508 (Hattons) - *10*	50	62
32-112	**D3336** BRc green hinged door - *04*	35	46
32-101A	**D3586** BRc green wasp stripes - *01*	35	45
32-101	**D3729** BRc green wasp stripes - *00*	30	40
32-117	**D3963** BRc green W wasp stripes - *12*	65	78
32-116	**D3986** BRc green wasp stripes - *not made*	NA	NA

BR Class 08 diesel shunter [L61]

Cat No	Description		
32-116A	**D3986** BRc green wasp stripes - *11*	50	64
32-101B	**D4192** BRc green wasp stripes - *03*	35	45
32-118	**08011/D3018** **Haversham** BRc green, hinged door, no ladders ** - *13*	NPG	NPG
32-115A	**08021** BRe blue hinged door, no ladders - *13*	NPG	NPG
32-335	**08173** BRe blue W hinged door, no ladders - *09*	45	57
32-111	**08243** BRe blue hinged door - *04*	35	46
32-111A	**08375** BRe blue hinged door - *05*	38	51
32-108V	**08410** FGW green Sp Edn 512 (Kernow Model Railway Centre) - *05*	45	59
32-108VDC	as above but with DCC decoder fitted (taken from above 512 models) - *07*	55	62
32-108VDCS	as above but with Lenz Silver DCC sound decoder fitted (taken from above 512 models) - *07*	63	70
32-102K	**08484** *Captain Nathaniel Darrell* Port of Felixstowe blue Sp Edn 504 (BCC) no ladders - *09*	45	57
32-102Z	**08507** BRe blue W Ltd Edn 1000 (BCC) - *03*	40	50
32-106	**08585** Freightliner green - *02*	35	45
32-102X	**08600** *Ivor* early NSE Sp Edn 500 (ModelZone) - *03*	40	50
32-102	**08623** BRe blue no ladders - *00*	30	40
32-102V	**08641** *Dartmoor* NSE bright blue Sp Edn 512 (The Signal Box) - *08*	50	60
32-107	**08648** BRe Rft departmental grey - *02*	35	45
32-104	**08653** Railfreight Distribution grey - *01*	35	45
32-108	**08683** EWS maroon+yellow - *05*	38	51
32-102B	**08748** BRe blue no ladders - *03*	35	45
32-102A	**08762** BRe blue no ladders - *01*	35	45
32-111Z	**08721** *Starlet* BRe Express Parcels blue with red stripe Sp Edn 508 (ModelZone) - *12*	62	74
32-105	**08800** InterCity swallow grey - *02*	40	50
32-111Y	**08833** GER lined blue Sp Edn 512 (Invictor) - *13*	68	83
32-103	**08921** EWS red air comp cabinet new front windows deep springs - *01*	35	45
32-116	**09006** Mainline blue - *02*	35	45
32-100Z	**(Cambridge)** RES grey+red Ltd Edn 500 (*Model Rail* magazine) * - *01*	40	55
32-102W	**97800** *Ivor* BRe blue+red Sp Edn 500 (ModelZone) - *04*	30	40
32-102U	**878** *Basra* Longmoor Military Railway blue+red Sp Ed 512 (ModelZone) - *11*	60	70

* This was sold through the magazine and came with a sheet of numbers by Modelmaster and a sheet by Shawplan with 'Cambridge' nameplates and logos. ** This was the oldest

Bachmann Branchline

working diesel on British Rail and was repainted in its original BR green and named Haversham by the staff at Bletchley. It was eventually withdrawn from service in 1991.

L62. Class 20 Bo-Bo (2004)
This is an English Electric designed freight loco of 1957, the first of 20 being built at their Vulcan Foundry works. Other batches followed until the final member of the class was delivered in 1968. 228 eventually arrived and were allocated to the Eastern, London Midland and Scottish Regions. It was now the standard BR Type 1 diesel and all of the other pilot scheme Type 1s were withdrawn. They were often seen operating in pairs, joined nose to nose so that their cabs were at the outer ends. This allowed them to drive the pair from either end and thus overcame the visual obstruction created by the long bonnet.

From the start, the model has been 'DCC ready'. It has a choice of bogies with NEM pockets, wire sand pipes and, like the real locomotives, some models have code discs at either end while others have code boxes. In 2005, Bachmann improved windscreen profiles and enhanced radiator grills. A version with tablet catcher recesses in the cab sides arrived in 2006.

Cat.	No.	Description		
32-027	D8000	BRc green, discs - 04	40	49
32-027Y	D8000 & D8001	BRc green, discs, in 504 twin pack Sp Edn (Ian Allan 50th Anniv.) - 07	NA	110
32-044	D8028	BRc green, discs, tablet catcher - 13	NPG	NPG

BR Class 20 [L62] (Tony Wright)

32-027A	D8046	BRc green, discs - 04	40	49
32-042DC	D8101	BRc green, tablet catcher, DCC chip fitted - 07	52	66
32-040DS	D8113	BRc green, discs, DCC sound chip fitted tc - 06	100	120
32-028	D8134	BRc green, codeboxes - 04	40	49
32-034DS	D8138	BRc green, codeboxes DCC sound chip fitted - 11	NPG	178
32-033DS	D8158	BRc green, codeboxes DCC sound chip fitted - 08	130	150
32-034	D8164	BRc green, codeboxes - 08	42	56
32-028A	D8169	BRc green, codeboxes - 04	40	49
32-032	D8307	BRe blue W, codeboxes - 05	42	55
32-029	20023	BReLL Railfreight grey, discs - 05	40	51
32-041	20028	BRe blue, discs, tablet catcher - 07	40	51
(32-027Z)	20030 *River Rother*	BRe green, discs, Sp Edn (Model Rail magazine) ex-pair - 05	65	NA
32-035DS	20034	BRe blue, discs, DCC sound chip fitted - 08	130	150
32-025TF	20042	Waterman Railways black, Ltd Edn 500 (2004 London Toyfair) - 04	80	100
32-031	20052	BRe blue W, discs - 05	42	55
32-031	20052	BRe blue W, codeboxes - *not made*	NA	NA
32-025A	20058	BRe blue, discs - 04	40	49
32-025	20063	BRe blue, discs - 04	40	49
(32-027Z)	20064 *River Sheaf*	BRe green, discs, Sp Edn (Model Rail magazine) ex-pair - 05	65	NA
32-027Z	20064 *River Sheaf* + 20030 *River Rother*	Sp Edn 500 (Model Rail magazine) - 05	NA	124
32-029A	20090	BReLL, Rft red stripe grey, discs - 10	50	61
32-038DS	20124	BRe blue W, discs, DCC sound chip fitted - 13	NPG	NPG
32-036	20128	BRe blue W, discs - 11	55	73
32-030	20132	BReLL red-stripe Rft grey, codeboxes - 05	40	51
32-035A	20136	BRe blue - 11	55	69
32-035	20164	BRe blue, domino headcode, DCC21 - 09	45	59
32-027Y	20188	Waterman Railways black Sp Edn 504 (Basement Models) - order cancelled and models released as BCC model 32-026K (below)	NA	NA
32-026K	20188	Waterman Railways black, Sp Edn 504 (BCC) - 07	65	80
32-026	20192	BRe blue, codeboxes - 04	40	50
32-026A	20217	BRe blue, codeboxes - 04	40	50
32-030Y	20227	LT red+white, codeboxes, Sp Edn 504 (London Transport Museum) - 13	NPG	NPG
32-037	20901	GBRf Europorte blue+yellow - 13	NPG	NPG
-	20901 *Nancy*	Hunslet-Barclay grey	60	NA
-	20904 *Janis*	Hunslet-Barclay grey	60	NA
32-027X	above two locomotives in twin pack Sp Edn 512 (Kernow Model Rail Centre) - 10		NA	140

L63a. Class 24 Bo-Bo (2001)
Built originally at BR Derby Works form 1957, the Class 24 locomotives were for mixed traffic and were introduced to British Railways in 1958. Subsequent orders also involved Crewe and Darlington workshops and 151 were built before the design was modified to produce the Class 25. Withdrawals of the class started in the late 1960s and had been completed by the Autumn of 1980. Four members of the class have been preserved.

The models include red fans seen beneath the roof exhaust grill. They are 'DCC ready' and a mixture of 8-pin (DC8) and 21-pin (DC21) sockets are fitted. Since 2002, they have had NEM pockets on the bogies. The models come with code discs on the cab fronts and some have digital sound chips fitted.

BR Class 24 [63a]

32-430	D5013	BRc green, discs - 06	38	51
32-429	D5011	BRc green - 03	35	45
32-430A	D5030	BRc green - 09	40	57
32-427	D5038	BRc 2-tone green - *not made*	NA	NA
32-426DS	D5038	BRc 2-tone green discs DCC sound chip fitted - 09	130	155
32-426	D5054	BRc green - 01	35	45
32-430B	D5061	BRc green - 10	45	59
32-425Y	D5072	BRc 2-tone green W Sp Edn 512 (Kernow Model Rail Centre) - 08	55	70
32-427	D5085	BRc 2-tone green - 02	35	45
32-429DS	D5100	BRc green discs DCC sound chip fitted - 11	NPG	174
32-428	5087	BRe blue - 02	35	45
32-429DS	D5100	BRc green DCC sound chip fitted - 10	130	157
32-425DS	24035	BRe blue DCC sound chip fitted - 07	100	113
32-431DC	24077	BRe blue, discs, DCC chip fitted - 13	75	90
32-425	24081	BRe blue - 01	35	45
32-425Z	97201 *Experiment*	BRe Research Department red+blue Sp Edn 750 (Rail Express) - 01	100	125
32-425X	97201	BRe Research Department red+blue Sp Edn 512 (ModelZone) - 11	60	72
32-425W	RDB968007	BRe Research Dept. (originally D5061) blue+red Sp Edn 512 (Invictor) - 13	78	93

L63b. Class 24/1 Bo-Bo (2013)
In all, 50 of the Class 24 were designated 24/1 and were delivered between February 1960 and January 1961. The last was withdrawn in 1976 and none has been preserved.
The models are fitted with a 21-pin DCC decoder socket.

32-440	D5135	BRc plain green - 13	NPG	86
32-441	D5149	BRc green with small yellow panels - 13	NPG	86
32-442	24137	BRe blue - 13	NPG	86

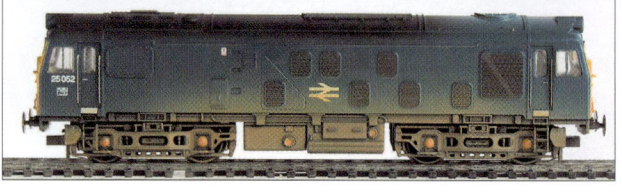

BR Class 25 (old body) weathered [L64a]

L64a. Class 25 (old body style) Bo-Bo (2003)
The Class 25s were introduced to Britain's railways in 1961 as mixed traffic locomotives and were a development of the Class 24. A total of 323 were built at Derby, Darlington and by private sector contractor Beyer Peacock, between 1961 and 1967. There were 4 subclasses, the main differences being in the electrical equipment incorporated in their

construction. There were also five slight body differences which affected the appearance of the cab fronts and the ventilation louvers on the sides. A fifth subclass was formed in 1986 by modification of some existing locos. Withdrawals started in the late 1970s, with the last member of the class going in 1987. At least 20 of the class survived into preservation.

The model was produced with alternative cab front styles, a see-through roof grill and visible fan beneath. Since 2005 they have been 'DCC ready' and the latest ones have been fitted with 21-pin DCC sockets. In the table below, the models are marked with a 25/1 or 25/2 according to the subclass to which they belong (if known). The bogies are fitted with NEM coupling pockets.
Sno = snow ploughs fitted.

32-328	D5182 BRc green 25/1 - *10*	45	59
32-330DS	D5183 BRc green 25/1 DCC sound chip fitted - *11*	145	177
32-325	D5211 BRc green 25/1 - *03*	35	45
32-325DC	D5211 BRc green 25/1 DCC chip fitted - *06*	50	63
32-326Z	D5218 BRe blue 25/1 Sp Edn 504 (ModelZone) - *07*	44	56
32-402	25034 *Castell Aberystwyth/Aberystwyth Castle* BRe blue 25/1 ex set - *08*	45	NA
32-331	25043 BRc green W - *13*	NPG	NPG
32-327	25052 BRe blue W - *08*	44	56
32-326	25054 BRe blue 25/1 - *03*	35	51
(30-050)DC	25058 BRe blue 25/1 DCC chip fitted ex-set - *08*	44	56
32-329	25231 BRe blue W 25/2 - *11*	NPG	66
32-326DS	25245 BRe blue 25/2 DCC sound chip fitted - *09*	130	155

L64b. Class 25 (new body style) Bo-Bo (2001)

The early members of the class had ventilation louvres dotted all over the locomotives' sides. The body was restyled around 1963, approximately when work started on the subclass 25/2. The new style body had the side vents transferred to the roof-line.

With the release of the model in 2001, both body styles were available from the start. Since 2005 they have been 'DCC ready' with 8-pin DCC sockets. As an early candidate for a sound chip, 21-pin sockets have been fitted since 2006. In the table below, the models are marked with a 25/2 or 25/3 according to the subclass to which they belong. From 2002, the bogies were fitted with NEM coupling pockets.
sno = snow ploughs fitted.

32-411	D5233 BRc 2-tone green 25/2 - *01*	35	44
(30-045)	As above but DCC chip fitted ex-set sno - *05*	45	NA
32-413	D5237 BRc 2-tone green 25/2 - *02*	35	44
32-406	D5255 BRc 2-tone green 25/3– *not made*	NA	NA
32-403	D5269 BRc 2-tone green W 25/2 - *02*	35	44
32-410	5293 BRe blue 25/2 - *not made*	NA	NA
32-406	D7502 BRc 2-tone green 25/3 - *10*	50	65
32-401DS	D7638 BRc 2-tone green DCC sound chip fitted 25/3 - *09*	130	155
32-400	D7645 BRc 2-tone green 25/3 - *01*	35	45
32-405	D7646 BRc 2-tone green 25/3 - *07*	38	56
32-404	D7667 BRe blue, sno 25/3 - *02*	40	50
32-402	D7672 *Tamworth Castle* BRc 2-tone green 25/3 - *01*	35	60
32-412	25083 BRe blue W 25/2 - *02*	35	43
32-410	25087 BRe blue 25/2 - *01*	35	43
32-400DS	25095 BRe blue with DCC sound chip fitted unique livery 25/3 - *06*	90	110
32-404DS	25276 BRe blue 25/3 DCC sound chip fditted - *11*	NPG	177
32-401	25279 BRe blue 25/3 - *01*	35	45
32-407	25279 BRe blue W 25/3 -*11*	55	69
32-402Z	25322 *Tamworth Castle* BRe blue, silver roof, yellow cabs 25/3 Sp Edn 750 (*Model Rail* magazine) - *02*	40	75
32-400TF	ADB97252 *Ethel 3* IC grey 25/3 Sp Edn 750 (2008 London Toy Fair) - *08*	45	58

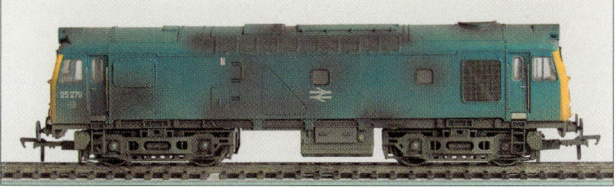

BR Class 25 (new body) [L64b]

L65a. Class 37/0 Co-Co (2002)

The Class 37 was an English Electric mixed traffic design, which entered service in 1960. It became the largest of the Type 3 classes with 309 built. Construction took place between 1957 and 1962, but, over the following years, modifications and refurbishments created six subclasses, four of which have been modelled by Bachmann. This table contains the models which reflect the diesel in its original condition i.e. the standard locomotive (37/0).

The model has working LED headlights, metal roof grill and fan, sprung buffers and cast or fabricated bogies. Upgraded bogies and wheels were fitted from the start of 2008 as appropriate. Since 2006, 21-pin DCC sockets have been fitted.
en = etched nameplates. sno = snow ploughs. ch = centre headcode. sh = split headcode. hye = half yellow ends.

32-375Z	D6607 *Ben Cruachan* BRc green 37/4 Sp Edn 900 (BCC) - *02*	80	95
32-776	D6707 BRc green sh - *04*	45	60
32-?	D6711 BRc green W sh Sp Edn (Ian Allan) - *11*	75	90
32-776K	D6717 BRc green W sh hye Sp Edn 1,000 (BCC) - *04*	45	60
32-782	D6801 BRc green sh hye - *11*	60	76
32-778	D6826 BRc green ch - *04*	45	60
32-782A	D6984 BRc green W ch hya - *12*	80	98
32-775Z	37003 BRe blue Sp Edn 512 (The Class 37 Locomotive Group) - *12*	NPG	NPG
32-780Y	37025 *Inverness TMD* BReLL blue Sp Edn 500 (Rails) - *06*	60	75
32-780Y	37025 *Inverness TMD* BReLL blue W Sp Edn 500 (Rails) - *07*	55	70
32-781A	37034 BRe blue W sh - *12*	80	98
32-779	37035 BRe Dutch grey+yellow 37/0 sh sno DCC21 - *06*	48	62
32-775	37038 BRe blue sh - *04*	45	60
32-780X	37038 DRS dark blue 37/0 Sp Edn 512 (Cheltenham Model Centre) - *?*	60	75
32-783DS	37049 BRe blue sh DCC sound chip fitted - *10*	150	174
32-781DS	37057 *Viking* BReLL blue DCC sound chip fitted - *07*	120	145
32-775DC	37114 *City of Worcester* EW&S maroon sno sh 37/1 DCC chip fitted - *06*	60	74
32-777Z	37142 BRe blue W ch Sp Edn 504 (Kernow Model Rail Centre) - *04*	60	73
32-777ZDC	as above but with DCC chip fitted (taken from above 504 models) - *07*	76	83
32-777ZDCS	as above but with Lenz Silver DCC sound decoder fitted (taken from above 504 models) - *07*	66	93
32-786	37174 EWS maroon+yellow - *13*	NPG	NPG
32-780Z	37207 *William Cookworthy* BRe blue + Cornish motifs Sp Edn (Kernow Model Rail Centre) - *07*	60	76
32-777	37238 BRe blue ch - *04*	45	60
32-780	37239 *The Coal Merchants Association* BRe Rft Coal triple grey 37/2 - *09*	54	55
32-784	37242 Mainline blue W ch - *13*	NPG	NPG
32-?	37248 West Coast Railways maroon, Sp Edn 504 (*Model Rail* magazine) - *10*	65	80
32-781	37251 BRe blue ch domino headcode - *11*	65	84
32-776DS	37254 BRe Rft Coal blue DCC sound chip fitted - *08*	140	164
32-785DS	37254 BR Eng (Dutch) grey+yellow W ch, DCC sound chip fitted - *13*	NPG	NPG
32-777Y	97303 Network Rail yellow Sp Edn 500 (Model Rail) – *09*	65	80

BR Departmental Class 37/0 [L65a]

L65b. Class 37/4 Co-Co (2003)

In 1984, refurbishment was seen as an alternative to locomotive replacement, as it would give the British Railways Board more up to date machines within the budget available. Of a class of 308, 135 underwent refurbishment at Crewe. The locomotives in this 37/4 subclass were modified for passenger work by the addition of an electric train supply (ETS) for heating the carriages.

The model has working LED headlights, metal roof grill and visible fan, sprung buffers and cast or fabricated bogies. The locomotives are 'DCC ready' and had upgraded bogies and wheels fitted from 2008. From the start these were fitted with an 8-pin DCC decoder socket but from 2009, some were described as having a 21-pin socket fitted.
en = etched nameplates. sno = snow ploughs.

32-384	37406 *The Saltire Society* Railfreight Distribution triple grey DCC21 - *09*	60	73
32-377	37408 *Loch Rannoch* BReLL blue Eastfield motif 700 made - *03*	40	50

Bachmann Branchline

32-?	37409 DRS (compass) blue Sp Edn (Model Rail magazine) - 10		NPG	NPG
32-382	37410 **Aluminium 100** BReLL blue scottie motif sno en - 07		48	62
32-375W	37411 **The Institution of Railway Signal Engineers** BReLL blue W Sp Edn (Model Rail magazine) - 03		50	60
32-381	37411 **Ty Hafan** EWS maroon en - 07		48	62
32-375K	37411/D6990 **Caerphilly Castle/Castell Caerffili** BRc green en Sp Edn 504 (BCC) - 07		60	75
32-385	37415 Intercity Executive grey+beige DCC21 - 10		60	76
32-377DS	37417 **Highland Region** BReLL blue + yellow cabs DCC sound chip fitted - 11		NPG	190
32-375	37419 EW&S maroon - 03		40	45
32-381X	37425 **Pride of the Valleys** BReLL Sp Edn (G. Allison) - 06		60	75
32-381W	37426 **Vale of Rheidol** BReLL blue Sp Edn 504 (Hereford Model Centre) - 10		60	75
32-381V	37427 **Highland Enterprise** Regional Railways/ ScotRail blue Sp Edn (Rails) - 07		60	72
32-388	37427 **Bont y Bermo** BReLL blue W DCC21 - 11		80	95
32-383	37428 **David Lloyd George** Railfreight Petroleum triple grey DCC21 - 09		60	73
32-780V	37428 **Loch Arkalg** West Coast maroon Sp Edn 500 (Model Rail magazine) - 10		65	80
32-376	37429 **Eisteddfod Genedlaethol** Regional Railways blue - 03		40	45
32-378	37431 **Bullidae** IC Mainline /petroleum grey+ white sno - 03		35	40

BR Weathered Class 37/4 [L65b]

L65c. Class 37/5 Co-Co (2003)

Members of the 37/5 subclass were originally refurbished Railfreight locomotives, some of which were fitted with slow speed control.

The models in this table used old tooling and, in 2008, Rail Express magazine commissioned the tooling of a more accurate model (see below). The models have working LED headlights, metal roof grill and fan, cast or fabricated bogies, sprung buffers and are 'DCC ready, ready with either an 8-pin or 21-pin DCC decoder socket fitted.'
en = etched nameplates.

32-387	37506 Railfreight red stripe grey BReLL Thornaby depot motif DCC21 - 11	68	84
32-386	37513 Railfreight triple grey Metals Sector Thornaby depot plates DCC21 - 10	60	76
32-386	37514 Railfreight triple grey Metals Sector Thornaby depot plates DCC21 - 11	68	84
32-387	37518 Railfreight red stripe grey BReLL Thornaby depot motif DCC21 - not made	NA	NA
32-781Z	37670 **St. Blazey T&RS MD** EWS maroon W en Sp Edn (Kernow Model Rail Centre) - 07	60	76
32-781P	37670 **St. Blazey T&RS MD** DB Schenker red en Sp Edn 1000 (Rail Express magazine) - 10	60	77
32-781P (DS)	37670 **St. Blazey T&RS MD** DB Schenker red en Sp Edn 1000 (Rail Express magazine) DCC sound chip fitted - 10	145	167
32-380	37671 **Tre Pol and Pen** BRe Rft Dist. triple grey sno en, St Blazey plates and nameplates - 03	40	50
32-375DC	37672 Transrail triple grey en 37/6 DCC 8-pin chip fitted - 07	60	74
32-379	37678 BRe Railfreight red stripe grey sno - 03	40	45
32-381Y	37692 **Lass of Ballochmyle** Railfreight grey Sp Edn (GMD Models) - 07?	60	76
32-376DS	37693 BReLL Railfreight grey, yellow cabs, DCC sound chip fitted - 08	140	164
32-380DS	37698 **Coedbach** BRe coal load triple grey, DCC sound chip fitted en - 07	120	145
32-?	37698 Loadhaul black+orange Sp Edn (G. Allison) - not made *	NA	NA

* The required tooling to produce this variation was unavailable and so it was dropped.

L65d. Class 37/5 (Retooled) Co-Co (2008)

The model was retooled exclusively for Rail Express magazine in 2008 to include detail not on the original model.

The model has working LED headlights, sprung buffers, metal roof grill and fan and cast or fabricated bogies. There are body variations including either EE or RSH grilles, as well as nose variations and the model is 'DCC ready'.
en = etched nameplates.

	37501 **Teesside Steelmaster** British Steel light blue en	60	NA
	37502 **British Steel Teesside** Rft red stripe en	60	NA
32-381T	above two locos Sp Edn 1000 (Rail Express magazine) - 08	NA	150
	37510 DRS dark blue	60	NA
	37688 **Kingmoor TMD** DRS dark blue	60	NA
32-381U	above 2 locos Sp Edn 1000 (Rail Express magazine) - 08	NA	150
32-381S	37507 **Hartlepool Pipe Mill** Railfreight Metals en Sp Edn 672 (Rail Express magazine) - 08	60	75
32-381R	37521 **English China Clays** EWS maroon+yellow W Sp Edn 512 (Kernow MRC) - 10	60	75
32-381P	37670 **St. Blazey T&RS MD** red en Sp Edn 1000 (Rail Express magazine) - 10	60	77
32-381PDS	as above but with a DCC21 sound chip fitted (Rail Express magazine) - 10	145	167

L65e. Class 37/7 'Heavyweight' Co-Co (2010)

The subclass was created in 1986 when 44 Class 37 locomotives were refurbished for heavy freight work and numbered in the 377xx and 378xx ranges.

The model of the 37/7 subclass was produced initially exclusively for specialist retailer Rail Exclusive. It has a modified body and some were being offered sound fitted. There are opening cab doors, etched fan grills working LED directional lights, all-wheel drive and they are fitted with 21-pin DCC sockets.

-	37702 **Taff Merthyr** Transrail tripe grey, Canton depot logos	70	NA
-	37798 Mainline blue, Stewarts Lane depot logos	70	NA
32-390X	above 2 locos, Sp Edn 512 (Rail Exclusive) pack E - 10	NA	170
32-390XDS	above set with locos fitted with a DCC sound chip	NA	330
-	37713 LoadHaul black+orange	70	NA
-	37884 **Gartcosh** LoadHaul black+orange	70	NA
32-390Y	above 2 locos, Sp Edn 512 (Rail Exclusive) pack D - 10	NA	170
32-?DS	above set with locos fitted with a DCC sound chip	NA	330

L65f. Class 37/9 'Slug' Co-Co (2010)

The subclass was created in 1986 and 1987 when refurbished Railfreight Class 37 locomotives were fitted with experimental power units.

This model of the 37/9 subclass was produced exclusively for Kernow Model Rail Centre. It has a modified body and roof. There are working LED headlights, metal roof grill and fan, cast or fabricated bogies and it is 'DCC ready'.

-	37905 Railfreight Metals triple grey	70	NA
-	37906 BReLL Railfreight grey with yellow cabs	70	NA
32-390Z	above two locos Sp Edn 512 (Kernow Model Rail Centre) - 10	NA	170

BR Class 40 [L66a]

L66a. Class 40 1Co-Co1 (2004)

Built by English Electric, they finally totalled 200. Construction had started in 1956 and the new locomotive was unveiled in the Spring of 1958. The first 134 locos were equipped with disc codes and the next 22 had split code boxes instead. From early in 1961 all new class members had a single codebox at each end as the communicating doors were no longer considered necessary. Some received names of ocean going ships and the class survived until 1985, after which they were considered to be obsolete. Seven Class 40s have survived in preservation.

In 2005, the body on the model was lowered slightly to reduce the gap between body and bogies. At the time it was recorded as being 'DCC ready' and from 2008 as having an

8-pin DCC decoder socket. The model was replaced in 2013 and those models are listed in the next table.

32-475Z	**D200/40122** BRe green split headcode, full yell ends Sp Edn 750 (*Model Rail* magazine) - *04*	75	95
32-478	**D210** *Empress of Britain* BRc green, discs, the first of the improved models - *05*	52	66
32-477	**D325** BRe green split headcode - *04*	50	63
-	**D326** BRc green Sp Edn (Rails) - *not made*	NA	NA
32-475 (30-090)	**D368** BRc green code boxes - *04* **D396** BRc green ex-Bachmann 15th Anniversary set - *04*	50 60	63 NA
32-476	**40075** BRe blue discs - *04*	50	63
32-475DC	**40129** BRe blue split codeboxes DCC chip fitted - *not made**	NA	NA
32-475Y	**40145** BRe blue Sp Edn 504 (Class 40 Preservation Society) - *05*	80	95
32-479	**40169** BRe blue domino codeboxes, minus water tanks - *05*	55	66

* Due to tooling issues, this model was not released in 2010 as planned but was later released as 40141.

L66b.   Class 40 1Co-Co1 (2013)

From 2010, all models were to have been fitted with 21-pin DCC sockets and have working LED headlights, metal roof grill and fan, etched metal frost grills and cast or fabricated bogies. These improvements are now due to arrive in 2013 with a new highly detailed model.
DS = fitted with digital sound.

32-480DS	**D211** *Mauretania* BRc green, disc, DCC sound chip fitted - *13*	NPG	NPG
32-481	**D369** BRc green centre headcode - *13*	NPG	NPG
32-475DC	**40141** BRe blue split codeboxes DCC chip fitted - *13*	NPG	NPG

BR Class 42 [L67]

L67.   Class 42 'Warship' B-B (1998)

Based largely on the German V200 Class, the 'Warships' were built at Swindon and introduced between 1958 and 1961. A total of 38 were constructed and all were allocated to the Western Region. The first 13 started life with three figure route indicator frames fitted to the cab fronts. The rest had the four digit code boxes, the original 13 being converted on works visits. None survived long enough to carry TOPS numbers. Being non-standard, withdrawals started in 1968 and were completed in 1972. Two have been preserved.

Instead of reintroducing the Mainline Railways model, Bachmann chose to retool it. The model came with an optional separate apron parts and a buffer beam accessory pack. Despite earlier plans to do so, it was not made DCC enabled until 2010 when the chassis was rebuilt to take a 21-pin DCC socket and, at this stage, LED cab-front lights were added. In previous editions of this book, 32-050DC and 32-061 were listed as having been released in 2006 but it now seems that these were delayed until 2010.

32-055	**D800** *Sir Brian Robertson* BRc green - *00*	35	50
32-053	**D804** *Avenger* BRe blue - *00*	35	48
32-056	**D806** *Cambrian* BRc maroon - *01*	35	48
32-050Z	**D808** *Centaur* BRc green full yellow front Sp Edn 504 (ModelZone) - *11*	60	75
32-050DC	**D809** *Champion* BRc maroon DCC chip fitted - *10*	60	73
32-060	**D810** *Vanguard* BRc maroon W - *04*	40	56
32-062	**810** *Cockade* BRe blue W - *13*	NPG	NPG
32-061	**D812** *The Royal Naval Reserve* 1859-1959 BRe blue - *10*	50	62
32-052	**D816** *Eclipse* BRc green - *99*	35	48
32-050	**D817** *Foxhound* BRc maroon - *98*	35	45
32-059	**D818** *Glory* BRc green - *04*	40	56
32-058	**D820** *Grenville* BRc green - *03*	35	55
32-052A	**D823** *Hermes* BRc green - *11*	60	72
32-056DC	**D827** *Kelly* BRe blue DCC chip fitted - *11*	70	85
32-054	**D831** *Monarch* BRe blue - *99*	35	48
32-051	**D832** *Onslaught* BRc green - *98*	35	48
32-051DC	**D867** *Zenith* BRc green DCC chip fitted - *11*	70	85
32-057	**D870** *Zulu* BRe blue - *02*	35	50

A small number of maroon bodies of D827 'Kelly' (not of Mainline origin) have been found.

L68.   Class 43 'Warship' (2013)

Built between 1960 and 1962, the class eventually totalled 33 and they were dedicated to the Western Region. The last was withdrawn in 1971 and none has been preserved.

This is a new highly detailed model. It is fitted with a 21-pin DCC decoder socket.

32-065	**D865** *Zealous* BRc maroon - *13*	NPG	90
32-066	**D835** *Pegasus* BRc green - *13*	NPG	90
32-067	**842** *Royal Oak* BRe blue - *13*	NPG	90

LMS designed 10001 in BR green [L69a] (Bachmann)

L69a.   LMS Prototype 'Twins' Main Line Diesels (2013)

A year before Nationalisation of the railways, the LMS had announced their intention to build two experimental main line diesel locomotives. No.10000 emerged from Derby Works in November 1947 and was the only one of the two to carry 'LMS' on its sides, which it retained until November 1951. No.10001 arrived in July the following year.

The model is being developed in association with Rails of Sheffield and they have a 21-pin DCC decoder socket fitted. The model has not been released at the time of writing.

?	**10000** LMS black Sp Edn (Rails) - *13*	NPG	NPG
?	also available with 10001 in earliest livery together in a wooden presentation case - *?*	NPG	NPG
?	**10000** BRb (large) black - *14*	NPG	NPG
?	**10000** BRb (small) black - *14*	NPG	NPG
31-995	**10000** BRc lined green - *13*	NPG	113
31-996	**10000** BRc green with partial egg-shell blue waistband - *13*	NPG	113
?	**10001** BRb (large) black - *14*	NPG	NPG
?	**10001** BRb (small) black - *14*	NPG	NPG
?	**10001** BRc lined out green - *14*	NPG	NPG
?	**10001** BRc green with partial egg-shell blue waistband - *?*	NPG	NPG
?	**10001** BRc green with full egg-shell blue waistband - *?*	NPG	NPG
31-997	**10001** BRc green with full egg-shell blue waistband + small warning panel - *13*	85	113

L69b.   Class 44 'Peak' 1Co-Co1 (2003)

The first 10 Type 4 'Peaks' to be built were later made the Class 44. They formed part of the 1955 Modernisation Plan and were required as mixed traffic locomotives. They were introduced in 1959 and 1960. Further locomotives were subsequently ordered but, due to technical differences in their construction, when TOPS classification came in, they became two further classes (45 and 46). All ten locomotives of the Class 44 were allocated to the London Midland Region but were quickly displace from their passenger duties by later built 'Peaks'. They spent the rest of their days on freight duties in the Nottingham area.

The model was 'DCC ready' from 2005 and a 21-pin DCC decoder socket was fitted by 2008. The model has a see-through roof grill showing the fan beneath. The buffers are mounted on the bogies and the model comes with etched nameplates.

32-650	**D1** *Scafell Pike* BRc green - *03, 05*	52	64
32-652	**44004** *Great Gable* BRe blue discs - *09*	55	74
32-652DS	**44005** BRe blue DCC sound chip fitted - *11*	NPG	197
32-651	**44008** *Penyghent* BRe blue - *03, 05*	45	55

L70a.   Class 45 'Peak' 1Co-Co1(ex-Mainline) (2002)

Following the building of the first 10 'Peaks' (Class 44), the British Railways Board decided that it wanted more of these engines but with a slightly more powerful motor installed. 127 were ordered and were built at Crewe and Derby between 1960 and 1963. They were allocated to the London Midland and Eastern Regions and became the Class 45. 50 members of the class had electric train supply fitted at Derby, during the period 1973-75, and became the subclass 45/1. Some had communicating doors in the cab fronts and split codeboxes while the rest had no doors and central codeboxes. Later, solid central codeboxes were fitted and, from 1985, the boxes received sealed beam headlights.

Initially using the Mainline tooling and unhappy with the results, Bachmann decided to retool the model and so only one of the three planned models was made. The models listed here were based on the Mainline tooling. The only one made had a roof grill and fan, buffers on the bogies and etched nameplates, but of course was not fitted with DCC decoder sockets.

31-125Z	**D55** *Royal Signals* BRc green W Sp Edn 500 (Southampton MC) - *02*	55	65
31-125	**D67** *The Royal Artilleryman* BRc green, cream band - *not made* *	NA	NA

Bachmann Branchline

31-126	45114 BRe blue, white roof - *not made* *	NA	NA

* These were originally planned in 2002 using the old tooling but not proceeded with as it was decided to retool the model.

BR Class 45 [L70b]

L70b.   Class 45 'Peak' 1Co-Co1 (2004)

In 2004, Bachmann introduced their first Class 45s from completely new tooling. The retooled model is 'DCC ready', now with 21-pin DCC decoder socket, and has a see-through roof grill and visible fan, buffers mounted on the bogies and etched nameplates. Some members of the public were unhappy with the nose end and so further retooling took place prior to releases in 2006. In 2009 the cabs were modified again to improve detail. The models have directional lighting, plated or exposed body steps and fly-wheel drive to both bogies.

32-679DS	**D27** BRc green, small yellow panels sh DCC sound chip fitted - *11*	150	196
32-675Z	**D55** *Royal Signals* BRc green W Sp Edn 500 (Southampton MC) (31-125Z on certificate) - *04*	65	80
32-678DS	**D55** *Royal Signals* BRc green DCC sound chip fitted - *09*	150	171
32-675	**D67** *The Royal Artilleryman* BRc green, cream band - *04*	50	64
32-679	**D95** BRc green - *09*	60	75
32-681	**D108** BRc green - *13*	NPG	NPG
32-680	45036 BRe blue, split cwntre headcode - *13*	55	74
32-676Z	45048 *The Royal Marines* BRe blue Sp Edn 504 (ModelZone) - *06*	55	70
32-677	45053 BRe blue split codeboxes - *09*	55	74
32-676	45114 BRe blue, off-white roof - *04*	50	64
32-677A	45120 BRe blue, blue roof sh - *10*	62	77

L71a.   Class 46 'Peak' 1Co-Co1 (ex-Mainline) (1994)

Construction of the first of the Class 46s started at Derby in 1961. Except for minor grill and battery box changes, they were identical to 45s in external appearance. They were initially deployed in the Midlands and North East but later a batch went to the Western Region to replace diesel-hydraulics. They were eventually displaced by HSTs. Deletions started in 1977 and were completed in 1984. Three of the locomotives have been preserved.

The Class 46 was amongst the first diesels in the Bachmann range. The first arrived in 1994 and was produced using modified Palitoy Mainline Railways tooling produced for the Class 45 by Kader in China. This was replaced by new tooling in 2002 to make better quality models of the Classes 44, 45 and 46. The models were not fitted with DCC decoder sockets. Later models had roof grill and fan, buffers mounted on the bogies and etched nameplates.

wpc - wooden presentation case.

31-076A	BRe blue - *95*	25	35
31-081*	**D163** *Leicestershire and Derbyshire Yeomanry* BRc green - *not made*	NA	NA
31-080	**D172** *Ixion* BRc green Ltd Edn 2000 (Waterman's Railway) wpc - *96*	60	75
31-078	**D181** BRe blue - *97*	25	35
31-077	**D193** BRc green - *97*	25	35
31-075	46026 *Leicestershire and Derbyshire Yeomanry* BRe blue - *94*	30	40
31-076	46045 BRe blue - *94*	25	35
31-0??	97403 *Ixion* BR Derby Centre blue/red Sp Edn (*Rail Express* magazine) - *02*	90	110

* This was originally planned for 2001 using the old tooling but was not proceeded with as it was decided to retool the model.

BR Class 46 [L71b] (Tony Wright)

L71b.   Class 46 'Peak' 1Co-Co1 (2004)

These are the models from the new tooling of 2004 and are 'DCC ready', with 21-pin DCC decoder sockets. They have a see-through roof grill with the fan visible below,

directional lighting and flywheel drive to both bogies. The buffers were mounted on the bogies and named models had etched metal nameplates. By 2005 the nose ends had been modified to include the distinctive seam line as seen first on the model of Ixion.

wpc - wooden presentation case.

32-700	**D163** *Leicestershire and Derbyshire Yeomanry* BRc green - *04*	50	64
32-702DC	**D188** BRc green DCC chip fitted - *09*	67	87
32-703	**D186** BRe blue W - *11*	73	88
32-701	46053 BRe blue - *04*	50	64
32-700Z	97403 *Ixion* BRe Derby Research Centre blue+ red Sp Edn 750 (ModelZone) - *05*	55	70

L72a.   Class 47 Co-Co (2007)

Designed by Brush Ltd, a total of 512 locomotives, of what later became the Class 47, were built between 1962 and 1967 by Brush and BR Crewe. They were designed as Type 4 mixed traffic locomotives, in a second phase of diesel locomotive building by the British Transport Commission, and became the British standard Type 4 design. Being a large class, which has had a long life, there are many variations due to modifications to batches and refurbishments. The 47/0s are in the original design and were built with steam heating. The 47/3s were built between 1964 and 1965 with no train heating and were for freight train use. The 47/4s are locomotives with electric or dual heating systems. The 47/7s were fitted with remote control equipment for push-pull operation, otherwise they are like the 47/4s (conversions took place in 1979 and 1984). The 47/9 subclass contained one member, used for testing new equipment. Some remain in traffic today with various operators and others have been rebuilt into Class 57 locomotives. At the last count, 36 have been preserved for use on heritage railways.

The model features 6-axle drive, 5-pole motor, directional LED lighting, etched nameplates, open cab window and from 2006 has been 'DCC ready' with a 21-pin socket.

32-800	**D1500** BRc green 47/0 - *07*	60	72
32-805	**D1547** BRe blue 47/0 - *11*	70	87
32-804	**D1572** BRc 2-tone green 47/0 - *11*	70	87
32-801DS	**D1746** BRc 2-tone green 47/0 DCC sound chip fitted - *09*	150	176
32-801	1764 BRc 2-tone green, yellow ends 47/0 - *07*	60	72
32-804	**D1825** BRc 2-tone green– *not made*	NA	NA
8732-802	47035 BRe blue illum. marker lights 47/0 - *07*	60	72
32-801Y	47079 *George Jackson Churchward* GW 150 green 47/0 Sp Edn 512 (Kernow MRC) - *not made* (see 31-650V in next table)	NA	NA

BR Class 47 [L72a]

32-803	47148 BRe blue illuminated headcode 47/0 - *07*	60	72
32-800Z	47163 BRe blue + Union Jacks, silver roof 47/0 Sp Edn 504 (ModelZone) - *07*	60	72
32-816	47365 *Diamond Jubilee* BRe Raifreight Distributrion triple grey 47/3 - *13*	85	105
32-800DS	47404 *Hadrian* BRe blue 47/4 DCC sound chip fitted - *08*	150	176
32-800W	47408 *Finsbury Park* BRe blue 47/4 Sp Edn 500 (Deltic Preservation Society) - *07*	65	80
32-800Y	47560 *Tamar* BRe blue W 47/4 Sp Edn 504 (Cheltenham Model Centre) - *07*	60	80
32-650X	47573 *The London Standard* NSE blue 47/4 Sp Edn (ModelZone) - *09*	78	92
?	47604 *Pendennis Castle* Brunswick Green 47/4 Sp Edn (Rail Exclusive) 47/6 - *11*	NPG	100
?	as above but fitted with a DCC sound chip	NPG	200
32-817	47734 *Crewe Diesel Depot* RES red+dark grey 47/7 - *not made*	NA	NA
32-817	47794 *Saint David/Dewi Sant* RES red+dark grey 47/7 - *not made*	NA	NA
32-817	47745 *Royal London Society for the Blind* RES red+grey 47/7, Crewe modified front - *12*	80	101
32-815Z	47798 *Prince William* Royal Train dark purple Sp Edn (National Railway Museum) - *13*	80	101
32-801Z	47815 *Abertawe Landore* BRc green 37/08 Sp Edn 512 (Kernow MRC) - *08*	65	87

Bachmann Branchline

32-815	47834 *Fire Fly* BR ICs grey+beige - *13*		NPG	NPG

L72b. Class 47 (Modified) Co-Co (2008)

This version has new roof detail, revised bogie frames and authentic fuel tanks. It has 6-axle drive, 5-pole motor, directional lighting, high intensity centre light, etched nameplates and is 'DCC ready', with a 21-pin DCC decoder socket.

32-656DC	**D1677** *Thor* BRc green, yellow ends 47/0 DCC chip fitted - *12*		80	101
31-650V	**47079** *George Jackson Churchward* BRc green GW150, 47/0 Sp Edn 512 (Kernow MRC) - *08*		65	87
31-650U	**47145** *Merddin Emrys* BRe Tinsley blue Sp Edn (Rails) - *10*		75	90
31-658	**47190** *Pectinidae* BR Railfreight Petroleum grey W 47/0 - *13*		95	115
31-658DS	**47190** *Pectinidae* BR Railfreight Petroleum grey 47/0 DCC sound chip fitted - *13*		200	246
31-655	**47301** *Centurion* BR Railfreight 'red stripe' grey 47/3 - *12*		80	101
31-650P	**47406** *Rail Riders Club* IC Executive grey 47/4 Sp Edn 512 (Gaugemaster) - *09*		65	80
31-650?	**47461** *Charles Rennie Macintosh* Scotrail 47/4 Sp Edn (Rails) - *10*		75	90
31-652	**47474** *Sir Rowland Hill* Parcels red+dark grey 47/4 - *08*		60	76
31-650R	**47475** Provincial Services blue DCC21 47/4 Sp Edn 500 (*Model Rail* magazine) - *12*		90	116
31-650	**47535** *University of Leicester* BReLL blue 47/4 - *08*		60	76
31-650T	**47541** *The Queen Mother* I-C/Scotrail grey Highland motif 47/4 Sp Edn (Rails) - *10*		75	90

BR Class 47 (modified) [L72b] (Tony Wright)

31.650Z?	**47572** *Ely Cathedral* BReLL blue 47/4 Sp Edn 504 (Hornby Magazine) - *10*		NPG	NPG
31-651	**47612** *Titan* BR IC grey 47/4 - *08*		60	76
31-654	**47707** *Holyrood* NSE bright blue 47/7 - *12*		80	101
31-653	**47710** *Sir Walter Scott* BRe ScotRail dark grey+buff 47/7 - *12*		80	101
31-657	**47715** *Haymarket* NSE bright blue 47/7 - *13*		NPG	NPG
31-650W	**47972** *The Royal Army Ordinance Corps* pale grey+red 47/9 Sp Edn 512 (ModelZone) - *11*		85	105
31-650S	**47975** *The Institution of Civil Engineers* 'Dutch' grey+yellow 47/9 Ltd Edn 512 - *10*		70	88

L73a. Prototype 'Deltic' Co-Co (2007)

This was produced for the National Railway Museum (NRM) and is unique in that it is the only example of commissioned tooling which Bachmann were unable to use for other models after the two year exclusive use agreement.

The 3300hp diesel prototype 'Deltic' was built in 1955, and was affectionately known as the 'Cat's Whiskers' and 'Ice Cream Cart' due to its characteristic cream stripes, French blue livery and prominent central headlamp. It was the most powerful diesel locomotive in the world and English Electric went on to supply 22 production 'Deltic' locomotives for the East Coast Main Line.

Bachmann used laser scanning equipment for the first time to measure the locomotive. Initially, there were 500 special limited edition commemorative models, in special packaging and available from December 2007. After this, a further 2,500 limited edition standard models available the following January. In 2009, it was voted best 00 scale model of the decade. The first three models in this table are in the present livery carried by the model in the museum. The next four models are in a slightly different livery and the one in which it ran when in service on the Eastern Region (ER blue).

32-520	*Deltic* light blue in special box with certificate Sp Edn 500 (NRM) - *07*		150	300
32-520	*Deltic* light blue Sp Edn 2500 (NRM) - *08*		150	250
32-520A	*Deltic* light blue W Sp Edn 750 (NRM) - *11*		130	149
32-520NRM	*Deltic* ER blue Sp Edn (NRM) - *13*		105	125
32-520NRMDC	*Deltic* ER blue Sp Edn (NRM) chip-fitted* - *13*		115	135
32-520NRMDS	*Deltic* ER blue Sp Edn (NRM) with sound* - *13*		220	250
32-52NRMA	*Deltic* ER blue W Sp Edn (NRM)* - *13*		115	135

* Very small quantities of these have been produced.

Prototype 'Deltic' [L73a] (Bachmann)

L73b. Class 55 'Deltic' Co-Co (2003)

English Electric developed these express passenger locomotives, which were introduced in 1961. 22 were built in 1961 and 1962 for the East Coast Main Line expresses, replacing some of the ex-LNER A4s and other Pacifics that had ruled this route for almost 40 years. The 'Deltics' were built at Vulcan Foundry and performed well, achieving speeds of up to 100mph. Besides pulling crack East Coast expresses, some were later used on Trans-Pennine services. They were ousted from their main function by the introduction of the High Speed Trains. Withdrawals started in 1980 and were completed in 1982. Six of the class have been preserved.

Since 2008 the model has been 'DCC ready' with a 21-pin DCC decoder socket fitted. It has four metal roof fans, a 5-pole motor with flywheel drive to both bogies and metal sprung buffers.

wpc = wooden presentation case, en = etched nameplate.

32-525A	**D9002** *The Kings Own Yorkshire Light Infantry* BRc green - not made		NA	NA
32-524NRM	**D9002** BRc green (1961 condition) part of a 2 x Deltic set for NRM but a few sold separately - *09*		110	NA
(32-525TMCH)	**D9003** *Meld* BRc green en part of Sp Edn ex-set of two100 (TMC) - *04*		60	NA
32-525U/A	**D9003** *Meld* BRc green en 1A16 Sp Edn 252 (Harburn Hobbies) - *05*		60	80
32-525U/B	**D9003** *Meld* BRc green W en 1A35 Sp Edn 252 (Harburn Hobbies) - *05*		60	80
32-525	**D9004** *Queen's Own Highlander* BRc 2-tone green small yellow panels en - *03*		40	50
32-531DC	**9005** *The Prince of Wales's own Regiment of Yorkshire* BRe blue DCC chip fitted en - *11*		80	105
(32-525TMCH)	**D9007** *Pinza* BRc green en part of Sp Edn ex-set of 2 locomotives 100 (TMC) - *04*		65	NA
32-525DS	**D9007** *Pinza* BRc green en DCC sound chip fitted - *06*		NPG	NPG
32-525TMCH	**D9003** *Meld* + **D9007** *Pinza* BRc green wpc en Sp Edn 100 sets (TMC) - *04*		NA	130
32-529B	**D9011** BRc 2-tone green W - *13*		80	97
TMC189D	**D9013** *The Black Watch* BRc green [1A35+1A06] Sp Edn 100 (TMC) - *05*		70	90
TMC189DW	as above but weathered Sp Edn 100 (TMC) - *05*		70	90
32-529A	**D9014** *The Duke of Wellington's Regiment* BRc 2-tone green en - *11*		70	89
32-529	**D9017** *The Durham Light Infantry* BRc two-tone green - *09*		60	77
32-529	**D9019** *Royal Highland Fusiliers* BRc green - not made		NA	NA
32-525X	**D9021** *Argyll & Sutherland Highlander* BRc green [1A16+1E15] Sp Edn 504 (TMC) - *04*		60	80
32-525Y	as above but weathered Sp Edn 504 (TMC) - *04*		60	70
32-530DS	**55001** *St. Paddy* BRe blue with sound chip fitted - not made		NA	NA
32-530DS	**55001** *St. Paddy* BRe blue DCC sound chip fitted - *08*		60	70
32-525A	**55002** *The Kings Own Yorkshire Light Infantry* BRc green* - *04*		40	50
32-525Z	**55009** *Alycidon* BRe blue en Sp Edn 500 (DPS) - *04*		60	100
31-530ZDS	**55011** *The Royal Northumberland Fusiliers* BRe DCC sound chip fitted Sp Edn (Rails) - *08*		150	170
32-527	**55012** *Crepello* BRe blue - *04*		40	50
32-528	**55013** *The Black Watch* BRe blue en ** - *05*		50	60
32-525V	**55015** *Tulyar* BRe blue Sp Edn 750 (DPS) - *05*		60	80
32-526DS	**55018** *Ballymos* s BRe blue DCC sound fitted en - *11*		NPG	190
32-525W	**55019** *Royal Highland Fusilier* BRe blue W Sp Edn 750 (DPS) - *04*		40	80
32-526	**55020** *Nimbus'* BRe blue - *03*		45	55

8th Edition

Bachmann Branchline

32-525T	55022/D9000 *Royal Scots Grey* BRe en blue Sp Edn 504 (Beaver Sports) - *06*	65	80

* Also issued as Heritage Range model. ** Upgraded diecast metal alloy buffers developed for the Class 66.

BR Class 55 'Deltic' [L73b] (Tony Wright)

L74. Class 57 Co-Co (2005)

The Class 57 fleet made its debut in 1998. Freightliner had asked Brush Traction to completely rebuild six former Class 47 locomotives and to fit reconditioned General Motors 645-12E3 engines. More were ordered, including 16 by Virgin Trains for hauling its new fleet of 'Pendolinos' when diverted over non-electrified routes. These were also available for rescuing trains in trouble and have become known as 'Thunderbirds', after the cult television series. First Great Western ordered four 57/6 locomotives and these have been named after West Country castles. These are used on the overnight sleepers and on some other services when required.

The models have differing fuel tank styles, working lights, etched roof profile grilles. They have been 'DCC ready' since 2005 and with an 8-pin or 21-pin DCC decoder socket fitted. Early models did not have the Dellner couplings fitted.

32-750DS	57003 *Freightliner Evolution* Freightliner green, 57/0 with DCC sound chip fitted - *11*	170	197
32-750	57008 *Freightliner Explorer* Freightliner green, DCC8 - *05*	55	68
32-750DC	57010 *Freightliner Crusader* 57/0 Freightliner green, DCC chip fitted - *06*	60	82
32-753	57011 *Freightliner Challenger* 57/0 Freightliner green, DCC8 - *06*	58	71
32-754	57011 DRS (compass) dark blue, 57/0 DCC21 - *09*	60	82
32-751	57301 *Scot Tracy* Virgin red and grey - *05*	55	68
32-760Z	57306 *Jeff Tracy* Virgin red and grey, Delner coupling Sp Edn 504 (Hereford Model Centre) - *06*	60	78
32-760	57307 *Lady Penelope* Virgin silver+red Delner coupling DCC8 - *06*	58	71
32-763	57309 *Pride of Crewe* DRS (compass) blue, Delner coupling DCC21 - *13*	58	71
32-762DS	57312 *The Hood* Virgin silver+red W, Delner coupling, DCC sound chip fitted - *06*	NPG	NPG
32-761	57312 Network rail yellow, DCC21 57/0 - *12*	80	101
32-755	57315 Arriva Trains Wales 2-tone blue, 57/3 Delner coupling, DCC8 - *10*	65	82
32-750K	57601 Porterbrook silver+mauve, 57/6, Sp Edn 504 (BCC) - *05*	55	68
32-750?	57601 West Coast maroon, 57/6, DCC21, Sp Edn 504 (Model Rail magazine) - *09*	65	85
32-752	57602 *Restormel Castle* FGW green, 57/6, DCC8 - *05*	58	71
32-752Y	57603 *Tintagel Castle* FGW purple, 57/6, DCC21 Sp Edn 512 (Kernow Model Rail Centre) - *not made*	NA	NA
32-752Y	57605 *Totnes Castle,* FGW purple, 57/6, DCC21, Sp Edn 512 (Kernow Model Rail Centre) - *10*	75	95

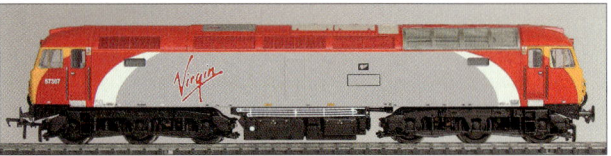

Virgin Trains Class 57 [L74]

L75a. Class 66 Co-Co (2005)

When the American backed EWS sought to replace the ageing locomotive fleet with highly reliable and efficient machines, it turned to General Motors to supply them. 250 of an updated Class 59 were ordered and built in Canada and these became the Class 66. Freightliner, Direct Rail Services (DRS) and GB Railfreight all followed suite and they have spread to mainland Europe. Few modifications have been made and each locomotive has a combination of couplings. One major change has been the introduction, since 2004, of low-emission technology. Locomotives so fitted have an extra external door on the 'A' side of the machine. There are six subclasses resulting from the specific needs of individual customers:

66/0s were supplied to EWS and are numbered 66001-66250.
66/4s are 30 locomotives supplied to DRS.
66/5s are the 99 standard Freightliner locomotives.
66/6s are 25 Freightliner locomotives that have modified gearing.
66/7s are 32 standard GB Railfreight locomotives.
66/9s are the 2 locomotives used for the development of the low-emission technology.

The models have been 'DCC ready' since 2005 and had 21-pin DCC decoder sockets fitted since 2007. They have directional lighting (options), 6-axle drive, different light cluster styles and etched roof grills.

en = etched nameplates.

32-725DS	66022 *Lafarge Charnwood* EWS maroon+yellow DCC sound chip fitted - *06*	NPG	NPG
32-733	66068 EWS maroon+yellow - *07*	65	80
32-725Z	66077 *Benjamin Gimbert* GC EWS maroon+ yellow Sp Edn 504 (Rails) - *05*	50	73
32-734A	66101 DB Schenker red - *13*	NPG	NPG
32-725	66135 EWS maroon+yellow - *05*	50	73
32-734	66152 DB Schenker red W - *09*	65	84
32-730	66200 *Railway Heritage Committee* EWS maroon+yellow - *05*	50	73
32-735	66209 EWS maroon+yellow W - *11*	80	109
32-725W	66249 EWS maroon+yellow W Sp Edn (Hereford Model Centre) - *06*	50	73
32-729	66405 DRS/Malcolm Logistics Services dark blue - *05*	50	73

Colas Rail Class 66 [L75a]

32-731	66407 DRS (compass) blue - *06*	50	76
32-726Z	66522 *East London Express* Freightliner/Shanks 2-tone green Sp Edn 504 (Kernow Model Railway Centre) - *05*	65	85
32-726DS	66522 Freightliner/Shanks 2-tone green 40th Anniversary, DCC sound chip fitted - *07*	120	157
32-732	66532 *P&O Nedlloyd Atlas* Freightliner green en - *06*	55	76
32-726K	66540 *Ruby* Freightliner green Ltd Edn 540 (BCC) - *06*	70	90
32-728DS	66546 Freightliner green DCC sound chip fitted - *11*	170	202
32-725Y	66552 *Maltby Raider* Freightliner green Sp Edn 504 (Rails) - *05*	50	73
32-726	66610 Freightliner green - *05*	50	73
32-728	66612 *ForthRaider* Freightliner green - *05*	50	73
32-726Y	66618 *Railways Illustrated* Freightliner green Sp Edn 504 (Ian Allan) - *05*	65	85
32-727	66701 GBRf blue - *05*	50	73
32-727DS	66702 *Blue Lightning* GBRf blue+yellow en, DCC sound chip fitted - *08*	150	176
32-727Y	66705 *Golden Jubilee* GBRf blue with Union Jack Sp Edn 512 (Kernow) - *08*	70	90
32-727Z	66709 GBRf 'Medite' blue Sp Edn (*Model Rail* magazine) - *06*	50	73
32-736	66744 Colas yellow+orange+black - *not made*	NA	NA
32-736	66846 Colas yellow+orange+black - *13*	85	101

L75b. Class 66/9 Co-Co (2007)

Freightliner Group Ltd placed an order for 30 Class 66 freight locomotives of a new design giving even greater hauling capacity and a significant improvement in fuel economy. 'Project Genesis', which was being developed in partnership with General Electric (GE), brought new technology to the UK rail freight market, enabling Freightliner to move longer and heavier trains, whilst reducing CO2 emissions per tonne moved.

The model is 'DCC ready', with a 21-pin DCC decoder socket fitted, and has directional lighting (options), etched nameplates, 6-axle drive, different light cluster styles and etched roof grill.

32-979Y	66301 Fastline Freight grey W Sp Edn (*Rail Express* magazine) - *09*	75	90
32-979Y(DS)	66301 Fastline Freight grey W Sp Edn (*Rail Express* magazine) DCC sound chip fitted - *09*	150	170

Bachmann Branchline

Malcolm Rail Class 66/9 [L75b]

32-977	**66411** *Eddie the Engine* DRS/Stobart blue - *08*		65	84
32-976DC	**66412** DRS (compass) violet-blue DCC chip fitted - *07*		75	92
32-979	**66412** DRS/Malcolm Rail violet-blue - *09*		70	85
32-979Z	**66623** *Bill Bolsover* Bardon Aggregates violet-blue Sp Edn 512 (Kernow Model Rail Centre) - *10*		80	100
32-979X	**66722** *Sir Edward Watkin* GBRf Metronet violet-blue Sp Edn 500 (*Model Rail* magazine) - *10*		80	98
32-978	**66725** *Sunderland AFC* FGBRf violet-blue en - *08*		65	80
32-975	**66952** Freightliner green 40th Anniversary - *07*		65	80
32-980	**66731** *InterhubGB* GBRf Europorte blue+yellow - *13*		85	101
32-?	**66062** Euro Cargo Rail red+yellow * Sp Edn 500 (*Model Rail* magazine) - *13*		NPG	122
32-?DC	**66062** Euro Cargo Rail red+yellow * with DCC sound, Sp Edn (*Model Rail* magazine) - *13*		NPG	262

* These have modified front skirts to take fitted snowploughs, as on the real locomotives operating in France.

L76.   Class 70 'Powerhaul' Co-Co (2011)

The new 75 mph 129 tonne Co-Co 'PowerHaul' locomotives, built by GE Transportation of America for heavy freight work, feature innovative designs such as 'Dynamic Braking' and AC traction technology. They are intended to be utilised across all parts of the extensive Freightliner route network. The first two locomotives arrived at Newport Docks on the 8th November 2009. The locomotives are leased to Freightliner Heavy Haul by the Lloyds Banking Group and their depot is Leeds Midland Road.

The model was developed in co-operation with General Electric and Freightliner and the models have elaborate fan detail, multifunctional lighting control, DCC 21-pin decoder sockets enabling sound to be added.

Freightliner Class 70 [L76]

31-585Z	**70001** *Powerhaul* Freightliner green+yellow Sp Edn 504 (Freightliner) - *11*	85	100
31-586	**70003** Freightliner green+yellow - *11*	80	95
31-587DC	**70004** Freightliner green+yellow, DCC chip fitted - *13*	115	140
31-588	**70005** Freightliner green+yellow W - *13*	110	135
31-585	**70006** Freightliner green+yellow - *11*	80	95

Electric Locomotives

L77.   Class 85 Bo-Bo (2012)

The Class 85 locomotives were built in the early 1960s for the electrification of West Coast Main Line services. They were originally classified as 'Class AL5'. With a capability of 100 mph, the locomotives were used on a variety of mixed traffic work. Later, to work freight trains for Railfreight Distribution, 14 of the class were downgraded to 80 mph capability and renumbered in the 85/1 series.

The models are fitted with DCC21 decoder sockets, enabling sound cips to be fitted. They have etched metal BR emblems and detailed roof equipment.

31-677	**E3056** BRd blue, single pantograph - *12*	90	112
31-676	**E3058** BRd bright blue, twin pantographs - *12*	90	112
31-679	**E3095** BRd bright blue, twin pantographs - *13*	NPG	NPG
31-678	**85026** BRe blue, single pantograph - *12*	90	112
31-676K	**85101** *Doncaster Plant 150* BRe Rft Distribution grey, single pantograph Sp Edn 504 (BCC) - *12*	95	118

Diesel Multiple Units

L78.   Class 101 2-Car DMU (2014)

The Class 101s were built in 1956-59 by Metro-Cammell Ltd for branch line and local services. They had a maximum speed of 75mph and were the most numerous of the first generation diesels. All regions received an allocation and the combination of the size of the class and the large geographical area of operation made them an obvious subject to model.

The models have directional and interior lighting and with alternative cab fronts and roof styles. Each is 'DCC ready' with an 8-pin DCC decoder socket fitted. At the time of writing, the first of the models has not yet been released.

32-285	**?** [?] + **?** [?] BRc green with speed whiskers - *14*	110	130
32-286	**?** [?] + **?** [?] BRc green half yellow ends - *14*	110	130
32-288	**?** [?] + **?** [?] BRe blue - *14*	110	130
32-287	**?** [?] + **?** [?] BRe blue+grey - *14*	110	130

L79a.   Class 105 2-Car DMU (2010)

The Class 105s were built in 1956 by Cravens Ltd of Sheffield, for branch line and local services. They built 402 vehicles from 1956 to 1960 and 275 of these were power cars. They were of all steel construction and the bodies were similar to Mk1 coaches. The 2-car units listed in this table were made up of a DMBS and a DTCL. Withdrawals started in the early 1980s and were completed by 1990. A few made it into blue and grey livery. Only three cars survive into preservation.

The models have directional and interior lighting and consist of a DMBS and a DTCL. Both early and late body styles have been modelled. Early versions feature large cab-front train number indicator boxes; models of later versions show them plated over. They also show the early type of exhaust system that passed through the coach from the motor compartment to the exhaust port on the roof. Models of the later versions show the exhaust relocated on the end of the power car, rising to roof level. The model is 8-pin 'DCC ready' and has lit destination boxes and interiors.

BR Class 105 DMU [L79a]

31-326	**E51254** [Welwyn Garden City] + **E56412** [Kings Cross York Road] BRc green + whiskers - *10*	75	89
31-326A	**E51276** [Cambridge] + **E56434** [Harwich] BRc green, speed wiskers, codeboxes - *11*	85	104
31-325	**E51289** [Lowestoft] + **E56463** [Norwich] BRe blue, yellow ends no codeboxes - *10*	75	89
31-327	**E51296** [Harwich] + **E56451** [Manningtree] BRc green half yellow ends - *10*	75	89
31-325DC	**E51277** [Peterborough] + **E56439** [Norwich] BRe blue, yellow ends, codeboxes, DCC chip fitted - *11*	NPG	118

L79b.   Class 105 'Power-Twin' 2-Car DMU (2011)

The Class 105 'Power Twins' had earlier been 3-car units with a driver motor brake second (DMBS) at one end and a driver motor composite with a lavatory (DMCL) at the other end and with a trailer composite with a lavatory (TCL) as a centre car. When the TCLs were done away with in 1970, what was left was two driving cars with motors. These differed from the 2-car Class 105s in the above table which had only one motorised driving car and a driving trailer.

The description of the models in the above table, also apply here.

31-536	**M50773** [Milnrow] + **M50806** [Oldham] BRc green with speed whiskers, codeboxes - *11*	90	109
31-537	**M50779** [Manchester] + **M50812** [Rochdale] BRc green half yellow ends, codeboxes - *11*	90	109
31-535	**M50762** [Colne] + **M50795** [Preston] BRe blue, codeboxes - *11*	90	109

BR 'Derby Lightweight' [L80]

L80.   Derby 'Lightweight' 2-Car DMU (2011)

This is the original Derby 'Lightweight' of which 97 were built by BR workshops at Derby between 1954 and 1956. They were pioneering units which sped up the retirement of steam locomotives by taking over branch line, cross-country and suburban routes. They had the comfort of a city bus and were not to be ridden in for long journeys. As newer units came on stream, they were withdrawn, the last unit disappeared in 1969, and too early to be designated a class under TOPS. They saw extensive use across the country, including the West Riding of Yorkshire, Cumbria, East London, West Midlands, South

Bachmann Branchline

Midlands, East Anglia and Lincolnshire. Some units passed into departmental service and a 2-car unit has been preserved at the Midland Railway Centre at Butterley.

DMBS and DTC cars have been modelled and all are 'DCC ready' with 6-pin and 8-pin decoder sockets fitted, one in each car. They have directional lighting.

32-516	**M79010** [Carlisle] + **M79602** [Maryport] BRb green with whiskers - 11	85	101
32-516A	**M79010**+? BRc green, speed whiskers - 12	NPG	NPG
32-515	**M79044** [Dereham] + **M79602** [Kings Lynn] BRc green with half yellow ends - 11	85	101
32-515A	**M79145** [Hayfield] + **M79226** [Manchester] BRc green small yellow panel - 12	90	110
32-517	**M79124** [Keswick] + **M79645** [Pemrith] BRe blue - 11	85	101

L81a. Class 107 3-Car DMU (2010)

BR Derby built these units in 1960-61 for Scottish local services. They were made up of DMBS+TSL+DMCL cars. 26 3-car sets were built and they are sometimes known as 'Derby Heavyweights', being of a more robust steel structure. The fleet was withdrawn in 1991-92 and 11 cars have been preserved.

This was basically the 3-car version of the Class 108 model below. Models are 'DCC ready' and have bi-directional lighting, detailed interior with lights and a concealed mechanism.

32-910Z	**107447** (**SC52029** [Edinburgh Waverley] + **SC59792** + **SC52008** [Glasgow]) Strathclyde PTE orange+black, large roof box Sp Edn 510 (Model Rail magazine & Harburn Hobbies) - 10	85	114

L81b. Class 108 2-Car DMU (2006)

These were also built at BR Derby and consisted of 147 2-car, five 3-car and six 4-car units, built between 1958 and 1961. This totalled 210 powered vehicles and 123 trailer cars and they were generically known as 'Derby Lightweights', not to be confused with the earlier batch (above) of similar name, built from 1954. A two-car set could accommodate 117 passengers and they were suitable for use on branch lines and local services. Most survived until the early 1990s, when major withdrawal took place with the arrival of the second generation units ordered by Regional Railways. A number carried Network SouthEast livery and the last unit was withdrawn in October 1993. Over 50 vehicles have passed to heritage railways.

The model is 'DCC ready', with 8-pin DCC decoder sockets fitted, has directional lighting, illuminated roof boxes, a fully detailed interior, with lights, and has full under-floor detailing. Both types of cab roof have been produced to allow the option of either type of headcode / destination boxes (large or small) to be produced. The model incorporates a heavy internal weight which negates the need for traction tyres and it has a concealed mechanism.

srb = small roof box. lrb = large roof box.

32-906	**M50626** [Nottingham] + **M56212** [Rugby] BRc green yell warning panel - 12	90	110
32-900	**M50628** [Liverpool] + **M56214** [Warrington] BRc green, whiskers srb - 06	60	78
32-900A	**M51928** [Liverpool] + **M52043** [St Helens] BRc green, lrb - 09	60	83
32-901	**51909** + **54271** NSE bright blue, lrb - 06	60	78
32-902	**54243** [Skipton] + **53959** [Carlisle] BRe blue+grey srb - 06	60	78
32-902A	**51939** [Exeter] + **52063** [Paighnton] BRe blue+grey lrb - 08	60	82
32-903	**M56231** [Manchester] + **M50948** [Chester] BR/GMPTE white+blue srb - 09	70	89
32-900Z	**M51908** [Hunts Cross] + **M56491** [Liverpool] AN276 BRe blue Sp Edn 504 (ModelZone) - 06	70	88
32-900Y	**C970** (56322 [Cheltenham] + **54205** [Cardiff]) BRe blue+grey, red bufferbeams, dragon motif Sp Edn 504 (Hereford Model Centre) - 06	70	86
32-900B	**M50979** [Bedford] + **M56262** [Hitchin] BRc green with whiskers, lrb, - 10	60	87
32-904DC	**56199** + ? BRe blue srb DCC chip fitted - 11	NPG	125
32-905	**53610** [Sheffield]+ **54198** [Doncaster] BRe West Yorkshire PTE Metrotrain blue+grey, lrb - 12	90	110

BR Class 108 DMU [C81c]

C81c. Class 108 3-Car DMU (2008)

These are the same as above but with a TSL car in the middle to make it a 3-car unit.
srd = small roof box. lrb = large roof box.

32-911	**E50620** [Scarborough] + **E50642** + **E59386** [York] BRc green, small yellow panel srb - 08	80	102
32-911A	**E50644** [Scarborough] + **E59388** + **E50622** [Middlesbrough] BRc green, small yellow panel srb - 09	85	104
32-913	**E50621** [Middlesbrough] + **E59387** + **E50643** [Scarborough] BRc green, speed whiskers - 12	110	135
32-912	**E59390** [Middlesbrough] + **E59390** + **E50646** [Newcastle] BRe blue - 12	110	135
32-910	**M52051** [Manchester Piccadilly] + **M51936** + **M59386** [Buxton] BR/GMPTE blue+grey lrb - 08	80	102

L82a. Class 150/1 2-Car DMU (2009)

These were the first of the 2nd generation DMUs and the contract for them was placed with BREL by BR Provincial Sector in 1983. They were based on the Mk3 coach design and were built, to new safety standards, at BR York. Much attention was paid to passenger comfort - in particular sound insulation and the use of anti-drumming compound. The most obvious difference between the two subclasses is the provision of gangway connections on the front ends of the 150/2s, so that units coupled together in longer trains have 'through' access, for staff and passengers, between units. Fifty of the 150/1 sets were built and 85 of the 150/2s. The latter are now owned by Angel Trains and Porterbrook.

Both subclasses 150/1 and 150/2 have been modelled by Bachmann and they have tinted glazing, metal-effect window frames, LED directional lighting and 5-pole motor with flywheel drive. All are 'DCC ready' with DC21 decoder sockets.

32-925K	**150123 *Richard Crane*** (**52123** [Bedford] + **57123** [Bletchley]) Silver Link violet+green Ltd Edn 504 (BCC) - 09	65	88
32-926	**150125** (**52125** [Dorridge via Solihull] + **57125** [Snow Hill via Solihull]) Central Trains light green +blue - 09	65	88
32-927	**150128** (**52128** [?] + **57128** [?]) FGW violet blue with red doors - 13	NPG	NPG
32-925Z	**150135** (**52135** [Peterborough] + **57135** [Birmingham New St]) BR Provincial Railways light blue Sp Edn 512 (Trains4U) - 10	75	95
32-925	**150144** (**52144** [Blackpool N] + **57144** [Preston]) FNW violet blue - 09	65	88
32-925A	**150144** (**52144** [Blackpool N] + **57144** [Preston]) FNW violet blue W - 13	NPG	NPG
32-928	**150150** (**52150** [?] + **57150** [?]) BRe Sprinter blue+grey W - 13	NPG	NPG

* This livery was carried from 1999 to 2004.

First North Western Class 150 [L82a]

L82b. Class 150/2 2-Car DMU (2008)

This is similar to the Class 150/1 (above) but has corridor connectors in the cab ends allowing units to be joined together. Descriptions in the above table apply here.

(30-046)	**150148** (**52148** [Preston] + **57148** [Liverpool]) BR Provincial Railways blue+grey ex-Dynamis Digital set - 09	65	NA
32-937	**150202** (**52202** [?] + **57202** [?]) Centro green+grey - 13	NPG	NPG
32-938	**150204** (**52204** [?] + **57204** [?]) Northern Rail blue+purple - 13	NPG	NPG
32-935Z	**150207** (**52207** [Liverpool] + **57207** (Manchester Victoria]) Regional Railways Merseyrail yellow+white Sp Edn 512 (Hattons) - 09	75	95
32-935Y	**150252** (**52252** [Perth] + **57252** [Edinburgh]) ScotRail (Whoosh) * violet+pale grey, Sp Edn 500 (Model Rail & Harburn Hobbies) - 12	85	104
32-935	**150256** (**52256** [Cardiff Central] + **57256** [Shrewsbury]) Arriva Trains Wales lt. blue - 08, 10	65	88
32-936	**150270** (**52270** [York] + **57270** [Leeds]) BR Regional Railways blue+grey - 08	65	81

* This livery was carried from 1999 to 2004.

L83a. Class 158 Express 2-Car DMU (1996)

In the late 1980s, British Railway's Provincial Sector needed a large fleet of DMUs for the outer suburban and cross-country trains. The competitive tender was won by BREL who

Bachmann Branchline

built both 2-car and 3-car formations at BR Derby. In all, 182 sets were built, comprising 381 vehicles and the first were ready for service in 1992. Many variations exist and, since privatisation, the fleet has been owned by Porterbrook and Angel Trains and leased to several TOCs. Rebuilds and refurbishments have also taken place. In 1991, BREL won the contract to supply Thailand with 20 Class 158 style vehicles, with metre gauge bogies, for Bangkok.

The model did not receive a DCC decoder socket until 2012 and now 21-pin sockets are fitted.

TPE = Trans- Pennine Express

Cat No	Description		
31-501	158702 Scotrail Express blue+white - 97	NPG	NPG
31-500Z	158725 (52725+57725) First ScotRail purple Sp Edn 504 (AMRSS) - 07	NPG	NPG
31-507	158726 (52726+57726) ScotRail (Whoosh!) livery - 02	50	70
31-517DC	158732 (?+?) Regional Railways white, DCC chip fitted - 12	NPG	NPG
31-508	158739 (52739+57739) First ScotRail (Whoosh!) - 05	60	75
31-506	158745 (52745+57745) Wales & West Alphaline silver - 00	50	70
31-506A	158746 (52746+57746) Wessex Trains Alphaline silver - 02	50	70
31-503	158757 (57757+52757) Regional Railways/ Express blue+white - 97	40	60
31-505	158758 (52758+57758) First North Western blue - 00	50	70
31-510	158768 (52768+57768) First TransPennine purple+blue - 05	60	75
31-518	158773 (52773+57773) East Midlands white+blue +red - 13	NPG	NPG
31-518DC	158780 (?+?) East Midlands white+red, DCC chip fitted - 12	NPG	NPG
31-504	158783 (52783+57783) Central Trains green - 00	50	70
31-500	158791 Regional Railways blue+white - 96	45	65
31-504A	158797 (52797+57797) Central Trains green - 02	50	70
31-510	158806 First TPE purple+blue - not made	NA	NA
31-511	158823 (52823+57823) Arriva Trains Wales light blue - 09	75	91
31-517DS	158849 (528492 + 57849) Regional Railways white, DCC sound chip fitted - 13	NPG	NPG
31-500A	158860 Regional Railways blue+white - 97	50	70
31-500B	158868 Regional Railways blue+white - 98	40	60
31-509	158905 Northern Rail W.Yorks PTE Metro red+ silver - 06	60	75
31-502	158906 BRe W.Yorks PTE Metro red - 97	40	60
31-515	158741 (52741+57741) First ScotRail violet - 08	65	82
31-514	158791 (52791+57791) Northern Rail purple+ violet - 08	65	82
31-516	158782 (52782+57782) Central Trains green - 08	65	82
(30-051)	2700 Iarnrod Eiraenn Class 2700 light green ex-set - 10	65	NA

Central Trains Class 158 [L83a] (Tony Wright)

L83b. Class 158 Express 3-Car DMU (1998)

Although the main production of Class 158 sets were 2-car, there was an order for 17 3-car units for TransPennine Express. These had a motor standard sandwiched between two driving cars.

This is the 3-rail version of the above model.

31-5??	158798 Reg Rlys Express blue+grey – not made	NA	NA
31-511	158809 Reg Rlys Express blue+white - 98	65	85
31-513	158811 TransPennine purple+gold - 99	65	80
31-513A	158799 Arriva TransPenine purple+gold? - 02	65	85

L83c. Class 159 3-Car DMU (1998)

With a need to upgrade services on the Waterloo-Salisbury-Exeter line, Network SouthEast ordered 22 3-car sets in the style of the Class 158, which were then coming into use. Once the Class 158 building programme was complete, Derby started building the Class 159s. After leaving Derby, the units were sent up to Babcock Rail at Rosyth Dockyard where they were rebuilt internally to NSE requirements. The result was some excellent DMUs. They were built in 1992 and 1993 and were finished in NSE livery. They started service in 1993 operating from a built-for-the-purpose depot at Salisbury.

The models are not fitted with DCC decoder sockets.

31-510	159001 **City of Exeter** NSE bright blue 3-car - 98	65	85
31-512	159009 SWT/Stagecoach white 3-car - 98	65	85
31-514	159019 SouthWest Trains white 3-car - 01	65	85

L84a. Class 165/1 'Network Turbo' DMU

Working LED lights and flywheel driven 5-pole motor. This was possibly dropped once Bachmann realised the amount of additional work that would be required to alter the Class 166 tooling.

31-035	165001 Chiltern Line white 2-car - not made	NA	NA

FGW - Link Class 166 [L84b]

L84b. Class 166 'Network Express Turbo' DMU (1999)

These were 3-car DMUs built by ABB York as semi-fast commuter trains and introduced from May 1993. An order was placed for 21 3-car sets for the Paddington-Worcester and Reading-Gatwick lines. These were virtually the same as the Class 165 units but had, amongst other things, full air-conditioning. When privatisation of the railways took place, the units passed to Angel Trains and the NSE livery was replaced by Thames (GoAhead) white and mid-blue livery.

The models have working LED lights and twin flywheel driven by 5-pole motors. They are not fitted with DCC decoder sockets.

31-025	166202 NSE white+blue+red - 99	65	85
31-029	166204 Thames Trains white+blue+green - 13	NPG	NPG
31-028	166205 FGW 2006 livery violet+red - not made	NA	NA
31-026	166209 Thames Trains Express white+blue - 06	80	96
31-026	as above but 166212	NA	NA
31-028	166213 FGW Neon livery violet+red - 08	80	102
31-027	166214 (58135+58614+58114) FGW/Link white+ blue+green - 06	80	96
31-025A	166216 (?+?) NSE bright blue - 13	NPG	NPG

L85. Class 168/1 'Clubman' 3-Car DMU (2003)

These are the post-Privatisation Adtranz built fast commuter DMUs for the Chiltern Line and were introduced in 2000. Five 3-car sets were ordered by Porterbrook for leasing to Chiltern Railways for the Marylebone-Birmingham service and they were built at Derby. They are effectively Adtranz 'Turbostars' but were named 'Clubmans' by the operator. The fleet had grown to 19 sets by 2008, as business on the line grew, and they are based at Aylesbury. The original five sets were built with cab fronts that resembled those of the classes 165 and 166. Thereafter, they were built with the style used on the Class 170.

The models have flywheel drive to both bogies and LED directional lighting. They are not fitted with DCC decoder sockets.

32-470	168110 (58160+58460+58260) Chiltern Railways white+violet - 03	75	90
32-471	168111 (58261+58461+58161) Chiltern Railways white+violet - 05	75	93

Cross Country Class 170 [L86a]

8th Edition

Bachmann Branchline

L86a. Class 170/171 'Turbostar' 2-Car DMU (2001)

Post-Privatisation, various TOCs were wanting new trains for medium and long distance travel and Adranz had their 'Turbostars' as supplied to Chiltern Railways (Class 168). The design was modified, to produce fast commuter and inter-regional trains, and given a new cab front. Having already been tested, they could be supplied quickly and so started to appear on the network in 1998. They were again built at Derby and aluminium was used in their construction. A large number of sets operate around the country and the interiors vary according to the requirements of the operating companies. Liveries carried are numerous.

On the model there is flywheel drive to both bogies and LED directional lighting. Prototypical ribbon glazing and different front apron styles have been produced. Despite suggestions to the contrary in the 2007 catalogue, the models are not fitted with DCC decoder sockets.

32-450	**170105** (50105+79105) Midland Mainline teal 170/1 - *01*	50	70
32-453	**170271** (50271+79271) Anglia Railways light blue+white 170/2 - *04*	65	80
32-452	**170301** (50301+79301) SouthWest Trains white+red 170/4 - *01*	50	70
32-452A	**170302** (50302+79302) SWT white+blue+red 170/3 - *04*	65	80
32-466	**170504** (50504+79504) LM City green+black+ pale grey - *09*	70	88
32-451A	**170514** (50514+79514) Central Trains green W 170/5 - *04*	65	80
32-451	**170515** (50515+79515) Central Trains green 170/5 - *01*	55	75
32-460Z	**171721** (50721+79721) Southern green+white 171/7 Sp Edn 504 (ModelZone) - *05*	60	87
32-40DC	Transpennine DC21 170/2 - *not made*	NA	NA

L86b. Class 170/171 'Turbostar' 3-Car DMU (2001)

ADtranx/Bombardier built fast commuter and inter-regional trains from 1998. Ten of the Midland Mainline 2-car sets were turned into 3-car ones. The largest user is First ScotRail who took delivery of 59 3-car sets between 1999 and 2005, but they were also the choice of other TOCs. Design details and model details are the same as for the 2-car units in the table above.

32-464	**170202** (50202+56202+79202) Anglia/One light violet 170/2 - *09*	80	104
32-463	**170413** (50413+56413+79413) First ScotRail purple 170/4 - *06*	65	80
32-461	**170424** (50424+56424+79424) ScotRail (Whoosh) livery 170/3 - *01*	65	85
32-467	**170434** (79434+56434+50434) Scotrail (Saltaire) 170/4 - *11*	90	112
32-462	**170470** (50470+56470+79470) Strathclyde PTE maroon+cream 170/3 - *03*	65	85
32-460	**170637** (50637+56637+79637) Central Trains green 170/6 - *03*	65	85
32-465	**170102** (50102+55102+79102) Cross Country grey+deep purple 170/2 - *09*	85	102

L87. Class 205 'Thumper' 2-Car DEMU (2013)

Known as either Class 205, 2-H, 'Hampshires', 'Berkshires' or 'Thumpers', these unique units operated for over 40 years on a great number of services across the BR Southern Region. They travelled to London on a daily basis from lines, such as the Uckfield branch, which were not part of the Southern Region's extensive electrified network, thus allowing a through service to be maintained.

A real 2-H, currently in preservation, was laser scanned and all tooling allows for backdating this model to 'as built' condition and a centre coach will be added during later production runs. Originally Kernow Model Railway Centre asked Dapol to produce this model for them but the commission was transferred to Bachmann who offered to accommodate a sound unit. Consequently, the models are fitted with 21-pin DCC sockets and were initially produced exclusively for Kernow MRC. The models have highly detailed interiors with lighting, directional headlight and directional indicator blinds.

31-236Z	**1108** (60107 + 60807) BRc green, whistles, original exhaust, alternative engine louvres, original bogies (K2003) - *13*	110	140
31-236ZDS	as above with sound - *13*	200	230
31-235Z	**1115** (60114 + 60814) BRc green 'V' (K2007) - *13*	110	140
31-235ZDS	as above with sound - *13*	110	140
K2006	**1119** (? + ?) BRc green with small yellow panel - *13*	NPG	150
K2004	**1121** (? + ?) BRc green with small yellow panel - *13*	NPG	150
K2005	**1120** (? + ?) BRe blue - *13*	NPG	110
K2005DC	**1120** (? + ?) BRe blue with sound chip fitted - *13*	NPG	200
31-237Z	**205012** (60111 + 60811) Connex white+yellow headlight, revised exhaust, warning horns and shock absorber bogies (K2002) - *13*	200	230
K2001	**205025** (? + ?) NSE bright blue - *13*	NPG	150

Virgin Trains Class 220 'Voyager' [L88a]

L88a. Class 220 'Voyager' DEMU (2002)

Built by Bombardier in 2000 for fast passenger service, they were part of Virgin Trains' commitment when they won the Cross-Country franchise in 1996. 34 non-tilting Class 220 'Voyagers' were built by Bombardier Transportation. The 5-car trains, replacing 8-10 car HSTs not surprisingly proved to be inadequate for the amount of passengers they needed to carry and problems followed their introduction. The stock transferred to Arriva when they took over the Cross Country franchise.

Listed here are 3- and 4-car packs which have a directional lighting and are not fitted with DCC decoder sockets.

32-600	**220001** *Maiden Voyager* (60301+ 60701+ 60201 + 60401) Virgin grey+red 4-car pack - *02*	80	100
(30-600)	**220017** *Bombardier Voyager* (60317+60717+ 60417) Virgin grey+red 3-car ex-set - *03*	80	NA
32-602	**220018** *Dorset Voyager* (60318+60718+60218+ 60418) Virgin grey+red 4-car pack - *07*	90	110
32-601	**220032** *Grampian Voyager* (60332+60732+ 60232+60432) Virgin grey+red 4-car pack - *04*	80	103
(30-601)	**220008** *Draig Gymreig Welsh Dragon* (60308+ 60208+60408) Virgin grey+red 3-car ex-set - *07*	70	NA
32-603	**220017** (60317+60717+60217+60417) Cross Country grey+deep purple - *09*	95	123

L88b. Class 221 'Super Voyager' DEMU (2004)

These are tilting 5-car sets which also formed part of Virgin Trains' commitment when they won the Cross-Country franchise in 1996. 44 tilting Class 221 'Super Voyagers' were built by Bombardier Transportation. It was thought that tilting trains would speed up the service, particularly between Oxford and Birmingham. With the change of franchise, Arriva took over the route and the 'Super Voyagers', bringing to them a new livery.

The models are not fitted with DCC decoder sockets.

32-626	**221101** *Louis Bleriot* (60451+60751+60851+ 60951+60351) Virgin grey+red 5-car pack - *04*	80	123
32-627	**221122** *Doctor Who* (60472+60772+60872+ 60972+60372) Virgin red+silver 4-car pack - *09*	110	130
32-625	**221130** *Michael Palin* (60480+60780+60880+ 60980+60380) Virgin grey+red 5-car pack - *04*	80	120
32-628	**221135** (60485+60785+60885+60985+60385) Cross Country grey+deep purple 5-car pack - *09*	80	138

BR 'Blue Pullman' Class 251 [L89]

L89. BR Class 251 'Blue Pullman' 6-car DMU (2012)

Constructed by Metro-Cammell in Birmingham, two all-first class Midland Pullman 6-car sets arrived in July 1960 and ran between London St Pancras and Manchester Central. On the old MR main line the journey took 3 hours. Three 8-car sets were also built for the Western Region but at present Bachmann have no plans to build these and would need to retool the cab front to accommodate multiple working cables. The trains were out-dated five years after their introduction by the electrification of the West Coast main line, which provided a better alternative journey to Manchester. In consequence, the two Midland sets were transferred to the Western Region. All five sets were withdrawn in 1973 and none of the cars was preserved.

Each six-car model comprises 2 power cars (both with motors), 2 kitchen first cars (type

4) and 2 parlour first cars (type 6) and is sold as a 6-car unit. In reality it is two 3-car trains joined in the middle by non-conductive couplers. The model has a new style close coupling, central coach ceiling lights and table lamp lighting, directional lighting, cab lights, etched fan grilles, flush glazing, a DCC socket and has provision for added sound.

31-255DC	BR Midland Pullman [A] **M60090**+ [B] **M60730**+ [C] **M60740**+ [D] **M60741**+ [E] **M60731**+ [F] **M60091** Nanking blue DCC Chip fitted - *12*	300	350
31-256DC	BR **Midland Pullman** [A] **M60092** + [B] **M60732** + [C] **M60742** + [D] **M60743** + [E] M60733 + [F] **M60093**, Nanking blue with yellow ends (as carried after transfer to the Western Region) DCC Chip fitted - *12*	300	350

Electric Multiple Units

L90. Class 350 'Desiro' 4-car EMU (2011)

Operating on the West Coast, the Siemens Class 350 EMUs are now in service with London Midland City and based at the depot at Northampton. There are 30 4-car units operating from the 25Kv catenary and the first batch originally also had third rail current collection capability. A further 37 units were ordered by London Midland and these do not have third rail provision and have different interiors. They are designated Class 350/2.

The Bachmann model represents both versions and models are 'DCC ready' for 21-pin decoders.

31-032	**350101** (**63761**+**66811**+**66861**+**63711**) London Midland grey+green [London Euston] 350/1 - *12*	110	132
31-030	**350111** *Apollo* (**?**+**?**+**?**+ **?**) blue unbranded Silverlink en, 350/1 - *11*	110	132
31-031	**350238** (**61438**+**65238**+**67538**+**61538**) London Midland grey+green, [Birmingham New Street] 4- 350/2 - *12*	110	132

London Midland Class 350 'Desiro' [L90]

L91. Class 411 4-CEP 4-Car EMU (2009)

The units were built in 1956-63 by BR at Eastleigh as express commuter trains. 111 of the 4-car units were built and were based on the Mk1 coach design. Also based on the 1937 SR built 4-COR units they were mainly built for the Kent Coast electrification scheme. The 4 cars in each unit were a motor brake second open (MBSO), trailer composite corridor (TCK), trailer second corridor (TSK) and another MBSO. All units were refurbished at Swindon Works in 1980-83 and renumbered. Post privatisation, the units saw service with Connex SouthEastern (later South Eastern Trains), Connex South Central and South West Trains. The last unit was withdrawn in 2005 and several vehicles have been preserved.

The Bachmann model initially depicts the vehicles in the original condition as running between delivery and refurbishment. It utilises many components from the Bachmann Mk1 CK and SCK vehicles, but has authentic bogies, lit indicator boxes and new roofs. In developing the model, Bachmann worked with the Southern Electric Group. It is 'DCC ready' with a 21-pin DCC decoder socket fitted and it is essential that the cars are assembled in the prescribed order for the unit to work, otherwise the continuous electrical circuit will be broken. In 2009, it was voted best 00 scale electric or diesel locomotive model of the year.

31-425	**7105** (**S61230**+**S70235**+**S70229**+**S61229**) BRc green, whistle - *09*	100	129
31-427	**7113** (**S61308**+**S70305**+**S70262**+**S61309**) BRe blue+grey, roof horns - *09*	100	129
31-426	**7126** (**S61335**+**S70318**+**S70275**+**S61334**) BRc green, yellow panel, roof horns - *09*	100	129
31-426A	**7128** (**S61338**+**S70277**+**S70320**+ **S61339**) BRc green, yellow panel, roof horns - *10*	100	133
31-426B	**71??** (**S613??**+**S702??**+**S703??**+ **S613??**) BRc green W, yellow panel, roof horns - *13*	NPG	NPG
31-427A	**7134** (**S61350**+**S70326**+**S70283**+ **S61371**) BRe blue+grey, roof horns - *10*	100	133
31-425A	**7141** (**S61365**+**S70290**+**S70333**+ **S61364**) BRc green, whistle - *10*	100	133
31-425B	**71??** (**S61367**+**S702??**+**S703??**+ **S616??**) BRc green W, whistle - *13*	NPG	NPG
31-427Z	**7119** (**S61321**+**S70268**+**S70311**+**S61320**) BRe blue full yellow ends Sp Edn 504 (ModelZone) - *09*	110	140

BR Class 411 (4-CEP) EMU [L91]

L92. Class 416 2-EPB 2-Car EMU (2011)

These were built between 1953 and 1956 at Eastleigh and Ashford. They were intended for suburban passenger services and were the first of a new generation of Southern Electrics. They were a descendant of the SR's SUB stock, incorporating new ideas. They were built on reclaimed underframes from SR 2NOL stock and were formed of a motor brake second open and a driving trailer second. Each 2-car set could hold 178 passengers. In the mid 1950s the need for more 2-car suburban units was realised and 79 2-car BR designed sets, based on Mk1 coach design, started to arrive in 1954. Major refurbishment of EPB stock took place in the 1970s and 1980s. Withdrawals started in the late 1980s and were completed in 1995. One 2-car unit has been preserved.

The model is sold in 2-car sets that are 'DCC ready' with 21-pin sockets. They have full under-floor detail, illuminated train headcode panels and internal lighting.

31-376	**5770** (**S65384**+**S77569**) BRc green - *11*	90	110
31-376?	**5759** (**S?**+**S?**) BRc green Sp Edn (Lord & Butler) - *11*	100	120
31-375Z	**5739** (**?**+**?**) BRe early blue Sp Edn 512 (ModelZone) - *11*	100	118
31-375	**5764** (**S65378**+**S77563**) BRe blue full yellow end - *11*	90	110
31-375*	**5764** (**S77563**+**S65378**) BRe blue full yellow end DCC21 - *11*	90	110
31-377	**6238** (**S65352**+**S77537**) BRe blue+grey Network SouthEast Kent - *11*	90	110

BR Class 416 (2-EPB) EMU [L92] (Lord & Butler)

* When released, it was found that the numbers on the two all blue cars had been transposed due to an error in the design office and Bachmann had a batch of correctly numbered bodies produced for those who wished to have them the correct way round. Thus, both arrangements will exist, this one being the original incorrect version.

L93. Class 419 MLV Motor Luggage Van (2012)

Found in the Eastern Section of the Southern Region, motor luggage vans formed part of the 13 coach electric boat trains, made up of 3 x 4-CEPs and an MLV. At the dock passenger terminal, at Folkstone for example, the MLV was detached from the back of the train and driven under its own battery power to the dockside for luggage to be transferred to the ship. The vehicles were built at Eastleigh in 1951-61.

The model, which has plenty of weight, has a detailed cab, considerable underfloor detail, illuminated headcode, internal lighting and is 'DCC ready' with 21-pin sockets.

31-265	**S68001** BRc green - *12*	65	81
31-269	**S68001** BRe 'Jaffa Cake' 2-tone grey - *13*	NPG	NPG
31-268	**S68004** NSE blue - *13*	NPG	NPG
31-266	**S68006** BRc green with yellow end panels - *12*	65	81
31-267	**S68009** BRe blue+grey - *12*	65	81

Bachmann Branchline

COACHES

The earliest Bachmann coaches were a number of GWR Colletts and LMS types from the former Mainline Railways range but with different stock numbers. Some of these had also been made for Replica Railways by the tool owners - Kader. They were followed by LNER coaches of Thompson design and Bulleid stock of the Southern Region, development of which had been started by Mainline owners - Palitoy. The finest development so far is an extensive range of Mk1 coaches, in the Blue Riband series, which first appeared late in 1999.

NPCCS - A fundamental change in this edition is that the non-passenger carrying coaching stock, that was previously listed under wagons, is now here with the coaches.

Running Numbers - Bachmann tend to give their coaches different stock numbers with each batch they produce and this is usually reflected in the addition of a letter suffix to the catalogue number to denote the change. There have, however, been a few cases where the suffix has been missed off the box and some newly numbered batches have been released in boxes which carry the number used on the earlier release. As always, it is as well to ensure that the contents of the box are what you expect them to be.

Cat No.	Company, Number, Colour, Date	£	£

GWR

Collett Stock

The Collett coaches were the final coach development by Palitoy before the drawing office was closed down in 1983 and only one batch of each livery was sold under the Mainline Railways name. It seems that there were none amongst the residue stock bought by Dapol when the Mainline warehouse was cleared out. This was because the original batches had completely sold out and Palitoy were about to reorder when the decision to closedown the operation came through.

Kader used the tooling to produce some Collett coaches for Replica Railways in 1987 and 1988. However, before doing so, Replica paid to have the tooling modified, as there was some distortion of the mouldings due to poor mould design, and the height of the windows had to be changed. The Replica and Bachmann Colletts are therefore slightly different from the original Mainline ones.

Collett all-3rd [Cla] GWR

C1a. GWR 60' Collett Coach (ex-Mainline) (1991)

This is the ex-Mainline model of a Collett C77 third corridor coach which changed its classification just by changing the printing. Thus it was an all-1st or an all-3rd or a composite coach. A lot of this style of coach were built by the GWR at the end of 1938. They had eight compartments with four doors on the corridor side and two on the other side. Some of the windows were fitted with sliding vents and the drop lights in the doors were shorter than the fixed windows.
H = Hawksworth livery

		3rd Class		
34-050B	**Great Western** 1118 brown+cream H - *97*		12	17
34-050C	**Great Western** 1155 brown+cream H - *01*		12	17
34-050D	**Great Western** ? brown+cream H - *not made*		NA	NA
34-052	**Great Western** 1115 brown+cream H - *05*		12	17
34-052A	**Great Western** 1124 brown+cream H - *10*		13	18
34-053	**Great Western** ? brown+cream H - *13*		NPG	NPG
34-051	**GWR** (button) 1145 brown+cream H - *95*		12	19
34-051A	**GWR** (button) 1127 brown+cream H - *95*		17	22
(30-021)	**GWR** (button) 1137 brown+cream H ex-set - *06*		14	NA
34-050	**GWR** 1107 brown+cream - *91*		12	22
34-050A	**GWR** 1104 brown+cream - *93*		12	20
34-055	**BR** W1123 red+cream - *95*		12	19
34-056	**BR** W1139W red+cream - *04*		12	17
34-056A	**BR** W?W red+cream - *13*		NPG	NPG
34-200	**BR** W562W maroon - *91*		12	22
34-201	**BR** W547W maroon - *11*		17	22
(30-052)	**BR** W510W maroon ex-'Western Rambler' set - *11*		17	NA
	1st Class			
34-100	**GWR** 8095 brown+cream H - *90*		12	22
34-100B	**Great Western** 8096 brown+cream H - *97*		12	18
34-100A	**GWR** 8099 brown+cream - *93*		12	17
34-101	**GWR** (button) 8101 brown+cream - *95*		12	19
34-101	**GWR** (button) 8109 brown+cream - *95*		12	19
	Composite			
34-127	**Great Western** 7026 brown+cream H - *05*		12	17
34-127A	**Great Western** 7045 brown+cream H - *10*		15	20
34-128	**Great Western** ? brown+cream H - *13*		NPG	NPG
34-125C	**Great Western** 7050 brown+cream H - *01*		12	17
34-125D	**Great Western** brown+cream H - *not made*		NA	NA
34-126	**GWR** (button) 7023 brown+cream - *95*		12	19
34-126A	**GWR** (button) 7055 brown+cream - *11*		17	22
34-125	**GWR** 7001 brown+cream - *90*		12	22
34-125A	**GWR** 7003 brown+cream - *93*		12	17
34-125B	**GWR** 7056 brown+cream H - *97*		12	18
34-076	**G()W** 7025 brown+cream - *04?*		12	17
34-130	**BR** W7021 red+cream - *95*		12	19
34-131	**BR** W7031W red+cream - *04*		12	17
34-131A	**BR** W?W red+cream - *13*		NPG	NPG
34-150	**BR** W7033W maroon - *90*		12	22
34-151	**BR** W7010W maroon - *11*		17	22

C1b. GWR 60' Collett Brake End (ex-Mainline) (1991)

This is the ex-Mainline model of a Collett E159 brake composite coach. These were built in the late 1930s with five 3rd class compartments off a corridor. Beyond these compartments there were two further independent compartments with their own access doors. Beyond these there was a half size compartment. According to Bachmann catalogue illustrations, on early models these three compartments were marked on their doors as 'Third', 'Guard' and 'Luggage'. At other times they were printed 'First', 'First' and 'Guard' or 'Third', First and 'Guard'. Somehow in the midst of this there was also a lavatory, as well as one at the other end of the coach. In any combination, there was little of no luggage space.
H = Hawksworth livery

Ex-GWR Collett brake 3rd [C1b]

		Brake 3rd(2nd) Class		
34-075	**GWR** 1655 brown+cream 3rd - *91*		12	22
34-075A	**GWR** 1657 brown+cream 3rd - *93*		NPG	NPG
34-075C	**Great Western** 6706 brown+cream 3rd H - *01*		12	17
34-075D	**Great Western** ? brown+cream 3rd H - *not made*		NA	NA
34-175	**BR** W1657W maroon 2nd - *91*		17	22
34-176	**BR** W1656W maroon 2nd - *11*		17	22
(30-052)	**BR** W1655W maroon 2nd ex-'Western Rambler' set - *11*		17	NA
	Brake Composite			
34-075B	**Great Western** 1656 brown+cream 1st/3rd H - *97*		12	18
34-076	**Great Western** 6543 brown+cream 1st/3rd H - *05*		12	17
34-076A	**Great Western** 6421 brown+cream 1st/3rd H - *10*		13	19
34-052A	**Great Western** ? brown+cream 1st/3rd H - *13*		NPG	NPG
34-076	**GWR** (button) 6600 brown+cream 1st/3rd H - *95*		12	19
34-077	**GWR** (button) 6609 brown+cream 1st/3rd H - *11*		17	22
(30-021)	**GWR** (button) 6356 brown+cream H ex-set - *06*		14	NA
34-078	**BR** W6550 red+cream 1st/2nd - *95*		12	19
34-081	**BR** W6608W red+cream 1st/2nd - *04*		12	17
34-081A	**BR** W?W red+cream 1st/2nd - *13*		NPG	NPG
	Miscellaneous			
(40-0190)	bright red, yellow lining, ex-US 'The Flying Scot' set - *86*		18	NA
(40-?)	bright blue, yellow lining, ex-US 'The Royal Scot' set - *85*		18	NA

8th Edition

Bachmann Branchline

C2. BR Auto Trailer (2013)

The BR Auto Trailer is listed here under GWR coaches because they were associated with the Western Region of British Railways and successors to the GWR auto trailer rather than being Mk1 stock.

The model was introduced to go with the Class 64xx pannier tank, which was being developed at the same time and neither had yet been released at the time of writing.

34-575	**BR** ? red+cream - *13*	NPG	NPG
34-577	**BR** ? red - *13*	NPG	NPG
34-576	**BR** ? maroon - *13*	NPG	NPG

LMS

Stanier Stock

This section includes models of LMS period 1 panelled stock, the period 3 Stanier parcel van and the district engineer's inspection saloon.

The panelled stock, a 57ft brake end and a 57ft composite coach, had already been made in large numbers for the Mainline Railways range, produced by Palitoy in 1977. In the closing days of Mainline development, the company was experimenting with livery variations and examples exist of the LMS livery with a post-war mid-grey roof and BR maroon coaches with variations to the lining.

C3a. LMS 57' Period 1 Composite (ex-Mainline) (1990)

The LMS paid much attention to the design of the 1st/3rd composite coach, experimenting with different layouts. These models are based on coaches built in the immediate post-Grouping era known as Period 1 in Stanier coach design. They were side corridor coaches and had an external door to each of their seven compartments, four of which were 3rd class and three were 1st class. On the corridor side of the coach there were four doors, two each marked 1st and 3rd.

34-251	**LMS** 3650 maroon + end boards - *96*	12	16
34-251A*	**LMS** 3572 maroon + end boards - *00*	12	15
34-251B	**LMS** 3650 maroon + end boards - *not made*	NA	NA
34-251B	**LMS** 3605 maroon + end boards - *06*	12	16
34-251C	**LMS** 3622 maroon + end boards - *08*	13	17
34-251D	**LMS** 3526 maroon + end boards - *11*	16	21
34-252	**LMS** 3705 maroon + end boards - *96*	12	16
34-252A	**LMS** 3591 maroon - *00*	12	15
34-252B	**LMS** 3650 maroon - *not made*	NA	NA

Ex-LMS Period 1 coach used as staff accommodation [C3a]

34-252B	**LMS** 3619 maroon - *03*	12	16
34-252C	**LMS** 3506 maroon - *08*	13	17
34-252D	**LMS** 3652 maroon - *11*	16	21
(?)	**LMS** ? maroon Sp Edn 100 ex-train set (NRM Shildon) - *12*	16	NA
(?)	**LMS** ? maroon Sp Edn 100 ex-train set (NRM Shildon) - *12*	16	NA
34-301	**LMS** 18997 maroon 1928 livery - *not made*	NA	NA
34-302	**LMS** maroon 1928 livery - *not made*	NA	NA
34-300	**BR** M3672 red+cream - *90*	12	18
34-250	**BR** M3565M maroon - *90*	12	18
34-253	**BR Departmental** KD M 395776 olive green 'Signal Box Construction Gang' - *13*	18	23
34-251X	**CIE** 2096 green Sp Edn 300 (Murphy's Models) - *01*	10	15
(00651)	**CIE** 2097 green (ex-US Irish set) - *04*	10	NA
(40-?)	bright blue & cream, gold lining, Royal Coach ex-US 'The Royal Scot' set - *85*	18	NA

* No 'A' suffix on box.

C3b. LMS 57' Period 1 3rd (ex-Mainline) (2001)

This is a variation of the Period 1, side corridor coach, that did not exist in the Mainline range and was produced by Bachmann specifically for the Irish and American markets.

34-251Y	**CIE** 1332 green Sp Edn 300 (Murphy's Models) - *01*	10	15
34-251Z	**CIE** 1336 green Sp Edn 300 (Murphy's Models) - *01*	10	15
(00651)	**CIE** 1333 green (ex-US Irish set) - *04*	10	NA
74700	**CIE** 1337 green (US solo release) - *?*	10	15

C3c. LMS 57' Period 1 Brake 3rd (ex-Mainline) (1990)

The model is based on a Stanier Period 1, side corridor, brake 3rd coach, built in the 1920s with panelled sides. It had five 3rd class compartments, each with its own external door. On the corridor side of the coach there were three passenger doors.

The brake van can be found with end boards which fit over the corridor connections when the vehicle is on the end of a train.

34-226	**LMS** 5312 maroon + end boards - *96*	12	16
34-226A*	**LMS** 5284 maroon + end boards - *00*	12	15
34-226B	**LMS** 5328 maroon + end boards - *03*	12	16
34-226C	**LMS** 5263 maroon + end boards - *08*	13	17
34-226D	**LMS** 5286 maroon + end boards - *11*	16	21
(?)	**LMS** ? maroon Sp Edn 100 ex-train set (NRM Shildon) - *12*	16	NA
34-276	**LMS** 10199? maroon 1928 livery - *not made*	NA	NA
34-275	**BR** M5267 red+cream - *90*	12	18
34-225	**BR** M5315M maroon - *90*	12	18
34-226Z	**CIE** 1095 green Sp Edn 300 (Murphy's Models) - *00*	10	15
34-226Y	**CIE** 1087 green Sp Edn 300 (Murphy's Models) - *01*	10	15
(00651)	**CIE** 1096 green (ex-US Irish set) - *04*	10	NA
74701	**CIE** 1088 green (US solo release) - *?*	10	15
(40-0190)	bright red, yellow lining, ex-US 'The Flying Scot' set - *86*	18	NA
(40-?)	bright blue, yellow lining, ex-US 'The Royal Scot' set - *85*	18	NA

* No 'A' suffix on box.

LMS Period 1 brake 3rd [C3c]

C4. LMS 50' Parcels Van (ex-Mainline) (1990)

Most of the Stanier Period 3 LMS 50' full brakes were built at Wolverton in the late 1930s and many had been scrapped by 1968. Some were successors to the 'Stove R' and became the most numerous LMS full brakes on the system. Most were rated as having a 12 ton carrying capacity.

The LMS 50ft parcels van was tooled by Kader and released in the last year of Mainline Railways and consequently had a shorter life in Mainline packaging. The parcels van can be found with end boards which fit over the corridor connections when the vehicle is on the end of a train.

34-327	**LMS** 31250 maroon + end board - *96*	12	16
34-327A	**LMS** 30989 maroon - *01*	12	15
34-327B	**LMS** 31250 maroon + end board - *06*	12	16
34-327B	**LMS** 30966 maroon - *?*	12	1634-
327C	**LMS** 30966 maroon - *not made*	NA	NA
34-327C	**LMS** 31027 maroon - *09*	13	18
34-327D	**LMS** 31200 maroon - *11*		21
34-325	**BR** M31340M red+cream - *90*	12	18
34-326	**BR** M31319M red+cream + LMS type end boards - *96*	12	16
34-326A	**BR** M?M red+cream + LMS type end boards - *13*	NPG	NPG

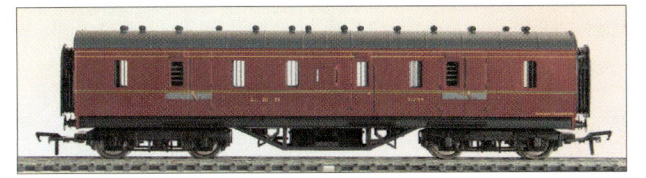

LMS parcels van [C4]

34-325	**BR** M31386M maroon + LMS type end boards - *96*	12	16
34-325A	**BR** M30980M maroon - *06*	12	16
34-325B	**BR** M31238M maroon - *08*	13	17
34-325C	**BR** M31386M maroon W - *not made*	NA	NA
34-325C	**BR** M31408M maroon W - *13*	20	24
34-350	**BR** M31261 maroon - *90*	12	18
34-328	**BR** M31198 blue - *10*	13	17
34-325Z	**BR** M31338M blue W internal used condemned Sp Edn 508 (ModelZone) - *12*	22	29

8th Edition

Bachmann Branchline

34-330	**BR Departmental** DM395665 black 'Electrification' - *12*	18	22
34-331	**BR Tartan Arrow** ? white - *13*	NPG	NPG
34-325Y	**BR Engineers** ADB975941 yellow QQW BTU tool van Sp Edn 508 (ModelZone) - *12*	20	26

C5.   LMS District Engineer's Inspection Saloon (2013)
This model is currently in development.

39-775	**LMS** ? lined maroon - *13*	NPG	NPG
39-776	**LMS** ? maroon - *13*	NPG	NPG
39-777	**LMS** ? blue+grey - *13*	NPG	NPG

Porthole Stock
The LMS 'Porthole' stock was the same as Stanier's Period 3 stock (as modelled by Hornby) but with a circular toilet windows. They therefore had steel walls on a wooden frame, were flush-sided without raised window surrounds, had sliding window vents and a ribbed metal roof with shell pattern vents.

The only vehicles to recieve a profile modification were in a batch of corridor composites which had a more pronounced tumblehome and a sharper junction of the sides and roof. The roof shape became closer to that adopted for the BR Mk1 coaches.

The coaches were built after Nationalisation to drawings prepared at Derby in 1947 and so did not run in LMS livery. Production ceased as the new BR Mk1 coaches took over.

The models had not been released at the time of writing.

C6a.   LMS Porthole 57' Corridor 3rd (2013)
These were built by Metro-Cammell in 1950 and totalled 100. They had post-war torpedo vents and it is believed that some survived into the BR blue period.

39-450	**BR** M?M red+cream - *13*	24	30

C6b.   LMS Porthole 57' Corridor 1st (2013)
These were built at Wolverton in 1950 and totalled 15 in all. Withdrawls took place in 1964 and 1965. Compared with earlier 1st class coaches, these had narrower compartments which allowed six to be provided on a 57ft underframe. They also had two extra doors on the compartment side and torpedo vents on the roof.

39-455	**BR** M?M red+cream - *13*	24	30

C6c.   LMS Porthole 57' Corridor Brake 3rd (2013)
These were built at Wolverton or Derby in 1949-50 and totalled 339. They had post-war BR type torpedo vents and it is believed that some survived into the BR blue period.

39-460	**BR** M26755M? red+cream - *13*	24	30

C6d.   LMS Porthole 60' Corridor Composite (2013)
These were the only 'Porthole' coaches to be built with a different profile and 240 were built at Derby in 1949-50. One lot of 75 received LMS livery and some survived into the blue period.

39-465	**BR** M?M red+cream - *13*	24	30

BR ex-LMS 'Porthole' composite coach [C6d] (Bachmann)

C6e.   LMS Porthole 60' Corridor Brake 1st (2013)
A total of 15 of these were built at Wolverton in 1949 and all were withdrawn in 1964-65. They also had smaller compartments than pre-war 1st class coaches and were fitted with the final style of sliding ventilators.

39-470	**BR** M?M red+cream - *13*	24	30

C6f.   LMS Porthole 60' Open Vestibule 1st (2013)
No information could be found on this design.

39-475	**BR** M?M red+cream - *13*	24	30

LNER

Thompson Stock
Thompson stock was longer than that of Gresley, being on 61.5ft underframes, and was built in steel on wooden frames. The internal layout was also completely different, having the entrance vestibules not at the ends but between groups of compartments. They coaches also had Thompson's trademark oval lavatory windows. The main windows, without toplights, looked large and stark, with their sharp corners. These were softened with rounder corners introduced by Peppercorn when he took over from Thompson.

The 1992-93 models were released in Thompson brown livery but those made in 2000 were in pre-war LNER brown.

C7aa.   LNER 63ft 3rd (2nd) (SK) (1991)
As a result of the different placement of the entrance vestibules, the coach was divided into three parts. The centre section between the vestibules contained three compartments in the all 3rd class coaches and the two end sections had two compartments apiece - making seven in all.

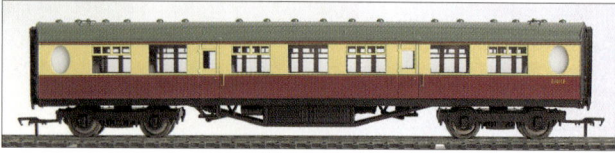

BR ex LNER Thompson 3rd class [C7aa]

34-377	**LNER** 1047 brown - *92*	12	19
34-375	**BR** E1098E red+cream - *91*	12	19
34-375	**BR** E1056E red+cream - *91?*	12	19
34-379	**BR** E1011E red+cream - *10*	12	19
(31-960)	**BR** E1516E maroon ex-'Elizabethan'* - *96*	14	NA
(31-960)	**BR** E1609E maroon ex-'Elizabethan'* - *96*	14	NA
(31-960)	**BR** E1600E maroon ex-'Elizabethan'* - *96*	14	NA
34-376	**BR** E1497E maroon - *91*	12	19
34-376	**BR** E1001E maroon - *91?*	12	19
34-378	**BR** E1550E maroon - *97*	12	18
34-378A	**BR** E1548E maroon - *not made*	NA	NA

* From the 'Elizabethan' limited edition set of which 1000 were made.

C7ab.   LNER All 2nd
Proposed for 2002 with flush end glazing but not made.

34-800	**BR** red+cream - *not made*	NA	NA

C7ac.   LNER 63ft All 3rd (2nd) Re-tooled (2013)
These models had not arrived at the time of writing.

34-385	**LNER** ? teak - *13*	NPG	30
34-386	**BR** E?E red+cream - *13*	NPG	30

C7ba.   LNER 59.5ft Composite (1991)
Like the all 3rd class coach, the interior of the composite coach was divided into three areas by the placing of the vestibules. The two end sections had two compartments each, as in the 3rd class coach, but, unlike the all-3rd, the composite coach had only two compartments in the centre section - making a total of six in the coach.

34-402	**LNER** 144 brown - *92*	12	19
34-400	**BR** E1207E red+cream - *91*	12	19
34-400	**BR** E1236E red+cream - *91?*	12	19
34-404	**BR** E1224E red+cream - *10*	12	19
34-401	**BR** E1228E maroon - *91*	12	19
34-401	**BR** E1240E maroon - *91?*	12	19
34-403	**BR** E1262E maroon - *97*	12	18
34-403A	**BR** E1266E? maroon - *not made*	NA	NA

C7bb.   LNER Composite
Proposed for 2002 with flush end glazing but not made.

34-825	**BR** red+cream - *not made*	NA	NA

C7bc.   LNER 59.5ft Composite Re-tooled (2013)
These models had not arrived at the time of writing.

34-410	**LNER** ? teak - *13*	NPG	30
34-411	**BR** E?E red+cream - *13*	NPG	30

C7ca.   LNER 63ft Brake Comp (1991)
The brake composite coaches had a large luggage section and two pairs of compartments. One pair was first class and the other pair was for third class passengers.

34-427	**LNER** 138 brown - *not made*	NA	NA
34-427	**LNER** 1142 brown - *92*	12	19
34-427/1	**LNER** 1112 brown - *not made*	NA	NA
34-425	**BR** E1146E red+cream - *91*	12	19
34-425	**BR** E1143E red+cream - *91?*	12	19
34-429	**BR** E1148E red+cream - *10*	12	19
(31-960)	**BR** E1161E maroon ex-'Elizabethan'* - *96*	14	NA

Bachmann Branchline

34-426	**BR** E1158E maroon - *91*	12	19
34-426	**BR** E1140E maroon - *91?*	12	19
34-428	**BR** E1151E maroon - *97*	12	18
34-428A	**BR** E1188E? maroon - *not made*	NA	NA

* From the 'Elizabethan' limited edition set of which 1000 were made.

C7cb.   LNER Comp Brake
Proposed for 2002 with flush end glazing but not made.

34-850	**BR** red+cream - *not made*	NA	NA

C7cc.   LNER 63ft Brake Comp Re-tooled (2013)
These models had not arrived at the time of writing.

34-435	**LNER** ? teak - *13*	NPG	30
34-436	**BR** E?E red+cream - *13*	NPG	30

C7da.   LNER 63ft Brake 3rd (2nd) (1991)
The brake 3rd had two pairs of compartments divided by a single vestibule. The rest of the coach was taken up by the guard's compartment and luggage area.

34-452	**LNER** 1908 brown - *92*	12	19
34-450	**BR** E1905E red+cream - *91*	12	19
34-450	**BR** E1925E red+cream - *91?*	12	19
34-454	**BR** E1936E red+cream - *10*	12	19
34-451	**BR** E1907E maroon - *91*	12	19
34-451	**BR** E1932E maroon - *91?*	12	19
34-453	**BR** E1910E maroon - *97*	12	18
34-453A	**BR** E1918E? maroon - *not made*	NA	NA

C7db.   LNER 2nd Brake
Proposed for 2002 with flush end glazing but not made.

34-875	**BR** red+cream - *not made*	NA	NA

C7dc.   LNER 63ft Brake 3rd (2nd) Re-tooled (2013)
These models had not arrived at the time of writing.

34-460	**LNER** ? teak - *13*	NPG	30
34-461	**BR** E?E red+cream - *13*	NPG	30

C7ea.   LNER 63ft All 1st (1991)
The layout of the all 1st coach was similar to that of the composite coach, with a total of six compartments.

34-477	**LNER** 1132 brown - *92*	12	19
34-477	**LNER** 138 brown - *92?*	12	19
34-475	**BR** E1315E red+cream - *91*	12	19
34-475	**BR** E1323E red+cream - *91?*	12	19
34-479	**BR** E1313E red+cream - *10*	12	19
34-476	**BR** E1322E maroon - *91*	12	19
(31-960)	**BR** E1328E maroon ex-'Elizabethan'* - *96*	14	NA
34-476	**BR** E1312E maroon - *91?*	12	19
34-478	**BR** E1320E maroon - *97*	12	18
34-478A	**BR** E1313E? maroon - *not made*	NA	NA

* From the 'Elizabethan' limited edition set of which 1000 were made.

C7eb.   LNER 1st Corridor
Proposed for 2002 with flush end glazing but not made.

34-900	**BR** red+cream - *not made*	NA	NA

C7ec.   LNER 63ft All 1st Re-tooled (2013)
These models had not arrived at the time of writing.

34-485	**LNER** ? teak - *13*	NPG	30
34-486	**BR** E?E red+cream - *13*	NPG	30

C7f.   LNER 63ft Full Brake BG (1994)
This model was fitted with end board and step board.

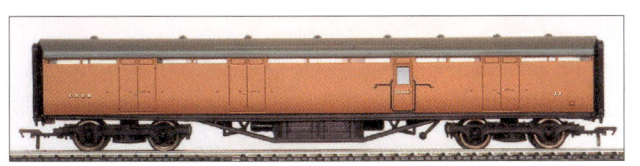

LNER Thompson full brake [C7f]

34-651	**LNER** brown - *not made*	NA	NA
34-655	**LNER** 11 brown - *00*	12	18
34-651	**BR** E12E red+cream - *95*	12	20
34-651A	**BR** E153E red+cream ** - *00*	12	18
34-651B	**BR** E162E red+cream - *00*	17	22
34-653	**BR** E16E red - *96*	12	18
34-653A	**BR** E16E red - *00*	12	18
(31-960)	**BR** E12E maroon also ex-'Elizabethan' pack (31-960)* - *96*	12	NA
34-651	**BR** E12E maroon - *96*	12	18
34-654A	**BR** E14E maroon - *00*	12	18
34-654B	**BR** E145E maroon - *11*	17	22
34-654C	**BR** E141E maroon - *12*	20	25
34-654	**BR** E16E maroon - *97*	12	20
34-650	**BR** E19E maroon - *94*	12	21
34-652	**BR** E18E blue - *95*	12	20
34-652A	**BR** E18E blue - *00*	12	18
34-652B	**BR** E155E blue W - *12*	20	25

* From the 'Elizabethan' limited edition set of which 1000 were made. ** 34-651A has a paler cream band than 34-651.

SR

SE&CR 60ft 'Birdcage' Stock
The coach design took its name from the guard's quarters which had a raised section in the roof, allowing the guard to see along the train. The windows in this raised section had vertical bars and it was thought to look like a birdcage.

C8a.   SE&CR 'Birdcage' Brake Composite (2013/14)
Newly proposed and details unavailable.

39-600	**SECR** maroon - *13/14*	NPG	NPG
39-601	**SR** olive green - *13/14*	NPG	NPG
39-602	**BR** red - *13/14*	NPG	NPG

C8b.   SE&CR 'Birdcage' Composite (2013/14)
Newly proposed and details unavailable.

39-610	**SECR** maroon - *13/14*	NPG	NPG
39-611	**SR** olive green - *13/14*	NPG	NPG
39-612	**BR** red - *13/14*	NPG	NPG

C8c.   SE&CR 'Birdcage' Comp Brake 3rd (2013/14)
Newly proposed and details unavailable.

39-620	**SECR** maroon - *13/14*	NPG	NPG
39-621	**SR** olive green - *13/14*	NPG	NPG
39-622	**BR** red - *13/14*	NPG	NPG

Bulleid Stock
Although designed by Bulleid's Southern Railway design team, prior to nationalisation of the railways, they arrived too late to run in SR livery. Instead, they started life in BR carmine and cream and, from 1956, they started to be painted Southern Coach Green.

Airfix had got as far as producing the drawings and some sample models of Bulleid coaches before the company went into liquidation. These would have been released in 1981, if circumstances had been different. Palitoy were about to introduce three types of Bulleid coach in 1985 but, again, closedown of production prevented this. With Bachmann, it was 'third time lucky' for the Bulleid coaches.

C9a.   BR(SR) 63ft Semi-Open Brake 3rd (2nd) (1993)
These were built at Eastleigh in 1949 and each consisted of two compartments and a 32 seat open saloon. The two compartments were at the guard's end of the coach. There were three passenger entrance doors on both sides of the coach.
be = brown end door

34-502	**BR** S3960 red+cream - *93*	12	21
34-502	**BR** S3960 red+cream no red cantrail - *93*	12	21
34-502A	**BR** S3960 red+cream - *00*	12	18
34-503	**BR** S3962S red+cream - *93*	12	21
34-503A*	**BR** S3957S red+cream - *93*	12	21
34-503A	**BR** S3951S red+cream - *97*	12	18
34-503A	**BR** S3957S red+cream, be - *02*	12	18
34-504	**BR** S3953S green - *06*	12	18
34-500	**BR** S3945S green - *93*	12	21
34-501	**BR** S3948S green - *93*	12	21
34-501A	**BR** S3949S green - *97*	12	19
34-500A	**BR** S3955S green - *97*	12	19
34-500B	**BR** S3962S green - *00*	12	18
34-504A	**BR** S3975S green - *10*	13	20
34-504B	**BR** S?S green - *11*	17	22
(34-500Z)	**BR** S3952S green ex-coach set 'S764' Sp Edn 504 (ModelZone) - *11*	13	NA

Bachmann Branchline

(34-500Z)	**BR** S3953S green ex-coach set 'S764' Sp Edn 504 (ModelZone) - 11		13	NA

* No suffix on box.

C9b. BR(SR) 63ft Composite (1993)

Built at Eastleigh in 1948, these were 7-compartment coaches with side corridors. They were built to diagram 2318 and had four 1st class compartments and three 3rd class ones.

be = brown end door

BR Bulleid composite coach [C9b]

34-550	**BR** S5871S green yellow 1st class line - 93	12	21
34-550A	**BR** S5870S green yellow 1st class line - 99	12	18
34-550A	**BR** S5870S green - 97	12	19
34-550B	**BR** S5810S green yellow 1st class line - 00	12	18
34-551	**BR** S5890S green - 93	12	21
34-551A	**BR** S5900S green - 97	12	19
34-554A	**BR** S5850S green - 10	13	20
34-554	**BR** S5874S green - 11	17	22
(34-500Z)	**BR** S5880S green ex-coach set 'S764' Sp Edn 504 (ModelZone) - 11	13	NA
34-552	**BR** S5907S red+cream - 93	12	21
34-522	**BR** S5???S red+cream no crimson red band - 99	12	18
34-552A	**BR** S5907 red+cream no red cantrail band - 00	12	18
34-552A	**BR** S5907 red+cream no red cantrail band, be - 02	12	18
34-553	**BR** S5868S red+cream - 93	12	21
34-553A	**BR** S5900S red+cream - 97	12	18

C9c. BR(SR) 63ft All 3rd (2nd) (1993)

These are 8-compartment side-corridor 3rd class coaches, which were built at Eastleigh between 1948 and 1950. They were built to diagram 2019.

be = brown end door

34-527	**BR** S101 red+cream no red cantrail - 93	12	21
34-527A	**BR** S101 red+cream - 00	12	18
34-528	**BR** S114S red+cream - 93	12	21
34-528A	**BR** S83S red+cream - 97	12	18
34-528A	**BR** S83S red+cream, be - 02	12	18
34-525	**BR** S82S green - 93	12	21
34-529	**BR** S105S green - 06	12	18
34-526A*	**BR** S108S green - 97	12	19
34-529A	**BR** S118S green - 08	13	19
34-529B	**BR** S?S green - 11	17	22
34-525B	**BR** S125S green - ?	12	18
34-525A*	**BR** S127S green - 97	12	19
34-526	**BR** S130S green - 93	12	21

* No suffix on box.

C9d.   BR(SR) 63ft Open 3rd (2nd) (1995)

This time the coaches were 8-bay open 3rds, built to diagram 2017. They were from a very late batch built at Eastleigh in 1950.

EB = SR end boards

34-576	**BR** S1493S red+cream EB - 95	12	20
34-576A	**BR** S1493S red+cream - 00	12	18
34-577	**BR** S1494S green - 06	12	18
34-577A	**BR** S1488S green - 08	13	19
34-577B	**BR** S?S green - 11	17	22
34-575A	**BR** S1493S green EB - 00	12	18
34-575	**BR S1504S green EB - 95**	**12**	**20**

SR Luggage Vans

C10.   SR 4-Wheel Utility Van (PLV/PMV/CCT) (2013)

This model was still under development at the time of writing. The real vehicle illustrated in the catalogue is a Parcels & Miscellaneous Van (PMV) No.2186 and this was built at Ashford in 1934.

39-525	**SR** ? green passenger luggage van (PLV) - 13	NPG	NPG
39-526	**BR** ? red parcels & miscellaneous van (PMV) - 13	NPG	NPG
39-527	**BR** ? green parcels & miscellaneous van (PMV) - 13	NPG	NPG
39-528	**BR** ? blue covered carriage truck (CCT) - 13	NPG	NPG

BR

Mk1 Non-Gangwayed Stock

Frequently called 'suburban' coaches, non-gangwayed stock was designed for the transportation of large numbers of people over short journeys and was used particularly around large conurbations by all four railway companies prior to Nationalisation. This section includes Bachmann's models of BR designed standard non-gangwayed stock.

BR non-gangwayed 2nd class [11a]

C11a.   BR Mk1 57ft 'Suburban' 2nd (1993)

The second class coaches each had nine compartments and could seat 108 passengers. With the absence of corridors, compartments were isolated from each other and necessitated nine doors on each side of the coach. The coaches were built at BR Wolverton and Derby in four separate lots during 1954 and 1955.

34-600	**BR** M46082 red - 93	12	19
34-600/1	**BR** E56128 red - 94	12	19
34-601	**BR** M46083 red - 93	12	19
34-601A*	**BR** M46083 red - 02	12	18
34-605	**BR** E46109 red - 96	12	19
34-605A*	**BR** E46109 red - 00	12	18
34-606	**BR** E46127 red - 96	12	19
34-606A*	**BR** E46127 red - 00	12	18
34-608	**BR** E48040 red W - 12	22	26
34-609	**BR** E46081 red W - 12	22	26
34-602	**BR** M46073 maroon - 93	12	19
34-602A*	**BR** M46073 maroon - 02	12	18
34-603	**BR** M46074 maroon - 93	12	19
34-603A*	**BR** M46074 maroon - 02	12	18
34-604	**BR** W46199 maroon - 96	12	19
34-604A*	**BR** W46199 maroon - 00	12	18
34-604B	**BR** W46086? maroon - 11	17	22
(30-016)	**BR** M46300 maroon ex-set - 06	12	NA
34-607	**BR** E46087 blue - 06	12	18
34-607A	**BR** E46200 blue - 06	12	18

* Straight reissue with later style box and it with slim-line couplings and metal wheels.

C11b.   BR Mk1 57ft 'Suburban' Brake 2nd (1993)

The brake 2nd had six compartments, with doors on either side and the coaches could each accommodate 72 passengers, with six people sat on each seat. Four lots were built during 1954 and 1955, the work being divided between BR coach works at York, Derby and Doncaster.

34-625	**BR** M43259 red - 93	12	19
34-625A	**BR** M43270 red - 01	12	18
34-626	**BR** E43130 red - 94	12	19
34-628	**BR** E53171 red - 96	12	19
34-628A*	**BR** E53171 red - 00	12	18
34-631	**BR** W43106 red W - 12	22	26
34-626	**BR** M43257 maroon - 93	12	19
34-627	**BR** W43102 maroon - 96	12	19
34-627A*	**BR** W43102 maroon - 00	12	18
34-627B	**BR** W43132? maroon - 11	17	22
34-630	**BR** E43133 maroon - 11	17	22
(30-016)	**BR** M43230 maroon ex-set - 06	12	NA
34-629	**BR** E43112 blue - 06	12	18
34-629A	**BR** E43138 blue - 07	12	18
34-730	**BR** blue - not made	NA	NA
34-632	**BR** W43106? blue W - 13	NA	NA
34-633	**BR** W? blue W - 13	NA	NA
34-625Z	**Network Rail** ADB963952 yellow QQV BTU tool van Sp Edn 504 (ModelZone) - 10	12	18

* Straight reissue with later style box and it with slim-line couplings and metal wheels.

Bachmann Branchline

BR non-gangwayed brake 2nd [C11b]

C11c. BR Mk1 57ft 'Suburban' Open 2nd (1996)
Two lots of open 3rd class coaches were built at Derby and Doncaster. They were partitioned into two separate uneven sized saloons. There was an off-centre isle with double seats on one side of it and triple seats on the other side. There were long seats across both ends of each of the two saloons, each holding six passengers. The total capacity was 94 and there were ten doors along each side.

34-676	**BR** M48037 red - 96	12	19
34-676A*	**BR** M48037 red - 01	12	18
34-675B	**BR** M48038? maroon - 11	17	22
34-675	**BR** W48029 maroon - 96	12	19
34-675A*	**BR** W48029 maroon - 00	12	18
34-677	**BR** M46081 blue W - 00	NPG	NPG
34-678	**BR** M? blueW - 00	NPG	NPG

* Straight reissue with later style box and it with slim-line couplings and metal wheels.

C11d. BR Mk1 57ft 'Suburban' Composite (1996)
These were built at Wolverton in 1954-55 and had 9 compartments with doors on both sides. The middle three compartments were first class with a total of 24 seats and the remainder were 3rd class with a total of 72 seats.

34-701	**BR** M41006 red - 96	12	19
34-701A*	**BR** M41006 red - 01	12	18
34-703	**BR** E41010 red W - 12	22	26
34-700	**BR** W41058 maroon - 96	12	19
34-700A*	**BR** W41058 maroon - 00	12	18
34-700B	**BR** M41008? maroon - 11	17	22
34-702	**BR** E? blue** - *not made*	NA	NA

* Straight reissue with later style box and it with slim-line couplings and metal wheels.
**This was cancelled when it was realised that the BR(ER) coach was to a different design. It was replaced by 34-730 at short notice.

Mk1 Main Line Corridor Stock
Main line stock had corridors and corridor connections between coaches. The first Mk1 main line coaches went into service in 1951 and remained in use for over forty years. When production of the standard British Railways coaches started, the existing system of seats being classified as 1st class and 3rd class was continued for a while. Then, in June 1956, 3rd class travel was abolition in Britain. From that time, 3rd class became 2nd class, and a lot later - standard class.

While of a standard design, there was a significant variety of Mk1 types to meet many different needs and Bachmann are unique in tackling so many of these variations in 00 scale ready-to-run models.

C12a. BR Mk1 Corridor 2nd (SK) (1999)
More of these 3rd class corridor coaches were produced than any other design in the history of Britain's railways. The first lot was built in 1952 at Eastleigh and the last in 1963 at the BR coach works at York. The coach had doors both sides at each end and in the centre and the centre vestibule split the compartments into two groups of four. Shared armrests were provided on seats making three positions each side of the compartment and providing space for 48 passengers per coach. With armrests raised out of the way, 4 people could sit each side and 64 passengers could be accommodated. There were two lavatories, one positioned either side of the corridor at one end of the coach.

34-727	**BR** red+cream - *not made*	NA	NA
39-027	**BR** M24446 red+cream - *99*	15	22
39-027	**BR** 24813 red+cream - *not made*	NA	NA
39-027A	**BR** M24467 red+cream - *00*	15	21
39-027B*	**BR** E24813 red+cream - *02*	15	20
39-027C	**BR** E24796 red+cream - *03*	15	20
39-027D	**BR** M24467 red+cream - *not made*	NA	NA
39-027D	**BR** E24240 red+cream - *06*	15	21
39-027E	**BR** E24159 red+cream - *08*	16	22
39-027F	**BR** M24135 red+cream - *10*	16	23
39-027G	**BR** W24746 red+cream - *11*	20	26
39-027H	**BR** E24813 red+cream W - *not made*	NA	NA
39-027H	**BR** W24166 red+cream W - *12*	23	29
39-028	**BR** S24311 green - *00*	15	21
39-028A*	**BR** S24327 green - *02*	15	20
39-028B	**BR** S24305 green - *05*	15	21

BR corridor 2nd [C12a]

39-028C	**BR** S24324 green - *07*	15	22
39-028D	**BR** S24317 green - *10*	15	22
39-028E	**BR** S24302 green - *11*	20	26
39-029	**BR** W24165 brown+cream - *00*	15	21
39-029A*	**BR** W25051 brown+cream - *02*	15	20
39-029B	**BR** W24747 brown+cream - *05*	15	20
39-029C	**BR** W24165 brown+cream - *not made*	NA	NA
39-029C	**BR** W25200 brown+cream - *06*	15	21
39-029D	**BR** W24328 brown+cream - *10*	16	23
39-029E	**BR** W24328 brown+cream - *12*	22	28
(31-2000)	**BR** W24750 brown+cream ex-set - *01*	15	NA
(31-2000)	**BR** W25189 brown+cream ex-set - *01*	15	NA
(39-000G)	**BR** W? brown+cream ex-'Cornish Riviera' coach set Sp Edn 500 (Kernow Model Rail Centre) - *11*	22	NA
34-726	**BR** maroon - *not made*	NA	NA
39-026	**BR** E24538 maroon - *99*	15	22
39-026A**	**BR** E25044 maroon - *00*	15	21
39-026B	**BR** M25400 maroon - *01*	15	21
39-026C	**BR** M25704 maroon - *02*	15	20
39-026D	**BR** M24679 maroon - *05*	15	21
39-026E	**BR** M24911 maroon - *06*	15	21
39-026F	**BR** W24165 maroon - *08*	16	22
39-026G	**BR** W24379 maroon - *10*	15	23
39-026H	**BR** Sc25861 maroon W - *12*	23	29
39-000W(A)	**BR** W25043 maroon Sp Edn 500 (*Model Rail*) ex-coach set - *06*	18	NA
34-725	**BR** ? blue+grey - *not made*	NA	NA
39-025	**BR** E25039 blue+grey - *99*	15	22
39-025A	**BR** E26140 blue+grey - *01*	15	21
39-025B	**BR** E26033 blue+grey - *02*	15	20
39-025C	**BR** E25832 blue+grey - *06*	15	21
39-025D	**BR** M24032 blue+grey - *08*	16	22
39-025E	**BR** E25704 blue+grey - *10*	16	23
39-025F	**BR** W24689 blue+grey - *12*	22	28
39-030	**BR** InterCity M18753 grey - *02*	15	21
39-031	**BR** NSE 18752 bright blue - *05*	15	20
39-031A	**BR** NSE 18601 bright blue - *06*	15	21

* Box label wrongly shows running number of the previous release. ** code on box has no suffix.

C12b. BR Mk1 Open 2nd (SO/TSO) (1999)
While the external appearance was the same, the SO seated 48 passengers (2+1 abreast) and the TSO seated 64 passengers (2+2 abreast). The positions of doors and lavatories were the same as for the SK described above, but, being open plan coaches, the gangway ran down the centre. Again, very large quantities of this type of coach were built between 1953 and 1963, the first ones at Derby and the last batch at York.

34-752	**BR** red+cream - *not made*	NA	NA
39-052	**BR** M3737 red+cream - *99*	15	22
39-052A	**BR** M3788 red+cream - *00*	15	21
39-052B	**BR** E3979 red+cream - *02*	15	20

BR open 2nd [C12b]

39-052C	**BR** M4899 red+cream - *not made*	NA	NA
39-052C	**BR** E4260 red+cream - *05*	15	21
39-052D	**BR** E4268 red+cream - *not made*	NA	NA
39-052D	**BR** E3858 red+cream - *06*	15	21
39-052E	**BR** M3741 red+cream - *10*	15	23
39-052F	**BR** W3789 red+cream - *11*	20	26
39-052G	**BR** W? red+cream - *13*	NPG	NPG
39-053	**BR** S3998 green - *00*	15	20

Bachmann Branchline

Code	Description		
39-053A*	BR S4040 green (also 39-053B) - 01	15	20
39-053B	BR S4375 green - 05	15	21
39-053C	BR S3840 green - 07	15	22
39-053D	BR S3824 green - 10	15	22
39-053E	BR S3825 green - 11	20	26
39-054	BR W3791 brown+cream - 00	15	20
39-054A	BR W4739 brown+cream - 03	15	21
39-054B	BR W3821 brown+cream - 10	16	23
39-054C	BR W3879 brown+cream - 12	22	28
34-751	BR maroon - not made	NA	NA
39-051	BR E4238 maroon - 99	15	22
39-051A**	BR E3850 maroon - 01	15	21
39-051B*	BR M4414 maroon - 01	15	20
39-051C	BR M4899 maroon - 03	15	20
39-051D	BR M4780 maroon - 05	15	21
39-051E	BR M4929 maroon - 06	15	21
39-051F	BR W3984 maroon - 08	16	22
39-051G	BR W4739 maroon - 09	15	22
39-051H	BR W3192 maroon W - 12	23	29
(39-000W)	BR W4746 maroon Sp Edn 500 (*Model Rail*) ex-coach set - 06	18	NA
(39-000R)	BR W3875 maroon Sp Edn 500 (Cheltenham Model Centre) ex-coach set - 09	20	NA
34-750	BR blue+grey - not made	NA	NA
39-050	BR E4357 blue+grey - 99	15	22
39-050A	BR E5001 blue+grey - 01	15	21
39-050B	BR E4112 blue+grey - 04	15	20
39-050C	BR E4298 blue+grey - 06	15	21
39-050D	BR E4243 blue+grey - 08	16	22
39-050E	BR E4439 blue+grey - 10	16	23
39-050F	BR S3840 blue+grey - 12	22	28
39-055	BR InterCity 4909 grey - 02	15	21
39-056	BR Regional Railways 4873 blue+white - 02	15	21
39-057	BR NSE 4920 bright blue - 05	15	20
39-057A	BR NSE 4901 bright blue - 06	15	21
39-058	BR NSE ? bright blue - 13	NPG	NPG
(39-000X)	BR ScotRail - West Highland 4050 green+cream see C12m coach sets	20	NA
(39-000X)	BR ScotRail - West Highland 4494 green+cream see C12m coach sets	20	NA
(39-000X)	BR ScotRail - West Highland 4601 green+cream see C12m coach sets	20	NA
(39-000Y)	West Highland Line IC3767C green+cream - see C12m coach sets	20	NA
(39-000Z)	West Highland Line IC4912C green+cream - see C12m coach sets	20	NA
(39-000Z)	West Highland Line IC4911C green+cream - see C12m coach sets	20	NA

* Box label wrongly shows running number of the previous release. ** code on box has no suffix.

C12c. BR Mk1 Brake Corridor 2nd (BSK) (1999)

Over the years 13 lots of them were built, the earliest at Derby in October 1952 and the last lot were constructed at Wolverton in April 1962. The coach was divided roughly into two, with four compartments and a lavatory in one end, followed by the guard's compartment and luggage space at the other end. There were doors both sides, at either end of the passenger section, and **two** sets of double doors in the luggage compartment. The guard had a private door either side of the coach.

Code	Description		
34-777	BR red+cream - not made	NA	NA
39-077	BR M34655 red+cream - 99	15	22
39-077A	BR E34226 red+cream - 99	15	20
39-077B	BR E34500 red+cream - 05	15	21
39-077C	BR M34096 red+cream - 06	15	21
39-077D	BR E34288 red+cream - 09	15	22
39-077E	BR W34139 red+cream - 11	20	26

BR brake corridor 2nd [C12c]

Code	Description		
39-077F	BR E? red+cream - 11	20	26
39-078	BR S35020 green - 00	15	21
39-078A	BR S35021 green - 00	15	20
39-078B	BR S34974 green - 05	15	21
39-078C	BR S34255 green - 07	15	22
39-078D	BR S34641 green - 10	15	22
39-078E	BR S34642 green - 11	20	26
39-079	BR W34290 brown+cream - 00	15	20
39-079A	BR W34751 brown+cream - 03	15	21
39-079B	BR W34885 brown+cream - 10	16	23
39-079C	BR W34303 brown+cream W - 12	23	29
(31-2000)	BR W34892 brown+cream ex-set - 01	15	NA
(31-2000)	BR W34773 brown+cream ex-set - 01	15	NA
(39-000G)	BR W? brown+cream ex-'Cornish Riviera' coach set Sp Edn 500 (Kernow Model Rail Centre) - 11	22	NA
(39-000G)	BR W? brown+cream ex-'Cornish Riviera' coach set Sp Edn 500 (Kernow Model Rail Centre) - 11	22	NA
34-776	BR maroon - not made	NA	NA
39-076	BR E34168 maroon - 99	15	22
39-076A	BR E34007 maroon - 00	15	21
39-076B*	BR M35180 maroon - 00	15	20
39-076C	BR M35486 maroon - 05	15	21
39-076D	BR M34140 maroon - 06	15	21
39-076E	BR W34152 maroon - 08	16	22
39-076F	BR W34315 maroon - 09	15	22
39-076G	BR E34225 maroon W - 12	23	29
(39-000W)	BR W34751 maroon Sp Edn 500 (*Model Rail*) ex-coach set - 06	18	NA
(39-000R)	BR W34151 maroon Sp Edn 500 (Cheltenham Model Centre) ex-coach set - 09	20	NA
39-000U	BR 99952 maroon Sp Edn 504 (NRM) - 07	15	25
34-775	BR blue+grey - not made	NA	NA
39-075	BR E35445 blue+grey - 99	15	22
39-075A	BR M35040 blue+grey - 03	15	20
39-075B	BR E35383 blue+grey - 06	15	21
39-075C	BR E35322 blue+grey - 10	16	23
39-075D	BR S35010 blue+grey - 12	22	28
(39-000K)	BR 35402, blue+grey W see C12m	16	NA
39-080	BR InterCity M35465 grey - 02	15	21
39-081	BR Regional Railways 35452 blue+white - 02	15	21
39-082	BR NSE 35339 bright blue - 05	15	20
39-082A	BR NSE 35464 bright blue - 06	15	21
(39-000X)	BR ScotRail - West Highland 9312 green+cream see C12m coach sets	20	NA
-	BR RTC ? 'Laboratory 10' red+blue	25	NA
-	BR RTC ? 'Laboratory 11' red+blue	25	NA
39-001	above two Tribolgy Test Train (TRIB) cars Sp Edn 504 (Invictor) - 13	NA	66
-	BR RTC RDB975136 'Laboratory 12' red+blue Sp Edn 504 (ModelZone) - 06	20	NA
-	BR RTC ADB975051 'Test Car 5' red+blue Sp Edn 504 (ModelZone) - 06	20	NA
39-000V	above two cars - 06	NA	50

* Box label wrongly shows running number of the previous release.

C12d. BR Mk1 Restaurant Unclassed (RU) (1999)

Two batches of RUs were built in 1957 and 1958. Ashford provided the underframe and Swindon built the body. There was seating for 33 passengers, in each coach, but later a table and four seats were removed, reducing the capacity to 29. The rest of the space in the coach was taken up with the pantry and kitchen, staff compartment and staff toilet, as well as corridor links for the public.

BR restaurant unclassed [C12d]

Code	Description		
39-105	BR W1900 red+cream - 08	16	22
39-105A	BR W1900 red+cream - 11	20	26
39-102	BR W1902 brown+cream - 01	15	20
39-102A	BR W1919 brown+cream - 06	15	21
39-102B	BR W34139 brown+cream - 11	20	26
34-801	BR maroon - not made	NA	NA

Bachmann Branchline

39-101	**BR** E1926 maroon Gresley bogies - *99*	15	20
39-101A	**BR** E1961 maroon - *03*	15	21
39-101B	**BR** E1930 maroon - *07*	15	22
39-101C	**BR** Sc1941 maroon - *10*	16	23
39-103	**BR** W1915 maroon - *01*	15	20
39-103A	**BR** W1944 maroon - *01*	15	21
39-103B	**BR** W1924 maroon - *10*	16	23
39-103C	**BR** W1917 maroon - *10*	16	23
34-800	**BR** blue+grey - *not made*	NA	NA
39-100	**BR** E1938 blue+grey Gresley bogies - *99*	15	20
39-100A	**BR** M1966 blue+grey - *04*	15	21
39-100B	**BR** M1966 blue+grey - *08*	16	22
39-104	**BR** InterCity 1981 grey RBR - *02*	15	21

C12e. BR Mk1 Corridor Composite (CK) (2000)

Eleven lots of CKs were built, the first at Derby in 1952 and the last lot, also at Derby, in 1963. There were three 3rd class compartments and four in the 1st class end of the coach. They were separated by a door in the corridor, as well as a central vestibule with outside doors. In addition, there were vestibules with external doors at both ends of the coach.

39-127	**BR** M15019 red+cream - *00*	15	20
39-127A	**BR** E15271 red+cream - *03*	15	20
39-127B	**BR** E15055 red+cream - *06*	15	21

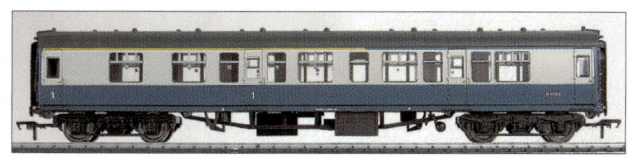

BR corridor composite [C12e]

39-127C	**BR** M15192 red+cream - *10*	16	23
39-127D	**BR** M15181 red+cream - *10*	16	23
39-127E	**BR** M? red+cream - *13*	NPG	NPG
39-128	**BR** S15904 green - *00*	15	20
39-128A	**BR** S15566 green - *03*	15	21
39-128B	**BR** S15904 green - *08*	16	22
39-128C	**BR** S15567 green - *11*	20	26
39-129	**BR** W15770 brown+cream - *00*	15	20
39-129A	**BR** W15777 brown+cream - *05*	15	21
39-129B	**BR** W15110 brown+cream - *10*	16	23
39-129C	**BR** W? brown+cream - *12*	22	28
(31-2000)	**BR** W15816 brown+cream ex-set - *01*	15	NA
(39-000G)	**BR** W? brown+cream ex-'Cornish Riviera' coach set Sp Edn 500 (Kernow Model Rail Centre) - *11*	22	NA
39-126	**BR** E15145 maroon - *00*	15	21
39-126A*	**BR** M16005 maroon - *01*	15	20
39-126B	**BR** M15684 maroon - *05*	15	21
39-126C	**BR** M15916 maroon - *06*	15	21
39-126D	**BR** W15077 maroon - *08*	16	22
39-126E	**BR** W16198 maroon - *10*	16	23
39-126F	**BR** E16244 maroon W - *11*	22	28
39-126G	**BR** E? maroon W - *13*	NPG	NPG
(39-000W)	**BR** W15426 maroon Sp Edn 500 (*Model Rail*) ex-coach set - *06*	18	NA
(39-000R)	**BR** W15066 maroon Sp Edn 500 (Cheltenham Model Centre) ex-coach set - *09*	20	NA
39-125	**BR** E16241 blue+grey - *00, 05*	15	20
39-125B	**BR** E15768 blue+grey - *06*	15	21
39-125C	**BR** M16153 blue+grey - *10*	16	23
39-125D	**BR** M? blue+grey - *13*	NPG	NPG
39-130	**BR NSE** 7232 bright blue - *05*	15	21
39-131	**BR NSE** ? bright blue - *13*	NPG	NPG

* Box label wrongly shows running number of the previous release.

C12f. BR Mk1 Corridor 1st (FK) (2000)

These were built in 8 lots, the first in 1952 at Swindon and it was there that the last lot was also built 10 years later. In each coach there were seven compartments, each with six seats, and there was a toilet at each end of the coach. Each end also had a vestibule with external doors and there was an additional door in the centre of the corridor side of the coach.

39-152	**BR** M13004 red+cream - *00*	15	20
39-152A	**BR** M13110 red+cream - *05*	15	21
39-152B	**BR** E13113 red+cream - *07*	15	22
39-152C	**BR** M13060 red+cream - *10*	15	23
39-152D	**BR** W13065 red+cream - *11*	20	26

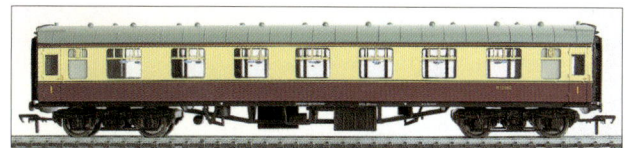

BR corridor 1st [C12f]

39-153	**BR** S13143 green - *00*	15	20
39-153A	**BR** S13003 green - *05*	15	21
39-153B	**BR** S13086 green - *08*	16	22
39-153C	**BR** S13003 green - *11*	20	26
39-154	**BR** W13074 brown+cream - *00*	15	20
39-154A	**BR** W13185 brown+cream - *06*	15	21
39-154B	**BR** W13074 brown+cream - *10*	16	23
39-154C	**BR** W? brown+cream - *12*	22	28
(31-2000)	**BR** W13187 brown+cream ex-set - *01*	15	NA
39-151	**BR** E13030 maroon - *00*	15	20
39-151A	**BR** M13223 maroon - *03*	15	20
39-151B	**BR** M13070 maroon - *06*	15	21
39-151C	**BR** W13127 maroon - *08*	16	22
39-151D	**BR** M13108 maroon - *10*	16	23
39-151E	**BR** E13333 maroon W - *11*	22	28
(39-000R)	**BR** W13132 maroon Sp Edn 500 (Cheltenham Model Centre) ex-coach set - *09*	20	NA
39-150	**BR** E13107 blue+grey - *00*	15	20
39-150A	**BR** E13234 blue+grey - *05*	15	21
39-150B	**BR** M13179 blue+grey - *08*	16	22
39-150C	**BR** M13085 blue+grey - *10*	16	23
39-155	**BR** InterCity M13341 grey - *02*	15	21
39-156	**BR** Regional Railways 13225 blue+white - *02*	15	21
39-157	**BR NSE** 13328 bright blue - *05*	15	21

C12g. BR Mk1 Full Brake (BG) (2000)

The full brake had a guard's compartment in the centre and two large areas either side of it for storing luggage. There were four pairs of doors in each side as well as a single door in the centre of each side for the guard. The standard Mk1 BG was shorter than other Mk1 coaches, being 57ft (17.37m) instead of 63ft (19.20m). Eight lots of them were built, the first batch at Derby in 1953 and the last lot were built in 1961, by Gloucester Railway Carriage & Wagon Ltd.

39-177	**BR** M80541 red+cream - *00*	15	20
39-177A	**BR** E80623 red+cream - *05*	15	21
39-177B	**BR** M81039 red+cream - *07*	15	22
39-177C	**BR** M85065 red+cream - *09*	15	22
39-177D	**BR** W80709 red+cream - *11*	20	26
39-178	**BR** S81510 green - *00*	15	20
39-178A	**BR** S81292 green - *05*	15	21
39-178B	**BR** S80893 green - *08*	16	22
39-178C	**BR** S80561 green - *11*	20	26
39-179	**BR** W81205 brown+cream - *00*	15	21
39-179A	**BR** W? brown+cream - *07*	15	22
39-179B	**BR** W80713 brown+cream - *10*	16	23
39-176	**BR** E80798 maroon - *00*	15	21
39-176A*	**BR** M80950 maroon - *01*	15	20
39-176B	**BR** M81300 maroon - *05*	15	21

BR Royal Mail full brake [C12g]

39-176C	**BR** W80708 maroon - *09*	15	22
39-176D	**BR** M80533 maroon - *10*	16	23
39-176E	**BR** W80725 maroon W - *11*	22	28
39-176F	**BR** W81266 maroon W - *12*	23	29
39-175	**BR** E80617 blue+grey - *00*	15	20
39-175A	**BR** M84281 blue+grey NDV - *03*	15	21
39-175B	**BR** M? blue+grey NDV - *08*	16	22
39-175C	**BR** M80906 blue+grey - *10*	16	23
39-175D	**BR** M80955 blue+grey Express Parcels - *12*	22	28
(39-000K)	**BR** 81221 blue+grey W Express Parcels, *see* C12m	16	NA
39-182A	**BR** M80689 blue+grey Newspapers - *06*	15	21

8th Edition

Bachmann Branchline

Cat. No.	Description		
39-182	**BR** 95211 blue Newspapers NCX - *02*	15	20
39-182B	**BR** M81124 blue Newspapers NCV - *10*	16	23
39-180	**BR** Inter-City 92151 grey+beige NEA - *02*	15	21
39-181	**BR** Regional Rlys E92058 blue+white NEA Parcels - *02*	15	21
39-176Z	**NSE** 92315 bright blue Sp Edn 504 (The Signalbox) - *08*	18	24
39-183	**RES** 92322 red+dark grey NEX - *03*	15	21
39-183A	**RES** 92418 red+dark grey NEX - *09*	16	22
39-184	**BR** Royal Mail 92131 red NEA - *03*	15	21
39-184A	**BR** Royal Mail 92233 red NEA - *11*	20	26
39-185	**BR** Departmental ADB975613 olive green QRX - *12*	23	28
39-175Z	**BR RD** 'Laboratory 23' red+blue Sp Edn 504 (ModelZone) - *11*	25	30
39-?	**NR** 6284 yellow generator van Sp Edn 750 (*Model Rail* magazine) - *13*	NPG	35

* Box label wrongly shows running number of the previous release.

C12h. BR Mk1 Corridor Brake Composite (BCK) (2001)

The earliest batch came from Derby in 1954 and the final lot, also from Derby, in 1963. There were five compartments, each with six seats with adjustable armrests. Three of the compartments were for 3rd class and two were 1st class. The corridor had a dividing door between them. There was a lavatory and vestibule, with external doors, at either end of the passenger section of the coach. Only a little over a quarter of the coach was left for the guard's compartment and luggage space. The latter had one double door each side and the guard also had a single door each side.

39-227	**BR** M21238 red+cream - *made?*	NPG	NPG
39-227	**BR** M21026 red+cream - *02*	15	20
39-227A	**BR** M21030 red+cream - *05*	15	21
39-227B	**BR** E21050 red+cream - *07*	15	22
39-227C	**BR** M21029 red+cream - *10*	15	23
39-227D	**BR** Sc21017 red+cream - *11*	20	26
39-228	**BR** S21268 green - *01*	15	20
39-228A	**BR** S21263 green - *05*	15	21

BR corridor brake composite [C12h]

39-228B	**BR** S21272 green - *09*	16	22
39-228C	**BR** S21264 green - *11*	20	26
39-229	**BR** W21067 brown+cream - *01*	15	21
39-229A	**BR** W21191 brown+cream - *07*	15	22
39-229B	**BR** W21080 brown+cream - *10*	16	23
39-229C	**BR** W? brown+cream - *13*	NPG	NPG
39-226	**BR** E21202 maroon - *01*	15	20
39-226A	**BR** M21030 maroon - *04*	15	21
39-226B	**BR** W21021 maroon - *09*	16	22
39-226C	**BR** M21026 maroon - *10*	16	23
39-226D	**BR** E21011 maroon W - *11*	22	28
39-226E	**BR** E? maroon W - *13*	NPG	NPG
39-225	**BR** M21241 blue+grey - *01*	15	20
39-225A	**BR** E21222 blue+grey - *05*	15	21
39-225B	**NSE** M21236 blue+grey - *08*	16	22
39-225C	**BR** 21247 blue+grey - *12*	22	28
39-230	**BR** InterCity 21266 grey - *02*	15	21
(39-000Y)	**West Highland** Line IC21241C green+cream - see C12m coach sets	20	NA
39-225Z	**NR** DB975280 yellow Sp Edn (*Model Rail*) ** - *12*	NPG	35

* Box label wrongly shows running number of the previous release. ** Formerly *Test Coach Mercury*, now used as a generator/staff car for the Structure Gauging Train (authentic printed details and B4 bogies).

C12i. BR Mk1 Restaurant 1st Open (RFO) (2001)

These were the very first BR standard restaurant cars and were built at York in 1951. They were designed to run with kitchen cars. They had seven 1st class bays seating 42 diners and only 11 were built.

39-252	**BR** M4 red+cream - *01*	15	20
39-252A	**BR** E10 red+cream - *05*	15	21
39-252B	**BR** W8 red+cream - *08*	16	22
39-252C	**BR** W8 red+cream W - *not made*	NA	NA

BR restaurant 1st [C12i]

39-252C	**BR** M9 red+cream W - *12*	23	29
39-253	**BR** S9 green - *01*	18	23
39-253A	**BR** green - *not made*	NA	NA
39-254	**BR** W7 brown+cream - *01*	15	21
39-251	**BR** E3 maroon - *01*	15	21
39-251A	**BR** M6 maroon - *07*	15	21
39-251B	**BR** M? maroon W - *11*	22	28
39-250	**BR** E3 blue+grey - *01*	15	20
39-250A	**BR** M5 blue+grey - *05*	15	21
39-250B	**BR** W9 blue+grey - *10*	16	23

C12j. BR Mk1 Restaurant Mini Buffet (RMB) (2007)

A total of 82 of these were built at York and Wolverton between 1957 and 1962. They were provided for shorter distance and cross country routes and had a small buffet counter offering light snacks and drinks. The first 12 vehicles had 48 seats but these were reduced to 44 to allow for additional stock storage. Numbers 1872 and 1873 were converted for use in Southern Region EMUs around 1975. During the 1980s, the RMBs were refurbished. After sectorisation, they passed to InterCity but most had been withdrawn by the time of privatisation. Three survived in service with Anglia Railways until the last was withdrawn in 2001 and many have been preserved.

BR restaurant mini buffet [C12j]

39-260	**BR** E1852 red+cream - *07*	15	21
39-262	**BR** S1852 green - *not made*	NA	NA
39-262	**BR** S1881 green - *07*	15	21
39-262A	**BR** S1849 green - *10*	16	23
39-263	**BR** W1814 brown+cream - *07*	15	21
39-261	**BR** E1854 maroon - *07*	15	21
39-261A	**BR** W1815 maroon - *09*	15	22
39-264	**BR** E1871 blue+grey - *07*	15	22

C12k. BR Mk1 Super Full Brake (BG) (2001)

These are 100mph high security brake vans with air brakes. TOPS coded NBA, they were rebuilt from gangwayed brakes. They have reinforced floors, sealed gangways and roller-shutter doors. They also have built-in tail lamps and are used to convey valuable cargo.

BR RES Super BG [C12k]

39-200	**RES** 94474 red+dark grey - *01*	15	20
39-200A	**RES** 94451 red+dark grey - *03*	15	21
39-200B	**RES** 94467 red+dark grey - *09*	16	22
39-200C	**BR** 94465 red+dark grey W NBA - *12*	24	29
39-201	**RES Royal Mail** 94420 red+dark grey - *01*	15	20
39-201A	**RES Royal Mail** 94520 red+dark grey NBA - *03*	15	21
39-201B	**RES Royal Mail** 94462 red+dark grey NBA - *09*	16	22

C12l. BR Mk1 Sleeping Cars (SLF & SLSTP) (2013)

BR 2nd class sleeping car [C12l]

Bachmann Branchline

The SLF was a 1st class sleeping car while the SLSTP was a 2nd class sleeping car with a pantry. As the models are physically the same externally, they share the same table.

Cat No	Description		
39-500	BR M2002 lined maroon SLF - 13	24	29
39-502	BR M2541 lined maroon SLSTP - not made	NA	NA
39-502	BR M2635 lined maroon SLSTP - 13	24	29
39-501	BR I-C E2054 blue+grey SLF - 13	24	29
39-503	BR M2527 blue+grey SLSTP - not made	NA	NA
39-503	BR I-C E2575 blue+grey SLSTP - 13	24	29

C12m.   BR Mk1 & Mk2 Coach Sets (2003)

Details of the coaches in the following sets will also be found under the coach type headings where they are individually listed in the tables.

Cat No	Description		
39-000Z	West Highland Line 2 x Mk1 SO green+cream Sp Edn 360 (Harburn Hobbies) - 03	NA	45
39-000Y	West Highland Line Mk1 SO + Mk1 BCK green+cream Sp Edn 360 (Harburn Hobbies) - 03	NA	45
39-000X	ScotRail - West Highland 3 x Mk1 SO + 1 x Mk1 BSK green+cream Sp Edn 500 (Model Rail) - 03	NA	90
39-000W	BR(WR) maroon Mk1 CK, SK, SO, BSK set of 4 Sp Edn 500 (Model Rail) - 06	NA	99
39-000V	BR RTC red+blue Mk1 BSK laboratory car & Mk1 BSK test car Sp Edn 504 (ModelZone) - 06	NA	50
39-000T	West Highland Line 3 x Mk2 TSO, 1 x Mk2 BSO green+ cream Sp Edn 500 (Model Rail) - 08	NA	NPG
39-000S	BR IC set of 2 Mk2 blue+grey MTA test coaches Sp Edn 504 (ModelZone) - 08	NA	55
39-000R	BR(WR) maroon Mk1 CK, SO, FK, BSK set of 4 Sp Edn 500 (Cheltenham Model Centre) - 09	NA	100
39-000L	Red Bank* Parcels Set 1 - BR blue+grey, weathered 2 x Mk1 GUVs, Sp Edn 500 (ModelZone) - 10	NA	55
39-000K	Red Bank* Set Parcels 2 - BR blue+grey, weathered Mk1 BG & BSK, Sp Edn 500 (ModelZone) - 10	NA	55
39-000G	BR(WR) Cornish Riviera brown+cream Mk1s: SK, CK & 2 x BSK set of 4 Sp Edn 500 (Kernow Model Rail Centre) - 11	NA	115
39-001	BR blue+grey Mk1s: 'Works Test Train' - 13	NA	NPG

* The name comes from the Red Bank Sidings outside Manchester (Victoria), where the empty coaches were kept.

C13.   BR Mk1 General Utilty Van (GUV) (2007)

General utility vans have been used for transporting parcels and mails. Several batches were built, the earliest at Doncaster in 1956 and the last ones in 1959 by Pressed Steel Ltd. Built without gangway connections, they had two large end doors and a bottom flap that rested on the buffers when open and thus allowed end-loading with motor vehicles. Some of the GUVs received 'Motorail' branding. The vans were built with three double doors along each side, each with a single window, and there were two intermediate windows between the sets of doors on each side.

Cat No	Description		
39-271	BR W85470 red - not made	NA	NA
39-273	BR S86724 green - 08	15	22
39-273A	BR S86791 green - 09	15	22
39-271	BR M86105 maroon - not made	NA	NA
39-271	BR W86253 maroon - 07	15	21
39-271A	BR W86148 maroon - 10	16	23
39-271B	BR W86442 maroon - 10	16	23
39-271C	BR E86123 maroon W - 11	22	28
39-271Z	BRe E86243 lined maroon, Parcels Express Sp Ed (ModelZone) - 10	20	26

BR general utility van [C13]

Cat No	Description		
39-272B	BR M86531 blue+grey Express Parcels - 10	16	23
39-272C	BR M86893 blue+grey W - 12	23	29
39-274	BR E93326 blue+grey, Motorail - 10	16	23
39-274A	BR E93736 blue+grey W Inter-City Motorail - 12	23	29
(39-000L)	BR ? blue+grey W Newspapers, see C12m	20	NA
(39-000L)	BR ? blue+grey W see C12m	20	NA
39-272	BR 95211 blue Newspapers NLX - 07	15	21
39-272A	BR W86479 blue Express Parcels - 09	15	22
39-272C	BR ? blue W - 12	23	29
39-270	BR W86078 blue Express Parcels - 07	15	21
39-270	RES 95199 red+dark grey NOX - 07	15	21
39-270A	BR 95146 red+dark grey NOX - 10	16	23
39-270Z	NSE 93852 bright blue Sp Edn 504 (The Signalbox) - 08	18	24
39-276	BR InterCity Motorail ? grey - 13	NPG	NPG
39-275	Royal Mail 93845 bright red - 13	NPG	NPG
39-270Y	Satlink KDB977557 red+yellow Sp Edn 504 (Model Rail) - 07	20	25

C14.   BR Mk1 TPO Sorting Van (POS) (2010)

This was used in a Travelling Post Office (TPO) and, during the journey, Royal Mail staff sort the mail ready for dropping off at points along the route. 96 of these vehicles were built by British Rail in small batches between 1959 and 1977, all to similar designs and based on the Mk1 coach. The early batches featured catching nets, which allowed mail bags to be collected from lineside apparatus while the train was still moving. Bags of sorted mail were also dropped off without a need for the train to stop. From the beginning of 1972, this practice was abandoned and the apparatus removed. However, being able to sort mail on the train was a great time saver and gave rail an advantage over road transport. Under the TOPS system the vans were coded 'NS'.

The Bachmann models, were initially produced exclusively for ModelZone stores and are based on diagram 720.

Cat No	Description		
39-420W	BR/Royal Mail W80300 red (late '50s) Sp Edn (ModelZone) - 10	28	32
39-420	BR/Royal Mail W80301 red (late '50s) - 11	30	36
39-420A	BR/Royal Mail W90300 red (late '50s) - 13	30	39
39-421	BR/Royal Mail W? red with nets - 13	NPG	43
39-420X	BR M80300 blue+grey (late '60s > late '80s) Sp Edn (ModelZone) - 10	28	32
39-425	BR M80301 blue+grey (late '60s > late '80s) - 11	30	36
39-426	BR M? blue+grey with nets - 13	NPG	43

BR MK1 Royal Mail travelling post office sorting van [C14]

Cat No	Description		
39-420Y	Royal Mail W80300 red (late '80s > early '90s) Royal Mail Letters, BR1 bogies, Sp Edn (ModelZone) - 10	28	32
39-430	Royal Mail 80301 red (late '80s > early '90s) Royal Mail Letters, BR1 bogies - 11	30	36
39-420Z	Royal Mail TPO80305 red (early '90s > 2004), Royal Mail Travelling Post Office B4 bogies, Sp Edn (ModelZone) - 10	28	32
39-435	Royal Mail TPO 80301 red (early '90s > 2004), Royal Mail Travelling Post Office B4 bogies - 11	30	36

C15a.   BR Mk1 TPO Stowage Van (POT) (2013)

A total of 40 Mk1 Post Office Stowage vans were built between 1954 and 1977. Most were built at York and a few at Wolverton but some were put out to private contractors, the principal one being Metro-Cammell who built 11 of them. Most contained a clear open space and high security sliding doors.

Cat No	Description		
39-750	BR Post Office ? red (as preserved) - 13	NPG	40
39-755	BR ? blue+grey - 13	NPG	40
39-760	Royal Mail (large Letters) ? red - 13	NPG	40
39-765	EWS Royal Mail ? red - 13	NPG	40

C15b.   BR Mk1 TPO Brake Stowage Van (BPOT) (2014)

Due to the need for guards accommodation on trains formed only of Post Office stock, a small batch of Stowage Vans was built with these facilities, which avoided the need to use passenger coaching stock. The vehicles were introduced in 1968, to diagram 733, in BR blue and grey livery, adopting both versions of the Royal Mail red in later years. They were withdrawn in 2003-04 and some vehicles have since been preserved.

Cat No	Description		
39-440Z	BR Post Office 80458 red (1960s as preserved) - 14	NPG	40
39-440Y	BR ? blue+grey (1970s NUX) - 14	NPG	40
39-440X	Royal Mail (large Letters) ? red 1980s NUX) - 14	NPG	40
39-440W	EWS Royal Mail ? red (1990s NUX) - 14	NPG	40

C16.   BR Mk1 CCT Parcels Van (2014)

The BR Mk1 4-wheel CCT is a much requested van, which was a common sight on the railway network. Used primarily for parcels traffic, many survived in departmental service

8th Edition

Bachmann Branchline

long after their parcel carrying days had ended.
 The van was commissioned by ModelZone and had not been released at the time of writing.

39-550Z	BR ? maroon - 14	NPG	20
39-551Z	BR ? blue - 14	NPG	20
39-552Z	BR ? blue Express Parcels W - 14	NPG	22
39-553Z	BR RCT ? red+blue Lt Edn 750 - 14	NPG	20
39-554Z	NR ? yellow rerailing Ltd Edn 750 - 14	NPG	20
39-555Z	BR Red Star ? blue Ltd Edn 500 - 14	NPG	20

C17. BR Mk1 Horsebox (2013)

This model is based on the standard horse boxes built using Mk1 coach principals and with accommodation for the grooms. The highly detailed model was commissioned by TMC but the tooling remained Bachmann property and available for them to use after an agreed period.

38-525Z	BR E96330 maroon Sp Edn 504 (TMC) - 13	20	25
-	BR E96346 maroon	20	NA
-	BR E96326 maroon	20	NA
38-525Y	above two models Sp Edn 504 (TMC) - 13	NA	49
38-525X	BR E96307 maroon Sp Edn 504 (TMC) - 13	20	25
38-526Z	BR S96359 green Sp Edn 504 (TMC) - 13	20	25
	BR S96366 green	20	NA
-	BR S96413 green	20	NA
38-526Y	above two models Sp Edn 504 (TMC) - 13	NA	49
38-526X	BR S96369 green (as presereved at the NRM) Sp Edn 504 (TMC) - 13	20	25
38-526W	BR S96403 green W (with chalk markings '4 Bales') Sp Edn 504 (TMC) - 13	22	27

Mk1 Pullman Stock

In 1948, the British Railways Board (BRB) took over responsibility for existing contracts with the Pullman Car Company. It purchased the ordinary shares in 1954, but the remaining preference shares were not acquired by the BRB until 1962, from which time the Pullman Car Company was a subsidiary of the board and fully nationalised.

 Unhappy about the great age of the Pullman cars being used on the East Coast services, it was decided to build some new ones and they would be based on the standard Mk1 coach design but with certain modifications to satisfy Pullman shareholders. This included recessed doors.

 The models of them, produced by Bachmann, have metal bearings within the bogie face and foil-plated window frames. The table lamps have fibre optic lighting, which light up when power is applied to the track.

C18a. BR Mk1 Pullman Kitchen 1st (FK) (2005)

There were 13 of the kitchen first cars built and all were given their names. They initially seated 20 passengers but, following refurbishment in 1967-68, it was possible to seat 26. Four of the seats were in the traditional Pullman coupe. There was a kitchen and servery at one end and a toilet at the other.

BR MK1 Pullman kitchen 1st [C18a]

39-280	BR Eagle brown+cream - 05	21	27
39-280A	BR Magpie brown+cream - 08	22	28
39-280B	BR Falcon brown+cream - 10	22	28
39-281	BR E315E grey+blue - 07	21	27
39-281A	BR E313E grey+blue - 11	26	32
39-281A	BR E325E grey+blue - 12	NPG	NPG
39-290Z	BR RTC Wren RDB975427 Laboratory 14 red+blue Sp Edn 504 (ModelZone) - 09	25	32

C18b. BR Mk1 Pullman Parlour 1st (FP) (2005)

A total of 8 of these were built and given the names of precious and semiprecious stones. As originally built, they had seating for 24 passengers in two banks of single seats facing in pairs across a table. With falling business, this was felt to be a wasteful use of space and the seating was doubled up down one side, bringing the capacity to 29. There was a coupe at one end and a lavatory at both ends of the car.

39-290	BR Emerald brown+cream - 05	21	27
39-290A	BR Amber brown+cream - 08	22	28
39-290B	BR Amethyst brown+cream - 10	22	28
39-291	BR E326E grey+blue - 07	21	27
39-291A	BR E327E grey+blue - 12	30	36
-	BR E353E blue+grey - 11	30	NA
-	BR E347E blue+grey - 11	30	NA
39-001z	above 2 coaches Sp Edn 512 (ModelZone) - 11	NA	72

C18c. BR Mk1 Pullman Kitchen 2nd (SK) (2005)

15 Pullman kitchen 2nds were built and these had seating for 30 passengers arranged in 1+2 (with tables) formation. There was a kitchen and servery at one end and a toilet at the other end. There were no coupes in the second class cars.

39-300	BR Car No.332 brown+cream - 05	21	27
39-300A	BR Car No.333 brown+cream - 08	22	28
39-300B	BR Car No.334 brown+cream - 10	20	30
39-300C	BR Car No.335 brown+cream - 12	30	36
39-301	BR E334E grey+blue - 06	21	27
39-301A	BR E332E grey+blue - 12	30	36

BR MK1 Pullman parlour 2nd [C18c]

C18d. BR Mk1 Pullman Parlour 2nd (SP) (2005)

7 Pullman parlour 2nds were built and had 42 seats in 1+2 (with tables) formation. There was a toilet adjacent to the end vestibule at each end. These later became open first class accommodation.

39-310	BR Car No.347 brown+cream - 05	21	27
39-310A	BR Car No.348 brown+cream - 08	22	28
39-310B	BR Car No. 349 brown+cream - 10	22	28
39-311	BR E352E grey+blue - 07	21	27
39-311A	BR E347E grey+blue - 12	30	36

C18e. BR Mk1 Pullman Bar 2nd (BSP) (2005)

This was a one-off vehicle which, when renumbered as M354E, received the name 'The Nightcap Bar'. It had seating for 24 passengers arranged in 1+2 (with tables) formation. There was also a lavatory at one end of the car.

39-320	BR The Hadrian Bar brown+cream - 05	21	27
39-320A	BR The Hadrian Bar brown+cream - 10?	26	32
39-321	BR M354E Nightcap Bar blue+grey - 07	21	27

Mk2 Main Line Stock

These had rounded ends, pressure ventilation and were of semi-integral construction. They had tungsten lighting and ran on B4 bogies. In the second class vehicles there was a different seating design and fluorescent lighting. Internal finishes were in wood and these Mk2 coaches were built between 1964 and 1966.

 Production then moved on to Mk2As which had aluminium compartment doors and partitions. They also had a new design of first class seating, sliding gangway doors were replaced by fold-away ones which were painted lime green and the toilets had foot pedal flushing. The Mk2As were made in 1967 and 1968.

 Production next moved on to air-conditioned Mk2F coaches, which had no opening toplights. The windows were long but shallow, looking completely different from those of the earlier Mk2s.

C19a. BR Mk2 Corridor 1st (FK) (2006)

These were built in 1963 and 1964 at BR Derby Carriage & Wagon Works. They have been scrapped now but the prototype coach is in the National Railway Museum.

BR MK2 corridor 1st [C19a]

39-332	BR E13373 maroon - 06	15	22
39-332A	BR W13432 maroon - 10	16	23
39-333	BR S13389 green - 06	15	22
39-333A	BR S13401 green - 10	16	23

Bachmann Branchline

39-330	**BR** S13393 blue+grey - *06*	15	22
39-330A	**BR** S13388 blue+grey - *10*	16	23
39-331	**BR IC** ? blue+grey – *made?*	NPG	NPG
39-330Z	**BR RTC** ADB975290 Test Car 6 red+blue Sp Edn 504 (ModelZone) - *12*	26	32

C19b. BR Mk2A Corridor 1st (FK) (2006)
Also built by BR Derby Carriage & Wagon Works, these were constructed in 1968. Many of them have found their way onto preserved lines. Others were renumbered in the 194xx sequence and some became departmental stock.

39-340	**BR** E13472 blue+grey - *06*	15	22
39-340A	**BR** E13468 blue+grey - *12*	22	28
39-341	**BR Inter-City** W13456 blue+grey - *06*	15	22
39-342	**NSE** 13443 bright blue - *06*	15	22
(39-000N)	**BR Trans-Pennine** 13445 blue+grey ex-coach pack Sp Edn (*Model Rail* magazine) - *12*	28	NA

C19c. BR Mk2 Open 2nd (TSO) (2006)
These were built between 1965 and 1968 at BR Derby Carriage & Wagon Works. A lot of the early members of the class were scrapped but many others have been preserved at heritage sites and a few were transferred to the Engineers Department. In the 2nd class vehicles, there was a different seating design and fluorescent lighting.

39-350	**BR** M5082 blue+grey - *06*	15	22
39-351	**BR Inter-City** E5311* blue+grey - *06*	15	22
39-352	**BR NSE** 5162 bright blue - *06*	15	22
(39-000N)	**BR Trans-Pennine** 5321 blue+grey ex-coach pack Sp Edn (*Model Rail* magazine) - *12*	28	NA
-	**BR** 5230 *Corriemoillie* green+cream TSO(T)	25	NA
-	**BR** 5212 *Capercaillie* green+cream	25	NA
-	**BR** 5166 *Clan MacKenzie* green+cream	25	NA
39-000T	above 3 coaches Sp Edn 500 (Model Rail) - *08*	NA	NPG
-	**BR** W5261 blue+grey NSE branded	20	NA
-	**BR** W5308 blue+grey NSE branded	20	NA
39-001T	above 2 Network SouthEast branded coaches Sp Edn 500 (Kernow Model Rail Centre) - *12*	NA	60
-	**BR** W5392 blue+grey ScotRail branded	20	NA
-	**BR** W5270 blue+grey ScotRail branded	20	NA
39-001U	above 2 ScotRail branded coaches Sp Edn 500 (Kernow Model Rail Centre) - *12*	NA	60
-	**BR** 977387 Brake Force Runner blue+grey (former brake end)	30	NA
-	**BR** 977337 Brake Force Runner blue+grey (former open coach)	30	NA
39-350Z	above 2 mobile track assessment coaches Sp Edn 504 (ModelZone) - *12*	NA	65

* Wrongly given a Mk2A number.

C19d. BR Mk2A Standard Open (TSO) (2006)
These were built at BR Derby Carriage & Wagon Works in 1967 and 1968. A greater proportion of these were scrapped with fewer going into preservation. Some, however, were exported to Ireland for re-gauging.

39-360	**BR** 5353 blue+grey - *06*	15	22
39-360A	**BR** E5284 blue+grey - *12*	22	28
39-360B	**BR** E5266 blue+grey - *12*	22	28
39-361	**BR Inter-City** E5361 blue+grey - *06*	15	22
39-362	**BR NSE** 5410 bright blue - *06*	15	22
39-363	**BR NSE** ? bright blue - *13*	NPG	NPG
-	**Regional Railways** 5316 blue+pale grey	20	NA
-	**Regional Railways** 5341 blue+pale grey	20	NA
39-000H	above two models in a twin pack, Sp Edn 500 (*Model Rail*) - *10*	NA	50
(39-000M)	**Regional Railways** 5385 blue+pale grey ex-pair with BSK 35510, Sp Edn (*Model Rail*) - *10*	20	NA

BR MK2A standard open [C19d]

C19e. BR Mk2 Brake Open 2nd (BSO) (2006)
These are from a batch of brake standard open coaches built at BR Derby Carriage & Wagon Works in 1966. Some were converted to brake standard micro-buffet open coaches between 1983 and 1986 and both converted and original coaches will be found on heritage lines.
MTA = mobile track assessment train

BR MK2 brake open 2nd [C19e]

39-370	**BR** E9399 blue+grey - *06*	15	22
39-371	**BR Inter City** E9400 blue+grey - *06*	15	22
39-372	**BR NSE** 9409 bright blue - *06*	15	22
(39-000T)	**BR** 9385 *Balmacara* green+cream Sp Edn 500 (*Model Rail*) - *08*	25	NA
39-370Z	**Network Rail** DB977337 yellow test coach Sp Edn (*Model Rail*) - *10*	20	28
-	**DRS** (compass) 9419 blue BSO	20	NA
-	**DRS** (compass) 9428 blue BSO	20	NA
39-000D	above two nuclear train support vehicles, Sp Edn (*Model Rail*) - *10*	NA	50

C19f. BR Mk2A Brake Open 2nd (BSO) (2006)
Also built at BR Derby Carriage & Wagon Works, these brake standard open coaches were out-shopped in 1967 and 1968. Some were converted to barrier vehicles for Mk4s and DMUs.

39-390	**BR** blue+grey - *not made*	NA	NA
39-391	**BR** IC grey - *not made?*	NA	NA
39-380	**BR** E9430 blue+grey - *06*	15	22
39-380A	**BR** E9418 blue+grey - *12*	22	28
39-381	**BR Inter City** Sc9424 blue+grey - *06*	15	22
39-382	**BR NSE** 9422 bright blue - *06*	15	22
39-000M	**Regional Railways** 35510 blue+pale grey BSK, ex-pair with TSO 5385, Sp Edn (*Model Rail*) - *10*	20	NA
39-381Z	**BR ScotRail** Sc9423 blue+pale grey Sp Edn 500 (Kernow Model Rail Centre) - *12*	25	30

C19g. BR Mk2 Brake Corridor 1st (BFK) (2006)
Built at Derby between 1966 and 1968, most of the Mk2 brake 1st corridor coaches were renumbered in the 17xxx sequence. Only a few were preserved.

39-400	**BR** 14033 blue+grey - *06*	15	22
39-401	**BR Inter City** 14080 blue+grey - *06*	15	22
39-401	**BR Regional Railways** blue+grey - *not made*	NA	NA
39-402	**NSE** 17040 bright blue - *06*	15	22

C19h. BR Mk2A Brake Corridor 1st (BFK) (2006)
These were built at BR Derby Carriage & Wagon Works in 1967 and 1968. Again, only a few were preserved. One lucky one was chosen for the Venice-Simplon Orient Express.
  The roof vents on models released early were incorrect and this was put right on subsequent batches.

39-410	**BR** 17063 blue+grey - *06*	15	22
39-411	**BR Inter City** 17093 blue+grey - *06*	15	22
39-421	**BR Regional Railways** blue - *not made*	NA	NA
39-432	**BR NSE** bright blue - *not made*	NA	NA
39-412	**NSE** 17079 bright blue - *06*	15	22
39-411Y	**BR NSE** 17070 blue+pale grey Sp Edn 500 (Kernow Model Rail Centre) - *12*	25	30

C19i BR Mk2z Test Coaches (2008)
These are former brake 2nd open vehicles.

-	**BR IC** DB977377 modified blue+grey MTA (dormitory coach)	20	NA
-	**BR IC** DB977378 modified blue+grey MTA (brake & stores coach)	20	NA
39-000S	above two coaches Sp Edn (ModelZone) - *08*	NA	55

C19j BR Mk2 Irish Coaches (2006)
These were produced for sale by Murphy Models of Dublin.

8th Edition   Visit the BRM website at: www.model-railways-live.co.uk

Bachmann Branchline

(MM4101)	**IR** 4101 orange+black - 06	18	NA
(MM4101)	**IR** 4108 orange+black - 06	18	NA
MM4101	above 2 coaches Sp Edn 504 (Murphy Models)	NA	50
(MM4101)	**IR** 4101 orange+black - 06	18	NA
(MM4101)	**IR** 4108 orange+black - 06	18	NA
MM4101	above 2 coaches Sp Edn 504 (Murphy Models)	NA	50
(MM4108)	**IE** 4101 orange+black - 06	18	NA
(MM4108)	**IE** 4108 orange+black - 06	18	NA
MM4108	above 2 coaches Sp Edn 504 (Murphy Models)	NA	50
(MM4110)	**IE** 4102 orange+black - 06	18	NA
(MM4110)	**IE** 4110 orange+black - 06	18	NA
MM4110	above 2 coaches Sp Edn 504 (Murphy Models)	NA	50
MM1072	**RPSI** 301 green (Mk2 TSO 2nd class) Sp Edn 500 (Murphy Models) - 08	25	NA
MM1071	**RPSI** 180 green (Mk2A FK 1st class) Sp Edn 500 (Murphy Models) - 08	25	NA
MM1073	**RPSI** 460 green (Mk2 BSO brake) Sp Edn 500 (Murphy Models) - 08	25	NA

<u>Mk2F Main Line Stock</u>
The Mk2Fs were introduced in 1973 and used the interior design of the Mk3s, which had been built the previous year for the High Speed Train (HST). However, the Mk2Fs had the external appearance of the Mk2Ds (modelled by Airfix and now by Hornby), which were introduced to the national network in 1970. They therefore had air-conditioning and long shallow windows, first seen on the Mk2Ds. Internally they had plastic panels and Inter-City seating. At the time of writing, these models have yet to be released.

C20a. BR Mk2F Open 1st FO (2013)
These were built at Derby in 1973 and contained 42 first class seats and two toilets. The seating was 2+1 with tables and an off-centre isle. Exit doors were at both ends of the coach.

39-650	**BR** ? blue+grey - 13	NPG	30
39-650DC	**BR** ? blue+grey, DCC chip fitted - 13	NPG	NPG
39-652	**BR InterCity** ? grey - 13	NPG	30
39-652DC	**BR InterCity** ? grey, DCC chip fitted - 13	NPG	NPG

C20b. BR Mk2F Tourist Open TSO (2013)
These were built at Derby from 1973 and have a cental isle with 2+2 seating at tables. Each coach contains 64 second class seats and two toilets, with a vestibule and outside doors at both ends.

39-675	**BR** ? blue+grey - 13	NPG	30
39-675DC	**BR** ? blue+grey, DCC chip fitted - 13	NPG	NPG
39-677	**BR InterCity** ? grey - 13	NPG	30
39-677DC	**BR InterCity** ? grey, DCC chip fitted - 13	NPG	NPG

C20c. BR Mk2F Restauvant 1st RFB (2013)
Converted at Derby in 1988 from former first open coaches, these had 26 first class seats and a toilet. The seating was in 2+1 format with tables and the coach consequently had an off-centre isle. The rest of the coach was taken up with the buffet area and corridor.

39-685	**BR** ? blue+grey - 13	NPG	30
39-685DC	**BR** ? blue+grey, DCC chip fitted - 13	NPG	NPG
39-686	**BR InterCity** ? grey - 13	NPG	30
39-686DC	**BR InterCity** ? grey, DCC chip fitted - 13	NPG	NPG

C20d. BR Mk2F Brake Standard Open BSO (2013)
These were built at Derby from 1974 and half the coach was taken up with an open seating area with 32 second class seats and a toilet. The seating was in 2+2 formation with tables and the rest of the coach contained the guard's cabin, a corridor and luggage space. There were doors to the outside at both ends of the seating area and double doors both sides of the luggage area.

39-700	**BR** ? blue+grey - 13	NPG	30
39-700DC	**BR** ? blue+grey, DCC chip fitted - 13	NPG	NPG
39-701	**BR InterCity** ? grey - 13	NPG	30
39-701DC	**BR InterCity** ? grey, DCC chip fitted - 13	NPG	NPG

C20e. BR Mk2F Driving Brake 2nd Open DBSO (2013)
These were built at Derby in 1974 and had the same layout as a BSO but with a driving cab in the far end of the luggage space.

39-725DC	**BR** ? blue+grey, DCC chip fitted - 13	NPG	NPG
39-726DC	**BR ScotRail** ? grey, DCC chip fitted - 13	NPG	NPG

Virgin Trains 'Voyager' trailer car [C21]

C21. 'Voyager' Centre Car (2005)
When Virgin introduced the 'Voyager' trains to their Cross-Country franchise, they ran as 5-car sets. The sets sold by Bachmann consist of either 3 or 4 cars. The coaches in this table allow you to complete sets.

30-625	**Virgin** 60217 (*Bombardier Voyager*) red+silver - 05	20	25
30-625A	**Virgin** 60708 (*Welsh Dragon*) red+silver - 07, 09	20	26

WAGONS
As with the locomotives and coaches, wagons started with Mainline originals reproduced in a selection of new liveries. A new development was the sets of themed coal wagons and petrol tankers which are likely to become more collectable than single wagons.

The Blue Riband wagons are amongst the best ready-to-run wagons available to 00 modellers and the range is expanding fast. Besides the greater body and chassis detail, the private owner open wagons now have the more correct 9ft wheelbase instead of the 10ft one. There have been many commissioned models (nearly all private owner open wagons) and some of these are already much sought after by collectors.

Several wagons were issued with detachable loads. These containers, transformers and boilers, used as loads on wagons in some cases, were also sold separately as accessories.

Confusion surrounds some of the wagons produced in 2000 and 2001 particularly as far as their catalogue numbering goes. This is because when ordered they were allocated a 33-XXX number but by the time they arrived their specification had been raised to that of the Blue Riband range although they had not been given catalogue numbers in the 37-XXX series.

NPCCS - A fundamental change in this edition is that the non-passenger carrying coaching stock, that was previously listed here under wagons, is now with the coaches.

Wagon Numbers - WARNING! Some of the numbers on wagons seen in catalogues are not the same as the ones carried by the models when they arrive.

Missing Wagons - People are often confused at not finding listed here certain wagons which have 'Bachmann Hong Kong' on the underside of the chassis. It could be that they will be found in the chapter titled **'Replica Railways'**. This is because the early Replica Railways models were made by Kader in Hong Kong who also owned and made Bachmann. To avoid making a new chassis for the wagons that Replica had ordered, they used ones from the Bachmann production line - thus the confusion.

Set of 3 - A lot of wagons are sold in sets of three different models. If you cannot find your model in the table you expect, have a look in the 'sets' tables. Also, the Midlander commissioned a number of private owner wagons for delivery in 2000 but the order was cancelled and the batches were split up to be sold by several other retailers. The supplier is shown as 'various' in the tables.

Prices - As we have seen, there is a rising demand for Bachmann's private owner open wagons and 14T tank wagons which is spilling over onto other wagons in the Bachmann range. Prices quoted are often based on actual prices achieved on eBay. Especially high climbers are wagons commissioned for release at Warley shows.

Bachmann Branchline

| Cat No. | Company, Number, Colour, Date | £ | £ |

Flat Wagons

W1a. 'Conflat A' (1996)

The 'Conflat A' was a post-war Swindon design and the first 400 were built at Swindon and Wolverton. Over the next ten years, 200,000 of them were built, most of them during the BR era. There is little difference between the GWR and BR versions.

This table includes the unloaded Conflat A' with its early underframe. Partly to economise on packaging, as one looked lost in a box on its own, the models were sold in pairs, carrying different numbers. Correctly boxed pairs are not easy to find. The Bachmann 'Conflat A' can be told apart from the Airfix one in having six pairs of fixing rings along the side of the body compared with four single rings on the Airfix wagon. There are of course other differences.

Cat No.	Description	£	£
-	**BR** B702201 brown - *96*	8	NA
-	**BR** B706709 brown - *96*	8	NA
33-335	above 2 'Conflats' - *96*	NA	18
-	**BR** B505461 brown - *98*	8	NA
-	**BR** B505432 brown - *98*	8	NA
33-335A	above 2 'Conflats' - *98*	NA	18

W1b. 'Conflat A' + BD Container (1995)

Each of the four railway companies had a door-to-door service, for house moving, using their own road vehicles and flat railway wagons to achieve this. This required co-operation between the companies as the road delivery at the other end might well involve the use of vehicles of a different company. Containers had their own number codes but, under BR, the containers in this table became known as 'B' type and a general merchandise container was a 'BD'. The 'Conflats' were XP rated for speedy distribution and containers were transferred between rail and road by a yard crane and so they had shackles in the roof for lifting chains to be attached.

In the following table we have the early 'Conflat' model (with its simpler underframe) and BD container.

GWR 'Conflat' with 'Door to Door' container [W1b]

33-329	**GW** 36876 dark grey + **GWR** dark brown container B1775 - *95*	10	12
33-325	**BR** B704789 brown + **BR** brown container BD42724B - *not made*	NA	NA
33-325	**BR** B704739 brown + **BR** brown container BD46724B - *95*	10	12
33-325A	**BR** B701283 brown + **BR** brown container BD46541B - *98*	9	11
33-326	**BR** B506033 brown + **BR** maroon container BD6600B - *95*	10	12
33-326A	**BR** B702326 brown W + **BR** maroon W container BD6698B - *99*	9	11

W1c. 'Conflat A' + AF Container (1995)

The small size container could be fitted two to a 'Conflat' and were known as 'A' type. The 'AF' container was for quick-frozen foods, ice cream etc. and had a rubber-sealed floating door. It could maintain a temperature of -15°F for 24 hours. There were doors at only one end.

The models in this table use the early 'Conflat A', with its simpler underframe, and with AF and AFU containers as a load. The latter were pallet containers, being fitted with eutectic plates.

BR 'Conflat A' & 2 AFU containers [W1c]

33-327	**BR** B703760 brown + **BR** light blue container AF66008B - *95*	10	12
33-327A	**BR** B704933 brown + **BR** light blue containers AF65137B + AF66187B - *98*	9	11
33-328	**BR** B704477 brown + **BR** white container AF65098B - *95*	10	12
33-330	**BR** B702201 brown + **BR** white containers AFU16320B, AFU16327B - *?*	10	12
33-330	**BR** B503829 brown + **BR** white containers AFU1632CB, AFU16327B - *96*	10	12

W1d. 'Conflat A' (2001)

When the improved Blue Riband 'Conflat A' wagon appeared in 2001, it too was sold in differently numbered pairs and these are tabled here.

1	**BR** B709437 brown Conflat A	9	NA
2	**BR** B737642 brown Conflat A	9	NA
37-980	above two wagons - *01*	NA	18
1	**BR** brown Conflat A	NA	NA
2	**BR** brown Conflat A	NA	NA
37-980A	above two wagons - *not made*	NA	NA
1	**BR** 704762 brown Conflat A	NPG	NA
2	**BR** ? brown Conflat A	NPG	NA
37-983	above two wagons - *13*	NA	NPG

37-980Z	**BR** TDB708135 pale yellow shunter's running wagon 'Norwich Loco' Sp Edn 500 (Pennine Models) - *01*	18	24
37-980Y	**BR** TDB736237 grey W shunter's running wagon (Hull Paragon Station 1981) Sp Edn 504 (TMC) - *11*	16	20
37-980W	**BR** TDB702702 yellow shunter's running wagon Sp Edn 504 (TMC) * - *13*	10	13

* Weathered versions have been produced by TMC.

W1e. 'Conflat A' + BD Container (2001)

As with the earlier 'Conflat A', the Blue Riband version of 2001 was matched with Bachmann's BD type container as listed below. Some second-hand BD containers ended up on the Isle of Man in 1967, providing a container service between Douglas and the port of Castletown. The Bachmann Man-tainor container was based on a photograph of one of these taken in 1968.

(30-075)	**GWR** 39612 light grey + **GWR** dark brown (shirt button) container B-1788 ex-Local Freight set - *10*	9	NA
37-950	**BR** B708315 brown + **BR** grey+yellow '**Speedfreight**' container BD47381B - *01*	9	11
37-950A	**BR** B505569 brown + **BR** grey+yellow '**Speedfreight**' container BD46491B - *05*	9	11
37-952	**BR** B737642 brown + **BR** grey+yellow '**Speedfreight**' container BD46491B - *05*	9	11
37-950Z	**BR** B705400 brown + '**Man-Tainor**' yellow+red container BD.105 Sp Edn 500 (Model Rail) - *05*	22	30

Bachmann Branchline

'Conflat A' with Man-tainor container [W1e]

BR 'Conflat A' with weathered AF container [W1f]

37-951	**BR** B705549 brown + **BR** maroon container BD48964B - *01*		9	11
37-951A	**BR** B704954 brown + **BR** maroon container BD479301B - *not made*		NA	NA
37-951A	**BR** B709708 brown + **BR** maroon container BD50150B - *05*		9	11
37-951B	**BR** B709076 brown + **BR** maroon container BD50165B - *10*		6	8
37-951C	**BR** B709007 brown + **BR** maroon container BD50311B - *11*		6	8
37-951D	**BR** B? brown + **BR** red container BD?B - *11*		7	9
-	**BR** B708303 brown W + **BR** brown W container BD46023B		8	NA
-	**BR** B708778 brown W + **BR** brown W container BD48488B		8	NA
-	**BR** B709179 brown W + **BR** brown W container BD50252B		8	NA
37-950Y	above 3 weathered wagons Sp Edn 1004 (ModelZone) - *11*		NA	31
-	**BR** 705490 brown W + **BR** maroon W container BD46233B		9	NA
-	**BR** 707707 brown W + **BR** maroon W container BD49109B		9	NA
-	**BR** 709009 brown W + **BR** maroon W container BD48848B		9	NA
37-982	above 3 weathered wagons with containers - *13*		NA	39

W1f. 'Conflat A' + AF Containers (2001)

Here we have the Blue Riband 'Conflat' with the half-size AF containers, either singly or in pairs.

37-975	**GW** 39354 dark grey + **GWR** white container AF-2098 - *01*		9	11
37-975A	**GW** 39326 dark grey + **GWR** white container AF-2111 - *05*		8	10
37-976	**BR** B704954 brown + **BR** white AF16098B + BR pale blue AF16392B containers - *01*		9	11
37-977	**BR** B706709 brown + **BR** pale blue container AF66008B - *08*		6	8
37-978	**BR** B734734 brown + **BR** pale blue container AF65999B - *12*		7	9
-	**BR** B740503 brown + 2 **'Birds Eye'** AFP66348B + AFP66358B		10	NA
-	**BR** B740736 brown + 2 **'Birds Eye'** AFP66390B + AFP66405B		10	NA
-	**BR** B740460 brown + 2 **'Birds Eye'** AFP66377B + AFP66378B		10	NA
37-975Z	above 3 wagons Sp Edn 504 (TMC) - *12*		NA	35
-	**BR** B505444 brown + **BR** pale blue W AF66108B		9	NA
-	**BR** B505544 brown + **BR** pale blue W AF66066B		9	NA
-	**BR** B505501 brown + **BR** pale blue W AF66021B		9	NA
37-981	above 3 weathered wagons with containers - *12*		NA	30

W1g. 'Conflat A' with BA Container

'Conflat' with improved chassis and sliding door container from Trix range.

37-985	**BR** B708315 brown + **BR** '**Speedfreight**' silver BA container - *not made*		NA	NA

W1h. 'Conflat A' with A Container (2013)

These containers were the wooden half-sized ones, with 'cupboard' doors and a dropdown flap at the ends and no side doors.

37-961	**BR** B707211 brown + **BRe** brown container A7579B 'door to door' - *not made*		NA	NA
37-961	**BR** B704762 brown + **BR** brown container A3391B 'door to door' - *13*		9	11
37-960	**BR** B707222 brown + **BR** maroon container A2575B - *13*		9	11

W2. GWR Shunter's Truck (2013)

These were allocated to individual yards and the name of the yard was painted on the sides of the central tool box. They had a short wheelbase and were built over a long period of time, some before 1900. Later ones were sometimes built on redundant chassis of other wagons.

The model was under development at the time of writing.

38-675	**GWR** 41736 dark grey 'Canons Marsh, Bristol' - *13*		NPG	12
38-676	**GWR** 41734 dark grey 'Newton Abbott' - *13*		NPG	12
38-677	**GWR** 94979 dark grey 'Old Oak Common' - *13*		NPG	12
38-678	**GWR** DW43960 dark grey 'Loco Dept.' - *13*		NPG	12
38-679	**GWR** DW41049 dark grey W 'Margam Jn' - *13*		NPG	12

W3. OTA BR Timber Carrier Wagon (2012)

The actual wagons were built to transport timber, which had been cut in the Scottish Highlands, to paper mills. Many ran in the livery of the paper company that was hiring the wagon, while others were in Railfreight red livery. By 1994, 165 of them were transferred to Transrail and thence to EWS. When built in the 1980s, most made use of the chassis of redundant air-braked open wagons (OCA) and, later, the chassis of VDA vans. Various batches were built and a variety of designs may be found, particularly regarding the number and arrangement of the stanchions.

The Bachmann model is based on a cut-down VDA van and is supplied with a lumber load.

OTA timber wagon [W3]

38-300	**BR Rft** 200974 red+grey with lumber load - *12*		17	20
38-301	**EWS** 200817 maroon with lumber load - *12*		17	20

Bachmann Branchline

Planked Open Wagons

W4a. 1-plank 10T/13T Wagon (ex-Mainline) (1990)

As its name implies, a 1-plank wagon had only a single narrow plank making up each side and this would be hinged along the bottom to allow it to drop down to make loading and unloading easier. All four railway companies had them and BR built 3150 'Lowfits', as they were called. The first 400 had wooden bodies but, after that, they were built in steel.

Bachmann have modelled a wooden bodied type, allowing it to be used for early liveries. The table here lists the wagons released without loads.

33-405	'Bath Stone Firms Ltd' 10T - cream - 97	14	16
33-401	'Corsham Quarrying Co.' 70 maroon - 92	12	15
33-400	'H Lees & Son' 101 red - 90	8	10
33-400A	'H Lees & Son' 96 red - 92	9	11
33-404	LMS 460531 brown - 97	8	10
33-402	BR M460648 brown Lowfit - 92	8	10
33-403	undecorated light grey - 91	5	7

W4b. 1-plank 12T Wagon + Vehicle Load (1997)

This table includes the original model with various vehicle loads, supplied from the Herpa range.

33-410	BR B450023 brown + white Ford Transit Van (Herpa) load - 97	13	15
33-411	BR B450050 brown, + blue or red Ford Capri (Herpa) load - 97	13	15
33-412	BR B450141 brown, + green Triumph TR3 (Herpa) load - 97	13	15

W4c. 1-plank 12T Wagon + Small Container (1991)

The original Bachmann 1-plank wagon came from Palitoy's Mainline Railways range and is listed here with the AF and AFU containers. The 1-plank wagon can represent an earlier container carrier than the 'Conflat A', which was a post-war design.

33-951	GW 70031 dark grey + GWR white container AF-2121 (box says LMS) - 91	10	12
33-953	LMS 209340 brown + LMS white container E5 - 93	10	12
33-950	BR B450027 brown + BR white container AFU16320B (box says LNER) - 91	10	12
33-952	BR B450300 brown + BR white container AF12 - 92	10	12

W4d. 1-plank Wagon 12T + Large Container (1992)

This is the early 1-plank model with the BD size container.

33-975	LMS 209341 grey + LMS maroon container BD1641 - 92	10	12
33-976	NE 203169 brown + LNER blue container BD1465 - 94	9	11
33-977	undecorated dark grey - not made *	NA	NA

* planned for the Crewe Open Day in 1996.

Private owner 1-plank wagon [W4e]

W4e. 1-plank 'Lowfit' Wagon (2001)

When Bachmann replaced the original 1-plank wagon model with the better detailed Blue Riband version, they resisted the temptation to produce the steel version and thereby kept their livery options open. To date, it has not been released with a load.

37-476	'H Lees & Sons' 105 red - 02	9	11
37-476A**	'Morris & Griffin' 1 brown - 03	8	10
37-475Z	G&KER 31 grey Sp Edn 504 (Toys 2 Save) - 03	11	13
37-475	LMS 200345 grey - 01	7	9
37-475A*	LMS 209346 grey - 03	6	8
37-478	LMS 460030 brown - 13	NPG	NPG
37-477	BR B450032 brown - 07	6	8
37-477A	BR B450262 brown - 09	5	7
37-477B	BR B450394 brown - 11	5	7
37-477C	BR B450130 brown - 13	6	8
37-479	BR B450270 brown - 13	6	8

* Boxes labelled 37-475. ** Also listed as 37-476B.

W5a. 3-plank Open Wagon (ex-Mainline) (1991)

The 3-plank wagon was a 'medium' goods wagon, as opposed to a low-sided one. But, despite this, amongst other things, it was used for the transportation of containers. They were particularly found on the LMS and had drop-down sides and fixed ends. New wagons to the LMS design continued to arrive in 1948 and 1949, totalling over 10,000 in all. In 1950 BR changed over to steel construction. They ended up as ballast carriers in the Engineers Department.

This model was originally tooled by Kader for the Mainline range and dates from 1982. It was an early re-release by Bachmann.

33-450	'Cammell Laird & Co.' 630 maroon - 92	9	11
33-451	'James Carter' 170 grey - 91	9	11
33-451A	'Evan Davies' 25 light grey - 96	9	11
33-450A	'Easter Iron Mines' 4 brown - 96	9	11
33-450Z	M&GN 470 brown + LNER container BD1466 On Loan to M&GN blue Sp Edn 500 (North Norfolk Railway) - 97	15	18
33-454	SR 62948 dark brown - 96	8	10
(30-200)*	LT BW231 dark grey ex-set - 91	15	NA
(30-077)	LT BW260 grey ex-'Midnight Metropolitan' train set - 13	12	NA
33-452	BR W36459 brown - 92	8	10
(30-100)	BR B478450 brown ex-set - 91	8	NA
33-453	undecorated light grey - 91	5	7

* Box unnumbered.

W5b. 3-plank Open Wagon (2001)

In 2001 the retooled Blue Riband model arrived, replacing the original one. The BR versions reflect the LMS origins.

(30-005)	'English China Clays' 490 red ex-set - 05	8	NA
37-925	'ICI Buxton Lime' 48 light grey - 02	9	11
37-928	'United Stone Firms' 41 pale grey - 05	8	10
37-933	LMS 471405 grey - 13	NPG	NPG
37-932	LMS ? brown - 13	NPG	NPG
37-926	BR M470105 brown - 01	7	9
37-926A*	BR M470105 brown (2nd batch) - 03	6	8
37-931	BR Departmental DM477207 olive green - 13	6	8

* No 'A' on box end label.

W5c. 3-plank Open Wagon + BD Container (2005)

This is the retooled model, upgraded to Blue Riband standard, now with a BD type container load.

LNER 3-plank with container [W5c]

37-929	NE 535962 brown + LNER dark blue container BD1460 - 05	8	10
37-927	BR M470105 brown + BR maroon container BD48592B - not made	NA	NA
37-927	BR B457200 brown + BR maroon container BD6534B - 05	8	10
37-930A	BR B457203 brown + BR brown container BD47324B - 10	6	8
37-930	BR M475184 brown + BR red container BD6534B - 08	7	9
37-930B	BR M457203? brown + BR red container BD50150B - 10	6	8
37-930C	BR M47197 brown + BR maroon container BD560151B - 12	8	10

8th Edition

Bachmann Branchline

W6a. 5-plank 13T China Clay Wagon + Hood (1991)

The model was based on real 13T china clay open wagons and those with a yellow stripe carried ball clay, which was of an inferior quality. The wagons were of a standard GWR design dating back to 1913 and BR made batches of them every year between 1954 and 1960. Wood had to be used in the construction to avoid rust contaminating the load.

The model was based on real china clay open wagons and correctly had an 9ft wheelbase. A larger one would not fit the turntable at the docks where the wagons were unloaded into ships. The hoods are made of stitched light blue canvas and kept in shape by a removable moulded plastic frame. The hoods are light blue and carry the English China Clay's logo.

33-075	BR B743267 brown - 91	9	12
33-075A	BR B743321 brown - 94	9	11
33-075B	BR B743169 brown W - 98	9	11
33-075C	BR B743197 brown W - 99	8	10
33-075D	BR B743615 brown W - 01	8	10
33-075E	BR B743124 brown W - not made	NA	NA
33-076	BR B743752 brown - 92	9	11
33-076A	BR B743238 brown - 94	9	11
33-076B	BR B743156 brown W - 98	9	11
33-076C	BR B743127 brown W - 99	8	10
33-076D	BR B743597 brown 7405 - 02	8	10
33-076E	BR B743597 brown - not made	NA	NA

China clay wagon with hood [W6a]

33-080	BR B743169 brown W - 04	7	9
33-080A	BR B743802 brown W 7405 - 09	6	7
33-080B	BR B743378 brown W 7405 - 10	6	8
33-080C	BR B743595 brown W 7405 - 11	6	8
33-080D	BR B743142 brown W 7405 - 13	7	9
33-081	BR B743141 brown W - 04	7	9
33-081A	BR B743420 brown W - 09	6	7
33-081B	BR B743155 brown W - 10	6	8
33-081C	BR B743053 brown W - 11	6	8
33-084	BR B? brown W - 13	NPG	NPG
33-085	BR B743357 brown W 7401 - 13	NPG	NPG
-	BR B743689 brown W	7	NA
-	BR B743790 brown W	7	NA
-	BR B743808 brown W	7	NA
33-080Y	above 3 wagons Sp Edn 512 (Kernow MRC) - 10	NA	30

W6b. 5-plank 13T China Clay Wagon Ex-hood (1992)

The hoods to protect the load were a much later addition on the real wagons and so it was logical for Bachmann to produce a range of clay wagons without hoods - including some GWR examples. Some wagons carried the yellow circuit working symbol.

33-078A*	GW 92873 dark grey (light grey inside) - 00	7	9
33-078B	GW 92947 dark grey W (heavy) - 02	7	9
33-079	GW 92971 dark grey - 96	8	10
33-079	BR B743096 grey - 03	6	8
33-079A	BR W42833 grey - 10	6	8
33-079B	BR W92810 grey 'Return to St Blazey' - 11	6	7
33-077	BR B743236 brown - 92	8	10
33-077A*	BR B743620 brown W - 00	7	9
33-077B	BR B743221 brown W 7449 - 02	7	9
33-078	BR P270732 brown - 92	8	10
33-082	BR B743357 brown W 7401 - 04	6	8
33-083	BR B? brown - 13	NPG	NPG

* No 'A' on box end label.

W7a. 5-plank Open Wagon (ex-Mainline) (1990)

5-plank wagons were considered to be 'high goods wagons' and were referred to as 'Highfits' or 'High NF'. Anything larger was probably specifically for the coal and mineral trade. They were once highly numerous and used for the transportation of general merchandise. They often had their load sheeted over and the British weather and the labour cost of protecting the load made them impractical and some were replaced by vans. Many were privately owned. Despite their decline in numbers, BR adopted outstanding orders from all four railway companies and these were not completed until the Summer of 1949. BR continued to produce 5-plank wagons until 1957 and these were based on an LMS design with pressed steel ends and many had tarpaulin bars ('Highbarfit').

The Bachmann model was based on a 17'6" planked open wagon and was originally tooled in 1976 by Kader for the Mainline Railways range, marketed by Palitoy. This table includes all the Bachmann models produced from that original tooling.

33-051	'Cefnmawr & Rhosymedre' 12 red - 92	10	12
33-054	'English China Clays' 490 red - 95	10	12
33-050	'Hinckley Gas Works' 4 red - 91	10	12
33-050A	'Pounsbery' 1 green, also ex 33-041set - 94	10	12

Original 5-plank wagon (10ft wheelbase) [W7a]

33-056	'Stevenson' 10 blue (see table W7c - 37-051) - not made	NA	NA
33-055	'Worcester New Coop' 20 red+black (see table W7c - 37-052) - not made	NA	NA
33-050Z	M&GN 822045 brown Sp Edn 500 (North Norfolk Railway) - 94	12	14
33-051A	SR 28422 dark brown (see table W5c - 37-050) - not made	NA	NA
33-052	BR Deptartmental DW280 dark grey - 90	8	10
33-053	unfinished light grey - 91	6	8

W7b. 5-plank Open Wagon - Steel Floor (1998)

When it came to replacing the original 5-plank wagon with a Blue Riband model, it was decided to produce two variants instead of the one design. Externally they look the same but, inside, one has the representation of a steel floor and the other, a wooden floor. This table lists the Blue Riband models with the representation of a steel floor.

37-026A	'Arenig Granite' 207 red - 03	7	9
37-033	'John Arnold & Sons' 156 red - 10	5	7
37-032	'Constable Hart' 1004 black ** - 07	8	10
37-034	'James Durnford' 30 black - 10	5	7
37-025A	'James Durnford' 37 black - 03	8	10
37-028	'ICI (Lime) Ltd' 3034 light grey * - 00	9	11
37-029	'Hopton-Wood Stone Firms' 2 grey - 00	9	11
37-025X	'WJ King' 38 black Sp Edn 504 (Buffers) - 06	9	11
37-031	'Lilleshall' 1750 red - 06	8	10
37-027A	'George Lovegrove' 215 red-brown - 03	8	10
37-038	'EB Mason' 26 grey - 13	NPG	NPG
37-027	'Penderyn Limestone' 336 grey - 99	9	11
37-025	'Quarrite' 306 red - 98	10	12
37-037	'Roberts' Tarmacadam' 461 black - 12	7	9
37-035	'Shap Tarred Granite' 354 black - 11	6	8
37-025Y	'SLB' 702 pale grey - (See under Covered Lime Wagon later in this section)	-	-
37-025Z	see below under 5-plank wagons with wooden floors	-	-
37-036	'Tarbitumac' 285 black - 11	6	8
37-026	'Tarslag' (1923) 836 grey - 98	10	12
37-030	'Harry Whitehouse' 16 red - 00	9	11

* Reappeared in 2004 in the 30-045 Digital Freight Set. ** Box label misprint 'SREEL' for 'STEEL'.

W7c. 5-plank Open Wagon - Wooden Floor (1998)

As explained in the introduction to the last table, there are two versions of the Blue Riband model of a 5-plank wagon. This table lists those with the representation of a wooden floor.

Bachmann Branchline

Cat. No.	Description	Price	
37-059	'Nathanial **Atrill**' 6 black - 07	8	10
37-062A	'Edwin W **Badland**' 50 grey - 12	7	9
(37-080N)	'S **Bookman**' 30 light grey Sp Edn (ModelZone) - 07	8	NA
37-050Z	'**Birmingham Railway Carriage & Wagon Co.**' 26892 brown Sp Edn (Warley MRC) - 00	30	38
37-050T	'A **Butler & Co.**' 6 black Sp Edn 500 (Pendon Museum) - 12	8	10
37-056Y	'**Cafferata**' 18 brown Sp Edn (Access Models) - 01	12	14
37-050V	'AF **Chainey**' 1 brown Sp Edn 504 (Buffers) - 06	10	12
(37-080P)	'**Chapman & Sons**' 22 black ex-pack - 06	8	NA

Replacement 5-plank wagon on 9ft wheelbase [W7c]

Cat. No.	Description	Price	
37-060	'R.Fred.**Cole**' 11 red - 08	7	9
37-064	'**Farndon**' 18 maroon - 13	NPG	NPG
37-050Z	'**Forfar Victoria Coal Society**' 24 dark brown Sp Edn 500 (Virgin Trains) - 05	22	30
37-050W	'**Goodland & Sons**' 1 black Sp Edn 504 (Buffers) - 06	8	10
37-056	'Joshua **Gray**' 3 red-brown also ex-set - 02	9	11
37-050Y	'TS **Hanson**' 1 red Sp Edn 500 (B&H Models) - 00	13	15
37-050W	'**Hill Craig**' 6 brown Sp Edn 500 (Harburn Hobbies) - 00	28	34
37-056Z	'**Hucknall**' 3422 red Sp Edn 500 (Sherwood Models) - 01	13	15
37-056W	'JC **Kew**' 14 grey Sp Edn (Access Models) - 01	12	14
37-050A*	'Hugh **Lumley**' 21 grey+red - 00	9	11
37-056A	'AE **Moody**' I dark brown - 03	8	10
37-050X	'**Newark Corporation**' 4 brown Sp Edn 500 (Access Models) - 00	13	15
37-025Z	'**Ogilvy Brothers**' 1 dark brown Sp Edn 500 (Virgin Trains) - 04	12	15
37-050X	'**Ralls & Son**' 51 grey Sp Edn 504 (Buffers) - 06	10	12
37-037	'**Roberts Tarmacadam**' 461 black - 12	7	9
37-062	'**Salt Union**' 91 grey - 10	5	7
37-050U	'J **Sheppard & Son**' 3 black Sp Edn 504 (Salisbury Model Centre) - 08	8	10
37-050A	'FH **Silvey**' 191 brown - not made	NA	NA
37-050B	'FH **Silvey**' 191 dark brown - 03	8	10
37-063	'J **Skinner**' 7 green - 11	6	8
37-051	'EA **Stevenson**' 10 blue - 98	7	9
37-057	'J&R **Stone**' 245 blue grey - 03	8	10
37-065	'**W** (Writhlington Kilmersdon Foxcote Collieries)' 91 maroon W - 13	NPG	NPG
37-055	'**Wadsworth & Sons**' 53 light grey - 00	9	11
37-050Y	'Fred **Whiteman**' 503 red-brown Sp Edn 500 (Virgin Trains) - 05	10	12
37-053	'JR **Wood**' 33 orange-yellow - 99	9	11
37-052	'**Worcester New Co-operative & Industrial Society**' 20 red - 98	9	11
37-050	SR 28422 dark brown - 99	7	9
37-054	**BR** P143165 grey - 99	7	9
37-058	**BR** M254661 grey - 06	6	8
37-061	**BR** M318256 grey - 09	7	9
37-061A	**BR** P252247 grey - 10	5	7
37-061B	**BR** M270335 grey - 11	6	8
37-061C	**BR** M360583 grey - 13	NPG	NPG

* No 'A' on the box end label.

W8a. 12T 'Shocbar VB' Shock Open Wagon (1992)

Shock-absorbing springs, to protect sensitive loads during shunting, were developed in the 1930s by the LMS, SR and GWR. The war stopped further development but new batches of wagons, so fitted, were beginning to appear in the lead up to Nationalisation. Some of the SR design carried a 'B' number prefix.

The three models listed in this table are of 'Shocbar VB' designs, two built in 1951 and the third in 1955 - all at Derby. This is the original Bachmann wagon of 1992 which had a sheet rail, shock-resisting chassis and was marked with three vertical stripes on each side and the ends.

Cat. No.	Description	Price	
33-225	**BR** B721326 brown Shock - 92	7	9
33-226	**BR** B721385 brown Hybar - 94	7	9
33-227	**BR** B724180 brown Hybar W - 94	7	9

W8b. 12T 'Shocbar VB' Shock Open Wagon (2006)

The Blue Riband version of the shock open wagon did not arrive until 2006 and was based on the same wagon design as the earlier model.

BR Shockbar VB wagon [W8b]

Cat. No.	Description	Price	
37-875	**BR** B721326 brown - not made	NA	NA
37-875	**BR** B722620 brown - 06	6	8
37-876	**BR** B721385 brown - not made	NA	NA
37-876	**BR** B723176 brown - 06	6	8
37-877	**BR** B721326 brown - 10	5	7
37-878	**BR** B723206 brown - 11	6	8
37-879	**BR** B? brown (late) - 13	NPG	NPG

W9a. 7-plank Open Wagon (ex-Mainline) (1991)

Coal mines had vast fleets of 7-plank wagons and many a local coal merchant had one or two. They were also owned by coal factors, who traded in coal on a large scale, supplying industry and ports and they all carried the livery of their owner or operator. At one time the 7-plank wagon was the most numerous type of wagon in Britain and almost all were involved in the coal business. Indeed, 75% of all privately owned wagons were operated by colliery companies. In the Second World War they were requisitioned and, with the nationalisation of the mines in 1947 and railways in 1948, they became state owned. A considerable number of them were acquired by the National Coal Board for internal use. Those that passed to British Railways were replaced by 16 ton all-steel mineral wagons so that, by the end of the '50s, few wooden 7-plank wagons remained on the railways.

The models in this table are those made from the original Mainline tooling of 1977 and reintroduced by Bachmann in 1991. They were replaced in 1998 with Blue Riband models.

Cat. No.	Description	Price	
33-105	'**Anderson**' Whitstable 76 brown - 95	10	13
33-101A	'**Barnsley Main**' 528 brown - 93	10	12
33-100U	'**Blidworth**' 2444 light grey Sp Edn 500 (The Midlander) - 97	14	16
33-100X	'**Bolsover**' 1190 brown Sp Edn 500 (The Midlander) - 96	14	16
33-100PP	'W **Clarke**' 100 red Sp Edn 500 (B&H Models) (also seen listed as 33-100c) - 96	14	16

Original 10ft 7-plank wagon [W9a]

Cat. No.	Description	Price	
33-100A	'JL **Davies**' 121 brown - 94	10	12
33-100T	'**Dinnington Main**' 641 blue Sp Edn 500 (Geoffrey Allison No3) - 97	14	16

8th Edition

Bachmann Branchline

Code	Description		
33-100XX	'**Eckington**' 2801 red-brown Sp Edn 500 (The Midlander) - *99*	13	15
33-100K	'**Firbeck**' 787 brown Sp Edn 500 (Geoffrey Allison) - *98*	18	30
33-104A	'**Flower & Sons**' 7 dark grey - *96*	10	12
33-100Q	'**Forth**' 104 light grey Sp Edn 500 (Harburn Hobbies No2) - *96*	16	21
33-100F	'WH **Garton**' 23 brown Sp Edn 500 (B&H Models) - *99*	13	15
33-100C	'**Gedling**' 2598 red Sp Edn 500 (Gee Dee Models No1) - *99*	13	15
33-100ZZ	'**Hardwick**' 637 brown Sp Edn 500 (The Midlander) - *99*	13	15
33-100	'**Hickleton**' 1408 red-brown - *91*	10	12
33-100D	'**Hucknall No1 Colliery**' 7071 brown Sp Edn 500 (Sherwood Models No1) - *99*	13	15
33-100H	'**Hull Corporation**' 112 light grey Sp Edn 500 (53A Models) - *98*	14	16
33-100M	'**J Kime & Son**' 5 black Sp Edn 500 (B&H Models) - *98*	14	16
33-100W	'**James Lewis**' 19 bright red Sp Edn 500 (B&H Models) - *97*	14	16
33-100E	'**Linby Colliery Co.**' brown Sp Edn 500 (Sherwood Models No2) - *99*	13	15
33-100V	'**Lincoln Corporation**' 9 brown Sp Edn 500 (B&H Models) - *97*	14	16
33-100N	'**Lincoln Wagon & Engine**' light grey Sp Edn 500 (B&H Models) - *97*	12	14
33-100B	'**Manton**' 891 red-brown Sp Edn 500 (Geoffrey Allison) - *95*	14	16
33-100WW	'**North Norfolk Railway**' 8572 green Sp Edn 500 (NNR) - *93*	18	25
33-100J	'**Nunnery**' 1574 black Sp Edn 500 (Geoffrey Allison) - *98*	14	16
33-100R	'**Ormiston Coal Coy.**' 199 blue Sp Edn 500 (Harburn Hobbies No3) - *96*	26	32
33-100G	'JW **Pinner**' 12 red-brown Sp Edn 500 (B&H Models) (also seen listed as 33-100K) - *99*	13	15
33-100S	'**Rossington**' 2054 light grey Sp Edn 500 (Geoffrey Allison No4) - *97*	14	16
33-100Y	'**Sheepbridge**' 5101 pale red Sp Edn 500 (The Midlander) (also listed as 33-100Y) - *96*	14	16
(30-006)	'**Sheepbridge**' 6091 red ex-train set - *?*	6	NA
33-101	'**Shirebrook Colliery**' 159 dark red - *91*	10	12
33-100Z	'**Shireoaks**' 4241 brown Sp Edn 500 (Geoffrey Allison No1) - *97*	18	25
33-100YY	'**Staveley Metal Spun Pipes**' 4994 black Sp Edn 500 (The Midlander) ('33-100' on box) - *99*	10	12
33-104	'R **Taylor & Sons**' 451 brick red - *92*	10	12
33-105A	'Richard **Webster**' 107 red (see table W5c) - not made	NA	NA
33-100L	'**Welbeck**' 2692 black Sp Edn 500 (The Midlander No3) - *97*	20	36
33-100NN	'WS **White & Co.**' 15 grey Sp Edn 500 (B&H Models) - *96*	14	16
33-100P	'**Woodhall**' 220 green Sp Edn 500 (Harburn Hobbies No1) - *96*	15	20
33-102	'**Wyken Colliery Co.**' 441 soft brown - *92*	10	12
33-102A	**LMS** 609545 soft brown - *96*	8	10
33-106	**NE** 138455 grey (see table W7c) - *not made*	NA	NA
33-101A	**BR** M608163 grey - *96*	8	10
33-103	undecorated light grey - *91*	6	8

W9b. 7-plank Open Wagon - End Door (1998)

This is the retooled model upgrading it to Blue Riband standard. As explained earlier in the book, the retooling of the wagon to Blue Riband quality enabled Bachmann to also change to the more accurate timber framed 9' wheelbase, correct for early coal wagons. As with the 5-plank wagons, two versions have been produced. These reflect differences with real wagons in that some have an end door (non-opening on the model) while others have both ends fixed. The end door was actually the whole end wall of the wagon which swung upwards from the bottom, being held in place by only the top corners on which it swivelled. This table contains those models produced with the end door.

Code	Description		
37-075K2	'**Aberpergwm**' 941 red-brown Sp Edn 750 (BCC) - *06*	20	25

Replacement 9ft wheelbase 7-plank wagon with end door [W9b]

Code	Description		
37-080Z	'**Annesley**' 195 brown Sp Edn 500 (Sherwood Models) - *01*	12	14
37-080T	'**Arniston**' 617 brown Sp Edn (Harburn Hobbies) - *01*	12	14
37-100Y	'**Babbington**' 3144 black Sp Edn 500 (Gee Dee Models) - *00*	13	15
37-078X	'**Bachmann**' 89-99 blue Ltd Edn (Bachmann 10th (X suffix not printed on box) - *99*	13	14
37-075Y	'**Balgonie**' 226 brown Sp Edn 500 (Harburn Hobbies) - *01*	13	14
(30-045)	'**Barnsley Main**' 528 brown ex-set - *04*	8	NA
37-084Z	'**Blaenavon**' 1457 grey W Sp Edn 504 (Pontypool & Blaenavon Railway Society) - *10*	6	8
37-080Y	'**Blidworth**' 2323 red Sp Edn 500 (Gee Dee Models) - *01*	12	14
37-083	'**Bradleys (Weardale)**' 246 brown - *06*	8	10
37-079V	'**Butterley**' 2301 brown Sp Edn (various)* - *01*	12	14
37-075K3	'**Cain Bros.**' 3 black Sp Edn 750 (BCC) - *06*	10	12
37-079U	'**Clay Cross**' Sp Edn 500 (various) * - *01*	12	14
37-080L	'**Coventry**' 1497 black Sp Edn 504 (Castle Trains) - *08*	8	10
37-085	'**Crane & Company**' 107 red - *10*	5	7
37-2011K	'W.R**,Davies & Co.**' 701 brown Sp Edn (BCC) - *11*	7	10
37-080W	'The **Derbyshire Carriage & Wagon**' 110 brown Sp Edn (BCC) - *01*	12	14
37-076A	'**Douglas Bank Colliery**' 454 brown - *03*	8	10
37-080K	'**Edward Eastwood**' 2 green Sp Edn (BCC) - *08*	8	10
37-080R	'**Edinburgh**' 313 grey Sp Edn (Harburn Hobbies) - *01*	12	14
37-075K1	'**Fife Coal**' 1655 dark brown Sp Edn 750 (BCC) - *06*	10	12
37-082	'**Firestone**' 2004 dark blue - *06*	8	10
37-076	'**Gellyceidrim**' 719 light grey - *98*	14	15
37-2012K	'**Gloucester RCW**' brown Sp Edn (BCC) - *12*	9	12

9ft wheelbase 7-plank wagon with end door [W9b]

Code	Description		
37-075A	'**Goldendale Iron**' 598 blue-grey - *03*	8	10
37-084	'**Harrisons**' 5038 grey - *08*	9	11
37-080G	'**Highley Mining Co.**' 425 brown Sp Edn 504? (Severn Valley Railway) - *09*	7	9
37-2009K	'**Thomas Hunter**' brown Sp Edn (BCC) - *09*	9	12
37-077	'**ICI Salt Works**' Stafford 326 red-brown - *99*	9	11
37-2003	James **Kenworthy**' 47 brown Ltd Edn (BCC) - *03*	11	13
37-075Z	'**Kinneil**' 189 brown Sp Edn 500 (Harburn Hobbies) - *00*	13	15
37-078	'**Kobo**' 15 grey - *99*	9	11
37-080H	'**Leadbeter**' 211 dark red Sp Edn 504 (Pontypool & Blaenavon Railway) - *08*	20	24

Bachmann Branchline

Cat. No.	Description		
37-075S	'Mickelfield Coal & Lime Co.' 423 red-brown Sp Edn (NRM) - 07	9	11
37-080S	'Moore' 113 brown Sp Edn (Harburn Hobbies) - 01	12	14
37-076U	'Newbattle Colliery' 41 black Sp Edn (Harburn Hobbies) - 13	10	12
37-075W	'Newstead' 2281 grey Sp Edn (Sherwood Models) - 00	12	14
37-080U	'Niddrie' 491 grey Sp Edn (Harburn Hobbies) - 01	12	14
37-085A	'North End' 110 black - 12	8	10
37-076W	'James Oakes & Co.' 328 grey Sp Edn 504 (Midland Railway Trust) - 12	10	13
37-082A	'Park Lane' 2060 brown - 12	8	10
37-2010K	'Pickering [R.Y.] & Co.' 1002 brown Sp Edn (BCC) - 10	12	15
(30-007)	'Pick 'N' Mix' yellow ex-'Jack The Saddle Tank' set - 11	6	NA
37-079T	'Raven Anthracite Collieries' 421 brown Sp Edn 512 (Midland Railex) - 11	8	10
37-080V	'Renwick, Wilton & Dobson' 77 red-brown Sp Edn 500 (Warley Show) - 03	11	13
(30-006)	'Sheepbridge' 6091 red ex Harry the Hauler set - 10	8	NA
37-075K	'Standard Wagon' (Cambrian Wagon Company Ltd) 1923 pale yellow Ltd Edn (Bachmann Times) - 99	25	33
37-080V	'Swanwick' 2383 brown Sp Edn 500 (various *) - 01	12	15
37-075X	'Thorne - Pease & Partners' 1336 brown Sp Edn (Rails) - 00	13	15
(30-007)	'Totally Toys' green ex-'Jack The Saddle Tank' set - 11	6	NA
37-086	'TPP' Tir Pentwys Pontypool 29 black - 11	6	8
37-078B	'Wimberry Colliery Co.' 2 black (also seen as '37-078A') - 03	8	10
37-075V	'Tom Wright' 19 brown Sp Edn 504 (Midland Railway Society) - 03	11	13
37-080	'JR Wood' 346 orange - 00	9	11
37-080A	'JR Wood' 346 orange - 03	NPG	NPG
37-079	GW 09244 dark grey - 00	7	9
37-075	NE 158486 light grey - 98	8	10
37-081A	BR M608163 grey - 06	7	9
37-081B	BR P60084 grey - 08	5	7
37-081C	BR P38099 grey - 09	5	7
37-081D	BR P36147 grey - 10	5	7
37-081E	BR P45129 grey - 11	6	8
37-081F	BR P153290 grey - 13	NPG	NPG

* Originally commissioned by The Midlander but order subsequently cancelled. The order was then taken over jointly by Sherwood Models, Geoffrey Allison, Gee Dee Models and C&B Models.

Cat. No.	Description		
37-104	'Birch Coppice' 927 red - 00	9	11
37-108	'Frederick Biss' 3 grey - 08	7	9
37-105X	'Butterley' 0820 grey Sp Edn 500 (various)* - 01	12	14
37-105W	'BW&Co. Moorgreen Colliery' 1466 light grey Sp Edn 500 (Gee Dee Models) - 01	12	14
37-100E	'Thos.J Clarke' 602 dark brown Sp Edn 504 (Buffers) - 06	11	14
37-100U	'Clifton' 2121 brown Sp Edn 504 (Sherwood Models) - 00	13	15
37-101Z	'Jebez Cole' 17 black Sp Edn 504 (Frizinghall Model Railways) - 07	8	10
37-109	'DV Costick' 1 blue - 08	7	9
37-111	'Eales & Roberts' 6 red-brown - 10	5	7
37-105	'George & Matthews' 5 black - 00	9	11
37-101A	'The Great Western Railwaymen's Coal Association' 1 light grey - 03	8	10
37-105U	'Kimberley' 4151 brown Sp Edn 500 (Warley MRC) - 01	12	14
37-100M	'Kirriemuir Coal Society' 2 brown Sp Edn 500 (Virgin Trains) - 04	20	27
37-105V	'Lakeside & Haverwaithe' Sp Edn (L&HR) - not made	NA	NA
37-100J	'S Loney & Co.' 50 dark grey Sp Edn 504 (Buffers) - 06	10	12
37-100	'Marcroft Wagons' 761 black Sp Edn (BCC) - 02	12	14
37-112	'North Sea Coaling Co.' 27 red-brown - 12	7	10
37-101	'Parkend' 312 black - 98	10	12
37-100V	'GE Parker' 1 brown Sp Edn 500 (British Railway Modelling) - 00	13	15
37-100D	'Thos.S Penny' 2 red Sp Edn 504 (Buffers) - 06	10	12
37-100X	'Pinxton' 718 black Sp Edn 500 (Gee Dee Models) - 00	13	15
37-075R	'HJ Redgate' 47 brown, Ltd Edn 504 (Sherwood Models) - 10	8	10
37-101U	'Ridley's Coal & Iron Co.' 1 grey Sp Edn 504 (Model Junction) - 08	8	10
37-106	'Royal Leamington Spa' 22 red-brown - 06	8	10
37-110	'Shaka Salt' 580 red-brown - 10	5	7
37-100N	'Shipley' 1522 red-brown Sp Edn 504 (Sherwood Models) - 03	11	13
37-101R	'Charles Sinclair' 7 dark green Sp Edn 504 (Frizinghall Model Railways) - 11	8	10
37-103	'James H Smart' 1 black - 00	9	11
37-113	'Snibson' 755 red - 12	8	10
37-100W	'TE Smith' 9 dark red Sp Edn 500 (B&H Models) - 00	13	15
37-150?	'Teifi Valley/Henllan' Sp Edn (Teifi Valley Railway) - not made	NA	NA
37-101V	'WH Thomas & Son' 119 olive green Sp Edn 504 (Buffers) - 06	8	10

W9c. 7-plank Open Wagon - Fixed End (1998)

This is the second of the two Blue Riband versions of the 7-plank coal wagon, this one having no end door.

9ft wheelbase 7-plank wagon with fixed end [W9c]

Cat. No.	Description		
37-101X	'The Arley Colliery Co.' 27 red Sp Edn 504 (Castle Trains) - 08	8	10
37-100L	'Awsworth' 86 light grey Sp Edn 504 (Sherwood Models) - 03	11	13
37-100G	'Bassil King & Co.' 5 red Sp Edn 504 (Buffers) - 06	10	12

9ft wheelbase 7-plank wagon with fixed end [W9c]

Cat. No.	Description		
37-100H	'WH Thomas & Son' 120 olive green Sp Edn 504 (Buffers) - 06	10	12
37-100F	'William Thomas & Co.' 2 black Sp Edn 504 (Buffers) - 06	11	14
37-105Y	'Waleswood' 606 red-brown Sp Edn (Geoffrey Allison) - 01?	NPG	NPG
37-101Y	'Walker & Rodgers' 3 red Sp Edn 504 (Castle Trains) - 08	8	10
37-2002	'NA Walton' 1 grey Sp Edn 500 (Warley MRC) - 02	12	14

Bachmann Branchline

37-101T	'Warwick Gas Light Co.' 6 grey Sp Edn 504 (Castle Trains) - 09	6	8
37-105A	'Webb, Hall & Webb' 19 blue - 03	8	10
37-100	'Richard Webster' 107 red - 98	10	12
37-100A	'WE Wise' 18 black - 03	8	10
37-100Z	'Wollaton' 79 red Sp Edn 500 (Gee Dee Models) - 00	13	15
37-102	BR P156142 grey - 99	7	9
37-107	BR E454941 grey - 06	6	8

* Originally commissioned by The Midlander but order subsequently cancelled. The order was then taken over jointly by Sherwood Models, Geoffrey Allison, Gee Dee Models and C&B Models.

W10a. Early Coal Trader Packs (1995)

The Coal Traders series brought together three 7-plank coal wagons in private owner liveries that might be seen together in a single geographical area. All three wagons were unique to the set and so did not also appear as solo models. The sets were sold in a single attractively decorated box, specially designed for the series and with 'Coal Traders' branding and some of them were commisioned by retailers.

The series started in 1995, before the arrival of the Blue Riband range and this table includes all 13 of the sets that were based on the original Mainline 7-plank model tooling.

33-025	'Ammanford Colliery' 48 brown	9	NA
33-025/1	'Cambrian Mercantile' 114 light grey	9	NA
33-025/2	'Berthlwyd' 385 dark green	9	NA
33-025	Wales Coal Traders above set of 3 - 95	NA	30
A	'Chapman, Fletcher & Cawood' 980 black	9	NA
B	'Rothervale' 2563 grey	9	NA
C	'Sheffield & Eccleshall' 13 red	9	NA
33-025W	Coal Traders above set of 3 Sp Edn 500 (Rails) 1st set - 97	NA	30
A	'Dearne Valley' 61 light blue	9	NA
B	'Cortonwood' 751 brown	9	NA
C	'Monkton' 1771 black	9	NA
33-025X	Dearne Valley Coal Traders above set of 3 Sp Edn 500 (Geoffrey Allinson No.8) - 99	NA	28

Coal Traders wagon set (Derby & Notts) [W10a]

A	'Thos. Black' 49 brown	9	NA
B	'Tinsley Park' 2241 brown	9	NA
C	'Thorncliffe' 3751 black	9	NA
33-025Y	Coal Traders above set of 3 Sp Edn 500 (Rails) 2nd set - 98	NA	28
A	'Staveley' Bleaching Powder 4728 grey	9	NA
B	'Staveley' Caustic Soda 7230 black	9	NA
C	'Staveley' Sand Spun Pipes 9249 grey	9	NA
33-025Z	Coal Traders above set of 3 Sp Edn 500 (The Midlander No.4) - 98	NA	30
-	'Oxcroft' 721 black	9	NA
-	'Sherwood' 575 brown	9	NA
-	'Ilkeston & Heanor' 17 dark blue	9	NA
33-026	Derby/Notts Coal Traders above set of 3 - 95	NA	30
-	'Phorpres' Bricks' London Brick 988 dark grey	8	NA
-	'Lowe & Warwick' 42 red+yellow	8	NA
-	'HC Bull & Co.' 101 dark red	8	NA
33-027	London Coal Traders above set of 3 - 95	NA	26
-	'Blackpool Cooperative' 32 dark grey	9	NA
-	'Wigan Coal' A147 red-brown	9	NA
-	'JB Scholes - Cosy Fires' 778 light grey	9	NA
33-028	North West Coal Traders above set of 3 - 96	NA	30
-	'Hartnell & Son' 22 black	9	NA
-	'Dunkerton' 1117 dark grey	9	NA
-	'Milton' 10 dark brown	9	NA
33-029	West Country Coal Traders above set of 3 - 96	NA	30
-	'H Fulcher' 10 brown	9	NA
-	'Mellonie & Goulder' 307 grey	9	NA
-	'Wrights' 135 red	9	NA
33-030	East Anglia Coal Traders above set of 3 - 96	NA	30

-	'Florence' 1017 dark grey	9	NA
-	'Grazebrook' 49 red	9	NA
-	'Lunt' 724 grey	9	NA
33-031	West Midlands Coal Traders above set of 3 - 97	NA	30
-	'Newbold & Martell' 180 red	9	NA
-	'Whitwick' G55 black	9	NA
-	'Stockingford' 9 dark grey	9	NA
33-032	East Midlands Coal Traders above set of 3 - 97	NA	30
-	'Wm Shaw & Sons' 137 red	9	NA
-	'Flockton Coal Co.' 94 grey	9	NA
-	'Sycobrite - The South Yorkshire Chemical Works' 650 black+yellow	9	NA
33-033	Yorkshire Coal Traders above set of 3 - 97	NA	30

W10b. Later Coal Trader Packs (2000)

From 2000 onwards, the Coal Traders triple wagon packs contained the new Blue Riband 7-plank wagons with the correct 9' wheelbase and simulated wooden frame - so look more accurate. Initially they continued to be released in the specially designed box, but sadly, more recent sets have been in standard Bachmann dark blue packaging and, as such, have lost some of their charm. All wagons listed here are of the 7-plank type unless otherwise stated.

37-075JA	'Parkend' 312 black W	6	NA
37-075JB	'Parkend' 374 black W	6	NA
37-075JC	'Parkend' 380 black W	6	NA
37-075J	above 3 wagons Sp Edn 504 (Totally Trains) - 09	NA	21
-	'Fleetwood Fish' 2 red-brown	10	NA
-	'Guard Bridge Paper Co.' 67 grey	10	NA
-	'Lewis Merthyr Navigation Colliery' 674 black	10	NA
37-075K4	set of above 3 Sp Edn 750 (BCC) - 07	NA	40
-	'St Helens Industrial Coal Department Co-operative Society' 17 grey 7-plank	6	NA
-	'Lochgelly' 1898 red-brown 5-plank	6	NA
-	'T Jenkerson & Sons' 277 black 8-plank	6	NA
37-075K5	set of above 3 Sp Edn 504 (BCC) - 08	NA	21

Coal Traders wagon set [W10b]

-	'J Manning & Sons' 2 black W	8	NA
-	'Geo Mills & Sons' 40 black W	8	NA
-	'A Vitti & Son' 9 red-brown W	8	NA
37-075T	Coal Traders set of above 3 lightly weathered wagons Sp Edn 500 (Froude & Hext) - 05	NA	30
-	'Lincoln Corporation' 200 maroon	9	NA
-	'Lincoln Corporation' 201 maroon	9	NA
-	'Lincoln Corporation' 202 maroon	9	NA
37-075U	set of above 3 Sp Edn 500 (B&H Models) - 04	NA	33
-	'Pilkington Brothers' 1412, red	8	NA
-	'Smith Anderson & Co'. 10, brown	8	NA
-	'Jones [David] & Sons' 650, black	8	NA
37-077K	set of 3, Sp Edn 500 (BCC) - 10	NA	21
X	'Walter Boynton' 982 red-brown	10	NA
Y	'Walter Woodthorpe' 15 red-brown	10	NA
Z	'Walter Boynton' 01029 red-brown	10	NA
37-079X	Coal Traders set of above 3 Sp Edn (B&H Models) - 01	NA	36
-	'Cambrian' 1410 black	6	NA
-	'Stuart Coal Coy' 95 dark brown	6	NA
-	'Victoria Coal Co.' 10 grey	6	NA
37-080J	Cardiff Coal Traders set of above 3 wagons Sp Edn 504 (Lord & Butler) - 08	NA	21
-	'S Bookman' 30 grey 5-plank	7	NA
-	'WW Milton' 6 black	7	NA
-	'Whitwill Cole & Co.' 708 black	7	NA
37-080N	West Country (Bristol) set of above 3 Sp Edn 500 (ModelZone) - 07	NA	27

Bachmann Branchline

Code	Name	Price	NA
-	'**Snibston**' 585 red-brown	7	NA
-	'**South Leicester**' 373 red	7	NA
-	'**Wood & Co.**' (5-plank) 15 grey	7	NA
37-080M	East Midlands (Leicester) set of above 3 Sp Edn 500 (ModelZone) - 07	NA	27
-	'**Chapman & Sons**' 22 black 5-plank	8	NA
-	'**Fear Bros.**' 95 brown	8	NA
-	'**H Syrus**' I red	8	NA
37-080P	Surrey & Sussex Coal Traders set of above 3 Sp Edn 504 (ModelZone) - 06	NA	30
-	'Fred C **Holmes**' 104 red-brown	8	NA
-	'MA **Ray & Sons**' 123 light grey	8	NA
-	'FW **Wacher**' 6 black 5-plank	8	NA
37-080Q	Kent Coal Traders set of above 3 Sp Edn 504 (ModelZone) - 06	NA	30
-	'**Denaby**' 900 red	8	NA
-	'**Nostell**' 375 black	8	NA
-	'**Wath Main**' 1320 red-brown	8	NA
37-080T	South Yorkshire Coal Traders set 4 of above 3 Sp Edn 500 (Geoffrey Allison) - 05	NA	30
-	'W **Clarke & Son**' 405 brown	9	NA
-	'W **Clarke & Son**' 101 black	9	NA
-	'Wm **Clarke & Son**' 281 brown	9	NA
37-080UU	set of above 3 Sp Edn (B&H Models) - 03	NA	33
-	'**Manchester**' 8697 brown	11	NA
-	'**Manchester**' 8725 brown	11	NA
-	'**Manchester**' 8780 brown	11	NA
37-080X	Coal Traders set of above 3 Sp Edn 500 (TMC) - 00	NA	39
-	'**Brodsworth Main**' 350 red	9	NA
-	'**Waleswood**' 606 red-brown	9	NA
-	'**Yorkshire Main**' 9417 red-brown	9	NA
37-080X	set of above 3 Sp Edn (G Allison) - 01	NA	27
-	'**Barkby Jolliffe**' 606 black	11	NA
-	'**Birley**' 662 grey	11	NA
-	'**Marshell Bros.**' 7 black	11	NA
37-080Y	Coal Traders set of above 3 Sp Edn 500 (Rails) - 00	NA	39
-	'**Bulcroft**' 288 dark red	11	NA
-	'**Kiveton**' 2041 dark grey	11	NA
-	'**Maltby Main**' 298 brown	11	NA
37-080Z	South Yorkshire Coal Traders set 1 of above 3 Sp Edn 500 (G Allison No9) - 00	NA	39
-	'**Murphy Brothers**' 29 brown	10	NA
-	'**Murphy Brothers**' 32 brown	10	NA
-	'**Murphy Brothers**' 33 brown	10	NA
37-105Z	Coal Traders set of above 3 Sp Edn 300 (Murphy Models) - 01	NA	36

Coal Traders wagon set (South Yorkshire) [W10b]

Code	Name	Price	NA
-	'**Murphy Brothers**' 14 red-brown	7	NA
-	'**Murphy Brothers**' 19 red-brown	7	NA
-	'**Murphy Brothers**' 22 red-brown	7	NA
MM1704	above three wagons Ltd Edn 504 (Murphy Models) - 08	NA	28
-	'**Barrow Barnsley**' 1708 yellow	9	NA
-	'**BW & Co.**' black 8-plank	9	NA
-	'**Hatfield Main**' 1213 brown 8-plank	9	NA
37-105Y	South Yorkshire Coal Traders set 3 of above 3 Sp Edn 500 (G Allison) - 03	NA	33

Code	Name	Price	NA
-	'**City of Bradford Co-operative Society**' 118 brown	8	NA
-	'**Cleckheaton Industrial Co-operative Society**' 61 brown	8	NA
-	'**Hillhouses Co-operative Society**' 29 black	8	NA
37-075N	above three Yorkshire area wagons Sp Edn 504 (Natiobal Railway Museum) - 10	NA	27
-	'**Birmingham Industrial Co-operative Society**' 13 black	8	NA
-	'**Derby Co-operative Provident Society**' 149 grey (8-plank)	8	NA
-	'**Melton Mowbrey Co-operative Society**' 3 red-brown (8-plank)	8	NA
37-075P	above three Midlands area wagons Sp Edn 504 (National Railway Museum) - 10	NA	27
-	'**CWS**' 85 red	8	NA
-	'**Neasden Co-operative Coal Society**' 3 black	8	NA
-	'**Royal Arsenal Co-operative Society**' 144 brown	8	NA
37-075Q	above three London area wagons Sp Edn 504 (National Railway Museum) - 10	NA	27
-	'**Fleetwood Industrial Co-operative Society**' 2 brown (5-plank)	9	NA
-	'**Blackpool Co-operative Society**' 48 grey (8-plank)	9	NA
-	'**Workington Beehive Industrial Co-operative Society**' 20 black (7-plank)	9	NA
37-076Z	above 3 NW Coact Area wagons Sp Edn (National Railway Museum) - 12	NA	29

Coal Traders Co-ops wagon set for NRM [W10b]

Code	Name	Price	NA
-	'**Chippenham Co-operative Society**' 4 brown	9	NA
-	'**Stroud Co-operative Society**' 22 black	9	NA
-	'**Gloucester Co-operative & Industrial Society**' 47 brown	9	NA
37-076X	above 3 Cotswold Area wagons Sp Edn (National Railway Museum) - 12	NA	29
-	'**Windsford Industrial Co-operative Society**' 22 grey	9	NA
-	'**Chester Co-operative Society**' 18 black	9	NA
-	'**Stockport Industrial & Equitable Co-operative Society**' 32 brown	9	NA
37-076Y	above 3 North West Area wagons Sp Edn (National Railway Museum) - 12	NA	29
-	'**Burnley Corporation Gas Dept.**' 17 black	8	NA
-	'**Earl of Rosslyn's Collieries**' 4550 red	8	NA
-	'**Crynant Colliery Company**' 330 grey	8	NA
37-075K6	above three wagons Sp Edn 504 (BCC) - 10	NA	27
-	'**Highley Mining Company**' 136 red brown	8	NA
-	as above but numbered 162	8	NA
-	as above but numbered 428	8	NA
37-080F	above three wagons Sp Edn 504 (Severn Valley Railway) - 10	NA	27
-	'**Huntley & Palmers**' 21 maroon	8	NA
-	'Isaiah **Gadd & Compy**' 4 grey	8	NA
-	'**Thomas & Green**' 10 red	8	NA
37-081Z	above 3 Berks & Bucks coal traders wagons Sp Edn 504 (ModelZone) - 11	NA	29
-	'**Kynoch**' 170 red-brown 8-plank end door	8	NA
-	'N **Hingley & Sons**' 14 dark brown 5-plank, wood floor	8	NA
-	'E.R.**Gell**' 29 red-brown 7-plank end door	8	NA
37-075L	above 3 Midland coal traders wagons Sp Edn 504 (ModelZone) - 11	NA	29

Bachmann Branchline

Cat. No.	Description		
-	'TWW' 2451 brown W & repaired	8	NA
-	'St Helens Industrial Co-op Society' 17 grey W & repared	8	NA
-	'Burnley Corporation Gas Department' 17 black W & repaired	8	NA
37-095	above 3 weathered & repaired wagons - 12	NA	30

Coal Traders Co-ops wagon set for NRM [W10b]

-	'Birmingham Co-operative Society Ltd (CO-OP)' 45 red fixed end	12	NA
-	'Birmingham Co-operative Society Ltd (BCS)' 41 red fixed end	12	NA
-	'Birmingham Co-operative Society Ltd (CO-OP)' 172 black end door	12	NA
37-081Y	above 3 wagons Sp Edn 504 (Warley Show) - 11	NA	40
-	'Annesley' 191 maroon	8	NA
-	'Annesley' 194 maroon	8	NA
-	'Annesley' 198 maroon	8	NA
37-081X	above 3 wagons Sp Edn 504 (TMC) - 12	NA	30
-	'South Western Railway Servants Coal Club' 8 black	8	NA
-	'A&H Betts' 45 grey	8	NA
-	'Associated Coal Consumers' 61 red-brown	8	NA
37-081W	above 3 wagons Sp Edn 504 (ModelZone) - 12	NA	29
-	'Balgonie' 1402 brown (fixed end)	8	NA
-	'T&C Scowcroft & Son' 789 red (end door)	8	NA
-	'The Bwlch Colliery Co.' 131 black (end door)	8	NA
37-075K8	above 3 wagons Sp Edn 504 (BCC) - 12	NA	27
-	'Oxcroft' P151518 black W + repaired	8	NA
-	'Carlton' P326408 black W + repaired	8	NA
-	'Wemyss' P272062 brown W + repaired	8	NA
37-096	above 3 weathered wagons - 13	NA	30

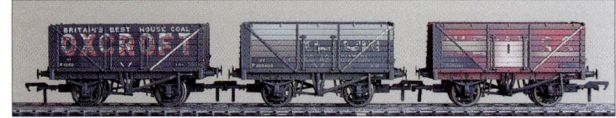

Set of weathered & repaired wagons with BR numbers [W10b]

W11a. 7-plank Coke Wagon + Top Rails (ex-Mainline) (1991)

Coke, being a lot lighter than coal, could be carried in greater volume and so the height of wagons was increased by the addition of extra planks, generally with small gaps between them.

These models are of 7-plank wagons with two extra rails fitted on top. This table lists the coke wagon models made using the original Mainline tooling of 1978.

33-150	'Abbott' 3607 grey - 91	9	10
33-155	'JA Bartlett' 2 red-brown - 94	9	10
33-152A	'Benzol & Byproducts' 1104 brown - not made (see table W11b - 37-177)	NA	NA
33-156	'Coalite' 401 red-brown - 95	9	10
33-151	'Flockton' 567 black - 92	9	10
33-152	'Lancashire Steel' 993 grey - 92	12	17
33-158	'Modern Transport' 1206 dark grey - not made (see table W12c - 37-204)	NA	NA
33-151A	'POP' 217 grey - not made (see table W11b - 37-176)	NA	NA
33-154	'Roberts Davy' 25 dark grey - 95	9	10
33-157	'Stringer & Jagger' 226 red - not made (see table W11b - 37-178)	NA	NA
33-150A	BR 368545 grey - not made (see table W11b - 37-175)	NA	NA
33-153	undecorated light grey - 91	4	6

W11b. 7-plank Coke Wagon + Top Rails (1998)

In contrast with the last table, here are the coke wagons made from the new Blue Riband tooling, first used in 1998. It will be noted that it includes examples of former privately owned coke wagons that were taken into British Railways stock at Nationalisation, painted grey and given a 'P' prefixed fleet number.

37-177	'Benzol & By-products' 1104 red - 98	10	12
37-175Z	'SJ Claye' 822 red Sp Edn 1000 (BCC) - 00	13	15
37-185.	'Cory Brothers & Co.' 9644 black - 11	6	8
37-183	'Dorchester Gas & Coke' 6 red-brown - 06	8	10
37-182	'Elders Navigation' 515 black - 06	8	10
37-182A	'Elders Navigation' 588 black - 09	7	9
37-186	'Exeter Gas Company' 5 grey - 11	6	8
37-184	'TL Hale (Tipton)' 1533 grey - 10	5	7
37-187	'TL Hale (Tipton)' 1718 grey - 13	5	7
37-179	'New Cransley' 166 red - 99	10	12
37-180	'S Mosley & Son' 58 grey+maroon - 00	9	11
37-188	'Moy' P150663 maroon W - 13	NPG	NPG
37-176	'POP' 217 grey - 98, 05	8	10
37-180	'POP' 217 grey - not sold with this cat.no.	NA	NA
37-180A	'POP' 215 grey - 08	7	9
37-181	'South Wales & Cannock Chase' 901 red-brown - 06	8	10
37-178	'Stringer & Jagger' 226 red - 98	10	12
37-2002	'NA Walton' 1 grey Sp Edn (Warley 2002) - 02	12	15
37-175	BR P368545 grey - 98	8	11
37-175A	BR P167248 grey - 01	7	10

7-plank coke wagon [W11b]

W12a. 8-plank Wagon - End Door (1998)

In order to carry greater loads, some companies ordered 8-plank coal wagons but these were far less common.

There was no Mainline equivalent tooling to use and so the 8-plank was not added to the Bachmann range until it launched its Blue Riband range in 1998. Once again, Bachmann produced two versions. In this table we have models based on the 8-plank with end doors.

37-130	'Bagley' 38 red - 00	9	11
37-125	'Boston [The] Deep Sea Fishing & Ice Co.' 86 blue (2 batches) - 98+99	10	12
37-125K	'T Burnett & Co.' 1907 red Sp Edn (BCC) - 07	8	10
37-125Z*	'Carlton' 4727 black Sp Edn 500 (The Midlander) - 00	13	15
37-131	'Great Mountain' 980 brown, also ex-37-075 'Local Freight' train set - 06	8	10
37-127	'Hinckley Gas Works' 19 red-brown - 99	9	11
37-135	'James & Emanuel' 451 black - 11	6	8
37-134	'Ketton Cement - Thos W Ward' S89 red+blue - 10	6	8
37-134	'Ketton Cement - Thos W Ward' S88 red+blue W - 11	7	9
37-129Z	'Manners' ? ? Sp Edn 504 (Railex 2013) - 13	10	12
37-175Z	'Charles Roberts' 70001 black Sp Edn (BCC) 1st version (no number on box label) - 98	10	12
37-129	'SC' 7961 grey - 99	8	10
37-129A	'SC' ? grey - 03	NPG	NPG
37-130Z	'Shelton' 2298 red Sp Edn 500 (Haslington Models) - 01	12	14
37-126	'Thorncliffe Izal' 2915 black - 98	10	12
37-132	'Thorne (Pease & Partners Ltd)' 740 red-brown - 06	10	12
37-125X	'JN Walker & Co.' 256 black, Ltd Edn 504 (Sherwood Models) - 10	7	9
37-128	BR P238934 grey - 99	7	10
37-133	BR P63984 grey - 06	6	8

* No 'Z' suffix on the box label.

Bachmann Branchline

W12b. 8-plank Wagon - Fixed End (1998)

The second version had no doors in the end and is referred to as a 'fixed end' wagon. Again we have some former private owner wagons in British Railways grey livery.

37-150Z*	'Cooperative Society' 71 brown Sp Edn 500		
	(The Midlander) - 00	13	15
37-156	'Firestone Tyres' - not made (see 37-082)	NA	NA
37-161	'Foster & Co.' 17 red - 11	6	8
37-163	'William Harrison' 674 grey - 13	NPG	NPG
37-162	'RW Hill & Son' 22 maroon - 13	NPG	NPG
37-160	'Isleworth Coal Co.' 10 dark blue - 11	6	8
37-160	'Ketton Cement' red+blue - (see table above)	NA	NA
37-150K	'Metropolitan' 188 red Sp Edn (BCC) - 06	10	12
37-154	'Musgrave' 2 dark grey - 00	9	11
37-156	'Osborne & Son' 10 green - 06	8	10
37-155	'Partington' 184 light grey - 00	9	11
37-153	'Quibell Brothers' 10 red - 00	9	11

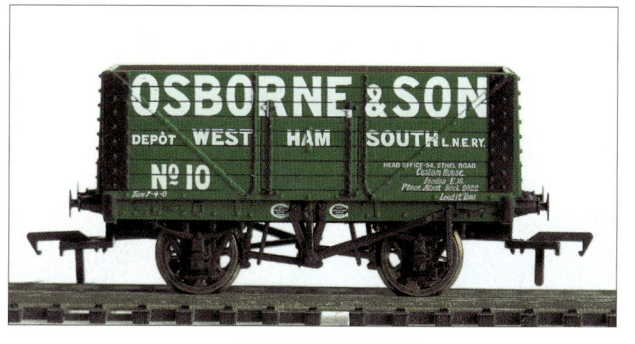

8-plank coal wagon [W12b]

37-152	'AJ Salter' 202 red-brown - 00	9	11
37-150	'Stewarts and Lloyds' 6159 grey - 98	9	11
37-157	'Stewarts & Lloyds' 6301 dark grey - 06	8	10
37-151	'Charles Ward' 4265 red - 98	9	11
37-159	'William Wood & Sons' 1006 maroon - 09	5	6
37-158	BR P308236 grey - 07	6	8
33-158A	BR P308328 grey - 10	7	9
33-158B	BR P322491 grey - 11	6	8
33-158C	BR P111136 grey - 13	NPG	NPG

* There was no 'Z' suffix on the box label.

W12c. 8-plank Coke Wagon + Top Rails (1998)

Some coke wagons were made by extending 8-plank wagons. Note the gas companies amongst the owners as they were important producers of coke. These were all Blue Riband wagons.

37-205	'Bedwas' 621 grey - 00	9	11
37-203	'Birley' 1605 black - 00	9	11
37-206	'Elders' - not made	NA	NA
37-202	'The Gas Light & Coke Co.' 821 grey - 99	9	11
37-207	'TL Hale' ? grey - not made (see table above)	NA	NA
37-204	'Modern Transport' 110 black - 00	9	11
37-206	'Reading Gas Company' 112 black - 06	8	10
37-200	'Stamford Gas Light & Coke' 101 light grey - 98	10	12
37-206A	'Stanton' 2477 red - 12	8	10
37-208	'Suncole' 5061 black - 13	NPG	NPG
37-201	'Suncole' 5062 black - 98	10	12
37-207	'TWW' Thos W Ward 1644A maroon - 11	6	8

W13. BR 5-plank 12T Pipe Wagon (2013)

These wagons were built for transportation of pipes from Stanton Ironworks at Ilkeston in Derbyshire, which was served by both the LNER and LMS. Both companies built wagons for this traffic and BR added further wagons of both designs. The model was under development at the time of writing but the illustration in the catalogue is of one built in 1957 at BR Wolverton and believed to be based on the LMS design.

38-700	BR ? brown (early) - 13	NPG	19
38-701	BR ? brown (late) - 13	NPG	19
38-702	BR Engineers DB? olive green - 13	NPG	19

W14. BR 5-plank 22T Tube Wagon STV (2013)

Originally seen as general merchandise wagons for long loads, both the LMS and GWR built them with drop-down doors in the centre of both sides.

This model was also under development as we went to press with this edition but the catalogue illustration is of a BR wagon built at Darlington in 1956. It was based on an LMS design but longer and with a longer wheelbase.

38-750	BR ? grey - 13	NPG	19
38-751	BR ? brown (early) - 13	NPG	19
38-752	BR ? brown (late) - 13	NPG	19

W15a. OBA 31t 5-plank Wagon - Low-Ends (B) (2006)

By 1967, the wagon fleet had fallen to about a third the size it had been in 1948. This was partly due to an improved road system and a reduction in demand for coal. British Rail launched a programme of vigorous marketing in the 1970s and backed this up with a fleet of new air-braked vehicles. These were larger and could travel faster than before. For merchandise, long wheelbase open wagons and vans with 45 tonnes loading capacity arrived. The wagons had an 'O' prefix and 'A' (for air-brakes) suffix and the middle letter denoted the type. The first OBAs were built at Shildon and Ashford in 1974 and had 5-plank sides with 4 drop-down sections each side, as well as higher ends.

OBA in EWS livery [W15a]

38-045	BR Engineers 110002 brown ZDA 'Bass' - 13	NPG	NPG
38-044	BRe Railfreight 110521 brown - 13	NPG	NPG
38-041	BRe Rft 110264 grey+red - 06	11	14
38-041A	BRe Rft 110583 grey+red - 09	12	15
38-041B	BRe Rft 110717 grey+red - 12	15	18
38-040Z	BR(S&T) Sat-Link KDC110588 ZDA red+yellow		
	Sp Edn 504 (Model Rail) - 06	14	17
38-040	EWS 110678 maroon+yellow - 06	11	14
38-040A	EWS 110332 maroon+yellow - 09	12	15

W15b. OBA 31t 5-plank Wagon - High-Ends (2006)

Some OBAs were built with the ends extended and Bachmann made both versions. This table contains the high-end ones. Plasmore Ltd makes building blocks from pulverised fuel ash at its plant at Heck, near Doncaster. They hired, and later bought, a fleet of OBA wagons.

38-042	BR 'Plasmore Blockfreight' 110547 red+grey		
	- 06	11	14
38-042A	BR 'Plasmore Blockfreight' ? red+grey - 13	NPG	NPG
38-042	as above but 110701 - 06	11	14
38-043	EWS 110436 maroon+yellow - 06	11	14
38-043	as above but 110636 - 06	11	14

Steel Merchandise Wagons

W16. OCA/ZDA 'Bass' Steel Open Wagon (2007)

Here we have the all-steel version of the OBA (above) built in the early 1980s. It was, in fact, a development of the SPA plate wagon and had three drop-down doors on each side and was known as a 'Bass'. They were the last air-braked open wagons built to a new design, as these were no longer required for general merchandise by the end of the decade.

38-055	BR Departmental 112115 grey+yellow - 07	10	13
38-059	BR Departmental ? grey+yellow - 13	NPG	NPG
38-056	BR Rft 112342 red - 07	10	13
38-056A	BR Rft 112391 red - 10	12	15
38-057	EWS 112256 maroon+yellow - 07	10	13
38-058	EWS 112260 maroon+yellow W - 11	12	16
38-055Z	BR S&T KDC112182 red+yellow Sp Edn		
	(Model Rail) - 10	16	20

W17a. LNER 'Highfit' Steel Wagon Type 1 (2010)

In 1945, the LNER started building open wagons with steel bodies. The side doors were made of either steel or wooden planks. The dimples, seen on the sides and ends of wagons in this table, accommodated rings on the inside of the wagon to which ropes could be tied when securing a load. They became 'Highfit' wagons under BR.

38-325	BR E480768 brown (early livery) - 10	6	8
38-326	BR E480215 brown (late livery) - 10	6	8

W17b. LNER High-Sided Steel Wagon Type 2 (2010)

The side doors on this type of wagon were made of steel and there were no dimples in the sides of the wagons.

Bachmann Branchline

38-327	**BR** E281227 brown (early livery) - *10*	6	8
38-328	**BR** E281604 brown (late livery) - *10*	6	8

W17c. LNER High-Sided Steel Wagon Type 3 (2010)
The side doors on this wagon type were made of wooden planks (six planks on iron straps).

38-329	**NE** 278785 grey - *10*	6	8

W17d. BR High-Sided Steel Wagon Sets (2011)
This table contains sets of three wagons of mixed type from the above 3 tables.

-	**BR Departmental** DE294009 olive green dimple sides	7	NA
-	**BR Departmental** DE281921 brown plain sides	7	NA
-	**BR Departmental** DE282529 olive green plain sides	7	NA
38-325K	above set of 3 wagons Sp Edn 504 (BCC) - *11*	NA	25
-	**BR** E281394 brown W	7	NA
-	**BR** E281460 brown W	7	NA
-	**BR** DE281515 brown W	7	NA
38-340	set of above 3 weathered wagons - *12*	NA	28

W18. BR Steel 'Highbar' Wagon (2012)
These were a BR conversion of LNER high-sided steel wagon design in 1951 and 1952 for the transportation of Soda Ash and were branded as such. In all, 80 were built at Shildon in two lots. A further batch was cancelled, as it was decided to convert some existing wagons instead.

ex-LNER 'Highbar' wagon [W18]

38-450	**BR** B483599 red-brown (early) - *12*	7	9
38-450A	**BR** B? red-brown (early) - *13*	NPG	NPG
38-451	**BR** B479390 red-brown W early style - *12*	9	11
38-452	**BR** B476496 red-brown (late) Soda Ash - *12*	7	9
38-452A	**BR** B? red-brown (late) Soda Ash - *13*	NPG	NPG

Steel Mineral Wagons

W19a. 16T Steel Mineral Wagon (ex-Mainline) (1990)
The original Bachmann 16T steel mineral wagons, listed in this table, are from the Mainline Railways tooling made by Kader in 1975. Interestingly, amongst the variations released by Bachmann are examples from the batch that were taken over by British Railways from the LMS in 1948.

33-751	**BR** M620248 grey - *92*	8	10
33-752C	**BR** M622128 brown Iron Ore - *98*	8	10
33-751/1	**BR** M620233 grey in London Transport sets 30-200 & 30-201 - *91*	14	NA
33-750	**BR** B88643 brown - *90*	8	10
33-750A	**BR** B88647 brown - *94*	8	10
33-750B	**BR** B68919 brown - *96*	8	10
33-750C	**BR** B160415 brown MCV - *98*	8	10
33-751A	**BR** B84198 grey - *94*	8	10
33-751B	**BR** B279900 grey - *95*	8	10
33-751C	**BR** B560287 grey - *96*	8	10
33-751D	**BR** B156124 grey - *97*	8	10
33-752	**BR** B68837 dark grey Coalight - *91*	9	11
33-752A	**BR** B68833 dark grey Coalite - *94*	9	11
33-752B	**BR** B68342 dark grey Coalite - *96*	9	11
33-753	undecorated - *not made*	NA	NA

W19b. 16T Steel Mineral - Top Flap (1998)
When Bachmann replaced the original Mainline 16T mineral wagon with a Blue Riband model, they did so with a selection of different mineral wagon designs. The ones listed here are of a very common variety with an end door and top flaps ('London Trader' flaps) above the side doors.

16T mineral wagon with top flaps [W19b]

37-227	**BR** B106979 grey W - *00*	6	8
37-227A	**BR** B106979 grey W - *02*	6	8
37-225	**BR** B100071 grey (2 batches) - *98+99*	7	9
37-225A*	**BR** B77701 grey - *02*	6	8
37-225B*	**BR** B80200 grey - *03*	6	8
37-225C	**BR** B106979 grey - *not made*	NA	NA
37-225C	**BR** B168553 grey - *06*	5	7
37-225D	**BR** B591270 grey - *08*	5	6
37-225E	**BR** B80285 grey - *09*	5	7
37-225F	**BR** B87019 grey - *11*	6	8
37-225G	**BR** B116801 grey - *13*	7	9
-	**BR** B569041 grey W	8	NA
-	**BR** B569023 grey W	8	NA
-	**BR** B569056 grey W	8	NA
37-225V	above set of three wagons Sp Edn 504 (TMC) - *11*	NA	30
-	**BR** B151711 grey W	7	NA
-	**BR** B151226 grey W	7	NA
-	**BR** B150998 grey W	7	NA
37-235	above set of 3 weathered wagons - *12*	NA	27
-	**BR** B? grey W	7	NA
-	**BR** B? grey W	7	NA
-	**BR** B? grey W	7	NA
37-235A	above set of 3 weathered wagons - *13*	NA	27
-	**NCB** 29 grey W	7	NA
-	**NCB** 100 grey W	7	NA
-	**NCB** 72413 grey W	7	NA
37-225W	above set of three NCB wagons Sp Edn 504 (ModelZone & Signal Box) - *11*	NA	28
-	**NCB** MCP442 grey W	7	NA
-	**NCB** MCP528 grey W	7	NA
-	**NCB** MCP95 grey W	7	NA
37-236	above 3 National Coal Board wagons - *13*	NA	31
-	**BR** B219829 grey W	7	NA
-	**BR** B571730 grey W	7	NA
-	**BR** B119161 grey W	7	NA
37-225X	above set of three Sp Edn 504 (TMC) - *09*	NA	27
-	**BR** B82219 grey W	7	NA
-	**BR** B257058 grey W	7	NA
-	**BR** B140952 grey W	7	NA
37-225Y	above set of three Sp Edn (Hattons) - *08*	NA	24
37-226	**BR** B68900 brown - *98*	7	9
37-226A	**BR** B69007 brown (37-226 on box) - *01*	6	8
37-226B	**BR** B68901 brown - *?*	5	7
37-226C	**BR** B47202 brown - *06*	5	7
37-226D	**BR** B64026 brown - *08*	5	7
37-226E	**BR** B68919 brown - *09*	5	7
37-226F	**BR** B551677 brown (early) - *11*	6	8
37-228	**BR** B69190 brown W - *00*	6	8
37-228A	**BR** B68998 brown W - *02*	6	8

* No suffix letter on box.

Bachmann Branchline

W19c. 16T Steel Mineral - End Door (1998)

This Blue Riband model is of a 16T steel mineral wagon that has an end door but no 'London Trader' flap above the side doors.

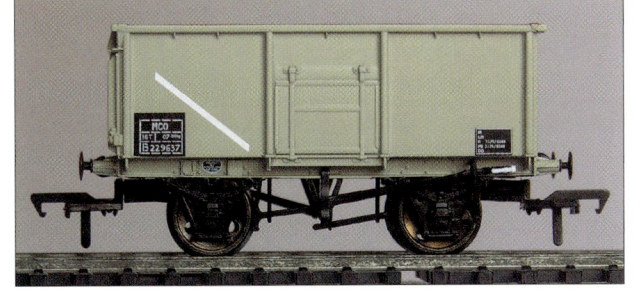

(30-077)	**LT** B37697 grey ex-'Midnight Metropolitan' train set - 13	6	NA
37-250	**BR** B38066 grey - 98	7	9
37-250A*	**BR** B22571 grey - 00	6	8
37-250B	**BR** B227229 grey - 03	6	8

16T mineral wagon [W19c]

37-250C	**BR** B25005 grey MCO - 02	6	8
37-250D	**BR** B60544 grey - 08	5	6
37-250E	**BR** B37236 grey - 09	5	7
37-250F	**BR** B27871 grey - 10	5	7
37-250G	**BR** B37697 grey - 11	6	8
37-250H	**BR** B27871 grey - *not made*	NA	NA
37-250H	**BR** B119610 light grey - 12	7	9
37-251	**BR** B258683 light grey MCO - 98	7	9
37-251A	**BR** B8258683 light grey MCO - *not made*	NA	NA
37-251A	**BR** B229637 light grey MCO - 01	6	8
37-251B	**BR** B121830 grey MCO - 02	5	7
37-251C	**BR** B229637 light grey MCO - 06	5	7
37-253	**BR** B24809 grey W - *not made*	NA	NA
37-253	**BR** B34807 grey W - 00	6	8
37-253A	**BR** B25311 grey W - 03	6	8
37-253B	**BR** B247055 grey W - 13	NPG	NPG
(37-225Z)	**BR** B203500 grey W Sp Edn (ex-ModelZone set see table 12b) - 07	7	NA
37-252	**BR** ADB562927 olive green ZHV - 99	6	8
37-252a	**BR** B77701 olive green ZHV - *not made*	NA	NA
37-252B	**BR** B561754 brown - 06	5	7
37-252C	**BR** B574829 brown MXV - 08	5	7
37-252D	**BR** B577541 brown MXV - 10	5	7
37-252E	**BR** B564000 brown MXV - 11	6	8
37-254	**BR** B266298 brown W Coal - *not made*	NA	NA
37-254	**BR** B564872 brown W Coal - 00	6	8
37-254A	**BR** B564872 brown W Coal - *not made*	NA	NA
37-254A	**BR** B561754 brown W Coal - 03	6	8
37-256	**BR** B551677 brown - 13	NPG	NPG
37-255	**BR** Departmental ADB 55?821 olive green - 12	7	9

* No 'A' on box label.

W19d. 16T Pressed Steel Mineral (1999)

This Blue Riband version is based on wagons which had their ends pressed out of sheets of steel. They include a number built for the Ministry of Transport during the Second World War.

37-375	**BR** B100768 grey - 99	6	8
37-375A	**BR** B101676 grey - 01	6	8
37-375B	**BR** B241057 grey - 03	6	8
37-377C	**BR** B61926 grey - 08	5	7
37-377D	**BR** B80220 grey - 09	5	7
37-378	**BR** B24890 grey - 13	NPG	NPG
37-377	**BR** B100245 grey W - 00	6	8
37-377A	**BR** B38751 grey W - 03	6	8
37-377B	**BR** B24890 grey W - 08	5	6
37-377E	**BR** B82688 grey W - 09	5	7
37-377F	**BR** B100925 grey W - 10	5	7
37-377G	**BR** B247055 grey W - 11	7	9
37-376	**MoT** 3308 brown - *not made*	NA	NA
37-376	**MoT** 33011 brown - 99	6	8
37-376C	**MoT** 33111 brown - 11	7	9
37-376A	**MoT** 3327 brown - 03	6	8
37-376B	**MoT** 33322 brown - 10	6	8

W19e. Mineral Mixed Wagon Set (2006)

This set contains models of steel mineral wagons of different types.

-	**BR** B84198 grey W top flaps	7	NA
-	**BR** B88430 grey W no top flaps	7	NA
-	**BR** B203500 grey W top flaps	7	NA
37-225Z	above set of three wagons Sp Edn 504 (ModelZone) - 06	NA	24

W20a. 16T Slope-Sided Pressed Steel Mineral (2001)

Here is a type built to the design of Charles Roberts of Wakefield (who built many for private owners) but this time it had pressed steel doors. The Ministry of Transport (MoT) ordered large quantities of them during the Second World War and they were built by various contractors. After nationalisation of the railways, many passed to British Railways and were given a 'B' prefix to their number.

16T pressed steel slope-sided mineral wagon {W20a}

37-425K	'**Charles Roberts**' 4 brown Sp Edn (BCC) * - 04	10	12
37-427	'**Denaby**' 9151 black - 04	10	12
37-425	**BR** B197525 grey - 01	6	8
37-425A	**BR** B8707 grey - 03	6	8
37-426	**MoT** 23743 brown - *not made*	NA	NA
37-426	**MoT** 23768 brown - 01	6	8
37-426A	**MoT** 31763 brown - *not made*	NA	NA
37-426A	**MoT** 24000 brown - 03	6	8
37-426B	**MoT** 23866 brown - 10	5	7
37-426	**MoT** 23866 brown - *not made*	NA	NA
37-426C	**MoT** 23763 brown - 12	7	9

* '37425 Club 2004' on the box label - no suffix.

W20b. 16T Slope-Side Riveted Steel Mineral (2001)

Here we have the Charles Roberts design constructed with rivets rather than welding. In the early days of steel wagon construction, some contractors did not trust welding and kept to the traditional way of joining steel plates. The Ministry of War Transport (MWT) came into being in 1941.

37-452	'**The Boston Deep Fishing Co.**' ? grey - 13	NPG	NPG
37-450	**BR** B11816 grey - *not made*	NA	NA
37-450	**BR** B8128 grey - 01	6	8
37-450A	**BR** B11532 grey - 03	6	8
37-451	**MWT** 11532 brown - 01	6	8
37-451A	**MWT** 9512 brown - 04	6	8
37-451B	**MWT** 9505 brown - 10	6	8

Riveted slope-sided mineral wagon [W20b]

Bachmann Branchline

Steel Tippler Wagons

W21. 13T Steel Sand Tippler Wagon (1999)

In 1957, BR built a batch of 100 13 ton all-steel wagons for the transportation of sand. As sand is heavier than coal, the wagons had lower sides, to avoid overloading. They had a 10' wheelbase chassis with vacuum brake gear, oil axleboxes and Oleo hydraulic buffers. They were in use up until the early 1970s and most were then soon scrapped.

-	'Taunton Concrete' ? ? W	7	NA
-	'Taunton Concrete' ? ? W	7	NA
-	'Taunton Concrete' ? ? W	7	NA
37-365	above 3 weathered wagons - 13	NA	NPG
37-351	**BR** B746609 grey Sand - 99	6	8
37-351A	**BR** B746576 pale grey Sand - 02	6	8
37-353	**BR** B746548 grey W Sand tare 9-6 - 02	6	8
37-353A	**BR** B746548 (smaller) grey W Sand tare 7-9 - 02	6	8
37-354	**BR** B746576 light grey Sand - not made	NA	NA
37-354	**BR** DB746638 light grey ZCO - 07	5	7
37-354A	**BR** B746724 grey - 09	5	6
37-354B	**BR** B746777 grey – not made	NA	NA
37-354B	**BR** B746674 grey - 10	5	6
37-354C	**BR** B746606 grey - 11	5	7
37-350	**BR** B746591 brown Sand - 99	6	8
37-350A	**BR** B746736 brown Sand - 02	6	8
37-352	**BR** B746426 brown W Sand - 00	6	8
37-352A	**BR** B746548 brown W Sand - 02	6	8
37-355	**BR** KDB746058 brown Sand - 07	5	7
37-355A	**BR** B746350 brown Sand - 09	5	6
37-355B	**BR** B746103 brown Sand - 10	5	7
37-355C	**BR** B746426 brown Sand - 11	5	7
37-356	**BR** Departmental DB746085 olive ZCO - 12	7	9

13T sand tippler [W21]

W22. 27T Steel 'Tippler' Wagon (1998)

Tippler wagons were not fitted with doors as they were emptied by the wagon being turned over in a cradle. Iron ore tippler wagons date back to 1939 when they were first used by Stewarts & Lloyds Ltd at their smelter at Corby. BR developed their own version and these were built in batches between 1951 and 1961. Some were built on 10' wheelbase chassis while most, like those in this table, had a 9' wheelbase. In 1956, BR entered into a contract with the Rugby Portland Cement Co. to transport chalk from a quarry at Totternhoe to the cement works at Rugby and Southby. Former iron ore tipplers were re-branded for this purpose.

Both types have been released by Bachmann and are listed below.

37-280	'Lancashire Steel Manufacturing' ? ? - 13	NPG	NPG
37-275	**BR** B381500 grey Iron Ore - 98	7	9
37-275A**	**BR** B381934 grey Iron Ore - 01	6	8
37-275B	**BR** B383560 grey Iron Ore - 03	6	8
37-275C	**BR** B382833 grey Iron Ore - 08	5	6
37-275D	**BR** B386369 grey Iron Ore - 08	5	6
37-275E	**BR** B381818 grey Iron Ore - 11	5	7
37-275F	**BR** B? grey Iron Ore - 13	NPG	NPG
37-277	**BR** B383476 grey W Iron Ore - 00	6	8
37-277A	**BR** B380005 grey W Iron Ore - 02	6	8
37-276	**BR** B381293 grey Chalk - 98	7	9
37-276A	**BR** B382888 grey Chalk - 02	6	8
37-276B	**BR** B380510 grey Chalk - 10	5	7
37-278	**BR** B381366 grey W Chalk tare 7-8 - 00	6	8
37-278A	**BR** B381366* grey W Chalk tare 7-4 - 02	6	8
37-279	**BR** B385866 brown MSV - 13	NPG	NPG

* Larger numbers. ** No 'A' on the box.

W23. 16T Slope-Sided Steel 'Tippler' (2001)

Slope-sided 16T mineral wagons were built for Stewarts & Lloyds immediately before the Second World War by Charles Roberts & Co.. They were bought to carry iron ore to the blast furnaces at Corby and were taken over by the British Steel Corporation in 1947, receiving the BSCO number prefix.

BSC 16 ton slope-sided steel tippler [W23]

37-400A	**BSCO** 9426 grey - 03	6	8
37-400	**BSCO** BSCO20142 grey - 01	6	8
37-401	**BSCO** BSCO20068 grey W - 01	6	8
37-401A	**BSCO** BSCO9446 grey W - 03	6	8
-	**BSCO** BSCO20206 grey W	8	NA
-	**BSCO** BSCO20490 grey W	8	NA
-	**BSCO** BSCO20651 grey W	8	NA
37-400Z	above 3 wagons Sp Edn 504 (ModelZone) - 12	NA	32

Steel Box Open Wagons

W24. MTA Open Box Mineral Wagon (2005)

These were built on the chassis of redundant TTA tank wagons and some were converted from ZKA 'Limpets'. The conversions were done by RFS Doncaster. They are used in engineers trains carrying ballast.

38-050	**EWS** 395112 maroon+yellow - not made	NA	NA
38-050	**EWS** 365154 * maroon+yellow - 05	6	8
38-050A	**EWS** 395118 maroon+yellow - 09	7	9
38-051	**EWS** 395090 maroon+yellow W - 09	7	9
38-052	**EWS** ? maroon+yellow - 13	NPG	NPG

* an erroneous number.

W25a. MFA Open Box Mineral Wagon (2002)

The MFA wagons were created by cutting down MEA wagons to restrict the loads they could carry. They are found in engineers' trains.

This table includes the models made from 2002, using the old MEA chassis of 1995. However, it was soon decided to start work on a new upgraded chassis for both models and this was first used on the MFA in 2004. These improved models will be found in the next table.

33-025	**EWS** 391102 blue+yellow (ex-Mainline) - 02	6	8
33-026	**EWS** 391572 maroon+yellow - 02	6	8
33-027	**EWS** 391070 grey (ex-Rft Coal) - 02	6	8
33-028	**EWS** 391223 black (ex-LoadHaul) - 02	6	8

W25b. MFA Open Box Mineral Wagon (2004)

The earlier MEA model chassis was not up to the standard now expected and so it was retooled, firstly for use on the MFA and later to upgrade the MEA. This table includes the upgraded MFAs.

38-010	**EWS** 391170 maroon W - 04	5	7
38-010A	**EWS** 391572 maroon W - 06	5	7
38-010B	**EWS** 391257 maroon W - 09	6	8
38-011	**EWS** ex-Mainline - not made	NA	NA
38-011	**EWS** 391225 black ex-LoadHaul - 04	5	7
38-011A	**EWS** 391222 black ex-LoadHaul - 09	5	7
38-011B	**EWS** 391223 black ex-LoadHaul - 12	9	11
38-012	**EWS** 391077 dark grey+yellow ex-Rft - 04	5	7
38-013	**EWS** 391374 maroon W - 09	6	8
38-013A	**EWS** 391271 maroon W - 10	6	8

W26a. MEA 45t Steel Box Body Mineral Wagon (1995)

Redundant HEA hopper wagon chassis were used in MEA construction and a steel box body fitted. Early conversions were ordered by Railfreight and these were subsequently divided up equally between Mainline Freight, Loadhaul and Transrail. Mainline and Loadhaul ordered further batches and, after they introduced all three fleets, EWS continued to place orders for them. The most recent were built in 2004.

This model was an early introduction by Bachmann and the early versions of it are listed here. However, in 2004 the model was upgraded to the Blue Riband standard and the next table lists these versions

b = Barry WRD motifs

Bachmann Branchline

MEA open box wagon [W26a]

33-375	**BR Rft** Coal 391045 grey+yellow b - *95*		7	9
33-375A	**BR Rft** Coal 391014 grey+yellow b - *96*		7	9
33-376	**BR Rft** Coal 391010 grey+yellow - *95*		7	9
33-376A	**BR** Rft Coal 391042 grey+yellow - *96*		7	9
33-375B	**Transrail** 391008 grey+yellow W b - *01*		6	8
33-377	**BR** M391158 blue - *96*		7	9
33-379	**BR** M391229 black+white - *97*		7	9
33-378	**Mainline** M391139 blue+yellow - *96*		7	9
33-378A	**Mainline** 391143 blue W - *02*		6	8
33-380	**EWS** Wagon ews 391262 maroon - *98*		7	9
33-380A	**EWS** Wagon ews 391250 maroon - *99*		6	8
33-380B	**EWS** Wagon ews 391444 maroon - *02*		6	8
33-380C	**EWS** Wagon ews 391389 maroon - *03*		5	7

W26b. MEA 45t Steel Box Mineral (2005)

This is the retooled model, upgraded to Blue Riband standard, which uses the new chassis produced the previous year for the MFA model.

38-061	**Mainline** M391155 blue - *05*		5	7
38-060	**EWS** 391327 maroon+yellow W - *05*		5	7
38-062	**EWS** 391374 maroon+yellow W - *09*		5	8
38-062A	**EWS** 391362 maroon+yellow - *11*		7	9
38-064	**EWS** ? maroon+yellow W - *13*		NPG	NPG
38-063	**Railfreight Coal** 391018 dark grey+yellow - *11*		7	9
38-063A	**Railfreight Coal** ? dark grey+yellow - *13*		NPG	NPG

W27a. PNA 34T Ballast/Spoil 5-Rib Wagon (2007)

These PNAs were converted in the late 1990s by Marcroft Ltd and are used in engineers' trains as low volume ballast carriers. Owned by CAIB, they were first leased to Railtrack and later to Network Rail.

Bachmann have modelled two designs - those built with five ribs to a side, as listed here, and those built with seven ribs in each side, as listed in the next table.

38-095	**Railtrack** CAIB3627 green - *07*		5	7
38-095A	**Railtrack** CAIB3727 green - *08*		6	8
38-095B	**Railtrack** CAIB3693 green - *10*		8	10
-	**Railtrack** CAIB? green W		8	NA
-	**Railtrack** CAIB? green W		8	NA
38-095Z	above 2 wagons Sp Edn 504 (ModelZone) - *11*		NA	22

W27b. PNA 34T Ballast/Spoil 7-Rib Wagon (2007)

These are a variation on the above wagons.

38-100	**Railtrack** CAIB-3619 green - *07*		5	7
38-100A	**Railtrack** CAIB-3603 green - *08*		6	8
38-100B	**Railtrack** CAIB-3611 green - *11*		8	10
38-100C	**Railtrack** CAIB-3636 green - *12*		9	11
38-100D	**Railtrack** CAIB-? green W - *13*		NPG	NPG

PNA ballast & spoil wagon [W27b]

W28. ZKA 34t Limpet Ballast Wagon (2006)

These are ballast wagons that were originally high sided open wagons built onto the chassis of redundant air-braked tank wagons, with roller bearings. They were later modified into 'Limpets' by introducing cut-outs high in the centre two panels of the sides, thus limiting the loads they could carry - ballast being heavy.

38-085	**BR** DC390153 grey+yellow - *06*		5	8
38-085A	**BR** DC390226 grey+yellow - *07*		6	8
38-085B	**BR** DC390312 grey+yellow - *10*		7	9
38-086	**BR** DC390168 grey - *06*		5	8
38-086A	**BR** DC390190 grey - *10*		7	9
38-087	**BR** DC390268 black+orange - *06*		5	8

W29. POA/MKA 46t Box Mineral Wagon (2005)

These were built by C.C.Crump Ltd of Connahs Quay in 1988, reusing redundant liquid chlorine and caustic soda railtank chassis. Owned by Tiger Rail Leasing, they were mostly used for stone traffic.

37-552	**ARC** TRL5323 yellow - *05*		6	8
37-552A	**ARC Tiger** TRL5321 yellow - *09*		6	8
37-552B	**ARC Tiger** TRL5322 yellow - *12*		9	11
37-550	**Tiger** TRL5157 pale grey - *05*		6	8
37-550A	**Tiger** TRL5377 pale grey - *09*		7	9
37-551	**Yeoman** TRL5352 light grey - *05*		6	8
37-554	**Yeoman Tiger** TRL5154 light grey POA - *05*		6	8
37-553	**Loadhaul** 393030 black+orange MKA - *05*		6	8

W30. POA/SSA 51t Iron & Steel Scrap Wagon (1995)

The model is based on 100 scrap metal wagons built by Standard Wagon Co. of Heywood in 1984. They were for Railease Ltd and were hired out to British Steel and sold to BR in 1990. The chassis were from redundant PGA hoppers owned by British Steel and the wagons carry the letters 'SR' which stands for 'Standard Railfreight', a subsidiary of the builders. On the British Rail network, the wagons were originally coded 'POA' but were later re-coded as steel carriers and given the 'SSA' code.
lsb = later style body.

POA iron & steel scrap wagon [W30]

33-425	**SR** 470068 pale blue POA - *not made*		NA	NA
33-425	**SR** RLS5098 pale blue POA - *97*		7	9
33-430	**SR** RLS5068 pale blue POA lsb SR - *99*		6	8
33-430A	**SR** RLS5091 pale blue POA lsb SR - *04*		5	7
33-432*	**SR** 470005 pale blue SSA lsb - *not made*		NA	NA
33-426	**SR** 470058 pale blue SSA - *not made*		NA	NA
33-426	**SR** 470096 pale blue SSA - *95*		7	9
33-426A	**SR** 470034 pale blue W SSA - **99**		**6**	**8**
33-431	**SR** 470005 pale blue SSA lsb - *99*		6	8
33-431A	**SR** 470181 pale blue SSA lsb - *not made*		NA	NA
33-431A	**SR** 470161 pale blue SSA lsb - *04*		5	7
33-433*	**SR** 470181 pale blue SSA lsb - *not made*		NA	NA
33-434	**SR** RLS5059 pale blue+yellow SSA lsb - *07*		6	8
33-436	**SR** RLS? pale blue+yellow SSA - *13*		NPG	NPG
33-435	**SR** 470014 pale blue+yellow W SSA - *09*		6	8
33-435A	**SR** 470084 pale blue+yellow W SSA - *11*		8	10
33-435B	**RLS5045** pale blue+yellow W SSA - *12*		8	10
33-437	**Transrail** T470158 grey SSA - *13*		NPG	NPG

Open & Covered Hopper Wagons

W31a. 12T/24T Ore Hopper Wagon (ex-Mainline) (1990)

Iron ore is a heavy material and only small hoppers were required for a 24 ton load. Steel iron ore hoppers were used by the LMS and LNER as well as private operators. Those built by BR were similar in design and were built by contractors. Some private owner hoppers passed to the British Iron & Steel Corporation (BISC).

In this table are listed the 24T iron ore hoppers produced by Bachmann from the original Mainline tooling.

33-252	**'BISC'** 665 black - *92*		10	12
33-254	**'South Durham Steel'** 1010 black - *97*		10	12

Bachmann Branchline

33-255	'Richard **Thomas**' 9451 brown - 97	10	12
33-252	**LMS** grey - not made	NA	NA
33-250	**BR** P209938 grey Iron Ore - 90	12	15
33-251	**BR** B435906 brown - 90	8	11
33-253	undecorated light grey - 91	6	9

W31b. 24T Ore Hopper Wagon (2002)
This is the retooled model upgrading it to Blue Riband standard. Once again, some private owner examples are included.

37-504	'**Millom Ironworks**' 261 brown - 07	7	9
37-501	'**RT & Co.**' 2016 brown - 02	8	10
37-503	'**Richard Thomas**' 9452 brown - 06	7	9
37-500	**BR** B437491 grey Iron Ore - 02	6	8
37-500A	**BR** B437491? Grey Iron Ore - made?	NPG	NPG
37-502	**BR** B436166 grey Iron Ore - 06	5	7
37-502A	**BR** B435339L grey Iron Ore - 09	5	7
37-502B	**BR** B436549 grey Iron Ore - 11	5	7
37-502C	**BR** B435549 grey Iron Ore - 11	6	8
37-502D	**BR** B435498 grey Iron Ore - 12	7	9
37-508	**BR** B? grey W - 13	NPG	NPG
37-507	**BR** B437221 brown Sand - 13	NPG	NPG
37-505	**BR** Civil Engineers DP101453 red ZEO - 10	5	7
-	**BR** B435331 grey W Iron Ore	7	NA
-	**BR** B435824 grey W Iron Ore	7	NA
-	**BR** B435079 grey W Iron Ore	7	NA
37-500Y	above 3 wagons Sp Edn 1004 (ModelZone) - 11	NA	28
37-506	**BISC** ? ? 'Iron Ore' - 13	NPG	NPG

W32a. HEA/HSA/HBA 46t Hopper (ex-Mainline) (1992)
These air-braked hoppers were built for coal traffic in their thousands at BREL (Shildon Works) between 1976 and 1979.

Although alike, the models carried any of the three TOPS codes. Those in this table are all from the original Mainline tooling of 1976.

33-550A	**BR** 360234 brown W HBA - 02	7	9
33-550	**BR Railfreight** 360075 brown HSA - 92	8	10

HEA Railfreight Scotland [W32a]

33-551	**BR Railfreight** 361862 red+grey HEA - 92	8	10
33-551A	**BR Railfreight** 360694 red+grey W - 94, 01	8	9
33-551B	**BR Railfreight** 361992 red+grey HSA has Scottish Saltaire flag marking - 94	8	10
33-551C	**BR Railfreight** 360320 red+grey W HEA - 02	8	9
33-551Z	**BR Railfreight** 36? Red+grey Sp Edn (Pennine Models) - 01	10	12
33-552	**Railfreight** 360601 grey+black HEA - 93	8	10
33-552A	**Railfreight** Coal 361554 grey+yellow W HES - 02	7	9
33-554	**Transrail** 361874 grey HEA - 96	8	10
33-553	**Mainline** 360955 blue HEA - 97	8	10
33-556	**ex-Mainline** 360940 blue W graffiti one side only HEA - 03	6	8
33-555	**EWS** 361870 maroon HEA - 98	8	10
33-555A	**EWS** 361328 maroon HEA - 99	7	9
33-555B	**EWS** 360677 maroon HEA - 02	7	9
33-555C	**EWS** 360042 maroon HEA - 03	6	8

W32b. HEA/HSA/RNA 46t Hopper (2004)
These are from the new tooling first used in 2004, upgrading the model to Blue Riband standard.

38-002	**BR** 360226 brown W HSA - 04	6	8
38-005	**BR** 360008 brown W HSA - 09	7	9
38-005A	**BR** 361257 brown W HSA - 10	7	9
38-005B	**BR** ? brown W HSA - 11	8	10
38-005C	**BR** 360613 brown W HSA - 12	10	13
38-001	**BR Railfreight** 391493 red+grey HEA - 04	6	8
38-006	**BR Railfreight** 391481 red+grey HEA - 09	7	9
38-006A	**BR Railfreight** 360166 red+grey HEA - 10	7	9
38-006B	**BR Railfreight** 360275 red+grey HEA - 12	8	10
38-006C	**BR Railfreight** 361303 red+grey HEA - 12	10	12
38-007	**BR Railfreight** 361990 red+grey RNA nuclear flask barrier wagon - 13	NPG	NPG
38-000Z	**BR Railfreight Coal** 360434 grey+yellow RNA Barrier Wagon Sp Edn 504 (ModelZone) - 12	10	13
38-003	**Mainline** 360643 blue HEA - 04	6	8
38-000	**EWS** 360392 maroon W HEA - 04	6	8
38-004	**EWS** 960392 maroon W HEA - not made	NA	NA
38-004	**EWS** 361859 maroon W HEA - 07	6	8

W33. CHV 'Covhop' 24T Covered Hopper (2013)
These were built to diagram 1/210 at BR Ashford in 1963 and their usage spans both the steam and diesel eras.

The model has replicated alternative braking systems and separately attached catwalk and filler lid. The models had not been released at the time of writing.

38-502	'**BIS**' Sand for Rockware Glass B870861 red-brown - 13	14	17
38-500	**BR** B870812 red-brown - 13	14	17
38-501	**BR** 886113 light grey Soda Ash - 13	14	17

W34a. CEA 46t Covered Hopper Wagon (2000)
This is a covered coal hopper introduced for dust control.

This table contains models which made use of the former Mainline HBA tooling, but adapted as a CEA. The opportunity had been taken to upgrade the chassis and incorporate NEM pockets for the couplings.

33-575	**LoadHaul** 361845 orange+black - not made	NA	NA
33-575	**LoadHaul** 361841 orange+black - 00	7	9
33-575A	**LoadHaul** 361845 orange+black W - 02	7	9
33-576	**EWS** 360791 maroon - not made	NA	NA
33-576	**EWS** 360726 maroon - 00	7	9
33-576A	**EWS** 361024 maroon - 01	7	9
33-576B	**EWS** 360955 maroon - 03	6	8
33-577	**EWS** 361024 maroon W - not made	NA	NA
33-577	**EWS** 361896 maroon W - 02	7	9

W34b. BR 46t Covered Hopper (2006)
This model features new underframe upgrade, using the one developed for the new HEA.

CEA covered hopper [W34b]

38-021	**LoadHaul** 360663 black + orange - 06	6	8
38-020	**EWS** 360726 maroon - not made	NA	NA
38-020	**EWS** 361087 maroon - 06	6	8
38-020A	**EWS** 360533 maroon - 12	10	12

W35. BR 21T Hopper Grain Van (2013)
BR adopted the final LMS design for their 21 ton all-steel hopper grain vans. Early ones were riveted and later ones welded. They were 21.5 feet long and on a 10.5 feet wheelbase.

38-600	**BR** ? grey - 13	NPG	NPG
38-601	**BR** ? brown (early) - 13	NPG	NPG
38-602	**BR** ? brown (late) - 13	NPG	NPG

W36. BRT 35T Bulk Grain Wagon (1994)
In the mid 1960s, The British Railway Traffic & Electric Company (BRTE) had constructed 300 of these PAF bulk grain carriers for hire. Early ones were built with eight ribs each side and later ones with five. They were all hired by the Distillers Group and most carried boards advertising their brands of whisky. They moved malted barley from East Anglia to Scotland. Most were displaced by 'Polybulks' from 1982. Some were converted for transporting imported Alumina and some were refurbished by Procor and returned to

Bachmann Branchline

grain traffic through Traffic Services Ltd (TSL) in 1984. The latter carry grain to a flour mill in Birkenhead where 'Polybulks' cannot be used.

The Bachmann model is based on the 8-rib type and was originally made by Lilliput and sold by British Trix from 1967. When Kader acquired Lilliput in 1993, they also acquired the tools for the grain wagon.

33-125	**BRT 'Grainflow'** BRT7690 green+grey - *94*	10	12
33-127A	**BRT 'Grainflow'** BRT7785 green+grey - *97*	10	12
33-130	**BRT 'Haig'** 5864 blue W - *02*	9	11
33-127	**BRT 'Johnnie Walker'** 5820 blue - *?*	10	12
33-127	**BRT 'Johnnie Walker'** 5819 blue - *94*	10	12

BRT bulk grain wagon [W36]

33-126A	**'The Maltsters Association'** 6026 yellow - *96*	10	12
33-126	**BRT 'Vat 69'** 5819 blue - *94*	10	12
33-129	**BRT 'White Horse'** 5818 blue - *97*	10	12
33-125A	**BRT** 7617 brown - *96*	9	11
33-125B	**BRT** 7586 brown - *06*	9	11
33-128	**BRT** 7580 grey - *94*	9	12

W37. 20T/22T CPV 'Presflo' Bulk Powder Wagon (2010)

Dating from 1953 many batches were made for BR between 1955 and 1964 for cement traffic. Some 'Presflos' were later modified for salt traffic and later still for slate powder traffic and eventually they carried fly-ash. Both Associated Portland Cement and Tunnel Cement ordered their own wagons based on the BR design. The 'Presflos' were replaced from 1984 onwards and all had gone by 1991.

These are very detailed models and Bachmann have included variations in their tooling which include either one vacuum cylinder (20T) or two (22T). Other differences will be found in buffers, brake levers and vacuum discharge pipes. Some also have an additional notice board on the solebars.

38-270	**'Blue Circle'** B873364 red-brown 22T - *10*	7	9
38-270A	**'Blue Circle'** B888723 red-brown 22T - *10*	7	9
38-260	**'Bulk Tunnel Cement'** B888113 red-brown 20T - *10*	7	9
38-260A	**'Bulk Tunnel Cement'** B888112 red-brown 20T - *10*	7	9
38-271	**'Cement Marketing Company'** ('Blue Circle') PF100 grey 22T - *10*	7	9
38-271A	**'Cement Marketing Company'** ('Blue Circle') APCM8688 grey 22T - *10*	7	9
38-261	**Bulk Cement** ('Crown Cement') B888229 red-brown 20T - *10*	7	9
38-261A	**Bulk Cement** ('Crown Cement') B888235 red-brown 20T - *10*	7	9
-	**'Blue Circle'** B873150 red-brown W 22T	8	NA
-	as above but numbered B887879	8	NA
-	as above but numbered B888803	8	NA
38-270Z	above 3 wagons Sp Edn 512 (Hattons) - *10*	NA	31
-	**Bulk Cement** B873110 brown	9	NA
-	as above but numbered B873344	9	NA
-	as above but numbered B873295	9	NA
38-275Y	above 3 wagons Sp Edn 504 (Lord & Butler)* - *10*	NA	31
-	**'Cement'** B873083 brown	9	NA
-	as above but numbered B873091 Pool 5647	9	NA
-	as above but numbered B887860	9	NA
38-270X	above 3 wagons Sp Edn 512 (Lord & Butler)* - *11*	NA	33
-	**'Blue Circle'** PF52 yellow 22T	9	NA
-	as above but numbered PF76	9	NA
-	as above but numbered PF109	9	NA
38-286	above 3 wagons - *11*	NA	31
-	**'Tunnel Cement'** TC8952 brown W 22T	9	NA
-	as above but numbered TC8955	9	NA
-	as above but numbered TC8956	9	NA
38-285	above 3 wagons - *12*	NA	33
-	**BR** ? brown W	14	NA
-	**BR** ? brown W	14	NA
-	**BR** ? brown W	14	NA
38-287	above 3 wagons - *13*	NA	47
38-261A	**'Rugby Cement'** ? ? - *13*	NPG	NPG

* Lord & Butler also offered these weathered, a finish provided at the shop and so, strictly speaking - code 3.

'Presflo' 22T bulk powder wagon [W37]

W38 PCA Metalair Bulk Powder Wagon (2013)

In 1984, powder tank specialists Metalair co-operated with Blue Circle and Powell Duffryn to produce this design. It had a lighter barrel and could carry a greater load and had faster discharge. These were the successors to the 'depressed-centre' cement tankers. This model had not been released at the time of writing.

38-651	unbranded ? pale grey - *13*	NPG	14
38-650	**'Blue Circle Cement'** ? ? - *13*	NPG	14
38-652	? ? pale grey W - *13*	NPG	14

Tank Wagons
33-500 Series Tank Wagons Guide

The numbering of small tank wagons became a little confusing and so I have provide here an index to show where you will find models numbered 33-500 to 33-512:

cat. No.	table	cat. No.	table	cat. No.	table
33-505	W39a	33-502	W39c	33-506	W39b
33-500A	W39b	33-502A	W39c	33-507	W39b
33-500W	W39c	33-502B	W39c	33-508	W39c
33-500X	W39x	33-503	W39c	33-509	W39c
33-500Z	W39c	33-504	W39b	33-510	W39d
33-500Z	W39c	33-504A	W39c	33-512	W39d
33-501	W39A	33-505	W38a		
33-501A	W39b	33-505A	W39d		

W39a. 14T Tank Wagon (Early Type 1) (ex-Mainline) (1990)

This model has broad ladders (8mm across), an 8' gantry (32mm long) and 'kettle' manhole cap (9mm across) either side of which there are two small projections (a hand wheel type control valve and a ring). The end stanchions are linked together by a horizontal wires which also tie them down to the frame. It was made using the original Mainline tooling.

33-505	**'Castrol Oil'** 131 green - *92*	15	20
33-501	**'Esso'** 3123 black - *90*	20	25
33-500	**'Royal Daylight'** 1534 red - *92*	15	20

W39b. 14T Tank Wagon (Early Type 2) (1992)

This second version has an 8' gantry (32mm long) and 'kettle' manhole cap (8mm across) but no ladders. The hand wheel control valve and ring projections are again either side of the cap but the wheel is extended higher than with type 1. The end stanchions are again linked together by a horizontal wire which also ties them down to the frame. This is the 2nd type of tank wagon based on the former Mainline tooling.

Bachmann Branchline

Early 14T tank wagon type 2 [W39b]

33-502A	'Berry Wiggins' 106 black - 95	14	16
33-502A	as above but name missing from tank sides (misprint) - 95	NPG	NPG
33-500A	'BP' 22 silver - 94	12	14
33-507	'DCL' 241 silver - 96	14	16
33-504	'Fina' 135 silver - 92	10	13
33-506	'Shell Electrical Oils' 3102 dark brown - 94	14	18
33-501A	'Swindon United Gas Co.' 5 maroon - 96	18	23

W39c.   14T Tank Wagon (Early Type 3) (1991)

This third version of the 14T tank wagon, from the Mainline tooling, has a 'kettle' manhole cap (7mm across) but no ladders or gantry. Beside the cap is a hand wheel control valve at the top of a column. This must have been particularly vulnerable as wagons are often found with this broken off short. The end stanchions are again linked together by a horizontal wire which also ties them down to the frame. Slimline couplings are now being used.

33-500W	(see 33-500Z in table W30e and footnote)	NA	NA
33-502B	'Berry Wiggins' 116 silver - 98	10	12
33-509	'BOCM' B7 brown - 98	10	12
33-500X	'Briggs' 18 black Sp Edn 750 (Harburn Hobbies) - 99	20	30
33-500Y	'Briggs' 38 black Sp Edn 750 (Harburn Hobbies) - 98	30	50
	'Briggs' 20 black (see table W39e)	NA	NA
33-500Z	'Esso' 1634 buff Dalkeith posters Sp End 750 (Harburn Hobbies) - 98	18	25
33-502	'NCB' Tar 597 black - 92	18	25
33-504A	'Trent Oil Products' 6 buff+brown - 97	15	18
33-508	'The Yorkshire Tar Distillers' 597 black - 98	15	18
33-503	undecorated light grey - 91	8	10

W39d.   14T Tank Wagon (Early Type 4) (1998)

This fourth version of the 14T tank wagon from the Mainline tooling has ladders which are much narrower (4.5mm), a 6' gantry (23mm) each side of the manhole the cover of which is flat rather than domed like the others. The cover appeares more detailed. It too has just a hand wheel control valve projection beside it. The end stanchions are again linked together by a horizontal wire which also ties them down to the frame.

33-505A	'Brotherton' 908 blue - 98	25	30
33-510	'M.O.S.' 195 buff - 98	17	22
33-512	'Shell BP Lubricating Oil' A7287 black - 99	20	27

W39e.   14T Tank Wagon (Early Type 5) (1999)

The fifth and final original version of the model has a raised manhole with a domed cap (10mm across). It has a short projection beside it that looks like a shortened hand wheel control valve column. However, the main difference between this and the other four early model types is that the tank is held in place by cross stays.

33-676	'BP Ethyl' 1448 buff - 99	12	15
33-675W	'Briggs' 20 black (see 37-675W)	-	-
33-677	'Esso' 981 black - 99	17	22
33-675Y	'Kalchester' 101 red Sp Edn 500 (TMC) - 00	30	40

Early 14T tank wagon model type 5 [W39e]

33-675Z	'Manchester & Sheffield Tar Works' 19 black Sp Edn 500 (Rails) (numbered 33-657) - 99	30	40
37-675A	'Mobil' 5294 black - 09	6	8
33-675X	'Michael Nairn' 503 yellow (see 37-675X)	-	-
33-675	'Power' 115 silver - 99	12	15
33-500Z*	'Sheffield Chemical Co.' 33 black Sp Edn 500 (Rails) - 00	25	37

* This was the number carried on the box although it had already been used on another tank wagon. Bachmann literature also recorded this tank wagon as 33-500W. To make matters worse, it was one of a number of tank wagons given 33-XXX numbers that should have been in the 37XXX series as they were to Blue Riband quality. It should have been 37-675V but this has now been used on something else.

W39f.   14T Tank Wagon (Revised Type 3) (2000)

This is the Blue Riband version of the early Type 3 and so it has a 7mm domed manhole cap, a tall hand wheel control valve and horizontal stays tieing the end stanchions together. The body appears to be from the old tooling and the chassis has had two modifications. The brake handles are now a separate moulding and the couplings are in NEM pockets allowing them to be easily changed.

37-651	'Bitumuls' 12 black - 00	15	23
37-679	'BP' 5075, buff - 03	9	11
37-679R	'BP Shell' 5075, buff * - 05	8	10
37-653	'Burmah' 118 black - 02	12	15
37-652	'Joseph Crosfield & Sons' 3 blue - 00	12	15
37-650	'ICI' 315 maroon - not made	NA	NA
37-650	'ICI' 313 maroon - 00	14	18
(30-045)	'ICI' 313 maroon, ex-set - 04	14	NA
37-661	'ICI' 311 maroon - 13	10	12
37-656	'ICI' 159 dark blue-green - 05	5	7
37-650V	'Lane Brothers' 101 black Sp Edn 500 (Warley 2008) - 08	30	50
37-650W	'Lane Brothers' 102 black W Sp Edn 500 (Warley 2008) - 08	30	65
37-675	'Mobil' 1624 black - 00	15	25
37-675A	'Mobil' 5294 black - 09	6	8
37-675B	'Mobil' 5291 black - 10	6	8
37-659	'National Benzole' 654 yellow? - not made	NA	NA
37-660	'National Fertilizers' 501 brown - 10	6	8
37-662	'Pease & Partners Limited' brown - 13	10	12
37-655	'Pratts Spirit' 1613 buff - 02	15	20
37-650K	'Charles Roberts' 9876 buff Sp Edn (BCC) - 05	10	12
37-665A	'Ronuk' 34 black+blue - 13	10	12
37-654	'Ronuk' 38 black+blue - 02	15	20
37-657	'Rothervale' 48 black - 05	8	10
37-679A	'Jas. Williamson & Son' 21 buff - 05	8	10

W39g.   14T Tank Wagon (Revised Type 4) (2002)

Here we have the Blue Riband version of the early Type 4 tank wagon but with the modified chassis as described above. So it has narrow ladders (4.5mm wide), a 6' gantry (23mm) each side of the flat 7.5mm detailed manhole cover, a hand wheel control valve projection beside it and horizontal stays tieing the end stanchions together.

Late 14T tank wagon model Type 4 [W39g]

37-690Y	'Brotherton' 900, blue+red, Sp Edn 500 (Warley 2007) - 07	35	40
37-690T	'Brotherton' 906, blue+red W, Sp Edn 500 (Warley 2010) - 10	8	10
37-690Z	'Brotherton' 806, red-brown, Sp Edn 500 (Warley 2007) - 07	35	40
37-690U	'Brotherton' 808, red-brown W, Sp Edn 500 (Warley 2010) - 10	8	10

Bachmann Branchline

37-656	'ICI' 159, dark blue-green - 05	5	7
37-650S	'Scottish & Newcastle' 113 red-brown Sp Edn 504 (Harburn Hobbies) - 13	12	15
37-500Z*	'Shell-Mex-BP' A5281, Sp Edn 500 (Pennine Models) - 02	25	34

* Box marked '37-500Z'. The label was stuck over one for '24T Hopper BR Grey'. Was this due to a change in the order?

W39h. 14T Tank Wagon (Type 4.5) (2009)

This is the same as Blue Riband Type 4 but has no ladders and may carry logo boards mounted on its sides.

37-659	'National Benzole' 755 silver - 09	6	8
37-659A	'National Benzole' 757 silver - 10	6	8
37-659B	'National Benzole' 752 silver - 11	7	9

W39i. 14T Tank Wagon (Revised Type 5) (2000)

We come finally to the Blue Riband version of the large cap tank (Type 5). It has the Type 5 body on the modified chassis with its separate brake handles and coupling NEM pockets. So it has the raised 10mm manhole cover and small hand wheel control valve column and cross stays.

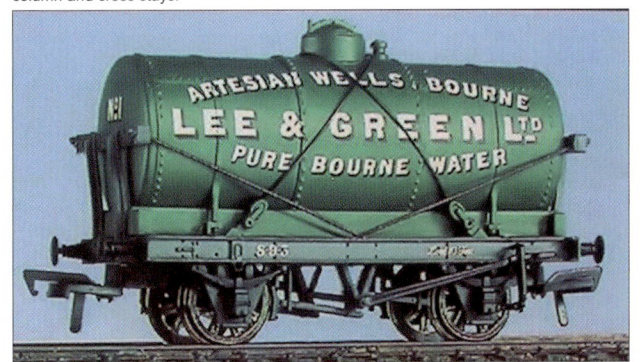

Late 14T tank wagon Type 5 [W39i]

37-676	'Acme Dominion' 25 lemon - 00	12	15
37-679	'BP Shell' 5075 buff - 02	9	11
37-679R	'BP Shell' 5075 buff * - 05	8	10
37-675W*	'Briggs' 20 black Sp Edn (Harburn Hobbies) (33-675W) - 00	15	25
37-677	'Carburine' Motor Spirit 6 buff - 01	12	15
37-682	'Crosfield Chemicals' 129 dark green - 10	10	12
37-680	'Esso' 1210 silver - 02	12	16
37-680R	'Esso' 1210 silver * - 05	8	10
37-684	'Esso' 2877 silver - 13	10	12
37-680A	'Fina' 136 silver - 05	8	10
37-658	'Fina' 140 black - 09	6	8
37-658A	'Fina' 141 black - 10	6	8
37-658B	'Fina' 114 black - 11	7	9
37-679	'Lancaster Tar' - not made	NA	NA
37-675S	'Lane Bros' 186 black Sp Edn 500 (Warley 2009) - 09	15	22
37-675T	'Lane Bros' 187 black W Sp Edn 500 (Warley 2009) - 09	12	20
37-650X	'Lee & Green' 1 blue-green Sp Edn 750 (British Railway Modelling) - 02	25	30
37-650Y	'Lindsey & Kesteven Chemical Co.' 2 black Sp Edn 500 (B&H Models) - 02	14	17
37-650Z	'Morris Little's Sheep Dips' 3 black Sp Edn 500 (B&H Models) - 01	14	17
-	above two wagons - 03	NA	24
37-675ZZ	'Major & Co.' 87 brown (Only one 'Z' printed on the box) Sp Edn (Warley 2005) - 05	30	42
37-685W	'Mex Lamp Oils' 336 black - 13	10	12
37-675Z	'Midland Tar Distillers' 278 black Sp Edn 500 (Warley 2004) (no 'Z' on box) - 04	40	55
37-675X	'Michael Nairn & Co.' 503 yellow Sp Edn (Harburn Hobbies) - 00	14	17
37-681	'OCO' (Olympic Cake & Oil) 202 brown - 07	10	12
37-683	'John Robinson & Co,' 3 brown - 10	7	9
-	'Sheffield Chemical Co.' 33 black (see table W39e)	NA	NA
37-678	'United Molasses' 13 brown - 02	12	15
37-675Y	'War Office A6' 86, buff, Sp Edn 504 (Castle Trains) - 09	6	8
37-675V	'The West Midlands Sugar Co.' 2 dark blue Sp Edn (Warley Show 2006) - 06	30	42

It seems these two wagons, in error, were sent instead of 'Lancaster Tar' and 'Fina' and so were given an 'R' suffix and sold as new models after the boxes had been re-labelled. Early releases from the store were not re-labelled and so do not carry the 'R' suffix and some retailers added the suffix by hand. 'Lancaster Tar' was then dropped and replaced by 'Jas. Williamson & Son'.

W39j. 14T Tank Traffic Classics Sets (Mixed) (1997)

These are pre-Blue Riband tank wagons of mixed types. In some cases, special illustrated 'Tank Classics' boxes were used and in other cases they came in a standard dark blue box.

-	'Shell BP' A5066 pale grey	8	NA
-	'Shell BP' 4886 black	8	NA
-	'Shell' 4417 silver	8	NA
33-525	Tank Traffic above set of 3 - 97	NA	30
-	'Esso' 301 buff	10	NA
-	'Power Ethyl' 116 green	10	NA
-	'Royal Daylight' 1531 red	10	NA
33-525Z	Tank Traffic above set of 3 Sp Edn 500 (Alton Model Centre) - 98	NA	35

Tank Traffic Set (early) [W39j]

-	'National Benzol' 734 silver	9	NA
-	'National Benzol' 2023 black	9	NA
-	'National Benzol Mixture' 576 buff	9	NA
33-526*	Tank Traffic above set of 3 - 98	NA	32
-	'Esso' 1829 black	8	NA
-	'Esso' 2232 silver	8	NA
-	'Esso' 303 buff	8	NA
33-527*	Tank Traffic above set of 3 - 98	NA	30
-	'Berry Wiggins' 150 black	10	NA
-	'Berry Wiggins' 119 silver	10	NA
-	'Berry Wiggins' 109 black	10	NA
33-528	Tank Traffic above set of 3 - 99	NA	35

The factory list gives the set number to the first wagon listed and a '1' suffix to the second and a '2' suffix to the third.

W39k. Sets of 14T Tank Wagons (2002)

These were sets of three railtank models, the same as in the last table, but all were fitted with Blue Riband chassis. The wagon set came in a single long box.

Tank Traffic Set (late) [W39k]

-	'BP' A3472 silver twin logos	10	NA
-	'BP' 36 silver single logo boards	10	NA
-	'BP/Shell' 1223 silver, words	10	NA
37-665	set of above 3 wagons - 02	NA	35
-	'British Tar Products' 102 black W	12	NA
-	'British Tar Products' 104 black W	12	NA
-	'British Tar Products' 105 black W	12	NA
37-672	set of above 3 weathered wagons - 13	NA	40
-	'Crosfield' 127 green W large cap	8	NA
-	'Crosfield' 128 green W large cap	8	NA
-	'Crosfield' 130 green W large cap	8	NA
37-682Z	set of above 3 weathered revised type 5 tank wagons Sp Edn 504 (Waltons) - 11	NA	29
-	'Esso' 1945 black W	9	NA
-	'Esso' 1343 black W	9	NA
-	'Esso' 1921 black W	9	NA
37-682	set of above 3 wagons - 05	NA	32

8th Edition

Bachmann Branchline

Cat No.	Description	Price	Value
-	**'Esso'** 1485 black W large cap	8	NA
-	**'Esso'** 2338 black W small cap	8	NA
-	**'Esso'** 2184 black W small cap	8	NA
37-666A	set of above 3 wagons - 06	NA	29
-	**'Esso'** 1231 black W large cap (type 5)	7	NA
-	**'Esso'** 1855 black W small cap (type 4)	7	NA
-	**'Esso'** 1869 black W small cap (type 4)	7	NA
37-666B*	set of above 3 wagons - 09	NA	26

Weathered Esso tank wagons [W39k]

Cat No.	Description	Price	Value
-	**'Esso'** 2878 silver W large cap	9	NA
-	**'Esso'** 303 silver W small cap	9	NA
-	**'Esso'** 3060 silver W gantry + ladder	9	NA
37-668	set of above 3 weathered wagons - 05	NA	32
-	**'Esso'** ? silver large cap	11	NA
-	**'Esso'** ? silver large cap	11	NA
-	**'Esso'** ? silver large cap	11	NA
37-684	above 3 wagons - 13	NA	39
-	**'Fina'** 138 black W large cap	11	NA
-	**'Fina'** 143 black W large cap	11	NA
-	**'Fina'** 146 black W large cap	11	NA
37-671	above 3 weathered wagons - 13	NA	39
-	**'National Benzole'** 762 silver W	8	NA
-	**'National Benzole'** 764 silver W	8	NA
-	**'National Benzole'** 766 silver W	8	NA
37-659Z	set of above 3 weathered wagons types 4 & 5 Sp Edn 504 (Hereford Model Centre) - 11	NA	30
-	**'Shell BP'** A4294 black W (Type 5)	8	NA
-	**'Shell BP'** 5101 black W (Type 4)	8	NA
-	**'Shell BP'** 3973 black W (Type 3)	8	NA
37-669Z	set of above 3 wagons Sp Edn (ModelZone & Signal Box) - 11	NA	30
-	**'Lion'** C15 black W	9	NA
-	**'Lion'** C24 black W	9	NA
-	**'Lion'** C66 black W	9	NA
37-665Z	set of above 3 weathered wagons Sp Edn 250 (Hereford Model Centre) - 07	NA	32

Tank Traffic set (late) [W39k]

Cat No.	Description	Price	Value
-	**'Power Petrol'** 106 buff	9	NA
-	**'Power'** 501 buff	9	NA
-	**'Power Petrol'** 505 buff	9	NA
37-665Y	above 3 tank wagons Sp Edn 504 (ModelZone) - 11	NA	32
-	**'Shell BP'** 3971 black small cap	8	NA
-	**'Shell BP'** 5103 black ladders	8	NA
-	**'Shell BP'** A4282 black large cap	8	NA
37-669	set of above 3 wagons - 06	NA	29
-	**'Tarmac'** 58 black W large cap (Type 5)	7	NA
-	**'Tarmac'** 60 black W large cap (Type 5)	7	NA
-	**'Tarmac'** 66 black W large cap (Type 5)	7	NA
37-670	set of above 3 wagons - 09	NA	24
-	**'Tarmac'** 55 black W large cap (Type 5)	7	NA
-	**'Tarmac'** 68 black W large cap (Type 5)	7	NA
-	**'Tarmac'** 69 black W large cap (Type 5)	7	NA
37-670A	set of above 3 wagons - 10	NA	26
-	**'War Office A6'** 83 buff	10	NA
-	**'War Office A6'** 84 buff	10	NA
-	**'War Office A6'** 85 buff	10	NA
37-675Y	above three models as a set Sp Edn 504 (Castle Trains) - 09	NA	28

* This set was released early in 2009 in the standard all-blue packaging and then reissued at the end of 2009 in the new blue and red box.

W40. 20T Tank Wagon (2013)

This was a 20 ton private owner wagon.

The model was under development as we went to press but the catalogue illustration suggests that it will be a larger version of the 14 ton tank wagons in the Bachmann range and have plenty of detail, including ladders and a gantry.

Cat No.	Description	Price	Value
38-776	**'Esso'** ? silver - 13	NPG	12
38-775	**'ICI'** ? ? - 13	NPG	12
38-777	**'NCB'** ? ? W - 13	NPG	14

W41. 45t TTA 'Monobloc' Tank Wagon (2005)

The 'Monobloc' tank wagon appeared on the railways in Britain in 1958 and was based on a French design. By lowering the tank between the solebars the centre of gravity was also lowered, thus allowing the accommodation of a larger tank. Wing plates welded to the solebars hold the tank in place.

'Monobloc' tank wagon [W41] (Tony Wright)

Cat No.	Description	Price	Value
37-575M	**'Amoco'** PR58123 pale grey Sp Edn 250 (Frizinghall Model Railways) - 08	10	13
37-575M/W	**'Amoco'** PR58123 pale grey W Sp Edn 250 (Frizinghall Model Railways) - 08	10	13
37-581	**'BP'** BPO53724 black (gas oil) - 06	6	8
37-575	**'BP'** BPO53774 green, petroleum logos - 05	7	9
37-575A	**'BP'** BPO37086 green, petroleum logos - 10	7	9
37-575B	**'BP'** BPO37263 green, petroleum logos - 13	8	10
37-575R	**'BP'** Chemicals 5557 grey W Sp Edn (Cheltenham Model Centre) - 07	10	12
37-575N	**'BP' Jet A1** *** BPO60880 green, aviation fuel Sp Edn 500 (Model Rail) - 07	10	12
37-575P	**'BP' Jet A1** BPO60586 green, aviation fuel Sp Edn 500 (Model Rail) - 07	10	12
37-575Q	**'BP' Jet A1** BPO60873 green, aviation fuel Sp Edn 500 (Model Rail) - 07	10	12
37-575J	**'BP' Jet A1** BPO60878 green W, aviation fuel Sp Edn 504 (Harburn Hobbies/D&F Models) - 11	9	12
37-576V(4)	**'Charringtons'** 53759 black W -12	9	12
37-576V(1)	**'Charringtons'** 53760 black W -12	9	12
37-576V(2)	**'Charringtons'** 53777 grey W -12	9	12
37-576V(3)	**'Charringtons'** 53775 grey W -12	9	12
37-576V	above 4 weathered wagons were to have been issued as a set but were sold individually Sp Edn 504 (ModelZone)	NA	NA
37-584	**'Ciba-Geigy'** ? light blue - 13	10	12
37-576	**'Esso'** 57575 light grey BRT - 05	7	9
37-576A	**'Esso'** 5961 light grey BRT - 10	7	9
37-576B	**'Esso'** 5955 light grey BRT - 11	8	10
37-576X	**'Esso'** 5925 pale grey W Sp Edn 504 (ModelZone)	10	12
37-576Y	**'Esso'** 5959 pale grey W Sp Edn 504 (ModelZone)	10	12
37-576Z	**'Esso'** 5970 pale grey W Sp Edn 504 (ModelZone)	10	12

Bachmann Branchline

37-576W	Above 3 Esso tank wagons individually boxed - *07*		NA	32
37-582	'**Fina**' 3 silver - *06*		7	9
37-575S	'**Gulf**' 731 grey W Sp Edn (Cheltenham Model Centre) - *07*		10	12
37-578A	'**ICI Methanol**' 54858 very pale grey - *13*		10	12
37-578	'**ICI Petrochemicals & Plastics**' 54365 white - *05*		8	10
37-583	'**Mobil**' 57305 pale grey - *09*		7	9
37-583A	'**Mobil**' 57303 pale grey - *11*		7	10
37-577	'**Shell BP**' 67391 light grey - *04*		7	9
37-577A	'**Shell BP**' 582 light grey - *11*		7	10
37-577Z	'**Shell BP**' 5165 black Sp Edn 504 (Hereford Model Centre) - *07*		10	12
37-577Y	'**Shell BP**' 5169 black Sp Edn 504 (Hereford Model Centre) - *10*		8	11
37-577W	'**Shell BP**' 5172 black Sp Edn 504 (Hereford Model Centre) - *10*		8	11
37-577X	'**Shell BP**' 5178 black Sp Edn 504 (Hereford Model Centre) - *10*		8	11

TTA 'Monobloc' tank wagon [W41]

37-582A	'**Shell BP**' 3452 black - *10*		7	9
37-582B	'**Shell BP**' 3029 black - *11*		8	10
37-582C	'**Shell BP**' 3410 black - *12*		10	12
37-575X	'**Shell**' 65537 black W Sp Edn (TMC)* - *05*		10	12
37-575Y	'**Shell**' 65543 black W Sp Edn (TMC)* - *05*		10	12
37-575Z	'**Shell**' 65709 black W Sp Edn (TMC)* - *05*		10	12
37-579	'**Shell**' SUKO60705 pale grey - *05*		7	9
37-580	'**Total**' PR58278 grey Caib - *06*		7	9
C	CC55526 black, 'Water Only'		10	12
B	CC55529 black, 'Water Only'		10	12
A	CC55530 black, 'Water Only'		10	12
D	CC55536 black, 'Water Only'		10	12
37-575L	above 4 wagons** Sp Edn 512 (Kernow MRC) - *10*			

Unbranded Grey

37-575T	56050 W		9	NA
37-575U	56039 W		9	NA
37-575V	56177 W		9	NA
37-575W	56103 W		9	NA
37-575T	set of above 4 wagons Sp Edn 512 (Kernow MR Centre) - *05*		NA	40

* Initially sold only as a set of the three.
** From a Chipman weedkilling train. Individually boxed.
***These wagons have been used to transport fuel from the oil refinery at Grangemouth to Prestwick Airport.

W42. TTA 45T Class B Tank Wagon (2013)

This is a more modern TTA tank wagon with conical ends. The model was under development at the time of writing.

37-560	'**?**' ? black - *13*		NPG	12
37-561	'**?**' ? black W - *13*		NPG	14
37-562	'**?**' ? black - *13*		NPG	12
37-563	'**?**' ? black W - *13*		NPG	14

Pitched Roof Vans

W43. Covered Lime Wagon (2004)

Lime was once carried in special wagons with steeply pitched roofs to throw off the water. Later dry powder tanks were used, with pressure unloading.
  This consisted of a Blue Riband 5-plank wagon (with a wooden type floor) and a separate moulded roof section in the box which converted it into a lime wagon.

37-025Y	'**SLB**' 702 grey Sp Edn 500 (Geoffrey Allinson) - *04*		11	13

W44. 10T Salt Van (1992)

Although called 'salt' vans, these peak roofed vehicles, which looked like garden shed on wheels, also carried other things. Similar designs in Scotland were used as the forerunners of steel grain hoppers and they were used for other loads. For example, 'LGW' stands for Leith General Warehousing. Most, however, were owned by salt companies in the Cheshire area.

33-177	'**Chance & Hunt**'* 333 dark brown - *92*		10	12
33-178	'**DCL**' 52 light grey - *02*		9	11
33-177V	'**DCL**' 52 light grey W Sp Edn 504 (Harburn Hobbies) - *11*		6	8
33-180	'**Falk Salt**' 2521 green - *06*		8	10
33-178	'**ICI Salt**' 3781 green blue - *92*		10	12
33-179	'**ICI Salt**' 326 maroon - *06*		8	10
33-179A	'**ICI Fleetwood Salt**' 12 maroon - *09*		5	7
33-183	'**ICI Tees Salt**' 71 red-brown - *12*		7	9
33-177X	'**Leith General Warehousing Co**.' ** 120 red-brown Sp Edn 500 (Harburn Hobbies) - *03*		10	12
33-177U	'**Leith General Warehousing Co.**' ** 184 brown W Sp Edn 504 (Harburn Hobbies) - *11*		6	8
33-177W	'**LGW**' ** 118 red-brown Sp Edn 500 (Harburn Hobbies) - *03*		10	12
33-177T	'**LGW**' ** 168 brown W Sp Edn 504 (Harburn Hobbies) - *11*		6	8
33-177	'**Mangers Salt**' 180 green - *not made*		NA	NA
33-177	'**Mangers Salt**' 121 green - *02*		9	11
33-177Y	'**North British Storage and Transit Company**' ** 56 grey Sp Edn 500 (Harburn Hobbies) - *03*		10	12
33-176	'**Saxa Salt**' 255 orange-yellow - *92*		10	12
33-176A	'**Saxa Salt**' 251 yellow - *96*		10	12
33-179	'**Shaka Salt**' 168 blue - *92*		10	12
33-182	'**Snowdrift Salt**' 306 light green - *09*		5	7
33-181	'**Stafford Salt Works**' C28 red - *94*		10	12
33-175	'**Stubbs Salt**' 35 maroon - *92*		10	12

Salt van [W44]

33-177Z	'**The Distillers Co**.' ** 46 light grey Sp Edn 500 (Harburn Hobbies) - *03*		11	13
33-184	'**Tollemache Pulverised Coal**' ? ? - *13*		NPG	NPG
33-180	'**Union Salt**' 2713 grey - *92*		10	12
33-177	'**Winsford Salt**' - *not made*		NA	NA

* sold in a box marked 'Winsford Salt'. ** This was based on the 10T covered salt wagon and not an accurate representation of the Scottish grain wagons, the models represent. These were in use between 1903 and 1969 and 'LGW' was the post-Nationalisation livery of 'Leith General Warehousing Co..

GWR Vans

W45. 8T/12T GWR/BR Cattle Wagon (2009)

The cattle wagon was an early development on the railways, allowing farmers to move cattle quickly to market and to take them over far greater distances than could previously be achieved by droving. They were a common sight parked in rural sidings. To load them, a cattle dock was usually required and these became a common feature at country stations. Many of the GWR cattle wagons dated back to the late Victorian period but, during the 1930s, there was a decline in livestock traffic on the railways some vans were rebuilt for fruit traffic or ale. BR inherited over 11,000 cattle wagons and, despite the continuing decline in traffic, carried on building them up until 1954 - 2300 of them at Swindon. Redundant vans were used for other purposes, including vegetables. The last

Bachmann Branchline

two cattle wagons are at the National Railway Museum.
  Compared with the LMS cattle wagon (below), the GWR model is finescale and superbly detailed.

37-711	GW 106881 dark grey - 09	6	7
37-711A	GW 106909 dark grey - 10	6	7
37-711B	GW 106766 dark grey - 11	6	8
37-711C	GW ? dark grey - 13	NPG	NPG
37-710	BR 134209 brown - not made	NA	NA
37-710	BR B893343 brown - 10	6	7
37-710A	BR B893111 brown - 10	6	7
37-710B	BR B893023 brown early livery - 11	6	8
37-712	BR B893085 brown XP - 10	6	7
37-712A	BR B893268 brown late livery - 10	6	7
37-712B	BR B893639 brown late livery - 11	6	8
37-712C	BR B893232 brown W - 12	9	11
37-713	BR B893429 brown late livery 'Ale' - 13	NPG	NPG
-	GWR 106699 dark grey W	7	NA
-	GWR 106855 dark grey W	7	NA
-	GWR 106901 dark grey W	7	NA
37-711Z	above 3 Sp Edn (Hereford Model Centre) - 10	NA	27
-	GWR 106750 dark grey	7	NA
-	GWR 106838 dark grey	7	NA
-	GWR 106917 dark grey	7	NA
37-711Y	above 3 Sp Edn (Hereford Model Centre) - 10	NA	27
-	BR B893603 brown W	7	NA
-	BR B893455 brown W	7	NA
-	BR B893682 brown W	7	NA
37-710Z	above 3 Sp Edn 504 (ModelZone) - 09	NA	26
-	BR B893007 brown W	7	NA
-	BR B893510 brown W	7	NA
-	BR B893370 brown W	7	NA
37-712Z	above 3 wagons Sp Edn 504 (TMC) - 10	NA	27
-	BR B893582 brown W	8	NA
-	BR B893401 brown W	8	NA
-	BR B893177 brown W	8	NA
37-715	above 3 weathered wagons - 11	NA	33

BR cattle wagon [W45]

W46a.   GWR 12T Goods Fruit Van (ex-Mainline) (1991)

This model is based on the GWR 'Goods Fruit A', 200 of which were built in 1938. They were also used for vegetables and general merchandise. They were vacuum braked and carried the XP branding for use in fast trains. 100 more were built to the same design at Swindon in 1949-50. Early in their lives they were largely used in the Vale of Evesham but later they were usually to be found in East Anglia.
  The models in this table were made using the original Mainline tooling.

33-202	GW 134209 dark grey - 94	8	10
33-202	LMS 134209 grey - not made	NA	NA
33-201	BR 'Fisons' W134195 brown * - 91	8	10
33-204	BR W134265 brown W - 99	7	9
33-200	BR B875274 brown + chalk marks - 90	8	10
33-203	undecorated light grey - 91	6	8

* box says BR grey with chalk marks.

W46b.   GWR 12T Goods Fruit Van (2001)

These examples are mounted on a Blue Riband chassis with NEM pockets for couplings and separate brake handles.

37-751	GW 134281 dark grey - 01	7	9
37-751A	GW 134209 dark grey - 02	7	9
37-751B	GW 134330 dark grey - 03	7	9
37-751C	GW 134139 dark grey - 05	6	8
37-750	BR W134143 brown - 01	7	9
37-750A*	BR W134143 brown - 02	7	9
37-750B	BR W134333 brown - 03	7	9
37-752	BR W134330 brown - 05	6	8
37-754	BR W134150 brown - 06	6	8
37-754A	BR W134214 brown - 09	5	7
37-754B	BR W134211 brown - 10	5	7
37-754C	BR W134277 brown - 11	6	8
(37-726Y)	BR W134201 brown W 'Pembroke Dock/ Carmarthen' ex-set of 3 Sp Edn 504 (Modelzone) - 06	9	NA

W47a.   12T GWR 'Mogo' Van (ex-Mainline) (1991)

'Mogo' motor car vans were fully planked and had doors at both ends to allow the cars to be end-loaded and passed van to van. They were fitted with end flaps, which folded down and rested on the buffer stocks to provided a bridge. Inside the van there were wheel chocks and fixing-down tackle which could be stowed when the vans were used for other merchandise.
  This table includes the models with the former Mainline chassis.

33-702	GW 126981 dark grey - 94	8	10
33-704	GW 126342 dark grey W - 99	7	9
33-700	BR W126981 brown - 91	8	10
33-700A	BR W126981 brown with chalk marks - ?	NPG	NPG
33-701	BR W126901* dark grey - 91	14	18
33-703	undecorated light grey - 91	6	8

W47b.   12T GWR 'Mogo' Van (2001)

This is the model with the upgraded chassis, which brought it into the Blue Riband range.

37-778	GW 127000 dark grey - 06	6	8
37-778A	GW 126450 dark grey - 09	5	7
37-778B	GW 123955 dark grey - 10	5	7
37-778C	GW 109705 dark grey - 12	7	9

GWR 'Mogo' van [W47b]

37-775	BR W133971 grey - 01	7	9
37-776	BR W126884 brown - 01	7	9
37-776	BR W123956 brown - 01	7	9
37-776A	BR W123954 brown - 02	7	9
37-776B	BR W124000 brown - 03	7	9
37-777	BR W105666 brown - 05	6	8
37-779	BR W105737 brown - 06	6	8
37-779A	BR W105666 brown - 09	5	7
37-779B	BR W126428 brown - 10	5	7
37-780	BR W? brown - 13	NPG	NPG
(37-726Y)	BR W126337 brown W 'Return to Cowley' ex-set of 3 Sp Edn 504 (ModelZone) - 06	9	NA
37-779Z	BR Satlink KDW65742 red+yellow Sp Edn 504 (*Model Rail* magazine) - 12 *	10	13

This wagon was distributed by Kernow Model Rail Centre.

W48a.   12T GWR Double Vent Van (ex-Mainline) (1991)

At Nationalisation, the former GWR had unfulfilled orders of unfitted ventilated vans. They were delivered to British Railways who ordered 330 more of them in 1949.

33-602	GW 134089 dark grey - 91	8	10
33-604	GW 35065 dark grey W - 99	7	9
33-600	BR W145548 brown with chalk marks - 91	8	10
33-601	BR W133977 grey - 91	8	10

Bachmann Branchline

33-603	undecorated light grey - 91		6	8

W48b. 12T GWR Double Vent Van (2001)
This is the retooled model upgrading it to Blue Riband standard.

37-725	GW 139956 dark grey - 01		7	9
37-725A	GW 112787 dark grey - 03		6	8
37-727	GW 112787 grey Parto - not made		NA	NA
37-727	GW 112754 dark grey Parto - 04		6	8
37-730	GW 126129 dark grey - 06		6	8
37-730A	GW 142335 dark grey - 09		5	7
37-730B	GW 134040 dark grey - 11		6	8
-	GW 142711 dark grey W		7	NA
-	GW 142101 dark grey W		7	NA
-	GW 133939 dark grey W		7	NA
37-730Z	above set of 3 Sp Edn 504 (Hereford Model Centre - 11	NA	25
37-775	BR W133971 light grey - 01		7	9
37-775A	BR W133971 light grey - not made		7	9
37-775B	BR W134030 light grey - 02		7	9
37-775C	BR W142220 light grey - 05		6	8
37-731	BR W133980 light grey - 09		5	7
37-731A	BR W142220 light grey - 10		5	7
37-726	BR W124480 brown - 01		7	9
37-726A	BR W142689 brown - 03		6	8
37-726B	BR W14150 brown - 05		6	8
37-728	BR W142689 brown - not made		NA	NA
37-728	BR W142218 brown - 04		6	8
37-729	BR W101090 brown - 06		6	8
37-729A	BR W126140 brown - 08		5	7
37-729B	BR W125987 brown - 11		6	8
(37-726Y)	BR W126725 brown W 'M/T Hither Green' ex-set of 3 Sp Edn 504 (ModelZone) - 06		9	NA

Ex-GWR double vent van [W48b]

-	BR W114521 brown W 'Plymouth/Bristol TM'		9	NA
-	BR W112818 brown W 'Crewe'		9	NA
-	BR W116296 brown W		9	NA
37-726Z	above three Sp Edn 500 (TMC) - 03		NA	32
37-800Z	Virgin Trains 220 white Sp Edn 500 (Virgin Trains) - 01	8	10

W49. Set of Mixed Ex-GWR Vans (2006)
So far there has been only one mixed set of GWR vans.

-	BR W134201 brown W fruit van		7	NA
-	BR W126725 brown W vent van		7	NA
-	BR W126337 brown W Mogo van		7	NA
37-726Y	above three vans Sp Edn 504 (ModelZone) - 06	NA	25

LMS Vans

W50a. LMS Cattle Wagon (ex-Mainline) (1991)
The LMS cattle van design seems to have been much influenced by Midland Railway design. Improved roads in the 1930s caused a decline in railway transportation and some LMS vans were converted to carry ale. After the war, surviving cattle vans needed replacing and the LMS placed an order resulting in 1350 being built by BR in 1949-50, mostly at Derby.

The models in this table are from the original Mainline tooling.

33-652	LMS M14400 grey small letters - 92		8	10
33-652A	LMS M14407 grey small letters - 94		8	10
33-652C	LMS 292372 grey large letters (boxed as 'LMS Brown') - 98		8	10
33-655	LMS 243606 grey W - not made		NA	NA
33-655	LMS M143820 grey W **** - 00?		NPG	NPG
33-652B	LMS 214875 brown medium letters - 95		8	10
33-651A	NE 502460 grey - 94		8	10
33-651A	NE 55787 grey (box says 'NE brown') - 95		8	10
33-651B	NE 55787 grey large letters - 96		8	10
33-651	NE 502680 brown large letters - 91		12	17
33-651.1	NE 502676 brown *** - made?		NPG	NPG
(30-100)	NE 502676 brown ex-set (33-650Z?) - ?		8	NA
33-655	BR M143820 brown W **** - 00		7	9
33-651A	BR B753894 grey ('NE Brown' on box) - 95		8	10
33-650	BR M14398 brown - 90		8	10
33-650A*	BR M14390 brown - 93		8	10
33-650B	BR M266640 brown - 95		8	10
33-650C	BR M14400 brown - 98		7	9
33-650.1	BR M14398 brown + chalk marks - 90		10	12
33-650.2	BR 12098 brown - made?		NPG	NPG
33-656**	BR M143820 brown W - made?		NPG	NPG
33-656	BR 243606 brown W - 00		7	9
33-652Z	BTU yellow tool van Sp Edn (ModelZone) - 10		NPG	NPG
33-653	undecorated light grey - 91		6	8

* No 'A' suffix on box label. ** 33-655 box relabelled. *** no number on box. **** The box was marked - 'BR B/GREY WEATHERED'.

W50b. 12T LMS 10T HBO Cattle Wagon (2002)
In 2002, the former Mainline cattle wagon was upgraded with a new chassis, making it a Blue Riband model. It now had slimline couplings clipped into NEM pockets. The new chassis had independent brake handles and tie-bar.

37-701	LMS M14390 grey - 02		7	9
37-701A	LMS 230909 grey - 04		6	8
37-703	LMS 12098 grey - 05		6	8
37-705	LMS 69453 grey - 07		6	8

ex-LMS cattle wagon [W50b]

37-708	LMS 214878 brown - 13		NPG	NPG
37-707	NE 626800 grey - 13		NPG	NPG
37-706	NE 602686 brown - 13		NPG	NPG
37-700A	BR M292722 brown - 04		6	8
37-702	BR M230909 brown - 05		6	8
37-704	BR M239381 brown - 07		6	8
37-700	BR B891416 brown - 02		7	9
-	BR M292750 brown W		6	NA
-	BR M301600 brown W		6	NA
-	BR M302349 brown W		6	NA
37-700Z	above 3 Sp Edn 504 (TMC) - 04		NA	22

W51a. LMS 12T Single Vent Van (ex-Mainline) (1992)
These had corrugated steel end walls and a single sliding door on both sides. Orders for 1300 plywood-sided and 1000 planked vans were placed immediately after Nationalisation and these carried a B prefix to the number.

The doors on the model are fixed shut as they are part of the single moulding. This table lists the early models without the Blue Riband chassis.

33-625	LMS 511470 grey - 92		8	10
33-626	BR M283322 light grey - 92		8	10
33-628	BR M504891 light grey W - 99		7	9
33-627	BR B751782 brown Sunday Times - 92		8	10

Bachmann Branchline

W51b. 12T LMS Single Vent Van (2001)
This is the same model as above, but with the retooled chassis, upgrading the model to Blue Riband standard.

LMS single vent van [W51b]

37-800	**LMS** 505969 grey (blue label on box) - *01*		7	9
37-800A	**LMS** 505969 grey (white label on box) - *02*		7	9
37-800B*	**LMS** 52946 grey - *03*		6	8
37-803	**LMS** 506818 grey - *07*		6	8
37-803A	**LMS** 518520 grey - *09*		5	7
37-803B	**LMS** ? grey - *13*		NPG	NPG
37-803	**LMS** 505969 brown - *not made*		NA	NA
37-801	**BR** M518972 brown - *01*		7	9
37-801A	**BR** M508587 brown ** - *03*		7	9
37-801B*	**BR** M508894 brown - *03*		6	8
37-802	**BR** M501723 brown - *05*		6	8
37-802A	**BR** M518113 brown - *09*		5	7
37-802B	**BR** M509355 brown - *10*		8	10
37-802C	**BR** M509509 brown - *11*		6	8

* shown with a 'B' suffix in the catalogue but an 'A' suffix on the box. ** Box marked as '37801' with no suffix. Reappeared in 2004 in the 30-045 Digital Freight Set.

LNER Vans

W52. 12T LNER Ventilated Fruit Van (2010)
For some time fruit vans on the LNER retained timber ends as it was easier to build-in louvres in the lower half of each end to ensure good air circulation. Later LNER fruit vans were built in plywood. Besides the end louvers, the models have six ventilators in the roof.

38-385	**BR** E222599 brown (early) - *10*	6	8
38-386	**BR** E222334 brown (late) - *10*	6	8

W53a. 12T LNER Vent Van (Planked Ends) (2010)
LNER standard ventilated vans, for general merchandise, were built on both timber and steel underframes, fitted and unfitted, with spoked or disc wheels and with timber or corrugated steel ends. They generally had a single sliding door on each side, similar to LMS ventilated vans.

The models in this table represent an early design with planked walls.

38-375Z	**'Shepherds Neame & Co.'** 3 cream Sp Edn 504 (Erith MRS 50th Anniv.) - *12*	9	12
38-375	**NE** 236824 brown - *10*	6	8
38-375A	**NE** ? brown - *12*	8	10
38-376	**BR** E236698 brown (early) - *10*	6	8
-	**BR** E235812 brown W	8	NA
-	**BR** E236115 brown W	8	NA
-	**BR** E236396 brown W	8	NA
38-390	set of above 3 weathered vans - *12*	NA	30

W53b. 12T LNER Vent Van (Corrugated Ends) (2010)
Around 1934, the decision was made to follow LMS practice and build ventilated vans with corrugated steel ends and on steel chassis. Many vans of this type were built and included a number of design variations. Some had a hooded ventilator added in each end and some were built two inches narrower for use in restricted sidings. Some were partitioned inside for specific traffic and some found themselves on fish trains. These became the standard design for LNER ventilated vans from the mid 1930s. By the outbreak of war, almost 3000 had been built and, by Nationalisation, the number had risen to 7700.

38-380	**BR** E256948 brown (early) - *10*	6	8
38-380A	**BR** E? brown (early) - *12*	8	10
38-381	**BR** E211308 brown (late) - *10*	6	8
-	**'Aristocraft Trains'** 1935 red+white	7	NA
-	**'Scenecraft'** 2008 grey+yellow	7	NA
-	**'Woodland Scenics'** 1975 dark green	7	NA
38-380K	above 3 vans Sp Edn 504 (BCC) - *11*	NA	25

W53c. 12T LNER Non-Vent Van (Corrugated Ends) (2011).
Referring to the description above, these represent the post-1934 LNER vans that were built without ventilators.

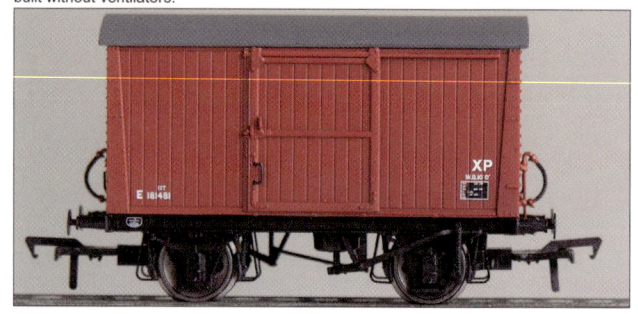

Ex LNER non-vent van [W53c]

38-475	**BR** E181497 brown (early) - *11*	8	10
38-476	**BR** E181481 brown (late) - *11*	8	10

W54. 12T LNER Fish Van (2013)
In the early days, fish was carried in open trucks with low sides but usually sheeted over. The passing of a fish train on a hot summer's day must have been quite an experience. From around 1900 vans started to be used.

38-575	**LNER** 174894 brown - *13*	8	10
38-576	**BR** E184090 brown (early) - *12*	8	10
38-577	**BR** E184090 brown (late) - *13*	8	10

SR Vans

W55a. 12T SR Planked Vent Van (2005)
Typical Southern Railway vans had a vari-curve roof (inherited from the SE&CR) which had tight curves at the edges but flatter on top. The design later proved to be problematical due to 'racking' which caused the roof boards to move, resulting in leakage.

38-072	**SR** 'Express Dairy Company English Eggs' 48323 dark brown - *13*	NPG	NPG
38-070	**SR** 48679 dark brown large letters - *05*	6	8
38-070A	**SR** 48501 dark brown large letters - *06*	6	8
38-070B	**SR** 48293 dark brown large letters - *08*	6	8
38-070C	**SR** 48329 dark brown large letters - *09*	6	8
38-070D	**SR** 48467 dark brown large letters - *10*	6	8
38-071	**BR** S49091 brown - *05*	6	8
38-071A	**BR** S49186 brown Parto - *06*	6	8
38-071B	**BR** S49230 brown - *08*	6	8
(38-071Z)	**BR** S49226 brown W ex-ModelZone set 'Waterloo-Nottingham Empty' - *05*	9	NA

W55b. 12T SR 2+2 Planked Vent Van (2005)
One very obvious style change, dating from late 1938, was the 2+2 planking. This consisted of two narrow planks followed by two wide ones, then two narrow, and so on. Before the war, 1800 were built with this design feature but more were built in a simplified form after hostilities. At least 67 vans went new to the War Department and more followed. Most ended up on various military railways after the war and some remained abroad. During the war over 1000 were ordered by the Railway Executive Committee for use on the LMS and GWR.

38-084	**SR** 65636 dark brown small letters - *13*	NPG	NPG
38-080	**LMS** 521202 light grey - *05*	6	8
38-083	**GWR** 144293 dark grey - *10*	5	7
38-080A	**LMS** 521191 light grey - *09*	6	8
38-080B	**LMS** 523423 light grey - *12*	8	10
38-081	**BR** M523538 light grey - *05*	6	8

Ex-SR vent van with 2+2 planking [W55b]

Bachmann Branchline

38-081A	**BR** M521144 light grey - 08	6	8
38-081B	**BR** M523351 light grey - 10	7	9
38-082	**BR** S54239 brown - 08	6	8
38-082A	**BR** S59123 brown - 09	6	8
38-082B	**BR** S65148 brown - 11	7	9
38-082C	**BR** S59379 brown - 13	8	10
(38-071Z)	**BR** S65981 brown W ex-ModelZone set 'Loaded Basingstoke' - 05	9	NA

W55c. 12T SR Plywood Vent Van (2005)

The shortage of timber later in the war led to some vans being built in plywood, the first appearing in 1945. The building of the vans continued for a while after nationalisation of the railways.

38-075Z	**'Arnold & Hancock'** 1 buff Sp Edn 504 (Buffers) - 06	10	12
38-075Y	**'Arnold & Hancock'** 2 buff Sp Edn 504 (Buffers) - 08	7	8
38-075X	**'Axminster Carpets'** B895008 pale grey Sp Edn 504 (Buffers) - 08	7	8
38-075	**SR** 54409 dark brown small letters - 05	6	8
38-075	**SR** 57002 dark brown small letters - not made	NA	NA
38-075A	**SR** 50933 dark brown small letters - 06	6	8
38-076	**BR** B752698 brown - 05	6	8
38-076A	**BR** S54273 brown - 06	6	8
38-076B	**BR** B752909 brown - 08	6	8
(38-071Z)	**BR** B753001 brown W ex-ModelZone set 'M/T Brighton' - 05	9	NA

W56. 12T BR(SR) Set of Vans (2005)

So far there has been only one mixed set of SR vans.

-	**BR** S49226 brown W 'Waterloo-Nottingham Empty'	9	NA
-	**BR** S65981 brown W 'Loaded Basingstoke'	9	NA
-	**BR** B753001 brown W 'M/T Brighton'	9	NA
38-071Z	above 3 vans with chalk marks Sp Edn 504 (ModelZone) - 05	NA	26

W57. SR 4-Wheel Utility Van (PLV/PMV/CCT) (2013)

This is a new model, due for release in 2013/14, and will be found in the Coaches section and at the end of the Southern Railway Coaches.

BR Vans

W58. 12T BR 'Vanwide' Box Van

This was to have been a Blue Riband model.

37-825	**BR** B784873 brown - not made	NA	NA
37-826	**Railfreight** 230506 red+grey - not made	NA	NA

W59a. 12T BR Planked Ventilated Van (2008)

By the early 1950s, BR started to design their standard wagons. The series of vans they developed had much in common with former GWR designs but with ideas borrowed from the other three companies. These included corrugated end walls (LMS & LNER), hinged double doors (GWR & SR) and a single vent at each end for the ventilated vans.

38-160	**BR** B763964 brown - not made	NA	NA

BR planked vent van [W59a]

38-160	**BR** B762361 brown - 08	6	8
38-160A	**BR** B755845 brown (early) - 09	6	8
38-160B	**BR** B756303 brown (early) - 11	7	9
38-161	**BR** B755180 brown - 08	6	8
38-161A	**BR** B758582 brown - 09	6	8
38-161B	**BR** B760289 brown (late) - 10	6	8
38-160X	**BR** KDB767014 brown W St Blazey Eng. Stores Sp Edn 504 (Kernow MRC) - 08	9	11
38-160Y	**BR** B755772 brown W St Blazey Eng. Stores Sp Edn 504 (Kernow MRC) - 08	9	11
38-162	**BR Departmental** DB7??? Olive green - 13	8	10
-	**'Bachmann'** 175 white+red	7	NA
-	**'Liliput'** 60 grey+blue	7	NA
-	**'Kader'** 60 grey+orange	7	NA
38-160K	above 3 vans Sp Edn 504 (BCC) - 09	NA	23
-	**BR** B758515 brown W	7	NA
-	**BR** B758948 brown W	7	NA
-	**BR** B759129 brown W	7	NA
38-160W	above 3 vans Sp Edn 504 (Hattons) - 09	NA	28
-	**BR** B755822 brown, 'ICI Fertilizer' posters	10	NA
-	**BR** B760065 brown, 'Blue Circle' posters	10	NA
-	**BR** B765001 brown, 'Carrs Biscuits' posters (Mogo van -see W36b)	10	NA
38-160Z	above 3 vans Sp Edn 504 (ModelZone) - 08	NA	43
-	**BR** B770968 brown W chalk marks Bedford	8	NA
-	**BR** B758185 brown W chalk marks Walsall	8	NA
-	**BR** B779954 brown W chalk marks Reading	8	NA
38-161Z	above 3 weathered vans Sp Edn 504 (TMC) - 09	NA	30
-	**BR** ? late brown W	NA	NA
-	**BR** ? late brown W	NA	NA
-	**BR** ? late brown W	NA	NA
38-185 *	set of above 3 weathered vans - not made	NA	NA
-	**BR** (Internal User) 041478 brown W, planked	8	NA
-	**BR** (Internal User) 042130 brown W, plywood	8	NA
-	**BR** (Internal User) 096047 brown W, plywood	8	NA
38-160U	set of above 3 weathered vans Sp Edn 504 (ModelZone) - 12	NA	31

* produced instead as plywood BR fruit vans (see below).

W59b. 12T BR Planked Vent Van (Plywood Doors) (2009)

There were many batches of standard ventilated vans built during the 1950s and this model is based on a batch built at BR Wolverton in 1957-58. The standard vans were either planked or built in plywood or, like these ones, in a combination of both.

38-230	**BR** B773727, brown - 09	6	8
38-230A	**BR** B774447, brown (early livery) - 10	6	8
38-231	**BR** B774238, brown - 09	6	8
38-231A	**BR** B777973, brown - 11	7	9
-	**'Bachmann Branchline'** 1989 20th Anniversary, blue+red	7	NA
-	**'Grafar'** 60th Anniversary 1949, blue+yellow	7	NA
-	**'Graham Farish'** 90th Anniversary 60, white+black	7	NA
38-230K	set of above 3 vans, Sp Edn 504 (BCC) - 09	NA	23
-	**BR** B773667 early brown	7	NA
-	**BR** B773642 early brown	7	NA
-	**BR** B773594 early brown	7	NA
38-230Z	set of above 3 weathered vans, Sp Edn 504 (Hattons) - 10	NA	28
-	**BR** B775312 late brown	7	NA
-	**BR** B774316 late brown	7	NA
-	**BR** B775058 late brown	7	NA
38-231Z	set of above 3 weathered vans, Sp Edn 504 (Hattons) - 10	NA	28

W59c. 12T BR Plywood Ventilated Van (2008)

Plywood bodywork, compared with the more traditional planked type, simplified van building and probably shortened the building time.

The model represents vans built at Wolverton, Darlington and Ashford between 1955 and 1957.

38-170	**BR** B772170 brown - 08	6	8
38-170A	**BR** B772139 brown - 09	6	8
38-170B	**BR** B777586, brown (early) - 10	6	8

Bachmann Branchline

38-170C	BR B775866 brown - *not made*	NA	NA
38-170C	BR B776001 brown (early) - *12*	8	10
38-171	BR B765477 brown - *not made*	NA	NA
38-171	BR B765759 brown - *08*	6	8
38-171A	BR B765351 brown - *09*	6	8
38-171B	BR B775719 brown (late) - *10*	6	8
38-171C	BR B775719 brown - *not made*	NA	NA
38-171C	BR B765995 brown - *12*	8	10
38-170Z	BR ADB766234 olive green 'Vanfit' (EMU spares) Sp Edn 504 (*Model Rail*) - *09*	8	10

W60.   12T BR Fruit Van (2008)

While these were built as fruit vans, they were also used for vegetable traffic and general merchandise. They had a 10ft wheelbase and were vacuum-braked and XP rated.

The model was based on the final version of the standard van, 100 of which were built at Darlington 1953-54.

38-180K	'Graham Farish' No.40 black+yellow Sp Edn ** (BCC) - *10*	7	9
38-180	BR B875800 brown - *08*	6	8
38-180A	BR B875726 brown - *09*	6	8
38-180B	BR B875716 brown (early) - *10*	6	8
38-181	BR B875640 brown - *08*	6	8
38-181A	BR B875649* brown - *09*	6	8
38-181B	BR B875823 brown (late) - *08*	6	8
38-181C	BR B875823 brown (late) - *not made*	NA	NA
38-181C	BR B875772 brown (late) - *12*	8	10
-	BR B875588 late brown W	9	NA
-	BR B875702 late brown W	9	NA
-	BR B875841 late brown W	9	NA
38-185	set of above 3 weathered plywood vans - *12*	NA	35

* Number correctly printed at an angle as on the original wagon.   ** This wagon commemorated the 40th Anniversary of the Graham Farish N gauge range.

W61.   10T BR Insulated Van (2008)

The insulated meat vans were to the same construction as the standard ventilated van but without the end vents. There being little use for them, many ended up in ale traffic and some were used for fish - although, with their short wheelbase, they were unsuitable for the fast Blue Spot fish trains. They were gradually absorbed into general traffic and broken up early.

38-190	BR B872208 pale blue - *08*	6	8
38-190A	BR B872016 pale blue - *09*	6	8
38-191	BR B872187 white - *08*	6	8

BR insulated van [W61]

38-191A	BR B872112 light cream - *09*	6	8
38-191B	BR B872112 white - *not made*	NA	NA
38-191B	BR B872117 white - *12*	8	10
-	BR B872011 white W	8	NA
-	BR B872039 white W	8	NA
-	BR B872129 white W	8	NA
38-191Z	above 3 wagons Sp Edn 504 (Frizinghall Model Railways) - *08*	NA	30
-	BR B872156 pale blue W	8	NA
-	BR B872072 pale blue W	8	NA
-	BR B872191 pale blue W	8	NA
38-190Z	above 3 wagons Sp Edn 504 (TMC) - *09*	NA	30

W62.   Sets of Mixed 12T BR Vans (2011)

In this table are sets of three vans of different types. Where sets are of the same type, they are listed in the appropriate table for that type.

-	BR B761885 brown W 'Cond' planked	7	NA
-	BR B772598 brown W 'Cond' plywood	7	NA
-	BR B765436 brown W 'Cond' plywood	7	NA
38-160V	above 3 condemned vans Sp Edn 504 (ModelZone) - *11*	NA	18
-	BR ? brown internal user vent van planked	9	NA
-	BR ? brown internal user vent van plywood	9	NA
-	BR ? brown internal user vent van plywood	9	NA
38-160U	above 3 internal user vans Sp Edn 508 (ModelZone) - *12*	NA	31

W63.   BR Mk1 Horsebox (2013)

This model will be found in the Coaches section at the end of the Mk1 coaches.

Shock Absorbing Vans

W64a.   12T GWR Shock-Absorbing Van (1995)

This is the original Palitoy designed GWR double vent van body with a shock absorbing chassis designed by Bachmann. It has 3 vertical white stripes on each end and side. Short fat stripes were used after 1963.

33-725	GW 139576 dark grey Shock Absorbing Van No.39 - *95*	15	20
33-726	BR W139556 brown 3 medium thin vertical stripes (return to Fishguard) - *95*	15	20
33-727	BR W139594 dark grey 3 long thin vertical stripes 'Shock Van No.57' (return to Britton Ferry) - *95*	15	20

GWR shock van with BR running number [W64a]

W64b.   12T GWR Shock Absorbing Van (2006)

This is the Blue Riband version of the above model.

37-904	GWR 139547 dark grey 'Shock Absorbing Van No.37' - *13*	NPG	NPG
37-900	BR B851440 brown - *not made*	NA	NA
37-900	BR B859554 brown - *not made*	NA	NA
37-900	BR W139600 brown - *06*	6	8
37-900A	BR W139641 brown - *11*	7	9
37-902	BR W139556 brown - *09*	5	7
37-902A	BR W139591 brown - *11*	7	9

W65a.   12T BR Standard Shock-Absorbing Van (1994)

This is the original Mainline BR vent van on a shock absorbing chassis. The van has corrugated ends and 3 vertical white identification stripes on ends and sides. Short fat stripes date the finish to 1964 onwards.

33-735	BR B852193 brown 3 short thick vertical stripes (post 1964) - *94*	15	20
33-736	BR B850605 brown 3 medium thin vertical stripes - *94*	15	20
33-737	BR brown 3 medium thin vertical stripes - *not made*	NA	NA

W65b.   12T BR Standard Shock Absorbing Van (2005)

This is the Blue Riband version of the above model.

37-901	BR B851778 brown - *not made*	NA	NA
37-901	BR B850005 brown - *05?*	8	10
37-901	BR B851692 brown - *05*	6	8
37-903	BR B852353 brown - *09*	5	7
37-903A	BR B851440 brown - *11*	7	9

Bachmann Branchline

Large Vans

W66a. VAA 45T BR Sliding Door Box Van (2007)

These 'modern' long wheelbase air-braked vans were built at BR Ashford and arrived in 1969. In all 209 were constructed in this first batch but the design was to go through several modifications as further batches were built. They became the mainstay of the general merchandise fleet.

38-120	**Railfreight** B200116 red+grey - *07*	12	15
38-120A	**Railfreight** B200102 red+grey - *09*	11	14
38-120B	**Railfreight** B200112 red+grey W - *12*	18	21
38-121	**Railfreight** B200119 red-brown - *07*	12	15
38-?	**BR RTC** 999000 red-brown Sp Edn 504 (Invictor) from TRIB train - *13*	NPG	NPG

W66b. VBA 45T BR Sliding Door Box Van (2007)

These were similar to the VAA/VAB vans but did not have end ventilators. They also had different suspension gear - the BR long-link type. They were originally coded COV AB. 75 were built at Ashford in 1970-71 and a further 100 were constructed at Shildon in 1974-75.

VBA sliding door van [W66b]

38-125K	**LoadHaul** 200600 black+orange Sp Edn 504 (BCC) - *07*	12	15
38-125	**EWS** 200241 maroon - *07*	12	15
38-125A	**EWS** 200628 maroon - *12*	16	19
38-126	**BR** 200289 red-brown - *07*	12	15
38-126A	**BR** 200228 red-brown W - *12*	16	19

W66c. VDA/ZDA 29T BR Sliding Door Box Van (2008)

The VDA was put into production after experimenting with different types of door in the mid-1970s. It had spaced out door release catches and centrally opening doors. A distinctive feature of the VDAs was the external bracing of the end walls, with two vertical braces and two horizontal ones. 750 vans were built at Ashford and Shilton in 1976-78.

38-141	**BR Rft** 200077 brown Cov AB - *08*	12	16
38-145	**BR Rft** ? brown Cov AB - *13*	NPG	NPG
38-140	**BR Rft** 210380 grey+red - *08*	12	16
38-144	**BR Rft** ? grey+red - *13*	NPG	NPG
38-142	**BR Rft** 200834 grey+yellow - *08*	12	16
33-140K	**Transrail** T210195 grey * Sp Edn 504 (BCC) - *08*	12	16
33-146	**BR Civil Link** DC? Grey+yellow ZRA - *13*	NPG	NPG
33-140Z	**BR Civil Link** DC200660 grey+yellow ZRA Sp Edn 504 (*Model Rail*) - *08*	15	19
33-140Y	**Satlink Western** KDC201122 red+yellow ZDA Sp Edn (*Model Rail* magazine) - *11*	17	22
38-143	**EWS** 200731 maroon - *09*	13	16
38-143A	**EWS** ? maroon - *11*	15	18

* Carries Carlisle Currock wagon shop motifs (running fox).

W67a. VGA 46t Sliding Wall Van (1998)

The next van design, after the larger VDA, was the VGA which began to appear in the early 1980s and showed a similarity with Continental designs. This saw a complete change in design and, instead of sliding doors, it had sliding sides, making access to the interior easier.

33-275	**BRe Speedlink** 210595 grey+red - *98*	12	15
33-276	**BR Rft Distrib** 210614 grey+yellow* - *98*	12	15
33-277	**Transrail** 210572 silver+yellow* - *98*	12	15

* carries Carlisle Currock wagon shop motifs (running fox).

W67b. VGA 46t Sliding Wall Van (2000)

This is the retooled model upgrading it to Blue Riband standard. Two of these vans were hired by Lovat who put their logo on them and models of both these were commissioned by Harburn Hobbies of Edinburgh.

37-601A	**BRe Rft Speedlink** 210595 grey+red - *not made*	NA	NA
37-601A	**BRe Rft Speedlink** 210452 grey+red - *02*	12	15
37-602	**Rft Distribution** 210614 grey+red - *00*	12	15
37-602A	**Rft Distribution** 210639 grey+yell W - *02*	12	15
37-603	**Rft Distribution** 210614 grey+yellow - *not made*	NA	NA
37-603	**Rft Distribution** 210632 grey+yellow - *00*	12	15
37-603A	**EWS** ? maroon W - *12*	NPG	NPG
37-604	**Rft Distribution** 210592 silver+yellow - *06*	11	14

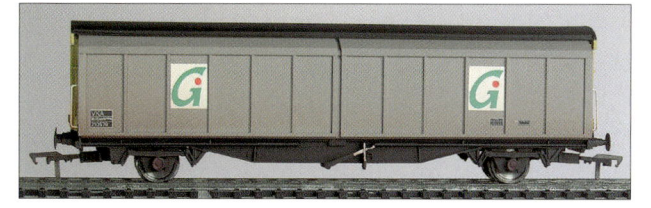

VGA sliding wall van [W67b]

37-605	**Rft Distribution/Gi** 210572 grey+yellow W + graffiti (one side) VKA - *07*	11	14
37-607	**Railfreight Dist.** 210493 silver+yellow W - *10*	13	16
37-601	**Transrail** grey+yellow - *00*	12	15
37-600	**EWS** 210444 maroon - *00*	12	15
37-600A	**EWS** 210626 maroon - *03*	11	14
37-603	**EWS** 210632 maroon - *06*	11	14
37-606	**EWS** 210430 maroon - *09*	12	15
37-606A	**EWS** 210632 maroon - *11*	14	17
37-607	**EWS** 210493 grey+yellow W - *10*	12	16
-	'Lovat Spring' 210527 grey+yellow	15	NA
-	'Lovat Spring' 210622 grey+yellow	15	NA
37-601Z	above 2 vans, Sp Edn (Harburn Hobbies) - *02*	NA	40

Brake Vans

W68. 20T GWR 'Toad' Brake Van (ex-Mainline) (1990)

The GWR 'Toad' brake van changed little in appearance down the years. They had a veranda at one end only and no side duckets. Later versions, which tend to be the subject of models, had a 16' wheelbase. They had mostly restricted use (RU) and generally carried the name of the yard to which they were allocated.

The model was introduced to the Mainline Railways catalogue in 1978 and the tools were later used for this Bachmann Branchline model.

33-300K	**BCC** W1997-12 dark blue Sp Edn (BCC) - *12*	8	10
33-300B	**GW** 56683 dark grey 'Severn Tunnel Junc' RU - *01*	7	9
33-300C	**GW** 68690 grey 'Dowlais Cae Harris' - *03, 05*	6	8
33-300D	**GW** 68690 grey 'Dowlais Cae Harris' - *06*	6	8
33-300E	**GW** 68751 dark grey 'Berkenhead' - *07*	6	8
33-301	**GW** 114926 grey 'Cardiff' - *90*	8	10
33-301A	**GW** 56368 dark grey 'Paddington RU' - *97*	8	10
33-301B	**GW** 114800 dark grey W 'Rhymney' - *99*	7	9
33-301Z	**GW** 56368 grey W 'Toddington' * Sp Edn 500 (Cotswold Steam Preservation) - *01*	7	9
(30-010)	**GW** 56590 dark grey 'Oswestry' ex-set - *04*	6	NA
30-301W	**GW** 68897 dark grey 'Stratford-Upon-Avon' Sp Edn 504 (Classic Train & M. Bus) - *05*	6	8
30-301W	**GW** 68897 dark grey 'Stratford-Upon-Avon' Sp Edn 504 (Classic Train & Bus) - *12*	7	9
33-301R	**GW** 68684, dark grey, 'Hayle RU', Sp Edn 504 (Kernow MR Centre) - *09*	7	10
(30-075)	**GW** 17410 dark grey 'Bewdley' ex-Local Freight set - *10*	7	NA

Ex-GWR brake van [W68]

8th Edition — Visit the BRM website at: www.model-railways-live.co.uk

Bachmann Branchline

33-300F	**GW** 114776 dark grey 'Merthyr (Plymouth St)' Sp Edn 750 (Hereford Model Centre) - *12*	8	11
33-300Z	**GW** 114777 dark grey 'Oldbury Town' Sp Edn 504 (Warley Show) - *12*	10	15
33-300	**BR** W68805 grey - *90*	8	10
33-300A	**BR** W68875 grey - *97*	8	10
33-301X	**BR** B950609 grey 'St Blazey RU' Sp Edn 504 (Kernow MR Centre) - *05*	9	11
33-301S	**BR** W68474 light grey 'Truro RU' Sp Edn 504 (Kernow MR Centre) - *09*	7	10
33-301U	**BR** W68568 grey 'St Erth & St Ives RU' Sp Edn 504 (Kernow MR Centre) - *07*	9	11
33-305	**BR** W35960 grey 'Shrewsbury (Cotton Hill) RU' - *01*	7	9
33-305A	**BR** W114925 grey 'Oxford RU' - *03*	7	9
33-306	**BR** W35918 grey 'Bristol West Depot RU', No.2 Western - *05*	6	8
33-306A	**BR** W68834 light grey 'Stourbridge RU' - *09*	5	7
33-306B	**BR** W68476 grey 'Roath Basin Junction RU' - *10*	8	10
33-306C	**BR** W68567 light grey 'Machynlleth No.3 RU' - *11*	6	8
33-301C	**BR** W17390 brown 'Westbury (Wilts)' - *04*	6	8
33-301D	**BR** W68870 brown 'Tavistock Jcn RU' - *06*	6	8
33-301E	**BR** W114854 brown 'Birkenhead RU' - *09*	5	6
33-301F	**BR** W17444 brown - *10*	8	10
33-307	**BR** W? brown - *13*	NPG	NPG
33-301T	**BR** W68856 brown 'Penzance RU' Sp Edn 504 (Kernow MR Centre) - *07*	9	11
33-302	**BR** DW17455 brown ST - *94*	8	10
33-304A	**BR** DW68786 brown W ZTP XP - *12*	9	11
33-304	**BR** W114961 brown - *98*	8	10
(30-700)	? brown ex-set - *?*	6	NA
33-301Y	**Virgin Trains** 2003 Warley red+silver Sp Edn 500 (Virgin Trains) - *03*	7	9
33-303	undecorated light grey - *91*	8	10

* This was also being offered by the Gloucester & Warwickshire Railway with bespoke different station names.

W69.   20T MR Brake Van (2013)

These brake vans marked the first change from the original Midland Railway design by the use of duckets on either side of the van. They had a 12ft wheelbase and were 20ft long over headstocks. 100 were built at Derby during 1926-27.

This model was under development at the time of writing.

38-552	**LMS** 2045 grey with duckets - *13*	NPG	14
38-553	**LMS** 280663 brown without duckets - *13*	NPG	14
38-551	**BR** M295516 grey with duckets - *13*	NPG	14
38-550	**BR** M? grey without duckets - *13*	NPG	14

W70.   20T LNER 12ft Brake Van (ex-Mainline) (1990)

This was a design built by the LNER from 1929. It had a central cabin with a veranda at each end, metal duckets on the sides but no platforms beyond the verandas, unlike later designs. They should have torpedo roof vents.

Model manufacturers generally use the body tooled for the BR standard brake van and mount it on a shorter chassis. This was from the original tooling.

33-800	**NE** 162030 brown large letters ex-sets - *90*	8	NA
33-800.1	**NE** 108001 brown - *90*	8	NA
33-802	**NE** 108061 brown small letters - *02*	8	10
33-802	**NE** E178513 brown small letters - *91*	8	10
33-801	**BR** E168064 grey ** - *91*	8	10
33-801B*	**BR** E167830 grey - *01*	7	9
33-801D	**BR** E178499 grey - *03*	7	9
33-803	**BR** E178510 grey unfitted - *04*	6	8
33-805	**BR** E175613 grey - *07*	6	8
33-801A*	**BR** E178569 brown unfitted - *00*	7	9
33-801C*	**BR** E167830 brown - *02*	7	9
33-802	**BR** E178513 brown - *02*	6	8
33-804	**BR** E178500 brown - *04*	6	8
33-806	**BR** E.178499 brown - *07*	6	8
(30-007)	red ex-'Jack The Saddle Tank' set - *11*	8	NA

* No 'A' on the box label. ** Reappeared in 2004 in the 30-045 Digital Freight Set.

W71.   25T SR 'Pill Box' Brake Van (2012)

The so called 'Pill Box' brake van was the standard design adopted by the Southern Railway and the original drawing was done at the Lancing Works. Modifications for a later batch were made to the drawings at Eastleigh but the vans were built at Lancing. The main change seen from outside was with regard to the position of the ducket which was in one side only. As one looked at the side of the van containing the ducket, early vans had the ducket on the left but later ones had it on the right. Another change came in BR days when the sand box that had been constructed on the outside of one verandah wall and painted red, was removed. It is interesting to note that this design, which incorporates a small van body placed centrally on a longer chassis, predates the similar LNER design which was later adopted by British Railways to be their standard design.

This is a well detailed model and Bachmann have modelled a number of the variations described here.

rhd = right-hand duckets, lhd = left-hand duckets.

SR 25T 'Pill Box' brake van [W71]

38-400	**SR** 55975 dark brown, red ends, white roof lhd - *12*	11	14
38-403	**SR** 56365 dark brown, red ends, grey roof rhd - *12*	11	14
38-401	**BR** S55953 grey lhd - *12*	11	14
38-401A	**BR** S? grey lhd - *13*	NPG	NPG
38-402	**BR** S55583 brown - *12*	11	14
38-402A	**BR** S? brown rhd - *13*	NPG	NPG
38-404	**BR Departmental** DS56400 olive green rhd - *12*	11	14

W72a.   20T 16ft LNER/BR Brake Van (ex-Mainline) (1990)

The BR standardised their brake van design on that developed by the LNER and, consequently, one normally finds one basic model used for both LNER and BR standard variations, as applies here. The van had a small cabin with a narrow veranda at both ends and, beyond each veranda, there was a platform giving the impression that the chassis was too large for the body. However, the longer chassis ensured a steadier ride and improved visibility. On BR standard brake vans a raised grab-rail was provided along the edges of the two platforms. Each van also had a ducket on either side to give the guard a view along the train.

This table contains the original model.

33-351	**NE** 182908 brown large letters - *92*	8	10
33-352	**NE** 260922 brown small letters, box labelled 'NE Grey' - *90*	8	10
33-352	**EN** (error) *** 260922 brown - *92*	15	18
(30-201)**	**LT** B582 dark grey also (30-200) - *91*	18	20
33-350	**BR** B950880 grey (error) (1st issue) - *90*	12	16
33-352A	BR B951759 grey unfitted - *96*	8	10
33-350	**BR** B950880 brown (1st issue) - *90*	8	10
33-350.1	**BR** B950880 brown with chalk marks - *made?*	NPG	NPG
33-350A*	**BR** B953087 brown (2nd issue) - *93*	8	10
33-350Aa	**BR** B955044 brown fitted - *96*	8	10
33-350B	**BR** B952103 brown fitted - *99*	7	9
33-354	**BR** B955136 brown+yellow - *92*	8	10
33-354	**BR** P0016149 brown+yellow - *made?*	NPG	NPG
33-355	**BR Rft Distribution** B964885 grey+red CAR - *not made*	NA	NA
33-355	**BR Rft Distribution** B954673 grey+red CAR - *94*	8	10
33-355A	**BR Rft Distribution** 201205 B954132 dark grey with yellow end panels CAR - *99*	7	9
33-353	undecorated light grey *** - *not made*	NA	NA

* No 'A' on box label. ** Box unnumbered. It also appeared in set 30-200. ***The wrongly printed bodies were withdrawn before issue but were later sold off to the public and so may turn up occasionally, possibly fitted to a spare chassis.

1990 version of the LNER brake van [W72A]

Bachmann Branchline

W72b. 20T 16ft LNER/BR Standard Brake Van (2002)
This was a Blue Riband version of the above model.

20T standard brake van [W72b]

37-527	**BR** NE260922 brown small letters, fitted - *02*	7	9
37-529	**NE** 178705 brown, large letters - *05*	6	8
37-529A	**NE** ? brown, large letters - *13*	NPG	NPG
(30-077)	**LT** B581 light grey with red ends ex-Midnight Metropolitan' train set - *13*	12	NA
37-527Z	**LT** B583 light grey with red ends Sp Edn 504 (Kernow MRC) - *07*	10	12
37-526	**BR** B950002 grey - *not made*	NA	NA
37-526	**BR** B951480 grey - *02*	7	9
37-528	**BR** B950884 grey - *05*	6	8
37-528A	**BR** B951504 grey - *11*	5	7
37-528B	**BR** B951148 grey - *11*	7	9
37-528C	**BR** B952241 grey - *12*	9	11
37-530	**BR** B? grey - *12*	NPG	NPG
37-525	**BR** B954762 brown fitted - *02*	7	9
37-528B	**BR** B950358 brown W - *11*	7	9
37-531	**BR** B? brown W - *13*	NPG	NPG
37-532	**BR** B? brown CAP/ZTV - *13*	NPG	NPG
37-527A	**Rft Dist** B954661 grey+yellow - *07*	5	7
37-527Y	**BR** KDB954164 red+yellow ZTR S&TD Sp Edn 504 (*Model Rail*) - *05*	6	8

* Despite its number, this has planked, not flush' ends.

W72c. 20T BR Standard Brake (flush ends) (2003)
The final batch of standard brake vans was built in 1963 and had vacuum pipes, roller bearings and hydraulic buffers. Later they were mostly converted to air brakes.

This model represents standard brake vans which had their lives extended by having their verandah walls sheeted over with plywood.

37-538	**BR Departmental** LDB954219, grey - *05*	6	8
37-537	**BR** B950388 brown fitted - *05*	6	8
37-537A	**BR** B953810 brown fitted - *08*	6	8
37-537B	**BR** B950358 brown fitted - *?*	6	8
37-537C	**BR** B950358 brown W fitted - *11*	6	8
37-537D	**BR** B952830 brown W (late) - *12*	9	11
37-537Z	**BR Rft** B954991 CAR brown+yellow W 'New Cross Gate' * Sp Edn 504 (ModelZone) - *11*	5	7
37-535	**BR Rft** B955247 CAR grey+red - *03*	7	9
37-535A	**BR Rft** B955143 CAR grey+red - *07*	5	7
37-5333	**BR Engineers** B951767 ZTO grey+yellow - *13*	NPG	NPG
37-535B	**BR Rft** B? CAR grey+red - *11*	6	8

W72d. 20T BR Standard Brake (flush sides) (B) (2002)
This is like the model above but while it has flush sides, it does not have flush ends.

37-536	**BR** B955055 CAP brown - *02*	7	9
37-535Z	**BR** B955010 RES CAR red+grey Sp Edn 500 (*Model Rail*) - *02*	10	12
37-535	**BR Rft** B955247 CAR grey+red - *not made*	NA	NA

W72e. 20T BR Standard Brake (flush sides & ends)(2002)
This model represents standard brake vans which had their lives extended by having all their sides sheeted over with plywood.

37-536	**BR** B955055 CAP brown - *02*	7	9
37-535Z	**BR** B955010 RES CAR red+grey Sp Edn 500 (*Model Rail*) - *02*	10	12
37-535	**BR Rft** B955247 CAR grey+red - *not made*	NA	NA

Bogie Wagons

W73. 25T SR 'Queen Mary' Brake Van (1996)
In 1933, the Southern Railway had used the chassis of redundant AC motor luggage vans to build some bogie brake vans for express freight trains. The success of these prompted the construction of a further 25 vans in 1936, with flat-sided wooden bodies on shortened standard carriage underframes. These were nicknamed 'Queen Marys' and were the subject of the Bachmann model. Not all had plain planked sides as on the model; around eight were partially clad in steel sheet from new and a few more gained sheeting later. The 'Queen Marys' remained in revenue use until the 1970s, six receiving air brakes in 1961. Their official name was 'Bogie Goods Brake Vans - Express Service' but the name 'Queen Mary' has stuck. Several remain in service and several more have been preserved.

Palitoy had planned to release this model in 1985 but ceased production in 1984 before they could develop one.

33-827	**SR** 56282 dark brown large letters - *96*	12	14
33-827B	**SR** 56294 dark grown large letters - *98*	12	14
33-827A	**SR** 56299 dark brown small letters - *97*	12	14
33-830A	**SR** 56301 dark brown - *04*	11	13
33-830B	**SR** 56291 dark brown - *07*	11	13
33-825	**BR** S56297 brown - *96*	12	14
33-825A	**BR** S56302 brown - *97*	12	14
33-825B	**BR** S56299 brown - *98*	12	14
33-825C	**BR** S56288 brown - *04*	11	13
33-825D	**BR** S56306 brown - *06*	11	13
33-825E	**BR** S56298 brown - *09*	12	15
33-825F	**BR** S56303 brown - *10*	14	17

BR departmental 'Queen Mary' brake van [W73]

33-825G	**BR** S56294 brown (early) - *12*	15	18
33-826	**BR S&T Department** ADS56296 olive green+yellow - *96*	15	18
33-826A	**BR S&T Department** ADS56299 green+yellow - *97*	15	18
33-826B	**BR Departmental** ADS56302 olive green - *13*	15	18
33-829	**BR** S56302 stone - *97*	14	17
33-828	**NSE** ADS56304 blue - *97*	15	18
33-825Z	**BR Satlink** KDS56305 red+yellow VZW Sp Edn 504 (*Model Rail* magazine) - *07*	15	18
33-830	**EWS** ADS56299 maroon - *99*	12	14

W74a. GWR 'Macaw B' Wagon (ex-Mainline) (1992)
30 ton bogie bolster wagons were used for carrying long loads, such as girders, rails and complete sections of track. The 'Macaw B' was pretty much the GWR's standard bogie bolster wagon and was being built before the First World War, some being converted to tank carriers for use in France. The LMS adopted a Midland Railway design for their 30 ton bogie bolsters and between 1926 and 1934, built 327 of them. The numbers on the LMS models here belong to wagons built in 1928 and 1929. British Railways adopted more than one design from the former railway companies and for its 30 ton 'Bogie C' wagons turned to the GWR 'Macaw B' design which had four moveable bolsters. Between 1949 and 1962, many batches of these were built

The model was designed by Palitoy and released in the Mainline Railways range in 1980.

cb = commonwealth bogies. db = diamond bogies.

	'Macaw B'		
33-852	**GW** 70247 dark grey db - *92*	10	12
33-852A*	**GW** 56302 dark grey db - *not made*	NA	NA
	LMS		
33-850A	**LMS** 314064 grey db - *02*	9	11
33-850B	**LMS** 720717 brown db - *04*	9	11
33-857	**LMS** 314000 grey db - *05*	8	10
33-857A	**LMS** 301326 grey db - *09*	7	8
	'Bogie Bolster C'		
33-850	**BR** ADB997648 dark grey S&T Dept. cb - *91*	10	12
33-851	**BR** B943134 grey cb - *?*	8	10
33-851A*	**BR** M290075 grey db - *97*	12	16
33-855	**BR** B940751 grey cb - *99*	9	11
33-856A	**BR** B922150 grey cb - *not made*	NA	NA
33-856A	**BR** B943405 grey - *05*	8	10
33-856B	**BR** B940050 grey - *09*	7	8
33-856C	**BR** B943501 grey - *10*	7	9

Bachmann Branchline

33-856D	**BR** B944183 grey -*12*	9	12
33-856	**BR** B943359 brown cb - *02*	9	11
33-853	**BR** B943293 brown (warped) - *97*	10	12
33-853A	**BR** B943293 brown db - *97*	10	12
'Prawn'			
33-854	**BR** KDB997653 red S&T cb - *97*	10	12
33-854A	**BR** DB997636 Gulf red S&T - *04*	9	11

* No 'A' on box label.

W74b. 30T Bogie Bolster + Load (ex-Mainline) (1991)
Using the above bogie bolster wagon model, the girder load from the Mainline models was reintroduced by Bachmann in their Branchline range.

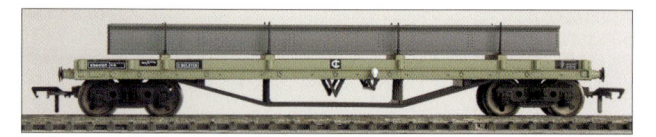

'Bogie Bolster C' with girder load [W74b]

33-927	**GW** 70240 grey + girder - *92*	14	16
33-926	**LMS** 301326 grey + brown girder - *92*	14	16
33-925	**BR** M290034 grey + girder - *91*	14	16
33-928	**BR** B946405 grey + brown girder – not made	NA	NA
33-928	**BR** B943500 grey + brown girder - *10*	8	10
33-928A	**BR** B940055 grey + brown girder - *11*	9	11
33-928B	**BR** B944165 grey + grey girder - *12*	10	12
33-929	**BR** B943439 grey + pipe load - *10*	8	10
33-929A	**BR** B940334 grey + pipe load - *11*	9	11
33-929B	**BR** B943860 grey + pipe load - *12*	10	12
33-930	**BR** B943999 grey + timber load - *12*	10	12

W75a. BDA 80T Bogie Bolster Wagon (2008)
British Railways built a large number of bogie bolster wagons between 1949 and 1962. The 52ft long version was originally known as a 'Bogie Bolster D'. Following the move to air braked trains, after 1964, 1250 of these were rebuilt to become BDA bogie bolster wagons under TOPS, the first vehicle being converted at Swindon in 1975. BDAs were used for the conveyance of mainly metal products such as steel rods but, with the decline of that traffic, those remaining are used in departmental service mainly for carrying rail to and from work sites. 388 BDA wagons remained in service on the national network in 2008.

The model is fitted with diamond bogies.

38-150	**BR Loadhaul** 950414 black+orange - *08*	12	16
38-150A	**BR Loadhaul** 950308 black+orange - *12*	18	21
38-151	**BR Railfreight** 950954 red, girder - *08*	12	16
38-151A	**BR Railfreight** 951163 red - *09*	12	16
38-151B	**BR Railfreight** 950791 red - *09*	18	21
38-150Z	**BR Departmemtal** DC950064 yellow YAA 'Brill' Sp Edn 504 (*Model Rail*) - *08*	14	18
38-152	**EWS** 950026 maroon - *08*	12	16
38-152A	**EWS** 950049 maroon - *10*	13	17

W75b. BDA 80T Bogie Bolster Wagon + Load (2010)
These are the same as the wagons in the above table but with a load added.

38-158	**BR** 950000 maroon + steel pipes - *10*	17	21
38-159	**BR Railfreight** 950991 + steel beams - *10*	17	21

W76a. GWR 'Crocodile H' Well Wagon (ex-Mainline) (1991)
The GWR used the code name 'Crocodile' for its trolley wagons and had a range of different designs, each identified by a letter suffix and some dating back to the start of the last century. The 'Crocodile H' dates from the 1920s and seems to have been small in number. This might explain the repeated use by Bachmann of the running numbers of two of a small batch of only three that were built in 1926 and fitted with commonwealth bogies. The wagon type became a 'Weltrol WH' in BR days and the floor was strengthened to increase its capacity from 45T to 65T. No new ones were built by British Railways; instead, they built 'Trestrols' in the late '50s for carrying steel plates.
A new shorter coupling was introduced to the model in 2004.

'Crocodile H'			
33-900	**GW** 41900 dark grey 45T - *92*	12	15
33-900A	**GW** 41973 dark grey 45T - *98*	10	12
33-900B	**GW** 41900 dark grey 45T - *02*	8	10
33-900C	**GW** dark grey - not made	NA	NA
33-900D	**GW** 41901 dark grey 45T - *05*	6	8
33-900E	**GW** 41974 dark grey 45T - *09*	6	8
33-901	**LMS** grey - not made *	NA	NA

GWR 'Crocodile' well wagon [W76a]

'Weltrol WH'			
33-901A	**BR** W41973 grey 65T - *98*	10	12
33-901B	**BR** W41900 grey 65T - *00*	8	10
33-901C	**BR** W41973 grey 65T - *04*	6	8
33-901D	**BR** W41974 grey * 65T - *04*	6	8
33-901E	**BR** W41900 grey * 65T - *10*	14	17
33-902	**BR** W41973 grey 65T - *91*	12	15
'Weltrol MX'			
33-902	**BR Departmental** ? black - *13*	8	10
33-901Z	**BR Satlink** KDB900935 red+yellow Sp Edn 504 (*Model Rail*) magazine - *13*	10	13

* Factory record says "planned for the Crewe Open Day in 1996".

W76b. 45T/65T Well Wagon with Load (ex-Mainline) (1991)
These were the above model with a load. The Palitoy practise of offering the well wagon with a load was adopted by Bachmann when they reintroduced the former Mainline model. Two loads were used, a transformer and a boiler.

33-875	**NE** 77823 grey 'Flatrol M' + boiler '**Riley Bros**' 3780 brown - *91*	18	23
33-879	**NE** 736919 grey 'Protrol E' + boiler brown - *11*	9	11
33-879A	**NE** 415296 grey 'Flatrol S' + boiler brown - *13*	9	12
33-876	**BR** W41975 black 'Weltrol WH' + boiler 1877 black 65T - *92*	17	20
33-877	**BR** W41843 grey 'Weltrol WH' + green transformer - *92*	17	20
33-878	**LMS** 299882 grey + grey transformer - *92*	17	20

W77. 'Warflat' Bogie Flat Wagon (2013)
These wagons were built to transport military equipment such as tanks. The model was under development at the time of writing.

38-725	**WD** ? khaki drab + tank - *13*	NPG	NPG
38-726	**WD** ? bronze green + tank - *13*	NPG	NPG
38-727	**BR** ? grey - *13*	NPG	NPG

W78. 'Intermodal' Bogie Wagon
Planned prior to the adoption of Blue Riband standards.

33-475	**BR** Railfreight Distribution with ISO dry freight steel container - not made	NA	NA

W79a. 'Intermodal' ('Euro Twin') + Containers (2001)
Like the real thing, these come as a pair of bogie flat wagons, which usually share the same European style running number. They are intended to be semi-permanently joined and are designed to carry 45ft 'Swap Body' containers. The models' frames are diecast, to lower the centre of gravity.

37-300	**Rft Dist.** 31 70 4938 115-8 + 3170 4938 121-1, green, plus two maroon 45ft **ECS European Containers**: ECBU452607[0] + ECBU450600[6] - *01*	22	27
37-300A	**Rft Dist.** 31 70 4938 002-3 + 3170 4938 002-5, green, plus two 45ft **Consent Leasing** containers: NEVU220181[8] + NEVU220200[7] - *02*	20	25
37-300B	**Rft Dist.** 31 70 4938 121-1, green, plus two 45ft **ECS** containers: ECDU450106[7] + ECDU850805[6] - *02*	20	25
37-301	**Rft Dist.** 33 70 4938 713-3, green, plus 45ft containers: **Power Box** PWRU450209[2] and **Sea Wheel** SWLU450001[3] - *01*	22	27
37-301A	**Rft Dist.** 33 70 4938 531-9, green, plus two 45ft **Axis** containers: AXIU716457[4] + AXIU716309 - *02*	20	25
37-301B	**Rft Dist.** 33 70 4938 713-3, black, plus two green 45ft **Sea Wheel** containers: SWLU451349[8] + SWIU965245[0] - *03*	22	27
37-302	**Rft Dist.** 33 70 4938 113-8, green, plus two 45ft **Seaco** containers: SCZU146450[1] + SCZU147551[1] - *01*	22	27
37-302A	**Rft Dist.** 33 70 4938 519-4, green, plus two 45ft **EFS** containers: EFSU452044[8] + EFSU452047[4] - *03*	20	25

Bachmann Branchline

37-302B	Rft Dist. 31 70 4938 113-8, green, plus two dark blue 45ft **Seaco** containers: SCZU146922[6] + SCZU147605[6] - 02		20	25
37-303	Rft Dist. 33 70 4938 523-6, green, plus two green+white 45ft **Asda** containers: (WHMU450819[1] + WHMU 450825[2]) - 07		20	27
37-310	Rft Dist. 31 70 4938 217-7, green, plus two 20ft **Hamburg Sud** containers: SUDU370512[2] + SUDU369632[9]) - 10		22	27
37-311	Rft Dist. 33 70 4938 319-9, green, plus two 20ft **P&O** containers: POCU050018[4] + POCU041942[6] - 02		20	25
37-312	Rft Dist. 31 70 4938 006-3, black, plus two 20ft **Mediterranean Shipping Co**. containers: MSCU116371[3] + MSCU251438[7] - 03		20	25
37-313	Rft Dist. 70.4938.202.9 Flats, green, plus two 45ft containers: '**Maersk**' MSKU 467101[8] grey + '**Maersk Sealand**' MSKU 454860[0] - 13		30	39

'Intermodal' ('Euro Twin') + containers [W79a]

37-314	Rft Dist. 70.4938.081-7, green, plus two 45ft dark blue '**Safmarine**' containers: MSKU462710[3] + MSKU462726[2] * - 12		30	39
37-315	Rft Dist. 70 4938 012 2 (two flats), black - 03		15	19
37-316	Rft Dist. 33 70 4958 135-0 (two flats), green, weathered - 06		15	19
37-308	EWS 33 70 4938 130-2, green, plus two dark blue 45ft **Geest** containers: GNSU597748[4] + GNSU451546[0] - 10		32	30
37-320	EWS 33 70 4938 300-9, plus two red 20ft **K Line** green+red containers: KKTU740516[4] + KKTU741006[2] plus two 20ft **MOL** grey containers: MOAU052613[8] + MOAU046387[3] - 10		25	31
37-320A	EWS 33 70 4938 197-1 green, plus two red 20ft **K Line** red containers: KKTU521875[9] + KKTU716136 [0] plus two 20ft **MOL** grey containers: MOAU065359[6] + MOAU057294[0] - 11		28	35
37-309	EWS 33 70 4938 324-9, green, plus two dark blue 45ft **Samskip** containers: SANU798868[0] + SANU799037[3] - 10		25	30

'Intermodal' ('Euro Twin') + containers [W79a]

37-321	EWS 33 70 4938 326-4, green + two red 20ft **Hyundi** containers: HDMU217810[1] + HDMU235691[8] plus two blue 20ft **CMA CGM** containers: ECMU196946[4] + ECMU217218[2] - 10		25	31
37-321A	EWS 33 70 4938 740-6, green + two red 20ft **Hyundi** containers: HDMU229050[7] + HDMU225393 [0] plus two dark blue 20ft **CMA CGM** containers: CMAU160078[7] + CMAU107672[5] - 11		28	35
37-304	EWS 33 70 4938 510-3, green, plus two 45ft, navy blue, **Malcolm Logistics** containers: WHMU450015[9] + WHMU450020[4] - 07		20	27
37-305	EWS 33 70 4938 535-0, green, plus two 45ft, yellow, **DHL** containers: DZ5141 KDG1 + DZ7005 LEG1 - 07		20	27
37-305A	EWS 33 70 4938 438-4, green, plus two 45ft, yellow, **DHL** containers: DZ5143 + DZ7003 - 11		28	33

* These numbers have also been recorded as MSKU 462725[2] and MSKU 462750[3].

W79b. 'Intermodal' ('Euro Twin') + Containers (2013)
These had not been released at the time of writing but will be like the models above but will have curtain-sided containers.

37-340	? ? ? + 2 45ft '**P&O Ferrymaster**' curtain-sided containers - 13		38	45
37-340	? ? ? + 2 45ft '**Geest**' curtain-sided containers - 13		38	45

W79c. 'Intermodal' ('Euro Twin') + Containers (2013)
These will be like the models above but will carry 20' tank-tainers. These also were awaited at the time of writing.

37-390	**InterBulk** ? ? tank-tainers - 13		38	45

W79d. 45ft 'Intermodal' Containers (only) (2002)
These containers were sold only in packs of two.

36-100	2 x yellow 45' containers **P&O Ferrymasters** FMBU 001799[1] + '**P&O Ferrymasters - Container Services**' FMBU 001260[2] - 02		5	8
36-101	2 x dark green 45' containers '**Eucon**' (45') EUCU 459120[1] + EUCU 459026[8] - 06		5	8
36-102	2 x blue 45' containers '**Dream Box**' JOKU 000921[3] + JOKU 450273[7] - 06		5	8
36-125	2 x green containers '**China Shipping**' CCLU 314404[5] + CCLU 304949[6] - 03		5	7
36-126	2 x grey containers '**Maersk**' APMO282700[1] + '**Maersk Sealand**' MSKU206820[0] - 03		5	7
36-127	2 x grey containers '**Cosco**' CBHU3281860[8] + CBHU328736[5] - 03		5	7

W80. IPA Car Transporter (2010)
In 1993 STVA introduced a fleet of 350 four axle, double-deck, car transporters. Following incidences of vandalism and theft, side blinds were fitted and these are included on the model.

38-250	'**STVA**'/**Wincar** 23 87 4392 692-1 TAL489 red - 10		23	29

W81. FNA Nuclear Flask Wagon (2011)
This is the DRS 'Flatrol' Atomic Flask Wagon. Originally 8 were built at Ashford in 1976 and 1978. Two more were built at Shildon in 1982, seven at Swindon in 1986 and the main batch of 34 were built by Procor (UK) Ltd in 1988. They are used to carry spent nuclear fuel in flasks from various BNFL power stations to the Sellafield reprocessing plant in Cumbria. The flask sits beneath the white hood.

Bachmann have modelled three different types of wagon: flat floor and round buffers, flat floor with external changeover valve and 'Oleo' buffers and a later sloping floor version with oval shaped buffers.

FNA nuclear flask wagon [W81]

38-345	**DRS** 550014 beige flat floor, round buffers - 11		20	24
38-345A	**DRS** ? beige flat floor, round buffers - 12		25	30
38-346	**DRS** 550023 beige flat floor round buffers - 11		20	24
38-346A	**DRS** ? beige flat floor, round buffers - 12		25	30
38-347	**DRS** 550038 beige sloping floor, oval buffers - 11		20	24
38-347A	**DRS** 550043 beige sloping floor, round buffers - 13		25	30
38-345K	**DRS** 550011 blue flat floor Sp Edn 504 (BCC) - 11		23	28

W82. MBA 'Megabox' (High-sided) (B) (2010)
EWS replaced BR wagons with high volume ones in 1998, when they ordered 300 of these from Thrall Europa at York. They came in two forms as they run in sets of five, made up of 'outers' (with buffers) and 'inners' (without). Within the sets, the wagons are linked with buckeye couplings. They have been used to carry scrap, timber, stone and coal.

Based on the original Thrall works drawings, the body and underframe of the model are highly detailed and have many separately fitted components. Knuckle couplers are included in the box.

38-240	**EWS** 500028 maroon with buffers - 10		15	20
38-241	**EWS** 500178 maroon without buffers - 10		15	20
38-242	**EWS** 500067 maroon W without buffers - 11		19	24

Bachmann Branchline

W83. MOA 'Megabox' (Low-sided) (2010)
Overloading of MBAs (above) had led to a cutting-down of the height of the sides of the last 100 MBAs delivered. These became MCAs ('outers') and MDAs ('inners'). These run in sets of five (2 MCAs and 3 MDAs). The MOAs are Czech built, low-sided 'Mega' bogie box wagons and similar to their British built MCA and MDA cousins. They are usually used by Network Rail for infrastructure work. Knuckle couplers are included in the box.

38-245	**EWS** 500327 maroon - *10*	15	20
38-245A	**EWS** ? maroon W - *13*	NPG	NPG

W84. BAA/BZA Open Steel Coil Carriers (2011)
BAA wagons for carrying semi-finished steel were built in four different designs between 1972 and 1976. Two batches were built at Ashford and two batches at Shildon. Bachmann models represent three of these design differences. The wagons were built with a 40ft long heavy-duty deck and FBT6 bogies. There were end and cradle variations according to requirements.

The models come with three model steel coils in place and a set of side pins to be attached.

BAA open steel carrier [W84]

38-350	**EWS** 900142 maroon + steel coil load BZA - *11*	16	21
38-350A	**EWS** 900158 maroon + steel coil load BZA - *12*	18	23
38-351	**Railfreight Metals** 900205 grey+yellow + steel coil load BAA - *11*	16	21
38-351A	**Railfreight Metals** 900177 grey+yellow + steel coil load BAA - *12*	18	23
38-352	**BR Railfreight** 900047 red+yellow + steel coil load BAA - *11*	16	21
38-352A	**BR Railfreight** 900102 red+yellow + steel coil load BAA - *12*	18	23

W85a. BYA 102t 'Thrall' Steel Coil Carriers (2002)
These are steel coil carriers, each fitted with a cradle and telescopic sliding roof. They were built in York in 1998 and look a bit like a load of Anderson shelters from the Second World War.

37-625	**EWS** 960015 maroon - *02*	16	20

W85b. BRA 102t 'Thrall' Steel Strip Carriers (2002)
These covered steel slab wagons are identical to the BYAs (above) in outward appearance but were built to transport steel strip, protected from the weather, and so are not fitted with cradles. They were also built at York, but in 1999. Several faults were found with them when they were first introduced and some ended up being used as barrier wagons for the movement of stock fitted with buckeye couplings.

37-626	**EWS** 964014 maroon - *02*	16	20
37-627	**EWS** 966018 maroon - *06*	16	20
37-628	**EWS** 964007 maroon W - *04*	16	21
37-628A	**EWS** 964040 maroon W - *09*	18	23
37-628B	**EWS** 964010 maroon W - *12*	24	28
37-629	**DB Schenker** ? red - *13*	NPG	NPG

W86. JGA 90t Bogie Hopper Wagon (2001)
The JGA TOPS code covers a number of large bogie hopper wagons of different designs.

The model is based on wagons built by Tatrastroj Poprad of Slovakia in the mid to late 1990s.

37-327	'**Buxton**' BLI19206 white+blue - *01*	17	19
37-327A	'**Buxton**' BLI19218 white+blue - *01, 05*	17	19
37-327B	'**Buxton**' BLI19211 white+blue - *02, 05*	17	19
37-327C	'**Buxton**' BLI19200 white+blue - *11*	18	23
37-326	'**RMC**' RMC19241 orange - *01*	17	19
37-326A	'**RMC**' RMC19228 orange - *01*	17	19
37-326B	'**RMC**' RMC19238 orange - *02*	17	19
37-328	'**Tarmac**' NACO19174 pale grey, green+yellow flash - *02*	17	19
37-328A	'**Tarmac**' NACO19177 off-white, blue line - *03*	17	20
37-328B	'**Tarmac**' NACO19199 off-white, blue line - *not made*	NA	NA
37-328B	'**Tarmac**' NACO19175 off-white, green+yellow flash - *10*	17	20
37-328C	'**Tarmac**' NACO19170 off-white, green+yellow flash - *11*	18	23
37-325	'**Tilcon**' **NACCO** NACO19184 grey - *01*	17	19
37-325A	'**Tilcon**' **NACCO** NACO19175 grey - *02*	17	19
37-325B	'**Tilcon**' **NACCO** NACO19188 grey - *02*	17	19

JGA bogie hopper wagon [W86]

W87. HTA 102t 'Thrall' Bulk Coal Hopper (2003)
The HTA was introduced by EWS to use on the coal mine/power station merry-go-round route. They represented the largest order for one specific design of wagon since the mid 1970s. 1162 were built and they have a maximum speed of 75mph.

37-850	**EWS** 310222 maroon - *03*	16	20
37-851	**EWS** 310223 maroon W - *04*	16	21
37-852	**EWS** 310077 maroon - *05*	16	21
37-853	**EWS** 310103 maroon - *06*	16	21
37-854	**EWS** 310384 maroon W - *09*	18	23
37-854A	**EWS** 310148 maroon W - *10*	20	26
37-854B	**EWS** 310395 maroon W - *12*	25	29

W88. HHA 100t Bogie Hopper Wagon (2007)
This is the Freightliner Heavy Haul bogie coal hopper wagon of which 446 were built by Wagony Swidnica in Poland and introduced in 2000. They have a maximum capacity of 73.6 tonnes and a top speed of 75mph. They were built to transport coal to power stations.

The model comes in two types of design, ones with hinged doors and those with sliding doors - although the doors on the models do not open.

sed = non-working sliding end door. hed = non-working hinged end doors.

	Freightliner Heavy Haul		
38-030	370258 silver+green sed - *07*	15	20
38-030B	370270 silver+green sed - *10*	17	22
38-030A	370429 silver+ green sed - *07*	15	20
38-031	370043 silver+green hed - *not made*	NA	NA
38-031	370001 silver+green hed - *07*	16	21
38-032	370169 silver+green W hed - *08*	18	23
	Colas Rail		
38-033	370233? silver+green - *13*	NPG	NPG
38-034	? pale brown W - *13*	18	23

W89. YGA/B/H 40t 'Seacow'/'Sealion' (2007)
These bogie ballast wagons were a development of the 'Walrus' bogie hopper wagon which originated on the Southern Railway.

The model is based on the earlier riveted type of 'Sea Cow'. The 'Sea Lion' and 'Sea Cow' were very similar in appearance but the former had two vacuum cylinders on one end while the latter had only one. The hand wheel below the solebars is a hand-brake while the three hand-wheels on the end platform were for controlling the ballast chutes which may be seen between the bogies.

38-130	**BR** DB982582 olive green YGH - *07*	14	18
38-130A	**BR** DB982651 olive green W YGH - *12*	24	28
38-131	**BR** DB982473 grey+yellow YGB - *07*	14	18
38-131A	**BR** DB? grey+yellow YGB - *07*	16	20
38-132	**EWS** DB982696 maroon YGA - *07*	14	18
38-132A	**EWS** DB980220 maroon YGA - *10*	16	20
38-133	**Loadhaul** DB982582 black+orange YBH - *10*	16	20

W90. 'Polybulk' Bulk Grain Hopper Wagon (2013)
The first Traffic Services 'Polybulks' arrived in 1974 and were 80 tonne all-steel bogie vehicles capable of carrying a 58 tonne load. They were built in France with the requirements to also be used in Continental Europe and were initially used for the transportation of china clay as well as grain. A second batch was built in 1981.

At the time of writing the model had not been released but it is understood that features will include detailed ends with an etched metal catwalk, brake and underfloor discharge equipment represented and individual hand wheels.

38-425	'**Traffic Services**' ? green W - *13*	25	34
38-426	'**Polybulk**' ? ? - *13*	25	32
38-427	'**Traffic Services Ltd**' ? ? - *13*	25	30

W91. JPA Bogie Cement Wagon (2010)

Bachmann Branchline

These are a new design of tank for the transportation of cement. They were built in 2007 by VTG Feldbinder in Germany.

JPA bogie cement wagon [W91]

38-201	'Castle Cement' VTG12461 pale grey - *10*		18	23
38-201A	'Castle Cement' VTG12459 pale grey - *11*		23	27
38-200	'Lafarge Cement' VTG12434 silver - *10*		18	23
38-200A	'Lafarge Cement' VTG12405 silver - *12*		24	30

W92. TEA 100T Bogie Tank Wagon (2007)

Where large quantities needed to be carried by rail, bogie tank wagons of 100 ton capacity could be used. These started to appear in 1966 when Shell-Mex, BP and Esso were forming block trains of them. They also rode better than the four-wheeled tank wagons. With the arrival of the new 100T bogie tank wagons, the small 2-axle tankers quickly disappeared from trains carrying petroleum products. The BP models are based on a batch built in 1967-69.

TEA 100T bogie oil tank wagon [W92]

38-112	'BP' BPO87467 grey - *07*	16	20
38-112A	'BP' BPO87469 black - *11*	24	29
38-111	'BP' BPO87887 green - *07*	16	20
38-111A	'BP' BPO80560? green - *10*	20	25
38-113	'Esso' 20059 pale grey - *09*	18	23
38-113A	'Esso' 20062 pale grey - *11*	24	29
38-115	'Fina' ? pale grey - *13*	NPG	NPG
38-114	'Gulf' GULF 85021 pale grey - *09*	18	23
38-114Z	'Gulf' GP628 black W Sp Edn 504 (TMC) - *10*	22	27
38-116	'Jet A1' BPO80562 green 'Aviation Fuel' - *13*	NPG	NPG
38-110	'Shell' SUKO87317 grey - *07*	16	20
38-110A	'Shell' SUKO87222 grey - *10*	20	25

W93. TEA 100T Crude Oil Bogie Tanker (2009)

These petrochemical bogie tank wagons, built by Charles Roberts to design code TE 021C, have conical ends. Like the TEA above, they have cranked solebars and Gloucester Mk3 bogies. BPO sold its fleet of TEAs to VTG and hired them back again and are of a batch of tankers built 1968-72.

38-222	'Amoco' AMOC85020 black - *09*	18	22
38-220	'BP' BPO83377 black - *09*	18	22
38-220A	'BP' BPO83383 black - *11*	20	25
38-221	'Shell/BP' BPO7500 black - *09*	18	22

TRACK MAINTENANCE EQUIPMENT

T1. Plasser 'Tamper' Machine (2001) (H0)

These machines pack the track to its correct longitudinal and transverse level and pull the track to correct alignment on both the straights and curves.
The model was produced by Lilput and is to H0 scale.

36-160	BRe DX73205 yellow no motor - *01*	12	18
36-160A	BRe DX73205 yellow no motor - *08*	12	19
36-165	EWS DX73205 yellow motorised - *03*	32	42
36-165A	EWS DX73205 yellow motorised - *08*	32	44

T2. Plasser OWB8 with Crane (2001) (H0)

These were the first examples of a new generation of engineers' trolley with a comfortable enclosed cab and a hydraulic lifting crane. DX68200 was introduced on the Southern Region in 1975 and was the only one of the DX682xx series to not have a trailer. This model was also produced by Liliput and to H0 scale.

36-150	BRe DX68200 yellow no motor - *01*	12	18
36-151	BRe DX68200 yellow motorised crane - *06*	25	32

T3. JJA Railtrack 'Auto-Ballaster' Mk2 (B) (2010)

These were conversions of Tiphook Rail 90 tonne aggregate wagons which had originally been built by AFR. Some had their height reduced so that they would safely pass under the loading hopper at Buxton Lime, which explains why some are flat topped and some are curved. At first they were in Tiphook blue and 10 of these were built as the Mark 1 type. The Mark 2 followed in RailTrack livery and 104 were built. The one in GE livery was built as a demonstration set.

JJA Railtrack 'Auto-Ballaster' Mk2 [T3]

38-210	Railtrack GERS12976 blue+buff (outer) with generator - *10*	22	29
38-210A	Railtrack GERS12945 blue+buff (outer) with generator - *12*	32	38
38-211	Railtrack GERS13005 blue+buff (inner) - *10*	22	29
38-212	Railtrack GERS12967 blue+buff (outer) - *10*	22	29
38-212A	Railtrack GERS12991 blue+buff (outer) - *12*	32	38
38-212K	GE Rail Services GERS13002 buff (outer) with generator Sp Edn 504 (BCC) - *12*	32	37
-	Iarnród Éireann 9960 9352 001-2 yellow with generator	38	NA
-	Iarnród Éireann 9960 9352 007-9 yellow	38	NA
38-210Z	above 2 in a set Sp Edn 507 (Marks Models) - *12*	NA	88

T4. MPV (Multi-Purpose Vehicle) Class 416 (2011)

These were built in 1998-2001 by Windhoff GmbH for use by Railtrack for general maintenance work. They consist of master and slave units, alternative on-board equipment and directional lighting. The models are DCC ready with 21-pin sockets. They allow for alternative autumn and winter configurations. They are highly detailed.

31-575	Network Rail DR98956+DR9806 blue+yellow - *11*	95	110
31-576DC	Network Rail DR98952+DR98902 blue+yellow - *11*	95	110
31-577	Railtrack DR98960+DR98910 blue+yellow - *11*	95	110
31-577A	Railtrack DR98960+DR98910 blue+yellow W - *13*	NPG	NPG

SETS

Initially, Bachmann sets were assembled at Barwell and came with a circle of track, an inexpensive controller, a standard range locomotive and rolling stock drawn from what was available in the store at the time. None of these are of particular interest to collectors but interest in them will almost certainly grow in future years as they were not sold in very great quantities and many sets were broken up by retailers in order to sell the contents separately.

An exception to the general run was the London Transport set (30-201) of 1991 which contained the early pannier tank in LT livery and three wagons. Another exception is the 'Cambrian Coast Express' set (31-2000), which was originally planned by Palitoy for their Mainline range. The Bachmann set had two locomotives and six coaches together with accessories.

Bachmann Branchline

In 2004, Bachmann introduced some special sets with a view to introducing beginners to a simple form of digital command control (DCC).

Underground Ernie

The Underground Ernie range was introduced in 2006 with the launch of the children's television series. However, this ran to only one series and, as such, could not establish itself as a marketable product worldwide. Without overseas sales, the project was abandoned and in the summer of 2009, Bachmann cleared their warehouse of remaining stock. It also meant that they did not complete their development plans and several of the models were not released.

Cat No.	Company, Number, Colour, Date	£	£

TRAIN SETS
S1. Sets (2006)
Containing train, track etc.

UE101	Circle Electric Train Set - *06*	NA	60

STOCK
L1. Trains (2007)

UE201	**(Hammersmith & City)** twins - *07*	28	35
UE202	**(Bakerloo)** & trailer car - *07*	28	35
UE203	**(Victoria)** & trailer car - *07*	28	35
UE204	**(Jubilee)** & trailer car - *07*	28	35
UE205	**(Circle)** & trailer car - *08*	28	35
UE207	**(Brooklyn)** & trailer car - *07*	28	35
UE208	**(Paris)** & trailer car - *not made*	NA	NA
UE209	**(Moscow)** & trailer car - *not made*	NA	NA
UE210	**(Osaka)** & trailer car - *not made*	NA	NA
UE211	**(Sydney)** & trailer car - *not made*	NA	NA

L2. Mobile Equipment (2008)

UE206	**(Ernie 1)** inspection vehicle - *08*	16	20

BUILDINGS ETC.
B1. Stations etc. (2007)

UE301	International station - *07*	NA	28
UE302	control centre - *not made*	NA	NA
UE303	train home - *not made*	NA	NA
UE304	Mr Rails' repair shop - *not made*	NA	NA
UE305	turntable - *not made*	NA	NA
UE306	Seaside station with cafe and bridge - *not made*	NA	NA
UE307	Botanical Garden station with trees - *not made*	NA	NA
UE308	Mystery Mansion station - *08*	NA	27
UE309	Sports Stadium station - *07*	NA	25
UE310	Airport station - *not made*	NA	NA
UE311	industrial units - *08*	NA	15
UE312	International tunnel - *not made*	NA	NA

TRACK
T1. Track Packs (2007)

UE201	track pack A - *07*	NA	20
UE201	track pack B - *07*	NA	14
UE201	track pack C - *07*	NA	16
UE201	track pack D - *07*	NA	12

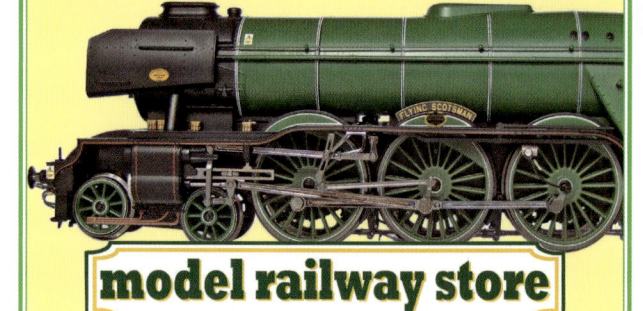

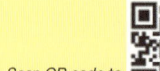

British Railways Steam
OO Scale Model Locomotives

BACHMANN BRANCH-LINE

31-146 — Class D11/1 62663 'Prince Albert' BR Black Early Emblem — 21 DCC — Era 4 (1948-1956)

32-550B — Class A1 BR Brunswick Green — 8 DCC — Era 9 (1995 onwards)

32-203A — 8750 BR Black L/Crest W'thrd — 8 DCC — Era 5 (1957-1966)

32-154A — N Class BR Black L/Crest W'thrd — 6 DCC — Era 5 (1957-1966)

31-626A — Class 3F BR Black E/Emblem — 21 DCC — Era 4 (1948-1956)

31-213DS — Patriot Class BR Green L/Crest — DCC SOUND — Era 5 (1957-1966)

31-967 — A4 BR Lined Green L/Crest — 8 DCC — Era 5 (1957-1966)

Era **4** signifies locomotives suitable for period 1948-1956 British Railways Early Emblem.
Era **5** signifies locomotives suitable for period 1957-1966 British Railways Late Crest.
Era **9** signifies locomotives suitable for period 1995 onwards - Post Privatisation

DCC SOUND Indicates models that are fitted with a DCC Sound decoder and speaker system

6 DCC Denotes that this locomotive is equipped with a 6pin DCC Socket.
8 DCC Denotes that this locomotive is equipped with an 8pin DCC Socket.
21 DCC Denotes that this locomotive is equipped with a 21pin DCC Socket.

OO Scale **Bachmann Europe Plc.** Moat Way, Barwell, Leicestershire. LE9 8EY
www.bachmann.co.uk

BACHMANN EUROPE Plc
A Bachmann Product

Bachmann Branchline

Bachmann Branchline Pocket Guide
1st Edition

Over 1500 Bachmann Branchline items inside!

Only £9.99

From the publishers of **BRITISH RAILWAY MODELLING**

by Pat Hammond

Bachmann Branchline contains listings of every known model and variation at the time of publication and provides suggested values of each and about 350 illustrations. There is a 20 year history of the famous 00 scale model range and the book describes how the models develop from idea to finished product. Included in the book are also the Underground Ernie and Bachmann Brassworks ranges.

To order call 01778 391180

www.model-railways-live.co.uk

Bachmann Brassworks

HISTORY

These high quality brass models are produced by San Cheng in China, exclusively for Bachmann Europe Plc. Randolph Cheng, the MD of San Cheng, is a former Vice-president of Bachmann USA. Painted versions are produced without numbers or insignia etc. They are supplied as ready to run, but allowing the owner to customise each model as required.

Gauge 0

LOCOMOTIVES

These are to 1:43 scale.

Cat No.	Company, Number, Colour, Date	£	£

L0-1. LNER J94 0-6-0T (2001)

Designed by Riddles, this was based on a Hunslet Class 50550 design and 391 were built for the government during the Second World War, using various locomotive builders. A further 93 were built for other customers. J94 was applied as a class code to the 75 locomotives bought by the LNER after the war and which passed to BR in 1948. Many others were sold to the National Coal Board and to private industry. Their high power and short wheelbase made them versatile machines. Of the 484 built, 70 are still in existance.

BW005	unpainted brass, high bunker - 06	250	324
BW006	black, high bunker - 06	280	369
BW007	unpainted brass, standard bunker (also YO94) - 01	250	324
BW008	black, standard bunker - 06	280	369

LNER Class J94 [L0-1]

L0-2. BR Standard 2-6-4T (2008)

Riddles designed this mixed traffic locomotive, which first made its appearance in 1951. A total of 155 locomotives were built between 1951 and 1957. They were used mainly for branch line and suburban passenger duties. The last was withdrawn in 1967 and 15 have been preserved.

BW065	unpainted brass - 08	750	830
BW066	unlined black - 08	780	865

L0-3. GWR 2251 Collett Goods 0-6-0 (2009)

Following the Grouping of 1923, the GWR found itself with a number of lightly constructed lines. The existing Dean 0-6-0s were getting old and so a new class of light 0-6-0 tender engines was required. The building of 120 of Collett's standard 0-6-0 class started at Swindon in 1930 and continued in batches until 1948. They were initially used for pick-up goods trains but, in BR days, they were acknowledged as mixed traffic engines, finding themselves on both cross-country routes and branch lines and pulling passengers as well as freight.

BW085	unpainted brass - 09?	NPG	NPG
BW086	unlined black - 09?	NPG	NPG
BW087	unlined green - 09?	NPG	NPG

L0-4. LMS 4F 0-6-0 (2002)

Designed by Sir Henry Fowler these locomotives were introduced in 1924 as a standard design for the LMS and as a variant of the Midland 4F. They were built for freight work and were occasionally used on branch passenger trains. The last was withdrawn in 1966 and three have been preserved.

BW015	unpainted brass (also YO4F) - 02	390	469
BW016	black (also YO4FP) - 05	475	549

L0-5. LMS Crab 2-6-0 (2005)

The 'Crab' Moguls were the first LMS standard locomotive, being based on a planned Caledonian Railway design. Also called 'Horwich Moguls', they were built at Horwich and arrived in 1926 with a Fowler tender. Building continued until 1932 and the class totalled 425. They were a short but powerful design, with large boilers, and were used for both passenger and freight workings, including express work. The last was withdrawn in 1967 and 3 were preserved, including one in the National Collection.

BW025	unpainted brass (also YOCRAB) - 05	600	685
BW026	black (also YOCRABP) - 05	635	712

LMS Ivatt Class 2MT [L0-6] (Tony Wright)

L0-6. LMS Ivatt 2MT 2-6-0 (2008)

This was the Ivatt mixed traffic design of 1946 and 128 of the class were built between 1946 and 1952. Construction continued under British Railways and light axle loadings allowed them to be used on branch line passenger and freight duties. Their almost enclosed cabs made them ideal for working tender first. The last was withdrawn in 1967 and 7 have been preserved.

BW075	unpainted brass - 08	945	1019
BW076	unlined black - 08	975	1057
BW077	unlined green - 09	975	1057

L0-7. LNER A3 Class 4-6-2 (2006)

The Class A3s of the LNER were a development of the A1s, which had been designed for the Great Northern Railway by Nigel Gresley in 1922. Almost all existing A1s were rebuilt, while later ones were built as A3s. One of the most visible changes was the new banjo shaped steam dome fitted to the top of the A3's boiler.

BW035	Flying Scotsman as preserved unpainted brass - 06	725	800
BW036	LNER Doncaster green as preserved Flying Scotsman - 06	890	964
BW041	LNER Doncaster green with GN tender, banjo dome, double chimney and smoke deflectors - 06	890	964
BW045	unpainted brass with non-corridor tender, banjo dome, single chimney - 06	725	800
BW046	BR green with non-corridor tender, banjo dome, single chimney - 06	890	964
BW047	Doncaster green with non-corridor tender, banjo dome, double chimney, smoke deflectors - 06	890	964
BW048	unpainted brass with GN tender, banjo dome, single chimney - 06	725	800
BW049	BR green with GN tender, banjo dome, single chimney - 06	890	965
BW050	Doncaster green with GN tender, banjo dome, single chimney - 06	890	965
BW052	BR Brunswick green with non-corridor tender, domed top feed, single chimney - 06	890	964
BW053	BR Doncaster green with non-corridor tender, domed top feed, single chimney - 06	890	964
BW055	BR Brunswick green with GN tender, domed top feed, double chimney - 06	890	964
BW056	LNER Doncaster green with GN tender, domed top feed, double chimney - 06	890	964
BW057	unpainted brass with non-corridor tender, domed top feed, double chimney - 07	725	800

Bachmann Brassworks

BW057PL	LNER Doncaster green supplied fully lined with non-corridor tender, domed top feed, double chimney - 07	1100	1175
BW058	BR green supplied fully lined with non-corridor tender, domed top feed, double chimney - 07	1100	1175
BW059	with non-corridor tender, domed top feed, double chimney and smoke deflectors - 07	890	964
BW059PL	with non-corridor tender, domed top feed, double chimney and smoke deflectors - 07	1100	1175
BW069	LNER Doncaster green with non-corridor tender, banjo dome, single chimney - 07	890	964
BW070	unpainted brass with GN tender, domed top feed, single chimney - 07	725	800
BW071	BR green with GN tender, domed top feed, single chimney - 07	890	964
BW072	LNER Doncaster green with GN tender, domed top feed, single chimney - 07	890	964

LNER Class A3 [L0-7]

L0-8. Class 03 (2006)

In all 230 of the Class 03 were built at Doncaster and Swindon between 1957 and 1962. They were used on all regions, initially, but later activity was concentrated on the Eastern and London Midland Regions. Eight locomotives on the Western Region, were given cut down cabs for working between Burry Port and Cwmmawr. The 03s were used for general shunting and pilot duties and, with a weight of just 30 tons, could be used on lines with severe weight limitations.

BW250	unpainted brass with flower pot chimney - 06	300	377
BW250A	unpainted brass with flower pot chimney, air tanks - 06	300	377
BW251	BR green with wasp stripes, flower pot chimney - 06	335	412
BW252	BR blue with wasp stripes, flower pot chimney - 06	335	412
BW253	unpainted brass, cone chimney, air tanks - 06	300	377

L0-9. Class 04 (2007)

The Class 04 diesel shunter was designed by Drewry in 1952 and it was ideal for dockyards and other confined spaces. 140 of these were built at Vulcan Foundry and Robert Stephenson & Hawthorn between 1952 and 1962. The class eventually totalled 142. They were used for shunting and pilot duties and on lines with severe weight limitations. Four of them side skirts and 'cowcatchers' fitted, to enable them to operate on the Wisbech & Upwell Tramway and other former LNER lines with on-street running. The last 04 was withdrawn from the national network in 1972, many being sold on for industrial use and 18 going for preservation.

BW260	unpainted brass - 07	300	377
BW261	BR blue with wasp stripes - 07	335	412
BW262	BR green with wasp stripes - 07	335	412
BW263	BR black - 07	320	395

L0-10. Class 08 (2002)

This was the standard BR diesel shunter and dated from 1952. It was based on an LMS design of 1945 and 894 were built between 1953 and 1962, for shunting and station pilot duties. As the fleet was reduced, due to shrinking freight traffic and pilot duties, many found their way into industry and at least 60 have found their way onto heritage lines.

Two types (A & B) were available. The A Type is the earlier version.

YO08	unpainted brass - 02	275	349
YO09	unpainted brass (type B) - 04	275	349
BW270	BR blue with wasp stripes (type B) - 07	425	505
BW169	BR green (type A) (also YO08PG) - 07	425	505

L0-11. Class 24/0 (2001)

Built originally at BR Derby Works form 1957, the Class 24 locomotives were for mixed traffic and were introduced to British Railways in 1958. Subsequent orders also involved Crewe and Darlington workshops and 151 were built before the design was modified to produce the Class 25. Withdrawals of the class started in the late 1960s and had been completed by the Autumn of 1980. Four members of the class have been preserved.

YO24	unpainted brass - 01	275	349
BW275	BR green - 09?	NPG	NPG
BW276	BR blue - 09?	NPG	NPG

L0-12. Class 25/3 (2001)

The Class 25s were introduced to Britain's railways in 1961 as mixed traffic locomotives and were a development of the Class 24. Between 1961 and 1967, a total of 323 were built at Derby, Darlington and by private sector contractor Beyer Peacock. There were 4 subclasses, the main differences being in the electrical equipment incorporated in their construction. There were also five slight body differences which affected the appearance of the cab fronts and the ventilation louvers on the sides. A fifth subclass was formed in 1986 by modification of some existing locos. Withdrawals started in the late 1970s, with the last member of the class going in 1987. At least 20 of the class survived into preservation.

YO25	unpainted brass - 01	275	349
BW285	BR green - 09?	NPG	NPG
BW286	BR blue - 09?	NPG	NPG

L0-13. Class 101 2-Car DMU (2008)

The Class 101s were built in 1956-59 by Metro-Cammell Ltd for branch line and local services. They had a maximum speed of 75mph and were the most numerous of the first generation diesels. All regions received an allocation and the combination of the size of the class and the large geographical area of operation made them an obvious subject to model.

These vehicles were supplied ready-to-run. They were unpainted brass and required painting, glazing and interiors to be fitted by the purchaser.

YO101	unpainted brass - 99	320	395
BW295	BR green - 08	570	645
BW296	BR blue - 08	570	645

L0-14. Class 106 2-Car DMU (2001)

These vehicles were supplied ready-to-run. They were unpainted brass and required painting, glazing and interiors to be fitted by the purchaser.

YO106	unpainted brass - 01	335	409
BW295	BR green - 08	570	645
BW296	BR blue - 08	570	645

L0-15. Class 121 ('Bubble Car') (2000)

In all 15 of the Class 121 DMBSs were introduced to the rail network in 1960 for high density local passenger transportation. At the time it was a modern version of the GWR AEC railcar. Derby designed, they were built by Pressed Steel and have 65 seats in a 2+3 pattern.

These vehicles were supplied ready-to-run. They were unpainted brass and required painting, glazing and interiors to be fitted by the purchaser.

BR Class 121 'Bubble Car' [L0-15] (Bachmann)

YO122	unpainted brass - 00	220	295
BW325	BR green - 08	435	510
BW326	BR blue - 08	435	510

L0-16. Wickham Trolley & Trailer (2009)

These were built between 1948 and 1990 and totalled over 600 in all. Many were exported and they ran on narrow gauge and broad gauge as well as standard gauge lines. They were used by engineers working on the railway and can travel at up to 30mph. Many are found on preserved lines.

BW305	unpainted brass - 09?	NPG	NPG
BW306	painted - 09?	NPG	NPG

Bachmann Brassworks

COACHES

These coaches were supplied ready-to-run. They were unpainted brass and required painting, glazing and interiors to be fitted by the purchaser. At the time of their introduction they were the first ready-to-run 0 gauge coaches to be introduced since the demise of the underscale Lima Mark 1 coaches and the only alternative had been kit built coaching stock.

The coaches were later available only through Tower Models and were incorporated into the Tower Brass range for a number of years.

Cat No.	Company, Number, Colour, Date	£	£

C0-1. BR MK1 Stock (1999)

Following the nationalisation of the railways at the start of 1948, most outstanding coach construction plans were completed by British Railways. This gave the Carriage Standard Committee time to design its own range of standard coaches that could be used throughout Britain. These were what we now refer to as BR Mk1 coaches, the prototypes for which arrived in 1950. They had much in common with final pre-nationalisation designs and visually they looked very like the Bulleid coaches of the Southern Railway. All are unpainted brass models.

Y7-96-001	SK corridor 2nd - 99	120	159
Y7-96-002	SO open 2nd - 99	120	159
Y7-96-003	FO 1st open - 99	120	159
Y7-96-004	FK corridor 1st - 99	120	159
Y7-96-005	RMB miniature buffet - 99	120	159
Y7-96-006	BSK corridor 2nd - 99	120	159
Y7-96-007	BCK corridor composite brake - 99	120	159
Y7-96-008	full brake - 99	120	159
Y7-96-009	CK corridor 2nd - 99	120	159
Y7-96-010	SO/SK suburban 2nd - 99	120	159
Y7-96-011	suburban 2nd brake - 99	120	159

WAGONS

These vehicles were supplied ready-to-run. They were unpainted brass and required painting by the purchaser

Cat No.	Company, Number, Colour, Date	£	£

W0-1. MEA 46t Steel Box Mineral Wagon (2000)

Redundant HEA hopper wagon chassis were used in MEA construction and a steel box body fitted. Early conversions were ordered by Railfreight and these were subsequently divided up equally between Mainline Freight, Loadhaul and Transrail. Mainline and Loadhaul ordered further batches and, after they inherited all three fleets, EWS continued to place orders for them. The most recent were built in 2004.

| Y555 | unpainted brass - 00 | 45 | 59 |

W0-2. HEA 46t GLW Hopper Wagon (2000)

These air-braked hoppers were built for coal traffic in their thousands at BREL (Shildon Works) between 1976 and 1979.

| Y380 | unpainted brass - 00 | 45 | 59 |

W0-3. 12T Tank Wagon (2001)

There are two things to know about tank wagons - the first is that there are few wagon types more diverse in design and secondly they are one type of railway wagon left almost exclusively to the private sector to provide. These 12 ton wagons were probably built between the wars and at one time were numerous. An improved road network led to their decline.

Y650	unpainted brass with ladder and cat walk - 01	45	59
Y651	unpainted brass with large filler and straps - 01	45	59
Y652	unpainted brass without ladder or cat walk - 01	45	59

W0-4. 20T Tank Wagon (2001)

These were larger than those in the table above and were used for a wide range of products, including many types of chemical. They were not usually used for petroleum products.

| Y675 | unpainted brass - 01 | 50 | 64 |

Gauge 1

LOCOMOTIVES

Cat No.	Company, Number, Colour, Date	£	£

L1-1. GWR Class 57xx 0-6-0PT (2007)

This was a Collett pannier tank design of 1929, but with a Churchward cab. A total of 863 locomotives were built between 1929 and 1950. The last was withdrawn in 1966. 13 had been sold to London Transport between 1957 and 1963 and the last of these worked on the London Transport network until 1971. 16 of the class have been preserved, including 6 of those sold to London Transport.

BW1021	unpainted brass - 07	580	655
BW1020	black - 07	650	722
BW1022	green - 07	650	722

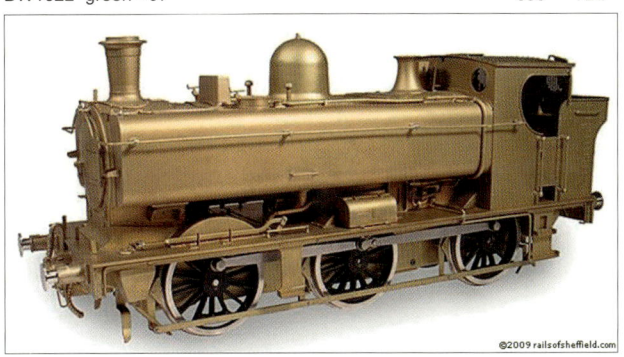

GWR Class 57xx pannier tank [L1-1] (Rails of Sheffield)

L1-2. GWR Class 8750 0-6-0PT (2009)

These are usually considered to be part of the Class 57xx and were introduced to the GWR in 1933 by Collett, as a heavier version. They had a modified cab, for better visibility by the crew, and better weather protection.

BW1005	unpainted brass - 09?	NPG	NPG
BW1005	black - 09?	NPG	NPG
BW1007	green - 09?	NPG	NPG

L1-3. LMS Johnson 1F 0-6-0T (2009)

The locomotives were built to an 1874 design between 1878 and 1879 for the Midland Railway. A large number were rebuilt from 1919 onwards with Belpaire fireboxes. The last was withdrawn in 1966 and one has been preserved.

BW1015	unpainted brass closed cab - 09?	NPG	NPG
BW1016	unlined black closed cab - 09?	NPG	NPG
BW1017	unpainted brass open cab - 09?	NPG	NPG
BW1018	unlined black open cab - 09?	NPG	NPG

L1-4. LMS Class 3F 'Jinty' 0-6-0T (2006)

This was based on a Johnson design of 1885, which was later modified by Deeley. It was a small goods engine which was introduced to the Midland Railway in 1903. The LMS took over 490 of the locomotives in 1923 and they were rebuilt by Fowler, giving them the distinctive Belpaire firebox. The last was withdrawn in 1964 and none was preserved.

| BW1010 | unpainted brass - 06 | 485 | 560 |
| BW1011 | unlined black - 06 | 535 | 610 |

L1-5. LNER J94 0-6-0T (2006)

Designed by Riddles, this was based on a Hunslet Class 50550 design and 391 were built for the government during the Second World War, using various locomotive builders. A further 93 were built for other customers. J94 was applied as a class code to the 75 locomotives bought by the LNER after the war and which passed to BR in 1948. Many others were sold to the National Coal Board and to private industry. Their high power and short wheelbase made them versatile machines. Of the 484 built, 70 are still in existence.

BW1000	unpainted brass, high bunker - 06	425	499
BW1001	black, high bunker - 06	485	560
BW1002	unpainted brass, standard bunker - 06	425	499
BW1003	black, standard bunker - 06	485	560

L1-6. GWR Class 45xx 2-6-2T (2008)

This is a Churchward designed tank dating from 1906 and was a development of his earlier Class 44xx, which they closely resembled. The most noticeable difference was the larger driving wheels. They were built at Wolverhampton or Swindon and construction continued until 1929, bringing the total to 175. In 1953 15 were fitted for push-pull work in the Cardiff area and those in the Taunton area were fitted with an automatic staff changing apparatus. The last of the class was withdrawn in 1965 and 14 have been preserved.

| BW1100 | unpainted brass - 08 | 650 | 725 |
| BW1102 | unlined green - 08 | 700 | 775 |

L1-7. GWR Class 4575 2-6-2T (2008)

These were 45xx tanks built to the modified design of 1927. They had larger side tanks, giving an extra 300 gallons water capacity and sloping tank tops to improve driver visibility. These later locomotives all had the larger bunker to increase coal capacity.

8th Edition

Bachmann Brassworks

BW1150	unpainted brass - 08		650	725
BW1152	unlined green - 08		700	775

L1-8. LMS Class 5MT ('Black Five') 4-6-0 (2008)

Stanier's Class 5 mixed traffic locomotive of 1934 was one of the most successful and influential designs. The fact that 842 were built between 1934 and 1951 meant that they were a common sight on the LMS. It was to form the basis of the Standard 5 class built by British Railways and 'Black 5s' remained on the network to the very end of steam. 18 have survived in preservation.

The model was paired with a 4,000 gallon Stanier tender and there was a choice between a riveted and a welded tender.

BW2001	unpainted brass riveted tender - 08	1100	1200
BW2002	unpainted brass smooth tender - 08	1100	1200

L1-9. Class 03 (2008)

In all 230 members of the Class 03 were built at Doncaster and Swindon between 1957 and 1962. They were used on all regions, initially, but later activity was concentrated on the Eastern and London Midland Regions. Eight locomotives on the Western Region, were given cut down cabs for working between Burry Port and Cwmmawr. The 03s were used for general shunting and pilot duties and, with a weight of just 30 tons, could be used on lines with severe weight limitations.

BW1075	unpainted brass, flower pot chimney, air tanks - 08	500	575
BW1077	unpainted brass, flower pot chimney, air brakes - 08	570	645
BW1077A	green, flower pot chimney - 08	570	645
BW1078	unpainted brass, conical exhaust - 08	570	645
BW1078A	unpainted brass, cone chimney, air tanks - 08	500	575
BW1080	blue, conical exhaust - 08	570	645

L1-10. Class 04 (2008)

Drewry Car designed this loco in 1952 and it was ideal for dockyards and other confined spaces. 140 of these were built by Drewry (but subcontracted to Vulcan Foundry) and Robert Stephenson & Hawthorn between 1952 and 1962. The total number of the fleet was 142. They were used for shunting and pilot duties and on lines with severe weight limitations. The last 04 was withdrawn from the national network in 1972, many being sold on for industrial use and 18 have been preserved.

BR Class 04 diesel shunter [L1-10] (Rails of Sheffield)

BW1024	BR green - 08	570	645
BW1025	BR blue - 08	570	645

Gauge 3

LOCOMOTIVES

Cat No.	Company, Number, Colour, Date	£	£

L3-1. GWR Class 45xx 2-6-2T (2008)

This is a Churchward designed tank dating from 1906 and was a development of his earlier Class 44xx, which they closely resembled. The most noticeable difference was the larger driving wheels. They were built at Wolverhampton or Swindon and construction continued until 1929, bringing the total to 175. In 1953 15 were fitted for push-pull work in the Cardiff area and those in the Taunton area were fitted with an automatic staff changing apparatus. The last of the class was withdrawn in 1965 and 14 have been preserved.

BW1160	green - 08		1350	1475

COACHES

This vehicle was supplied ready-to-run. They were unpainted brass and required painting, glazing and interiors to be fitted by the purchaser. They normally ran in pairs.

Cat No.	Company, Number, Colour, Date	£	£

C3-1. GWR B Set (2009)

'B Set' coaches were brake ends which were built by the GWR in 1933 to run in two car sets. Each contained five 3rd class and one 1st class non-corridor compartments and a guards/luggage area at one end.

BW1161	unpainted brass - 09	750	840

Narrow Gauge

These were built to 1:19th scale to run on garden railways. Both 32mm and 45mm track gauge options were available

LOCOMOTIVES

Cat No.	Company, Number, Colour, Date	£	£

LN-1. Double Fairlie 0-4-4-0 (2008)

This takes its inspiration from the Double Fairlies that run on the Festiniog Railway.

Double Fairlie 0-4-4-0 [LN-1] (Malcolm Pugh)

BW1500	green 32mm gauge - 08	1100	1220
BW1545	green 45mm gauge - 08	1100	1220

BRM — BRITISH RAILWAY MODELLING

Subscribe today to guarantee your copy!

Call our hotline on 01778 392002

Bassett-Lowke 0

HISTORY

Wenman Joseph Bassett-Lowke was born in December 1877 and was a member of the boiler making family, J T Lowke & Co Ltd. After the death of Tom Lowke, his wife had married one Absalom Bassett who adopted her son Joseph Tom Lowke. He got on well with his stepfather and when he married and had three sons of his own he gave them all 'Bassett' as their middle name. The two surviving sons grew up using the surname Bassett-Lowke. Wenman, for some reason, took the name Whynne but was often referred to simply as 'WJ'.

Standard 'Compound' of 1928 [L48]

Whynne Bassett-Lowke trained in the family business but wanted to strike out on his own. With his father's book keeper, Harold Franklin, he founded his own model engineering company in 1899 while still serving an apprenticeship with his father. This became a limited company in 1910 with a factory base in Northampton. The Company was never large although its output was considerable. This was achieved by contracting out work to other companies that Bassett-Lowke became associated with. One of these was Winteringham Ltd, which had been established by George Winteringham in 1908 as a subsidiary, and this became Bassett-Lowke's main manufacturer.

WJ had been to the 1900 Paris Exhibition and been much impressed by the products of German manufacturers such as Marklin, Carette and Bing. A year later, all three had agreed to manufacture models to Bassett-Lowke's designs for the latter to sell in the UK. The first supply arrived in 1901 and the first locomotive was a gauge 3 model of a LNWR 4-4-0 named *Black Prince*. WJ supplemented the supplies he received from Germany with models built within his limited facilities although, initially, these were mainly freelance subjects. By 1904 a range of 40 locomotives was being offered!

In 1913, when James Carson & Co. abandoned model engineering, Bassett-Lowke purchased their stock but the only 0 gauge locomotive in this range was an LNWR 4-6-0 'Experiment'. Since 1910, they had been marketing some of Carson's larger scale models which remained in the Bassett-Lowke catalogue until 1925. They also advertised the Carson roller test-rig in the early '20s.

The same thing happened in 1916 when C Butcher & Co. of Watford, who had previously been making high quality models for Bassett-Lowke, gave up model railway production and sold Bassett-Lowke their remaining stock.

The German supplies ceased during the First World War but Bing and Marklin both produced models to Bassett-Lowke's requirements after the war. However, it took Germany sometime to recover from the war and there was now considerable anti-German feeling in Britain, particularly among Bassett-Lowke's affluent middle class whose boyhood ranks had been so tragically decimated.

When German supplies did resume, Bassett-Lowke removed German trademarks and stamped the models 'Foreign Made'. Any models marked 'Bing' or 'Marklin' are likely to be from stocks supplied before the First World War. They even supported the sentiments againts German products in their advertising! Eventually, around 1930, Winteringhams took over production and Bassett-Lowke became less reliant on imported products.

Model railways in gauges 0, 1, 2 and 3 were only part of the Bassett-Lowke business. They also made stationary engines, model ships and miniature railways. A man who became closely linked with Bassett-Lowke for many years was Henry Greenly and he was responsible for the design of some of their engines as well as the British liveries used on German models made for the British market. Another famous name associated with Bassett-Lowke was the model maker E.W.Twining who illustrated catalogues for them and later joined the company.

Year-by-year the Bassett-Lowke catalogue grew and was split into different interest sections. Besides the large range of railway locomotives, rolling stock, accessories, track and sets being offered, there were the drawings and parts to enable you to construct your own models in one of a number of gauges. Models were also available with a choice of power units; namely steam, clockwork or electric.

The range of locomotives available before and immediately after the First World War was considerable and some were available for many years. Amongst the favourites were the 'Precursor' tank, *George the Fifth*, *Sydney*, Deeley Compound (which was also available as a kit from 1909), GNR 'Atlantic' and the Great Central locomotive *Sir Sam Fay*.

In the early 1920s, Bassett-Lowke and Henry Greenly were instrumental in introducing 00 scale to Britain in the form of the Bing Table Top Railway. This started life as a clockwork system but was soon available with electric motors. In the mid 1930s they assisted Trix to establish a company in Britain and this became closely associated with Winteringhams where the models were made.

A different approach to marketing had been made in 1927 through Godfrey Phillips BDV cigarettes, where sons were encouraged to get their fathers to smoke themselves to death to collect enough tokens for the Bassett-Lowke model Duke of York! Bassett-Lowke made 30,000 locomotives for this promotion. It was in October this year that Bassett-Lowke opened a shop at 28 Corporation Street, Manchester. A branch they had opened earlier in Fredrick Street, Edinburgh, was closed in 1930.

LMS 'Jubilee' Class Newfoundland [L74a] (Tony Wright)

Bassett-Lowke 0

Milestones

- 1899 Bassett-Lowke sets up his company with Harry Franklin.
- 1899 B-L produces his first mail order catalogue at the age of just 22.
- 1900 Paris Exhibition and B-L enters into an import agreements with Stefan Bing and Georges Carette.
- 1901 B-L takes delivery of his first supply from Bing.
- 1901 Henry Greenly appointed Consulting Engineer and Designer to B-L.
- 1902 Track developed by George Winteringham.
- 1902 First comprehensive catalogue produced containing railway items.
- 1905 First exhibition stand at the Model Engineering Exhibition in London.
- 1905 *Model Railway Handbook* first published.
- 1907 'Lowko' motor introduced.
- 1908 Winteringham Ltd formed as a subsidiary.
- 1908 B-L opens his first shop in Holborn, London.
- 1910 Bassett-Lowke Ltd becomes a public company.
- 1912 First Continental retail agency opens in Paris.
- 1913 Acquires Carson models etc.
- 1916 Acquires C Butcher's stock.
- 1919 Mass production plant installed for small gauge models.
- 1920-23 Winteringham's trademark appears on some items.
- 1922 Introduction of Bing 'Table Top Railway'.
- 1922 Edinburgh shop opens.
- 1922 First American agency established in New York.
- 1924 Smallest model railway in the world made for Queen's dolls house.
- 1925 Cast loco paperweights.
- 1927 BDV gift coupon scheme sells 30,000 locos.
- 1927 Manchester shop opened.
- 1931 Robert Bindon Blood joins B-L, later to design many of the better models.
- 1932 Franz Bing emigrates to England.
- 1932 Trix Ltd founded in the UK with W J Bassett-Lowke as a Director.
- 1935 Launch of Trix Twin Railway.
- 1941 Founding of Precision Models Ltd.
- 1946 Reappearance of models after the war.
- 1949 50th Anniversary celebrations.
- 1950 New BR livery appears on a B-L locomotive.
- 1953 Death of W J Bassett-Lowke.
- 1963 Last Bassett-Lowke catalogue released.
- 1965 Bassett-Lowke Ltd ceases trading.
- 1968 Bassett-Lowke Railways produce some prototype models.
- 2000 Corgi Classics re-launch the range.
- 2008 Hornby acquire the brand.

As the years passed, the demand for the larger gauges fell away and 0 gauge became the mainstay of Bassett-Lowke Ltd, especially after the First World War. Likewise, interest in electric traction grew and that in steam and clockwork lessened especially after the Second World War.

Some of the finest and most famous Bassett-Lowke locomotives were built during the late 1920s and 1930s; many designed by Robert Bindon Blood. Popular subjects included *Flying Scotsman*, *Royal Scot*, *Lord Nelson*, a 'Jubilee', *Princess Elizabeth*, a 'Duchess', a range of A4s with different names, a Midland 'Compound', the 0-6-0 and 0-4-0 Standard tanks and, of course, the much loved 'Moguls'.

Carette for Bassett-Lowke short bogie coach GNR [C3] (Keith Bone)

Production in Northampton ceased during the Second World War and restarted sometime after the cessation of hostilities. The new British Railways livery made its appearance on Bassett-Lowke models in 1950 and, the following year, the 4-4-0 *Princess Elizabeth* was replaced by *Prince Charles*. Notable post-war locomotives were the rebuilt 'Royal Scot', *Spitfire* ('Castle'), *Britannia*, the Classes 5, 8F and 9F and a 'Deltic'. These were mostly built in brass for Bassett-Lowke by Mr V Hunt and some were later rebuilt to a higher quality by Mr V Reader. These compare favourably with today's finescale 0 gauge models.

The final catalogue was published in 1963 and trading ceased in 1965; although there was a short lived attempt at reviving the company in the late 1960s under the name Bassett-Lowke Railways.

In the mid 1990s, a range of white metal models, in 1:43 scale, was produced under the Bassett-Lowke name by the then owners. These were of steam land vehicles such as a 'Clayton' steam lorry, a 'Burrell' steam roller and others. A showman's engine had been planned but deposits for this had to be returned when the name and intellectual assets of the company were acquired by Corgi. This acquisition provided an interesting link with the past. Corgi had been a product of Mettoy, a company which started life in 1933 in the basement and ground floor of the Winteringham factory. At the time Winteringham Ltd was, of course, the production arm of Bassett-Lowke Ltd!

At the 2000 British Toy and Hobbies Fair at Olympia, Corgi Classics launched the first of a new range of Bassett-Lowke 0 gauge locomotives and the subject chosen for the re-launch was a steam powered 'Mogul'. All subsequent models produced by Corgi were electric powered.

In 2008, Hornby bought Corgi Classics and with it Bassett-Lowke. While Hornby initially released a few new models, by 2013 it appeared that their interest in developing the Bassett-Lowke range had waned

FURTHER READING

The standard work is *The Bassett-Lowke Story* by Roland Fuller, published by New Cavendish Books (ISBN 0-904568-34-2). This is out of print but available through the public library service. A book of value to researchers is *Wenman Joseph Bassett-Lowke* by his late niece Janet Bassett-Lowke and published by Rail Romances (ISBN 1-900622-01-7). This same publisher has also released a video tape showing footage taken by WJ himself which includes factory scenes. In 2013 Graham de Chastelain released his pictorial album *Bassett-Lowke - The Gauge 0 Locomotives*.

COLLECTORS CLUB

The Bassett-Lowke Society caters for those who collect and operate Bassett-Lowke models. The Society publishes a quarterly magazine called Lowko News and organises events to which members may take their stock to run. For further information about the Society, ring the secretary on 01473 437713.

Prices - There is very limited information about prices of Bassett-Lowke models except through auctions. Where auction prices are known, the latest is given but it should be remembered that some of these are now 4 or 5 years old. These will be added to as more information becomes available. The two prices suggest a range for a model in good condition.

Codes - The following codes are peculiar to this section:
(F) = Freelance design. Also, 'Standard' normally implies freelance.
(B) = Made by Bing for Bassett-Lowke.
(C) = Made by Carette for Bassett-Lowke.
(H) = Made by Hunt for Bassett-Lowke.
(L) = Made by Leeds Model Company for Bassett-Lowke.
(M) = Made by Marklin for Bassett-Lowke.
litho = lithographed (printed as opposed to painted) locomotives.

Dates - The dates when models were available are very difficult to determine so long after the event and should not be taken too seriously. They also ignore breaks in availability during the two World Wars when the company was engaged in war work.

Bassett-Lowke 0

LOCOMOTIVES

Pre-WW1 - Not listed here are a number of imported 0 gauge locomotives listed in Bassett-Lowke's catalogues before the First World War. These bore little resemblance to any real locomotives and included 0-4-0Ts, 0-4-0s, 2-2-0Ts, 2-2-0s and 4-4-0s. However, in the larger gauges 1, 2, 3 and 4, greater realism could be found as early as 1902 including quite authentic British liveries. Both steam powered and clockwork versions were available from the start.

Hand-Built Locomotives - In 1933, Bassett-Lowke announced a range of hand-built locomotives which could be made to order. The models would be to a very high specification including all solder construction, all external and visible details and full painting and lining. Locomotives could be had either with variable speed clockwork drive, 8-10v DC or 20v AC electric mechanisms. These are listed together below in a table at the end of the section on steam locomotives.

LNER 'Flatrol M' trolley wagon with Callender Cable load. [W8] (Tony Wright)

'Nu-Scale' - In 1957, Bassett-Lowke introduced both a 2-rail electric control system and a 'Nu-Scale' service. 'Nu-Scale' was Bassett-Lowke's response to a changing market which required an improved, more scale, appearance for model railway locomotives which would run on BRMSB gauge 0 scale track, as well as standard Bassett-Lowke track. The changes, which increased prices by 30 to 40%, included replacing the alloy wheels with 10-spoke iron ones on the front bogies, thinner driving wheel profiles (.200"), Stuart Turner wheel castings and iron ones on the tender. It also meant sprung close-coupled tender drawbars, lamp brackets and lamps, whistles and extra handrails. All the standard range of locomotives, in 2 or 3-rail, were available with these improvements except for *Prince Charles*.

<u>Warning!</u> - Be careful when buying models alleged to be 'Nu-Scale' versions as the term is often misused to describe a locomotive which has had some or all of its wheels changed or thinned down, has been converted to 2-rail electric or has had non-standard details added. These conversions could actually reduce the value of the model on the collector's market, rather than increase it as would be the case with a genuine 'Nu-Scale' model.

The 'Nu-Scale' service does not appear to have been well used judging by the infrequency with which these models turn up at auction. That said, particularly the iron 10 spoke front bogie wheels, do appear on 'Compounds', *Prince Charles* and *Flying Scotsman* locomotives where these have been obtained separately by individual customers. Collectors are advised to check the provenance most carefully.

Loco Search

The following table might help you to trace that elusive model. If you know the running number on the side of the locomotive or its tender you can look it up in the following table and the adjacent column may tell you in what section you will find it.

Loco Nos.	Tables	Loco Nos.	Tables	Loco Nos.	Tables
1	L2	1442	L53	4844	L66
10	L4	1448	L56a	4853	L73b
11	L14	1456	L57	5071	L71
23	L92	1652	L97	5320	L32
25	L4	1864	L62	5374	L15
33	L63	1902	L31	5524	L67
36	L4	1927	L44	5552	L73a
41	L12	1930	L44	5573	L73a
44	L12	1931	L44	5600	L75
45	L11	1931	L56	5701	L73a
63	L4	2066	L63	5712	L73a
77	L37	2241	L13	5765	L18
78	L15	2265	L45	6000	L72
78	L21	2350	L29	6027	L72
88	L4	2495	L67	6100	L19b
89	L14	2509	L84	6100	L76
94	L20	2510	L84	6101	L19b
100	L1	2511	L84	6105	L19a
101	L1	2512	L84	6200	L80
103	L83	2524	L22a	6201	L80
112	L3	2526	L22a	6202	L80
142	L36	2531	L22a	6220	L81
211	L3	2531	L22b	6225	L81
251	L53	2536	L22a	6232	L82
298	L16	2603	L22a	6285	L43
335	L15	2603	L22b	6508	L58
433	L15	2663	L32a	6508	L68
440	L42	2663	L32b	6560	L96
441	L8	2664	L32a	6750	L26
483	L47	2664	L32b	6810	L12
504	L11	2670	L23	7100	L15
504	L50	2700	L59	7083	L96
504	L32c	2838	L70	8851	L26
513	L30	2848	L70	8851	L58
513	L32c	2871	L67	8872	L54
596	L11	2945	L62	8937	L15
601	L49	3064	L98	9405	L51
650	L25	3400	L48	13000	L59
773	L54	3410	L40	13007	L61
773	L58	3433	L32c	41109	L48
850	L78	3433	L40	41125	L48
851	L67	3536	L22a	41611	L15
864	L60	3611	L9	41613	L15
866	L60	3611	L11	42603	L22b
903	L65	3800	L41	42608	L22b
910	L52	3801	L41	42980	L61
930	L55	4072	L56	43871	L57
947	L15	4079	L71	45126	L77
955	L28	4256	L57	45295	L67
982	L62	4331	L64	46100	L74
999	L33	4390	L50	46232	L82
1000	L34	4417	L59	48209	L88
1000	L32	4420	L26	60103	L83
1017	L1	4431	L64	61324	L79
1036	L45	4460	L58	62078	L45
1063	L48	4460	L79	62136	L45
1067	L48	4472	L58	62453	L45
1082	L48	4472	L69	62759	L43
1106	L5	4472	L83	63871	L57
1108	L48	4481	L1	64193	L57
1113	L48	4489	L84	68211	L15
1190	L48	4490	L84	70000	L85
1425	L53	4498	L84	92220	L90

Bassett-Lowke 0

Cat No.   Company, Number, Colour, Date   £   £

Tank Engines
0-4-0T

L1a.   Peckett 0-4-0ST (by Bing) (1907)
The Peckett saddle tank engine was sold in the No.0P train set. It also contained two bogie coaches and a circle of large radius track - the equivalent of today's 'starter sets'.

Cat No.	Details	£	£
0P	**100** MR maroon c/w - ?	450	650
0P	**101** LNWR black c/w - 07-09-?	400	550
0P	**101** MR maroon c/w - 07-09-?	350	550
0P	**101** GNR green c/w - 07-?	500	650

L1b.   Peckett 0-4-0ST (by Carette) (1924)
This would have been produced from former Carette tooling acquired by Bassett-Lowke after the First World War. It was slightly smaller than the Bing one.

Peckett tank by Carette [L1b] (Special Auction Services)

Cat No.	Details	£	£
3104/0	**1017** green c/w - 24-34	300	400
3104/0	**1017** electric - 24-34	500	600
-	**4481** green electric - 24-34	400	450

L2.   SECR Steam Railmotor (by Carette) (1907)
This was introduced at the time that the real steam motor-coaches were beginning to appear on the railways. It consisted of a 4-wheel tank engine with a passenger car attached piggy-back to the bunker and supported at the other end by a bogie. It was sold in a set with a circle of rails.

-	**1** litho steam brown - 07-09-?	1600	1900

L3.   L&SWR Class S14 0-4-0T (by Bing) (1921)
The S14 was a passenger tank of which 4 were built originally as a 2-2-0T for motor train srvices and classified as C14. Rebuilding of them into S14 0-4-0Ts started in 1913 and only 3 survived into SR ownership - and then passing to BR. Two more were built as S14s but were sold to the Ministry of Munitions in 1917.
In 1921, Bassett-Lowke introduced the model as their standard clockwork 0-4-0 tank, initially in 4 liveries.

Cat No.	Details	£	£
	Clockwork		
21/0	**112** LNWR black - 21-29	NPG	NPG
21/0	**112** GNR green - 21-29	NPG	NPG
21/0	**112** MR red - 21-29	NPG	NPG
21/0	**112** CR blue - 21-29	NPG	NPG
21/0	**112** GWR green - 21-29	400	600
21/0	**112** LMS maroon - 24-29	NPG	NPG
21/0	**112** L&NER green - 24-29	NPG	NPG
	Steam		
53/0	**112** LNWR black - 21-29	NPG	NPG
53/0	**112** GNR green - 21-29	NPG	NPG
53/0	**112** MR red - 21-29	NPG	NPG
53/0	**112** NER brown - 21-29	NPG	NPG
53/0	**112** CR blue - 21-29	NPG	NPG
	Electric		
21/0	**112** GNR green - 21-29	NPG	NPG
31/0	**112** CR blue - 21-29	NPG	NPG
37/0	**211** LNWR black - 21-29	325	350
37/0	**211** GNR green - 21-29	NPG	NPG
37/0	**211** MR red - 21-29	NPG	NPG
37/0	**211** CR blue - 21-29	NPG	NPG

L4.   Standard Tank 0-4-0T (1937)
This was a freelance design by Bassett-Lowke which had wide appeal and became the standard 0-4-0T design in their catalogue. It did not have outside cylinders. The models were available with clockwork, 8v DC or 20v AC drives and in black LMS, LNER and SR livery. Listed below are known versions.

Standard 0-4-0 tank [L4] (Vectis)

Cat No.	Details	£	£
	Clockwork		
4730/0	**25** LMS black litho - 37-?	NPG	NPG
4730/0	**36** LMS black litho - 37-?	200	250
4730/0	**36** LNER black litho - 37-?	NPG	NPG
4730/0	**63** Southern black litho - 37-?	NPG	NPG
	Electric		
4309/0	**10** LMS black DC 8v - 37-?	300	360
-	**25** LMS black litho - 37-?	NPG	NPG
5509/0	**36** LMS black litho AC 20v - 37-?	300	450
-	**36** LNER black - 37-?	NPG	NPG
4309/0	**88** LNER green DC 8v - 37-?	NPG	NPG
4309/0	**88** LNER black DC 8v - 37-?	300	400
-	**63** Southern black litho - 37-?	NPG	NPG

L5.   GWR Class 11xx Class Dock Tank 0-4-0T (1961)
The GWR needed new locos at Swansea in the aftermath of the Grouping, when the GWR gained control of the Swansea docks and needed to replace the shunters working there.
These models were made to order.

-	**1106** GWR green (only about 3 made) electric - 61-63	NPG	NPG

0-4-4T

L6.   GNR Suburban Tank 0-4-4T (by Marklin) (1907)
Information about this prototype could not be found, nor could a picture of the model

-	GNR c/w - 07-?	NPG	NPG

L7.   L&SWR Class M7 Tank 0-4-4T (by Bing) (1909)
Designed by Drummond for the LSWR in 1897, over 100 were built and became important part of the Southern Railway's fleet as light passenger suburban locomotives.

-	**109** LSWR yellow-green c/w - 09-13	750	900

L8.   NER Class 0 Passenger Tank 0-4-4T (by Bing) (1914)
This is thought to be the 0-4-4T designed by W.Worsdell who was CME of the North Eastern Railway during the period 1890-1910. They became the G5 Class under the LNER. The model has large sand boxes forward of the side tanks and a large railed bunker.

-	**441** NER light green c/w - 14-19	NPG	NPG

2-4-2T

L9.   GWR Clas 36xx 2-4-2T (by Bing) (1911)
A 2-4-2T was an unusual wheel arangement on the GWR and the model appears to have been based on a Class 36xx of 1900. 31 were eventually built.

-	**3611** GWR green c/w - 11-13	1900	2800
-	as above electric - 13-16	1900	2800

Bassett-Lowke 0

4-4-0T

L10. 4-4-0T (Freelance) (by Bing) (1920)
Also known as a 'Short Precursor'.

-	GNR green c/w - 20-26	NPG	NPG
23593/0	L&NWR black c/w - 20-26	NPG	NPG
-	MR red c/w - 20-26	NPG	NPG
-	CR blue c/w - 20-26	NPG	NPG
-	GWR green c/w - 20-26	NPG	NPG
-	NBR brown c/w - 20-26	NPG	NPG

L11. L&NWR Short 'Precursor' 4-4-0T (by Bing) (1921)
The 'Precursors' were designed by George Whale who succeeded Webb as CME at Crewe. The name applied to his 4-4-0 tender locomotives but by association his 4-4-2 tank engines were similarly named by those who drove them. The model listed here is based on the correct 4-4-2T in the next table, but was shortened with a smaller bunker and did not need the rear pony.

L&NWR short 'Precursor' by Bing [L11] (Vectis)

-	GNR lined green c/w - 21-?	360	500
-	CR blue c/w - 21-?	NPG	NPG
-	Great Western green c/w - 21-?	450	550
-	MR red c/w - 21-?	NPG	NPG
-	NBR pale brown c/w - 21-?	NPG	NPG
-	3611 L&NWR black c/w - 21-?	NPG	NPG
-	45, 4221 LMS maroon c/w - 23-?	400	600
-	504 LNER green c/w - ?	550	900
-	3611 LNER black c/w - 23-?	400	450
-	596 SR lined green - ?	600	1000

4-4-2T

L12a. L&NWR 'Precursor' Tank 4-4-2T (by Marklin) (1909)
Built as a tank version of Whale's 4-4-0 'Precursor' class, they were passenger tanks working in the London, Birmingham and Manchester suburbs. They started to appear in 1906.

-	44 L&NWR black c/w - 09-10	450	550
-	as above electric - 09-10?	450	550

L12b. L&NWR 'Precursor' Tank 4-4-2T (by Bing) (1911)
This version by Bing had an enamelled finish. It is interesting that both Marklin and Bing adopted No.44 for their model as this was the subject chosen by the L&NWR for an official photograph of the class. 44 was the first of a batch built in 1907.

3101/0	44 L&NWR black c/w - 11-19?)	350	450
-	as above 3-rail 4-8v DC - 11-14?	350	450

L12c. L&NWR 'Precursor' Tank 4-4-2T (by Bing)
Later Bing changed to lithographed finishes and this is the later model. Considering that German imports were restricted after the First World War, the suggested date of 1920 seem inappropriate, unless this was a pre-war order that was late arriving.

3101/0	L&NWR black c/w - 20?	350	450
-	as above 3-rail 4-8v DC - 20?	350	450

L12d. L&NWR 'Precursor' Tank 4-4-2T (1921)
After the First World War, Bassett-Lowke produced their own model of the 'Precursor' tank and at last introduced some alternative numbers. This model has a large block under the smoke box.

3101/0	44 L&NWR black c/w - 21-c23	300	400
-	as above electric - 21-c23	300	400
-	6810 L&NWR black c/w - 21-?	NPG	NPG
-	as above electric - 21-c23	NPG	NPG
-*	as above electric over-painted 'LMS' - c25	400	500
3101/0	6810 LMS red c/w - 25-28	250	400

2/0	as above electric 3-rail 12vDC - 25-28	300	450
-	41 M&GN yellow electric - 64	NPG	NPG
-	9* M&GN yellow electric - ?	NPG	NPG

* Special order

L13. GWR 22xx Class 'County' Tank 4-4-2T (1950)
The 30 County Class 22xx tank engines were introduced in 1905 and were to gradually replace the smaller 2-4-2 tanks of the 36xx class. They were heavy and their driving wheels were the largest and used on a standard gauge tank engine.

-	2241 GWR green one-off electric - c50	NPG	NPG

L14a. LBSCR I2 Class 4-4-2T (by Bing) (1911)
The 10 Class I2 4-4-2 tank engines were suburban traffic tanks. They were poor performers and had a short life. Built in 1908, they had all been scrapped before the outbreak of the Second World War.

LBSC I2 Class suburban tank by Bing [L14a] (Vectis)

4/0	11 LB&SCR umber c/w - 11-25	350	550
-	as above electric - 11-25	450	600

L14b. LBSCR I3 Class 4-4-2T (1969)
These were built between 1907 and 1913 and were more successful than the I1s and I2s. 27 were built and all but one survived briefly in BR ownership.

-	89 LB&SCR umber electric - 69	500	650

0-6-0T

L15. Standard Tank 0-6-0T (Freelance) (1933)
These popular and long surviving models had outside cylinders and a large boiler, remenicent of LNER design. All the 0-6-0 standard tanks were lithographed. Some electric locomotives were fitted with a super reduction gear (40:1) for shunting and locos can be found with automatic (track operated) couplings. Likewise, some models are found with smoke units driven by a cam on the front axle. The LMS versions had a capuchon on the chimney. Pre-war electric models did not have key holes or control rod holes in the cab rear plate while post-war examples usually did, until late production orders. Catalogue number 4305/0 was used until 1940 for electric locos fitted with junior permag mechanisms.

3305/0	5374 LMS black lined red c/w - 33-38	250	350
4305/0	as above electric - 33-38	350	450
4305/0	as above with Walschaerts valve gear electric - 33-38	450	650
3305/0	61 LMS black lined red c/w - 38-50	250	350
5305/0	as above electric - 38-50	350	450
5505/0	as above electric 20vAC - 38-50	350	450
3305/0	78 LMS black lined red c/w - 38-50	250	350

Standard 0-6-0 Tank [L15] (Vectis)

8th Edition

Bassett-Lowke 0

5305/0	as above electric - *38-50*	350	450
3305/0	**7100** LMS black lined red electric - *?*	250	350
3305/0	**335** LNER black lined red c/w - *33-38*	250	350
5305/0	as above electric - *33-38*	350	450
3305/0	**433** LNER black lined red c/w - *38-50*	250	350
5305/0	as above electric - *38-50*	350	450
3305/0	**533** LNER black lined red c/w - *47-50*	250	350
5305/0	as above electric 12vDC - *47-50*	250	350
5305/0	**8937** LNER black lined red electric 12vDC - *47-50*	300	430
5305/0	**9033** LNER black lined red electric - *48-50*	450	550
3305/0	**947** Southern black lined green c/w - *38-50*	350	400
5305/0	as above electric 12vDC - *38-50*	400	500
3305/0	**68211** BRb black lined red c/w - *51-67*	250	350
5305/0	as above electric 12v DC 3-rail - *51-67*	300	350
2305/0	as above 2-rail electric - *51-67*	350	400
3305/0	**41611** BRb black lined red c/w - *51-67*	250	350
5305/0	as above electric - *57-67*	400	500
2305/0	as above 2-rail electric - *51-67*	400	500
-	as above electric Nu-Scale** - *57-65*	550	650
3305/0	LMS black lined red c/w - *59-61*	400	450
5305/0	as above electric - *59-61*	450	550
2305/0	as above 2-rail electric - *59-61*	450	550
3305/0	LNER black lined red c/w - *59-63*	400	450
5305/0	as above electric - *59-63*	450	550
2305/0	as above 2-rail electric - *59-63*	450	550
-	**41613-41617*** Longmoor Military Railway (LMR) blue electric - *?*	450	750

* used for training at Longmoor Military Railway. It is understood that they were numbered in sequence from 41613 to 41617. ** See note on Nu-Scale in the Introduction to this chapter.

L16. Hudswell Clarke Ex-Burry Port 0-6-0T (1968)

All of the 15 Burry Port & Gwendraeth Valley Railway locomotives handed over to the GWR in 1922 were 0-6-0 tanks and most were built by Hudswell Clarke.

-	**298** black prototype only, steam - *68*	NPG	NPG

L17. GWR Class 27xx Pannier 0-6-0PT

This class was introduced in 1896 during William Dean's time as CME of the Great Western Railway.

-	GWR green 2/3 rail electric - *?-50-57?*	NPG	NPG

L18. GWR 57xx Pannier 0-6-0PT (by Hunt) (1958)

This was Collett's pannier tank design of 1929 and 863 were built between 1929 and 1950. The last was withdrawn in 1966 and 16 have been preserved, including 6 of the 13 that were sold to London Transport between 1957 and 1963 and which survived in use until 1971.

-	**5765, 5775** * Great Western green electric - *58-63*	1600	2000

* Made to order. Other numbers probably exist.

2-6-2T

L19a. GWR 61xx Class 'Prairie' 2-6-2T (1937)

This was a Collett Prairie tank design of 1931 and 70 were built. They were the GWR's London suburban tank engines and were required to pull heavy suburban trains from Paddington at fairly high speeds.

GWR Class 61xx 2-6-2T [L19a] (Vectis)

3609/0	**6105** GWR button green c/w - *37-41?*	1100	2200
A4609/0	as above electric AC - *37-41?*	1100	2200
5609/0	as above electric DC - *37-41?*	1100	2200

L19b. GWR 61xx Class 'Prairie' 2-6-2T (by Hunt) (1955)

This is the post-war version hand-built by Hunt and to order. It is not known how many were made but other running numbers probably exist.

-	**6100, 6101** Great Western green electric 2/3 rail - *55-63*	800	2400

L20. LMS Fowler 3P Class 'Prairie' Tank 2-6-2T

Designed by Fowler, the class first appeared on the rail network in 1930 and 70 of them passed into BR ownership in 1948. None has been preserved. The number 94 belonged to an LMS Stanier 'Prairie' dating from 1935.

-	**94** LMS black lined red c/w - *?*	2100	2900
-	as above electric 3-rail AC - *?*	2100	2900

L21. LMS Class 3P Suburban Tank 2-6-2T (1941)

This model was listed only in the 1941/42 catalogue and did carry a running number that belonged to a 3P class of 139 Stanier 'Prairie' tanks.

3620/0	**78** LMS black lined red c/w - *41-42*	1800	2200
5620/0	**78** LMS black lined red 8-10vDC - *41-42*	1800	2200
5720/0	**78** LMS black lined red 20v AC - *41-42*	1800	2200

2-6-4T

L22a. Stanier 3-Cylinder 4P 2-6-4T (by Marklin) (1935)

This was an early Stanier design and had a combined dome and water feed pipe on top of the boiler, a taper to the front footplating and a pronounced curve to the rear of the cab doorway aperture.

913/0/C	**2524** LMS black c/w - *35-?*	1800	2100
913/0/A	as above electric AC - *35-?*	1800	2400
913/0/D	as above electric DC - *35-?*	1800	2400
913/0/C	**2526** LMS black c/w - *c37*	2300	2800
913/0/A	as above electric AC - *c37*	2300	2800
913/0/D	as above electric DC - *c37*	2300	2800
913/0/C	**2531** LMS black c/w - *c39*	1100	1600
913/0/A	as above electric AC - *c39*	1100	1600
913/0/D	as above electric DC - *c39*	1100	1600
913/0/C	**2536** LMS black c/w - *c37*	1800	2300
913/0/A	as above electric AC - *c37*	1800	2300
913/0/D	as above electric DC - *c37*	1800	2300

L22b. LMS Stanier 2-Cylinder 4P Tank 2-6-4T (1940)

This was a later Stanier design with separate dome and water feed manifold on top of the boiler and parallel framing to the footplating. The upper edge of the cab doorway had a pronounced recess.

LMS 2-cylinder Class 4P tank [L22b] (Vectis)

3618/0	**2531** LMS black c/w - *40-c50*	1000	1200
5618/0	as above electric 12vDC - *40-c50*	1100	1700
5718/0	as above electric 20vAC - *40-c50*	1100	1700
913/0	**2602** LMS black electric AC - *40-c50*	750	900
913/0	as above electric DC - *40-c50*	750	900
-	**2603, 2606** LMS black c/w - *40-c50*	1100	1700
913/0	as above electric AC - *40-c50*	1100	1700
913/0	as above electric DC - *40-c50*	1100	1700
-	**42603** BRb black c/w - *c50-?*	1300	1900
-	as above electric - *c50-?*	1600	1900
3618/0	**42608** BRb black c/w - *c52-c59*	850	1400
5618/0	as above electric 2/3 rail - *c52-63*	1100	1400
-	as above * Nu-Scale - *57-60*	1600	2200

* See note on Nu-Scale in the Introduction to this chapter.

Bassett-Lowke 0

4-6-2T

L23. Bowen-Cooke Superheater 4-6-2T (by Bing) (1914)
This was a tank version of the LNWR 'Prince of Wales' Class built in 1911.
-	**2670** L&NWR black c/w - *14*	800	1100

Tender Engines

2-2-2

L24. Der Adler 2-2-2 (by Marklin) (1935)
This was the first steam locomotive to operate in Germany and was a Robert Strphenson design of 1833. It was built at Stephenson's Newcastle works in 1835 and ran on the Nuremberg-Furth Railway. The 20v AC model was sold with three coaches - one open and two enclosed - and filled with passengers.
-	***Der Adler*** electric - *35-?*	NPG	NPG

4-2-2

L25. MR Johnson 'Spinner' 4-2-2 (by Bing) (1914)
At one time 'single wheelers' pulled express trains and Johnson's 'Spinners' were famous in their day. They were built between 1887 and 1900 and formed a class of 95. One is preserved in the National Collection.
-	**650** MR maroon litho c/w - *14-20*	800	1600
-	**650** MR maroon litho 4V electric - *20*	1000	1800
-	**650** MR red litho c/w - *14*	1400	1500

0-4-0

L26. Freelance 0-4-0 (by Bing?) (1928)
This is a subject that is difficult to attribute to any prototype.
4734/0	**4420** GWR green c/w - *c28*	NPG	NPG
4735/0	**6750** LMS maroon c/w - *c28*	NPG	NPG
4732/0	**8851** LNER green c/w - *c28*	NPG	NPG
4733/0	Southern c/w - *c28*	NPG	NPG

L27. Freelance 0-4-0 (ex-Carette) (1928)
This model was produced from Carette tooling acquired after Carette closed down in 1917. All were steam driven.
6460/0	green lined in yellow - *c28*	NPG	NPG
6460/0	maroon lined in yellow - *c28*	NPG	NPG
6460/0	blue lined in white - *c28*	NPG	NPG
6460/0	black lined in red - *c28*	NPG	NPG

2-4-0

L28. L&NWR 'Precedent' 2-4-0 (by Marklin) (1903)
Ramsbottom and Webb both built 2-4-0 tender locomotives for the L&NWR. The 'Precedents' started to appear in 1874 and *Charles Dickens* knocked up a high milage working a return trip from Manchester to London six days a week.
-	**955** *Charles Dickens* L&NWR black c/w - *03 -?*	1600	2200
-	as above electric - *03 -?*	1600	2200

4-4-0

L29. NYC Vauclain 'Compound' 4-4-0 (by Carette) (1905)
There is no information about this hard to find model.
2350C/0	**2350** NYC c/w - *05-?*	NPG	NPG

L30. L&NWR 'Precursor' Class 4-4-0 (by Marklin) (1907)
The iconic 'Precursor' was George Whale's first design, dating from 1904, and had a steel framed tender design used for all Whale's tender locos.
-	**513** *Precursor* L&NWR black c/w - *07-?*	450	550

L31. L&NWR Webb 'Jubilee' Class 4-4-0 (by Bing) (1910)
This class, designed by Webb, dated from 1897 and the first two were *Iron Duke* and *Black Prince*. The model has a lubricator in the smokebox and reversing motion in the cab.
26/0	**1902** *Black Prince* L&NWR black steam - *10-19**	700	900

* Remainer stock was being cleared in 1927.

L32a. L&NWR 'George the Fifth' 4-4-0 (by Bing) (1911)
C.J. Bowen-Cooke suceeded Whale as CME of the L&NWR in 1909 and his first design arrived the following year when two locomotives of a new class were built at Crewe. These two locomotives were named after the new King and Queen.
This original model by Bing was of soldered construction and was hand painted.
11/0	**2663** *George the Fifth* L&NWR black c/w - *11-13*	300	350
11/0	as above electric - *11-19*	300	350
-	**2664** *Queen Mary* L&NWR black painted c/w - *11*	NPG	NPG
-	as above electric - *11*	NPG	NPG

L&NWR 'George the Fifth' by Bing [L32a] (Vectis)

L32b. L&NWR 'George the Fifth' 4-4-0 (by Carette) (1911)
That same year a litho model of the same subject was also developed for Bassett-Lowke by Carette, who were more extravagant with rivet detail than Bing.
-	**2663** *George the Fifth* L&NWR black c/w - *11*	NPG	NPG
-	as above electric - *11*	NPG	NPG

L32c. L&NWR 'George the Fifth' 4-4-0 (by Bing) (1919)
This litho model was also sold in the UK under the Bing name and also under the Gamages name and by other shops that imported it. These included other names such as Apollo, GWR 3343 Mercury, LMS 513 Mercury, LNER 8551, LNER 504 King George V and LMS 1924 as well as versions similar to those listed below. Marklin also made a rather ugly 'George V' which too was not marketed through Bassett-Lowke.
2663/0	**2663** *George the Fifth* L&NWR black c/w - *19-23*	250	300
2663/0	as above electric - *19-23*	250	300
-	**1000** MR red c/w - *19-23*	NPG	NPG
-	**2664** *Queen Mary* L&NWR black painted c/w - *21?-?*	800	950
-	as above electric - *21?-?*	800	950
61/4710/0	**5320** *George the Fifth* LMS maroon c/w - *24-27*	300	400
61/BL/0	as above electric - *24-27*	350	450
	5320 LMS maroon no name c/w - *24-27*	300	400
	1924 LMS maroon no name electric - *?*	300	400
	513 *George the Fifth* LMS maroon c/w - *26?*	NPG	NPG
	as above electric - *26?*	NPG	NPG
	3433 *City of Bath* GWR green c/w - *24-27*	250	300
	as above electric - *24-27*	250	300
	504 LNER green c/w - *24-27*	250	300
	as above electric - *24-27*	250	300

L33. MR 'Compound' 4-4-0 (by Bing) (1910)
On the Midland Railway, Samuel Johnson's first 'Compound' was introduced in 1902 and modified versions were produced by Richard Deeley in 1905. The 45 locos were originally classified as Class 4 but this was later changed to 4P, as their primary function was express and local passenger services
17/0	**999** MR maroon c/w - *10-14, ?-30*	1100	1600
No.0	**1000** MR maroon steam - *10-14**	850	1300

* Remainer stock was being cleared in 1927.

L34. MR Deeley 4P 'Compound' 4-4-0 (by Bing) (1912)
Here is the Midland Railway 'Compound' as modified by Richard Deeley in 1905.
-	**1000** MR maroon c/w - *c21-23*	NPG	NPG
-	as above steam - *12-14?, c21-23*	NPG	NPG
-	as above electric - *c21-23*	NPG	NPG

L35. SE&CR Wainwright Class D 4-4-0 (by Bing) (1914)
The D Class was designed by Wainwright and nicknamed 'Coppertops'. 51 were built between 1901 and 1907 and 21 were rebuilt by Maunsell as D1s. One is preserved in the National Collection.
-	SE&CR green c/w - *14*	1900	2700

L36. CR McIntosh 'Dunalastair IV' 4-4-0 (1911)
The 'Dunalastairs were designed by J.F.McIntosh and arrive on the Caledonian Railway in 1896. The Dunalastair IV was the fourth development of this great class of express

8th Edition

Bassett-Lowke 0

locomotives. Incidentally, the name was that of the Highland home of the CR Chairman.

CR 'Dunalastair IV' [L36] (Vectis)

-	**142** C()R blue (B) c/w - *11-16*	1600	1900
142/0	**142** C()R blue c/w - *25-35*	1500	1800
142E/0	as above electric - *25-35*	1600	1900

L37. CR Pickersgill Class 72 4-4-0 (by Leeds) (1922)
48 of these locomotives were built for the Caledonian Railway and introduced in 1916. They were a development of the 'Dunalastair' family, introduced by J.F.McIntosh.

This model had a 6-wheel tender and was built for Bassett-Lowke by the Leeds Model Company.

77/0	**77** C()R blue c/w - *22*	NPG	NPG
77E/0	as above electric - *22*	NPG	NPG

L38. Bogie Express 4-4-0 (Freelance) (by Bing) (1911)
The inspiration for this model has not been established and may contain bits of a number of 4-4-0s, which were common at the time. All were steam driven.

61/250/0	GWR green - *11*	NPG	NPG
61/250/0	LMS red - *24-26*	NPG	NPG
61/250/0	LNER green - *24-26*	NPG	NPG
61/250/0	GWR green - *24-26*	NPG	NPG

L39. GWR 'Atbara' Class 4-4-0 (by Bing) (1904)
The 'Atbara' Class dates from the time of the Boer War and took names associated with it. These included *Mafeking*, *Kimberley* and *Kitchener*. All had been withdrawn by 1930. Typical of GWR locomtives, they had outside frames, which have been reproduced on this model.

-	**3410** *Sydney* GWR green c/w - *04-10*	750	1100

L40. GWR 'City' Class 4-4-0 (by Bing) (1913)
Ten locomotives of the 'City' Class were built at Swindon in the Spring of 1903. A further ten were rebuilt from locomotives of the 'Atbara' Class between 1902 and 1909 to make a total of 20.

The models had outside frames and cranks and were of an all soldered construction. Brass bogie wheels, nameplates and safety valve cover. They had typical Bing buffers with tapered shank and were nickel plated.

-	**3433** *City of Bath* Great Western green with incorrect yellow and black lining c/w - *13-15*	4200	6000
-	as above electric - *14*	4200	6000

L41. GWR Churchward 'County' 4-4-0 (by Leeds) (1922)
This is the original 'County' Class introduced by Churchward in 1904 for express passenger duties. None made it into BR ownership as the last was withdrawn in 1933.

3800/0	**3800** *County of Middlesex* GWR green c/w - *22-25*	NPG	NPG
3800E/0	as above electric - *22-25*	NPG	NPG
3800/0	**3801** *County of Carlow* GWR green c/w - *22-25*	400	550

Other names exist.

L42. Standard Express 4-4-0 (Freelance) (by Bing) (1922)
Early Bassett-Lowke models had been steam driven, but in post-First World War Britain, the demand was for clockwork and electric drive. However steam enthusiasts continued to be catered for with freelance steam powered locomotives like this one.

48/0	**440** LSWR green - *22-29*	NPG	NPG
48/0	**440** *Greater Britain* CR blue -*22-29*	NPG	NPG
48/0	**440** L&NWR black - *22-27*	NPG	NPG
48/0	**440** MR red - *22-29*	NPG	NPG
48/0	**440** GNR green - *22-29*	NPG	NPG
48/0	**440** GWR green - *22-29*	NPG	NPG

L43. Enterprise Express 4-4-0 (Freelance) (1931)
Here is another steam driven freelance 4-4-0, this time produced by Bassett-Lowke.

Enterprise live steam freelance loco [L43] (Vectis)

Many of them sold as kits and many of the ready-to-run examples that turn up at auction may well have started life as a kit.

?	loco kit - *31-?*	NPG	NPG
?	SR green lined white - *31-40?*	NPG	NPG
6690/0	**6285** on tender red - *31-40*	250	300
6690/0	as above black - *31-40*	350	550
6690/0	as above green - *31-40*	250	270
6690/0	as above LNER green - *31-40*	250	400
6690/0	**62759** BRb green lined white - *c54*	300	350
6690/0	as above blue lined orange - *c54*	400	450
6690/0	as above black lined orange - *c54*	300	350
6690/0	as above black lined white - *c54*	250	300

L44. 'Duke of York' 4-4-0 (Freelance) (1927)
This model was the start of a succession of freelance 4-4-0s produced by Bassett-Lowke and named after a future monarch. All examples of this model have a lithographed body. Only LMS versions carried a company designation. The 1927 locos had coupling rods with 'marine' Bing style big ends while later coupling rods were of a simplified shape. Electric models with a key hole have been converted to electric operation after purchase. The running number denotes the year each batch was released.

1927 Duke of York			
61/4710/0	light green lined black+white c/w - *27-29*	300	450
61/4710/0	as above electric - *27-29*	300	650
61/4710/0	dark green lined black+white c/w- *27-29*	300	450
61/4710/0	as above electric - *27-29*	300	650
61/4710/0	olive green lined black+white c/w - *27-29*	300	450
61/4710/0	as above electric - *27-29*	300	600
61/4710/0	red lined black+yellow c/w - *27-29*	300	450
61/4710/0	as above electric - *27-29*	300	650
1930 Duke of York			
3301/0	light green lined black+white c/w - *30*	350	550
4301/0	as above electric - *30*	400	650
3301/0	dark green lined black+white c/w - *30*	350	550
4301/0	as above electric - *30*	400	650
3301/0	olive green lined black+white c/w - *30*	350	550
4301/0	as above electric - *30*	400	650
3301/0	red lined black+yellow c/w - *30*	350	550
4301/0	as above electric - *30*	400	650
1931 Duke of York			
3301/0	light green lined black+white c/w - *31-32*	300	450
4301/0	as above electric - *31-32*	300	650
3301/0	dark green lined black+white c/w - *31-32*	300	450
4301/0	as above electric - *31-32*	300	650
3301/0	olive green lined black+white c/w - *31-32*	300	450
4301/0	as above electric - *31-32*	400	650
3301/0	red lined black+yellow c/w - *31-32*	300	450
4301/0	as above electric - *31-32*	300	650

The green 'Duke of Yorks' were intended to represent the LNER (Apple [light] green), GWR (Brunswick [dark] green) and SR (olive green). None had any distinctive company features such as a copper capped chimney for the GWR version. The red models represented LMS ones.

L45. 'Princess Elizabeth' 4-4-0 (Freelance) (1932)
Here we have the successor to the 'Duke of York' models. The alloy wheels on this model were prone to metal fatigue and disintegration with the result that many have been re-wheeled. In such a case, if original period Bassett-Lowke iron replacement wheels have been fitted, add £50 to the value. Electric models with a key hole have been converted to electric operation after purchase. All models are lithographed.

3301/0	**2265** *Princess Elizabeth* LMS red crest on cab c/w - *32-35*	250	350
4301/0	as above electric - *32-35*	300	550
3301/0	**2265** *Princess Elizabeth* LNER green c/w - *32-35*	250	350

Bassett-Lowke 0

4301/0	as above electric - 32-35	300	550

Freelance Princess Elizabeth [L45] (Lacy, Scott & Knight)

L46. 'Prince Charles' 4-4-0 (Freelance) (1951)
Here is the third in the line of 'heir apparent' freelance 4-4-0s, coming onto the market with Princess Elizabeth's accession to the throne. All models were lithographed and all had a key hole whether clockwork or electric.

3313/0	**62078** *Prince Charles* BRb blue c/w - *51-53*	250	400
4313/0	as above electric - *51-53*	300	550
3313/0	**62136** *Prince Charles* BRb dark green lined black+white c/w - *52-54*	250	400
4311/0	as above electric - *52-54*	300	550
3313/0	**62453** *Prince Charles* BRb dark green lined black+white c/w - *51-55*	250	400
4311/0	as above electric - *51-55*	300	500
3313/0	**62453** *Prince Charles* BRb Brunswick green lined black+orange c/w - *54-64*	250	350
4311/0	as above electric 3r - *54-64*	300	450
2311/0	as above electric 2r - *57-64*	300	550

L47. LMS Class 2P 4-4-0 (1926)
This was Johnson's Midland Railway 4-4-0 design which in 1928 was rebuilt by Fowler. Most were built at Derby from where at least three, built in 1928, went straight into S&DJR Prussian blue livery.

17/0	**483** LMS maroon c/w - *26?-28-?*	NPG	NPG
66/0E	as above electric - *c26-28-?*	NPG	NPG

L48. LMS Standard 'Compound' 4-4-0 (1928)
This was a freelance design by Bassett-Lowke which had wide appeal and sold well. Pre-war electric models did not have key holes and had their handrails cranked where they passed over the front edge of the firebox. After the war, all 'Compounds' had key holes whether clockwork or electric and the handrails were straight. Pre-war models could be had with 20v AC mechanisms (Cat. No. A5502/0).
sBt = small Bing type tender. B-Lst = Bassett-Lowke standard tender. crt = coal rail tender

Rare GWR standard 'Compound' [L48]

3302/0	**3400** GWR dark green painted over 1190 litho c/w - *34-35*	450	850
5302/0	as above electric - *34-35*	450	850
3302/0	**3400** GWR dark green painted over 1108 litho c/w - *36-39*	450	850
5302/0	as above electric - *36-39*	450	850
3302/0	**1190** LMS maroon litho sBt c/w - *28-35*	300	450
4302/0	as above 6-8v DC - *28-35*	300	650
-	as above 20v AC - *28-35*	300	650
3302/0	**1108** LMS maroon litho B-Lst c/w - *36-40*	300	450
4302/0	as above 6-8v junior premag - *36-40*	300	650
5302/0	as above 8-10v stand premag - *36-40*	300	650
A5502/0	as above 20vAC - *36-40*	300	650
3302/0	**1108** LMS maroon litho crt c/w - *36-40*	300	450
4302/0	as above electric - *36-40*	300	650
3302/0	**1108** LMS maroon litho crt c/w - *46-47*	300	450
5302/0	as above electric - *46-47*	300	650
3302/0	**1036** LMS maroon litho crt c/w - *48-50*	300	450
5302/0	as above electric - *48-50*	300	650
3302/0	**1036** LMS brown litho crt c/w - *48-50*	300	450
5302/0	as above electric - *48-50*	300	650
3302/0	**1063** LMS brown litho crt c/w - *48-50*	300	450
5302/0	as above electric - *48-50*	300	650
3302/0	**1063** LMS maroon litho crt c/w - *48-50*	300	450
5302/0	as above electric - *48-50*	300	650
3302/0	**1082** LMS maroon litho crt c/w - *48-50*	300	450
5302/0	as above electric - *48-50*	300	650
3302/0	**1082** LMS black painted over 1082 litho red lined c/w - *48-50*	300	450
5302/0	as above electric - *48-50*	300	650
3302/0	**1082** LMS black painted over 1063 litho red lined c/w - *48-50*	300	450
5302/0	as above electric - *48-50*	300	650
3302/0	**41109** BRb black litho lined red+grey c/w - *51-65*	300	450
5302/0	as above electric 3-rail - *51-65*	300	650
2302/0	as above electric 2-rail - *57-68*	350	750
5312/0	**41109, 41125** BRb black litho electric Nu-Scale* - *57-68*	500	850
3302/0	**41125** BRb black litho lined red+grey c/w - *60-64*	300	450
2302/0	as above electric 3-rail 12vDC - *60-64*	300	650

Pre-war hand-built quality models of the 'Compound' will be found in the table at the end of the steam locomotives section. These had numbers to the customer's choice as could post-war 'Compounds' and 41107 and 41108 are known to exist. * See note on 'Nu-Scale' in the introduction to this chapter.

L49. LMS Class 2P 4-4-0 (altered 'Compound') (1936)
These were former 1108 'Compound' models (above table) that were over-painted. They have had their outside cylinders removed and plated over, and steam chest fairings on each side of the smokebox mounting also removed (the tin tab slots for the fairings can still be seen). The electric models were often fitted with lamp brackets not found on the 'Compounds'.

3306/0	**601** LMS black c/w - *36-40*	300	450
4306/0	as above electric - *36-40*	300	600
5506/0	as above electric - *36-40*	300	600
4306/0AC	as above electric 20vAC - *36-40*	300	600
4306/0P	as above electric - *36-40*	300	600

L50. GNR Ivatt Class D1 4-4-0 (by Bing) (1924)
Designed by H.A.Ivatt for the Great Northern Railway, the D1s first appeared in 1898. In LNER ownership they became the Class D2. They were used for express passenger and suburban passenger duties and the last was withdrawn in 1951.

L2103/0	**504** LNER green litho c/w - *24-25*	550	850
LE2103/0	as above electric - *24-25*	550	850
L2103/0	**4390** LNER green litho c/w - *27-30*	330	400
LE2103/0	as above electric - *c26-28-?*	330	400

L51. LNER 'Glen' Class 4-4-0
This was a model built by the reformed Bassett-Lowke Railways in the late 1960s.

-	**9405** *Glen Spean* LNER green 3-rail - *late 60s?*	NPG	NPG

L52. SR 'Schools' Class 4-4-0 (by Marklin) (1934)
Britain's most powerful 4-4-0 class of locomotive was designed by Maunsell in 1930 for the Southern Railway as his Class V. It was an express passenger locomotive and the last class of 4-4-0s to be built.

SR 'Schools' Class [L52] (Vectis)

910/0/C	**910** *Merchant Taylors* Southern green c/w - *34-37-?*	950	1600
910/0/A	as above electric AC - *34-36-?*	1100	1700
910/0/D	as above electric DC - *34-36-?*	1100	1700

Bassett-Lowke 0

4-4-2

L53. GNR C1 'Atlantic' 4-4-2 (by Carette or Bing) (1907)

With the nickname 'Klondykes', this was the Great Northern Railway's Class C1, which became Class C2 under the LNER. They were designed by H.A.Ivatt and the last was withdrawn in 1950. No.251 is in the National Collection.

251/0	**251** GNR green (C) c/w - *07-09*	800	1100
-	as above (C) electric - *07-?*	NPG	NPG
9/0	**1425** GNR green (B) c/w - *13-14?*	500	650
-	as above (B) electric - *12-14?*	500	650
-	**1442** GNR green litho (C) c/w - *11-?*	500	850
-	as above (C) electric - *11-?*	500	850

L54. NBR Class H 'Atlantic' 4-4-2 (1955)

Designed by W.P.Reid, these locomotives were built between 1906 and 1920. Their nickname was 'Whippets' and they became Class C10 in LNER ownership. The fitting super-heaters transformed them into powerful engines and all were named. *Auld Reekie* was based at Aberdeen.

-	**8872** *Auld Reekie* LNER green elec - *c55*	NPG	NPG

0-6-0

L55. L&NWR 'Cauliflower' 0-6-0 (by Bing) (1912)

The famous 'Cauliflower' express goods 0-6-0 tender locomotives were introduced by Webb in 1880. They underwent a number of modifications during the LMS days.

-	**930, 1269** L&NWR black c/w - *12-14*	NPG	NPG
-	GNR black c/w - *12-14*	NPG	NPG

L56. MR Fowler 4F 0-6-0 (1927)

This was a Fowler Midland Railway design of 1911. They became a standard design adopted by the LMS and the building of them carried on until 1942. A total of 772 were produced.

This model was of soldered construction with a paint finish.

3204/0	**4072** LMS black lined red c/w - *27-33*	400	650
4204/0	as above electric - *27-33*	400	750
5302/0	**1931** GWR green lined + copper capped chimney elec. - *27-33*	350	500

L57. LNER Gresley J39 0-6-0 (1927)

Built between 1926 and 1941, this was Gresley's standard small freight design for the LNER and replaced many of the 800 plus 0-6-0 locomotives that the LNER inherited in 1923. This model was of soldered construction with a paint finish.

LNER Class J39 [L57] (Vectis)

3205/0	**1448** LNER black lined red c/w - *27-35*	350	350
4205/0	as above electric 12v - *27-35*	350	350

L58. Goods Loco 0-6-0 (by Bing) (1927)

It is not known what was the inspiration for this Bing model.

4736/0	**773** Southern green litho c/w - *28-?*	NPG	NPG
4736/0	**4460** GWR green litho c/w - *28-?*	NPG	NPG
-	**4472** LNER green litho c/w - *27-?*	NPG	NPG
4736/0	**6508** LMS maroon litho c/w - *28-?*	NPG	NPG
4736/0	**8851** LNER green? c/w - *28-?*	NPG	NPG

L59. Standard Goods Locomotive 0-6-0 (1936)

This was a freelance design by Bassett-Lowke which had wide appeal and sold well. This model was of tab construction and lithographed. The LMS version had a capuchon on the chimney. The non-BR locos had a Bing type tender without the horizontal fluting found on passenger locomotives. The BR model has the later standard Bassett-Lowke tender.

	The following were lined in red		
?	**4256** black c/w - *36?*	250	450
3307/0	**4256** LMS black c/w - *36-40*	300	500
4307/0	as above 12vDC - *36-40*	350	500
A4307/0	as above 20vAC - *36-40*	350	550
5307/0	as above spur drive - *36-40*	350	550
?	**4417** LMS black c/w - ?	250	450
4308/0	**156** LNER black electric - *36-40*	350	550
4308/0	**1448** LNER black 3-rail 12vDC - *36-40*	450	600
3308/0	**1456** LNER black c/w - *36-40*	300	450
4308/0	as above electric - *36-40*	350	550
A4308/0	as above 20vAC - *36-40*	350	550
5308/0	as above spur drive - *36-40*	350	550
	The following were unlined		
3308/0	**63871** BRb black c/w - *55-67*	250	450
5308/0	as above electric 3-rail - *55-67*	300	500
3308/0	**64193** BRb black c/w - *55-67*	250	450
5308/0	as above electric 3-rail - *55-67*	300	500
2308/0	as above electric 2-rail - *55-67*	300	500
-	as above electric * - *55-67*	550	650
3308/0	**43871** BRb black c/w - *55-67*	250	450
5308/0	as above electric 3-rail - *55-67*	300	500
2308/0	as above electric 2-rail - *55-67*	300	500

* See note on Nu-Scale in the Introduction to this chapter.

2-6-0

L60. GWR Churchward Class 43xx 'Mogul' 2-6-0 (1925)

This was Churchward's mixed traffic design of 1911 and 342 were built up to 1925, They had wide duties and were found throughout the GWR network. Some even saw service in France during the First World War and 80 were rebuilt as 'Granges' and 20 as 'Manors'. The last was withdrawn in 1965 and one has been preserved.

All models carried Great (crest) Western on their tenders.

GWR Churchward Mogul Class 43xx [L60] (Vectis)

6680/0	**4431** green steam - *25-28-?*	420	450
3603/0	as above c/w - *25-36?*	500	550
4603/0	as above electric - *25-36?*	500	550
6680/0	**4431** black steam - *25-28-?*	NPG	NPG
3603/0	as above c/w - *25-28?*	NPG	NPG
4603/0	as above electric - *25-28?*	NPG	NPG
3603/0	**4331** green c/w - *25-36?*	500	550
4603/0	as above electric - *25-36?*	500	550

L61. LMS Hughes 'Crab' 'Mogul' 2-6-0 (1925)

These were easily recognised due to their instantly and steeply angled cylinders, which gave them their nickname. They were the first LMS standard locomotive, being based on a planned Caledonian Railway design. Also called 'Horwich Moguls', they were built at Horwich and arrived in 1926 with a Fowler tender. Building continued until 1932 and totalled 425. The last was withdrawn in 1967 and 3 were preserved, including one in the National Collection.

-	**2700** LMS maroon steam - *25-?*	NPG	NPG
-	as above c/w - *25-?*	NPG	NPG
-	as above electric - *25-?*	NPG	NPG
-	**2700** LMS black steam - *25-?*	NPG	NPG
-	as above c/w - *25-?*	NPG	NPG
-	as above electric - *25-?*	NPG	NPG
6660/0	**13000** LMS maroon steam - *25-39*	600	750
6670/0	as above steam - *25-39*	600	750
3601/0	as above c/w - *25-33*	550	700
4601/0	as above electric - *25-33*	700	900
4602/0	as above electric - *25-33*	700	900
4601/0	as above number on cabsides and tender 3-rail		
4602/0	12vDC - *25-33*	700	900
6660/0	**13000** LMS black steam - *25-39*	650	900
6670/0	as above steam - *25-39*	650	900
3601/0	as above c/w - *25-33*	600	800

Bassett-Lowke 0

4601/0	as above electric - *25-33*		800	1100
4602/0	as above electric - *25-33*		800	1100

L62. LMS Stanier 'Mogul' 2-6-0 (1934)

Stanier's Moguls dated from 1933 and 40 were built at Crewe for lighter mixed traffic duties. They arrived in 1934 and were widely distributed within the LMS. Unlike the 'Crabs', these had the Stanier tapered boiler.

Bassett-Lowke's standard models had the Greenly derived motion, but both clockwork and electric models were available with full Walschaerts valve gear.

2945 LMS Maroon

6660/0	steam - *34-c41*	350	550
-	steam kit - *c39-c49*	650	800
-	c/w - *34-c41*	300	400
-	c/w kit - *c39-c49*	400	500
6660/0	c/w with Walschaerts valve gear - *35-40*	450	550
4601/0	electric - *34-c41*	300	400
-	electric kit - *c39-c49*	400	500
4601/0	electric with Walschaerts valve gear - *35-40*	650	750

2945 LMS Black

6660/0	steam - *34-c41*	350	550
-	steam kit - *c39-c49*	650	800
-	c/w - *34-c41*	300	400
-	c/w kit - *c39-c49*	400	500
6660/0	c /w with Walschaerts valve gear - *35-40*	450	550
4601/0	electric - *34-c41*	300	400
-	electric kit - *c39-c49*	400	500
4601/0	electric with Walschaerts valve gear - *35-40*	650	750

42980 BRb Black

6661/0	lined grey+red steam - *c52-64*	550	800
-	as above c/w - *?*	NPG	NPG
-	as above electric - *?*	NPG	NPG
-	**5524** LMS maroon steam Fowler tend - *?*	NPG	NPG
-	**13007** LMS maroon steam - *68-69*	NPG	NPG
-	**42981** BRb black steam - *?*	NPG	750

L63. LNER Gresley Class K3 'Mogul' 2-6-0 (1925)

This was Gresley's 3-cylinder heavy freight and occasional passenger locomotive of 1924 and 183 were built between 1924 and 1937. They were widely used on express goods and passenger duties. The arrival of the V2s displaced some K3s from their normal work but until the great cull of 1962, which wiped out the class, they continued to pull the fish trains out of Grimsby. None survived into preservation.

LNER Class K3 [L63]

6670/0	**33** LNER green steam - *25-41*	1100	1400
3602/0	as above c/w - *25-41*	850	1400
4602/0	as above electric 12vDC - *25-41*	850	1400
6670/0	**33** LNER black steam - *25-41*	1600	1900
3602/0	as above c/w - *25-41*	1300	1700
4602/0	as above electric - *25-41*	1100	1500
6670/0	**982** LNER green steam - *26-c38*	NPG	NPG
3602/0	as above c/w - *26-28-?*	NPG	NPG
4602/0	as above electric - *26-28-?*	NPG	NPG
6670/0	**982** LNER black steam - *26-c38*	NPG	NPG
3602/0	as above c/w - *26-28-?*	NPG	NPG
4602/0	as above electric - *26-28-?*	NPG	NPG
-	**1864** LNER green steam - *46-?*	400	550
-	as above c/w - *46-?*	450	550
-	as above electric - *46-?*	450	550
-	**1864** LNER black steam - *46-50-?*	550	1050
-	as above c/w - *46-50-?*	550	1050
-	as above electric - *46-50-?*	550	1100

Another model described which fits this section was numbered '56' but the colour and type of drive are unrecorded.

L64. LNER Gresley Class K4 'Mogul' 2-6-0

This was a late Gresley design and built in 1937-38 and a development of the K3, which was unsuitable for the West Highland Line. Consequently 6 K4 locomotives were built with a specially designed boiler. One has been preserved.

-	**2066** *Deer Stalker* LNER green elec - *c69*	450	550

L65. SR Maunsell Class N 'Mogul' 2-6-0 (1926)

Maunsell designed these 'Woolwich' mixed traffic locomotives for the SE&CR and the first took to the rails in 1917. Despite a number of teething problems, it proved to be a very successful design. To provide work for unemployed munitions workers at the end of the First World War, it was agreed that 100 of the locomotives should be built at Woolwich Arsenal.

6685/0	**864** Southern green steam - *26-c38*	NPG	NPG
3644/0	as above c/w - *26-28-?*	NPG	NPG
4644/0	as above electric - *26-28-?*	NPG	NPG
6685/0	**864** Southern black steam - *26-c38*	NPG	NPG
3644/0	as above c/w - *26-28-?*	NPG	NPG
4644/0	as above electric - *26-28-?*	NPG	NPG
6685/0	**866** Southern green steam - *26-c38*	NPG	NPG
3644/0	as above c/w - *26-c38*	NPG	NPG
4644/0	as above electric- *26-c38*	NPG	NPG

2-6-2

L66. LNER Gresley Class V2 2-6-2

This was Gresley's express passenger and freight locomotive of 1936. They were built at Doncaster or Darlington and totalled 184. They did sterling work throughout the Second World War with heavy freight and troop trains to pull, including 700 ton trains of 24 coaches! The last one was withdrawn in 1966 and *Green Arrow*, in the National Collection, is the only survivor.

These models were made to order.

-	**4844** *Coldstreamer* LNER green c/w - *?*	NPG	NPG

4-6-0

L67. CR 'Cardean' 4-6-0 (floor model) (by Carette) (1909)

This was one of a class of 5 locomotives built 1906 and was specifically allocated to the Anglo-Scottish expresses between Glasgow and Carlisle, where the L&NWR took the train on to London.

-	**903** *Cardean* C()R blue c/w - *09-?*	450	550

L68. L&NWR 'Prince of Wales' 4-6-0 (by Bing) (1924)

These were a super-heated development of a Whale design and became the most useful passenger class the L&NWR owned. Introduced by Bowen-Cooke in 1911, 245 of the class were in service by 1923.

49/0	**5600** *Prince of Wales* LMS maroon c/w - *24-25*	NPG	NPG

L69. Freelance 4-6-0 (by Bing) (1928)

All were litho printed and clockwork.

Freelance - LNER Flying Fox [L69] (Vectis)

4737/0	**4460** *Windsor Castle* GWR green - *28-32*	NPG	NPG
4737/0	**4472** *Flying Fox* LNER green - *28-32*	NPG	NPG
4737/0	**6508** *Royal Scot* LMS maroon - *28-32*	NPG	NPG
4737/0	**773** *King Arthur* Southern green - *28-32*	1100	1300

L70. GWR 'Castle' Class 4-6-0 (1930)

The 'Castles' were a post-Grouping design by Collett and were made over many years (1923-1950) to produce a class of 166 locomotives. The design was a development of Churchward's excellent 'Star' Class of 1907.

-	**4079** *Pendennis Castle* GWR green using Mogul parts c/w - *30-?*	1350	1600
-	**4079** *Pendennis Castle* GWR green c/w - *39-51*	1600	2100
-	as above electric - *39-51*	1600	2100
-	as above electric (H) - *c55*	2100	2600
-	**5071** *Spitfire* GWR green electric 2/3 rail - *55-63*	2100	2600
-	**5071** *Spitfire* BRb green (H) - *c55*	2100	2600
-	**5015** *Kingswear Castle* * Great Western green electric 3-rail 12vDC - *50s?*	3200	3700

Bassett-Lowke 0

-	5003 *Lulworth Castle* * Great Western green electric 3-rail 12vDC - *50s?*	3200	4200

* Examples of special order models that have been sold at auction.

L71.   GWR 'County' Class 4-6-0 (by Hunt) (1957)

Hawksworth succeeded Collett as CME of the GWR and tinkered with the 'Castle' Class to produce his 'County' Class. These started to appear in 1945 and a total of 30 of them were built between 1945 and 1947 and the last was withdrawn from service in 1964. None escaped the cutter's torch but one is currently being built.

-	1003 *County of Wilts* BRc green electric 3-rail 12vDC *57-63?*	NPG	NPG

L72.   GWR 'King' Class 4-6-0 (1935)

The 'Kings' formed Collett's 'top of the range' express class and a total of 30 were built at Swindon. The class might not have been built had not the Southern Railway correctly claimed that their new 'Lord Nelson' locomotives were the most powerful locomotives in the country, beating the GWR 'Castles' into second place.

GWR 'King' Class [L72] (Vectis)

912/0/C	6000 *King George V* Great()Western green (M) c/w - *35-37-?*	3200	4700
612/0/A	as above electric AC (M) - *35-37-?*	4200	5450
912/0/D	as above electric DC (M) - *35-37-?*	4200	5450
-	6027 *King Richard* GWR green electric 2/3 rail hand built - *c60-63**	2700	3200

* Made to order.

L73a.   LMS 'Black 5' 4-6-0 (1935)

Stanier's Class 5 mixed traffic locomotive of 1934 was one of Britain's most successful and influential designs. The fact that 842 were built between 1934 and 1951 meant that they were a common sight on the LMS. 18 have survived in preservation.

Some of the Bassett-Lowke models were rebuilt from Marklin 'Jubilees' but others are clearly Bassett-Lowke originals.

-	4853? LMS black c/w - *35-c40*	800	1100
-	5294 LMS black elec 12vDC 3-rail - *35-c40*	800	1100
-	5241 LMS black elec 12vDC 3-rail - *35-c40*	NPG	2500

L73b.   LMS 'Black 5' 4-6-0 (1959)

This would have been a hand-built model and built to order and to the customer's requirements.

-	45126 BR black electric 2/3 rail - *59-63*	NPG	NPG

L74a.   LMS 'Jubilee' Class 4-6-0 (by Marklin) (1935)

Designed by Sir William Stanier for the LMS, 191 locomotives were built between 1934 and 1936. This was his Class 5 express passenger locomotive for all but the heaviest duties. Originally classified 5XP, the class was later reclassified 6P, the same as the 'Royal Scots'. The last was withdrawn in 1967 and 4 have been preserved.

911/0	5552 *Silver Jubilee* LMS black + silver c/w - *35*	3100	4200
911/0/A	as above electric AC - *35*	3100	4200
911/0/D	as above (M) electric DC - *35*	3100	4200
911/0	5610 *Gold Coast* LMS maroon c/w - *35-?*	2850	3700
911/0/A	electric AC - *35-?*	2850	3700
911/0/D	electric DC - *35-?*	2850	3700
911/0	5573 *Newfoundland* LMS maroon c/w - *35-40?*	2850	3700
911/0/A	as above electric AC - *35-40?*	2850	3700
911/0/D	as above electric DC - *35-40?*	2850	4700
911/0/C	5682 *Trafalgar* LMS maroon c/w (also 3607/0) - *36-40-?*	4200	5500
5607/0	as above electric - *36-40-?*	4200	5500

L74b.   LMS 'Jubilee' Class 4-6-0 (1936)

The 'Jubilee' model built by Bassett-Lowke had a top-feed projection on top of the boiler which was missing from the Marklin model. The locomotive looked longer and the tender a more realistic shape.

911/0/C	5701 *Conqueror* LMS maroon c/w (also 3607/0) - *36-40?*	2700	5200
911/0/A	as above electric AC - *36-40?*	3000	5700
911/0/D	as above electric DC - *36-40?*	3000	5700
911/0/C	5712 *Victory* LMS maroon c/w (also 3607/0) - *36-40-?*	3900	5200
5607/0	as above electric DC - *36-40-?*	4200	5700

L75.   LMS 'Royal Scot' Class 4-6-0 (1929)

This was Fowler's express passenger design of 1927 and 71 were built between 1927 and 1930. They were mainly used on express passenger services, until replaced by Stanier's Pacifics. From 1947, smoke deflectors were fitted and all of them were rebuilt with tapered boilers between 1943 and 1955.

Ft = Fowler tender.   St = Stanier tender.   sd = smoke deflectors fitted.

LMS 6100 *Royal Scot*

LMS 'Royal Scot' Class [L75] (Walis & Wallis)

3303/0	maroon litho Ft c/w - *29-37*	850	1450
3611/0	maroon St c/w - *37-52*	850	1450
3622/0	black St c/w - *c48-52*	1300	1900
A4303/0	maroon litho Ft AC - *29-37*	550	700
4303/0	maroon litho Ft DC - *29-37*	550	700
5611/0	maroon St and sd AC - *37-52*	750	950
5711/0	maroon St and sd DC - *37-52*	750	950
5622/0	black St and sd 3-rail 12vDC - *c48-52*	1300	1600

L76.   LMS Rebuilt 'Royal Scot' 4-6-0 (1953)

Stanier commenced rebuilding the whole of the 'Royal Scot' Class in 1943 and this process continued until 1955. Throughout the class the original single chimneys were replaced by double ones and from 1947 smoke deflectors started to appear on members of the class. The last locomotive was withdrawn in 1965 and two have been preserved.

BRb 46100 *Royal Scot*

-	green c/w - *53-?*	1300	1800
5622/0	green 3-rail 12vDC - *53-56-?*	2600	3200
-	green 2-rail 12vDC - *57-?*	2600	3200
-	green electric* Nu-Scale - *57-60*	2100	3700

* See note on 'Nu-Scale' in the Introduction to this chapter.

L77.   LNER Class B17 4-6-0 (1936)

The early B17 locomotives were built to help out the ageing B12s on passenger trains on the Great Eastern Division of the LNER. Those built later, with larger Group Standard tenders, were for use on the Great Central Division.

-	2838 *Melton Hall* LNER green c/w - *36-c39*	4700	6200
-	as above electric 3-rail 12vDC - *36-c39*	4600	6200
3608/0	2848 *Arsenal* LNER green c/w - *36-c39*	5000	9200
A4608/0	as above electric AC - *36-c39*	5200	9200
5608/0	as above electric DC - *36-c39*	5200	9900
3608/0	2853 *Huddersfield Town* LNER green c/w - *36-c39*	4200	5200
A4608/0	as above electric AC - *36-c39*	4200	5200
5608/0	as above electric DC - *36-c39*	4200	5200

L78.   SR 'Lord Nelson' 4-6-0 (from litho Royal Scot) (1935)

This was Maunsell's express passenger locomotive of 1926, in its final form as rebuilt by Bulleid. 16 had been were built at Eastleigh with Belpaire fireboxes, but conversion to larger boilers was started by Bulleid in 1937.

-	850 *Lord Nelson* Southern green c/w - *35-?*	1300	1600
-	as above electric - *35-?*	1300	1600

L79.   Super Enterprise 4-6-0 (Freelance) (1937)

This was the largest version of Bassett-Lowke's freelance live steam locomotives.

6655/0	851 Southern green steam *37-?*	NPG	NPG
6655/0	2495 black steam *37-40*	NPG	NPG
6655/0	2871 LNER green steam *37-40*	NPG	NPG
6655/0	5524 LMS maroon steam *37-40*	350	NPG
-	45295 BRb green steam ?	250	400
-	45295 BRb black steam *51-56*	250	420

Bassett-Lowke 0

| | 61324 | BRb black steam ? | 250 | 400 |

Super Enterprise live steam model [L79]

4-6-2

L80. LMS 'Princess Royal' Class 4-6-2 (1935)

The prototype 'Princess Royal' Class had been designed by William Stanier and introduced to the LMS in 1933 for express duties. Only 13 were built, each of them named after a female member of the Royal Family. The last was withdrawn from service in 1962 and two of the class were bought by Butlins for their holday camps, as static exhibits. These were later sold for restoration and preservation.

	LMS 6200 *The Princess Royal*		
3605/0/C	maroon c/w - *35-?*	3100	4200
3605/0/A	maroon electric AC Fowler tender - *35-?*	3100	4200
3605/0/D	maroon electric DC Fowler tender - *35-?*	3100	5000
	LMS 6201 *Princess Elizabeth*		
3605/0	maroon c/w - *36-39-?*	3100	5200
A4605/0	maroon electric AC - *36-39-?*	3100	4700
5605/0	maroon electric DC - *36-39-?*	3600	4700
-	**6202** LMS maroon 'Turbomotive' c/w - *36-c50*	NPG	NPG
-	as above but 3-rail 12v electric (only one known) - *c37*	10000	12000

L81. LMS Streamlined 'Princess Coronation' (1937)

The LMS released their first streamlined 'Princess Coronation' in 1937. They were upgraded 'Princess Royals' (see above) to handle heavier loads on the London-Scotland West Coast Main Line and were built at Crewe. Some were named after members of the Royal Family and others after British cities. In all, 24 streamline locomotives ('Coronations') were built, the last in 1943.

-	**6220 *Coronation*** LMS blue c/w - *37-c48*	4200	7200
-	as above electric - *37-c48*	4200	8700
3606/0	**6225 *Duchess of Gloucester*** LMS maroon c/w - *38?-c48*	4200	5200
4606/0	as above electric AC - *38?-c48*	4200	7200
5606/0	as above electric DC - *38?-c48*	4200	7200
-	**6227 *Duchess of Devonshire*** LMS maroon c/w made to order* - ?	NPG	8700

* Made for Harold Elliott's sea-front layout at Scarborough.

L82. LMS 'Princess Coronation' Class 4-6-2 (1939)

These are the same class as the 'Coronations' but were either built without streamlined cladding or with the cladding later removed. The first batch built without cladding dated from 1938 and the last 'Coronation' to become a 'Duchess', by removal of its cladding, was *City of Lancaster* in 1949. There were 38 members of the class and the last was withdrawn in 1964. Three of the class have been preserved, the one in the National Collection having been returned to a streamlined 'Coronation' by popular demand.
sd = with smoke deflectors fitted.

	LMS 6232 *Duchess of Montrose*		
3613/0	maroon c/w - *39-49*	2100	3200
5613/0	maroon electric 12vDC 3-rail - *39-49*	2100	3200
	BRb 46232 *Duchess of Montrose*		
3613/0	blue sd c/w - *c52*	3700	5200
3613/0	green sd c/w - *c54-c58*	2600	3200
-	blue sd electric - *c52*	4200	5200
2613/0	green sd electric 2-rail - *c57-c58*	3000	4500
5613/0	green sd electric 3-rail - *c54-c58*	3100	4700
-	green sd electric Nu-Scale ** 2-rail - *57-63*	3000	4500
-	green sd electric Nu-Scale ** 3-rail - *57-65*	3000	4500
-	**46245 *City of London*** * BRb black smoke deflectors 3-rail 12vDC - *50s*	3100	3700
-	**46257 *City of Salford*** * BRb black smoke deflectors 3-rail 12vDC - *50s*	1300	1500

* Special order. ** See note on Nu-Scale in the Introduction to this chapter.

L83. LNER A1/A3 'Pacific' 4-6-2 (1933)

The Class A3s of the LNER were a development of the A1s, which had been designed for the Great Northern Railway by Nigel Gresley in 1922. Almost all existing A1s were rebuilt, while later ones were built as A3s. One of the most visible changes was the new banjo shaped steam dome fitted to the top of the A3's boiler.

LNER A1 4472 *Flying Scotsman*

LNER Class A1 [L83] (Wallis & Wallis)

3304/0	green litho c/w - *33-c41*	750	1400
4304/0	green litho electric 8vDC - *33-c41*	850	1400
5304/0	green litho 8vAC - *33-c41*	850	1400
5504/0	green litho electric 20vAC - *33-c41*	850	1400
6304/0	green litho electric 20vAC - *33-c41*	850	1400
-	green litho electric Nu-Scale - *57-65*	1600	2000
	LNER A3 103 *Flying Scotsman*		
-	green litho c/w - *c47-c50*	1300	1900
-	green litho electric - *c47-c50*	1300	1900
	BRb A3 60103 *Flying Scotsman*		
3310/0	blue litho - *50-52*	1300	1600
-	blue litho electric 12vDC 3r - *50-52*	1300	1600
3310/0	green litho c/w - *c53-c58*	800	1300
5310/0	green litho electric 12vDC 3-rail - *c53-c58*	800	1300
2310/0	green litho electric 12vDC 2-rail - *c57-c58*	1300	1700
-	green litho electric 12v DC 3-rail Nu-Scale* - *57-c63*	2000	2500
-	green litho electric 12v DC 2-rail Nu-Scale* - *57-c63*	2000	2500

* See note on Nu-Scale in the introduction to this chapter.

L84. LNER A4 'Pacific' 4-6-2 (1936)

The A4 was Gresley's ultimate express engine development and arrived in 1935. It was one of the most successful streamlined railway engine designed in Britain and one of the class (*Mallard*) still holds the world speed record for a steam locomotive. For easy maintenance, side valances were removed during the war and early examples were given corridor tenders to allow for a change of crew on the journey.

2507/0	**2509 *Silver Link*** LNER silver c/w - *36-c40*	4700	8200
4606/0	as above electric AC - *36-c40*	4700	8200
5606/0	as above electric DC - *36-c40*	4700	8200
2507/0	**2510 *Quicksilver*** LNER silver c/w - *36-c40*	4700	8200
4606/0	as above electric AC - *36-c40*	4700	8200
5606/0	as above electric DC - *36-c40*	4700	8200
2507/0	**2511 *Silver King*** LNER silver c/w - *36-c40*	4700	8200
4606/0	as above electric AC - *36-c40*	4700	8200
5606/0	as above electric DC - *36-c40*	4700	8200
2507/0	**2512 *Silver Fox*** LNER silver c/w - *36-c40*	4700	8200
4606/0	as above electric AC - *36-c40*	4700	8200
5606/0	as above electric DC - *36-c40*	4700	8200
2507/0	**4489 *Dominion of Canada*** LNER blue c/w - *c38-c40*	4700	8200
4606/0	as above electric AC - *c38-c40*	4700	8200
5606/0	as above electric DC - *c38-c40*	4700	8200
2507/0	**4490 *Empire of India*** LNER blue c/w - *c38-c40*	4700	8200
4606/0	as above electric AC - *c38-c40*	4700	8200
5606/0	as above electric DC - *c38-c40*	4700	8200
2507/0	**4498 *Sir Nigel Gresley*** LNER blue c/w - *c38-c40*	4700	8200
4606/0	as above electric AC - *c38-c40*	4700	8200
5606/0	as above electric DC - *c38-c40*	4700	8200

L85. BR 'Britannia' Class Pacific 4-6-2 (by Hunt) (1958)

The 'Britannia' Class was introduced in 1951 as the standard express passenger locomotive design for the newly formed British Railways. Designed by R.A.Riddles, 55 of them were built at Crewe and distributed to all of the regions. Only two survived into preservation.

| - | **70000 *Britannia*** BRc green hand built electric 2/3-rail - *58-?* | 5200 | 8200 |

8th Edition

Bassett-Lowke 0

BR 'Britannia' Class & 9F [L85 & L90]

L86. German State Railways 4-6-2 (by Marklin) (1934)
The model of a late 1920s German State Railways locomotive had a pacific wheel arrangement and an 8-wheel bogie tender. It was finished in matt black with gold lining and sported two working lights below the smokebox door.

MG/0	12920	black+red German State Railways, electric - 34-38	NPG	NPG

L87. New York Central 'Hudson' 4-6-4 (by Marklin) (1934)
In 1935 this J1E Class baltic type locomotive was only briefly offered by Bassett-Lowke but remains one of the best examples of a coarse scale model of the prototype. It was very well detailed. The model was produced by Marklin for overseas markets and was not readily available in Germany. The model had a single light in the centre of the smokebox door.

AK/0	5273	black, New York Central black, electric - 34-35	NPG	NPG

2-8-0

L88. LMS Class 8F 2-8-0 (1960)
The class was introduced by William Stanier in 1935 to fill a serious gap in the LMS stud. It was based on the highly successful 'Black 5s' and became the standard heavy freight design adopted by the War Department during the Second World War. In all, 666 locomotives were built and 9 of the class have been preserved.
Any models made would have been made to order and to the customer's specification.

-	48209	BRc black electric 2/3-rail - 60-63	NPG	NPG

4-8-2

L89. French 'Mountain' 4-8-2 (by Marklin) (1934)
The locomotive had an 8-wheel bogie tender and was finished in French grey with black lining. It had a working pair of hadlights. The model was fitted with a Fornereau 5-pole 12v DC motor.

MF/0	12920	ETAT lined pale grey, simple valve gear - 34-35	NPG	NPG
MF/0	12920	ETAT pale grey, full Heusinger valve gear, 'ME' (Mountain Etat) on smoke deflectors - 35-38	NPG	NPG
MF/0	12920	ME (Mountain Etat) pale grey, full Heusinger valve gear,- 35-38	NPG	NPG

2-10-0

L90. BR Class 9F 2-10-0 (by Hunt) (1961)
This was the ultimate locomotive development by Riddles for his BR standard classes and the 2-10-0 wheel arrangement was influenced by the success Riddles had had with the WD 2-10-0 locomotives during the war. The last was withdrawn in 1968 and 9 have been preserved.
Any models made would have been made to order and to the customer's specification.

-	92220	*Evening Star* BRc green electric 2/3-rail - 61-63	2300	3200
-		BRc black electric - 61-63	NPG	NPG

Miscellaneous

L91. Hand-Built Locomotives (1933)
In 1933, Bassett-Lowke announced a range of hand-built locomotives which could be made to order. The models would be to a very high specification including all solder construction, all external and visible details and full painting and lining. Locomotives could be had either with variable speed clockwork drive, 8-10v DC or 20v AC electric mechanisms. Customers could choose their own running numbers and those given below are examples seen or advertised.

-		GWR 2-6-0 'Mogul' - 33-35	NPG	NPG
-		GWR 2-6-2T - 33-35	NPG	NPG
-	2793	GWR 0-6-0T - 33-35	NPG	NPG
-		LMS 2-6-0 'Mogul' - 33-35	NPG	NPG
-	6100	LMS 4-6-0 'Royal Scot' Class - 33-39	NPG	NPG
-		LMS 4-6-0 'Patriot' Class - 33-39	NPG	NPG
-		LMS 4-6-0 Rebuilt 'Claughton' Class - 33-35	NPG	NPG
-	1067	LMS 4-4-0 Midland 'Compound' - 33-35	450	650
-		LMS 4-6-2T CR Pickersgill - 33-35	NPG	NPG
-		LMS 2-6-2T - 33-39	NPG	NPG
-		LMS 2-6-4T - 33-39	NPG	NPG
-		LMS 0-6-0 goods tender loco - 33-39	NPG	NPG
-	4472	*Flying Scotsman* LNER 4-6-2 A1/A3 Class - 33-39	NPG	NPG
-		LNER 0-6-0 goods tender loco - 33-35	NPG	NPG
-	453	*King Arthur* SR N15 Class - 33-35	NPG	NPG
-	850	*Lord Nelson* SR LN Class - 33-35	NPG	NPG
-		PLM French 'Windcutter' 'Pacific' - 33-35	NPG	NPG
-	2300	CP 4-6-2 Canadian Pacific loco - 33-35	NPG	NPG

Diesel and Electric Locomotives

L92. Steeplecab Electric 0-4-0 (by Bing & Marklin) (1903)
The catalogue described this as the 'Twopenny Tube' clockwork locomotive and said that it was a model of the electric locos in use on the Central London Electric Railway. It was a short 4-wheel model with a large cab and a small bonnet at each end.

-	23	CLR blue (M) electric - 03-?	1600	1900
-	23	CLR blue (B) electric - 04-?	500	650

Prototype 'Deltic' by Reader [L93] (Tony Wright)

L93. 'Deltic' Diesel Co-Co (by Reader) (1959)
This was a model of the English Electric express passenger locomotives introduced in 1961. These were built by Vic Reader, as just two batches each of 6 models.

-		*Deltic* electric blue twin electric motor bogies 2- or 3-rail 12vDC - 59-63	2100	4700
-		*Deltic* BRc green twin electric motor bogies 2- or 3-rail 12vDC - 59-63	NPG	NPG

L94. Swiss Pantograph Electrics (by Marklin) (1935)
There are no further details of this model.

-		SBB 4-6-2 electric - 35-?	NPG	NPG
-		SBB 4-4-2 electric - 35-?	NPG	NPG
-		SBB 0-4-0 electric - 35-?	NPG	NPG

L95. LT London Underground Standard EMU (1937)
This was a three-car unit hand-made initially in brass but later wood was used. They were hand-painted in London Transport colours. The models worked off a 8v DC centre-rail supply and were based on units that worked between the Bakerloo Tube and Watford on the LMS.

-		7073+?+7072 London Transport red +cream brass 3-car electric - 37-38	2600	5200
-		7073+?+7072 London Transport red +cream wood 3-car electric - 37-38	2600	5200
-		7073+?+7072 London Transport red +cream with blue horizontal band wood 3-car electric - 37-38	2600	5200

L96. LMS Suburban Electric Train EMU (1930)
This model was based on Euston-Watford 1927 LMS suburban electric stock. The models were built of steel plate and based on drawings loaned by the LMS. They were sold as a 3-car unit.

104/0	1652+3416+6560	LMS maroon 3-car * litho electric 3-rail 12vDC - 30-35	1100	2000

* The centre car was a 1st/3rd.

Bassett-Lowke 0

LMS suburban electric [L96] (Tony Wright)

L97. Southern EMU (by Bing) (1928)
This was a single car built in tinned steel plate and fitted with a new motor specially designed for it. The assembled model was hand-enamelled and lined. The customer would need to make up the rest of the train with standard SR coach stock which matched the design.

Cat No.	Description	£	£
1457/0	**2601** Southern green 3-car set elec - *c28*	1400	1600

L98. Southern EMU (by Exley) (1953)
These were post-war Exley 3-car sets with 12V DC Bassett-Lowke motor bogies and B-L coach bogies.

	Description	£	£
?	**3072/3086 (11165 + ?)** Southern green Portsmouth 3-car set - ?	1300	1600
?	**3072/3074** Southern green 4RES 3-car suburban set - *53-57*	1300	1600
?	**3091/3071** Southern green 4RES 3-car suburban set - *53-57*	1600	2100
?	LMS maroon ex-Southern 4RES 3-car EMU (fictional) about 10 sets made as a special order - *c55*	1600	2200

L99. 'Brighton Belle' Pullman EMU
The cars were made-to-order and had metal sides, metal window frames, wooden floors and roof, brass handrails, B-L bogies and full internal fittings.

	Description	£	£
-	**88** Pullman dark brown+cream driver	NA	NA
-	**87** Pullman dark brown+cream driver	NA	NA
-	***Hazel*** Pullman dark brown+cream 1st	NA	NA
-	***Doris*** Pullman dark brown+cream 1st	NA	NA
-	**86** Pullman dark brown+cream 3rd	NA	NA
-	the above 5 cars	2600	4200

COACHES

As with the locomotives, many of the early coaches were imported from Germany where they were made by Bing, Marklin or Carette but, by the 1930s, Bassett-Lowke were manufacturing their own.

Carette coaches produced for Bassett-Lowke were all made before the First World War and, consequently were all in pre-Grouping liveries. Some of these were toy-like but so-called 'scale' model coaches arrived in 1910. Some of Carette tools were later acquired by Bassett-Lowke to produce the LNWR and LMS travelling post offices and 12-wheeled diners in the 1920s.

Bing lithographed coaches dominated the '20s and are known as the '1921 Series'. These were all steel and were produced in the pre-Grouping liveries of GNR, LNWR, MR and GWR (lake). A year after the Grouping of 1923, the coaches were produced in the liveries of the 'Big Four', namely LMS, LNER (teak), SR and GWR (chocolate and cream) and were fitted with corridor connections.

The first coach made by Bassett-Lowke themselves appeared in 1930 and was part of the Watford EMU set. First class corridor and brake thirds were made in the liveries of all four railway companies but the LMS and SR EMUs (see 'Locomotives' section) also received a pair of suburban coaches. These were available separately as too was an LMS travelling post office.

A new design of coach was introduced after the Second World War in BR red and cream. These new coaches were made by Precision Models in Northampton who were also manufacturing the Trix Twin system at that time. Exley also made coaches for Bassett-Lowke from 1936 and these had the Exley trademark carefully removed and were packed in Bassett-Lowke boxes. More about these later.

Cat No.	Company, Number, Colour, Date	£	£

C1. Early Coaches (by Carette) (1908)
These coaches were 10" and 12" long respectively and fitted with Mansell type wheels and double windows. All but the GNR ones had clerestory roofs.

	Description	£	£
-	**GNR** 1321 teak 1st/3rd - *08-19*	200	230
-	**GNR** 1331 teak brake - *08-19*	200	230
	With Clerestory Roof		
-	**MR** 1323 maroon 1st/3rd - *10-19*	200	230
-	**MR** 1333 maroon brake - *10-19*	200	230
-	**GWR** 1324 dark brown+cream 1st/3rd - *08-19*	200	230
-	**GWR** 1334 dark brown+cream full brake - *08-19*	200	230
-	**GWR** 1334 dark brown+cream full brake red cross hospital coach - *14-19*	1000	1500
-	**LNWR** 1322, 1325 brown+cream 1st/3rd - *08-19*	200	230
-	**LNWR** 1334, 133 brown+cream full brake - *08-19*	200	230

C2. 6-Wheel 'Clemenson' Coaches (by Carette) (1910)
These coaches had embossed sides and three pairs of wheels. The centre pair were the Clemenson type and so slid from side to side to allow for tight curves. The coaches were also available as a set of three permanently close coupled and had standard couplings at the end of the trio. The set consisted of a composite coach with a brake 3rd at both ends. The coaches had clerestory roofs.

6-wheel Carette coach for Bassett-Lowke [C2] (Vectis)

	Description	£	£
-	**LNWR** 13212 black+crm 1st/3rd composite - *10-?*	200	230
-	**LNWR** 13312 black+cream brake/3rd - *10-?*	200	230
-	**LNWR** 13312 black+cream full brake - *?*	200	230
-	**MR** 13213 red 1st/3rd composite - *10-?*	300	350
-	**MR** 13313 red brake/3rd - *10-?*	300	350
-	**MR** 13313 red full brake - *?*	300	350
-	**GNR** 13211 teak1st/3rd composite - *10-?*	300	350
-	**GNR** 13311 teak brake/3rd - *10-?*	300	350
-	**GNR** 13211 teak 1st/3rd composite - *10-?*	300	350

C3. Short Bogie Coaches (by Carette) (1910)
These were to a similar specification as the later 1921 and 1924 Series coaches but were only 9.5" long. They were fitted with folded tinplate Carette style bogies and a transverse mounted single gas cylinder.

	Description	£	£
-	**GWR** brown+cream coach - *10-?*	NPG	NPG
-	**GWR** 13324 brown+cream brake van - *10-?*	NPG	NPG
-	**GNR** 13221 teak coach - *10-?*	NPG	NPG
-	**GNR** 13321 teak brake van - *10-?*	NPG	NPG

C4. Early Freelance Coaches
These were designed to be whatever you wanted them to be and were finished for the customer accordingly. They had a curved roof which was fitted with torpedo ventilators. The windows were glazed with glass, including ground glass for the lavatory compartments. They were 13" long and the bodies and underframes were made from hard wood, the door handles were gold plated brass. The doors did not open but the coaches could be bought in kit form.

Cat No.	Description	£	£
601E	teak various 1st/2nd/3rd - *?-19*	200	230
602E	teak various brake - *?-19*	200	230

C5. '1921 Series' Bogie Coaches (by Bing) (1921)
These coaches were 13" long and of tinplate construction. They had embossed sides

Bassett-Lowke 0

and compensated heavy gauge steel bogies. The black painted wheels were a heavy alloy, Mansell type, with thick flanges and ran loose on crimped axles which were retained in covered axle boxes by crimped on washers. The roofs were clipped on and there was no provision for corridor connectors. They were fitted with Bing couplings with long single drop links, cast oval alloy buffers riveted on, with two gas cylinders and underframe stays. The coaches could be had with turned cast iron wheels and are often found with the later superior Bassett-Lowke 612/0 bogies with large diameter turned cast iron Mansell pattern wheels and cast axle boxes. Stocks lasted well after the introduction of the later '1924 Series' coaches.

Series 1921 coach GWR brake 3rd [C5] (Vectis)

60/0	**MR** lake 1st corridor - *22-26*	170	250
61/0	**MR** 2783 lake 3rd/brake - *22-26*	170	250
62/0	**GWR** 132 lake 1st corridor - *22-26*	170	250
63/0	**GWR** 133 lake 3rd/brake - *22-26*	170	250
64/0	**LNWR** 1921 brown+cream 1st corridor - *21-26*	170	250
65/0	**LNWR** 1921,1334 brown+cream 3rd/brake - *21-26*	170	250
65/0	**LNWR** 1334 brown+cream full /brake - *21-26*	170	250
66/0	**GNR** teak 1st (12" long) - *21-26*	170	250
67/0	**GNR** teak full brake (12" long) - *21-26*	170	250
64/0	**LSWR** 1308? brown+salmon 1st/3rd corridor - *21-26*	170	250
65/0	**LSWR** brown+salmon 3rd/brake - *21-26*	170	250

C6. 12-Wheel Dining Cars (Carette design) (1921)

14" long, these had uncompensated folded tinplate bogies, a battery box (instead of gas cylinders), no axle boxes, cast alloy buffers riveted on, recessed vestibules, a clip-on roof, underframe stays, heavy alloy wheels running loose on crimped axles and embossed tinplate sides. The tooling was acquired by Bassett-Lowke after the First World War.

94/0	**LNWR** 13210 cream+brown - *21-24*	250	370
94/0	**GNR** 3040 teak - *21-24*	250	370
94/0	**LMS** 13210 maroon - *24-34*	250	370

C7. Prototypical Scale Wooden Coaches (1921)

Bassett-Lowke offered a high quality range of wooden coaches, of scale length, at least until around 1938. By this time, Edward Exley Ltd were supplying top of the range quality coaches. Most of the models in the Bassett-Lowke quality range were made to customer's own specifications including choice of livery and panelled and moulded sides. Bogies were the current top of the range ones consisting of 601/0, 607/0 (6-wheel) or 612/0 as appropriate. 57' and 70' coaches were available in LMS, LNER and GWR livery.

G621/0	brake 3rd - *21-38*	NPG	NPG
G621/0	1st/3rd composite corridor - *21-38*	NPG	NPG
G621/0	dining car - *21-38*	NPG	NPG
G621/0	sleeping car - *21-38*	NPG	NPG

C8. Post Office Mail Vans (Carette design) (1911)

The length of these vans was 12.25" and they had no corridor connections. They had 4-wheel uncompensated folded tinplate bogies, gas cylinders, no underframe stays, cast buffers riveted on and a long ducket along one side. The coach had an operating pickup 'net' and delivery arm and an activating trigger beneath the coach which engaged with a ramp which was operated by the lineside delivery apparatus. Coaches came complete with mail bags and ground apparatus, electric or clockwork. The ground apparatus could be either on tinplate or wooden sleepered track.

95/0	**LNWR** 1339 cream+brown - *11*	220	240
95/0	**LMS** 1924 Royal Mail maroon *24?*	220	240
95/0	**LMS** 1924 maroon - *24-31*	180	200

Carette design travelling post office [C8] (Lacy, Scott & Knight)

C9. '1924 Series' Bogie Coaches (by Bing) (1924)

These were also 13" long and were to the same specification as the Bing '1921 Series' (above) except for livery and provision of corridor connections. Each coach had one overscale bellows type coach connector made in black camera cloth which spanned between adjacent coaches. The connections were hollow and brake end coaches were provided with a clip-on closure plate. Early examples had brass buffers and brass Bing couplings and, again, improved bogies and cast iron wheels could be fitted.

60/0	**LMS** 2784 maroon 1st - *24-31*	170	200
61/0	**LMS** 2783 maroon 3rd/brake - *24-31*	170	200
62/0	**GWR** 132, 1235N, 8271 cream+dark brown 1st - *28-31*	200	230
63/0	**GWR** 133, 1921, 3251 cream+dark brown 3rd/brake - *28-31*	200	230
66/0	**Southern** 2601, 5180, 7001 green 1st * - *26-31*	220	270
67/0	**Southern** 7000, 7716 green 3rd/brake* - *26-31*	220	270
68/0	**LNER** 1235N teak 1st - *24-31*	170	200
68/0	**LNER** 601 teak all 1st - *24-31*	170	200
69/0	**LNER** 1234N teak 3rd/brake - *24-31*	170	200

*SR coaches introduced in 1926 were repaints of GWR lake coloured ones.

C10. Short Bogie Coaches (Carette design) (1925)

These Bassett-Lowke made coaches from Carette tooling were to a similar specification as the '1921 and 1924 Series' coaches but were only 9.5" long. They were fitted with folded tinplate Carette style bogies and reduced size Bing style couplings. They were also fitted with a transverse mounted single gas cylinder.

Carette design short bogie coach [C10] (Vectis)

100/0	**LNER** 524 teak full brake - *25-32*	120	250
101/0	**LNER** 525 teak 1st - *25-32*	120	250
103/0	**LNER** 526 teak 3rd - *25-32*	120	250
160/0	**LNER** teak 1st/3rd - *30-32*	120	250
160/0	**LMS** maroon 1st/3rd - *30-32*	120	250
260/0	**LNER** teak full brake, opening doors - *30-32*	120	250
260/0	**LMS** maroon full brake, opening doors - *30-32*	120	250

C11. Short Pullman Coaches (by Bing) (1928)

These were 12.25" long and were of tinplate construction with hinged roofs. They were interior fitted with tables and chairs and had vestibule ends, underframe trusses with two transverse gas cylinders and battery box as well as brass couplings and buffers. Bing style bogies with axles retained by press-on washers in axle covers and heavy alloy spoked wheels, were fitted. There were similar GWR, LMS and LNER coaches in this range but they were not listed in the Bassett-Lowke catalogues.

195/0	Pullman *Minerva* brown+cream - *28-32*		100	120
195/0	Pullman *Cassandra* brown+cream - *28-32*		100	120

C12. Wooden Modern Coaching Stock Bodies (1928)

These were quality coach bodies that could be bought and finished by the purchaser. They were supplied without bogies and the body and roof were made of wood. They came ready for painting.

625/8/0	LMS 54' corridor 3rd/brake, old type - *28-32*	NPG	NPG
623/7/0	LMS 54' corridor 1st/3rd, old type - *28-32*	NPG	NPG
625/5/0	LMS 57' centre corridor 1st - *28-32*	NPG	NPG
625/1/0	LMS 57' centre corridor 1st/3rd - *28-32*	NPG	NPG
625/2/0	LMS 57' centre corridor 3rd/brake - *28-32*	NPG	NPG
625/3/0	LMS 57' centre corridor 3rd - *28-32*	NPG	NPG
625/4/0	LMS 50' kitchen car - *28-32*	NPG	NPG
625/28/0	LMS sleeping car 1st - *30-32*	NPG	NPG
625/29/0	LMS passenger brake van - *30-32*	NPG	NPG
625/13/0	GWR 57' corridor 1st/3rd - *28-32*	NPG	NPG
625/14/0	GWR 57' corridor 3rd/brake - *28-32*	NPG	NPG
625/15/0	GWR 57' diner 1st/3rd - *28-32*	NPG	NPG
625/25/0	GWR 70' corridor 1st/3rd - *28-32*	NPG	NPG
625/26/0	GWR 70' 3rd/brake - *28-32*	NPG	NPG
625/27/0	GWR 70' diner 1st/3rd - *28-32*	NPG	NPG
627/1/0	GWR 57' corridor 1st/3rd, old type - *28-32*	NPG	NPG
627/2/0	GWR 57' 3rd/brake, old type - *28-32*	NPG	NPG
627/10/0	LNER 60' corridor 1st/3rd - *28-32*	NPG	NPG
627/11/0	LNER 60' corridor 3rd/brake - *28-32*	NPG	NPG
627/12/0	LNER 60' diner 1st/3rd - *28-32*	NPG	NPG
628/1/0	GWR 38'9" suburban 1st/3rd - *28-32*	NPG	NPG
628/2/0	GWR 38'9" suburban 3rd/brake - *28-32*	NPG	NPG
626/1/0	Pullman 76' saloon car - *28-32*	NPG	NPG
626/2/0	Pullman 76' kitchen car - *28-32*	NPG	NPG

C13. Post Office Mail Van - Wooden (1930)

This was to a similar specification to that used for the 1922 post office mail van model made from Carette tooling, with identical mechanical features, but with the coach body made of wood and with the livery transferred on. The roof was solidly fixed in place and there appeared to be no easy way of retrieving mail bags from inside the coach.

-	LMS 1930 maroon - *30*	300	330

C14. '1931 Series' Coaches (by Winteringham) (1932)

These were 13" long and of a similar specification as the earlier steel '1921 and 1924 Series'. They had a lower roof line, simplified non-compensated bogies, battery box (instead of gas cylinders), underframe trusses and lighter diecast alloy wheels pressed onto splined axles. The clip-on roofs had under-scale ventilators and rain strips. The buffers were cast alloy, riveted on and the couplings were Bing style with the long link. They also had detachable concertina corridor connections at each end of the coach. At extra cost, the coaches could be bought with improved bogies (612/0) and cast iron wheels.

-	GWR 9174 dark brown+cream 1st corridor - *32-40*	170	220
-	GWR 9310 dark brown+cream 3rd brake corridor - *32-40*	170	220
-	LMS 3490 maroon 1st corridor - *32-40*	140	170
-	LMS 9343 maroon 3rd brake corridor - *32-40*	140	170
-	LNER 36232 teak 1st corridor - *32-40*	140	170
-	LNER 62362 teak 3rd brake corridor - *32-40*	140	170
-	LMS 3416 maroon suburban 1st/3rd (13.75") - *32-40*	140	170
-	LMS 6560 maroon suburban 3rd/brake (13.75") - *32-40*	140	170
-	Southern 7411 green 1st corridor - *32-40*	200	240
-	Southern 3722 green 3rd brake corridor - *32-40*	200	240

Winteringham 1931 Series coach [C14] (Vecttis)

C15. LMS Post Office Mail Van (by Winteringham) (1932)

This was 13" long and of a similar specification to the '1931 Series' coaches in table above. However the pickup and delivery mechanism was the same as that for the earlier Carette mail van. The concertina clip-on corridor connections were offset from the centre and the coach came with mail bags and ground operating apparatus which were the same as those for earlier TPOs. The coaches could be bought separately and were suitable for both electric and clockwork systems. There were no underframe trusses and one battery box. Bogies and wheels were the same as for the '1931 Series'. It seems that the royal cipher of 'G(crown)R' on a red post box, carried on the sides of the coach, was not changed in 1937 with the change of monarch.

107/0	LMS 3251 maroon - *32-40*	200	220

C16. Standard BR Coaches (by Precision Models) (1950)

These were 13.75" long and featured tinplate concertina corridor connections. They had the simplified Fox pattern bogies (611/0) with MFD/0 disc pattern alloy wheels although they are often found with the better running TS/0 turned steel disc wheels or synthetic plain disc wheels for 2-rail running which was available from 1957. A particular characteristic of these coaches was the overlong, blackened, round-headed, turned brass buffers. Standard Bassett-Lowke black hook and short single link couplings were used. Curiously, these coaches did not carry a Bassett-Lowke trademark.

110/0*	BR 3995 red+cream 1st corridor - *50-61*	140	200
112/0	BR 26233 red+cream 3rd/brake - *50-61*	140	200
113/0	BR 9272 red+cream 3rd corridor - *50-61*	140	200

* 1st class coaches (110/0) are sometimes found in boxes labelled '111/0 1st Class Corridor Coach', but it is clear that the number '111/0 was never used for this series of coaches.

Precision Models BR 3rd class coach [C16] (Vectis)

Coaches by Edward Exley Ltd

Bassett-Lowke bought in complete coach bodies from Exley, fitted their own bogies and wheels, removed any Exley labelling and sold them in Bassett-Lowke labelled boxes. Towards the end of production, the LMS maroon lake was becoming distinctly red and plastic components were being used. For example, battery boxes, coach ends, dynamos and vacuum tanks were introduced and, right at the end (1963-65), Bassett-Lowke (617/0) plastic bogies were used.

There were two types of coach, the K5 and the K6. The differences, for the Bassett-Lowke marketed Exley coaches, were principally the windows. The earlier K5s had the window ventilators painted on whereas the later K6s had them punched out. On K5s and K6s coaches they sold themselves, Exley used their own bogies whereas Bassett-Lowke fitted to them with 616/0 Fox or 618/0 Gresley pattern bogies with turned steel disc wheels (Mansell MCF/0 or plain disc TS/0). From 1957, synthetic plain disc wheel sets were available for 2-rail operation.

The following tables list the Exley coaches sold by Bassett-Lowke in their own boxes. They were produced in batches and were not all available at the same time. The running numbers varied and, because Exley coaches were sold through various retail outlets, it is not easy to determine whether any particular running numbers were unique to Bassett-Lowke.

C17. Pre-WW2 Coaches (by Exley) (1936)

These were quality coaches made for Bassett-Lowke by Edward Exley Ltd. The original labels were removed and the coaches were sold in Bassett-Lowke boxes, fitted with the appropriate Bassett-Lowke bogies and wheels (usually 612/0). These coaches continued to be shown in the catalogues after the Second World War until 1950 but availability would have been both doubtful and, at best, intermittent.

	Pullman Dark Brown & Cream		
-	*Hazel* 1st class 19" - *36-40*	250	270

Bassett-Lowke 0

-	3rd class 19" - *36-40*	250	270
-	3rd/brake 19" - *36-40*	250	270
LMS Maroon			
-	Royal Mail TPO 17" with non-working apparatus - *36-40*	250	270
-	1st corridor 15.5" - *36-40*	250	270
-	3rd corridor 15.5" - *36-40*	250	270
-	1st corridor brake 15.5" - *36-40*	250	270
-	3rd corridor brake 15.5" - *36-40*	250	270
-	dining/kitchen car 2050 16.5" - *36-40*	250	270
SR Green			
-	1st corridor 16.5" - *36-40*	320	350
-	3rd corridor 16.5" - *36-40*	320	350
-	1st corridor brake 16.5" - *36-40*	320	350
-	3rd corridor brake 16.5" - *36-40*	320	350
LNER Teak			
-	dining/kitchen 16.5" - *36-40*	250	270
-	1st corridor 15.5" - *36-40*	250	270
-	3rd corridor 15.5" - *36-40*	250	270
-	1st corridor brake 15.5" - *36-40*	250	270
-	3rd corridor brake 15.5" - *36-40*	250	270
GWR Dark Brown & Cream			
-	corridor 16.5" long - *36-40*	300	320
-	corridor brake end (16.5" long) - *36-40*	300	320

C18. Early Post-WW2 Coaches (by Exley) (1947)
These early post-war coaches predate the introduction of the K5 and K6 types.

Early post-war LMS coach by Exley [C18] (Vectis)

LMS Maroon			
-	57' open - *47-50*	120	170
-	57' open brake - *47-50*	120	170
-	5091 54' 5091 corridor 3rd - *47-50*	120	170
-	3921 54' 3921 corridor brake comp - *47-50*	120	170
-	restaurant car - *47-50*	140	200
-	sleeping car - *47-50*	120	170
LNER Teak			
-	54' corridor - *47-50*	120	170
-	54' corridor brake end - *47-50*	120	170
-	54' luggage van and brake end - *47-50*	120	170
-	restaurant car - *47-50*	140	200
GWR Dark Brown & Cream			
-	2791 57' corridor 3rd - *47-50*	120	150
-	7172 57' corridor 1st - *47-50*	120	150
-	57' corridor brake - *47-50*	120	150
-	full brake - *47-50*	120	170
-	restaurant car - *47-50*	140	200

C19. Post-WW2 LMS Coaches (by Exley) (1950)
There were no listed LMS side-corridor 1st/brakes (K6) version from Bassett-Lowke, neither was there an LMS Engineer's inspection saloon. The LMS livery was crimson lake (maroon) of late style lined in yellow and black. The LMS decal was carried in the centre of each side. The roofs and underframing were black.

LMS Maroon			
-	54' corridor 3rd - *50-54*	120	230
-	54' corridor 1st - *50-54*	120	230
-	54' corridor brake/3rd - *50-54*	120	230
-	54' corridor brake/1st - *50-54*	120	230
-	57' open 3rd (K5) - *50-54*	120	230
-	57' open 1st (K5) - *50-57*	170	320
-	57' open brake/3rd (K5 - *50-57*	170	320
-	57' open brake/1st (K5) - *50-57*	170	320
-	57' sleeper, 1st/3rd 716 - *50-67*	140	280
-	TPO 30244 (K6) - *54-65*	170	470
-	suburban non-corridor 3rd - *54-62*	140	280

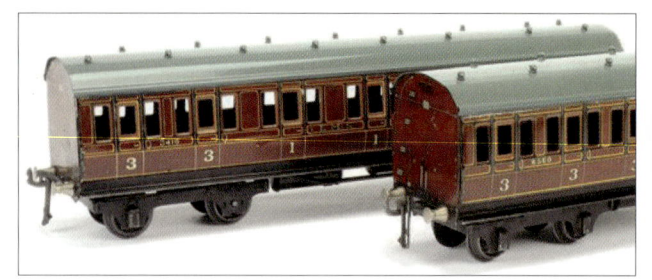

Post-war suburban coaches by Exley [C19] (Vectis)

-	suburban non-corridor brake/3rd - *54-62*	140	280
-	suburban non-corridor 1st/3rd - *54-62*	140	280
-	corridor full brake (K5) - *54-57*	140	280
-	corridor kitchen (K5) - *54-57*	200	320
-	non-gangwayed full brake - *54-57*	140	280
-	non-gangwayed parcels van - *54-57*	140	280
-	buffet car + pantry (K5 & K6) - *54-60*	200	300
-	suburban 6-wheeled 3rd - *54-57*	170	310
-	suburban 6-wheeled 1st/3rd - *54-57*	170	310
-	suburban 6-wheeled brake/3rd - *54-57*	170	310
-	corridor 3rd (K5) - *54-57*	140	320
-	corridor 1st (K5) - *54-57*	140	270
-	corridor brake/3rd (K5) - *54-57*	140	290
-	corridor brake/1st (K5) - *54-57*	140	280
-	corridor 1st (K6) - *57-67*	140	280
-	corridor 3rd (K6) - *57-67*	140	280
-	corridor brake/3rd (K6) - *57-67*	140	280
-	restaurant 1st/3rd 44 (K5) - *54-57*	170	320
-	restaurant 1st (K5) - *54-57*	170	310
-	restaurant 1st (K6) - *57-65*	200	300
-	open 3rd (K6) - *57-62*	200	300
-	open 1st (K5&K6) - *57-62*	200	320
-	open brake/3rd (K6) - *57-62*	200	300
-	open brake/1st (K6) - *57-62*	200	300
-	corridor 1st/3rd composite - ?	200	300

C20. Post-WW2 GWR Coaches (by Exley) (1950)
There was no listed GWR K6 corridor 1st/brake from Bassett-Lowke. The GWR livery was chocolate brown and cream with 'Great(crest)Western' at the centre of the coach sides. Roofs and underframing were black.

GWR Dark Brown & Cream			
-	57' corridor 3rd (K5) - *50-57*	120	260
-	57' corridor 1st (K5) - *50-57*	120	210
-	57' corridor 3rd/brake (K5) - *50-57*	120	220
-	57' corridor 1st/brake - *50-54*	120	220
-	57' restaurant car 1st/3rd (K5) - *50-62*	170	310
-	57' restaurant car 1st/3rd (K6) - *50-62*	170	310
-	57' open 3rd (K5) - *54-57*	120	220
-	suburban 3rd - *54-64*	120	220
-	suburban 3rd/brake - *54-64*	120	220
-	suburban 1st/3rd - *54-64*	120	220
-	Ocean Mail parcel van - *54-57*	120	220
-	parcels train full brake - *54-57*	120	220
-	corridor full brake - *54-57*	140	280
-	sleeping car 5550? 1st - *54-57*	140	310
-	sleeping car 3rd - *54-57*	140	280
-	buffet car with pantry - *54-57*	140	280
-	TPO - *54-57*	200	310
-	6-wheel suburban 3rd - *54-57*	200	310
-	6-wheel suburban 3rd/brake - *54-57*	140	280
-	6-wheel suburban 1st/3rd - *54-57*	150	300
-	57' corridor 3rd (K6) - *57-62*	210	310
-	57' corridor 1st (K6) - *57-62*	210	310
-	57' corridor 3rd/brake (K6) - *57-62*	210	310
-	57' open 3rd - *57-62*	230	330

C21. Post-WW2 LNER Coaches (by Exley) (1950)
LNER coaches were not listed in Bassett-Lowke catalogues but details could be supplied on request. Two separate liveries are known to exist - Gresley/Thompson teak and LNER tourist stock green and cream. Note that the LNER Exley coaches have square cornered windows (any found with round cornered windows may be repainted LMS or GWR coaches which are more common). LNER coaches should be fitted with Gresley

Bassett-Lowke 0

-	type bogies (618/0).		
-	LNER teak 50-59	140	270
-	LNER green+cream 55-5?	550	750

C22. Post-WW2 SR Coaches (by Exley) (1954)

The Southern Railway coaches had green sides and black ends, roofs and underframes. The name 'Southern' was printed in yellow as a logo in the centre of the coach sides.

Post-war SR 3rd class coach by Exley [C22] (Lacy, Scott & Knight)

	SR Green		
-	corridor 3rd - *54-57*	230	390
-	corridor 1st - *54-57*	230	390
-	5600 open 1st - *54-57*	230	390
-	corridor 3rd/brake - *54-57*	230	390
-	suburban 3rd - *54-57*	210	330
-	suburban 3rd/brake - *54-57*	210	330
-	suburban 1st/3rd - *54-57*	210	330

C23. Post-WW2 BR Coaches (by Exley) (1955)

British Railways coaches by Exley were not listed in the Bassett-Lowke catalogues but for a short period (1955-57) Bassett-Lowke offered to supply any of the post-grouping coaches painted in BR livery, to order. Examples are known to exist in both carmine & cream and crimson lake (maroon) livery. Look out for crimson lake examples as they are easy to miss as they look similar to LMS stock. They have slightly different lining and have no decals. The coaches should be fitted with the standard Bassett-Lowke Fox pattern bogie (616/0) and either steel turned wheels or post 1957 synthetic plain disc wheels for 2-rail operation.

	BR Red & Cream		
-	standard open 9272 - *55-57*	280	380
-	1st class - *55-57*	280	380
-	brake end - *55-57*	280	380
-	full brake - *55-57*	280	380
-	restaurant car - *55-57*	280	380
-	M660 sleeping car (K5) - *55-57*	280	380
	BR Maroon		
-	open standard - *55-57*	200	300
-	1st class - *55-57*	200	300
-	brake end - *55-57*	200	300
-	full brake - *55-57*	200	300
-	restaurant car - *55-57*	200	300
-	sleeping car - *55-57*	200	300

WAGONS

An early example of the series of Bassett-Lowke branded open wagons [W1] (Special Auction Services)

Up until the First World War, Carette of Nuremberg produced wagons in tinplate to Bassett-Lowke's order in 0 gauge and gauge 1. They were first introduced in 1909 with new additions to the range, and reissues, appearing each year until 1913. A photograph showing these wagons has survived in the Bassett-Lowke archives and they are listed and individually illustrated in the early catalogues.

Carette went out of business at the time of the First World War but Bassett-Lowke must have acquired the tooling and litho-printing artwork because most of the range was reissued after the war with the Bassett-Lowke name in the tinprinting, usually on the ends.

Both wooden and tinplate wagons were produced and were available side by side. The former were mostly post-grouping examples and in wood. You could buy a range of scale handmade wagons at a price four times that of a tinplate equivalent. Even the standard wooden wagons could be twice the price of tinplate ones. After the Second World War, some wooden wagons were available in kit form.

Today, the value of wagons has reversed with tinplate ones selling for twice the price of wooden ones. Look particularly for the 2-rail versions fitted with synthetic wheels and the 3-rail ones which have top quality Bassett-Lowke iron spoked wagon wheel sets.

Cat No.	Company, Number, Colour, Date	£	£

W1. Pre-WW1 Tinplate Wagons (by Carette) (1909)

These wagons had the 'grotesque' style large Carette couplings and separate cast iron axleguards. They could be supplied with either heavy iron spoked wheels or lighter tinplate wheels. Although slightly underscale in length, the tin-printing was particularly fine and accurate to prototype. Most wagons carried the 'drop-signal' Bassett-Lowke emblem on the solebars and the date of issue was included in the tin-printing. Thus it is possible to have variations of the wagons showing different issue dates (e.g. the MR cattle van was issued in 1909 and 1913). The Bassett-Lowke catalogue number was also included in the tin-printing in tiny numbers, usually on the wagon end but sometimes on the solebars. In this table is given the catalogue numbers and decoration of each wagon to which it relates. .

Cat No.	Company, Number, Colour, Date	£	£
	Un-Lettered		
1349/35	No.1909 black Tar Wagon - *09-14*	200	250
	Private Owner		
13411/35	'Anglo American Oil Co.' 405 red tanker - *09-14*	120	150
13413/35	'Bassett-Lowke', Northampton' 165 red-brown 8-plank - *09-10*	450	550
13413/35	'Bassett-Lowke', Northampton' 165 black 8-plank - *13-14*	100	120
13413/35	'Bassett-Lowke Ltd', London & Northampton' 6285 red-brown, diagonal stripe, 8-plank lithographed in England - *11-12*	150	250
13413/35	'Bassett-Lowke Ltd', London & Northampton' 6285 light grey, diagonal stripe, 8-plank - *13-14*	150	250
13425BL/35	'WJ Bassett-Lowke & Co.' yellow 8T van - *09-14*	900	1200
13428/35	'City of Birmingham Gas Dept.' 1201 red-brown 12T 8-plank coal wagon Sp Edn (Hull & Son) - *09-14*	250	350
13430/35	'City of Birmingham Gas Dept.' 779 grey steel coke hopper - *09-14*	250	350
13425M/35	'Colman's Mustard Traffic' yellow van - *09-14*	800	1000
13425S/35	'Colman's Starch Traffic' yellow van - *09-14*	800	1000
1348/35	'EWJ Greaves Blue Lias Lime/Portland Cement' 130 grey pitched roof wagon - *09-14*	200	250
13418/35	'WH Hull & Son' 405 light grey 10T 7-plank - *09-14*	250	300
	Pre-Grouping		
13443/35	CR 71908 brown 4-plank wagon lithographed in England - *?-14*	100	150
13443/35	CR 71908 brown 4-plank wagon - *13-14*	150	200
13432/35	GCR grey 8T 4-plank wagon - *11-14*	100	150
13446/35	GER 14096 grey 4-plank wagon - *11-14*	100	150
13423/35	GNR 18335 brown 15T 6-plank wagon - *09-14*	150	200
13412/35	GNR 1909 red-brown van - *09-14*	150	200
13422/35	GNR 39284 brown 8T banana van - *09-14*	150	200
13424/35	GNR 27451 brown 5T fish van - *09-14*	150	200
13421/35	GNR 10959 brown 10T brake van - *09-14*	200	250
13416/35	GWR 23464 grey 8T 4-plank Loco coal wagon - *09-14*	50	80
13415/35	GWR 16613 grey ventilated van - *09-14*	100	150
13416/0	GWR 8T banana van - *not made*	NA	NA

Bassett-Lowke 0

GNR fish van of 1909 [W1] (Lacy, Scott & Knight)

Cat. No.	Description		
13420/35	**GWR** 59761 off-white Mica B refrigerated meat van - *09-14*	150	200
13414/35	**GWR** 56452 grey brake van 'Paddington' - 'Guard Greenly' - *09-14*	100	150
13436/35	**LB&SCR** 9083 light grey open wagon + sheet rail + LB&SCR tarpaulin - *11-14*	250	350
13429/35	**LNWR** 1043 dark brown open carriage truck - *09-14*	100	150
13410/35	**LNWR** 1909 grey 2 x timber bolster trucks - *09-14*	200	250
1346/35	**LNWR** 530 grey 4-plank 7T goods wagon 1914 - *09-14*	50	80
13449/35	**LNWR** 640 grey 4-plank 10T Loco Coal wagon - *13-14*	50	80
13427/35	**LNWR** 329 dark brown horse box - *09-14*	450	550
13445/35	**LNWR** 13445 dark brown motor car van - *11-14*	700	900
1344/35	**LNWR** light grey van - *09-14*	100	150
13448/35	**LNWR** grey van - *11-14*	100	150
13426/35	**LNWR** 670 dark brown 'Fruit & Milk Traffic' van - *09-14*	450	550
1345/35	**LNWR** off-white refrigerator van - *09-14*	100	150
1341/35	**LNWR** grey brake van 'Crewe' - *09-14*	100	150
13447/35	**LNWR** grey brake van 'Camden' - *11-14*	100	150
13444/35	**LNWR** 15591 brown gunpowder van lithographed in England - *11-14*	300	400
13434/35	**LYR** 418 grey 3-plank ballast wagon - *11-14*	150	200
13438/35	**MR** grey 3-plank ballast wagon - *11-14*	150	200
13442/35	**MR** 68 brown Eng. Dept. (ED) ballast wagon lithographed in England - *11-14*	100	150

MR loco coal wagon of 1909 [W1] (Lacy, Scott & Knight)

Cat. No.	Description		
1347/35	**MR** grey 5-plank wagon - *09-14*	150	200
13433/35	**MR** dark grey 7-plank Loco Coal - *11-14*	80	120
13434/0	**MR** open wagon loco coal - *11-14*	NPG	NPG
13436/35	**MR** 35626 grey ventilated van - *11-14*	150	200
13443/35	**MR** grey large cattle truck - *09-14*	150	200
1342/35	**MR** grey brake van one open and one closed verandah - *09-14*	100	150
13417/35	**MR** bogie steel loco coal wagon grey - *09-14*	200	250
13431/35	**NBR** grey 8T 4-plank wagon - *11-14*	100	150
13439/35	**NER** 3192 grey Flatrol M + brown boiler 'JT Lowke & Sons' - *11-14*	600	900

W2. Pre-WW1 Cheap Tin Wagons (by Carette) (1912)

In 1912, a cheaper range of wagons, very similar to those listed in the previous table, was supplied by Carette for Bassett-Lowke. These wagons had tin-printed axleguards integral with the solebars and were supplied only with tinplate wheels. They were, therefore, lighter than the wagons listed above but appear very similar in general style. This range was restricted to the eleven vehicles listed here. The '35' at the end of the catalogue number refers to the gauge in millimetres.

Pre-Grouping		
13471-35 **GNR** 18335 brown 15T open wagon - *12*	40	60
13472-35 **GNR** brown covered van - *12*	120	150
13492-35 **GNR** 13492 brown 20T brake van - *13*	150	180
13476-35 **LNWR** grey 7T open wagon - *12*	40	60
13474-35 **LNWR** grey goods van - *12*	120	150
13475-35 **LNWR** white refrigerator van - *12*	120	150
13493-35 **LNWR** grey 10T brake van, Willesden - *13*	150	180
13477-35 **MR** grey open wagon - *12*	40	60
13473-35 **MR** grey short 'Large' cattle van - *12*	120	150
13470-35 **MR** 35626A grey ventilated van - *12*	120	150
13479-35 **MR** grey 10T brake van - *13*	150	180

W3. Wagon Tarpaulins (1920)

Wagon sheets, made either by Bing or Bassett-Lowke, were available for several pre- and post-grouping companies and would fit any tinplate or wooden 4-wheeled open wagon . Each company's sheet had its own number and initials and RCH diamonds parallel with the long edges. The Bing sheets also had a St Andrew's cross stretching to the corners. They were made of black linen and the printing was in white. Strings, with which to tie the sheet to the wagon's buffers, were sewn into short edges but some early sheets had elasticated ends.

	Pre-Grouping		
-	**GNR** 17220 black by Bing - *20-36*	10	12
-	**GNR** 1922 black - *20-36*	10	12
-	**GWR** 5231 black - *20-36*	10	12
-	**L&NWR** black - *20-27*	10	12
-	**L&SWR** 1343 black by Bing - *20-27*	10	12
-	**MR** 1922 black - *20-36*	10	12
-	**MR** 139197 black by Bing - *20-36*	10	12
	Post-Grouping		
-	**LMS** 5231 black - *?*	10	12

W4. Methylated Spirit Tanker (1922)

This was 5.25" long and consisted of a brass tank on a wooden base. It had cast WAG/0 axle guards screwed to the solebars, cast buffers screwed to the buffer beams and standard heavy alloy spoked wheels, which were painted black and mounted on splined axles. The tank was secured by wire cables to the end stanchions and the wooden base. The tank carried either water or methylated spirits for operating live steam locomotives. Removing the loose cap from the top, disclosed a spring valve which, when operated, allowed the contents to flow out of the outlet pipe beneath the tank.

Colas tank wagon [W4] (Vectis)

?	**'Colas'** black - *?*	80	120
3112/0	**'Lowko Spirit'** red - *22-37*	80	120

W5. Scale LMS (MR) High Capacity Bogie Wagon (1923)

This wagon, which was 12" long, was the type used by the Midland Railway for transportation of rails, girders and other cumbersome items. It was offered for a short period only. The bogies were cast in white metal and could be bought separately as

Bassett-Lowke 0

509/0. The wagon had low stretchers to hold loads in place.
- **LMS** grey - *23-24* 80 120

W6. Post-WW1 Tinplate Wagons (B-L/Carette) (1923)

These tinplate wagons were made by Bassett-Lowke using Carette tooling and so resemble the pre-WW1 Carette wagons. They were a restricted range having the Bassett-Lowke name included in the tinprinting at their ends. They had a mixture of Bassett-Lowke and Carette style couplings with cast spoked wheels. The issue of these wagons spanned the Grouping of the railways and so pre- and post-Grouping designs were used. The wagons were of an excellent quality but had distinctly short proportions - 5" long and 2.25" wide.

Private Owner
13413/0	**'Bassett-Lowke'** London & Northampton 6285 red-brown 8-plank - *23-30*	80	100
13413/0	**'Bassett-Lowke'** London & Northampton 6285 light grey 7-plank - *23-30*	80	100
13413/0	**'Bassett-Lowke'** London, Northampton & Edinburgh 6285 light grey 8-plank - *23-30*	80	90

Pre-Grouping
13416/0	**GW** (large) 91694 light grey 10T 5-plank open wagon - *23-30*	20	30
13416/0	**GW** (small) 91694 light grey 10T 5-plank open wagon - *23-30*	20	30
?	**GW** 35642 green 16T brake van 'Exeter' - *23-30*	35	45
1346/0	**LNWR** 850, 44865 grey 10T 5-plank open wagon - *23-26*	20	30
13448/0	**LNWR** grey covered goods van - *23-26*	45	55
13447/0	**LNWR** grey 10T brake van, single end verandah - *23-26*	35	45
13433/0	**MR** 45321 grey 12T 7-plank open wagon, Loco Coal - *23-26*	20	30

Post-Grouping
1346/0	**LMS** 24320 grey 10T 5-plank open wagon - *26-30*	20	30
13433/0	**LMS** 45321 grey 12T 7-plank open, Loco Coal Only - *26-30*	45	55
13448/0	**LMS** 4132 grey 10T covered goods van - *26-30*	35	45
13447/0	**LMS** 152540 grey 10T brake van, single end verandah - *26-30*	35	45

W7. Cheap Tinplate Wagons (by Bing) (1928)

These tinplate wagons were 5" long and 2.25" wide and were of a simplified appearance but with good quality litho printing. They had either Bing automatic couplings or standard Bing drop link hooks with a drop link at one end only. The bases were common for both vans and wagons and carried a running number on the solebars. 73923 was the number often used but 163581, 356204 and 425071 are also found. The wheels were tinplate on spragged axles but some had Bassett-Lowke heavy alloy spoked wheels. The vans were issued with either opening or non-opening doors. The wagons are also found without any company lettering, sometimes with a solebar number on the lower left planking.

Unlettered
593/0	dark grey 7-plank *, number on solebars - *28-32*	50	60
593/0	231462 dark grey 7-plank * - *28-32*	50	60

Post-Grouping
592/0	**GW** dark grey 7-plank - *28-32*	25	35
593/0	**GW** dark grey van - *28-32*	30	40
592/0	**LMS** dark grey 7-plank - *28-32*	25	35
593/0	**LMS** dark grey van - *28-32*	30	40
592/0	**NE** dark grey 7-plank - *28-32*	25	35
593/0	**NE** dark grey van - *28-32*	30	40
592/0	**SR** dark grey 7-plank - *28-32*	25	35
593/0	**SR** dark grey van - *28-32*	30	40

* Bassett-Lowke may have ordered some blank wagons so that customers could add their own lettering.

Several of the Bing tinplate wagons were not listed in the Bassett-Lowke catalogues including 'Explosives', NE 'Refrigerator', NE cattle, LMS fish and the bogie vans - 'Fish Traffic' and 'Milk Traffic'.

W8. Tinplate Standard Wagons (by Winteringham) (1930)

These were 5.75" long and 2.25" wide and made in tinplate. They were of scale proportions with Bing style hook and long link couplings. The wagons had heavy metal spoked wheels on splined axles and cast buffers that were riveted on. There was no representation of brake gear or vee-hangers and the wheels were painted black. The range, with the exception of the LMS open wagon, covered van and guards van, ceased in 1940 with the outbreak of the Second World War. The design of the LMS wagons was changed in 1938 and continued after the war until 1960. The wheels on these changed to the new post-war design which had a neater, more scale, appearance. They carried the Loko logo on the sole bars.

Mobiloil tanker [W8] (Vectis)

Private Owner
1356/0	**'Bassett-Lowke Ltd** London Northampton & Manchester' 6285* green-grey 12T 7-plank - *30-40*	70	90
1404/0	**'Esso'** 21774 cream petrol tanker (also 1042/0) - *3?-40*	450	700
1404/0	**'Mobiloil Vacuum Oil'** dark green-grey tanker (also 1042/0) - *36-40*	450	700
1402/0	**'Pratts Spirit'** 1852, 21774 buff petrol tanker - *30-35*	500	650
1406/0	77823 brown bogie well wagon + orange+green cable drum and coil **'Enfield Cable Works Ltd. London'** - *30-40*	850	950

Post-Grouping
1354/0	**GW** 91694 green 5-plank - *30-40*	35	40
1354/0	as above but light grey - *30-40*	35	40
1401/0	**GW/'United Dairies'** 2007 white milk tanker - *30-40*	480	650
1372/0	**GW** 103873 dark green 12T van - *30-40*	35	40
1362/0	**GW** 35642 grey 20T brake Toad van Exeter - *30-40*	60	100
1352/0	**LMS** 24468 grey 5-plank - *30-38*	35	40
1380/0	**LMS** 17741, 14548 grey cattle wagon - *30-40*	60	70
1370/0	**LMS** 29850, 291859 grey 12T van - *30-38*	60	70
1360/0	**LMS** 62306 grey 20T brake van verandah both ends - *30-38*	60	70
1353/0	**NE** 130911 green 5-plank - *30-40*	35	40
1371/0	**NE** 138971 grey-green** 12T luggage van - *30-40*	50	60
1390/0	**NE** 54849, 153180 white 8T Refrigerator van - *30-40*	120	140
1361/0	**NE** 140517 grey 20T brake van verandah both ends - *30-34*	80	100
1361/0	**NE** 140517 red-brown 20T brake van verandah both ends - *34-40*	90	100

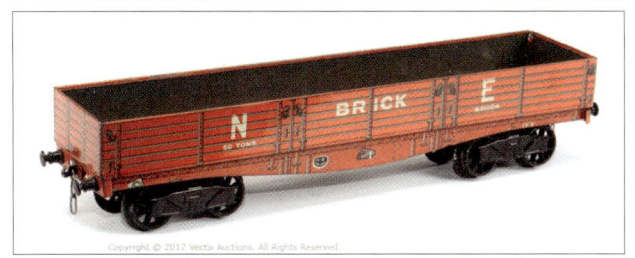

LNER bogie brick wagon [W8] (Special Auction Services)

1406/0	**NE** 77823 brown standard Flatrol bogie wagon 12" long *** - *32-40*	650	750
1406/0	**NE** 77823 grey Flatrol M + brown 'Callender' cable drum - *30-40*	850	950
1406/0	**NE** 77823 grey standard 'Flatrol' bogie wagon + brown boiler **'Bassett-Lowke Ltd'** 12" - *32-40*	450	950
1400/0	**NE** 451004 brown bogie Brick wagon - *30-40*	80	100

8th Edition

Bassett-Lowke 0

1355/0	SR 9232, 9871, 10252, dark brown 12T open wagon 6-plank - *30-40*	40	45
1373/0	SR 15757, 17741 dark brown van - *30-40*	80	90

* 6285 was the telephone number of the Bassett-Lowke shop at 112 high Holborn, London. ** The NE van tinplate printing suffered a production problem resulting in almost all the survivors having a crazed appearance. The number also frequently appears as '13897' as the final '1' is lost in a surface groove. *** The load bed was plain having no tinplate tab slots for the attachment of either the cable drum or the boiler.

Wooden Goods Vehicles

Bassett-Lowke continued to offer, throughout their existence, a bespoke service for top quality, museum standard, rolling stock. However, just prior to the First World War, the company introduced a standard range of vehicles made of best quality materials for discerning clients who preferred something rather better than the mass produced tinplate wagons. The clients also preferred models made of the same materials as the prototypes i.e. wooden tops, steel wheels and three link couplings.

The specification of the standard range of goods vehicles changed over the period. Some were plain while others had representations of sides and ends printed on. There may have been several suppliers, such as Mills Bros. and the Leeds Model Company, who produced the bodies to which Bassett-Lowke fitted the wheels, couplings and buffers. The Bassett-Lowke wooden vehicles may be recognised by the WAG/O axle guards or the use of box or pine wood with butt joins (as opposed to combed or dovetail joints). Theirs had a one piece wooden base with the tops and solebars pinned and glued on. Except for roofs, Bassett-Lowke never used plywood.

Three link couplings when fitted were not normally sprung. The coupling shanks were twisted through 90º and pinned to small wooden blocks under the wagon's floor. Other couplings included Bing style hook and long link and Stedman LF/16 single hook and single link. Wheels were generally the period Bassett-Lowke heavy alloy spoked wheels mounted on splined axles.

W9. Wooden Pre-Grouping Wagons - Pre-WW1 (1919)

These were 5" long and had printed and/or painted sides.

	Pre-Grouping		
3323	GN brown 15T 6-plank - *20-22*	20	25
3311	LNWR grey 7T 4-plank - *19-22*	20	25
3321	LNWR grey 10T 5-plank - *19-22*	20	25
3331	LNWR grey box van - *19-22*	25	30
3341	LNWR grey brake van, Crewe - *19-22*	25	30
3322	MR grey 10T 6-plank Loco Coal - *20-22*	20	25

Pre-grouping wooden wagons (Vectis)

W10. Wooden Pre-Grouping Wagons - Post-WW1 (1919)

The unlettered wagons could be lettered at the request of the purchaser and at extra cost. These were also available as kits.
db = dumb buffers

	Unlettered		
G507E	grey unlettered pair of timber bolster wagons with db - *19-22*	30	35
G561E	grey unlettered 8T open - *21-22*	15	20
G561E	grey unlettered 10T open - *21-22*	15	20
G583E	grey unlettered cattle wagon - *21-22*	35	45
G562E	grey unlettered 10T box van - *21-22*	20	25
	Private Owner		
G561E	'Bassett-Lowke Ltd London & Northampton' 10T 8-plank - *19*	15	20

	Pre-Grouping		
G501E	GC 10T 5-plank db - *19*	30	35
G501E	GN brown 10T 5-plank db - *19*	30	35
G582E	GN 10T box wagon - *19*	30	35
G505E	GN refrigerator van - *19-22*	45	55
G534E	GN brown 4-wheel 10T brake van, 2 verandas - *19*	30	35
G535E	GN brown 6-wheel 20T brake van, 2 verandas - *19*	35	45
G501E	GW green 10T 5-plank db - *19*	30	35
G516E	GW green 4-wheel 10T brake van, 1 veranda - *19-22*	30	35
G501E	LNWR grey 10T 5-plank db - *19*	30	35
G582E	LNWR grey 10T box wagon - *19*	30	35
G505E	LNWR white refrigerator van - *19-22*	45	55
G585E	LNWR grey 4-wheel 10T brake van, 1 veranda - *19*	30	35
G586E	LNWR grey 6-wheel 20T brake van, 1 verandah - *19*	35	45
G501E	MR grey 10T 5-plank db - *19*	30	35
G582E	MR grey 10T box wagon - *19*	30	35
G514E	MR grey 4-wheel 10T brake van, 1 veranda + 1 platform - *19-22*	30	35
G515E	MR M1907 grey 6-wheel 20T brake van, 1 veranda + 1 platform - *19-22*	35	45
G504E	MR grey high capacity bogie mineral wagon 504/0 bogies - *19*	45	55
G582E	NBR 10T box wagon - *19*	30	35
G513E	NBR brown 4-wheel brake van, ducket, no veranda - *19-22*	30	35
G505E	NER 90652 white refrigerator van - *19-22*	45	55
G511E	NER 17827 brown 4-wheel 10T brake van, 2 verandas + duckets - *19-22*	30	35
G504E	NER grey high capacity bogie mineral wagon 504/0 bogies - *19-22*	45	55
G510	North Eastern 108340 brown high capacity bogie box van - *19-22*	45	55

W11. Wooden Scale Prototypical Models (1920)

These were 5" long and similar to those in the table above but were of a better quality - perhaps having come from a different supplier. They were fitted with cast iron turned wheels and detailed fittings; especially the guards vans. They were forerunners to further series of quality wagons. It seems that none of the models were fitted with brake gear or vee-hangers.

	Unlettered		
-	** open wagons - *27-40*	35	45
-	** open wagons - *27-40*	35	45
-	** brake vans - *27-40*	35	45
-	** high capacity bogie mineral wagons - *27-40*	70	80
	Private Owner		
	'Schweppes' Summer Cordials grey open, Sp Edn (Schweppes Ltd) * - *25*	NPG	NPG
	Pre-Grouping		
03309/0	GN 18335? brown 15T high-sided - *23-26*	25	30
03311/0	LNWR 1503? grey 7T open - *20-28*	25	30
03321/0	LNWR grey 10T open - *20-28*	25	30
03331/0	LNWR 1911? grey van - *23-26*	30	35
03341/0	LNWR 1809? grey brake van, 1 verandah - *20-26*	30	35
03322/0	MR 1311? grey 12T open, Loco Coal - *23-26*	25	30

Schweppes wooden wagon [W11] (Vectis)

Bassett-Lowke 0

* The wagons were made for Schweppes publicity department and could be obtained from the company's head office or from Bassett-Lowke shops.
** These had liveries painted to order.

W12. Wooden Standard Wagons (1928)

This was a cheaper range of wooden wagons released later and it is not known whether they were made by Bassett-Lowke or bought in from another manufacturer.

	Private Owner		
3113/0	'Colas' grey black tank no valve and pipe - *30-36*	120	140
	Post-Grouping		
3354/0	GW green 8T 5-plank - *30-36*	15	25
3362/0	GW green brake van, 7.37" - *30-36*	20	30
3352/0	LMS grey 10T 5-plank - *30-36*	15	25
3370/0	LMS grey van - *30-36*	20	30
3360/0	LMS 646 grey 10T brake van, 7.5" long - *30-36*	20	30
3353/0	NE brown 10T 5-plank - *30-36*	15	25
3371/0	NE brown van - *30-36*	20	30
3371/0	NE 138971 grey van - *30-36*	30	40
3361/0	NE 451091 grey 10T ** brake van, 5.5" long - *30-36*	20	30
3327/0	SR 3753 brown 12T 7-plank - *28-36*	15	25
3333/0	SR 15757 brown 12T van - *28-36*	20	30
3344/0	SR 11892 brown 20T brake van 2 verandahs - *28-36*	15	25

** Catalogue picture shows '20T'.

W13. Wooden Standard Wagons (1937) (by Milbro)

These wagons were 5.5" long. They had no trademark showing but were almost certainly made for Bassett-Lowke by Milbro. They had Milbro axle guards screwed to the solebars and cast wheels, turned brass buffers, 3-link unsprung couplings and Milbro style wood construction. The wagons were not normally fitted with brake gear or vee-hangers although these may have been fitted at the customer's request or have been done so retrospectively. The brake vans had footboards.

	Unlettered		
-	black 20T tube wagon - *37-40*	35	45
-	grey cattle wagon - *37-40*	45	60
	Post-Grouping		
-	GW green? Eng. Dept. low-sided - *37-40*	35	45
-	GW green 12T 5-plank - *37-40*	35	45
-	GW green van - *37-40*	45	60
-	GW 98014 green 10T brake van 2 verandahs - *37-40*	35	45
-	LMS grey? Eng. Dept. low-sided - *37-40*	35	45
-	LMS grey 12T 5-plank - *37-40*	35	45
-	LMS red gunpowder van - *37-40*	60	70
-	LMS 1906 grey van - *37-40*	45	60
-	LMS grey 10T 4-wheel brake van 2 verandahs 5.5" long - *37-40*	35	45
-	LMS grey 20T 6-wheel brake van 2 verandahs - *37-40*	60	70
-	NE grey? Eng. Dept. low-sided - *37-40*	35	45
-	NE grey 12T 5-plank - *37-40*	35	45
-	NE grey van - *37-40*	45	60
-	NE grey 10T, brake van, 1 verandah - *37-40*	35	45
-	SR brown? Eng. Dept. low-sided - *37-40*	35	45
-	SR brown 12T 5-plank - *37-40*	35	45
-	SR brown van - *37-40*	45	60
-	SR brown 10T brake van - *37-40*	45	60

LMS low-sided wooden wagon (Lacy, Scott & Knight)

Bakelite Wagons

These were made in self-coloured bakelite with standard Leeds Model Company axle guards mounted on separate tinplate double brackets which were tabbed to the floor of the wagon. They had non-locking alloy buffers and sprung 3-link couplings. The wagons were fitted with LMC alloy spoked or 4-hole disc wheels and had super details included on the bakelite moulding. Metal fatigue is a common problem with the buffers and wheels on these wagons and these items have often been replaced. Although dropped from the catalogue in 1940, some remained on sale in Bassett-Lowke's shops as late as 1948. (see also the chapter on the Leeds Model Company and the wagons tables).

W14. Bakelite Wagons (Leeds for Bassett-Lowke) (1938)

	Post-Grouping		
P30	GW grey 12T 7-plank - *38-40*	15	20
P10	LMS brown 12T 7-plank - *38-40*	15	20
P80	LMS 606521 brown 12T van - *38-40*	15	20
P90	LMS 606521 brown 12T van, ventilators, brake pipes - *38-48*	20	25
P100	LMS maroon 6T fish van, passenger brake - *38-40*	25	30
P20	NE 37042 grey 12T 7-plank - *38-40*	15	20
P50	NE red 12T 7-plank - *38-40*	20	25
P110	NE grey 12T van - *38-40*	15	20
P120	NE grey 12T van, ventilators, brake pipes - *38-48*	20	25
P130	NE red 12T fruit van, ventilators, brake pipes - *38-48*	20	25
P40	SR brown 12T 7-plank - *38-40*	20	25

Post-war Wagons

The tinplate wagons in the following three tables used WF/0 8-spoked alloy wheel sets as standard but could be had with the better running WCF/0 8-spoked turned steel wheels at extra cost. From 1957, the vehicles could be had with Tri-ang manufactured synthetic 3-hole disc wheels, at a reduced cost, for 2-rail operation (these wheels have the word 'Tri-ang' moulded into the back of the wheels). All these vehicles featured standard, later pattern, Bassett-Lowke black hook and short single link couplings but Bassett-Lowke offered a replacement conversion kit (601/13/0) for scale 3-link couplings which are sometimes found on these wagons. So too are track operated hook and loop remotely controlled automatic couplings.

Tarpaulin covers (or 'sheets') were not available for the open wagons after the war.

W15. Post-war Tinplate Wagons (1938)

Although pre-war tinplate rolling stock appeared in the early post-war catalogues, none was produced except for the later 0 gauge LMS brown goods series which was introduced in 1938 and continued, albeit with modifications, until 1960. These had a brown base until 1950, when it changed colour to black. Until 1948 the wagons had black integral axle guards, but from sometime in 1948 these changed to black separate axle guards.

	Post-Grouping		
1352/0	LMS 36721, 3672 * brown 13T open wagon - *38-60*	20	30
1370/0	LMS 91375 brown 12T van - *38-60*	25	45
1360/0	LMS 730273 brown 20T brake van - *38-53*	30	55
	Post-Nationalisation		
1364/0	BR B37354 grey LWB, black base - *51-68*	25	35

* Due to a litho printing error, some wagons have the last digit ('1') missing on one or both sides making the running number '3672'.

W16. Post-war Wooden Wagons and Kits (1948)

These wagons were available factory made or as sets of parts, for home assembly and finishing, at approximately half the price of factory made vehicles. The specification included parts made of good quality seasoned wood cut to size with planking scribed as necessary. Included in each kit were WAG/0 axle guards, WO/12 or WO/10 oval or round buffers, 601/15/0 3-link couplings, strapping, WF/0 alloy wheel sets, screws, pins, transfers and instructions. Turned steel wheels (WCF/0) were available at extra cost and synthetic 3-hole disc wheels for 2-rail operation were available from 1957 and reduced

Bassett-Lowke 0

the price of the kit by 2/-. Prices are provided in this table for factory made models built from these kits and (at the bottom) any unmade kit with all parts still intact.

Wooden bodied LMS wagons (Vectis)

	Post-Grouping		
-	GW green 12T 5-plank - *48-50*	15	20
-	GW green 12T van - *48-50*	25	30
-	GW green 20T brake van - *48-50*	25	30
-	LMS 672149* brown 12T 5-plank - *48-56*	15	20
-	LMS brown 12T van - *48-56*	25	30
-	LMS brown 20T brake van - *48-56*	25	30
-	NE 36720* grey 12T 5-plank - *48-56*	15	20
-	NE 14972* grey 12T van - *48-56*	25	30
-	NE 13758* grey 20T brake van - *48-56*	25	30

Wooden bodied LNER wagons (Vectis)

	Post-Nationalisation		
-	BR 837483* grey 12T 5-plank - *50-65*	15	20
-	BR grey cattle wagon - *52-60*	20	30
-	BR 108283* grey 12T van - *52-60*	25	30
-	BR 37463* grey 20T brake van - *52-60*	25	30
-	any kit complete - *48-68*	NPG	25

* The numbers given are for known examples, however, these changed over the years and depended on the production batches.

W17. Long Wheelbase Special Load Wagons (1957)

These wagons used the base of the 1364/0 guards van. All bases were black.

Vehicle A black chained metal plates - *57-65*		30	60
Vehicle B black + strung and wedged 2 '**Hornby Liverpool Cables**' drums - *57-65*		30	60
Vehicle E black + chained large metal tube - *57-65*		30	60
Vehicle M large log chained black - *57-65*		30	60
Vehicle N black + chained lg square timber - *57-65*		30	60

W18. Standard Wheelbase Special Load Wagons (1957)

1957 improvised wagon loads [W18] (Vectis)

These wagons used the base of 1352/0, 1370/0 and 1360/0 standard wagons; all with black bases.

Vehicle C black + pinned '**Hornby**' insulated meat container - *57-65*		30	60
Vehicle D black + chained machinery casting (varied) - *57-65*		30	60
Vehicle F black + chained 12 '**Bassett-Lowke**' wooden sleepers - *57-65*		30	60
Vehicle G black + chained 4 '**Bassett-Lowke**' loco driving wheels - *57-65*		30	60
Vehicle H black + strung and wedged '**Hornby Liverpool Cables**' drum - *57-65*		30	60
Vehicle K black + pinned '**Hornby**' furniture container - *57-65*		30	60
Vehicle L black + 2 chained ship propellers - *57-65*		30	60

ACCESSORIES

Bassett-Lowke produced quite an extensive range of accessories, not least their various series of track which offered the public different standards according to what they could afford. Lineside equipment included stations, goods depots, level crossings, signals and platform personnel and equipment.

SETS

Train sets did not play a big part in the company's marketing policy but starter sets were available.

Bassett-Lowke post-war passenger set (Vectis)

Visit the BRM website at: www.model-railways-live.co.uk

Bassett-Lowke
by Corgi & Hornby

HISTORY

Corgi Classics purchased the tools and intellectual assets of Bassett-Lowke in 1996 and decided to introduce a range of 0 gauge models, in 1999, based on earlier Bassett-Lowke designs with the Greenly valve gear. The first was released as a steam driven model but only one steam version was made. After that all new models have had 12v electric mechanisms fitted with smoke generators. All electric steam outline locomotives were able to run in either 2-rail or 3-rail control through a unique switching system. This included an 'off' setting operated by a control rod in the cab. A second control rod operated the smoke unit.

The models were individually made in brass using soldered construction. The plan from the start was to develop each new model, release it in a range of liveries and then move on to a new model. The recommended smallest radius for the locomotives is 3 feet.

With mounting financial worries, due largely to over production in the diecast model industry, late in 2004, Corgi decided to pull out of locomotive production and terminated the employment of their designer and engineer, Len Mills, who transferred to Ace Trains to work on their future locomotives. It was rumoured that the Bassett-Lowke name was available for sale. However, a year later, the Bassett-Lowke range was still alive and moving forward.

There followed an LNER/BR Class A3 and a prototype for the LMS 6202 'Turbomotive' was made and displayed at various venues in 2004. A Great Western 'Castle' class loco was also announced but Len Mills developed this for Ace Trains instead.

In 2006, Corgi Classics turned to ETS, in The Czech Republic, and commissioned some models from them. These started to arrive in 2007 and were made in tinplate using ETS manufacturing and design technology. They had no generic or common features with the earlier locomotives and, moreover, the new models were made to Continental European 1:45 scale rather than British 0 gauge 1:43 scale.

In May 2008, Hornby purchased the Corgi Classics brand, tooling and intellectual assets and with them the Bassett-Lowke business. Initially, Hornby saw the link with ETS continuing but by 2012 had realised that the range did not fit in with their high volume production program and no further development was planned.

LOCOMOTIVES

In the cab, each model carries an identity plate with its production number. The locomotives can be switched between 2-rail and 3-rail operation and from 2007 they were advertised as having smoke generators fitted.

Peckett 0-4-0ST by Hornby [L1] (Tony Wright)

Cat No.	Company, Number, Colour, Date	£	£

Locomotives by Corgi

L1. Peckett 0-4-0ST (2011)

Work on this started under Corgi's management and the project was taken over by Hornby. Models are fitted with smoke generators.

BL99053	**Wenman** red Ltd Edn 250 - *11*	200	268
BL99063	**Joseph** green Ltd Edn 250 - *11*	200	268

L2. LNER Class J39 0-6-0 (2009)

The Gresley standard 0-6-0 freight locomotive of 1926 was the first post-Grouping LNER 0-6-0 locomotives to be built and replaced many of the 800 plus 0-6-0 locomotives that the LNER inherited in 1923.

These models are branded 'Bassett-Lowke' and are made in tinplate to 1:45 scale. They have a 12-14V motor and a 2-rail/3-rail switch in cab. All are fitted with smoke generators.

99032	**2714** LNER black Ltd Edn 250 - *not made*	NA	NA
99032	**1532** LNER black Ltd Edn 50 - *09*	450	590
99032A	**1563** LNER black Ltd Edn 50 - *09*	450	590
99032B	**1580** LNER black Ltd Edn 50 - *09*	350	460
99032C	**1588** LNER black Ltd Edn 50 - *09*	350	460
99032D	**1875** LNER black Ltd Edn 50 - *09*	450	590
99031	**64744** BRc black Ltd Edn 130 - *09*	450	590
99031A	**64757** BRc black Ltd Edn 40 - *09*	450	590
99031B	**64781** BRc black Ltd Edn 40 - *09*	450	590
99031C	**64816** BRc black Ltd Edn 40 - *09*	450	590

L3. LMS Stanier 'Mogul' 2-6-0 (2000)

Stanier's Moguls dated from 1933 and 40 were built at Crewe for lighter mixed traffic duties. They arrived in 1934 and were widely distributed within the LMS.

This was steam powered when first released, but it was soon found that the market demanded electic powered locomotives and so steam was soon dropped.

99002	**2945** LMS lined maroon Ltd Edn 750 - *00*	200	250
99001	**42981** BRb black steam powered Ltd Edn 520 - *00*	200	250

L4. SR Maunsell N Class 'Mogul' 2-6-0 (2001)

Most of the initial releases of the SR N Class 'Mogul' locomotives were marred by the wheels being out of gauge at 29mm back-to-back, instead of 28mm and they had a very noisy mechanism. Corgi arranged a 'return to works' programme for a replacement redesigned mechanism and wheels of the correct gauge. Intending purchasers of locomotives from the 2001 batches are strongly advised to ascertain the status of the locomotives mechanism as the upgrade is essential. The Hornby batch of 2009 have enhanced detail, new low resonance gearboxes as standard and are fitted with smoke generators.

SR Class N 2-6-0 [L4] (Vectis)

99042	**810** SECR Austerity grey Ltd Edn 50 - *09*	300	386
99064	**?** LSWR lined green Ltd Edn 75 – *not made*	NA	NA
99003	**1864** SR lined green Ltd Edn 500 - *01*	220	240
99054	**?** SR Ltd Edn 75 - *09*	300	386
99004	**31407** BRb lined black Ltd Edn 500 - *01*	220	240
99064	**?** BRb lined black Ltd Edn 500 - *09*	300	386
99005	**372** CIE lined green Ltd Edn 60 - *01*	330	350

L5. LMS 'Rebuilt Patriot' Class 4-6-0 (2004)

The rebuilt loco looked very much like a 'Rebuilt Royal Scot' but while the 'Scots' retained their Fowler cabs, the 'Patriots' were given a 'Jubilee' cab. The Fowler tender was also disposed of and a Stanier 4,000 gallon tender provided in its place.

99017	**45527** *Southport* BRb green Ltd Edn 200 - *04*	430	450
99041	**45534** *E.Tootal Broadhurst* BRc green Ltd Edn 180 smoke generator - *09*	300	376

Bassett-Lowke by Corgi

L6. LMS 'Rebuilt Royal Scot' Class 4-6-0 (2003)

This was Fowler's express passenger, parcel or fitted freight design of 1927. A total of 71 'Royal Scots' were built and, between 1943 and 1955, all of them were rebuilt with No.2a tapered boilers. They were mainly used on express passenger services, competing with the Gresley Pacifics in the race to the North, until replaced by Stanier's Pacifics.

The model is fitted with a 12-14v electric motor and has sprung buffers, lamp irons and lamps and a smoke generator.

99015	**6162** *Queens Westminster Rifleman* LMS black Ltd Edn 200 - *04*	480	500
99016	**6100** *Royal Scot* LMS maroon (as preserved) Ltd Edn 100 - *04*	580	600
99056	**6100** *Royal Scot* LMS maroon Ltd Edn 100 - *09*	NPG	700
99011	**46100** *Royal Scot* BRb green Ltd Edn 500 - *03*	350	370
99012	**46102** *Black Watch* BRb green ex-Thames-Clyde set* Ltd Edn 350 - *04*	480	500

* Sold in a set with Ace Trains C5 crimson and cream coaches.

L7. LMS 'Princess Royal' Class 4-6-2 (2002)

The prototype 'Princess Royal' Class had been designed by William Stanier and introduced to the LMS in 1933 for express duties. Only 13 were built, each of them named after a member of the Royal Family, before the LMS switched to a more powerful design known as the 'Princess Coronation' Class or perhaps better known today as the 'Duchesses'. The last of the 'Princess Royals' was withdrawn in 1962 and two of the class, 46201 *Princess Elizabeth* and 46203 *Princess Margaret Rose*, have survived into preservation.

Ex-LMS 'Princess Royal' Class [L7] (Modelfair)

99006	**6201** *Princess Elizabeth* LMS maroon Ltd Edn 480 - *02*	440	460
99010	**6210** *Lady Patricia* LMS black Ltd Edn 200 - *03*	480	500
99014	**46205** *Princess Victoria* BRa black Ltd Edn 100 - *04*	440	460
99008	**46203** *Princess Margaret Rose* BRb blue Sp Edn 100 (Much Ado About Toys) - *02*	480	500
99009	**6206** *Princess Marie Louise* LMS black Ltd Edn 100 - *02*	480	500
99007	**46200** *The Princess Royal* BRb green Ltd Edn 396 - *02*	480	500
99013	**46208** *Princess Helena Victoria* BRc maroon Ltd Edn 200 - *04*	480	500

L8. LNER Class A3 4-6-2 (2005)

The Class A3s of the LNER were a development of the A1s, which had been designed for the Great Northern Railway by Nigel Gresley in 1922. All existing A1s, with the exception of one, had been converted to A3s by the end of 1948 and the final 27 of the class were built as A3s.

The LNER/BR A3 series models are fitted with a red fireglow lamp in the firebox. dc = double chimney.

90018	**2751** *Humorist* SR green* dc Ltd Edn 100 - *05*	550	575
99021	**4472** *Flying Scotsman* LNER polished brass Ltd Edn 100 - *06*	350	375
99022	**4472** *Flying Scotsman* LNER green double tender Ltd Edn 400 - *06*	470	490
99023	**4472** *Flying Scotsman* LNER green Australian Tour Sp Edn (Much Ado) - *06*	480	500
99024	**4472** *Flying Scotsman* LNER green USA Tour** Sp Edn 100 (Modelzone) - *06*	780	800
99040	**4472** *Flying Fox* LNER green Ltd Edn 180 - *09*	600	750
90019	**60052** *Prince Palatine* BRb blue* Sp Edn 50 (Much Ado About Toys) - *05*	580	600
99026	**60103** *Flying Scotsman* BR green, double chimney, German smoke deflectors, high sided tender Ltd Edn 350 - *07*	NPG	NPG
99024	**60103** *Flying Scotsman* BRc green, smoke deflectors Ltd Edn 350 - *07*	500	700
99068	**60046** *Diamond Jubilee* BR green, smoke deflectors Ltd Edn 50 - *09*	550	685
99069	**60048** *Trigo* BR green, smoke deflectors Ltd Edn 50 - *09*	550	685

* The livery is best described as Maunsell Southern green with Southern lining. Some were returned by dissatisfied customers. ** This has the headlight, cowcatcher, whistle, hooter, red backed nameplates, smoke unit, green cylinders and double tender.

Models by E.T.S.

L9. Class 20 Diesel Bo-Bo (2007)

This is an English Electric designed freight loco of 1957, the first of 20 being built at their Vulcan Foundry works. Other batches followed until the final member of the class was delivered in 1968. In all, 228 eventually arrived and were allocated to the Eastern, London Midland and Scottish Regions.

The model was branded 'Bassett-Lowke' and the body was made in tinplate to 1:45 scale. It was fitted with a 12-14V motor and had a switch allowing the operator to change between 2-rail and 3-rail. The model also had directional lights (also changeable to allow nose to nose double heading).

BR Class 20 diesel [L9]

99027	**8001** BRc green + goods, vent and insulated van Ltd Edn train pack 150 - *07*	NA	350
-	above loco on its own - *07*	250	NA
99028	**20227** Traction BRe Railfreight red stripe grey + 3 12T vent vans Ltd Edn train pack 100 - *07*	NA	350
-	above loco on its own - *07*	250	NA

WAGONS

These are all made by ETS of The Czech Republic but branded 'Bassett-Lowke'

Cat No.	Company, Number, Colour, Date	£	£

W1. 3-plank 8-Ton Wagon (2007)

The 3-plank wagon was considered to be a 'medium' goods wagon, as opposed to a low-sided one. But, despite this, amongst other things, it was used for the transportation of containers. They were particularly found on the LMS and had drop-down sides and fixed ends.

99037	'Bassett-Lowke' 6207 green - *07*	22	28
99060	'Bassett-Lowke' 9062 brown - *09*	22	28
99071	LMS 99071 grey - *09*	22	28
99059	LNER 99059 grey - *09*	22	28
99066	SR 99066 dark brown - *09*	22	28
-	BR M268922 grey	25	NA
-	BR M268923 grey	25	NA
-	BR M268924? grey	25	NA
99034	set of 3 above wagons - *07*	NA	102

W2. 7-plank Wagon (2007)

7-plank wagons were mostly privately owned and used for the transportation of coal. Between the wars they were the most numerous wagon type on Britain's railways. They were requisitioned by the government during the Second World War and passed to BR in 1948. During the 1950s the aging fleet was gradually replaced by steel mineral wagons.

99036	'Bassett-Lowke' 6285 green - *07*	22	28
99057	'Bassett-Lowke' 99057 brown - *09*	22	28
99079	'Firestone' 99079 dark blue - *09*	22	28
99078	'DR Llewellyn' 55 brown - *09*	22	28
99073	LMS 99073 grey - *09*	22	28
99072	LNER 99072 grey - *09*	22	28
99074	SR 99074 dark brown - *09*	22	28
-	BR E4659451 grey	25	NA
-	BR E698264 grey	25	NA
-	BR E4659452 grey	25	NA
99033	set of 3 above wagons - *07*	NA	107

Bassett-Lowke by Corgi

W3. Tank Wagons (2009)

Tank wagons formed the largest sector of wagon provision that British Railways left to the private sector to provide. Their purpose is to carry liquids and many kinds travel this way, including petrol, oil, tar, milk, bitumen, industrial chemicals etc..

Bassett-Lowke tank wagon [W3] (Tony Wright)

99038	**'Bassett-Lowke'** 6288 green - *09*	35	53
99062	**'Bassett-Lowke'** 6388 brown - *09*	35	53
99065	**'Esso'** 21774 buff - *09*	35	53
99067	**'Pratt's Spirit'** 1852 buff - *09*	30	40
99070	**'United Dairies'** GW 2007 white - *09*	35	53
-	**'National Benzole Mixture'** 827? silver	30	NA
-	**'BP Motor Spirit'** 1449 buff	30	NA
-	**'Shell Motor Spirit'** ? red	30	NA
99035	set of 3 above tank wagons – *09*	NA	161

W4. Vans (2007)

Vans protected the merchandise and gradually replaced open wagons fitted with tarpaulins. Many vans were built for specifit loads, such as bananas, fruit, meat, fish etc.

99076	**LMS** 99076 grey - *09*	NPG	28
99075	**LNER** 99076 grey - *09*	NPG	28
99077	**SR** 99077 dark brown - *09*	NPG	28
-	**BR** M32385 white 8T goods van	28	NA
-	**BR** maroon ventilated meat van	28	NA
-	**BR** B872056 white 10T Insulmeat van	28	NA
99029	set of above 3 vans - *07*	NA	85
-	**BR** B785753 brown 12T ventilated van	28	NA
-	**BR** B785436 brown 12T ventilated van	28	NA
-	**BR** B785159 brown 12T ventilated van	28	NA
99030	set of above 3 ventilated vans Ltd Edn 150 - *07*	NA	97

W5. 20T Standard Brake Van (2009)

The BR standard brake van was based on the LNER standard design. This had a small cabin, which was placed centrally on a long chassis with a veranda at each end This left a clear platform at each end of the vehicle. In BR days grab rails were fitted along the sides of each platform.

These had white platform rails and working red rear light run off 2 AAA batteries.

99043	**LNER** 259501 brown - *09*	35	42
99039	**BR** B95542 brown - *09*	35	40

The Bachmann Class 7F No.53809 on the Somerset & Dorset Joint Railway - a computer enhanced photograph by Robbie McGavin

WANTED

Don't Delay Call Today

No Cheques / No Posting / Just a Top Cash Deal

Top Prices Paid for Your collection of
Hornby, Bachmann, Heljan, Farish, Wrenn, DJH and Other Kits Built & Unbuilt, Exley, LGB

WE PURCHASE YOUR WHOLE COLLECTION

Layouts dismantled - Distance No Object

We also require O gauge and above R.T.R or Kitbuilt Locos, Coaches, Wagons etc.

VISIT WWW.SANDJMODELS.CO.UK

For Discontinued Mint Boxed Hornby & Bachmann Locos, Coaches, Wagons etc.

100s of items listed who knows you may just find that elusive item!

**S&J Models,
20 Winnington Lane,
Northwich,
Cheshire CW8 4DE**

Call Now Tel: 01606 872786 Mobile: 07531 949 069
Email: sjmodels@tiscali.co.uk

Bond's 0

HISTORY

Bond's are primarily known as a manufacturer of mechanisms, locomotives, rolling stock and track parts as well as being agents for other manufacturer's products. They were established in 1887, in the London N.W.1 area, by Arthur Bond, trading mainly in bicycles and cars, but also, to a lesser extent, engineering models and tools. Bond moved his premises to 245 -247 Euston Road, in the early days of the last century and then across the road to No.254 in 1923. The business now became Bonds Ltd, with the name Bond's O'Euston Road Ltd, finally being adopted in April 1926. Their final London location was No.357 Euston Road.

They catered principally for the 0 gauge and larger scales but made small quantities of 00 scale models from 1925. The pre-war catalogues show a wide selection of model railway items by both British and Continental manufacturers. Materials, castings, tools, lathes, milling machines and boilers were also offered for those interested in model engineering.

LMS 'Jinty' 0-6-0T [L2] (Special Auction Services)

Bond's electric motors and gearboxes are highly regarded; in fact, they are often found fitted to other makers' locomotives. Some will have been changed during the life of the engine but others may have been installed when new, as many manufacturers were quite pleased to fulfil extra requirements, such as a Bond's motor, at extra cost. Bond's also made brass framed motor bogies as well as sprung coach bogies.

Arthur Bond retired in 1929, leaving the running the business to his manager Sydney Phillips. The latter progressively increased the range of the company's own products, but also retained the sales agencies of several other product lines.

Sydney Phillips eventually bought the business in 1942 and continued to run it until he died in 1966. Bonds was left in the capable hands of his son Robert.

Following the Second World War, things had not got back to normal until late in 1947. The company, by then, had changed direction, becoming more retail orientated, and during the 1950s their catalogues listed the Hornby Dublo, Tri-ang and Trix ranges as well as a wide selection of parts for not only model railways but also aircraft and boats. Phillips increasingly concentrated on tools and raw materials and, by the early 1970s, models took up no more than 25 pages at the back of the 100 page Bond's catalogue, and just 9 pages dealt with model railway items.

In 1973, Robert Phillips moved the business from Euston Road to Rumbolds Hill in Midhurst as the whole London site was to be redeveloped. At Midhurst he concentrated on sales of quality tools, both for the trade and DIY markets. The stocks of model engineering and railway items, found at the rear of the shop, were slowly ran down and were not replenished when exhausted.

In 2010, Robert Phillips decided to retire and what remained of the railway spares were acquired by the Bassett-Lowke Society.

Collectors Club
There is no collector's society for Bond's equipment but the Bassett-Lowke Society may be able to help or indicate sources of information (see details under 'Bassett-Lowke').

Prices - It is difficult to assess the value of Bond's locomotives as they are not often found for sale. The two prices shown represent the likely range for one in good condition.

New Information - We would welcome information on other locomotives and rolling stock by this manufacturer.

LOCOMOTIVES

Bond's own locomotives were offered in gauges 00, 0 and 1, as well as 2.5" and 3.5" and many were made to special order. Indeed, their catalogues offered to quote for building any type "from the tiny 4mm 00 gauge electric model to a 1.5" scale garden steam locomotive".

Other Gauges - The locomotives listed below were also available in gauge 1 electric and in live steam in gauges 1, 2.5" and 3.5".

Cat No.	Company, Number, Colour, Date	£	£

L1. Peckett Dockyard Tank 0-6-0ST (1927)

Referred to as the 'Bonzone', the model was based on a Peckett design and had six balanced, all flanged, wheels in a short wheelbase. It also had a toolbox with a lid that opened to reveal the winding key. This box varied in position and there were slight variations in the shape of the body. It had a copper top chimney and brass dome and the numbering was progressive. Post-war mechanisms were 12V.

1, 2, 3, 4, 6 Bonzone

'Bonzone' 0-6-0ST [L1] (Vectis)

Cat No.	Company, Number, Colour, Date	£	£
-	Great Western green c/w - *27-56?*	250	350
-	Great Western green 6-8V DC - *28-56?*	250	350
-	black c/w - *27-56?*	250	350
-	black 6-8V DC - *28-56?*	250	350
-	deep yellow c/w - *28-56?*	250	350
-	deep yellow 6-8V DC - *28-56?*	250	350
-	red-brown - *28-56?*	250	350
Unnamed			
-	Great Western green - *28-56?*	225	300
-	Southern green - *28-56?*	250	350
-	6 dark green - *28-56?*	250	350

L2. LMS 'Jinty' Type 3F Tank Engine 0-6-0T (1938)

The class was designed for the LMS by Henry Fowler but owes its origins to a Midland Railway 0-6-0 tank engine designed by Johnson. The 'Jinty' became the LMS's standard 0-6-0T shunting engine and 422 were built between 1924 and 1931. So large was the order that much of the work was contracted out.

Post-war mechanisms were 12V.

-	7118 LMS black 6-8V DC electric - *38-60*	300	350

L3. LNER J39 Goods 0-6-0 (by Vulcan) (1964)

The Gresley standard 0-6-0 freight locomotive of 1926 was the first post-Grouping LNER 0-6-0 locomotive to be built and replaced many of the 0-6-0 locomotives that the LNER inherited in 1923 and which were approaching retirement age.

Bond's 0

This model was made by Harry D'Arcy of Vulcan of Kendal.

		£	£
-	4811 LNER black 12V DC electric - *64-69*	150	250
-	47260 BR black 12V DC electric - *64-69*	150	250

L4. Bond's Special Order Locomotives (1935)

The following is a list of locomotives that Bond's would build to order and to the customer's specification. The post-war mechanisms were 12V.

GWR

		£	£
-	4-4-0 Dean 'City' Class GWR 3440 *City of Truro* green 6-8V DC - *35-c55*	NPG	NPG
-	4-6-0 Collett 'King' Class GWR 6000 *King George V* green 6-8V DC - *35-c55*	2100	2300

LMS

Ex-CR 0-4-4T special order model [L4]

		£	£
-	0-4-4T LMS ex-CR 15201 black - ?	NPG	NPG
-	2-4-2T LMS ex-L&Y 1384 black 6-8V DC - *35-c55*	250	350
-	2-6-0 Stanier Mogul LMS red 6-8V DC - *35-c55*	NPG	NPG
-	4-6-0 Stanier Class 5MT LMS 5020 black 6-8V DC - *35-c55*	750	1300
-	4-6-2 Bowen-Cooke LMS ex-LNWR 6798 black 6-8V - *35-c55*	350	450
-	as above but red - *35-c55*	350	450
-	4-6-2 Stanier 'Princess Royal' Class LMS maroon 6200 *The Princess Royal* 6-8V DC - *35-c55*	2100	2300

LNER

		£	£
-	2-6-2T Gresley V1 Class LNER black 6-8V DC - *35-c55*	850	1100
-	0-6-2 Worsdell Class N10 LNER black - *35-c55*	NPG	NPG
-	4-6-2 Gresley A3 Class LNER 4472 *Flying Scotsman* green 6-8V DC - *35-c55*	NPG	NPG
-	as above but black - *35-c55*	2100	2300

SR

		£	£
-	0-6-0T Stroudley Class E1 SR 0-6-0T - ?	NPG	NPG
-	0-4-4 LSWR 73 green - ?	NPG	NPG
-	4-6-0 Urie N15 Class SR A767 *Sir Valence* green 6-8V DC - *35-c55*	NPG	NPG
-	4-6-0 Maunsell LN Class SR 850 *Lord Nelson* green 6-8V DC - *35-c55*	NPG	NPG

Bond's continued to build models to order in gauges 0 and 1 and, in their catalogues during the 1970s, illustrated an LMS 6247 *City of Liverpool* they had built for a Mr Liverpool.

L5. Hunslet Diesel Shunter 0-6-0DS (1932)

The diesel shunter had a short wheelbase making it very versatile in railway yards, dock yards and on industrial sites. When the model was introduced in 1932, the real locomotives were new on the railway scene.

		£	£
-	3 black electric - *32-40?*	250	300
-	3 green electric - *32-40?*	250	300

L6. LMS Main Line Diesel Twins Co-Co (1956)

Ex-LMS main line diesel 10001 [L6] (Vectis)

A year before Nationalisation of the railways, the LMS announced its intention to build two experimental main line diesel locomotives. No.10000 emerged from Derby Works in November 1947 and No.10001 arrived in July the following year. They worked main line passenger services on both the London Midland Region and the Southern Region, as well as freight trains. They were eventually scrapped in the mid 1960s.

Only a small batch of models was made.

		£	£
-	10000 BR black electric - *56*	3500	4000
-	10001 BR black electric - *56*	3500	4000

COACHES

In the 1920s, Bond's sold a range of coach bodies of their own manufacture, but also stocked coaches by Marklin, Bing, Bassett-Lowke, Leeds and others. Those of German origin (especially Marklin) had their identity concealed after the First World War. In the 1930s the company offered its own range of wooden bodied hand-painted coaches which were of a good quality. After the Second World War the 0 gauge range stocked by Bond's was limited to Exley's and kits by CCW and Ratio. However, they continued to sell their own coach fittings into the 1960s.

Cat No.	Company, Number, Colour, Date	£	£

C1. 1927 Wooden Coach Bodies

These unpainted wooden bodies were sold without bogies but were glazed. They were based on real prototypes and varied in length according to the subject modelled - 15", 16" and 17". Fittings including bogies were available separately.

Cat No.	Description	£	£
C8/Q	Pullman coach - *27-32*	15	20
C8/R	Pullman kitchen - *27-32*	15	20
C8/I	GWR 57' corridor 1st/3rd - *27-32*	15	20
C8/J	GWR corridor brake 3rd - *27-32*	15	20
C8/K	GWR 57' 1st/3rd diner - *27-32*	15	20
C8/L	GWR 70' corridor 1st/3rd - *27-32*	15	20
C8/M	GWR 70' brake 3rd - *27-32*	15	20
C8/N	GWR 70' 1st/3rd diner - *27-32*	15	20
C8/O	GWR 57' old type corridor 1st/3rd - *27-32*	15	20
C8/P	GWR 57' old type brake 3rd - *27-32*	15	20
C8/A	LMS 57' corridor 1st - *27-32*	15	20
C8/B	LMS 57' corridor 1st/3rd - *27-32*	15	20
C8/C	LMS 57' brake 3rd - *27-32*	15	20
C8/D	LMS 50' all 3rd - *27-32*	15	20
C8/E	50' kitchen car - *27-32*	15	20
C8/F	GNR LNER 60' corridor 1st/3rd - *27-32*	15	20
C8/G	GNR LNER 57' corridor brake 3rd - *27-32*	15	20
C8/H	GNR LNER 57' 1st/3rd diner - *27-32*	15	20

C2. 1932 Ready-made Coaches

Between 1932 and the outbreak of the Second World War, Bond's advertised 'New Super Detail Coaches' in their catalogues but little detail of the types available was given. They were a range of corridor and 'suburban' coaches, the latter term applying to non-corridor coaches without gangway connections. It is assumed that the models were built to order in their own workshop.

We know that the wooden and hand-painted bodies were not all of a standard design but were specific to the companies whose livery they carried and varied in length accordingly. They had glass in the windows, corridor compartments and separate door handles fitted. They also had bogies of special construction, metal wheels, oval brass buffers and corridor coaches had corridor connections, where appropriate. They were not quite so heavy in proportion as the Milbro coaches and sold at a standard price of £1-18-6. The listing below is based on very limited evidence and the author would welcome further information.

GWR

		£	£
-	dark brown+cream corridor 1st/3rd - *32-40*	120	170
-	dark brown+cream corridor brake - *32-40*	120	170
-	dark brown+cream suburban coach - *32-40*	120	170
-	dark brown+cream suburban brake - *32-40*	120	170

GWR all-3rd corridor coach [C2]

Bond's 0

LMS		
crimson corridor 1st/3rd - *32-40*	120	170
crimson corridor all 3rd - *32-40*	120	170
crimson corridor brake 3rd - *32-40*	120	170
crimson suburban coach - *32-40*	120	170
crimson suburban brake - *32-40*	120	170
LNER		
teak Gresley corridor 1st/3rd - *32-40*	120	170
teak Gresley corridor brake - *32-40*	120	170
teak suburban coach - *32-40*	120	170
teak suburban brake - *32-40*	120	170
SR		
green corridor coach - *32-40*	120	170
green corridor brake end - *32-40*	120	170
green suburban coach - *32-40*	120	170
green suburban brake - *32-40*	120	170

WAGONS

From the mid 1920s, these were listed as 'True Scale Model Wagons' and described as 'models of lesser known types of goods stock'. The original dozen or so, dated at least from 1923 and could have been earlier. However, it is thought that it was not until 1926 that they were identified as having been made by a Sheffield company known as the Miniature Reproductions Company (MRCo). Earlier ones may have been made by Bonds.

The MRCo wagons were sold almost exclusively by Bond's between the mid '20s and the outbreak of the Second World War. Sixteen more models were added to the range from 1932 and are assumed to have come from the same supplier, but may have been made in Bond's workshop.

The majority were made of wood and fitted with sprung 3-link couplings and oval head buffers (3/6 extra). All had turned cast iron wheels and some had metal chassis; the hopper and well wagons were all metal. It seems that while a stock of finished wagons was kept in the shop, the models could be finished to the customer's requirements, involving a few days delay and, until 1931, this included private owner liveries (1/- extra).

Bond's also sold wagons of other manufacturers including Marklin, Bing, Hornby, Jubb and the Leeds Model Company..

Cat No.	Company, Number, Colour, Date	£	£

Flat Wagons

W1. Machinery Flat Wagon (by MRCo.) (1928)
This was a 5.75" long flat wagon without superstructure, bolsters or sides but with a horizontal plank effect on the surface.

	flat top machinery truck - *28?-31*	25	30
	ditto with spring buffers/couplings - *28?-31*	25	30

W2a. Pre-Grouping Single Bolster Wagons (1923)
This was a shorter wagon than the later double bolster wagon and they were sold as a pair for long loads.

	H&BR 2 single bolster wagons with tree trunk load - *23-?*	25	30

W2b. Single Bolster Wagons (by MRCo.) (1929)
This was a shorter wagon than the double bolster wagon being 5.75" long.

	NE with single bolster - *29-33*	25	30
	as above with spring buffers/couplings - *29-33*	28	32

W3a. Pre-Grouping Double Bolster Wagons (1923)
Some will be found with company lettering and some without.

	CR double bolster with tree trunk load - *23-?*	25	30
	same wagon without the bolsters - flat truck (this was unusual in having an underframe) - *23-?*	25	30

W3b. Double Bolster Wagons (by MRCo.) (1926)
This was 8" long and both the 4-wheel and 6-wheel versions were shown in the catalogue.

	LMS double bolster timber wagon - *26-33*	25	30
	LMS 20T 6-wheel double bolster timber wagon - *26-40*	30	35
	ditto with spring buffers/couplings - *28-33*	32	37

W4. Pulley Wagon (by MRCo.) (1934)
This was a 12 ton flat wagon with side structures which supported a ship's propeller. The model was fitted with sprung buffers and couplings

	LNER 46470 + ship's propeller - *34-40*	70	80

W5. Trestle Wagon (by MRCo.) (1934)
This was a long wheelbase flat wagon with a trestle to support sheets of glass or metal. The model was fitted with sprung buffers and couplings.

	LNER 14710 - *34-40*	70	80

Open Wagons

W6. 1-plank Container Wagons (by MRCo.) (1932)
The models were fitted with all metal chassis, ladders, vacuum pipes, sprung buffers and couplings. The containers differ in style.

	GWR + **GWR** closed meat container - *34-40*	35	40
	LMS + **LMS** open container - *32-40*	35	40
	LMS + **LMS** closed container - *32-40*	35	40
	LNER + **LNER** open container - *32-40*	35	40
	LNER + **LNER** closed container - *32-40*	35	40

W7a. Pre-Grouping Ballast Wagon (1923)
This looked like a short 3-plank wagon with lettering and a number on its sides and the letters 'ED'. It was claimed to be 'in all leading railways' liveries', but only the LNWR one was illustrated.

	LNWR 3031? dropside Engineers' Dept - *23-?*	25	30

W7b. Ballast and Low-Sided Wagons (by MRCo.) (1926)
These were low-sided wagons and appear to have been shorter than other open wagons. They also had opening sides.

	private owner wagons - *36-40*	30	35
	LMS 15T ballast wagon - *26-40*	25	30
	as above but two end doors - *26-40*	25	30
	LNER 3-plank dropside fish truck with vacuum pipes - *28-40*	25	30
	as above with Westinghouse pipes - *28-40*	25	30
	LNER 12T ballast dropside - *26-40*	25	30

W8a. Pre-Grouping 5-plank Wagons (1923)
Like the rest of the early Bonds wagons, these had no brake gear..

	CR brown - *23-?*	25	30
	GCR grey - *23-?*	25	30
	GNR brown - *23-?*	25	30
	GWR grey - *23-?*	25	30
	LNWR grey - *23-?*	25	30
	MR grey - *23-?*	25	30

W8b. Post-Grouping 5-plank Wagons (by MRCo.) (1928)
This model had drop-down side doors.

	GWR 1171 dark grey - *28-40*	25	30
	LMS grey - *32-40*	25	30
	LNER grey - *32-40*	25	30
	SR dark brown - *32-40*	25	30

W9a. Pre-Grouping 7-plank Wagons (1923)
Like the rest of the early Bonds wagons, these had no brake gear..

	CR brown - *23-?*	25	30
	GCR grey - *23-?*	25	30
	GNR brown - *23-?*	25	30
	GWR grey - *23-?*	25	30
	LNWR 1177 grey 'Loco' - *23-?*	25	30
	MR grey - *23-?*	25	30

W9b. Post-Grouping 7-plank Wagons (by MRCo.) (1926)
End doors on these wagons were made so that they would open.

	private owner - various - *26-40*	25	30
	GWR 1171 dark grey - *28-40*	25	30
	LMS grey - *32-40*	25	30
	LNER grey - *32-40*	25	30
	SR dark brown - *32-40*	25	30

Hoppers & Tankers

W10. Small Hopper Wagons (by MRCo.) (1932)
This model was fitted with an all metal body and chassis, had an opening hopper door and had sprung buffers and couplings.

Bond's 0

-	'Roberts & Co.' - *32-40*	80	90
-	'City of Birmingham Gas Dept.' - *32-40*	80	90

W11. LMS Coke Hopper Wagon (by MRCo.) (1933)
This was a large all metal model of a 20 ton wagon, fitted with sprung buffers and couplings. It had rails around the top to increase its capacity for coke.
- **LMS** grey - *33-40* — 70 80

W12. GWR Hopper Wagon (by MRCo.) (1928)
The model illustrated in the catalogue had been specially made for a customer and it is implied that it would be made to order.
- **GWR** grey 'Loco' - *28-31* — 60 70

W13. 14T Tank Wagon (1923)
The model illustrated in the early catalogues was beautifully detailed and most likely was built to a customer's specification. By 1926 it was no longer listed.
- **'Mex Fuel Oil'** black Shell Mex - *23-?* — 80 100

Vans

W14. Lime Wagon (by MRCo.) (1932)
These were of all metal construction with a sliding roof door.
- various private owner names could be applied - *32-40* — 35 40

W15. Cattle Wagon (by MRCo.) (1932)
The model had correct open plank sides, dummy swing doors and flap (ramp). It was fitted with an all metal chassis, vacuum pipes, sprung buffers and couplings.
- **LMS** - *32-40* — 25 30
- **LNER** - *32-40* — 25 30

W16. Horse Box (by MRCo.) (1932)
The model had an all metal chassis.
- **LMS** - maroon? *32-40* — 25 30

W17a. Small Vans (1923)
These were short vans and looked as though they were on a 9ft chassis.
- **L&Y** brown? - *23 - ?* — 25 30
- **NER** 1531? white, refrigerator but with no end ladders - *23-?* — 25 30

W17b. Goods Vans (1928)
These had four opening and fastening doors. A refrigerator version was available with end ladders, built to order.
- **NE** van, 2 doors each side - *28-40* — 25 30
- as above but ventilated van - *28-40* — 25 30
- ditto + pipes + torpedo vents - *28-40* — 27 32
- ditto with dual braking - *28-40* — 27 32
- refrigerator van with end ladders - *28-40* — 30 35

W18. Ferry Wagon (by MRCo.) (1932)
This model was based on a real one on the Harwich-Zeebrugge ferry. The model had an all-metal chassis, sprung buffers and couplings and glazed windows.
- grey - *32-40* — 70 80

W19. Refrigerator Vans (by MRCo.) (1932)
The vans were fitted with all metal chassis, ladders, vacuum pipes, sprung buffers and couplings. The LNER and GWR versions had vents at each end.
- **LMS** - *32-40* — 25 30
- **SR** - *32-40* — 25 30
- **LNER** 139284 white - *32-40* — 25 30
- **GWR** white - *36-40* — 25 30

W20. Meat Van (by MRCo.) (1932)
These vans were fitted with an all-metal chassis.
- **LMS** - *32-40* — 25 30

W21. Fish Vans (by MRCo.) (1932)
These were fitted with all-metal chassis, ladders, vacuum pipes, sprung buffers and couplings.
- **LNER** dummy louvres - *32-40* — 25 30
- **LMS** dummy sliding doors - *32-40* — 25 30

Brake Vans

W22. Pre-Grouping Brake Vans (1923)
These were available in different company designs and varied considerably in shape.

- **GWR** typical 4-wheel 'Toad' - *23-?* — 25 30
- **NER** short 4-wheel, 2 verandas - *23-?* — 25 30
- **NBR** short 4-wheel, 1 veranda - *23-?* — 25 30
- **MR** 5943 short 4-wheel, 2 verandas (1 open) - *23-?* — 25 30

Wooden MR brake van [W22] (Vectis)

W23. Post-Grouping Brake Vans (by MRCo.) (1926)
These models were of a more recent style with a longer wheelbase, metal chassis, sprung buffers and couplings and glazed windows.
- **GWR** 20T - *33-40* — 27 32
- **LMS** (modern) - *32-40* — 27 32
- **LNER** short 4-wheel, 2 verandas - *26-33* — 25 30
- **LNER** with platforms - *32-40* — 27 32
- **SR** dark brown with platforms - *32-40* — 30 35
- 6-wheel - *28-33* — 30 35

Bogie Wagons

W24. Bogie Bolster Wagon (1923)
This early model was fitted with sprung buffers and couplings.
- bogie bolster wagon with a girder load - *23-40* — 80 100

W25. Well Wagons (by MRCo.) (1929)
This was a superb model with sprung bogies and buffers and a removable girder load. The model was 15.5" long.
- **LMS** with girder frame - *29-40* — 60 70
- ditto with brake wheels - *31-40* — 60 70
- ditto with LMS brakes fitted - *31-32* — 60 70
- **LNER** grey - *32-40* — 70 80
- 'H' section girder load - *32-40* — 25 30
- **GWR** grey - *32-40* — 70 80
- diesel road roller load - *33-40* — 25 30

W26. Bogie Open Wagon (by MRCo.) (1932)
The model was fitted with sprung buffers and couplings.
- bogie open wagon - *32-40* — 60 70

W27. LNER Bogie Hopper Wagon (by MRCo.) (1932)
This was an all-metal model of a 40 ton hopper wagon with sliding hopper doors. It had equalised bogies, end ladders, sprung buffers and couplings.
- **LNER** 100011 - *32-40* — 70 80

W28. Bogie Vans (by MRCo.) (1932)
These had 8 opening doors, but there is very little detail about them and they were not illustrated in the catalogues..
- bogie covered van - *32-40* — 70 80
- ditto with vents - *32-40* — 70 80
- ditto with vacuum pipes - *32-40* — 70 80
- ditto with brake gear - *32-40* — 70 80

Bowman

HISTORY

Although Bowman built locomotives for only 10 years, this firm's products had a major impact on the live steam locomotive market and many enthusiasts are continuing to run these engines.

Geoffrey Bowman Jenkins (born in 1891) took out his first patent in 1919. This was for driving a toy locomotive with elastic. He had also patented a number of ideas for toy steam boats, which he was successfully making in London and in 1923 he was invited to join forces with the well established firm of Hobbies Ltd at Dereham in Norfolk, who traded in materials and tools for keen amateur woodworkers. With Jenkins' ideas and Hobbies machinery and marketing, the firm Bowman Models was established.

'Baby Bowman' 0-4-0T [L1] (Vectis)

The powerful single-acting oscillating-cylinder engines were first placed in a series of successful steamboats and then developed onto horizontal stationary engines. In 1925, the first of three non-reversing model railway locomotives was placed on the market, most being powered by two oscillating cylinders. In 1927 a patent was obtained for his design of track and the following year Jenkins exhibited his models at the British Industries Fair. During this, a 4-4-0 locomotive with six Bowman coaches behind it clocked up 183 miles. It was refuelled every 40 minutes and the success of this exercise lead directly to Bassett-Lowke developing their Enterprise 4-4-0 model to achieve a similar performance.

The scale of these locomotives was really gauge 1 which allowed for the use of a large boiler and burner (meths fired) but the wheels were set to gauge 0. At this stage, gauge 1 was on the decline so it was advantageous to have models which would run on the more popular 0 gauge track.

Most of the brass parts were made in Birmingham but assembly and finishing was done at Dereham. It was there also that the wooden parts such as sleepers and rolling stock parts were made. Initially the models were packed in wooden boxes but, later, card ones were used. These could be identified by their brown and cream striped finish.

The production of Bowman trains was run down during the early 1930s and had ceased by 1935, when Jenkins started the Jentique furniture-making firm and the following year parted company with Hobbies Ltd. The only post-war production of Bowman was stationary and marine engines done at Luton. These were made until about 1950. Jenkins died in 1959. The withdrawal of Jenkins from Hobbies Ltd left a gap which was filled by Geoffrey Malins and this lead to the Mamod range.

Bowman items used to be very cheap but the market has risen over recent years.

Prices - The two prices shown represent the likely range for one in good condition.

Small 0-4-0T [L2] (Vectis)

LOCOMOTIVES

The largest locomotive was a 4-4-0 tender engine whilst the other three were 0-4-0 tanks, one being smaller in size and a bit nearer 0 scale. Strictly speaking, the wheel arrangements were not as just described, as the locomotives had no coupling rods, only connecting rods to the rear set of wheels.

Although you will go a long way before you will find a real locomotive looking quite like a Bowman, with its long thin cylinders and distinctive safety valve, Bowman locomotives were characterised by their simple design, sound engineering and superb performance.

Power and speed were effectively controlled by blanking off up to three of the burner wicks with burner caps, making the engine quite docile and able to trundle round 2ft curves without a load. Unfortunately the wick caps were often lost and in later years operated on full throttle unless substitute wick caps or plugs were fitted. This gave them a reputation for being too fast and needing plenty of stock behind them to slow them down and keep them on the track.

Most models carried an oval badge on cabside marked 'Bowman Patent' or, on later models, 'Bowman Models'

Large 0-4-0T [L3] (Vectis)

Cat No.	Company, Number, Colour, Date	£	£

L1. Small 0-4-0 Tank Engine (Freelance) (1932)

This model had a single oscillating cylinder on the cab floor driving the rear axle by gearing. It is sometimes called the 'Baby Bowman' and it had an oversize bunker. It did not carry company identification lettering and the most common colour was the light green used by the LNER.

Cat No.	Company, Number, Colour, Date	£	£
410	light green with black & white lining - *32-34*	175	250
410	black - *32-34*	200	275

L2. Small 0-4-0 Tank Engine (Freelance) (1927)

This was the neatest looking of the three tank engines and had the smallest bunker. It also had outside cylinders.

Cat No.	Company, Number, Colour, Date	£	£
300	**300** LNER green with black & white lining - *27-35*	100	140
300	**300** LMS black - *27-35*	120	160
300	**300** LMS maroon with yellow & black lining - *27-35*	100	140
30	**30** LMS maroon - *27-35*	150	200

Bowman

L3. Large 0-4-0 Tank Engine (Freelance) (1927)

This was a larger tank engine with outside cylinders and a bunker size between that of the other two.

Cat	Description	£	£
265	**265** LNER green with black & white lining - *27-35*	100	140
265	**265** LNER black with red double lining - *27-35*	120	160
265	**265** LMS maroon with yellow double lining - *27-35*	100	140
265	**265** LMS black with red double lining - *27-35*	120	160

4-4-0 tender loco [L4] (Vectis)

L4. 4-4-0 Tender Locomotive (Freelance) (1927)

The finishes changed over the years but it is not known when these changes occurred. The dates given therefore indicate the period over which the model was made and not the specific dates of the livery style. Incorrect numbering appears on some models.

Cat	Description	£	£
234	**4073** GWR green also numbered - *27-35*	250	350
234	**13000** (on cabsides) LMS (on tender) black with heavy double red lining - *27-35*	200	275
234	**13000** LMS (both on tender) black with thinner double red lining - *27-35*	175	250
234	**13000** LMS (both on tender) red with thinner double yellow lining - *27-35*	160	210
234	**4472** LNER (both on tender) light green with doulble thinner black and white lining - *27-35*	150	200
234	**4472** LNER black - *27-35*	NPG	NPG
234	**453** SR green also numbered - *27-35*	250	350

COACHES

Without doubt the passenger coach was the most attractive model made by Bowman. It was a bogie coach with a heavy wooden base and ends but with nicely lithographed tin sides. It had opening doors and a pair of large gas cylinders under the floor. No brake coach was made. Like the locomotives, the coach was built to gauge 1 proportions but for 0 gauge track. They are not common and consequently can be more expensive to buy than the locomotives.

Cat No.	Company, Number, Colour, Date	£	£

LNER coach [C1] (Vectis)

C1. 1st/3rd Composite (1927)

The same model was available in three different liveries.

Cat	Description	£	£
551	**LNER** 17172 teak - *27-35*	180	260
551	**GWR** 10152 dark brown+cream - *27-35*	180	260
551	**LMS** 10153 maroon - *27-35*	180	260

WAGONS

Bowman produced wagons to go with the locomotives and again, although 0 gauge, they were built to gauge 1 proportions. A range of 0 scale wagons was planned but never made. In June 1933 retailers were informed that the wagons were no longer available. The open wagon and brake van had the 'Bowman Models' badge on each end, the tank wagon was badged on the side and the timber wagons carried no badge.

The wagons were made of wood with neatly printed detail which was probably printed onto thin paper and well stuck on so that it appeared to have been printed onto the surface of the wood. The light grey of the wagons had a greeny tinge, probably due to a discolouration of the varnish used to seal it.

Cat No.	Company, Number, Colour, Date	£	£

4 wagons made by Bowman [W1-W4] (Lacy, Scott & Knight)

W1. Timber Wagon (1927)

This consisted of the wooden chassis used for the open wagon and brake van but with flat tin 'bolster pins' holding in place six pieces of sawn timber. The wagon had brass buffers.

Cat	Description	£	£
664	**LMS** light grey - *27-35*	30	40
664	**LNER** light grey - *27-35*	30	40

W2. 5-plank Open Wagon (1927)

The wagon body and the wagon frame on which it sat, were in wood with a printed paper covering. It had brass buffers and printed pressed tin axle boxes.

Cat	Description	£	£
661	**LMS** light grey - *27-35*	35	50
661	**LNER** light grey - *27-35*	35	50

W3. Tank Wagon (1927)

This wagon also used the standard wooden chassis on which a wooden cradle held the tank, which appears to have been the boiler of the Baby Bowman tank engine.

Cat	Description	£	£
663	**Shell** red - *27-35*	60	75

W4. Brake Van (1927)

The wooden brake van body had cut-out windows at one end of the sides and a window in each end wall. It had brass buffers and a tin roof. The frame and solebars were also made of wood and the axle hangers were a printed tin pressing.

Cat	Description	£	£
662	**LMS** light grey - *27-35*	40	55
662	**LNER** light grey - *27-35*	40	55

Dapol 00

HISTORY

David Boyle, of Highfield Birds & Models, who in 1981 had been unsuccessful in a bid to buy the model railway division of Airfix when the company was being broken up and sold off, founded a company with his wife Pauline called Dapol. This was established to handle a large amount of Airfix stock and spares that he had been able to acquire. Boyle's ambition all along was to produce a range of a British outline locomotives and rolling stock of a quality in performance and detail that previously had been foud only in some Continental ranges.

L&Y 'Pug' 0-4-0ST [L1]

Research and development had already commenced with a L&Y 'Pug', a GWR 'County' Class 4-6-0 and an Austerity (J94) saddle tank to the extent that plans had been drawn and the tools manufactured.

When Airfix stock ran low, Boyle had new moulds made of some of the old Airfix wagons, which went on the market in November 1983. His company also commenced the production of the ex-L&Y 'Pug' which was released the following year, and the Hawksworth 'County' which arrived soon after.

When Palitoy closed down in 1985, David Boyle was finally offered the Airfix tools as well as the intellectual assets of Palitoy's Mainline Railways range and unsold stock. There followed a merging of Airfix, Mainline and Dapol products under the Dapol name. In fact, very few Mainline designs were used, except for old stock, as the vast majority of the tools for them belonged to the production company in Hong Kong - Kader.

Dapol next took over the remnants of some of the Trix Trains/Liliput UK range in the late '80s and these included the tooling for bodies of the E3000 and 'Transpennine' DMU, the chassis remaining with Liliput in Austria and ending up with Bachmann.

Dapol also bought the tools and intellectual assets of G&R Wrenn in 1992 and some wagons from the Wrenn ranged joined the Dapol catalogue. Some of these were sold on chassis purchased from Bachmann when the latter turned over their production to the Blue Riband range. Dapol also make plastic kits from the former Airfix and Kitmaster tools and have added one or two of their own. At one time they also made kits from former Tri-ang Model-Land tools.

Stock was stored in various places including Boyle's own home. From time to time, forgotten boxes of obsolete stock emerged and the contents sold, often through Dapol's shop - especially at their Windsford addresses in Cheshire. Some of this stock was never advertised, making it difficult to record what and when models were released.

In 1994, Dapol started to move their entire operation to Llangollen, in Wales, where they opened an exhibition called 'Model Railway World', which at one time included some of the former Wrenn machines and tools which had started life in the Hornby Dublo production line at the Meccano factory in Liverpool. It was while this move was in progress during 1995 that a servere fire at the Winsford factory destroyed much of the stock and damaged a number of tools.

To raise much needed capital, some of the Dapol and former Airfix tools were offered to Bachmann but, subsequently, were sold to Hornby in 1996. Almost all of these are back in production out in China, having undergone further improvements. Dapol, however,

Photo of a Hornby 'Battle of Britain' Class model Computer enhanced by Robbie McGavin and titled 'Blower On'

Dapol 00

continued to produce limited runs of some of these models from their stock of parts.

In April 1999, Dapol Ltd parted company with its founder, David Boyle, and came under the management of Pauline Boyle with George Smith as Director of Corporate Affairs. Later, following the death of Pauline Boyle, George Smith took over direction of the company as Managing Director.

At the 2000 Warley National Model Railway Exhibition, Dapol announced one of their largest projects for several years - the production of a model of a 'Pendolino'. The model was in the shops a year later. At about the same time, having extracted what they wanted from the Wrenn tooling, the company sold the remainder, the archives and intellectual assets of G&R Wrenn to Mordvale Ltd.

In January 2004, the company moved once more, this time to an industrial unit at Chirk on the Welsh/English border. This gave them the opportunity to dispense with much of the clutter from the past and consolidate on what had become their main products - 00 gauge private owner wagons and a new and serious bid for part of the N gauge market. In 2005 they started to upgrade the 00 wagon range with new tooling. By 2006 they had established themselves as a major competitor to Bachmann's Graham Farish range and were now showing that they could also compete with models of modern wagons in 00 scale.

GWR Castle Class [L20]

Confusion - This is a very difficult range to record as there was such a mix-up of old stock from other manufacturers, that was repackaged, and new batches made by Dapol from the old tooling - often with the same running number. There were also models made from duplicate tools produced for Dapol in the Far East.

An example of this problem may be seen with Dapol's coaches which are a mixture of ex-Airfix, ex-Mainline and Dapol manufactured. Some of the 'Dapol' variety have 'Dapol' printed on the underside. However, several have the Mainline arc with 'Railways' printed below it. The word 'Mainline' has been blanked out and 'Dapol' printed above the arc. To make matters more difficult, there are two versions of the (now blank) arc. In the case of one, it looks as if the name 'Mainline' has been removed from the mould using a file, as there are vertical striations where the word had been. In the case of the other, the arc is totally smooth and appears never to have had any writing on it. I have not attempted to seperate out these variations in the following listing.

Also, beware of strange locomotives with swapped tenders, wrong numbers and even carrying a different name on each side. This seems to be particularly prevalent amongst the 'Counties' and 'Castles'. This suggests that quality control was not a high priority in the early days of Dapol production, especially that done by Dapol themselves. This is a far cry from the standards set today.

Confusion is sometimes caused today due to the company changing its plans on detail (catalogue numbers, running numbers, livery etc.) after its initial announcement. It is very difficult to know whether the new information published refers to extra batch or is a replacement for the original one. There will be quite a few models in the tables in this chapter which were substituted and so were never made. The information is as accurate as that available at the time of publication.

Dates - I have found little information about when early models first became available or when they were no longer being produced. The dates quoted are based largely on press advertising and model reviews in magazines. They are for rough guidance only. One of the reasons for uncertainty is the haphazard stock control in the early days. It resulted in boxes of stock being discovered and offered for sale long after they were thought to have sold out. Collectors are advised to exercise caution in using catalogues when attempting to date models and to not take too literally the dates quoted in the lists below.

The only date provided below is the year that the model is thought to have first become available in the shops, through Dapol.

Packaging - Items in the following lists shown as 'ex-Airfix stock' or 'ex-Mainline stock' were, as far as is known, sold in their original packaging.

(A) = ex-Airfix stock
(M) = ex-Mainline stock

Further Reading

There was a series of articles by Graham Smith-Thompson in *Model Railway Enthusiast* magazine in August to November 1999 issues. This profiled the Airfix and Mainline ranges and other systems that later used the tools.

Weathering - This is popular with many modellers today, giving models a more realistic appearance. 'Weathered' models have been given a light spay with a thin grey or brown paint to give the appearance of dirt blown up from the track. To save space, weathered models are coded in the text with a 'W' after the colour.

LOCOMOTIVES

Cat No.	Company, Number, Colour, Date	£	£

Tank Engines

0-4-0T

L1. L&Y Class B7 'Pug' 0-4-0ST (1984)

Aspinall designed these tiny locomotives, which were built at Horwich, and the first of the 57 built started work in 1891. They were usually found in dock areas where the short wheelbase was essential for the tight curves. The last was withdrawn by BR in 1963 and two have been preserved.

The model was developed by Dapol in 1984 and the tools sold to Hornby in 1996 and the model is still made by them. The 1999 released models listed in this table were made from a stock of parts held by Dapol.

D10	**19** L&Y black - *90*	28	38
D1	**11217** LMS black - *84*	30	40
D?	**821** WD black, spark arrester fitted to chimney, Ltd Edn 100 - *99?*	65	85
D?	**402** black Ltd Edn 100 - *03*	40	60
D2	**51241** BRb black - *84*	28	38

L2. Y1/3 Class Sentinal 100hp 4wVBT (2011)

This is made exclusively for Model Rail magazine, with a 5-pole super-creep motor with flywheel, low gear, 8-pin DCC socket, NEM couplers, wire handrails, flush glazing and various detail changes.

Y1/3 Class Sentinal [L2] (Model Rail)

Dapol 00

MR-001	**13** GWR plain green - *11*	60	72
MR-006	**7161** LMS plain black - *12*	60	72
MR-002	**150** LNER plain black - *11*	60	72
MR-003	**68184** BRb plain black - *11*	60	72
MR-007	**68150** BRb plain black - *12*	60	72
MR-008	**54** BRb plain black (Y1 Departmental) - *12*	60	72
MR-004	**57** BRc Departmental plain black - *11*	60	72
MR-009	***Isebrook*** (industrial) lined black Ltd Edn 300 - *12*	60	72
MR-005	**281** Great Southern Railway (Ireland) black - *12*	60	72

0-4-2T

L3. GWR Class 14xx 0-4-2T (ex-Airfix) (1985)

The model is based on Collett's 1932 design of a small locomotive suitable for light branch lines. 95 were built, the first 75 with push-pull equipment. The last was withdrawn in 1965 and four have been preserved.

The model first appeared in the Airfix catalogue in 1978 and two versions were made. The tooling passed to Palitoy in 1981 and to Dapol (along with unsold Airfix stock) in 1985. Those produced by Dapol are listed in this table. In 1996, Dapol sold the tools to Hornby who solved its running problems and they still make the model. Some stored parts were used by Dapol for a batch of locomotives in 1999 and 2002.

D19	**1466** GWR green (A) - *85*	20	30
D19	**1420** GWR (button) green, new chassis - *95*	22	35
D97	**1459**** GWR black, new chassis - *95*	25	35
D97	**1466** GWR black, new chassis - *95*	25	35
D97S1	**4803** GWR green, Ltd Edn 1200 - *99*	65	90
D96	**1438***BRb black, new chassis - *95*	25	35
?	**1401** BR black, from film Titfield Thunderbolt, Ltd Edn 100 *** - *02*	50	70
D20	**1466** BRc lined green (A) - *85*	22	32

* also shown in catalogue as 1442. **also shown as black 1456 in 1989 catalogue.
*** this model was claimed by Dapol to be their last limited edition locomotive.

2-4-0T

L4. LSWR 0289 Beattie Well Tank 2-4-0WT (2011)

These were built by Beyer Peacock in 1874 to a design by W.G.Beattie, which was based on one by his father Joseph. 85 were built as suburban tanks for the London & South Western Railway and were based at Nine Elms. As suburban loads increased, they were replaced by more powerful locomotives and were moved out to rural areas. Two of those passed to BR in 1948 have been preserved.

This model was sponsored by Kernow Model Railway Centre. It has a 5-pole motor with a flywheel, 8-pin DCC socket with provision for a sound chip and load speaker. It has NEM coupling pockets, opening smokebox door and modelled smokebox interior and an accessory pack for individualising the model.

K2054	**3329** SR black, Maunsell lettering - *11*	78	92
K2055	**3314** SR black, 'Sunshine' lettering - *11*	80	95
K2051	**30587** BRb black - *11*	75	90
K2052	**30586** BRb black - *11*	75	90
K2053	**30585** BRc black - *11*	75	90

0-4-4T

L5. LSWR Class O2 0-4-4T (2013)

These Adams 0-4-4 tank engines were built by the L&SWR at Nine Elms in 1889. Between then and 1889, 60 were built and were a lighter version of Adams' T1 tanks. They were built for secondary passenger traffic and goods on lighter routes, replacing worn out Beattie tanks. First withdrawals took place in the 1930s and most survived into the 1950s. One survives in preservation on the Isle of Wight.

At the time of writing the model had not been released.

K2105	**225** SR black - *13*	NPG	120
K2101	**24** *Calbourne* BRb black - *13*	NPG	120
K2103	**30182** BRb black with push-pull equipment - *13*	NPG	120
K2106	**30193** BRb black - *13*	NPG	120
K2102	**16** *Ventnor* BRc black - *13*	NPG	120
K2104	**20225** BRc black - *13*	NPG	120

0-6-0T

L6. GWR Class 57xx 0-6-0PT (ex-Mainline) (1985)

This was Collett's pannier tank design of 1929, but with a Churchward cab. 863 were built, the first in 1929 and the last in 1950. 13 were sold to London Transport between 1957 and 1963. The last was withdrawn by BR in 1966 and by LT in 1971. 16 of the class have been preserved, including 6 of those sold to London Transport.

Dapol had only remnant Mainline Railways stock to sell, having bought it on the closure of Palitoy production, as the tools belonged to Kader in China.

D61	**5768** BRb black (M) - *85*	30	38

L7. LNER Class J72 0-6-0T (ex-Mainline) (1985)

This was Wilson Worsdell's 1898 design for the North Eastern Railway, for goods yard shunting. They were built over a long period of time, initially at Darlington but also contracted out to Armstrong Whitworth & Co. The LNER built some at Doncaster and BR built a batch at Darlington between 1949 and 1951. The last was withdrawn in 1966 and one has been preserved.

Again, Dapol did not receive the tooling for this model as the tools were owned by Kader. They did, however, buy the unsold stock which is what features here.

D56	***Joem*** North Eastern green (M) - *85*	20	28
D54	**581** LNER green (M) - *85*	20	28
D55	**68745** BRa black, Ross pop safety valves (M) - *85*	20	28
D57	**69001** BRb black, enclosed safety valves (M) - *85*	18	26

L8. LBSCR 'Terrier' 0-6-0T (1988)

This is based Stroudley's Class A1 'Terrier' tank engine of 1872, as redeveloped by Marsh in 1911, to form the Class A1X. 50 were built as suburban and branch line passenger locomotives and for shunting duties. As they were replaced by more powerful engines, their lightness proved useful to others and several were sold to other railway companies and some to industry. The last was withdrawn in 1963 and 10 have been preserved.

The Terrier tank model was designed and tooled by Dapol and first released in 1989. It was a good choice of subject as the little tanks had long been favourites with British enthusiasts. The tooling was sold to Hornby in 1996 who still make the model. However, before the tooling was handed over, Dapol produced a stock of parts for future use and these were used to produce the limited edition versions of the model released between 1997 and 1999.

SR 'Terrier' tank [L8]

D69	**662** LBSC Marsh Umber - *89*	35	45
D100	**82** *Boxhill* LBSC yellow-brown - *89*	35	45
D101	**82** *Boxhill* LBSC yellow-brown as D100 but Ltd Edn - *99*	50	75
D102	**55** *Stepney* LBSC yellow-brown - *90*	50	65
D70	**2635** SR lined green - *89*	35	45
D6A	**2655** SR dark green Ltd Edn 100 - *98*	75	90
D101S2	**B636** SR black Ltd Edn - *99*	75	90
D?	**2647** SR plain black Ltd Edn 100 - *01*	85	130
D101S1	**2659** SR black, wartime 'Sunshine' lettering Ltd Edn 100 - *97*	75	90
D72	**6** GWR (button) green - *88*	35	45
D101S3	**5** *Portishead* GWR (button) green Ltd Edn 100 - *11*	80	95
D71	**32640** BRb lined black - *89*	30	40

L9. SR Class USA 0-6-0T

This model was commissioned by Model Rail magazine. However, in August 2013 it was announced that the model would no longer be developed by Dapol and the contract had been given to Bachmann.

L10. WD Austerity J94 0-6-0ST (1985)

This was Riddles powerful and versitile tank engine based on a Hunslet Class 50550 design. 391 were built for the government during the Second World War, using various builders. A further 93 were built for other customers. The J94 class code was applied to 75 locomotives bought by the LNER after the war and which passed to BR in 1948. Many others were sold to the National Coal Board and to private industry. Of the 484 built, 70 are still in existance, mostly on railway heritage sites.

The model was designed by Dapol and was revolutionary at the time in having sprung buffers. In need of money after a devistating fire, it was amongst tooling sold to Hornby in 1996. However, before the tooling was handed over, Dapol produced a stock of parts for future use and these were used to produce the limited edition versions of the model released in 1998.

Dapol 00

LNER Class J94 [L10]

D7	**WD150** *Warrington* WD* deep grey - *85*		25	40
D?	**8049** LNER 'Desert Sand' livery Ltd Edn 125 - *98*		65	85
D?	**8054** LNER black Ltd Edn 125 - *98*		65	85
D8B	**68034** BRb black - *86*		25	40
D9	**68080** BR black ** - *90*		22	38
D8A	**68077** BRc black, rectangular windows - *86*		25	40
D8C	**68068** BRc black, round windows - *86*		25	40

* Under-feeder stoker type chimney, preserved livery. ** With extended bunker kit and corrected balance weights. An EM wheel conversion kit was available.

0-6-2T

L11.   GWR Class 56xx 0-6-2T (ex-Mainline) (1985)

200 of these Collett designed heavy freight tanks were built at Swindon between 1924 and 1928. They were mostly to work coal trains in the Welsh valleys and gradually replaced older tank engines that had been absorbed by the GWR in 1923. In the Welsh Valleys they were also used on passenger trains and this led to some being given a lined Brunswick green livery in later years. The last was withdrawn from BR service in 1966 and 9 have been preserved.

With the closure of Palitoy production, Dapol bought the remnant stock which is listed here.

D60	**6697** GWR green (M) - *85*		30	35
D59	**6652** BRb black (M) - *85, 98*		30	35

L12.   LNER Class N2 0-6-2T (ex-Airfix) (1985)

This was a Gresley design of suburban tank introduced on the Great Northern Railway in 1920. A total of 107 were built and most of them worked out of Kings Cross and Moorgate. 40 of these were built without the condensing pipes for use in Scotland, in particular the Glasgow suburbs, but only one member of the class has been preserved.

The model was designed by Airfix and tooled in China, but the models arrived after Airfix had gone into receivership. They passed to Palitoy who sold them in their Mainline range. On the demise of Palitoy, the tooling and outstanding stock was bought by Dapol who sold the stock but did not reuse the tooling before they sold it to Hornby. The model is still made by Hornby.

D51	**4744** LNER lined black (M) - *85*		28	38
D53	**9522** LNER lined green (M) - *85*		22	30
D52	**69532** BRb lined black (M) - *85*		22	30

2-6-2T

L13.   GWR Class 61xx 'Prairie' 2-6-2T (ex-Airfix) (1985)

This was a Collett Prairie tank design of 1931 and 70 were built. They were the GWR's London suburban tank engines and were required to pull heavy suburban trains from Paddington at fairly high speeds. Like most suburban tank engines, they were displaced by diesel multiple units and were moved on to parcel trains and empty stock duties.

The model dates from 1977 when it joined the Airfix range. It passed to Palitoy in 1981 and to Dapol in 1985, along with outstanding Airfix and Mainline stock. Dapol sold the stock and did not make any additional models before they sold the tools to Hornby, who still make it.

D22*	**6110** Great Western green (A) - *85*		18	32
D24*	**6169** GWR green (M) - *85*		27	35
D21	**6167** BRb liner black (A) - *85*		20	32
D23	**6167** BRc lined green (M) - *85*		27	35

* Some confusion exists as to which number applied to which loco.

Tender Engines

4-4-0

L14.   LMS Class 2P 4-4-0 (ex-Mainline) (1985)

Here we have Fowler's 1928 version of a 2P Class, which was a rebuild of Johnson's Midland Railway 4-4-0 design. Most were built at Derby from where at least three, built in 1928, went straight into S&DJR Prussian blue livery. The locomotives were found on suburban and country services, but all had gone by the end of 1962. None was preserved.

The model was developed by Palitoy for their Mainline Railways range, using the former Airfix Fowler 4F tender, and it was released in 1984. This was the year Palitoy went out of business and some were sent to shops without their outer boxes. As a Palitoy model which was not tooled by Kader, it was amongst the assets purchased by Dapol, along with unsold stock, which then went out in Dapol packaging. Dapol produced their own versions of the model and the tooling was sold to Hornby in 1996 and is still made by them.

Ex-LMS Class 2P [L14]

D15	**635** LMS lined black (M) - *85*		32	42
D17	**563** LMS lined maroon - *86*		30	38
D67	**45** SDJR very dark blue - *88*		32	40
D16	**40568** BRb lined black (M) - *85*		30	40
D16A	**40567** BRb lined black - *90*		30	38
D16B	BRb lined black - *90*		NPG	NPG
D16C	**40569** BRb lined black - *90*		32	40

L15.   U.S. 4-4-0 (ex-Bachmann/Airfix) (1985)

This was outstanding stock of the model Airfix had bought from Bachmann for their 1977 train sets.

D33	*Jupiter* red+silver (A) - *85-94*		25	35

0-6-0

L16.   GWR 2301 'Dean Goods' 0-6-0 (ex-Airfix) (1985)

This was Dean's standard 0-6-0 goods locomotive of 1883. Although it was designed for goods traffic, it also undertook light passenger duties. Their lightness meant that they could go anywhere on the GWR network. 62 saw service in France during the First World War and 108 were sent abroad during the Second World War. Only 54 of the class passed to British Railways and these were soon being replaced by standard 2-6-0s. One of Dean's locos has been preserved.

Airfix designed the model around 1980 and the tools were made by Heller in France. The model had tender drive and a single batch were produced before Airfix went into receivership. Palitoy inherited the stock and released it as part of their Mainline range. The tools and remaining stock passed to Dapol on the demise of Palitoy and they sold the remaining stock and produced the four new versions also listed in this table. Dapol sold the tools to Hornby in 1996 and the model is still available.

D18A	**3329** Great Western green - *86*		25	38
D018S1	**3314** Great Western green Ltd Edn - *99*		65	90
D18	**30587** GWR green (M) - *85*		28	38
D18B	**30586** GWR green - *86*		25	38
D18C	**30585** GWR (button) green - *86*		25	38
D50	**2538** BRb black (M) - *85*		28	38

L17.   LMS Class 4F 0-6-0 (ex-Airfix) (1985)

This was Fowler's Midland Railway design of 1911, based on Johnson's smaller loco of similar form, built for the Midland Railway. The building of them carried on until 1942 and a total of 772 were produced. Some later ones were made for the S&DJR. Some briefly were oil burners in 1947-48 but converted back again and some were fitted with tender cabs for running tender first.

The model was based on later built ones and was designed by Airfix and released in 1978. It had tender drive and the tender was semi-permanently attached to the loco. The tooling passed to Palitoy, who had planned to release their own versions of it, but closed down production before they could. The tools passed to Dapol in 1985, along with unsold stock. Dapol also planned to produce their own versions of the model but with the Airfix stock unsold, they did not proceed. In 1996 they sold the tooling to Hornby and the model is still in production.

D25	**4454** LMS black (A) - *85*		25	30
D25	**4312** LMS lined black - *not made*		NA	NA
D98	**LMS** maroon - *not made*		NA	NA
D99	**SDJR** very dark blue - *not made*		NA	NA
D26	**44454** BRb (small or large) black (A) - *85*		30	40

Dapol 00

2-6-0

L18. GWR Class 43xx 2-6-0 (ex-Mainline) (1985)

This was designed by Churchward as a mixed traffic locomotive. A total of 342 of these were built between 1911 and 1925, the final 20 as Class 93xx. They were numbered in the 43xx, 53xx, 63xx and 73xx series. Members of the class undertook a wide range of duties and were found throughout the GWR network. Some saw service in France during the First World War. In the 1930s, 80 were dismantled to build 'Granges' and 20 became 'Manors', but the Second World War brought the project to a close. The last was withdrawn from service in 1965 and one of the original class has been preserved.

On the closure of Palitoy, Dapol purchased the unsold stock which is listed in this table.

D48	5322 Great Western green (M) - 85	32	40
D47	5328 BRb black (M) - 85	37	45
D49	43583 BRb lined green (M) - 85	32	40

4-6-0

L19. GWR 'Manor' Class 4-6-0 (ex-Mainline) (1985)

Arriving in 1938, Collett's 'Manor' Class was quite a late introduction for the GWR. The 30 locomotives were built at Swindon between 1938 and 1950 for mixed traffic duties, on cross-country routes and lightly constructed branch lines. They were a lighter version of a 'Grange'. The last was withdrawn in 1966 and 8 have been preserved.

Dapol bought the remaining stock when Palitoy closed and this is listed in this table.

D44	7808 Cookham Manor GWR green (button) (M) - 85	32	40
D45	7819 Hinton Manor GWR green (M) - 85	32	40
D46	7827 Lydham Manor BRc green (M) - 85	32	40

L20. GWR Class 4073 'Castle' 4-6-0 (ex-Airfix) (1983)

GWR 'Castle' Class [L20]

The 'Castles' were a post-Grouping design by Collett and were made over many years (1923-1950) to produce a class of 166 locomotives. The design was a development of Churchward's excellent 'Star' Class of 1907 and included some members of that earlier class that were rebuilt as 'Castles'.

This was the Airfix model with tender-drive, which passed to Palitoy and thence to Dapol. It was Dapol who developed the Hawksworth tender and produced the 'County' variation of the model (see next table). They also bought and sold the outstanding Airfix stock and renamed and renumbered some of them before selling them. Of these renamed models, some were sold in their original Airfix boxes while others were put into new Dapol packaging, once the polystyrene trays had been trimmed with a large knife. In 1996 the tools for both the 'Castle' and 'County' were sold to Hornby.
H = Hawksworth tender.

D30	4073 Caerphilly Castle Great () Western green (A) - 83	35	50
-	4080 Powderham Castle Great () Western green (Airfix 54124 renamed by Dapol) - 83	75	100
-	4078 Pembroke Castle Great () Western green (Airfix 54124 renamed by Dapol) - 83	75	100
D107	5090 Isambard Kingtom Brunel GW green - not made	NA	NA
D6	5090 Neath Abbey G()W green H - 85	40	50
-	4080 Powderham Castle BRb green (Airfix 54125 renamed by Dapol) - 83	75	100
D29	4079 Pendennis Castle BRb green (A) - 85	35	50
-	4078 Pembroke Castle BRb green (Airfix 54125 renamed by Dapol) - 83	75	100
D5	4090 Dorchester Castle BRb lined green, optional double chimney H - 85	40	50

L21. GWR Class 1000 'County' 4-6-0 (1985)

Hawksworth succeeded Collett as CME of the GWR and tinkered with the 'Castle' Class to produce his 'County' Class. These started to appear in 1945 and were the final development of Churchward's award winning design that had for decades influenced the design of GWR locomotives. Particular visual features that make them stand out amongst other GWR classes are the continuous splashers over all three driving wheels and the straight nameplates. A total of 30 of them were built between 1945 and 1947 and the last was withdrawn from service in 1964. None escaped the cutter's torch.

It was Dapol who developed the Hawksworth tender and produced the 'County' variation of the Airfix 'Castle'. This model had loco-drive and a Hawksworth flat-sided tender. The tooling was sold to Hornby in 1996 and the model reintroduced by them.
sc = single chimney. dc = double chimney.

GWR 'County' Class [L21]

D3	1029 County of Worcester G()W green sc - 85	40	50
D3	1027 County of Worcester S - ?	NPG	NPG
D3	1029 County of Worcester/County of Stafford ** BRb green sc - ?	NPG	NPG
D103	1011 County of Chester S - 90	40	50
D?	1000 County of Middlesex S - 02	80	95
D68	1019 County of Merioneth S - 88	40	50
D4	1027 County of Stafford S - 85	40	50

* Remodelled boiler and firebox, improved finish. ** This was almost certainly a one-off factory error.

L22. LMS 'Royal Scot' 4-6-0 (ex-Mainline) (1985)

This was Fowler's express passenger design of 1927 and 71 were built between 1927 and 1930. They were mainly used on express passenger services, until replaced by Stanier's Pacifics. From 1947, smoke deflectors were fitted and all of them were rebuilt with tapered boilers between 1943 and 1955. (see below).

Dapol bought the unsold stock on the demise of Palitoy.

D34	6127 Old Contemptibles LMS maroon (M) - 85	32	40
D35	46137 Prince of Wales Volunteers, South Lancashire BRb green (M) - 85	32	40

L23a. LMS Rebuilt 'Royal Scot' 4-6-0 (ex-Airfix) (1985)

Stanier commenced rebuilding the whole of the 'Royal Scot' Class in 1943 and this process continued until 1955, when the last one received its No.2a tapered boiler.

Both Airfix and Palitoy released models of the 'Rebuilt Royal Scot' Class and Dapol should have been able to buy the Airfix tooling but it was not found. Dapol did, however, buy the unsold Airfix stock and sold it through their own catalogue.

D28	6103 Royal Scots Fusilier LMS lined black (A) - 85	25	40
D27	46100 Royal Scot BRb green (A) - 85	25	40

L23b. LMS Rebuilt 'Royal Scot' 4-6-0 (ex-Mainline)

In the case of the Mainline 'Rebuilt Royal Scot', the tooling belonged to Kader in Hong Kong, but Dapol did buy the unsold stock from Palitoy in 1985.

D58	6100 Royal Scot LMS maroon with bell on front, name on smokebox door (M) - 85	30	38
D36	6115 Scots Guardsman LMS lined black (M) - 85	30	38
D41	46115 Scots Guardsman BRc green (M) - 85	35	42

L24. LMS Rebuilt 'Patriot' 4-6-0 (ex-Mainline) (1985)

This was Ivatt's 1946 rebuild of Fowler's 'Patriot' Class. The rebuilt loco looked very much like a 'Rebuilt Royal Scot' but while the 'Scots' retained their Fowler cabs, the 'Patriots' were given 'Jubilee' cabs. They were given a Stanier 4,000 gallon tender. The last loco was withdrawn in 1965.

Once again it was Palitoy's unsold stock of this model which Dapol bought in 1985 and sold through their own catalogues.

D39	45536 Private W. Wood BRa lined black (M) - 85	35	42
D40	45532 Illustrious BRc green (M) - 85	35	42

L25. LMS 'Jubilee' 4-6-0 (ex-Mainline) (1985)

Designed by Sir William Stanier for the LMS, 191 locomotives were built between 1934 and 1936. This was his Class 5 express passenger locomotive for all but the heaviest duties and they were named after countries and states within the British Empire, as well as former admirals and warships. The last was withdrawn in 1967 and 4 have been preserved.

The Mainline model was released in 1979 and members of the class named after ships had been chosen. In 1985 Dapol bought the unsold stock when Palitoy closed down.
FT = Fowler tender. ST = Stanier tender.

D37	5687 Neptune LMS lined black, ST (M) - 85	30	38
D42	45700 Amethyst BRb lined black, FT (M) - 85	30	38
D43	45698 Mars BRb green, FT (M) - 85	35	42
D38	45691 Orion BRc green, ST (M) - 85	35	42

Dapol 00

4-6-2

L26. LNER Class A2 4-6-2 (ex-Trix)
Boyle thought that he had been able to acquire the tooling that produced the Liliput UK models, when Ernst Rozsa retired in 1992, but the following year Kader of Hong Kong bought the Austro-German company that owned the tooling.

D89	525 **A.H.Peppercorn** LNER light green - *not made*	NA	NA
D90	60532 **Blue Peter** BRc green - *not made*	NA	NA

L27. LNER Class A3 4-6-2 (ex-Trix)
This was also sought by Boyle but was unavailable for the reason given above. Boyle had gone as far as advertising the ex-Trix models in the Dapol catalogue before realising that they were not for sale.

D87	4472 **Flying Scotsman** LNER light green - *not made*	NA	NA
D88	60103 **Flying Scotsman** BRc green - *not made*	NA	NA

L28. LNER Class A4 4-6-2 (ex-Trix)
Once again, this was advertised by Dapol but the tooling was not available. In the end this model joined the Bachmann Branchline range in 1995, Liliput and Bachmann both being owned by Kader.

D85	2512 **Silver Fox** LNER grey with valances - *not made*	NA	NA
D84	4468 **Mallard** LNER blue with valances - *not made*	NA	NA
D86	60027 **Merlin** BRc green - *not made*	NA	NA

L29. Beyer-Garratt 2-6-0+0-6-2
Garratt licensed the British firm of Beyer, Peacock and Company to build locomotives to his patent design. After the original Garratt patents expired in 1928, Beyer, Peacock continued to market Garratts under its own brand, Beyer-Garratt, at their Gorton Foundry. The model was announced by Dapol in 1985, but no more was heard of it. These were to have been catalogued as D9 and D10.

L30. WD 2-8-0
In 1985, D11 was allocated to a WD 2-8-0, also due for release in 1987, but about which no more was heard.

Diesel & Electric Locomotives

L31. Class 22 B-B (2011)
These were Type 2 locomotives introduced between 1959 and 1962 and were built by the North British Locomotive Company. The class totalled 58 and they were used on secondary passenger duties and goods. They were phased out between 1968 and 1971.

This model contains a new 5-pole skew-wound 'Supercreep' can motor and has a 21-pin DCC decoder board fitted It has directional lighting, cab lights, lit headcode boxes, alternative headcode characters to fit, metal split-frame chassis and roof fan grille with fan detail below. The tooling was revised, probably in 2012.

sb = split code box.

Class 22 [L31] (Tony Wright)

D1000E	D6313 BRc green, small yellow panels sb - *not made*	NA	NA
D1000C	D6314 BRc green, small yellow panels sb Ltd Edn - *not made*	NA	NA
D1000X	D6315 BRc green W, small yellow panels sb Sp Edn 250 (Kernow MR Centre) - *11*	110	140
D1000G	D6316 BRc green, small yellow panels - *12*	125	150
4D012001	D6316 BRc green, small yellow panels, disc headcode - *12*	100	125
D1000B	D6318 BRe blue, full yellow ends sb Ltd Edn 300 - *11*	100	125
D1000V	D6318 BRc green W, small yellow panels sb Sp Edn 250 (Kernoe MR Centre) - *12*	125	150
D1000D	D6319 BRc green, small yellow panels sb Ltd Edn 300 - *not made*	NA	NA
D1000D	D6319 BRc green, full yellow fronts sb Ltd Edn 300 - *11*	100	125
D1000C	D6320 BRc green, small yellow panels sb Ltd Edn 300 - *11*	100	125
D1000W	D6321 BRc green W, small yellow panels sb Sp Edn 250 (Kernow MR Centre) - *12*	125	150
D1000Y	D6323 BRc green W, small yellow panels sb Sp Edn 250 (Kernow MR Centre) - *11*	110	140
D1000A	D6324 BRe blue, full yellow ends sb Ltd Edn 300 - *11*	100	125
D1000B	D6326 BRe blue, full yellow ends sb Ltd Edn 300 - *not made*	NA	NA
4D012000	6326 BRc greeb no warning panels, disc headcode - *13*	100	125
D1000E	D6327 BRc green, small yellow panels sb Ltd Edn 300 - *not made*	NA	NA
4D012002	D6327 BRc green, amended yellow panels, disc headcode - *13*	100	125
D1000E	D6327 BRc blue, full yellow panels sb Ltd Edn 300 - *11*	100	125
D1000U	D6328 BRc green W, small yellow panels sb Sp Edn 250 (Kernow MR Centre) - *12*	125	150
D1000H	D6328 BRc blue, full yellow ends - *12*	100	125
D1000Z	D6330 BRe blue W, full yellow ends sb Sp Edn 250 (Kernow MR Centre) - *11*	100	125
D1000F	D6332 BRc green sb Ltd Edn 300 - *11*	100	125

L32. Class 29 Bo-Bo (2012)
The Class 29s were rebuilds of the Class 21 with a more powerful Paxman motor replacing the original MAN motor. They served most of their lives in Scotland, eventually all being scrapped in 1971.

This model contains a new 5-pole skew-wound 'Supercreep' can motor, 21-pin DCC decoder board, directional lighting, cab lights, lit head code boxes, alternative head code characters to be fitted, metal split-frame chassis and roof fan grille with fan detail below.

D1002C	D6100 BRe blue, full yellow panels - *not made*	NA	NA
D1001A	D6112 BRc green - *not made*	NA	NA
D1002B	D6114 BRc green, full yellow panels - *not made*	NA	NA
4D014001	D6114 BRc green, full yellow panels - *12*	110	130
4D014003	D6123 BRc green, small yellow panels - *12*	110	130
D1002A	D6130 BRc green, full yellow panels - *not made*	NA	NA
4D014000	D6130 BRc green, full yellow panels - *12*	110	130
4D014002	D6130 BRe blue, full yellow panels - *12*	110	130
D1001B	D6134 BRc green - *not made*	NA	NA
D1001C	D6150 BRc green - *not made*	NA	NA

L33. Class 31/4 A1A-A1A (ex-Airfix) (1985)
263 members of the class were built between 1957 and 1962 and were intended for mixed traffic duties, originally on the Eastern Region. They were built at the Brush Electrical Engineering Company plant at Loughborough and 28 have been preserved.

The model was released by Airfix in 1977 as the first British outline locomotive in the Airfix range. It passed to Palitoy and and then Dapol who planned to produce their own versions of it. However, they had also bought the remainder stock in 1985. A further batch of unsold stock was uncovered in 1988. The tooling was offered to Hornby in 1996, but was not required by them.

D31**	D5531 BRc green (A) - *85*	15	30
D62	D5531 BRc green (A) - *88*	15	30
D32	31217 BRe Railfreight Distribution grey - *not made*	NA	NA
D30	31226 BReLL Railfreight plain grey - *not made*	NA	NA
D31	31247 BReLL Railfreight red stripe grey - *not made*	NA	NA
D61	31401 BRe blue (A) - *88*	15	30
D30**	31401 BRe blue, new bogie (A) - *85*	15	30
D73	BR3 Railfreight Distribution grey - *not made*	NA	NA

** Early code numbers used for D61 and D62.

L34. Class 41 'Warship' B-B (2013)
The A1A-A1A 'Warships' were built by the North British Locomotive Co. and introduced to the Western Region in 1958. Only 5 were built and all of them have been modelled exclusively for Kernow Model Railway Centre. Production of each is limited to 750 models and they come with numbered certificates.

The models have a 5-pole skew-wound can motor with two large brass flywheels. They have a 21-pin DCC board fitted, directional lighting, cab lights, heavy metal split frame chassis, lit headcode boxes, alternative headcode characters provided and roof fan grille with fan detail below. Two different front ends and two side variations are being modelled.

mg = mesh grilles. hd = headcode discs. hb = headcode boxes.

K2600	D600 **Active** BRe blue, full yellow ends, mg hb - *13*	110	133
K2601	D601 **Ark Royal** BRc green, louvres hd - *13*	110	133

Dapol 00

K2602	**D602** *Bulldog* BRc green, louvres hd - *13*		110	133
K2603	**D603** *Conquest* BRc green, small yellow panels, hb mg - *13*		110	133
K2604	**D604** *Cossack* BRc green, hd mg - *13*		110	133

L35.   Class 42 'Warship' B-B (ex-Mainline) (1985)

38 of these diesel hydraulic locomotives were built by the North British Locomotive Company between 1958 and 1961 for the Western Region of British Railways.

In 1985, Dapol purchased the remaining stock of Mainline models and added them to their own catalogue.

D66	**D824** *Highflyer* BRc green (M) - *85*	22	30
D65	**827** *Kelly* BRe blue (M) - *85*	20	30
D64	**827** *Kelly* BRe blue with diesel sound and klaxon (M) - *85*	30	40

L36.   LMS 'Twins' Main Line Diesels (2011)

In 1947 the LMS had announced their intention to build two experimental main line diesel locomotives. No.10000 emerged from Derby Works in November 1947 and was the only one of the two to carry 'LMS' on its sides. No.10001 arrived in July the following year.

The model was produced exclusively for Hattons of Liverpool. It has all-wheel pick-ups and drive and sprung buffers. There is a centrally mounted Dapol 5-pole acute skew-wound motor, flywheels, separate handrails and wipers, etched see-through roof grille and detailed side grilles yellow and red LED lighting, a 21-pin DCC decoder socket, split frame chassis, pin-point axles, separately fitted roof horns, cab lights and brass workplate.

Ex-LMS prototype main line diesel [L36] (Hattons)

10000AP	**10000** LMS black - *11*	100	125
10000BP	**10000** BRb (large) black - *11*	100	125
10000CP	**10000** BRb (small) black - *11*	100	125
10000DP	**10000** BRc lined green - *11*	100	125
10000EP	**10000** BRc green, light blue waist band - *11*	100	125
10000FP	**10001** no insignia, black - *11*	100	125
10000GP	**10001** BRb (large) black - *11*	100	125
10000HP	**10001** BRb (small) black - *11*	100	125
10000HAP	**10001** BRc lined green - *11*	100	125
10000IP	**10001** BRc green, partial light blue waist band - *11*	100	125
10000JP	**10001** BRc green, light blue waist band - *11*	100	125
10000KP	**10001** BRc green, light blue waist band, small yellow warning panel - *11*	100	125

L37.   SR Bulleid 1-Co-Co-1 (2013)

Designed by Oliver Bulleid for the Southern Railway, the loco did not appear until after Nationalisation. 10201 and 10202 were built at Ashford works in 1950 with 10203 being built at Brighton Works in 1954. The diesel engine and transmission were supplied by English Electric.

Kernow Model Railway Centre commissioned the model and, at the time of writing, it had not been released.

K2701	**10201** BRb black - *13*	NPG	140
K2702	**10202** BRb black - *13*	NPG	140
K2703	**10203** BRb black - *13*	NPG	140

L38.   DP2 Co-Co (2013)

This was an experimental loco when the search was on for a second generation Type 4 locomotive. It was designed by English Electric and built at their Vulcan Foundry. It used a production 'Deltic' body but had totally different equipment inside. Internally it was closer to the later Class 50.

The model has a new 5-pole can motor with heavy large brass flywheels. It has directional lighting, cab lights, DCC 21-pin DCC decoder socket, a large space for a speaker, etched roof fan grilles and separate cab steps. Further details of it are awaited.

?	**DP2** BRc green - *13*	NPG	NPG

L39.   Class 52 'Western' C-C (2013)

The 'Western' had diesel hydraulic drive and was designed and constructed at Swindon, while some were built at Crewe. They were introduced to the Western Region in 1962 to provide high powered mixed traffic locomotives to the region. They were expensive to maintain and this led to their early replacement by the Class 50s and HSTs. The last was withdrawn in 1978 and seven have been preserved.

This is reckoned to be the most accurately shaped 00 scale 'Western' on the market. The models have a new 5-pole skew-wound motor with two large brass flywheels. They have a 21-pin DCC socket fitted, room for a speaker, detailed cab interiors, directional lighting, cab lights, heavy metal split frame chassis, yellow glow headcode panels, alternative headcode characters provided, replacement front valances, etched brass nameplates supplied and etched fan grille with fan detail below.

-	**D1000** *Western Enterprise* BRc buff, in a presentation box & GWR badge, Sp Edn 400 (Steam Museum) - *13*	130	160
D?	**D1005** *Western Venturer* BRe blue - *13*	110	130
-	**D1009** *Western Invader* BRc maroon Sp Edn 200 (Lord & Butler) - *13*	110	130
D?	**D1029** *Western Legionaire* BRc maroon - *13*	110	130
4D003003	**D1030** *Western Musketeer* BRe blue, small yellow panel - *13*	110	130
D1003Z	**D1030** *Western Musketeer* BRe chromatic blue W Sp Edn 250 (Kernow MR Centre) - *13*	130	160
D?	**D1038** *Western Sovereign* BRc green - *13*	110	130
D1003X	**D1042** *Western Princess* BRc maroon - *not made*	NA	NA
4D003001	**D1042** *Western Princess* BRc maroon, small yellow panel - *13*	110	130
D1003Y	**D1045** *Western Viscount* BRc maroon, full yellow panel - *not made*	NA	NA
4D003002	**D1045** *Western Viscount* BRc maroon W Sp Edn 250 (Kernow MR Centre) - *13*	110	130
D?	**D1056** *Western Sultan* BRc maroon - *13*	110	130
-	**D1062** *Western Courier* maroon Sp Edn 150 (The Western Locomotive Association) - *13*	125	150
4D003000	**1068** *Western Reliance* BRe blue, full yellow panel - *13*	110	130
D1003W	**1068** *Western Reliance* BRe blue W Sp Edn 250 (Kernow MR Centre) - *13*	130	160

L40.   Class 56 Co-Co (ex-Mainline) (1985)

The first 30 Class 56 locomotives were built by Electroputere at Craiova in Romania but the remaining 105 machines came from BREL at Doncaster and Crewe. They were introduced between 1976 and 1984.

The model was designed by Palitoy and was not tooled by Kader. Consequently the tools were amongst the assets bought by Dapol in 1985. Palitoy had released two versions in 1983, the year before the Receiver was called in. Dapol took over the unsold stock and manufactured several new versions. In 1996 they sold the tooling to Hornby who produced a large number of variations before replacing it with a new model.

Class 56 diesel [L40]

D81	unpainted grey - *89*	25	35
D80	**56001** BRe Railfreight Construction grey - *89*	30	40
D14A	**56064** Railfreight grey - *89*	30	40
D14B	**56068** Railfreight grey - *89*	30	40
D14	**56075** *West Yorkshire Enterprise* Railfreight red stripe grey - *85*	35	45
D12*	**56077** BRe blue - *?*	30	40
D14	**56077** BRe blue - *94*	25	35
D12	**56079** BRe blue (M) - *85*	25	35
D13	**56086** BReLL blue (M renumbered) - *85*	22	35
D14C	**56090** Railfreight grey - *89*	30	40
D104	**56094** Railfreight Coal Sector grey - *91*	30	40

* Also shown as D14. The tooling was sold to Hornby in 1996 and the model reintroduced by them.

L41.   Class 73/1 Electro-Diesel (2013)

The Class 73 electro-diesels have been a very successful mixed traffic locomotives. They were built especially for the Southern Region and designed to make use of the third

Dapol 00

rail electrified routes, but also be able to operate using diesel power. The first 6 locomotives were built at Eastleigh in 1962 and form the JA type subclass 73/0 and the remaining 43 were built by English Electric between 1965 and 1967, becoming JB type subclass 73/1. Some 73/1s were transferred to InterCity and renumbered to became subclass 73/2. At the last count, 15 had been bought for preservation.

The model has 22-pin decoder sockets fitted, authentic lighting, etched metal grilles and all wheel drive.

-	E6047 BRe blue Sp Edn 150 (The Hobby Shop Faversham) - 13	95	116
4D010000	73102 *Airtour Suisse* Intercity grey - 13	100	125
4D010001	73105 BRLLe blue - 13	100	125
4D010002	73124 BRe blue - 13	100	125
-	73128 *O.V.S.Bulleid C.B.E* * BRe Departmental 'Dutch' grey+yellow Sp Edn 150 (Model Rail magazine) - 13	110	135
4D010003	73135 BRe blue - 13	100	125
K2800	73212 Network Rail yellow Sp Edn 250 (Kernow MR Centre) - 13	100	125

* This marks the 130th Anniversary of the birth of Oliver Bulleid.

L42. Class 81 Bo-Bo (ex-Trix)

The 25 members of the AL1 class were built in 1959-64. They were supplied by AEI Ltd and mechanically constructed by Birmingham Railway Carriage & Wagon Ltd.

Dapol had expected to be able to buy the former Trix tooling in 1993 and advertised these models in their catalogue, Instead, the owner of the tools, Liliput, was taken over that year by Kader.

D91	E3000 BRd electric blue - *not made*	NPG	NPG
D92	BRe rail blue - *not made*	NPG	NPG
D93	BRe executive grey - *not made*	NPG	NPG

Railcars & Multible Units

L43. GWR Diesel Railcar (2013)

Introduced to the GWR in 1933, they were the forerunner of the branch line DMUs, which superceded them.

The model has yet to be released at the time of writing but will have a 5-pole skew-wound 'Supercreap' motor, a DCC 21/22 pin (22-21 pin conversion board), directional lighting and interior lighting, fully modelled cab and saloon interior and sprung buffers. It will have all-wheel drive and power contact.

L44. Class 121 Pressed Steel Railcar (2013)

In all, 15 of the Class 121 DMBSs were introduced to the rail network in 1960 for high density local passenger transportation. At the time it was a modern version of the GWR AEC railcar. Derby designed, they were built by Pressed Steel and have 65 seats in a 2+3 pattern.

These will have a 5-pole skew wound underfloor mechanism, a close coupling mechanism, DCC 21/22 pin DCC compatibility (22-21 pin conversion board), independent cab lighting and saloon lighting, directional lighting and headcode lighting, rotating and lit headcode panels (where applicable) with different destinations, fully modelled cab and saloon interior, 2 digit reporting panels (where applicable) and original 'joined' exhausts (where applicable). Slides within tools allow for alternate bodyside window version, high intensity headlight, alternate exhausts and underframe detail, and also the trailer variant. At the time of writing the model had not been released.

4D-009-001	W55020 BR green with whiskers - 13	NPG	130
4D-009-004	W55023 BR blue - 13	NPG	130
4D-009-002	W55028 BR green with small yellow panel - 13	NPG	130
4D-009-003	W55029 BR blue/grey 13	NPG	130

L45. Class 122 Gloucester R.C.&W. Railcar (2013)

These were built by the Gloucester RC&WC in 1958. There were 20 in the class and they were very like the Class 119 the members of which were built at the same time. They had side doors to each seating bay. Survivors became sandite units and 7 have been preserved.

Details for the Class 121 (above) apply also to this model At the time of writing the model had not been released.

4D-015-002	W55000 BR green with whiskers - 13	NPG	130
4D-015-001	55002 BR blue/grey - 13	NPG	130
4D-015-005	SC55007 BR green with small yellow panel - 13	NPG	130
4D-015-003	55012 Regional Railways - 13	NPG	130
4D-015-004	SC55013 BR blue - 13	NPG	130

L46. Class 124 'Transpennine' DMU (ex-Trix) (1994)

These were six-car units built at Swindon in 1960. They had a wrap-round cab fronts, which made them visually the most attractive DMU of their time. 51 cars were built including 17 driving motor composites, 17 motor brake corridor 2nds, 9 trailer 2nds and 8 buffet 1sts. These formed 8 six-car sets with a spare left over of each car type except the buffet car. They were withdrawn in 1984.

These were assembled using mouldings made at Dapol's Winsford factory and fitted with their 'Sprinter' motor bogie with side frames clipped on. The units were adapted to take Dapol coach weights to give them extra stability.

D95	NE51953 + NE51954 BRc green 2-car, single motor - 94	75	90
D105	NE51953 + NE51954 BRc green 2-car, 2 motors, 221 made - 00	80	100
D94	BRe blue 2-car, single motor - *not made*	NA	NA

L47. Class 150/2 'Sprinter' DMU (1992)

The Class 150 was the first of the 2nd generation DMUs and the contract for them was placed with BREL by BR Provincial Sector in 1983. They were based on the Mk3 coach design and were built at BR York. Fifty of the 150/1 sets were built and 85 of the 150/2s. The latter are similar to the Class 150/1 but have corridor connectors in the cab ends allowing units to be joined together. They are now owned by Angel Trains and Porterbrook.

The model was not very reliable, nor accurate, particularly at the front end and the body side windows. Although the tooling was among those of other models that Hornby bought in 1996, it has not been brought back into production.

D82+D82A	150237 (57237 + 52237) BRe Provincial grey+blue 2-car - 92	50	70
D82+D82A	150237 (57237 + 52237) BRe Provincial grey+blue 2-car improved - 93	50	70
D108	Centro 2-car - *not made*	NA	NA
D109	PTE 2-car - *not made*	NA	NA

L48. Class 155 'Super Sprinter' DMU (1992)

Class 155 'Super Sprinter' DMU [L48]

These were 3-car DMUs built by ABB York as semi-fast commuter trains and introduced from May 1993. An order was placed for 21 3-car sets for the Paddington-Worcester and Reading-Gatwick lines. These were virtually the same as the Class 165 units but had, amongst other things, full air-conditioning. When privatisation of the railways took place, the units passed to Angel Trains.

The tooling was sold to Hornby in 1996 and reintroduced by them.

D83+D83A	155329 (57237 + 52329) BRe Provincial grey+blue 2-car - 92	50	70
D83+D83A	155329 (57237 + 52329) BRe Regional Railwaysl grey+blue 2-car improved - 93	50	70
D110	155345 (57325 + 52345) NRe Metro PTE maroon 2-car - ?	NPG	NPG
D106	BRe Regional Railways grey+blue - *not made*	NA	NA

L49. Class 205 2-H 'Thumper' 2-car EMU (2010)

These were to be made by Dapol for Kernow Model Railway Centre but in March 2010 the order was switched to Bachmann who released it in 1913.

L50. Class 390 'Pendolino' 4-car EMU (2001)

The tilting Pendolinos were ordered by Virgin Trains for the West Coast Main Line as soon as the operator was granted the franchise. They replaced loco hauled trains with fixed formation multiple units, based on trains running in mainland Europe which were built by Fiat/Alstom. A total of 53 9-car units were initially delivered by Alstom and they came on stream between 2001 and 2005. The fleet was further extended in 2008 and now 11-car units are run.

	Virgin Red & Grey		
D390-1	390001 *Virgin Pioneer* Ltd Edn 2000 - *01*	50	80
D390-2	390002 *Red Revolution* Ltd Edn 2000 - *01*	50	80
?	390002 *Red Revolution* motorless power car Sp Edn * - *01*	50	90

Dapol 00

Cat No.	Company, Number, Colour, Date	£	£
D390-3	390006 *Mission Impossible* Ltd Edn 200 - *03*	50	80
D390-4	390007 *Virgin Lady* Ltd Edn 200 - *03*	50	80
D390-5	390010 *Commonwealth Games* Ltd Edn 200 - *03*	50	80
D390-6	390011 *City of Preston* Ltd Edn 200 - *03*	50	80
D390-7	390014 *City of Manchester* Ltd Edn 200 - *03*	50	80
-	*Pen y darren/Pendolino* Sp Edn for Railfest 2004 (Virgin Trains) - *04*	NPG	NPG

* This was a launch special in an Angel Trains/Alstrom/Virgin Trains sleeve and given to the staff involved.

COACHES

For its coaches, Dapol depended principally on old Airfix and Mainline stock and Airfix tooling. Initially they sold the large surpluses of stock they had acquired in 1985, but then produced variations using the Airfix tools. These included Mk2D coaches in Executive livery and the 12-wheel LMS diner which was planned by both Airfix and Palitoy, but not actually released until Dapol took it over. The coaches were given catalogue numbers with an 'E' prefix and E41 seems to have been the highest number reached.

(A) = ex-Airfix stock
(M) = ex-Mainline stock

Cat No.	Company, Number, Colour, Date	£	£

Pre-Nationalisation

GWR

C1. GWR Suburban 'B Set' Coach (ex-Airfix) (1985)

'B Set' coaches were brake ends which were built by the GWR in 1933 to run in two-car sets. Each contained five 3rd class and one 1st class non-corridor compartments and a guards/luggage area at one end.

Airfix had released the model in 1977 and, as with other models, the tooling passed to Palitoy in 1981 and the model added to the Mainline range. Dapol acquired the tooling from Palitoy in 1985, along with unsold stock. They did not use the tooling before it was sold to Hornby in 1996.

E22	GWR 6896 dark brown+cream (A/M) - *85*	8	14
E23	BR W6894W maroon (A) - *85*	8	14
E24	BR W6447W lined maroon (M) - *85*	12	18

C2. GWR Auto Trailer (ex-Airfix) (1985)

Auto trailers were used for push-pull operation on branch lines and many small batches were built by the GWR. They were eventually displaced by DMUs.
The Airfix model had been released in 1978 and was taken over by Palitoy for their Mainline range. Dapol bought the tools and residue stock and added them to their catalogue. The tooling was sold to Hornby in 1996.

E25	GWR 187 dark brown+cream (M) - *85*	12	18
E25	GWR 188 brown+cream - *?*	12	18
E27	BR W176W red+cream (M) - *85*	12	18
E26	BR W187W maroon (A) - *85*	8	14

C3a. GWR 'Centenary' Composite (ex-Airfix) (1985)

Just four 'Centenary' composite coaches were built at Swindon in 1938 and they carried 48 passengers in 7 compartments. These were made up of four 1st class compartments with 6 seats each and three 3rd class with 8 seats each.
The model had been released by Airfix in 1980 and the tooling passed to Palitoy the following year and the GWR 'Centenary' coaches were added to their Mainline Railways range. With the closedown of Palitoy in 1985, Dapol acquired the tooling as well as remaining stock. The latter must have sold well as by 1988 Dapol had the tooling back in use. In 1996, Dapol sold the tools to Hornby.

E16	GWR 6659 dark brown+cream ** (M) - *85*	8	14
E20	BR W6562W, W6662W red+cream * - *90*	10	16
E18	BR W6659W maroon (A) - *85*	10	17
E18	BR W6661W maroon * - *88*	10	16

* 'Paddington Newport Cardiff and Swansea' coach boards. ** 'Cornish Riviera' coach boards.

C3b. GWR 'Centenary' Brake 3rd (ex-Airfix) (1985)

In 1938, six brake 3rd coaches were built at Swindon and they each had 2 compartments and seating for 16 passengers. There was a guard's compartment and most of the coach was given over to luggage space.
The history of the model was the same as that for the one in the table above.

E17	GWR 4575 dark brown+cream ** (M+A) - *85*	8	14
E21	BR W4576W red+cream * - *90*	10	16
E19	BR W4576W maroon * - *88*	10	17

* 'Paddington Newport Cardiff and Swansea' coach boards. ** 'Cornish Riviera' coach boards.

LMS

C4a. LMS 57' Non-Corridor Comp (ex-Airfix) (1985)

Airfix released a pair of non-gangwayed coaches in 1981, which was the year the Receiver was called in. The tooling passed to Palitoy and although models were planned and included in the Mainline catalogue, none was made. The tooling passed to Dapol, along with remaining Airfix stock and the tooling was later put back into use.

LMS non-corridor composite coach [C4a] (Dapol)

E28	LMS 19195 maroon (A) - *85*	8	14
E28	LMS 19191 maroon - *88*	10	16
C097C	LMS 19194 maroon, kit - *12*	10	14
4P010003	LMS 19194 maroon - *12*	NA	9
E41	BR M16456M red - *02*	10	16
E42	BR M16161M red (all 2nd) - *02*	10	16
4P010002	BR M16685 red - *12*	10	14
C095C	BR M16685 red - *12*	NA	9
4P010013	BR M16615 red - *13*	10	14
E30	BR M19199M maroon - *88*	10	16
E31	BR M19195M maroon (A) - *85*	10	16
E31	BR M16161M maroon - *88*	10	16
4P010006	BR M16658 lined maroon - *12*	10	14
C099C	BR M16658 lined maroon, kit - *12*	NA	9

C4b. LMS 57' Non-Corridor Brake 3rd (ex-Airfix) (1986)

This non-gangwayed brake 3rd was also released by Airfix in 1981 and its history is the same as that for the model in the above table.

E29	LMS 15185 maroon (A) - *87-?*	10	14
E29	LMS 25250 maroon - *95*	12	16
4P010004	LMS 25252 lined maroon - *12*	10	14
C098C	LMS 25252 lined maroon, kit - *12*	NA	9
E40	BR M16370 red - *02*	12	16
4P010001	BR M25248M red - *made?*	NPG	NPG
4P010001	BR M20562 red - *12*	10	14
C096C	BR M25248M red - *made?*	NPG	NPG
C096C	BR M20562 red - *12*	NA	9
E30	BR M25250M maroon (A) - *86*	12	17
E30	BR M16161M maroon - *94*	12	16
4P010005	BR M20562 lined maroon - *made?*	NPG	NPG
4P010005	BR M25248M lined maroon - *12*	10	14
C100C	BR M20562 lined maroon, kit - *made?*	NPG	NPG
C100C	BR M25248M lined maroon, kit - *12*	NA	9

C5. LMS 68' Period 2 Dining Car (ex-Airfix) (1985)

The model was based on an LMS Period 2 coach.
Initially planned by Airfix, it was in the design stage when Airfix went into receivership in 1981. Palitoy took over the project and probably made the tools which were taken over by Dapol when Mainline Railways production ceased in 1964. Dapol were the first to produce a model but parted with the tools to Hornby when they needed to raise money following a disastrous fire at their warehouse. Hornby upgraded the tooling and released their first model in 1999.

LMS Period 2 12-wheel dining car [C5]

E1	LMS 10440 * maroon - *87*	15	25
E1A	LMS 10440 * maroon panelled - *88*	15	25
E1A	LMS 238 * maroon panelled - *88*	15	25

Dapol 00

E3	**BR** 10440 red+cream - *85*	20	35
?	**BR** maroon+cream - *not made*	NA	NA
E2	**BR** M239M maroon - *86, 98*	15	25
E2A	**BR** M239M maroon *98*	15	25

C6a. LMS 60' Period 3 Composite (ex-Airfix) (1985)

This was an LMS Period 3 1st/3rd composite coach, developed during Stanier's time as CME.

The model was released by Airfix in 1978 and the tooling reused by Palitoy in 1983. In 1985, Dapol bought the tools and the unsold stock and later reused the tooling. It was not bought by Hornby, who already had a similar model, but in 2013 the tools were once again used by Dapol.

E4	**LMS** 3935 maroon (A) - *87*	8	14
E4	**LMS** 3936 maroon - *88*	10	16
4P010007	**LMS** ? maroon - *13*	10	14
C101C	**LMS** ? maroon, kit - *13*	NA	9
E6	**BR** M3935M red+cream (A) - *85*	8	14
4P010011	**BR** ? red+cream - *13*	10	14
C105C	**BR** ? red+cream - *13*	NA	9
E8	**BR** M3868M maroon (M) - *87*	8	14
E8	**BR** M3868 maroon - *91*	10	16
4P010009	**BR** M3870M maroon - *13*	10	14
C103C	**BR** M3870M maroon, kit - *13*	NA	9

C6b. LMS 57' Period 3 Brake 3rd (ex-Airfix) (1985)

This is also an LMS Period 3 coach designed by Stanier. The history of the model is the same as that for the Stanier coach in the above table.

LMS corridor brake 3rd [C6b] (Dapol)

E5	**LMS** 5542 maroon (A) - *85*	8	14
E5	**LMS** 5545 maroon - *89*	10	16
4P010008	**LMS** 5543 lined maroon - *13*	10	14
C102C	**LMS** 5543 maroon, kit - *13*	NA	9
E7	**BR** M5542M red+cream (A) - *85*	8	14
E7	**BR** M5542M red+cream - *97*	10	16
4P010012	**BR** M5530M red+cream - *13*	10	14
C106C	**BR** M5530M red+cream - *13*	NA	9
E9	**BR** M3868M maroon (M) - *85*	12	20
E9	**BR** M5648M maroon - *87*	10	16
4P010010	**BR** M5650M maroon - *13*	10	14
C104C	**BR** M5650M maroon, kit - *13*	NA	9

C7. LMS 50' Parcels Van BG (ex-Mainline) (1985)

Most of the Stanier Period 3 LMS 50' full brakes were built at Wolverton in the late 1930s and virtually all had been scrapped by 1968. They were successors to the 'Stove R' and became the most numerous LMS full brakes on the system. Most were rated as having a 12 ton carrying capacity.

The LMS 50ft parcels van was tooled by Kader and released in the last year of Mainline Railways and consequently had a short life in Mainline packaging. Dapol bought the unsold stock in 1985 and added it to their catalogue. The tooling was put back into use by Bachmann.

E37	**LMS** 30965 maroon (M) - *86*	8	12
E35	**BR** red+cream (M) - *86*	15	18
E36	**BR** lined maroon (M) - *86*	15	18
E33	**BR** M31262M blue+grey NFV (M) - *85*	10	15
E34	**BR** M31398 blue NFV - *85*	10	15

C8. LMS 'Stove R' (2010)

This was a period 3 LMS designed full brake and 75 were built at Wolverton in 1932 and 1933. All survived into BR ownership and most were withdrawn between 1963 and 1968.

This model is the result of a joint project with *Hornby Magazine*. It has separately fitted footboards and steps, brass handrails, gangway connections and good underframe detail. The chassis features a floating centre axle and pivoting outer axles to allow it to negotiate tight curves. Initial orders were for 500 of each but further orders were placed for some of the popular BR versions.

BR 'Stove R' [C8] (Ian Allan)

HM001	**LMS** 32919 lined maroon with maroon ends - *11*	NPG	28
HM002	**LMS** 32925 lined maroon with black ends - *11*	NPG	28
HM002A	**LMS** 32919 lined maroon with black ends (500 produced in error) instead of maroon end ones - *11*	NPG	28
HM003A	**BR** M32962M red - *10*	NPG	28
HM003B	**BR** M32927M red - *10*	NPG	28
HM004A	**BR** M32928M maroon - *11*	NPG	28
HM004B	**BR** M32929M maroon - *11*	NPG	28
HM005	**BR** M32930 blue - *10*	NPG	28

SR

C9. LSWR Gate Stock Push-Pull Sets (2013)

The tooling for these is the property of Kernow Model Railway Centre and the sets are produced by Dapol exclusively for them. Each set consists of a driving brake composite (which was downgraded to a driving brake 3rd in 1939) and an all-3rd coach.

-	**SR** 6546 lined green driving brake composite	50	NA
-	**SR** 727 lined green all-3rd coach	50	NA
K1001	above 2 form set 363, Sp Edn (Kernow MR Centre) - *13*	NA	100
-	**SR** 2622 plain light green driving brake 3rd	50	NA
-	**SR** 738 plain light green all-3rd coach	50	NA
K1002	above 2 form set 373, Sp Edn (Kernow MR Centre) - *13*	NA	100
-	**BR** 2624 plain red driving brake 3rd	50	NA
-	**BR** 739 plain red all-3rd coach	50	NA
K1003	above 2 form set 374, Sp Edn (Kernow MR Centre) - *13*	NA	100
-	**BR** 2622 plain green driving brake 3rd	50	NA
-	**BR** 738 plain green all-3rd coach	50	NA
K1004	above 2 form set 373, Sp Edn (Kernow MR Centre) - *13*	NA	100

BR

Post-Nationalisation

C10a. BR Mk1 Corridor 2nd (SK) (ex-Mainline) (1985)

The first two numbers used suggest a 2nd class corridor coach built in the late 1950s or early 1960s at either Wolverton or Derby.

The model, released in 1976, came from the Mainline range and the tooling belonged to Kader. Dapol bought the unsold stock when Palitoy closed down but what happened to the tooling remains a mystery as it was not used for the Bachmann Branchline range.

E38	**BR** S25915 green (M) - *86*	14	17
E39	**BR** M25390 maroon (M) - *86*	10	15
E32	**BR** M1709 * blue+grey (M) - *85*	9	13

* This number belonged to a restaurant car.

C10b. BR Mk1 Brake 2nd (BSK) (ex-Mainline) (1985)

The number in this case belonged to a brake corridor 2nd, built at Gloucester in 1957. It had 4 compartments, each seating six passengers. Half the coach was given over to a luggage area, guard's quarters and corridor connection.

This model was released at the same time as the one above and had the same history.

E40	**BR** M35040 maroon (M) - *85*	10	15

C11a. BR Mk2D Open 2nd (TSO) (ex-Airfix) (1985)

The model is thought to be based on a Mk2D tourist standard open coach built by BR Derby Carriage and Wagon Works, sometime in 1971-72.

Airfix had released the model in 1980 and the tooling passed to Palitoy in 1981. In 1985 the coach passed to Dapol along with remaining stock of a version Palitoy had made for their Mainline Railways. Dapol also used the tooling to produce InterCity coaches. Later they sold the tooling to Hornby.

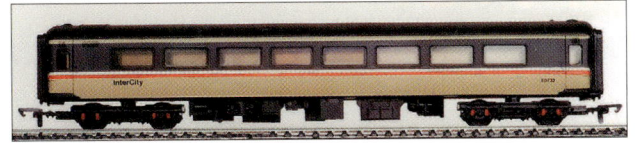

BR Mk2D standard class [C11a]

E11	BR E5690 blue+grey (M) - 85	10	20
E14	BR ICs E5732 executive grey - 86	10	16

C11b. BR Mk2D Open 1st (FO) (ex-Airfix) (1985)

This model was based on a Mk2D open first class coach design and built at BR Derby Carriage and Wagon Works in 1970-71. This had 7 windows each side.

The model was introduced by Airfix in in 1977 and the tooling passed to Palitoy in 1981. In 1985 the tooling was bought by Dapol, having previously bought the old Airfix stock. Again, the model was sold to Hornby in 1996.

E10	BR E3170 blue+grey (A) - 85	8	14
E13	BR OCs E3207 executive grey - 86	10	16

C11c. BR Mk2D Open Brake 2nd (BSO) (ex-Airfix) (1985)

The model was based on Mk2D brake standard coaches built at Derby between 1971 and 1974.

The history of the tooling is the same as that for the last model above.

E12	BR E9479 blue+grey (M) - 85-02	10	14
E15	BR ICs E9483 executive grey - 86-02	12	16

C12a. 'Pendolino' Standard Class (2003)

This was produced by Dapol for their 'Pendolino' sets and the model makes coaches AD and AJ for sets 390-001 and 390-002 and coaches AC, AD and AJ for sets 390-006, 390-007, 390-010, 390-011 and 390-014.

DPC-01	Virgin red+grey with transfers for any set - 03	12	15

C12b. 'Pendolino' 2nd Class (2003)

Again, this was produced for the Dapol 'Pendolino' sets and makes coach AF for sets 390-001 and 390-002

DPC*02	Virgin red+grey with transfers for either set - 03	15	20

C13. U.S. Passenger Car (ex-Airfix) (1985)

A stock of these American coaches came with the remnant stock that Dapol bought on the demise of Airfix.

E41	CPRR 3 red saloon car with trapdoor in roof (A) - 85	8	14

NPCCS: Non-passenger carrying coaching stock, such as the GWR Passenger Fruit D Van and SR CCT should in theory be listed here but they were treated as freight wagons in the Dapol catalogues and so are for the time being left with the wagons below.

Coach Gift Sets

CS1. Mixed Coaches (1999)

To help dispose of the large quantity of unsold coaches that Dapol took into stock in 1985, many were offered in sets as below and some show strange pairing.

E100	2 x E10 - 99	NA	25
E200	2 x E12 - 99	NA	25
E300	2 x E14 - 99	NA	25
E400	E13 + E15 - 99	NA	25
E500	E30 + E31 - 01	NA	25
E600	E40 + E41 - 01	NA	25
E700	E8 + E9 - 01	NA	25

WAGONS

Private owner wagons were colourful and model versions of them have become very popular. They have consequently become the principal subject for specially commissioned models and Dapol have commanded this market due to their willingness to supply quite small numbers of each type chosen. This has been possible because they have kept the work close to home and as a semi-cottage industry.

While quite a lot of the models produced are colourful, in reality 53% of private owner wagons were finished in red oxide (red-brown but sometimes called 'red' in early descriptions) and 30% in black as these were the two cheapest pigments being based on iron oxide and carbon, respectively. White paint was made with lead and by mixing brown, black and white you could produce a whole range of shades. White mixed with black gave you grey and this was the next most common colour. Rare colours were green, blue and yellow. The lettering was normally applied with lead based paint and therefore white - again for cheapness.

Former Airfix and Mainline Wagons - Dapol had hoped to acquire the Airfix wagon tooling when Airfix collapsed, but it went to Palitoy with much of it being put back into use to produce new Mainline wagons. Instead, Dapol had a series of wagons tooled up for them in Hong Kong from proprietary samples sent out there. These seem to have included the 12T tanker, 'Mogo' van, 7-plank wagon, 5-plank wagon, double vent van, SR box van, LMS and GWR brake vans, 'Conflat' and container, 12T hopper wagon, the large steel mineral wagon and a PCA depressed centre tank. These copies are difficult to tell from the the originals. Later, Dapol acquired the Airfix tools but also tooled up at least five new wagons themselves. Further newly tooled, better detailed ones have more recently been produced by Dapol and some of these have replaced earlier ones.

The first wagons marketed under the Dapol name were released in 1984 and were numbered with a 'B' prefix. Dapol did acquire surplus Airfix and Mainline stock from Palitoy which they sold through their own catalogue, under the Dapol name. Dapol also obtained Airfix and Mainline wagon parts and assembled some of the wagons themselves, packaging them as Dapol wagons. No records have come to light to show the origins of these wagons and so a 'B' number can include repackaged Airfix or Mainline stock, models assembled from factory clearance parts, replica parts made by Dapol or a mixture of all these. Thus, the listing here has had to be done on a generic basis but with divisions made in the tabling only where detective work suggests that these should be. Much more research is needed and I would welcome further information on this subject.

In addition to the above, Dapol used the Airfix tooling they had acquired in 1985 to produce more of them, often taking the opportunity to change the running number, but the printing on these early reissues was sometimes of a poorer quality which helps to identify them. They also reissued some Mainline wagons but using the equivalent Dapol replica or Airfix body but with Mainline artwork.

SR double vent van [W40b] (Tony Wright)

Former Wrenn Wagons - In 1993, Dapol purchased G&R Wrenn on the retirement of George Wrenn. While on this occasion they did not receive any completed stock, they did have all the unassembled parts from which wagons were made up and sold. From 1997 these were sold in three different categories. Where all Wrenn parts were used, they was sold as Wrenn models with a 'WR1' prefix to the catalogue number. If the wagons were made up from Wrenn bodies fitted to a Dapol chassis they were sold as Dapol wagons with a 'WR2' prefix and if new bodies were made from the acquired Wrenn tools they were sold as Dapol models with a 'WR3' prefix. Once original parts were used

Dapol 00

up, the WR1 and WR2 categories disappeared and WR3 wagons were absorbed into the main wagon series and given 'B' prefixes.

Unfortunately, I had no production records when compiling this list and depended to a large extent on catalogues and price lists. Thus, the inclusion of a wagon in the following tables is not evidence that it was actually made. It is merely an indication that Dapol listed it.

When, in 2001, Dapol sold G&R Wrenn Ltd to Mordvale, they retained all but 9 of the former HD/Wrenn wagon body tools including the following: utility van, gunpowder van, 'Presflo', 5-plank wagon, banana van, mineral wagon, grain wagon, salt van and cattle van.

WRCC Models - Dapol produced wagon bodies for the Wrenn Railways Collectors Club and these were supplied in Dapol boxes and with two gold printed labels. The pairs of labels carried a unique number and indicated the size of the run. The idea was that members would fit these special edition bodies to any spare Wrenn chassis they had and, if they wished, box them in Wrenn boxes to which they affixed the gold label. The bodies sold for about £6 each. Later produced special editions for the club were complete wagons. In all there were ten of these releases by Dapol.

Special Editions - In recent years, Dapol has established itself as the leading manufacturer of special edition wagons commissioned by shops and organisations. These are often produced in numbers no greater than 100 and quickly sell out. Due to the vast number of variations produced, we have not been able to trace every one of them and the absence of one from the tables below is not an indication that the model is rarer than others. I am always interested to learn of ones I have missed and, in each case, would like to know inscription, colour, running number, production quantity, year of release and who it was made for, etc. - if known.

(A) = ex-Airfix stock
(M) = ex-Mainline stock

Cat No.	Company, Number, Colour, Date	£	£

Flat Wagons

W1. 'Lowmac MS' (ex-Airfix) (1985)

This was a British Railways design which seems to have been influenced by the LNER 'Mac' machinery wagons.

Airfix had introduced the model in 1977 and the tools passed to Palitoy, who did not use them. The models in this table are made from the Airfix tools and include unsold Airfix stock which Dapol added to their own catalogue. The Hornby Dublo 'Lowmac' tool was damaged and not used by Dapol. It was later sold, with others, to Morevale Ltd with most of the G&R Wrenn Ltd assets. The Airfix tooling was sold to Hornby in 1996 and the model reintroduced by them.

Cat No.	Description	£	£
B57	BR dark grey + crate - 89	7	12
B57	BR B904662 red brown + crate (A) - 85	8	12
B58	BR B904662 red brown + 'Sea Land' container (A) - 8515		15

W2a. 'Conflat A' (ex-Airfix) (2007)

The 'Conflat A' was a post-war Swindon design and the first 400 were built at Swindon and Wolverton. Over the next ten years, 200,000 of them were built, most of them during the BR era. There is little difference between the GWR and BR versions.

The model was the same as that used for the wagon listed in the next table.

Cat No.	Description	£	£
-	BR B737759 brown Sp Edn 100 (Alexandra Models) - 07	9	16

W2b. 'Conflat A' with BD Container (ex-Airfix) (1986)

This was an attractive model released by Airfix in 1978. The tooling was acquired by Palitoy in 1981, who sent it to Kader in Hong Kong to be altered to take the AF container. It is thought that Dapol had duplicate tooling made of the Airfix wagon and subsequently received the former Airfix tools in 1985 for just the 'Conflat B', but not the container which was mislaid in China. Their replica 'Conflat B' and container they sold to Hornby, who are still making versions of it. Meanwhile, Dapol having the container-less original 'Conflat B' wagon, matched it with a new container and the results are listed here.

Cat No.	Description	£	£
A4	brown container on a grey wagon - unfinished - 86	5	10
A4	black container on a grey wagon - unfinished - ?	5	10
A20	light grey+light grey unfinished - 11	6	8
-	LB&SRC 7160 grey + 'Curtiss & Sons' container pale brown SP Edn 168 (Wessex Wagons) - 08	9	12
-	LB&SCR 7986 grey + 'White & Co.' container 200 brown+cream Sp Edn 128 (Wessex Wagons) - 09	15	19
-	LSWR 32245 brown + 'White & Co.' container 200 brown+cream Sp Edn 139 (Wessex Wagons) - 09	15	19

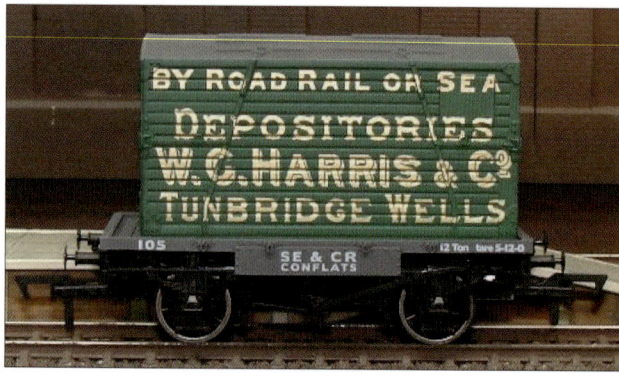

SE&CR conflat container [W2b] (Dapol)

Cat No.	Description	£	£
-	SE&CR 105 grey + 'W G Harris' container dark green Sp Edn (Ballards) - 09	7	9
-	SECR 105 dk.grn + 'W G Harris' container dark green Sp Edn 1000 (Ballards) - 03	10	12
B91	GW 39324 dark grey + 'C&G Ayers' container 37 green (M) - 87	8	12
B399	GW 39005 dark grey + 'C&G Ayers' container 37 dark blue (also boxed as B91) - 02	8	10
4F037104	GW 39024 dark grey + 'C&G Ayers' container 35 green - 12	10	13
4F037105	GW 39024 dark grey W + 'C&G Ayers' container 35 green W - 12	11	14
-	GW 39029 brown + 'VJ Blew' container 23 dark blue Sp Edn 167 (Wessex Wagons) -08	10	12
-	GW 39005 grey + 'W&A Chapman' container brown Sp Edn 270 (Wessex Wagons) - 05	10	12
-	GW 39029 grey + 'JM Davis & Son' container 2 dark brown Sp Edn (Burnham & District MRC - 11	11	14
-	GW 39024 dark grey + 'GH German' container brown Sp Edn 145 (Burnham & District MRC - 12	11	14
-	GW 39024 grey + 'GW&H Gibbs & Sons' container red-brown Sp Edn 150 (Burnham & District MRC - 11	11	14
-	GW 39024 grey + 'Hawkes, Freeman' container 4 brown Sp Edn 93 (Buffers) - 10	9	11
No.10	GW 39050 dark grey + 'Jane's' 50 container cream Sp Edn 97 (West Wales Wagon Works) - 03	10	12
-	GW 39024 grey + 'Lane & Hawkes' green Sp Edn 180 (Wessex Wagons) - 07	10	12
-	GW 39024 dark grey + 'Lewis & Sons' container green Sp Edn 125 (Burnham & District MRC - 13	9	12
-	GW 39005 grey + 'Llangollen International Musical Eisteddfod' green container Sp Edn 1 08 (Llangollen Railway GW Loco Group) - 07	10	12
-	GW 39005 grey + 'Medway Queen' 37 dark green Sp Edn 80 (Medway Queen PS) - 08	10	12
-	GW 39024 grey + 'New Medway' 66 green Sp Edn 60 (Medway Queen PS) - 07	10	12
-	GW 39005 grey + 'Peace' container 2 blue Sp Edn 74 (Burnham & District MRC) - 09	10	12
-	GW 39024 grey + 'F.R.Purchase' container 3 green Sp Edn 141 (Burnham & District MRC) - 10	11	14
-	GW 39029 grey + 'Shirer & Haddon' container dark brown Sp Edn 145 (Burnham & District MRC - 11	11	14
B119	GW 39324 dark grey + GWR container BK1828 brown - 88	10	12
B119	GW 39005 dark grey + GWR container BK1828 dark brown - 95	10	12
B531	GW 39005 dark grey + GWR container BK1828 dark brown - 03	7	9
B650	GW 39024 dark grey + GWR container K1691 dark brown - 06	7	9

Dapol 00

GWR 'conflat' + GWR container [W2b] (Dapol)

Cat	Description		
B1006	GW 39024 dark grey + **GWR** container K1691 dark brown 'Furniture Removal Service' - *11*	10	13
B1006W	GW 39024 dark grey W + **GWR** container K1691 dark brown 'Furniture Removal Service' W - *11*	11	14
4F037003	GW 39024 dark grey + **GWR** container K1691 dark brown 'Furniture Removal Service' - *12*	10	13
4F037004	GW 39024 dark grey W + **GWR** container K1691 dark brown 'Furniture Removal Service' W - *12*	11	14
B162	**LMS** 300478 light grey + **LMS** container K1 maroon - *91*	9	11
B544	**LMS** N300478 grey + **LMS** container K1 maroon - *03*	7	9
-	NE 240748 light grey + **'Bollingbroke & Wenley'** container 08 red-brown Sp Edn 243 (Chelmsford & District MRC) - *08*	9	11
B120	NE 240747 grey + **'J Miles'** container red (A) - *88*	9	12
B383	NE 240748 grey + **'J Miles'** container 3 red - *02*	7	9
B120	NE 240749 grey + **'J Miles'** container red (A) - *88*	8	12
B121	NE 240747 brown + **LNER** container dark blue BK1828 - *88*	5	7
B121	NE 240749 brown + **LNER** container dark blue BK1828 - *88*	5	7

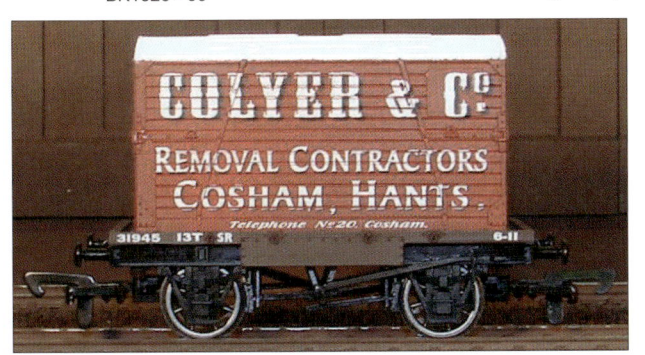

SR 'Conflat' & container [W2b] (Dapol)

Cat	Description		
B563	NE 240748 grey + **LNER** container BK1828 dark blue - *03*	3	5
-	SR 31955 dark brown + **'T.Browning & Sons'** container white Sp Edn 145 (E.Kent MRS) - *05*	9	12
-	SR 31945 dark brown + **'Colyer & Co.'** maroon Sp Edn 188 (Wessex Wagons) - *06*	10	12
-	SR 31873 dark brown + **'JM Davis & Son'** container 2 brown Sp Edn 136 (Burnham & District MRC) - *11*	8	10
-	SR 31927 dark brown + **'Day & Co.'** container cream Sp Edn 280 (Wessex Wagons) - *06*	9	12
-	SR 31955 dark brown + **'Gadd'** container red-brown Sp Edn 147 (Burnham & District MRC) - *12*	11	14
4F037101	SR 31955 dark brown + **'WG Harris & Co.'** container green - *12*	10	13
4F037102	SR 31955 dark brown W + **'WG Harris & Co.'** container green W - *12*	11	14
-	SR 31955 grey + **'Hawkes, Freeman'** container 4 brown Sp Edn 101 (Buffers) - *10*	9	11
-	SR 31927 dark brown + **'Medway Queen'** container 37 blue Sp Edn 80 (Medway Queen PS) - *08*	10	12
-	SR 31875 brown + **'New Medway'** container 66 blue Sp Edn 60 (Medway Queen PS) - *07*	10	12
-	SR 31875 dark brown + **'JC Nutt'** container green Sp Edn 280 (Wessex Wagons) - *06*	9	12
-	SR 31927 grey + **'Peace'** container 2 blue Sp Edn 63 (Burnham & District MRC) - *09*	10	12
No.44	SR 31952 brown + **'Pimm & Son'** container brown Sp Edn 108 (West Wales Wagon Works) - *07*	10	12
No.16	SR 39050 dark brown + **'Reeves'** container brown Sp Edn 93 (West Wales Wagon Works) - *04*	11	13
-	SR 31876 dark brown + **'Reynolds & Co.'** container 3 cream Sp Edn 150 (Richard Essen) - *10*	12	15
-	SR 31875 dark brown + **'James Sayers'** container cream Sp Edn 200 (Wessex Wagons) - *06*	10	12
-	SR 7986 dark brown + **'Shepard Bros.'** container 6 green Sp Edn 198 (Buffers) - *11*	10	13
B129	SR 39115, 39155 dark brown + **SR** container K591 - *94*	9	11
B530	SR 31955 dark brown + **SR** container K591 green - not made	NA	NA
B530	SR 31955 dark brown + **SR** container K595 green - *03*	7	9
B1007	SR 31955 grey + **SR** container K598 green - *11*	11	13
B1007W	SR 31955 grey W + **SR** container K598 green W - *11*	12	14
4F037001	SR 31955 dark brown + **SR** container K598 green - *12*	10	13
4F037002	SR 31955 dark brown W + **SR** container K598 green W - *12*	11	14
-	SR 39028 dark brown + **SR** container B255 dark brown Sp Edn 1000 (Ballards) - *04*	10	12
B118	BR W36507 brown + **'Pickfords'** 1666 container dark blue - *87*	9	11
4F037102	BR W16305 dark brown + **'Pickfords'** container dark blue - *12*	10	13
4F037103	BR W16305 dark brown W + **'Pickfords'** container dark blue W - *12*	11	14
-	BR W36507 brown + **'Trago Mills'** container dark brown Sp Edn 250 (Trago Mills) - *06*	10	13
-	BR B737759 red-brown + **'Beale & Piper'** container yellow Sp Edn (Strathspey Railway) - *06*	11	13
B100	BR B735700 red-brown + **BR** furniture container (A) - *86*	8	12
-	BR MU60001 dark brown + tractor load (yellow, blue or grey [equal split] by Oxford Diecasts) Sp Edn 100 (Modellbahn Union**) some sold with continental couplings - *13*	14	18
-	MHR 02004 dark grey + **'Watercress Line'** container K904 green Sp Edn 100 (Mid Hants Railway) - *04*	10	12
-	GNR(I) 1997 brown + **GNR** Furniture Removals container No.1 dark blue Sp Edn 129 (Provincial Wagons) - *08*	10	13
-	GNR(I) 4287 brown + **GNR(I)** Furniture Removals container No.4 dark blue Sp Edn 136 (Provincial Wagons) - *08*	10	13
-	GNR(I) 728 brown Sp Edn (Alexandra Models) - *12*	9	16
-	grey + **'Reg Stickells'** container green Sp Edn 110 1st issue (Hythe Models) - *02*	11	13

GNR (1) 'Conflat' & container [W2b] (Dapol)

** Modellbahn of Germany is also known as Japan Model Railways of Kamen, Germany.

W2c. 'Conflat A' & Resin Containers (2010)

This is the former Airfix 'Conflat A' (as above) but sold with a resin container, commercially produced for the Irish market, but not by Dapol. The containers were made for Provincial Wagons by Smallbrook Studios on the Isle of Wight. Two containers can be carried on one 'Conflat A'.

Dapol 00

-	**GNR(I)** 772 brown + resin bread containers SP Edn 142 (Provincial Wagons) * - *10*	20	25
-	**GNR(I)** 1957 grey + resin bread containers Sp Edn 160 (Provincial Wagons) * - *10*	20	25
-	**GNR(I)** N728 brown + Guiness 2 small silver resin containers Sp Edn 100 (Provincial Wagons) - *12*	20	26

* These two wagons were issued with a choice of Irish bread containers which were cast in resin, painted and with transfers applied, as they were unique to this traffic. Purchasers had a choice of combinations of any of four bread containers produced so far. The containers came as follows: 'Windsor' (red), 'McCone' (red), 'Ingle' (red) and 'Highes' Bread' (black). The values suggested reflect the price of a 'Conflat' with containers.

Planked Goods Wagons

W3a. 1-plank Wagon (ex-Wrenn) (1995)

As its name implies, a 1-plank wagon had only a single narrow plank making up each side and this was hinged along the bottom to allow it to drop down to make loading and unloading easier. All four railway companies had them and BR built 3150 'Lowfits', as they were called. The first 400 had wooden bodies but, after that, they were built in steel.

This is a plastic moulding of a separate body that fits on the standard plastic chassis. Wrenn must have produced the tool for the body themselves.

B241	**'Auto Trader'** 115 red brown - *c95*	12	15
WR1-30	**'Auto Spares'** 115 brown + 4 tyres - *99*	12	20
WR2-29	as above Dapol chassis - *99*	12	15
B239	**BR** B459325 grey - *c95*	10	15
WR1-31	as above - *99*	10	17

W3b. 1-plank Wagon + Container (ex-Mainline) (1986)

This is the Mainline 1-plank model with the BD size container which was released by Palitoy in 1982. The models sold by Dapol were old Mainline stock bought by them in 1985.

B240	**LMS** + **LMS** container - *not made*	NA	NA
B90	**BR** B450023 red brown + **'Bird's Eye'** BD container (M) - *86*	8	12

W4. 3-plank Open Wagon (ex-Mainline) (1985)

3-plank wagons were low-sided wagons for merchandise and were particularly common on the LMS. Many found use as container wagons.

It seems that this was a wagon that Airfix had been working on at the time they went into receivership and that the work was completed by Palitoy. It was released in the Mainline range in 1982 and the unsold stock was bought by Dapol when Palitoy closed down. However, from the table it seems that Dapol had access to tooling to produce more 3-plank wagons themselves. This may have been a duplicate body tool produced at the same time as the other copies.

A8	brown - unfinished - *85*	5	10
	Private Owner		
B47	**'Carter'** 172 grey (M) - *85*	6	10
B96	**'E.Turner'** 26 cream (M) - *86*	6	10
	Railway Company		
B48	**LMS** 471624 grey - *85*	8	10
B24	**LMS** 471194 grey - *?*	8	10
B24	**LMS** 473449 red brown - *85*	8	10
B49	**NE** 535962 grey (M) - *85*	6	10
B23	**BR** M471363 light grey - *85*	8	10
B50	**BR** M473453 red brown, new chassis (M) - *85*	6	10

W5. 4-plank Open Wagon (2006)

This model is based on a GWR design of the early 1900s and was a general-purpose open wagon. A single batch of 200 was built before it was decided that a 5-plank design would be more versatile.

The model was tooled by Dapol to widen the range of subjects that could be used for private owner wagons. It has NEM pocket couplings, correctly profiled wheels and each comes with a suitable load.

A005	unfinished grey - *10*	4	10
	Private Owner		
-	**'Abercriban Quarries'** 57 red with granite load Sp Edn 109 (David Dacey) - *08*	7	9
BE5	**'Arnold Sands'** 503 brown sand load Sp Edn 150 (1E Promotionals) - *07*	7	9
-	**'BCWW'** 159 yellow Sp Edn 165 (Wessex Wagons) - *10*	7	10
-	**'Beswick's Lime Works'** 216 cream Sp Edn 400 (Bagnall Locomotive Group) - *12*	8	10

4-plank open wagon 'Arnolds Sands' [W5]

-	**'Blue Circle Cement'** 5 yellow Sp Edn 113 (Wessex Wagons) - *09*	7	9
-	**'Blue Circle Cement'** 18 yellow Sp Edn 100 (Wessex Wagons) - *09*	7	9
B665	**'The Bold Venture Lime Co.'** 24 grey - *06*	6	8
No.8	**'Willm H Booth'** 701 red-brown Sp Edn 200 (Mid-Suffolk Light Railway) - *08*	7	9
B755	**'BW Co.'** 1100 red + grey load - *08*	6	8
4F-040001	**'BW Co.'** 1100 red + grey load - *13*	7	9
4F-040002	**'BW Co.'** 1100 red W + grey load - *13*	7	10
SY2	**'Cadbury Co.'** 10 red Sp Edn 350 (1E Promotionals) - *08*	7	9
-	**'Ceiriog Granite Co.'** 195 brown Sp Edn (Dapol Shop) - *08*	7	9
B743	**'Clee Hill Granite'** 331 light blue - *08*	6	8
4F-040003	**'Clee Hill Granite'** 331 grey + granite load - *12*	7	9
4F-040004	**'Clee Hill Granite'** 331 grey W + granite load - *12*	7	10
No.82	**'Corris Railway'** 343 light grey with brick, coal, sand or planks load Sp Edn 120 (West Wales Wagon Works) - *09*	7	10
No.82	**'Corris Railway'** 343 light grey W with brick, coal, sand or planks load Sp Edn 120 (West Wales Wagon Works) - *09*	8	11
E06A	**'Cranmore Granite'** 346 lt grey Sp Edn 150 (East Somerset Models) ex-pair - *07*	7	NA
E06B	**'Cranmore Granite'** 347 lt grey Sp Edn 150 (East Somerset Models) ex-pair - *07*	7	NA
-	above pair - *07*	NA	16
-	**'Cwmbran Brick Co.'** 15 dark brown Sp Edn 106 (David Dacey) - *09*	6	8
-	**'Deane & Son'** 2 black Sp Edn 150 (Buffers) - *12*	8	11
-	**'East Downshire Steamship Co.'** (Irish) 14 grey Sp Edn 110 (Provincial Wagons) - *07*	7	9
-	**'East Downshire Steamship Co.'** (Irish) 2 grey Sp Edn 143 (Provincial Wagons) - *07*	7	9
B883	**'Ellis & Everade'** 23 yellow - *11*	7	9
B883W	**'Ellis & Everade'** 23 yellow W - *12*	7	10
No.56	**'C&F Gaen'** 4 grey + black tar load Sp Edn 120 (West Wales Wagon Works) - *07*	7	9
No.56	**'C&F Gaen'** 4 grey W + black tar load Sp Edn 40 (West Wales Wagon Works) - *07*	7	9
-	**'Great Wheal Prosper'** 22 orange Sp Edn 137 (Wessex Wagons) - *12*	8	10
-	**'Hard Stone Farms'** 105 white Sp Edn 159 (Burnham & District MRC) - *11*	7	9
B905	**'Walter Harper'** 1 red-brown + road slag load - *11*	7	9
B905W	**'Walter Harper'** 1 red-brown W + road slag load - *12*	7	10
B882	**'The Harts Hill Iron Company'** 8 dark brown+ grey load - *11*	7	9
B882W	**'The Harts Hill Iron Company'** 8 dk brown W + grey load - *12*	7	10
-	**'Holms Sand & Gravel Co.'** 20 black Sp Edn 163 (Wessex Wagons) - *07*	7	9
ANT 031	**'Hore Brothers'** 60 black Sp Edn 250 (Antics) - *08*	7	9
B682	**'Hudson Bro.'** 10 grey + brick load - *07*	6	8
-	**'Richard Hughes'** 10 red-brown Sp Edn 157 (Wessex Wagons) - *10*	8	10
E07A	**'Foster Yeoman'** 126 light grey Sp Edn 175 (East Somerset Models) - *08*	7	9
E07B	**'Foster Yeoman'** 130 light grey Sp Edn 175 (East Somerset Models) - *08*	7	9
-	**'WJ King'** 39 black Sp Edn (West Somerset Railway) - *12*	9	12

Dapol 00

-	'AE **Lavender & Sons**' 12 red Sp Edn 159 (Burnham & District MRC) - *13*	8	11
-	'**Llanharry**' 37 cream W Sp Edn * (Barry & Penarth MRS) - *07*	8	10
-	'E **Marsh**' 1 grey with stone load Sp Edn 146 (West Wales Wagon Works) - *07*	7	9
-	'**Mendip Granite Works**' 8 buff Sp Edn 167 (Wessex Wagons) - *08*	7	9

4-plank open wagon - Mid Suffolk [W5] (Dapol)

-	**Mid Suffolk** 5 light grey Sp Edn (Middy Trading Co.) - *09*	7	9
-	**Mid Suffolk** 18 grey Sp Edn (Middy Trading Co.) - *09*	8	11
B718	'**New Cransley Iron & Steel**' 76 grey - *08*	6	8
-	'**T.Pearson**' 2 white Sp Edn (St Albans Signal Box Preservation Trust) - *10*	9	12
-	'**Pentrefelin Slab & Slate Works**' 3 light grey Sp Edn 109 (Llangollen Railway GWR group) - *07*	7	9
-	'**Penwyllt Silica Works**' 19 grey Sp Edn 103 (David Dacey) - *08*	7	9
-	'**Portland Cement**' 13 yellow Sp Edn 145 (Wessex Wagons) - *11*	7	10
B662	'**Pwllheli Granite Co.**' 155 grey - *06*	5	6
-	'**Radstock Coal Co.**' 1379 black Sp Edn 244 (Wessex Wagons) - *06*	8	10
-	'**RNCF**' N63 grey Sp Edn 129 (Wessex Wagons) - *12*	8	10
-	'**RVR**' 1 grey Sp Edn 108 (K&ESR) - *07*	8	12
B674	'**Stonehouse Brick & Tile**' 10 red - *06*	7	9
B736	'**Teign Valley Granite**' 1145 black - *08*	6	8
-	'**Timsbury Collieries**' 118 grey Sp Edn 116 (Wessex Wagons) - *08*	7	9
-	'**Timsbury Collieries**' 126 grey Sp Edn 112 (Wessex Wagons) - *08*	7	9
ANT032	'**The Covertry Ordnance Work**' 2 red-brown Sp Edn 250 (Antic) - *08*	7	9
-	'**The Earl Waldegrave Radstock Collieries**' 563 blacl Sp Edn 147 (Burnham & District MRC) - *10*	7	9
CMM003	'**Threlkeld Granite Co.**' 103 grey + granite load Sp Edn 150 (C&N Models) - *10*	9	11
092AM	'**Tonfanau Granite Quarries**' 5 black Sp Edn 83 (West Wales Wagon Works) - *10*	8	11
092AW	'**Tonfanau Granite Quarries**' 5 black W Sp Edn 83 (West Wales Wagon Works) - *10*	9	12
092BM	'**Tonfanau Granite Quarries**' 9 black Sp Edn 83 (West Wales Wagon Works) - *10*	8	11
092BW	'**Tonfanau Granite Quarries**' 9 black W Sp Edn 83 (West Wales Wagon Works) - *10*	9	12
092PM	2 of above pristine wagons 5 & 9 Sp Edn 18 (West Wales Wagon Works) - *10*	NA	20

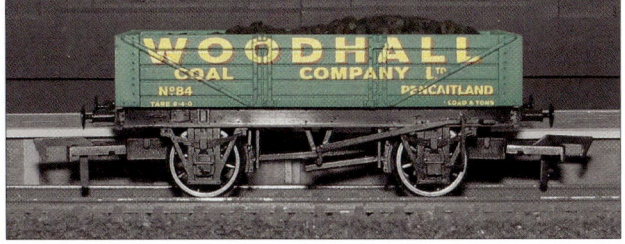

4-plank open wagon - 'Woodall Coal Co.' [W5] (Dapol)

092PW	2 of above weathered wagons 5 & 9 Sp Edn 17 (West Wales Wagon Works) - *10*	NA	20
-	'**Toyne Carter & Co.**' 71 grey Sp Edn 163 (Wessex Wagons) - *10*	8	10
B714	'**Weardale**' 805 brown - *07*	6	8
-	'**Robert Whitehead & Co.**' W41 grey Sp Edn 76 (Wessex Wagons) - *13*	8	10
-	'**Robert Whitehead & Co.**' W41 grey with red corners Sp Edn 46 (Wessex Wagons) - *13*	8	10
-	'F **Wilkinson**' 11 red-brown Sp Edn 135 (Crafty Hobbies) - *07*	7	9
B877	'**Woodall Coal Company**' 84 dark green - *11*	7	9
-	'**Writhlington & Kilmersdon Colliery**' 'W' 93 black Sp Edn 204 (Wessex Wagons) - *07*	7	9
-	'**Writhlington & Kilmersdon Colliery**' 'K' 342 black Sp Edn 206 (Wessex Wags) - *07*	7	9
-	'**Ynydybwl Pennant Stone**' 12 red-brown Sp Edn 106 (South Wales Coalfields) - *07*	8	10

Railway Company

-	**BCDR** (Belfast & County Down Railway) 107 dark grey Sp Edn 156 (Provincial Wagons) - *09*	7	9
-	**BCDR** (Belfast & County Down Railway) 2A dark grey Sp Edn 156 (Provincial Wagons) - *10*	9	12
B761	**GW** 45504 grey with timber load - *09*	7	9
B761A	**GW** 44404 grey with timber load ** - *10*	7	9
B761AW	**GW** 44404 grey W with timber load ** - *10*	7	9
4F-040005	**GW** 45506 grey with timber load - *12*	7	9
4F-040006	**GW** 45506 grey with timber load - *12*	7	10
-	**GNR(I)** 3164 grey Sp Edn 100 (Provincial Wagons) - *07*	7	9
-	**GNR(I)** 5558 grey Sp Edn 115 (Provincial Wagons) - *08*	7	9
-	**GNR(I)** 3616 grey with timber load Sp Edn 164 (Provincial Wagons) - *09*	8	11
-	**HM&STy** grey Sp Edn (Colonel Stephens Railway Enterprise) - *11*	8	12
-	**UT** (Ulster Transport) C85 red-brown Sp Edn 150 (Provincial Wagons) - *09*	7	9
-	**WC&PR** grey Sp Edn 100 (Kent & East Sussex Railway) - *08*	8	11

4-plank open wagon - HM&STy [W5]

* Short run weathered by Dapol for an eBay retailer. ** Possibly renumbered old stock.

W6. 5-plank Open Wagon 9ft WB (2009)

5-plank wagons were considered to be 'high goods wagons' and were referred to as 'Highfits' or 'High NF'. Anything larger was probably specifically for the coal and mineral trade. They were once highly numerous and used for the transportation of general merchandise.

Early 5-plank wagons had a 9ft wheel base and many of the private owner wagon liveries are more suited to these shorter wooden framed wagons. The introduction of this model by Dapol was part of an attempt at improving their wagon range.

A015	grey - unfinished - *11*	4	10

Private Owner

B870	'**Nath Atrill**' 6 black - *11*	7	9
B870W	'**Nath Atrill**' 6 black W - *12*	7	10
B906	'**Caves Coals**' 303 red - *11*	7	10
B838	'**Chipping Norton Co-op**' 10 black - *10*	7	10
-	'**Dean & Son**' 2 black Sp Edn 156 (Buffers) - *12*	9	11
B812	'J **James & Co.**' 98 red-brown - *09*	7	10
-	'**Hocknulls**' 1 grey Sp Edn 150 (Wessex Wagons) - *10*	8	10
B901	'**ICI**' 75739 blue-grey - *11*	7	9
B901W	'**ICI**' 75739 blue-grey W - *12*	7	10
B767	'**Marshall**' 2 red-brown - *09*	7	10
4F052001	'**Marshall**' 2 red-brown - *13*	7	9
4F052002	'**Marshall**' 2 red-brown W - *13*	7	10

Dapol 00

-	'John **Milligen**' 50 red-brown Sp Edn (Leslie NcAllister) - 11	8	10
-	'FW **Pinniger**' 2 black Sp Edn 152 (Burnhan & District MRC) - 10	7	9
B813	'EA **Robinson**' 1905 red-brown - 09	7	10
4F052005	'EA **Robinson**' 1905 red-brown - 12	7	9
4F052006	'EA **Robinson**' 1905 red-brown W - 12	7	10
B814	'FH **Silvey & Co.**' 196 dark brown - 09	7	10
4F052007	'FH **Silvey & Co.**' 196 dark brown - 12	7	9
4F052008	'FH **Silvey & Co.**' 196 dark brown W - 12	7	10
B818	'**Stevens & Co.**' 3 red - 09	7	9
4F052003	'**Stevens & Co.**' 3 red - 12	7	9
4F052004	'**Stevens & Co.**' 3 red W - 12	7	10
-	'**Taylot & Anderson**' 900 dark green Sp Edn 150 (Wessex Wagons) - 10	8	10
ANT44	'**Worcester New Co-operative & Industrial Society**' 20 red-browm Sp Edn 140 (Antics) - 10	8	11

9ft wheelbase 5-plank wagon [W6] (Hattons)

W7a. 5-plank Open Wagon 10ft WB (ex-Airfix) (1984)

Airfix released their 5-plank wagon in 1978 and the tools were later used by Palitoy to add variety to their Mainline Railways range. Dapol bought the Airfix tooling from Palitoy as well as unsold Airfix and Mainline models produced from it. It seems that they also had duplicate tooling previously produced for them in China. We have no record as to which models were done with which tool but one was sold to Hornby in 1996 and the other retained by Dapol.

A2	grey - unfinished - 84	5	10
	Private Owner		
B160	'**Alloa**' 1124 yellow (A) - 89	6	10
B160	'**Alloa**' 1125 yellow - ?	8	10
B38	'**Arnold**' 156 red brown (A) - 86	6	10
B45	'**BAC**' 4253 red brown (M) - 85	6	10
B46	'**Black Rock**' 46 black (M) - 85	6	10
B268	'**Black Rock**' 46 black - 98	7	9
B515	**Corporation of Dundee Gas Dept.**' 67 red-brown - not made	NA	NA
B39	'**Devizes Sand**' 1 grey (A) - 85	6	10
B41	'**Harts Hill**' 2 brown (A) - 85	6	10
B41	'**Harts Hill**' 2 brown - 95	7	9
B199	'**Higginbotham**' 521 dk.brown - 91, 95	8	11
-	'JP **Higgs**' 4 dark brown Sp Edn 120 (Wessex Wagons) - 12	8	10
-	'**HMS Excellent**' 6 black Sp Edn 117 (Wessex Wagons) - 12	8	10
-	'Alfred **Horsman**' 1 red-brown Sp Edn 139 (Wessex Wagons) - 12	8	10
-	'**Kent & East Sussex Railway**' 2 grey Sp Edn 100 (K&ESR) - 13	9	12
-	'**London Brick Company Limited (Phorpes Bricks)**' 632 black Sp Edn 143 (Burnham & District MRC) - 12	7	9
B101	'**James Marriott**' 14 brown - not made	NA	NA
B183	'**James Marriott**' 14 brown - 91, 97	9	11
-	'John **North & Son**' 18 red-brown, Sp Edn 200+ (Geoff Osborn) - 99	11	13
(3)	'**Old Radnor Lime**' 126 grey Sp Edn 200 (Hereford Model Centre) - 02	11	13
(5)	'**Old Radnor Co.**' 159 grey Sp Edn (Hereford Model Centre) - 02	11	13
(04)	'**Old Radnor Co.**' 238 grey Sp Edn 200 (Hereford Model Centre) - 02	11	13
B40	'**Spencer**' 24 red (A) - 85	6	10
-	'Wm **Tompkins & Son**' 1 grey Sp Edn 125 (Wessex Wagons) - 12	8	10
B163	'**Warrener**' 3 green - 94	9	11
B126	'**Webster**' 341 dark brown (M) - ?	6	10
B267	'**Wolverton Mutual Society**' ** 29 grey Sp Edn 500 (Chris Wright) - 88	11	13

Railway Company

5-plank ex-Airfix wagon [W7a]

B18	**GW** (thick) 109458 dark grey (A) - 84	6	10
B18	**GW** (thin) 109459 dark grey (A) - 84	6	10
B3	**LMS** 413833 red brown - 84	6	8
B42	**LMS** 404104 grey (A) - 86	6	10
B42	**LMS** 404105 grey - 95	6	8
B177	**NE** 535962 grey - 89	6	8
B13	**NE** 104021 red brown - 84	6	8
B13	**NE** 214021 red brown - ?-03	6	8
B179	**SR** 27348 dark brown - 89	6	8
4F051003	**SR** 27348 dark brown - 12	7	9
4F051004	**SR** 27348 dark brown W - 12	8	10
B11	**BR** M407562 light grey (A) - 84	6	10
B11	**BR** M407565 light grey - 84	6	8
B11	**BR** M407580 light grey - 84	6	8
B19	**BR** M411455 red brown - 84	6	8

W7b. 5-plank Open Wagon 10ft WB (ex-Mainline) (1985)

Palitoy had also modelled their own 5-plank wagon before receiving the Airfix tools. In 1985, when Palitoy closed down, Dapol received all the unsold Mainline models and these are listed here.

B164	'**Ellis & Everard**' 136 red+black (M) - ?	6	10
B67	'**Timpson**' 5 blue grey (M) - 85, 97	6	10
B99	'**Wadworths**' 66 black (M) - 86	6	10
B163	'**Warrener**' 3 - green - (M) - 89	6	10

W7c. 5-plank Open Wagon 10ft WB (ex-HD/Wrenn) (1995)

When Dapol bought the G&R Wrenn assets, on the retirement of George Wrenn, it was the wagon tools that they most wanted. These had been tooled by Meccano Ltd in the late 1950s and early 1960s for their Hornby Dublo model railway system.

This is the former Hornby Dublo 5-plank wagon, which was first released in 1958. It was amongst the tooling that Wrenn bought and re-released in 1968. It became Dapol's main 5-plank wagon and, as will be seen from the table here, it has been produced in great variety. Almost without exception, the models in this table were sold with a coal (or other) load infill.

A2	grey - unfinished - 02-03	4	6
A001	grey - unfinished - 04	4	10
	Private Owner		
-	'**Abrem Coal Co.**' 462 red-brown Sp Edn 150 (Astley Green Colliery Museum) - 10	7	9
-	'C **Addicott & Son**' 30 black Sp Edn 152 (Wessex Wagons) - 05	9	11
-	'**Affleck F Fyfe**' 1 brown Sp Edn 100 (Strathspey Railway) - 03	10	12
-	'**Affleck F Fyfe**' 2 brown Sp Edn 100 (Strathspey Railway) - 06	9	11
-	'**Albion Dockyard**' 9 black Sp Edn 60 (Medway Queen Preservation Society) - 09	7	9
-	'**Albion Dockyard**' 9 dark green Sp Edn 90 (Medway Queen Preservation Society) - 09	7	9
-	'**Alexander Brothers**' 37 brown Sp Edn 100 (West Wales Wagon Works) - 12	10	12
-	'**Alexander Brothers**' 37 brown W Sp Edn 20 (West Wales Wagon Works) - 12	10	12
B369	'**Alloa**' 1125 cream - 02-03	8	10

Dapol 00

-	'William **Ambrose**' 4 black Sp Edn 191 (Wessex Wagons) - 06	9	11
No.5A	'Wm. **Aplin**' 2 black Sp Edn 120 (West Wales Wagon Works) - 03	9	11
No.5B	'Wm. **Aplin**' 5 black Sp Edn 110 (West Wales Wagon Works) - 03	9	11
-	'**Arbroath** Friendly Coal Soc.' 295 light grey Sp Edn 500 (Virgin Trains) for Glasgow Show - 03	9	11
B591	'**Arenig** Granite' 207 red - 04	7	9
-	'**Arnell**' black Sp Edn 250 (Colonel Stevens Railway Enterprises) - 11	9	13
-	'EJ **Astin**' 1 brown 102 Sp Edn (Nene Valley Railway) - 09	7	9

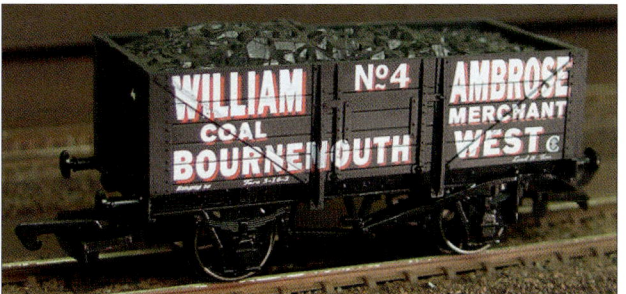

5-plank wagon 'William Ambrose' [W7c] (Dapol)

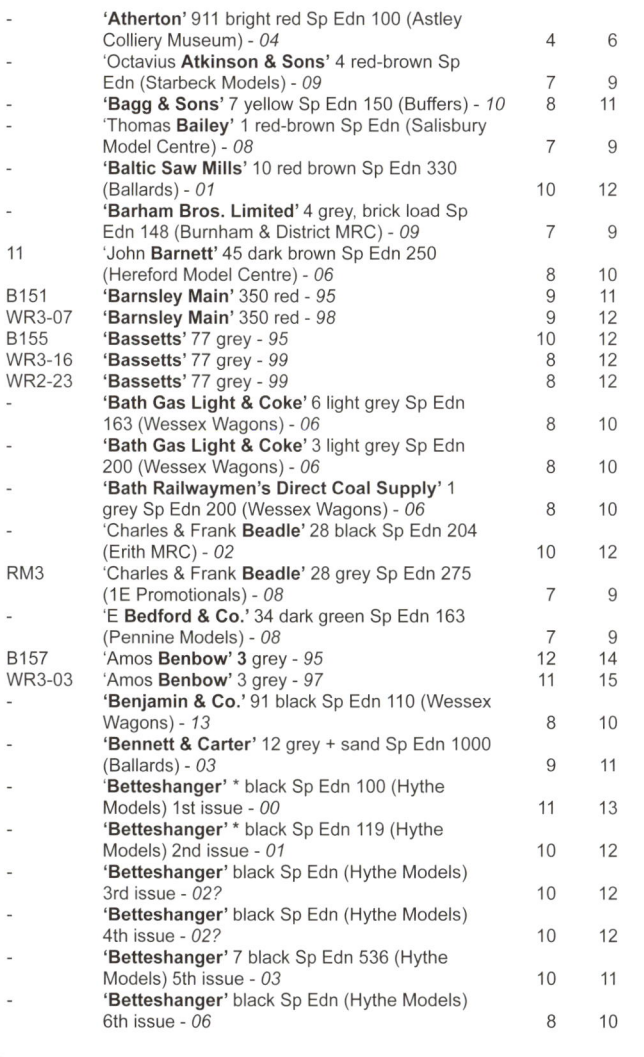

-	'**Atherton**' 911 bright red Sp Edn 100 (Astley Colliery Museum) - 04	4	6
-	'Octavius **Atkinson & Sons**' 4 red-brown Sp Edn (Starbeck Models) - 09	7	9
-	'**Bagg & Sons**' 7 yellow Sp Edn 150 (Buffers) - 10	8	11
-	'Thomas **Bailey**' 1 red-brown Sp Edn (Salisbury Model Centre) - 08	7	9
-	'**Baltic** Saw Mills' 10 red brown Sp Edn 330 (Ballards) - 01	10	12
-	'**Barham** Bros. Limited' 4 grey, brick load Sp Edn 148 (Burnham & District MRC) - 09	7	9
11	'John **Barnett**' 45 dark brown Sp Edn 250 (Hereford Model Centre) - 06	8	10
B151	'**Barnsley** Main' 350 red - 95	9	11
WR3-07	'**Barnsley** Main' 350 red - 98	9	12
B155	'**Bassetts**' 77 grey - 95	10	12
WR3-16	'**Bassetts**' 77 grey - 99	8	12
WR2-23	'**Bassetts**' 77 grey - 99	8	12
-	'**Bath** Gas Light & Coke' 6 light grey Sp Edn 163 (Wessex Wagons) - 06	8	10
-	'**Bath** Gas Light & Coke' 3 light grey Sp Edn 200 (Wessex Wagons) - 06	8	10
-	'**Bath** Railwaymen's Direct Coal Supply' 1 grey Sp Edn 200 (Wessex Wagons) - 06	8	10
-	'Charles & Frank **Beadle**' 28 black Sp Edn 204 (Erith MRC) - 02	10	12
RM3	'Charles & Frank **Beadle**' 28 grey Sp Edn 275 (1E Promotionals) - 08	7	9
-	'E **Bedford & Co.**' 34 dark green Sp Edn 163 (Pennine Models) - 08	7	9
B157	'Amos **Benbow**' 3 grey - 95	12	14
WR3-03	'Amos **Benbow**' 3 grey - 97	11	15
-	'**Benjamin & Co.**' 91 black Sp Edn 110 (Wessex Wagons) - 13	8	10
-	'**Bennett & Carter**' 12 grey + sand Sp Edn 1000 (Ballards) - 03	9	11
-	'**Betteshanger**' * black Sp Edn 100 (Hythe Models) 1st issue - 00	11	13
-	'**Betteshanger**' * black Sp Edn 119 (Hythe Models) 2nd issue - 01	10	12
-	'**Betteshanger**' black Sp Edn (Hythe Models) 3rd issue - 02?	10	12
-	'**Betteshanger**' black Sp Edn (Hythe Models) 4th issue - 02?	10	12
-	'**Betteshanger**' 7 black Sp Edn 536 (Hythe Models) 5th issue - 03	10	11
-	'**Betteshanger**' black Sp Edn (Hythe Models) 6th issue - 06	8	10

-	'**Bickershaw**' 555 red-brown Sp Edn 100 (Astley Colliery Museum) - 04	9	11
-	'AH&S **Bird**' 27 grey Sp Edn 149 (Wessex Wagons) - 06	8	10
-	'**Bispham** Hall' 74 red-brown Sp Edn 100 (Astley Green Colliery Museum) - 12	8	11
-	'Wm **Black & Sons**' 849 black Sp Edn 220 (Ayr Glass & Glazing) - 03	9	11
B715	'**Black** Rock Quarries' 49 black - 07	6	8
#32	'**Blake**' 112 bright red Sp Edn 250 (Hereford Model Shop) - 06	9	11
B387	'**Blake**' 136 red - 02	8	10

5-plank wagon 'Bletchley & District Co-Op' [W7c]

-	'John **Bland & Co.**' 7 red-brown Sp Edn 141 (Burnham & District MRC) - 09	7	9
-	'John **Bland & Co.**' 5 red-brown Sp Edn 145 (Burnham & District MRC) - 12	7	9
B575	'H **Blandford**' 7 light grey - 04	9	11
BY5	'**Bletchley** & Dist Co-op' 86 black Sp Edn 250 (1E Promotionals) - 06	8	10
-	'VJ **Blew**' 03 black Sp Edn 177 (Wessex Wagons) - 07	7	9
B154	'J **Bly**' black - 95	12	14
W5000	'J **Bly**' black Sp Edn 250 (Wrenn Railways Collectors Club WRCC1) - 99	12	15
-	'John **Board & Co.**' 11 black Sp Edn 208 (Wessex Wagons) - 06	8	10
-	'**Bobbett**' 7 dark brown Sp Edn 1000 (Ballards) - 09	9	11
-	'**Bonnell**' 12 red-brown Sp Edn 1000 (Ballards) - 05	8	10
-	'**Bottrill**' 12 black Sp Edn 100 (Richard Essen/Wicor Models) - 07	7	9
-	'**Bowden** Bros.' 16 grey Sp Edn 100 (Henford Halt) - 05	8	10
-	'**Bradford** & Sons' 194 black Sp Edn 110 (Wessex Wagons) - 12	8	10
BY4	'A **Bramley**' 16 dark brown Sp Edn 250 (1E Promotionals) - 05	8	10
B152	'A **Bramley**' 6 red-brown - 95	15	20
-	'Henry **Bramwell**' 2 red-brown Sp Edn 389 (Bignall 2746 Locomotive Society) - 11	7	10
-	'**Braysdown** Colliery' 97 black Sp Edn 237 (Wessex Wagons) - 08	7	9
B150	'**British** Soda' 14 brown - 95	12	15
WR1-10	as above grey or white load - 99	12	15
WR2-26	as above, Dapol chassis - 99	12	15
WR3-02	'**British** Soda' 14 brown - 97	7	11
-	'S **Brookman**' 30 light grey Sp Edn 200 (West & Wales Assn. of MRCs) - 06	8	10
-	'RJ **Broughton**' 24 grey Sp Edn 100 (Nene Valley Railway) - 08	7	9
B300	'**Broughton** & Plas' 630 olive green, Ltd Edn 600 - 98	4	6
-	'George **Bryant** & Son' 4 black Sp Edn 100 (Burnham & District MRC) - 08	7	9
-	'G **Bryant** Coal & Coke' 17 black Sp Edn 90 (Burnham & District MRC) - 08	7	9
WO7	'CH **Burt**' 1 black Sp Edn 200 (Wessex Wagons) - 06	7	9
-	'Walter **Burt**' 2 dark brown Sp Edn 150 (1E Promotionals) - 10	8	10
(20)	'W **Butler**' 29 light grey Sp Edn 250 (Hereford Model Shop) - 05	8	10
-	'**Cam** Rys' grey Sp Edn 120 (Cambrian Railway Society) - 01	10	15
-	'The **Cardi-Bach**' (see 'DG Thomas' below)	-	-
CMM004	'**Carlisle** Southend Co-operative Society' 21 red-brown Sp Edn 150 (C&M Models) - 11	7	10

Dapol 00

-	'Carriage & Wagon Dept. - Dover Marine' 4121 black Sp Edn 200 (Carriage & Wagon Models) - 08	7	10
-	'Carter & Co.' 7 red-brown Sp Edn 195 (Wessex Wagons) - 07	7	9
B392	'Cefn Mawr & Rhosymedre' 12 red-brown - 02	7	9
-	'AF Chainey' 2 dark brown Sp Edn 164 (Wessex Wagons) - 05	8	10
-	'Champion Brothers' 4 black Sp Edn 200 (Wessex Wagons) - 05	8	10
-	'Chichester Coal Co.' 50 red-brown Sp Edn 149 (Richard Essen) - 11	9	12
OX2	'Chipping Norton Co-op' 9 black Sp Edn 250 (1E Promotionals) - 05	8	10
No.6	'Christie & Son' 103 black Sp Edn 200 (Middy Trading Company) - 06	8	10
-	'Clarke Sharp & Co.' 400 black Sp Edn 300 (Ballards) - 10	9	11
-	'Clee Hill Granite' 350 pale grey Sp Edn 95 (Dartmoor Railway) - 04	12	15

5-plank wagon 'Chipping Norton Co-Op' [W7c]

F4051009	'Cliffe Hill Granite Co.' 805 grey - 13	7	9
F4051010	'Cliffe Hill Granite Co.' 805 grey W - 13	8	10
B658	'The Cliffe Hill Stone Pavement' 805 pale blue-grey - 06	8	10
4F051009	'The Cliffe Hill Stone Pavement' 805 pale blue-grey - 12	7	9
4F051010	'The Cliffe Hill Stone Pavement' 805 pale blue-grey W - 12	7	9
21	'Edward R Cole' 6 red-brown Sp Edn 250 (Hereford Model Shop) - 05	8	10
-	'Colliery Supply Co.' 10 red-brown Sp Edn 240 (Wessex Wagons) - 12	8	10
-	'Colliery Supply Co.' 10 red-brown W Sp Edn 65 (Wessex Wagons) - 12	8	11
-	'Conduit Colliery' 124 red-brown Sp Edn 250 (Tutbury Jinny) ex-set of 2 - 02	10	NA
B149	'Consolidated Fisheries' 76 grey - 95	12	15
WR1-36	as above - 99	12	15
WR2-02	as above but Dapol chassis - 97	8	12
B515	'Corporation of Dundee Gas Dept.' 67 red-brown - 03	7	9
B515	'Corporation of Dundee Gas Dept.' 67 dark brown - 03	7	9
-	'Corrall & Co.' 401 red Sp Edn 1000 (Ballards) - 07	7	9
-	'Correll & Co.' 514 red Sp Edn 1000 (Ballards) - 07	7	9
ANT013	'Alexander Crane' 103 brown Sp Edn (Antics Online) - 04	9	11
B161	'Cranston' 347 red - 95	10	15
-	'Critchlow & Shepperd' 3 grey Sp Edn (Cotswold Steam Preservation Ltd) - 08	7	9
-	'Crook & Greenway' 2 blue Sp Edn 600 (Glouc/Warks Railway) - 03	9	11
-	'Crook & Greenway' 10 dark brown Sp Edn (Glouc/Warks Railway) - 07	7	9
-	'Crook & Greenway' 29 dark green+red Sp Edn 200 (Cotswold Steam Preservation) - 08	7	9
-	'Cudham' pale grey Sp Edn 500 (MRE Magazine) - 9910	7	12
-	'Cudham' red brown Sp Edn 500 (MRE Magazine) - 99	10	12
CMM001	'Cumberland Tarred Slag' 22 black Sp Edn 150 (C&M Models) - 09	7	10

5-plank wagon 'E.E. Davies & Co.' [W7c] (Dapol)

B726	'Cumberland Granite' 22 black - 08	6	8
-	'Dapol 2000' green Sp Edn (Dapol) - 00	11	13
-	'EE Davies & Co.' 9 black Sp Edn (Dapol Shop) - 08	6	8
-	'Dawson Bros.' 22 black Sp Edn 160 (Wessex Wagons) - 06	8	10
26	'Dean Forest Coal Co.' 311 red-brown Sp Edn 250 (Hereford Model shop) - 06	8	10
-	'Denton Colliery Co.' 180 red-brown Sp Edn 100 (Astley Green Colliery Museum) - 12	8	11
RM1	'R Deveson & Co.' 8 black Sp Edn 200 (1E Promotionals) - 07	7	9
-	'Devon Trading Company' 7 red-brown Sp Edn 150 (Buffers) - 11	8	11
-	'Didcot Railway Centre' 817200 green Sp Edn 110 (DRC) - 01	10	12
-	'Albert Down' 1 dark brown Sp Edn 150 (Burnham & District MRC) - 10	7	10
-	'Dunball Steam Pottery Tile & Brick Company' 10 brown Sp Edn 141 (Burnham & District MRC) - 09	6	8
-	'EA Early' 105 pale blue Sp Edn 156 (Wessex Wagons) - 10	8	10
-	'ECLP' 1614 red-brown no load Sp Edn (Mevagissey Model Railway) - 02	10	NA
-	'ECLP' 1707 red-brown no load Sp Edn (Mevagissey Model Railway) - 02	10	NA
-	'Eglwyseg Quarries Limestone' 5 yellow Sp Edn 150 (Llangollen Railway Locomotive Group) - 10	8	10
-	'English China Clays Lovering Pochin & Co.' 163 red-brown no load Sp Edn (Mevagissey Model Railway) - 02	10	NA
-	'English China Clays Lovering Pochin & Co.' 318 red-brown no load Sp Edn (Mevagissey Model Railway) - 02	10	NA
-	'John Evans' 4 red-brown Sp Edn 109 (Welshpool & Llanfair Railway) - 07	7	9
(9)	'W Evans' 2 black Sp Edn 250 (Hereford Model Centre) - 05	8	10
-	'Executors of Colonel Hargreaves' (Burnley Collieries) 262 red-brown Sp Edn 100 (Red Rose Steam Society) - 09	7	9

5-plank wagon 'B.F. Faulkner' [W7c] (Dapol)

-	'GE Farrant' 21 brown Sp Edn 550 (Ballards) - 02	9	11
-	'GE Farrant' 20 brown Sp Edn 500 (Ballards) - 07	6	8
-	'BF Faulkner' 1 dark brown Sp Edn 1000 (Gloucester Warwickshire Railway) - 06	6	8
-	'Ferry Brick & Tile Co.' 5 black Sp Edn 100 (Richard Essen) - 12	10	12

Dapol 00

-	'Field & Mackay' 4 red-brown Sp Edn 103 (SVR Erlestoke Manor Fund) - 09	6	8
-	'H Finch & Son' 16 red-brown Sp Edn 225 (Cotswold Steam Preservation) - 09	7	9
-	'Fogwills Seeds' 98 grey (all grey body) Sp Edn (Wessex Wagons) - 09	6	8
-	'Fogwills Seeds' 98 grey (corner irons in black) Sp Edn (Wessex Wagons) - error (not released)	NA	NA
E01A	'Foster Yeoman' 36 black, stone load Sp Edn 125 (East Somerset Models) - 01	10	12
E01B	'Foster Yeoman' 74 black, stone load Sp Edn 125 (East Somerset Models) - 01	10	12
E01C	'Foster Yeoman' 39 black, stone load Sp Edn 150 (East Somerset Models) - 03	9	11
E01D	'Foster Yeoman' 61 black, stone load Sp Edn 150 (East Somerset Models) - 03	9	11
-	'Thomas Fowler' 3 light grey Sp Edn (Cotswold Steam Preservation Ltd) - 07	7	9
-	'Thomas Fowler' 4 light grey Sp Edn 200 (Cotswold Steam Preservation Ltd) - 09	7	9
-	'James Frame' 30 red Sp Edn (Strathspey) - 04	9	11
NR1	'H Fulcher' 5 brown Sp Edn 250 (1E Promotionals) - 04	9	11
No.13	'Isaiah Gadd' 29 black Sp Edn 155 (West Wales Wagon Works/Loddon Vale Railway Club) - 03	9	11
-	'Garswood Hall Collieries' 1600 red-brown Sp Edn 100 (Red Rose Steam Society) - 09	7	9
-	'General Refractories' 85 pale cream Sp Edn 200 (TAG Models) - 02	10	12
B577	'W.C.Gethen' 14 bright red - 04	7	9
BE4	'Godden & Rudd' 10 red-brown Sp Edn 250 (1E Promotionals) - 06	8	10

5-plank wagon 'Godden & Rudd' [W7c]

-	'J Greatorex & Son' 131 grey Sp Edn 400 (Bagnall 2746 Locomotive Society) - 10	7	9
B301	'J B Gregory' 37 red brown, Ltd Edn 600 - 98	10	12
No.27	'Gresford Colliery' 631-638 black Sp Edn 229 (West Wales Wagon Works) - 05	8	10
B378	'Groby Granite Co.' 471 grey - 02	8	10
-	'Charles Gush & Son' 30 black Sp Edn 150 (Buffers) - 10	8	11
N0.57	'Gwili Railway' 2 pale grey W Sp Edn ***** (West Wales Wagon Works) - 07	8	10
No.57	as above with bricks Sp Edn 15 (West Wales Wagon Works) - 07	8	10
No.57	as above with sand Sp Edn 15 (West Wales Wagon Works) - 07	8	10
No.57	as above with planks Sp Edn 15 (West Wales Wagon Works) - 07	8	10
-	'W Stanley Gwilt' 17 light grey Sp Edn 115 (Welshpool & Llanfair Railway) - 09	7	9
-	'Hamworth Wharf' 300 black Sp Edn 181 (Wessex Wagons) - 06	8	10
B156	'S Harris' 14 black - 95	10	15
WR1-53	as above - 99	10	18
WR1-20	as above - 99	10	15
ANT012	'Hathway Stonehouse' 1 grey Sp Edn 100 (Antics Online) - 05	8	10
-	'Hatton's' light grey Sp Edn (Hattons) - 88	10	15
-	'Haydock' 3841 red-brown Sp Edn (Red Rose Society) - 11	8	10
-	'Heal & Son' 9 light blue with timber load Sp Edn 105 (Buffers) - 13	8	11

-	'TG Hearnden' 12 red-brown Sp Edn 1000 (Ballards) - 09	7	9
-	'C Heywood & Sons' 1 black Sp Edn 150 (Burnham & District MRC) - 10	7	9
WR1-38	'Higgs' light grey - 99	10	15
WR2-04	as above but with Dapol Chassis -98	8	10
-	'Charles Hill' 2 dark brown Sp Edn 150 (Wessex Wagons) - 09	7	9
-	'Hingley' 14 dark brown Sp Edn 100 (Modellers Mecca) - 01	10	NA
-	'T Hogarth' 2 red-brown Sp Edn 150 (1E Promotionals) - 11	8	10
31	'S Holmes, Kidnalls & Nags Head Collieries' 317 blackSp Edn (Hereford Model Shop) - 06	8	10
-	'Homewood' 1 black Sp Edn 140 (Carriage & Wagon Models) - 11	8	11
B702	'Hopton-Wood Stone Firms' 2 grey - 07	6	8
-	'Hulton' 982 red-brown Sp Edn 100 (The Red Rose Steam Society) - 08	7	9
-	'J.H.Hutt & Sons' 1 red Sp Edn 148 (Wessex Wagons) - 07	7	9
-	'Huxford & Co.' 153 red-brown Sp Edn 320 (Hythe Kent Models + KESR) 2nd issue - 01	9	11
-	'Huxford & Co.' 153 red-brown Sp Edn 664 (Hythe Kent Models + KESR) - 03	8	10
-	'Huxford & Co.' 153 red-brown Sp Edn (Colonel Stevens Railway Enterprise) - 11	8	10
B347	'ICI' L3102 grey blue - 01	8	10

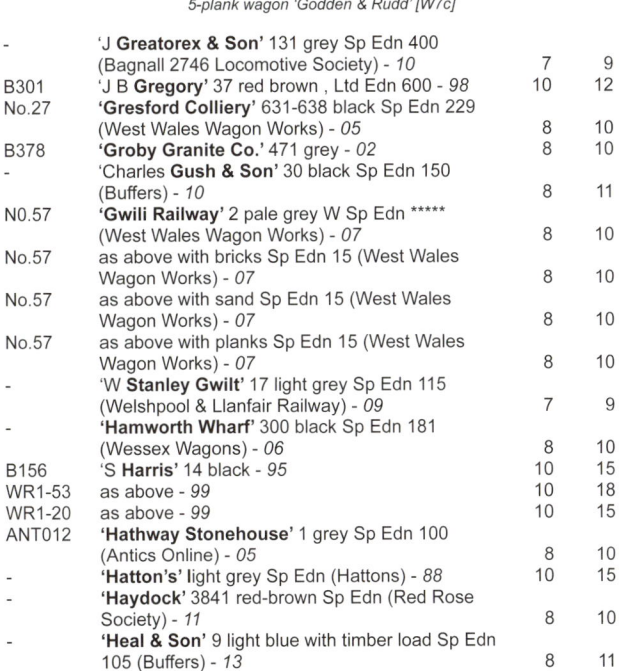

5-plank wagon 'Itters Brick Co.' [W7c]

4F051100	'I.C.I. (Lime) Ltd' 3034 grey - 13	7	9
4F051101	'I.C.I. (Lime) Ltd' 3034 grey W - 13	7	9
IP7	'Ipswich Gas Company' 1 brown Sp Edn 150 (1E Promotionals) - 10	7	9
WO6	'Itters Brick Co.' 151 red-brown with brick load Sp Edn 200 (1E Promotionals) - 08	7	9
HMC42	'Basil Jayne & Co.' 120 grey Sp Edn 250 (Hereford Model Centre) - 07	7	9
B569	'Samuel Jeffries' 7 red - 04	7	9
-	'Jeram & Co.' 60 red Sp Edn 234 (Wessex Wagons) - 08	7	9
HMC 46	'Jones & Co.' 14 light grey Sp Edn 250 (Hereford Model Centre) - 08	7	9
HMC 40	'Jones & Co.' 20 light grey Sp Edn 250 (Hereford Model Centre) - 07	7	9
ANT020	'CW Jones' 14 gry Sp Edn 250 (Antics) - 07	7	9
-	'Maurice Jones' 40 brown Sp Edn 158 (Wessex Wagons) - 08	7	9
-	'Kent & East Sussex Rly' * grey Sp Edn 1st issue of 210 (Hythe Models + KESR) - 02	10	12
-	'Kent & East Sussex Rly' 1 grey Sp Edn 100 (KESR) - 12	10	13
-	'Kent & East Sussex Rly' 10 grey Sp Edn 100 (KESR) - 11	10	13
B656	'Ketton Cement' 9 buff - 06	9	11
4F051007	'Ketton Cement' 9 cream - 12	7	9
4F051008	'Ketton Cement' 9 cream W - 12	7	9
-	'WJ King' 39 black Sp Edn 200 (Crowcombe Community Shop) - 04	12	15
-	'WJ King' 150 black Sp Edn (Wessex Wagons) - 04?	8	10
-	'WJ King' 37 black Sp Edn 150 (Wessex Wagons) - 05	8	10

Dapol 00

Code	Description		
-	'**Lanemark** Coal Co.' 20 pale grey Sp Edn 110 (Ayr Glass & Glazing) - 04	9	11
ANT021	'Edward **Langford**' 6 grey Sp Edn 250 (Antics) - 07	7	9

5-plank wagons 'Leighton Buzzard Sand' and 'A.Sharpe' [W7c]

BE7	'**Leighton** Buzzard Sand' 2 red-brown + sand load Sp Edn 150 (1E Promotionals) - 08	7	9
-	'**Llanfyllin** Coal & Lime Co.' 15 black Sp Edn 112 (Welshpool & Llanfair Rlway) - 05?	8	10
-	'**Llay** Hall' 491 black Sp Edn (Dapol Shop) - 08	6	8
B305	'**Llay** Hall' 492 black - 98	9	11
28	'Samuel **Llewellyn**' 9 black Sp Edn (Hereford Model shop) - 06	8	10
-	'A T **Locke**' 4 red-brown Sp Edn 110 (Astolat MRC) - 03	10	12
-	'James **MacPherson**' 12 brown Sp Edn (Strathspey Railway) - 03?	10	12
-	'James **Macpherson**' 14 brown Sp Edn (Strathspey Railway) - 04	10	12
-	'**Maloney** & Co.' 50 grey Sp Edn 150 (Buffers) - 11	8	11
-	'**Manchester** Collieries' 2810 red-brown Sp Edn 100 (Astley Green Colliery Museum) - 13	8	11
-	'**Mapperley**' 72 brown Sp Edn 250 (Tutbury Jinny) ex-set of 2 - 04	9	11
-	'**Marsh**' ? ? Sp Edn 144 (West Wales Wagon Works) - 07	9	11
-	'**Martin**' 25 grey Sp Edn 180 (Wessex Wagons) - 05	8	10
-	'EB **Mason**' 30 grey Sp Edn 150 (Wyre Forest MRC) - 05	12	16
-	'**May** & Hassell' 7 yellow Sp Edn 130 (Burnham & District MRC) - 12	7	9
-	'WH&HL **May** - Hop Factors' 10614 SE&CR dark grey Sp Edn 1000 (Ballards) - 05	7	9
E04A	'**Mendip** Mountain Quarries' 342 light grey Sp Edn 150 (East Somerset Models) - 06	8	10
E04B	'**Mendip** Mountain Quarries' 335 light grey Sp Edn 150 (East Somerset Models) - 06	8	10

5-plank wagon 'Mid Suffolk' [W7c]

No.1	'**Mid** Suffolk' 16 grey Sp Edn 200 (Mid-Suffolk Light Railway) - 02	10	12
No.2	'**Mid** Suffolk' 17 grey Sp Edn 200 (Mid-Suffolk Light Railway) - 03	9	11
No.2	'**Mid** Suffolk' 17 dark brown Sp Edn (Mid-Suffolk Light Railway) - 02	10	15
B314	'Tom **Milner**' 2 grey - 00	8	10
ANT019	'WW **Milton** & Co.' 19 grey Sp Edn 250 (Antics) - 07	7	9
B393	'The **Minera** Lime Company' 125 brown - 02	8	10
-	'**Moira** Collieries' 1340 brown Sp Edn 500 (Tutbury Jinny) - 00	10	12
12	'**Morgan** Bros.' 16 dark brown Sp Edn 250 (Hereford Model Centre) - 05	8	10
4th	'WE **Morgan**' ? ? Sp Edn (Welshpool & Llanfair Railway) - 07	7	9
-	'**MOY**' 9431 red-brown Sp Edn 201 (Mid-Suffolk Light Railway) - 12	9	11
-	'**MOY**' 9431 red-brown W Sp Edn 201 (Mid-Suffolk Light Railway) - 12	9	11
No.60	'F G **Mullis** & Co.' 31 black Sp Edn 85 (West Wales Wagon Works) - 07	7	9
No.60	'F G **Mullis** & Co.' 31 black W Sp Edn 85 (West Wales Wagon Works) - 07	7	9
OX5	'EW **Nappin**' 1 red Sp Edn 250 (1E Promotionals) - 06	8	10
-	'Walter E **Neate**' 2 red-brown Sp Edn 150 Wessex Wagons) - 05	8	10
-	'**Newcastle** Main' 415 grey Sp Edn 500 (G Allison) - 99	11	13
-	'**Newcastle** Main' 415 brown Sp Edn 12 (G Allison) - 99	18	20
-	'**New** Hem Heath' 22 grey Sp Edn 100 (Tutbury Jinny) - 07	7	9
-	'**New** Medway' 13 grey Sp Edn (Medway Queen Preservation Society) - 13	9	12
-	'**New** Medway' 13 grey W Sp Edn (Medway Queen Preservation Society) - 13	9	12
-	'**Norley** Coal & Cannel Co.' 205 blue Sp Edn 100 (Red Rose Steam Society) - 08	7	9
-	'**North** Devon Clay Co.' 114 black Sp Edn (P.McAllister) - 07	7	9
-	'The **North** London Clay Co.' 114 black Sp Edn (P.McAllister) - not made	NA	NA
B313	'W&W **Nunnerley**' 1 grey - 00-02	8	10
-	'WJ **Oldacre**' 3 black Sp Edn (Gloucester Warwickshire Railway) - 05	7	9
-	'**Outwood**' 644 red-brown Sp Edn 100 (Astley Green Colliery Museum) - 13	8	11
B595	'**Palmer** & Sawdye' 16 grey - 04-05	8	10
-	'**Par** Harbour' 3 light grey Sp Edn (World of Model Railways, Mevagissey) - 10	8	10
-	'**PD&SW**' 41 red Sp Edn 191 (Wessex Wagons) - 07	7	9

5-plank wagon 'Nathaniel Pegg' [W7c] (Dapol)

-	'J. LL **Peate** & Sons' 1 brown Sp Edn 400 (Welshpool & Llanfair Railway) - 02	9	11
-	'Nathaniel **Pegg**' 155 bright red Sp Edn 210 (Hythe Models) 1st issue - 02	10	12
-	'Nathaniel **Pegg**' 155 bright red Sp Edn 100 (K&ES Railway) 2nd issue - 06	8	10
B397	'**Penderyn** Limestone' 336 grey + limestone load - 02-03	8	10
-	'**Pepper** & Son' 49 light grey Sp Edn (Amberley Museum) - 10	7	10
-	'**Pepper** & Son' 17 light grey Sp Edn (Amberley Museum) - 10	8	11
-	'**Perry** & Perry' 7 dark green Sp Edn 150 (Buffers) - ?	12	15
-	'D **Petrie**' 65 red Sp Edn (Strathspey Railway) - 04	9	11
B586	'The **Phoenix** Coal Co.' 10 black - 04	7	9
25	'**Phoenix** Coal Co.' 50 black Sp Edn 250 (Hereford Model shop) - 06	8	10
24	'**Phoenix** Coal Co.' 520 black Sp Edn 250 (Hereford Model shop) - 06	8	10
-	'**Pierce** Foundry' 1911 grey Sp Edn 510 (Wexford MRC) - 11	9	11
-	'**Pilch** Collard' * light grey Sp Edn 200 (Hythe Models) 1st issue - 01	10	12
-	'G&F **Pitts** & Co.' 14 grey Sp Edn 157 (Burnham & District MRC) - 11	7	9

Dapol 00

Code	Description		
ANT022	'Wm **Playne & Co.**' 1 brown Sp Edn 250 (Antics Online) - 06	8	10
-	'**Pompey Royal (United Breweries)**' N48391 dark blue Sp Edn 144 (Wessex Wagons) - 12	8	10
-	'**Poppit Sands**' 710 deep cream Sp Edn 121 (West Wales Wagon Works for Teifi Valley Railway) - 02	10	12
No.7	'**Poppit Sands**' 711 deep cream Sp Edn 99 (West Wales Wagon Works for Teifi Valley Railway) - 03	9	11
TVR No.6	'**Poppit Sands**' 712 deep cream Sp Edn 121 (West Wales Wagon Works for Teifi Valley Railway) - 02	10	12
-	'**Portland Cement**' 31 yellow Sp Edn 110 (Wessex Wagons) - 11	8	10
-	'**Portsea Island Gaslight Company**' red-brown Sp Edn 110 (Wessex Wagons) - 12	8	10
-	'**Pothywaen Lime Co.**' 3 grey Sp Edn 108 (Welshpool & Llanfair Railway) - 05?	8	10
B307	'**Pounsbury**' 1 green - 00	8	10
B543	'H **Preston**' 1 dark brown + coal - 03	7	9
-	'**Robert Pugh**' 8 grey+red Sp Edn 158 (Burnham & District MRC) - 12	8	10
-	'W **Ramsden & Sons**' 139 red-brown Sp Edn 100 (Red Rose Steam Society) - 08	7	9

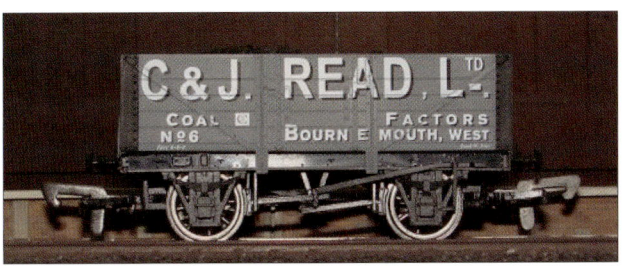

5-plank wagon 'C&J Read' [W7c] (Dapol)

Code	Description		
-	'George **Randle**' 5 dark brown Sp Edn 158 (Burnhan & District MRC) - 11	7	9
-	'**Raunds Co-operative Society**' 14 bright blue Sp Edn 100 (Kitmaster Club) - 04	9	11
-	'C&J **Read**' 6 grey Sp Edn 150 (Somerset & Dorset Railway Trust) - 08	7	9
-	'**Reese & Co.**' 23 black Sp Edn 150 (Hereford Model Centre) - 13	7	10
B611	'**Renwick & Wilton**' 107 light grey - 05	7	9
4F051005	'**Renwick & Wilton**' 107 light grey - 12	7	9
4F051006	'**Renwick & Wilton**' 107 light grey W - 12	7	10
-	'John **Reynolds**' 5 black, brick load Sp Edn 220 (Wessex Wagons) - 07	7	9
-	'**Rickett Smith & Co.**' 8501 red-brown Sp Edn 1000 (Ballards) - 07	7	9
-	'**Ringwood Coal Co.**' (see Thomas Bailey)	-	-
-	'Cuthbert **Ritson**' 4 dark brown Sp Edn 154 (Burnham & District MRC) - 11	7	9
-	'**RNAD**' 189 grey Sp Edn 100 (Wessex Wagons) - 12	8	10
-	'**RNAD**' 261 grey Sp Edn 170 (Wessex Wagons) - 12	8	10
-	'The **Road Supplies & Construction Co.**' red-brown each with different transfer number (1-50) 4 different loads, different text either side Sp Edn 50 (Oliver Leetham) - 02	9	11
-	same but black and numbered 51-100 - 04	9	11
-	'**Roberts & Maginnis**' 7 grey Sp Edn 90 (Llangollen Railway GW Loco Group) - 09	7	9
-	'EA **Robinson**' 1907 red-brown Sp Edn 100 (Ballards) - 08	6	8
-	'James **Roscoe & Sons**' 601 red-brown Sp Edn 199 (Astley Green Colliery Museum) - 12	8	11
4F080120	'**Rose, Smith & Co.**' 8243 red - 12	7	9
4F080121	'**Rose, Smith & Co.**' 8243 red W - 12	7	10
-	'**Royal Welsh Whiskey**' 9 dark brown Sp Edn 103 (Llangollen Rly GWR Loco Gp) - 07	7	9
-	'Edward **Russell**' 140 grey Sp Edn 100 (Modellers Mecca) - 01	10	NA
B733	'Hannah **Samwell & Co.**' 060 grey - 08	6	8
-	'**Scatter Rock**' 88 grey Sp Edn 100 (The Model Shop Exeter) - 03	9	11
6	'**Settle Speakman**' 2143 black Sp Edn 200 (Haslington Models) - 03	9	11
-	'**Shap Tarred Granite**' black, each with different gold transfer number (1-50) Sp Edn 50 (Oliver Leetham) - 04	9	11
-	as above but white numbers (101-160) - 04	9	11
BY9	'A **Sharp**' grey Sp Edn 150 (1E Promotionals) - 08	7	9
B572	'F.H.**Silvey**' 205 light grey - 04	7	9

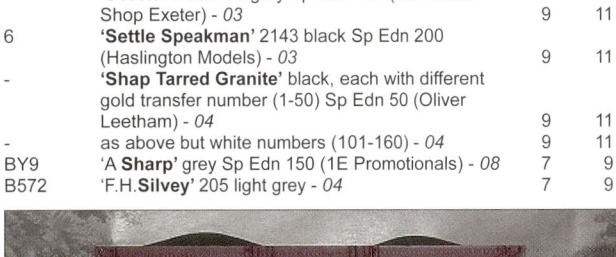

5-plank wagon 'J.E. Smith' [W7c] (Dapol)

Code	Description		
B547	'**Simmonds**' 23 dark brown + coal - 03	7	9
-	'JE **Smith**' 102 brown Sp Edn 170 (Wessex Wagons) - 10	8	9
-	'R **Smith**' & Son grey Ltd Edn (West Wales Wagon Works) for Corwen Eisteddfodd) - 03	9	11
-	'John **Snow**' 201 light grey + timber load Sp Edn 204 (Wessex Wagons) - 06	8	10
-	'**Somerset County Council**' 71 red-brown Sp Edn 139 (Burnham & District MRC) - 10	7	9
B551	'**Somerset Trading Company**' 56 red + coal - 03	9	11
-	'**Spalding**' 52 light grey Sp Edn 200 (Tutbury Jinny) ex-set of 2 - 02	10	NA
-	'**Stafford Corporation Gas**' 33 red Sp Edn 100 (Trident Trains) - 07	7	9
WO2	'JG **Stanton**' 22 red-brown Sp Edn 250 (1E Promotionals) - 05	8	10
No.39	'**Stephens Silica Brick Co.**' 22 brown sand load Sp Edn 109 (West Wales Wagon Works) - 06	8	10
No.39	'**Stephens Silica Brick Co.**' 22 brown brick load Sp Edn 109 (West Wales Wagon Works) - 06	9	11
No.39	'**Stephens Silica Brick Co.**' 22 brown coal load Sp Edn 109 (West Wales Wagon Works) - 06	8	10
B632	'**Stevenson**' 10 blue - 05	7	9
-	'H **Stone**' 1 dark green + wood load Sp Edn 113 (Wessex Wagons) - 09	7	9
-	'**Sussex Brick Co.**' 115 red-brown Sp Edn 90 (Richard Essen) - 09	7	9
-	'**Swan Lane Collieries**' 42 red-brown Sp Edn 100 (Red Rose Steam Society) - 09	7	9
-	'James **Taylor**' 19 brown Sp Edn 250 (Cotswold Steam Preservation Ltd) - 03?	9	11
-	'James **Taylor**' 23 brown Sp Edn 250 (Cotswold Steam Preservation Ltd) - 03?	9	11
-	'James **Taylor**' 24 brown Sp Edn 250 (Cotswold Steam Preservation Ltd) - 03?	8	10
-	'James **Taylor**' 25 red-brown Sp Edn (Cotswold Steam Preservation) - 06	8	10
-	'James **Taylor**' 26 dark brown Sp Edn (Cotswold Steam Preservation) - 08	7	9
-	'**Tilmanstone Colliery**' 155 grey Sp Edn 200 (Colonel Stevens Railway Enterprises) - 09	9	13
-	'DG **Thomas**' 50 yellow Sp Edn 90 (West Wales Wagon Works) - 12	9	12
-	'DG **Thomas**'/'The Cardi-Bach' (the two sides printed differently) 50 yellow Sp Edn 56 (West Wales Wagon Works) - 12	9	12
No.21	'William **Thomas**' **** grey Sp Edn 170 (West Wales Wagon Works) - 04	8	11
No.58	'**Thomas & Jones**' 2 light grey Sp Edn 160 (West Wales Wagon Works) - 07	7	9
-	'F **Thorndike**' 2 dark brown Sp Edn 200 (Carriage & Wagon Models) - 09	7	10

Dapol 00

Code	Description		
No.18	'Richard **Trevithick**' 200 brown Sp Edn 106 (West Wales Wagon Works) - 04	9	11
-	'John **Toomer & Sons**' 35 red-brown Sp Edn 200 (Froude & Hext) - 08	7	9
-	'John **Toomer & Sons**' 35 red-brown W Sp Edn 146 (Froude & Hext) - 08	7	9
-	'W&J **Turner (Wigan Junction Colliery)**' 301 grey Sp Edn 100 (Red Rose Steam Society) - 09	7	9
BY6	'James **Turney**' 28 red-brown Sp Edn 200 (1E Promotionals) - 06	8	10
B153	'**Twining**' 95 red-brown - 95	10	15
WR1-25	as above ochre and no shading - 99	40	50

5-plank wagon 'J.O' Vinter' [W7c]

Code	Description		
B618	'**Twining**' 150 light grey - 05	7	9
-	'**Tyldesley**' 49 grey Sp Edn 100 (The Red Rose Steam Society) - 05	8	10
B302	'**Vauxhall**' 292 green-grey, Ltd Edn 600 - 98	9	11
-	'**Vectis**' 34 grey Sp Edn 200 (I of W Model Railways) ex-set of 2 - 02	10	NA
CA5	'JO **Vinter**' 315 light grey Sp Edn 150 (1E Promotionals) - 09	7	9
B303	'**Vron**' 175 black, Ltd Edn 600 - 98	9	11
OX8	'**Wade**' 11 dark brown Sp Edn 150 (1E Promotionals) - 07	7	9
PE1	'L **Wagstaff**' 22 red Sp Edn 150 (1E Promotionals) - 08	7	9
-	'John **Wainwright & Co.**' 268 black 418 Sp Edn 200 (Wessex Wagons) - 06	8	10
B126	'**Webster**' 47 grey - 95	12	15
WR3-17	'**Webster**' 47 green - 99	7	9
(B522)	'R **Webster**' 303 red-brown - 03	9	NA
-	'**Weedon Brothers**' 131 grey Sp Edn (Wessex Wagons) - 09	8	10
No.86M	'George **West**' 4 red-brown Sp Edn 100 (West Wales Wagon Works) - 10	8	10

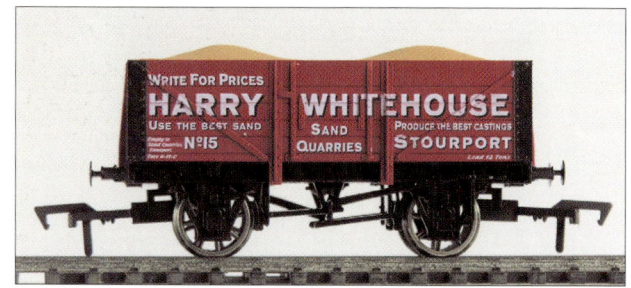

5-plank wagon 'Harry Whitehouse' [W7c]

Code	Description		
No.86W	'George **West**' 4 red-brown W Sp Edn 40 (West Wales Wagon Works) - 10	9	11
-	'**Western Coal Co.**' 37 grey Sp Edn 193 (Wales & West Assn of MRCs) - 05	8	10
-	'**Westhoughton**' 240 black Sp Edn 150 (Red Rose Steam Society) - 10	7	9
-	'**Westleigh Stone & Lime Co.**' 48 red-brown Sp Edn 120 (Burnham & District MRC) - 12	7	9
B304	'**Westminster**' 74 grey, Ltd Edn 600 - 98-02	9	11
-	'**Willcock & Co.**' 8 grey Sp Edn 200 (Bagnall Locomotive Group) - 13	10	13

Code	Description		
-	'John S **White & Son**' 31 bright ed Sp Edn 160 (Wessex Wagons) - 07	7	9
OX4	'HO **White**' 16 red-brown Sp Edn 250 (1E Promotionals) - 06	8	10
SY4	'Harry **Whitehouse**' 15 red-brown + sand load Sp Edn 300 (1E Promotionals) - 10	7	10
B663	'Harry **Whitehouse**' 16 red-brown + sand load - 06	7	9
4F051001	'Harry **Whitehouse**' 16 red + sand load - 12	7	9
4F051002	'Harry **Whitehouse**' 16 red W + sand load - 12	7	10
-	'William **Whitemore**' 26 red-brown Sp Edn 120 (Wessex Wagons) - 09	7	9
-	'William **Whitemore**' 56 red-brown Sp Edn 120 (Wessex Wagons) - 09	7	9
-	'**Wigan Coal & Iron Co.**' 584 grey Sp Edn 100 (Astley Green Colliery Museum) - 13	8	11
-	'**Wigan Coal Corporation**' 126 red-brown Sp Edn 150 (Astley Green Colliery Museum) - 10	7	9
-	'Amos **Williams**' 1 red Sp Edn 110 (Llangollen Railway GW Loco Group) - 08	7	9
-	'L **Williams & Son**' 1 ochre, white load Sp Edn 107 (Barry & Penarth MRC) - 03	9	11
(2)	'Robt **Williams & Sons**' 9 light grey Sp Edn 250 (Hereford Model Centre) - 03	10	12
-	'**Wilmer**' 83 grey Sp Edn 160 (Froude & Hext) - 07	7	9
-	'**Wincanton Coal Gas Co.**' 18 red-brown Sp Edn 150 (S&D Railway Trust) - 08	7	9
-	'**Wolverton Mutual Society**' 29 grey Sp Edn 500 (Wolverton Railway Works 150th Anniversary) - 97	10	12
BY7	'**Wolverton Mutual Society**' 29 dark grey Sp Edn 150 (1E Promotionals) - 07	7	9
No.80	'S **Woodcock**' 7 grey Sp Edn 85 (West Wales Wagon Works) - 09	7	10
No.80	'S **Woodcock**' 7 grey W Sp Edn 46 (West Wales Wagon Works) - 09	8	11
WD1	'**Woodman Bros.**' 75 red-brown Sp Edn 250 (1E Promotionals) - 05	8	10
-	'FT **Woolway**' 16 black Sp Edn 100 (The Model Shop, Exeter) ex set - 04	9	NA
-	'AC **Woolway**' 26 black Sp Edn 100 (The Model Shop, Exeter) ex set - 04	9	NA
ANTO16	'**Wyken & Craven**' 72 dark brown Sp Edn 250 (Antics Online) - 05	8	10
B306	'**Wynnstay**' Q551 brown - 00	8	10

Railway Company

Code	Description		
-	**CIE** 412d grey Sp Edn (Mark's Models) - 02?	9	11
-	**CM&DP** (Cleobury Mortimer & Ditton Priors Light Railway) 2 grey Ltd Edn 100 (Dapol Shop) - 02	7	9
-	**CV** 46 grey Sp Edn 90 (Colne Valley Railway) - 07	8	10

5-plank wagon 'GE' [W7c]

Code	Description		
-	**GE** 7748 grey (Chalk marks - 'Prent. Bros 2227') + coal load Sp Edn 62 (Stowmarket Railway Club) - 02	14	16
-	**GE** 7748 grey (Chalk marks - 'Prent. Bros 2227') + sand load Sp Edn 23 (Stowmarket Railway Club) - 03	16	18
-	**GE** 7748 grey (Chalk marks - 'Prent. Bros 2227') + packing cases Sp Edn 20 (Stowmarket Railway Club) - 03	16	18
-	**GE** 7748 dark brown (Chalk marks - 'Prent. Bros 2227') Sp Edn 62 (Stowmarket Railway Club) - 03	12	15
WRCC16	**GW** 109438 dark green Sp Edn 100 (Wrenn Railways Collectors Club) - 08	12	14
-	**HM&STy** (Hundred of Manhood & Selsey Tramway) grey Sp Edn 100 (K&ESR) - 11	9	13

Dapol 00

-	**IWC** 117 black Sp Edn 100 (I of W Model Railways) ex-set of 2 - *01*	10	NA
-	**IWC** 68 grey Sp Edn 100 (I of W Model Railways) ex-set of 2 - *01*	9	NA
-	**IWC** 68 grey Sp Edn 178 (Upstairs Downstairs) - *13*	9	12
-	**IWC** 115 black Sp Edn 150 (Upstairs Downstairs) - *13*	9	12
-	**IWR** 29 brown Sp Edn 200 (I of W Model Railways) ex-set of 2 - *02*	10	NA
-	**SE&CR** ('WH&HJ May Hop Factors') 10614 grey Sp Edn 1000 (Ballards) - *05*	7	9
-	**SECR** 50899 grey Sp Edn 101 (Bluebell Railway) - *09*	7	9
-	**S&DJR** 356 grey Sp Edn 140 (Burnham & District MRC) - *10*	7	9
B338	**LMS** 404102 light grey - *01*	7	9
WRCC19	**LMS** 24364 dark brown Sp Edn 100 (Wrenn Railways Collectors Club) - *12*	10	13
WRCC18	**LNER** 214150 blue Sp Edn 100 (Wrenn Railways Collectors Club) - *11*	10	13
-	**NE** 600002 blue Loco Sand Sp Edn 100 (Stowmarket Railway Club) - *03*	8	10
WRCC17	**SR** 12785 bright green Sp Edn 100 (Wrenn Railways Collectors Club) - *09*	8	10
4F051003	**SR** 27348 dark brown - *12*	7	9
4F051004	**SR** 27348 dark brown W - *12*	7	10
-	**SR** (IOW SME) 64394 black Sp Edn 110 (Wessex Wagons) - *13*	8	10

* These were delivered unnumbered and were individually numbered by Steve Skelton of Hythe (Kent) Models. ** Produced to celebrate the 150th anniversary of Wolverton Railway Works. *** A spelling error and the wagons were sold abroad in sets. **** Individually numbered. + Real sand from Poppet Sands beach (on the estuary of the Afon Teifi, near Cardigan) was used as a layer over the coal insert.

W8. 7-plank Open Wagon 9ft WB (2009)

Before the 1923 standardisation of wagon design by the Railway Clearing House (RCH) wagons varied in design according to the builder and to a certain extent this continued for a while after 1923. However, a disadvantage in not building to RCH specifications was the time it took to get your own design registered by each of the railway companies that would in future be asked to handle it. RCH designs were universally accepted for registration. A common variant was a 7-plank wagon on a wooden under-frame and with a 9ft wheelbase and internal bracing. This was an early design, before a 10ft wheelbase and steel under-frame became the preferred design.

Until 2009, all 7-plank wagons by Dapol used the 10ft chassis. This new 9ft wheelbase chassis has deeper frames and a brake handle fitted to one side only. It is more suited to the early private owner liveries.

A014	unfinished grey - *11*	4	10

Private Owner

7-plank with 9 foot wheelbase 'Antelope Coal Co.' [W8] (Dapol)

B869	**'Antelope Coal Company'** 31 black - *11*	7	9
B821	**'The Arley Colliery'** 27 red - *10*	7	9
-	**'The Avon India Rubber Ltd'** 3 black Sp Edn 84 (West Wales Wagon Works) - *13*	10	14
-	**'The Avon India Rubber Ltd'** 3 black W Sp Edn 24 (West Wales Wagon Works) - *13*	10	14
B890	**'John Bennett & Co.'** 2 grey - *11*	7	9
B890W	**'John Bennett & Co.'** 2 grey W - *11*	7	10
DAGM03	**'Bangor Coal & Transport Co'** 3 red-brown Sp Edn 150 (Gaugemaster) - *10*	9	12
B860	**'Bradbury'** 2018 black, (misspelt Southampton and model was withdrawn from sale) - *10*	12	14
ANT41	**'Bristol & District Co-operative Society'** 12 black Sp Edn 160 (Antics) - *10*	9	12
ANT40	**'Cainscross & Ebley Co-operative Society'** 1 black Sp Edn 160 (Antics) - *10*	9	12
-	**'CJ Cole'** 31 red-brown Sp Edn 145 (Burnham & District MRC) - *11*	7	9
DAGM06	**'The Country Gentleman's Association'** 4 red-brown Sp Edn 150 (Gaugemaster) - *11*	9	11
-	**'Francis Davis'** 17 blue Sp Edn (The Hobby Shop, Faversham) - *12*	12	16
B810	**'Dickinson Prosser & Cox'** 21 grey - *09*	7	9
B884	**'Samuel Evers & Sons'** 34 grey - *11*	7	9
B884W	**'Samuel Evers & Sons'** 34 grey W - *11*	7	10
4F072001	**'Glazebrook'** 49 red-brown - *12*	7	9
4F072002	**'Glazebrook'** 49 red-brown W - *12*	8	9
B766	**'M&W Grazebrook'** 49 red-brown - *09*	7	9
ANT42	**'Gloucester Co-operative & Industrial Society'** 47 dark brown Sp Edn 150 (Antics) - *10*	9	12
-	**'The Gloucester Direct Coal Supply Co.'** 108 dark brown Sp Edn 214 (Cotswold Steam Preservation) - *11*	7	9
B875	**'S Healing & Sons'** 5 brown - *11*	7	9
-	**'C Heywood & Sons'** 10 black Sp Edn 169 (Burnham & District MRC) - *10*	7	9
-	**'Wm Cordon Jameson's'** 47 buff Sp Edn 164 (Wessex Wagons) - *11*	8	10
-	**'Phil Johnson'** 8 grey Sp Edn 150 (The Hobby Shop, Faversham) - *11*	10	16
B832	**'Kingsbury Collieries'** 700 green - *10*	7	9
DAGM05	**'A Munday'** 6 red-brown W Sp Edn 150 (Gaugemaster) - *11*	9	12
-	**'Portsmouth Dockyard'** 10 black Sp Edn 155 (Wessex Wagons) - *10*	8	10
-	**'Issac Roberts'** 19 black Sp Edn 130 (West Wales Wagon Works) - *11*	8	10
-	**'HE Rugg'** 2 red-brown Sp Edn 160 (Buffers) - *11*	12	15
-	**'Sheffield & Eccleshall'** 12 red Sp Edn 140 (Antics) - *10*	9	12
B771	**'Small & Son'** 17 grey - *09*	7	9
4F072003	**'Small & Son'** 17 grey - *12*	7	9
4F072004	**'Small & Son'** 17 grey W - *12*	8	10
DAGM08	**'Stalybridge Corporation Gas Department'** 18 red-brown Sp Edn 150 (Gaugemaster) - *11*	10	13

7-plank wagon with 9 foot wheelbase 'Stockingford Colliery Co.' [W8] (Dapol)

-	**'GE Stevens'** 2 red-brown Sp Edn 74 (West Wales Wagon Works) - *12*	9	12
-	**'GE Stevens'** 2 red-brown W Sp Edn 33 (West Wales Wagon Works) - *12*	9	12
ANT43	**'Stevens & Co.'** 298 dark green Sp Edn 140 (Antics) - *10*	8	11
B842	**'Stockingford Colliery Co.'** 9 grey - *10*	7	9
-	**'John Symons & Co.'** 6 ochre Sp Edn 150 (Buffers) - *12*	8	11
DAGM07	**'R Taylor & Sons'** 451 red-brown Sp Edn 150 (Gaugemaster) - *11*	10	13
-	**'C Gething Turner'** 100 grey Sp Edn 160 (Wessex Wagons) - *11*	8	10
DAGM04	**'Usher & Sons'** 19 red-brown Sp Edn 150 (Gaugemaster) - *10*	9	11
-	**'Vallance'** 1910 black Sp Edn 152 (Buffers) - *10*	9	11
-	**'WA Vallis'** 31 black Sp Edn 156 (Wessex Wagons) - *10*	7	10
-	**'Wheeler & Gregory'** 324 buff Sp Edn 144 (Wessex Wagons) - *10*	7	10

Dapol 00

B772	'John **Yates**' 3 grey - 09		7	9
-	'Yeovil Gas Works' 22 red-brown Sp Edn 150 (Buffers) - 11		12	16

W9a. 7-plank Open Wagon 10ft WB (ex-Mainline) (1984)

7-plank wagons were mostly privately owned and used for the transportation of coal. Between the wars they were the most numerous wagon type on Britain's railways. They were requisitioned by the government during the Second World War and passed to BR in 1948. During the 1950s the aging fleet was gradually replaced by steel mineral wagons.

The model, with its 10ft wheelbase and steel type under-frame, was released by Palitoy in the Mainline Railways range in 1977 and private owner liveries had to be stretched to fit the longer body. The residue stock was bought by Dapol when Palitoy production closed down. These then are models made in China by Kader for Palitoy, which Dapol sold through their own catalogues. The reason for some having altered numbers is not known. The tooling was later used by Bachmann.

Private Owner

B171	'**Bass**' 65 grey (M) - c89	4	6
B171	'**Bass**' 56 grey - ?	4	6
B174	'**Cambrian**' 1078 (M) black - ?	4	7
B174	'**Cambrian**' 107 black - ?	4	7
B167	'**Colman's**' 35 yellow (M) - c89	4	6
B169	'**Courtaulds**' 18 green (M) - c89	4	6
B69	'**CWS**' 1941 dark brown (M) - 85	4	6
B173	'**Diamond**' 34 red (M) - c98	4	7
B170	'**Emlyn**' 813 grey (M) - c89	4	7
B170	'**Emlyn**' 811 grey - ?	4	7
B80	'**Horlicks**' 1 brown (M) - 85	4	7
B166	'S.J.**Moreland**' 1 red+black (M) - c89	4	7
B82	'**Parkinson**' 107 dark blue (M) - 85	5	8

Former Mainline 7-plank wagon re-packaged by Dapol [W9a]

B82	'**Parkinson**' 100 dark blue - ?	5	8
B172	'**Patent Nut & Bolt Co.**' 658 dark brown (M) - c89	4	7
B70	'**Perfection Soap**' 82 brown (M) - 85	4	7
B168	'**Persil**' 258 dark green (M) - c89	4	6
B172	'**Persil**' 258 dark green (M) - c89	4	6

Railway Company

B14	GW 06515 dark grey (M) - 84	4	7
B81	NE 'Loco Coal' HB4333 grey (M) - 85	4	6
B10	BR P130288 grey (M) - 84	4	7

Although 'SJ Moreland', 'Colman's', 'Persil', 'Courtaulds', 'Emlyn', 'Bass', 'Patent Nut & Bolt Co.', 'Diamond' and 'Cambrian' were illustrated in catalogues, we have found no evidence that any of them was sold in Dapol packaging although some were reissued using the Airfix body (see Wagons introduction).

W9b. 7-plank Open Wagon 10ft WB (ex-Airfix) (1985)

This is an end door wagon and typical of the design specifications laid down by the Railway Clearing House in 1923. It is based on a wagon with a 10ft wheelbase and a steel under-frame and, again, private owner liveries have often had to be stretched to fit the longer body.

Airfix launched the model in 1978 and the tooling passed to Palitoy in 1981 and to Dapol in 1985, along with unsold stock. Previously Dapol had arrange for a duplicate tool to be made for the wagon's body and sold one of the pair to Hornby in 1996. The other tool became Dapol's principal one for 7-plank wagons. This table includes models made from the Airfix body tool (or the copy). Almost without exception, the models in this table were sold with a coal (or other) load in-fill. This is almost certainly the largest list of variations made of any British model.

A3	brown or grey unfinished - 86	4	10
A3	black unfinished - ?	4	10
A002	grey unfinished - 04	4	10
-	blue with brick load - 12?	6	NA
-	dull red with coal load - 12?	5	NA

Private Owner

-	'**A&T**' 1000 red Sp Edn 100 (Astley Green Colliery Museum) - 12	8	11
-	'**Abbott**' 1028 grey Sp Edn (Warley Show) - 03	12	15
BE2	'James **Abbott**' 20 red Sp Edn 250 (1E Promotionals) - 05	4	10
-	'**Aberbeeg Colliery**' 569 light grey Sp Edn 90 (South Wales Coalfield) - 04	10	12
-	'**Abercrave**' 331 red-brown Sp Edn 105 (South Wales Coalfields) - 04	9	11
-	'**Aberdare Graig Coal**' 2 red-brown Sp Edn 90 (South Wales Coalfields) - 03	10	12
-	'**Aberdeen MRC 35th Anniversary**' light grey Sp Edn 250 (Aberdeen MRC) - 06	8	10
-	'**Aberpergwm**' 1 black Sp Edn 110 (Roger Mileman) - 03	9	11
No.77	'**Abingdon on Thames Gas Dept.**' **** red Sp Edn 104 (West Wales Wagon Works) - 09	7	9
-	'Ed T **Agius & Co.**' 91 dark brown Sp Edn 252 (Wessex Wagons) - 08	7	9
-	'Ed T **Agius & Co.**' 91 dark brown W Sp Edn (Wessex Wagons) - 11	7	9
-	'Thomas C **Allan**' 3 black Sp Edn 1000 (Ballards) - 05	7	9
-	'Thomas C **Allan**' 3 black Sp Edn 1000 (Ballards) - 05	7	10
-	'**Allerdale Coal Company**' 10 red Sp Edm 160 (Crafty Hobbies) - 12	8	11
-	'The **Alton Brewery Co.**' 4 buff Sp Edn 310 (Wessex Wagons) - 11	8	11
-	'**A M**' (Ashton Moss Colliery) 16 red-brown Sp Edn 150 (Astley Green Colliery Museum) - 11	8	11
-	'**Amalgamated Anthracite**' 7520 black Sp Edn 108 (South Wales Coalfields) - 07	7	9
B375	'**Ammanford**' 24 - dark brown - 02	8	10
B375A	'**Ammanford**' 48 - dark brown - 02	8	10
B893	'**Ammanford Colliery Co. Anthracite**' 48 dark brown - 11	7	9
RM4	'**Anderson & Co.**' 4 red-brown Sp Edn 275 (1E Promotionals) - 08	7	9
-	'**Andover Co-operative Society**' 4 red-brown Sp Edn 135 (Burnham & District MRC) - 12	7	9
D006A	'**Annesley**' 162 brown, Sp Edn 100 (The Model Centre) - 03	9	11
D006B	'**Annesley**' 173 brown, Sp Edn 100 (The Model Centre) - 03	9	11
D006C	'**Annesley**' 195 brown, Sp Edn 100 (The Model Centre) - 03	9	11
-	'**Arnell**' 1 dark brown Sp Edn 100 (Richard Essen/Wicor Models) - 07	7	9
-	'**Arscott Collieries**' 21 light grey Sp Edn (Shrewsbury Model Centre) - 07	7	9
B546	'**Asquith & Tompkins**' 21 red - 03	9	11
-	'**Astley Green Colliery**' 245 red-brown 'M' Sp Edn 100 (Astley Green Mining Museum) - 02	10	12
-	'**Astley Green Colliery**' 229 red-brown 'M' Sp Edn 100 (Astley Green Mining Museum) - 03	9	11
-	'**Astley Green Colliery**' 337 red-brown 'M' Sp Edn 100 (Astley Green Mining Museum) - 03	9	11
-	'**A T** (Astley & Tyldesley Collieries Ltd)' 1473 red-brown Sp Edn (Astley Green Mining Museum) - 07	7	9
-	'**Atherton**' 1980 red Sp Edn 100 (Red Rose Steam Society) - 09	8	10
-	'**Atkinson & Prickett**' 1518 red-brown Sp Edn (D.Hewins) - 03?	9	11
-	'**Atkinson & Prickett**' P238288 red-brown (overprinted BR 1516) Sp Edn (D.Hewins) - 03?	9	11
CA3	'**Austin & Co.**' 602 red-brown Sp Edn 200 (1E Promotionals) - 06	8	10
-	'**Avan Hill**' 128 black Sp Edn (Jenny's) - 03?	9	11

Private owner 7-plank open wagon 'A.G. Bailey' [W9b]

Dapol 00

Code	Description		
-	'Babbington Colliery' 80 black Sp Edn 100 (Paul Freer) - 03	9	11
-	'BC' 222 red-brown Sp Edn 100 (Astley Green Colliery Museum) - 12	8	11
-	'AG Bailey' 18 red-brown Sp Edn 200 (1E Promotionals) - 09	7	9
-	'AG Bailey' * brown Sp Edn 200 (Hythe Models Kent) - 04	9	11
-	'E Bailey & Son' 15 black Sp Edn 178 (Wessex Wagons) - 08	7	9
-	'Baird's & Dalmellington' 550 red-brown Sp Edn 92 (Ayr Glass & Glazing) - 04	9	11
No.36	'Baker & Kernick' 410 black Sp Edn 151 (West Wales Wagon Works) - 05	8	10
57	'IW Baldwin & Co.' 22 dark brown Sp Edn 250 (Hereford Model Centre) - 09	6	8
PBR13	'Baldwins' 132 black Sp Edn 250 (Pontypool & Blaenavon Railway) - 05	8	10
-	'Robert Balfour' 161 red-brown Sp Edn 190 (Crafty Hobbies) - 06	8	10
-	'C Ball' 1 Sp Edn (Wessex Wagons) - not made	NA	NA
OX7	'C Ball' 1 red Sp Edn 150 (1E Promotionals) - 07	7	9
-	'Bamfurlong' 1540 red-brown Sp Edn 100 (Astley Green Colliery Museum) - 13	8	11
B603	'CT Bamfurlong & Mains' 1482 red - 04	8	10
No.83M	'Banbury Gas Co.' 200 black Sp Edn 110 (West Wales Wagon Works) - 09	7	9
No.83W	'Banbury Gas Co.' 200 black W Sp Edn 40 (West Wales Wagon Works) - 09	7	9
-	'Bannings' 13 red-browd Sp Edn 127 (Wessex Wagons) - 11	7	10
-	'Ed Bannister' 1500 light grey Sp Edn 100 (D Hewins) - 00	11	13
SWL11	'Barrow' 623 red Sp Edn 120 (Midlander) - 01	10	12
-	'Barrow' 623 grey Sp Edn 212 (Crafty Hobbies) - 11	8	
SWL28	'Barrow Barnsley' cream Sp Edn 140 (Midlander) - 03	9	11
-	'Barry Coal Coy.' 14 black Sp Edn 116 (Barry & Penarth MRC) - 04	9	11
-	'Barry Rhondda' 148 black, Sp Edn 130 (South Wales Coalfields) - 03	9	11
-	'WH Bartlett' E34 bright red Sp Edn 100 (The Model Shop Exeter) - 03	9	11
-	'WH Bartlett' E34 dark red Sp Edn 150 (Wessex Wagons) - 09	9	11
B171	'Bass' 56 light grey - 90	8	10
-	'Bass' 56 light grey Sp Edn 200 (Tutbury Jinny) ex-2-wagon pack - 02	10	NA
-	'Bass' 32 light grey Sp Edn 200 (Tutbury Jinny) - 09	7	9
-	'Bassil King & Co.' 6 grey Sp Edn 209 (Wessex Wagons) - 05	8	10
D005A	'Archd Bathgate & Sons' 201 red, Sp Edn 100 (The Model Centre) - 03	9	11
D005B	'Archd Bathgate & Sons' 205 red, Sp Edn 100 (The Model Centre) - 03	9	11
D005C	'Archd Bathgate & Sons' 211 red, Sp Edn 100 (The Model Centre) - 03	9	11
B574	'S.J.Baverstock' 51 black - 04	9	11

Private owner 7-plank open wagon 'Beaumont' [W9b]

Code	Description		
No.11	'Charles Bazzard & Son' 192 black Sp Edn 261 (West Wales Wagon Works) - 03, 05	8	10
B519	'Beaumont' 665 red-brown - 03	7	9
IP6	'Beaumont & Co.' 665 red-brown Sp Edn 150 (1E Promotionals) - 09	7	9
-	'Beeby & Son' 1735 red-brown Sp Edn 99 (Nene Valley Railway) - 08	7	9
-	'Beili-Glas' 25 black Sp Edn 92 (David Dacey) - 06	8	10
B903	'Benzol & Byproducts' 1044 grey - 11	7	9
-	'Berry Hill Collieries' 1505 red-brown Sp Edn 100 (Trident Trains) - 06	8	10
-	'Berry Hill Collieries' 1505 red-brown Sp Edn 150 (Tutbury Jinny) - 08	7	9
B524	'Berthlwyd' 966 black - 03	7	9
NR3	'Bessey & Palmer' 743 grey Sp Edn 250 (1E Promotionals) - 05	8	10
-	'Betteshanger' 81 black Sp Edn 70 (Carriage & Wagon Models) 11	9	12
-	'Betteshanger' 81 black W Sp Edn 35 (Carriage & Wagon Models) - 11	10	14
-	'T Beynon & Co.' 3 black (see Newport & Abercarn)	-	-
-	'Bickershaw' 970 red-brown Sp Edn 100 (Red Rose Steam Society) - 08	7	9
-	'Bickershaw' 960 red Sp Edn 100 (Red Rose Steam Society) - 09	8	10
-	'Bickerstaffe' 51 grey Sp Edn 150 (Astley Green Colliery Museum) - 11	8	11
-	'Billingsley' 17 dark brown Sp Edn 150 (Foot Plate) - 05	8	10
-	'John T Bingham & Co.' 10 black Sp Edn 1000 (Ballards) - 03	8	10
7	'Birchenwood Colliery' 53 red-brown Sp Edn 200 (Haslington Models) - 05	8	10
B377A	'Black Park' Ruabon 329 brown	8	NA
B377B	'Black Park' Chirk 2021 red-brown	8	NA
B377	above 2 wagons in a twin pack - 02	NA	18
-	'Black Park Colliery' 324 red-brown	6	NA
-	'Black Park Colliery' 2024 red-brown	6	NA
B912	above 2 wagons in a twin pack Ltd Edn (Dapol Shop) - 11	NA	15
No.17	'Blackwell' 1836 red brown Sp Edn 130 (Midlander) - 01	10	12
No.24	'Blackwell' 1298 red-brown Sp Edn 115 (Midlander) - 02	10	12
PBR4	'Blaenavon' 1530 grey Sp Edn 150 (Pontypool & Blaenavon Railway) - 03	9	11
PBR8	'Blaenavon' 1472 pale grey Sp Edn 200 (Pontypool & Blaenavon Railway) - 04	9	11
PBR11	'Blaenavon' 1378 grey Sp Edn 300 (Pontypool & Blaenavon Railway) - 05	8	10
-	'Blaen-Cae-Gurwen Colliery Co.' 61 dark brown Sp Edn 98 (David Dacey) - 06	9	11
-	'Blaendare Co.' 254 grey with brick load Sp Edn 100 (David Dacey) - 08	7	9
-	'Blaen-Graigola' 29 red Sp Edn 94 (South Wales Coalfields) - 03	10	12
-	'The Blaenmawr Colliery' 163 black Sp Edn 106 (David Dacey) - 05	8	10
-	'Blaina Colliery Co.' 1004 black Sp Edn 106 (David Dacey) - 05	8	10
B521	'Blidworth' 2323 grey - 03	7	9
No.12	'Bliss Tweed Mills' 6 green Sp Edn 160 (Banbury MR Show + West Wales Wagon Works) - 03	9	11
-	'Blisworth Tunnel' 1805-2005 pale blue Sp Edn 200 (Blisworth Bygones) - 05	8	10
B316	'Blue Circle' 173 yellow - 00	7	9
B693	'Joseph Boam' 510 red-brown - 07	7	9
-	'Wm Body & Sons' deep green Sp Edn (Colonel Stevens Railway Enterprises) - 09	10	13
-	'FJ Bonner & Mason & Toogood' 1 light grey Sp Edn 208 (Wessex Wagons) - 06	8	10
No.81	'Bonvilles Court Coal Coy.' 13 grey Sp Edn 114 (West Wales Wagon Works) - 09	7	10
No.81	'Bonvilles Court Coal Coy.' 13 grey W Sp Edn 114 (West Wales Wagon Works) - 09	8	11
B322	'John G Boreland & Peat' 317 pale grey - 01	8	10
B680	'Bourne Fisher & Co.' 21 brown - 06	7	9
B680	'Bourne Fisher & Co.' 21 red-brown W - 08	6	8
38	'Bowson' 1334 red-brown Sp Edn 250 (Hereford Model Centre) - 06	8	10

8th Edition

Dapol 00

-	'Bradford & Sons' 1 brown Sp Edn 100 (Buffers) - 03	9	11
-	'Bradford & Sons' 2 brown Sp Edn 100 (Buffers) - 03	9	11

Private owner 7-plank open wagon 'Bramley & Son' [W9b]

-	'Bradford & Sons' 4 brown Sp Edn (Buffers) - 04	9	11
-	'Bradford & Sons' 5 brown Sp Edn (Buffers) - 05	8	10
-	'Bradford Colliery Co.' 249 red-brown Sp Edn 100 (Red Rose Steam Society) - 08	7	9
BY11	'Bramley & Son' 5 dark brown Sp Edn 175 (1E Promotionals) - 09	7	9
-	'Breeze' 23 dark blue Sp Edn 100 (Shrewsbury Model Centre) - 08	7	9
B94	'Brentnall & Cleland' 3000 black (M) - 86	6	10
-	'BC Bridgewater Collieries' 1870 black Sp Edn 100 (Astley Green Collieries Museum) - 09	7	9
B323	'Brightmore' 113 grey - 01	8	10
-	'G Briyer Ash' 1110 black Sp Edn 100 (Buffers) - 04	9	11
B175	'Broadoak' 460 brown (A) - 89	6	10
B175	'Broadoak' 406 brown - ?	8	10
-	'Brynn Hall' 748 red-brown Sp Edn 100 (Astley Green Mining Museum) - 07	7	9
-	'Brynhenllys' 337 black Sp Edn 100 (David Dacey) - 06	8	10
-	'BT' (Bridgewater Trustees) 837 black Sp Edn 183 (Red Rose Steam Society) - 04	9	11
39	'Budd & Company' 3175 black Sp Edn 250 (Hereford Model Centre) - 06	8	10
B566	'Bullcroft' 288 bright red - 04	7	9
LB3	'Burnyeat, Brown & Co.' 335 black Sp Edn 100 (Lord & Butler Model Railways) ex- double pack. - 02	10	NA
-	'Burton-on-Trent Co-op' 11 red-brown Sp Edn 250 (Tutbury Jinny) - 01	10	12
-	'FW Butcher' 3 dull green Sp Edn 1000 (Ballards) - 02	7	9
ANT008	'Bute' 115 black Sp Edn 250 (Antics) - 04	9	11
-	'TF Butler' ? ? Sp Edn 275 (Crafty Hobbies) - 05	8	10
ANT028	'T Butt & Sons' 2 black Sp Edn 250 (Antics) - 07	7	9
ANT028A	'T Butt & Sons' 3 black Sp Edn 250 (Antics) - 06	7	9
No.1	'Butterley' 2322 red brown Sp Edn 102 (Midlander) - 00	11	13
SWL14	'Butterley' 01702 dark grey Sp Edn 105 (Midlander) - 01	10	12
No.2	'Butterley' 5513 grey Sp Edn 130 (Midlander) - 01	10	12
-	'Bwlch Colliery Co.' 131 black Sp Edn 101 (David Dacey) - 05	8	10
IP2	'Byford' 88 red-brown Sp Edn 250 (1E Promotionals) - 05	8	10
-	'HP Byrne' 5 red-brown Sp Edn 120 (Wessex Wagons) - 12	8	10
No.25	'Caerbryn Colliery' 219 black Sp Edn 220 (West Wales Wagon Works) - 04	9	11
-	'Caerphilly Coal Co.' red-brown Sp Edn 107 (David Dacey) - 07	7	9
B638	'Cain' 3 black - 05	7	9
B174	'Cambrian' 107 black - 89	10	12
ANT005	'Cambrian Standard' 1923 cream Sp Edn 100 (Antics) - 04	9	11
CA2	'Cambridge Gas Co.' 19 black Sp Edn 250 (1E Promotionals) - 05	8	10
-	'Came & Storey' 8 black Sp Edn 150 (Burnham & District MRC) - 08	7	9
E02A	'Camerton Collieries' 175 black	8	NA
E02B	'Camerton Collieries' 199 black	8	NA
-	above 2 wagons in a double box, Sp Edn 125 (E.Somerset Models) - 02	NA	22
-	'Camerton Collieries' 169 black Sp Edn 115 (Wessex Wagons) - 05	8	10

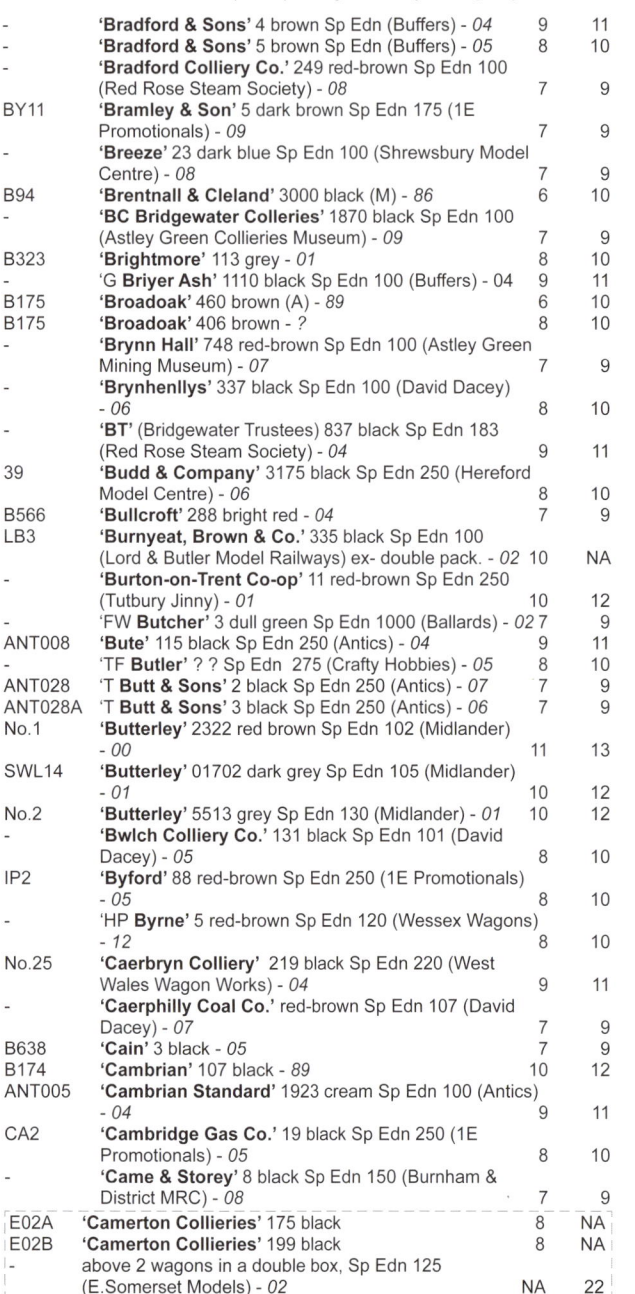

Private owner coal wagon 'Camerton Colleries' [W9b] (Dapol)

-	'Camerton Collieries' 325 black Sp Edn 147 (Burnham & District MRC) - 12	7	9
-	'Cannock & Leacroft Colliery' 4129 brown Sp Edn 200 (Tutbury Jinny) ex set of 2 - 04	9	NA
-	'Cannock Rugeley' 648 grey+red Sp Edn 200 (Tutbury Jinny) ex-set of 2 - 01	10	NA
-	'Cannock & Rugeley' 465 red Sp Edn 200 (Tutbury Jinny) ex-set of 2 - 04	9	NA
51	'Cannop' 27 black Sp Edn 300 (Hereford Model Centre) - 09	6	8
-	'Cardiff Navigation' 256 black Sp Edn 110 (South Wales Coalfields) - 04	9	11
No.17	'Cardigan Mercantile Co.' various numbers carried black Sp Edn 174 (West Wales Wagon Works) - 04	9	11
No.90	'Cardigan Mercantile Co.' 900 black Sp Edn 150 (West Wales Wagon Works) Cardigan 900th Anniversary - 10	9	11
-	'Cardox' (see Wolstanton Cardox)	-	-
B122	'Carlton' 4372 black (A) - ?	6	10
B550	'Carpenter & Son' 4 red-brown - 03	7	9
-	'Carpenter & Sons' 27 red-brown Sp Edn 135 (P.McAllister) - 06	8	10
S2056	'R.J & M Carr' 369 black Sp Edn 107 (The Model Clearing House) - 13	9	12
-	'Carterhatch Brick & Tile Co.' 2 dark brown Sp Edn 100 (Peter Paye) - 06	8	10
-	'Cefn-Y-Bryn' 76 dark brown Sp Edn 110 (David Dacey) - 06	8	10
-	'Chadwick & Smith' 2 red-brown Sp Edn 100 (Colwyn Model Railway Club) - 04	9	11
-	'Chadwick & Smith' 5 red-brown Sp Edn 100 (Colwyn Model Railway Club) - 04	9	11
B319	'Chatterley-Whitfield' 1822 grey - 00	8	10
-	'Chatterley-Whitfield' 1822 pale grey, re-run of B319 Sp Edn 100 (Trident Trains) - 06?	8	10
-	'Chislet' * 440 black Sp Edn 520 (Hythe Models) 1st issue - 01	9	11
-	'Chislet' * black Sp Edn (Hythe Models) - 05	8	10
-	'Chislet' * 65 brown Sp Edn 65 (Carriage & Wagon Models) - 11	9	12
-	'Chislet' * 65 brown W Sp Edn 35 (Carriage & Wagon Models) - 11	10	14
SWL20	'City of Birmingham' 1747 black Sp Edn 140 (Midlander) - 01	10	12
No.61	'City of Liverpool' 800 grey Sp Edn 128 (West Wales Wagon Works) - 07	7	9
No.61	'City of Liverpool' 800 grey W Sp Edn 46 (West Wales Wagon Works) - 07	9	11
-	'Thos. J Clarke' 603 brown Sp Edn 210 (Wessex Wagons) - 05	8	10
SWL3	'Claycross' 1254 red brown Sp Edn 140 (Midlander) - 0011	13	
B101	'S J Claye' 825 red-brown - 86	9	11
-	'S J Claye' 825 red-brown Sp Edn (Railway & Barter Shop) - 08	7	9
RTR4	'Clement's Tump' 2 black Sp Edn 250 (RD Whyborn) - ?	12	14
-	'Clevedon Gas Company' 21 light grey Sp Edn 200 (Wessex Wagons) - 05	8	10

Dapol 00

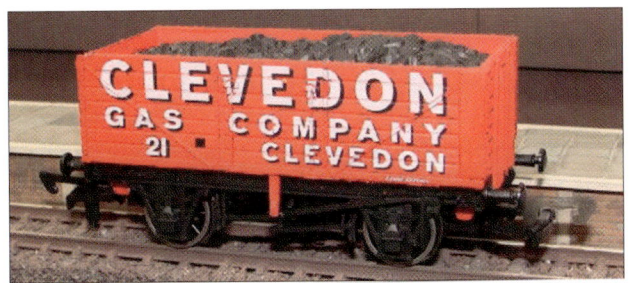

Private owner 7-plank coal wagon 'Clevedon Gas Company' [W9b] (Dapol)

Ref	Description		
-	'Clevedon Gas Company' 21 red Sp Edn (Col.Stevens Railway Enterprise) - 08	7	10
-	'Clifton & Kersley' 2224 bright red Sp Edn 337 (Red Rose Steam Society) - 03	9	11
-	'Clifton & Kersley' 2250 red-brown Sp Edn 150 (Astley Green Colliery Museum) - 10	8	10
-	'Clifton Colliery' 2121 red Sp Edn 110 (Paul Freer) - 03	9	12
-	'Clutton (The Earl of Warwick's Collieries)' 533 black Sp Edn 120 (Burnham & District MRC) - 09	7	9
-	'Clyde shipping Co.' green? Sp Edn (Ayr Glass & Glazing) - not made	NA	NA
B181	'Coal Agencies' 42 black - 89	8	10
BY12	'Frs Coales' 8 grey Sp Edn 150 (1E Promotionals) - 10	8	10
-	'Geo. J Cockerell & Co.' 5375 red-brown Sp Edn 1000 (Ballards) - 08	7	9
-	'Coleford Red Ash' 6 black Sp Edn 250 (RD Whyborn) - ?	12	14
52	'Coleford Red Ash' 6 black Sp Edn 250 (Hereford Model Centre) - 09	6	8
-	'R Coller & Sons' 55 red-brown Sp Edn 151 (Nene Valley Railway) - 10	7	9
No.74A	'C Collett & Sons' 5 brown Sp Edn 75 (West Wales Wagon Works) - 08	7	9
No.74A	'C Collett & Sons' 5 brown W Sp Edn 25 (West Wales Wagon Works) - 08	7	9
-	'C Collett & Sons' 6 green Sp Edn (Bourton -on-the-Water Model Railway) - 04	9	11
No.74B	'C Collett & Sons' 7 brown Sp Edn 84 (West Wales Wagon Works) - 08	7	9
No.74B	'C Collett & Sons' 7 brown W Sp Edn 22 (West Wales Wagon Works) - 08	7	9
-	as above but red (error)	20	24
33	'D Colley' 49 bright red Sp Edn 250 (Hereford Model Centre) - 06	8	10
RM2	'JT Collins & Sons' 35 black Sp Edn 200 (1E Promotionals) - 07	7	9
B384	'Collins Green' 417 brown - 02	8	10
B167	'Colman's' 35 yellow - 91	9	11
-	'Colthurst, Symons & Co.' 7 light grey Sp Edn 160 (Burnham & District MRC) - 09	6	8
-	'Coltness Kinghill Colliery' 349 orange-red Sp Edn 200 (Model Rail Scotland) - 08	9	12
-	'Cooke & Nuttall' 11 red Sp Edn 100 (Trains & Diecast) - 06	8	10
-	'Co-operative Society - Twerton' 1 maroon Sp Edn 182 (Wessex Wagons) - 08	7	9
-	'Co-operative Society - Trowbridge' 1 maroon Sp Edn 167 (Wessex Wagons) - 08	7	9
WO1	'Coote & Warren' 2176 dark brown Sp Edn 250 (1E Promotionals) - 05	8	10
-	'Cope & Baker' 4 dark brown Sp Edn 250 (Hereford Model Centre) - 05	8	10
-	'Corrall & Co.' 1341 grey-green Sp Edn 100 (Richard Essen) - 09	7	9
B186	'Cory Bros.' 9644 black - 91	8	10
-	'W Counsell & Co.' 7 black Sp Edn 171 (Wessex Wagons) - 05	8	10
B169	'Courtaulds' 18 green - 90	8	10
SWL19	'Coventry Collieries' The Warwickshire Coal Co 334 black Sp Edn 143 (Midlander) - 01	10	12
-	'Coventry Collieries' 1404 black Sp Edn (Castle Trains) - made?	NPG	NPG
2nd	'Coventry Collieries' 1436 black Sp Edn 150 (Castle Trains) - 07	7	9
-	'Wm Coward & Co.' 4 dark green Sp Edn 109 (Llangollen Railway GWR Loco Group) - 08	7	9
ANT006	'Alexander Crane' 102 brown Sp Edn 100 (Antics) - 04	9	11
-	'Crane & Company' 107 bright red Sp Edn 185 (Wales & West Assn MRCs) - 04	9	11
-	'Crawshay Bros.' 1120 black Sp Edn 107 (South Wales Coalfields) - 03	9	11
PRB14	'Crawshay's' 15 cream Sp Edn 250 (Pontypool & Blaenavon Railway) - 06	8	10
-	'Cribbwr Fawr Collieries' 468 red Sp Edn 112 (South Wales Coalfields) - 03	9	11
-	'Crippins Arley Coal' 1048 red Sp Edn 100 (Astley Green Colliery Museum) - 09	7	9
ANT011	'Critchlow & Sheppard' 15 red-brown Sp Edn 250 (Antics) - 05	8	10
-	'W. Crocker' 40 red-brown 40th Anniversary Sp Edn 220 (Hampton Court MRS) - 02	9	11
B536	'Crosfields' Perfection Soap' 84 red - 03	10	12
-	'Crow Catchpole & Co.' 208 black Sp Edn 160 (Wessex Wagons) - 11	7	10
PBR10	'Crumlin Valley Collieries' 15 black Sp Edn 300 (Pontypool & Blaenavon RS) - 05	8	10
No.70A	'Crynant Colliery' 332 grey+red Sp Edn 172 (West Wales Wagon Works) - 08	7	9
No.70A	'Crynant Colliery' 332 grey+red W Sp Edn 37 (West Wales Wagon Works) - 08	9	11
No.70B	'Crynant Colliery' 335 grey+red Sp Edn 187 (West Wales Wagon Works) - 08	7	9
No.70B	'Crynant Colliery' 335 grey+red W Sp Edn 36 (West Wales Wagon Works) - 08	9	11
-	'Crystalate' 1262 bright yellow Sp Edn 1000 (Ballards) - 04	8	10
-	'Cwmaman' 541 black, Sp Edn 130 (South Wales Coalfields) - 03	9	11
-	'Cwmteg' 152 black Sp Edn 99 (South Wales Coalfields) - 04	9	11
-	'Cwmtillery' 2660 black Sp Edn 200+ (Geoff Osborn) - 01?	15	18
PBR2	'Cwmtillery' 2537 black Sp Edn 100 (Pontypool & Blaenavon Railway) - 03	9	11
-	'Cynon' 221 black Sp Edn 90 (Jenny's) - 04	10	12
-	'Dalmellington Iron Co.' 351 bright red Sp Edn 350 (Ayrshire Railway Pres Group) - 01	8	10
-	as above but brighter red, now with steel wheels, narrow couplings abd name less curved - 11	7	9
-	'Darkhill & Elwood' 50 black Sp Edn (RD Whyborn) - 97?	12	14
B324	'Darton' 145 red - 01	8	10
-	'Davies Brothers' 60 black Sp Edn 110 (Barry & Penarth MRC) - 04	9	11

Private owner 7-plank coal wagon 'Cope & Baker' [W9b] (Dapol)

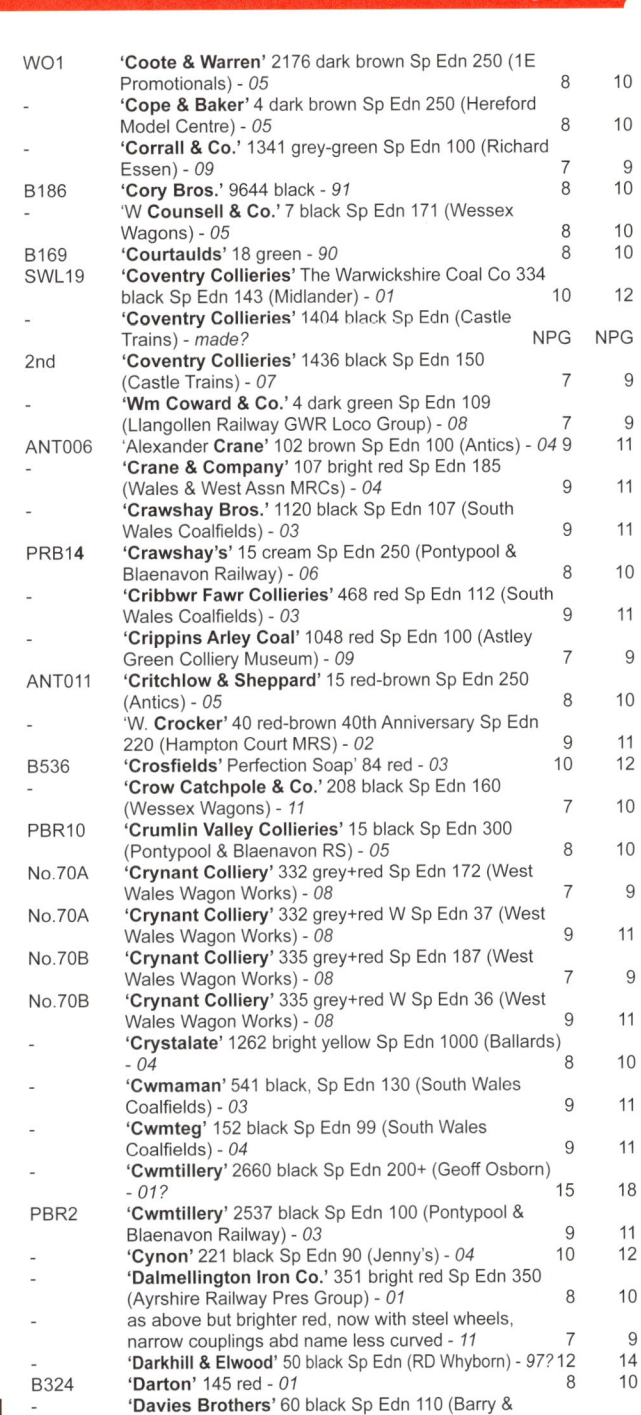

Coal Merchant's 7-plank wagon 'Devereux' [W9b]

Dapol 00

Code	Description		
BY2	'FJ **Davis**' 1 green+yellow Sp Edn 250 (1E Promotionals) - 04	9	11
No.63	'JL **Davis**' 125 red Sp Edn 80 (West Wales Wagon Works) - 07	9	11
No.63	'JL **Davis**' 125 red W Sp Edn 42 (West Wales Wagon Works) - 07	9	11
-	'**Davis & Co.**' 7 black Sp Edn 127 (Wessex Wagons) - 12	8	10
-	'**Deal & Walmer**' 6 dark brown Sp Edn 195 (East Kent MRS) - 11	9	12
-	'**Dean Forest Coal**' 607? bright red Sp Edn 110 (Dean Sidings) - 04	9	11
(10)	'**Dean Forest Coal**' 437 black Sp Edn 250 (Hereford Model Shop) - 05	8	10
10	'**Dean Forest Coal**' 437 black Sp Edn 250 (Hereford Model Shop) - 08	7	9
B514	'**Dearne Valley**' 61 bright blue - 03	7	9
NR10	'JI **Dennick**' 123 red-brown Sp Edn 225 (1E Promotionals) - 09	7	9
No.22	'**Derbyshire Fumeless Coke**' (HO White) C1>C9**** grey Sp Edn 175 (West Wales Wagon Works/Banrail MREx) - 04	9	11
BY8	'GH **Deveraux & Son**' 1 grey Sp Edn 150 (1E Promotionals) - 07	7	9
WD2	'John **Dickinson**' 46 grey Sp Edn 250 (1E Promotionals) - 05	7	9
B545	'**Dinington Main**' 641 grey blue - 03	7	9
-	'Walter J **Dixon**' 3 red-brown Sp Edn 191 (Wessex Wagons) - 06	8	10
-	'**Doncaster New Royal Infirmary**' 3 red-brown Sp Edn 1020 (BRM magazine) - 02	9	11
-	'**Doncaster Plant Works 1853-2003 Anniv.**' brown Sp Edn 100 (Wabtec Ltd) - 03	9	11
No.29	'**Drake & Mount**' **** grey Sp Edn 101 (West Wales Wagon Works) - 05	8	10
ANT007	'**Dudley & Gibson**' 101 dark brown Sp Edn 100 (Antics) - 04	9	11
-	'**Duffryn Aberdare**' 548 black Sp Edn 106 (David Dacey) - 07	7	9
-	'**Duffryn Rhondda Co.**' 305 black Sp Edn 100 (Jenny's) - 03	9	11
B335	'**Dunkerton**' 1117 grey - 01	8	10
-	'**Dunkerton Colliery**' 10 blue Sp Edn 200 (Buffers) - 049	9	11
-	'**Dunkerton Colliery**' 12 blue Sp Edn 200 (Buffers) - 058	8	10
E05A	'**Dunkerton Coal Factors**' 1207 grey Sp Edn 150 (East Somerset Models) - 06	8	10
E05B	'**Dunkerton Coal Factors**' 1213 grey Sp Edn 150 (East Somerset Models) - 06	8	10
-	'**Eaglesbush**' 1 black Sp Edn 109 (David Dacey) - 07	7	9
WO4	'**Eales & Roberts**' 6 red-brown Sp Edn 200 (1E Promotionals) - 06	8	10
-	'**East Cannock**' 4916 black Sp Edn 200 (Tutbury Jinny) ex-set of 2 - 02	10	NA
PBR5	'**Eastern Valleys**' 125 black Sp Edn 150 (Pontypool & Blaenavon Railway) - 03	9	11
-	'**Eastleigh**' 1 red-brown Sp Edn 125 (Wessex Wagons) - 11	7	10
33	'Edward **Eastwood**' Sp Edn (Midlander) - made?	NPG	NPG
No.66	'Edward **Eastwood**' 2 grey-green Sp Edn 126 (West Wales Wagon Works) - 08	7	9
B539	'**Eccleshall Industrial & Provident Society**' 4 dark brown - 03	7	9
-	'**Economic Coal Co.**' 3 red-brown Sp Edn (Footplate Models) - 07	7	9
-	'**ED**' 675 red brown Sp Edn 100 (Modellers Mecca) - 01	10	NA
-	'**Edmunds Brothers**' 33 black Sp Edn 94 (David Dacey) - 06	8	10
D008A	'WH **Edwards**' 10 red-brown Sp Edn (TMC) - 04	9	11
D008B	'WH **Edwards**' 18 red-brown Sp Edn (TMC) - 04	9	11
D008C	'WH **Edwards**' 25 red-brown Sp Edn (TMC) - 04	9	11
-	'O **Edwards & Son**' 148 pale brown Sp Edn 300 (Hythe Models - Copyright passed to KESR in 2005) - 01	10	12
-	'**Eifionyd Farmers Association**' 17 grey Sp Edn 117 (West Wales Wagon Works) - 06	8	10
-	'**Elders Steam Navigation**' 466 black Sp Edn 250 (RD Whyborn) - 98?	12	14
-	'G&G **Ellis**' * blue Sp Edn 100 (Hythe Models 30th Anniversary) - 02	10	12
SWL12	'**Elsecar**' 771 bright red Sp Edn 130 (Midlander) - 01	10	12
CA1	'**Ely Gas Co.**' 4 brown-red Sp Edn 250 (1E Promotionals) - 04	9	11
B170	'**Emlyn**' 811 olive green - 90	8	10

Gas Company 7-plank coal wagon 'Ely Gas' [W9b]

Code	Description		
ANT004	'**Empire**' 1673 black Sp Edn 250 (Antics) - 04	9	11
BY1	'JH & E **Essen**' 4 dark brown Sp Edn 250 (E1 Promotionals) - 04	9	11
B192	'Wm **Evans**' 174 black - 90	8	10
B320	'**Evans & Bevan**' 386 grey - 01	8	10
HMC 41	'**Evans & Jones**' 4 mid-grey Sp Edn 250 (Hereford Model Centre) - 07	7	9
-	'**Evans, Adlard & Co.**' No.1 black Sp Edn 200 (Glos. & Warks Railway) - 00	11	13
-	'W **Evans**' Sp Edn (Antics) - made?	NPG	NPG
-	'Samuel **Evers**' 34 dark grey Sp Edn 200 (Modellers Mecca) ex-set - 02	10	NA
B884	'Samuel **Evers & Sons**' 34 grey - 11	7	9
B884W	'Samuel **Evers & Sons**' 34 grey W - 11	7	10
32	'**Eveson**' 343 red-brown Sp Edn 140 (Midlander) - 03	9	11
-	'**Ewens Brothers**' 1 red Sp Edn 180 (Wessex Wagons) - 90	8	10
-	'W **Fairclough**' 32 brown-red Sp Edn 219 (Toys2Save) - 04	9	11
-	'W **Fairclough**' 28 brown-red Sp Edn 200 (Toys2Save) - 04	9	11
-	'**Fairweather & Son**' 37 red-brown Sp Edn 124 (Nene Valley Railway) - 07	7	9
-	'Allan **Feaver**' 10 red-brown Sp Edn 100 (Henfold Halt) - 04	9	11
No.35	'**Felinfoel Brewery**' **** black Sp Edn 160 (West Wales Wagon Works) - 05	8	10
-	'**Fernhill**' 670 red-brown Sp Edn 105 (David Dacey) - 05	8	10
-	'**Firbeck Main Colliery**' 751 red-brown Sp Edn 100 (Richard Essen) - 08	7	9
B723	'**Flower & Sons**' 1 grey - 08	6	8
-	'A **Flowers & Co.**' 16 red-brown Sp Edn 200 (Wessex Wagons) - 06	8	10
-	'**Fosdick**' 251 red-brown Sp Edn 200 (The Middy Trading Company) - 05	8	10
25	'**Fountain & Burnley**' 104 red-brown Sp Edn 120 (Midlander) - 02	10	12
35	'John **Fowler**' 125 grey Sp Edn 250 (Hereford Model Shop) - 06	8	10
NR9	'W **Fowler**' 301 red-brown Sp Edn 225 (1E Promotionals) - 09	7	9
-	'**Fox**' 458 black Sp Edn 200 (Tutbury Jinny) ex set of 2 - 04	9	NA
-	'**Foxfield Colliery**' 2 red Sp Edn 250 (Alsager Toys & Models) - 02	10	12
-	'**Foxfield**' 101 red-brown Sp Edn 100 (Nostalgic Memories of Trentham) - 10	7	9
-	'**Foxfield**' 538 red-brown Sp Edn 100 (Nostalgic Memories of Trentham) - 07	7	9
BE8	'Henry **Francis**' 7 red Sp Edn 175 (1E Promotionals) - 09	7	9
BE3	'**Franklin**' 203 black Sp Edn 250 (1E Promotionals) - 05	8	10
No.34	'JU **Freeman**' 3 black Sp Edn 120 (West Wales Wagon Works/Banrail 2005) - 06	8	10
-	'TR **Freeman & Sons**' 5 grey Sp Edn 214 (Wessex Wagons) - 05	8	10

Dapol 00

Ref	Description		
GA1	'Galashiels Gas Light Co.' 249 black Sp Edn 150 (1E Promotionals) - 10	7	9
01, 04	'Gann & Brown' * grey-blue Sp Edn 323 (Hythe Kent Models) 1st issue - 01	10	12
NR9	'Gann & Brown' 211 red-brown Sp Edn 150 (1E Promotionals) - 09	7	9

Private owner 7-plank coal wagon 'Gardner' [W9b]

Ref	Description		
NR5	'Gardner' 306 red Sp Edn 250 (1E Promotionals) - 06	8	10
-	'KG&NA Gay' 73226 black Sp Edn 158 (Wessex Wagons) - 09	8	10
-	'GCG' 269 black Sp Edn 105 (South Wales Coalfields) - 08	7	9
B581	'Gedling' 2598 bright red - 04	7	9
-	'Gellyonen Collieries' 510 pale grey Sp Edn 99 (South Wales Coalfields) - 03	9	11
-	'Gilwen' 532 dark red Sp Edn 92 (South Wales Coalfields) - 03	9	11
HMC 44	'Gittings & Sons' 4 mid grey Sp Edn 250 (Hereford Model Centre) - 07	7	9
No.85	'Glan-Garnant' 292 black Sp Edn 141 (West Wales Wagon Works) - 09	7	9
No.85W	'Glan-Garnant' 292 black W Sp Edn 70 (West Wales Wagon Works) - 09	7	9
-	'Glascote' 255 pale grey Sp Edn 200 (Tutbury Jinny) - 04	9	11
-	'Glasgow Iron & Steel Co.' 952 grey Sp Edn 100 (Model Rail Scotland) - 07	12	20
-	'Glenavon' 1063 black Sp Edn (Jenny's) - 04	9	11
BRM/0046	'Gloucester Gas Light Company' 37 black Sp Edn 500 (BRM magazine) - 05	8	10
BRM/0048	'Gloucester Gas Light Company' 51 black Sp Edn 500 (BRM magazine) - 05	8	10
B43	'Gloucester Gas Light' 51 black (A) - 85	6	10
-	'Glyncoed' 162 dark brown, Sp Edn 130 (South Wales Coalfields) - 03	9	11
-	'Glyncorrwg Collieries' 276 black Sp Edn 79 (Jenny's) - 02	10	12
-	'Glyncorrwg Colliery' 535 black Sp Edn (Jenny's) - 05	8	10
B359	'Glynea & Castle' 191 brown - 01-02	8	10
No.15	'Goldthorpe' 2744 red-brown Sp Edn 122 (Midlander) - 01	10	12
-	'Goodland' 30 black Sp Edn 150 (Wessex Wagons) - 05	8	10
-	'WT Goodland & Co.' (uniquely numbered with transfers 1-77) dark red, 5 different loads used Sp Edn 77 (Oliver Leetham) - 03	10	12
B541	'Gortac' 29 yellow - 03	7	9
-	'Granville' 227 grey Sp Edn 200 (Tutbury Jinny) ex-set of 2 - 02	10	NA
23	'Grassmoor' 940 black Sp Edn 115 (Midlander) - 02	10	12
-	'Great Grimsby Coal Salt' 1180 black Sp Edn 100 (D Hewins) - 00	11	13
-	'Great Treverbyn' 48 red-brown no load Sp Edn (Railtronics) ex-set - 01	10	NA
-	'Great Treverbyn' 48 red-brown + chalk Sp Edn (Railtronics) ex-set - 01	10	NA
-	'Great Western Colliery Co.' 650 black Sp Edn 95 (David Dacey) - 05	8	10
*	'Victor Grey' 54 bright red Sp Edn 130 (South Wales Coalfields) - 03	9	11
36	'James Griffin' 5 grey Sp Edn 250 (Hereford Model Shop) - 06	8	10
-	'AE Griffiths' 35 light grey, choice of 5 loads*** Sp Edn 96 (O Leedham) - 03	10	12
(ANT003)	'Matthew Grist' 2 grey Sp Edn 100 (Antics) ex-set of 2 - 03	9	NA
(ANT014)	'Matthew Grist' 2 grey Sp Edn 250 (Antics) - 05	8	10
No.88	'Grumbly Gas Works' 1 grey (based on Ivor the Enginestories) Sp Edn 116 (Gwii Railway) - 08	7	9

Coal merchant's 7-plank open wagon 'S.P. Gunn & Sons' [W9b]

Ref	Description		
-	'Guest, Keen & Nettlefolds' 0747 black, Sp Edn 151 (South Wales Coalfields) - 03	9	11
-	'SP Gunn & Sons' 1 bright red Sp Edn (Dartmoor Railway) - 04	9	11
NA1	'SP Gunn & Sons' 1 bright red Sp Edn 150 (1E Promotionals) - 09	9	11
-	'Gwili Railway' 1 pale grey+red Sp Edn 120 (West Wales Wagon Works) - 06	8	10
PBR7	'Hafodyrynys' 729 brown Sp Edn 200 (Pontypool & Blaenavon Railway Soc.) - 05	8	10
B44	'Hales Fuels' 241 grey (A) - 85	6	10
-	'Hall & Co.' 161 red LBSC Sp Edn (Ballards) - 09	8	10
-	'Hall & Co.' 161 red-brown Sp Edn 100 (Ballards) - 09	8	10
-	'Hall & Co.' 510 red-brown Sp Edn (Richard Essen) - 12	9	12
SWL7	'Hall's Collieries' 1401 black Sp Edn 132 (Midlander) - 01	10	12
-	'FJ Hall' 65 brown Sp Edn 200 (Tutbury Jinny) ex set of 2 - 04	9	NA
-	'Herbert Hall' 111 maroon Sp Edn 200 (Modellers Mecca) ex-set - 02	10	NA
B182	'Halls Swadlincote' 711 brown - 89, 95	9	11
-	'Halstead Co-operative Society' 11 red-brown Sp Edn 95 (Colne Valley Railway) - 07	8	10
-	'Edwin Hammond' 1 black Sp Edn 101 (David Dacey) - 05	8	10
-	'Hampson & Co.' dark brown Sp Edn 108 (Richard Hampson) - 04	9	11
B535	'Fred Hardisty' 2 red-brown - 03	7	9
-	'Harecastle' 55 brown Sp Edn 200 (Tutbury Jinny) - 03	9	11
ANT003	'Harris & Co.' 21 black Sp Edn 100 (Antics) ex-set of 2 (with 'Matthew Grist') - 03	9	NA
B334	'Hartnell' 22 black - 01	7	9
-	'Hartnell & Son' 23 black Sp Edn 183 (Wessex Wagons) - 08	7	9
-	'Hartnell & Son' 25 black Sp Edn (West Somerset Railway) - 13	9	12
-	'Harwood Rake' 20 black Sp Edn 106 (DavidDacey) - 05	8	10
-	'Hatton's' brown Sp Edn (Hattons) - ?	8	10
-	'Haverhill UDC' 4 red-brown Sp Edn 98 (Colne Valley Railway) - 09	6	8
-	T A Hawkins' 271 red-brown Sp Edn 200 (Tutbury Jinny) ex-set of 2 - 01	10	NA
-	'Haydock' 561 black Sp Edn 100 (Trains & Diecast) - 04	9	11
-	'Haydock' 3841 red-brown Sp Edn 150 (Red Rose Steam Society) - 11	8	11
IP1	'Heath' 20 grey Sp Edn 250 (1E Promotionals) - 04	9	11
8	'Samuel Heath Jnr.' 24 black Sp Edn 200 (Haslington Models) - 06	8	10
B542	'John Heaton' 101 grey - 03	7	9
B200	'Hendy Merthyr' 1862 brown - 91	9	11
ANT017	'Henry Heaven' 1 dark brown Sp Edn 250 (Antics) - 05	8	10
-	'Helston Gas Company' 10 black Sp Edn (Kernow MR Centre) ex-set of 2 - 03	9	NA

Dapol 00

-	'Helston Gas Company' 20 black Sp Edn (Kernow MRCentre) ex-set of 2 - 04	9	NA	SWL27	'Houghton Main' 2029 red-brown Sp Edn 120 (The Midlander) - 03	9	11
-	'Helston Gas Company' 30 black Sp Edn (Kernow MRCentre) ex-set of 2 - 03	9	NA	SY1	'HP Sauce Works' 1 red-brown Sp Edn 350 (1E Promotionals/Warley Show 2007) - 07	7	9
-	'Helston Gas Company' 40 black Sp Edn (Kernow MRCentre) ex-set of 2 - 04	9	NA	No.7	'Wm Hubbard' 30 black, Sp Edn 294 (Teifi Valley Railway) - 02	10	12
				No.59	'Wm Hubbard' 200 black Sp Edn 100 (West Wales Wagon Works - Aberaeron's Bicentenary) - 07	7	9
				No.098	'Wm Hubbard' 100 black, Sp Edn 117 (West Wales Wagon Works) - 11	10	12
				B190	'Huddersfield Co-op' 14 black - 90	9	11
				Ant 027	'AP Hudson' 21 red Sp Edn 250 (Antics) - 07	7	9
				-	'Hulton Colliery Co.' 164 black Sp Edn 150 (Red Rose Steam Society) - 10	7	9
				-	'Hulton Colliery Co.' 542 red Sp Edn 100 (Red Rose Steam Society) - 12	9	11
				B557	'Humber' 100 red - 03	7	9
				-	'Hunstanton Models' brown Sp Edn 150 (Hunstanton Model Shop) - 04	9	11
				No.46	'Hunt Edmunds & Co.' 8 light grey Sp Edn 166 (West Wales Wagon Works) - 06	8	10
-	'Helston Gas Company' 50 black Sp Edn (Kernow MRCentre) - 05	8	10	-	'Hunting & Co.' 61 red-brown Sp Edn (Nene Valley Railway) - 09	7	9
-	'Hempsted' 37 black Sp Edn 500 (*BRM* magazine) - 058		10	No.28	'Huntley & Palmers' **** black Sp Edn 147 (West Wales Wagon Works) - 05	8	10
34	'Hereford Corporation Gas Works' 7 grey Sp Edn 250 (Hereford Model Shop) - 06	8	10	No.55	'CJ Hyslop' 12 red-brown Sp Edn 70 (West Wales Wagon Works) - 07	7	9
-	'Hertingfordbury' 1 buff Sp Edn 100 (Great Eastern Railway Society) - 03	9	11	No.55	'CJ Hyslop' 12 red-brown W Sp Edn 70 (West Wales Wagon Works) - 07	7	9
B367	'Hickleton' 3166 brown - 02	7	9	-	'Imperial Chemical Industries - Buxton Lime' ? grey Sp Edn 200 (Bagnall Locomotive Group) - 13	10	13
-	The High Brooms' red Sp Edn 300 (Ballards) - 01	10	12	-	'Imperial Chemical Industries - Buxton Lime' ? grey Sp Edn 200 (Bagnall Locomotive Group) - 13	10	13
-	The High Brooms' 12 red Sp Edn 1000 (Ballards) - 057		9	B880	'ICI Salt Works' 326 red - 11	7	9
B176	'Highley Mining' 245 brown - ?	8	10	B380	'Ilkeston & Heanor Water Board' 14 blue-grey - 02	7	9
B176	'Highley Mining' 425 brown (A) - 89	6	10	-	'International Colliery' French Anthracite 400 red-brown Sp Edn 100 (South Wales Coalfield) - 04	9	11
-	'Highley Mining Co.' 246 red-brown Sp Edn 100 (Severn Valley Railway) - 05?	8	10	-	'Ipswich Co-operative Society' 115 red Sp Edn 99 (Old Wagon Works) - 04	9	11
-	'Highley Mining Co.' 247 brown Sp Edn 100 (Severn Valley Railway) - 06	8	10	-	'Itshide' 265 black Sp Edn 1000 (Ballards) - 03	8	10
-	'Hill Bros.' 3 red-brown Sp Edn 1000 (Ballards) - 07	6	8	PBR6	'James & Emanuel' 189 black Sp Edn 170 (Pontypool & Blaenavon RS) - 04	9	11
-	'Hind, Chesterfield' blue Sp Edn (Geoff Osborn's Railway & Model Shop) - 06	12	15	WD4	'James Kasner & Co.' 121 red-brown Sp Edn 150 (1E Promotionals) - 07	7	9
-	'A Hinxman & Co.' 75 grey Sp Edn 176 (Wessex Wagons) - 08	8	10	-	'G.E.Jenkins - Master Engineer' light blue Sp Edn 100 (Tywyn & District MRC) - 08	7	9
-	'HM Office of Works' 172 grey Sp Edn 160 (Wessex Wagons) - 10	7	10	No.23	'T Jenkerson & Sons' 274 black Sp Edn 189 (West Wales Wagon Works) - 04	9	11
B555	'Hockaday & Co.' 4 black - 03	7	9	-	'Ann Jones' 4 black Sp Edn 150 (Llangollen Railway GWR Loco Group) - 09	7	10
30	'John Hollins' 6 black Sp Edn 250 (Hereford Model shop) - 06	8	10	B873	'David Jones' 7 black - 11	7	9
-	'Holly Bank' 62 brown Sp Edn 200 (Modellers Mecca) ex set - 02	10	NA	B89	'David Jones' 650 red-brown (M) - 86	6	10
-	'Holly Bank' 62 brown Sp Edn 100 (Tutbury Jinny) - 049		NA	B89	'David Jones' 650 red-brown - 95	8	10
-	'Hood & Son' 2 green Sp Edn (Salisbury Model Centre) - 08	7	9	No.48	'David Jones' Pencader 1 black Sp Edn 121 (West Wales Wagon Works) - 06	8	10
-	'Hood & Son' 3 dark green Sp Edn 162 (Salisbury Model Centre) - 07	7	9	No.49	'David Jones' Llandyssul 5 black + brick load Sp Edn 129 (West Wales Wagon Works) - 06	9	11
No.53	'Hook Anthracite' 602 black Sp Edn 175 (West Wales Wagon Works) mis-spelt Pembrokshire one side like prototype - 07	7	9	NR11	'H Jones' 1 grey Sp Edn 150 (1E Promotionals) - 10	7	9
No.67	'Horlicks' 2 red-brown Sp Edn 133 (West Wales Wagon Works) - 08	7	9	No.97M	'William Jones' 5 dark grey Sp Edn 88 (West Wales Wagon Works) - 11	9	12
No.67	'Horlicks' 2 red-brown W Sp Edn 40 (West Wales Wagon Works) - 08	7	9	No.97W	'William Jones' 5 dark grey W Sp Edn 88 (West Wales Wagon Works) - 11	10	13
-	'Horwich Industrial Co-operative Society ' 12 red-brown Sp Edn 100 (Trains & Diecast) - 09	7	9	-	'Alfred Jukes' 29 red-brown Sp Edn 104 (West Wales Wagon Works) - 11	9	12
				-	'Alfred Jukes' 29 red-brown W Sp Edn 25 (West Wales Wagon Works) - 11	10	13
				-	'Jury Brick Co.' 4 black Sp Edn 100 (Richard Essen) - 08	7	9
				B623	'Sir John LL Kaye Bart.' 9 blue - 05	7	9
				No.093M	'John Kerkin' 1 grey Sp Edn 125 (West Wales Wagon Works) - 10	8	11
				No.093W	'John Kerkin' 1 grey W Sp Edn 125 (West Wales Wagon Works) - 10	9	12
				-	'C Kerry & Sons' 10 red+white+blue Sp Edn 186 (Wessex Wagons) - 12	9	12
				NR4	'ET Ketteringham' 30 red-brown Sp Edn 250 (1E Promotionals) - 05	8	10

Coal merchant's 7-plank wagon 'Henry Heaven' [W9b] (Dapol)

Industrial 7-plank coal wagon 'H.P. Sauce' [W9b]

Dapol 00

-	'**Kilmersdon Colliery**' 22 green Sp Edn (Buffers) - *04*	8	10
-	'**Kilmersdon Colliery**' 24 green Sp Edn 100 (Buffers) - *04*	9	11

Coal merchant's 7-plank wagon 'E.T. Ketteringham' [W9b]

-	'**Kilmersdon Colliery**' 26 Sp Edn (Buffers) - *04*	9	11
-	'**K&K (A.Knowles)**' 360 red-brown Sp Edn 100 (Red Rose Steam Society) - *05*	8	10
-	'**Kingsbury Collieries**' 699 dark green Sp Edn 100 (The UK Model Shop Directory) - *07*	10	12
B589	'**Kinneil**' 118 red-brown - *04*	7	9
-	'**Kinneil**' 189 red-brown Sp Edn (Scottish Railway Preservation Society) - *08*	7	9
-	'**Kirby-in-Furness Co-operative Society**' 4 light grey Sp Edn 159 (Crafty Hobbies) - *08*	7	9
-	'**Kirkland & Perkins**' 18 bright red Sp Edn 370 (Peak Rail) - *04*	9	11
-	'**Lachlan Grant**' 1 buff Sp Edn 100 (Strathspey Railway) - *03*	9	12
-	'**Lachlan Grant**' 2 beige Sp Edn (Strathspey Railway) - *06*	9	10
-	'**Lachlan Grant**' 3 beige Sp Edn (Strathspey Railway) - *069*		10
-	'**Lamb Brewery**' 1 brown Sp Edn 150 (Wessex Wagons) - *05*	8	10
-	'**Lamdin & Sons**' 11 red-brown Sp Edn 160 (Wessex Wagons) - *09*	8	10
PBR3	'**John Lancaster & Co.**' 1063 black Sp Edn 100 (Pontypool & Blaenavon Railway) - *03*	9	11
-	'SV **Lancey**' 20 blue Sp Edn 145 (Wessex Wagons) - *077*		9
-	'RS **Langford & Sons**' 10 red Sp Edn 127 (Burnham & District MRC) - *12*	7	9
-	'AE **Lavender & Sons**' 1 red Sp Edn 110 (Burnham & District MRC) - *12*	8	10
-	'AE **Lavender & Sons**' 2 red Sp Edn 116 (Burnham & District MRC) - *13*	8	10
B390	'**Lawley**' 391 grey - *02-03*	7	9
-	'**Lawrence & Co.**' 12 black Sp Edn 167 (Wessex Wagons) - *08*	7	9
-	'**Leadbeter**' 105 light grey Sp Edn 103 (Barry & Penarth MRC) - *04*	9	11
22	'**Leadbeter**' 211 bright red Sp Edn 250 (Hereford Model Centre) - *05*	8	10
-	'**Leadbeter**' 211 bright red Sp Edn 500 (The Pontypool & Blaenavon Railway) - *08*	7	9

Co-operative Society 7-plank coal wagon 'Leek & Moorlands' [W9b] (Dapol)

-	'**Leek & Moorlands**' 175 grey Sp Edn (Tutbury Jinny) ex-set of 2 - *05*	8	NA
-	'**Leek & Moorlands**' 175 cream Sp Edn 92 (Tutbury Jinny) - *07*	8	10
-	'**Leek & Moorlands**' 167 cream Sp Edn (Tutbury Jinny) - *09*	7	9
-	'**L.E.P.**' 358 red-brown Sp Edn 100 (Red Rose Steam Society) - *12*	9	11
B374A	'**Lewis**' 0199 black - *02*	7	9
-	'**Lewis' Merthyr**' 955 black Sp Edn 103 (David Dacey) - *07*	7	9
LB3	'**Lewis' Merthyr Navigation**' 768 black Sp Edn 100 (Lord & Butler Model Railways) ex double pack - *02*	10	NA
-	'**Lightmoor**' 263 grey, Sp Edn 200+ (Geoff Osborn) - *9912*		14
ANT029	'RA **Lister**' 1 dark brown Sp Edn 250 (Antics) - *07, 08*	7	9
-	'**Llanbradach**' 252 black Sp Edn 100 (David Dacey) - *05*	8	10
-	'**Llantrisant Railwaymen's Coal Association**' 1 red-brown Sp Edn 110 (South Wales Coalfields) - *04*	9	11
-	'Samuel **Llewellyn**' 122 grey Sp Edn 179 (South Wales Coalfields) - *03*	9	11
-	'Samuel **Llewellyn Carw**' 58 red-brown Sp Edn 100 (South Wales Coalfields) - *07*	7	9
-	'**Lockets**' 72 black Sp Edn 200+ (Geoff Osborn) - *01?*15		18
-	'**Lockets Merthyr**' 362 black Sp Edn 150 (David Dacey) - *10*	7	9
BE1	'Wm **Lockhart**' 63 black Sp Edn 250 (1E Promotionals) - *04*	9	11
No.16	'Henry **Lodge**' 214 bright red Sp Edn 159 (Midlander) - *01*	10	12
-	'Frank **Lomas**' 4 pale grey Sp Edn 520 (Peak Rail Stock Fund) - *04*	9	11
D007A	'**Longbottom & Co.**' 703 red, Sp Edn 100 (The Model Centre) - *03*	9	11
D007B	'**Longbottom & Co.**' 716 red, Sp Edn 100 (The Model Centre) - *03*	9	11
D007C	'**Longbottom & Co.**' 728 red, Sp Edn 100 (The Model Centre) - *03*	9	11
-	'S **Loney & Co.**' 51 grey Sp Edn 150 (50 used in set with 'William Thomas') (Wessex Wagons) - *05*	8	10
IP3	'**Lowestoft Coaling Co.**' 4567 dark red Sp Edn 250 (1E Promotionals) - *06*	8	10
-	'**Lydney Coal Co.**' 9 grey Sp Edn (Dean Sidings) - *03*	9	11
-	'**Lydney Coal Co.**' 9 grey Sp Edn 250 (Hereford Model Shop) - *09*	7	9
-	'John **Lysaght's**' 1471 black 40th Anniv. Sp Edn 100 (Scunthorpe District MRS) - *03*	9	11
B525	'**Macclesfield**' 10 red-brown - *03*	7	9
B570	'**Macclesfield Co-op**' 41 brown - *04*	7	9
No.96M	'**Maidenhead Industrial Co-operative Society**' 5 red Sp Edn 95 (West Wales Wagon Works) - *11*	9	12
No.96W	'**Maidenhead Industrial Co-operative Society**' 5 red W Sp Edn 95 (West Wales Wagon Works) - *11*	10	13
-	'**Main Colliery Co.**' 568 black, Sp Edn 110 (D Dacey) - *04*9		11
-	'**The Mains Coal & Canal Co.**' 475 grey Sp Edn 200 (Buffers) - *04*	9	11
B677	'**Maltby Main**' 298 red W - *06*	6	8
D004A	'**Manchester Collieries**' 8692 brown, Sp Edn 100 (The Model Centre) - *03*	9	11
D004B	'**Manchester Collieries**' 8743 brown, Sp Edn 100 (The Model Centre) - *03*	9	11
D004C	'**Manchester Collieries**' 8785 brown, Sp Edn 100 (The Model Centre) - *03*	9	11

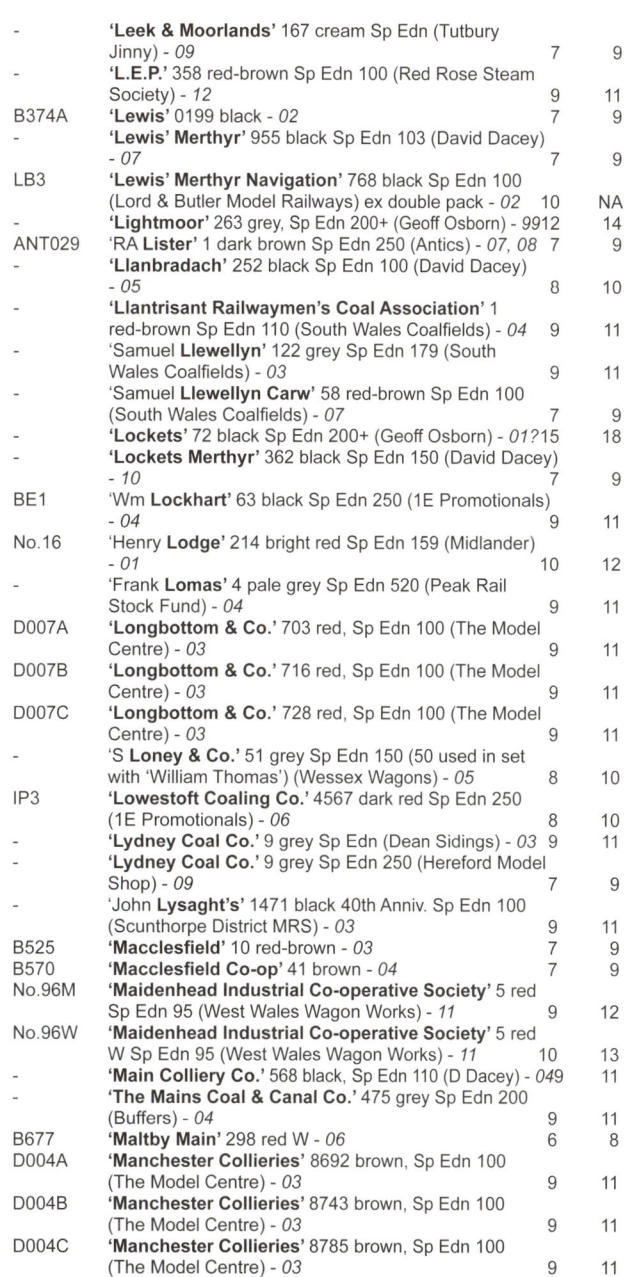

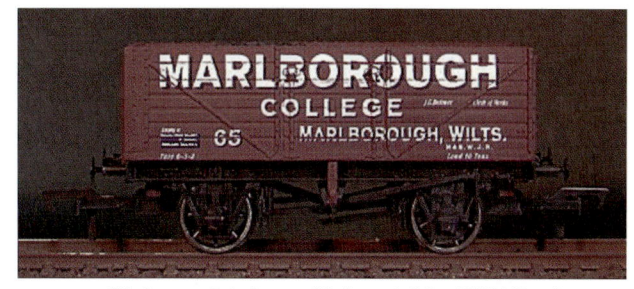

Private owner 7-plank wagon 'Marlborough College' [W9b] (Dapol)

-	'**Manchester Corporation**' 85 red-brown Sp Edn 150 (Astley Green Colliery Museum) - *11*	8	11

Dapol 00

-	'**Mansfield Bros.**' Sp Edn (Dean Sidings) - made?	NPG	NPG
B394	'**Manton**' 891 brown - *02*	7	9
22	'**Manvers Main**' 3044 red-brown Sp Edn (Midlander) - *0210*		12
-	'**Manx Tails**' brown, Dapol for show Ltd Edn - *03*	9	11
-	'**Marlborough College**' 65 dark brown Sp Edn 127 (Wessex Wagons) - *11*	7	10
B362	'**Marlborough Gas Co.**' 4 black - *01*	8	10
OX6	'James **Marriott**' 91 black Sp Edn 200 (1E Promotionals) - *06*	8	10
-	'**Marshall Bros.**' 7 black Sp Edn (?) - *06*	8	10
-	'**Martin Bros.**' 26 brown no load Sp Edn (Mevagissy Model Railways) ex-set - *01*	10	NA
-	'**Martin Bros.**' 26 brown + chalk load Sp Edn (Mevagissy Model Railways) ex-set - *02*	10	NA
-	'**Massey Bros. (Feeds) Ltd**' light green Sp Edn 100 (David Wild) - *12*	7	10
-	'**MC**' (Manchester Collieries) 10743 black Sp Edn 150 (Astley Green Colliery Museum) - *10*	7	9
-	'W **McMichael & Son**' 5 red-brown Sp Edn 120 (Nene Valley Railway) - *07*	7	9
-	'F **Meaker**' 1 grey Sp Edn 132 (Burnham & District MRC) - *12*	7	9
SWL8	'**Measham**' 1305 black Sp Edn 123 (Midlander) - *01*	10	12
-	'**Medway Coal Co.**' 17 black Sp Edn 1000 (Ballards) - *06*	7	9
-	'Charles **Meehan & Son**' 20>29 black, Sp Edn 160 (West Wales Wagon Works) - *06*	8	10
-	'**Mein, Wooding & Co.**' 250 black Sp Edn 120 (Barry & Penarth MRC) - *03*	9	11
No.7	'**Mellonie**' 244 grey Sp Edn 214 (Middy Trading Company) - *07*	7	9
-	'**Mellonie & Goulder**' 303 grey Sp Edn 229 (Mid Suffolk Light Railway) - *13*	8	11
-	'**Mellonie & Goulder**' 303 grey W Sp Edn 80 (Mid Suffolk Light Railway) - *13*	8	11
-	'**Mells Colliery**' 156 grey Sp Edn 170 (Burnham & District MRC) - *12*	7	9
No.20	'Elizabeth **Meredith Jones**' 1>9 red-brown Sp Edn 160 (West Wales Wagon Works) - *04*	9	11
4	'**Midland Coal, Coke & Iron**' 5004 red Sp Edn 200 (Haslington Models) - *02*	10	12
-	'**Midland Coal, Coke & Iron**' 2234 red-brown Sp Edn 200 (Tutbury Jinny) ex-set of 2 - *04*	9	NA
ANT001	''Wm **Miles**' 5 black Sp Edn 100 (Antics) - *03*	9	11
ANT001	''Wm **Miles**' 4 black Ltd Edn 160 (Gaugemaster) - *09*	8	10
B351	'**Miller & Lilley**' 66 black - *01*	7	9
No.091M	'**MM [Ministry of Munitions]**' 5141 red So Edn 116 (West Wales Wagon Works) - *10*	9	11
No.091W	'**MM [Ministry of Munitions]**' 5141 red W So Edn 45 (West Wales Wagon Works) - *10*	10	12
ANT026	'WW **Milton & Co.**' 6 grey Sp Edn 250 (Antics) - *07*	7	9
ANT026A	'WW **Milton & Co.**' 6 dark brown Sp Edn 250 (Antics) - *07*	7	9
-	'MM **Mitchell**' 573 red-brown Sp Edn 196 (Middy Trading Co.) - *11*	7	10
ANT015	'T **Mitchell**' 1902 black Sp Edn 250 (Antics) - *05*	8	10
-	'**Moger & Co.**' 576 red-brown Sp Edn 1000 (Ballards) - *08*	7	9
-	'**Moira**' 267 red-brown Sp Edn 200 (Tutbury Jinny) - *00*	11	13
-	'**Moira**' 467 red brown Sp Edn 500 (Tutbury Jinny) - *00*	11	13
B599	'**Mold Collieries**' 258 blue grey - *04*	7	9
-	'**Mold Collieries**' (overprinted with 'P') P12963 blue-grey W Sp Edn 100 (Wirral Models) - *08*	20	25
(18)	'**Monmouth Steam Saw Mills**' 1 light grey Sp Edn 250 (Hereford Model Centre) - *05*	8	10
(16)	'**Monmouth Steam Saw Mills**' 7 black Sp Edn 250 (Hereford Model Shop) - *05*	8	10
(17)	'**Monmouth Steam Saw Mills**' 13 grey Sp Edn 250 (Hereford Model Centre) - *06*	8	10
(15)	'**Monmouth Steam Saw Mills**' 18 grey Sp Edn 250 (Hereford Model Shop) - *05*	8	10
CMM005	'**Moresby Coal Company**' 180 grey Sp Edn 150 (C&M Models) - *12*	7	10
(14)	'**Morgan Bros.**' 14 light grey Sp Edn 250 (Hereford Model Centre) - *05*	8	10
23	'**Morgan Bros.**' 2 grey Sp Edn 250 (Hereford Model Centre) - *06*	8	10
(13)	'**Morgan Bros.**' 6 dark grey Sp Edn 250 (Hereford Model Centre) - *05*	8	10
-	'**Morgan Lloyd Williams**' 1072 grey Sp Edn 111 (Albatross Models) - *07*	7	9
-	'DE **Morgan**' 29 dark green + sand load Sp Edn (Albatross Models) - *08*	7	9
54	'EP&RL **Morgan**' 154 red-brown Sp Edn 250 (Hereford Model Shop) - *09*	6	8
No.79	'**Morris Bros.**' 22 red-brown Sp Edn 104 (West Wales Wagon Works) - *09*	6	8
No.79	'**Morris Bros.**' 22 red-brown W Sp Edn 104 (West Wales Wagon Works) - *09*	6	8
CA4	'Wm **Morris**' 100 black Sp Edn 175 (1E Promotionals) - *08*	7	9
(8)	'**Morris & Holloway**' 4 grey Sp Edn 250 (Hereford Model Centre) - *05*	8	10
-	'**Mortimore**' red-brown 56 Sp Edn 187 (Wessex Wagons) - *06*	8	10
-	'**Mossfield Colliery**' 874 black Sp Edn 200 (Trident Trains) - *13*	8	10
31	'**Mottramwood**' 2021 red-brown Sp Edn (Midlander) - *03*	9	11
-	'**Mountsorrel Granite**' 539 grey Sp Edn 100 (West Wales Wagon Works) - *12*	9	12
-	'**Mountsorrel Granite**' 539 grey W Sp Edn 20 (West Wales Wagon Works) - *12*	10	13
No.4	'**Moy**' 4194 red-brown Sp Edn 200 (Mid Suffolk Light Railway) - *04*	9	11
B553	'A **Munday**' 6 red-brown - *03*	7	9
No.47	'**Mwrwg Vale Colliery**' 26 black Sp Edn 124 (West Wales Wagon Works) - *06*	8	10
-	'**Mynydd Maen Colliery**' 105 light grey Sp Edn 110 (South Wales Coalfields) - *04*	8	11

A 'Mold Collieries' wagon after nationalisation [W9b]

National Coal Board 7-plank coal wagon [W9b] (Dapol)

-	'**Napier & Co.**' 25 black Sp Edn 110 (Roger Mileman) - *04*	9	11
-	'**Naval Colliery**' 540 black Sp Edn 108 (David Dacey) - *05*	8	10
CMM 006	'**Naworth Colliery Co.**' 140 brown Sp Edn 150 (C&M Models - Carlisle) - *13*	8	11

Dapol 00

Code	Description	Col1	Col2
-	'NCB - Bowes' 406 red-brown Sp Edn 100 (Bowes Railway) - 03, 08	7	9
-	'Neath Abbey' 15 black Sp Edn 101 (David Dacey) - 04	9	11
-	'Neath Merthyr Colliery' 259 red-brown Sp Edn 107 (David Dacey) - 05	8	10
SWL6	'Netherseal' 881 red brown Sp Edn 109 (Midlander) - 01	10	12
-	'Newbury' 327 grey Sp Edn 175 (Burnham & District MRC) - 12	7	9
No.32	'New Cross Hands Colliery' 391>399*** grey Sp Edn 143 (West Wales Wagon Works) - 05	8	10
No.9	'New CwmGorse Colliery' *** brown Sp Edn 150 (West Wales Wagon Works) - 03	9	11
-	'New Hey Industrial Co-operative' 21 yellow Sp Edn 100 (Paul Devlin) - 04	9	12
-	'New Medway' 19 red-brown Sp Edn 100 (Medway Queen) - 03, 04	9	11
-	'New Medway' 19 black Sp Edn 100 (Medway Queen) - 03, 04	9	11
-	'New Medway' 19 green Sp Edn 30 (Medway Queen) - 04	12	14
-	'New Medway' 24 black Sp Edn 65 (Medway Queen) - 04	11	13
-	'New Medway' 24 brown Sp Edn 65 (Medway Queen) - 04	11	13
-	'New Medway' 24 green Sp Edn 30 (Medway Queen) - 04	12	14
-	'Newport & Abercarn' 3 black Sp Edn 100 (David Dacey) - 08	7	9
E03A	'New Rock' 207 black Sp Edn 150 (East Somerset Models) ex-set - 04	9	11
E03B	'New Rock' 212 black Sp Edn 150 (East Somerset Models) ex-set - 04	9	11
-	'F. J. Newton' 37 grey Sp Edn 200 (Modellers Mecca) ex set - 02	10	NA
B363	'Nicholsons' 1 black - 01	8	10
HMC 60	'Norchard' 801 grey Sp Edn 250 (Hereford Model Centre) - 10	6	8
B265	'Normans Super Warehouse' brown - 97	9	11
B395	'Norstand' 376 maroon - 02-03	7	9
-	'North Cornwall' 3 brown no load Sp Edn (Mevagissy Model Railways) ex-set - 01	10	NA
-	'North Cornwall' 3 brown + chalk Sp Edn (Mevagissy Model Railways) ex-set - 02	10	NA
-	'North End' 42 black Sp Edn 104 (David Dacey) - 05	8	10
-	'North & Rose' 19 brown no load Sp Edn (Mevagissy Model Railways) ex-set - 00	11	NA
-	'North & Rose' 19 brown + chalk Sp Edn (Mevagissy Model Railways) ex-set - 01	10	NA
-	'North Rhondda' 21 very dark brown Sp Edn 110 (Jenny's) - 04	9	11
37	'Northern United' 220 black Sp Edn 250 (Hereford Model Centre) - 06	8	10
-	'North's Navigation Collieries' 7 maroon Sp Edn 220 (MIB models) - 04	9	15
-	'Norton & Biddulph' 3237 black Sp Edn 200 (Haslington Models) - 02	10	15
-	'Norton & Biddulph' 3237 black Sp Edn 100 (Trident Trains) - 07	7	9
No.4	'Norton & Co.' 176 black Sp Edn 213 (W.Wales Wagon Works) - 02	9	11
NR7	'Norwich Co-operative Society' 16 red-brown Sp Edn 200 (1E Promotionals) - 08	7	9
-	'Notts & Derby' 3601 black Sp Edn 195 (Sherwood Models) - 03	9	11
-	'Nottingham Corporation Gas' 169 black Sp Edn 200 (Sherwood Models) - 02	10	12
-	'Novis & Son' 1 bright red Sp Edn 1000 (Ballards) - 02	6	8
5	James **Oakes & Co.'** 772 black Sp Edn 200 (Haslington Models) - 02	10	12
B331	'Old Silkstone' 2401 bright red - 01	8	10
B565	'Oldham Corporation Gas' 019 red-brown - 03	7	9
B558	'Old Roundwood Collieries' 312 red-brown - 03	7	9
-	'Orrell Colliery' 443 bright red Sp Edn 100 (Red Rose Steam Society) - 05	8	10
No.2	'GD **Owen**' 16 red-brown Sp Edn 247 ** (West Wales Wagon Works) - 02, 03	9	11
No.62	'Palmer & Sons' 7 black Sp Edn 120 (West Wales Wagon Works) - 07	7	9
RTR3	'Parc-y-Bryn' 58 black Sp Edn 250 (RD Whyborn) - ?	12	14
-	'Parkers' 2 red-brown Sp Edn 100 (Richard Essen) - 11	9	12
-	'Parkhall & Foxfield' 1143 red-brown Sp Edn 170 (Trident Trains) - 10	9	11
-	'Parkhouse Colliery' 2993 brown Sp Edn 200 (Haslington Models) - 01	10	12
B82	'Parkinson' 100 dark blue - ?	9	11
-	'Parkyn & Peters' 35 red no load Sp Edn (Mevagissy Model Railways) ex-set - 00	11	NA
-	'Parkyn & Peters' 35 red + chalk Sp Edn (Mevagissy Model Railways) ex-set - 01	10	NA
-	'Allen **Parsons & Co.**' 20 dark red, Sp Edn 1000 (Ballards) - 06	7	10
-	'Pates & Co.' 18 bright red Sp Edn 200 (Cotswold Steam Preservation) - 08	7	9
-	'Pates & Co.' 22 bright red Sp Edn 250 (Cotswold Steam Preservation) - 04	9	11
-	'Pates & Co.' 24 bright red Sp Edn 250 (Cotswold Steam Preservation) - 05	9	11
(19)	'Payne & Son' 2 bright red Sp Edn 250 (Hereford Model Centre) - 05	8	10
WD3	'F **Payne**' 14 red-brown Sp Edn 250 (1E Promotionals) - 06	8	10
-	'PD' (Powell Duffryn) 1853 grey Sp Edn (Bristol 2008 Model Railway Exhibition) - 08	7	9
-	'Peacock Bros. & Harris' 6 brown Sp Edn 1000 (Ballards) - 04	7	9
OX9	'AT **Pearse**' 7 maroon Sp Edn 200 (1E Promotionals) - 08	7	9
-	'Pemberton & Co.' 25 dark brown Sp Edn 100 (Osbornes Models) - 05	8	10
RG1	'Pemberton & Co.' 25 dark brown Sp Edn 150 (1E Promotionals) - 09	8	10
No.65A	'Penlan Colliery' 114 black Sp Edn (West Wales Wagon Works) - 08	7	9
No.65A	'Penlan Colliery' 114 black W Sp Edn (West Wales Wagon Works) - 08	7	9
No.65B	'Penlan Colliery' 117 black Sp Edn (West Wales Wagon Works) - 08	7	9
No.65B	'Penlan Colliery' 117 black W Sp Edn (West Wales Wagon Works) - 08	7	9
-	'Pennington Mining Co.' 17 green Sp Edn 144 (Crafty Hobbies) - 09	7	10
-	'Thos S **Penny**' 1 red-brown Sp Edn 180 (Wessex Wagons) - 05	8	10
SWL9	'Pentrich' 1674 black Sp Edn 127 (Midlander) - 01	10	12
-	'Travis **Perkins**' dark green Sp Edn 155 (Travis Perkins) - 06	8	10
-	'WH **Perkins**' 3 red-brown Sp Edn 80 (West Wales Wagon Works - 13	9	13
-	'WH **Perkins**' 3 red-brown W Sp Edn 20 (West Wales Wagon Works - 13	9	14
-	'John **Perry**' 13 red-brown Sp Edn 345 (East Kent MRS) - 02	10	12
-	'Peterborough Coal & Coke Co.' 143288 red-brown Sp Edn 750 (Osbornes) - 99	10	12
-	'Peterborough Coal Co.' 404 black Sp Edn 95 (Nene Valley Railway) - 09	6	8
-	'Peterborough Co-op Society' 138 grey Sp Edn 96 (Nene Valley Railway) - 08	7	9

Co-operative society 7-plank coal wagon [W9b] 'Norwich Co-op'

Dapol 00

No.6	'SJ **Phillips**' 7 black Sp Edn 269 (West Wales Wagon Works) - 03	10	12
B325	'**Phorpes Bricks**' 988 black - 01	8	10
	'**Phorpes Bricks**' 938 black Sp Edn (Burnham & District MRC) certificate says '5-plank' - 01	7	9

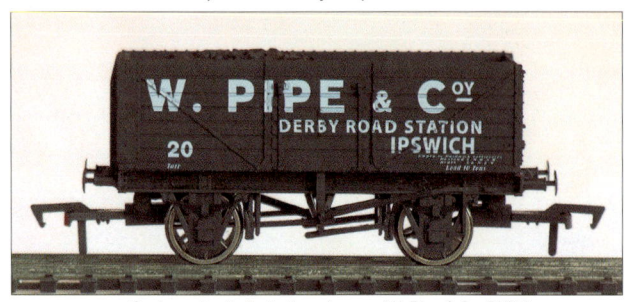

Coal merchant's 7-plank coal wagon 'W. Pipe & Co. [W9b]

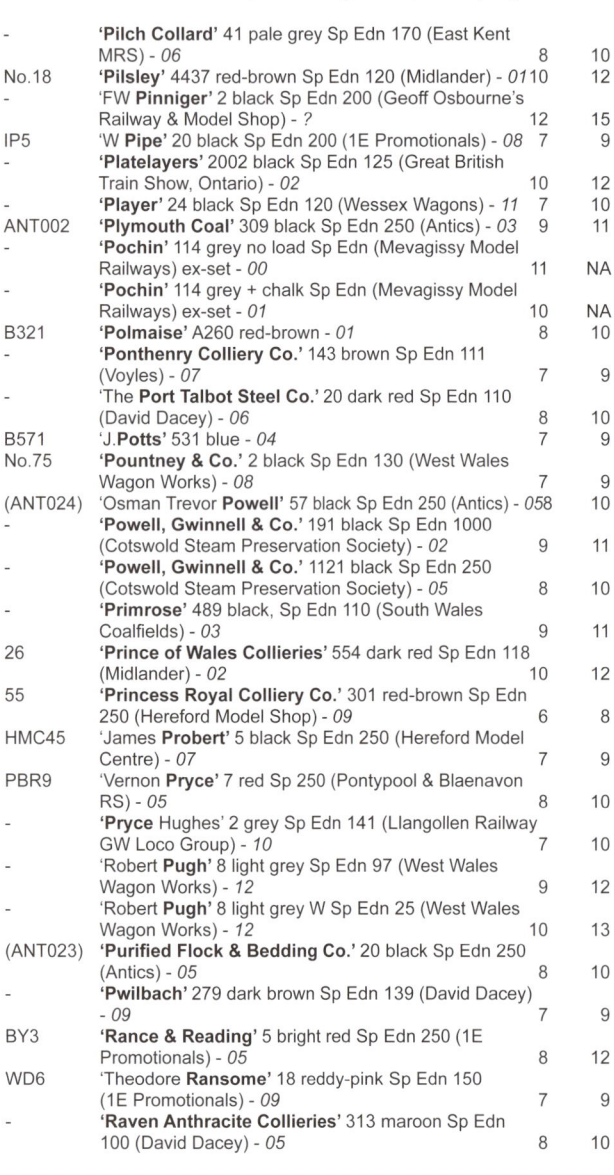

Lime Works 7-plank wagon 'Theodore Ransome' [W9b]

-	'**Pilch Collard**' 41 pale grey Sp Edn 170 (East Kent MRS) - 06	8	10
No.18	'**Pilsley**' 4437 red-brown Sp Edn 120 (Midlander) - 01	10	12
-	'FW **Pinniger**' 2 black Sp Edn 200 (Geoff Osbourne's Railway & Model Shop) - ?	12	15
IP5	'W **Pipe**' 20 black Sp Edn 200 (1E Promotionals) - 08	7	9
-	'**Platelayers**' 2002 black Sp Edn 125 (Great British Train Show, Ontario) - 02	10	12
-	'**Player**' 24 black Sp Edn 120 (Wessex Wagons) - 11	7	10
ANT002	'**Plymouth Coal**' 309 black Sp Edn 250 (Antics) - 03	9	11
-	'**Pochin**' 114 grey no load Sp Edn (Mevagissy Model Railways) ex-set - 00	11	NA
-	'**Pochin**' 114 grey + chalk Sp Edn (Mevagissy Model Railways) ex-set - 01	10	NA
B321	'**Polmaise**' A260 red-brown - 01	8	10
-	'**Ponthenry Colliery Co.**' 143 brown Sp Edn 111 (Voyles) - 07	7	9
-	'**The Port Talbot Steel Co.**' 20 dark red Sp Edn 110 (David Dacey) - 06	8	10
B571	'J.**Potts**' 531 blue - 04	7	9
No.75	'**Pountney & Co.**' 2 black Sp Edn 130 (West Wales Wagon Works) - 08	7	9
(ANT024)	'Osman Trevor **Powell**' 57 black Sp Edn 250 (Antics) - 058		10
-	'**Powell, Gwinnell & Co.**' 191 black Sp Edn 1000 (Cotswold Steam Preservation Society) - 02	9	11
-	'**Powell, Gwinnell & Co.**' 1121 black Sp Edn 250 (Cotswold Steam Preservation Society) - 05	8	10
-	'**Primrose**' 489 black, Sp Edn 110 (South Wales Coalfields) - 03	9	11
26	'**Prince of Wales Collieries**' 554 dark red Sp Edn 118 (Midlander) - 02	10	12
55	'**Princess Royal Colliery Co.**' 301 red-brown Sp Edn 250 (Hereford Model Shop) - 09	6	8
HMC45	'James **Probert**' 5 black Sp Edn 250 (Hereford Model Centre) - 07	7	9
PBR9	'Vernon **Pryce**' 7 red Sp 250 (Pontypool & Blaenavon RS) - 05	8	10
-	'**Pryce** Hughes' 2 grey Sp Edn 141 (Llangollen Railway GW Loco Group) - 10	7	10
-	'Robert **Pugh**' 8 light grey Sp Edn 97 (West Wales Wagon Works) - 12	9	12
-	'Robert **Pugh**' 8 light grey W Sp Edn 25 (West Wales Wagon Works) - 12	10	13
(ANT023)	'**Purified Flock & Bedding Co.**' 20 black Sp Edn 250 (Antics) - 05	8	10
-	'**Pwilbach**' 279 dark brown Sp Edn 139 (David Dacey) - 09	7	9
BY3	'**Rance & Reading**' 5 bright red Sp Edn 250 (1E Promotionals) - 05	8	12
WD6	'Theodore **Ransome**' 18 reddy-pink Sp Edn 150 (1E Promotionals) - 09	7	9
-	'**Raven Anthracite Collieries**' 313 maroon Sp Edn 100 (David Dacey) - 05	8	10
-	'**Raunds Cooperative Society**' 2 bright blue Sp Edn 97 (Kitmaster Club) - 03	9	12
-	'G **Rawlings & Sons**' 1 black Sp Edn 171 (Wessex Wagons) - 08	7	9
-	'John **Read**' 1913 red Sp Edn 140 (Wessex Wagons) - 06	8	10
B332	'**Redgrave**' 1386 grey - 01	8	10
SWL4	'**Renishaw Park Collieries**' 379 red-brown Sp Edn 118 (Midlander) - 01	10	12
B699	'**Renwick & Wilton**' 124 black - 07	6	8
B552	'**Renwick, Wilton & Co.**' 521 brown - 03	7	9
-	'**Renwick, Wilton & Dobson**' 1020 black - made?	NPG	NPG
B333	'**Rhymney**' 1927 grey - 01	8	10
-	'AET **Richards**' 2 black Sp Edn 110 (David Dacey) - 06	8	10
-	'Rose **Richards**' 114 black Sp Edn 100 (Richard Essen) - 08	7	9
-	'W **Rickman & Sons**' 8 red-brown Sp Edn 206 (Wessex Wagons) - 07	7	9
-	'**Ripponden Industrial Society**' 10 black Sp Edn 250 (Sutcliff's Model Shop?) - ?	8	10
B540	'**Rix & Groom**' 21 red - 03	7	9
-	'**RNCF**' 15 grey Sp Edn 160 (Wessex Wagons) - 10	7	10
B360	'**Charles Roberts**' 1910 red-brown - 01	8	10
-	'DA **Roberts**' 1 grey Sp Edn (?) - ?	6	8
No.094M	'Issac **Roberts**' 19 black Sp Edn 130 (West Wales Wagon Works) - 11	8	11
No.094W	'Issac **Roberts**' 19 black W Sp Edn 130 (West Wales Wagon Works) - 11	9	12
-	'**Rock Colliery**' 153 red-brown Sp Edn 143 (David Dacey) - 10	7	9
-	'**Rock Veins**' 61 red-brown Sp Edn 96 (South Wales Coalfields) - 05	8	10
ANT033	'John **Rogers & Son**' 3 light grey Sp Edn 250 (Antics) - 09	7	9
-	'James **Roscoe & Sons**' 130 red-brown Sp Edn 100 (Red Rose Steam Society) - 08	7	9
-	'**Rose Bridge Colliery**' 901 black Sp Edn 199 (Astley Green Colliery Museum) - 12	8	11
-	'**Rowe Camborne**' 14 red-brown Sp Edn 97 (Kernow MR Centre) - 05	8	10
IP4	'**Rowland Manthorpe Co.**' 1400 red-brown Sp Edn 150 (1E Promotionals) - 07	7	9
-	'**Rowland Manthorpe & Co.**' 20 red-brown Sp Edn 182 (Mid-Siffolk Light Railway) - 10	7	10
-	'**St Leger**' 225th Aniviversary 86451 grey Peco extension planks supplied Sp Edn 225 (Oliver Leetham) - 01	10	12
No.73	'Thomas **Saunders**' 6 black Sp Edn 115 (West Wales Wagon Works) - 08	7	9
No.73	'Thomas Rees **Saunders**' 6 black W Sp Edn 40 (West Wales Wagon Works) - 08	9	11
-	'**SC**' 5046 pale grey Sp Edn 100 (Richard Essen) - 12	15	20
-	'John **Scowcroft**' 1380 grey Sp Edn 100 (Red Rose Steam Society) - 08	7	9
-	'J **Settle**' 25 grey Sp Edn 170 (Alsager Railway Association) - 04	9	11
ANT037	'**Severn Valley Gas Corporation**' 105 grey Sp Edn 140 (Antics) - 09	9	12
B361	'**Sharlston**' 1420 brown - 01	8	10
B318	'**Sheepbridge**' 6091 red-brown - 00	8	10

Dapol 00

Code	Description		
-	'Sheffield & Eccleshall Co-op Soc.' 13 maroon Sp Edn 100 (TAG Models) - 02	10	12
-	'Sheffield & Eccleshall' 12 red 140 (Antics) - 10	9	12
B710	'Sherwood' 6089 maroon W - 07	6	8
SWL13	'Shipley' 1254 red-brown Sp Edn 130 (Midlander) - 01	10	12
-	'Shrewsbury Co-op Society' 16 pale grey Sp Edn 150 (Shrewsbury Railway Heritage Trust) - 11	7	10
-	'Siddons & Sons' 12 red-brown Sp Edn 137 (Nene Valley Railway) - 10	7	9
-	'Silverdale Co.' 175 red-brown Sp Edn 137 (Tutbury Jinny) ex-set of 2 - 05	8	NA
-	'Charles Skeates' 51 red-brown Sp Edn 122 (Wessex Wagons) - 12	8	10
-	'Sleight' P201194 grey Sp Edn 50 (D Hewins) - 02	12	14
-	'Sleight' P201083 grey Sp Edn 50 (D Hewins) - 02	12	14
B594	'Small & Son' 17 black - 04-05	7	9
-	'Small & Son' 17 black (this is B594 over sprayed in thin grey wash in the factory and over printed with a large white 'P' and the running number 'P12957' Sp Edn 34 (Wirral Models) - 08	20	25
ANT030	'Alfred J Smith' 260 red-brown Sp Edn 250 (Antics) - 08	7	9
-	'AW Smith & Son' 8 black Sp Edn 223 (Wessex Wagons) - 07	7	9
-	'AW Smith & Son' 8 black Sp Edn 40 (Wessex Wagons) - 10	7	9
-	'GH Smith & Son (Fuel)' 24 black Sp Edn 1000 (Ballards) - 02	8	10

Private owner 7-plank coal wagon 'James Smith' [W9b] (Dapol)

Code	Description		
B520	'HG Smith' 24 red-brown - 03	9	11
(ANT010)	'James Smith' 819 grey Sp Edn 250 (Antics) - 05	8	10
-	'WJ Snelling' 9 red-brown Sp Edn (Simply Southern) - 13	8	10
-	'WJ Snelling' 9 red-brown W Sp Edn (Simply Southern) - 13	8	10
SWL5	'Sneyd' 1414 red-brown Sp Edn 104 (Midlander) - 01	10	12
-	'Snowdon' 48 grey Sp Edn 107 (Hythe Kent Models) - 00	6	8
-	'Snowdown' 42 light grey Sp Edn 70 (Carriage & Wagon Models) - 11	9	12
-	'Snowdown' 42 light grey W Sp Edn 35 (Carriage & Wagon Models) - 11	10	14
-	'Snowdown' * grey Sp Edn 574 (Hythe Models) 3rd issue - 00	11	13
NR2	'P Softley' 11 grey Sp Edn 250 (1E Promotionals) - 04	9	11
BI1	'South & Gasson' 105 dark brown Sp Edn 225 (1E Promotionals) - 09	7	9
-	'South Ayrshire Collieries' 68 red brown Sp Edn 110 (Ayr Glass & Glazing) - 04	9	11
-	'South Crofty Mine' 26 blue Sp Edn 110 (Blewetts of Hayle) - 02	10	12
-	'South Herefordshire' 4 brown Sp Edn 250 (Hereford Model Centre) - 05	8	10
-	'South Leicester' 2120 red Sp Edn 200 (Tutbury Jinny) ex-set of 2 - 02	10	NA
B576	'South Wales' 20 grey - 04	7	9
SWL30	'South Yorkshire Chemical Works' 330 red-brown Sp Edn 140 (Midlander) - 03	9	11

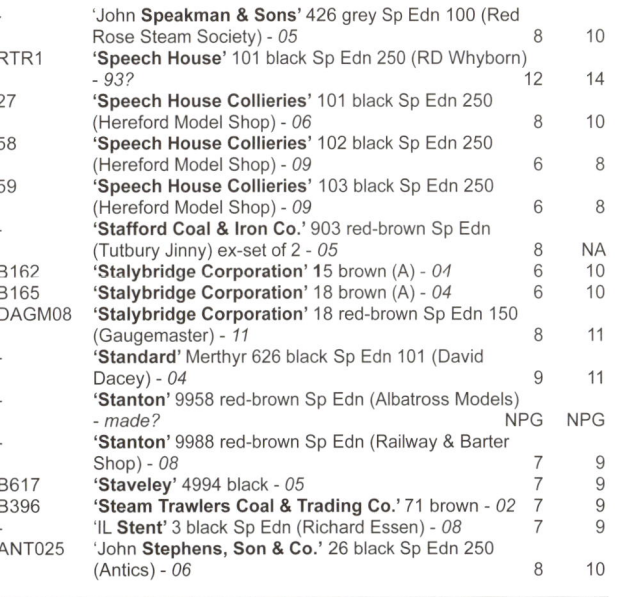

Code	Description		
-	'John Speakman & Sons' 426 grey Sp Edn 100 (Red Rose Steam Society) - 05	8	10
RTR1	'Speech House' 101 black Sp Edn 250 (RD Whyborn) - 93?	12	14
27	'Speech House Collieries' 101 black Sp Edn 250 (Hereford Model Shop) - 06	8	10
58	'Speech House Collieries' 102 black Sp Edn 250 (Hereford Model Shop) - 09	6	8
59	'Speech House Collieries' 103 black Sp Edn 250 (Hereford Model Shop) - 09	6	8
-	'Stafford Coal & Iron Co.' 903 red-brown Sp Edn (Tutbury Jinny) ex-set of 2 - 05	8	NA
B162	'Stalybridge Corporation' 15 brown (A) - 04	6	10
B165	'Stalybridge Corporation' 18 brown (A) - 04	6	10
DAGM08	'Stalybridge Corporation' 18 red-brown Sp Edn 150 (Gaugemaster) - 11	8	11
-	'Standard' Merthyr 626 black Sp Edn 101 (David Dacey) - 04	9	11
-	'Stanton' 9958 red-brown Sp Edn (Albatross Models) - made?	NPG	NPG
-	'Stanton' 9988 red-brown Sp Edn (Railway & Barter Shop) - 08	7	9
B617	'Staveley' 4994 black - 05	7	9
B396	'Steam Trawlers Coal & Trading Co.' 71 brown - 02	7	9
-	'IL Stent' 3 black Sp Edn (Richard Essen) - 08	7	9
ANT025	'John Stephens, Son & Co.' 26 black Sp Edn 250 (Antics) - 06	8	10

Coal merchant's 7-plank wagon 'F.D. Stigwood & Sons' [W9b]

Code	Description		
OX1	'Stevens & Co.' 31 bright red Sp Edn 250 (1E Promotionals) - 04	9	11
-	'Stevens & Son' 1 black Sp Edn 140 (Buffers) - 10	8	10
-	'Stewart Coal Co.' 2320 brown Sp Edn 107 (Barry & Penarth MRC) - 03	8	10
CA6	'FD Stigwood & Sons' 2 black Sp Edn 150 (1E Promotionals) - 10	7	9
-	'Stirrup & Pye' 848 black Sp Edn 150 (The Hobby Goblin) - 10	7	9
-	'Stuart Coal Co.' 95 dark brown Sp Edn 107 (Barry & Penarth MRC) - 03	9	11
-	'GS Sturgeon' 465 black Sp Edn 330 (Ballards) - 01	10	12
-	'Sully & Co.' 596 black Sp Edn 186 (Wessex Wagons) - 05	8	10
-	'Sully & Co.' 470 red-brown Sp Edn 138 (Burnham & District MRC) - 12	8	10
B370	'Summers' 69 black - 02	7	9
No.88M	'Edward Sutcliffe' 75 red-brown Sp Edn 124 (West Wales Wagon Works) - 10	8	11
No.88W	'Edward Sutcliffe' 75 red-brown W Sp Edn 38 (West Wales Wagon Works) - 10	9	12
ANT039	'Sutton' 48 red-brown Sp Edn 170 (Antics) - 09	9	12
-	'Sutton Heath Collieries' 1186 grey Sp Edn 100 (Astley Green Colliery Museum) - 09	7	9
B195	'Sutton Manor' 1075 light grey - 90, 95	8	10
-	'Sutton Manor' 1480 grey Sp Edn 100 (Red Rose Steam Society) - 09	8	10
-	'Swansea Navigation' 247 black Sp Edn 100 (David Dacey) - 03	9	11
SWL10	'Swanwick' 551 bright red Sp Edn 137 (Midlander) - 01	10	12
-	'Symes' 21 black Sp Edn (?) - 09	8	10
-	'H Syrus' 1 pale grey Sp Edn 1000 (Ballards) - 05	7	9
-	'Talk-O'Th Hill Colliery' 5 red-brown Sp Edn (Tutbury Jinny) ex-set of 2 - 05	8	NA

Dapol 00

No.40	'GW **Talbot**' 703 brown Sp Edn 141 (West Wales Wagon Works) - 06		8	10	-	'**Tunbridge Wells Co-operative Society**' 1 red-brown Sp Edn 1000 (Ballards) - 04	9	11
-	'AF **Tapp & Son**' 5 red-brown Sp Edn 192 (Wessex Wagons) - 05		8	10	OX3	'B **Turner**' 20 red-brown Sp Edn 250 (1E Promotionals) - 05	8	10
NR8	'**Tassell**' 107 red-brown Sp Edn 200 (1E Promotionals) - 08		7	9	B587	'E **Turner & Sons**' 25 cream - 04	7	9
-	'A **Taunt**' 3 blue Sp Edn 190 (Hythe Models - copyright passed to KESR) - 04		9	11	53	'E **Turner & Sons**' 25 cream Sp Edn 250 (Hereford Model Shop) - 04	7	9
B529	'C H **Taylor**' 3 grey - 03		7	9	-	'**Tyldesley Coal Co.**' 289 red-brown Sp Edn 100 (Astley Green Mining Museum) - 07	7	9
B368	'R.**Taylor**' 451 red-brown - 02		7	9	-	'**Tyldesley Coal Co.**' 598 red-brown Sp Edn 150 (Astley Green Mining Museum) - 10	7	9
DAGM07	'R **Taylor & Sons**' 451 red-brown Sp Edn 150 (Gaugemaster) - 11		8	11	-	'**Tynygraig**' 28 black Sp Edn 108 (David Dacey) - 06	8	10
B604	'S.**Taylor, Firth**' 731 red - 04		7	9	43	'**Underwood & Co.**' 100 red Sp Edn 250 (Hereford Model Centre) - 07	7	9
TVR1	'**Teifi Valley**' 1 dark green Sp Edn 108 (TVR) - 00		11	13	B516	'**United Collieries**' 1505 black - 03	7	9
TVR2	'**Teifi Valley**' 285 black Sp Edn 121 (TVR) - 01		10	12	B516	'**United Collieries**' 1505 dark grey - 03	10	15
TVR3	'**Teifi Valley**' 28 black Sp Edn 97 (TVR) - 01		10	12	-	'**Vale of Glamorgan**' Sp Edn (Vale of Glamorgan Railway) - 05	8	10
No.8	'**Teifi Valley**' 20 green Sp Edn 91 (West Wales Wagon Works) - 03		9	11	-	'**V&S Morfa Colliery**' 142 black Sp Edn 165 (David Dacey) - 10	7	9
No.14	'**Thomas** Thomas' various numbers black + filled with builders materials Sp Edn 198 (West Wales Wagon Works) - 04		9	11	-	'**Varteg Collieries**' 312 black, Sp Edn 130 (David Dacey) - 05	9	11
					-	'**Victoria Coal - Wales**' Best Productions' 10 grey Sp Edn 102 (David Dacey) - 06	8	10

Paper mill 7-plank coal wagon 'Thomas & Green' [W9b]

Coal merchant's 7-plank wagon 'F.W. Wachar' [W9b]

B708	'William **Thomas**' 1 black - 07		6	8	No.33	'W **Vincent & Co.**' **** red Sp Edn 160 (West Wales Wagon Works) - 05	8	10
-	'William **Thomas & Co.**' 1 black Sp Edn 167 (Wessex Wagons) - 03		8	10	PBR12	'John **Vipond**' 814 brown Sp Edn 280 (Pontypool & Bleanavon Rly Soc) - 05	8	10
BY10	'**Thomas & Green**' 10 red-brown Sp Edn 150 (1E Promotionals) - 08		8	10	-	'John **Vipond**' 877 dark brown Sp Edn 101 (South Wales Coalfields) - 03	9	11
B103	'**Thrutchley**' 2212 red - 86, 96		8	10	RM8	'FW **Wacher**' 6 black Sp Edn 275 (1E Promotionals) - 09	7	9
-	'**Tilmanstone**' * red-brown Sp Edn 100 (Hythe Kent Models) - 00		11	13	ANT018	'**Walker & Rogers**' 3 bright red Sp Edn 250 (Antics) - 05	8	10
-	'**Tilmanstone**' * dark brown Sp Edn 200 (Hythe Kent Models) 2nd issue numbered 101-200 - 00		11	13	1st	'John **Walker**' 2 black Sp Edn 150 (Castle Trains) - 07	7	9
-	'**Tilmanstone**' *dark brown Sp Edn 310 (Hythe Kent Models) - 00		11	13	-	'**Ward & Son**' 14 red-brown Sp Edn 1000 (Ballards) - 02	8	10
-	'**Tilmanstone**' * dark brown Sp Edn 514 (Hythe Kent Models) - 00		11	13	ANT009	'ET **Ward**' 4 black Sp Edn 100 (Antics) - 04	9	11
-	'**Tilmanstone**' 21 grey Sp Edn 70 (Carriage & Wagon Models) - 11		9	12	D003A	'**Waterloo**' 853 black, Sp Edn 100 (The Model Centre) - 03	9	11
-	'**Tilmanstone**' 21 grey W Sp Edn 70 (Carriage & Wagon Models) - 11		10	14	D003B	'**Waterloo**' 932 black, Sp Edn 100 (The Model Centre) - 03	9	11
B888	'John J **Tims**' 191 brown - 11		7	9	D003C	'**Waterloo**' 949 black, Sp Edn 100 (The Model Centre) - 03	9	11
B371	'John J **Tims**' 413 brown - 02		7	9	SWL21	'**Wath Main**' 1875 red brown Sp Edn 159 (Midlander) - 02	10	12
-	'**Timsbury Colliery**' 14 red Sp Edn 200 (Buffers) - 04		9	11	-	'**William Watkeys**' 465 dark brown Sp Edn (Voyles) - 07	7	9
-	'**Timsbury Colliery**' 15 red Sp Edn 200 (Buffers) - 05		8	10	-	'G **Watkinson & Son**' 10 red-brown Sp Edn 80 (Southport MRS) - 13	9	12
PBR1	'**Tirpentwys**' 121 black Sp Edn 100 (Pontypool & Bleanavon Railway) - 02		10	12	-	'G **Watkinson & Son**' 10 red-brown W Sp Edn 20 (Southport MRS) - 13	9	12
PBR15	'**Tirpentwys**' 457 black Sp Edn 250 (Pontypool & Bleanavon Rly Soc) - 08		7	9	B608	'**Webbs**' Coals' 86 black - 04	7	9
-	'**Ton Hir Colliery**' 217 black Sp Edn 117 (David Dacey) - 04		9	11	(B522)	'R **Webster & Sons**' 302 maroon - 03	7	NA
-	'**Ton Phillip Rhondda**' 277 black Sp Edn 102 (David Dacey) - 05		8	10	-	'W **Welford**' 7 blue Sp Edn (West Wales Wagon Works) - 11	9	12
No.54	'R **Toomers & Co.**' **** black Sp Edn 87 (West Wales Wagon Works) - 07		10	12	-	'W **Welford**' 7 blue W Sp Edn (West Wales Wagon Works) - 11	10	13
No.54	'R **Toomers & Co.**' black W Sp Edn 86 (West Wales Wagon Works) - 07		10	12	-	'**Wellingborough**' 29 grey Sp Edn 128 (Kitmaster Collectors Club) - 06	8	10
-	'**Tredegar**' 3410 grey Sp Edn 140 (David Dacey) - 10		7	9	-	'**West Goonbarrow**' 28 grey no load Sp Edn (Mevagissy Model Railways) ex-set - 01	10	12
-	'**Treoch Granite Co.**' blue-grey Sp Edn 120 (Model Rail magazine) - 06		8	9				
-	'**Trimsaram Anthracite**' 295 dark blue Sp Edn 96 (David Dacey) - 08		7	9				
-	'**Trojan Engineering**' 4 red-brown Sp Edn 100 (Richard Essen) - 12		10	12				

Dapol 00

Code	Description		
-	'West Goonbarrow' 28 grey no load Sp Edn (Mevagissy Model Railways) ex-set - 01	10	NA
-	'West Goonbarrow' 28 grey + chalk Sp Edn (Mevagissy Model Railways) ex-set - 02	10	NA
-	'West of England' 126 light grey no load Sp Edn (Mevagissy Model Railways) ex-set - 00	11	NA
-	'West of England' 126 light grey + chalk Sp Edn (Mevagissy Model Railways) ex-set - 01	10	NA
-	'WLC West Leigh Collieries' 868 red Sp Edn 100 (Astley Green Colliery Museum) - 09	7	9
-	'West Wales Wagon Works' 60 ? Sp Edn (West Wales Wagon Works) - not made	NA	NA
B596	'Western Valleys' 670 dark brown - 04	7	9
-	'Wetmore' 27 dark red Sp Edn 183 (Association of Model Railway Clubs Wales & West England) - 07	7	9
SWL29	'Wharncliffe Woodmoor' 1540 red-brown Sp Edn 140 (Midlander) - 02	7	9
4F071102	'Arthur Wharton' 3018 grey - 12	7	9
4F071103	'Arthur Wharton' 3018 grey W - 12	8	10
-	'Wheeler & Gregory' 324 ochre no load Sp Edn 144 (Wessex Wagons) - 10	7	10
B614	'White & Beeny' 17 black - 05	7	9
-	'White Beeny' 304 black Sp Edn (Simply Southern) - 13	8	10
-	'White Beeny' 304 black W Sp Edn (Simply Southern) - 13	8	10
ANT035	'Richard White & Sons' 109 light blue Sp Edn 250 (antics) - 08	7	10
-	'Whitehaven' 11 light grey Sp Edn 180 (Crafty Hobbies) - 10	8	11
-	'White, Winchester & Eastley' Sp Edn (Wessex Wagons) - not made	NA	NA
RM7	'Whitstable Shipping' 21 black Sp Edn 275 (1E Promotionals) - 09	9	11
-	'Whitstable Shipping' 22 brown Sp Edn 110 (East Kent MRS) - 02	10	12
-	'Whitstable Shipping' 24 grey Sp Edn 130 (East Kent MRS) - 03	9	11
No.45	'Whitwell Cole & Co.' **** black Sp Edn 176 (West Wales Wagon Works) - 06	8	10
-	'Whitwick Colliery' 1046 black Sp Edn 200 (Tutbury Jinny) ex-set of 2 - 02	10	NA
B649	'Whitwood' 1583 grey+red - 06	7	9
B598	'Wigan Coal & Iron' A147 grey - 04	7	9

Private owner 7-plank coal wagon 'Wiggins & Co.' [W9b]

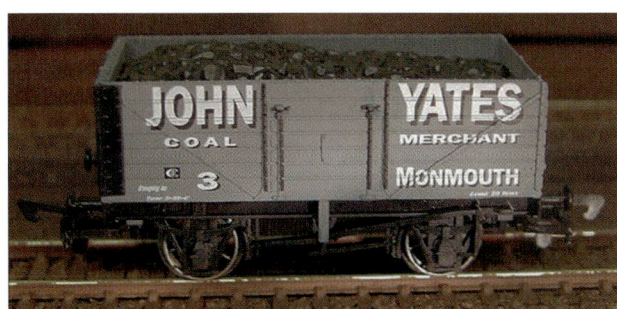

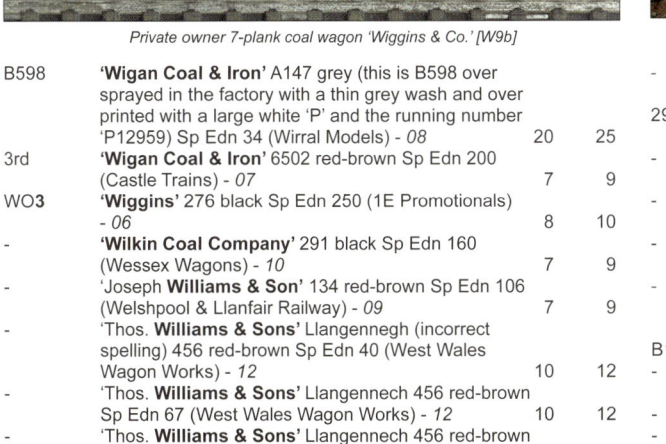

Code	Description		
B598	'Wigan Coal & Iron' A147 grey (this is B598 over sprayed in the factory with a thin grey wash and over printed with a large white 'P' and the running number 'P12959') Sp Edn 34 (Wirral Models) - 08	20	25
3rd	'Wigan Coal & Iron' 6502 red-brown Sp Edn 200 (Castle Trains) - 07	7	9
WO3	'Wiggins' 276 black Sp Edn 250 (1E Promotionals) - 06	8	10
-	'Wilkin Coal Company' 291 black Sp Edn 160 (Wessex Wagons) - 10	7	9
-	'Joseph Williams & Son' 134 red-brown Sp Edn 106 (Welshpool & Llanfair Railway) - 09	7	9
-	'Thos. Williams & Sons' Llangennegh (incorrect spelling) 456 red-brown Sp Edn 40 (West Wales Wagon Works) - 12	10	12
-	'Thos. Williams & Sons' Llangennech 456 red-brown Sp Edn 67 (West Wales Wagon Works) - 12	10	12
-	'Thos. Williams & Sons' Llangennech 456 red-brown W Sp Edn 25 (West Wales Wagon Works) - 12	11	13
-	'TL Williams' 29 red Sp Edn 120 (Barry & Penarth MRC) - 03	9	11
(1)	'WT Williams' 6 brown Sp Edn 500 (Hereford Model Centre) - 01	10	12
-	'Williams, Foster & Co.' 203 dark grey Sp Edn 106 (South Wales Coalfields) - 04	9	11
WO5	'Williams' 13 brown Sp Edn 200 (1E Promotionals) - 07	7	9
-	'Willmer & Son' 3069 red-brown Sp Edn 100 (Wicor Models) ex-set of 2 - 07	7	NA
-	'Willmer & Son' 3073 red-brown Sp Edn 100 (Wicor Models) ex-set of 2 - 07	7	NA
-	'Wimberry' 2 black Sp Edn (Dean Sidings) - 03	9	11
-	'Winchcombe Coal Co.' 12 grey Sp Edn 1000 (Glous & Wark Railway) - 98	10	12
-	'Winchcombe Coal Co.' 10 grey Sp Edn 1000 (Glous & Wark Railway) - 00	9	11
-	'Winchcombe Coal Co.' 7 grey Sp Edn (Glous & Wark Railway) - 03?	9	11
-	'Winchcombe Coal Co.' 5 grey Sp Edn (Cotswold Steam Preservation) - 12	7	9
-	'Windsor' 1584 black Sp Edn 124 (South Wales Coalfield) - 04	9	11
-	'Winstanley Collieries' 592 grey Sp Edn 90 (Red Rose Steam Society) - 08	8	10
B867	'WE Wise' 18 black - 11	7	9
-	'WM' (White Moss Colliery) 174 red-brown Sp Edn 100 (Red Rose Steam Society) - 09	7	9
-	'Wolstanton Cardox Mined Coals' 601 grey Sp Edn 100 (Trident Trains) - 07	7	9
No.78	'Woolcombers' 15 red-brown Sp Edn 72 (West Wales Wagon Works) - 09	6	8
No.78	'Woolcombers' 15 red-brown W Sp Edn 72 (West Wales Wagon Works) - 09	6	8
-	'Tom Wright' 19 red-brown Sp Edn 500 (Peak Rail Stock Fund) - 03	9	11
B554	'Wright's' 14 brown - 03	7	9
-	'Writhlington Colliery' 160 dark grey Sp Edn 200 (Buffers) - 04	9	11
-	'Writhlington Colliery' 140 dark grey Sp Edn (Buffers) - 05	8	10

Coal merchant's 7-plank wagon 'John Yates' [W9b] (Dapol)

Code	Description		
-	'Writhlington Colliery' 144 dark grey Sp Edn (Buffers) - not made	NA	NA
29	'John Yates' 3 grey Sp Edn 250 (Hereford Model shop) - 06	8	10
-	'Yeovil Gas Works' 24 dark brown Sp Edn 200 (Buffers) - 04	9	11
-	'Yeovil Gas Works' 25 dark brown Sp Edn 200 (Buffers) - 04	9	11
-	'Ynisgynon' 160 black Sp Edn 90 (South Wales Coalfields) - 05	8	10
-	'Ystradgynlais & Yniscedwyn' 779 black Sp Edn 100 (West Wales Wagon Wks) - not made	NA	NA

Commemoratives

Code	Description		
B178	'Dapol' black Sp Edn (Dapol) - c89	10	15
-	'Deltic Preservation Society' 1977-1997 black Sp Edn (DPS) - 97	12	14
-	as above but blue Sp Edn 500 (DPS) - 97	12	14
-	'Didcot Railway Centre - Great Western Society' brown Sp Edn (GWS) - ?	7	10

Dapol 00

-	'Great Western Society' green Sp Edn (GWS) - ?	10	15
-	'Great Western Society' 1 red-brown Sp Edn (GWS) - ?	10	15
-	'Howes Models' 1 blue Sp Edn 110 (Howes Models) - 02	10	12
-	'Monk Bar' deep blue 40th Anniv. Sp Edn (Monk Bar Model Shop) - 03	9	11
D009	NRM 2004 maroon Sp Edn 200 (TMC) - 04	9	11
D012	NRM Keep Scotsman Steaming black Sp Edn 4472 (TMC) - 05	8	10
-	'Railway Enthusiasts Club' grey Sp Edn 19 (Cove Models) - 04	9	12
-	'Silverhills Models & Toys' crimson 25th Anniv. Sp Edn (Silverhill Models) - 03	9	11
-	'Southwold MRE' blue-grey Sp Edn 500 (Southwold MRC) - 03	9	11
-	'Steamtown' black Sp Edn (Steamtown Museum Shop) - ?	8	10
-	'Ten Commandments' bright red Sp Edn 100 (Ten Commandments) - 02	10	12
-	'Barrow Hill' 1870 brown Sp Edn 94 (Barrow Hill Ltd) - 06	8	10
-	'Barrow Hill' 1998 maroon Sp Edn 209 (Barrow Hill Engine Shed Soc.) - 06	8	10
-	'Barrow Hill' 2008 dark brown Sp Edn 2008 (Barrow Hill Engine Shed Society) - 08	7	9
-	'Bideford 150' 1855 grey Sp Edn 100 (P.McAllister) - 05	8	10
-	'Yeovil Railway Centre' black Sp Edn 200 (Buffers) - 04	9	11

Railway Company

-	'Mid-Hants Rly' green Sp Edn 110 (Mid-Hants Railway) - 03?	9	11
-	Moors Valley Railway 2006 red Sp Edn 247 (Moors Valley Railway) - 06	8	10
-	North Norfolk Railway brown Sp Edn (NNR) - ?	8	10
-	NYMR 454491 grey Sp Edn (North Yorkshire Moors Railway) - 01	11	12
-	NYMR 454491 grey Sp Edn (North Yorkshire Moors Railway) letters small - 03	9	11
-	NYMR 454491 grey Sp Edn (North Yorkshire Moors Railway) letters larger - 05	8	10
-	G&KERy 67 grey Sp Edn 200 (Toys2Save) - 03	9	11
-	G&SW (Ayr Glass & Glazing) - not made	NA	NA
No.3	GE 5043 grey Sp Edn 200 (Mid-Suffolk Light Railway) - 03	9	11
-	GN 39850 brown Sp Edn 92 (Old Wagon Works) - 03	9	11
4F071001	GW 06479 dark grey - 13	7	9
4F071002	GW 06479 dark grey W - 13	8	11
B14	GW (thick) 06515 dark grey - 95	8	10
B14	GW (thin) 29019 dark grey - 95	8	10
B348	GW 06512 grey - 01	6	8
B348a	GW 06577 grey (possibly renumbered old stock) - 10	6	8
B348AW	GW 06577 grey W (possibly renumbered old stock) - 10	6	8
4F071001	GW 06577 grey - 12	7	9
4F071002	GW 06577 grey W - 12	76	10
-	GW 45,51,64,451,645,864,6451,8645 and 86851 dark grey part hand painted from St Ledger wagon + Peco extensions horse wagon Sp Edn 33 (Oliver Leetham) - 04	12	15
B6	LMS 609525 red brown - 84	9	11
B337	LMS 602504 light grey - 01	8	10
B111	LMS 602604 grey - 89	6	10
B111	LMS 602508 grey - ?	8	10
B758	LMS 302511 grey - 09	6	8
B758A	LMS 302511 grey (possibly renumbered old stock) - 10	6	8
B758AW	LMS 302511 grey W (possibly renumbered old stock) - 10	7	10
4F071005	LMS 302081 light grey - 12	7	9
4F071006	LMS 302081 light grey W - 12	8	10
-	LWR LW114 grey Sp Edn 100 (Leadhills & Wanlockhead Railway) - 01	9	11
B12	NE 171519 grey - 84	9	11
B356	NE Loco HB4333 grey - 01	8	10
-	NE Loco Coal 454941 dark grey Sp Edn 100 (Grantham Railway Society) - 08	7	9

-	SECR various numbers dark grey part hand painted from above + Peco extension, sheep wagon Sp Edn 20 (Oliver Leetham) - 04	12	15
-	SER various numbers dark grey part hand painted ex-St Ledger + Peco exten'n, sheep wagon Sp Edn 40 (Oliver Leetham) - 04	12	15
B205	SR 37427 dark brown - 94	9	11
B328	SR 37423 dark brown - 01	7	9
4F051003	SR ? brown - 12	NPG	NPG
4F051004	SR ? brown W - 12	NPG	NPG
4F071007	SR 37429 brown - 12	7	9
4F071008	SR 37429 brown W - 12	8	10
-	SR 'Beachy Head Quarry Co.' 2012 & 1103 grey Sp Edn 77 (Simply Southern) - 11	8	11
-	SR 'Beachy Head Quarry Co.' 2012 & 1103 grey W Sp Edn 40 (Simply Southern) - 11	8	11
4	WHR 20 grey Sp Edn (Welsh Highland Railway) - 08	7	9
B568	BR P238864 grey - 04	5	6
B568A	BR P238832 grey (possibly renumbered old stock) - 106		8
B568AW	BR P238832 grey W (possibly renumbered old stock) - 10	6	8
4F071003	BR P238832 grey - 12	7	9
4F071004	BR P238832 grey W - 12	76	10
B10	BR P130288 grey (M) - 84	9	11

* These were delivered unnumbered and were individually numbered by Steve Skelton of Hythe (Kent) Models. ** 200 were sold as solo models and the other 200 came in wagon sets. *** The 5 loads are Dapol coal, real coal, crushed brick rubble, limestone and crystaline salt. Just 96 of each load were made. **** These were individually numbered by W.Wales Wagon Works. ***** 3 alternative numbers.

W10.   7-Plank Coke Wagon (ex-Mainline) (1985)

This was a 7-plank wagon with a pair of extra planks on top, to allow extra room for coke, which is a light substance and could be carried in larger quantities.

The wagon was released by Palitoy in 1978 and the residue of its stock was sold to Dapol in 1985 and sold through their catalogues.

Private Owner

B152	'Baldwin' 2030 black (M) - c89	6	10
B148	'Bedwas' 621 light grey (M) - c89	6	10
B154	'Carpenter' 28 red (M) - c89	6	10
B156	'CCC' 105 dark red (M) - c89	6	10
B150	'Coalite' 552 dk.brown new chassis (M) - c89	6	10
B71	'Dinnington' 254 red brown (M) - 85-89	6	10
B151	'MOY' 1851 red brown (M) - c89	6	10
B153	'Arthur H.Stabler' 21 grey (M) - c89	6	10
B149	'TCD' 171 dark brown (M) - c89	6	10
B155	'TWW' 1746 brown (M) - c89	6	10

Although a number of other coke wagons were illustrated in catalogues we have found no evidence that any were sold in Dapol packaging.

W11.   8-plank Open Wagon with 10ft Chassis (2006)

In order to carry greater loads, some companies ordered 8-plank coal wagons but these were far less common in the coal industry.

Dapol added the 8-plank wagon to their catalogue at a time when they were creating new and better models and the appeal of this one was that it could be used for private owner liveries.

A006	unfinished grey - 09	4	10

Private Owner

-	'Aberthaw & Bristol Channel' 39 red-brown Sp Edn 98 (David Dacey) - 08	7	9
B885	'Adler & Allan' 107 red-brown - 11	7	9
B863	'Banks' 351 light grey - 10	7	9
B681	'H.C.Bull & Co.' 101 brown - 06	6	8

8-plank wagon 'J.T. Burton & Sons' [W11]

Dapol 00

Code	Description		
4F080001	'HC **Bull & Co.**' 103 red - 12	7	9
4F080002	'HC **Bull & Co.**' 103 red W - 12	7	9
CR1	'JT **Buxton & Sons**' 1930 red-brown Sp Edn 200 (1E Promotionals) - 08	7	9
B696	'**Chatterley**-**Whitfield**' 4055 grey - 07	6	8
SY3	'**City of Birmingham Gas Dept.**' 1225 red-brown Sp Edn 300 (1E Promotionals) Warley Charity Link) - 10	7	9
-	'**Colliery Supply Co.**' 7 red-brown Sp Edn 306 (Wessex Wagons) - 08	7	9
-	'Hiram **Cox**' 10 beige Sp Edn 286 (Wessex Wagons) - 08	7	9
-	'J **Cramer & Sons**' 23 black Sp Edn 258 (Wessex Wagons) - 08	7	9
-	'J **Cramer & Sons**' 23 black W Sp Edn 40 (Wessex Wagons) - 10	7	9
B879	'**Embling & Son**' 15 red-brown - 11	7	9
BE6	'John **Facer & Son**' 120 maroon Sp Edn 150 (1E Promotionals) - 07	7	9
-	'**Florence Coal & Iron Co.**' 1018 grey Sp Edn (Tutbury Jinny) - 11	9	12
B840	'**Hatfield Main**' 1213 red-brown - 10	7	9
B891	'**Enoch Haythorne**' 105 light blue - 11	7	10
-	'RW **Hearn & Son**' 105 red-brown, brick load, Sp Edn 270 (Wessex Wagons) - 07	7	9
BE9	'B **Laporte**' 55 black, white Barite load, Sp Edn 150 (1E Promotionals) - 10	7	9
4F080003	'**Leamington Priors Gas Co.**' 24 red-brown - 12	7	9
4F080004	'**Leamington Priors Gas Co.**' 24 red-brown W - 12	8	10
B730	'**LC**' (Littleton Collieries) 151 black - 08	5	7
WD5	'**Letchworth Electricity Works**' 11 red-brown Sp Edn 150 (1E Promotionals) - 08	7	9
-	'**Measham Collieries**' 1308 black Sp Edn 200 (Tutbury Jinny) - 08	7	9
-	'**Minehead Gas Light & Coke Co.**' 73 light grey Sp Edn 325 (Wessex Wagons) - 09	7	9
4F080100	'**Modern Transport**' 1206 grey - 12	7	9
4F080101	'**Modern Transport**' 1206 grey W - 12	7	10
B705	'**Osborne & Son**' 11 grey W - 07	6	8
-	'WT **Parkes**' 19 dark brown Sp Edn 195 (Wessex Wagons) - 07	7	9
B825	'**Partington Steel & Iron Co.**' 184 grey - 10	7	9
No.87AM	'**Porter & Son**' 60>69 * red-brown Sp Edn (West Wales Wagon Works) - 10	8	10
No.87AW	'**Porter & Son**' 60>69 red-brown W Sp Edn 28 (West Wales Wagon Works) - 10	9	11
No.87BM	'**Porter & Son**' 120>129 grey Sp Edn (West Wales Wagon Works) - 10	8	10
No.87BW	'**Porter & Son**' 120>129 grey W Sp Edn 27 (West Wales Wagon Works) - 10	9	11
No.87PM	No.87am + No.87bm Sp Edn 17 (West Wales Wagon Works) - 10	NA	18
No.87PW	No.87aw + No.87bw Sp Edn (West Wales Wagon Works) - 10	NA	19
-	'**Pugh & Co.**' 380 red-brown Sp Edn 1000 (Ballards) - 08	7	9
-	'**Railway Employees Coal Club - St Albans City**' 2 black Sp Edn 85 (David Dacey) - 10	9	12
-	'**Railway Employees Coal Club - St Albans City**' 3 black Sp Edn 85 (St Albans Signal Box Preservation Trust) - 08	7	9
-	'**Railway Employees Coal Club - St Albans City**' 3 black W Sp Edn 85 (St Albans Signal Box Preservation Trust) - 08	8	10
NR6	'B **Raywood & Son**' 1933 black Sp Edn 150 (1E Promotionals) - 07	6	8
4F080102	'**Rose Smith**' ? ? - 13	7	9
4F080103	'**Rose Smith**' ? ? W - 13	7	10
B669	'**Royal Leamington Spa**' 24 brown - 06-07	6	8
B889	'T&C **Scowcroft & Son**' 789 red-brown - 11	7	9
-	'**Shelton Iron Steel & Coal**' 2298 red Sp Edn 100 (Trident Trains) - 07	7	9
-	'**Shelton Iron Steel & Coal Co.**' 2299 red Sp Edn (Tutbury Jinny) - 11	9	12
B671	'**Smith Parkinson & Cole**' 5009 black - 06	6	8
B820	'**South Wales & Cannock Chase Coal & Coke Co.**' 977 light grey - 10	7	9
-	'**Tenterton Brewery Co.**' 148 red-brown Sp Edn (Col. Stephens Railway Enterprise) - 08	8	10
B675	'**Thorncliffe Izal**' 2915 black - 06	6	8
-	'**Twickenham Coal Co,**' 7 red-brown Sp Edn 160 (Wessex Wagons) - 11	8	10
-	'**Westbury Iron Works**' 51 dark brown Sp Edn 236 (Wessex Wagons) - 07	7	9
-	'TW **Woolford**' 1908 grey Sp Edn 182 (Wessex Wagons) - 08	7	9

* Various numbers applied by West Wales Wagon Works.

W12a. NE 20T 9-plank Mineral Wagon (ex-Airfix)(1985)

This model was based on the first coal wagons built by the LNER around 1928. They had a 20 ton capacity and were constructed in wood. They were built with end and bottom doors and with twin drop-down doors in each side.

This was another former Airfix wagon which was released in 1981. Palitoy produced two versions of it before the tooling passed to Dapol, who also received the unsold Airfix and Mainline models to sell. The tools were sold to Hornby in 1996 and the model reintroduced by them.

Code	Description		
A9	brown or grey - unfinished - 85	4	10
A007	unfinished grey - ?	4	10
Private Owner			
B54	'**Charringtons**' 257 brown (M) - 85	7	11
B55	'**Gas Light & Coke**' 794 grey (M) - 85	7	11
B114	NE 31273 grey (A) - ?	7	11
Railway Company			
B266	NE 31285 grey ex-set B402 - 97	6	8
B115	BR E10995, E30995 grey (A) - 86	7	11
B115	BR E30996 grey - ?-02	6	8

W12b. NE 20T 9-plank Mineral Wagon (2005)

The 20 ton 9-plank mineral wagon was retooled by Dapol in 2005 and was one of four new wagons released by them that year.

Code	Description		
Private Owner			
B864	'**Baldwin**' 4602 black - 12	9	12
B670	'Lowell **Baldwin**' 4301 black - not made	NA	NA
B670	'Lowell **Baldwin**' 4601 black - 06	7	9
4F090001	'Lowell **Baldwin**' 4601 black - 12	7	9
4F090002	'Lowell **Baldwin**' 4601 black W - 12	7	10
B661	'**Bedwas Coke**' 331 brown - 06	7	9
B641	'**Charringtons**' 259 red-brown - 05	7	9
B689	'**Co-operative Society Ltd - Dovercourt Bay**' red-brown - 07	7	9
B907	'**Dovercourt Bay Co-op Society**' 7 grey - 11	7	9
B907W	'**Dovercourt Bay Co-op Society**' 7 grey W - 11	7	10
B637	'The **Gas Light & Coke Co.**' 766 pale grey - 05	7	9
4F090003	'The **Gas Light & Coke Co.**' 766 pale grey - 13	7	9
4F090004	'The **Gas Light & Coke Co.**' 766 pale grey W - 13	7	10
S1153	'**Geoscenics Natural Scenic Products**' dark green, coal in-fill + bag of natural stone Sp Edn 100* (Geoscenics) - 07	8	10
ANT 036	'**Gloucester**' 3 black Sp Edn 250 (Antics) - 07	7	9
-	'**Harrogate Gas Co.**' 14 black Sp Edn 94 (Starbeck Models) - 08	7	9
No.38	'**Isambard Kingdom Brunel**' 1806 green Sp Edn 120 (West Wales Wagon Works) - 06	8	10
TVR4	'**Teifi Valley**' 25 dk.green Sp Edn (TVR/West Wales Wagon Works) - 08	7	9
B651	'**Wellingborough Gas Light Company**' 5 grey - 06	7	9
B878	'**Wellingborough Gas Light Company**' 9 grey - 11	7	9

8-plank wagon 'B. Raywood & Sons' [W11]

Dapol 00

B878W	'Wellingborough Gas Light Company' 9 grey W - 11	7	10

9-plank wagon [W12b] (Dapol)

	Railway Company		
B631	BR E30994 grey - 05	6	8
B631A	BR E30910 grey - 10	7	9
B631AW	BR E30910 grey W - 10	7	10

* Actually 117 made but 17 retained by shop.

Steel Open Wagons

W13.   13T Steel Sided Wagon (1995)

This was based on an LNER, design even though it was built by British Railways. The projections on the outside of the wagon body housed fastening rings on the inside of the wagon.

The original Hornby Dublo tooling was lost and the one used today by Dapol is a replica.

Ex-LNER design steel-sided wagon [W13]

	Private Owner		
B237	'BAC' 4253 red-brown - c95	10	15
WR1-26	as above - ?	10	15
WR3-06	as above - 98	10	15
D011	NRM 2004 maroon Sp Edn 200 (TMC) - 04	12	18
B236	'NTG' B486863 buff - c95	10	15
WR1-19	as above - 99	10	15
WR2-17	as above Dapol chassis - 99	10	12

	Railway Company		
No.19	TVR Extension Project Department 120>129 grey Sp Edn 162 (West Wales Wagon Works) - 04	12	18
BY13	024185 grey (Wolverton Works) Sp Edn 150 (1E Promotionals) - 10	7	9
B238	BR B466865 brown - c95	10	15
WR1-50	as above - 99	10	15
WR2-32	BR B468865 red-brown + coal 12T - 99	10	12
B354	BR Soda Ash B745543 grey + grey load - 01	8	10
B358	BR B490563 grey + coal - 01	8	10
B559	BR B489177 red-brown Sand - 03	7	9
B691	BR B480202 red-brown - 07	6	8
B826	BR B478605 red-brown - 10	7	9

W14.   'Grampus' Ballast Wagon (2008)

From the early 1950s, the versatile Grampus was a major ballast and spoil carrier in the BR Engineer's fleet until the beginning of the 1980s. Almost 4,800 were built by outside firms during the 1950s and included several design variations. They were to be found all over the British network but were replaced by higher capacity and sturdier vehicles as the industry modernised. The wagon had removable end planks and drop-down sides.

The model has self-centring couplings in NEM pockets and steel buffers. They are supplied with an imitation granite load. The original chassis has grease type axleboxes but in 2009 Dapol introduced a chassis modelled on one with roller bearing axleboxes. The new moulding has shorter and slimmer buffers, a vacuum cylinder underneath and steel bar across the chassis to the brake handles, which are also different.

A018	unfinished black - 11	4	10

	Private Owner		
B742	'Taunton Concrete Works' DB986428 dark green + grey load - 08	10	13
B742A	'Taunton Concrete Works' DB986700 dark green + grey load - 10	10	13
B742AW	'Taunton Concrete Works' DB986700 dark green W + grey load - 10	12	15

	Railway Company		
B734	BR DB990488 black 'Grampus' - 08	10	13
4F060007	BR DB990488 black 'Grampus' - 12	11	14
4F060008	BR DB990488 black 'Grampus' W - 12	12	15
B734/5	BR DB988393 black 'Grampus' * Sp Edn 275 (Hattons) - 09	9	12
B734/6W	BR DB988393 black 'Grampus' * Sp Edn 250 (Hattons) - 09	9	12
B734/1	BR DB988395 black 'Grampus' * Sp Edn 250 (Hattons) - 09	10	13
B734/2W	BR DB988395 black W 'Grampus' * Sp Edn 250 (Hattons) - 09	10	13
4F060007	BR DB990488 black + white load - 12	11	14
4F060008	BR DB990488 black W + white load - 12	12	15
B734/3	BR DB990173 olive green 'Grampus' * Sp Edn 250 (Hattons) - 09	10	12
B734/4W	BR DB990173 olive green W 'Grampus' * Sp Edn 250 (Hattons) - 09	10	12
B822A	BR Eng. DB990644 brown - 10	10	13
B822B	BR Eng. DB990646 brown - 10	10	13
B836A	BR Eng. DB990648 brown W - 10	10	14
B836B	BR Eng. DB990641 brown W - 10	10	14
4F060001	BR Eng. DB990648 brown + grey load - 12	11	14
4F060002	BR Eng. DB990648 brown W + grey load - 12	12	15
B836A	BR Eng. ? red-brown W - made?	NPG	NPG
B836B	BR Eng. ? red-brown W - made?	NPG	NPG

'Grampus' ballast wagon [W14] (Dapol)

B749A	BR Eng. DB988456 grey+yellow - 09	10	13
B749B	BR Eng. DB991640 grey+yellow - 09	10	13
B749C	BR Eng. DB991571 grey+yellow - 09	10	13
B749D	BR Eng. DB991500 grey+yellow - 09	10	13
B749E	BR Eng. DB988546 grey+yellow - 09	10	13
4F060003	BR Eng. DB988546 grey+yellow + grey load - 12	11	14
4F060004	BR Eng. DB988546 grey+yellow W + grey load - 12	12	15
B749F	BR Eng. DB991487 grey+yellow - 09	10	13
B749G	BR Eng. DB988237 grey+yellow - 09	10	13
B749H	BR Eng. DB991747 grey+yellow - 09	10	13
B756A	BR Eng. DB988458 grey+yellow W - 09	10	13
B756B	BR Eng. DB991643 grey+yellow W - 09	10	13
4F060005	BR Eng. DB8981487 grey+yellow + grey load - 13	11	14
4F060006	BR Eng. DB8981487 grey+yellow W + grey load - 13	12	15

* New roller bearing chassis.

W15a.   16T Steel Mineral Wagon (ex-Mainline) (1985)

The wagon was of a type produced in their thousands during the 1950s. It had an end door and side doors with 'London Trader' flaps above the side doors.

The wagons sold by Dapol in the 1980s were residue stock from the closure of Palitoy.

	Private Owner		
B28	'ICI' 776 dark blue (M) - 86	6	10

Dapol 00

		Railway Company		
B27	BR B118301 grey (M) - 86		6	10
B73	BR B595150 red-brown + coal (M) - 85		6	10

W15b. 16T Steel Mineral Wagon (ex-HD/Wrenn) (1995)

This is a model of the ubiquitous 1950s 16 ton steel mineral wagon built in vast numbers by BR to replace scrapped timber bodied wagons. Like the above model, it had an end door with side doors and 'London Traders' flaps. Over 300,000 steel mineral wagons were built and involved several different wagon builders, each with their own variation in style.

The model was first released in the Hornby Dublo range in 1958 and was bought by G&R Wrenn in the late 1960s. In 1993, Dapol bought the body tooling, which is still in use.

A008	unfinished grey - ?		4	10
-	black with sand load in grey - 12?		5	NA
		Private Owner		
B655	'Atkinson & Prickett' 1609 grey - 06		7	9
B843	'Atkinson & Prickett' 1611grey - 10		7	9
4F030007	'Atkinson & Prickett' 1611 grey - 12		7	9
4F030008	'Atkinson & Prickett' 1611grey W - 12		7	10
B229	'Esso' silver - c95		15	18
WR1-14	as above - 99		15	20
WR2-31	as above but with Dapol chassis		NPG	NPG
B346	'ICI' 268 blue-grey + coal - 01		8	10
B728	'ICI' 268 blue-green - 08		6	8
B364	'NCB' 30 pale grey + coal - 01		8	10
-	'A Oakes' 100 years white Sp Edn 100 (A.Oakes) - 04		9	11
B90	'Park Ward' 7 brown - c95		10	15
WR1-15	as above - 99		10	18
B230	'Shell' silver - c95		8	12
WR2-10	as above - 98		10	12

Former Hornby Dublo Mineral Wagon 'TCS' [W15b]

		Commemoratives		
PR4	'TCS' light grey Sp Edn 175 (Train Collectors Society/1E Promotionals) - 09		7	9
-	'Virgin & Dapol' 'Pendolino' red Sp Edn 500 (Virgin Trains) - 01		25	30
-	'Virgin & Dapol' 'Pendolino' white Sp Edn 100 (Dapol for dealers) - 01		35	40
		Railway Company		
B228	GW 110265 dark grey - c95		10	15
B350	GW 'Loco' 18810 grey + coal - 01		8	10
4F030100	GW 'Loco' 18618 grey - 12		7	9
4F030101	GW 'Loco' 18618 grey W - 12		7	10
B27	BR B54884 grey - c95		9	11
WR2-11	as above - 98		8	10
B73	BR B54884 brown - c95		10	15
WR2-06	as above - 98		10	20
B352	BR B54882 grey + coal - 01		8	10
B353	BR B54884 brown + coal - 01		8	10
WR2-11	as above - 01		10	12
B398	BR 105530 grey Coal - 02		8	10
B398A	BR 105534 grey Coal - 02		8	10
B523	BR B480215 red-brown + coal - 03		7	9
B686	BR M620623 brown - 07		6	8
B701	BR B550220 brown (1st batch - door stripe at wrong end) - 07		6	8
B701	BR B550220 brown (2nd batch - door stripe correct) - 07		6	8
B706	BR M620248 grey W - 07		6	8

B748	BR M620638 W - 09		6	8
4F030001	BR M620623 brown - 12		7	9
4F030002	BR M620623 brown W - 12		8	10
4F030003	BR M620248 grey - 12		7	9
-	BR M620619 brown		7	NA
-	BR M620622 brown		7	NA
-	BR M620721 brown		7	NA
-	BR M620734 brown		7	NA
-	BR M620676 brown		7	NA
4F030005	above 5 wagons - 12		NA	40
-	BR M620619 brown W		7	NA
-	BR M620622 brown W		7	NA
-	BR M620721 brown W		7	NA
-	BR M620734 brown W		7	NA
-	BR M620676 brown W		7	NA
4F030006	above 5 wagons - 12		NA	40

W16a. GWR 20T Steel Mineral Wagon (ex-Airfix) (1984)

Here we have another former Airfix wagon, but this time based on a GWR design of the 1930s, many of which were built for locomotive coal transportation. BR continued to construct similar looking wagons after Nationalisation.

The model was tooled by Airfix in 1979. The tooling passed to Palitoy in 1981 and to Dapol in 1985. From the latter it passed to Hornby in 1996. Dapol had also received unsold stocks of both the Airfix and Mainline produced models and these are also listed in this table.

A5	brown unfinished - 84		5	10
A5	dark grey unfinished - ?		5	10
A009	unfinished - ?		4	10
		Private Owner		
B51	'Avon Tyres' 1 black (M) - 85, 97		7	10
B53	'Blaenavon' 2441 red brown (M) - 85, 97		7	10
B52	'Glenhafod' 2277 black (M) - 85		7	10
B83	'PJ&JP' 3619 black (M) - 85		7	10
B95	'SC' 25503 dark grey (M) - 86		7	11
B56	'Stewart & Lloyds' 3506 grey (M) - 85		7	10
		Railway Company		
B25	GW Loco 83516 grey (A) - 85, 97		7	10
B25	GW Loco 83517 grey - ?		7	9
B8	BR P339371K grey (A) - 84		7	11
B8	BR P339377K grey (brown inside) - 89?		7	9
B8	BR P339377K dark grey - 89?		7	9

W16b. 20T Steel Mineral Wagon (2006)

These wagons came into service in the 1920s as a more economical alternative to the wooden coal wagons. They had two doors each side and one at an end.

This is a replacement wagon for the above.

		Private Owner		
-	'AAC Anthracite' (Amalgamated Anthracite) T300 black Sp Edn 101 (David Dacey) - 09		6	8
B727	'Bolsover' 6490 red-brown - 08		6	8
B727B	'Bolsover' 6390 red-brown W - 08		6	8
-	'BQC' 99 red Sp Edn 130 (Wessex Wagons) - 11		9	12
B735	'Cilely' 12 black - 08		6	8
-	'Ebbw Vale' 17103 black Sp Edn 112 (David Dacey) - 08		7	9

20T steel mineral wagon [W16b] (Dapol)

-	'Emlyn Anthracite' 5000 grey Sp Edn 106 (South Wales Coalfields) - 07		7	9
B861	'Emlyn Anthracite' 2000 - 10		7	9
4F038001	'Emlyn Anthracite' 2000 grey - 12		8	10
4F038002	'Emlyn Anthracite' 2000 grey W - 12		8	11

Dapol 00

B698	'Glenhafod' 2277 black - 07	6	8
B685	'Gloucester Corporation' 3 grey - 07	6	8
B887	'Marriott' 920 black - 11	7	9
B872	'PJ&JP' 3619 black - 11	7	9
B694	'SC' 25506 olive green - 07-08	6	8
-	'Scatter Rock Macadams' 9 blue-grey, stone load, Sp Edn 276 (Wessex Wagons) - 07	7	9
B659	'Stevens' 1001 red - 06	7	9
B703	'Richard Thomas' 23301 black - 07	6	8
B672	'West Midlands Joint Electricity Authority' 16 black - 06	6	8
Railway Company			
-	'NVR' 272 grey Sp Edn (Nene Valley Railway) - 10	7	9
B712	GW 33152 grey - 07	6	8
B712A	GW 33225 grey ** - 10	7	9
B712AW	GW 33225 grey W ** - 10	7	10
B664	GW 33156 grey Loco - 06	7	9
B770	GW 33156 grey Loco - 09	7	9
B823	GW 33159 grey - 10	7	9
No.64	GW (Ebbw Vale) 10972 * grey Sp Edn 97 (West Wales Wagon Works) - 07	6	8
No.64	GW (Ebbw Vale) 10995 * grey Sp Edn 115 (West Wales Wagon Works) - 07	6	8
E08	GW 'Fredk Bendle' 63066 dark grey Sp Edn 150 (East Somerset Models) - 10	8	11
B679	BR B315748 grey Coal 21 - 06	6	8
B679A	BR B315739 light grey Coal 21 ** - 10	7	9
B679AW	BR B315739 light grey W Coal 21 ** - 10	8	11

* These should have been 6 figure numbers and, although transfers for a 6th digit were produced to correct them, there was insufficient room and the wagons were sold with the incorrect numbers as manufactured. ** These appear to be renumbered old stock.

Hopper & Dry Powder Wagons

W17a. 12T/24T Ore Hopper Wagon (ex-Mainline) (1985)

This is the small hopper wagon of a type built to carry small quantities of heavy materials such as iron ore.

The model was released in the Mainline range in 1978 and in 1985 Dapol bought the unsold stock when Palitoy production closed down and that is what is listed here.

Private Owner			
B142	'Cadbury Bournville' 156 blue (M) - 91	7	10
B143	'Clay Cross' 72 red-brown (M) - ?	7	11
B68	'Hoare Bros.' 101 black (M) - 85	7	10
B139	'Sheepbridge' 8251 red-brown (M) - 91	7	9
British Steel			
B97	'BISC' 776 dark grey Iron Ore (M) - 86, 91	7	10
Railway Company			
B72	BR Sand B437319 grey + sand (M) - 91	8	10
B140	BR B435925 red-brown (M) - ?	7	11
B141	BR B435475 grey Ore Hop (M) - 91	7	10

W17b. 12T/24T Ore Hopper Wagon (2005)

This model was one of four new wagons tooled up in 2005, the Mainline residue stocks (above) having sold out.

Private Owner

Small hopper wagon [W17b] (Dapol)

B713	'Bell Brother' 1 black - 07	7	9
B868	'Bell Brother' 3 black - 11	8	10
B1013	'Bell Brother' 1 brown - 11	8	10
B1013W	'Bell Brother' 1 brown W - 11	9	11
4F033003	'Bell Brother' 1 brown - 12	8	10
4F033004	'Bell Brother' 1 brown W - 12	8	11
B902	'Cadbury Bournville' 128 yellow - 11	8	10
B639	'Clay Cross Iron Ore Co.' red-brown - 05	7	9
4F033009	'Clay Cross Iron Ore Co.' red-brown - 13	8	10
4F033010	'Clay Cross Iron Ore Co.' red-brown W - 13	8	11
B707	'DL (Cleveland)' Dorman Long A224 red-brown - 07	7	9
4F033007	'DL (Cleveland)' Dorman Long A224 red-brown - 12	8	10
4F033008	'DL (Cleveland)' Dorman Long A224 red-brown W - 12	8	11
B628	'Hoare Bros.' 102 black - 05	8	10
-	'Hoare Bros.' 103 black Sp Edn 111 (Burnham & District MRC) - 13	8	10
B628	'Hoare Bros.' 105 black - 10	9	12
B633	'Millom Iron Works' 261 red-brown - 05	8	10
B690	'Millom Iron Works' 271 red-brown - 07	8	10
4F033005	'Millom Iron Works' 261 red-brown - 13	8	10
4F033006	'Millom Iron Works' 271 red-brown - 13	8	11
Railway Company			
B643	BR B433472 light grey Ore Hop - 05	7	9
B833	BR B433472 light grey Ore Hop - 10	7	9
B645	BR B437316 light grey Sand - 06	8	10
B1012	BR B433472 grey - 11	8	10
B101W	BR B433472 grey W - 11	9	11
4F033001	BR B433472 grey - 12	8	10
4F033002	BR B433472 grey W - 12	8	11

W18. Ore Hopper Wagon (ex-Wrenn) (c1995)

This model uses the lower half of the 'Presflo' wagon body.

Private Owner			
B243	'Wm.Carter' 7 black - c95	10	15
WR1-41	as above - 99	10	17
B249	'Clay Cross' black - c95	50	60
WR1-24	'Hinchley' blue - 99	10	18
B605	'NCB' 69 grey - 05	6	8
B607	'Sheepbridge' 2149 brown Coal & Iron - 04	6	8
B250	'Southdown' 17 blue - c95	15	18
British Steel			
B593	'BISC Iron Ore' 398 dark grey - 04	6	8

W19a. NE 21T Hopper Wagon (ex-Airfix) (1984)

There is confusion between this former Airfix model and the former Wrenn hopper wagon. Listing here is divided between the two according to catalogue illustrations - some models may be in both lists. After acquisition of the Wrenn tooling in 1993, it seemed that the Wrenn tools were used instead of the Airfix ones. Three years later, in 1996, the Airfix tools were sold to Hornby, but it is known that some of the tools, before going to Hornby, were used to build up a stock of mouldings for future use. Five years later, in 2001, the former Wrenn hopper wagon tooling was sold when the G&R Wrenn intellectual assets and some of the Wrenn tools were sold to Mordvale Ltd. According to catalogue illustrations, an Airfix style hopper reappeared in several versions around 2004. These may have used mouldings previously stored and, if so, this stock seems to have run out by 2007, after which the model was dropped from the catalogue. Of course, Dapol could have retooled the model based on the Airfix version, or maybe they had duplicate tooling that was not sold to Hornby. However, neither of these would explain the disappearance of the wagon in 2007.

A1	grey - unfinished - 84	5	10
A003	grey - unfinished - 04-07	5	10
A03	grey - unfinished - 11	4	10
Private Owner			
No.26	'Blaenavon' 2051, 2053, 2055 (39 made), 2060, 2061* grey Sp Edn 40 (West Wales Wagon Works) - 05	8	10
B668	'Borough of Bedford Electricity' 42 black - 06	6	8
B692	'Cadbury Bournville' 156 pale blue - 07	7	9
4F034001	'Cadbury Bournville' 156 pale blue - 13	8	10
4F034002	'Cadbury Bournville' 156 pale blue W - 13	9	11
B113	'Charringtons' B421814K grey+red (M) - 89	7	13
B113	'Charringtons' B461818K grey+red - 89	9	11
B646	'Charringtons' B441834K grey+red - 06	7	9
4F034003	'Charringtons' B441834K grey+red - 12	8	10
4F034004	'Charringtons' B441834K grey+red W - 12	9	11

Dapol 00

21T hopper [W19a] (Hattons)

-	'Locomotion' B345872 orange-brown Sp Edn (NRM Shildon) - 07	8	10
-	'Trago Mills Shopping Centre' grey Sp Edn 250 (Trago Mills) - ?	8	10
-	'Trago Mills Shopping Centre' black Sp Edn 250 (Trago Mills) - ?	8	10
	Railway Company		
-	MHR S2007 grey Sp Edn 90 (Mid Hants Railway) - 07	7	9
-	North Norfolk Railway grey Sp Edn 250 (NNR) - ?	8	10
-	TVLR B345921 cream Sp Edn 110 (Tanat Valley Light Railway Co.) - 07	8	10
B592	NE 193264 pale grey - 04	7	9
B112	NE 193258 grey (M) - 88	7	11
B1004	NE 193264 light grey - 11	7	9
B1004W	NE 193264 pale grey W - 11	8	11
B1	BR E289595K light grey (A) - 84	7	13
B1	BR E289592K light grey - 89	9	11
B1	BR E289593K light grey - 89	9	11
B128	BR - ? - red brown - ?	NPG	NPG
B201	BR B??6398 grey - ?	NPG	NPG
B585	BR E289595K grey - 04	7	9
B1005	BR E289595K grey - 11	7	9
B1005W	BR E289595K grey W - 11	8	11
-	BR B419322 grey W	8	NA
-	BR B419317 grey W	8	NA
-	BR B419262 grey W	8	NA
-	BR B419249 grey W	8	NA
-	BR B419254 grey W	8	NA
B1005MHOPW	above 5 weathered wagons in boxed set - 12	NA	45

B124	'House Coal Concentration' B429816K red-brown (M) - 89	7	13
B676	'House Coal Concentration' 429911 brown - 06	7	9
4F034005	'House Coal Concentration' 429911 brown - 12	8	10
4F034006	'House Coal Concentration' 429911 brown W - 12	9	11
B59	'Norman Jackson' 10 black (M) 85	9	13
B59	'Norman Jackson' 10 black - ?-99	8	10
-	'London Brick Company - Phorpes Bricks' 1012 black Sp Edn 101 (Burnham & District MRC) - 13	9	12
-	'Meldon Quarry' 291 brown + white ore load Sp Edn 110 (Dartmoor Railway) - 03?	20	25
-	'Meldon Quarry' 291 brown, no load Sp Edn 100 (Dartmoor Railway) - 03	10	15
B657	'The Northampton Electric Light & Power Co.' 80 brown - 06	7	9
B622	'Simpson' 72 grey - 05	7	9
B610	'Sykes' 10 pale grey - 05	7	9
B203	'G Weaver Transport' 152 brown - 94	8	10
B616	'G Weaver' 154 brown - 05	7	9
	British Gas		
B201	'British Gas' 142 dark grey - c95	8	10
B579	'British Gas' 142 red-brown - 04	7	9
4F034102	'British Gas' 147 black - 12	8	10
4F034103	'British Gas' 147 black W - 12	9	11
	British Steel		
B201	'British Steel' 28 brown - 98-99	8	10
B602	'British Steel' 26 red-brown - 04	7	9
4F034100	'British Steel' 32 brown - 12	8	10
4F034101	'British Steel' 32 brown W - 12	9	11

21T hopper wagon [W19a] (Dapol)

	Ministry of Transport		
B60	'MOT' 1324 black (M) - 85	7	13
B588	'MOT' 1328 black - 04	7	9
	National Coal Board		
B606	'NCB' 128 dark grey - 04	7	9
B1003	'NCB' 128 grey - 11	7	9
B1003W	'NCB' 128 grey W - 11	8	11
	Commemorative		
S1154	'Geoscenics Natural Scenic Products' B345875 dark green, coal infill + bag of natural stone Sp Edn 97 (Geoscenics) - 07	8	10

W19b. 21T Hopper Wagon (ex-HD/Wrenn) (c1995)

This is the former short-lived Hornby Dublo 21 ton hopper wagon which dates from 1963. The tooling was bought by G&R Wrenn. The fuller model history is told in the introduction to the above table.

	Private Owner		
B187	'Hoveringham' red-brown - c95	10	15
WR1-09	as above - 99	10	15
B189	'Sykes' 7 light grey - c95	10	15
WR1-23	as above - 99	10	45
B188	'Tarmac' M82 beige - c95	10	15
WR1-07	as above - 98-99	10	15
	British Gas		
B202	'British Gas' 142 dark grey - c95	15	25
WR1-44	as above - 99	15	30
	National Coal Board		
WR1-08	'NCB' black - c99	20	45
	Railway Company		
WR1-48	BR B413021 dark grey - 99	15	30

W20. HBA/HEA Hopper Wagon (1991)

These air-braked hoppers were built for coal traffic in their thousands at BREL (Shildon Works) between 1976 and 1979.

This is one of a few wagons that Dapol originated in the early 1990s. The tooling was sold to Hornby in 1996 and the model reintroduced by them.

B158	BR 360634 red-brown HBA - 91	8	10
B159	BR 360394 red+grey Railfreight HEA - 91	8	10
B159	BR 361874 red+grey Railfreight HEA - ?	8	10

W21. BR 20T Grain Wagon (ex-HD/Wrenn)(1995)

Grain wagon [W21] (Hattons)

Dapol 00

The model is of a Grain 'Hopvan' built at BR Derby in 1951; British Railways had standardised on the LMS design.

This was the first model to be made for the Hornby Dublo range with a plastic body and was a good choice. The clean polystyrene moulding proved the superiority of the material used. The tooling was bought by G&R Wrenn in the late 1960s and sold to Dapol in 1993.

Private Owner

-	'Bass' 3 blue Sp Edn (Tutbury Jinny) - 08	7	10
-	'Bass' 11 blue Sp Edn (?) - ?	10	15
B252	'Bass Charrington' 24 maroon - c95	10	15
WR1-42	as above - 99	10	35
B548	'Bass Charrington' 9 brick red - 03	7	9
-	'A Bowering' 2 grey Sp Edn 139 (Burnham & District MRC) - 12	9	12
B254	'Kelloggs' B885040 grey - c95	10	15
B255	'Quaker Oats' red-brown - c95	10	15
B517	'SGD' 18 grey - 03	7	9
B517	'SGD' 18 pale grey - 03	10	12
B765	'SGD' 16 grey - 09	8	10
-	'Worthington' 8 bright green Sp Edn (?) - ?	10	15
-	'Worthington' 2 green Sp Edn (Tutbury Jinny) - 08	7	10

Railway Company

B503	GW dark grey 'Grano' - 02	6	8
B503A	GW dark grey 'Grano' (small 'GW' and newer couplings) - 10	7	9
B503AW	GW dark grey W 'Grano' (small 'GW' and newer couplings) - 10	8	11
4F036005	GW 2886 dark grey - 12	8	10
4F036006	GW 2886 dark grey W - 12	8	11
B528	GW 42315 dark grey 'Grano' - 03	6	8
B534	LMS 701314 grey 'Bulk Grain' - 03	6	8
B562	LMS 710351 red-brown 'Bulk Grain' - 03	6	8
4F036007	LMS 701351 brown - 12	8	10
4F036008	LMS 701351 brown W - 12	9	12
B251	BR B885040 light grey - c95	10	15
WR1-49	as above - 99	10	15
B502	BR B885044 grey - 02	6	8
B502A	BR B885364 grey - 02	6	8
B502A	BR B885302 grey - 10	7	9
B502AW	BR B885302 grey W - 10	7	10
4F036003	BR B885312 grey - 12	8	10
4F036004	BR B885312 grey W - 12	8	11
-	BR B885304 grey	7	NA
-	BR B885309 grey	7	NA
-	BR B885314 grey	7	NA
-	BR B885323 grey	7	NA
-	BR B885337 grey	7	NA
4F036001	above 5 pristine grain wagons - 11	NA	40
-	BR B885304 grey W	7	NA
-	BR B885309 grey W	7	NA
-	BR B885314 grey W	7	NA
-	BR B885323 grey W	7	NA
-	BR B885337 grey W	7	NA
4F036002	above 5 weathered grain wagons - 11	NA	40

W22. BR 'Presflo' Wagon (ex-HD/Wrenn) (c1995)

The first 'Presflo' appeared in 1953 and those that followed were for the bulk handling of cement. Many batches were made by or for British Railways between 1955 and 1964. Some 'Presflos' were modified for salt traffic and later slate powder traffic and eventually carried fly-ash. They were loaded through two top hatches and unloaded under pressure. They were replaced from 1984 onwards and all had gone by 1991.

The Hornby Dublo model arrived in 1961 and the tooling was bought from Meccano Ltd in the late 1960s by G&R Wrenn, passing finally to Dapol in 1993.

Private Owner

B600	'ARC' AR12640 yellow - 04	7	9
4F035100	'ARC' AR12645 yellow - 12	7	10
4F035101	'ARC' AR12645 yellow W - 12	8	11
B242	'Blue Circle' grey - c95	10	15
B578	'Blue Circle Cement' grey - 04	7	9
B683	'Blue Circle' yellow - 07	6	8
B683W	'Blue Circle' yellow W - 10	8	11
-	'Brierfield' dark green Sp Edn 90 (St Luke's MRC) - 08	7	9
B248	'Bulk Cement' 52 orange - c95	10	15
B720	'Bulk Cement' 32 brown - 08	6	8
B1011	'Bulk Tunnel Cement' 32 grey - 11	7	10
B1011W	'Bulk Tunnel Cement' 32 grey W - 11	8	11
4F035003	'Bulk Tunnel Cement' grey - 12	7	10
4F035004	'Bulk Tunnel Cement' grey W - 12	8	11
-	'Bulk Tunnel Cement' 8617 brown	6	NA
-	'Bulk Tunnel Cement' 8653 brown	6	NA
-	'Bulk Tunnel Cement' 8681 brown	6	NA
-	'Bulk Tunnel Cement' 8790 brown	6	NA
-	'Bulk Tunnel Cement' 8803 brown	6	NA
B1005MULTI	above 5 pristine wagons - 11	NA	40
-	'Bulk Tunnel Cement' 8617 brown W	7	NA
-	'Bulk Tunnel Cement' 8653 brown W	7	NA
-	'Bulk Tunnel Cement' 8681 brown W	7	NA
-	'Bulk Tunnel Cement' 8790 brown W	7	NA
-	'Bulk Tunnel Cement' 8803 brown W	7	NA
B1005MULTIW	above 5 weathered wagons - 11	NA	45
B246	'Cerebos Salt' orange - c95	15	18
B582	'Cerebos Salt' red - 04	7	9
B725	'ICI Bulk Salt' green - 08	6	8
B615	'Pozzoianic' 41094 brown - 05	7	9
-	'Old Delabole Slate Co.' 71 grey+light blue Sp Edn 175 (Wessex Wagons) - 11	9	12
B609	'Readymix Concrete' 66 grey - 05	7	9
B1010	'Readymix Concrete' 66 grey - 11	7	10
B1010W	'Readymix Concrete' 66 grey W - 11	8	11
4F035001	'Readymix Concrete' 66 grey - 12	7	10
4F035002	'Readymix Concrete' 66 grey W - 12	8	11
B247	'RMC' 68 grey - c95	30	35
B620	'Rugby Cement' brown - 05	7	9
-	Sittingbourne & Kemsley Light Railway 100 grey Sp Edn 92 (S&KLR) - 05	8	10
B739	'Slate Powder' 4888189 * dark grey - 08	6	8
B244	'Tunnel Bulk' grey - c95	10	15
B601	'Tunnel Cement' grey - 04	7	9
B621	'Bulk Tunnel Cement' grey - 05	7	9

Commemoratives

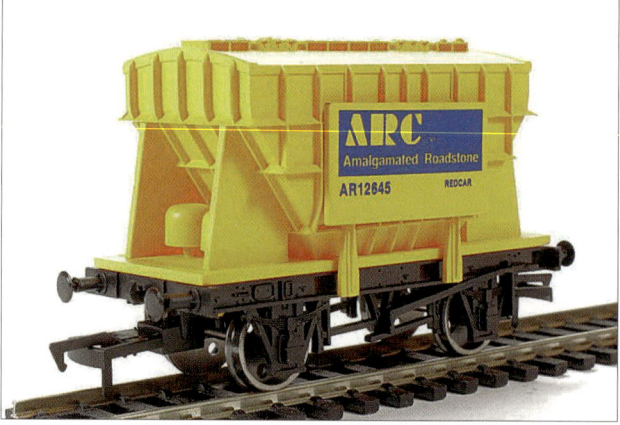

'Presflo' bulk powder wagon 'ARC' [W22] (Hattons)

'Presflo' bulk powder wagon 'Milton Keynes' [W22]

Dapol 00

H560	'Hattons of Liverpool' red - 05	7	9
-	'Hattons' brown W - 09	7	9
PR3	'Milton Keynes Model Railway Society 40th' 40 brown Sp Edn 110 (1E Promotionals) - 09	6	8
-	'Model Rail Scotland' pale grey Sp Edn (Model Rail Scotland) - 06	7	9
-	'Virgin Trains' Warley 2004 red - 04	7	9
Railway Company			
B245	BR 'Presflo' 72 brown - c95	10	15
B763	BR 'Presflo' 75 brown - 09	8	10
B763	BR 'Presflo' 75 brown W Sp Edn (Hattons) - 09	8	10

* Incorrectly numbered - it should have been B888189. The box label has the same error printed.

W23. BR 'Prestwin' Silo Wagon (ex-HD/Wrenn) (c1995)

It had been found that the angular shape of earlier 'Presflo' wagons created a tendency for powder to catch in the corners, and so the 'Prestwin' was introduced. It was based on a Continental design and around 130 were built. The conical shape of the bottom half of the silos was largely hidden by cladding on British wagons. Loads carried included cement and sand.

The model is another from the former Hornby Dublo range, having originally been released in 1962. The tooling passed to G&R Wrenn in the late 1960s and to Dapol in 1993.

B191	'Fisons' B873000 brown - c95	10	15
B190	BR B873000 brown - c95	10	15

W24. PCA 'Presflo' ('V-Tank) (ex-Lima/Dapol) (1995)

These were used for carrying dry powders to be released under pressure.

It is thought likely that the PCA that was introduced by Dapol in 1995 was tooled in China using the Lima model as a guide. Dapol sold the tools to Hornby in 1996 who in 2004 acquired the Lima tooling as well.

Private Owner			
B197	'Albright & Wilson' PR10126 greeny-blue - 95	7	9
B198	'APCM' 9344 very pale grey - 95	7	9
B196	'BOC' 1066 very pale grey - 95	7	9

The tooling was sold to Hornby in 1996 and the model reintroduced by them.

Tank Wagons

W25. Rectangular Tank (2008)

The rectangular tank wagon predates the cylindrical ones but survived on Britain's railways at least up until 1930. They were often seen around gas works and used for the transportation of tar as well as other chemicals. The ability to produce curved plated and cylindrical tanks was developed in the late 1920s.

A022	unpainted - 12	5	8
Private Owner			

Rectangular tank wagon [W25] (Dapol)

B751	'ACC' 436 black - 09	9	12
B871	'Bromley Gas Consumers' 1 black - 11	10	13
B871W	'Bromley Gas Consumers' 1 black W - 12	10	14
-	'The Burnden Tar Oil Co.' black Sp Edn (Trains & Diecast) - 10	8	10
-	'Burt, Boulton & Hayward' T12 black Sp Edn 200 (Buffers) - 11	8	11
B738	'Wm Butler & Co.' 64 black - 08	8	10
4F032005	'Wm Butler & Co.' 64 black - 13	10	13
4F032006	'Wm Butler & Co.' 64 black W - 13	10	14
B816	'RS Clare & Co.' 12 grey - 09	9	12
4F032009	'RS Clare & Co.' 12 grey - 13	10	13
4F032010	'RS Clare & Co.' 12 grey W - 13	10	14
B876	'Henry Ellison' 8426 black - 11	10	13
B876W	'Henry Ellison' 8426 black W - 12	10	14
ANT038	'TH Harvey Chemical Works' 7 black Sp Edn 150 (Antics) - 09	11	14
B731	'Imperial Chemical Industries' 50 grey - 08	8	10
B731A	'Imperial Chemical Industries' 60 grey - 10	9	12
B731AW	'Imperial Chemical Industries' 60 grey W - 10	11	14
-	'Railton & Son' 3 red+grey Sp Edn 200 (AMRCWWE) - 11	9	12
B835	'Rimer Bros.' 5 grey - 10	9	12
4F032001	'Rimer Bros.' 5 grey - 12	10	13
4F032002	'Rimer Bros.' 5 grey W - 12	10	14
-	'Scottish Fish Oil & Guano & Co.' 3 red-brown Sp Edn (Harburn Hobbies) - 10	9	12
B744	'Smith & Forrest' 2 red - 08	8	10
B815	'Smith & Forrest' 2 red W - 09	9	12
4F032007	'Smith & Forrest' 2 red - 12	10	13
4F032008	'Smith & Forrest' 2 red W - 12	10	14
B865	'South Eastern Tar Distillers' R9 black - 10	9	12
-	'South Eastern Tar Distillers' 45 blue Sp Edn (East Kent Model Railway Society) - 10	10	14
B775	'Walkers' 25 black - 09	9	12
B757	'Yorkshire & Lincolnshire Tar Distillation Co.' 6 black - 09	9	12
Commemorative			
-	'Model Rail Scotland' black Sp Edn (Model Rail Scotland) - 09	9	12
Rail Company			
4F032003	BR 21 black - 12	10	13
4F032004	BR 21 black W - 12	11	14

W26. 14T Tank Wagon (ex-Mainline) (1985)

This table includes remnant Mainline stock as well as tank wagons produced by Dapol from tools that were made for them in China. The latter models are virtually identical to the original Mainline ones and this tooling was sold to Hornby in 1996 and they now produce the model.

14T tank wagon [W26]

Private Owner			
B136	'Benzole By-Products' 1 buff - 91	10	12
B131	'BP' 5049 grey - 91	10	12
B133	'Crossfield' 49 green-grey - 91	10	12
B134	'Esso' 3066 silver White Spirit - 91	10	12
B137	'ICI' 895 dark blue - 91	10	12
B132	'National Benzol' 731 silver - 91	10	12
B138	'Ronuk' 38 blue - 91	9	11
B130	'Royal Daylight' 1534 black (M) - 91	8	12
B135	'Shell' 4492 silver - 91	10	12
B86	'Shell Electrical Oils' SM2202 brown (M) - 86	8	14
B86	'Shell Electrical Oils' SM2202 very dark grey - 90	9	11
B32	'United Molasses' 128 red-brown (M) - 85	10	14
B32	'United Molasses' 128 red-brown larger letters - 91	8	11
Railway Company			
B87	LMS Creosote 304592 grey (M) - 86	8	14
B87	LMS Creosote 304592? grey - 90	9	11

W27. 12T Tank Wagon (2004)

This was a tank wagon that Dapol has had tooled up and is the size of a 14 ton tank wagon and has a large dome. It has horizontal bracing and, compared to the 14 ton versions by Mainline and Bachmann, it lacks detail.

Private Owner			
B583	'Anglo Persian Oil Co.' 1595 red-brown - 04	8	10

Dapol 00

B597	'Barrow' 4 bright red - 04	8	10
-	'Esso' silver Sp Edn 50 (Llangollen Railway Preservation Society) - made?	NPG	NPG
No.24*	'Express Dairy' 041348 off-white + additional ladders Sp Edn 100 (Buffers) - 04	10	12
No.24*	'Express Dairy' 744 off-white, numbers on tank ends, Sp Edn 75 (West Wales Wagon Works) - ?	12	14
-	'Fothergill Brothers' 2 bright red Sp Edn 100 (The Model Shop, Exeter) - 04	10	12
-	'Pendle Forest MRS' yellow Sp Edn 90 (Pendle Forest MRS) - 04	11	13
-	'John Samper Dairy' 1 white Sp Edn 186 (East Kent MRS) - 04	10	12
-	'Tunbridge Wells Gas, Light & Coke, Tar' 34 black Sp Edn 400 (Ballards) - 04	9	11
No.23	'United Dairies' 634 white, print blue Sp Edn 135 (West Wales Wagon Works) - 04	8	10
-	'United Dairies' 041882 white + additional ladders, print black Sp Edn 200 (Buffers) - 04	8	10
B590	'United Molasses' 13 maroon - 04	8	10
B580	'Yorkshire & Lincolnshire Tar Distillation Co.' 4 red - 04	8	10

* These came from the same batch which was shared.

12t tank wagon [W27]

W28.   20T Tank Wagon (ex-Airfix) (1985)

This was an authentic model of a 12' chassis tank wagon, produced from Railway Clearing House drawings, but the liveries are not strictly authentic, belonging as they do to other styles of tanker.

The model was released by Airfix in 1979 and the tooling passed to Palitoy in 1981. In 1985, Dapol bought the tooling and left-over Airfix and Mainline stock and also produced their own versions of the model. The tooling was sold to Hornby in 1996 and they have produced many more versions of it.

A13	unfinished - 98	5	10
	Private Owner		
B85	'Crosfield' 15 dark green (M) - 86	8	14
B133	'Crosfield' 15 green and no number on ends of tank - 97	10	12
B29	'ICI' 499 dark blue (M) - 85	8	14
B29	'ICI' 400 dark blue - ?-87	10	12
B107	'Newcastle & Gateshead' 18 black also ex set B404 - 87, 96	10	12
B106	'Rainford Tar Prods.' 1 black - 87	10	12
B106	'Rainford Tar Prods.' 1 brown - 97	9	11
B20	'Shell' 2373 buff (A) - ?	8	14
B21	'Shell BP' 3967 black (A) - ?	8	12
B116	'United Molasses' 86 red-brown - 88	10	12

W29a.   6-wheel Tank Wagon (ex-HD/Wrenn) (c1995)

It was found that milk travelled better in six-wheeled tank wagons and so these were built especially for milk traffic. As the body belonged to the dairy and the chassis to the railway company, they each had their own numbering system, which explains why two numbers may be found on some milk tank wagons.

The Hornby Dublo 6-wheeled milk tank wagon was released in 1962 and sold well over the 2 years before production ended. G&R Wrenn bought the tooling and produced several versions of it. In 1993 the tools passed to Dapol, who also produced their own versions. The model was replaced in 2005 (see below).

	Private Owner		
B214	'Co-op' 172 white - c95	40	45
B220	'Double Diamond' red-brown - c95	20	25
B215	'Express Dairies' 50 blue - c95	25	30
B222	'Guinness' silver - c95	20	25
B218	'Milk Marketing Board' blue - c95	20	25
B217	'St Ivel Gold' white - c95	50	55
B221	'Skol Lager' red-brown - c95	20	25
B219	'UD' white also W4657P - c95	15	20
B216	'Unigate' 220 white - c95	50	55

W29b.   6-wheel Tank Wagon (2005)

This model was one of four new wagons tooled up in 2005 and is believed to be based on an LMS design. In 2009, new wheels were being fitted.

A021	unfinished light grey - 11	5	10
	Private Owner		
B673	'Alpin & Barrett' brown - 06	11	13
-	'Boat of Garten Dairy' 7 silver Sp Edn 200 (Strathspey Rly Co Ltd) - 07	13	15
-	'Boat of Garten Dairy' 7 silver W Sp Edn 100 (Strathspey Rly Co Ltd) - 07	13	15
-	'British Vinigars' T10 red Sp Edn 135 (Buffers) - 09	10	13
-	'British Vinigars' T12 red Sp Edn 140 (Buffers) - 10	9	12

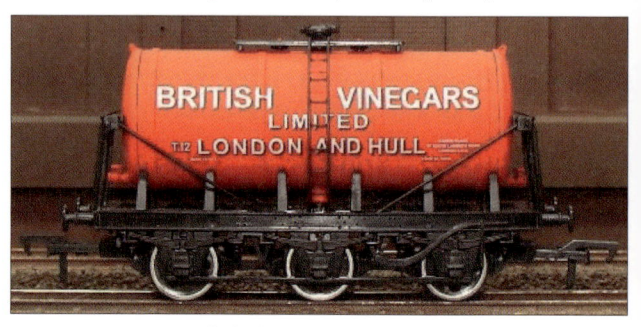

6-wheel tank wagon [W29b] (Dapol)

-	'Classic Trains - 10th Anniversary' dark blue Sp Edn 150 (Classic Trains, Models & Buses) - 08	13	15
-	'Coates Cider' 2 white Sp Edn 169 (Burnham & District MRC) - 10	10	13
B654	'Co-op Milk' 169 white - 06	10	13
B841	'Co-operative Wholesale Society' (Pure New Milk) red - 10	10	13
S1950P	'Co-operative Wholesale Society' 017 green Sp Edn 80 (Simply Southern) - 12	10	14
S1950W	'Co-operative Wholesale Society' 017 green W Sp Edn 23 (Simply Southern) - 12	12	15
S1966P	'Co-operative Wholesale Society' 010 green Sp Edn 83 (Simply Southern) - 12	11	14
S1966W	'Co-operative Wholesale Society' 010 green W Sp Edn 41 (Simply Southern) - 12	11	14
S1967P	'Co-operative Wholesale Society' 008 green Sp Edn 84 (Simply Southern) - 12	11	14
S1967W	'Co-operative Wholesale Society' 008 green W Sp Edn 49 (Simply Southern) - 12	11	14
-	'Cottesmore Dairy' 1 white Sp Edn 162 (Burnham & District MRC) - 11	11	14
-	'Culm Valley Dairy Company' 19 silver Sp Edn 162 (Wessex Wagons) - 10	10	13
B678	'CWS' green - 06	10	13
B866	'CWS' red - 11	10	13
-	'CWS Pure Milk' 020 green Sp Edn 80 (Simply Southern) - 12	10	13
-	'CWS Pure Milk' 020 green W Sp Edn 80 (Simply Southern) - 12	10	13
-	'Daws Creamery' 17 white Sp Edn 136 (Burnham & District MRC) - 12	11	14
-	'Dorset & Devon Dairy Co.' 4 cream Sp Edn 136 (Burnham & District MRC) - 12	11	14
B634	'Express Dairy' dark blue - 05	10	13
B667	'Express Dairy' 45 dark blue - 06	10	13
B732	'Express Dairy' dark blue - 08	10	13
B697	'Express Dairy' silver - 07	9	11
-	'Express Dairy' 1 white Sp Edn 180 (Burnham & District MRC) - 10	10	13
4F031009	'Express Dairy' dark blue - 13	10	13
4F031010	'Express Dairy' dark blue W - 13	10	14

Dapol 00

6-wheel tank wagon [W29b] (Dapol)

6-wheel tank wagon [W29b] (Hattons)

-	'Felin Foel Brewery' dark green Sp Edn 154 (Voyles) - *10*	11	14
-	'Glenboble Dhu' 1 buff Sp Edn 100 (Strathspey Railway Co Ltd) - *06*	12	14
-	'Glenboble Dhu' 1 buff W Sp Edn 100 (Strathspey Railway Co Ltd) - *07*	12	14
B908	graffiti on silver tank - *11*	10	13
B640	'IMS' 23 light blue - *05*	10	13
B892	'IMS' 23 light blue - *11*	10	13
4F031007	'IMS' 23 light blue - *13*	10	13
4F031008	'IMS' 23 light blue W - *13*	10	14
B660	'Independent Milk Supplies' red-brown - *06*	10	13
B741	'Independent Milk Supplies' red-brown - *08*	10	13
4F031011	'Independent Milk Supplies' red-brown - *13*	10	13
4F031012	'Independent Milk Supplies' red-brown W - *13*	10	14
-	'Kent & Sussex Dairies' 012 cream Sp Edn 93 (Simply Southern) - *12*	10	14
-	'Kent & Sussex Dairies' 012 cream W Sp Edn 32 (Simply Southern) - *12*	12	15
-	'Kent & Sussex Dairies' 072 cream Sp Edn 62 (Simply Southern) - *11*	10	14
-	'Kent & Sussex Dairies' 072 cream W Sp Edn 44 (Simply Southern) - *11*	12	15
-	'Kent & Sussex Dairies' 070 cream Sp Edn 91 (Simply Southern) - *11*	10	14
-	'Kent & Sussex Dairies' 070 cream W Sp Edn 18 (Simply Southern) - *11*	12	15
-	'Kent & Sussex Dairies' 074 cream Sp Edn 91 (Simply Southern) - *11*	10	14
-	'Kent & Sussex Dairies' 074 cream W Sp Edn 18 (Simply Southern) - *11*	12	15
B648	'Milk Marketing Board' dark blue - *06*	10	13
B817	'Milk Marketing Board' dark blue - *09*	9	11
4F031005	'Milk Marketing Board' dark blue - *12*	10	13
4F031006	'Milk Marketing Board' dark blue W - *12*	11	14
B719	'MMB' 113 dark blue - *08*	6	8
-	'MMB' dark grey Sp Edn 100 (Barry & Penarth Railway) - *06*	10	13
-	'National Smelting Company' 295 grey Sp Edn 300 (Burnham & District MRC) - *10*	10	13
-	'Nestles' blue Sp Edn 177 (Burnham & District MRC) - *10*	10	13
-	'Nestles' 6 blue + Swiss flag Sp Edn 200 (Burnham & District MRC) - *10*	11	14
-	'Newcastle Emlyn' black Sp Edn (West Wales Wagon Works) - *06*	11	14
-	'RS Norris & Sons' white Sp Edn 185 (Burnham & District MRC) - *11*	11	14
S2134P	'Polegate Treacle Mines' 101 yellow Sp Edn 67 (Simply Southern) - *13*	10	13
S2134W	'Polegate Treacle Mines' 101 yellow W Sp Edn 76 (Simply Southern) - *13*	10	13
S1969P	'Polegate Treacle Mines' 103 yellow Sp Edn 76 (Simply Southern) - *12*	10	13
S1969W	'Polegate Treacle Mines' 103 yellow W Sp Edn 76 (Simply Southern) - *12*	10	13
-	'Royal Arsenal Co-op Society' - Pure New Milk bright red Sp Edn 186 (Wessex Wagons) - *06*	12	15
-	'Royal Arsenal Co-op Society' - Pure New Milk bright red W Sp Edn 260 (Wessex Wagons) - *08*	14	20
-	'Satlink Western' red+yellow Sp Edn 100 (Model Rail magazine) - *08*	10	13
-	'Scottish Cables Ltd' T1 black Sp Edn 150 (Buffers) *09*	9	12
-	'Somerset, Dorset & Devon Dairy Co.' 62 cream Sp Edn 119 (Burnham & District MRC) - *12*	11	14
-	'South Coast Dairies' 16 **** orange Sp Edn 127 (Burnham & District MRC) - *13*	11	14
-	'Sheppy's Cider' 7 light brown Sp Edn 275 (Burnham & District MRC) - *10*	10	13
-	'Taunton Cider' 11 cream Sp Edn 260 (Wessex Wagons) - *07*	15	18
-	'Taunton Cider' 23 bright green Sp Edn 150 (Burnham & District MRC) - *10*	11	14
-	'Taunton Cider' 27 bright green Sp Edn 150 (Burnham & District MRC) - *11*	11	14
-	'Thatchers' 3 brown Sp Edn 150 (Burnham & District MRC) - *12*	11	14
-	'The Cheddar Valley Dairy Co.' 3 cream Sp Edn 150 (Burnham & District MRC) - *10*	10	13
-	'The Totnes Dairy Co.' 271 pale blue Sp Edn 120 (Wessex Wagons) - *12*	11	14
-	'The Totnes Dairy Co.' 271 pale blue W Sp Edn 120 (Wessex Wagons) - *12*	11	14
-	'Turners Dairies' 3 white Sp Edn 147 (Burnham & District MRC) - *13*	9	12
B1009	'Unigate Creameries' 700351 + 219 silver - *11*	10	13
B1009W	'Unigate Creameries' 700351 + 219 silver W - *11*	11	14
B709	'United Creameries' 70351 219 silver - *07*	10	13
SBB3	'United Creameries' 70351 219 silver W Sp Edn 300 (Signal Box) - *09*	10	12
4F031003	'United Creameries' 70351 219 silver - *13*	10	13
4F031004	'United Creameries' 70351 219 silver W - *13*	10	14
B629	'United Dairies' white - *05*	8	13
-	'United Dairies' silver Sp Edn 133 (Barry & Penarth MRC) - *05*	8	13
B629S	'United Dairies' 107 white W Sp Edn 300 (Signal Box) - *07*	10	13

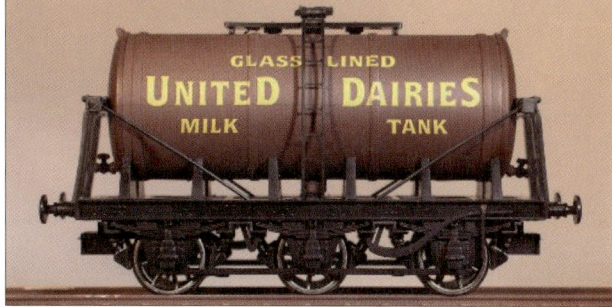

6-wheel tank wagon [W29b] (Dapol)

B687	'United Dairies' SR white - *07*	10	13

8th Edition

Dapol 00

B1008	'United Dairies' SR white - 11	10	13
B1008W	'United Dairies' SR white W - 11	10	14
B759	'United Dairies' white heavily weathered - 09	9	11
-	'United Dairies - Wilts' 25 cream Sp Edn 150 (Burnham & District MRC) - 10	10	13
-	'United Dairies' brown with yellow lettering Sp Edn 300 (Wessex Wagons) - 11	10	14
-	'United Dairies' cream Sp Edn (Hattons) - 09	10	14
4F031001	SR 'United Dairies'? white - 13	10	13
4F031002	SR 'United Dairies'? white W - 13	10	14
B762	'UD' white - 09	9	11
-	'UD(W)' 6 red Sp Edn 220 (Buffers) - 11	9	12
No.72	'Wensleydale Creamery' * cream Sp Edn 162 (Wensleydale Creamery/Wesy Wales Wagon Works) - 08	20	30
B644	'West Park Dairy Co.' 2 brown - 05	10	13
B831	'West Park Dairy Company' 175 brown - 10	9	11
-	'West Somerset Dairy & Bacon Co.' 1 white Sp Edn 139 (Burnham & District MRC) - 12	11	14
-	'Whiteways Cyder Co.' 17 cream Sp Edn 146 (Wessex Wagons) - 10	10	13
-	'Wilts. United Daries' 21 cream Sp Edn 131 (Burnham & District MRC) - 09	10	12
-	'Wilts. United Dairies' 24 cream Sp Edn 140 (Burnham & District MRC) - 12	11	14
-	'Wilts. United Dairies' 25 cream Sp Edn 150 (Burnham & District MRC) - 11	10	12
-	'Wilts. United Dairies' 41 cream Sp Edn 192 (Buffers) - 11	10	12
-	'Whitstable Bitumen' 5 red-brown Sp Edn 188 (East Kent MRS) - 08	10	11
-	'Robert Wiseman' 3 white+black Sp Edn 209 (Burnham & District MRC) - 11	11	14

	Railway Company		
2	WHR Ltd black Sp Edn (Welsh Highland Railway) - 05	10	14
-	WHR Ltd black Sp Edn 192 (Welsh Highland Railway) - 06	10	14
No.37	plain black Sp Edn 205 (West Wales Wagon Works) - 06	10	13
-	BR(ER) Loco Dept 101 brown Sp Edn 151 (Wessex Wagons) - 13	11	14
-	BR(WR) Drinking Water 105 brown Sp Edn 233 (Wessex Wagons) - 07	14	19
SBB2***	BR Diesel Fuel Only black Ltd EDn (Dapol Shop) - 10	15	20
SBB2**	BR Diluted Antifreeze silver W with blue band Sp Edn 300 (Signal Box) - 09	8	11

*Various numbers on ends of tank as transfers. Those with numbers less than 200 (or 300>) were sold by West Wales Wagon Works and those numbered between 200 and 299 were sold by the creamery who received 100 wagons in all (in 2 batches of 50). ** Box marked 'S882' in error. *** A cancelled order which was sold through the Dapol shop. **** This can be mistaken for 6.

Lime & Salt Vans

W30. Lime Van (2005)

This model was one of four new wagons tooled up in 2005. It is also sometimes referred to as a 'salt' wagon by Dapol, but it differs from the Dapol salt wagon, developed originally for Hornby Dublo in 1958, in having a detailed roof, suggesting roof hatches, and having no wire grab-rails either side of the doors.

	Private Owner		
B?	'The Bovey Pottery Company' 5 black Sp Edn 307 (Wessex Wagons) - 07	7	9
B653	'Richard Briggs & Sons' 187 red - 06	7	9
B819	'Richard Briggs & Sons' 189 red-brown - 10	7	9
4F017005	'Richard Briggs & Sons' 189 red-brown - 12	7	9
4F017006	'Richard Briggs & Sons' 189 red-brown W - 13	8	10
-	'George Brown & Sons' 1 grey Sp Edn 98 (Severn Valley Railway - Erlestoke Manor Fund) - 09	7	9
B630	'Crawshay Brothers' 138 pale yellow - 05	7	9
B837	'Crawshay Brothers' 134 cream - 10	7	8
4F017009	'Crawshay Brothers' 134 cream - 12	7	9
4F017010	'Crawshay Brothers' 134 cream W - 12	8	10
B904	'John Delaney' 155 grey - 11	7	9
-	'Dorking Creystone Lime Co.' 8 buff Sp Edn 151 (Burnham & District MRC) - 12	8	10
-	'Evercreech Lime & Stone Co.' 6 light grey Sp Edn 137 (Burnham & District MRC) - 09	8	10
-	'Gainsborough MRS Diamond Jubilee 1943-2006' white with blue roof Sp Edn (Gainsborough MRS) - 06	12	15
No.52	Gwili Railway 30 grey Sp Edn 160 (West Wales Wagon Works) - 07	7	9
No.31	'Llywernog Silver-Lead Mining Co.' * grey Sp Edn 160 (West Wales Wagon Works) - 05	8	10
B717	'The Minera Lime Co.' 125 brown - 07	6	8
4F017001	'The Minera Lime Co.' 125 brown - 12	7	9
4F017002	'The Minera Lime Co.' 125 brown W - 12	8	10
-	'North Devon Clay Co.' 107 grey Sp Edn 162 (Wessex Wagons) - 09	8	10
-	'Oxstead Greystone Lime' 15 beige Sp Edn (Burnham & District MRC) - 11	8	10
B624	'Peak Lime Co.' 45 pale grey - 05	7	9
B624	'Peak Lime Co.' 45 pale grey W - 05	7	9
B830	'Peak Lime Co.' 48 pale grey - 10	6	8
4F017007	'Peak Lime Co.' 48 pale grey - 13	7	9
4F017008	'Peak Lime Co.' 48 pale grey W - 13	8	10
-	'Pepper & Son' 10 light grey Sp Edn (Amberley Museum) - 10	8	10
B619	'Porthywaen Lime Co.' pale grey - 05	7	9
4F017003	'Porthywaen Lime Co.' pale grey - 12	7	9
4F017004	'Porthywaen Lime Co.' pale grey W - 12	8	10

Lime van [W30] (Dapol)

No.76	'Salt Union' 639 dark red Sp Edn. 78 (West Wales Wagon Works) - 08	7	9
No.76	'Salt Union' 639 dark red W Sp Edn. 78 (West Wales Wagon Works) - 08	7	9
B626	'SLB' 527 pale grey - 05	7	9
B626	'SLB' 527 pale grey W - 11	8	11
B874	'SLB' 527? pale grey? - 11	8	10
B874W	'SLB' 527? pale grey? W - 11	8	11
-	'Statfold' 21 dark green Sp Edn (Statfold Barn Railway) - 09?	12	15
-	'Stoneycombe' 15* grey Sp Edn 150 (Wessex Wagons) - 05	8	10
-	'D Thomas & Son' 10 buff with white roof Sp Edn 90 (David Dacey) - 03	9	11
B729	'Whitecliff Lime Co.' 6 buff - 08	6	8

* various numbers carried.

W31. Salt Van (ex-HD/Wrenn) (c1995)

Salt is an important commodity in industry and especially the chemical industry. Most of it has come from Cheshire, but is found in other counties in the North and Midlands. The salt was carried in these vans, in bags, the pitched roof being particularly effective in throwing off rain water. Private owner liveries on salt vans were once common.

The Hornby Dublo model was released in 1958 and the opportunity to produce other liveries was not taken. The tooling passed to G&R Wrenn in the late 1960s and to Dapol in 1993. Originally sold as 'WR3' stock it was absorbed from the Wrenn range when G&R Wrenn was sold to Mordvale in 2001. It is most easily distinguished from the Lime Van (above) in having a plain non-detailed two-way pitched roof. It also has wire handrails either side of the side doors.

	Private Owner		
-	'Aspect' grey Sp Edn 250 (?) - ?	7	10
-	'George Brown' 1 grey Sp Edn 100 (Modellers Mecca) - 01	10	NA
B308	'Chance & Hunt' 333 maroon - 00	8	10

Dapol 00

Code	Description		
-	'Chance & Hunt' 100 brown Sp Edn 100 (A Oakes) - 05	8	10
4F018100	'Chance & Hunt' 171 maroon - 12	8	10
4F018101	'Chance & Hunt' 171 maroon W - 12	8	11
B223	'Jas. Colman' 15 pale green - c95	10	15
B225	'DCL' 87 grey - c95	10	15
WR3-04	'DCL' 87 grey - 98	8	10
B881	'Falk Salt' 2019 red-brown - 11	7	9
-	'ICI Fleetwood Salt' 12 maroon Sp Edn 232 (Toys2Save) - 04	9	11
-	'ICI Fleetwood Salt' 14 maroon Sp Edn 250 (Toys2Save) - 04	9	11
-	'Glan-Yr-Afon' 11 cream Sp Edn (David Dacey) - 08	7	9
B224	'ICI Bulk Salt' 25 grey - c95	10	12
WR3-05	'ICI Bulk Salt' 25 grey - 98	10	12
W5101	'ICI Salt' 25 white (body only) Sp Edn 70* (Wrenn Railways Collectors Club) WRCC5 - 01	30	35
-	'Llanharry Limestone & Gravel Coy' 33 cream Sp Edn 109 (Barry & Penarth MRC) - 03	9	11
-	'Llanharry Limestone & Gravel Coy' 37 cream Sp Edn 100 (Barry & Penarth MRC) - 04	9	11
No.15	'Llywernog Silver-Lead Mining Co.' 12 grey Sp Edn 160 (West Wales Wagon Works) - 04	9	11
No.31	'Llywernog Silver-Lead Mining Co.' ? grey Sp Edn (West Wales Wagon Works) - 05	9	11
B894	'Lymm Pure Salt' 128 brown - 11	8	12
-	'New Explosives Co' 10 black Sp Edn 100 (Stowmarket MRC) - 02	10	12
-	'North Cornwall China Clay Co.' 3 dark brown Sp Edn 148 (Wessex Wagons) - 12	10	12
No.3	'GD Owen' 12 red-brown Sp Edn ** 250 (West Wales Wagon Works) - 02	9	11
B226	'Saxa Salt' 248 lemon yellow - c95	10	15
B226	'Saxa Salt' 248 yellow - 00	8	10
B505	'Saxa Salt' 248 yellow - 02	7	9
B612	'Saxa Salt' 242 yellow - 05	7	9
B612B	'Saxa Salt' 235 yellow - ?	7	9
B612B	'Saxa Salt' 247 yellow - not made?	NPG	NPG
WR3-01	'Saxa Salt' 248 yellow - 97	10	12
W4665	'Saxa Salt' 25 white (body only) Sp Edn 70 * (Wrenn Railways Collectors Club - WRCC4) - 01	20	30
B1014	'Saxa Salt' 242 yellow - 12	7	9
B1014W	'Saxa Salt' 242 yellow W - 12	8	10
4F018001	'Saxa Salt' 242 yellow - 12	8	10
4F018002	'Saxa Salt' 242 yellow W - 12	8	11
B895	'Seddon's Salt' 22 brown - 11	7	9
B366	'Shaka Salt' 119 blue - 02	7	9
B811	'Snowdrift Salt' 309 green - 09	8	10
-	'South Wales Portland Cement & Lime Co.' 115 grey Sp Edn 120 (Barry & Penarth MRC) - 03	9	11
-	'South Wales Portland Cement & Lime Co.' 110 grey Sp Edn 150 (Barry & Penarth MRC) - 03	9	11
B635	'Stafford Salt Works' C,25 red - 05	7	9
B647	'Star Salt' 108 red - 06	7	9
B647B	'Star Salt' 11274 red - 07	6	8
B1015	'Star Salt' 105 red - 12	7	9
B1015W	'Star Salt' 105 red W - 12	8	10
4F018003	'Star Salt' 105 red - 12	8	10
4F018004	'Star Salt' 105 red W - 12	8	11
B886	'Stubbs & Compy' 37 orange - 11	7	9
B309	'Stubbs Salt' 37 orange-red - 00	8	10
-	'D Thomas Lime' 10 pink/stone Sp Edn 90 (David Dacey) - 03	9	11
-	'Tollemache' 1000 black Sp Edn 90 (South Wales Coalfields) - 08	7	9
B827	'Union Salt' 2169 grey - 10	7	9
4F018005	'Union Salt' 2169 grey - 12	8	10
4F018006	'Union Salt' 2169 grey W - 12	8	11

Commemoratives

Code	Description		
1	'AMETIA Eurotrack' yellow Sp Edn 100 (Solent Model Railway Group) - 04	10	12
1	'Baldwin Locomotive Works' 590 red Sp Edn 103 (Welsh Highland Railway) - 05	6	8
-	'Dapol' 20th Anniversary 2003 silver Ltd Edn 200 - 03	16	20
-	'Marks Models 1987-2007' white - 07	8	12
D010	'NRM' 2004 maroon Sp Edn 200 (TMC) - 04	9	11
D013	'NRM Keep Scotsman Steaming' black Sp Edn (TMC) - 05	9	11
-	'St Matthews School' Tuck Shop Supplies 8 yellow Sp Edn 100 (St Matthews) - 04	9	11
-	'UK Train Sim' 3103 light grey Sp Edn 117 (Atomic Systems - UK Train Sim) - 04	12	16
-	'Virgin Trains' Warley 2004 white+red Sp Edn 500 (Virgin Trains) - 04	9	11
-	'West Wales Wagon Works' 100 sand yellow GWR Sp Edn (West Wales Wagon Works) - 11	12	15

Railway Company

Code	Description		
-	G&KERy 15 dark grey Sp Edn 110 (Toys2Save) - 03	9	11

* 125 of each body were produced but only about 70 of each were usable due to faults with the others. These were returned to the factory. ** 100 were sold in wagon sets.

Vans

GWR

W32. GWR 8T Y10 Fruit Van (ex-Wrenn) (c1995)

This was the Hornby Dublo cattle wagon converted by Wrenn to a fruit van and represents one of 130 so converted by the GWR in 1939, by boarding in the open upper sides of the walls.

Code	Description		
A011	unfinished grey - 11	5	10

Private Owner

Code	Description		
-	'Felin Foel Brewery' 1 black Sp Edn 124 (Voyles) - 08	9	11
-	'George Gale & Co.' 6 dark green Sp Edn 228 (Wessex Wagons) - 10	9	11

Railway Company

Salt van [W31] (Dapol)

Ex-GWR Y10 fruit van [W32] (Hattons)

Code	Description		
B212	GW 38200 grey - c95	12	14
B504	GW 38231 grey - 02	6	8
4F015001	GW 38231 grey - 13	7	9
4F015002	GW 38231 grey W - 13	7	10
B504A	GW 38218 grey - 02	7	9

Dapol 00

B504A	GW 38228 grey * - 10	7	9
B504AW	GW 38228 grey W *- 10	7	10
B211	BR B872181 grey - c95	15	18
WR1-33	as above - 99	15	75
B213	BR B872181 brown - c95	10	15
WR1-32	as above - 99	10	20
B584	BR B833341 brown Mex - 04	6	8
B584A	BR B833340 brown Mex * - 10	7	9
B584AW	BR B833340 brown W Mex * - 10	7	10
4F015003	BR B833347 grey - 13	7	9
4F015004	BR B833347 grey W - 13	7	10
-	BR W106133 red-brown Evesham Sp Edn 300 (Classic Train & Motor Bus) - 03	9	11
-	BR W106147 brown, Sp Edn 100 (Classic Train & Motor Bus) - 05	8	10

* possibly renumbered old stock.

W33a. GWR Passenger 'Fruit D' Van (ex-HD/Wrenn)(1998)

This was a 10T van with a long wheelbase (18') built by the GWR for transporting fruit. It was the largest of their fruit vans and was built in 1938. It had 3 pairs of hinged doors along each side and was originally painted dark brown, as they ran with passenger trains. They were also used for parcel traffic.

The Hornby Dublo model was released in 1960 and reintroduced by Wrenn in 1970. Dapol offered it in their catalogues for ten years before replacing it with a model with a better chassis (see below).

WR1-05	BR W28720 blue - 98	10	22
WR1-51	BR B517112 grey - 99	30	60

W33b. GWR Passenger 'Fruit D' Van (2008)

This used a slightly adapted body from the above Hornby Dublo/Wrenn model but with a new well-detailed chassis.

A013	unfinished black - 11	5	10
Private Owner			
-	'Weald of Kent Hops' 1898 brown Sp Edn 100 (Carriage & Wagon Models) - 12	17	22
Railway Company			
B746	GWR (large GW) 2877 dark brown - 08	12	15
B746A	GWR (large GW) 2882 dark brown * - 10	12	15
B746AW	GWR (large GW) 2882 dark brown W * - 10	14	17
4F014005	GWR (large GW) 2886 dark brown - 12	12	16
4F014006	GWR (large GW) 2886 dark brown W - 12	13	17
B737	GWR (button) 2881 dark brown - 08	12	15
B737A	GWR (button) 2878 dark brown * - 10	12	15
B737AW	GWR (button) 2878 dark brown W * - 10	14	17
B737W	GWR (button) 2878 dark brown W * Sp Edn 300 (Hattons) - 10	12	15

'Fruit D' van in BR blue livery [W33b] (Hattons)

4F014001	GWR (button) 2881 dark brown - 12	12	16
4F014002	GWR (button) 2881 dark brown W - 12	13	17
B745	BR W2915 maroon - 08	12	15
B745A	BR W2010 maroon * - 10	12	15
B745AW	BR W2010 maroon W * - 10	14	17
B745W	BR W2010 maroon W * Sp Edn 300 (Hattons) - 10	12	15
4F014003	BR W2023 red-brown - 12	12	16
4F014004	BR W2023 red-brown W - 12	13	17
B753	BRe W38129 greeny-blue - 09	12	15
B753A	BRe W38103 greeny-blue * - 10	12	15
B753AW	BRe W38103 greeny-blue W * 10	14	17
4F014007	BRe W38107 greeny-blue - 12	12	16
4F014008	BRe W38107 greeny-blue W - 12	13	17
SBB5	BRe W38129 greeny-blue W (with chalk marks on both sides) Sp Edn 300 (Signal Box) - 09	14	17

W34. GWR 12T Goods Fruit Van (ex-Mainline) (1989)

This model is based on the GWR 'Goods Fruit A', 200 of which were built in 1938. They were also used for vegetables and general merchandise. They were vacuum braked and carried the XP branding for use in fast trains. 100 more were built to the same design at Swindon in 1949-50. Early in their lives they were largely used in the Vale of Evesham but later they were usually to be found in East Anglia.

This van is of standard length and has louvered panels along the top of each side, either side of the doors. Dapol bought the residue of the Mainline models when Palitoy closed. As Dapol did not have the tooling, which belonged to Kader and was used by Bachmann, the B261 van remains a mystery.

B81	GW 134149 grey (M) - 89	7	9
B98	BR W134251 brown (M) - 91	8	10
B261	BR grey - not made	NA	NA

W35. GWR 12T 'Mogo' Van (ex-Mainline) (1991)

'Mogo' vans were built by the GWR for transporting motor vehicles. To facilitate this they had a pair of doors at each end and drop-down flaps that rested on the buffer stocks and closed the gap between wagons. Vehicles were driven in from a platform on the end of the siding and were driven through the train from one van to the next

This model was based on the Mainline 'Mogo' van, a copy of which was tooled in China. Despite having the tooling, Dapol did not use it and later sold it to Hornby. Dapol had, however, bought the remnant Mainline stock and sold this through their catalogue.

B146	GW 126342 grey Mogo (M) - 91	7	8
B145	BR W105682 red-brown Mogo (M) - 91	7	9

W36. GWR 12T Planked Double Vent (ex-Mainline) (1984)

The van had two ventilators in each end and no angled braces on the doors. They were built at Swindon, many of them after Nationalisation.

This model was based on the Mainline Railways GWR double vent van and was tooled in China for Dapol, who made little use of it. Instead they sold the remnant Mainline stock and Hornby bought the duplicate tooling.

Private Owner			
B147	'Shepherd Neame' 3 cream (M) - ?	7	11
Railway Company			
B144	GW 123507 grey (M) - 91	7	9
B4	LMS 521202 red-brown - 84	9	11
B92	BR W141826 red-brown (M) - 86, 91	8	10
B93	BR W133971 grey (M) - 86	8	10

W37. GWR 6T 'Mica B' Refrig. Van (ex-HD/Wrenn) (c1995)

The Mica B was a refrigerated meat van, already being used by the GWR in the early days of the last century. It had wide ventilators at each end which could be opened or closed. With them open it was an ordinary meat van but with them closed and the addition of ice it was a refrigerator.

The Hornby Dublo model was released in 1958 and the tools were in the first batch bought by G&R Wrenn. Dapol acquired them in 1993.

Private Owner			
B234	'Birds Eye' 312 blue - c95	10	15
WR2-07	'Eskimo' W59850 white - 98	9	11
WR1-12	'Young's' 78 white - 99	10	15
Railway Company			
WR1-13	W59850 plain green - 99	25	35
B233	GW 59828 white 'Mica B' - c95	10	15
B231	BR 150721 grey 'Insulmeat' - c95	10	15
B232	BR W145207 white 'Mica B' - c95	15	18

LMS

W38. LMS Cattle Wagon (ex-Mainline) (1986)

The LMS cattle van design seems to have been much influenced by Midland Railway design. Improved roads in the 1930s caused a decline in railway transportation and some LMS vans were converted to carry ale.

As Dapol did not have the tooling for this model and it seems that a copy was not made, it is probable that this single model was Mainline stock acquired in 1985. The slightly different running number may be due to a listing error.

B157	BR M12098 red-brown (M) - 86	9	11

W39a. LMS 12T Single Vent Van (ex-Mainline) (1984)

The model had a single sliding door on each side which could be opened. This model, sold by Dapol, would be former Mainline stock acquired by Dapol in 1985.

B7	LMS 511476 grey doors slide (M) - 84	7	11

Dapol 00

W39b. LMS 12T Single Vent Van (ex-Airfix) (1984)

This is like the Mainline model above but the doors are part of a single body moulding and so do not slide. In this case, Dapol had bought the Airfix tooling and made the models themselves and did not sell it to Hornby.

A6	unfinished grey - *84*		5	10
A6	unfinished brown - *?*		5	10
A6	unfinished black - *?*		5	10
A019	unfinished grey - *11*		5	10

Private Owner

-	'The **Alton Brewery Co.**' 23 ochre Sp Edn 151 (Wessex Wagons) - *13*	10	12
-	'**Anglo Swiss Condensed Milk**' 23 cream Sp Edn 181 (Burnham & District MRC) - *10*	8	10
-	'**Bass**' 15 grey Sp Edn 200 (Tutbury Jinny) - *10*	8	10
-	'**Bass**' 16 olive green Sp Edn (Tutbury Jinny) - *?*	10	12

LMS single vent van [W39b] (Dapol)

-	'**Bass**' 17 olive green Sp Edn 200 (Tutbury Jinny) ex-set of 2 (with Bass 7-plank) - *02*	10	NA
-	'**Bass**' 19 olive grey Sp Edn (Tutbury Jinny) - *08*	7	9
-	'**Bass**' 23 olive green, Sp Edn 200 (Tutbury Jinny) ex-set of 2 - *02*	10	NA
-	'**Bass**' 24 grey, Sp Edn 200 (Tutbury Jinny) ex-set of 2 - *05*	8	NA
-	'**Bass**' 28 grey Sp Edn 200 (Tutbury Jinny) ex-set of 2 (with Worthington 88) - *05*	8	NA
-	'**Bass**' 29 light grey, Sp Edn 200 (Tutbury Jinny) ex-set of 2 - *03*	9	NA
-	'**Battle Wine Estate**' 5 cream Sp Edn 119 (Burnham & District MRC) - *11*	8	10
-	'**Battle Wine Estate**' 2 cream Sp Edn 137 (Burnham & District MRC) - *12*	8	11
-	'**BPCM**' 143 pinkish-brown Sp Edn 229 (Wessex Wagons) - *06*	8	10
-	'**Breeds & Co.**' 4 buff Sp Edn 118 (Burnham & District MRC) - *12*	7	10
-	'**Brickwoods Brewery**' 29 dark brown Sp Edn 191 (Wessex Wagons) - *08*	7	10
-	'**Brutton, Mitchell & Toms**' 2 red Sp Edn 140 (Burnham & District MRC) - *12*	8	11
-	'**Brutton, Mitchell & Toms**' 4 red Sp Edn 100 (Burnham & District MRC) - *13*	9	12
-	'**Burts of Ventnor**' 1 cream Sp Edn 189 (Wessex Wagons) - *10*	8	10
-	'**Carson's Chocolates**' 3 light blue Sp Edn 164 (Burnham & District MRC) - *10*	8	10
-	'The **Charlton Brewery**' 22 green Sp Edn 185 (Burnham & District MRC) - *10*	8	10
-	'**Devenish Weymouth Ales**' 43 green Sp Edn 210 (Wessex Wagons) - *09*	9	11
-	'The **Duchess of Devonshire Dairy Co.**' 15 cream So EDn 230 (Burnham & District MRC) - *10*	8	10
-	'**Eady & Dulley**' 2 dark brown Sp Edn 143 (Burnham & District MRC) - *11*	8	10
-	'The **Eclipse Peat Co.**' 23 dark brown Sp Edn 153 (Burnham & District MRC) - *09*	8	10
-	'**Elworthy Brothers & Co.**' 3 yellow Sp Edn 122 (Burnham & District MRC) - *13*	9	12
B64	'**English Eggs**' 506150 dark blue (A) - *85*	9	14
B376	'**English Eggs**' deep blue - *02*	7	9
-	'**English Eggs**' blue Sp Edn (The Train Shop, Morecombe) re-run of B376 - *06*	5	6
-	'**English Eggs**' (Westmoreland) dark blue Sp Edn (The Train Trains) - *06*	8	10
-	'**Faversham Hop Festival 2012**' blue Sp Edn (The Hobby Shop - Faversham) - *12*	9	12
-	'**Fox Brothers & Co.**' 3 yellow Sp Edn 179 (Burnham & District MRC) - *11*	8	10
-	'**Fox Brothers & Co.**' 9 yellow Sp Edn 108 (Burnham & District MRC) - *13*	9	12
-	'**Friary Meux Brewery**' 47 cream Sp Edn 206 (Wessex Wagons) - *11*	8	12
-	'Wm **Furze & Sons**' 23 cream Sp Edn 217 (Wessex Wagons) - *10*	7	10
-	'Henry **John Gasson**' 20 black Sp Edn 213 (Wessex Wagons) - *11*	9	12
-	'**Georges & Co.**' 12 red-brown Sp Edn 120 (Burnham & District MRC) - *13*	9	12
-	'**Gibbs, Mew & Co.**' 3 dark blue Sp Edn 178 (Wessex Wagons) - *08*	7	10

LMS single vent van [W39b] (Dapol)

-	'**Grey & Church St Breweries**' 1 cream Sp Edn 190 (Wessex Wagons) - *07*	7	9
-	'**Grey & Church St Breweries**' 2 cream Sp Edn 152 (Wessex Wagons) - *05*	8	10
-	'**Hall & Woodhouse**' 5 green Sp Edn 197 (Wessex Wagons) - *06*	8	10
-	Hall & Woodhouse - Badger Brewery' 7 white Sp Edn (Burnham & District MRC) - *12*	8	10
-	'**Harveys of Hayle**' 81802 brown Sp Edn 100 (Blewetts of Hayle) - *04*	9	11
-	'**Harveys (Sussex Brewers - Lewes)**' 2 light blue Sp Edn 178 (Burnham & District MRC) - *11*	8	10
-	'**Heavitree Brewery**' 131 red-brown Sp Edn 230 (Wessex Wagons) - *10*	9	11
-	'**Henty & Constable's Brewery**' 17 pale blue Sp Edn 160 (Wessex Wagons) - *12*	10	12
-	'**Holts Brewery Co.**' 4 buff Sp Edn (Burnham & District MRC) - *09*	8	10
B161	'**Huntley & Palmer**' 566327 green (A) - *?*	7	12
-	'**Huntley & Palmer**' 566325 green Sp Edn 104 (West Wales Wagon Works) - *13*	10	14
-	'**Huntley & Palmer**' 566325 green W Sp Edn 36 (West Wales Wagon Works) - *13*	10	14
B65	'**ICI Salt**' 2300 maroon doors fixed (M) - *85*	9	11
-	'Joseph **Jones**' 15 red Sp Edn 202 (Burnham & District MRC) - *11*	8	10
-	'**Kelsey**' dark brown Sp Edn 300 (Ballards) - *10*	8	11
-	'**Kemp Town Brewery**' 9 blue-grey Sp Edn 120 (Burnham & District MRC) - *13*	8	11
-	'**King & Barnes**' 9 red-brown Sp Edn 185 (Burnham & District MRC) - *11*	8	10
-	'**Knotty Ash Brewery**' 15 red Sp Edn 202 (Burnham & District MRC) - *11*	8	10
-	'AE **Langley & Co.**' 1 dark blue Sp Edn 100 (Burnham & District MRC) - *12*	8	11
-	'**Marks & Spencer**' 15 light green Sp Edn 153 (Burnham & District MRC) - *11*	8	10

Dapol 00

-	'W&H **Marriage & Sons**' 2007 light grey Sp Edn 315 (Chelmsford & District MRC) - *07*	8	10
-	'**Marstin's Brewery**' 9 white Sp Edn 149 (Burnham & District MRC) - *12*	8	10
-	'**Mellesh & Neale**' 4 green Sp Edn 146 (Burnham & District MRC) - *13*	8	11
-	'**Miles Tea & Coffee**' 3 white Sp Edn 167 (Burnham & District MRC) - *11*	8	10
B66	'**Nestle's Milk**' 531179 blue (A) - *85*	8	12
-	'**Oakhill Brewery Coy.**' 14 green Sp Edn 240 (Burnham & District MRC) - *10*	8	10
-	'**Otter Brewery**' 3 cream Sp Edn 190 (Buffers) - *10*	8	11
-	'**Otter Brewery**' 4 light blue Sp Edn 204 (Burnham & District MRC) - *12*	8	11
-	'**Packer's Chocolets**' 6 blue Sp Edn 143 (Buffers) - *10*	8	10
B62	'**Persil**' 547921 green (A) - *85*	8	12
-	'**Petter & Sons Anchor Brewery**' 5 light blue Sp Edn 195 (Buffers) - *10*	8	11
-	'**P.D. & S.W.**' 51 red Sp Edn 155 (Wessex Wagons) - *12*	10	12
-	'JW **Phipp & Sons**' 43 grey Sp Edn 300 (Wessex Wagons) - *08*	7	9
-	'The **Pilchard Works**' 5 light blue Sp Edn 179 (Burnham & District MRC) - *11*	8	10

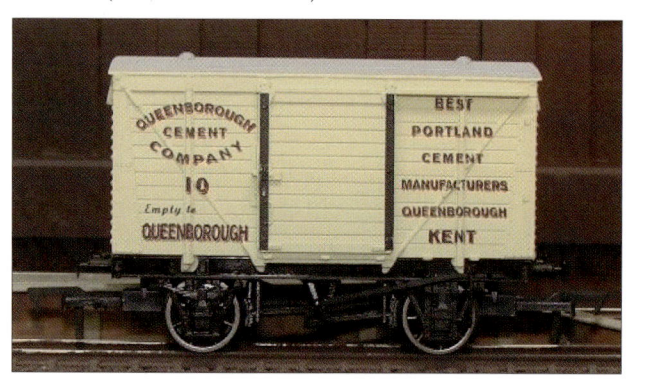

LMS single vent van [W39b] (Dapol)

-	'**Plymouth Breweries**' 7 cream Sp Edn 122 (Burnham & District MRC) - *13*	9	12
-	'**Plymouth Breweries**' 11 green Sp Edn 117 (Burnham & District MRC) - *13*	8	11
-	'**Queenborough Cement Co.**' 10 cream Sp Edn 1000 (Ballards) - *09*	8	10
-	'**Red Tape**' red Sp Edn 165 (Elmet Images) - *11*	8	11
-	'**Red Tape**' red W 39 (Elmet Images) - *11*	9	12
-	'**Sheppy's Somerset Cyder**' 11 buff Sp Edn 154 (Burnham & District MRC) - *11*	8	10
-	'**Simonds Brewery**' 15 brown Sp Edn 125 (Burnham & District MRC) - *11*	8	10
-	'**Somerset, Dorset & Devon Dairy Co.**' 1 dark blue Sp Edn 105 (Buffers) - *13*	8	11
-	'**Southdown & East Grinstead Breweries**' 2 yellow Sp Edn 132 (Burnham & District MRC) - *13*	11	14
-	'**Star Mineral Waters**' white Sp Edn 164 (East Kent MRS) - *12*	10	12
-	'**Starkey, Knight & Ford**' 3 buff Sp Edn 250 (Wessex Wagons) - *07*	7	9
-	'**Starkey, Knight & Ford**' 7 buff Sp Edn 167 (Wessex Wagons) - *13*	8	11
-	'**Style & Winck - Medway Brewery**' 6 yellow Sp Edn (Burnham & District MRC) - *12*	8	10
-	'**Tamplin & Sons - Phoenix Brewery**' 6 pale brown Sp Edn (Burnham & District MRC) - *12*	8	10
-	'**Taunton Cider**' 4 green Sp Edb 150 (Burnham & District MRC) - *11*	8	11
B61	'**Tizer**' 561772 yellow (A) - *85*	8	12
-	'**Trago Mills**' yellow Sp Edn 250 (Trago Mills) - *89*	12	14
-	same but blue Sp Edn 250 - *89*	12	14
-	same but green Sp Edn 250 - *89*	12	14
-	same but red Sp Edn 250 - *89*	12	14
-	same in brown Sp Edn 250 - *89*	20	24
-	'**United Kingdom Tea Company**' 1 red Sp Edn 163 (Burnham & District MRC) - *11*	8	10
-	'**Westerham Ales (Black Eagle Brewery)**' 3 cream Sp EDn 117 (Burnham & District MRC) - *12*	8	10
-	'**Weston's Cyder**' 3 blue Sp Edn 150 (Burnham & District MRC) - *12*	8	10

LMS single vent van [W39b] (Dapol)

-	'**Wilts United Daries**' 3 cream Sp Edn 136 (Burnham & District MRC) - *09*	7	9
-	'**Wilts United Daries**' 4 cream Sp Edn 160 (Burnham & District MRC) - *10*	8	10
-	'**Worthington**' 3 brown, Sp Edn 200 (Tutbury Jinny) ex-set of 2 - *03*	9	NA
-	'**Worthington**' 8 brown, Sp Edn 200 (Tutbury Jinny) - *10*	8	10
-	'**Worthington**' 30 brown Sp Edn (Tutbury Jinny) - *08*	7	9
-	'**Worthington**' 33 brown, Sp Edn 200 (Tutbury Jinny) ex-set of 2 - *05*	8	NA
-	'**Worthington**' 88 brown Sp Edn 200 (Tutbury Jinny) ex-set of 2 (with Bass 28) - *05*	8	NA

Commemoratives

PR2	'**BBRUA**' 25th Anniversary maroon Sp Edn 250 (1E Promotionals) - *05*	8	10
PR1	'**Bletchley TMD 40th Anniversary**' white Sp Edn 250 (1E Promotionals) - *05*	8	10
-	'**Faversham Hop Festival 2012**' red Sp Edn (The Hobby Shop - Faversham) - *12*	9	12
-	'**Faversham Hop Festival 2012**' white Sp Edn (The Hobby Shop - Faversham) - *12*	9	12
-	'**Great Western Society**' dark brown Sp Edn (GWS) - *06*	5	6
-	'**Saltley Depot Commemoration**' 150 years DM514921 black, Sp Edn 180 (Classic Train & Motor Bus) - *04*	9	11
-	'**SMR War Department**' 30 light grey Sp Edn 100 (Shresbury Model Centre) - *08*	7	9
-	**SVR 40th Anniv.** white Sp Edn (SVR Wolverhampton Branch) - *07*	7	9

Railway Companies

-	**TVLR** M632154 cream Sp Edn 96 (Tanat Valley Light Railway Co.) - *07*	7	10
B4	**LMS** 520212 brown - *?*	8	10
B7	**LMS** 501086 grey - *84*	8	10
B7	**LMS** 508587 grey (M) - *88*	8	12
B9	**LMS** 511840 red-brown - *84*	8	10
B382	**LMS** 508587 light grey - *02*	7	9
B382A	**LMS** 508579 light grey - *02*	7	9
No.30	**LMS** 282093 brown LMS Salvage Campaign Sp Edn 119 (West Wales Wagon Works) - *05*	8	10
B839	**LMS** 511235 rey , Egg Van - *10*	7	9
B829	**LMS** 511239 grey, Fruit Van - *10*	7	9
B526	**LMS** 511240 grey, Egg Van - *03*	7	9
B527	**LMS** 511246 grey, Fruit Van - *03*	7	9
4F011005	**LMS** 511235 grey Egg Van - *12*	7	9
4F011006	**LMS** 511235 grey W Egg Van - *12*	7	10
4F011007	**LMS** 511239 grey Fruit Van - *12*	7	9
4F011008	**LMS** 511239 grey W Fruit Van - *12*	7	10
B567	**LMS** 611846 brown - *04*	7	9
B752	**LMS** 538864 grey - *09*	6	8

Dapol 00

4F011001	**LMS** 538864 grey - *12*	7	9
4F011002	**LMS** 538864 grey W - *12*	8	10
B22	**BR** M501085 light grey - *84*	8	10
B63	**BR** B753722, B751707 red-brown (M) - *85*	8	12
B386	**BR** M283328 grey - *02*	7	9
B386A	**BR** M283331 grey - *02*	7	9

LMS single vent van [W39b] (Dapol)

B764	**BR** M183317 grey - *09*	6	8
4F011003	**BR** M183317 grey - *12*	7	9
4F011004	**BR** M183317 grey W - *12*	8	10
-	**UT** (Ulster Transport Authority) 2478 red-brown Sp Edn 152 (Provincial Wagons) - *08*	7	9

* These were delivered unnumbered and were individually numbered by Steve Skelton of Hythe (Kent) Models..

SR

W40a.   SR 12T Double Vent Box Van (ex-Airfix) (1984)

This van has an elliptically curved roof, the sharpest curves being just above the sides. For B17, two sizes of 'SR' may be found. Airfix had released the model in 1979 and it was used once by Palitoy before passing to Dapol in 1985. Dapol used the tooling as seen in this table before selling it to Hornby in 1996. For 2005, Dapol produced their own tooling for a new model, the variations of which are listed in the next table.

A7	unfinished grey with a brown roof - *84*	5	10
B15	**GW** 144888 dark grey - *84*	9	11
B16	**SR** 44433 grey - *84*	9	11
B16	**SR** 44434 grey - *?*	9	11
B17	**SR** 273843 dark brown - *84*	9	11
B17	**SR** 44393 dark brown - *?-94*	9	11
B327	**SR** 273840 dark brown - *01*	9	10
B16	**BR** S44434 grey - *84*	9	11

W40b.   SR 12T Double Vent Box Van (2005)

This van was retooled in 2005.

A7	unfinished grey with a brown roof - *?*	5	10
A012	unfinished grey - *11*	5	10

SR double vent van [W40b] (Dapol)

Private Owner

-	'Thomas **Amey & Co.**' 3 red Sp Edn 100 (Burnham & District MRC) - *13*	9	12
No.69	'**Baldwins**' 841 dark brown Sp Edn 114 (West Wales Wagon Works) - *08*	7	9
-	'**Battle Brewery**' 1 dark blue Sp Edn 149 (Burnham & District MRC) - *11*	8	10
-	'George **Beer & Rigden**' 8 buff Sp Edn 127 (Burnham & District MRC) - *13*	9	12
-	'**Bryant & Son**' 1 red-brown Sp Edn 193 (Buffers) - *10*	8	11
-	'Alfred **Day**' 273836 dark blue (Colonel Stevens Railway Enterprises) - *09*	10	13
-	'**Dover Packet Yard - Stores**' 3 grey Sp Edn 150 (Carriage & Wagon Models) - *10*	9	12
-	'**Eldridge, Pope & Co.**' 48345 green Sp Edn 250 (Wessex Wagons) - *07*	7	9
-	'**Eldridge, Pope & Co.**' N48402 green Sp Edn 150 (Wessex Wagons) - *13*	10	12
-	'**Express Dairy Co. English Eggs (Devonshire)**' 48323 dark blue Sp Edn 230 (Wessex Wagons) - *06*	8	10
-	'**Express Dairy Co. English Eggs (Devonshire)**' 49168 dark blue Sp Edn 180 (Wessex Wagons) - *08*	8	10
-	'**Express Dairy Co. English Eggs (Devonshire)**' 48359 dark blue Sp Edn 165 (Wessex Wagons) - *11*	9	12
-	'**Express Dary Co. English Eggs**' (Fine Cheeses) 49345 blue-grey Sp Edn 302 (Wessex Wagons) - *07*	7	10
-	'**Flint & Co.**' 3 green Sp Edn 135 (Burnham & District MRC) - *13*	9	12
-	'**RH&J Follett**' 2 red-brown Sp Edn 149 (Buffers) - *09*	8	11
-	'**RH&J Follett**' 4 red-brown Sp Edn 213 (Buffers) - *10*	8	11
-	'John **Groves & Son**' 3 pale brown Sp Edn 200 (Buffers) - *10*	8	11
-	'**Highbridge Bacon Co.**' 7 brown Sp Edn 179 (Burnham & District MRC) - *11*	8	10
-	'JS & JL **Hilder**' 273849 red-brown Sp Edn (Colonel Stevens Railway Enterprises) - *10*	8	11
-	'John **How & Co.**' 8 red Sp Rdn (Buffers) - *12*	8	11
-	'**Leney's Dover Pale Ale**' 2 grey Sp Edn 3 (Carriage & Wagon Models) - *13*	11	14
-	'**Leney's Dover Pale Ale**' 5 cream Sp Edn 100 (Carriage & Wagon Models) - *13*	11	14
-	'**Longford Engineering Company**' S59262 grey Sp Edn 100 (Richard Essen) - *12*	10	12
-	'**Mitchell Toms & Co.**' 3 green Sp Edn 230 (Wessex Wagons) - *09*	7	9
-	'**New Medway**' 40 blue-grey Sp Edn 95 (Medway Queen Preservation Society) - *07*	7	9
-	'**New Medway**' 53 blue-grey Sp Edn 90 (Medway Queen Preservation Society) - *07*	7	9
-	'**New Medway**' 12 dark blue Sp Edn (Medway Queen Preservation Society) - *12*	9	12
-	'**New Medway**' 12 dark blue W Sp Edn (Medway Queen Preservation Society) - *12*	9	12
-	'**New Medway**' 20 dark blue Sp Edn (Medway Queen Preservation Society) - *12*	9	12
-	'**New Medway**' 20 dark blue W Sp Edn (Medway Queen Preservation Society) - *12*	9	12

SR double vent van [W40b] (Dapol)

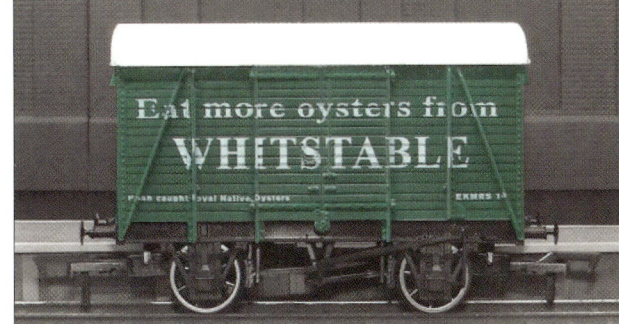

-	'**Oysters from Whitstable**' EKMRS07 pale blue Sp Edn 171 (East Kent MRS) - *07*	7	9
-	'**Oysters from Whitstable**' EKMRS14 dark green Sp Edn 182 (East Kent MRS) - *10*	8	10

8th Edition

Dapol 00

-	**'Page & Overton'** 42 orange-brown Sp Edn 167 (Burnham & District MRC) - *11*	8	10
-	**'Pride of Sussex'** bright green Sp Edn 185 (Kent & East Sussex Railway) - *07*	7	9
-	**'Rother Valley Brewery'** bright green Sp Edn 200 (Colonel Stephens Railway Enterprises KESR) - *06*	7	9
*	**'Scutt Bros Stogumber Brewery'** 19 cream Sp Edn 280 (Wessex Wagons) - *07*	9	11
*	**'Seccotine'** blue with orange roof Sp Edn 150 (McDiamid) - *10*	9	11
-	**'Shepherd Neame & Co.'** 1 cream Sp Edn 236 (East Kent MRS) - *09*	7	9
-	**'Star Brewery Co.'** 3 red Sp Edn 135 (Burnham & District MRC) - *12*	7	10
-	**'Strong & Co.'** 7 dark blue Sp Edn 240 (Wessex Wagons) - *07*	7	9
-	**'Vallance Brewery Co.'** 1 dark green Sp Edn 143 (Buffers) - *09*	8	11
-	**'Vallance Brewery Co.'** 2 dark green Sp Edn 200 (Buffers) - *11*	9	11
	Railway Company		
-	**'Moors Valley Railway'** 2009 red MaintenanceV Sp Edn 232 (Moors Valley Railway) - *09*	8	10
3	**WHR** 60 grey Sp Edn (Welsh Highland Railway) - *08*	7	9
B636	**GW** 144859 grey - *05*	6	8
B636A	**GW** 144852 grey * - *10*	7	9
B636AW	**GW** 144852 grey W * - *10*	7	10
B642	**LMS** 611819 brown - *05*	6	8
4F021003	**LMS** 611421 brown - *12*	7	9
4F021004	**LMS** 611421 brown W - *12*	7	10
B627	**SR** 273849 brown - *05*	6	8

SR double vent fish van [W40b] (Dapol)

B627A	**SR** 273830 brown * - *10*	7	9
B627AW	**SR** 273830 brown W * - *10*	7	9
-	**SR** 46946 dark brown' Fish Traffic Only' Sp Edn 1000 (Ballards) - *07*	6	8
-	**SR - 'Sovereign Harbour Port Authority'** 070 grey Sp Edn 64 (Simply Southern) - *11*	8	11
-	**SR - 'Sovereign Harbour Port Authority'** 070 grey W Sp Edn 64 (Simply Southern) - *11*	10	13
-	**SR - 'Royal Atlantic Cruises'** 053 silver Sp Edn 62 (Simply Southern) - *11*	8	11
-	**SR - 'Royal Atlantic Cruises'** 053 silver W Sp Edn 51 (Simply Southern) - *11*	10	13
-	**SR - 'Sussex Fisheries'** 053 pale blue Sp Edn (Simply Southern) - *11*	8	13
-	**SR - 'Sussex Fisheries'** 053 pale blue W Sp Edn (Simply Southern) - *11*	10	14
B625	**BR** B753848 grey - *05*	6	8
-	**BR** S45756 brown Sp Edn 100 (KESR) - *12*	10	13
4F021005	**BR** 753846 grey - *12*	7	9
4F021006	**BR** 753846 grey W - *12*	7	10

* Possibly renumbered old stock.

W41. SR CCT Utility Van (ex-HD/Wrenn) (2001)

All four pre-1948 railway companies had covered carriage trucks (CCT) which were used with passenger trains to carry parcels, milk, newspapers and other commodities that needed urgent delivery. This former Hornby Dublo model was of one type built by the Southern Railway and had been depicted in BR passenger green. It was built as a luggage van in 1931 at Ashford.

The Hornby Dublo model was released in 1961 and the tooling was in the first batch acquired by Wrenn. It was reintroduced by them in 1970 and the model passed to Dapol in 1985.

-	**Mid Hants Railway** S2005 green Sp Edn (Mid Hants Railway) - *05*	10	14
B341	**SR** S2279S green - *01*	10	12
B388	**BR** S2380S green - *02*	10	12
B342	**BR** M527071 red - *01*	10	12
B342	**BR** M527042 red - *01*	10	12
B340	**BR** S2514S blue - *01*	10	12
SBB4	**BR** S25148 blue W Sp Edn 300 (Signal Box) - *09*	14	17

BR

W42. BR Gunpowder Van (ex-HD/Wrenn) (c1995)

The gunpowder transported in these GPV vans was usually for the mining and quarrying industries, although they may well have been used for transporting stocks of fireworks in the lead up to November 5th. The 11 ton capacity vans, built by British Railways, were to the GWR design.

The Hornby Dublo wagon was released in 1962 and was amongst the models bought by Wrenn. The tooling passed to Dapol and the model originally sold as 'WR3' stock. However, it was absorbed into the Dapol range when G&R Wrenn was sold to Mordvale in 2001. While the prototype of this model was the BR Standard gunpowder van it has been used to represent a GW Iron Mink van. Several of these were either owned by, or carried the livery of, the Associated Portland Cement Company, whose brands included 'Blue Circle', 'Ferrocrete' and 'Sandtex'.

A016	unfinished grey - *11*	4	10
	Private Owner		
-	**'Arnold & Hancock'** 3 brown Sp Edn 150 (Wessex Wagons) - *05*	8	10
-	**'Axminster Carpets'** B895006 light grey Sp Edn 150 (Buffers Model Railways) - *03*	9	11
-	**'Axminster Carpets'** B895006 white Sp Edn (Buffers Model Railways) - *05*	8	10
-	**'Battle Gunpowder Mills'** 1 black Sp Edn 110 (Burnham & District MRC) - *11*	8	11
-	**'Battle Gunpowder Mills'** 2 black Sp Edn 150 (Burnham & District MRC) - *11*	8	10
-	**'BC Railway'** 24 grey Ltd Edn 150 (Dapol Shop) - *07*	7	9
-	**'Bear's Beers'** - purple Sp Edn 100 (*Model Rail* magazine) - *05*	8	10
B750	**'Blue Circle'** 173 yellow - *09*	6	8
B315	**'Blue Circle'** 177 yellow - *00*	7	9
-	'John **Board & Co.**' 12 cream Sp Edn 153 (Burnham & District MRC) - *09*	8	10

Gunpowder van [W42] (Hattons)

4F013100	**'BPCM'** 168 grey - *12*	7	9
4F013101	**'BPCM'** 168 grey W - *12*	7	10
W5200	**'Brock's Fireworks'** B887008 black Sp Edn 100 (Wrenn Collectors Club - WRCC8) - *02*	20	30
WRCC14	**'Brock's Fireworks'** B887008 bright green Sp Edn 100 (Wrenn Collectors Club) - *04*	10	14
B209	**'BSA'** B887002 brown - *c95*	10	15
-	'Joe Miller **Buggleskelly**' 1937 red-brown Sp Edn 107 (Aslan Associates) - *07*	7	9
B372	**Cambrian Railways** 139 black - *02*	7	9
-	**'Cotton Powder Co.'** various numbers brown		

Dapol 00

-	Sp Edn 310 (Hythe Models) - 02		10	12
-	'Cotton Powder Co.' 2 brown Sp Edn 1,000 (Ballards) - 08		7	9
B556	'Elterwater Gunpowder' 11 light grey - 03		7	9
B311	'Ferrocrete' 167 - yellow - 00		7	9
B688	'Ferrocrete' 262 yellow - 07		6	8
-	'Marley Tile Co.' 7 dark green Sp Edn 1000 (Ballards) - 05		7	9
-	'Mevagissey Model Railways' 1 blue Sp Edn (Mevaguissey Models) - ?		10	12
No.095	'Middleton' 2011 violet Sp Edn (West Wales Wagon Works) - 11		10	13

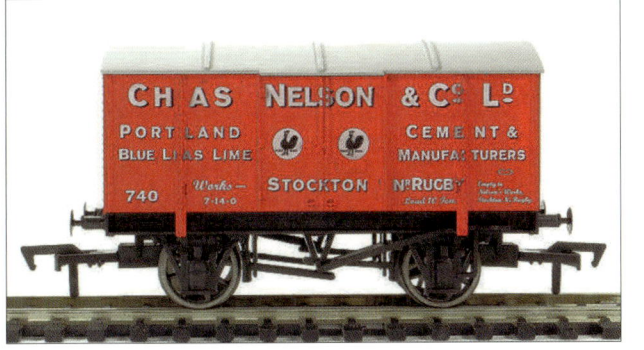

Gunpowder van [W42] (Hattons)

-	'Minitry of Munitions' red-brown 4159 Sp Edn 200 (Wessex Wagons) - 06		8	10
-	'Morgan **Lloyd Williams**' 388 dark brown Sp Edn (Albatross Models) - 09		8	10
4F013102	'Chas **Nelson**' 740 red - 12		7	9
4F013103	'Chas **Nelson**' 740 red W - 12		7	10
B652	'ROF' M12 grey + red cross - 06		7	9
-	'Royal Leamington Spa' DB887499 brown Enparts van Sp Edn 200 (Classic Train & Motor Bus) - 02		10	12
-	'Royal Leamington Spa' DB887499 faded blue Enparts van Sp Edn 50 (Classic Train & Motor Bus) - 04		14	17
B365	'Rugby' 13 black - 02		7	9
B760	'Rugby' 13 black - 09		6	8
-	'Simonds Brewery' 16 dark red Sp Edn 218 (Wessex Wagons) - 06		8	10
B573	'Spillers Flour' 175 white - 04		7	9
B824	'Spillers Flour' 179 white - 10		7	9
B210	'Standard Fireworks' B887002 brown - c95		12	15
W4313P	'Standard Fireworks' B887007 light blue Sp Edn 100 (Wrenn Railways Collectors Club - WRCC7) - 02	20	30
WRCC13	'Standard Fireworks' B887007 bright red Sp Edn 100 (Wrenn Railways Collectors Club) - 04	20	30
WRCC15	'Standard Fireworks' B887007 black Sp Edn 100 (Wrenn Railways Collectors Club) - 06/08	20	30
-	'Taunton Cider Co'. 17 cream Sp Edn 275 (Wessex Wagons) - 06		8	10

Commemoratives

B513	'2002 Golden Jubilee' 1952 purple - 02		8	10
B513	'2002 Golden Jubilee' 1952 blue - 02		8	10
WCC10	'Golden Anniversary' gold Sp Edn 150 (Wrenn Railways Collectors Club) - 03		10	14
TVR4	'Jiwbili' 2002 white, Welsh flag Sp Edn 111 (Teifi Valley Railway) * - 01		10	12
TVR5	'Jubilee' 1952 blue, Union Jack Sp Edn 100 (Teifi Valley Railway) * - 01		10	12
-	above 2 wagons in a set Ltd Edn 50 *** - 01		NA	22
-	'N'Gaugers Club 2012' No.6 silver - 12		9	11
-	'Platelayers' dark grey Sp Edn 125 (The Great British Train Show 2004) 04		9	11
-	'R&D Models 1977-2002' dark green Sp Edn 100 (R&D Models) - 02		10	12
-	'Rialtronics' Sp Edn (Railtronics) - ?		8	10
-	'Square Wheels' yellow Sp Edn100 (Square Wheels) - 03		9	12
-	'TMC' blue Sp Edn 180 (The Model Centre) - 03		9	11
-	'Trains, Models & Hobbies' white Sp Edn 108 (TM&H) - 01		10	12

Railway Companies

-	**Talyllyn Railway** Sp Edn (Talyllyn Railway) - 05		8	10
B310	**LNWR** light grey - 00		8	10
4F013003	**LNWR** light grey - 12		7	9
4F013004	**LNWR** light grey W - 12		7	10
B518	**NB** bright red gunpowder van - 03		7	9
B518	**NB** maroon gunpowder van - 03		7	10
B330	**LSWR** 1379 red - 01		7	9
B909	**LSWR** 1904 bright red - 11		8	10
B207	**GW** W105780 black, red X - c95		12	15
WR1-52	as above - 99		12	15
WR2-01	as above (Dapol chassis) - 99		8	10
4F013001	**GW** W105739 black, red X - 12		7	9
4F013001	**GW** W105739 black W, red X - 12		7	10
B349A	**GW** W105743 black? - 12		7	9
B349W	**GW** W105743 black? W - 12		7	10
B312	**GW** 37985 dark grey - 00		7	9
LB4	**GWR** Salvage 47305 light blue Iron Mink Sp Edn 250 (Lord & Butler) - 03?		9	11
-	**GWR** Salvage 47303 light blue Sp Edn 132 (Burnham & District MRC) - 12		8	10

Gunpowder van [W42] (Hattons)

B336	**LMS** 299031 light grey - 01		6	8
4F013005	**LMS** 299031 light grey - 12		7	9
4F013006	**LMS** 299031 light grey W - 12		7	10
B355	**NE** grey - 01		6	8
B560	**NE** 71418 bright red gunpowder van - 03		6	8
4F013007	**NE** 71418 red - 12		7	9
4F013008	**NE** 71418 red W - 12		7	10
B329	**SR** 61204 brown - 01		6	8
B722	**SR** GPV(Improvised) 59061 black - 08		6	8
B349	**BR** W105780 black, red cross - 01		6	8
B349A	**BR** W105743 black, red cross ** - 10		7	9
B349AW	**BR** W105743 black W, red cross ** - 10		7	10
B208	**BR** B887002 red-brown - c95		10	15
B510	**BR** B887002 red-brown - 02		8	10
WR3-15	**BR** B887002 red-brown - 99		9	11
B510	**BR** B887002 red-brown - 02		7	9
B700	**BR** M701058 brown - 07		6	8
B700A	**BR** M701048 brown ** - 10		7	9
B700AW	**BR** M701048 brown W ** - 10		7	10
4F013009	**BR** M701048 light brown - 12		7	9
4F013010	**BR** M701048 light brown W - 12		7	10
-	**BR** B887049 black (trencher train) Sp Edn 100 (Alexandra Models) - 07		7	9

* See also boxed wagon sets (below).

W43. BR 8T Cattle Wagon (ex-HD/Wrenn) (c1995)

British Railways inherited 11,089 cattle wagons in 1948 and, despite the continuing decline in traffic, it carried on building them up until 1954. 2,300 of these were built at Swindon. The Hornby Dublo model was based on one of these that was built in 1951.

The original model was released in 1958 and the tooling sold to G&R Wrenn in the late 1960s. Dapol bought the model in 1993 and from 2007 these were fitted with a new chassis.

Dapol 00

Code	Description		
A010	unfinished grey - 11	4	10

Railway Company

Code	Description		
-	**CV** 140 grey Sp Edn 92 (Colne Valley Railway) - 08	8	10

LBSCR cattle wagon [W43]

Code	Description		
-	**K&ESR** 13 light grey Sp Edn 200 (Col. Stephens Rly Enterprise KESR) - 06	8	10
-	**K&ESR** 2 grey Sp Edn 100 (K&ESR) - 13	9	12
-	**LBSC** 7479 dark grey Sp Edn 1000 (Ballards) - 06	8	10
-	**Mid Hants Railway** S2006 brown Ale Wagon Sp Edn 101 (Mid Hants Rly) - 06	8	10
-	**NYMR** B894178 grey Sp Edn (NYMR) - 07	7	9
-	**TR** 2004 dark grey Sp Edn (Talyllyn Railway) - 04	9	11
No.89AM	**TVR** 115 (GW13815) black	9	NA
No.89BM	**TVR** 115 (GW13875) black	9	NA
No.89PM	above two pristine wagons Sp Edn (West Wales Wagon Works) - 10	NA	17
No.89AW	**TVR** 115 (GW13815) black W	10	NA
No.89BW	**TVR** 115 (GW13875) black W	10	NA
No.89PW	above two weathered wagons Sp Edn (West Wales Wagon Works) - 10	NA	18
B58	**GW** 103240 grey - c95	10	15
WR1-03	as above - 97	10	25
B500	**GW** 13813 dark grey - 02	6	8
B500a	**GW** 13818 dark grey * - 10	7	9
B500AW	**GW** 13818 dark grey W * - 10	7	10
4F020003	**GW** 13824 dark grey * - 12	7	9
4F020004	**GW** 13824 dark grey W * - 12	7	10
B549	**GW** 38659 grey Ale Wagon - 03	6	8
B549a	**GW** 38618 grey Ale Wagon * - 10	7	9
B549AW	**GW** 38618 grey W Ale Wagon * - 10	8	11
B549A	**GW** 38618 grey Ale Wagon * - 10	7	9
4F020007	**GW** 38621 grey Ale Wagon * - 13	8	11
4F020008	**GW** 38221 grey W Ale Wagon - 13	6	8
-	**SR** 53172 dk.brown Sp Edn 1000 (Ballards) - 05	6	8
-	**BR** B893874 dark grey	6	NA
-	**BR** B893771 dark grey	6	NA
-	**BR** B893786 dark grey	6	NA
-	**BR** B893792 dark grey	6	NA
-	**BR** B893777 dark grey	6	NA
B500MULU	above 5 pristine cattle wagons - 11	NA	40
-	**BR** B893874 dark grey W	7	NA
-	**BR** B893771 dark grey W	7	NA
-	**BR** B893786 dark grey W	7	NA
-	**BR** B893792 dark grey W	7	NA
-	**BR** B893777 dark grey W	7	NA
B500MULTIW	above 5 weathered cattle wagons - 11	NA	45
B47	**BR** B893344 red-brown - c95	10	15
WR1-04	as above - 98	10	15
B501	**BR** B893380 red-brown - 02	6	8
B501	**BR** B893344 red-brown - 02	7	9
B501A	**BR** B893373 red-brown - 02	7	9
B501A	**BR** B893373 red-brown * - 10	7	9
B501AW	**BR** B893373 red-brown W - 10	7	10
B501A	**BR** B893369 red brown - 02	4	6
4F020005	**BR** B893375 red-brown - 12	7	10
4F020006	**BR** B893375 red brown W - 12	4	6
-	**BR** Bass W102208 brown Ale Wagon Sp Edn 200 (Tutbury Jinny) - 06	8	10
-	**BR** Bass W102200 brown Ale Wagon Sp Edn 200 (Tutbury Jinny) - 09	8	10

Ireland

Irish Cattle Wagon [W43] (Dapol)

Code	Description		
-	**SLNC** (Sligo, Leitrim & Northern Counties Railway) 158 grey Sp Edn 143 (Provincial Wagons) - 08	8	10
-	**SLNC** (Sligo, Leitrim & Northern Counties Railway) 110 grey Sp Edn 145 (Provincial Wagons) - 10	8	10
-	**CIE** 510 pale grey Sp Edn (Marks Models) - 04, 06	8	10

* possibly renumbered old stock.

W44. BR 'Yellow Spot' Banana Van (ex-HD/Wrenn) (c1995)

This is based on a BR van with plywood sides and corrugated ends and with no protruding vents in the ends. It was released in 1962 and it was in the first batch of tools bought from Meccano Ltd by G&R Wrenn. When Wrenn was bought by Dapol, the model was originally sold by Dapol as 'WR3' stock but it was absorbed into the Dapol range when G&R Wrenn was sold to Mordvale in 2001.

Code	Description		
A017	unfinished grey - 11	5	10

Private Owner

Code	Description		
-	'Brixham Fish' 1 green Sp Edn 133 (Burnham & District MRC) - 12	8	10
-	'Buffers' 50 white Sp Edn 150 (Buffers) - 12	9	12
-	'Fresh Fish from Hastings Fleet' 1 dark brown Sp Edn 113 (Burnham & District MRC) - 13	8	11
-	'JS **Fry & Sons**' 59741 white Sp Edn 145 (Wessex Wagons) - 08	8	10
-	'JS **Fry & Sons**' 105870 white Sp Edn 130 (Wessex Wagons) - 08	8	10
-	'Macfisheries' 96 dark blue Sp Edn 129 (Burnham & District MRC) - 12	8	11
-	'B **Sawtell & Sons**' 22 yellow Sp Edn 150 (Burnham & District MRC) - 11	8	10
-	'Stogumber Brewery' 19 cream Sp Edn 280 (Wessex Wagons) - 07	7	9
-	'Thompson & Son' 6 yellow Sp Edn 154 (Burnham & District MRC) - 11	8	10
B263	'Tropical Fruit Co.' M40 grey - ?	10	15
B716	'Tropical Fruit Co.' M40 grey - 07	6	8
WR1-54	as above - 99	10	15
WR2-08	as above Dapol chassis - 98	8	10
B263	'Tropical Fruit Co.' M45 grey - 10	7	9
B862	'Tropical Fruit Co.' M45 grey - 11	7	9
-	'Ushers Ales' 83 buff Sp Edn 162 (Wessex Wagons) - 11	9	12
-	'Walmer Brewery' 6 yellow Sp Edn 154 (Burnham & District MRC) - 11	8	10
-	'Whiteways Cyder Co.' 31 cream Sp Edn (Wessex Wagons) - 08	8	10

Railway Companies

Code	Description		
-	**GN** (Irish) 2229 grey Sp Edn 155 (Provincial Wagons) - 07	7	9
B357	**NE** 158677 light grey - 01	7	9
4F016001	**NE** 158677 light grey - 12	7	9
4F016002	**NE** 158677 light grey W - 12	7	10
B326	**SR** 41536 dark brown, dark grey roof - 01	8	10
B326	**SR** 41536 dark brown, light grey roof, box marked 'Ventilated Van' - 01	7	9
B325	**SR** 41535? dark brown - 07	7	9

Dapol 00

LNER banana van [W44] (Hattons)

B373	BR B784879 brown - 02	7	9
B373A	BR B784870 brown - 02	7	9
B385	BR B753479 grey - not made	NA	NA
B385	BR B753498 grey - 02	7	9
B385A	BR B753487 grey - 02	7	9

Ireland

-	CIE 2017 brown Sp Edn (Marks Models) - 08	7	9
-	CIE 2017 brown W Sp Edn (Marks Models) - 08	7	9

W45a. BR Ventilated Van (ex-HD/Wrenn) (1995)

This van is very like the Dapol single vent planked van (below) but has no bolt protruding downwards from the point where the doors join. It joined the Hornby Dublo catalogue in 1958 and was also used as their packing van to go with the large rail crane. It was an early model acquired by Wrenn and rereleased in 1968. Dapol took over the tooling in 1993.

A11	unfinished grey - 02	5	10
A004	unfinished grey - 04	5	10

Private Owner

-	'Albion Dockyard' 11 black Sp Edn 75 (Medway Queen Preservation Society) - 11	8	11
-	'Albion Dockyard' 11 dark green Sp Edn 150 (Medway Queen Preservation Society) - 11	8	11
-	'Ales from the Isle of Malts' 1 cream Sp Edn (Japan Model Railways) - 11	10	15
-	'Anglo Bavarian Brewery' 12 dark blue Sp Edn 275 (Wessex Wagons) - 07	7	10
-	'Budden & Briggs Brewery' 1 grey Sp Edn (Wessex Wagons) - 12	10	12
WECC11	'Camerons' B757051 white Sp Edn (Wrenn Railways Collectors Club) - 03	10	12
B613	'Carricks' 181 grey - 05	7	9
-	'The Cheddar Valley Brewery Co.' 11 cream Sp Edn 176 (Burnham & District MRC) - 12	8	10
-	'Culm Valley Dairy Company' 5 cream Sp Edn 180 (Burnham & District MRC) - 12	8	10
-	'Dee Valley Eggs' 1 brown Sp Edn 111 (Llangollen Railway) - 08	7	9
-	'Fremlin Bros.' 1 white, grey roof Sp Edn 1000 (Ballards) - 02	6	8
-	'Fremlin Bros.' 2 white Sp Edn 1000 (Ballards) - 09	8	11
-	'Hall & Woodhouse' 7 white Sp Edn 150 (Burnham & District MRC) - 12	8	11
-	'C&T Harris (Caine)' 8 ochre Sp Edn 174 (Burnham & District MRC) - 10	8	10
-	'HM Dockyard Plymouth' 11 blue Sp Edn 162 (Wessex Wagons) - 09	9	11
B317	'ICI Salt' 2653 red - 00	8	10
-	'Islay Ales' 1 cream Sp Edn (Japan Model Railways) - 11	8	10
-	'Wm. Lee, Son & Co.' 78 black Sp Edn 159 (Wessex Wagons) - 12	9	12

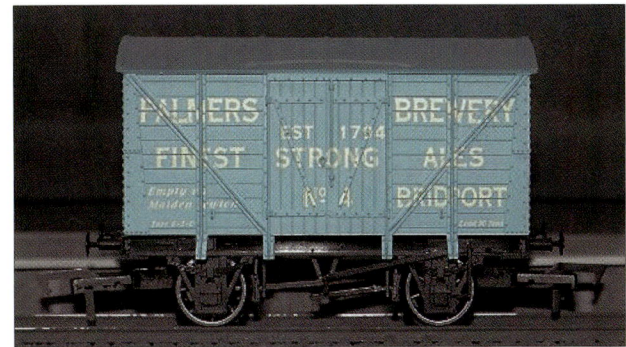

B182	BR 'Jaffa' B881902 grey - c95	12	15
B379	BR 'Jaffa' B881902 grey - 02	7	9
W5105	BR 'Jaffa' B881867 orange Sp Edn (Wrenn Railways Collectors Club - WRCC6) - 02	20	30
WRCC9	BR 'Jaffa' B881867 lemon yellow Sp Edn 100 (Wrenn Railways Collectors Club -) - 02	20	30
B180	BR 'Fyffes' B881687 brown - 89	10	15
B381	BR 'Fyffes' B881620 brown - 02	7	9
B381	BR 'Fyffes' B881967 brown - 02	7	9
B721	BR 'Fyffes' B881804 brown - 08	6	8
B264	BR 'Fyffes' B881867 yellow (also B263) - c95	12	15
WR1-27	as above - 99	12	15
B511	BR 'Fyffes' 881902 yellow - 02	7	9
WR3-18	BR 'Fyffes' 881902 yellow - 00	8	10
B754	BR 'Fyffes' B861846 yellow - 09	7	9
4F016001	BR 'Fyffes' B881933 brown - 12	7	9
4F016002	BR 'Fyffes' B881933 brown W - 12	7	10
4F016100	BR 'Fyffes' B240745 yellow - 12	7	9
4F016101	BR 'Fyffes' B240745 yellow - 12	7	10
B204	BR 'Geest' B881902 grey - 94	10	15
WR1-28	as above - 99	10	50
B512	BR 'Geest' B881967 grey - 02	8	10
WR3-19	BR 'Geest' B881967 grey - 00	8	10
W5007A	BR 'Geest' B881902 black (body only) Sp Edn 135 (Wrenn Railways Collectors Club - WRCC2) - 00	20	30
W5007A	BR 'Geest' B881902 dark grey (body only) SP Edn 115 (Wrenn Railways Collectors Club - WRCC3) - 00	20	30
B561	BR 'Geest' B881632 brown - 04	7	9
-	BR 'Lec' B881904 white Sp Edn 100 (Richard Essen) - 12	9	12
B178	BR B881902 brown Banana - ?	10	15
WR1-18	BR B881902 brown - 99	10	35
B345	BR B881802 brown Banana - 01	6	8

BR yellow spot banana van [W44] (Hattons)

B345	BR B881632 brown Banana - 01	7	9
B345A	BR B881900 brown Banana * - 09	7	9
B345AW	BR B881900 brown W Banana * - 09	7	10
4F016003	BR B881905 brown Banana - 13	7	9
4F016004	BR B881905 brown Banana W - 13	7	9
B561	BR B882117 brown Geest - 03	7	9
B711	BR B882128 brown Geest - 07	6	8

BR vent van [W45a] (Dapol)

-	'John Norton & Son' 9 * dark green Sp Edn 194 (Hythe Kent Models) 1st issue - 01	10	12
-	'The Norton Mills Company' 6 dark green Sp Edn 160 (Burnham & District MRC) - 10	8	10
-	'Palmers Brewery' 4 pale blue Sp Edn 264 (Buffers) - 10	8	11
-	'PSTO(N) Portland' 373 dark grey Sp Edn 154 (Wessex Wagons) - 12	10	12

8th Edition

Dapol 00

WRCC12	'Rebellion Beer Co. 1993 The Marlow Brewery' white Sp Edn 100 (Wrenn Railway Collectors Club) - 03	30	45
WR2-03	'Robertson's' B757051 brown - 98	10	15
-	'Rother Valley Brewery' 49225 dark green Sp Edn 198 (Hythe Kent Models) - 02	10	12
-	'Rother Valley Brewery' 49225 dark green Sp Edn 113 (Hythe Kent Models) - 03	9	11
-	'Royal Navy Stores' * dark blue Sp Edn 200 (Hythe Kent Models) - 04	7	9
-	'Shepherd Neame' 3 cream Sp Edn 400 (East Kent MRS) - 02	9	11
-	'SNSO' 419 navy blue Sp Edn 240 (Wessex Wagons) - 10	7	10
-	'A&R Sommerville & Co.' 4 pale brown Sp Edn 156 (Burnham & District MRC) - 11	8	10
-	'Style & Winch' 6 yellow Sp Edn 143 (Burnham & District MRC) - 12	8	11
-	'John Symons & Co.' 6 ochre Sp Edn 150 (Buffers) - 12	8	11
-	'Tamplin & Sons' 6 ochre Sp Edn 154 (Burnham & District MRC) - 12	8	11
-	'Th. Tolchard & Son' 19 blue Sp Edn 161 (Wessex Wagons) - 12	10	12
-	'Vickery's Pure Cider' 5 buff Sp Edn 147 (Burnham & District MRC) - 09	8	10
No.84A	'Wensleydale Creamery' 1984 cream Sp Edn 82 (West Wales Wagon Works) - 09	7	10
No.84A	'Wensleydale Creamery' 1984 cream W Sp Edn 79 (West Wales Wagon Works) - 09	8	11
No.84B	'Wensleydale Creamery' 1989 cream Sp Edn 85 (West Wales Wagon Works) - 09	7	10
No.84B	'Wensleydale Creamery' 1989 cream W Sp Edn 853 (West Wales Wagon Works) - 09	8	11
No.84C	'Wensleydale Creamery' 1982 cream Sp Edn 85 (West Wales Wagon Works) - 09	7	10
No.84C	'Wensleydale Creamery' 1982 cream W Sp Edn 84 (West Wales Wagon Works) - 09	8	11
No.84D	'Wensleydale Creamery' 1997 cream Sp Edn 85 (West Wales Wagon Works) - 09	7	10
No.84D	'Wensleydale Creamery' 1997 cream W Sp Edn 84 (West Wales Wagon Works) - 09	8	11
Commemoratives			
D001	'CLA Game Fair' green Sp Edn 137 (TMC) - 03	9	11
-	'Great Western Society' dark brown Sp Edn (Great Western Society) - 06	8	10
-	'Mevagissey Model Railway' 20061 dark red Sp Edn (Mevagissey Models) - 06	8	10
D002	'TMC 5th Anniversary' blue Sp Edn 173 (The Model Centre) - 03	9	11
Railway Company			
-	'MHR' S2009 light grey Sp Edn 96 (Mid Hants Railway) - 09	7	9
-	'Nene Valley Railway' 402 grey Sp Edn (Nene Valley Railway) - 09	7	9
-	NYMR NE133971 dark grey Sp Edn 200 (North Yorkshire Moors Railway) - 01, 04, 05	8	10
-	IWCR 297 light grey Sp Edn 175 (Wessex Wagons) - 08	7	9
-	S&DJR 756 grey road van Sp Edn (Wessex Wagons) - 09	9	11
No.50	GW 2356 dark brown Sp Edn 150 (West Wales Wagon Works - 07	6	8
B532	GW 95444 grey Steam Banana - 03	8	10
4F12003	GWR 123507 dark grey - 13	7	9
4F12004	GWR 123507 dark grey W - 13	8	10
B339	LMS 511840 light grey - 01	4	6
B339	LMS 59673 red - ?	10	12
WR1-39	as above - 99	10	15
WR2-05	as above but Dapol chassis - 98	9	11
B235	SR 41596 dark brown - c95	10	15
WR1-61	as above - 99	10	15
WR2-09	as above Dapol chassis - 98	8	10
WR1-35	BR 57 brown - 99	25	30
WR1-22	BR B545523 brown - 99	10	35
WR1-34	BR W145207 grey - 99	25	30

S+DJR road van [W45a] (Dapol)

B389	BR B753889 grey - 02	7	9
B389A	BR B753896 grey - 02	7	9
B391	BR B760561 brown - 02	7	9
B391A	BR B760579 brown - 02	7	9
4F12001	BR B768103 brown - 12	7	9
4F12002	BR B768103 brown W - 12	8	10
Ireland			
-	CIE 315 pale grey Sp Edn (Mark's Models) - 02	10	12

* These were individually numbered by Hythe Models.

W45b. BR 12T Planked Single Vent Van (1984)

This model was designed and tooled by Dapol. It has one vent each end and has angled braces on the doors. The corner irons are also tapered and it differs from the HD/Wrenn vent van in having a bolt protruding downwards from the point where the doors join.

A11	? - unfinished - 98	5	10
B16	BR M501085 grey - 84	9	11
B109	BR B760563 red brown - 88	8	10
B110	BR B753894 grey - 89	9	11

W46. BR 12T Plywood Single Vent Van (1986)

This wagon was designed and tooled by Dapol. It has no plank effect on the sides but has vents in the ends. It also has a raised data panel near the bottom left hand corner of the sides.

A10	unfinished brown or grey - 95	5	10
Commemoratives			
-	'Cathcart Railway Exhib.' 1968-1992 brown Sp Edn (Cathcart MRS) - 92	12	14
-	'Crewe Heritage Centre' grey Sp Edn (Crewe Centre Models) - ?	10	15
Railway Company			
-	North Norfolk Raiway brown Sp Edn (NNR) - ?	8	10
B204	BR 'Geest' B881902 grey - 94	10	15
B102	BR B784873 red-brown, also ex set B404 - 86	8	10
B108	BR B753498 grey - 89	9	11

W47. BR 10T Quad Vent Meat Van (1985)

The model was designed by Dapol and was modelled on 100 vans built by British Railways at Wolverton Works in 1952. These were built despite there being adequate meat containers already in use. The van was a standard design with planked sides and corrugated steel end walls. The latter each had four large ventilators and there were smaller vents in the sides. In 1996, Hornby bought the tooling from Dapol, but had problems with it and only two versions were made by them.

A14	red - unfinished - 98	6	10
B102	LMS 173127 brown - ?	10	12
B26	BR B870074 red also ex-set B402 - 85	8	10
B180	BR B670006 red-brown - 89	9	11

W48a. BR 'Blue Spot' Fish Van (ex-HD/Wrenn) (c1995)

These were built in the early 1950s to transport fish from the East Coast ports and whole trains of 'Blue Spot' vans would be seen hauled by 9Fs and 'Britannias'. Many were later converted to parcels vans (SPVs) and painted blue. These were in use until the 1980s.

The van was introduced to the Hornby Dublo range in 1961 and was in the first batch of models sold to G&R Wrenn. In Dapol's ownership, these were originally sold as 'WR3' stock, but were absorbed from the Wrenn range when G&R Wrenn was sold to Mordvale in 2001.

Private Owner			
WR3-12	'Findus' E87232 white - 00	8	10
B257	'North Sea Fish' E67840 blue - c95	10	15

Dapol 00

B509	'North Sea Fish' E87642 white - 02		7	9
WR3-11	'North Sea Fish' E87642 white - 00		8	10

Virgin Trains promotional van {W48a}

B258	'Ross' white - c95		10	15
WR3-13	'Ross' E87234 white - 00		8	10

Commemoratives

-	'Virgin Trains' red + silver Sp Edn 500 (Virgin for Crewe Open Day) - 03		9	11
-	'York Model Railway' 2002 light blue Sp Edn 100 (YMR) - 02		10	12
-	as above but numbered 2003 - 03		9	11
-	as above but numbered 2004 - 04		9	11

Railway Company

B256	BR E87231 white Insulfish - c95		10	12
B507	BR E87234 white Blue Spot - 02, 07		6	8
WR3-09	BR E87232 white Blue Spot - 99		8	10
-	BR(SR) * white LNER design Insulfish Sp Edn 61 (Oliver Leetham) - 05		8	10
B538	BR E87488 light blue Insulvan - 03		7	9
-	BR E87464 ice blue with black lettering Sp Edn 70 (O.Leetham) - 02		11	13
-	BR E87464 ice blue with white lettering Sp Edn 70 (O.Leetham) - 02		11	13
B259	BRe E87003 blue Red Star - c95		15	18
B508	BRe E87160 blue Red Star - 02		8	10
WR3-10	BRe E87537 blue Red Star - 99		8	10
WR3-10	BRe E87160 blue Red Star - 99		8	10
B262	BRe E87003 blue Exp. Parcels - c95		15	18
B506	BRe E87160 blue Exp. Parcels - 02		8	10
WR3-08	BRe E87537 blue Exp. Parcels - 99		8	10
B533	BRe E88005 blue Exp Parcels NRV - 03		7	9
-	BR 041317 blue Express Parcels Sp Edn 110 (Alexandra Models) - 07		9	12
SBB6	BRe E88005 blue W Express Parcels Sp Edn 300 (Signal Box) - 09		8	11
B537	BR E75575 brown 'Van Fit' - 03		7	9
B564	BR DE75575 brown 'Van Fit' ballast cleaner van - 03		7	9
B260	BRe E67840 beige BRT - c95		10	15
WR1-06	as above - 98		10	20
WR3-14	BRe E87539 ochre BRT - 00		8	10
-	BRe ADB975419 red Barrowhill Depot Tool Van Sp Edn 90 (O.Leetham) - 01		11	13
B704	BRe ADB975424 red (Barrowhill Depot MPD tool van) - 07		6	8
-	BR ADB975418 yellow (Shirebrook Depot) Sp Edn 120 (O.Leetham) - 01		11	13
B695	BR ADB975436 yellow (Shirebrook Depot packing van) - 07		6	8
-	BR M87793 red-brown RBV barrier wagon Sp Edn 93 (O.Leetham) - 02		11	13
-	9 of above had unique numbers** applied by Oliver Leetham - 04?		10	12
-	3 of above but solebars and bufferbeams brown + brake handle white Sp Edn - 04?		13	15
-	BRe ADE75415 rail blue boiler van Sp Edn 59 (Oliver Leetham) - 05		9	11
-	BR ADB975329 red ZQV Frodingham Tool Van Sp Edn 134 (Oliver Leetham) - 05		8	10
B773	BR ADB975324 red with wasp stripes on ends ZQV Frodingham Packing Van - 09		8	10
-	BR ADB975350 yellow Immingham tool van Sp Edn 107 (O.Leetham) - 05		8	10

Frodingham packing van [W48a] (Dapol)

B769	BR ADB975356 yellow Immingham Tool Van - 09		8	10
-	BR ADW87706 yellow (Shirebrook Depot) tool van Sp Edn 91 (Oliver Leetham) - 05		8	10

* Each wagon had a different running number in the E75xxx series. The first four digits were put on by Dapol and the rest by Oliver Leetham. ** These were M87707/34/52/59/6 3/75/76/77/90 also shown on modified certificates.

W48b.   BR 'Blue Spot' Fish Van   (2013)

This is a completely retooled model.

4F019000	BR E87221 white - 13		10	13
4F019001	BR E87221 white W - 13		10	14
4F019002	BR E87242 white - 13		10	13
4F019003	BR E87242 white W - 13		10	14
4F019004	BR E87009 white - 13		10	13
4F019005	BR E87009 white W - 13		10	14
4F019006	BR E87324 white - 13		10	13
4F019007	BR E87324 white W - 13		10	14
4F019008	BR Express Parcels E87007 blue - 13		10	13
4F019009	BR Express Parcels E87007 blue W - 13		10	14
4F019010	BR ADB9753538 yellow Immingham tool van - 13		10	13
4F019011	BR ADB9753538 yellow W Immingham tool van - 13		10	14

Brake Vans

W49a.   GWR 20T Goods Brake Van (ex-Airfix) (1985)

Like so much on the GWR, the 'Toad' brake van changed very little in appearance over time. It had a veranda at only one end and no side duckets. The 'Toads' had mostly restricted use ('RU' painted on their sides) and generally carried the name of the yard to which they allocated.

This model was introduced by Airfix in 1977 and passed to Palitoy, who already had a similar model in their Mainline range and so did not use the tooling. It passed to Dapol in 1985 along with left-over Airfix stock. Three GWR versions were produced by Dapol. The tooling was sold to Hornby in 1996 and the model reintroduced by them.

B104	GW 56835 grey 'Rhymney' - 87		9	11
B105	GW 114925 grey 'Saltney' - 86, 98		8	10
B117	GW 68796 dark grey 'Park Royal' - 88		9	11
B33	BR 114926 grey (A) also - 85		8	12

W49b.   GWR 20T Brake Van (ex-Mainline) (1985)

Besides acquiring the Airfix tooling and unsold Airfix stock, in 1985 Dapol also received the remnant stock of the Mainline GWR brake van, which was made from tooling developed by Kader and used by Mainline, which was later used by Bachmann.

B34	BR W68855 light grey (M) - 85		8	12
B35	BR W68816 red-brown (M) - ?		8	12

W50a.   LMS 20T Goods Brake Van (ex-HD/Wrenn) (1984)

The model was based on a design built at Derby between 1935 and 1941 and was the final style of LMS brake van.

The Hornby Dublo model was released in 1958 and the tooling was in the first batch of models that Meccano Ltd sold to G&R Wrenn. Listed here are the models that Dapol produced from the tools.

B2	LMS 730670 red-brown - 84		10	12
B2	LMS 730973 red-brown - 84		10	12
WR1-46	as above - 99		10	15

W50b.   LMS 20T Brake Van (ex-Airfix) (1984)

The body was typical of brake vans built at Derby in the 1930s. In 1981 the model, which had its own chassis, passed to Palitoy and they made a few of them in 1984. Dapol received the tooling in 1985, having already received unsold Airfix stock, and used the

Dapol 00

tools for their own brake vans. Today it is the LMS brake van in Hornby's range.

B123	**LMS** 730097 grey (A) - *92*	4	8
B5	**BR** M730836 grey - *84*	9	11
B5	**BR** M? grey - *97*	9	11
B127	**BR** B950016 brown + yellow (A) - *92*	8	13
B185	**BR** M732148 red-brown - *94*	9	11

W51a.   Short Brake Van (ex-Mainline) (1985)

This is a typical LNER cabin, mounted on a short wheelbase, and is thought to be based on an LNER 'Toad E', which dated from the mid-1930s. The same body was sometimes mounted on the longer chassis to give a smoother ride on long goods trains. It had a veranda at both ends and pressed steel duckets on both sides.

The model was released by Palitoy in 1975, in their first batch of models and the stock of unsold models was bought by Dapol in 1985 and added to their catalogue that year.

B37	**NE** 182030 red-brown (M) - *85*	9	11
B31	**BR** E168064 grey (M) - *85*	8	12

W51b.   BR Short Brake Van (ex-HD/Wrenn) (c1995)

Meccano Ltd had used a red BR brake van body on a short plastic chassis for the Hornby Dublo starter train sets that it produced near the end of production and Wrenn had produced a grey version from the same tooling. The Dapol version used the same body but on a diecast chassis.

B31	**NE** 128105 grey - *c95*	10	18
WR1-02	as above - *97*	10	18

W52a.   LNER/BR Goods Brake Van (ex-Mainline) (1985)

Having produced the short LNER 'Toad E' in 1975, Palitoy produced the long wheelbase version the following year. The tooling belonged to Kader and so was not acquired by Dapol in 1985, however, the unsold stock was bought by them.

B30	**BR** B951480 dark brown (M) - *85*	8	12
B36	**BR** B950880 grey (M) - *85*	8	12

W52b.   LNER/BR Goods Brake Van (ex-HD/Wrenn) (c1995)

The BR standard brake van was based on the LNER standard 'Toad E' design with the long wheelbase. This had a small cabin, which was placed centrally on a long chassis with a veranda at each end of the cabin. This left a clear platform at each end of the vehicle. There were also pressed steel duckets in the side of the cabin. This had a diecast chassis and had initially been released in the Hornby Dublo range in 1959.

B206	**SR** 32831 dark brown - *c95*	10	18
WR1-01	as above - *97*	10	18
B30	**BR** B950350 red-brown - *c95*	10	18
B36	**BR** B932103 grey - *c95*	15	20
WR1-47	as above - *99*	15	40

Bogie Flat & Container Wagons

W53.   GWR 'Macaw H' Bogie Bolster (ex-Airfix) (1986)

The 20 ton 'Macaw H' was smaller than the standard 'Macaw B' which was more widely used. It was built in the late 1930s and, when taken over by British Railways in 1948, the wagons were recoded as 'Bogie Bolster A'.

The model was released by Airfix in 1981 and immediately afterwards, Airfix went into receivership. The tooling passed to Palitoy and then to Dapol, along with the unsold Airfix and Mainline stock. The latter were probably the same model but some were in Airfix boxes and some in Mainline ones. The tooling was sold to Hornby in 1996 and the model reintroduced by them. Airfix sold the models two in a box but they were sold singly in the Mainline range.

A12	unfinished grey - *98*	5	10
A12	unfinished black (in early grey box) - *?*	5	10
B88	**BR** W107364 grey (A) * - *86*	9	22

* Possibly in Mainline boxes.

W54.   GWR 'Macaw B' Bogie Bolster (ex-Mainline) (1985)

As we saw above, the 'Macaw B' was a more common bogie bolster wagon on the GWR and BR versions based on it were classified as 'Bogie Bolster C'. These were longer than the 'Macaw H' and had been built in the early years of the last century.

The mainline model had been released in 1980. Dapol sold only Mainline residue stock as they did not have access to the tooling.

B125	**GW** 107291 dark grey Macaw B (M) - *90*	8	10
B75	**BR** W84921 grey + girder (M) - *85*	8	12

W55.   BBA Bogie Steel Wagon (2013)

Designed at BR Shildon and built at BR Ashford between 1973 and 1981, the BBA was a development of the BAA wagon. 550 were built and were mainly seen in steel production areas. They usually operated in blocks of ten and carried various liveries during their lives. In later years, when no longer required for their original use, they were converted for other uses.

This is a new model which had not been released at the time of writing.

4F042001	**BR** 910414 Railfreight red - *13*	NPG	NPG
4F042002	**BR** 910008 Railfreight red - *13*	NPG	NPG
4F042003	**BR** 910023 Railfreight red - *13*	NPG	NPG
4F042004	**BR** 910106 Railfreight red - *13*	NPG	NPG

W56.   GWR 'Crocodile H' Wagon (ex-Mainline) (1985)

The GWR used the code name 'Crocodile' for its trolley wagons and had a range of different designs, each identified by a letter suffix and some dating back to the start of the last century. The 'Crocodile H' dates from the 1920s and seems to have been small in number. The wagon type became a 'Weltrol WH' in BR days and the floor was strengthened to increase its capacity from 45T to 65T. No new ones were built by British Railways.

The Mainline model was released in 1980 and with the boiler load in 1981. Dapol received the residue stock in 1985, following the closedown of Palitoy production.

B74	**GW** 41973 dark grey Crocodile H + marine boiler (M) - *85*	10	14

W57a.   FEA-B Spine Wagon (2008)

This was a French built design with a low floor for high capacity containers and swap-bodies.

Containers are available separately. The models have been sold in pairs and with a close-coupling system and a diecast deck for a low centre of gravity. Only 250 of each pair of numbers are produced. They come with a pack of add-on detail.

Railway Company			
-	**Fastline** Freight ? + ? grey Sp Edn (Rail Express Modeller magazine) - *09*	20	25
B853	**Freightliner** 640101 + 640102 green FEA-B - *10*	16	20
B854	**Freightliner** 640103 + 640104 green FEA-B - *10*	16	20
B724A	**Freightliner** 640121 + 640122 green - *08*	16	20
B724B	**Freightliner** 640209 + 640210 green - *08*	16	20
B724C	**Freightliner** 640213 + 640214 green - *09*	16	20
B724D	**Freightliner** 640353 + 640354 green - *09*	16	20

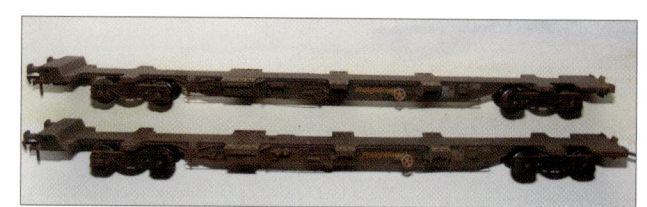

FEA-B spine wagon [W57a] (Dapol)

B724E	**Freightliner** ? + ? green - *09*	16	20
B724F	**Freightliner** ? + ? green - *09*	16	20
B724M	**Freightliner** 640709 + 640710 dark green - *09*	20	25
B724N	**Freightliner** 640499 + 640500 dark green - *09*	20	25
-	**Freightliner** 640351 + 640352 olive green W Sp Edn 250 (Trainlines) - *08*	18	23
B724P	**Freightliner** 640707 + 640708 green - *11*	16	20
B724Q	**Freightliner** 640721 + 640722 green - *11*	16	20
B724R	**Freightliner** 640719 + 640720 green - *11*	16	20
B724S	**Freightliner** 6401011+ 640012 green - *11*	16	20
B913C	**Freightliner** ? + ? - *11*	16	20
B193D	**Freightliner** ? + ? - *11*	16	20
B740A	**GBRf** 640603 + 640604 blue - *08*	15	19
B740B	**GBRf** 640619 + 640620 blue - *08*	15	19
B740C	**GBRf** ? + ? blue - *08*	15	19
B740D	**GBRf** 640601 + 640602 blue - *08*	15	19
B900A	**Balfour Beatty** 640511+640512 ? - *11*	16	20

W57b.   FEA-B Spine Wagon + Containers (2012)

This wagon is a French design with a low floor for high capacity containers and swap-bodies. Built in Poland by Wagony Swidinica, they were Introduced to the British rail network in 2003. FEA-B is one of seven FEA designs and the body has a central spine with out-riggers branching off it. The out-riggers carry the 'twistlock' container fixings. The FEA-Bs are semi-permanently joined in 301 pairs with a bar and usually have consecutive running numbers. The main user has been Railfreight, although Balfour Beatty had some for infrastructure work. Some used by Jarvis Fastline are now with DRS.

Containers are available separately. The models are sold in pairs and with a close-coupling system and a diecast deck for a low centre of gravity. Only 250 of each pair of numbers are produced. They come with a pack of additional detail for the purchaser to fit.

Private Owner			
B913A	**GBRf** 640623+ 640624 dark blue + **'C&CL'** (40ft) PGRU913161[7] red-brown + **'GE Seaco'**		

Dapol 00

	(20ft) GESU332867[8] dark blue + **'ZIM'** (40ft) ZCSU838467[-] orange-brown + **'CMA CGM'** (20ft) CAMU020896[1] dark blue - *12*	NA	35

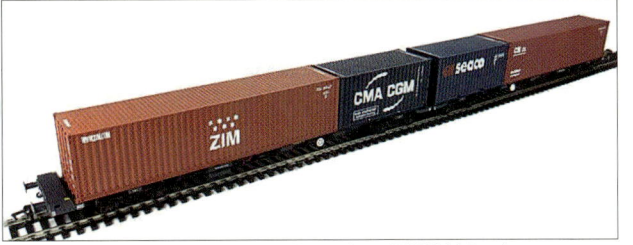

FEA-B spine wagon with containers [W57b] (Hattons)

B913B	**GBRf** 640627+640628 dark blue + **'C&CL'** (40ft) PGRU913161[7] red-brown + **'GE Seaco'** (20ft) GESU332867[8] dark blue + **'ZIM'** (40ft) ZCSU838467[-] orange-brown + **'CMA CGM'** (20ft) CAMU020896[1] dark blue - *12*	NA	35
B913C	**Freightliner** 640163+640164 green + **'C&CL'** (40ft) PGRU913161[7] red-brown + **'GE Seaco'** (20ft) GESU332867[8] dark blue + **'ZIM'** (40ft) ZCSU838467[-] orange-brown + **'CMA CGM'** (20ft) CAMU020896[1] dark blue - *12*	NA	35
B913D	**Freightliner** 640313+640314 + **'C&CL'** (40ft) PGRU913161[7] red-brown + **'GE Seaco'** (20ft) GESU332867[8] dark blue + **'ZIM'** (40ft) ZCSU838467[-] orange-brown + **'CMA CGM'** (20ft) CAMU020896[1] dark blue - *12*	NA	35
4F044001	**Freightliner** 640707+640708 + containers - *13*	NA	35
4F044002	**Freightliner** 640721+640722 + containers - *13*	NA	35
4F044003	**Freightliner** 640719+640720 + containers - *13*	NA	35
4F044004	**Freightliner** 640011+640012 + containers - *13*	NA	35

W58. FIA 'Megafret' Intermodal Twin Flat (2010)

Built by Arbel Fauvet in France in the 1990s, these operate in pairs, joined together with a bar coupling and treated as a single wagon with one running number. Effectively it is an articulated flat wagon for carrying containers. The official term is an 'Intermodal Twin Container Flat'. Some have been fitted with a frame to carry steel.

The model has a diecast body to lower the centre of gravity when carrying containers and NEM coupling pockets with self-centring couplings.

	Private Owner		
B782A	**Crawshay Brothers** 33 68 4943 179 light blue - *11*	20	25
B782B	as above 33 68 4943 083 light blue - *11*	20	25
B782C	as above 33 68 4943 059 light blue - *11*	20	25
B782D	as above 33 68 4943 091 light blue - *11*	20	25
B782E	as above 33 68 4943 094 black Ltd Edn (Dapol shop) - *11*	22	28
B782F	as above 33 68 4943 088 black Ltd Edn (Dapol shop) - *11*	22	28
	Railway Company		
	EWS 33 70 4938 ??? Sp Edn (Trainlines) - *10*	NPG	NPG

W59. IKA 'Megafret' Intermodal Low Platform Flat (2010)

Built by Arbel Fauvet in France, these were designed to carry containers on UK W9 loading gauge track, including 9ft 6ins high containers, which were becoming increasingly common. The first batch ordered by Freightliner arrived in 2001 and subsequently batches were received by EWS and DRS. Height is reduced by the use of small wheels and they are permanently coupled together in pairs and share a running number. The design is officially known as an 'Intermodal Low Platform Flat'. Some are adapted to carry vehicles.

The model has a diecast body to lower the centre of gravity when carrying containers and NEM coupling pockets with self-centring couplings.

-	**'Stobart Rail/AAE'** 33 68 4943 076-8 light blue + container TESU450011[0] dark blue	15	NA
-	**'Stobart Rail/AAE'** 33 68 4943 076-9 light blue + container TESU450031[5] dark blue	15	NA
B909A	above 2 wagons and containers - *?*	NA	35
-	**'Stobart Rail/AAE'** 33 68 4943 055-1 light blue + container TESU450077[9] dark blue	15	NA
-	**'Stobart Rail/AAE'** 33 68 4943 055-6 light blue + container TESU450022[8] dark blue	15	NA
B909B	above 2 wagons and containers - *?*	NA	35

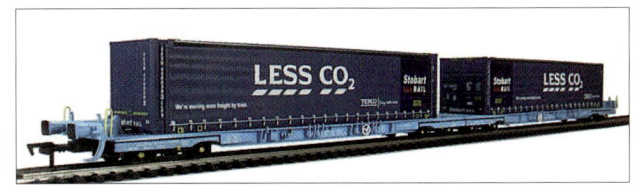

IKA 'Megafret' with containers [W59] (Hattons)

-	**'Stobart Rail/AAE'** 33 68 4943 061-? light blue + container TESU450043[9] dark blue	15	NA
-	**'Stobart Rail/AAE'** 33 68 4943 061-? light blue + container TESU450056[8] dark blue	15	NA
B909C	above 2 wagons and containers - *?*	NA	35
-	**'Stobart Rail/AAE'** 33 68 4943 0??-? light blue + container TESU4500??[?] dark blue	15	NA
-	**'Stobart Rail/AAE'** 33 68 4943 0??-? light blue + container TESU4500??[?] dark blue	15	NA
B909D	above 2 wagons and containers - *?*	NA	35
-	**'Stobart Rail/AAE'** 33 68 4943 0??-? light blue + container TESU4500??[?] dark blue	15	NA
-	**'Stobart Rail/AAE'** 33 68 4943 0??-? light blue + container TESU4500??[?] dark blue	15	NA
B909E	above 2 wagons and containers - *12*	NA	35
-	**'Stobart Rail/AAE'** 33 68 4943 0??-? light blue + container TESU4500??[?] dark blue	15	NA
-	**'Stobart Rail/AAE'** 33 68 4943 0??-? light blue + container TESU4500??[?] dark blue	15	NA
B909F	above 2 wagons and containers - *12*	NA	35
-	**'Stobart Rail/AAE'** 33 68 4943 0??-? light blue W + 45ft 'High Cube' container TESU4500??[?] dark blue W	15	NA
-	**'Stobart Rail/AAE'** 33 68 4943 0??-? light blue W + 45ft 'High Cube' container TESU4500??[?] dark blue W	15	NA
4F046001	above 2 weathered wagons and containers - *13*	NA	35

W60. KTA/KQA 'Pocket' Wagon (2010)

With the increase in the use of 9'6" ('High Cube') containers during the 1990s, there was a problem in transporting them in the UK due to the tighter loading gauge. Tiphook Rail produced a wagon with a low lattice platform between the bogies and the structure was strengthened with slab steel sides. 75 of the wagons were built by Rautaruuki in Finland, in two batches, and came into operation in 1997.

The model features close coupling, NEM coupling pockets, profile wheels, weighting to lower the centre of gravity and etched steel parts. It is a modern Intermodal wagon which carries a 40ft container.

KTA 'Pocket' wagon and container [W60] (Hattons)

	Private Owner		
B779A	**GERRS** 97705 blue - *11*	20	25
B779B	**GERRS** 97716 blue - *11*	20	25
B779C	**GERRS** 97721 blue - *11*	20	25
B779D	**GERRS** 97771 blue - *11*	20	25
B910A	**GERRS** 97771 blue + **'Cosco'** 40ft container CBHU822427[2] grey - *11*	22	28
B910B	**GERRS** 97762 blue + **'Florens'** 40ft container FSCU912108[6] red-brown - *11*	22	28
B779B	**Tiphook Rail** 84 70 4907 019-9 - *10*	22	28
B779C	**Tiphook Rail** 84 70 4907 015-3 - *10*	20	25
B779D	**Tiphook Rail** 84 70 4907 070-3 - *10*	22	28
B779A	**Tiphook Rail** 84 70 4907 017-4 - *10*	20	25
B779E	**Tiphook Rail** 84 70 4907 ?-? - *11*	22	28
B779F	**Tiphook Rail** 84 70 4907 ?-? - *11*	22	28
B779sh1	**Tiphook Rail** ? blue W - *10*	20	25
B779sh2	**Tiphook Rail** 84 70 4807 061-5 dark grey W - *10*	20	25

Dapol 00

B779sh3	**Tiphook Rail** 84 70 4807 023-7 dark grey W - *10*	20	25	
B779sh4	**Tiphook Rail** 84 70 4807 052-2 dark grey W - *10*	20	25	

W61a. 20ft Containers (2009)
Only 250 of each number are produced.

-	**'EWL'** EWLU230196 light blue	4	NA	
-	**'Hanjin'** HJCU829660 blue	4	NA	
-	**'MSC'** GLDU222133 buff	4	NA	
-	**'Triton'** TTNU150118 brown	4	NA	
B776A	above 4 containers - *09*	NA	18	
-	**'China Shipping'** CCLU237754 green	4	NA	
-	(unbranded) NPCU700741 brown	4	NA	
-	**'Hanjin'** HJCU829620 blue	4	NA	
-	**'Water Front'** WFCL1247165	4	NA	
B776B	above 4 containers - *09*	NA	18	
-	**'MSC'** GLDU505229[2] red-brown	4	NA	
-	**'Triton'** TRIU398477 brown	4	NA	
B776C?	above 2 containers - *10*	NA	9	
-	**'ZIM'** ZIMU253692	4	NA	
-	**'ZIM'** ZIMU253681	4	NA	
B776D	above 2 containers - *11*	NA	9	
-	**'CMA CGM'** ECMU141481[0]	4	NA	
-	**'CMA CGM'** ECMU142148[2]	4	NA	
B776E	above 2 containers - *11*	NA	9	

W61b. 40ft Containers (2009)
These containers have opening doors and are fully compatible with existing 'Intermodal' wagons.

-	(unbranded) APZU431656 blue	4	NA	
-	**'Evergreen'** EMCU127934 green	4	NA	
-	**'Tiphook'** TPHU577349 dark brown	4	NA	
-	**'UASC'** UACU807236 green	4	NA	
B775A	above 4 containers - *09*	NA	18	
-	**'Genstar'** GSTU836120 red-brown	4	NA	
-	**'Hanjin'** HJCU755528 blue	4	NA	
-	**'Italia'** IMTU109833[0] blue	4	NA	
-	**'MSC'** MSCU422133 cream	4	NA	
B775B	above 4 containers - *09*	NA	18	
-	**'MSC'** MSCU484614 cream	4	NA	
-	**'TEX'** TGHU438578[3] red-brown	4	NA	
B775C	above 2 containers - *10*	NA	10	
-	**'CMA CGM'** ECMU141481[0] dark blue	5	NA	
-	**'Hanjin'** HJCU755545[1] blue	5	NA	
B775D	above 2 containers - *12*	NA	13	
-	**'OOCL'** OOLU755223[0] pale grey	5	NA	
-	**'CMA CGM'** ECMU461430[2]	5	NA	
B775E	above 2 containers - *12*	NA	13	

W62. 40ft Curtain-sided Container (2009)
These containers have not yet been seen.

?	? ? - *09*	NPG	NPG	

W63a. 45ft 'Hi Cube' Containers (2009)
These containers have opening doors and are fully compatible with existing 'Intermodal' wagons.

-	**'Cosco'** CBHU822817[5] grey	4	NA	
-	**'Florens'** FSCU912374[6] red-brown	4	NA	
-	**'MSC'** MSCU994560[0] red-brown	4	NA	
-	(unbranded) TRLU707834[8] red-brown	4	NA	
B780	above 4 containers - *09*	NA	19	

W63b. 45ft 'Hi Cube' Containers (2010)
This table contains models of 9.5ft containers.

B896A	**'CMA & CGM'** FSCU638511[0] red-brown + 'GTS' MUCU002308[0] dark blue - *10*	NA	12	
B896B	**'ECS'** ECBU462709[7] maroon + **'Deanside'** DSCU000762[-] - *10*	NA	12	
B857A	**'Stobart'** TESU450099[5] + TESU450124[5] dark blue twin pack - *10*	NA	12	
B857B	**'Stobart'** TESU450057[3] + TESU450083[0] dark blue twin pack - *10*	NA	12	
B857C	**'Stobart Rail'** TESU450146[1] + TESU450166[7] dark blue blister pack - *10*	NA	12	
B857D	**'Stobart Rail'** TESU450194[1] + TESU450151[7] dark blue blister pack - *10*	NA	12	
B857E	**'Stobart'** TESU450123[3] + TESU450157[0] dark blue twin pack - *11*	NA	12	
B857F	**'Stobart'** TESU450165[1] + TESU450197[0] dark blue twin pack - *11*	NA	12	
B844B	**'ESC'** ECBU453585[3] + ECBU467551[4] maroon twin pack - *12*	NA	12	

Bogie Open Wagons

W64. IOA-E NR Bogie Box Wagon (2010)
This is a wagon used to carry ballast to virtual quarry sites.

Network Rail

IOA-E bogie box wagon [W64] (Hattons)

B856A	NR 3170 5992 002-3 bright yellow - *10*	16	20
B856B	NR 3170 5992 014-8 bright yellow - *10*	16	20
B856C	NR 3170 5992 021-2 bright yellow - *10*	16	20
B856D	NR 3170 5992 026-2 bright yellow - *10*	16	20
B856E	NR 3170 5992 ? bright yellow - *10*	16	20
B856F	NR 3170 5992 ? bright yellow - *10*	16	20
B856G	NR 3170 5992 ? bright yellow - *10*	16	20
B856H	NR 3170 5992 ? bright yellow - *10*	16	20
4F045001	NR 3170 5992 028-4 bright yellow - *13*	16	20
4F045002	NR 3170 5992 041-7 bright yellow - *13*	16	20
4F045003	NR 3170 5992 065-6 bright yellow - *13*	16	20
4F045004	NR 3170 5992 081-3 bright yellow - *13*	16	20

Hatton's Special Editions

B856A	NR 3170 5992 102-1 bright yellow 500 - *10*	16	20
B856AW	NR 3170 5992 030-4 bright yellow W 250 - *10*	16	20
B856B	NR 3170 5992 045-3 bright yellow 500 - *10*	16	20
B856BW	NR 3170 5992 043-7 bright yellow W 250 - *10*	16	20
B856C	NR 3170 5992 077-1 bright yellow 500 - *10*	16	20
B856CW	NR 3170 5992 067-6 bright yellow W 250 - *10*	16	20
B856D	NR 3170 5992 033-3 bright yellow 500 - *10*	16	20
B856DW	NR 3170 5992 083-3 bright yellow W 250 - *10*	16	20

W65. JNA NR 'Falcon' Ballast Wagon (2010)
These wagons are used on engineering work throughout the rail network, carrying ballast and spoil. A total of 555 of them were built by Astro Vagone in Romania. They came into use in 2004 and incorporate a reinforced central door in each side to facilitate cleaning. They operate in rakes of five and are all in Network Rail yellow livery.

Network Rail

B855A	NR MLU29003 bright yellow - *10*	16	20
B855B	NR MLU29012 bright yellow - *10*	16	20
B855C	NR MLU29047 bright yellow - *10*	16	20
B855D	NR MLU29064 bright yellow - *10*	16	20
B855E	NR MLU? bright yellow W Sp Edn 250 (Hattons) - *10*	16	20
B855F	NR MLU? bright yellow W Sp Edn 250 (Hattons) - *10*	16	20
B855G	NR MLU? bright yellow W Sp Edn 250 (Hattons) - *10*	16	20
B855H	NR MLU? bright yellow W Sp Edn 250 (Hattons) - *10*	16	20
B855K	NR MLU29276 bright yellow - *11*	16	20
B855L	NR MLU29299 bright yellow - *11*	16	20
B855M	NR MLU29348 bright yellow - *11*	16	20
B855N	NR MLU29391 bright yellow - *11*	16	20

Dapol 00

W66. MBA EWS 'Monsterbox' High-sided Wagon (2009)

The real wagons entered service with EWS in 1999 and were used for aggregates, slag and scrap metal. They have also been used for coal, wood and spoil. 300 were built and run in semi-permanent sets of five, consisting of 2 'outers' with buffers and 3 'inners' without. The models have self-centring couplings, buffers to suit the livery carried and a removable ballast load.

	Railway Company		
B777J	EWS 500002 maroon - 09	16	20

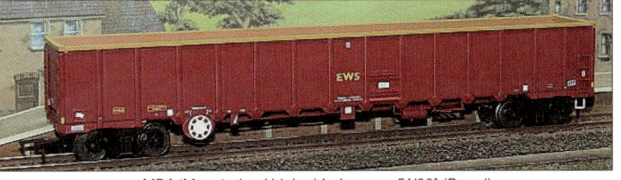

MBA 'Monsterbox' high-sided wagon [W66] (Dapol)

B777A	EWS 500003 maroon - 09	16	20
B777B	EWS 500017 maroon - 09	16	20
B777C	EWS 500045 maroon - 09	16	20
B777D	EWS 500098 maroon - 09	16	20
B777E	EWS 500112 maroon Sp Edn 200 (Hattons) - 09	16	19
B777K	EWS 500113 maroon - 09	16	20
B777M	EWS 500118 maroon - 09	16	20
B777N	EWS 500133 maroon - 09	16	20
B777H	EWS 500199 maroon - 09	16	20
B777F	EWS 500234 maroon W Sp Edn 250 (Trainlines) - 09	17	22
B777G	EWS 500238 maroon W Sp Edn 250 (Trainlines) - 09	17	22

W67. MCA EWS 'Megabox' Low-sided Wagon (2009)

100 of the MBAs (above) were later cut down in height to give easier access and to reduce load capacity by two thirds. The MCAs were outer wagons with buffers. The inner wagons in the set were MDAs. The models have self-centring couplings, buffers to suit the livery carried and a removable ballast load.

	Railway Company		
B778F	EWS 500153 maroon W Sp Edn 250 (Trainlines) - 09	20	23
B778G	EWS 500161 maroon W Sp Edn 250 (Trainlines) - 09	20	23

MCA 'Monsterbox' low-sided [W67] (Dapol)

B778J	EWS 500204 maroon - 11	17	22
B778K	EWS 500206 maroon - 11	17	22
B778A	EWS 500207 maroon - 09	15	20
B778M	EWS 500207 maroon - 11	17	22
B778B	EWS 500213 maroon - 09	15	20
B778C	EWS 500221 maroon - 09	15	20
B778D	EWS 500229 maroon - 09	15	20
B778N	EWS 500231 maroon - 11	17	22
B778E	EWS 500231 maroon Sp Edn (Hattons) - 09	15	19
B778H	EWS 500240 maroon Sp Edn (Hattons) - 09	14	19

W68. MJA Freightliner Heavy Haul Box Twin (2013)

The bogie box wagons were built in Poland in 2003 at Wagony Swidnica exclusively for Freightliner. They run permanently bar coupled in pairs with buffers at the outer ends. They are used to carry stone to sites where there is no hopper unloading facility.
The model was originally commissioned by Hattons.

	Railway Company		
?	Freightliner Heavy Haul ? green - *not made*	NA	NA
?	Freightliner Heavy Haul ? white - *not made*	NA	NA
4F025001	Freightliner Heavy Haul ? green - *13*	24	29
4F025002	Freightliner Heavy Haul ? green - *13*	24	29
4F025003	Freightliner Heavy Haul ? green - *13*	24	29
4F025004	Freightliner Heavy Haul ? green - *13*	24	29

W69. MLA Bogie Low Open Ballast Wagon

These were built in 2008 by Wagony Swidnica in Poland.
The models will have the correct bogies for the livery they are finished in. The model was proposed in 2011.

	Railway Company		
B854B	EWS 503505 maroon	NPG	NPG
?	EWS ? maroon W Sp Edn (Hattons)	NPG	NPG
B854A	GBRf Metronet 503103 yellow	NPG	NPG
?	GBRf Metronet ? yellow W Sp Edn (Hattons)	NPG	NPG
	Network Rail		
B854C	NR 503097 yellow	NPG	NPG
?	NR ? yellow W Sp Edn (Hattons)	NPG	NPG

W70. MRA Bogie Side Tippler Wagon (2012)

These ballast wagons were built by Thrall Europa, the first 200 in 2001 and the second batch of 100 in 2004. The wagons run in sets of five, the outer ones with conventional couplings and inner ones being connected by bars. Each wagon has two ballast containers and each container is divided in two. One wagon at a time is emptied sideways, both boxes together in the same direction. One of the outer wagons has smaller containers with a generator fitted in the middle between them. This provides air and power to the whole set.

The models have finely detailed bodies and are sold in sets of five. Beneath the removable ballast boxes is a finely detailed underframe. The side flaps may be lowered on representations of the hydraulic arms and a bag of extra detail comes with each wagon. The models have metal bases and weigh around 200 grams each, giving them good stability.

	Railtrack & Network Rail		
B859B	Railtrack 501068, 501128, 501125, 501124 + 501051 (generator), blue+grey set of 5 wagons - *13*	100	125
B859E?	Railtrack ? blue+grey W set of 5 wagons Sp Edn (Hattons) - *12*	100	125
B859A	NR ? yellow set of 5 wagons - *12*	100	125
B859D	NR 501315 (generator), 501383, 501384, 501385, 501332 yellow set of 5 wagons - *12*	100	125
	Private Owner		
B859C	Metronet ? yellow set of 5 wagons - *12*	100	125

MRA bogie side-tipper wagon [W70] (Dapol)

W71. YCV 'Turbot' Ballast Wagon (2013)

Over 900 wagons were rebuilt in the early 1980s from bogie bolsters for ballast and spoil transportation.

4F043003	BR Eng. DB978371 grey+yellow - *13*	NPG	18
4F043004	BR Eng. DB978371 grey+yellow W - *13*	NPG	18
4F043001	EWS 08978354 maroon - *13*	NPG	18
4F043002	EWS 08978354 maroon W - *13*	NPG	18

Bogie Hopper & Dry Powder Wagons

W72. HIA Freightliner Heavy Haul Hopper (2013)

Freightliner Heavy Haul acquired a fleet of HIAs in 2005-06 for bulk limestone, sand and aggregate traffic. Their maximum carrying capacity is 24 tonnes.

Hattons commissioned Dapol to model these and have exclusive use of the tooling.

4F026004	Freightliner Heavy Haul ? grey? - *13*	17	22
4F026004	Freightliner Heavy Haul ? grey? - *13*	17	22
4F026004	Freightliner Heavy Haul ? grey? - *13*	17	22
4F026004	Freightliner Heavy Haul ? grey? - *13*	17	22

W73. ICA 'Silver Bullet' China Clay Tank Wagon (2010)

These widely seen chrome bodied V-tanks were first produced by Arbel Fauvet in France between 1989 and 1990 but a later batch was produced in 2007 for Channel Tunnel traffic between Belgium and Scotland. They are used for the transportation of clay slurry, for example, from Cornwall to paper mills in Scotland. Although originally with bright metal tanks, due to rusting, these have later turned brown

The models carry NACCO branding and have NEM pockets for couplings and darkened profile wheels.

8th Edition

Dapol 00

B076A	'ECC' 33 87 789 8046-0 chrome - *not made*		NA	NA
B076B	'ECC' 33 87 789 8047-8 chrome - *made?*		NPG	NPG
B076C	'ECC' 33 87 789 8057-7 chrome - *made?*		NPG	NPG
B076D	'ECC' 33 87 789 8062-7 chrome - *made?*		NPG	NPG

'Silver Bullet' china clay tank wagon [W73] (Hatons)

B850A	'ECC' 33 87 789 8102-4 chrome - *10*	22	27
B850B	'ECC' 33 87 789 8066-? chrome - *10*	22	27
B850C	'ECC' 33 87 789 8147-? chrome - *10*	22	27
B850D	'ECC' 33 87 789 8076-? chrome - *10*	22	27
B850K	'ECC' 33 70 789 0102-8 chrome - *11*	22	28
B850M	'ECC' 33 70 789 8066-? chrome - *11*	22	28
B850N	'ECC' 33 70 789 8047-7 chrome - *11*	22	28
B850P	'ECC' 33 70 789 8046-9 chrome - *11*	22	28

Commissioned by Hattons

B850E	'ECC' 33 87 789 8093-5 chrome - *10*	22	27
B0850F	'ECC' 33 87 789 8055-3 chrome - *10*	22	27
B850G	'ECC' 33 87 789 8100-0 chrome - *10*	22	27
B850H	'ECC' 33 87 789 8105-5 chrome - *10*	22	27

Commissioned by Kernow MR Centre

B850O	'ECC' 33 87 789 8054-7 chrome - *10*	24	29
B850P	'ECC' 33 87 789 8057-0 chrome - *10*	24	29
B850Q	'ECC' 33 87 789 8042-2 brown W - *10*	24	29
B850R	'ECC' 33 87 789 8041-4 brown W - *10*	25	33
B850S	'ECC' 33 87 789 8091-1 brown W - *10*	25	33
B850T	'ECC' 33 87 789 8087-4 brown W - *10*	25	33
B850U	'ECC' 33 87 789 8083-6 brown W - *10*	25	33
B850V	'ECC' 33 87 789 8080-5 brown W - *10*	24	29
B850W	'ECC' 33 87 789 8063-? brown W - *10*	24	29
B850X	'ECC' 33 87 789 8064-? brown W - *10*	24	29
B850Y	'ECC' 33 87 789 8061-? brown W - *10*	24	29
B850Z	'ECC' 33 87 789 8060-? brown W - *10*	24	29

W74. JIA NACCO China Clay Covered Hopper (2011)

The real wagons were built by Fauvet Girel in 1982 for Tiger Rail Leasing and English China Clays International.

The models have etched handrails, steps and walkways and are fitted with NEM pockets for couplings. The tooling belongs to Kernow Model Rail Centre and so all models released are special editions for them.

SB001A	'Imerys' 33 70 089 4020-3 light blue - *11*	22	29
SB001B	'Imerys' 33 70 089 4000-5 light blue - *11*	22	29
SB001C	'Imerys' 33 70 089 4001-3 light blue - *11*	22	29
SB001D	'Imerys' 33 70 089 4002-1 light blue - *11*	22	29
SB001E	'Imerys' 33 70 089 4003-9 light blue W - *11*	23	30
SB001F	'Imerys' 33 70 089 4004-7 light blue W - *11*	23	30
SB001G	'Imerys' 33 70 089 4005-4 light blue W - *11*	23	30
SB001H	'Imerys' 33 70 089 4006-2 light blue W - *11*	23	30

W75. PBA Tiger China Clay Covered Hopper (2013)

This model is proposed. The real wagons were built by Fauvet Girel in 1982 for Tiger Rail Leasing and English China Clays International.

The models will have etched handrails, steps and walkways and be fitted with NEM pockets for couplings. The tooling will belong to Kernow Model Rail Centre and so all models released will be special editions for them.

SB002A	'ECC International' TRL11600 white - *13*	20	27
SB002B	'ECC International' TRL11602 white - *13*	20	27
SB002C	'ECC International' TRL11605 white - *13*	20	27
SB002D	'ECC International' TRL11609 white - *13*	20	27
SB002E	'ECC International' TRL11626 white W - *13*	23	30
SB002F	'ECC International' TRL11628 white W - *13*	23	30
SB002G	'ECC International' TRL11629 white W - *13*	23	30
SB002H	'ECC International' TRL11631 white W - *13*	23	30

Other Bogie Wagons

W76. KIA Telescopic Steel Hood Wagon (2009)

This was a 1980s air-braked wagon used for the protected transportation of steel coil. Only 250 of each number have been produced and 4 'steel coils' in plastic are supplied with each model.

B747E	'Tiphook Rail' 0899 024-0 blue - *09*	21	25
B747F	'Tiphook Rail' 0899 089-9 blue - *09*	21	25
B747G	'Tiphook Rail' 0899 042-0 blue - *09*	21	25
B747H	'Tiphook Rail' 0899 066-0 blue - *09*	21	25
-	'Tiphook Rail' 089-9-046-3 blue W Sp Edn 300 (Trainlines) - *09*	22	27
B747A	'VTG' 589-9-087-6 grey+blue - *09*	21	25
B747B	'VTG' 589-9-082-7 grey+blue - *09*	21	25
B747C	'VTG' 589-9-077-7 grey+blue - *09*	21	25
B747D	'VTG' 589-9-076-9 grey+blue - *09*	21	25
-	'VTG' 474-6-442-9 grey+blue W Sp Edn 250 (Trainlines) - *09*	22	27
B747I	'VTG' 589-9-080-1 grey+blue Sp Edn 320 Hattons - *11*	18	22
B74jD	'VTG' 589-9-088-4 grey+blue Sp Edn 320 Hattons - *11*	18	22
B7k7D	'VTG' 589-9-074-4 grey+blue Sp Edn 320 Hattons - *11*	18	22
4F039001	'VGT Ferrywagon' 589-9-061-5 grey+blue - *12*	21	25
4F039002	'VGT Ferrywagon' 589-9-091-2 grey+blue - *12*	21	25
4F039003	'VGT Ferrywagon' 589-9-098-4 grey+blue - *12*	21	25
4F039004	'VGT Ferrywagon' 589-9-058-5 grey+blue - *12*	21	25

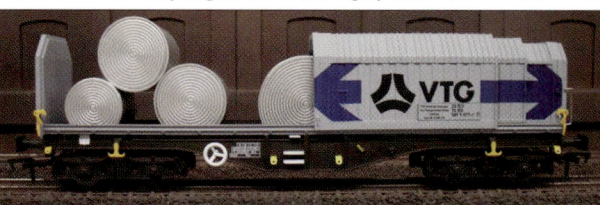

KIA telescopic hood steel carrier [W76] (Dapol)

W77. GWR 'Siphon G' Bogie Milk Van (ex-Airfix)(1985)

This is a GWR built van, with corridor connections, for transporting milk in churns. They were built in batches between 1913 and 1927.

As a cost cutting exercise, the two GWR 'Siphons' were fitted with bogies from the GWR 'Centenary' coaches. While authentic, examples on the railways with these bogies were rare. They should have been a 9' American type. Airfix released the model in 1980 and the tooling was taken over by Palitoy the following year. Palitoy released their own versions in 1982. In 1985, Dapol purchased the tooling and residue Airfix and Mainline stock and eventually sold the tools to Hornby in 1996. The model is still in production.

B77	**GW** 1478 brown (A) - *?*	10	14
B78	**BR** W1478 maroon (A) - *85*	10	14
B78	**BR** W1457 maroon (M) - *85*	10	15
B78	**BR** W1452 maroon - *88*	10	15

W78. GWR 'Siphon H' Bogie Milk Van (ex-Airfix)(1985)

This is a GWR designed milk van with end doors, built in 1919. Besides being used for milk, they could be used as scenery vans or for the transportation of motor vehicles.

The history of this model is the same as the one above.

B76	**GW** 1435 brown - *85*	9	14
B76	**GW** 1437 brown (M) - *85*	10	15
B76	**GW** 1437 brown - *90*	10	15
B262	**GW** 1437 brown - *?*	NPG	NPG
B79	**BR** W1429 maroon (A) - *85*	9	14
B79	**BR** W1429 maroon - *88*	10	15

W79. American Caboose (ex-Bachmann/Airfix) (1985)

These were originally made by Bachmann and sold to Airfix for incorporation in their first train sets. Dapol received the unsold Airfix stock.

B84	**Union Pacific** yellow - (A) - *85*	4	6

PACKS

In 1999, Dapol offered a range of wagon packs in an attempt to move some of the more stagnant items in their stock. They also had a rather large number of the GWR and BR Class 14XX locos and used up some of these in 'loco and wagon' packs which contained one of three versions of the loco, a BR liveried toad brake van and two other wagons.

Dapol 00

P1. Wagon Packs (1999)

This was an attempt in 1999 to clear mounds of unsold stock.

Ref	Description		
B400	BR 'Toad', -plank **'B&C',** BR plywood van, **BR** 9-plank mineral - 99	NA	20
B401	BR 'Toad', 7-plank **'Thrutchley',** 10T **BR** meat, 20T **'Rainford Tar'** brown - 99	NA	20
B402	BR 'Toad', 7-plank **'Coal Agencies'**, 10T **BR** meat, **NE** 9-plank mineral - 99	NA	20
B403	BR 'Toad', 7-plank **'Broadoak'**, 10T **BR** meat, 20T **'Joseph Crosfield'** - 99	NA	20
B404	BR 'Toad', BR plywood van, 7-plank **'Emlyn',** 20T **'Newcastle Gas'** - 99	NA	20
B405	BR 'Toad', 7-plank **'Emlyn',** BR plywood van, BR + **NE** 9-plank minerals - 99	NA	20
B409S	4 Welsh wagon set - 01	NA	20
B522	**'Webster'** brown twin pack 7-plank 302 + 5-plank 303 - 03	NA	15
-	5-plank **'Spalding Colliery'** 52 light grey + 7-plank **'Granville'** 227 grey Sp Edn 200 (Tutbury Jinny) - 02	NA	14
-	set of 4 - 7-plank **'Edward Russell'** 140 grey + 5-plan**k 'N Hingley & Sons'** 14 brown + 7-plank **'ED'** 14 red-brown + salt wagon **'George Brown & Sons'** 1 grey Sp Edn 100 (Modellers Mecca) - 01	NA	20

Weathered KIA wagon [W76] (Dapol)

-	2 x 7-planks **'Whitwick Colliery'** 1046 black **+ 'South Leicester'** 2120 red-brown Sp Edn 200 Tutbury Jinny) - 02	NA	14
-	7-plank **'East Cannock'** 4916 black + 5-plank **'Conduit Colliery'** 124 brown Sp Edn 200 (Tutbury Jinny) - 02	NA	14
-	2 x 7-planks **'Cannock Rugeley'** 248 grey + **'Hawkins'** 271 red-brown Sp Edn 200 (Tutbury Jinny) - 02	NA	14
-	4 x 7-planks **'Herbert Hall'** 111 brown + **'FJ Newton'** 37 grey + **'Holly Bank'** 62 brown + **'Samuel Evers'** 34 grey Sp Edn 200 (Modellers Mecca) - 02	NA	20
-	4 x 7-planks **'North & Rose'** 9 brown + **'Parkyn & Peters'** 35 red + **'Pochin'** 114 grey + **'West of England'** 126 light grey Sp Edn (Mevagissy Models) - 00	NA	25
-	4 x 7-planks **'Great Treverbyn'** 48 red-brown + **'Martin Bros.'** 28 brown + **'North Cornwall'** 3 brown + **'West Goonbarrow'** 28 grey Sp Edn (Mevagissy Models) - 01	NA	25
-	2 wagons - **'Camerton Collieries'** 175+199 black + coal Sp Edn 125 (East Somerset Models) - 02	NA	14
-	7-plank **'GD Owen'** 16 dark red + salt van **'GD Owen'** 12 Sp Edn 200 (West Wales Wagon Works) - 02	NA	15
-	2 x Mink vans **'Jubilee'** 1952 + **'Jiwbili'** 2002 Sp Edn 50 (Teifi Valley Railway) - 01	NA	15
-	2 x 5-planks IWC 117 + 68 grey Sp Edn 100 (I of W Model Railways) - 01	NA	15
-	2 x 5-planks IWR 29 brown + **'Vectis Cement Co.'** 34 grey Sp Edn 200 (I of W Model Railways) - 02	NA	25
-	2 x 7-planks **'Lewis, Merthyr Navigation'** 768 black + **'Burnyeat, Brown & Co.'** 335 black Sp Edn 100 (Lord & Butler Model Railways) - 02	NA	15
-	4 x 5-planks **'English China Clays Lovering Pochin & Co.'** 318 + 163, **'ECLP'** 1614 + 1707 Sp Edn (Mevagissey Model Railway) - 02	NA	27
-	7-plank **'Bass'** 56 grey + vent van **'Bass'** 23 grey Sp Edn 188 (Tutbury Jinny) - 02	NA	15
-	7-plank **'Bass'** 56 grey + vent van **'Bass'** 17 grey Sp Edn 200 (Tutbury Jinny) - 02	NA	15
-	2 LMS style vent vans * **'Worthington'** 3 brown + **'Bass'** 29 grey Sp Edn 200 (Tutbury Jinny) - 03	NA	15
-	2 LMS style vent vans * **'Worthington'** 33 brown + **'Bass'** 24 grey Sp Edn 200 (Tutbury Jinny) - 05	NA	15
ANT003	7-plank **'Harris & Co.'** 21 black + 7-plank **'Mathew Grist'** 2 grey Sp Edn 250 (Antics) - 03	NA	14
-	2 x 7-planks **'FJ Hall'** 65 red-brown + **'Cannock & Leacroft Colliery'** 4129 red-brown Sp Edn 200 (Tutbury Jinny) - 04	NA	15
-	5-plank **'Mapperley'** 72 and 7-plank **'Fox'** 458 black Sp Edn 200 (Tutbury Jinny) - 04	NA	15
-	**'FT Woolway'** 16 black **'AC Woolway'** 26 black Sp Edn 100 (The Model Shop, Exeter) - 04	NA	13
-	**'New Rock'** 207 + 212 black Sp Edn 150 (East Somerset Models) - 04	NA	14
-	**'Cannock & Rugeley'** 7-plank + **'Midland Coal'** 7-plank Sp Edn 150 (Tutbury Jinny) - 05	NA	14
-	2 x 7-plank **'Helston Gas Company'** 10 + 30 black Sp Edn (Kernow MRC) - 03	NA	14
-	**'Helston Gas Company'** 20 + 40 black Sp Edn (Kernow MRC) - 04	NA	14
-	2 x 7-plank **'Leek & Moorlands'** grey + **'Silverdale Co.'** brown Sp Edn 175 (Tutbury Jinny) - 05	NA	15
-	2 x 7-plank **'Stafford Coal & Iron'** 903 brown + **'Talk-O'Th Hill Colliery'** 5 brown Sp Edn (Tutbury Jinny) - 05	NA	15

P2. Loco + Wagon Gift Sets (1999)

Again, these were introduced to help shift stock.

B406	**GWR** 14xx + 'Toad' + 2 wagons - 99	NA	45
B407	as above but shirt button - 99	NA	45
B408	as above but BR black tank - 99	NA	45

SETS

Dapol sets went under the prefix 'F' in their catalogue numbering scheme and tended to be made up with surplus stock, including Airfix, Mainline and Dapol models (often mixed). In selling sets, like other companies, Dapol found it difficult to compete with Hornby whose name was familiar to first-time buyers. In 1983 there were just three sets but these rose to ten by 1987. While a few were added as more were dropped, the sets were not pushed very hard from this time on and were soon dropped from the advertising. If they did not sell well they are likely to become collectable in the future and prices are only now beginning to rise as Dapol becomes more collectable. Do not be surprised if you get offered little more than the value of their contents, for one. If this is the case, the best advice is to hang on to them and hope that their value will rise.

Dapol track cleaner (Tony Wright)

Bonhams 1793

Fine Bassett-Lowke locomotives sold by Bonhams.

Toys & Trains at Auction

Bonhams hold two sales a year devoted to Toys and Trains at our Oxford saleroom, offering for sale trains and models by famous manufactures such as: Hornby '0' and Dublo, Bassett-Lowke, Marklin, Bing, Tri-ang and many others.

For a free confidential valuation with a view to selling at Bonhams or for further details regarding our auctions please contact:

+44 (0) 20 8963 2839
leigh.gotch@bonhams.com

Catalogues
+44 (0) 1666 502200

Or visit our web site www.bonhams.com/toys three weeks prior to the sale for full catalogue descriptions and illustrations.

International Auctioneers and Valuers - **bonhams.com/toys**
Prices shown include buyer's premium. Details can be found at bonhams.com

Dapol N

HISTORY
Dapol N gauge (1:148) was launched in 2003 at the Warley National Model Railway Exhibition at the National Exhibition Centre in Birmingham and was the talk of the show.

Initially, the subjects chosen had all been ones previously made in 00 gauge by Airfix and Hornby Dublo/Wrenn and subsequently produced by Dapol after their acquisition of the Airfix and Wrenn tooling. Tooling is done in China and the mechanisms bought in. Indeed, it is believed that the motors come from the same company that supplies Bachmann for their Graham Farish models. The models are completed in the Dapol factory at Chirk on the Wales/England border. No more than 1,000 of each standard release are produced and in some cases a lot less.

First East Midlands HST [L28] (Dapol)

Weathering - This is popular with many modellers today, giving models a more realistic appearance. 'Weathered' models have been given a light spay with a thin grey or brown paint to give the appearance of dirt blown up from the track. To save space, weathered models are coded in the text with a 'W' after the colour.

LOCOMOTIVES
Early locos had bright metal wheels but following suggestions from their customers Dapol had all metalwork darkened in subsequent batches. From April 2005, no more than 500 of each finish on a diesel locomotive were made.

Cat No.	Company, Number, Colour, Date	£	£

Tank Engines
0-4-2T

L1. GWR Class 14XX 0-4-2T (2004)
The model is based on Collett's 1932 design of a small locomotive suitable for light branch lines. 95 were built, the last 20 without push-pull equipment. The last was withdrawn in 1965 and four have been preserved.

When first released, the model had bright metal wheels but later these were darkened.

Cat No.	Details	£	£
ND-017	**1403** GWR green - *05*	38	45
ND-001	**1425** GWR green - *04*	38	45
ND-080-1	**1466** GWR green ex-set - *08*	38	NA
ND-080-3	**1467** GWR green + autocoach - *09*	NPG	NPG
ND-009	**1472** GWR green - *05*	38	45
ND-004	**1420** GWR (button) green - *04*	38	45
ND-010	**1433** GWR (button) green - *05*	38	45
ND-080-4	**4865** GWR (button) green + autocoach - *09*	NPG	NPG
ND-080-2	**4866** GWR (button) green ex-set - *08*	38	NA
ND-104A	**1438** BRb black - *09*	NPG	NPG
ND-104B	**1414** BRb black - *09*	NPG	NPG
ND-002	**1458** BR black - *04*	38	45
ND-003	**1466** BR lined green - *04*	38	45
ND-016	**1462** BR green - *05*	38	45
(Nsteam1)	**4866** BRc lined green ex-train set - *13*	38	NA

0-4-4T

L2. SR Class M7 0-4-4T (2005)
Designed by Drummond for the LSWR in 1897, over 100 were built and became an important part of the Southern Railway's fleet as light passenger suburban locomotives.

The model has NEM coupling pockets and Dapol chain/shackle interchangeable decorative fitting. There is extra fine in-cab detail. Following criticism, the dome was restyled and the chimney shortened. Batches made after May 2006 should have these modifications.

SR Class M7 0-4-4T [L2] (Dapol)

Cat No.	Details	£	£
ND-057	**245** LSWR light green - *07*	50	65
ND-046	SR plain Maunsell green - *not made*	NA	NA
ND-046	**676** SR malachite green * - *06*	50	65
ND-026	**37** SR lined Maunsell green - *05*	50	65
ND-058	**30241** BRa green - *07*	50	65
ND-025	**30031** BRb lined black - *05*	50	65
ND-045	**30128** BRc lined black * - *06*	50	65

* Reshaped dome, shortened chimney and added weight under coal load.

0-6-0T

L3. GWR Class 57xx 0-6-0PT (2012)
This was Collett's pannier tank design of 1929, with a Churchward cab. 863 locomotives were built between 1929 and 1950. The last was withdrawn in 1966 and 16 have been preserved, including 6 of the 13 that were sold to London Transport between 1957 and 1963 and which survived in use until 1971.

The model features the correct cabs, whistle shield etc. for the relevant production numbers and Dapol have a riveted water tank available for those members of the class that were fitted with them. The model is 'DCC ready', with a 6-pin NEM socket in the cab below door height. The model has see-through wheels, a tungsten chassis, 50-1 gear ratio, etched sanding levers and factory fitted etched brass number plates. It is sold with a pair of magnetic couplers within the packaging for those that wish to fit them.

Cat No.	Details	£	£
ND-204B	**5764** Great Western green - *not made*	NA	NA
ND-204B	**6739** Great Western green - *12*	50	66
2S-007-003	**8762** GWR green - *12*	50	66
ND-204C	**9659** GWR green - *12*	50	66
2S-007-000	**L94** LT lined red - *12*	50	66
2S-007-004	**9741** BRa green - *12*	50	66
2S-007-002	**5799** BRb black - *12*	50	66
ND-204A	**7734** BRb black - *not made*	NA	NA
ND-204A	**6713** BRb black - *12*	50	66
ND204D	**3716** BRc black - *not made*	NA	NA
ND204D	**3616** BRc black - *12*	50	66
2S-007-001	**5758** BRc black - *12*	50	66

L4. SR Class A1 'Terrier' 0-6-0T (2009)
This is based Stroudley's Class A1 'Terrier' tank engine of 1872, as redeveloped by Marsh in 1911 to form the Class A1X. 50 were built as suburban and branch line passenger locomotives and for shunting duties. Several were sold to other railway companies and some to industry. The last was withdrawn in 1963 and 10 have been preserved.

This is a model with NEM coupling pockets, profiled wheels, 40:1 gearing and add-on accessories. Because of the model's small size, an extra small motor had to be found and it is believed that the one in use is a development of a motor used in mobile phones.

Cat No.	Details	£	£
ND-100J	**53** *Ashtead* LBSCR orange-brown - *10*	52	65
ND-100K	**54** *Waddon* LBSCR orange-brown - *11*	52	65
ND-100B	**55** *Stepney* LBSCR orange-brown - *09*	50	62
ND-100M	**62** *Martello* LBSCR orange-brown - *11*	52	65
ND-100A	**82** *Boxhill* LBSCR orange-brown - *09*	50	62
ND-100H	**84** *Crowborough* LBSCR orange-brown - *10*	52	65
ND-100I	**DS377** *Brighton Works* - LBSCR orange-brown Ltd Edn 250 – *not made*	NA	NA

Dapol N

LB&SCR 'Terrier' 0-6-0T [L4] (Dapol)

Cat No	Description		
DAGM01	**32635 Brighton Works** - LBSCR orange-brown Sp Edn 250 (Gaugemaster) - *09*	55	70
ND-OSB-001	**5** *Portishead* GWR green Sp Edn 250 (Osborn's Models) - *09*	55	70
ND-100F	**8** *Freshwater* SR lined green - *09*	50	62
ND-100C	**2662** SR black - *09*	50	62
ND-100E	**32640** BRb lined black - *09*	50	62
ND-100N	**32677** BRb lined black - *11*	50	62
(ND-146)	**32678** BRb lined black ex-set - *11*	50	NA
ND-100D	**32667** BRc lined black – *not made*	NA	NA
ND-100D	**32642** BRc lined black – *not made*	NA	NA
ND-100D	**32662** BRc lined black - *09*	50	62
ND-100G	**32646** BRc lined black - *09*	50	62
ND-100D	**32646** BRc lined black – *not made*	NA	NA
ND-100P	**32661** BRc lined black - *11*	50	62

2-6-2T

L5a. GWR Class 45xx 2-6-2T (2005)

This is a Churchward designed tank dating from 1906 and was a development of his earlier Class 44xx. They were built at Wolverhampton or Swindon and construction continued until 1929, bringing the total to 175. In 1953 15 were fitted for push-pull work in the Cardiff area and those in the Taunton area were fitted with an automatic staff changing apparatus. The last of the class was withdrawn in 1965 and 14 have been preserved.

The model has much detail, including brake rigging beneath the chassis, whistles, rivet detail, glazed cab and tank top fittings.

Cat No	Description		
ND-014	**4523** Great Western green - *05*	50	65
ND-020	**4567** GWR (button) green - *05*	50	65
ND-023	**4527** GWR green - *05*	50	65
ND-024	**4571** BRa plain black - *05*	50	65
ND-013	**4580** BRb unlined green - *05*	50	65
ND-013	**4570** BRb unlined green - *05*	50	65
ND-019	**4554** BRb plain black - *05*	50	65
ND-035	**4565** BRc lined green - *05*	50	65

L5b. GWR Class 4575 2-6-2T (2006)

This is a model of a Collett modified 45xx tank dating from 1927. They had larger side tanks with sloping tops for better driver visibility.

The model has much detail, including brake rigging beneath the chassis, whistles, rivet detail, glazed cab and tank top fittings.

Cat No	Description		
ND-047	**5531** GWR green - *06*	50	65
ND-059	**5529** GWR (button) green - *06*	50	65
ND-048A	**5511** BRb plain black Ltd Edn 100 - *06*	50	65
ND-048B	**5521** BRb plain black Ltd Edn 100 - *06*	50	65
ND-048C	**5532** BRb plain black Ltd Edn 100 - *06*	50	65
ND-048D	**5539** BRb plain black Ltd Edn 100 - *06*	50	65
ND-048E	**5542** BRb plain black Ltd Edn 100 - *06*	50	65
ND-048F	**5572** BRb plain black Ltd Edn 100 - *06*	50	65
ND-048G	**5574** BRb plain black Ltd Edn 100 - *06*	50	65
ND-048	**5576** BRb plain black - *not made*	NA	NA
ND-060	**5552** BRc lined green - *not made*	NA	NA
ND-060A	**5522** BRc lined green Ltd Edn 100 - *06*	50	65
ND-060B	**5524** BRc lined green Ltd Edn 100 - *06*	50	65
ND-060C	**5530** BRc lined green Ltd Edn 100 - *06*	50	65
ND-105	**5532** BRc lined green - *09*	50	65
ND-106	**5538** BRc lined green - *09*	50	65
ND-060D	**5541** BRc lined green Ltd Edn 100 - *06*	50	65
ND-060E	**5552** BRc lined green Ltd Edn 100 - *06*	50	65
ND-060F	**5553** BRc lined green Ltd Edn 100 - *06*	50	65
ND-060G	**5573** BRc lined green Ltd Edn 100 - *06*	50	65

L6. LMS Ivatt 2MT 2-6-2T (2006)

This was an Ivatt mixed traffic design of 1946 and was a tank version of his 6400 Class tender engines. Only 8 were built by the LMS before nationalisation, but BR continued building them until 1952. With modifications, it then became the BR standard 84xxx 2-6-2T Class. The class became a common sight on branch lines and 60 were fitted with push-pull equipment. The last was withdrawn in 1967. Of the 130 built, four have survived into preservation.

Both push-pull and non-push-pull versions of the tank were developed. NEM coupling pockets were fitted and supplied with optional buckeye and decorative chain and shackle couplings. This was a limited to 500 produced of each number.

LMS Class 2MT 2-6-2T [L6] (Dapol)

Cat No	Description		
ND-062A	**1200** LMS plain black - *06*	50	65
ND-062B	**1205** LMS plain black - *06*	50	65
ND-064A	**41225** BRb lined black push-pull - *08*	50	65
ND-064B	**41265** BRb lined black push-pull - *not made*	NA	NA
ND-064D	**41271** BRb lined black push-pull - *08*	50	65
ND-064A	**41285** BRb lined black push-pull - *not made*	NA	NA
ND-061B	**41312** BRc lined black – *not made*	NA	NA
ND-061B	**41258** BRc lined black - *06*	50	65
ND-061A	**41234** BRc lined black - *06*	50	65

Tender Locomotives
4-4-0

L7. SR 'Schools' Class 4-4-0 (2013)

Britain's most powerful 4-4-0 class of locomotive was designed by Maunsell in 1930 for the Southern Railway as his Class V. It was an express passenger locomotive and smoke deflectors were added in 1932. Half of the class were fitted with double chimneys and Lemaitre blast pipes. The last was withdrawn in 1963 and three have been preserved.

This model features the 'Super Creep' motor, tender drive, traction tyres, etched nameplates, both standard and 'Easi-fit' magnetic couplings, comes with a bag of extra detail pieces to add and is 'DCC ready'. An extra D suffix to the catalogue number will indicate that a DCC decoder has been fitted.

Cat No	Description		
2S-002-001	**905** *Tonbridge* SR malachite green - *13*	100	120
2S-002-003	**929** *Malvern* SR malachite green - *13*	100	120
-	**925** *Cheltenham* SR lined green Sp Edn (Osborn's Models) - *13*	NPG	NPG
2S-002-002	**921** *Shrewsbury* BRb lined black - *13*	100	120
2S-002-0003	**0926** *Repton* BRc lined green - *13*	100	120

0-6-0

L8. SR Class Q1 0-6-0 (2007)

This was Bulleid's war-time austerity design of 1942. It incorporated many material saving features and was both light and powerful. 40 of the locomotives were built and they were used for freight and later on some passenger trains. The last of them was withdrawn in 1965 and one has been preserved.

The model is tender powered, with loco drive through a drive shaft between tender and loco. It is 'DCC ready', has see-through wheels on the loco and tender, wire handrails, removable coal load, all-axle power contacts and headcode discs supplied. Only 250 of each version have been made. An extra D suffix to the catalogue number will indicate that a DCC decoder has been fitted.

Cat No	Description		
ND-207C	**C1** SR black - *12*	85	105
ND-207D	**C7** SR black - *12*	85	105
ND-092A	**C11** SR black - *08*	70	90
ND-092B	**C16** SR black - *08*	70	90
ND-092C	**C21** SR black - *08*	70	90
ND-092D	**C28** SR black - *08*	70	90
ND-207B	**33011** BRb black - *12*	85	105

Visit the BRM website at: www.model-railways-live.co.uk

8th Edition

Dapol N

ND-076A	33030 BRb black - 07		70	90
ND-076B	33040 BRb black - 07		70	90
ND-094	33002 BRc black - 08		70	90
ND-075A	33004 BRc black - 07		70	90
ND-207A	33005 BRc black - 12		85	105
ND-075B	33009 BRc black - 07		70	90

Ex-SR Class Q1 0-6-0 [L8] (Dapol)

4-6-0

L9. GWR 'Manor' Class 4-6-0 (2010) (Ex-Ixion)

This model was developed by Ixion Model Railways Ltd, an Anglo-Australian company registered in the United Kingdom. Later the tooling was acquired by Dapol.

The Class 78xx model has darkened see-through wheels and stainless steel rods. It also has 12-wheel pick-ups and stainless steal coupling and connecting rods, a highly detailed loco body and 3500 gallon tender, NEM coupling pockets with alternate couplers, spare air pipes and coupling chains, etched brass factory fitted nameplates and cab-side number plates, backhead detail, fire irons, 2 man crew, hand lamps and front steps (for customer fitting). The model has a Dapol 'Super Creep' 5-pole skew-wound motor, 40:1 gear ratio, phosphor-bronze self-lubricating wheel axle bearings and a positively sprung front bogie.

INS-7816	7816 *Frilsham Manor* GWR plain green - 10		80	105
INS-7819	7819 *Hinton Manor* GWR plain green - 11		80	105
INS-7808	7808 *Cookham Manor* GWR (button) plain green - 10		80	105
INS-7823	7823 *Hook Norton Manor* BRb plain black - 10		80	105
INS-7800	7800 *Torquay Manor* BRc lined green - 10		80	105
INS-7822	7822 *Foxcote Manor* BRc lined green - 10		80	105

L10. GWR 'Hall' Class 4-6-0 (2011)

Designed in 1928, the 49xx Class was one of Collett's mixed traffic locomotives of which 259 were built, based on the earlier 'Saint' Class. Production started in 1928 when 80 of the new class were built and a further 178 were ordered.

The model has a 'Super Creep' motor, 40:1 gearing, NEM coupling pockets and is 'DCC ready'. The model has a split-frame chassis, traction tyres, etched nameplates to fit and an accessory pack with spare parts. An extra D suffix to the catalogue number will indicate that a DCC decoder has been fitted.

GWR 'Hall' Class 4-6-0 [L10] (Dapol)

2S-010-0004	4937 *Lanelay Hall* GWR green - 12		95	115
2S-010-0034	4958 *Priory Hall* GWR green - 12		95	115
ND-135B	6953 *Leighton Hall* Great()Western green - 11		85	105
ND-1350 SB1	5900 *Hinderton Hall* Great()Western green Sp Edn 500 (Osborn's Models) - 11		85	105
ND-1350S B1/Ba	s above but with the wheels painted black - 11		90	110
ND-135A	5935 *Norton Hall* GWR green - 11		85	105
ND-135?	6956 *Mottram Hall* GWR green Sp Edn (Dapol N'thusiasts Club) - 12		NPG	NPG
ND-135C	6910 *Gossington Hall* BRb lined black - 11		85	105
2S-010-0024	4914 *Cranmore Hall* BRc green - 12		95	115
2S-010-0014	4951 *Pendeford Hall* BRc green - 12		95	115
ND-135B	6952 *Kimberley Hall* BRc green - 11		85	105

L11. GWR 'Modified Hall' Class 4-6-0

In 1944, Hawksworth modified the design of the 'Hall' Class and built a further 70 locomotives, which are known as 'Modified Halls' or Class 6959.

When announced, it was said that the model will have a 'Super Creep' motor, 40:1 gearing and NEM pockets. It will has a split-frame chassis, traction tyres, etched nameplates to fit, an accessory pack with spare parts and will be 'DCC ready'. No further news has been received.

ND-135D	6969 *Wraysbury Hall* Great()Western green – not made		NA	NA
-	6960 *Raveningham Hall* GWR lined green Sp Edn (Osborn's Models) - ?		NPG	NPG
ND-135B	6996 *Blackwell Hall* Great Western green – not made		NA	NA
ND-135C	6962 *Soughton Hall* GWR (button) green – not made		NA	NA
ND-135A	6991 *Acton Burnell* Hall BRc green – not made		NA	NA

L12. Class B1 4-6-0 (2010)

This was Edward Thompson's 'Antelope' Class of 1942 and 410 were built as mixed traffic locomotives. Construction of the class went on for a number of years, ending with a final batch in 1950. The last was withdrawn in 1967 and two have been preserved.

This model has a 'Super Creep' motor, 30:1 gearing, NEM coupling pockets alternative coupling bar for closer coupling, sprung power transfer from engine to tender, traction tyres, square axle ends for perfect quartering and an accessory pack with spare parts. The model is 'DCC ready'.

ND-120C	1230 LNER light green - 10		85	100
ND-120D	1234 LNER light green - 10		85	100
ND-120G	1252 LNER light green - 11		85	100
ND-120H	1225 LNER light green - 11		85	100
ND-120B	61097 BRb lined black - 10		85	100
ND-120F	61363 BRb lined black - 11		85	100
ND-120A	61099 BRc lined black - 10		85	100
ND-120E	61406 BRc lined black - 11		85	100
ND-148	61000 *Springbok* BRb? lined black + 3 Gresley coaches - 11		NPG	NPG
(ND-148)	above loco on its own ex-set - 11		90	NA

L13. LNER Class B17/4 'Footballer' 4-6-0 (2008)

The early B17 locomotives were built to help out the ageing B12s on passenger trains on the Great Eastern Division of the LNER. Those built later, with larger Group Standard tenders, were for use on the Great Central Division and named after football clubs, which gave them the nickname - 'Footballers'.

This model has a 'Super Creep' motor, tender drive, 40:1 gearing, etched nameplates, is 'DCC ready' and has NEM coupling pockets.

LNER Class B17 'Footballer' 4-6-0 [L13] (Dapol)

ND-079A	2850 *Grimsby Town* LNER light green - 09		80	100
(ND-079C)	2854 *Sunderland* LNER light green - not made		NA	NA
ND-079D	2869 *Barnsley* LNER light green - 10		80	100
(ND-079-1)	2857 *Doncaster Rovers* LNER light green - 08		80	NA
ND-079F	2863 *Everton* LNER light green - 11		80	100
ND-079E	61655 *Middlesbrough* BRb green - not made		NA	NA
ND-079E	61655 *Middlesbrough* BRc green - 11		80	100
ND-079A	61660 *Hull City* BRc green - 09		80	100
(ND-079-2)	61652 *Darlington* BRc green - 08		80	NA
(ND-079-3)	61665 *Leicester City* BRc green ex train pack - not made		NA	NA
ND-079C	61647 *Helmingham Hall* BRc green - 10		85	102

4-6-2

L14. LNER Class A3 4-6-2 (2012)

The Class A3s of the LNER were a development of the A1s, which had been designed for the Great Northern Railway by Nigel Gresley in 1922. Almost all existing A1s were rebuilt, while later ones were built as A3s. One of the most visible changes was the new banjo shaped steam dome fitted to the top of the A3's boiler.

The model is fitted with a 'Super Creep' motor, 14 wheel power contacts, tender drive, traction tyres, etched nameplates, standard and magnetic couplings and a 6-pin DCC decoder socket and can be supplied with a Gaugemaster DC23 decoder fitted. An extra

Dapol N

D suffix to the catalogue number will indicate that a DCC decoder has been fitted. There are variations of the chimney, dome, smoke deflector and tender.
dc = double chimney, sc = single chimney, rd = round dome, bd = banjo dome, sd = smoke deflectors, GN = GNR style tender, nst = non-streamlined tender, ct = corridor tender.

ND129G	2744 *Grand Parade* LNER light green - 12	100	120
ND-129B	2750 *Papyrus* LNER light green sc nst - 12	100	120
ND-129D	4470 *Flying Scotsman* LNER light green sc bd ct - 12	100	120
ND129E	60070 *Gladiateur* BRb green - 12	100	120
ND-129C	60079 *Bayardo* BRb green sc GN - 12	100	120
ND129H	60094 *Colorado* BRb green - 12	100	120
ND-129A	60045 *Lemberg* BRc green dc bd GN - 12	100	120
ND129F	60106 *Flying Fox* BRc green - 12	100	120
(Nsteam2)	60103 *Flying Scotsman* BRc green ex-train set - 13	100	NA

L15. LNER Class A4 4-6-2 (2012)

The A4 was Gresley's ultimate express engine development and arrived in 1935. A total to 34 were built. Early examples were given corridor tenders to allow for a change of crew on the journey and, for easy maintenance, side valances were removed during the war.

This model is fitted with a 'Super Creep' motor, tender-drive, both standard and 'Easi-fit' magnetic couplings and a 6-pin DCC decoder socket. DCC fitted models being available with a Gaugemaster DC23 decoder and an extra D suffix to the catalogue number will indicate that one has been fitted. There are chimney and tender variations, 14-wheel power contact, traction tyres, etched nameplates and a bag containing extra detail.
dc = double chimney, sc = single chimney.

LNER Class A4 4-6-2 [L15] (Dapol)

ND-128E	2509 *Silver Link* LNER grey sc Sp Edn (N'thusiasts Club) - 12	80	95
ND128H	8 *Dwight D Eisenhower* LNER blue - 12	100	120
ND-128A	4494 *Andrew K McCosh* LNER blue sc - 12	80	95
2S-008-002	4498 *Sir Nigel Gresley* LNER blue, as preserved, double chimney - 13?	100	120
2S-008-003	60004 *William Whitelaw* BRa Garter blue - 13?	100	120
ND-128D	60022 *Mallard* BRb blue - 12	80	95
2S-008-001	60005 *Dwight D Eisenhower* BRb green - 13?	100	120
ND128F	60016 *Silver King* BRb green - 12	100	120
ND-128B	60017 *Silver Fox* BRb green sc - 12	80	95
ND122G	60005 *Sir Charles Newton* BRc green - 12	100	120
2S-008-000	60019 *Bittern* BRc green, double chimney - 13?	100	120
ND-128C	60021 *Wild Swan* BRc green dc - 12	80	95

L16. SR Class WC/BB Un-Rebuilt 4-6-2 (2014)

The locomotive was designed by Oliver Bullied and the first of the class arrived in 1945. The rebuilding of some them started in 1957. Those for service in the eastern sector had been given 'Battle of Britain' names and the rest were named after places in the West Country. The last member of the class was withdrawn in 1967 and 20 of the class have survived in preservation.

The model is fitted with a 'Super Creep' motor, traction tyres, tender drive and 12-wheel power connection. Both standard and 'Easi-fit' magnetic couplings are provided as well as etched nameplates and a bag of extra detail is provided. A 6-pin DCC decoder socket is fitted and DCC fitted models are available with the Gaugemaster DC23 decoder.

ND-208G	21C113 *Okehampton* SR light green - 14	100	130
ND-208A	21C164 *Fighter Command* SR light green - 14	100	130
ND-208D	34066 *Spitfire* BRc green - 14	100	130
ND-208H	34030 *Watersmeet* BRc green - 14	100	130
-	34019 *Bideford* BR green Sp Edn (Osborn's Models) - 14	NPG	NPG

L17. BR Class WC/BB 4-6-2 Rebuilt (2014)

Some of Bulleid's Light Pacific design of 1945 were rebuilt by British Railways and the result was some attractive looking locomotives.

The model is fitted with a 'Super Creep' motor, traction tyres, tender drive, 12 wheel power connection, both standard and 'Easi-fit' magnetic couplings provided, etched nameplates and a bag of extra detail is provided. A 6-pin DCC decoder socket is fitted and DCC fitted models are available with the Gaugemaster DC23 decoder.

ND-208C	34042 *Dorchester* BRc green - 14	100	130
ND-208F	34052 *Lord Dowding* BRc green - 14	100	130
ND-208E	34088 *213 Squadron* BRc green - 14	100	130
ND-208B	34098 *Templecombe* BRc green - 14	100	130

L18. BR 'Britannia' 4-6-2 (2010)

The 'Britannia' Class was introduced in 1951 as the standard express passenger locomotive design for the newly formed British Railways. Designed by R.A.Riddles, 55 of them were built at Crewe and distributed to all of the regions. Only two survived into preservation.

The model has a 'Super Creep' skew wound 5-pole motor, 30:1 gearing for quieter mechanism, is 6-pin 'DCC ready', has see-through darkened wheels, tractions tyres on each rear driver, squared off axle ends to allow for perfect quartering, NEM coupling pockets, etched nameplates and close coupling between cab and tender. An accessory pack includes air pipes, coupling chains, 'knuckle couplers' and 2 replacement traction tyres.

BR 'Britannia' Class 4-6-2 [L18] (Dapol)

ND-095A	70000 *Britannia* BR green - 10	90	110
ND-095B	70013 *Oliver Cromwell* BRb green - 11	90	110
ND-OSB-002	70014 *Iron Duke* BRb green + Golden Arrow insignia Sp Edn (Osborn Models) - 10	100	122
ND-095C	70038 *Robin Hood* BRb green - 11	100	120
ND-095D	70050 *Firth of Clyde* BR green - 10	90	110
ND-095E	70004 *William Shakespeare* BR green - 10	90	110
ND-095F	70030 *William Wordsworth* BRc green - 11	90	110
ND-095G	70022 *Tornado* BRc green - 11	100	120
ND-095H	70048 *The Territorial Army* BR green - 10	90	110

2-8-0

L19a. GWR Class 28xx 2-8-0 (2012)

This was Churchward's heavy long distance freight locomotive of 1903 and 84 of them were built at Swindon to his original design between 1903 and 1919. A further 83 were later built there to a revised design by Collett as the 38xx Class (see next table). The last of the 28xx Class was withdrawn from service in 1965 and 4 have survived into preservation.

This model has a 'Super Creep' motor, tender drive, traction tyres, 40:1 gearing, is 6-pin DCC ready, has NEM coupling pockets, both standard and 'Easi-fit' magnetic couplings, fitted etched brass number plates and has a bag containing other extra detail. An extra D suffix to the catalogue number will indicate that a DCC decoder has been fitted.

2S-009-002	2872 Great()Western green - *not made*	NA	NA
2S-009-000	2884 GWR (shirt button) green - *not made*	NA	NA

L19b. GWR Class 2884 (Class 38xx) 2-8-0 (2012)

More commonly called the Class 2884 (as numbering started at that number) these were built at Swindon in the period 1938-42 by Collett. They were almost identical to the Class 28xx, and are often treated as part of the same class, but had windows in the cab sides and continuous covers over the two back pairs of driving wheels. 7 of the class survived into preservation.

This model has a 'Super Creep' motor, tender drive, traction tyres, 40:1 gearing, is 6-pin DCC ready, has NEM coupling pockets, both standard and 'Easi-fit' magnetic couplings, fitted etched brass number plates and has a bag containing other extra detail. An extra D suffix to the catalogue number will indicate that a DCC decoder has been fitted.

2S-009-000	2884 GWR green - 13	100	120
2S-009-002	2892 GWR (shirt button) green - 12	100	120
-	3850 GWR green Sp Edn (Osborn's Models) - 12	100	119
2S-009-003	3832 BRb plain black - 12	100	120
2S-009-001	3836 BRc plain black - 12	100	120

Dapol N

2-10-0

L20.   BR Class 9F 2-10-0 (2008)

This was the ultimate locomotive development by Riddles for his BR standard classes and the 2-10-0 wheel arrangement was influenced by the success he had with the WD 2-10-0 locomotives during the war. A total of 251 were built, most of them at Crewe, the rest were built at Swindon - including Evening Star. Later members of the class had double chimneys and the last was withdrawn in 1968 - nine being preserved.

The model has a 5-pole skew-wound motor, NEM 651 coupling sockets, 16 wheel power contacts, see-through wheels and 10 wheels driving. The model is tender mounted and 'DCC ready'.

sc = single chimney. dc = double chimney.

ND-090J	92001 BRb black BR1G tender dc - 09	85	105
ND-090B	92002 BRb black BR1G tender sc - 08	85	105
ND-090F	92100 BRc black BR1C tender sc - 08	85	105
ND-090K	92233 BRb black BR1G tender dc - 09	85	105
ND-090D	92247 BRb black BR1G tender dc - 08	85	105
ND-090A	92008 BRc black BR1G tender dc - 08	85	105
ND-090E	92050 BRc black BR1C tender sc - 08	85	105
ND-090R	92052 BRc black BR1B tender - 11	NPG	NPG
ND-090S	92082 BRc black BR1B tender - 11	NPG	NPG
ND-090P	92088 BRc black BR1C tender - 11	NPG	NPG
ND-090M	92133 BRc black W BR1C - 10	NPG	NPG
ND-090G	92208 BRc black BR1C tender dc - 08	85	105
ND-090I	92220 *Evening Star* BRc black dc - 08	85	105
ND-090C	92226 BRc black BR1G tender dc - 08	85	105
ND-090Q	92226 BRc black BR1G tender - 11	NPG	NPG
ND-090H	92231 BRc black BR1C tender dc - 08	85	105
ND-92203	92203 *Black Prince* BRc black BR1G tender dc *Sp Edn 150 (TMC) - 09	85	110

BR Class 9F 2-10-0 [L20]

* Etched brass nameplates and headboards for both 'Pines Express' and 'The David Shepherd Wildlife Foundation'. David Shepherd signed each box sleeve.

Diesel & Electric Locomotives

L21.   Class 03 Drewry 0-6-0DS

Planned for 2006 but dropped after Bachmann announced their plan to introduce one.

L22.   Class 04 Drewry 0-6-0DS

Planned for 2006 but dropped after Bachmann announced their plan to introduce one.

L23.   Class 22 B-B (2013)

This class of diesel-hydraulic locomotives was introduced in 1959-1962 and they were built by the North British Locomotive Co.. The class totalled 58 and were for the Western Region. The fleet was phased out between 1968 and 1971. A few of them made it into blue livery but none has been preserved.

Featuring Dapol's established heavy split frame tungsten chassis and 'Super Creep' motor, the model has lots of detail. An extra D suffix to the catalogue number will indicate that a 6-pin DCC decoder has been fitted.

2D-012-004	D6313 BRc green, yellow warning panels - 13	100	135
2D-012-001	D6318 BRe blue full yellow ends - 13	100	135
2D-012-003	D6319 BRc green, yellow warning panels - 13	100	1350
2D-012-002	D6320 BRc green, yellow warning panels - 13	100	120
2D-012-000	6326 BRe blue full yellow ends - 13	100	120
2D-012-005	D6331 BRc green small yellow panel - 13	100	120

L24.   Class 26 Bo-Bo (2011)

Birmingham RC&W Co. built 47 of these Type 2 locos. The first ones arrived in 1958 and were allocated to semi-fast and suburban duties in North London. From early 1960 they were all moved to Scotland.

Both 26/1 and 26/2 versions are planned by Dapol. Round or oval buffers are provided, as appropriate. They have all-wheel power connection and drive, 40:1 gearing, etched nameplates and body grilles, a bag of detail extras, separate handrails, directional lights, a 6-pin DCC socket fitted and NEM coupling pockets to take either standard or magnetic couplings, both of which are provided with the model. An extra D suffix to the catalogue number will indicate that a DCC decoder has been fitted.

BR Class 26 diesel [L24] (Dapol)

ND-145B	D5301 BRc green, small yellow panels - 11	85	108
ND-145H	D5307 BRc green with headcode discs - 12	85	108
ND-145J	D5326 BRc green small yellow panels - 12	95	115
-	26001 BR green with yellow panels	NA	NA
-	26007 BR green with yellow panels	NA	NA
ND145 Rails 1	above 2 locomotives Sp Edn (Rails of Sheffield) - not made	NA	NA
-	D5300 BR green with yellow panels	90	NA
-	D5301 BR green with yellow panels	90	NA
ND145	Rails 1 above 2 locomotives Sp Edn (Rails of Sheffield) - 11	NA	110
ND-145J	26003 BRe blue - not made	NA	NA
ND-145D	26007 Railfreight Coal grey - 11	85	108
ND145E	26011 grey+yellow + 5 'Dogfish' wagons train pack Sp Edn (Dapol N'thusiasts Club) - 11	NA	100
ND-145A	26015 BRe blue - 11	85	108
ND-145F	26026 BRe blue with snowploughs & discs - 12	80	100
ND-145D	26027 Railfreight Coal grey – not made	NA	NA
ND-145C	26038 BRe Railfreight 'red stripe' grey, Eastfield totems - 11	85	108
ND145G	26040 blue with snowploughs & discs - 12	80	100

L25.   Class 27 Bo-Bo (2013)

These locomotives were basically the same as the Class 26 but more powerful. They were also built by Birmingham RC&W at Smethwick and the first joined the BR fleet in the Summer of 1961. A total of 8 of the class have been preserved.

The model has working headlights, headcode panels and marker lights, along with Dapol's now standard chassis and 'DCC ready' or fitted options, a 6-pin DCC decoder socket. The model weighs 78 grams and has a 5-pole motor and flywheel, with shaft-drive to both bogies. It has directional marker lights and an extra D suffix to the catalogue number will indicate that a DCC decoder has been fitted, in which case it is likely to be a Gaugemaster DC23 decoder

ND-205A	D5356 BRc green, yellow warning panels - 13	85	105
ND-205A	D5381 BRc green, yellow warning panels - not made	NA	NA
ND-205B	D5411 BRc green, full yellow ends - 13	85	105
ND-205C	27008 BRe blue - 13	85	105
ND-205D	27032 BRe blue - 13	85	105
ND-205D	27046 BRe blue - not made	NA	NA

L26.   Class 33 Bo-Bo (2013)

98 Class 33 locomotives were built by the Birmingham Railway Carriage & Wagon Co. during 1961-62. At least 26 of them have been preserved.

The model will have working headlights, headcode panels and marker lights, etched metal grilles, both standard and 'Easi-fit' magnetic couplings provided, a 5-pole 'Super Creep' motor, all-wheel drive and power contact, along with Dapol's now standard chassis. It will be 'DCC ready' with a 6-pin decoder socket. An extra D suffix to the catalogue number will indicate that a DCC decoder has been fitted.

2D-001-001	D6571 BRc green, no warning panels 33/0 - 13	100	120
2D-001-003	D6597 BRc green small yellow panels 33/0 - 13	100	120
2D-001-000	33030 BRe blue 33/0 - 13	100	120
2D-001-002	33046 *Merlin* BR Eng. grey+yellow 33/0 -13	100	120
2D-001-020	33102 BRe blue 33/1 - 13	100	120
2D-001-021	33103 BR Engineering grey+yellow 33/1 - 13	100	120

L27.   Class 35 'Hymek' B-B (2008)

This is based on the Western Region diesel hydraulic, the first of which started to appear on the rail network in 1961. They were built by Beyer Peacock between 1961 and 1964

Dapol N

and the last was withdrawn from service in 1973.

The model has a 5-pole skew-wound motor, wire handrails, yellow-glow marker lights, air-pipes and snowploughs to add. It is 'DCC ready' and produced as limited editions of 250.

BR Class 35 'Hymek' diesel [L27] (Dapol)

Cat No	Description	Price 1	Price 2
ND-084R	D7001 BRe blue, yellow ends, non-powered - *11*	20	25
ND-084Q	D7005 BRe blue, yellow ends - *11*	72	90
ND-084B	D7008 BRc green - *08*	75	95
ND-084D	D7011 BRe blue - *08*	75	95
ND-084Z	D7017 BRe green, no yellow panels, Sp Edn 150 (Kernow Model Centre) - *08*	75	95
ND-084F	D7018 BRe green Sp Edn 150 (Kernow Model Centre) - *08*	75	95
ND-084C	D7023 BRe green, yellow ends - *08*	75	95
ND-084Y	D7036 BRe chromatic blue, small yellow panels, Sp Edn 150 (Kernow Model Centre) - *08*	75	95
ND-084M	D7042 BRc 2-tone green non-powered - *11*	20	25
ND-084Z	D7048 BRe green W + 5 'NCB' mineral wagons Sp End (Dapol Club) - *09*	NA	100
(ND-084Z)	above loco only - *09*	75	NA
ND-084j	D7057 BRc 2-tone green, half yellow ends - *10*	85	108
ND-084A	D7066 BRc green - *08*	75	95
ND-132	D7071 BRc 2-tone green non-powered (also referred to as ND-084n) - *11*	20	25
ND-084H	D7083 BRc 2-tone green, half yellow ends - *10*	85	108
ND-084P	D7084 BRc 2-tone green - *11*	75	90
ND-084G	D7093 BRe green Sp Edn 150 (Kernow Model Centre) - *08*	75	95
(ND-084E)	D7099 BRe blue W ex-pack - *08*	75	NA
ND-084E	above with 6 x 6-wheel milk tanks - *08*	NA	125

L28. Class 43 InterCity 125 (2010)

The High Speed Train, or IC125, has been one of the most successful and influential designs ever to run in the British rail network. The first HSTs went into service on the Western Region main line in October 1976 and were still very much in evidence in Britain at the turn of the century. The HST sets were made up with Mk3 coaches without buffers and classified as Mk3A. They had as their power units one of these Class 43 diesel locomotives at each end.

The model has a 5-pole 'Super Creep' motor, all-wheel power contact and drive, directional lights, 40:1 gearing, a 6-pin DCC decoder socket, NEM coupling pockets and a bag of additional detail to add. There are exhaust differences between models.

Cat No	Description	Price 1	Price 2
	Inter-City		
ND-111A	43006+43007 InterCity blue+grey - *10*	NPG	NPG
ND-111B	43120+43114 ICs Executive grey - *10*	NPG	NPG
ND-122A	253024 (43048+W41121+W42288+43049) IC125 blue+grey -*10*	NPG	150
ND-122B	43194+41086+42161+43118 ICs grey - *10*	NA	150
ND-122C	253028 (43056+41029+42281+43057) IC Exec * grey - *10*	NPG	150
ND-122H	?+? BR blue+grey - *12*	130	160
	Virgin Trains		
ND-111C	43098+43102 red+black - *10*	NPG	NPG
ND-122D	43008+41079+42154+43092 red+black - *10*	NA	150
ND-122J	43094+43104 (+ 2 Mk3 coaches) red+black - *12*	NA	150
	Miscellaneous		
ND-111E	43014+43062 Network Rail (NMT) - *11*	NPG	125
ND-122E	43423+41204+42401+43484 Grand Central black - *11*	NA	160
ND-122F	43015+43168 (+ 2 Mk3 coaches) First Great Western purple - *11*	NA	155
ND-122G	43378+41194+42371+43285 (+ 2 Mk3 coaches) Cross Country grey - *11*	NPG	NPG
ND-122L	43044+41076+42149+43059 (+ 2 Mk3 coaches) East Midlands Trains - *12*	NA	160

L29. Class 50 Co-Co (2013)

The Class 50s were built by English Electric during 1967 and 1968 and were initially hired out to the British Railways Board. Later, all 50 locos were bought by them. Although normally associated with the Western Region, they started life on the LMR on the West Coast Main Line. To this day, the class has had a cult following which may explain why 18 of the locomotives have been preserved.

The model has the 5-pole 'Super Creap' motor, all wheel power contacts and drive, both standard and 'Easi-fit' magnetic couplings provided, etched nameplates and body grilles, working headlights, headcode panels and marker lights, along with Dapol's now standard chassis and a bag of detail extras. The model is 'DCC ready' with a 6-pin decoder socket fitted. An extra D suffix to the catalogue number will indicate that a DCC decoder has been fitted.

Cat No	Description	Price 1	Price 2
2D-002-000	D406 BRe blue unrefurbished - *13*	100	120
2D-002-003	50037 *Illustrious* NSE bright blue - *13*	100	120
2D-002-002	50040 *Leviathan* BReLL blue - *13*	100	120
2D-002-001	50043 BRe blue unrefurbished - *13*	100	120

L30. Class 52 'Western' C-C (2013)

The 'Westerns' were diesel hydraulics and were designed and constructed at Swindon, while some were built at Crewe. The class of 74 had a very distinctive shape and attracted a cult interest. They were introduced to the Western Region in 1962 to provide high powered mixed traffic locomotives to the region. The last was withdrawn in 1978 and seven have been preserved.

This is a 'DCC ready' model with a 'Super Creep' 5-pole skew wound motor, darkened wheels, partial low friction mechanism, twin flywheels, directional lighting, lit yellow glow headcode panels, accessory bag, fully detailed cab interior, etched name and number plates, split frame tungsten chassis and NEM coupling box. An extra D suffix to the catalogue number will indicate that a DCC decoder has been fitted. Both standard and 'Easi-fit' magnetic couplings are supplied with the model.

Cat No	Description	Price 1	Price 2
ND-OSB3	D1000 *Western Enterprise* ochre Sp Edn (Osborn Models) - *13*	100	112
ND-202A	D1005 *Western Venturer* BR blue - *13*	85	105
ND-202C	D1005 *Western Venturer* BR maroon - *not made*	NA	NA
ND-202B	D1029 *Western Legionaire* BRc maroon - *13*	85	105
ND-202C	D1038 *Western Sovereign* BRc green - *13*	85	105
ND-202D	D1056 *Western Sultan* BRc maroon full yell front - *made?*	85	105

L31. Class 56 Diesel (Romanian) (2012)

The first 30 Class 56 locomotives were built by Electroputere at Craiova in Romania but the remaining 105 machines came from BREL at Doncaster and Crewe. They were introduced between 1976 and 1984.

This is a 'DCC ready' model with 6-pin 'decoder socket, sound capability, a 'Super Creep' motor with 2 flywheels and low friction mechanism, NEM coupling pockets, directional lighting, cab interior detail, separate handrails all round and a bag of extras to fit. An extra D suffix to the catalogue number will indicate that a DCC decoder has been fitted.

EWS Class 56 diesel [L31] (Dapol)

Cat No	Description	Price 1	Price 2
(Ndiesel2)	56003 Loadhaul triple grey ex-train set - *not made*	NA	NA
(Ndiesel2)	56003 Loadhaul black+orange ex-train set - *13*	85	NA
ND-203B	56013 Railfreight Coal triple grey - *12*	85	105
ND-203D	56018 EWS maroon+yellow - *12*	85	105
ND-203A	56005 red stipe Railfreight grey - *12*	85	105
ND-203A	56019 red stipe Railfreight grey - *not made*	NA	NA
ND-203C	56006 BR blue - *12*	85	105
ND-203C	56026 BR blue - *not made*	NA	NA

Dapol N

L32. Class 58 Co-Co (2009)

These heavy freight locomotives were built at Doncaster between 1983 and 1987 and totalled 50 in all. They had been designed at Derby and were cheap to build. They spent their lives hauling merry-go-round coal trains between the coal stockpile depots and power stations. Some of them were named after the industrial sites they served.

The model has a 'Super Creep' motor with flywheel, low friction mechanism and is 6-pin 'DCC ready'.

ND-103A	58012 Railfreight 'red stripe', grey - 10	85	105
ND-103F	58017 Railfreight triple-grey Coal - 11	85	105
ND-103E	58021 Mainline blue - 11	85	105
ND-103B	58023 Railfreight 'red stripe', grey - 10	85	105
ND-103G	58027 Mainline triple-grey - 11	85	105
ND-103J	58033 EWS maroon+yellow - 12	85	105
ND-103D	58037 EWS maroon+yellow - 09	85	105
ND-103C	58042 BRe triple grey Coal Sector - 10	85	105
ND-103H	58044 unbranded triple-grey - 11	85	105
-	5811 ACTS dark blue+yellow Sp Edn 100 (Modelbahn Union) - 10	90	110

L33. Class 59 Co-Co (2013)

The Class 59s were a forerunner of major changes that were coming to the railways. For the first time since the war we had foreign built locomotives in regular use on Britain's railways. They were also the first to be supplied and owned by the commercial sector and not by British Railways. Foster Yeoman started the trend but others followed, also buying them from General Motors. They were the forerunners of the Class 66 fleet. The Class 59 quickly established itself as a powerful and reliable performer.

Dapol's model will feature working headlights, painted and detailed cab, the 'Super-Creep' motor, a split frame tungsten chassis, low fiction mechanism, alternate lights and solebar detail etc. and will be 'DCC ready' with DCC fitted option. In this respect, an extra D suffix to the catalogue number will indicate that a DCC decoder has been fitted.

2D-005-000	59002 *Alan J Day* Foster Yeoman silver - 13	105	120
2D-005-001	59103 *Village of Great Elm* ARC yellow - 13	105	120
2D-005-003	59204 National Power blue - 13	105	120
2D-005-002	59206 *John F Yeoman* DB Schenker red - 13	105	120

L34a. Class 66 Co-Co (2005)

When the American backed company EWS took over most of the freight business in Britain in the mid '90s, they needed to replace the ageing locomotive fleet with highly reliable and efficient machines. For these they turned to General Motors and 250 of an updated Class 59 were ordered and built in Canada, becoming the Class 66. They were introduced in 1998 and other freight operators followed. Many are also now found on the European mainland.

The model has working white lights in direction of travel, working red lights at rear, day and night settings, separate metal handrails and wipers, skew-wound twin flywheel motor, NEM pocket couplings (Rapido or Buck-eye), imitation screw couplings, cab interior detail, split and insulated chassis and etched roof detail. After the first 8 EWS models, the light cluster on the cab fronts was modified. Also, the detail on the model was improved with smaller lamp irons, reshaped cab front lifting plates, weathered bodyside grilles, white handrails and factory fitted etched nameplates. A more powerful motor was introduced for the Freightliner locomotives in 2006 and, from mid 2007, the model received highly detailed bogies. 2009 models were retooled to take the NEM 651 6-pin socket for DCC control and weathered oxidised chrome exhaust.

EWS Maroon

ND-027	66008 Ltd Edn 250 - 05	65	80
ND-028	66014 Ltd Edn 250 - 05	65	80
ND-144A	66017 non-powered - 11	25	30
ND-029	66050 Ltd Edn 250 - 05	65	80
ND-030	66072 Ltd Edn 250 - 05	65	80
ND-065A	66081 Ltd Edn 250 no motor or lights - 07	25	30
ND-065B	66106 Ltd Edn 250 no motor or lights - 07	25	30
ND-108B	66111 maroon+yell W Sp Edn 500 (Hattons) - 09	55	65
ND201C	66115 powered - 11	70	85
ND-031	66121 Ltd Edn 250 - 05	65	80
ND-108	66181 - 09	55	65
ND-032	66155 Ltd Edn 250 - 05	65	80
ND-144B	66173 non-powered - 11	25	30
ND-033	66204 Ltd Edn 250 - 05	65	80
ND-109	66222 Ltd Edn 250 - 09	55	65
ND-034	66225 Ltd Edn 250 - 05	65	80
ND-134	66250 non-powered - 11	25	30

EWSi Maroon

ND-066B	66022 new EWS-i livery - 07	65	70
ND-066A	66215 new EWS-i livery - 07	65	70

DB Schenker Red

ND-110	66152 - 09	55	65

Freightliner Green

ND-144C	66512 non-powered - 11	25	30
ND-144D	66524 non-powered - 11	25	30
ND-049	66539 Ltd Edn 250 - not made	NA	NA
ND-049	66540 *Ruby* 40th Anniversary model - 06	65	80
ND-050	66545 Ltd Edn 250 - 06	65	80
ND-051	66554 40th Anniversary Ltd Edn 250 - 06	65	80
ND-052	66566 Ltd Edn 250 - 06	65	80
ND-053	66578 40th Anniversary Ltd Edn 250 - 06	65	80
ND-054	66581 Ltd Edn 250 - 06	65	80
ND-055	66610 40th Anniversary Ltd Edn 250 - 06	65	80
ND-056	66613 Ltd Edn 250 - 06	65	80

Freightliner Class 66 diesel [L34a] (Dapol)

GBRf Blue

ND-037	66702 *Blue Lightning* Ltd Edn 250 - 06	65	80
ND-038	66703 *Doncaster Spa* Ltd Edn 250 - 06	65	80
ND-039	66705 *Golden Jubilee* Ltd Edn 250 - 06	65	80
ND-040	66706 *Nene Valley* Ltd Edn 250 - 06	65	80
ND-041	66709 *Medite* Ltd Edn 250 - 06`	65	80
2D-007-000	66709 *Sorrento* MSC/GBRf - 12	60	70
ND-042	66713 *Forest City* Ltd Edn 250 - 06	65	80
ND-043	66714 *Cromer Lifeboat* Ltd Edn 250 - 06	65	80
ND-044	66716 *Willesden Traincare* Ltd Edn 250 - 06	65	80
-	66841 Colas Rail orange+yellow	65	NA
-	66842 Colas Rail orange+yellow non-powered	25	NA
ND-126	above two models in twin pack - 10	NA	100

* Revised group standard light cluster.

L34b. Class 66 Low Emission Co-Co (2007)

Specification for these low emission Class 66 models include new ultra high detail bogie frames and piping, fully retooled body with 3rd door, altered cab side windows, 'DCC ready' 'plug and play' board and NEM coupler sockets.

ND-125	66305 Fastline grey DC6 - 10	65	84
ND-067	66411 *Eddie the Engine* DRS/Stobart Rail blue Ltd Edn 250 - 07	65	80
ND-?	as above non-powered - 08	25	30
ND-069A	66413 DRS dark blue Ltd Edn 250 - 07	65	80
ND-069B	66417 DRS dark blue Ltd Edn 250 - 07	65	80
ND-201A	66562 Freightliner green powered - 11	70	85
ND-085A	66585 Freightliner green non-powered - 08	25	30
ND-077	66594 *Spirit of Kyoto* Freightliner green Ltd Edn 250 - 07	65	80
ND-068	66623 Freightliner/Bardon Aggregates blue - 07	65	80
ND-085B	66718 GBRf/Metronet blue, non-powered - 07	25	30
ND-078A	66719 *Metro-Land* GBRf/Metronet blue - 07	65	80
ND-078B	66720 *Metronet Pathfinder* GBRf/Metronet - 07	65	80
ND-201E	66720 Children's livery - 12	70	85
ND-074A	66723 First/GBRf blue Ltd Edn 250 - 07	65	80
ND-102	66725 *Sunderland* First GBR blue DC6 'Footballer' nameplate, Sp Edn 500 (Dapol 25th Anniversary) - 08	45	50
ND-074B	66727 First/GBRf blue Ltd Edn 250 - 07	65	80
ND-201D	66729 *Derby County* GBRf Europorte blue - 12	70	85
ND-201A	66953 Freightliner green powered - not made	NA	NA
ND-201B	66956 Freightliner green – 11	65	80

L35. Class 67 Bo-Bo (2009)

The 30 members of the Class 67 were made by Alstom at Valencia in Spain and introduced to Britain in 1999 and 2000. They were built for EWS for its Royal Mail trains but EWS lost the Royal Mail contract in 2003. Since then, the locomotives have been

Dapol N

used on various duties, including express passenger trains, rail tours, over-night sleepers, rescue work and for the Royal Train.

This is a model with new high-torque 5-pole skew-wound 'Super Creep' motor. It is 'DCC ready' with a NEM 651 socket. It has NEM coupling pockets, directional lighting, darkened wheels, all-wheel power contacts, etched see through grilles and etched nameplates. An extra D suffix to the catalogue number will indicate that a DCC decoder has been fitted.

EWS

EWS Class 67 diesel [L35] (Dapol)

ND-101M	67001 maroon+yellow non-powered - 11	85	105
ND-101H	67002 maroon+yellow - 11	85	105
ND-101E	67008 maroon+yellow – not made	NA	NA
ND-088	67008 maroon+yellow - 10	80	100
ND-101B	67009 maroon+yellow (ND-088) – not nade	NA	NA
ND-101F	67024 maroon+yellow - 10	85	105
ND-101G	67026 maroon+yellow non-powered - 10	20	25
ND-101C	67027 Rising Star maroon+yellow - 09	80	95
ND-101-1	67029 Royal Diamond silver + DVT 82146 - 09	NA	115
ND-101J	67030 maroon+yellow - 11	85	105

Wrexham & Shropshire

ND-101?	67010 grey+silver non-powered Ltd Edn (W&S) - 09	20	25
ND-101D	67012 grey+silver + 2 x Mk3s + Mk3 DVT train pack - not made	NA	NA
-	67012 A Shropshire Lad grey+silver, non-powered Sp Edn (W&S) - 09	15	20
ND-101D	67013 * grey+silver + 2 x Mk3s + Mk3 DVT train pack - 09	NA	100
(ND-101D)	above loco on its own - 09	85	NA

Miscellaneous

2D-010-000	67003 Arriva Trains Wales blue -12	85	105
ND-101K	67005 Royal Train purple non-powered - 11	20	25
ND-101A	67006 Royal Sovereign Royal Train purple - 09	80	95
ND-200A	67018 DB Schenker red - 11	NPG	NPG

* Was to have been 67012 but when the train pack arrived it contained 67013.

L36. Class 73 ED Electro-Diesel Bo-Bo (2004)

The Class 73 electro-diesels were built especially for the Southern Region and designed to make use of the third rail electrified routes, but also be able to operate using diesel power. The first 6 locomotives were built at Eastleigh in 1962 and form the JA type subclass 73/0 and the remaining 43 were built by English Electric between 1965 and 1967, becoming JB type subclass 73/1. Some 73/1s were transferred to InterCity and renumbered to become subclass 73/2. At the last count, 15 had been bought for preservation.

The model has constant brightness directional lights and illuminated headcode panels which light-up in the direction of travel. It is powered by the Mabuchi, self-lubricating, 5-pole Macro-motor, driving all 4 axles via twin flywheels and has a diecast chassis, flush glazing, cab interiors, air horns and high level jumper cables. Early examples have over-long couplings making close-coupling difficult. This was later changed in 2005 with 73138 and, since 2007, this model has been 'DCC ready'.

SBD1	E6003 BRc green (73/0) half yellow panels Sp Edn 300 (Signal Box) DCC - 07	65	75
ND-999	E6005 BRe blue (73/0) Sp Edn 92 (Dapol Club) DCC - 08	70	80
?	E6007 BRe blue Sp Edn 100 (Nsprays) - 06	NPG	90
NSPEC3	E6007 BRe light blue Sp Edn 125 (Hattons) - 10	75	90
ND-036D	E6033 BRe blue - 06	60	75
(Ndiesel1)	73001 BRe blue ex-train set - 13	22	28
SBDN3	73002 BRe blue non-powered Sp Edn 300 (Signal Box) - 09	22	28
SBDN2	73005 Mid-Hants Watercress Line BR blue Sp Edn 300 (Signal Box), etched nameplates - 09	55	68
ND-011A	73101 Brighton Evening Argus Pullman livery - 05	60	75
ND-011B	73101 The Royal Alex Pullman livery - 05	60	75
ND-036B	73108 BRe blue - 06	60	75

BR Class 73 electro-diesel [L36] (Tony Wright)

ND-006	73109 Battle of Britain 50th Anniversary NSE bright blue (South West) - 04	60	75
ND-022B	73110 BR Dutch grey+yellow - 05	60	75
ND-036C	73111 BRe blue - 06	60	75
ND-021A	73114 Stewarts Lane Mainline - 05	60	75
ND-022A	73119 Kentish Mercury BR Dutch grey+ yellow - 05	60	75
ND-005	73128 EW&S maroon - 04	60	75
ND-012A	73129 City of Winchester NSE bright blue - 05	60	75
ND-005	73131 EW&S maroon - not made	NA	NA
ND-021B	73133 Mainline blue - 05	60	75
ND-007	73134 Woking Homes 1885-1985 InterCity Executive grey * - 04	60	75
ND-012B	73136 Kent Youth Music NSE bright blue - not made	NA	NA
ND-012B	73136 NSE bright blue - 05	60	75
ND-008	73138 BReLL blue - 05	60	75
ND-036A	73142 Broadlands BRe blue, light grey roof - 06	60	75
ND-071	73202 Dave Berry Gatwick Express grey - 07	60	75
ND-070A	73204 Janice GBRf blue+yellow DCC + non-powered 73205 Jeanette - 07	NA	100
ND-070B	73206 Lisa GBRf blue+yellow DCC + non-powered 73209 Alison - 07	NA	100
ND-072	73211 Gatwick Express grey - 07	60	75
-	73212+73213 Railtrack Sp Edn 100 (N-thusiast Resprays) - 06	NA	180
-	73212 Railtrack non-powered ex- above Sp Edn pair - 06	50	NA
-	73213 Railtrack powered ex- above Sp Edn pair - 06	80	NA
ND-008A	(unnumbered) BReLL blue + transfer sheet - 04	55	75

* May also be available with a wrong coloured roof.

L37. Class 86 Bo-Bo (2009)

In 1965, the first 100 of a new class of 25kv AC electric locomotives started to arrive. The AL6 (later Class 86) took the best features of the five earlier classes (AL1-AL5) and became the largest class of main line electric locomotives built in Britain. Some were built by BR Doncaster and the rest by English Electric. Many were rebuilt in 1972 when they were given new motors and improved suspension, becoming subclass 86/2 and were renumbered accordingly.

This model was announced at the 2008 N Gauge Society AGM. It has a 5-pole 'Super Creep' motor, flywheels, all-wheel power connection and drive, directional lighting, NEM pockets for couplings and a bag containing extra detail pieces. It is 'DCC ready' with a 6-pin decoder socket and has non-powered but movable pantographs. A new improved pantograph was fitted from 2011.

Freightliner Class 86 electric [L37] (Dapol)

ND-099?	86204 City of Carlisle BRe blue Sp Edn 125 (C+M Models) - 09	85	105
ND-099B	86213 ICs grey - 09	85	105

Dapol N

Code	Number	Description		
ND-099G	86219	Intercity grey + 2 x MK3 + Mk3 DVT train pack - 09	NA	160
ND-099A	86229	*Sir John Betjeman* Virgin Trains red+black - 09	85	105
ND-099?	86241	*Glenffidich* BRe blue Sp Edn 125 (C+M Models) - 09	85	105
ND-099P	86241	Royal Mail red+grey – *not made*	NA	NA
ND-099E	86259	Virgin Trains red+black + 2 x MK3 + Mk3 DVT train pack - 09	NA	160
ND-099N	86261	EWS maroon+yellow - 11	85	105
ND-099M	86401	*Northampton Town* NSE blue - 10	85	105
ND-099K	86415	BR Railfreight Distribution triple grey - 11	85	105
ND-099D	86425	RES red+dark grey - 09	85	105
ND-099S	86605	Freightliner triple grey non-powered - 12	32	40
ND-099P	86606	Freightliner triple grey - 11	90	110
ND-099C	86621	Freightliner green - 09	85	105
ND-099R	86628	Freightliner green+yellow non-powered - 12	32	40
ND-099F	86633	Freightliner grey + 3 Freightliner 'Spine' wagons train pack - 09	NA	150
(ND-099F)		above loco only -09	85	NA
ND-099Q	86637	Freightliner Powerhaul green+yellow with new style pantograph - 11	85	110
(ND-147)	86901	N-R yellow	32	NA
(ND-147)	86902	N-R yellow non-powered	32	NA
ND-147		above 2 locos - 11	NA	125

L38. Class 92 Co-Co (2013)

This class was built for Railfreight Distribution, Eurostar and SNCF, for use on services through the Channel Tunnel. 46 locos were built by Brush Traction and are able to operate from 4 different power systems.

Work had started on this at the time of going to press. The model will be 'DCC Ready'.

Code	Number	Description		
ND-???	92???	Railfreight Distribution grey - 13	NPG	NPG
ND-???	92???	unbranded triple grey - 13	NPG	NPG
ND-???	92???	EWS maroon+yellow - 13	NPG	NPG
ND-???	92???	DB Schenker red - 13	NPG	NPG

Railcars & Multiple Units

L39. Class 121 'Bubble Car' (2011)

15 of the Class 121 DMBSs were introduced to the rail network in 1960 for high density local passenger transportation. At the time it was a modern version of the GWR AEC railcar. Designed at Derby, they were built by Pressed Steel and have 65 seats in a 2+3 pattern.

The model has a 'Super Creep' 5-pole motor, low friction mechanism, flywheels, all-wheel power contacts and drive, 6-pin DCC socket, NEM coupler pockets, both standard and 'Easi-fit' magnetic couplings, alternate exhausts, light bar ready, directional lighting, darkened wheels and an accessory pack containing air pipes, coupling chain etc. An extra D suffix to the catalogue number will indicate that a DCC decoder has been fitted.

BR Class 121 'Bubble Car' [L39] (Dapol)

Code	Number	Description		
ND-118Z	55020	GWR brown+cream Sp Edn (Kernow MR Centre) - 13	88	103
2D009101	W55020	BR green with whiskers - 12	90	110
ND-118B	55021	BR green small yellow panel powered – *not made*	NA	NA
ND-118A	W55021	BR green with wiskers powered - 11	88	103
2D009000	W55022	BR green small yellow panel - 12	90	110
ND-118D	55022	Network SouthEast bright blue powered - 11	88	103
ND-119B	55023	BR green small yellow panel non-powered – *not made*	40	50
Nd-119A	W55023	green with wiskers non-powered - 11	40	50
ND-118C	55024	BR blue powered - 11	88	103
ND-118A	55027	BR green with whiskers powered – *not made*	NA	NA
2D009001	W55027	BR green with whiskers - 12	90	110
ND-118B	W55027	BR green with yellow panels powered - 11	88	103
2D009100	W55028	BR green with small yellow panels - 12	90	110
ND-119D	55028	Network SouthEast blue non-powered - 11	40	50
ND-119C	55029	BR blue non-powered - 11	40	50
2D009102	W55030	BR blue+grey - 12	90	110
ND-119A	55032	BR green with whiskers non-powered – *not made*	NA	NA
ND-119B	W55032	BR green with yellow panels non-powered - 11	40	50
2D009002	W55032	BR blue+grey - 12	90	110

L40. Class 122 Gloucester RCW 'Bubble Car' (2012)

Built by the Gloucester Railway Carriage and Wagon Co. in 1958, 20 were delivered. The railcars had side doors to each seating bay. They were initially allocated to the Western Region, London and the Midlands but later some moved to Scotland. The closure of many branch lines reduced their usefulness and the last was withdrawn in 1994. Three were converted into motor parcels vans (Class 131). Some later became engineer's inspection saloons and some have been preserved.

The model has a similar specification to the Class 121 'Bubble Car' (above).

Code	Number	Description		
ND-209A	55000	(122100) BR Regional Railways - *not made*	NA	NA
ND-209B	55000	(122100) BR Regional Railways - 12	90	110
ND-209A	55005	BR blue+grey - 12	90	110
ND-209B	55006	BR blue+grey - *not made*	NA	NA
ND-209D	55009	BR green with whiskers - 12	90	110
ND-210B	55011	BT blue+grey non-powered - 12	42	50
ND-210A	55012	(122112) BR Regional Railways non-powered - 12	42	50
ND-210C	55016	BR green with whiskers non-powered - 12	42	50
ND-209Z	960015	(975042) NR yellow - 13	42	50
ND-209C	TDB975023	(55001) BR blue (route learning car) - 12	90	110

L41. Class 142 'Pacer' DMU (2013)

Initially 50 sets were ordered but this later rose to almost 100. They were built using Leyland National bus parts and came into operation between 1985 and 1987. The 'Pacers' were popular with local passenger transport executives (PTEs) and consequently appeared in a number of colourful liveries.

The model will have directional lighting, a DCC decoder socket, under floor 'Super Creep' motor, power contact and drive on all wheels, working Scharfenburg couplers to allow compatibility with the class 153 and 156 models and a bag of detail parts to add. An extra D suffix to the catalogue number will indicate that a DCC decoder has been fitted.

Code	Number	Description		
ND-116E	142021	Tyne & Wear PTE - 13	90	105
ND-116C	142025	Northern Spirit light blue - 13	90	105
ND-117A	142026	Northern Rail purple non-powered - 13	45	55
ND-117C	142050	Northern Spirit light blue - 13	90	105
ND-116A	142065	Northern Rail purple - 13	90	105
ND-117D	142069	Arriva Trains Wales lt. blue non-powered - 13	45	55
ND-117B	142077	Regional Railways blue non-powered - 13	45	55
ND-116B	142081	Regional Railways blue - 13	90	105
ND-116D	142085	Arriva Trains Wales light blue - 13	90	105

L42. Class150/2 2-Car 'Sprinter' DMU

Planned for 2006 but dropped after Bachmann announced their plan to introduce one.

L43. Class153 'Super Sprinter' Railcar (2009)

For use on secondary and branch lines, 35 2-car Class 155 units were rebuilt into 70 single car Class 153 railcars. The work was undertaken in Kilmarnock by Hunslet-Barclay Ltd and the units came into service during 1991 and 1992.

The model is 'DCC ready', with a 6-pin decoder socket, 5-pole 'Super Creep' motor, all-wheel power contact and drive, directional lights, 2 on/off switches on the underside and a bag of additional detail. It also has a light bar connection in the roof. An extra D suffix to the catalogue number will indicate that a DCC decoder has been fitted.

Code	Number	Description		
ND-114A	153302	East Midlands blue - 09	90	107
ND-115D	153307	Northern Rail purple+violet non-powered - 11	28	35
ND-114F	153320	Arriva Trains Wales light blue - 10	90	107
ND-115A	153321	East Midlands blue non-powered - 09	28	35
ND-115B	153328	Regional Railways non-powered - 10	28	35
ND-114Z	153329	'St Ives Bay Belle' light blue Sp Edn 150 (Kernow MRC) DC6 - 10	100	120

8th Edition

Dapol N

Northern Rail Class 153 railcar [L43] (Dapol)

Cat No.	Number	Description	£	£
ND-114D	153332	Northern Rail purple+violet - *11*	90	107
ND-114C	153333	Central Trains green - *09*	90	107
ND-114E	153334	London Midland grey+green - *09*	90	107
ND-115H	153358	Northern Transpennine dark blue non-powered - *11*	28	35
ND-114G	153360	Northern Spirit - *not made*	NA	NA
ND-114H	153360	Northern Transpennine dark blue - *11*	90	107
ND-114B	153377	Regional Railways - *10*	90	107
ND-114J	153380	First Great Western purple (neon) - *12*	90	107
ND-115C	153383	Central Trains green non-powered - *09*	28	35

L44. Class 156 2-car 'Super Sprinter' DMU (2009)

The Class 156 2-car 'Super Sprinters' were built by Metro-Cammell in Birmingham between 1987 and 1989. 114 sets were ordered by the British Railway Board's Provincial Sector for outer suburban use with a top speed of 75mph. They are amongst the most reliable units operating in Britain today.

This model has the new high-torque 5-pole under-floor motor, DCC 6-pin decoder socket, close coupling, light switch, NEM coupling pockets with working BSI couplings on outer ends, directional lighting, RP25 darkened wheels and seats painted to match the livery.

Cat No.	Number	Description	£	£
ND-112B	156404	Regional Railways blue powered - *11*	NPG	NPG
ND-097B	156405	East Midlands blue non-powered - *09*	35	39
ND-097A	156406	East Midlands blue powered - *09*	85	105
ND-113C	156409	Regional Railways blue non-powered - *10*	NPG	NPG
ND-113B	156411	Regional Railways blue non-powered - *11*	NPG	NPG
ND-082A	156418	Regional Railways 2-car - *09*	85	102
ND-096A	156418	Central Trains green 2-car - *09*	85	104
ND-112C	156419	Nat. Express East Anglia powered - *10*	NPG	NPG
ND-096B	156422	Central Trains green non-powered - *09*	35	39
ND-083B	156435	Strathclyde PT non-powered - *09*	35	39
ND-098B	156438	Northern Spirit blue non-powered - *09*	35	39
ND-081A	156440	First Northern Rail purple+violet 2-car - *09*	85	105
ND-113A	156444	Northern Rail pur+violet non-powered - *11*	NPG	NPG
ND-082B	156448	Regional Railways non-powered - *09*	35	39
ND-112A	156468	Northern Rail purple+violet powered - *11*	NPG	NPG
ND-spec1	156484	Northern Rail Settle & Carlisle - *09*	95	122
ND-098A	156498	Northern Spirit blue+green 2-car - *09*	85	105
ND-081B	156492	First Northern Rail purple+violet non-powered - *09*	35	39
ND-097B	156502	Strathclyde PT non-powered - *not made*	NA	NA
ND-097A	156504	Strathclyde PT 2-car - *not made*	NA	NA
ND-083A	156506	Strathclyde PT 2-car - *09*	85	102

L45. Class 220 'Voyager' 4-car DMU (2006)

34 non-tilting Class 220 'Voyagers' were built by Bombardier Transportation in 2000 for fast passenger service. They were part of Virgin Trains' commitment when they won the Cross-Country franchise in 1996. The 5-car trains, replaced 8-10 car HSTs and, not surprisingly, proved inadequate for the amount of passengers they needed to carry and problems followed their introduction. The stock transferred to Arriva when they took over the Cross Country franchise.

The model is 'DCC ready' with a 6-pin decoder socket fitted and ready for a digital sound chip. The model also has directional lights, close coupling, etched metal nameplates and sprung pantographs.

Cat No.	Number	Description	£	£
ND-063C	220002	*Forth Voyager* (60302+60202+60702+60402) Virgin red+silver Ltd Edn 250 - *07*	NA	NPG
ND-063A	220004	*Cumbrian Voyager* (60304+60204 +60704+60404) Virgin red+silver Ltd Edn 250 - *06*	NA	140
ND-063B	220007	*Thames Voyager* (60307+60207+60707+60407) Virgin red+silver Ltd Edn 250 - *06*	NA	140
ND-063G	220016	*Midland Voyager* Virgin (60316+60216+60716+60416) red+silver Ltd Edn 250 - *07*	130	150
ND-063H	220019	*Mersey Voyager* (60319+60219+60719+60419) Virgin red+silver Sp Edn 250 (Hattons) - *07*	NA	150
ND-063E	220023	*Mancunian Voyager* (60323+60223+60723+60423) Virgin red+silver Ltd Edn 250 - *07*	NA	150
ND-063Z	220029	*Vyajer Kernewek/Cornish Voyager* (60329+60229+60729+60429) Sp Edn 150 (Kernow Models) - *07*	NA	150
ND-063D	220032	*Grampian Voyager* (60332+60232+607232+60432) Virgin red+silver Ltd Edn 250 - *07*	NA	NPG
ND-063F	220034	*Yorkshire Voyager* (60334+60234+60734+60434) Virgin red+silver Ltd Edn 250 - *07*	NA	NPG

L46. Class 221 'Super Voyager' 4-car DMU (2007)

These are tilting 5-car sets which also formed part of Virgin Trains' commitment when they won the Cross-Country franchise in 1996. 44 tilting Class 221 'Super Voyagers' were built by Bombardier Transportation. It was thought that tilting trains would speed up the service, particularly between Oxford and Birmingham. With the change of franchise, Arriva took over the route and the 'Super Voyagers', bringing to them a new livery.

The model is 'DCC ready' with a 6-pin decoder socket fitted and ready for a digital sound chip. The model also has directional lights, close coupling, etched metal nameplates and sprung pantographs.

Virgin 'Super Voyager' [L46] (Dapol)

Cat No.	Number	Description	£	£
ND-073A	221109	*Marco Polo* (60359+60759+ 60959+60459) Virgin red+silver - *07*	85	105
ND-073B	221110	*James Cook* (60360+60760+ 60960+60460) Virgin red+silver - *07*	85	105
ND-087A	221120	(60470+60970+60770+60370) X Country - *08*	85	119
ND-121B	221128	X Country non-powered car - *10*	NPG	NPG
ND-073C	221130	*Michael Palin* (60380+60780+ 60980+90480) Virgin red+silver - *07*	85	105
ND-121A	221134	X Country non-powered car - *10*	NPG	NPG
ND-087B	221135	(60485+60985+60785+60385) X Country - *08*	85	119
ND-073D	221144	*Prince Madoc* (60394+60794+ 60994+60494) Virgin red+silver - *07*	85	105
ND-073F	221122	*Doctor Who* (60372+60772+60972+60472) Virgin red+silver non-motorised Sp Edn (Dapol 25th Anniversary) - *08*	45	50

L47. Class 390 'Pendolino' EMU

This model is still on the proposals list.

COACHES

All Dapol coaches have highly detailed interiors and are produced with a range of running numbers. The Collett main line coaches are of a late '30s design.

NPCCS - Railway vans that are technically non-passenger carrying coaching stock, in this chapter are listed under wagons.

Cat No.	Company, Number, Colour, Date	£	£

GWR Stock

C1. GWR 'Suburban B' Set Coach (2003)

'B Set' coaches were brake ends which were built by the GWR in 1933 to run in two car sets. Each contained five 3rd class and one 1st class non-corridor compartments and a guards/luggage area at one end.

The models have NEM coupling pockets.

Cat No.	Company, Number, Colour, Date	£	£
-	GWR (arms) 6363 brown+cream, grey roof	11	NA

Dapol N

	GWR (arms) 6367 brown+cream, grey roof	11	NA
NC-OSB-001	above 2 coaches Sp Edn (Osborn Models) - 11	NA	24
NC-007	GWR 6736 brown+cream - 03	8	12
NC-008	GWR 6738 brown+cream - 03	8	12
NC-023*	GWR 6736 brown+cream - 05	8	12
NC-024*	GWR 6738 brown+cream - 05	8	12
(2P003000)	GWR (button) 6736 brown+cream - 12	11	NA
(2P003000)	GWR (button) 6738? brown+cream - 12	11	NA
NC-005	BR W6907W maroon - 03	8	12
NC-006	BR W6970W maroon - 03	8	12
(2P003001)	BR W?W maroon - 12	11	NA
(2P003001)	BR W?W maroon - 12	11	NA

* These differ from NC-007 and NC-008 in having revised bogies.

C2. GWR Auto Trailer (2004)

Auto trailers were used for push-pull operation on branch lines and many small batches were built by the GWR. They were eventually displaced by diesel multiple units. The model features wire handrails and a pack of extra detail.

(ND-080-3)	GWR (arms) 178 brown+cream ex-train pack	9	NA
(ND-080-4)	GWR (button) 185 brown+cream ex-train pack - 08	9	NA
NC-009	GWR 187 dark brown+cream - 04	8	12
(ND-080-1)	GWR 187 dark brown+cream ex-train pack - 08	8	NA
NC-047B	GWR (button) 187 dark brown+cream * - 09	8	10
NC-012	GWR 189 dark brown+cream - 04	8	12
2P004001	GWR (arms)189 dark brown+cream - 12	10	14
NC-047A	GWR 190 dark brown+cream * - 09	8	10
(ND-080-2)	GWR (button) 190 dark brown+cream ex-train pack - 08	8	NA
NC-019	GWR 191 dark brown+cream - 05	8	12
NC-OSB-003	GWR (button) 192 brown+cream Sp Edn (Osborn Models) - 11	9	11
NC-013	GWR 193 dark brown+cream - 05	8	12
NC-025	GWR 195 dark brown+cream - *not made*	NA	NA
2P004002	GWR (arms) 195 dark brown+cream - 12	10	14
NC-OSB-004	GWR (button) 195 brown+cream Sp Edn (Osborn Models) - 11	9	11
NC-026	BR W190W red+cream - 06	8	12
NC-011	BR W192W red+cream - 04	8	12
NC-018	BR W194W red+cream - 05	8	12
2P004004	BR W197W red+cream - 12	10	14
(Nsteam1)	BR W174W lined maroon ex-train set - 13	10	NA
2P004003	BR W193W maroon - 12	10	14
NC-025	BR W195W maroon - 06	8	12
NC-010	BR W196W lined maroon - 04	8	12
SBCN1	BR RTC Test Car 1 red+blue Sp Edn 300 (The Signal Box) - 09	12	16

Ex-GWR auto-trailer [C2] (Dapol)

* sold in card-headed plastic bags instead of the usual plastic boxes.

C3. GWR Collett Stock

These models, introduced in 2006, have well detailed bodies and liveries, good underframe detail, NEM coupling pockets and, from 2009, they have been ready for fitting a lighting bar in the roof. (lb = light bar ready.) This offers a choice between yellow for incandescence or white for more modern lighting. Dapol's Collett coach models, in 2006, were Model Rail Model of the Year.

C3a. GWR Collett Corridor Brake 3rd (2006)

These were built in the late 1930s with five 3rd class compartments off a corridor. Beyond these compartments there were two further independent compartments with their own access doors. Beyond these there was a small guard's compartment with very little space for luggage.

NC-017A	GWR 6485 dark brown+cream - 06	14	18
NC-017B	GWR 6543 dark brown+cream - 06	14	18
NC-035	GWR (button) 6487 dark brown+cream - 07	14	18
NC-042	GWR (arms) 6486 lb dark brown+cream - 09	16	20
NC-057A	GWR (button) 6552 lb dark brown+cream - *not made*	NA	NA
NC-057A	GWR (button) 6539 lb dark brown+cream - 09	16	20
OSB-012	GWR (button) 6482 brown+cream Sp Edn 250 (Osborn's Models) - 13	15	18
NC-057B	GWR (arms) 6603 lb dark brown+cream - 09	16	20
NC-057C	GWR (arms) 6543 lb dark brown+cream - 10	16	20
NC-022A	BR W6355 red+cream - 06	14	18
2P000200	BR W6549 maroon - 13	16	20
NC-022B	BR W6562 red+cream - 06	14	18
NC-029A	BR W6562 maroon - 06	14	18
NC-029B	BR W6605 maroon - 06	14	18

C3b. GWR Collett Corridor Composite (2006)

A lot were built of this style of coach by the GWR at the end of 1938. They had eight compartments with four doors on the corridor side and two on the other side. Half the coach was 1st class and the other half 3rd class, until the change to 2nd class in 1957. Some of the windows were fitted with sliding vents and the drop lights in the doors were shorter than the fixed windows.

GWR Collett corridor 3rd [C3b] (Dapol)

NC-015A	GWR 7050 dark brown+cream - 06	14	18
NC-015B	GWR 7021 dark brown+cream - 06	14	18
NC-034	GWR (button) 7321 dark brown+cream - 07	14	18
NC-041	GWR (arms) 7052 lb dark brown+cream - 09	16	20
NC-056A	GWR (button) 7029 lb dark brown+cream - *not made*	NA	NA
NC-056A	GWR (button) 7056 lb dark brown+cream - 09	16	20
OSB-011	GWR (button) 7003 brown+cream Sp Edn 250 (Osborn's Models) - 13	15	18
NC-056B	GWR (arms) 7045 lb dark brown+cream - 09	16	20
NC-056C	GWR (arms) 7059 lb dark brown+cream - 10	16	20
NC-020A	BR W7038 red+cream - 06	14	18
NC-020B	BR W7014 red+cream - 06	14	18
2P000001	BR W7016 maroon (NC-222A) - 13	16	20
NC-027A	BR W7019 maroon - 06	14	18
2P000002	BR W7021 maroon (NC-222B) - 13	16	20
NC-027B	BR W7034 maroon - 06	14	18

C3c. GWR Collett Corridor 3rd (2006)

A lot of these coaches were built by the GWR at the end of the 1930s. They had eight compartments with four doors on the corridor side and all were 3rd class, until 1957 when they became 2nd class. Some of the windows were fitted with sliding vents and the drop lights in the doors were shorter than the fixed windows.

NC-016A	GWR 1086 dark brown+cream - 06	14	18
NC-016B	GWR 1146 dark brown+cream - 06	14	18
NC-036	GWR (button) 1080 dark brown+cream - 07	14	18
NC-043	GWR (arms) 1084 lb dark brown+cream - 09	16	20
NC-058A	GWR (button) 1089 lb dark brown+cream - 09	16	20
NC-058B	GWR (arms) 1063 lb dark brown+cream - *not made*	NA	NA
NC-058B	GWR (arms) 1115 lb dark brown+cream - 09	16	20
OSB-010	GWR (button) 1126 brown+cream Sp Edn 250 (Osborn's Models) - 13	15	18
NC-058C	GWR (arms) 1112 lb dark brown+cream - 10	16	20
NC-021A	BR W1087 red+cream - 06	14	18
NC-021B	BR W1116 red+cream - 06	14	18
2P000100	BR W1089 maroon (NC-223A) - 13	16	20
NC-028A	BR W1092 maroon - 06	14	18
2P000101	BR W1117 maroon (NC-223B) - 13	16	20
NC-028B	BR W1138 maroon - 06	14	18

C3d. GWR Collett Buffet Car

This was referred to in the 2012/2013 catalogue as NC-224B but missing from the later price list. It is not known whether Dapol plan to produce a model.

C4. GWR Hawksworth Full Brake (2013)

Although designed by the GWR during Hawksworth's time as CME, it is thought that they did not see full service until after nationalisation of the railways in January 1948.

Dapol N

Representing a 64' coach, 45 were built between 1949 and 1951. During the 1960s they were transferred to parcels and departmental service.

This model is being produced exclusively for the N Gauge Society. It will have a lot of added detail, expanding close couplers in NEM pockets and flush glazing.

-	**GWR** 156 lined dark brown+cream - *13*	14	18
-	**GWR** 114 unlined dark brown+cream - *13*	14	18
-	**BR** W181W red+cream - *13*	14	18
-	**BR** W272W unlined red - *13*	14	18
-	**BR** W142W lined maroon - *13*	14	18
-	**BR** W161W blue - *13*	14	18
-	**BR** Eng. ADB975157 olive green 'Enparts' - *13*	14	18

LMS Stock

The LMS Stanier passenger stock originally planned for 2006 was dropped after Bachmann announced their plan to introduce them.

C5.   LMS 6-wheeled 'Stove R' (2009)

This was a LMS 'Period 3' design of a full brake and 75 were built at Wolverton in 1932 and 1933. All survived into BR ownership and most were withdrawn between 1963 and 1968.

This model is produced exclusively for the N Gauge Society, for sale to its members.

-	unpainted (50 made) - *13*	18	23
-	**LMS** 32975 maroon - *09*	14	18
-	**LMS** 32977 maroon - *09*	14	18
-	**LMS** 33000 maroon - *09*	14	18
-	**BR** M32957M red+cream - *09*	14	18
-	**BR** M32988M red+cream - *09*	14	18
-	**BR** M33006M red - *09*	14	18
-	**BR** M32905M maroon - *09*	14	18
-	**BR** M32991M maroon - *09*	14	18
-	**BR** M33018M maroon - *09*	14	18
-	**BR** M32957M maroon - *12*	14	18
-	**BR** M32990 blue - *09*	14	18
-	**BR** Departmental 975249 red - *09*	14	18
-	**Pullman** 32975 brown - *11*	14	18

Ex-LMS 'Stove R' [C5] (Tony Wright)

LNER Stock

C6.   LNER Gresley Stock

These were produced with new high definition tools and feature a new close coupling system. They are fitted with NEM pockets for couplings and come with optional buckeye close couplings in the box. Initially, only 750 of each unit were made per running number. Those made from 2009 onwards have provision for fitting light bars in the coach. Dapol's Gresley coaches were declared Model Rail Model of the Year in 2007.

C6a.   LNER Gresley Corridor 3rd (2006)

These all-3rd side-corridor coaches were built between the mid-1920s and the mid-1930s and each contained of eight compartments and a lavatory at each end of the coach.

(ND-079-1)	**LNER** 364 teak ex-train pack - *08*	20	NA
NC-046	**LNER** 384 teak - *not made*	NA	NA
NC-045A	**LNER** 258 teak - *09*	16	20
NC-045B	**LNER** 4173 teak - *09*	16	20
NC-045C	**LNER** 60657 teak - *09*	16	20
NC-045D	**LNER** 23853 teak - *09*	16	20
NC-209A	**LNER** 60654 teak - *11*	16	20
NC-209B	**LNER** 60643 teak - *11*	16	20
NC-209C	**LNER** 60656 teak - *11*	16	20
NC-209D	**LNER** 60651 teak - *11*	18	23
NC-209E	**LNER** 60648 teak - *11*	18	23
NC-209F	**LNER** 60647 teak - *11*	18	23
(ND-079-2)	**BR** E12101E red+cream ex-train pack - *not made*	NA	NA
(ND-079-2)	**BR** E12279E red+cream ex-train pack - *08*	NA	20
NC-060A	**BR** E12285E red+cream - *09*	16	20
NC-060B	**BR** E12691E red+cream - *09*	16	20
NC-060C	**BR** E12706E red+cream - *10*	16	20
NC-060D	**BR** E12614E red+cream lb - *10*	16	20
NC-201A	**BR** E12683E red+cream - *11*	18	23
(Nsteam2)	**BR** E12687E red+cream ex-train set - *13*	18	NA
(Nsteam2)	**BR** E12693E red+cream ex-train set - *13*	18	NA
NC-031C	**BR** E12002E maroon - *06*	20	25
NC-031D	**BR** E12071E maroon - *06*	20	25
NC-031A	**BR** E12279E maroon - *06*	20	25
NC-031B	**BR** E12704E maroon - *06*	20	25

C6b.   LNER Gresley Corridor 1st (2007)

These 1st class side-corridor coaches were built between the mid-1920s and the mid-1930s. Each had seven compartments and a lavatory at each end of the coach. The compartments were larger than those in the 3rd class coach - thus the smaller number of them.

(ND-079-1)	**LNER** 31879 teak ex-train pack - *08*	20	NA
NC-044	**LNER** 31878 teak - *not made*	NA	NA
NC-044A	**LNER** 31869 teak - *09*	16	20
NC-044B	**LNER** 22356 teak - *09*	16	20
NC-044C	**LNER** 52401 teak - *09*	16	20
NC-044D	**LNER** 4151 teak - *09*	16	20
NC-208A	**LNER** 31872 teak - *11*	18	23
NC-208B	**LNER** ? teak - *11*	18	23
(ND-079-2)	**BR** E11020E red+cream ex-train pack - *08*	20	NA
NC-059A	**BR** E11023E red+cream - *09*	16	20
(Nsteam2)	**BR** E11025E red+cream ex-train set - *13*	16	NA
NC-059B	**BR** E12028E red+cream - *09*	16	20
NC-059C	**BR** E11015E red+cream - *10*	16	20
NC-059D	**BR** E11027E red+cream lb - *10*	16	20
NC-200A	**BR** E11019E red+cream - *11*	18	23
NC-030B	**BR** E11020E maroon - *07*	20	25
NC-030A	**BR** E11023E maroon - *07*	20	25

C6c.   LNER Gresley Brake Composite (2007)

These brake composite side-corridor coaches were built between the mid-1920s and the mid-1940s. There were four 3rd class compartments, two 1st class and a very small guards and luggage area.

(ND-079-1)	**LNER** 32558 teak ex-train pack - *08*	20	NA
NC-045	**LNER** 32556 teak – *not made*	NA	NA
NC-048A	**LNER** 5550 teak - *?*	16	20
NC-048B	**LNER** 4472 teak - *?*	16	20
NC-211A	**LNER** 5536 teak - *11*	18	23
NC-211B	**LNER** 5531 teak - *11*	18	23
(ND-079-2)	**BR** E10097E red+cream - *not made*	NA	NA
(ND-079-2)	**BR** E10077E red+cream ex-train pack - *08*	20	NA
NC-061C	**BR** E10100 red+cream - *10*	16	20
ND-061D	**BR** E10112E red+cream lb - *10*	16	20
(Nsteam2)	**BR** E?E red+cream ex-train set - *13*	18	NA
NC-032A	**BR** E10077E maroon - *07*	20	25
NC-032B	**BR** E10080E maroon - *07*	20	25

C6d.   LNER Gresley Buffet Car (2007)

25 buffet cars were built between 1933 and 1937. They had open seating for 24 in a 1 + 2 arrangement and consequently had an off-centre corridor. At one end of the car was a kitchen and between that and the seating area was a bar. In some of the kitchens, cooking was done on gas and, others had electric cookers. Some of the Gresley buffet cars lasted long enough to make it into blue and grey paintwork.

Gresley buffet car [C6d] (Dapol)

NC-046A	**LNER** 9113 teak - *09*	16	20
NC-046B	**LNER** 9126 teak - *09*	16	20

Dapol N

NC-210A	**LNER** 2124 teak - *11*	18	23
NC-210B	**LNER** 2128 teak - *11*	18	23
NC-202A	**BR** E9122E red+cream - *12*	18	23
NC-061A	**BR** E9126E red+cream - *09*	16	20
NC-061B	**BR** E9128E red+cream - *09*	16	20
NC-033	**BR** E9132E maroon - *07*	30	35

C6e. LNER Gresley Sleeping Car
Proposed

SR Stock

These coaches will have highly detailed bodies, adjustable internal lighting, NEM coupling pockets, new corridor connectors and a finely printed finish.

C7a. SR Maunsell First Class Coach
Proposed.

C7b. SR Maunsell Composite Coach
Proposed.

C7c. SR Maunsell Brake End
Proposed.

C7d. SR Maunsell Brake Van C
Proposed.

BR Stock

Initially this was limited to two Mk3 coaches and a DVT but in 2012 a Mk3 catering car was added. They are released in both Mk3 (loco hauled) and Mk3A (HST) forms, the latter without buffers. They have moulded plastic bodies with separate glazing inserts. Door release lights are moulded into the body and footsteps are separate fittings. Each type of carriage has the appropriate interior fitting. The models are fitted with NEM pockets for couplings and are ready for the fitting of a light bar, with electric pick-ups on all wheels. Alternative buckeye couplings are provided.

C8a. Mk3 Trailer First (TF) (2009)
The prototype on which this model was based was made in Derby in 1985.

The model's interior has a 2+1 seating format and the seats are orange in the blue and grey model.

NC-037E	**BR** blue with buffers - *not made*	NA	NA
NC-037F	**BR** blue - *not made*	NA	NA
NC-050C	**BR** M11064 blue+grey with buffers - *09*	16	20
NC-051C	**BR** W41136 blue+grey - *09*	16	20
NC-051?	**BR** W41137 blue+grey – *not made*	NA	NA
NC-069A	**BR** M11081 blue+grey with buffers - *10*	16	20
NC-069B	**BR** M11077 blue+grey with buffers - *10*	16	20
(ND-122A)	**BR** W41121 blue+grey ex-train pack - *11*	16	NA
NC-037C	**Intercity** ? grey with buffers - *not made*	NA	NA
NC-037D	**Intercity** ? grey - *not made*	NA	NA
NC-050B	**Intercity** 11031 grey with buffers - *09*	16	20
NC-051B	**Intercity** ? grey - *09*	16	20
NC-051B	**ICs** 41095 - *?*	16	NA
NC-050B	**ICs** 11031 with buffers - *?*	16	NA
(ND-122B)	**ICs** 41086 ex-train pack - *11*	16	NA
(ND-122C)	**ICs** 41029 ex-train pack - *11*	16	NA
NC-037A	**Virgin** red+black with buffers - *not made*	NA	NA
NC-037B	**Virgin** red+black - *not made*	NA	NA
NC-050A	**Virgin** 11017 red+black with buffers - *09*	16	20
NC-051A	**Virgin** 41100 red+black - *09*	16	20
(NC-067)	**Virgin** 11007 red+silver ex-Virgin Relief pack - *10*	16	NA
(NC-067)	**Virgin** 11018 red+silver ex-Virgin Relief pack - *10*	16	NA
(NC-067)	**Virgin** 11048 red+silver ex-Virgin Relief pack - *10*	16	NA
(ND-122D)	**Virgin** 41079 red+black ex-train pack - *11*	16	NA
(ND-122E)	**Grand Central** 41204 black ex-train pack - *11*	16	NA
(ND-122F)	**FGW** 41132 purple ex-train pack - *11*	16	NA
4P005000	**FGW** 41103 [G] purple - *12*	16	20
(ND-122L)	**East Midlands** 41076 - *12*	16	NA
ND-226A	**East Midlands** 42384 - *not made - see TS*	16	20
NC-226B	**Cross Country** 45002 silver - *12*	16	20
(ND-122G)	**Cross Country** 41194 silver ex-train pack - *12*	16	NA

Arriva Cross-Country Mk3 1st class [C8a] (Hattons)

C8b. Mk3 Trailer Open Standard (TS) (2009)
The prototype used for this model was a Mk3 HST Trailer Open Standard which was built at Derby between 1976 and 1982.

The model has 2+2 seating format and the seats are blue in the blue and grey model.

NC-038E	**BR** blue with buffers - *not made*	NA	NA
NC-038F	**BR** blue - *not made*	NA	NA
NC-053C	**BR** W42252 blue+grey - *09*	16	20
NC-053?	**BR** W42251 blue+grey – *not made*	NA	NA
NC-053F	**BR** W42280 blue+grey - *09*	16	20
NC-053?	**BR** W42279 blue+grey - *09*	16	20
NC-064A	**BR** ? blue+grey – *11?*	16	20
NC-064B	**BR** ? blue+grey – *11?*	16	20
(ND-122A)	**BR** W42288 blue+grey ex-train pack - *11*	16	NA
NC-052C	**BR** 12043 blue+grey with buffers - *09*	16	20
NC-052F	**BR** M12047 blue+grey with buffers - *?*	16	20
NC-068A	**BR** M12119 blue+grey with buffers - *10*	16	20
NC-068B	**BR** M12095 blue+grey with buffers - *10*	16	20
NC-068C	**BR** M12063 blue+grey with buffers - *10*	16	20
NC-068D	**BR** M12068 blue+grey with buffers - *10*	16	20
NC-038C	**Intercity** grey with buffers - *not made*	NA	NA
NC-038D	**Intercity** grey - *not made*	NA	NA
NC-053B	**Intercity** 42101 grey - *09*	16	20
(ND-122C)	**ICs** 42284 ex-train pack - *11*	16	NA
NC-052B	**ICs** 12067 grey with bufferes - *09*	16	20
NC-052E	**ICs** 12079 grey with bufferes - *09*	16	20
NC-053E	**ICs** 42148 grey - *?*	16	20
(ND-122B)	**ICs** 42161 grey ex-train pack - *11*	16	NA
(ND-122C)	**ICs** 42281 grey ex-train pack - *11*	16	NA
NC-212A	**ICs** 42180 grey - *?*	16	20
NC-212B	**ICs** 42235 grey - *?*	16	20
NC-063A	**ICs** ? grey - *11?*	16	20
NC-063B	**ICs** ? grey - *11?*	16	20
NC-065A	**IC Executive** ? grey – *11?*	16	20
NC-065B	**IC Executive** ? grey – *11?*	16	20
NC-226C	**Inter-City** Executive 42283 grey - *12*	16	20
NC-227C	**Inter-City** Executive 42284 grey - *12*	16	20
NC-038A	**Virgin** red+black with buffers - *not made*	NA	NA
NC-038B	**Virgin** red+black - *not made*	NA	NA
NC-052A	**Virgin** 12085 red+black with buffers - *09*	16	20
NC-052D	**Virgin** 12032 red+black with buffers - *?*	16	20
NC-053A	**Virgin** 42235 red+black - *09*	16	20
NC-053D	**Virgin** 42207 red+black - *?*	16	20
(ND-122D)	**Virgin** 42154 red+black ex-train pack - *11*	16	NA
NC-062A	**Virgin** ? red+black - *11?*	16	20
NC-062B	**Virgin** ? red+black - *11?*	16	20
NC-066A	**Virgin** Charter Relief 12011 red+silver - *10*	16	NA
NC-066B	**Virgin** Charter Relief 12078 red+silver - *10*	16	NA
NC-066C	**Virgin** Charter Relief 12133 red+silver - *10*	16	NA

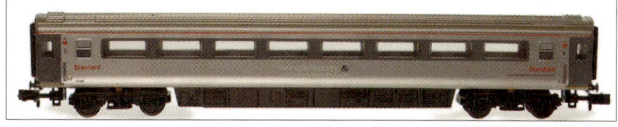

Wrexham & Shropshire standard open Mk3 coach [C8b] (Dapol)

(2P005002)	**Virgin** ? red+silver - *12*	16	NA
(ND-101D)	**Wrexham & Shropshire** 12127 greys with buffers ex-train pack - *09*	16	NA
(ND-101D)	**Wrexham & Shropshire** 12145 greys with buffers ex-train pack - *09*	16	NA
(2P005002)	**Wrexham & Shropshire** ? silver+grey - *13*	16	NA
(ND-122E)	**Grand Central** 42401 black ex-train pack - *11*	16	NA
NC-214A	**Grand Central** 42405 black - *11*	16	20

Dapol N

Cat No.	Description	£	£
NC-214B	Grand Central 42402 * black - 11	16	20
(ND-122F)	FGW 42073 purple ex-train pack - 11	16	NA
NC-213A	FGW 42038 purple ex-train pack - 11	16	20
4P005001	FGW 42083 [E] purple - 13	16	20
NC-213B	FGW 42296 purple ex-train pack - 11	16	20
NC-221A	BR RTC ADB97514 red+blueTest Coach 10 Ltd Edn - 11	20	24
(ND-122L)	East Midlands 42149 - 12	16	NA
ND-226A	East Midlands ** 42384 - 12	16	20
ND-227A	East Midlands ** 42341 - 12	16	20
ND-227B	Cross Country ? - 12	16	20
(ND-122G)	Cross Country 42371 ex-train pack - 12	16	NA

*Some early boxes were incorrectly labelled '42401'. ** Name missing off sides of coach!

C8c. Mk3 Restaurant 1st Modular RFM (2012)

Known running numbers used on the model suggest that the prototype was an HST Trailer Buffet Standard which was built in 1976 or 1977 at BR Derby.
This model has four large saloon windows, good interior detail, NEM pockets for couplings and is ready for the fitting of a light bar.

Cat No.	Description	£	£
NC-039E	BR ? blue with buffers - not made	NA	NA
NC-039F	BR ? blue - not made	NA	NA
NC-216A	BR ? blue+grey - 13	16	20
NC-039C	Intercity ? grey with buffers - not made	NA	NA
NC-039D	Intercity ? grey - not made	NA	NA
NC-216E	Intercity ? grey - 13	16	20
NC-039A	Virgin ? red+black with buffers - not made	NA	NA
NC-039B	Virgin ? red+black - not made	NA	NA
NC-216B	Virgin ? red+black - 13	16	20
NC-216D	Virgin ? red+silver - 13	16	20
(2P005002)	Virgin ? red+silver - 13	16	NA
NC-216J	Grand Central 40426 black+orange - 12	18	23
NC-216C	Wrexham & Shropshire ? silver+grey - 13	16	20
(2P005002)	Wrexham & Shropshire ? silver+grey - 13	16	NA
NC-216H	FGW 40210 purple - 13	16	20
NC-216K	East Midlands 40728 - 13	16	20

First Great Western Mk3 restaurant car [C8c] (Dapol)

C8d. Mk3 TGS

Proposed.

Cat No.	Description	£	£
NC-?	BR blue - not made	NA	NA
NC-?	Intercity grey - not made	NA	NA
NC-?	Virgin red+black - not made	NA	NA

C9. Mk3b DVT (2009)

The real vehicles were part of BR's plan to introduce unit train operation to its InterCity fleet on the WCML. 52 of the cars were built between 1988 and 1990 and they greatly increased the efficiency of trains powered by the AC electric locomotives. They were taken over by Virgin Trains but eventually the 'push-pull' trains that used them were replace by 'Pendolinos'. Some of the displaced DVTs found new life with One Anglia on trains between Norwich and Liverpool Street. Others went to the Wrexham & Shropshire operation.
The model is 'DCC ready' (NEM 651 socket) and has NEM coupling pockets with choice of couplings. It also has directional lighting and darkened wheels.

Cat No.	Description	£	£
ND-089C	Intercity 82116 grey - 09	20	25
ND-089D	Intercity 82132 grey - 09	20	25
ND-089A	Virgin 82106 red+black - 09	20	25
ND-089B	Virgin 82125 red+black - 09	20	25
NC-067	Virgin Charter Relief 82126 red+silver + 3 Mk3 FOs DC6 - 10	60	75
(ND-101-1)	EWS 82146 silver with buffers ex-train pack – 11	18	NA
(ND-101D)	Wrexham & Shropshire 82304 silver+grey with buffers ex-train pack – 11	18	NA

C10. 'Super Voyager' Car (2007)

Each model was supplied with a sheet of transfers for numbering.

Cat No.	Description	£	£
ND-073E	Virgin un-numbered silver+red - 07	12	15
ND-087C	X Country un-numbered silver+black+red - 08	12	15

WAGONS

Cat No.	Company, Number, Colour, Date	£	£

Planked Wagons

W1. 3-Plank Wagon

Proposed but no longer in the catalogue.

W2. 7-Plank Open Wagon (end door) (2005)

7-plank wagons were mostly privately owned and used for the transportation of coal. Between the wars they were the most numerous wagon type on Britain's railways. They were requisitioned by the government during the Second World War and passed to BR in 1948. During the 1950s the aging fleet was gradually replaced by steel mineral wagons.
This model serves the same purpose as the 7-plank wagon in the 00 range and is being well used for commissions.

Cat No.	Description	£	£
2F071000	unpainted - ?	4	8
No.N022	'Abingdon on Thames Gas Dept.' red Sp Edn (West Wales Wagon Works) - 09	6	8
No.N022	'Abingdon on Thames Gas Dept.' red W Sp Edn (West Wales Wagon Works) - 09	6	8
-	'Ace of Clubs Brewery' brown Sp Edn 100 (Modelbahn Union) ex-twin pack with Albion Brewery - 08	6	NA
-	'Ace of Clubs Brewery' grey Sp Edn (Japan Model Railways Germany) ex-set of 3 - 10	7	NA
-	'Ackton Hall Colliery' 25 black Sp Edn (Pennine Wagons) - 08	6	9
-	'Albion Brewery' 12 blue Sp Edn 100 (Modelbahn Union) ex-twin pack with Ace of Clubs - 08	6	NA
-	'Albion Brewery' dark grey Sp Edn (Japan Model Railways Germany) ex-set of 3 - 10	7	NA
-	'Albion Dockyard' 10 black Sp Edn (Medway Queen Preservation Society) - 10	6	8

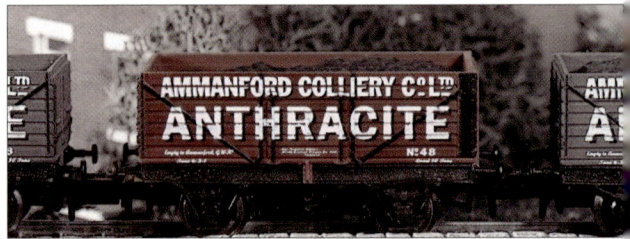

7-plank wagon 'Ammanford Colliery' [W2] (Dapol)

Cat No.	Description	£	£
NB-109	'Ammanford Colliery Co. Anthracite' 48 black - 11	7	9
2F071010	'Ammanford Colliery Co. Anthracite' 48 dark brown - 13	7	8
2F071011	'Ammanford Colliery Co. Anthracite' 48 dark brown W - 13	7	8
-	'Arscott' light grey Sp Edn (Midland Model Products) - 08	5	7
-	'MC Ashwin & Son' 24 red Sp Edn (Stephen Braund) - 07	5	7
No.N004	'Baker & Kernick' 410 black Sp Edn 110 (West Wales Wagon Works) - 05	5	8
-	'C Ball' 1 red Sp Edn (Osbourn Models) - 06	6	9
-	'Baltic Sawmills' 10 red-brown Sp Edn 100 (Ballards) - 05	5	7
-	'Bennett & Carter' 12 light grey with sand load Sp Edn 100 (Ballards) - 07	6	9
-	'Billingsley' 17 brown Sp Edn (DMB Footplate) - 06	5	7
-	'John T Bingham' 10 black Sp Edn (Ballards) - 07	5	8
-	'Fredrick Biss' 3 grey 200 Sp Edn (Bristol East MRC) - 06	5	8
(ND-146)	'Blackman, Pavie & Ladden' 577 brown – ex-set - made?	NPG	NA
2F071009	'Blackman, Pavie & Ladden' 577 Brown - 12	10	12
-	'Black Park' 324 red	6	NA
-	'Black Park' 2024 red	6	NA
NB-912	above 2 wagons in a twin pack Ltd Edn (Dapol Shop) - 11	NA	12
(NB-OSB-004)	'Black Rock Quarries' 49 black Sp Edn (Osborn's Models) ex-twin pack with Clevedon Gas - 09	5	NA

Dapol N

No.	Description		
No.N003	'Bliss Tweed Mills' 6 green Sp Edn 150 (West Wales Wagon Works) - 05	5	8
NB-020	'Blue Circle' 173 yellow - 05	5	7
NB-071	'Bourne Fisher '21 red Ltd Edn 250 - 08	5	7
-	'Britannic' 1346 black Sp Edn (Lord & Butler) - 07	5	8
-	'FW Butcher' 3 green Sp Edn 100 (Ballards) - 05	5	8
-	'Burton-on-Trent Co-op' 11 maroon Sp Edn 150 (Tutbury) - 05	5	7
-	'FW Butcher' 3 green Sp Edn 100 (Ballards) - 05	5	8

7-plank wagon 'Bute Merthyr' [W2] (Dapol)

7-plank wagon 'Fear Bros' [W2] (Dapol)

No.	Description		
-	'Bute 115 black Sp Edn (Lord & Butler) - 07	5	8
NB-034	'Bute Merthyr' 325 black - 06	5	7
-	'TF Butler' 129 red Sp Edn (Craft Hobbies) - 10	6	8
-	'T Butt & Son' black Sp Edn (Antics) - 07	6	8
No.N013	'Caerbryn Colliery' 219 black Sp Edn (West Wales Wagon Works) - 07	5	7
No.N013	'Caerbryn Colliery' 219 black W Sp Edn (West Wales Wagon Works) - 08	5	7
-	'R Carder & Co.' brown Sp Edn (Pennine Models) - 07	6	9
-	'Cardigan Mercantile Co.' black Sp Edn (West Wales Wagon Works) - 09	5	8
PW001	'CFC (Chapman Fletcher & Cawood)' 980 black Sp Edn 96 (Pennine Wagons) - 05	6	8
NB-OSB-004	'Clevedon Gas Company' 21 grey Sp Edn (Osborn's Models) ex-twin pack with Black Rock Quarries - 09	5	NA
-	'Corrall & Co.' 401 brown Sp Edn (Ballards) - 07	6	8
-	'Corrall & Co.' 514 brown Sp Edn (Ballards) - 09	7	9
-	'Crane & Co.' 107 red Sp Edn 195 (Bristol East MRC) - 05	6	8
-	'Alexander Crane' 102 brown Sp Edn (Antics) - 06	6	8
-	'Coventry Collieries' 1404 black Sp Edn (Castle Trains) - 07	6	8
CCN-N	'Crynant Colliery' Sp Edn (West Wales Wagon Works) - not made	NA	NA
-	'Crystalate' 1262 yellow Sp Edn 100 (Ballards) - 07	5	8
-	'Dapol Club' 1 purple Sp Edn (Dapol) - 07	5	8
-	'Dapol Club Open Days' grey Sp Edn (Dapol) - 07	5	8
NB-057	'Dinnington Main' 641 dark blue - 07	6	8
-	'Drake & Mount' 6 grey Sp Edn (West Wales Wagon Works) - 12	7	9
-	'Economic Coal Co.' 3 red Sp Edn (DMB Footplate Models) - 07	6	8
-	'BF Falkner' 1 brown Sp Edn (Gloucester & Warwickshire Railway) - 06	6	9
-	'G E Farrant' 21 brown Sp Edn 100 (Ballards) - 05	6	8
No.N007	'Fear Bros.' 41 red-brown Sp Edn 84 (West Wales Wagon Works) - 06	5	7
No.N020	'JU Freeman' 3 black Sp Edn 69 (West Wales Wagon Works) - 08	6	8
No.N020	'JU Freeman' 3 black W Sp Edn 29 (West Wales Wagon Works) - 08	7	9
No.N010	'Isaiah Gadd' 29 Sp Edn (West Wales Wagon Works) - 07	5	7
No.N023	'Glan-Garnant' 392? black Sp Edn 75 (West Wales Wagon Works) - 09	8	11
No.N023W	'Glan-Garnant' 392? black W Sp Edn 35 (West Wales Wagon Works) - 09	9	12

No.	Description		
BRM/N47	'Gloucester Gas Light Company' 37 black Sp Edn 500 (BRM Magazine) - 05	6	8
BRM/N49	'Gloucester Gas Light Company' 51 black Sp Edn 500 (BRM Magazine) - 05	6	8
No.N006	'Gresford Colliery' 638 black Sp Edn 129 (West Wales Wagon Works) - 06	5	8
No.N011	'Gwili Railway' 1 grey+red Sp Edn (West Wales Wagon Works) - 07	5	8
-	'Hall & Co.' 499 red-brown Sp Edn (E Surrey N Gauge Group) - 07	5	8
-	'Hall & Co.' 597 red-brown Sp Edn (E Surrey N Gauge Group) - 07	5	8
NB-025	'Hartnell & Son' 22 black - 05	5	7
-	'Hempsted' 37 black Sp Edn 500 (BRM) - not made	NA	NA
-	'Helston Gas Company' 10 black Sp Edn (Kernow Models) - 06	6	NA
-	'Helston Gas Company' 30 black Sp Edn (Kernow Models) - 06	6	NA
NB-001K	above two models	NA	15
-	'The High Brooms Brick & Tile Co.' maroon Sp Edn (Ballards) - 05	6	8
-	'Highley Mining' 246 brown Sp Edn (Severn Valley Railway) - 06	5	7
-	'Hills Bros' 3 red-brown Sp Edn (Ballards) - 09	5	7
No.N014	'Hind & Fisher' 2007 brown Sp Edn (West Wales Wagon Works) - 07	5	7
No.N014	'Hind & Fisher' 2007 brown W Sp Edn (West Wales Wagon Works) - 07	5	7
-	'Hood & Sons' 1 green Sp Edn (Salisbury Model Centre) - 07	5	7
-	'Hood & Sons' 2 green Sp Edn (Salisbury Model Centre) - 07	5	7
No.N017	'Horlicks' 2 red Sp Edn 80 (West Wales Wagon Works) - 08	5	7
No.N017	'Horlicks' 2 red W Sp Edn 20 (West Wales Wagon Works) - 08	6	8
No.N027M	'Wm Hubbard' 30 black Sp Edn 81 (West Wales Wagon Works) - 11	9	11
No.N027W	'Wm Hubbard' 30 black W Sp Edn 20 (West Wales Wagon Works) - 11	10	12
-	'AP Hudson' 21 red-brown Sp Edn (Antics) - 07	5	7
No.N001	'Huntley & Palmer' 21 black Sp Edn 100 (West Wales Wagon Works) - 05	5	7
NB-102	'ICI' 326 red - made?	NPG	NPG
2F071012	'ICI' 326 red - 13	7	8
2F071013	'ICI' 326 red W - 13	7	8
-	'Samuel Jeffries' 14 red Sp Edn (Antics) - 06	6	8
No.N024M	'John Kerkin' 1 grey Sp Edn 90 (West Wales Wagon Works) - 10	9	11
No.N024W	'John Kerkin' 1 grey W Sp Edn 20 (West Wales Wagon Works) - 10	10	12
PW003	'Lancashire Foundry Coke Co.' 322 grey Sp Edn 96 (Pennine Wagons) - 05	6	8
-	'SV Lancey' 20 blue Sp Edn 112 (Stephen Braund) - 07	6	8
-	'Leamington Priors Gas Co.' 10 red - 10	6	8
-	'Leamington Priors Gas Co.' 10 red W - 10	6	8
-	'Lewis Merthyr Navigation' 768 black Sp Edn (Lord & Butler) - 06	5	7

Dapol N

7-plank wagon 'Lewis Merthyr Navigation' [W2] (Dapol)

Code	Description		
-	'RA **Lister**' 1 brown Sp Edn (Antics) - *07*	6	8
(NB1S)	'**Llay Main**' 588 black from set of 2 - *06*	6	9
(NB1S)	'**Llay Main**' 591 black from set of 2 - *06*	6	9
NB-073	'**Maltby Main**' 298 red-brown Ltd Edn 250 - *08*	5	8
-	'**Medway Coal**' 17 black Sp Edn (Ballards) - *08*	5	8
-	**Mid Hants Rly** black Sp Edn (Mid-Hants Railway) - *05*	5	7
-	**Mid Suffolk** 25 grey Sp Edn (Middy Trading Company) - *09*	5	7
NB-021	'**Miller & Lilley**' 66 black - *05*	5	7
-	'WW **Milton & Co.**' 6 brown Sp Edn (Antics) - *07*	5	8
-	'WW **Milton & Co.**' 6 grey Sp Edn (Antics) - *07*	5	8
-	**Ministry of Munitions** ? black? Sp Edn 150? (West Wales Wagon Works) - *10*	6	8
No.N009	'**Mwrwg-Vale**' 26 brown Sp Edn (West Wales Wagon Works) - *06*	6	9
No.N008	'**New Cross Hands Collieries**' 392 grey Sp Edn 100 (West Wales Wagon Works) - *06*	5	7
No.N002	'**New Cwmgorse**' 42 brown Sp Edn 100 (West Wales Wagon Works) - *05*	5	7
-	'**New Medway Steam Packet Co.**' 24 green Sp Edn 109 (Medway Queen PS) - *06*	6	8
No.N005	'G D **Owen**' 16 red-brown Sp Edn 93 (West Wales Wagon Works) - *05*	5	8
-	'**Peacock Bros. & Harris**' 6 red-brown Sp Edn (Ballards) - *08*	6	9
-	'**Pemberton & Co.**' 25 brown Sp Edn 100 (Osborne Models) - *06*	6	9
MLS?	'**Pilkington Brothers Ltd**' 1489 red with sand load Sp Edn 115 (Mill Lane Sidings) - *08*	6	9
MLS?	'**Pilkington Brothers Ltd**' 1489 red W with sand load Sp Edn 20 (Mill Lane Sidings) - *08*	6	9
-	'**Renwick & Wilton**' 1020 black Sp Edn 100 (Osborne Models) - *05*	5	7
-	'**Ringwood Coal - Thomas Bailey**' ? ? Sp Edn (Salisbury Model Centre) - *08*	6	9
No.N019	'Issac **Roberts**' 19 black Sp Edn (W Wales Wagon Works) - *08*	6	9
No.N019	'Issac **Roberts**' 19 black W Sp Edn (W Wales Wagon Works) - *08*	6	9
(ND-146)	'**Sargent Longstaff & Co.**' 1047 brown ex-set - made?	NPG	NA
2F071008	'**Sargent Longstaff & Co.**' 1047 brown - *12*	10	12

7-plank wagon 'Seddon's Salt' [W2] (Dapol)

	'**Seddon's Salt**' 224 red-brown Sp Edn (Pennine Wagons) - *06*	6	9
Ant09	'**Sheffield & Eccleshall Co-op**' 12 Sp Edn (Antics) – *08?*	6	9
-	'J **Shepherd**' 3 grey Sp Edn (Salisbury Model Centre) - *08*	6	9
-	'J **Skinner**' 8 green+red	8	NA
-	'S **Skinner**' 1 green+red	8	NA
-	above 2 wagons Sp Edn 107 (Stephen Braund) - *07*	NA	18
Ant08	'**Alfred J Smith**' ? red Sp Edn (Antics) - *08*	7	9
-	'GH **Smith & Son**' 24 black Sp Edn 100 (Ballards) - *06*	5	8
NB-019	'**Somerset Trading**' 58 red - *05*	5	7
NB-058	'**South Wales**' 20 grey - *07*	6	8
(ND-146)	'**South Western Railway Servants Coal Club**' 8 black ex-set - made?	NPG	NA
2F071007	'**South Western Railway Servants Coal Club**' 8 dark grey - *12*	10	12
-	'**Stevens**' 2001 red Sp Edn (Dapol N'thusiasts Club) - *11*	12	15
-	'**Stevens Silica Brick Co.**' 24 brown Sp Edn 80 (West Wales Wagon Works) - *11*	6	8
-	'**Stevens Silica Brick Co.**' 24 brown W Sp Edn 19 (West Wales Wagon Works) - *11*	6	8
-	'GS **Sturgeon**' 465 black Sp Edn 100 (Ballards) - *08*	5	8
No.N024M	'**Edward Sutcliffe**' 75? red-brown Sp Edn (West Wales Wagon Works) - *10*	9	11
No.N024W	'**Edward Sutcliffe**' 75? red-brown W Sp Edn (West Wales Wagon Works) - *10*	10	12
-	'H **Syrus**' 1 light grey Sp Edn 100 (Ballards) - *08*	6	9
NB-024	'**Taylor**' 3 grey - *05*	5	7
-	'**Tilmanstone Colliery**' 120 brown Sp Edn 100 (Hythe Kent Models) - *05*	5	7
No.N012	'**Thomas Thomas**' 1 black Sp Edn (West Wales Wagon Works) - *07*	6	8
No.N012	'**Thomas Thomas**' 1 black W Sp Edn (West Wales Wagon Works) - *08*	7	9
-	'**Tunbridge Wells Co-op**' 1 red-brown Sp Edn 100 (Ballards) - *06*	5	8
No.N018	'**Vincent**' 31 red Sp Edn (West Wales Wagon Works) - *08*		
-	'John **Walker**' 2 black Sp Edn (Castle Trains) - *07*	6	8
-	'**Warwick Gas Light Co.**' 6 grey - *10*	6	8
-	'**Warwick Gas Light Co.**' 6 grey W - *10*	6	8
-	'**Wetmore**' 27 red 100 Sp Edn (Bristol East MRC) - *08*	6	8

7-plank wagon 'Richard White' [W2] (Dapol)

-	'**Richard White & Sons**' 109 light blue Sp Edn 250 (Antics) - *08*	7	9
-	'**Willow Brewery**' green Sp Edn (Japan Model Railways Germany) ex-pack of 3 - *10*	7	NA
NB-072	'**Whitwood**' 1583 grey+red Ltd Edn 250 - *08*	5	7
NB-026	'**Wigan Coal**' A147 grey - *05*	5	7
-	'**Winchcombe Coal Co.**' 7 grey Sp Edn (Gloucester & Warwickshire Railway) - *05*	5	7
No.N021	'**Woolcombers**' 15 red-brown Sp Edn (West Wales Wagon Works) - *09*	5	7
No.N021	'**Woolcombers**' 15 red-brown W Sp Edn (West Wales Wagon Works) - *09*	5	7
-	**WSNG** 250100 green Sp Edn (West Sussex Group of N Gauge Society) – *11*	6	8
-	**WSNG** 250200 blue Sp Edn (West Sussex Group of N Gauge Society) – *11*	6	8

Dapol N

-	**WSNG** 250300 red-brown Sp Edn (West Sussex Group of N Gauge Society) – *11*	6	8
-	**WSNG** 250400 brown Sp Edn (West Sussex Group of N Gauge Society) – *11*	6	8
NB-105	**GWR** 06577 grey - *11*	6	8
2F071014	**GWR** ? dark grey - *13*	6	8
2F071015	**GWR** ? dark grey - *13*	6	8
2F071003	**LMS** 302078 grey - *12*	6	8
2F071004	**LMS** 302078 grey W - *12*	6	8
2F071003	**SR** 37423 dark brown - *not made*	6	8
2F071004	**SR** 37423 dark brown W - *not made*	6	8
2F071005	**SR** 37423 dark brown - *12*	6	8
2F071006	**SR** 37423 dark brown W - *12*	6	8
2F071001	**BR** P238832 pale grey - *12*	6	8
2F071002	**BR** P238832 pale grey W - *12*	6	8

W3. 8-Plank Wagon 9' Wheelbase (2010)

This is a model of the Railway Clearing House (RCH) design of 1923 with timber frames and a 9ft wheelbase. The 8-plank wagons were also generally built for coal and had a slightly larger capacity.

The model has good internal detail, a high definition body and chassis moulding, darkened wheels, turned brass buffers, NEM coupler boxes and separately applied brake rigging and lever. The models are produced for Dapol by Helixon in China.

8-plank wagon 'LC' [W3] (Dapol)

FMR-N1	'Jabez **Cole**' 151 black Sp Edn (FMR) - *10*	5	7
-	'Jabez **Cole**' 17 black Sp Edn (Frizinghall) - *10*	6	8
NB-095A	'**Colthorp**' 123 black - *09*	5	7
NB-094A	'**Gas Company Pennistone**' 7 red - *10*	5	7
NB-085**A**	'**Hatfield Main**' 1213 brown - *09*	5	7
NB-083A	'**LC**' (Littleton Collieries) 151 black - *10*	5	7
NB-091A	'**Leamington Spa**' 24 red - *10*	5	7
NB-084A	'**Partington Steel & Iron Co.**' 184 brown - *10*	5	7
NB-092A	'**Smith Parkinson & Cole**' 5009 black - *10*	5	7
NB-096A	'**Stewarts & Lloyds**' 6301 grey - *10*	5	7
NB-093A	'**Thorncliffe Izal**' 2915 black - *10*	5	7

W4. 8-Plank Coke Wagon 9' Wheelbase
Proposed but no longer in the catalogue.

Steel & Hopper Wagons

W5. 'Sea Urchin' Engineers Wagon
Proposed but no longer in the catalogue.

W6. BR 'Grampus' Open Wagon (2013)

From the early 1950s, the versatile Grampus was a major ballast and spoil carrier in the BR Engineer's fleet until the beginning of the 1980s. Almost 4,800 were built by outside firms during the 1950s and included several design variations. They were to be found all over the British network but were replaced by higher capacity and sturdier vehicles as the industry modernised. The wagon had removable end planks and drop-down sides.

These models have NEM coupling pockets, ballast loads and close coupling.

NB-080D	'**Taunton Concrete Works**' ? green - *13*	10	13
2F060007	'**Taunton Concrete Works**' DB986703 green - *13*	10	13
2F060008	**BR** DB991391 black - *13*	10	13
2F060009	**BR** DB991391 black - *13*	10	13
2F060009	**BR** DB991601 black - *13*	10	13
NB-080B	**BR Eng** ? brown - *13*	10	13
NB-080C	**BR Eng** ? grey - *13*	10	13
2F060001	**BR** DB991601 red - *not made*	10	13
2F060001	**BR** DB990641 red-brown - *13*	10	13
2F060002	**BR** DB990648 red-brown - *13*	10	13
2F060003	**BR Civil Eng.** DB988546 grey+yellow - *13*	10	13
2F060004	**BR Civil Eng.** DB981487 grey+yellow - *13*	10	13
2F060005	**BR Civil Eng.** DB991643 grey+yellow - *13*	10	13
2F060006	**BR Civil Eng.** DB991570 grey+yellow - *13*	10	13

W7. BR 20T Steel Mineral Wagon (2006)

This is a model based on a GWR design of the 1930s, many of which were built for locomotive coal transportation. BR continued to construct similar looking wagons after Nationalisation.

Initially, 500 of each number were made.

2F038000	unpainted - ?	4	8
NB-060A	'**Blaenavon**' 2438 brown - *07*	8	10
NB-060B	'**Blaenavon**' 2441 brown - *07*	8	10
NB-060C	'**Blaenavon**' 2449 brown - *07*	8	10
NB-060D	'**Blaenavon**' 2450 brown - *07*	8	10

20T steel mineral wagon 'Bolsover' [W7] (Dapol)

NB-108	'**Bolsover**' 6390 brown - *11*	8	10
2F038013	'**Bolsover**' 6390 brown - *13*	8	10
2F038014	'**Bolsover**' 6390 brown W - *13*	8	10
No.N015	'**Cicely**' 23 black Sp Edn (West Wales Wagon Works) - *07*	8	10
No.N015	'**Cicely**' 23 black W Sp Edn (West Wales Wagon Works) - *08*	9	11
NB-113	'**Cicely**' 12 black - *11*	8	10
2F038011	'**Cicely**' 12 black - *13*	8	10
2F038012	'**Cicely**' 12 black W - *13*	8	10
-	'**Dapol**' 3 purple Sp Edn (Dapol N'thusiasts Club) - *09*	12	15
NB-104	'**Emlyn Anthracite**' 2000 grey - *11*	8	10
2F038009	'**Emlyn Anthracite**' 2000 grey - *12*	8	10
2F038010	'**Emlyn Anthracite**' 2000 grey W - *12*	8	11
No.N016	GW '**Ebbw Vale Steel Works**' 109728 grey Sp Edn (West Wales Wagon Works) - *08*	8	10
No.N016	GW '**Ebbw Vale Steel Works**' 109728 grey W Sp Edn (West Wales Wagon Works) - *08*	9	11
-	'**New Medway Steam Packet Co.**' 37 green Sp Edn (Medway Queen Preservation Society) - *08*	8	10
\	'**New Medway Steam Packet Co.**' 37 black Sp Edn (Medway Queen Preservation Society) - *08*	8	10
NB-041A	'**PJ&JP**' 3619 black - *06*	8	10
NB-041B	'**PJ&JP**' 3621 black - *06*	8	10
-	'**Stevens**' 1001 red Sp Edn (Dapol N'thusiasts Club) - *11*	10	12
NB-112	'**West Midlands Joint Electricity Authority**' 18? black - *11*	8	10
2F038007	'**West Midlands Joint Electricity Authority**' 18 black - *13*	8	10
2F038008	'**West Midlands Joint Electricity Authority**' 18 black W - *13*	8	11
NB-059A	**GWR** 33156 grey - *07*	8	10
NB-059B	**GWR** 33147 grey - *07*	8	10
NB-059C	**GWR** 33153 grey - *07*	8	10
NB-059D	**GWR** 33162 grey - *07*	8	10
2F038003	**GWR** 33223 dark grey - *12*	8	10
2F038004	**GWR** 33223 dark grey W - *12*	8	11
NB-040A	**BR** P339377K grey - *06*	8	10
NB-040B	**BR** P339354K grey – *06*	8	10
NB-040C	**BR** P339391K grey – *06*	8	10
NB-040D	**BR** P339324K grey – *06*	8	10
2F038005	**BR** B315764 grey - *13*	8	10
2F038006	**BR** B315764 grey W - *13*	8	11

W8. BR 21T Hopper Wagon (2006)
The model was based on an LNER 20 ton coal hopper wagon design of 1936 for use in

Dapol N

the North East. At Nationalisation, the LNER handed over more than 8000 of them to BR, who continued to build more as their standard 21 ton hopper wagon. They were built by a number of different firms and later by BR Shildon Wagon Works, so there were detail differences. They all had two bottom doors for gravity unloading.
Initially, 500 of each number were made.

2F034000	unpainted - ?	4	8
NB-046A	'British Steel' 26 brown - 07	8	10
NB-046B	'British Steel' 22 brown - 07	8	10
2F034005	'British Steel' 32 brown - 12	7	9
2F034006	'British Steel' 32 brown W - 12	7	9
NB-047A	House Coal B421943 brown - 07	8	10
NB-047B	House Coal B421957 brown - 07	8	10
NB-0?	Locomotion B429897 brown - 07	8	10

NCB 21T hopper wagon [W8] (Dapol)

NB-039A	'NCB' 128 grey - 06	8	10
NB-039B	'NCB' 198 grey - 06	8	10
NB-039C	'NCB' 136 grey - 06	8	10
NB-039D	'NCB' 154 grey - 06	8	10
(ND-084Z)	'NCB' 128 grey W Sp End (Dapol Club) - 09	8	10
(ND-084Z)	'NCB' 135 grey W Sp End (Dapol Club) - 09	8	10
(ND-084Z)	'NCB' 136 grey W Sp End (Dapol Club) - 09	8	10
(ND-084Z)	'NCB' 154 grey W Sp End (Dapol Club) - 09	8	10
(ND-084Z)	'NCB' 198 grey W Sp End (Dapol Club) - 09	8	10
2F034003	'NCB' 128 grey - 12	7	9
2F034004	'NCB' 128 grey W - 12	7	9
-	MHR 52007 grey Sp Edn (Mid Hants Railway) - 07	8	10
-	'Pilkington Brothers' 1973 red Sp Edn 112 (Mill Lane Sidings) - 09	7	8
NB-106	'Sykes' 10 grey - 11	9	11
2F034007	'Sykes' 10 grey - 13	7	9
2F034008	'Sykes' 10 grey W - 13	7	9
NB-110	'G Weaver' 154 brown - 11	9	11
NB-110W	'G Weaver' 154 brown W - 11	9	11
2F034009	'G Weaver' 154 brown - 13	7	9
2F034010	'G Weaver' 154 brown W - 13	7	9
2F034001	NE 193264 pale grey - 12	7	9
2F034002	NE 193264 pale grey W - 12	7	9
NB-038A	BR E289595K grey - 06	8	10
NB-038B	BR E307163K grey - 06	8	10
NB-038C	BR B414050? grey - 06	8	10
NB-038D	BR B414038? grey - 06	8	10
NB-118	BR E289535 grey - 11	9	11
CRS-003P	BR B429487 brown Sp Edn (County Rolling Stock) - 10	9	11
CRS-003W	BR B429487 brown W Sp Edn (County Rolling Stock) - 10	9	12
2F034011	BR E289595K grey - 12	7	9
2F034012	BR E289595K grey W - 12	7	9
-	MoT 1328 black Iron Ore Sp Edn (Dapol 'N'Thusiasts Club) - 12	10	12

W9. ZFV 'Dogfish' Hopper Wagon (2005)

The 'Dogfish' and 'Catfish' were British Rail's standard small ballast hopper wagons of which around 2000 were built from 1955 onwards and survived in service well into the current century.

Unless otherwise stated, 500 of each running number were made. The brown wagons are sprayed to appear rusty with parts of the lettering missing and all 10 wagons are different and so too are the two sides of each wagon. Five of the 10 black hoppers have Scottish ESC markings.

NB-029A	BR DB993315 grey - 05	8	10
NB-029B	BR DB993037 grey - 05	8	10
NB-029C	BR DB993024 grey - 05	8	10
NB-029D	BR DB993111 grey - 05	8	10
NB-029E	BR DB993318 grey - 05	8	10
NB-029F	BR DB993177 grey - 05	8	10

ZFV 'Dogfish' hopper wagon [W9] (Dapol)

NB-029G	BR DB992924 grey - 05	8	10
NB-029H	BR DB992938 grey - 05	8	10
NB-029J	BR DB992944 grey - 05	8	10
NB-029K	BR DB992902 grey - 05	8	10
NB-030A	BR DB993292 black - 06	8	10
NB-030B	BR DB993149 black - 06	8	10
NB-030C	BR DB993307 black - 06	8	10
NB-030D	BR DB993188 black - 06	8	10
NB-030E	BR DB983019 black - 06	8	10
NB-030F	BR DB983021 black - 06	8	10
NB-030G	BR DB992873 black - 06	8	10
NB-030H	BR DB992859 black - 06	8	10
NB-030J	BR DB992898 black - 06	8	10
NB-030K	BR DB993058 black - 06	8	10
NB-033A	BR DB993311 brown - 06	8	10
NB-033B	BR DB993367 brown - 06	8	10
NB-033C	BR DB993380 brown - 06	8	10
NB-033D	BR DB993203 brown - 06	8	10
NB-033E	BR DB993309 brown - *not made*	NA	NA
NB-033E	BR DB983098 brown * - 06	8	10
NB-033F	BR DB993457 brown - 06	8	10
NB-033G	BR DB993470 brown - 06	8	10
NB-033H	BR DB993401 brown - 06	8	10
NB-033J	BR DB993422 brown - 06	8	10
NB-033K	BR DB993450 brown - 06	8	10
NB-070A	BR DB983587 grey+yellow Ltd Edn 250 - 08	8	11
NB-070B	BR DB982958 grey+yellow Ltd Edn 250 - 08	8	11
NB-070C	BR DB982961 grey+yellow Ltd Edn 250 - 08	8	11
NB-070D	BR DB983314 grey+yellow Ltd Edn 250 - 08	8	11
NB-070E	BR DB983556 grey+yellow - 10	8	11
NB-070F	BR DB993312 grey+yellow - 10	8	11
NB-070G	BR DB992902 grey+yellow - 10	8	11
NB-070H	BR DB992972 grey+yellow - 10	8	11
(ND145E)	BR DB983092 grey+yellow - 12	9	NA
(ND145E)	BR DB983583 grey+yellow - 12	9	NA
(ND145E)	BR DB986586 grey+yellow - 12	9	NA
(ND145E)	BR DB993337 grey+yellow - 12	9	NA
(ND145E)	BR DB993411 grey+yellow - 12	9	NA
(ND145E)	BR DB993611 grey+yellow - 12	9	NA

* Box label gives the number as B993098.

W10. BR Bulk Grain Wagon (2006)

The model is of a Grain 'Hopvan' built at BR Derby in 1951; British Railways had standardised on the LMS design.
Initially, 500 of each number were made.

2F036000	unpainted - ?	4	8
NB-037A	'Bass Charington' 24 brown - 07	8	10
NB-037B	'Bass Charington' 28 brown - 07	8	10
NB-037C	'Bass Charington' 32 brown - 07	8	10
2F036002	'Bass Charington' 24 red, brake wheel now painted white - 13	9	11
2F036006	'Bass Charington' 24 red W, brake wheel now painted white - 13	9	12
NB-037D	'Bass Charington' 36 brown - 07	8	10
?	'Dapol' 2 purple - 08	5	6

Dapol N

NB-042A	GWR 42302 grey - 07	8	10
NB-042B	GWR 42303 grey - 07	8	10
NB-042C	GWR 42316 grey - 07	8	10
NB-042D	GWR 42318 grey - 07	8	10
2F036003	GWR 42302 dark grey, brake wheel now painted white - 12	9	11
2F036007	GWR 42302 dark grey W, brake wheel now painted white - 12	9	12
NB-043A	LMS 701351 brown - 06	8	10
NB-043B	LMS 701347 brown - 06	8	10
NB-043C	LMS 701359 brown - 06	8	10
NB-043D	LMS 701362 brown - 06	8	10
2F036004	LMS ? brown - 13	9	12
NB-036A	BR B885364 grey - 06	8	10
NB-036B	BR B885280 grey - 06	8	10
NB-036C	BR B885040 grey - 06	8	10
NB-036D	BR B885143 grey - 06	8	10
NB-037A	BR ? brown - not made	NA	NA
NB-037B	BR ? brown - not made	NA	NA
2F036001	BR ? brown? - 13	NPG	NPG

BR grain wagon [W10] (Dapol)

Tank Wagons

W11.   6-Wheel Milk Tank Wagon (2005)

It was found that milk travelled better in six-wheeled tank wagons and so these were built especially for milk traffic. As the body belonged to the dairy and the chassis to the railway company, they each had their own numbering system, which explains why two numbers may be found on some milk tank wagons.

Initially, 500 of each running number are made.

NB-044	'Co-op Milk' 169 white - 07	10	13

Co-op milk tank wagon [W11] (Dapol)

NB-115A	'Co-op Milk' (Newcastle) 174 white - 11	10	12
2F031005	'Co-op (London)' 172 white - 12	10	12
NB-032	'CWS' T44 green - 06	10	13
NB-028	'Express Dairy' blue - 05	10	13
NB-053	'Express Dairy' 45 light blue - 07	10	13
NB-115C	'Express Dairy' (Ruislip) 49 light blue - 11	10	12
2F031002	'Express Dairy' (Milk for London) SR4409 ? dark blue - 13	10	12
-	'Express Dairy' 35 blue	10	NA
-	'Express Dairy' 49 blue	10	NA
-	above 2 wagons Sp Edn (Osborn's Models) - 12	NA	21
NB-054	'IMS' 23 blue - 07	10	13
NB-115D	'IMS' 27 red? - 11	10	12
NB-031	'Independent Milk Supplies' red - 06	10	13
2F031003	'Independent Milk Supplies' red - 12	10	13
NB-045	'Milk Marketing Board' blue - 07	10	13
NB-115B	'Milk Marketing Board' ? blue? - 11	10	12
NB-056	'Pure New Milk' Co-op London red - 07	10	13
NB-?	'Satlink Western' red+yellow Ltd Edn 250 - not made *	NA	NA
NB-?	'Unigate Creameries' 220 silver W Sp (Dapol Club) - 07	12	14
(ND-084E)	'Unigate Creameries' 2992, 2995 silver W 6 wagons ex-pack (tank Nos.182, 191, 196, 207, 225) - 08	10	NA
NB-050	'United Creameries' 2969 silver (tank No.219) - 07	10	13
2F031004	'United Creameries' 2963 (& 213 on ends) silver - 12	10	13
NB-027	'United Dairies' white - 05	10	13
2F031001	'United Dairies' white - 12	10	13
NBS-002	'United Dairies' white W (red lettering) Sp Edn 500 (Hattons) - 10	10	12

* Too few orders were received.

Vans

W12.   GWR GPV Gunpowder Van (2004)

Once common on the railways, the gunpowder van carried explosives for mining and quarrying. The vans had a steel body which was lined internally with wood. Non-ferrous metals were used for catches and internal fittings.

2F013000	unpainted - ?	4	8
NB-035	'Blue Circle' 177 yellow - 06	8	10
NB-107	'Blue Circle' 173 yellow - 11	6	8
2F013007	'Blue Circle' 173 yellow (same as NB-107) - 12	6	8
2F013008	'Blue Circle' 173 yellow W - 12	6	9
-	'Cotton Powder Co.' 2 brown Sp Edn (Ballards) - 09	7	9
-	'Dapol' 2 purple * - 08	9	NA
NB-006	'Elterwater Gunpowder Co.' 11 light grey - 04	8	10
NB-018	'Ferrocrete' 167 yellow - 05	8	10
-	'Fremlin Bros.' 1 white Sp Edn 100 (Ballards) - 06	8	10
-	'Marley Tiles' 7 green Sp Edn 100 (Ballards) - 09	8	10
No.N026	'Middleton' 2011 blue Sp Edn 112 (West Wales Wagon Works) - 11	9	12
-	'New Medway Steam Packet Co.' 53 blue Sp Edn 108 (Medway Queen PS) - 07	7	9
-	'Palmers Brewery' 4 pale blue Sp Edn 200 (Buffers) - 10	8	10
-	'Queensborough Cement Co.' 10 white Sp Edn (Ballards) - 10	8	10
-	'ROF' M12 light grey Sp Edn (Dapol Club) - 10	8	10

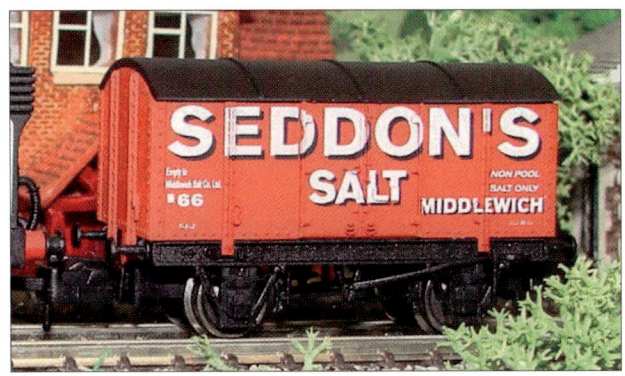

GPV - 'Seddon's Salt' [W12] (Dapol)

NB-103	'Rugby Portland Cement' 13 black - 11	6	8
2F013011	'Rugby Portland Cement' 13 black - 12	6	8
2F013012	'Rugby Portland Cement' 13 black W - 12	6	9
-	'Seddon Salt' 66 red-brown Sp Edn (Pennine Wagons) - 06	8	10
MU34000	'Willow Brewery' green Sp Edn (Modellbahn Union) - 10	9	11

8th Edition

Dapol N

Code	Description		
NB-005	**LNWR** light grey - *04*	6	8
2F013003	**LNWR** light grey - *12*	6	8
2F013004	**LNWR** light grey W - *12*	6	9
NB-010	**NB** red - *04*	4	6
NB-009	**NB** red - *not made*	NA	NA
-	**GNR** 1899 cream Sp Edn (Going Loco) - *10*	7	9
NB-017	**LSWR** 1379 - *05*	4	6
NB-010	**LSWR** 1379 - *not made*	NA	NA
NB-001	**GWR** 37985 grey - *04*	8	10
NB-012	**GWR** W105753 black with red cross - *04*	8	10
PW002	**GWR** Salvage Save For Victory 47305 pale blue Sp Edn (Pennine Wagons) - *06*	8	10
-	**GWR** Salvage Save For Victory 47305 pale blue Sp Edn (Modelbahn Union) - *13*	8	10
CRS-001P	**GWR** 175 black with red cross Sp Edn 99 (Country Rolling Stock) - *10*	7	9
CRS-001W	**GWR** 175 black W with red cross Sp Edn 50 (Country Rolling Stock) - *10*	7	10
CRS-002P	**GWR** 35374 grey Sand Van Sp Edn 100 (Country Rolling Stock) - *10*	7	9
CRS-002W	**GWR** 35374 grey W Sand Van Sp Edn 50 (Country Rolling Stock) - *10*	7	10
2F013004	**LMS** 299031 grey - *not made*	NA	NA
2F013004	**LMS** 299031 grey W - *not made*	NA	NA
2F013001	**LMS** 299031 grey - *12*	6	8
2F013002	**LMS** 299031 grey W - *12*	6	9
NB-011	**NE** grey - *04*	8	10
2F013005	**NE** 71418 red - *12*	6	8
2F013006	**NE** 71418 red W - *12*	6	9
NB-009	**SR** S61204 dark brown - *04*	8	10
-	**SR** S9061 dark brown W G.P.V. Improvised Gunpowder Van Sp Edn (Richard Dallimore) - *12*	8	10
NB-002	**BR** B887002 brown - *04*	8	10
NB-111	**BR** M701058 brown - *11*	6	8
NB-111W	**BR** M701058 brown W - *11*	6	9
2F013009	**BR** M701058 brown (same as NB-111) - *12*	6	8
2F013010	**BR** M701058 brown W - *12*	6	9

* A few of these were produced by visitors to the trade open days in October 2008 and may well appear on the market.

W13. GWR 'Fruit D' Van (2013)

This was an 18' long wheelbase van of which 50 were built by the GWR in 1939. More of them were built by British Railways up until 1955.

The model has profiled wheels and NEM coupling pockets for close coupling. The couplers are mounted on swivelling, self-centring brackets. The colour for the GWR models is incorrect and the branding should be the 'shirt-button' monogram.

Code	Description		
2F014002	**GWR** (big GW) 2886 maroon - *13*	10	13
2F014001	**GWR** (shirt button) 2881 maroon - *13*	10	13
2F014004	**BR** W2023 maroon - *13*	10	13
2F014003	**BR** W38107 blue - *13*	10	13

W14a. SR CCT Utility Van (2004)

All four pre-1948 railway companies had covered carriage trucks (CCT) which were used with passenger trains to carry parcels, milk, newspapers and other commodities that needed urgent delivery. This model was of one type built by the Southern at Ashford as a luggage van in 1931.

This was an early release which has now been replaced with a better model which will be found in the next table.

SR utility van [W14a] (Dapol)

Code	Description		
NB-016	**SR** S2279S Malachite green - *05*	8	12
NB-023	**SR** S2283S Malachite green - *05*	8	12
NB-003	**BR** S2380S green - *04*	8	12
NB-007	**BR** S2385S green - *04*	8	12
NB-013	**BR** S2394S green - *05*	8	12
NB-022	**BR** S2396S green - *05*	8	12
NB-015	**BR** S2388S green - *05*	8	12
NB-004	**BR** M527042 * maroon - *04*	8	12
NB-014	**BR** M527467 maroon - *05*	8	12
NB-008	**BR** S2514S blue - *04*	8	12

* The running number on the box was shown as M527402.

W14b. SR CCT Utility Van (New Body) (2013)

This is the replacement model for the one in the above table. It has flush glazing, profiled wheels, NEM coupling pockets and close coupling.

Code	Description		
NB-080A	**SR** ? Malachite green - *13*	11	14
NB-080B	**BR** S?S maroon - *13*	11	14
NB-080C	**BR** ? blue - *13*	11	14
NB-080D	**BR** ? Engineer's red - *13*	11	14

W15. BR 'Blue Spot' Van (2007)

These were built in the early 1950s to transport fish from the East Coast ports and whole trains of 'Blue Spot' vans would be seen on the East Coast Main Line. Many were later converted to parcels vans (SPVs) and painted blue. These were in use until the 1980s. Initially, 250 of each running number were made.

Code	Description		
NB-051A	**BR** E87234 white - *07*	7	9
NB-051B	**BR** E87228 white - *07*	7	9
NB-051C	**BR** E87002 white - *07*	7	9
NB-051D	**BR** E87329 white - *07*	7	9
NB-051E	**BR** E87221 white - *10*	7	9
NB-051F	**BR** E87009 white - *10*	7	9
NB-051G	**BR** E87242 white - *10*	7	9
2F019001	**BR** E87582 white - *12*	7	9
2F019001	**BR** E87706 white - *12*	7	9
NB-051H	**BR** E87324 white - *10*	7	9
NB-068A	**BR** E88005 blue - *08*	7	9
NB-068B	**BR** E88001 blue - *08*	7	9
2F019003	**BR** E87663 blue SPV Express Parcels - *12*	7	9
2F019004	**BR** E87505 blue SPV Express Parcels - *12*	7	9
NB-052A	**BR** ADB975436 yellow - *07*	7	9
NB-052B	**BR** ADB975402 yellow - *07*	7	9
NB-069A	**BR** ADB974524 red - *08*	7	9
NB-069B	**BR** ADB975417 red - *08*	7	9
(ND-079-3)	**BR** E? white ex-train pack - *not made*	NA	NA

BR-SPV express parcels van [W15] (Hattons)

Bogie Wagons

W16. FEA 'Megafret' Intermodal Wagon (2008)

These are a French built design with a low floor for high capacity containers and swap-bodies. The wagons were introduced in 2001, leased to Freightliner for Channel Tunnel and trans-Europe traffic. The low floor allows them to carry much taller 40' and 45' containers that were not possible before in Britain because of its tighter loading gauge. They operate in permanently coupled pairs and are painted blue.

The models are sold in pairs and have a close-coupling system and a diecast deck for a low centre of gravity. Containers are available separately.

Code	Description		
NB-067	basic Megafret wagon – *not made*	NA	NA
NB-076A	33 68 490 9 796-7P - *not made*	NA	NA
NB-076A	33 68 494 3 073-9P - *08*	20	25
NB-076B	33 68 490 9 915-3 - *not made*	NA	NA
NB-076B	33 68 490 9 351-1P - *08*	20	25

Dapol N

NB-076C	33 68 490 9 889-0 - *not made*	NA	NA
NB-076C	33 68 490 9 985-6P - *08*	20	25
NB-076D	33 68 490 9 360-2P - *not made*	NA	NA
NB-076D	33 68 494 6 263-5P - *08*	20	25
NB-076E	33 68 490 9 361-5P - *09*	20	25
NB-076F	33 68 490 9 351-1P - *09*	20	25
NB-076G	33 68 494 3 076-2 blue W with 45ft containers Tesco/Stobart 'Less CO2' Nos.11 & 13 – *11?*	24	30
NB-076W	33 68 490 9 918-4P ? W - *10*	20	25
NB117A	Megafret & container twin pack - *12?*	24	30
NB117B	Megafret & container twin pack - *12?*	24	30

FEA 'Megafret' intermodal wagon [W16] (Dapol)

W17. FEA-B 'Spine' 2-Car Container Wagons (2008)

In all 301 of these wagons were manufactured by Wagony Swidinica in Poland for use by Freightliner. They have two Intermodal platforms with a permanent coupling bar and can accommodate 20', 30' and 40' containers with standard 'twistlock' fittings. They were found mainly on Channel Tunnel trains with a maximum operating speed of 75mph.
The models come in pairs.

NB-062A	**Freightliner** 640121+640122 green - *07*	16	20
NB-062B	**Freightliner** 640209+640210 green - *07*	16	20
NB-062E	**Freightliner** 640212+640213 green - *08*	16	20
NB-062F	**Freightliner** 640352+640353 green - *08*	16	20
NB-062G	**Freightliner** 640303+640304 green - *08*	16	20
NB-062H	**Freightliner** 640353+640354 green - *08*	16	20
NB-062I	**Freightliner** 640499+640500 green - *09*	16	20
NB-062J	**Freightliner** 640327+640328 green - *09*	16	20
NB-116C	**Freightliner** 640163+640164 green with ZIM, CMA. C&CL and Seaco containers - *11*	22	30
NB-116D	**Freightliner** 640313+640314 green with containers - *11*	22	30
NB-062C	**GBRf** 640603+640604 blue - *07*	16	20
NB-062D	**GBRf** 640603+640604 blue - *not made*	NA	NA
NB-062D	**GBRf** 640619+640620 blue - *07*	6	20
NB-062K	**GBRf** 640601+640602 blue - *10*	6	20
NB-062M	**GBRf** 640621+640622 blue - *10*	6	20
NB-116A	**GBRf** 640623+640624 blue - *11*	22	30
NB-116B	**GBRf** 640627+640628 blue - *11*	22	30

FEA-B 'Spine' 2-car container wagons [W17] (Dapol)

W18a. 20' Containers (2008)

These 8' high containers are for the 'Spine' wagon and are sold in packs of one 40' and one 20' container, with the liveries and combinations changing.

(NB-063)	'Cosco' grey - *08*	5	NA
(NB-063)	'Eurofreight' green - *08*	5	NA
(NB-063)	'Hamburg Lines' black - *08*	5	NPG
(NB-063)	'MSC' buff - *08*	5	NA
(NB-063)	'Nordic' dark brown - *08*	5	NPG
(NB-063)	'Zim' orange-brown - *08*	5	NA
?	? red - *08*	5	NPG
(NB-063)	unbranded brown - *08*	5	NPG

W18b. 40' Containers (2008)

These 8' high containers are for the 'Spine' wagon and sold in packs of one 40' and one 20' container with liveries and combinations changing.

(NB-063)	'American Lines' white - *08*	5	NA
(NB-063)	'China Worldwide' blue - *08*	5	NA
(NB-063)	'Globestar' brown - *08*	5	NA
(NB-063)	'Hanjin' blue - *08*	5	NA
(NB-063)	'Italia' blue - *08*	5	NA
(NB-063)	'MSC' buff - *08*	5	NA
(NB-063)	'Trans Asia' green - *08*	5	NA
(NB-063)	'Triton' brown - *08*	5	NA

W18c. 40' 'High Cube' Containers (2009)

Proposed but dropped from the catalogue.

W18d. 45' Containers for FEA (2008)

The Tesco/Stobart containers are inscribed 'Less CO2'.
'curtain' = curtain sided container.

NB-077B	'Arei Van Donge' blue - *08*	4	NA
NB-077A	'Deanside International' blue + 'GTS' blue- *08*	4	NA
NB-077C	'GTS' blue - *08*	4	NA
NB-077G	'K-Line' red - *09*	4	NA
NB-077D	'MOL' green - *09*	4	NA
NB-067K	'**Tesco/Stobart**' Stobart 57 blue, curtain - *10*	4	5
NB-067M	'**Tesco/Stobart**' Stobart 83 blue, curtain - *10*	4	5
NB-067N	'**Tesco/Stobart**' Stobart 99 blue, curtain - *10*	4	5
NB-067P	'**Tesco/Stobart**' Stobart 124 blue, curtain - *10*	4	5
NB-067B	'**Tesco/Stobart**' Stobart 06 blue - *08*	4	5
NB-067C	'**Tesco/Stobart**' Stobart 10 blue - *08*	4	5
NB-067D	'**Tesco/Stobart**' Stobart 17 blue - *08*	4	5
NB-067E	'**Tesco/Stobart**' Stobart 21 blue - *08*	4	5
NB-067F	'**Tesco/Stobart**' Stobart 01 blue - *08*	4	5
NB-067G	'**Tesco/Stobart**' Stobart 07 blue - *08*	4	5
NB-067H	'**Tesco/Stobart**' Stobart 16 blue - *08*	4	5
NB-067J	'**Tesco/Stobart**' Stobart 26 blue - *08*	4	5
NB-077E	'Triton' orange - *09*	4	NA
NB-077F	unmarked blue - *09*	4	NA

W19. KQA 'Pocket' Wagon (2009)

Proposed but dropped from the catalogue.

W20. IOA 'Mussel' Ballast Wagon (2013)

Designed to carry ballast and spoil, the IOA is a large bogie open wagon built of steel and first appeared on the British network in 2009 in Network Rail yellow livery.
The model will have NEM coupling pockets and come with an accessory bag of extra detail for the purchaser to attach. The model had not been released at the time of writing.

NB-101A	**N-R** 70 5992 002-3 yellow - *13*	14	18
NB-101B	**N-R** 70 5992 014-8 yellow - *13*	14	18
NB-101C	**N-R** 70 5992 021-3 yellow - *13*	14	18
NB-101D	**N-R** 70 5992 026-2 yellow - *13*	14	18

W21. JNA 'Falcon' Ballast Wagon (2013)

A total of 555 of these were built in 2004 by Trinity in Romania for ballast and spoil transportation. They are used in sets of 5 and all are in Network Rail livery.
The models will have NEM coupling pockets and come with an accessory bag of extra detail. The model had not been released at the time of writing.

NB-100A	**N-R** NUL29003 yellow - *made?*	NPG	NPG
NB-100B	**N-R** NUL29012 yellow - *made?*	NPG	NPG
NB-100C	**N-R** NUL29047 yellow - *made?*	NPG	NPG
NB-100D	**N-R** NUL29064 yellow - *made?*	NPG	NPG
2F010001	**N-R** ? yellow - *13*	15	20
2F010002	**N-R** ? yellow - *13*	15	20
2F010003	**N-R** ? yellow - *13*	15	20
2F010004	**N-R** ? yellow - *13*	15	20

W22. EWS MBA 'Monsterbox' (2009)

Proposed but dropped from the catalogue.

Dapol N

W23. EWS MOA 'Megabox' (2009)
Proposed but dropped from the catalogue.

W24. MJA Freightliner Heavy Haul Box Twin (2013)
Built for Freightliner by Wagony Swidnica of Poland, these bogie box wagons run permanently coupled in pairs with buffers on the outer ends. Introduced in 2003, they are used to carry stone to sites where there is no hopper unloading facility.

The model had not been released at the time of writing.

NB-114A	**Freightliner Heavy Haul** ? green - *13*	20	28
NB-114B	**Freightliner Heavy Haul** ? green - *13*	20	28
NB-114C	**Freightliner Heavy Haul** ? green - *13*	20	28
NB-114D	**Freightliner Heavy Haul** ? green - *13*	20	28

W25. SR 'Seacow' Bogie Ballast Hopper
Planned for 2006 but dropped after Bachmann announced their plan to introduce one.

W26. HIA Freightliner Limestone Hopper (2013)
Freightliner Heavy Haul acquired a fleet of HIAs limestone hoppers in 2005-6 for bulk limestone, sand and aggregate traffic. Each hopper will carry up to 90 tonnes with a tare weight of 25 tonnes.

The model had not been released at the time of writing.

NB-086A	**Freightliner Heavy Haul** ? pale grey? - *13*	15	20
NB-086B	**Freightliner Heavy Haul** ? pale grey? - *13*	15	20
NB-086C	**Freightliner Heavy Haul** ? pale grey? - *13*	15	20
NB-086**D**	**Freightliner Heavy Haul** ? pale grey? - *13*	15	20

W27. PBA Tiger China Clay Covered Hoppers (2010)
Built by Fauvet Girel in 1982 for Tiger Rail Leasing and English China Clays International.

The model has etched handrails, steps and walkways and is fitted with NEM pockets for couplings.

NB?	'**ECC International**' TRL116? white *10*	20	27
NB?	as above but numbered TRL116? - *10*	20	27
NB?	as above but numbered TRL116? - *10*	20	27
NB?	as above but numbered TRL116? - *10*	20	27
NB?	'**ECC International**' TRL116? white W - *10*	23	30
NB?	as above but numbered TRL116? - *10*	23	30
NB?	as above but numbered TRL116? - *10*	23	30
NB?	as above but numbered TRL116? - *10*	23	30

W28. JIA NACCO Covered Hoppers (2010)
Built by Fauvet Girel in France in 2001 for NACCO and used for the transportation of china clay, potash and lime.

The model has etched handrails, steps and walkways and is fitted with NEM pockets for couplings.

NB?	'**Imerys**' 33 70 089 4 ? blue - *10*	22	29
NB?	as above but numbered 33 70 089 4 ? - *10*	22	29
NB?	as above but numbered 33 70 089 4 ? - *10*	22	29
NB?	as above but numbered 33 70 089 4 ? - *10*	22	29
NB?	'**Imerys**' 33 70 0894 ? blue W - *10*	23	30
NB?	as above but numbered 33 70 089 4 ? - *10*	23	30
NB?	as above but numbered 33 70 089 4 ? - *10*	23	30
NB?	as above but numbered 33 70 089 4 ? - *10*	23	30

W29. ICA 'Silver Bullet' Tank Wagon (2010)
These widely seen chrome bodied V-tanks were first produced by Arbel Fauvet in France between 1989 and 1990 but a later batch was produced in 2007 for Channel Tunnel traffic between Belgium and Scotland. They are used for the transportation of clay slurry, for example, from Cornwall to paper mills in Scotland. Although originally with bright metal tanks, due to rusting, these have later turned brown.

The models have NEM pockets and darkened profiled wheels. The model won a Model Rail Model of the Year award in 2010.

NB-076A	'**ECC**' 33 70 789 8 046-0 chrome - *not made*	NA	NA
NB-076B	as above numbered 33 70 789 8 047-8 - *not made*	NA	NA
NB-076C	as above numbered 33 70 789 8 057-7 - *not made*	NA	NA
NB-076D	as above numbered 33 70 789 8 062-7 - *not made*	NA	NA
-	'**ECC**' 33 87 789 8 101-2 chrome Sp Edn 250 (Hattons) - *10*	20	25
-	as above numbered 33 87 789 8 088-3 - *10*	20	25
-	as above numbered 33 87 789 8 071-2 - *10*	20	25
-	as above numbered 33 87 789 8 044-5 - *10*	20	25
NB-074A	'**ECC**' 33 70 789 0 102 chrome - *not made*	NA	NA
NB-074A	'**ECC**' 33 87 789 8 040 rust brown W - *10*	20	25
NB-074B	as above numbered 33 70 789 8 066 - *not made*	NA	NA
NB-074B	as above numbered 33 87 789 8 053 - *10*	20	25
NB-074C	as above numbered 33 87 789 8 102 - *10*	20	25
NB-074D	as above numbered 33 70 789 8 046 - *not made*	NA	NA
NB-074D	as above numbered 33 87 789 8 107 - *10*	20	25
NB-074E	'**ECC**' 33 70 789 8 060-6 rust brown W - *10*	20	25
NB-074F	as above numbered 33 70 789 8 063-5 - *10*	20	25
NB-074G	as above numbered 33 70 789 8 064-5 - *10*	20	25
NB-074H	as above numbered 33 70 789 8 061-6 - *10*	20	25
NB-074P	'**ECC**' 33 70 789 8 100 rust brown W - *11*	21	26
NB-074R	as above numbered 33 70 789 8 105 - *11*	21	26
NB-074S	as above numbered 33 70 789 8 093 - *11*	21	26
NB-074T	as above numbered 33 70 789 8 055 - *11*	21	26
NB-074P	'**ECC**' 33 70 789 8 100 rust brown W - *11*	21	26
2F027001	'**ECC**' 33 70 789 8 ? chrome - *13*	20	25
2F027002	as above numbered 33 70 789 8 ? - *13*	20	25
2F027003	as above numbered 33 70 789 8 ? - *13*	20	25
2F027004	'**ECC**' 33 70 789 8 ? rust brown W - *13*	22	27
-	'**ECC**' 33 87 789 8 111-2 rust brown W	20	NA
-	as above numbered 33 87 789 8 047-5	20	NA
NB-074W	above two weathered wagons in a twin pack - *11*`	NA	NPG

Weathered version of a 'Silver Bullet' tank wagon [W29] (Hattons)

W30. KIA Telescopic Hood Steel Carrier (2007)
A total of 104 of these were built in Germany by Linke Hofmann Busch in 1979 and were originally operated by VTG. More recently, Tiphook Rail took them over and they are often seen in trains of ten or more.

They feature sliding cover sections to give access to the contents and this feature has been partly replicated on the model. The models have a close coupling system, NEM pockets, optional buckeye couplings and an opening rear cover. Initially, 500 models have been made of each number.

NB-061A	'**VTG**' 589 9 087 6 silver+blue - *07*	15	20
NB-061B	'**VTG**' 589 9 082 7 silver+blue - *07*	15	20
NB-061C	'**VTG**' 589 9 077 7 silver+blue - *07*	15	20

KIA telescopic hood steel carrier [W30] (Dapol)

NB-061D	'**VTG**' 589 9 076 9 silver+blue - *07*	15	20
NB-075A	'**VTG**' 589 9 068 ? silver+blue - *07*	15	20
NB-075B	'**VTG**' 589 9 078 ? silver+blue - *07*	15	20
NB-075C	'**VTG**' 589 9 055 ? silver+blue - *07*	15	20
NB-075D	'**VTG**' 589 9 057 ? silver+blue - *07*	15	20
NB-075E	'**VTG**' 589 9 068 ? silver+blue - *10*	15	20
NB-075F	'**VTG**' 589 9 078 ? silver+blue - *10*	15	20
NB-075G	'**VTG**' 589 9 055 ? silver+blue - *10*	15	20
NB-075H	'**VTG**' 589 9 057 ? silver+blue - *10*	15	20
NB-066A	'**Tiphook Rail**' 338 0 4667 017 blue - *not made*	NA	NA
NB-066B	'**Tiphook Rail**' 338 0 4667 023 blue - *not made*	NA	NA
NB-066C	'**Tiphook Rail**' 338 0 4667 028 blue - *not made*	NA	NA
NB-066D	'**Tiphook Rail**' 338 0 4667 046 blue - *not made*	NA	NA
NB-066A	'**Tiphook Rail**' 337 0 0899 024 blue - *08*	15	20
NB-066B	'**Tiphook Rail**' 337 0 0899 037 blue - *08*	15	20
NB-066C	'**Tiphook Rail**' 337 0 0899 042 blue - *08*	15	20

Dapol N

Code	Description		
NB-066D	'Tiphook Rail' 337 0 0899 066 blue - 08	15	20
2F039000	'Tiphook Rail' 337 0 ? ? blue - 13	15	20
2F039001	'Tiphook Rail' 337 0 ? ? blue - 13	15	20
2F039002	'Tiphook Rail' 337 0 ? ? blue - 13	15	20
2F039003	'Tiphook Rail' 337 0 ? ? blue - 13	15	20

This wagon was also produced for Japan Model Railways and Modelbahn Union with mainland DB and SBB liveries and running numbers. These are not listed here.

W31. GWR 'Siphon G' Bogie Milk Van (2003)

This is a GWR built van, with corridor connections, for transporting milk in churns. They were built in batches between 1913 and 1927.

From 2010 these featured restyled bogies, profile wheels and NEM coupling pockets.

Code	Description		
2F024000	unpainted - ?	4	8
?	'Dapol N'thusiasts Club' No.4 yellow Sp Edn (Dapol club) - 10	8	10
Sclubsph2	GWR 1477 dark brown Sp Edn 200 (Dapol club) - 11	8	10
Sclubsph1	GWR 1479 dark brown Sp Edn 200 (Dapol club) - 11	8	10
NB-002	GWR 1443 dark brown - 03-06	9	12
NC-002B	GWR 1448 dark brown - 04	9	12
NB-081A	GWR 1447 dark brown - 10	10	13
NB-081B	GWR 1451 dark brown - 10	10	14
2F024001	GWR 1447 dark brown - 12	10	13
2F024005	GWR 1447 dark brown W - 12	10	14
2F024002	GWR 1451 dark brown - 12	10	13
2F024006	GWR 1451 dark brown W - 12	10	14
NB-001	BR W1449 maroon - 03	9	12
NB-081C	BR W1445 maroon - 10	10	13
NB-081D	BR W1457 maroon - 10	10	14
2F024003	BR 1445 maroon - 12	10	13
2F024007	BR 1445 maroon W - 12	10	14
2F024004	BR 1457 maroon - 12	10	13
2F024008	BR 1457 maroon W - 12	10	14

W32. GWR 'Siphon H' Bogie Milk Van (2003)

This is a GWR designed milk van with end doors and was built in 1919. Besides being used for milk, they could be used as scenery vans or for the transportation of motor vehicles.

From 2010 these featured restyled bogies, profile wheels and NEM coupling pockets.

Code	Description		
2F023000	unpainted - ?	4	8
NB-004	GWR 1435 dark brown - 03	8	12
NC-004B	GWR 1432 dark brown - 04	8	12

GWR 'Siphon H' milk van [W32] (Dapol)

Code	Description		
NB-082A	GWR 1424 dark brown - 10	8	12
NB-082B	GWR 1430 dark brown - 10	8	12
2F023001	GWR 1424 dark brown - 12	10	13
2F023005	GWR 1424 dark brown W - 12	10	14
2F023002	GWR 1430 dark brown - 12	10	13
2F023006	GWR 1430 dark brown W - 12	10	14
NB-003	BR W1431 maroon - 03	8	12
NB-082C	BR 1428 maroon - 10	8	12
NB-082D	BR 1434 maroon - 10	8	12
2F023003	BR 1428 maroon - 13	10	13
2F023007	BR 1428 maroon W - 13	10	14
2F023004	BR 1434 maroon - 12	10	13
2F023008	BR 1434 maroon W - 12	10	14

W33. IWA 'Cargowaggon' Bogie Van (2006)

These are bogie 'Cargowaggon' vans used for both domestic and trans-channel traffic. They were built by Waggon Union in Germany during 1988-1990.

Initially, 500 were made per running number. They have a close-coupling system, NEM pockets and come with optional buckeye couplings.

GE Rail Services

Code	Description		
NB-048A	279 7 604-6 silver+ blue - 06	12	18
NB-048B	279 7 671-5 silver+ blue - 06	12	18
NB-048C	279 7 607-5 silver+ blue - 06	12	18
NB-048D	279 7 617-6 silver+ blue - 06	12	18

CargoWaggon

Code	Description		
NB-049A	279 7 589-9p grey - 07	12	18
NB-049B	279 7 632-7p grey - 07	12	18
NB-049C	279 7 650-9p grey - 07	12	18
NB-049D	279 7 663-2p grey - 07	12	18
NB-065A	279 7 619-4p grey - 08	12	18
NB-065B	279 7 661-6p grey - 08	12	18
NB-065C	279 7 710-2p grey - 08	12	18
NB-065D	279 7 716-4p grey - 08	12	18

IWA 'Cargo Wagon' bogie van [W33] (Dapol)

Blue Circle

Code	Description		
NB-055A	279 7 611-9p yellow+*blue* - 07	12	18
NB-055B	279 7 613-9p yellow+*blue* - 07	12	18
NB-055C	279 7 649-9p yellow+*blue* - 07	12	18
NB-055D	279 7 683-9p yellow+*blue* - 07	12	18
NSPEC2	279 7 669-9p yellow+blue W Sp Edn (Dapol Club) - 07	12	18
-	'Taunton Cider' 2797-664-9p beige Sp Edn 750 (N Gauge Society) - 07	12	16
-	'CargoWaggon' 2797-664-0p slate blue Sp Edn 690 (N Gauge Society) - 07	12	16
-	'CargoWaggon' 2797-664-0p slate blue W Sp Edn 60 (N Gauge Society) - 07	12	16

W34. Snowplough

These were produced exclusively for the N Gauge Society.

Code	Description		
NGK42-1	BR DB965205 black (early 1960s) -10, 13	NPG	NPG
NGK42-9	BR ? black (1960s) -11	NPG	NPG
NGK42-2	BR DB965224 black with hazard stripes (mid-1960s) -10, 13	NPG	NPG
NGK42-10	BR ? black with hazard stripes (1960s) -11	NPG	NPG
NGK42-5	BR ADB965196 black (1970s/'80s) - 10	NPG	NPG
NGK42-3	BR ADB965240 blue (1970s-90s) - 10	NPG	NPG
NGK42-6	Rft Distribution ADB965308 Snow King grey (1980s) Tinsley Depot Special - 10	NPG	NPG
NGK42-12	Rft Distribution ADB965309 Snow Queen grey (1980s) Tinsley Depot Special - 11	NPG	NPG
NGK42-4	BR ADB965208 black (Inverness Stag) - 10	NPG	NPG
NGK42-11	BR ? black (Eastfield Scotty dog) - 11	NPG	NPG
NGK42-7	Railtrack * ADB965210/ADB965236 black ZZA - 10	NPG	NPG
NGK42-13	Network Rail ? black - 11	NPG	NPG
NGK42-8	Network Rail * ADB965232/ADB965243 black - 10	NPG	NPG

* In the first run of models, the Railtrack and Network Rail versions had different numbers on each side to allow the customer to appear to have different vehicles when running prototypically back-to-back.

SAS
Est. 1991

specialauctionservices.com

SELL YOUR COLLECTION THROUGH THE AUCTION HOUSE WITH THE BEST TRACK RECORD

We are pleased to accept fine toy and model trains from Z Gauge to 7¼in. for our sales throughout the year, rounded off by Trains Galore every December. In 2012, this ever-popular sale realised a record total in excess of £350,000.

Contact: Hugo Marsh or Bob Leggett on 01635 580595

81 Greenham Business Park, Newbury RG19 6HW   hugo@specialauctionservices.com

Dapol 0

HISTORY

Dapol was founded in 1981 by David Boyle, of Highfield Birds & Models and his wife Pauline. Initially the company sold Airfix and Mainline residue stock, after both ceased trading, but later it went into production using former Airfix tooling and some new models of their own creation.

In 2003, Dapol launched an N gauge range and the good quality of its models soon established it as a major competitor in the N gauge market. Then, in November 2011, it announced its intention to expand its range to include 0 gauge, starting with a range of 0 gauge open wagons.

LOCOMOTIVES

The locomotive was announced in March 2012. The first O gauge locomotive is a much requested one as well. The Class 08 diesel shunter is a model that has not been manufactured in ready-to-run 0 gauge before and this one, it was said, would benefit from the 'Dapol way of thinking' with slides in the tooling that allow for other versions, lighting differences, with or without ladders etc.

GWR 5-plank wagon [W1] (Dapol)

WAGONS

Initially they will be 5-plank, 7-plank and 8-plank types, with versions of each released and a lot more versions are promised. The wagons have sprung buffers, metal sprung coupling hooks, 3-link chains, brass axle cups, profile darkened metal wheels, opening side doors and internal floor and wall paintwork. They are handmade and printed at Chirk. As with the N and 00 wagon ranges, commissions for special editions are undertaken as and when requested, with a minimum quantity of just 25.

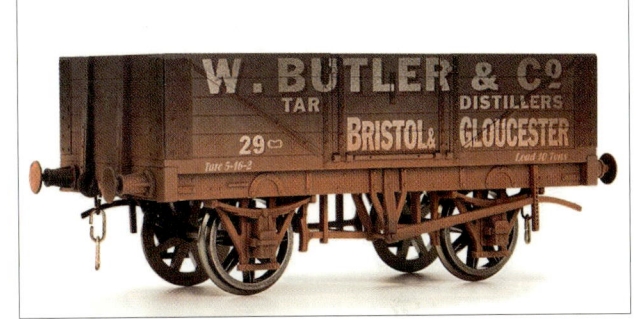

Weathered 5-plank wagon [W1] (Dapol)

W1. 12T 5-plank Wagon (2012)

5-plank wagons were considered to be 'high goods wagons' and were referred to as 'Highfits' or 'High NF'. Anything larger was probably specifically for the mineral trade.

Cat No.	Company, Number, Colour, Date	£	£
7F051001	'S **Allen**' 7 grey - 12	35	40
POW01	'**Birmingham Railway Carriage & Wagon**' 26892 red-brown Sp Edn 100 (Tower Models) - 13	35	40
7F051003	'**Butler**' ? ? - 13	35	40
POW08	'R Fred **Cole**' ? red Sp Edn 100 (Tower Models) - 13	35	40
-	'**Cumberland Granite Co.**' 24 black Sp Edn (Crafty Hobbies & C&M Models) - 13	NPG	NPG
POW07	'Joshua **Grey**' ? brown Sp Edn 100 (Tower Models) - 13	35	40
7F051002	**GW** 25134 grey - 12	35	40
7F051004	**BR** M318256 grey - 12	35	40

W2. 7-plank Wagon (2012)

7-plank wagons were mostly privately owned and used for the transportation of coal. Between the wars they were the most numerous wagon type on Britain's railways. They were requisitioned by the government during the Second World War and passed to BR in 1948. During the 1950s the aging fleet was gradually replaced by steel mineral wagons.

7-plank wagon [W2] (Dapol)

L1. SR 'Terrier 0-6-0T (2013)

This is based Stroudley's Class A1 'Terrier' tank engine of 1872, as redeveloped by Marsh in 1911 to form the Class A1X. 50 were built as suburban and branch line passenger locomotives and for shunting duties. Several were sold to other railway companies and some to industry. The last was withdrawn in 1963 and 10 have been preserved.

The model will have a 5-pole skew-wound motor and be 'DCC ready' with a PluX 22 socket fitted. It will have sprung buffers and coupling bar and a 3-link metal coupler. The model will also have firebox glow and flicker, etched nameplates, all-wheel power contacts and come with an accessory bag containing further detail parts. The model is to have an internally painted cab.

Cat No.	Company, Number, Colour, Date	£	£
7S010004	5 *Ashstead* LBSCR orange - 13	NPG	200
7S010003	W8 *Freshwater* SR green - 13	NPG	200
7S010001	32640 BRb black - 13	NPG	200
7S010002	32646 BRc black - 13	NPG	200

L2. Class 08 0-6-0DS (2013)

BR built 1,193 of these diesel shunting engines over a ten year period, but as railway yards disappeared and pilots were no longer required for railway stations, due to the disappearance of loco hauled trains, the fleet was steadily reduced - many going to industry and preserved lines.

A 5-pole motor allied to a flywheel and a DCC interface makes this a DCC sound compatible locomotive. It also features sprung buffers, sprung coupling hook and 3-link chain, internally painted cab detail and directional lighting correct for the livery depicted.

Cat No.	Company, Number, Colour, Date	£	£
7D008000	**D3048** BRc green - 13	NPG	200
7D008003	**D3084** BRc green wasp stripes - 13	NPG	200
7D008001	**13115** BRb green - 13	NPG	200
7D008002	**08529** BRe blue, wasp stripes - 13	NPG	200
7D010004	**08708** EWS maroon, wasp stripes - *not made*	NA	NA

Cat No.	Company, Number, Colour, Date	£	£
7F071004	'**Ammanford Colliery Co.**' 535 dark brown - 12	35	40
-	'**Bickershaw**' 964 red-brown Sp Edn 25 (Red Rose Steam Society) - 13	38	46
7F071003	'**Edinburgh**' ? ? - 13	35	40
POW03	'**Edward Eastwood Railways Wagon & Wheel Works**' 2 green Sp Edn 100 (Tower Models) - 13	35	40
POW02	'**Gloucester Railway Carriage & Wagon**' red-brown Sp Edn 100 (Tower Models) - 13	35	40

Dapol 0

POW04	'Lincoln Engine & Wagon Co.' dark grey Sp Edn 100 (Tower Models) - 13		35	40
POW05	'R.Y.Pickering Carriage & Wagons' 1002 red-brown Sp Edn 100 (Tower Models) - 13		35	40
POW10	'Ruabon Coal & Coke Co.' ? black Sp Edn 100 (Tower Models) - 13		35	40
POW09	'South Wales & Cannock' ? red Sp Edn 100 (Tower Models) - 13		35	40
POW11	'R.J.Wood & Co.' ? orange Sp Edn 100 (Tower Models) - 13		35	40
7F071001	GW 06515 grey - 12		35	40
7F071002	BR ? grey - 13		35	40

W3. 8-plank Wagon) (2012)

The 8-plank wagons were also generally built for coal and had a slightly larger capacity.

BR 8-plank wagon [W3] (Dapol)

7F081003	'Chatterley-Whitfield' 4055 grey - 12		35	40
POW06	'Metropolitan Railway Carriage & Wagon' 188 red-brown Sp Edn 100 (Tower Models) - 13		35	40
7F081001	'Stewarts and Lloyds' 6301 grey - 12		35	40
POW12	'Osborne & Son' ? green Sp Edn 100 (Tower Models) - 13		35	40
7F081002	'Thorncliffe Izal' 2915 black - 12		35	40
7F081004	BR P73148 grey - 12		35	40

W4. BR HEA Coal Hopper Wagon (2013)

These air-braked hoppers were built for coal traffic in their thousands at BREL Shildon during the period 1976-79.

7F047001	BR Railfreight 360104 red+grey - 13	NPG	64
7F047002	BR Railfreight 360000 red+grey - 13	NPG	64
7F047043	BR 360114 brown - 13	NPG	64
7F047001	EWS 360354 maroon - 13	NPG	64

W5. BR HAA/HBA MGR Hopper Wagon (2013)

A total of 10,701 of these wagons were constructed over a period of 20 years, mostly at Shildon. They were introduced to the British rail network in 1964 in an effort to revolutionise the bulk movement of coal.

7F048001	BR 358363 silver+red HAA - 13	NPG	70
7F048002	BR 355799 silver+brown HAA - 13	NPG	70
7F048003	BR Railfreight Coal 356202 silver+yellow HAA - 13	NPG	70
7F048004	BR 368389 silver+red HBA - 13	NPG	70

W6. 6-Wheel Milk Tank Wagon (2013)

It seems that milk travelled better in six-wheeled tank wagons and so these were built specially for milk traffic. As the body belonged to the dairy and the chassis to the railway company, they each had their own numbering system, which explains why two numbers may be found on milk tank wagons.

7F031000	'United Daries' ? ? - 13	65	74
7F031001	'Express Dairy' ? ? - 13	65	74
7F031002	'CWS' ? ? - 13	65	74
7F031003	'Milk Marketing Board' ? ? - 13	65	74
7F031004	'United Creameries' ? ? - 13	65	74

W7. BR VEA 'Vanwide' 12T Vent Van (2013)

Around 1980, several of the existing 10' wheelbase 'Vanwide' vans were converted to air brakes and re-coded VEA. They were intended for use carrying military supplies - their double sliding doors allowed the loading of quite large objects - thus their name. The short wheelbase was thought to be better suited to the tight curves in military establishments, but by the mid 1990s these were all in departmental service and coded ZSA or ZRA.

7F049001	BR 230012 brown - 13	NPG	50
7F049002	BR 230030 brown - 13	NPG	50
7F049003	BR Railfreight 230074 red+grey - 13	NPG	50
7F049004	BR Eng. 230142 olive green - 13	NPG	50

W8. SR 25T Pillbox Brake Van (2013)

7F100002	SR 55965 dark brown - 13	NPG	50
7F100001	BR Eng. D556400 olive green - 13	NPG	50
7F100003	BR Eng. DS55148 red - 13	NPG	50
7F100004	BR Eng. DS55597 dark grey, yellow panels - 13	NPG	50

Photo of the Hornby A3 60052 Prince Palatine, computer enhanced by Robbie McGavin

Darstaed & Vintage Trains
Trains-de-Luxe

HISTORY
The Darstaed brand was established in 1966 by Marcel Darphin of Zug, Switzerland, to reproduce accurate replicas of the famous pre-war 40cm Marklin coaches. Actual fabrication was by the Swiss firm of Twerenbold. No locomotives were produced. Today, these Darstaed examples are very keenly sought after in auction rooms world-wide. In 1993 Andries Grabowsky, a Dutch national and award winning modeller, bought the name and tooling from M. Darphin with the object of continuing and expanding the range. During the period 1995 to 2008, Andries Grabowsky was the manufacturing arm of the entire Ace Trains range, a story well recorded elsewhere.

In 2008, the two companies decided to go their separate ways. Darstaed's philosophy is to produce models within the budget that the customer is prepared to pay, giving him the best value. Models that were already in development for release in the Ace Trains range, at the time of the split, were subsequently released by Darstaed under the Vintage Trains label, as they did not strictly conform to the Darstaed philosophy. The first of these was the LNER Class J19 tender locomotive, which was released late in 2008.

The first item to be issued under the Darstaed name was a classic pre-war Pullman coach to honour the 40th Anniversary of the Hornby Railway Collectors Association (HRCA), celebrated in July 2009. Since then the range has expanded.

LOCOMOTIVES

Cat No.	Company, Number, Colour, Date	£	£

Steam Locomotives

L1. GWR Class 57xx 0-6-0PT (2012)
This was a Collett pannier tank design of 1929, but with a Churchward cab. A total of 863 locomotives were built between 1929 and 1950. The last was withdrawn in 1966. Thirteen had been sold to London Transport between 1957 and 1963 and the last of these worked on the London Transport network until 1971. Sixteen of the class have been preserved, including 6 of those sold to London Transport.

1	5764 Great Western green - 12	NPG	325
2	7741 GWR (shirt button) green - 12	NPG	325
3	? GWR (shirt button) black - 12	NPG	325
4	? GWR green - 12	NPG	325
5	? GWR black - 12	NPG	325
6	? BRa green - 12	NPG	325
7	? BRa black - 12	NPG	325
8	? BRb black - 12	NPG	325
9	? BRc black - 12	NPG	325
10	? LT maroon - 12	NPG	325
11	? NCB green - 12	NPG	295

L2a. LMS Class 3F 'Jinty' 0-6-0T (2012)

Ex-LMS Class 3F 'Jinty' [L2a]

The War Department acquired 8 LMS 0-6-0T Jinties which it numbered 8-15 before sending them over to France in late 1939/early 1940. Three were lost in the retreat at Dunkerque in 1940 and the remaining 5 sequestered by the SNCF, who renumbered them 030 TW 026/7 and 042-4, all apparently used on the East network. They were returned to the UK between October and December 1948 to the London Midland Region. The shed which applied the SNCF numbers did not have a W stencil but used a VV instead. White stripes were applied to the vertical edges of the bunker to render them more visible during blackout conditions.

?	7117 LMS lined red - 12	NPG	325
?	SNCF black - 13	NPG	325

L2b. NCB Class 3F 'Jinty' 0-6-0T (2013)
This version of the model will have no handrails and other small differences.

?	? NCB ? - 14?	NPG	325

L3. LBSCR Class A1X 'Terrier' 0-6-0T
This had been proposed but the project was dropped late in 2012 as ETS were planning to produce one for Ace Trains.

L4 2-6-2T Freelance Tank Engine (2010)
This was a generic design, modified to include the key features of each railway company represented. All carry full lining and crest, where suitable, and have a new 20v DC 3-rail mechanism, working lamps and an on/off switch in cab.

120201	316 LNWR black - 10	NPG	325
120401	950 CR blue - 10	NPG	325
121001	64 GER blue – 10	NPG	325
120601	753 SECR dark green - 10	NPG	325
120101	705 LBSCR Marsh umber - 10	NPG	325
120701	516 LSWR green - 10	NPG	325
120301	8118 GWR green - 10	NPG	325
120501	58 LMS maroon - 10	NPG	325
120502	6939 LMS black with black wheels - 10	NPG	325
120503	6939 LMS black with red wheels - 10	NPG	325
120901	4515 LNER black with black wheels - 10	NPG	325
120901	4515 LNER black with red wheels - 10	NPG	325
120801	2712 SR olive - 10	NPG	325
120802	429 SR black with black wheels - 10	NPG	325
120803	429 SR black with red wheels - 10	NPG	325
120901	2009 BRc green - 10	NPG	325
120902	5577 BRb black - 10	NPG	325

Freelance 2-6-2T [L4] (Lacy, Scott & Knight)

L5. Caledonian Railway 'Single' 4-2-2
These were being made exclusively for Wynford Classics. Despite quite a lot of progress having been made on tooling this model, in February 2013 it was announced that further work on it would not be done for the time being because of the economic situation.

130101	123 CR light blue - ?	NPG	NPG
130102	123 CR dark blue - ?	NPG	NPG
130103	123 CR black - ?	NPG	NPG

L6. LMS 'Black 5' Class 4-6-0
Development put on hold in February 2013.

L7. LMS 'Jubilee' Class 4-6-0
Development put on hold in February 2013.

L8. LNER Class B12 4-6-0
Development put on hold in February 2013.

L9. LMS Streamlined 'Coronation' 4-6-2
Development put on hold in February 2013.

L10. LNER Class A1 'Peppercorn' 4-6-2 (2013)
This model is produced and marketed exclusively by agreement with the A1 Trust, the

Darstaed & Vintage Trains

owners of new-build A1 locomotive. The model is in 3-rail only.

115001	**60163** *Tornado* grey - *13*	NPG	685
115002	**60163** *Tornado* BR apple green - *13*	NPG	685
115003	**60163** *Tornado* BR Brunswick green - *13*	NPG	685
110101	various (see below) - *13*	NPG	685

110101 offers customers a choice of names from 60113 Great Northern to 60162 Saint Johnstoun.

Diesel Locomotives

L11. Class 42 'Warship' (2013)
Under development.

EMU Sets

L12. 5-BEL 'Brighton Belle' (2009)

These are 5-coach units based on the prototype sets numbered 3051-3 which ran between London Victoria and Brighton from 1934 until 1972. They are in the umber and cream livery and were inspired by the pre-war Leeds Model Company (LMC), with support of the Leeds Stedman Trust. Each car is 35cm long, fully fitted inside with LED table lamps, white or grey roofs with accurately modelled detail, illuminated indicator board, insulated wheel sets and a working rear light. They were manufactured as 3-rail models but 2-rail conversion was available in 2010. The power car had a 24v DC motor with an on/off switch underneath. They are suitable for 2ft radius curves and are fitted with push/pull couplings between cars and drop link couplings at the ends.

	'Brighton Belle' Set 3051		
213009	*Car No.88* 3rd parlour driving car	90	NA
213002	*Doris* 1st kitchen	90	NA
213002	*Hazel* 1st kitchen	90	NA
213007	*Car No.86* 3rd parlour	90	NA
213009	*Car No.89* 3rd driving trailer	90	NA
219951	above set of 5 forming unit 3051 - *09*	NA	495
	'Brighton Belle' Set 3052		
213109	*Car No.90* 3rd parlour driving car	90	NA
213102	*Vera* 1st kitchen	90	NA
213102	*Audrey* 1st kitchen	90	NA
213107	*Car No.87* 3rd parlour	90	NA
219909	*Car No.91* 3rd driving trailer	90	NA
213152	above set of 5 forming unit 3052 - *09*	495	495
	'Brighton Belle' Set 3053		
213920	*Car No.92* 3rd parlour driving car	90	NA
213202	*Mona* 1st kitchen	90	NA
213202	*Gwen* 1st kitchen	90	NA
213207	*Car No.85* 3rd parlour	90	NA
213209	*Car No.93* 3rd driving trailer	90	NA
219953	above set of 5 forming unit 3053 - *09*	NA	495

COACHES

Cat No.	Company, Number, Colour, Date	£	£

Pullman Cars

These are in the umber and cream livery with lit table lamps, sprung bogies, a working rear light and there was a choice of Pewter grey or Ivory white roofs. Spare sets of roofs and alternative roof indicator boards were available to order. Electrical connection between the cars was by Marklin style jumper leads. Early sets were issued with drop link couplings and without lampshades. Later sets had L-shaped, variable distance, couplings fitted between cars and also had red lampshades. There were working rear lamps on brake cars. Variable couplings and lampshades were available to order for retro fitting to the early sets.

Some Pullman singles may have been available, subject to agents' availability and these are valued at £90 each when new, or £100 if fitted with lighting.

C1a. Pullman Parlour Car (2009)
Sold solo, this car is 35cms long.

310101	*Michaela* 1st parlour car Sp Edn 250 (HRCA 40th Anniversary) - *09*	NPG	NPG

C1b. Sets of Pullman Cars of Mixed Types (2009)
These have been sold in sets of five cars, specific to a specified loco hauled Pullman express train as indicated. All cars are 35cms long.

	Golden Arrow		
310212	*Cecelia* 1st kitchen car	75	NA
310201	*Lydia* 1st kitchen car	75	NA
310102	*Onyx* 1st parlour car	75	NA
310702	*Car No.194* 3rd parlour car	75	NA
310301	*Montana* 1st brake parlour car	75	NA
319901	above set of 5 - *09*	NA	395
	Yorkshire Pullman		
310202	*Belinda* 1st kitchen car	75	NA
310801	*Car No.171* 3rd kitchen car	75	NA
310103	*Sheila* 1st parlour car	75	NA
310701	*Car No.64* 3rd parlour car	75	NA
310902	*Car No.248* 3rd brake parlour car	75	NA
319902	above set of 5 - *09*	NA	395
	The Queen of Scots		
310203	*Joan* 1st kitchen car	75	NA
310204	*Aurelia* 1st kitchen car	75	NA
310104	*Zena* 1st parlour car	75	NA
310702	*Car No.194* 3rd parlour car	75	NA
310901	*Car No.77* 3rd brake parlour car	75	NA
319903	above set of 5 - *09*	NA	395
	Torbay Pullman/Bournemouth Belle		
Supplied with both sets of coachboards			
310205	*Loraine* 1st kitchen car	75	NA
310105	*Eunice* 1st parlour car	75	NA
310206	*Evadne* 1st kitchen car	75	NA
310106	*Juana* 1st parlour car	75	NA
310302	*Juno* 1st brake parlour car	75	NA
319904	above set of 5 - *09*	NA	395
	Tees-Tyne Pullman		
310207	*Aries* 1st kitchen car	75	NA
310505	*Car No.303* 2nd kitchen car	75	NA
310107	*Ursula* 1st parlour car	75	NA
310402	*Car No.66* 2nd parlour car	75	NA
310605	*Car No.82* 2nd brake parlour car	75	NA
319905	above set of 5 - *09*	NA	395
	Devon Belle		
310208	*Fingall* 1st kitchen car	75	NA
310108	*Minerva* 1st parlour car	75	NA
310501	*Car No.32* 2nd kitchen car	75	NA
310401	*Car No.35* 2nd parlour car	75	NA
310602	*Car No.65* 2nd brake parlour car	75	NA
319906	above set of 5 - *09*	NA	395
	South Wales Pullman		
310209	*Chloria* 1st kitchen car	75	NA
310504	*Car No.171* 2nd kitchen car	75	NA
310102	*Onyx* 1st parlour car	75	NA
310404	*Car No.84* 2nd parlour car	75	NA
310603	*Car No.67* 2nd brake parlour car	75	NA
319907	above set of 5 - *09*	NA	395
	Cunarder		
310210	*Rosamund* 1st kitchen car	75	NA
310211	*Argus* 1st kitchen car	75	NA
310109	*Agatha* 1st parlour car	75	NA
310403	*Car No.74* 2nd parlour car	75	NA
310604	*Car No.69* 2nd brake parlour car	75	NA
319908	above set of 5 - *09*	NA	395
	Thanet Belle/Kentish Belle		
310213	*Maid of Kent* 1st kitchen car	75	NA
310303	*Isles of Thanet* 1st parlour car	75	NA
310502	*Car No.132* 2nd kitchen car	75	NA
310503	*Car No.133* 2nd kitchen car	75	NA
310601	*Car No.16* 2nd brake parlour car	75	NA
319909	above set of 5 - *10*	NA	395

Darstaed & Vintage Trains

Pullman 3rd class parlour brake [C1b] (Darstead)

C1c. Pullman Bar Cars (2010)

Originally built by the BRC&W Co. in 1925 as a parlour first class for the Pullman Car Company, it was named *Octavia*. It was renamed several times, being rebuilt as a bar car after the war. *Daffodil Bar* was its final name.

311001	**The Trianon Bar** (Golden Arrow) - *10*		75	89
311002	**The Hadrian Bar** (Tees-Tyne) - *10*		75	89
311003	**Daffodil Bar** (South Wales) - *10*		75	89
311004	**The New Century Bar** (Golden Arrow) - *10*		75	89

Vintage Suburban Stock

C2. 6-Wheel Coaches (2013)

These are sold in sets of four. They have ready installed interior detail with curtains and interior lighting. Current collection on the 2-rail version is with plungers and on the 3-rail version with spoons at the brake end.

-	? GWR composite coach	50	NA
-	? GWR all 1st class coach	50	NA
-	? GWR all 3rd class coach	50	NA
-	? GWR brake 3rd coach	50	NA
-	? GWR full passenger brake	50	NA
?	4 of the above GWR coaches - *13*	NA	245
-	? CR composite coach	50	NA
-	? CR all 1st class coach	50	NA
-	? CR all 3rd class coach	50	NA
-	? CR brake 3rd coach	50	NA
-	? CR full passenger brake	50	NA
?	4 of the above CR coaches - *13*	NA	245
-	? LNWR composite coach	50	NA
-	? LNWR all 1st class coach	50	NA
-	? LNWR all 3rd class coach	50	NA
-	? LNWR brake 3rd coach	50	NA
-	? LNWR full passenger brake	50	NA
?	4 of the above LNWR coaches - *13*	NA	245
-	? MR composite coach	50	NA
-	? MR all 1st class coach	50	NA
-	? MR all 3rd class coach	50	NA
-	? MR brake 3rd coach	50	NA
-	? MR full passenger brake	50	NA
?	4 of the above MR coaches - *13*	NA	245
-	? LMS composite coach	50	NA
-	? LMS all 1st class coach	50	NA
-	? LMS all 3rd class coach	50	NA
-	? LMS brake 3rd coach	50	NA
-	? LMS full passenger brake	50	NA
?	4 of the above LMS coaches - *13*	NA	245
-	? GCR composite coach	50	NA
-	? GCR all 1st class coach	50	NA
-	? GCR all 3rd class coach	50	NA
-	? GCR brake 3rd coach	50	NA
-	? GCR full passenger brake	50	NA
?	4 of the above GCR coaches - *13*	NA	245
-	? LNER composite coach	50	NA
-	? LNER all 1st class coach	50	NA
-	? LNER all 3rd class coach	50	NA
-	? LNER brake 3rd coach	50	NA
-	? LNER full passenger brake	50	NA
?	4 of the above LNER coaches - *13*	NA	245
-	? SE&CR composite coach	50	NA
-	? SE&CR all 1st class coach	50	NA
-	? SE&CR all 3rd class coach	50	NA
-	? SE&CR brake 3rd coach	50	NA
-	? SE&CR full passenger brake	50	NA
?	4 of the above SE&CR coaches - *13*	NA	245
-	? LB&SCR composite coach	50	NA
-	? LB&SCR all 1st class coach	50	NA
-	? LB&SCR all 3rd class coach	50	NA
-	? LB&SCR brake 3rd coach	50	NA
-	? LB&SCR full passenger brake	50	NA
?	4 of the above LB&SCR coaches - *13*	NA	245
-	? LSWR composite coach	50	NA
-	? LSWR all 1st class coach	50	NA
-	? LSWR all 3rd class coach	50	NA
-	? LSWR brake 3rd coach	50	NA
-	? LSWR full passenger brake	50	NA
?	4 of the above LSWR coaches - *13*	NA	245
-	? SR composite coach	50	NA
-	? SR all 1st class coach	50	NA
-	? SR all 3rd class coach	50	NA
-	? SR brake 3rd coach	50	NA
-	? SR full passenger brake	50	NA
?	4 of the above SR coaches - *13*	NA	245

6-wheel 3rd class Metropolitan Railway coach [C2] (Darstead)

-	? Met composite coach	50	NA
-	? Met all 1st class coach	50	NA
-	? Met all 3rd class coach	50	NA
-	? Met brake 3rd coach	50	NA
-	? Met full passenger brake	50	NA
?	4 of the above Metropolitan coaches - *13*	NA	245
-	? LT composite coach	50	NA
-	? LT all 1st class coach	50	NA
-	? LT all 3rd class coach	50	NA
-	? LT brake 3rd coach	50	NA
-	? LT full passenger brake	50	NA
?	4 of the above London Transport coaches - *13*	NA	245
-	? composite coach	50	NA
-	? all 1st class coach	50	NA
-	? all 3rd class coach	50	NA
-	? brake 3rd coach	50	NA
-	? full passenger brake	50	NA
?	4 of the above S&DJR coaches - *13*	NA	245
-	? NZR composite coach	50	NA
-	? NZR all 1st class coach	50	NA
-	? NZR all 3rd class coach	50	NA
-	? NZR brake 3rd coach	50	NA
-	? NZR full passenger brake	50	NA
?	4 of the above NZR coaches - *13*	NA	245
-	? PLM composite coach	50	NA
-	? PLM all 1st class coach	50	NA
-	? PLM all 3rd class coach	50	NA
-	? PLM brake 3rd coach	50	NA
-	? PLM full passenger brake	50	NA
?	4 of the above PLM coaches - *13*	NA	245

Darstaed & Vintage Trains

-	? SNCF composite coach	50	NA
-	? SNCF all 1st class coach	50	NA
-	? SNCF all 3rd class coach	50	NA
-	? SNCF brake 3rd coach	50	NA
-	? SNCF full passenger brake	50	NA
?	4 of the above SNCF coaches - 13	NA	245

C3. 35cm Non-Corridor Sets (2010)

These are non-corridor suburban sets. Originally introduced in the Edwardian era, many of them lasted well into BR days.

Only the SR and BR sets list a sixth coach, a composite, which is available only unboxed. There should have also been a CR composite coach but the printing of this failed. All standard 5-coach sets come in a large carrying box containing 2 identical 3-coach set boxes. One of these 3-coach boxes contains a brake end (with power pick-up and end lamp), a third class and a first class coach. The other 3-coach box contains a brake end (without pick-up and lamp), another third class coach and an empty space. This means that a further coach can be added and also dealers could split a 5-coach set into a 3-coach and a 2-coach set for selling separately. The power pick-up bogie and rear lamp are available on their own for upgrading brake ends without them. The composite coach, where one exists, is designed to fit in the empty space. The suggested value of 3 cars, if sold separately is £210 and that for 2 cars is £140 (or £150 with power pick-up and a rear lamp). The extra composite coach is valued at £70. The pick-up/lamp unit on its own is valued at £20.

The models have sprung bogies, sole bar detail, interior compartment detail (including pictures on the walls above the seats) and ceiling lighting, glazed windows, rear lamp on brakes (rl), some with glazed lit clerestory roofs (c). In all 20 liveries are planned.

LNWR non-corridor brake end coach [C3] (tony Wright)

	LNWR		
320301	**1059** 1st purple-brown+white	55	75
320302	**875** 3rd purple-brown+white	55	75
320303	**912** 3rd purple-brown+white	55	75
320304	**958**, **967** brake 3rd purple-brown+white	55	75
320305	**967**, **958** brake 3rd purple-brown+white, rl	55	75
329903	set of 5 coaches limited run of only 34 sets - 10	NA	325
	CR		
320501	**571** 1st purple lake+white	55	75
320502	**136** composite purple lake+white - not made	NA	75
320503	**135** 3rd purple lake+white	55	75
320504	**541** 3rd purple lake+white	55	75
320505	**754**, **678** brake 3rd purple lake+white	55	75
320506	**678**, **754** brake 3rd purple lake+white, rl	55	75
320507	**127** brake composite purple lake+white	55	75
329905	set of 5 coaches - 10	NA	325
	GER		
321201	**84** 1st teak	55	75
321202	**93** 3rd teak	55	75
321203	**206** 3rd teak	55	75
321204	**542**, **207** brake 3rd teak	55	75
321205	**207**, **542** brake 3rd teak, rl	55	75
329912	set of 5 coaches - 10	NA	325
	SECR		
320801	**3028** 1st maroon	55	75
320802	**758** 3rd maroon	55	75
320803	**3824** 3rd maroon	55	75
320804	**3571**, **803** brake 3rd maroon	55	75
320805	**803**, **3571** brake 3rd maroon	55	75
329908	set of 5 coaches - 10	NA	325
	LBSCR		
320201	**610** 1st brown+cream	55	75
320202	**540** 3rd brown+cream	55	75
320203	**556** 3rd brown+cream	55	75
320204	**85**, **205** brake 3rd brown+cream	55	75
320205	**205**, **85** brake 3rd brown+cream, rl	55	75
329902	set of 5 coaches - 10	NA	325
	LSWR		
320901	**504** 1st salmon+brown	90	100
320902	**205** 3rd salmon+brown	90	100
320903	**372** 3rd salmon+brown	90	100
320904	**302**, **275** brake 3rd salmon+brown, rl	90	100
320905	**275**, **302** brake 3rd salmon+brown	90	100
329909	set of 5 coaches Ltd Edn of 34 sets (only 34 sets made due to problems with the 'peach' colour) - 10	NA	500
	GWR		
320401	**1059** 1st brown+cream, c	55	75
320402	**856** 3rd brown+cream, c	55	75
320403	**987** 3rd brown+cream, c	55	75
320404	**1952**, **1942** brake 3rd brown+cream, c	55	75
320405	**1942**, **1952** brake 3rd brown+cream, c, rl	55	75
329904	set of 5 coaches - 10	NA	325
	LMS		
320601	**5049** 1st maroon, c	55	75
320602	**2501** 3rd maroon, c	55	75
320603	**7125** 3rd maroon, c	55	75
320604	**2142** brake composite maroon, c	55	75
320605	**1904** brake 3rd maroon, c, rl	55	75
329906	above set of 5 - 10	NA	325
	LMS		
320701	**3330** (a) composite maroon	55	75
320702	**2502** (a) 3rd maroon	55	75
320703	**7126** (a) 3rd maroon	55	75
320704	**1904** (a) brake 3rd maroon	55	75
320705	**2142** (a) brake composite maroon, rl	55	75
329907	above set of 5 - 10	NA	325

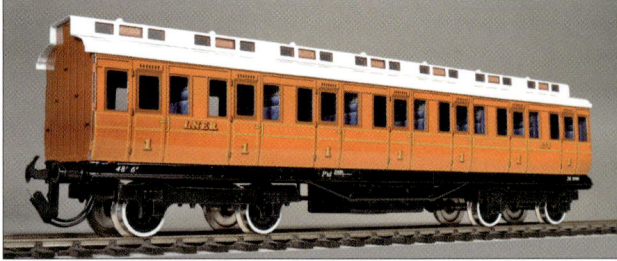

LNER clerestory non-corridor 1st class coach [C3] (Tony Wright)

	LNER		
320101	**573** 1st teak, c	55	75
320102	**459** 3rd teak, c	55	75
320103	**945** 3rd teak, c	55	75
320104	**354**, **395** brake 3rd teak, c	55	75
320105	**395**, **354** brake 3rd teak, c, rl	55	75
329901	set of 5 coaches - 10	NA	325
	SR		
321001	**461** 1st olive green	55	75
321002	**2046** 3rd olive green	55	75
321003	**1025** 3rd olive green	55	75
321004	**384** composite olive green	55	76
321005	**825**, **705** brake 3rd olive green	55	75
321006	**705**, **825** brake 3rd olive green, rl	55	75
329910	set of 5 coaches excluding composite - 10	NA	325
	BR		
321101	**M41005** composite maroon	55	75
321102	**M41012** composite maroon	55	75
321103	**M42568** 3rd maroon	55	75
321104	**M46105** composite maroon	55	76
321105	**M42312**, **M46852** brake 3rd maroon	55	75
321106	**M46852**, **M42312** brake 3rd maroon, rl	55	75
329910	set of 5 coaches excluding composite - 10	NA	325

C4. Main Line Coaches

Production of these has been put on hold with effect from February 2013.

Darstaed & Vintage Trains

WAGONS

Cat No.	Company, Number, Colour, Date	£	£
W1.	**16T Steel Mineral Wagon (2012)**		

These are diecast with diecast chassis and available in grey or brown. They are sold in sets of six all differently numbered and there are two sets of each colour. They are suitable for 2-rail or 3-rail. And have sprung buffers

Cat No.	Company, Number, Colour, Date	£	£
-	B266409 grey	25	NA
-	? grey	25	NA
-	? grey	25	NA
-	? grey	25	NA
-	? grey	25	NA
-	? grey	25	NA
?	above 6 wagons - 12	NA	150
-	? grey	25	NA
-	? grey	25	NA
-	? grey	25	NA
-	? grey	25	NA
-	? grey	25	NA
-	? grey	25	NA
?	above 6 wagons - 12	NA	150
-	B577502 brown	25	NA
-	? brown	25	NA
-	? brown	25	NA
-	? brown	25	NA
-	? brown	25	NA
-	? brown	25	NA
?	above 6 wagons - 12	NA	150
-	? brown	25	NA
-	? brown	25	NA
-	? brown	25	NA
-	? brown	25	NA
-	? brown	25	NA
-	? brown	25	NA
?	above 6 wagons - 12	NA	150

W2.	**Pre-Grouping Advertising Vans (2009)**		

This first series of 10 advertising vans was inspired by some of the small enamelled advertising signs made and marketed by Bassett-Lowke and others during the period before the Grouping, i.e. 1905 to 1923. Each van carries a livery and return station based on the location of the factory, firm or products advertised on each van. The weight of each van 500 grams or 1.1lbs. The vans have a cast plank effect roof, detailed brake gear and sprung buffers. Each design contains the artist's hidden logo, as with Cuneo paintings, and each is a limited edition of 500.

Cat No.	Company, Number, Colour, Date	£	£
110109	'Bass' 91201 MR - 09	40	45
110104	'Burgoyne's Australian Wines' 4255 GE - 09	40	45
110105	'Henry Murton's Waterproofers' 501735 NE - 09	40	45
110101	'Melrose's Tea' 1408 CR - 09	40	45
110107	'Rocket Lubricating Oil' 7429 GE - 09	40	45
110103	'Rowntree's Elect Cocoa' 3217 NE - 09	40	45
110110	'Spratt's Dog Food' 1087 SECR - 09	40	45
110108	'The Captain Magazine' 8384 GW - 09	40	45
110106	'Wood Milne Rubber Heels' 6008 LNWR - 09	40	45
110102	'Wright's Coal Tar Soap' 27741 SECR - 09	40	45

W3.	**Horton Darstaed Ad Vans (2012)**		

These were designed in Australia by Rob Horton of Wessex Transfers. The vans have a traditional Vintage Trains chassis, detailed brake gear and sprung buffers. They are suitable for both 2-rail and 3-rail. A second series was planned, but, before details of it were released, Rob Horton decided to transfer it to Ace Trains to produce through their manufacturing contacts.

Cat No.	Company, Number, Colour, Date	£	£
?	'Coleman's Mustard' ? yellow Sp Edn (Raylo) - 12	36	40
?	'Coleman's Starch' 43 yellow Sp Edn (Raylo) - 12	36	40
HP06	'Cydrax' 7 green - 12	35	39
HP05	'Ever Ready' 34 blue - 12	35	39
HP?	'Heinz' 3 yellow - 12	35	39
HP?	'Lyons Swiss Rolls' 5 blue - 12	35	39
HP?	'Ovaltine' 48 blue+ white - 12	35	39
HP?	'Palethorpes' 26 maroon Sp Edn (Raylo) - 12	36	40
HP?	'Robertson's Golden Shred' 2 red - 12	35	39
HP?	'Slumberland' 24 red - 12	35	39
HP?	'Weetabix' 25 yellow - 12	35	39

Advertising van - 'Cydrax' [W3] (David Upton)

VINTAGE TRAINS

HISTORY

Vintage Trains, previously known as Ace Trains Co. Ltd., was the manufacturer of the Ace range from its inception in 1995 until 2008, when the two companies parted. As a result, Vintage was left with an amount of stock and parts which will be re-issued from time to time.

LOCOMOTIVES

VL1.	**LNER Class J19 0-6-0 (2008)**		

The locomotives were designed by Hill for the Great Eastern Railway and were built between 1912 and 1920. They were originally built with Belpaire fireboxes but were all rebuilt by Gresley with round-topped boilers.

LNER Class J19 0-6-0 [VL1] (Darstead)

Cat No.	Company, Number, Colour, Date	£	£
010109	8145 LNER green extra cab lining - 10	300	345
010101	8245 LNER green - 08	300	345
010110	8262 LNER green extra cab lining - 10	300	345
010102	8281 LNER green - 08	300	345
010103	8141 LNER lined black - 08	300	345
010103	8141 NE lined black (only a few made) - ?	300	365
010104	64649 BRa black - 08	250	299
010105	64670 BRb black - 08	250	299
010106	NZR black - 09	300	345
010107	SAR black - 09	300	345
010108	NSWGR green – 09	300	345

VL2.	**GWR 'Castle' Class 4-6-0 (2013)**		

These have a diecast metal body and are fitted with a 20V DC Mabuchi motor. They have lit buffer beam mounted lamps of the correct colour, firebox glow, an on/off switch in the cab, a route availability indicator and are claimed to run on all types of track. They will be available with a wide range of names and liveries (including wartime black and experimental 'pea' green. Some will have the 1947 oil fired tenders and some will have Hawksworth tenders. There will be single and double chimneys as well as scollop and square inside cylinder covers.

Cat No.	Company, Number, Colour, Date	£	£
?	? GWR green - 13	NPG	525
?	? GWR (button) black - 13	NPG	525
?	? BR green - 13	NPG	525

Darstaed & Vintage Trains

VL3. LNER Class A4 4-6-0 (20113)

The A4 was Gresley's ultimate express engine development and arrived in 1935. It was one of the most successful streamlined railway engine designed in Britain and one of the class (*Mallard*) still holds the world speed record for a steam locomotive.

This has a diecast body produced from new tooling and new heavy-duty gearbox.

?	? LNER blue with valances - *13*	NPG	685
?	? LNER blue without valances - *13*	NPG	685
?	? LNER black - *13*	NPG	685
?	?		NPG	685

WAGONS

VW1. Milk Tanker (2010)

This was a limited run of 340 examples, with cream lettering on a blue background.

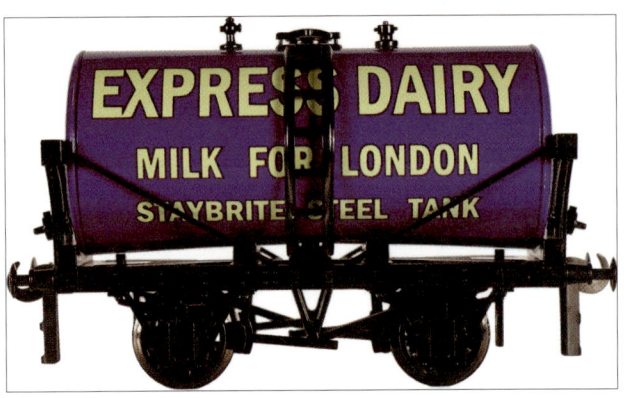

040101	'Express Dairies' blue - *10*	30	35
046001	a set of 3 of the above wagon - *10*	NA	99

VW2. 20T Guards Van (2010)

This is a 4-wheel tinplate vehicle with a working rear lamp, internal light, ducket and sprung buffers. The model is based on the long wheelbase LNER 'Toad E' design which was adopted as a standard by British Railways.

040201	LNER 178717 brown - *10*	32	39
040202	BR E178717 brown - *10*	32	39

'Express Daries' milk tank wagon [VW1] (Darstead)

1st issue - advertising vans [VW2] (Vectis)

Exley 0

HISTORY

This firm is primarily known for its coaching stock in 00 and 0 gauge and was founded at Bradford by Edward Exley in 1923 but did not become a limited company until 1947. Initially the products were locomotives, in live steam, clockwork and electrically powered, in gauges 0 and 1, which some were made to order.

By the 1930s, 0 gauge coaches had joined the range of products, and both locos and coaches were available 'off the shelf' as well as to order. During this period the company started supplying Bassett-Lowke with models, including the range of 0 gauge coaches which the latter company sold as their 'scale range'! It should be remembered that this was in the days before current consumer legislation, and as we have seen elsewhere in this catalogue, Bassett-Lowke bought in much of their range of products from other manufacturers and sold them through their catalogues under their own name. At the same time a business relationship was formed with J S Beeson, Mills Bros., Leeds Model Company and others, with much cross-fertilisation of products between the parties involved.

GWR Royal Mail Sorting Coach [C10] (Barry Potter)

In the later 1930s, partly as a result of Vivien Boyd-Carpenter having joined the company, high quality 00 coaching stock was added to feed a growing market in this new scale.

During the Second World War, work turned to the war effort and scale model ships for naval recognition use were made. With the return of peace, the company retooled in 1945 to produce their railway models again. The underframes and bogies of the early post war coaches were improved from those of the pre-war era, and around 1950 the tooling for the coach bodies was also upgraded to the style most commonly found today.

Edward Exley Ltd also produced industrial models to commissioned orders, which included charabancs, industrial installations, large diesel engines, etc., and continued to supply Bassett-Lowke with 'scale' coaches.

In the early post war years the sales department was in Worksop, Nottinghamshire, with Boyd-Carpenter running this part of the business, although the works were still in Bradford. By 1952, however, Edward Exley (Sales) Ltd had moved to Baslow in Derbyshire and Edward Exley had resigned as a director of the sales company in July 1955 after a disagreement. Indeed, it seems that the directors were continually changing due to boardroom squabbles. Edward continued to manage the works in Bradford and the Edward Exley (sales) Ltd catalogue carried the statement 'This company is not now a manufacturing undertaking'. Lists of coaches in 00 and 0 scale were issued by the factory but these were headed 'Exley of Bradford'.

An interesting link is worth mentioning here. Both before and after the Second World War, there was close association between Exley and Mills Bros.. Indeed, Frank Mills was, for some time in the '50s, a director of Edward Exley Ltd. and the two companies were known to build for each other. This can cause some confusion for collectors and historians.

Locomotives had continued to be available after the war, mainly to order, including a number of highly detailed and large scale display models for companies such as Hudswell Clarke, Ruston & Hornsby and British Railways. But, in the late 1950s Edward Exley sold the loco construction part of the business to Stanley Beeson, who had made locos for a number of Exley clients. Coaches were listed until 1962, when there was a terrible fire on 24th June which destroyed the Bradford premises and most of the tools. At this point Edward Exley decided to retire. A note in the 1962-63 catalogue, reporting the fire, indicated the company's intention to rebuild the factory but it seems that this did not happen.

In 1962 Edward Exley Ltd took over Mills Bros. stock and the Milbro name and became the sole suppliers of Milbro products which are covered elsewhere in this book.

The company at Baslow continued to offer coaches but discontinued the 00 gauge range as the manufacturing facility was lost in the fire. The 7mm models were listed as available until the death of Boyd-Carpenter in January 1995, but were being made to order by outside workers. It has to be said that quality of the coaches made after 1962, once a hallmark of the company name, was variable, and to the purist no true Exleys were made after the destruction of the Bradford factory.

After the death of Boyd-Carpenter in 1995, Edward Exley Ltd ceased trading at Baslow, and all the shares and remnants of the company were purchased by Quentin and Tricia Lucas from Fife. In the latter half of the 1990s they rebuilt the company, trading in original Exley models, carrying out restorations, and selling modern finescale 0 gauge kits, models and components. Quentin specialised in the 0 gauge Exley market, and Tricia in 00. They were a familiar sight at model railway exhibitions and at selected Train Fairs and Auctions, and operated a mail order service too. In January 1999 they moved the business to near Berwick-upon-Tweed, and not long after this wound up the company when they retired.

In August 2004, Edward Exley Limited was sold by Quentin and Tricia Lucas to Richard Gordon-Brown and Joe Brown. Work began on developing a new range of ready-to-run 0 gauge coaching stock.

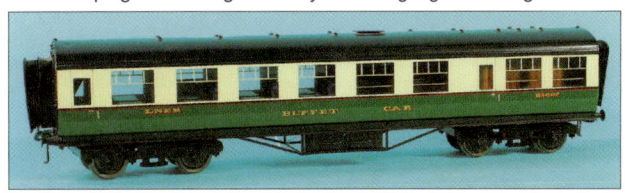

LNER tourist kitchen buffet [C6] (Special Auction Services)

Dates - Only post-war coaches are listed here at present as more research is required on pre-war production. Approximate dates of availability (for guidance only) are given in the tables and none are given after the factory burnt down in 1962.

LOCOMOTIVES

The majority of the Exley locomotives were hand-built, true to prototype and made to order. In the early days of the company many of them were built by Edward himself, as this was his first love in the business, but by the 1930s many were built by employees in the factory, and by other contemporary builders such as Mills Bros. and Stanley Beeson. As a result of almost no records being kept, exact production details have been impossible to obtain.

Pre-war, the Exley catalogue listed the following locos as available in both 0 gauge and gauge 1: 'Royal Scot', LNER A3, LMS 'Compound', LNWR *Hardwicke*, LNER N2, LMS 'Prince of Wales', LNER 10000, LMS 'Princess Royal', GNR 'Single', GWR 'King', Caledonian 4-6-0, SR 'Lord Nelson', GWR 2-6-2T, GWR 'Castle' and a freelance steam 0-4-0 saddle tank. All of these were listed as stock items, and others were advertised as built to order.

Post-war catalogues show an LNER *Flying Scotsman*, a Southern 4-6-0 'Lord Nelson', a Southern 'Schools' Class, a 36XX Class GWR 2-4-2T and a number of overseas locomotives for special purposes. Further known products were a NBR J35 and an LMS 2-6-4T. Catalogue illustrations post-war were usually of locos that had been supplied to customers, rather than an indication of what may be available from stock. As mentioned above, the locomotive building part of the Bradford business was sold to Stanley Beeson in the late 1950s.

Exley 0

Private owner 0-4-0 saddle tank [L1]

Prices - It is difficult to assess the value of Exley locomotives as they are not often found for sale, nor are they easy to identify. They are very well crafted models with nicely finished detail but they rarely carry the makers mark and when buying, one relies more on the provenance. The price for an Exley locomotive model is entirely dependent upon this as well as originality, condition and the price the buyer and seller are prepared to negotiate. Naturally locos identified positively as 'Beeson for Exley' attract premium prices. The two prices shown represent the likely range for one in good condition.

Cat No.	Company, Number, Colour, Date	£	£
L1.	**0-4-0ST (Freelance)**		
This model had the same body as the diesel shunter at L3 but different fittings to make it look like a steam engine and with outside cylinders.			
?	'Newman Bros.' orange - ?	100	150
L2.	**Miscellaneous Locomotives**		
These were high quality models built by hand, including ones that were made to order. MTO = made to order			
?	0-6-0ST (freelance) private owner - ?	150	200
	GWR Group		
?	GWR 4-6-0 'King' Class green - ?	850	1300
	LMS Group		
-	LNWR 2-4-0 *Hardwick* MTO - ?	2000	3500
?	LMS 2-6-4T black - ?	500	700
?	LMS 4-4-0 'Compound' 1126 red - ?	400	600
-	LMS 4-6-0 'Patriot' 5504 *Royal Signals* maroon MTO - 30-50	NPG	NPG
?	LMS 0-8-0 9500 black MTO - ?	500	700
	LNER Group		
-	GNR 4-2-2 Stirling 'Single' No.1 MTO - ?	2000	3500
?	NBR 0-6-0 Class J35 848 dark blue - ?	400	600
?	GCR/LNER Class 04/05 'ROD' 2-8-0 5012, 5412 black - 30-50	670	750
-	LNER Sentinel steam railcar *Fair Maid* green+ cream - ?	NPG	NPG
-	LNER A1 2573 *Harvester* green 3-rail 12V DC, brass, MTO - 57	2700	4300
-	LNER A1 4472 *Flying Scotsman* green MTO - ?	2500	4000
-	LNER A4 4498 *Sir Nigel Gresley* blue 3-rail 12V DC, brass, MTO - 57	2600	4300
	SR Group		
-	SR 4-4-0 'Schools' Class 923 *Bradfield* green - ?	2000	3500
-	Portsmouth 2-car EMU set 331+313 green - ?	650	750

'Schools' Class locomotive [L2] (Exley)

L3.	**0-4-0DS (Freelance)**		
This was the same model as that at L1 but had a square bonnet and radiator.			
?	LMS black - ?	150	200
?	LNER 717 green - ?	150	200
?	private owner livery - ?	150	200
L4.	**Southern EMU (Exley for Bassett-Lowke)**		
These were sold as 2-car sets with 12V DC Bassett-Lowke motor bogies and B-L coach bogies. Although made for Bassett-Lowke, they were also sold by Exley. The motor and trailer cars of the Portsmouth set were 3rd class centre corridor brake ends suitably modified, and many were sold with normal SR corridor coaches in the middle, to create the image of the prototype train. A similar suburban set was made from two suburban coaches in the same way, again often with additional non corridor coaches added. The suburban set is much rarer than the Portsmouth set. Values quoted should be adjusted where additional coaches have been added to the basic 2-car sets.			
?	LMS* 9020+9020 maroon all 3rd - c55	1600	2200
?	Southern green 3080 (11157+11171) Portsmouth 2-car set - 53-60?	1100	1500
?	Southern green 3064, 3074 (3990+?), 2186 (11161+?) 2-car suburban set - 53-60?	1300	1700

* A very small number of the corridor EMUs were turned out to special order in LMS livery (thought to be less than 10 sets). This was entirely a fictional subject and did not represent any known LMS prototype EMU but, nevertheless, makes a fine looking set.

Southern Electric driving car [L4]

COACHES

Exley coaches were made from aluminium using a wrap-round technique so that roof, sides and solebars were one. This was attached to a wooden floor which during the pre- and early post-war period sat high inside the coach body, but from about 1950 sat just above solebar level.

Pre-war, the ends were an alloy casting showing the end planking detail, which was bowed, if the prototype had bowed ends. They incorporated a cast lug which screwed to the underside of the floor. From around 1950, using a heavier alloy, the end castings were changed to a more modern pattern which was based on the LMS Stanier coach end. These were retained by copper wires cast into the end at solebar level. The heavier cast ends, with integral buffers also were replaced by plastic in the late 1950s.

The windows were glass, held in place by spring clips and should not be taken apart - unless by someone experienced in doing so.

Before the war, battery boxes were usually blocks of wood with little or no underframe detail. Post-war, pressed metal battery boxes were introduced, initially with an open bottom and an indication of truss rodding. Bogies were mounted on a central spigot bolted through the wooden floor.

These construction methods were modified with the introduction of the K5 and K6 series of the '50s. There has been much speculation about the significance of K5 and K6 but, suffice to say, the principal difference between them is that K5 and earlier coaches have the window ventilators painted onto the glass, whereas K6, and the plastic range, have window ventilators stamped out from the metal of the coach side. However, this is not an infallible rule, as many K5 coaches have stamped metal vents! K6 coaches, and K5 metal vents, do attract a price premium over those with painted vents. The K5 and K6 series also had different bogies but we have not distinguished between them here.

Exley 0

Apart from modified bogie fittings with the advent of the split pin, the underframes became more detailed and were an all metal construction. The bodies were lowered on the bogies so that no daylight showed underneath and material for the interiors changed in the late 1950s so that they now had coloured seats in metal. The final modification to the coaches themselves was the utilisation of plastic for coach ends, bogies and parts of the underframe, and they now carried the 'BFD EXLEY MODDEX' trade mark.

A variety of bogies have been used with Exley coaches over the years. Pre-war the Exley bogie had pressed steel and cast side frames. They had a central spigot socket and wire bracing and the axle ends were suspended on spring steel wire. Exley coaches sold by Bassett-Lowke were fitted with their range of bogies.

Post-war, Exley bogies developed to the familiar 'V' shaped central stretcher for split pin attachment. These had cast side frames and wire end stretchers, but still with spring steel wire support to the axle ends. Again, coaches sold by Bassett-Lowke were fitted with their post-war compensated bogie. Today, post-war coaches appearing on the market are about evenly divided between the two bogie types, and this has no effect upon value.

Quite a variety of coaches were made in the liveries of the 'Big Four' railway companies and latterly in the crimson & cream and maroon BR colour schemes; although BR coaches generally are far less common. Available to special order were coaches for the pre-grouping companies and freelance concerns. The rare availability on the market of these specials makes it impossible to provide a realistic valuation guide for them, however, good to excellent examples have changed hands at prices between £500 and £1200 each, depending upon the livery they carried and their rarity.

The coaches made before 1940 tend to be more accurate to the prototype whereas after the introduction of the K5 series, which were largely based upon the LMS Stanier profile, it became a matter of changing livery, rainstrips and window positions.

Exley coaches are always impressive, run well and, in their day, were the leaders in their field. More recently, hand-built scale coaches have overtaken Exleys for the finescale enthusiast, but they still have a major following amongst operators, as well as among collectors.

Numbers - It seems that a very large range of running numbers were used on each coach type and it is near impossible to find two identical coaches identically numbered. The tables below contain only known examples but many other numbers are sure to exist.

Values - We cannot give a suggested value to all the types of coach made but we have given an indication of value, of coaches manufactured after the 2nd World War. The values given refer to coaches in good to excellent condition. Those in poor, altered and well used condition are worth much less.

We apologise for the incompleteness of this section but much more research is required - and help with this is needed.

Cat No.	Company, Number, Colour, Date	£	£

'Suburban' Stock

C1. 'Suburban' 6-Wheel 31' Coaches
It is thought that few of these would still be in use after the grouping of the railway companies in 1923.

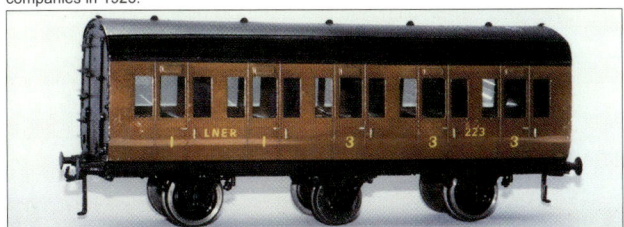

LNER 6-wheel surburban composite coach [C1]

	3rd Class		
-	GWR a dark brown+cream - 54?	250	350
-	LMS maroon - 54?	250	350
-	LNER 222 teak - 54?	250	350
-	SR green - 54?	250	500
	Composite		
-	GWR dark brown+cream - 54?	250	350
-	LMS maroon - 54?	250	350
-	LNER 223 teak - 54?	250	350
-	SR green - 54?	250	500
	Brake 3rd		
-	GWR 233 brake 3rd dark brown+cream - 54?	250	350
-	LMS 271 brake 3rd maroon - 54?	250	350
-	LNER brake 3rd teak - 54?	250	350
-	SR brake 3rd green - 54?	250	500

C2. 'Suburban' 50' Bogie Coaches
Called 'Suburban' coaches, because they had no corridor connection, no side corridor and, unless open coaches, no toilets, in fact they were used much more widely than the suburbs. They were a common sight in frequently stopping trains on cross-country routes and branch lines.

	1st Class		
-	LMS 10002 maroon - ?	250	300
	3rd Class		
-	GWR 223, 443, 6561 dark brown+cream - 50?-62	250	350
-	LMS 10033, 12225, 19161, 20011, 21537 maroon - 50?-62	200	250
-	LNER brown - 53?-62	300	375
-	SR 1999 green - 50?-62	400	650
-	BR maroon - 59?-62	NPG	NPG

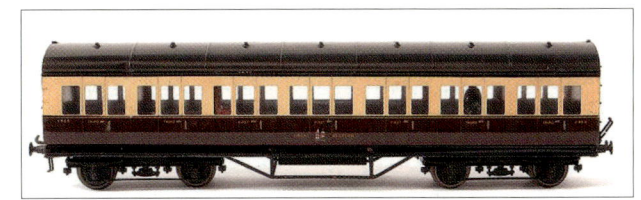

GWR surburban composite coach [C2] (Vectis)

	Composite		
-	GWR 1071, 2315, 3232, 3555, 8017 dark brown+cream - 50?-62	200	250
-	LMS 1620, 2420, 19992 maroon - 50?-62	200	250
-	LNER 223, 3224 brown - 53?-62	300	375
-	SR 7632 green - 50?-62	400	650
-	BR maroon - 59?-62	NPG	NPG
	Brake 3rd		
-	GWR 5111, 5588, 6661 dark brown+cream - 50?-62	250	350
-	LMS 2681, 2721, 18777, 20078, 23322 maroon - 50?-62	200	250
-	LNER 3330 brown - 53?-62	300	375
-	SR 3805, 3806, 3807, 4442 green - 50?-62	400	650
-	BR maroon - 59?-62	NPG	NPG
	Brake Composite		
-	LMS 478 maroon - 50?-62	250	350
	Full Brake		
-	LMS 25, 31181, 31187, 31321 maroon - 50?-62	200	250
-	LNER brown - 53?-62	300	250
-	SR 441 green - 50?-62	350	650
-	BR red+cream - 58?	375	450
-	BR maroon - 59?-62	NPG	NPG

Main Line Passenger Stock

C3. 57' Main Line Corridor Coaches
Main line stock had gangway connections, corridors and toilets. These ones had side corridors and compartments, with facing bench seats.

	1st Class		
-	GWR 720, 1071, 4200, 8100 dark brown+cream - 50?-62	250	300
-	LMS 6727, 8001, 8035, 8037, 8228, 8333, 8777		

Exley 0

-	maroon - *50?-62*	200	250
-	**LNER** 8004, 8001 brown - *53?-62*	350	380
-	**SR** 8103, 8531, 8771 green - *50?-62*	375	650
-	**BR** red+cream - *57?-58?*	475	550
-	**BR** maroon - *59?-62*	350	400
	3rd Class		
-	**GWR** 212, 2220, 2702, 3000, 5120, 6444, 6604, 6626, 8027, 8066, 8083, 8107, 9132, 9991 2220 dark brown+cream - *50?-62*	200	250
-	**LMS** 121, 1592, 1834, 2001, 2033, 2111, 2222, 2288, 2344, 2555, 3546, 4563, 6345, 6668, 7001, 19286 maroon - *50?-62*	200	250
-	**LNER** 8000, 8107, 8882 brown - *53?-62*	350	400
-	**SR** 5480?, 6055?, 8000, 8400, 8673, 8881, 8883, 8888 green - *50?-62*	200	250
-	**BR** M2210, M2211M, M2221 red+cream - *57?-58?*	425	500
-	**BR** maroon - *59?-62*	350	400
	Composite		
-	**GWR** 2120, 2255, 4722, 8892, 8989, 9555 dark brown+cream - *50?-62*	200	250
-	**LMS** 1111?, 1119, 3032, 3113, 3232, 3333, 3862, 4044, 4224, 4440, 8278, 10774, 22707 maroon - *50?-62*	200	250
-	**LNER** 7207 brown - *?*	250	350
-	**BR** M3322W red+cream - *59?-62*	250	350
	Brake 1st		
-	**LMS** 888, 1221, 6536 maroon - *?*	250	300
	Brake 3rd		
-	**GWR** 1900, 2220, 2323, 2720, 4018, 4077, 5518?, 6241, 7207, 10707 dark brown+cream - *50?-62*	200	250
-	**LMS** 888, 2284, 2288, 3000, 6000, 6266, 6300, 6464, 6656, 6660, 6661, 6666, 6668, 6888, 8616, 8723, 67777 maroon - *50?-62*	200	250
-	**LNER** 1553 brown - *53?-62*	350	300
-	**SR** 4447 green - *50?-62*	375	650
-	**BR** S4410 red+cream - *57?-58?*	425	500
-	**BR** maroon - *59?-62*	350	400
	Brake Composite		
-	**LMS** 3760 maroon - *?*	200	250
	Full Brake Class		
-	**GWR** 29, 202, 224,1120, 1178, 16 dark brown+cream - *50?-62*	325	350
-	**BR** maroon - *59?-62*	NPG	NPG

BR side-corridor brake end [C3] (Vectis)

C4. K5 Ex-LMS Side Corridor Stock
This was a late introduction of BR red and cream stock based on former LMS coaches but with the window top lights cut out and not painted onto the glazing.

-	**BR** M3030M, M3040M, M3044M red+cream composite - *?*	500	650
-	**BR** M3040M red+cream 3rd class - *?*	400	500
-	**BR** M6432M red+cream brake 3rd - *?*	450	600
-	**BR** M3344M red+cream brake composite - *?*	400	600

C5. 57' Main Line Open Coaches
These did not have a side corridor with compartments but had open saloons with a central, or off-centre, corridor with seats on either side of it. At the time the models were made, they were known as 'Centre Corridor Coaches'.

	1st Class		
-	**LMS** 7778 maroon - *50?-62*	200	250
-	**BR** maroon - *59?-62*	NPG	NPG
	3rd Class		
-	**GWR** 2033?, 6000 dark brown+cream - *50?-62*	300	380

-	**LMS** 1114?, 4424, 6616, 6667, 6777, 9000, 9200 maroon - *50?-62*	200	250
-	**LNER** 45001 green+cream - *53?-62*	475	550
-	**SR** 6611 green - *50?-62*	400	680
-	**BR** red+cream - *58?*	525	600
-	**BR** maroon - *59?-62*	350	400
	Brake 1st		
-	**LMS** 3032, 8811 maroon - *50?-62*	200	250
	Brake 3rd		
-	**LMS** 9955, 26141 maroon - *50?-62*	200	250
-	**LNER** green+cream - *53?-62*	475	550
-	**SR** green - *50?-62*	700	650
-	**BR** M11721M red+cream - *58?*	525	600
-	**BR** maroon - *59?-62*	350	400

C6. Catering Cars
Even when it came to designing the BR standard Mk1 coaches in the 1950s, a number of different types of catering cars were needed, according to the type of train. Many restaurant cars had their own kitchen, but for some long distance trains it was not uncommon to have two restaurant cars and a kitchen car serving them. Although cars are grouped together under headings, this does not mean that they had the same layout - only the same function.

	Buffet Car		
-	**LMS** 112 maroon - *50?-62*	300	400
-	**LNER** 21601, 21602, 21603, 21607, 30710 green+cream - *50?-62*	200	250
-	**SR** 1250, 1254, 1259 green - *50?-62*	450	900
-	**BR** M200M maroon - *59?-62*	NPG	NPG
	Restaurant/Dining Car 1st		
-	**GWR** 3280, 4721, 5005 choc+cream - *50?-62*	300	375
-	**LMS** 4279 maroon - *?*	300	375
	Restaurant Car 3rd		
-	**LMS** 1834 maroon - *?*	300	375
	Restaurant Car Unclassified		
-	**GWR** 2027, 9200 choc+cream - *?*	300	375
	Queen Mary Restaurant Car		
-	**GWR** 9112 choc+cream - *?*	300	375
	12-wheeled Dining Car		
-	**LMS** 5042 maroon 3rd - *prewar*	400	500
	50' Kitchen Car		
-	**GWR** 2060 dark brown+cream - *50?-62*	325	400
-	**LMS** 364, 3002, 30088, 31221, 37771, 30075, 41115 maroon - *50?-62*	200	250
-	**BR** 30075, M31131 red+cream - *61?-62*	400	500
	Restaurant 1st Kitchen 57'		
-	**LMS** 31, 33, 42, 45, 4203, 5081 maroon - *50?-62*	200	250
-	**SR** 6011, 6577 green - *50?-62*	450	900
-	**BR** red+cream - *61?-62*	500	600
	Restaurant 1st Kitchen 69'		
-	**LMS** 20, 41?, 42, 66 maroon - *?*	NPG	NPG
	Restaurant Unclassified Kitchen 57'		
-	**GWR** 3280, 4721, 5005 choc+cream - *50?-62*	300	375
-	**LMS** 16 maroon - *50?-62*	300	375

SR restaurant car [C6] (Vectis)

C7. Sleeping Cars
The first class sleeping car would have had a single berth in each compartment and may well have had communicating doors between pairs of compartments. The third class car probably had double berths in each compartment. A composite sleeping car would have had a mixture of cabins.

	1st Class		
-	**GWR** 5522, 6560? dark brown+cream - *50?-62*	375	620
-	**LNER** 6461, 6463 brown - *57?-62*	350	430
-	**BR** maroon - *59?-62*	NPG	NPG

Exley 0

3rd Class		
GWR 9040 dark brown+cream - *50?-62*	375	450
LNER brown - *57?-62*	350	425
BR maroon - *59?-62*	NPG	NPG
Composite 57'		
GWR 9075 dark brown+cream - *prewar*	380	430
LMS 250? maroon 57' *-50?-62*	250	350
BR M660 red+cream - *59?-62*	375	450
Composite 69'		
LMS 2?0, 737, 744, 3425 maroon 69' - *60?-62*	200	250

LMS sleeping car [C7] (Special Auction Services)

Non-Passenger Carrying Coaching Stock

C8. 'Stove R' 6-Wheel Full Brake 31'
This was a period 3 LMS designed full brake and 75 were built at Wolverton in 1932 and 1933. All survived into BR ownership and most were withdrawn between 1963 and 1968.

LMS Brake Stove R maroon - *54?*	300	400

C9. Parcels Train Brake Van 57'
Parcels vans were added to certain trains to increase luggage capacity, for example trains connecting with ocean liners. They were also used to make up parcels only trains or were added to trains to deliver newspapers.

LMS parcels van [C9] (Vectis)

50' Non-Gangwayed Full Brake		
GWR 200, 202 dark brown+cream - *50?-62*	250	325
LMS maroon - *50?-62*	250	300
LNER 303, 101 brown - *53?-62*	250	350
SR 113, 441 green - *53?-62*	350	650
BR crimson+cream - *58?-59?*	350	400
BR maroon - *59?-62*	NPG	NPG
50' Non-Gangwayed Parcels Van		
GWR 6196 dark brown+cream - *57?-62*	300	350
LMS 31322 maroon - *50?-62*	250	300
LNER brown - *59?-62*	250	350
SR green - *50?-62*	350	650
57' Parcels Train Brake Van		
GWR 151, 6295 dark brown+cream - *50?-62*	300	350
BR maroon - *59?-62*	NPG	NPG
Ocean Mails Van		
GWR 1110, 1111, 1196?, 1199 dark brown+cream - *50?-62*	400	475
BR maroon - *59?-62*	NPG	NPG

C10. Travelling Post Office 57'
This had folded-away collection nets and the representation of two floodlights low on the side of the coach.

GWR 818?, 910? dark brown+cream - *50?-62*	370	525
LMS 20007, 30220?, 30234 maroon - *50?-62*	200	250
LNER 808, 988 brown - *57?-62*	800	1000
BR M?M red+cream - *58?*	500	575
BR maroon - *59?-62*	NPG	NPG

Departmental Stock

C11. LMS Engineer's Inspection Saloon 50'
This would have been used by railway staff for track and other inspections.

LMS maroon - *57?-62*	400	450
BR maroon - *59?-62*	NPG	NPG

Other coaches in pre-grouping and private liveries were available to order.

Photo of a renamed Hornby 'Britannia' on the 'Night Parcels', computer enhanced by Robbie McGavin

ELLIS CLARK TRAINS

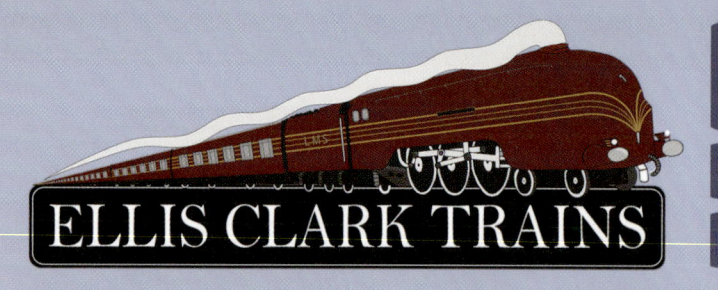

For info on upcoming fairs and exhibitons visit our website or find us on Facebook

www.ellisclarktrains.com

www.facebook.com/ellisclarktrains

WANTED

Top prices paid for your collections of trains, diecast & tinplate

Anything considered, all makes, gauges and ages, including all British, Continental and American, all gauges of Kit/scratch built and live steam All diecast & tinplate cars, lorries, busses, planes, soldiers etc...

Happy to travel nationwide and collect

Large collections a speciality

Will pay in your preferred method

A friendly & professional service

☏ 07799554491

✉ ellis@ellisclarktrains.com

Post a list to: Ellis Clark, Unit 13 Baildon Mills, Northgate, Baildon, Shipley, West Yorkshire, BD17 6JX

Exley 00

HISTORY

For a history of Edward Exley Ltd, see the Exley 0 gauge chapter.

In the late 1930s (1938 is assumed for our purpose), partly as a result of Vivien Boyd-Carpenter having joined the company, high quality 00 coaching stock was added to feed a growing market in this new scale.

It is assumed that the post-war Standard coaches were a revival of the pre-war range. All changed in December 1956 when Exley brought out their cheaper Zenith and Popular ranges. Major wholesalers such as W&H promptly dropped the Standard models and, by the end of 1957, were offering only the Zenith range. 00 scale coach production continued until the Exley works was burnt down in 1962.

LOCOMOTIVES

While we always think of coaches when the name Exley is mentioned, they also marketed a few locomotives as well. In many cases the majority of pre-war 00 gauge locomotives were made for Exley by Holtzappfel and later by Cimco. These included a 'Duchess' and a 'Royal Scot'. Little is known about these but those that are, are listed here.

Cat No.	Company, Number, Colour, Date	£	£
L1.	**Steam Locomotives (by Cimco)**		

This is a list of models that we know about but there were sure to have been more, including those built by Holtzappfel. As with the 0 gauge locomotive models, 00 scale locomotives would have also been built to order.

GWR 'Star' Class [L1]

-	3835 *County of Devon* GWR 4-4-0 'Country' Class green - *51*	60	80
-	1127 LNER 2-6-0 black - *52*	60	80
-	4016 *Knight of the Golden Fleece* GWR 4-6-0 'Star' Class green - *51*	60	80
-	6100 *Royal Scot* LMS 4-6-0 maroon - *37?*	60	80
-	6230 *Duchess of Buccleuch* LMS 4-6-2 maroon - *37*	60	80

Cat No.	Company, Number, Colour, Date	£	£
L2	**DMUs (1959)**		

Unfortunately the running numbers used were fictitious and so it is not possible to identify the prototype for this model.

-	M58642+M59286+M58242 BR green Leyland 3-car DMU - *59*	120	150

Cat No.			
L3.	**EMUs (1938)**		

These were 2-car sets consisting of a open 3rd class motor car and trailer car - both 57' vehicles. The powered car was fitted with a Romford flywheel motor bogie. It was 12v DC and available in 2-rail, outer third rail and inner third rail versions.

-	? (?+?) SR green main line set- *38*	100	120
-	3083 (11128+11113) SR green main line set - *55*	100	120
-	? (11150+?) LMS maroon main line set- *56*	100	120
-	2614? (5374+?) Great()Western brown+ cream main line set - *56*	100	120
-	? (?+?) SR green suburban set - *38*	100	120

COACHES

These had correct ventilators on the roof and doors, correct type bogies, roof gutters, accumulator boxes, tie rods, window rails, rain strips, compartment partitions and seats, a new type of corridor connection, glass in the windows, oval non-locking buffers and gold lacquered door and commode handles. They had brass wheels on steel axles and every coach was differently numbered and was appropriately lined and lettered.

Production ceased during the war and it seems that the LMS and SR ranges were the first to reappear in 1947. These were followed by the GWR range and then LNER in 1951

They also underwent structural changes and a cheaper Zephyr and Popular ranges were available from December 1956 (see below), which gradually replaced the Standard coaches in the late 1950s.

From the early 1950s, coaches could be supplied to special order in MR, LNWR, SE&CR, LB&SCR, L&SWR, CR, NBR, HR, G&SWR and LMSR (NCC) livery.

The tables below are based on lists in Exley catalogues during the 1950s and are not evidence that everything listed was made. We just don't know. The problem is that the lists are extensive but few is the number of models to be found today. This suggests to me that not many were made and, if that is the case, one can assume that not all the subjects listed below reached production.

Cat No.	Company, Number, Colour, Date	£	£

Pre-Grouping Coaches

C1.	**LNWR Brown & White Stock (1959)**		

These were also available in LMS livery on request. This stock had elliptical roofs.

57' Stock			

LNWR all-3rd coach [C1] (Vectis)

-	LNWR corridor 3rd - *59*	35	60
-	LNWR corridor 1st - *59*	35	60
-	LNWR corridor brake 3rd - *59*	35	60
-	LNWR sleeping car - *62*	NPG	NPG
-	LNWR dining car - *62*	NPG	NPG

C2.	**Midland Railway Maroon Stock (1959)**		

The Reid stock in the table had elliptical roofs.

34'Bain Clerestory 4-wheel Stock			
-	MR non-corridor 3rd - *60*	30	50
-	MR non-corridor 1st - *60*	30	50
-	MR non-corridor brake 3rd - *60*	30	50
-	MR full brake - *60*	30	50
54' Bain Clerestory 'Suburban' Stock			
-	MR non-corridor 3rd - *59*	30	50
-	MR non-corridor 1st - *59*	30	50
-	MR non-corridor brake 3rd - *59*	30	50
54' Clerestory Corridor Stock			
-	MR full brake - *60*	30	50
-	LMS full brake - *60*	30	50

MR 3rd class clerestory coach [C2] (Vectis)

8th Edition

Exley 00

	54' Reid 'Suburban' Stock		
-	MR non-corridor 3rd - 59	30	50
-	MR non-corridor 1st - 59	30	50
-	MR non-corridor brake 3rd - 59	30	50
	57' Clerestory Stock		
-	MR corridor 3rd - 59	30	50
-	MR corridor 1st - 59	30	50
-	MR corridor brake 3rd - 59	30	50
	65' Clerestory 12-Wheeled Stock		
-	MR dining carriage maroon - 59	30	50
-	LMS dining carriage maroon - 59	30	50

Pre-war Coaches

C3. Pullmans Umber & Cream (1938)
It would seem that the Pullman cars did not return after the war.

-	Pullman 1st class - 38	30	50
-	Pullman 3rd class - 38	30	50
-	Pullman brake 3rd - 38	30	50

C4. GWR Brown & Cream Stock (1938)
This was either a popular railway company with modellers who bought Exley 00 scale coaches or Exley made many more of them than some of the other liveries.

	50' 'Suburban' Stock		
-	GWR non-corridor - 38	22	35
-	GWR non-corridor brake end - 38	22	35
-	GWR brake - 38	22	35
	57' Stock		
-	GWR 'Ocean Mails' parcels van - 38	25	40
-	GWR corridor coach bow end - 38	20	30
-	GWR corridor brake bow end - 38	20	30
-	GWR corridor coach straight end - 38	20	30
-	GWR corridor brake straight end - 38	20	30
-	GWR corridor full brake bow ended - 38	20	30
-	GWR restaurant car - 38	22	35
-	GWR sleeping car 3rd 8-wheel - 38	22	35
-	GWR sleeping car 1st 12-wheel - 38	25	40
-	GWR buffet car - 38	25	40
	60' Stock		
-	GWR sleeping car 1st - 38	30	50
	65' Stock		
-	GWR Queen Mary Pullman car - 38	30	50
	70' Stock		
-	GWR corridor coach - 38	25	40
-	GWR corridor brake end - 38	25	40

C5. LMS Maroon Stock (1938)
As well as the GWR coaches above, many of the models found today are in this LMS maroon livery. It is thought that many more maroon coaches were made than some of the other liveries.

	42' Stock		
-	LMS motor car van - 38	20	30
	50' Stock		
-	LMS 50 non-corridor full brake - 38	22	35
-	LMS kitchen car - 38	25	40
-	LMS non-corridor coach - 38	20	30
-	LMS non-corridor brake end - 38	20	30
-	LMS luggage van - 38	22	35
	54' Stock		
-	LMS corridor coach - 38	20	30
-	LMS corridor brake end - 38	20	30
-	LMS Dynamometer car - 38	25	40

LMS 61ft restaurant car [C5] (Alan Farrow)

	60' Stock		
-	LMS open low waisted - 38	20	30
-	LMS open low waisted brake end - 38	20	30
-	LMS open coach - 38	20	30
-	LMS dining car low waisted 8-wheel - 38	22	35
-	LMS dining car low waisted 12-wheel - 38	25	40
-	LMS corridor low waisted - 38	20	30
-	LMS corridor low waisted brake end - 38	20	30
-	LMS mails stowage van - 38	25	40
-	LMS sleeping car 1st 12-wheel - 38	25	40
-	LMS sleeping car 3rd 8-wheel - 38	22	35
	Articulated Stock		
-	LMS twin excursion set maroon - 38	65	100

C6. LMS Blue Coronation Stock (1938)
These were for use in the prestigious 'Coronation Scot' train.

-	LMS 60' corridor - 38	35	60
-	LMS 60' corridor brake end - 38	35	60
-	LMS 60' open coach - 38	35	60
-	LMS 65' open coach - 38	35	60
-	LMS 50' kitchen car - 38	35	60

C7. LNER Teak Stock (1938)
This was a very difficult livery to replicate and tended to be a light brown colour.

	50' 'Suburban' Stock		
-	LNER non-corridor - 38	22	35
-	LNER non-corridor brake end - 38	22	35
	54' Stock		
-	LNER corridor bow end drop roof - 38	22	35
-	LNER corridor bow end drop roof brake end - 38	22	35
-	LNER luggage van and brake - 38	22	35
	60' Stock		
-	LNER corridor bow end - 38	22	35
-	LNER corridor brake bow end - 38	22	35
-	LNER restaurant car - 38	22	35
-	LNER sleeping car - 38	25	40

C8. LNER Silver Stock (1938)
Called 'Silver Link' coaches in the catalogue, these were for the LNER Silver Jubilee service which was pulled by the four silver grey A4 Class locomotives.

	Silver Link Stock		
-	LNER coach - 38	40	65
-	LNER brake end - 38	40	65

C9. LNER Green & Cream Stock (1938)
This livery was chosen for the special stock built for tourist trains.

LNER tourist stock buffet car [C9] (Vectis)

	Buffet Car		
-	LNER buffet car - 38	25	40
	Articulated Stock		
-	LNER triple buffet car - 38	80	130
-	LNER twin extention set - 38	70	110

C10. SR Green Stock (1938)
These tended to be in a mid green and not Malachite green.

	50' Stock		
-	SR non-corridor - 38	28	45
-	SR non-corridor brake end - 38	28	45
-	SR luggage van - 38	28	45
	54' Stock		
-	SR corridor coach - 38	28	45

Exley 00

-	SR 1616 corridor brake end - 38	28	45
	57' Stock		
-	SR 1258? buffet car - 38	28	45
	60' Stock		
-	SR corridor high window - 38	28	45
-	SR corridor high window brake - 38	28	45
-	SR dining car 8-wheel - 38	28	45
-	SR dining car 12-wheel - 38	30	50

Post-War Standard Coaches

After the Second World War the coaches were sold without bogies and wheels, which you bought separately and fixed to the wooden floor of the coach. Single link couplings were normal but Exley would fit other types if you preferred. All had interior fittings except for the sleeping cars, full brakes, parcels vans, TPOs and GWR Ocean Mails. Seats were now metal and coloured blue for 1st class and maroon for 3rd class. The 60' coaches had disappeared by 1957.

C11. 32' 4-wheel Van (1953)
Wheels ready fitted.

-	GWR brown+cream - 53	30	45
-	LMS maroon - 53	30	45
-	LNER teak - 53	30	45
-	SR green - 53	30	45

C12. 32' 4-wheel 'Suburban' Stock (1953)
Wheels ready fitted.

-	GWR brake 3rd brown+cream - 53	30	45
-	LMS brake 3rd maroon - 53	30	45
-	LNER brake 3rd teak - 53	30	45
-	SR brake 3rd green - 53	30	45
-	GWR composite brown+cream - 53	30	45
-	LMS composite maroon - 53	30	45
-	LNER composite teak - 53	30	45
-	SR composite green - 53	30	45
-	GWR 3rd brown+cream - 53	30	45
-	LMS 3rd maroon - 53	30	45
-	LNER 3rd teak - 53	30	45
-	SR 3rd green - 53	30	45

LNER teak 4-wheel and 6-wheel coaches [C11 + C13] (Lacy, Scott & Knight)

C13. 34' 6-wheel Corridor Full Brake (1953)
Wheels ready fitted.

-	GWR brown+cream - 53	30	45
-	LMS maroon - 53	30	45
-	LNER teak - 53	30	45
-	SR green - 53	30	45

C14. 34' 6-wheel 'Suburban' Stock (1953)
Wheels ready fitted.

-	GWR brake 3rd brown+cream - 53	30	45
-	LMS brake 3rd maroon - 53	30	45
-	LNER brake 3rd teak - 53	30	45
-	SR brake 3rd green - 53	30	45
-	GWR composite brown+cream - 53	30	45
-	LMS composite maroon - 53	30	45
-	LNER composite teak - 53	30	45
-	SR composite green - 53	30	45
-	GWR 3rd brown+cream - 53	30	45
-	LMS 3rd maroon - 53	30	45
-	LNER 3rd teak - 53	30	45
-	SR 3rd green - 53	30	45

C15. GWR Brown & Cream Stock (1949)

These were in traditional chocolate and cream livery in which the shade of brown varied from a mid-brown to dark brown.

	50' 'Suburban' Stock		
-	GWR non-corridor composite - 49	22	35
-	GWR non-corridor 3rd - 49	22	35
-	GWR non-corridor brake 3rd - 49	22	35
-	GWR non-corridor full brake - 49	25	40
-	GWR non-corridor parcel van - 49	25	40
	57' Stock		
-	GWR 'Ocean Mails' - 50	25	40
-	GWR parcels train brake van - 50	25	40
-	GWR corridor full brake - 49	20	30
-	GWR corridor brake 3rd - 49	20	30
-	GWR corridor 3rd - 49	20	30
-	GWR corridor composite - 49	20	30
-	GWR corridor 1st - 50	20	30
-	GWR sleeping car 3rd - 51	22	35
-	GWR sleeping car 1st - 51	22	35
	Special Vehicles		
-	GWR centre corridor 3rd - 51	20	30
-	GWR restaurant 1st/3rd kitchen - 51	22	35
-	GWR traveling post office 57' - 53	25	40

Post-war, coach bodies were sold without bogies. [C15] (Vectis)

C16. LMS Maroon Stock (1947)

Again, many more coach models were produced in this livery and that of the GWR than any other.

	50' 'Suburban' Stock		
-	LMS non-corridor composite - 47	20	30
-	LMS non-corridor 3rd - 47	20	30
-	LMS non-corridor 1st - 47	20	30
-	LMS non-corridor brake 3rd - 47	20	30
-	LMS non-corridor brake 1st - 47	20	30
-	LMS non-corridor brake composite - 47	20	30
-	LMS non-corridor full brake - 47	22	35
-	LMS non-corridor parcel van - 49	22	35
	Main Line Stock		
-	LMS corridor full brake 50' - 47	20	30
-	LMS corridor brake 3rd 57' - 47	20	30
-	LMS corridor brake 1st 57' - 47	20	30
-	LMS corridor 3rd 57' - 47	20	30
-	LMS corridor 1st 57' - 47	20	30
-	LMS corridor brake composite 57' - 47	20	30
-	LMS kitchen car 50' - 51	22	35
-	LMS composite sleeping car 57' - 51	22	35
	Special Vehicles		
-	LMS open brake 3rd - 50	20	30
-	LMS open 3rd - 50	20	30
-	LMS open 1st - 50	20	30
-	LMS restaurant kitchen 1st 57' * - 57	25	40
-	LMS dining car/kitchen 1st - 50	22	35
-	LMS dining /kitchen 3rd - 50	22	35
-	LMS buffet car 57' - 53	22	35
-	LMS traveling post office 57' - 51	25	40
-	LMS Engineers' inspection saloon - 57	30	50

* This car should have 6-wheeled bogies but may be fitted with 4-wheel ones.

8th Edition

Exley 00

C17. LNER Teak Stock (1951)
These coaches were in teak livery unless otherwise stated.

	50' 'Suburban' Stock		
-	LNER non-corridor 3rd - *51*	20	30
-	LNER non-corridor composite - *51*	20	30

LNER surburban coaches (Lacy, Scott & Knight)

-	LNER non-corridor brake 3rd - *51*	20	30
-	LNER non-corridor full brake - *51*	22	35
-	LNER non-corridor parcel van - *51*	22	35
	Main Line Stock		
-	LNER corridor full brake 50' - *53*	20	30
-	LNER corridor brake 3rd 57' - *53*	20	30
-	LNER corridor 3rd 57' - *53*	20	30
-	LNER corridor 1st 57' - *53*	20	30
-	LNER sleeping car 3rd 57' - *53*	22	35
-	LNER sleeping car 1st 57' - *53*	22	35
	Special Vehicles		
-	LNER buffet car 57' green+cream - *53*	22	35
-	LNER open full 3rd green+cream - *54*	20	30
-	LNER open brake 3rd green+cream - *54*	20	30
-	LNER traveling post office 57' - *54*	25	40

C18. SR Green Stock (1947)
Those examples seen have been in a mid-green similar to BR coach green.

	50' 'Suburban' Stock		
-	SR non-corridor 3rd - *47*	25	40
-	SR non-corridor full 1st - *47*	25	40
-	SR non-corridor composite - *47*	25	40
-	SR non-corridor brake 3rd - *47*	25	40
-	SR non-corridor full brake - *47*	25	40
-	SR non-corridor parcel van - *47*	25	40
	Main Line Stock		
-	SR corridor full brake 50' - *47*	25	40
-	SR corridor 3rd 57' - *47*	25	40
-	SR corridor composite 57' - *47*	25	40
-	SR corridor 1st 57' - *53*	25	40
-	SR corridor brake 3rd 57' - *47*	25	40
	Special Vehicles		
-	SR centre corridor 3rd - *51*	25	40
-	SR centre corridor 1st - *53*	25	40
-	SR centre corridor brake 3rd - *53*	25	40
-	SR dining car/kitchen 1st - *51*	28	45
-	SR buffet car - *53*	28	45
-	SR restaurant kitchen 1st maroon * - *57*	30	50

* This car should have 6-wheeled bogies but may be fitted with 4-wheel ones.

C19. BR Crimson & Cream Stock
These standard coaches would not have appeared in BR maroon as the change to that revised livery did not occur until after production of these ceased.

	57' Stock		
-	BR corridor brake 3rd - ?	30	50
-	BR corridor 3rd - ?	30	50
-	BR corridor 1st - ?	30	50

Zephyr (Type A) Coaches

These were available from December 1956. The mainline stock was 57' long and suburban stock was 50' in length. Unlike the Standard range of coaches, these were all sold complete with 2-rail bogies and wheels or as complete, ready-painted, kits. They had single link couplings but would take a Peco coupling and they were fitted with full interiors. The coaches could be supplied fully lit.

C20. GWR Brown & Cream Stock (1956)
These were in traditional chocolate and cream livery in which the shade of brown varied from a mid-brown to dark brown.

	34' 6-Wheel Stock		
-	GWR non-corridor brake 3rd - *60*	25	35
-	GWR non-corridor 3rd - *60*	25	35
-	GWR non-corridor 1st - *60*	25	35
	34' 6-Wheel Clerestory Stock		
-	GWR non-corridor brake 3rd - *60*	25	35
-	GWR non-corridor 3rd - *60*	25	35
-	GWR non-corridor 1st - *60*	25	35
-	GWR corridor full brake - *60*	25	35
	50' Stock		
-	GWR non-corridor brake 3rd - *56*	20	30
-	GWR non-corridor 3rd - *56*	20	30
-	GWR non-corridor 1st - *56*	20	30
-	GWR non-corridor full brake - *60*	20	30
-	GWR non-corridor parcels van - *60*	20	30
	54' 'Suburban' Stock		
-	GWR non-corridor brake 3rd - *61*	20	30
-	GWR non-corridor 3rd - *61*	20	30
-	GWR non-corridor 1st - *61*	20	30
	57' Stock		
-	GWR corridor full brake - *56*	18	28
-	GWR non-corridor full brake - *56*	20	30
-	GWR corridor brake 3rd - *56*	18	28
-	GWR corridor 3rd - *56*	18	28
-	GWR corridor 1st - *56*	18	28
-	GWR open brake 3rd - *56*	18	28
-	GWR open 3rd - *56*	18	28
-	GWR open 1st - *56*	18	28
-	GWR composite sleeping car - *56*	20	30
-	GWR restaurant kitchen 1st/3rd - *56*	20	30
-	GWR Ocean Mails van - *60*	22	35
-	GWR traveling post office - *60*	25	40

GWR 'Ocean Mails' (Lacy, Scott & Knight)

C21. LMS Maroon Stock (1956)
Again, many more coach models were produced in this livery and that of the GWR than any other.

	34' 6-Wheel Stock		
-	LMS non-corridor brake 3rd - *60*	25	35
-	LMS non-corridor 3rd - *60*	25	35
-	LMS non-corridor 1st - *60*	25	35
	34' Clerestory Stock		
-	LMS non-corridor brake 3rd - *60*	25	35
-	LMS non-corridor 3rd - *60*	25	35
-	LMS non-corridor 1st - *60*	25	35
-	corridor full brake - *60*	25	35
	50' Stock		
-	LMS kitchen car - *56*	20	30
-	LMS non-corridor brake 3rd - *56*	20	30
-	LMS non-corridor 3rd - *56*	20	30
-	LMS non-corridor 1st - *56*	20	30
-	LMS corridor full brake - *56*	20	30
-	LMS non-gangwayed full brake - *60*	20	30
-	LMS Engineers' inspection saloon - *60*	25	40
-	LMS non-corridor parcels van - *60*	22	35
	54' 'Suburban' Stock		
-	LMS non-corridor brake 3rd - *61*	20	30

Visit the BRM website at: www.model-railways-live.co.uk

Exley 00

LMS Inspector's saloon (Vectis)

-	LMS non-corridor 3rd - *61*	20	30
-	LMS non-corridor 1st - *61*	20	30
	57' Stock		
-	LMS non-corridor full brake - *56*	18	28
-	LMS corridor brake 3rd - *56*	18	28
-	LMS corridor 3rd - *56*	18	28
-	LMS corridor 1st - *56*	18	28
-	LMS open brake 3rd - *56*	18	28
-	LMS open 3rd - *56*	18	28
-	LMS open 1st - *56*	18	28
-	LMS composite sleeping car - *56*	20	30
-	LMS restaurant kitchen 1st - *56*	20	30
-	LMS buffet car - *56*	20	30
-	LMS traveling post office - *60*	22	35
	68'/69' Stock		
-	LMS 12-wheel restaurant car - *60*	25	40
-	LMS 12-wheel sleeping car - *60*	25	40

C22. LNER Teak Stock (1956)

The green and cream tourist stock livery did not occur this time.

	50' Stock		
-	LNER non-corridor brake 3rd - *56*	20	30
-	LNER non-corridor 3rd - *56*	20	30
-	LNER non-corridor 1st - *56*	20	30
-	LNER corridor full brake - *56*	20	30
-	LNER non-corridor full brake - *60*	20	30
-	LNER non-corridor parcels van - *60*	20	30
	57' Stock		
-	LNER non-corridor full brake - *56*	18	28
-	LNER corridor brake 3rd - *56*	18	28
-	LNER corridor 3rd - *56*	18	28
-	LNER corridor 1st - *56*	18	28
-	LNER open brake 3rd - *56*	18	28
-	LNER open 3rd - *56*	18	28
-	LNER open 1st - *56*	18	28
-	LNER composite sleeping car - *56*	20	30
-	LNER restaurant kitchen 1st - *56*	20	30
-	LNER buffet car - *56*	20	30
-	LNER traveling post office - *60*	22	35

C23. SR Green Stock (1956)

Those examples seen have been in a mid-green similar to BR coach green.

Various SR stock (Vectis)

	34' 6-Wheel 'Suburban' Stock		
-	SR non-corridor brake 3rd - *60*	28	40
-	SR non-corridor 3rd - *60*	28	40
-	SR non-corridor 1st - *60*	28	40
	50' 'Suburban' Stock		
-	SR non-corridor brake 3rd - *56*	22	35
-	SR non-corridor 3rd - *56*	22	35
-	SR non-corridor 1st - *56*	22	35
-	SR non-corridor full brake - *56*	22	35
-	SR non-corridor full brake - *60*	22	35
-	SR non-corridor parcels van - *60*	22	35
	54' 'Suburban' Stock		
-	SR non-corridor brake 3rd - *61*	22	35
-	SR non-corridor 3rd - *61*	22	35
-	SR non-corridor 1st - *61*	22	35
	57' Stock		
-	SR non-corridor full brake - *56*	20	30
-	SR corridor brake 3rd - *56*	20	30
-	SR corridor 3rd - *56*	20	30
-	SR corridor 1st - *56*	20	30
-	SR open brake 3rd - *56*	20	30
-	SR open 3rd - *56*	20	30
-	SR open 1st - *56*	20	30
-	SR restaurant kitchen 1st - *56*	22	35

C24. BR Stock (1956)

It is noticeable that more open stock was listed in the British Railways section, which perhaps reflecting a greater use of them in the 1950s. Also, there is no indication of the liveries used on BR stock bearing in mind the changes occuring on the real raiways at this time.

	50' Stock		
-	BR kitchen car - *56*	22	35
-	BR non-corridor brake 3rd - *56*	22	35
-	BR non-corridor 3rd - *56*	22	35
-	BR non-corridor 1st - *56*	22	35
-	BR corridor full brake green - *60*	22	35
-	BR non-corridor full brake - *60*	22	35
-	BR non-corridor parcels van - *60*	22	35
	57' Stock		
-	BR corridor full brake - *56*	22	35
-	BR non-corridor full brake - *56*	22	35
-	BR open brake 3rd - *56*	22	35
-	BR open 3rd - *56*	22	35
-	BR open 1st - *56*	22	35
-	BR open brake 3rd - *56*	22	35
-	BR open 3rd - *56*	22	35
-	BR open 1st - *56*	22	35
-	BR composite sleeping car - *56*	25	40
-	BR restaurant kitchen 1st - *56*	25	40
-	BR buffet car - *56*	25	40
-	BR Ocean Mails van - *60*	28	45
-	BR traveling post office - *60*	28	45
-	BR Engineers' inspection saloon maroon - *60*	30	50
	68'/69' Stock		
-	BR 12-wheel restaurant car maroon - *60*	28	45
-	BR 12-wheel sleeping car maroon - *60*	28	45

Popular (Type B) Coaches

The Popular (also called 'B Type') range was 50' for all stock and was also available from December 1956. These were also sold complete with 2-rail bogies and wheels or as complete, ready-painted, kits. They also had single link couplings and would take a Peco coupling. They were fitted with full interiors. This was obviously and attempt to break into the Hornby Dublo and Tri-ang market with coaches that were fine on tight curves and were not too expensive.

C25. GWR Brown & Cream Stock (1956)

These were in traditional chocolate and cream livery and there may have been some produced in Western Region brown and cream.

	50' Stock		
-	GWR bullion van - *?*	25	35
-	GWR corridor full brake - *56*	20	30

8th Edition

Exley 00

-	GWR non-corridor full brake - *56*	20	30

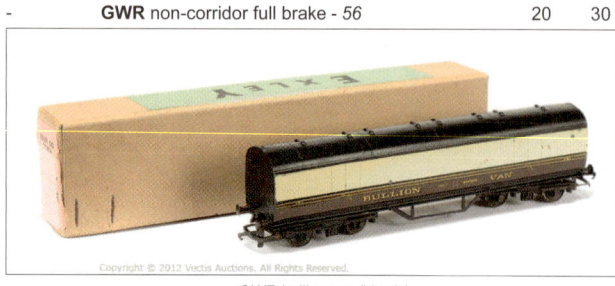

GWR bullion van (Vectis)

-	GWR corridor brake 3rd - *56*	20	30
-	GWR corridor 3rd - *56*	20	30
-	GWR corridor 1st - *56*	20	30
-	GWR open brake 3rd - *56*	20	30
-	GWR open 3rd - *56*	20	30
-	GWR open 1st - 56	20	30
-	GWR composite sleeping car - *56*	22	35
-	GWR restaurant car - *56*	22	35
-	GWR non-corridor brake 3rd - *56*	22	35
-	GWR non-corridor 3rd - *56*	22	35
-	GWR non-corridor 1st - *56*	22	35

C26. LMS Maroon Stock (1956)

Again, many more coach models were produced in this livery and that of the GWR than any other.

50' Stock			
-	LMS corridor full brake - *56*	20	30
-	LMS non-corridor full brake - *56*	20	30
-	LMS corridor brake 3rd - *56*	20	30
-	LMS corridor 3rd - *56*	20	30
-	LMS corridor 1st - *56*	20	30
-	LMS open brake 3rd - *56*	20	30
-	LMS open 3rd - *56*	20	30
-	LMS open 1st - *56*	20	30
-	LMS composite sleeping car - *56*	22	35
-	LMS restaurant car - *56*	22	35
-	LMS buffet car - *56*	22	35
-	LMS kitchen car - *56*	22	35
-	LMS non-corridor brake 3rd - *56*	22	35
-	LMS non-corridor 3rd - *56*	22	35
-	LMS non-corridor 1st - *56*	22	35

C27. LNER Teak Stock (1956)

Once again I have not seen evidence that suggests that Tourist stock green and cream coaches were included.

50' Stock			
-	LNER corridor full brake - *56*	20	30
-	LNER non-corridor full brake - *56*	20	30
-	LNER corridor brake 3rd - *56*	20	30
-	LNER corridor 3rd - *56*	20	30
-	LNER corridor 1st - *56*	20	30
-	LNER open brake 3rd - *56*	20	30
-	LNER open 3rd - *56*	20	30
-	LNER open 1st - *56*	20	30
-	LNER composite sleeping car - *56*	22	35
-	LNER restaurant car - *56*	22	35
-	LNER buffet car - *56*	22	35
-	LNER non-corridor brake 3rd - *56*	22	35
-	LNER non-corridor 3rd - *56*	22	35
-	LNER non-corridor 1st - *56*	22	35

C28. SR 50' Stock (1956)

These tended to be in a mid green and not Malachite green.

50' Stock			
-	SR corridor full brake - *56*	22	35
-	SR non-corridor full brake - *56*	22	35
-	SR corridor brake 3rd - *56*	22	35
-	SR corridor 3rd - *56*	22	35
-	SR corridor 1st - *56*	22	35
-	SR open brake 3rd - *56*	22	35
-	SR open 3rd - *56*	22	35
-	SR open 1st - *56*	22	35
-	SR composite sleeping car - *56*	25	40
-	SR restaurant car - *56*	25	40
-	SR non-corridor brake 3rd - *56*	25	40
-	SR non-corridor 3rd - *56*	25	40
-	SR non-corridor 1st - *56*	25	40

C29. BR 50' Stock (1956)

These would have been mostly in BR maroon livery although red and cream may also have been used, as too may BR coach green.

50' Stock			
-	BR corridor full brake - *56*	22	35
-	BR non-corridor full brake - *56*	22	35
-	BR corridor brake 3rd - *56*	22	35
-	BR corridor 3rd - *56*	22	35
-	BR corridor 1st - *56*	22	35
-	BR open brake 3rd - *56*	22	35
-	BR open 3rd - *56*	22	35
-	BR open 1st - *56*	22	35
-	BR composite sleeping car - *56*	25	40
-	BR restaurant car - *56*	25	40
-	BR buffet car - *56*	25	40
-	BR kitchen car - *56*	25	40
-	BR non-corridor brake 3rd - *56*	25	40
-	BR non-corridor 3rd - *56*	25	40
-	BR non-corridor 1st - *56*	25	40

BR restaurant car (Alan Farrow)

Have you seen the NEW LOOK BRM BRITISH RAILWAY MODELLING

Order your copy today!

Visit

www.model-railways-live.co.uk

Fleischmann H0 (British)

HISTORY

Fleischmann was founded in 1887 and acquired the German company, Doll, in 1938. They first made trains under the Fleischmann name in 1949, starting with 0 gauge and adding H0 to their range of products in 1952.

The German model manufacturer decided to attempt a break into the UK market in 1977 and produced a model of a 'Warship' diesel locomotive and three Bulleid coaches. This was a strange combination but apparently they could have been seen together when they ran the out of Waterloo in the mid 1960s.

'Warship' with head nameboards [L2] (Fleischmann)

Unfortunately, Fleischmann produced their models in H0 scale and not the slightly larger British 00 scale. As a result of this, the models did not sell well in Britain. However, in both liveries, and with their original catalogue numbers, they have remained in the Fleischmann catalogue and were still being advertised in the 2000/2001 German edition and on the Fleischmann website until fairly recently.

The only evidence I have seen that further batches were made is that there was a second design of mechanism, taken from their V200 and used in the 'Warship' model. This would have required a redesigned chassis and underframe in the 1980s.

The locos and coaches were available separately and were not available in a set.

Included in the boxes of both locomotives were three alternative headboards. These were for the 'Torbay Express', 'Cornish Riviera Express' and 'The Mayflower'.

An H0 scale 'West Country' locomotive was also planned in 1977. This was to have been *Blackmore Vale* but, with sales of the 'Warship' being so poor, the project was abandoned.

'Warship' class locomotive in BR green livery [L2] (Fleischmann)

LOCOMOTIVES

Cat No.	Company, Number, Colour, Date	£	£

L1. 'West Country' 4-6-2

The 'West Country/Battle Britain' Class was one of the largest classes of Pacific locomotives built in Britain and today 20 of the class have survived in preservation.

-	*Blackmore Vale* green - not made	NA	NA

L2. Class 42 'Warship' Diesel-Hydraulic B-B (1977)

Greyhound is one of only two of the Swindon built class of 38 locomotives that have been preserved.

| 4247 | D818 *Glory* BRe blue - 77-04 | 50 | 110 |
| 4246 | D821 *Greyhound* BRc green - 77-04 | 50 | 110 |

'Warship' class in BR blue livery [L2] (Fleischmann)

COACHES

These were based on BR built stock preserved on the Bluebell Railway in Sussex. The models had snap-in corridor end boards and a sheet of rub-down transfers representing 'set' numbers.

Cat No.	Company, Number, Colour, Date	£	£

C1. Bulleid Coaches (1977)

Although designed by Bulleid's Southern Railway design team, prior to Nationalisation, they arrived too late to run in SR livery. Instead, they started life in BR carmine and cream and, from 1956, they started to be painted Southern Coach Green.

5146	BR S5715S green 1st/3rd composite - 77-01?	10	25
5147	BR S130S green corridor 3rd - 77-01?	10	25
5148	BR S4279S green open brake 3rd - 77-01?	10	25

Bulleid coaches [C1] (Fleischmann)

WE WANT YOUR Model Railways

We will buy almost any Railway Collection, large or small. All gauges will be taken, in any condition. We always give an honest price and will collect and dismantle any layout.

Telephone: **01302 371623**
Mobile: **07526 768178**
or email: anoraksanonymous@googlemail.com

Graham Farish 00

HISTORY

The Company was founded by Thomas Graham Farish in 1919, at the end of the Great War, with a view to cashing in on the new interest in radio. In those days, if you wanted a wireless, you built your own and there was, therefore, a market for radio components. Remember, this was six years before the BBC came into being. Marconi, the radio pioneer, was a personal friend of Graham Farish.

The business was initially in Catford but in 1922 it moved to Masons Hill in Bromley, Kent. At its peak, the company was producing over 35,000 radio components per day. The boom lasted for about fifteen years, before competition from off-the-shelf radio sets took away much of their business. The company gradually turned over to other products, such as electric fires, of which over 8,000,000 were made and it is interesting to note that two of the company's senior managers were Donal Morphy and Charles Richards who later left to form Morphy-Richards. The company developed the first successful submarine aerial and were one of the first to use the early type of plastic known as Bakelite.

GWR class 94xx pannier tank [L1] (Special Auction Services)

During the Second World War they made hand grenades, shell and land mine casings, electronic equipment and an important sideline was 'Snap Vacuum Closures'. These consisted of a tinned lid, a rubber sealing ring and a reusable clip and they were used for sealing glass jars for storing preserved fruit. These were particularly useful during the war and over 1,000,000,000 were made! Other items manufactured up to 1949 included water pumps for ornamental fountains, underwater lights, lightning conductors for buildings, metal flower baskets and, in 1949, the Plantoid plant food pellets! Much sought after today are 60 or more figures that were made in 1953 to celebrate the Coronation.

With peace had come the need to look for new products for the company's fourteen toolmakers and four hundred production workers, not to mention the diecasting and other machines that had grown in number during the war. The steel and chromium needed for electric fire production were in short supply but alloy for casting and the new plastics were available. Like others, Graham Farish saw the potential of the model railway market and in particular they saw a need for a 2-rail electric system and good quality 2-rail flexible track. Here were products which required the available materials, the design and electrical skills within the company and which were labour intensive - in other words, ideal for Graham Farish to tackle.

In 1948 Graham Farish announced their proposed 'Scale Model Railroads' and demonstrated their new 'Formo' flexible track on a massive layout at the 1948 British Industries Fair at Earls Court. This type of track was a first in the British market and track production became a very big part of the company's output in those early days and right through the 1960s, when 'Formoway' was one of the best on the market. It was said that 60 miles of track was sold by them each year and at one stage the company was manufacturing 13 types of point.

The GP5 train sets of 1949, with their 'Black 5' locomotives, were Britain's first 2-rail ready-to-run 00 model railways. They came in four versions - goods or passenger (with 4-wheel coaches) and with or without track and the set's contents were available separately the following year together with transfers for the rolling stock.

No sooner had the company started train set production, than it was hit by material shortages due to the Korean War. It is also possible that some staff were directed back onto war work. The GWR 'Prairie', when it arrived in March 1952, was initially available only as a kit and a 3-rail version of the kit was also proposed. The body casting for the 'Prairie' was contracted out to Universal Engineering of Nottingham and it is possible that other early work was contracted out.

The GP5 loco was also followed by a Bulleid 'Pacific', a GWR 'King' and a New York 'Hudson' 4-6-4. Early wagons were diecast, the first series of five being released in 1949 but had gone by March 1951. They were replaced by three low-sided or flat wagons in 1952. Perhaps the best remembered item of early rolling stock was the cellulose acetate bodied Pullman car which distorted with age to give it a double bow to the roof. These were particularly attractive models and remained firm favourites over the years. It was claimed that over 100,000 of them were made in the early '50s. There were also bogie suburban coaches and the first Brookdale building kits arrived in 1951 and West's metal figures in 1952.

By the summer of 1953, stocks in shops were not moving and everywhere prices were being slashed. At the factory, production of 2-rail models was halted and, in November, a 3-rail train set with an oval of track was released onto the market. After being the first in the market with a 2-rail system, this move has surprised historians for many years but, with difficulty in selling the 00 system, Graham Farish had turned to what other companies such as Meccano Ltd and Trix were successfully selling - 3-rail! It should be born in mind that Tri-ang Railways, with their successful 2-rail system, had been launched only a year before and it was too early to see the impact of this.

The new 3-rail system was sold under the 'Formo' name, rather than that of Graham Farish, possibly because they were successfully selling their track under that name and hoped that success would rub off. Literature was published carrying the name 'Formo Ltd' but with the Bromley address. The range consisted of a Southern 0-6-0 Q Class loco, some wagons and tinplate track which looked rather like that made at the time by Marklin. The loco and rolling stock were available separately or in a boxed set. The wagons were from the same moulds as the earlier Graham Farish 2-rail vehicles but had diecast non-insulated wheels and the name 'Formo' cast into the underside of the chassis. The 3-rail system did not sell and was quickly dropped but not before there had been some preparations made to release the 'King' and 'Merchant Navy' in 3-rail forms. One could see that the 'Merchant Navy' would have been of interest to Hornby Dublo modellers, had it gone into production.

Ex-LMS 'Black 5' locomotive [L5] (Special Auction Services)

Possibly the company had hoped to develop the 2-rail system further but the poor motor design made the stocks they were holding difficult to sell. In 1958 Graham Farish disposed of their remaining complete and unmade stock through one of their subsidiaries, Hutchinson Roe of Bromley, who sold the models and parts cheaply to the public. The 'Formo' set for example was offered at £2.17.6 instead of £5.12.3. They also invited orders for Pullman coaches they could assemble from parts in stock. It seems that S. French & Sons Ltd. of Tolworth had bought a lot of the remaining stock by the following year and offered it to the public. Hutchinson Roe & Co. had the same address

Graham Farish 00

(Masons Hill, Bromley) as Graham Farish Ltd. Indeed, the latter had no fewer than ten subsidiaries in 1951 including Formo Products Ltd, Grafar Products Ltd, and West & Short Ltd who made the platform accessories.

After a break of eight years, and having cleared the factory of the old stock, the return to serious 00 modelling for Graham Farish came in 1961 with the release of the 'Prairie' tank with a much improved motor and chassis and a new Pannier tank. The revised range also included the first series of four plastic wagons and the Pullman cars, now in rigid polystyrene. Suburban and mainline coach kits were also available in the 1960s and mail and baggage coaches were also planned. By now the company was selling a much improved quality Formoway track which had a moulded plastic sleeper web and a good range of points.

In 1964, Graham Farish moved to a former armaments factory at Holton Heath in Dorset, not far from Poole. Here a number of factory units were developed. Throughout the 1960s the company published their handbook which both contained modelling tips and promoted their products. A 21st Anniversary edition of this was published in 1969 to celebrate the 21 years Farish had been involved in the model railway industry. At this time Peter Graham Farish was Sales Director and Dudley Dimmock (who had previously been associated with Bassett-Lowke) was General Manager of the Models Division.

In 1970, Graham Farish launched their N gauge system and a range of nicely printed 00 rolling stock followed in 1973. However, in 1975, it was decided to phase out production of 00 models after Peter Graham Farish had visited the Brighton Toy Fair and learned of the plans by both Airfix and Palitoy to enter the 00 gauge market. It was decided that the 00 market was about to be flooded and that Graham Farish would do better to concentrate all its efforts on N gauge. The last 00 model to be made at Holton Heath was a special edition van in 1980. 00 stock was no longer advertised after 1981.

Ex-SR 'Merchant Navy' Class [L6] (Vectis)

Tom Graham Farish's son Gordon, who was a naval architect, had established the Romney Boats business in 1959 and this occupied one of the factory units at Holton Heath. When Tom retired in 1973, Gordon disposed of the boat business and joined his brother Peter in running Graham Farish Ltd. Gordon retired first and moved to South Africa and Peter Graham Farish continued with the business on his own. Wishing to retire, himself, in the summer of 2000, Peter sold Graham Farish Ltd to Bachmann Industries Europe Ltd. Today, the Graham Farish name is solely associated with their dominant N gauge system which is described elsewhere in this book.

'Metal Fatigue' - Like some other manufacturers, Graham Farish had problems with diecast components due to impurities in the alloy used. Chassis are especially prone to mazak disintegration which results in the 'growth' of parts. This can result in the distortion of the chassis or body and breakage of small components. The problem cannot be cured but if not evident now may well never occur. It may be restricted to, say, a pony truck which can be replaced. It is advisable to check carefully for any evidence of this problem: our guide values assume that the item is in good sound condition with no trace of 'fatigue'.

Further Reading
To date we are unaware of any books published on the Graham Farish system but there have been a number of magazine articles including a series by Dennis Lovett in *TCS News*.

Dates - we have found little evidence of when models first became available and particularly when they were out of production. Those quoted in the tables below are based on this limited knowledge, coming largely from catalogues and press advertising, and are for guidance only.

Listing - The models are now arranged in the order adopted elsewhere in this book.

Couplings - These were like a cross between the early type IIb Tri-ang couplings and their later tension-lock type which were adopted as the British standard after 1965. Consequently Graham Farish models will couple to most British post 1965 makes.

LOCOMOTIVES
The first locomotive, an LMS 'Black 5', was initially available only in train sets. As a scale model it was not bad for the time, even if mechanically poor and lacking a good finish - not helped by the embossed cabside numbers. It had a diecast body but the tender body was a plastic moulding. It was claimed that it was designed to BRMSB standards and it has been suggested that some components were war surplus.

The tender drive motor unit of this model, as well as in the Bulleid, 'King' and 'Hudson' locomotives, was revolutionary. It consisted of an enclosed permanent magnet rotor with two coils of wire both above and below which, in turn, were connected to two contact blades which oscillated via the rotor shaft between four electrical contacts. These were connected to the two electrical plunger pick ups situated below the tender side frames. Two pieces of steel rod were situated either side of the coils which, in theory, returned the rotor to its starting point. The drive from the tender in later models was via a spring drive and centrifugal clutch to reduction gears and by pinion shaft to the locomotive's driving wheels.

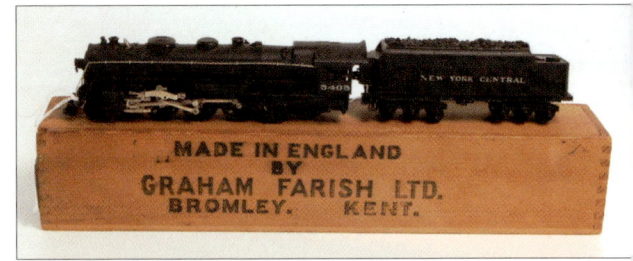

New York Central 4-6-4 [L7] (Lacy, Scott & Knight)

3-Rail Operation - The 3-rail Q Class 0-6-0 had a 5-pole conventional design motor with easily replaceable brushes. It was said at the time to be similar to the Pittman DC.60 motor. It had a 30:1 reduction worm set with a single-start square thread steel worm running in a 15mm diameter brass wheel. The model also had plunger type power collectors.

Evidence that later models of the 'King', Bulleid 'Pacific' and 'Prairie' tank were being prepared for 3-rail operation comes in the form of later models having the gear bracket extended backwards, ending in a vertical cylindrical boss bored to accept a pickup plunger similar to those on tenders. Some tender base plates also carry a marking which would be where the power supply wire would pass. However, there is no evidence of these models actually being sold fitted for 3-rail operation.

Later Mechanisms - The 5-pole motor used in the later 'Prairie' and Pannier tanks was developed in 1957 and was very like the Tri-ang X04 in design. It employed Alcomax magnets, a drum commutator, bronze bearings and carbon brushes. The chassis had plated, see-through, wheels, Tufnol worms for quiet running and phosphor bronze power collectors There was a choice of scale (BRMSB standards) or

Graham Farish 00

universal wheels. The bodies were diecast and fitted with nickel handrails, connecting rods and crossheads.

Cat No.	Company, Number, Colour, Date	£	£

L1. GWR Class 94xx Pannier Tank 0-6-0 (1961)

This was an excellent model with a choice of scale or universal wheels. The early mechanism used for this model had an open frame motor, whereas later models had a modified chassis with a can motor and finer wheels. The subject was also chosen early on for the N gauge range.

BE1W	9410 GWR green - *61-79*	25	40
-	GWR green no number - *?*	30	45
BE1BR	9410 BRb black - *75-79*	40	60

L2. GWR Class 81xx 'Prairie' Tank 2-6-2 (1951)

This started life as a kit and was initially a poor performer, possibly because the metal body shell interfered with eddy currents, from the unorthodox motor, restricting the available power. Due to this, few of the early '50s models have survived in working order and on many, the cast drive gearbox suffers from metal fatigue. The 1960s model, fitted with a conventional motor, was a good performer and a nice looking model, especially with scale wheels. 1950s models had plunger pickups but the 1960s models had wipers on the wheels.

-	8103 black kit - *51-53*	NA	60
-	8103 green kit - *51-53*	NA	60
-	8103 kit - *51-53*	NA	60
-	8103 BRb black - *52-53*	40	65
-	8103 GWR green - *52-53*	30	55
-	8105 Great Western green new motor and chassis - *61-71*	30	55
-	8105 BR green new motor and chassis - *61-71*	30	55

Ex-GWR 'Prairie' tank [L2] (Vectis)

L3. SR Class Q 0-6-0 (1953)

This was the only 3-rail locomotive made by Graham Farish and was strongly built to withstand heavy use and performed well. It had a 5-pole conventional motor and a diecast mazak body for loco and tender. Power collection was with plungers on the centre rail and, in effect, it offered Dublo operators a fourth locomotive to run. The name 'Formo' was cast into the smokebox and the cabsides.

-	Formo BRb black - *53*	80	NA
-	Formo BRb green - *53*	125	NA
-	Formo BRb black rear splashers extended to cab - *53*	100	NA

L4. GWR 'King' Class 4-6-0 (1951)

Mechanically, this model was similar to the Bulleid 'Pacific'. The safety valve cover was strange in having only the top half with a copper finish. All models, irrespective of the name they carried, had '6000' cast into the cab sides. Some suffer from 'metal fatigue' to the gearbox casting. 3-rail versions also exist which have a plunger pickup beneath the tender.

-	6000 *King Charles* Great () Western green - *51-53*	70	120
-	6000 *King Charles* BRb blue - *51-53*	80	140
-	6000 *King John* Great () Western green - *51-53*	70	120
-	6000 *King John'* BRb blue - *51-53*	80	140
-	6000 *King Henry V* Great () Western green - *51-53*	70	120
-	6000 *King Henry V* BRb blue - *51-53*	80	140
-	6000 *King George V* Great () Western green + bell - *51-53*	70	120
-	6000 *King George V* BRb blue + bell - *51-53*	80	140
-	6000 *King George V* Great () Western green no bell - *51-53*	70	120
-	6000 *King George V* BRb blue no bell - *51-53*	80	140
-	6000 BRb green - *?*	NPG	NPG
-	6000 BRb black - *?*	NPG	NPG
-	6000 kit - *?*	NPG	NPG

Ex-GWR 'King' class [L4] (Vectis)

L5. LMS 'GP5' Class 5MT ('Black 5') 4-6-0 (1949)

Known by Graham Farish as the 'GP5', the locomotive was propelled by a tender-mounted motor driven as described above. It had strangely designed central drivers with thicker rims and traction tyres and also had poor representation of valve gear. Power was collected from the track by a single sprung pickup each side. On the numberless first batch, the valve gear top pin was secured in a hole in part of the footplate casting and the cab floor brace plate was initially too thin to carry the chassis and subsequently snapped within a few months. This problem was overcome by strengthening the brace and, at the same time, the cabside number 44753 was cast into the body shell and the valve positioning hole became a slot. The chassis was also modified regarding its fixing to the cab floor and one of the pinions driving the wheels was deleted. The incorrect number '44753' belonged to a member of the class fitted with Caprotti valve gear and yet a more suitable number '44758' was used in illustrations.

-	44753 BRb black thin cab floor brace plate - *49*	35	60
-	BRb black unpainted numbers - *49-51*	30	50

L6. SR Bulleid 'Pacific' 4-6-2 (1950)

The same model was passed-off as a 'West Country', 'Battle of Britain' and a 'Merchant Navy' Class although in real life the first two should have been smaller. Mechanically, the model was originally similar to the GP5 but a revised version of the model soon followed which was completely different, both mechanically and in its body casting. Some models suffer from 'metal fatigue' to the gearbox casting. You could have any Bulleid 'Pacific' finished as a Golden Arrow locomotive for an extra 5/-. 3-rail versions of the Bulleid 'Pacific' were also made. These had a central plunger pickup on the underside of the tender.

-	21C25 *Brocklebank Line* SR green - *50-53*	90	170
-	21C103 *Plymouth* SR green - *50-53*	100	180
-	21C90 *Sir Eustace Missenden* SR green - *50-53*	80	170
-	21C90 *Sir Eustace Missenden* SR green Golden Arrow** + flags - *50-53*	140	220
-	34090 *Sir Eustace Missenden* BRb green 'Golden Arrow' + flags - *50-53*	150	250
-	34090 *Sir Eustace Missenden* BRb blue ** 'Golden Arrow' + flags - *50-53*	150	250
-	as above but numbered 34090 with BRb decals	NPG	NPG
-	35017 *Belgian Marine* SR green 'Golden Arrow' + flags - *?*	NPG	NPG
-	35017 *Belgian Marine* BRb blue - *50-53*	100	200
-	35027 *Port Line* BRb blue - *50-53*	100	200
-	35027 *Port Line* BRb green 'Golden Arrow' + flags - *50-53*	150	250
-	34101 *Exeter* BRb blue * - *50-53*	100	200
-	kit - *?*	NPG	NPG

Ex-SR 'Battle of Britain' class for the Golden Arrow service [L6]

* None of the West Country Class was painted blue and the number should have been '34001'. This was just one of several numbering errors which included models with SR numbers that were built post Nationalisation. ** It is understood that one of these was presented by Graham Farish to O V Bulleid when he left the Southern/BR.

Graham Farish 00

L7. New York Central 'Hudson' 4-6-4 (H0) (1952)
This model was noted for its scale wheels, Baker's valve gear detail and considerable body detail. Unlike its predecessors, the model had power collection from the tender wheels and axles. It was sold in a wooden box with a sliding lid.

Cat No.	Company, Number, Colour, Date	£	£
-	5405 New York Central black - *52-53*	120	200
-	5405 New York Central blk with 5-pole motor - *54*	130	240

COACHES

Coaches came in three phases - 1950s, 1960s and 1970s. In the early 1950s there were heavy plastic bodied 4-wheel and bogie suburbans, Pullman cars and a coach for the New York Central 'Hudson'. The suburban bogie coaches survived as kits into the 1960s phase when main line coach kits arrived and improved versions of the Pullman cars were introduced. The final phase came in the 1970s when the coaches were produced as ready-to-run models in a lighter all-plastic form and with tampo printed liveries.

The coaches in the final stage had plug-fit reversible bogies. One end had a Farish version of the hook and bar coupling while the other end would take a Tri-ang coupling unit and there was a centre hole which would take a Peco or Dublo coupling.

Cat No.	Company, Number, Colour, Date	£	£

4-Wheel Coaches

C1. 4-wheel 'Suburban' Stock (1949)
These coaches were 6" long and made for only a few months. They had a Bakelite body, tin roof and metal sideframes.

-	**BR** red 1st - *49*	35	45
-	**BR** red 3rd - *49*	35	45
-	**BR** red composite - *49*	35	45
-	**BR** red 3rd luggage - *49*	35	45

Pullman Cars

C2a. Pullmans (Early) (1950)
After some time, these developed a strange double bow to the roof. This has been caused by the use of cellulose acetate for the plastic mouldings and the vehicle having a solid diecast chassis and floor unit which, due to 'metal fatigue', had grown in length over the years, distorting the plastic roof in the process. The prices below recognise that Pullmans in perfect condition are virtually unheard of and, if found, would sell for quite a bit more. Pullmans made before late 1952 had no printed surround to the name board. The Golden Arrow (GA) versions have 'Golden Arrow' at one end and 'Fleche D'Or' at the other. Early Pullman cars were issued ready named and had the name rubber-stamped on the end of the box. A little later they were issued unnamed but supplied with a sheet of name transfers (as was also the case later when the Pullmans were reissued- table C2b).

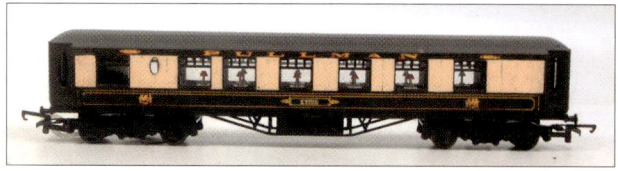

Pullman car [C2a] (Lacy, Scott & Knight)

-	Iolanthe dark brown+cream - *50-53*	25	40
-	Lydia dark brown+cream - *50-53*	25	40
-	Minerva dark brown+cream - *50-53*	25	40
-	Pauline dark brown+cream - *50-53*	25	40
-	Phyllis dark brown+cream - *50-53*	25	40
-	Iolanthe dark brown+cream GA - *51-53*	30	50
-	Lydia dark brown+cream GA - *51-53*	30	50
-	Minerva dark brown+cream GA - *51-53*	30	50
-	Pauline dark brown+cream GA - *51-53*	30	50
-	Phyllis dark brown+cream GA - *51-53*	30	50
-	**Wagon Lits** blue - *51-53*	30	50
-	**Pullman** TC No.94 dark brown+cream - *52-53*	25	40

C2b. Pullmans (Later) (1962)
This was the early 1960's version is type C2a with solid metal bogie casting and three part plastic wheels with a more stable polystyrene body. These are obviously employing the same production techniques as the third series wagons. The box was blue and yellow non-window type. The saloons came with blank nameboards and a choice of names as transfers. The choice of names was: Alice, Belinda, Fingall, Gladys, Ibis, Iolanthe, Joan, Lydia, Minerva, Niobe, Penelope, Phyllis and Rosamunde. The choice of numbers for the brake car was: No. 27, No. 36, No. 54, No. 55, No. 62, No. 63, No. 67, No. 68, No. 69, No. 70, No. 71, No. 72, No. 77, No. 78, No. 79, No. 80, No. 81 and No. 82.

B64	dark brown+cream 1st parlour - *62-?*	20	40
B65	TC No.94 dk.brown+cream brake end - *62-?*	20	40

C2c. Pullmans (Final)
These had plastic bogies, steel pinpoint axles, plastic wheels and came in transparent window box.

B64	dark brown+cream 1st parlour - *?-75*	20	40
B65	TC No.94 dark brown+cream brake end - *?-75*	20	40

Overseas Stock

C3. Stainless Steel Stock (H0) (1952)
These had plastic bodies and the same metal bogies as the tender of the 'Hudson' loco in table L7. These are very rarely found in perfect condition and this is recognised in the prices suggested below.

-	**New York Central** 3029 silver - *52-53*	30	40
-	**Chesapeake & Ohio** 3029 blue+cream - *not made**	NA	NA

* This was due to be released late in 1952 and a pre-production model was painted up and featured in adverts; however, they were not released.

Early Suburban Coaches

C4a. Bogie Non-Corridor 'Suburban' Coach (1952)
These were similar in appearance to the 4-wheel coaches but were twice as long. They were probably based on an LMS design and were well-detailed models, complete with seats, compartment partitions and fittings in relief - all part of the basic body moulding. They had a metal roof and floor and most had 'LMS', 'Southern', '1st', '3rd' etc. heat printed onto their sides. Early ones had a riveted fixing for Pullman type bogies while later ones (and the kits) had a nut and bolt attachment and smaller, improved, bogies. They were made in large quantities and collectors should be aware that many have received subsequent alterations by their owners.

-	**LMS** maroon 1st - *52-53*	10	18
-	**LMS** maroon 3rd - *52-53*	10	18
-	**LMS** maroon composite - *52-53*	10	18
-	**SR** green 1st - *52-53*	10	18
-	**SR** green 3rd - *52-53*	10	18
-	**SR** green composite - *52-53*	10	18
-	**BR** red 1st - *52-53*	10	18
-	**BR** red 3rd - *52-53*	10	18
-	**BR** red composite - *52-53*	10	18

LMS 'Surburban' 3rd class coach [C4a]

C4b. Bogie Non-Corridor 'Suburban' Brake End (1953)
The same details apply to this model as applied to the model above in table C4a.

-	**LMS** maroon brake 3rd - *53*	10	18
-	**SR** green brake 3rd - *53*	10	18
-	**BR** red brake 3rd - *53*	12	20

C5a. 'Suburban' Kits (1963?)
These kits used the original suburban coach one-piece body moulding, steel floor and diecast under-gear but had a lighter tinplate roof and bogies simplified for home construction.

A40*	black composite kit - *63?-74*	NA	20
A41*	black brake end kit - *63?-74*	NA	20

C5b. Main Line Kits (1970?)
Although substantially similar to the C5a kits (above), they used a new body moulding which was fractionally longer and with different window spacing.

A42	black composite kit - *70?-74*	NA	20
A43	black brake end kit - *70?-74*	NA	20

Graham Farish 00

All Plastic Coaches

C6a. Bogie Non-Corridor 'Suburban' Composite (1975)

These were outwardly similar to the earlier coaches (table C4 above) but were of a much lighter construction with all plastic parts. They were reduced in height and weight by removal of the solebar and the use of a new design of plug-in solebar/bogie mounting and side truss/battery box. They also had a plastic roof, reversible bogies and were issued in the liveries of the big four and BR. Catalogue numbers changed and both are provided. 'Shirt button' type logos were used on GWR coaches.
dl = detailed livery.

10601	LMS 16385 maroon (also BR60M) - 75-81	10	18
10602	LNER ? teak (also BR60N) - 77-81	10	18
BR60W	GWR ? brown+cream, simple livery - 75-77	10	18
10604	GWR 7053 brown+cream, dl (also BR60W) - 77-81	10	18
10603	SR ? green (also BR60S) - 75-81	10	18
10605	BR ? red (also BR60) - 77-81	12	20

C6b. Bogie Non-Corridor 'Suburban' Brake (1975)

The details described in C6a above also apply to this model. Catalogue numbers changed and both are provided. 'Shirt button' type logos were used on GWR coaches.

10611	LMS 20485 maroon (also BR61M) - 75-81	10	18
10612	LNER ? teak (also BR61N) - 76-81	10	18
BR61W	GWR 7294 brown+cream simple livery - 75-77	10	18
10614	GWR 7294 brown+cream detailed livery (BR61W) - 77-81	10	18
10613	SR 2697 green (also BR61S) - 75-81	10	18
10615	BR ? red (also BR61) - 77-81	12	20

C7a. Main Line Composite (1975)

These were almost identical to the suburban stock in table C6a above, but one side showed the larger corridor. 'Shirt button' type logos were used on GWR coaches.

LNER teak main line composite coach [C7a]

10621	LMS ? maroon (also BR62M) - 75-81	10	18
10622	LNER 75674 teak (also BR62N) - 76-81	10	18
BR62W	GWR ? brown+cream, simple livery - 75-77	10	18
10624	GWR (button) 7053 brown+cream, dl (also BR62W) - 77-81	10	18
10624	GWR (button) 9003 brown+cream, dl (also BR62W) - 77-81	10	18
10623	SR 1787 olive green (also BR62S) - 75-81	10	18

C7b. Main Line Brake (1975)

These were almost identical to the suburban stock in table C6b above but one side showed the larger corridor windows. Catalogue numbers changed and both are provided. 'Shirt button' type logos were used on GWR coaches.
dl = detailed livery.

10631	LMS ? maroon (also BR63M) - 75-81	10	18
10632	LNER ? teak (also BR63N) - 76-81	10	18
BR63W	GWR ? brown+cream simple livery - 75-77	10	18
10634	GWR 7094 brown+cream dl (BR63W) - 77-81	10	18
10631	SR 2763 or 2783 olive green (BR63S) - 75-81	10	18

WAGONS

The first series of wagons was released with the couplings in their original nickel-silver condition. Apart from being overscale they were rather obtrusive and within a few months were painted black prior to assembly. Further diecast wagons arrived in 1952 but a year later, production had ceased. Besides coupling and body colour variations, all early rolling stock could have either plain plastic or nickel-silver rimmed plastic wheels.

Although some publicity material showed wagons and vans with markings implying the existence of a fruit van, refrigerated van, insulated van, fish van and wagons with company lettering, it is understood that only the eight plain unmarked wagons and vans listed in tables W1 to W8 below were released.

Another series of wagons came with the revival of the system in 1961 and these had plastic bodies on diecast chassis and came non-printed but with transfers you could apply. The final series started in the 1970s and was quite extensive. The wagons were all plastic except for the couplings and had factory finished liveries.

Cat No.	Company, Number, Colour, Date	£	£

Diecast Wagons

All except the brake van had a realistic looking brake lever each side and the separate underframe on the surviving examples sometimes suffers from metal fatigue. The buffers and stocks, as well as the couplings, were bright metal and probably nickel-plated. Those released in 1951, 1952 or 1953 were produced in lower numbers with the result that they are harder to find. They had a tinplate floor, no handbrake gear and were very prone to metal fatigue.

W1. Match Truck (1952)

These were used with rail cranes, providing a support for the jib. This model was a plain flat wagon, in a single casting, which incorporated a planked effect on the floor and a central bolster without pins.

-	brown - 52-53	8	NA
-	dark brown - 52-53	8	NA
-	light grey - 52-53	8	NA

W2. Bolster Wagon (1952)

Single bolster wagons were usually used in pairs and could carry girders or logs as long as their combined length. The model was similar to the match truck (above), with a single bolster cast into the body, but this also had two pins and a chain.

-	brown - 52-53	8	NA
-	dark brown - 52-53	8	NA
-	light grey - 52-53	8	NA

W3. 3-plank Wagon (1952)

Three-plank wagons had limited use on the real railways, but the LMS had quite a lot of them. Loads included containers, other large objects and ballast. They had sides that could be lowered to allow easy loading and unloading. This model was announced and illustrated in the first catalogue but not made until the 1952.

-	brown - 52-53	8	NA
-	dark brown - 52-53	8	NA
-	light grey - 52-53	8	NA

W4. High-sided Wagon (1949)

As is the case here, the high-sided wagon on the real railways was usually a 5-plank and was used for the transportation of general merchandise. They were gradually replaced by vans which gave better protection to their contents.

Diecast high-sided wagon [W4] (Rails of Sheffield)

8th Edition

Graham Farish 00

-	light grey - *49-51*	4	10
-	dark grey - *49-51*	4	10
-	light brown - *49-51*	4	10
-	dark brown - *49-51*	4	10
-	red brown - *49-51*	4	10

W5.   Coal Wagon (1949)
This was a fixed-end 7-plank wagon typical of those used for the transportation of coal. The model incorporated the chassis within the body casting and it had the representation of over-large side drop-down doors.

-	light grey - *49-51*	4	10
-	dark grey - *49-51*	4	10
-	light brown - *49-51*	4	10
-	dark brown - *49-51*	4	10
-	red brown - *49-51*	4	10

W6.   Steel Mineral Wagon (1949)
The detail on the body of this model was poorly defined and, besides ribbing, showed the representation of side doors without top flaps and one hinged end for end tipping. The solebars and buffer beams were part of the body casting.

-	light grey - *49-51*	4	10
-	dark grey - *49-51*	4	10
-	light brown - *49-51*	4	10
-	dark brown - *49-51*	4	10
-	red brown - *49-51*	4	10

W7.   Goods Van (1949)
This was a model of a double vent van with the representation of narrow double hinged side doors. It had a separate tin roof.

-	red brown, grey roof - *49-51*	5	10
-	light grey, white or cream roof - *49-51*	5	10
-	grey, white or cream roof - *49-51*	5	10
-	'Formo' * - *53*	6	12

*This has 'Formo' cast into box on the underside of the body which is of a slightly different construction, the dummy underframe now being incorporated in the body moulding with separate coupling and axle carrier unit at one end.

W8.   Brake Van (1949)
The model was of a double veranda, short wheelbase, brake van, typical of early ones seen on the LMS and LNER. It has duckets in both sides and was constructed with vertical planking. The body and chassis on this model was a single casting and a separate tin roof was added.

-	red brown - *49-51*	4	10
-	black - ?	NPG	NPG
-	'Formo'* brown - *53*	5	10

*This was the same as the Formo wagon described above in table W4.

1960s Plastic Wagons

The first plastic wagons of the 1960s were fairly short lived. They had non-printed self-coloured polystyrene bodies and were not unlike Trackmaster or early Tri-ang wagons in appearance. Transfer sheets were available allowing the purchaser to apply the finish of one of the big four companies, but not BR!

1960's plastic tarpaulin wagon [W9]

Some of the bodies were later used in the later 1970s series of plastic wagons. They had a two-part diecast chassis which had been chemically blackened and which had four vertical locating pins for the body (again like Trackmaster or Tri-ang). Unnecessarily they had open axleboxes which rather spoilt the appearance. The chassis may be identified by a small 'GF' on the back of the solebar. The wagons were sold in a roll of corrugated paper and a thin printed outer paper wrapper.

W9.   Tarpaulin Wagon (1962)
Tarpaulin wagons were a step between open merchandise wagons and vans. Tarpaulins were stretched over wagons to protect the contents from rain and a central rail was added to raise the centre of the canvas to prevent water from pooling. This model was a fixed-end 7-plank wagon with a wire tarpaulin rail, but a 5-plank wagon would have been a better choice.

-	grey - *62-64*	8	12
-	red brown - *62-64*	8	12

W10.   Steel Mineral Wagon (1962)
Steel mineral wagons date from before the Second World War but were manufactured by British Railways in vast numbers during the 1950s to replace its adopted fleet of wooden mineral wagons that were nearing the end of their useful lives.

-	grey - *62-64*	8	12
-	red brown - *62-64*	8	12

W11.   Fast Goods Van (1962)
I have not seen one of these models but Graham Farish made a habit of modelling their vans with a slightly exaggerated height and this may have also been the case here.

-	grey - *62-64*	8	12
-	red brown - *62-64*	8	12

W12.   Brake Van (1962)
If this was like the previous and later brake van models, it will have been on a short wheelbase and have a veranda at each end, side duckets and vertical planking.

-	grey - *62-64*	8	12
-	red brown - *62-64*	8	12

1970s Plastic Wagons

This final series was of all plastic construction. Early examples had the axles in clips which were part of the floor moulding but later ones had the axles held by the side frames. Vans and brake vans may be found either with excessive roof heights or with later corrected ones. This time they were released from the factory already decorated but, again, no BR liveries were produced.

W13.   5-plank Wagon (1974)
These had wide side-doors and angled corner plates. They had timbered end walls and where catalogue numbers changed, both are provided here.

5-plank wagon 'A. Sharpe' [W13]

12001	**LMS** 165417 grey (also B20M) - *74-81*	5	8
12002	**NE** red brown (also B20N) - *74-81*	5	8
12003	**SR** dark brown (also B20S) - *74-81*	5	8
12004	**GW** 15082 dark grey (also B20W) - *74-81*	5	8
12011	**'D.Pitt'** 2 grey - *79-81*	5	8
12012	**'Spiers'** 513 yellow-orange - *79-81*	5	8
12013	**'Snow'** black - *76-81*	5	8
-	**'Sharpe'** grey Sp Edn (Neal's Toys) - *80-81*	8	12

W14.   7-plank wagon (1973)
The body moulding on this coal wagon model had the representation of drop-down doors on either side and a fixed end - i.e. no hinged end for end unloading. Catalogue numbers changed and both are provided.

12101	**LMS** 312154 brown (also B21M) - *73-81*	5	8

Graham Farish 00

12102	**NE** 131457 red brown (also B21N) - *73-81*	5	8
12103	**SR** 5079 dark brown (also B21S) - *73-81*	5	8
12104	**GW** 102784 dark grey (also B21W) - *73-81*	5	8
12111	**'Frost'** 31 black (also B21/1) - *75-80*	5	8
12112	**'Pritchard'** 26 green (also B21/2) - *75-81*	5	8
12113	**'Bullcroft'** 9471 red (also B21/3) - *75-81*	5	8
12114	**'Joseph Ellis'** 150? red brown (also B21/4) - *75-80*	5	8
12115	**'South Leicester'** 373 red brown (also B21/5) - *75-80*	5	8
12116	**'Wood'** 1410 yellow (also B21/6) - *75-81*	5	8
12122	**'Sleight'** 79 grey - *79-81*	5	8
12123	**'Powell Gwinnell'** 111 black - *79-81*	5	8
12124	**'Ocean'** 918 black - *79-81*	5	8
12125	**'Ormiston'** 54 blue - *made?*	NPG	NPG
12126	**'Staveley'** 8716 black - *79-81*	5	8

W15. 16T Steel Mineral Wagon (1973)
This was a better version of earlier Graham Farish steel mineral wagons. Catalogue numbers changed and both are provided.

12201	**LMS** 616014 red brown (also B22M) - *73-81*	5	8
12204	**GW** 110134 dark grey (also B22W) - *73-81*	5	8
12211	**'SC'** 07217 grey - *79-81*	5	8

W16a. Single Vent Van (tall) (1973)
There were two body forms for the single vent van as the original was too tall and a shorter version replaced it. The tall version had an extra plank above the door. At present it is assumed that the change of body occurred in 1975 and a split has been made accordingly. If this date is incorrect, I would would be interested to hear of an alternative. Catalogue numbers changed and both are provided.

12301	**LMS** 7701 grey (also B23M) - *73-75*	5	8
12302	**NE** 186547 red brown (also B23N) - *73-75*	5	8
12303	**SR** 50567 dark brown (also B23S) - *73-75*	5	8
12311	**'Bass'** 14 grey (also B23/1) - *74-75*	5	8
12312	**'Worthington'** 5 dark brown (also B23/2) - *74-75*	5	8

W16b. Single Vent Van (short) (1975)
The single vent van had corrugated end walls, vertical planking on the sides and the doors were of the single sliding type particularly associated with the LMS. Catalogue numbers changed and both are provided. There were two body forms (see table above).

12304	**GW** 95253 dark grey (also B23W) - *75-81*	5	8
12304	**GW** 95677 dark grey (also B23W) - *75-81*	5	8
12313	**'Knorr'** white (also B23/3) - *75-81*	5	8
12314	**'Terrys'** dark brown (also B23/4) - *75-81*	5	8
12315	**'Zoflora'** green (also B23/5) - *75-80*	5	8
12316	**'Fyffes'** yellow (also B23/6) - *75-80*	5	8
B23/7?	**'Railmail'** yellow Sp Edn - *77*	5	8
-	**'Beatties'** black Sp Edn - *80*	5	8

W17. Twin Vent Van (1974)
The double vent van had two vents at each end, horizontally planked walls and with the representation of a pair of hinged doors on either side. This model had much in common with GWR designs. Catalogue numbers changed and both are provided.

Packaged twin vent van [W17] (Ebay)

12401	**LMS** 7126 grey (also B24M) - *74-81*	5	8
12403	**SR** 64346 dark brown (also B24S) - *74-81*	5	8
12404	**GW** 95253 dark grey (also B24W) - *74-81*	5	8
12411	**'Sportsman'** white - *77-80*	5	8
12412	**'Gibbs SR'** blue - *77-80*	5	8
12413	**'John West'** green+pink - *77-80*	5	8
-	**'Beatties'** black Sp Edn - *80*	5	8

W18. Short Brake Van (1973)
Like previous Graham Farish brake vans, this model had a short wheelbase, verandas at both ends, vertical planking and a ducket in the centre of each side. Catalogue numbers changed and both are provided.

13021	**LMS** 159132 grey (also B31M) - *73-80*	5	8
13022	**NE** 157691 red brown (B31N) - *73-80*	5	8
13023	**SR** 158732 dark brown (B31S) - *73-80*	5	8

ACCESSORIES
Various model railway ancillary items were released between 1949 and 1952 which included a series of three building kits. These were:

Brookdale passenger station
Brookdale goods depot and signal cabin
'Red Roofs' and 'Timbers' (villas)

Each kit included a full set of building papers and supplementary sheets consisting of brick papers, doors and windows etc. and all that was required to complete each kit was balsa wood and glue.

Up until 1950, only a battery control unit was available but the introduction of the new controller/transformer finished in chromium plate and black stove enamel made operating the railway more practical. It had a reverse lever and a four position speed lever which, although it gave much better overall control of running trains, slow running was still a problem. This was overcome by the 'fingertip controller' which used in conjunction with the transformer/controller unit made engine movements and especially shunting more practical.

West & Short Ltd made a range of diecast accessories that were exclusively marketed by Graham Farish. The range included railway personnel, passengers, a railway horse wagon, platform seats, a range of signals, street lamps and a goods depot crane. These were sold in brightly illustrated card boxes. The Graham Farish connection was printed on the packaging and this adds to the value of these.

By the late '60s, the company was selling printed card shop fronts, plastic tunnel mouths and moulded station roofs. There were also six sets of building papers. These later accessories in original packaging are of interest to collectors.

SETS
The first four sets all contained the GP5 LMS 'Black 5' locomotive, which explains why this is the most common locomotive of that period to be found today. The choice was between six wagons or three 4-wheeled coaches and these combinations were available with or without track. Of these the goods set with track is the most common and sells for £80- £120. It seems that very few passenger sets were made and hardly any of the sets released without track have survived.

In 1953, a hard to find 3-rail set was sold under the name 'Formo' and this contained the Q Class 0-6-0 locomotive, 7-plank wagon, steel mineral wagon, van, brake van and an oval of tinplate track. In very good condition this would be expected to sell at between £120 and £150.

First Graham Farish train set (Vectis)

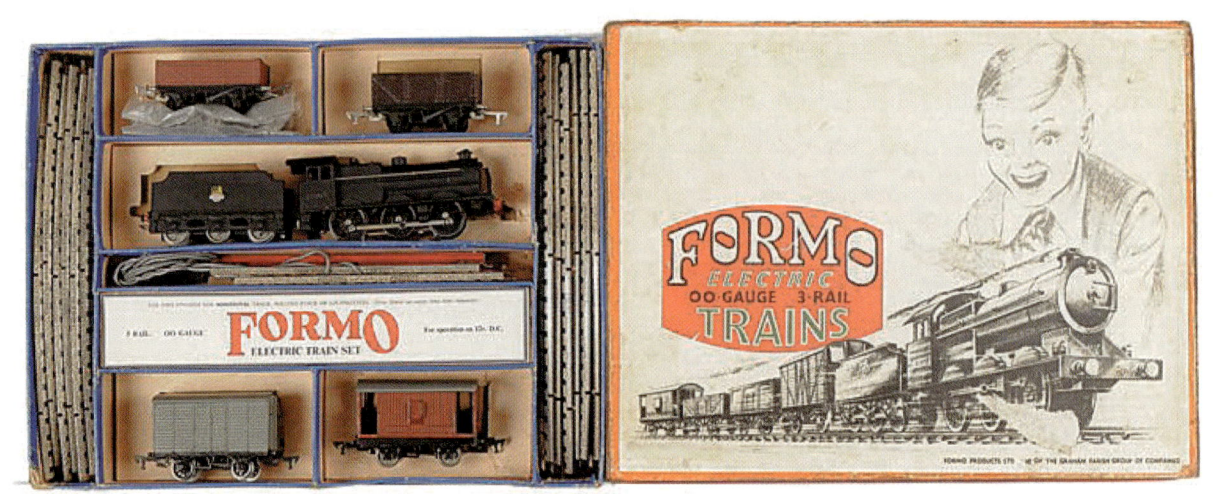

The Formo 3-rail train set (Vectis)

Photo of a renumbered Bachmann Class 4F with mineral empties, computer enhanced by Robbie McGavin

Graham Farish N

HISTORY
The history of the Graham Farish company has been covered elsewhere in this book (see 'Graham Farish 00') and we pick up the story in 1970.

What had previously been referred to as 000 gauge (being approximately half the size of 00) was renamed 'N' gauge in the early 1960s. By 1970 there were already Continental N gauge systems catering for the British market but these were a sideline to larger ranges for customers in Continental Europe and America. All were sold through British companies (Lima/Wrenn, Minitrix/Trix Trains and Rivarossi/Peco). All too often they involved compromises, including those of scale and use of common parts not strictly correct in a British setting.

The Gaffer and its coach [L2]

Dating Models from their Packaging
71-73 alphanumeric numbering and blue and yellow packaging.
73-77 now called 'Grafar'.
78 all figure catalogue numbers used and return to 'Graham Farish' name. Gold on black packaging using a clear plastic tube with rigid plastic ends.
79-80 black card window boxes used.
81-92 the same but colour scheme now yellow on black.
93-00 the same but an additional yellow stripe on the box.

What was needed was a complete N gauge system made specifically for the British Market. Graham Farish recognised this need and the opportunity it provided them with, at a time when they were struggling to maintain a toehold in the British 00 market. There had been the pioneering Lone Star in the late '50s and early '60s but this did not provide the quality that serious modellers were seeking, especially the N Gauge Society which had been founded in 1967. The Society set standards for Graham Farish to work to.

By now, the company were based at Holton Heath near Poole in Dorset and their main product at the time was 'Formoway' track which was a principle competitor for Peco track. The public heard little of the company's N gauge plans until its advertisement appeared in the model railway press in the autumn of 1970. Initially, 32 wagons and a Pannier tank were planned but many other accessories were proposed including an N gauge handbook.

The Pannier tank was released early in 1971 and a GER Holden 0-6-0 tank and some 4-wheel coaches followed in time for Christmas. Early wagons and coaches came non-printed but there were dry transfers (made by Lettraset) available to detail them. Suburban bogie and main line coaches followed in 1972, but by September that year the non-printed wagons and coaches were being supplanted by so called 'Superstock' which left the factory with a paint finish and ready printed by the silicone pad method. The first wagons in private owner liveries quickly followed but were initially available only in mixed sets of three.

The range of locomotives and rolling stock quickly expanded and included diesel and electric locomotives in the liveries of the privatised companies and modern rolling stock to go with them. An interesting innovation was the range of 'Magnum' layouts which were large printed cards which included a set design onto which you could lay your track. A large range of N gauge card buildings was also available in their 'Scenecraft' series. Five buildings in the archives have been found which never went into production - one was a terminus station building! Some special limited runs for industrial companies were also produced to be used as promotional aids.

In the summer of 2000, Peter Graham Farish took a well deserved retirement and sold Graham Farish Ltd to Bachmann Industries Europe Ltd. Production was transferred to China and work now started on upgrading the range. The resulting models are listed separately in this book.

Catalogue Numbers - The numbering system changed two or three times in the early days, causing confusion, but settled down to a simple four-figure number in 1978. It is therefore likely that models released before 1978 may be found with differing catalogue numbers although the box content remains the same.

The four-digit system worked on the basis that the last digit referred to the variation. This worked well for up to 9 variations but after this letters of the alphabet were used or, alternatively, the numbering continued into five digits for '10', '11' etc. Near the end, an 'FA' prefix was being used and some boxes had a 'FA' number on a printed yellow label one end of the box and a cut out sticker with a Bachmann number on the other end. These were amongst the last models made at Holton Heath.

Variations meant livery changes and not changes in names and running numbers. Thus a given catalogue number could be applied to models with different names and numbers, so long as the livery was the same.

An additional '0' was sometimes added in front of three figure numbers to bring them up to four digits. Here we have tended to leave out the surplus '0'.

Couplings - The European standard N gauge coupling was adopted from the start and this was altered towards the end of 1972. Initially these were sprung but, in order to avoid paying a license fee for use of the design which was owned by Arnold, the springs were dropped after a while, the sprung coupling returning in 1981.

LNER class A4 in post-war condition and with corridor tender [L19] (David Wild)

Graham Farish by Bachmann
Following their purchase of Graham Farish Ltd in 2000, Bachmann released a list of planned locomotives as follows:

Class 4P 'Compound' 4-4-0 41147 black BRb lined
'Castle' Class 4-6-0 7033 *Hartlebury Castle* green BRb (transfer no.14411)
'Duchess' Class 4-6-2 46255 *City of Hereford* blue BRb
Class A3 4-6-2 60051 *Blink Bonny* green BRc double chimney
Class A3 4-6-2 60080 *Dick Turpin* blue BRb
Class A4 4-6-2 60017 *Silver Fox* blue BRb
Class 8F 2-8-0 3107 black LNER (number on buffer beam)
Class 8F 2-8-0 48045 black BRc with Fowler tender
Class 20 Bo-Bo 20312 blue DRS yellow ends
Class 20 Bo-Bo D8163 green BRc small yellow ends
Class 25 Bo-Bo 25322 *Tamworth Castle* green BRc 2-tone
Class 31 diesel A1A-A1A 31601 *Bletchley Park* black Fragonset
Class 33 Bo-Bo 33109 *Captain Bill Smith RN* blue BRe, yellow ends
Class 37 Co-Co 37609 blue DRS, yellow ends
Class 37 Co-Co 37428 *Great Scottish* maroon EWS LMS type livery
Class 40 1-Co-Co-1 D306 *Atlantic Conveyor* green BRc half yellow ends
Class 43 43047+43058 jade Midland Mainline 3-car
Class 43 43096+43109 navy GNER 3-car
Class 47 Co-Co 47708 *Waverley* black Fragonset
Class 50 Co-Co 50017 maroon VSOE Northern Pullman (LMS 'Royal Scot' type livery)

Graham Farish N

Class 57 Co-Co 57011 *Freightliner Challenger* green
Class 158 DMU 1525 Northern Spirit 3-car
Class 158 DMU 1550 Central Trains 2-car
Class 158 DMU 1551 dark blue First North Western 2-car
Class 159 DMU 1526 Southwest Trains 3-car

Many of these models, and some refinished rolling stock, were produced at the Holton Heath works using parts available. Some went out with four figure catalogue numbers hand-written on a cut out gummed label while others were given Bachmann six figure numbers printed onto gummed labels using a computer. We understand from Bachmann that, with so much going on at the time when British production was wound down, no comprehensive record of these batches was kept. The question of what was produced during the closing days will make an interesting study and models made during this period are going to be the most sought after by collectors in years to come. This includes some locomotives with blackened rims on the driving wheels which Bachmann requested. Unfortunately the bogie and tender wheels remained in their former bright metal condition.

Bachmann discovered that much work would have to be done to the existing tooling to upgrade the models to a standard expected of their company and so work started on this. At the same time, development of new models started, albeit at a slower pace. All new and improved models are made by Bachmann's parent company, Kader, in China and these started to appear during late 2001.

As far as this guide is concerned we have included in this section all those models that were made at Holton Heath including a few sold under the Bachmann numbering system. Any models made in China will appear in the next section - **'Graham Farish by Bachmann'.**

LOCOMOTIVES

Except for Class 94xx pannier tanks made in 1971, the locomotives had a split chassis design. The combined motor and chassis unit was used from 1978, with the prairie tank being the first model to use it. The locomotives had 3-pole motors until March 1984, after which, 5-pole motors were fitted to all Graham Farish locomotives.

During the period 1996-97, there was an unsuccessful experiment with unpainted locomotives.

Cat No.	Company, Number, Colour, Date	£	£

Tank Locomotive
0-6-0T

L1.	Standard Tank 0-6-0T (Freelance) (1975)		
	This was made from the former Holden tank tooling which was altered for the purpose. It consequently looked very like a J69 but with slight structural changes.		
NE3M	583 LMS lined maroon - *75-76*	25	40
NE3S	187 Southern lined green - *75-76*	25	40

L2.	Promotional Tank 0-6-0T (Freelance) (1989)		
	This was a cheap to produce, non-powered model.		
-	'The Shredded Wheat Co.' black non-powered - *89-99*	25	NA
-	No1 *The Gaffer 1994* bright red powered ex-8530 set - *94*	25	NA

L3.	General Purpose Tank 0-6-0T (Freelance) (1978)		
	This replaced the Standard tank (above) as the 'all things to all men' model in the range and was larger than its predecessor.		
NE7M	16389 LMS lined maroon - *78*	25	40
1701	16389 LMS lined maroon- *78-00*	25	40
1706	7313 LMS black - *78-00*	25	40
NE7N	2801 LNER lined green - *78*	25	40
1702	2801 LNER lined green - *78-00*	25	40
-	2801 LNER blue ex set 85311 - *?*	30	NA
NE7S	2579 Southern lined green - *78*	25	40
1703	2579 Southern lined green - *78-00*	25	40
NE7BR	47313 BRb lined black - *78*	25	40
1705	47313 BRb lined black - *78-00*	25	40

Large general purpose 0-6-0T in LNER livery [L3]

L4.	GWR Class 94xx 0-6-0PT (1971)		
	This was based on a Hawksworth design. The tanks were built between 1947 and 1956 - most of them by British Railways and so did not run in GWR livery. A total of 210 were constructed and two have been preserved.		
	Early models had a Mabuchi can motor fitted and a cast metal chassis. From 1972, a split chassis design was used.		
NE1	*GWR green * - *71*	30	45
NE1GN	*GWR green * - *72-74*	30	45
NE1W	*GWR green * - *75-77*	30	45
1104	9405 GWR green - *78-00*	35	50
NE1BK	*BRb black * - *72-74*	30	45
NE1BR	*BRb black * - *75-77*	30	45
1105	9401 BRb black - *78-00*	35	50

* These models were supplied unnumbered and with a sheet of transfers with the following numbers: 8427, 9400, 9406, 9410, 9426, 9427.

L5a.	GWR Class 57xx 0-6-0PT (1995)		
	This much modelled subject was Collett's pannier tank design of 1929, with a Churchward cab. In all, 863 locomotives were built between 1929 and 1950. The last was withdrawn in 1966 and 16 have been preserved, including 6 of the 13 that were sold to London Transport between 1957 and 1963 and which survived in use until 1971.		
	This is identical to the model below but has a Churchward cab.		
1114	5768 Great Western green - *95-00*	35	50
111A	L99 London Transport maroon Ltd Edn 500 (red label) - *96*	55	77
1115	7777 BRb black - *95-00*	35	50

L5b.	GWR Class 8750 0-6-0PT (1996)		
	These are usually considered to be part of the Class 57xx and were introduced to the GWR in 1933 by Collett, as a heavier version. They had a modified cab, for better visibility by the crew, and better weather protection.		
	This is identical to the above model but has a Collett cab.		
1124	6752 GWR green - *96-00*	35	50
1124	8751 GWR green - *96-00*	35	50
1125	4782 BRc black - *96-00*	35	50
1125	4672 BRc black - *96-00*	35	50

L6.	LMS Class 3F 'Jinty' 0-6-0T (1996)		
	The class was designed for the LMS by Henry Fowler, based on an earlier Johnson design. The 'Jinty' became the company's standard 0-6-0 tank shunting engine and 422 were built between 1924 and 1931, much of the work being contracted out. They were highly versatile engines and found themselves on both freight and passenger trains. Seven spent a period on the S&DJR and two went to Northern Ireland in 1944. Some survived to the last days of steam and 10 have been preserved.		

LMS 'Jinty' 0-6-0T [L6]

Graham Farish N

1731	7277 LMS black - *96-00*		35	50
1731A	47268 LMS black - *99-00*		35	50
1735	47394 BRb black - *96-00*		35	50

L7. LNER Holden Class J69 0-6-0T (1972)

These were built for the Great Eastern Railway to a design by Holden as a Class S56. The first were built in 1890 and the last in 1904. The class finally totalled 126 (including several rebuilt from LNER J67s). One has been preserved in the National Collection.

The body tool was altered in 1975 to provide a standard tank that could be passed off in various liveries (see L1).

NE2BL	372 GER lined blue - *72-74*		30	45
NE2E	372 GER lined blue - *75*		30	45
NE2GN	1672 LNER lined green - *72-74*		30	45
NE2NE	1672 LNER lined green - *75*		30	45
NE2BK	? BRb lined black - *72-74*		30	45
NE2BR	? BRb lined black - *75*		30	45

L8. WD/LNER Class J94 0-6-0ST (1986)

Designed by Riddles, this was based on a Hunslet Class 50550 design and 391 were built for the government during the Second World War, using various locomotive builders. A further 93 were built for other customers. J94 was applied as a class code to the 75 locomotives bought by the LNER after the war and which passed to BR in 1948. Many others were sold to the National Coal Board and to private industry. Their high power and short wheelbase made them versatile machines. Of the 484 built, 70 are still in existence.

1016	68079 BRb black - *86-00*		35	50
1017	61 NCB blue, red rods - *86-00*		35	50
(8540)	07 *Robert* Industrial green ex-sets - *86-00*		35	50
?	196 LMR blue ex-set 8531 - *99-00*		35	50
101A	NS8811 Dutch dull green - *96*		40	50
101B	NS8826 Dutch dull green - *96*		40	50

2-6-2T

L9. GWR Class 61xx 2-6-2T (1977)

This was a Collett prairie tank design of 1931 and 70 were built. They were the GWR's London suburban tank engines and were required to pull heavy suburban trains from Paddington at fairly high speeds. Like most suburban tank engines, they were displaced by diesel multiple units and were moved on to parcel trains and empty stock duties.

The Class 81xx was a rebuild of the Class 61xx and had smaller wheels but there is no difference to be seen on the models.

1603	6104 GWR (button) green - *00*		35	50
1604	3112 GWR lined green - *77-00*		35	50
NE6W	8106 GWR lined green - *78*		35	50
1604	8106 GWR green - *78-00*		35	50
16012	6104 GWR (button) green - *00*		35	50
?	6105 BRb unlined green - *84*		40	60
16011	6135 BRb lined green - *00*		NPG	NPG
16011	6127 BRb lined green - *00*		35	50
0661	6113 BRb lined black - *?*		35	50
NE6BR	8100 BRc lined green - *78*		35	50
1605	8100 BRc lined green - *78-00*		35	50
1605	6115 BRc lined green - *77-00*		35	50
1606	8102 BRc lined black - *79-00*		40	55

2-6-4T

L10. BR Class 4MT 2-6-4T (1991)

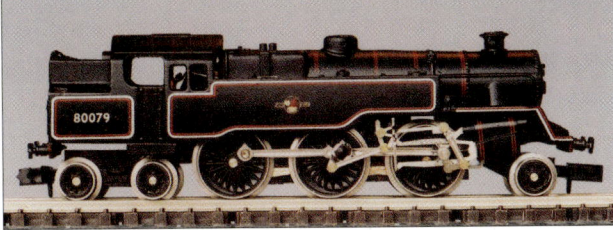

BR class 4MT 2-6-4T [L10]

Riddles designed this mixed traffic locomotive which first made its appearance in 1951. A total of 155 locomotives were built between 1951 and 1957. They were used mainly on branch line and suburban passenger duties. The last was withdrawn in 1967 and 15 have been preserved.

1655	80064 BRb lined black - *91-00*		40	55
1656	80079 BRc lined black - *91-00*		40	55

Tender Locomotive

4-4-0

L11. LMS Class 4P 'Compound' 4-4-0 (1980)

Johnson's first 'Compound' for the Midland Railway was introduced in 1902 and modified versions were produced by Deeley in 1905. Their primary function was express and local passenger services. The LMS adopted it as a standard design and the building of them continued until 1927. Much of their work was later taken over by the 'Jubilee' and 'Black 5' classes and the last was withdrawn in 1961.

1207	67 SDJR dark blue - *82-90*		65	80
1217	375 Caledonian Railway blue - *81-90*		60	75
1201	1111 LMS lined maroon - *80-00*		40	55
1206	1118 LMS black - *80-00*		40	55
1205	40938 BRb lined black - *80-00*		40	55
12011	? BRc black - *00*		40	55

0-6-0

L12. LMS Class 4F 0-6-0 (1993)

Here we have a Fowler Midland Railway design of 1911, based on Johnson's smaller loco of similar form, built for the Midland Railway. The building of them carried on until 1942 and a total of 772 were produced. Some later ones were made for the S&DJR. Some briefly were oil burners in 1947-48 but were converted back again and some were fitted with tender cabs for running tender first.

1841	4232 LMS black - *93-00*		40	55
1841	4269 LMS black - *93-00*		40	55
-	4210? LMS black ex-set 8524 - *98-99*		45	NA
1845	44370 BRc black - *93-00*		40	55

2-6-0

L13. LMS Class 5F 'Crab' 2-6-0 (1993)

The 'Crab' Moguls were easily recognisable locos due to their prominent and angled cylinders, which gave them their nickname. They were the first LMS standard locomotive, being based on a planned Caledonian Railway design. Also called 'Horwich Moguls', they were built at Horwich and arrived in 1926 with a Fowler tender. Building continued until 1932 and the class finally totalled 425. They were a short but powerful design, with large boilers, and were used for both passenger and freight workings, including express work. The last was withdrawn in 1967 and 3 were preserved, including one in the National Collection.

1851	2715 LMS lined black - *93-00*		40	55
185A	13071 LMS maroon Ltd Edn 500 (red label) - *94*		45	60
1855	42806 BRb black - *93-00*		40	55
18511	? BRc black - *00*		45	60

4-6-0

L14. GWR 'Hall' Class 4-6-0 (1975)

Production started in 1928 when 80 of the new class were built and a further 178 were ordered. They were mixed traffic locomotives and sometimes found themselves on express services when larger locomotives were unavailable. They were seen with various tenders including the small 3,500 gallon ones but most had the 'Castle' 4,000 gallon tenders. The last was withdrawn in 1966 and 10 have been preserved.

NE4W	6998 *Burton Agnes Hall* ** Great () Western green - *75-77*		50	65
1404	6998 *Burton Agnes Hall* ** Great () Western green - *78-80*		50	65
1404	6960 *Raveningham Hall* Great () Western green - *80-00*		50	65
NE4BR	7915 *Mere Hall* BRb black - *75-77*		50	65
1405	7915 *Mere Hall* BRb black - *78-00*		50	65
140A	6994 *Baggrave Hall* BRc green Sp.Edn (silver label) - *99-00*		60	80
14011	5955 *Garth Hall* BRc green - *00*		NPG	NPG

** an unfortunate choice as Burton Agnes Hall was built in 1949 and so did not receive GWR livery until it was preserved.

L15a. GWR 'Castle' Class 4-6-0 (1982)

The 'Castles' were a post-Grouping design by Collett and were made over many years (1923-1950) to produce a class of 166 locomotives. The design was a development of Churchward's excellent 'Star' Class of 1907 and included some members of that earlier class that were rebuilt as 'Castles'.

1444	7029 *Clun Castle* Great () Western green - *82-00*		55	70
1446	5042 *Winchester Castle* Great () Western green - *83-00*		55	70

Graham Farish N

14411	7033 *Hartlebury Castle* BRb green - *00*		60	80
1447	5037 *Monmouth Castle* BR grn - *83-00*		55	70
1442	5014 *Goodrich Castle* BRc green - *99-00*		55	70
1445	4082 *Windsor Castle* BRc green - *82-85*		55	70
1446	7029 *Clun Castle* BRc green - *?*		55	70

L15b. GWR 'King' Class 4-6-0 (2000)

The 'Kings' formed Collett's 'top of the range' express class and 30 were built at Swindon. It is said that the class was built when the GWR discovered that their 'Castle' Class was no longer Britain's most powerful class, having been overtaken by Maunsell's new 'Lord Nelson' locomotives on the Southern Railway.

This was the same model as the 'Castle' but had a 'King' Class front bogie specially tooled for it.

1414	6023 *King Edward II* GWR button green - *00*	60	80
1415	6023 *King John* BRb green - *00*	60	80

L16. LMS 'Black 5' Class 4-6-0 (1978)

Stanier's Class 5 mixed traffic locomotive of 1934 was one of the most successful and influential designs. The fact that 842 were built between 1934 and 1951 meant that they were a common sight on the LMS. It was to form the basis of the Standard 5 class built by British Railways and 'Black 5s' remained on the network to the very end of steam. 18 have survived in preservation.

1806	4806 LMS lined maroon - *81-89*	55	70
1806	5041 LMS lined maroon - *81-89*	55	70
1801	5041 LMS black - *78-00*	55	70
18011	5303 LMS lined black - *00*	60	80
18012	44896 BRb lined black - *00*	60	80
1805	44911 BRc lined black - *79-00*	55	70
1805	44923 BRc lined black - *78-00*	55	70
1805	45296 BRc lined black - *78-00*	55	70

4-6-2

L17. LMS 'Duchess' Class 4-6-2 (1982)

These are the same class as the streamlined 'Coronations', but were either built without streamlined cladding or with the cladding later removed. The first batch built without cladding dated from 1938 and the last 'Coronation' to become a 'Duchess', by removal of its cladding, was City of Lancaster in 1949. There were 38 members of the class and the last was withdrawn in 1964. Three of the class have been preserved, the one in the National Collection having been returned to a 'Coronation' by popular demand.

Ex-LMS 'Duchess' in late BR livery [L17]

1811	6242 *City of Glasgow* LMS black - *82-00*	60	75
1811	6255 *City of Hereford* LMS black - *83-00*	60	75
18111	46255 *City of Hereford* BR blue - *00*	65	80
1817	46221 *Queen Elizabeth* BRb blue - *82-90*	60	75
1814	46244 *King George VI* BRc green - *00*	60	75
1815	46247 *City of Liverpool* BRc maroon Sp Edn (silver label) - *00*	65	80
1816	46229 *Duchess of Hamilton* BRc maroon - *82-00*	60	75

L18. LNER Class A3 4-6-2 (1987)

The Class A3s of the LNER were a development of the A1s, which had been designed for the Great Northern Railway by Nigel Gresley in 1922. Almost all existing A1s were rebuilt, while later ones were built as A3s. One of the most visible changes was the new banjo shaped steam dome fitted to the top of the A3's boiler.

Gsd = German smoke deflectors.

1822	4472 *Flying Scotsman* LNER light green - *87-00*	60	75
18211	60080 *Dick Turpin* BRb blue - *00*	65	80
1827	60052 *Prince Palatine* BRc green, Gsd - *87-?*	60	75
1827	60052 *Prince Palatine* BRb green, Gsd - *?-00*	60	75
1825	60103 *Flying Scotsman* BRc green -*87-00*	60	75
18212	60051 *Blink Bonny* BRc green Gsd - *00*	65	80

L19. LNER Class A4 4-6-2 (1999)

The A4 was Gresley's ultimate express engine development and arrived in 1935. One of the class (Mallard) still holds the world speed record for a steam locomotive. For easy maintenance, side valances on the locomotive were removed during the war. Early examples were given corridor tenders to allow for a change of crew on the journey. They were renumbered in 1946 and there was quite a lot of renaming pre-Nationalisation.

1862	4498 *Sir Nigel Gresley* LNER blue as preserved - *99-00*	60	75
18611	60017 *Silver Fox* BRb blue - *00*	60	75
1865	60025 *Falcon* BRc green - *99-00*	60	75
1865	60003 *Andrew K McCosh* BRc green + 'The Capitals Ltd' headboard ex-set - *00*	65	NA
1865	60003 *Andrew K McCosh* BRc green - *00*	60	95

L20. SR 'Merchant Navy' Class 4-6-2 (1977)

Between 1941 and 1949, 30 of Bulleid's heavy pacific 'Merchant Navy' Class were built at Eastleigh with air smoothed casing, but all had this removed at Eastleigh between 1956 and 1959, as part of the rebuild. 11 of the class have survived into preservation.

This model was passed off as a heavy pacific but was in fact the same model that was sold as a 'Battle of Britain' light pacific in a table later. The body tool was damaged and later replaced by an improved one. The old version had the two cab windows each side the same size.

NE5S	21C17 *Belgian Marine* SR green - *77*	60	75
1503	21C17 *Belgian Marine* SR green - *78-92*	60	75
NE5SR	21C1 *Channel Packet* SR green - *77*	60	75
1503	21C1 *Channel Packet* SR green - *78-80*	60	75
NE5GA	21C1 *Channel Packet* SR green, Golden Arrow Ltd Edn - *77*	70	85
1513	21C1 *Channel Packet* SR green, Golden Arrow Ltd Edn - *85*	70	85
1523	21C4 *Cunard White Star Line* SR green - *00*	70	85
1507	35001 *Channel Packet* BRb blue - *80-92*	65	80

L21. BR 'Rebuilt Merchant Navy' 4-6-2 (1997)

This is a model of Bulleid's 'Heavy Pacific' design of 1941, as they looked after being rebuilt in BR days. 30 had been built at Eastleigh with air smoothed casing, like the WC/BB class, but all had this removed at Eastleigh between 1956 and 1959, as part of the rebuild. 11 of the class have survived into preservation.

BR 'Rebuilt Merchant Navy' in late BR livery [L21]

1513	35028 *Clan Line* BRc green - *97-00*	60	75
-	35027 *Port Line* BRc green ex set 8526 - *00*	65	NA

L22. SR 'Battle of Britain' Class 4-6-2 (1977)

The 'West Country/Battle of Britain' Class (WC/BB) was designed by Oliver Bullied as a smaller and lighter version of the 'Merchant Navy' Class. The first of the class arrived in 1945 and the rebuilding of some of them as more conventional looking locomotives was started by British Railways in 1957. Those for service in the eastern sector had been given 'Battle of Britain' names and the rest, for use further west, were named after places served by the Southern Railway. The last member of the class was withdrawn in 1967, however, 20 of the class have survived in preservation.

This model was passed off as both a light pacific and a 'Merchant Navy' Class (above), but was the same basic model. The body tool was damaged and later replaced by an improved one. The old version has the two cab windows each side the same size.

1525	34065 *Hurricane* BRb green - *00*	65	80
NE5BR	34066 *Spitfire* BRb green - *77*	60	75
1505	34066 *Spitfire* BRb green - *78-92*	60	75

L23. BR 'Rebuilt WC/BB' 4-6-2 (1997)

As with the streamlined 'Merchant Navy' heavy pacifics, BR had started rebuilding the light pacific 'West Country/Battle of Britain' Class in 1957. However, following the decision to phase out steam locomotives in Britain, the rebuilding programme was ended in 1961 and the non-rebuilt members of the class lived out the rest of their lives with their cladding in place. Of the 20 members of the class that have survived in preservation, 10 are as originally built and 10 are rebuilt ones.

1515	34089 *602 Squadron* BRc green - *97-00*	60	75
151A	34012 *Launceston* BRc green Sp Edn (silver label) - *99-00*	65	80

2-8-0

L24. LMS Class 8F 2-8-0 (1986)

The class was introduced by William Stanier in 1935 to fill a serious gap in the LMS stud. It was based on the highly successful 'Black 5s' and became the standard heavy freight design for the LMS and was adopted by the War Department during the Second World War. In all, 666 locomotives were built, including 331 that the LMS had ordered. The LMS ones were mostly built at Crewe and Horwich but with batches from Vulcan Foundry and North British as well. A batch of the wartime 8Fs was allocated to the LNER for one year (1947) and was known as the Class O6. Others went overseas for war service and some stayed there after the war. The last of the class was not withdrawn from service in Britain until 1968. Nine of the class have been preserved, including three recently repatriated from abroad.

1901	**8177** LMS black - *86-00*	55	70
1902	**3537** LNER black - *87*	55	70
19011	**3107** LNER black - *00*	60	75
1905	**48476** BRc black - *86-00*	55	70
1905	**48331** BRc black - *86-00*	55	70
19012	**48473** BRc black - *00*	60	75

Diesel Locomotive

L25. Class 08 0-6-0DS (1979)

What later became the Class 08 diesel shunter was based on a pre-war LMS development. British Railways went on to build 1,193 of these small shunting engines over a ten year period - making them the most numerous design to ever run on the British network. As railway yards disappeared and pilots were no longer required for railway stations, due to the disappearance of loco hauled trains, the fleet was steadily reduced - many going to industry and preserved lines.

BR Class 08 diesel shunter [L25]

1003	**54** Southern black - *79-80*	40	55
1001	**7130** LMS black - *79-85*	30	45
1005	**D4019** BRc red rods green - *79-00*	35	50
1007	**08113** BRe blue, yellow rods - *79-00*	35	50
1007	**08493** BRe blue, yellow rods - *79-00*	35	50
1006	**08500** *Thomas 1* BR red York Wagon Repair Depot - *91-99*	35	50
1008	**08834** BRe Rft Distribution grey - *91-00*	35	50
100G	**08921** EWS maroon+yellow Sp Edn (silver label) - *99*	40	55
100F	**08957** EWS maroon+yellow Sp Edn (silver label) - *99*	40	55
1001	**523** NS (Dutch Railways) grey+yellow - *84*	NPG	NPG
1001	**610** NS (Dutch Railways) grey+yellow - *84*	NPG	NPG
1001	**622** NS (Dutch Railways) grey+yellow - *84*	NPG	NPG
1001	**644** NS (Dutch Railways) grey+yellow - *84*	NPG	NPG
1001	**657** NS (Dutch Railways) grey+yellow - *84*	NPG	NPG

L26. Class 20 Bo-Bo (1982)

This is an English Electric designed freight loco of 1957, the first 20 being built at their Vulcan Foundry works. Other batches followed until the final member of the class was delivered in 1968. This brought the total to 228 and they were allocated to the Eastern, London Midland and Scottish regions. They were often seen operating in pairs, joined nose to nose so that their cabs were at the outer ends. This allowed the pair to be driven from either end.

8204	**D8144** BRc green, yellow ends - *82-00*	40	55
8205	**20142** BRe blue - *82-00*	40	55
8205	**20139** BRe blue - *82-00*	40	55
8205	**20215** BRe blue - *made?*	NPG	NPG
8208	**20137** BRe Rft red stripe, grey - *91*	45	60
8208	**20215** BRe Rft red stripe, grey Sp Edn - *91-93*	45	60
82011	**?** BRc green half ends Sp Edn - *00*	45	60
82012	**?** DRS blue Sp Edn - *00*	45	60

L27. Class 25 Bo-Bo (1983)

The Class 25s were introduced in 1961 as mixed traffic locomotives for the secondary routes. They were a development of the Class 24 and 323 were built at Derby, Darlington and by Beyer Peacock, between 1961 and 1967. Withdrawals started in the late 1970s, with the last member of the class going in 1987. At least 20 of the class survived into preservation.

8304	**D7645** BRc 2-tone green - *83-00*	40	55
83011	**D7672** BRe blue - *00*	45	60
8305	**25288** BRe blue - *83-00*	40	55
8305	**25326** BRe blue - *83-00*	40	55

L28. Class 31 A1A-A1A (1995)

263 members of the class were built between 1957 and 1962 and were intended for mixed traffic duties, originally on the Eastern Region. They were built at the Brush Electrical Engineering Company plant at Loughborough and 28 have been preserved.

Class 31 diesel in EWS livery [L28]

8064	**D5558** BRc green - *95-00*	45	60
8065	**31140** BRe blue - *95-00*	45	60
8066	**31205** BR Raiffreight red stripe grey - *00*	50	65
8067	**31421** *Wigan Pier* Regional Railways blue+grey - *95-00*	45	60
806B	**31466** EWS maroon+yellow Sp Edn (silver Label) - *99*	45	60
806A	**31552** BRe Civil Engineering grey+ yellow Sp Edn (silver label) - *97*	50	65
8011	**31601** *Bletchley Park Station X* Fragonset - *00*	50	65

L29. Class 33 Bo-Bo (1987)

98 Class 33 locomotives were built by the Birmingham Railway Carriage & Wagon Co. during 1961-62. At least 26 of them have been preserved.

83111	**D6525** *Captain Bill Smith RNR* BRe blue (also 371-125) - *00*	45	60
8314	**D6572** BRc green - *87-00*	45	60
8315	**33012** BRe blue - *87-00*	45	60
8312	**33025** *Sultan* BRe Civil Engineering grey+yellow Sp Edn (silver label) - *96*	50	65
831A	**33030** EWS maroon Sp Edn (silver label) - *99*	50	65
8315	**33035** BRe blue - *87-00*	45	60
8316	**33056** *The Burma Star* BRe Rft Construction grey - *90-00*	45	60
8317	**33205** BRe Raiffreight Distribution grey - *90-00*	50	65

L30. Class 37 Co-Co (1981)

Built by English Electric (subcontracted to Vulcan and Robert Stephenson & Hawthorns), 309 were built between 1960 and 1964. Intended mainly for freight, the class also did sterling service on passenger trains. The Class 37s became the definitive type 3 design for British Railways.

There are two main variants - the original split-headcode body and a refurbished centre-headcode version. The split-box one was not particularly good. The tumblehome was rather overdone and it sat too high. Early versions had Class 47 side-frames. The later, refurbished, body shell was much better and captured the look of the prototype.

Class 37 diesel in Mainline livery [L30]

8014	**D6736** BRc green split head code - *81-88*	45	60
8015	**37035** BRe blue split head code - *81-98*	45	60
803D	**37055** *Rail Celebrity* Mainline blue Sp Edn (silver label) - *97*	50	65
803E	**37408** *Loch Rannoch* EWS maroon+yellow Sp Edn - *99*	50	65
8035	**37408** *Loch Rannoch* BReLL blue - *00*	50	65

Graham Farish N

Code	Description		
8036	37696 BRe Rft Coal grey Canton motifs - 99-00	45	60
8036	37699 BRe Rft Coal grey Canton motifs - 90-98	45	60
8037	37887 BRe Rft Petroleum grey Ripple Lane motifs - 90-00	45	60
8038	37906 BRe Rft Metals grey Canton motifs - 90-00	45	60
80311	? DRS blue - 00	50	65
80312	37428 Great Scottish LMS maroon - 00	50	65

L31. Class 40 1-Co-Co-1 (1986)

Some 200 Class 40s were built by English Electric between 1958 and 1962. At the last count, 7 of them had been preserved.

Code	Description		
8115	D348 BRc green - 86-00	50	65
8116	40015 Aquitania BRe blue - 86-99	50	65
8114	40106 Atlantic Conveyor BRc green, yellow nose Sp Edn - 86-88	50	65
81111	40106/D306 Atlantic Conveyor BRc green - 00	50	65
8117	40145 BRe blue - 86-99	50	65

L32. Class 43 'HST 125' (1981)

The High Speed Train, or IC125, has been one of the most successful and influential designs ever to run in the British rail network. The HSTs went into service on the Western Region main line in October 1976 and are still very much in evidence at the turn of the century. The HST sets were made up with Mk3 coaches without buffers, classified as Mk3A. They had as their power units a Class 43 diesel locomotive at each end.

Early power bogies were unsatisfactory on the model and a new centrally mounted motor was introduced in 1984.

Code	Description		
8122	43185 Great Western+41007+43031 FGW green+ivory 3-car - 99-00	55	70
8165	BRe blue+grey driving car only - 84-00	35	50
0735	BRe blue+grey dummy driving car only - 84-00	10	14
8166	BRe I-C Executive grey driving car only - 84-00	35	50
0736	BRe I-C Executive grey dummy driving car only - 84-00	10	14
81211	Midland Mainline green 3-car - 00	70	85
81212	GNER navy 3-car - 00	70	85
8125	253007(W43015+W41015+W43014) *BRe I-C blue+grey 3-car - 81-98	55	70
8125	253007(W43015+W42263+W43014) BRe I-C blue+grey 3-car - 81-98	55	70
8126	W43014+?+W43014 BRe I-C Executive grey 3-car - 83-90	55	70
8127	43170+42219+43171 ICs grey 3-car - 90-00	60	75
8127	43080+42219+43081 ICs grey 3-car - 90-00	60	75
8128	43062+42108+43084 County of Derbyshire Virgin red 3-car - 99-00	60	75
8126	43129+W42023+43130 BRe I-C Executive grey 3-car - 83-90	55	70
8126	43129+W41015+43130 BRe I-C Executive grey 3-car - 83-90	55	70

* both end cars powered.

L33. Class 47 Co-Co (1981)

The class had been introduced in 1961 and became the mainstay of British Railway's main line diesel fleet. The locomotives were built by the Brush Electrical Engineering Co. Ltd and the Class was later split up into five subclasses. Many survived into the 21st Century but, within a short time, their numbers were decimated as the new Class 66 locomotives took over the freight business and loco hauled passenger trains were replaced by multiple units. At the last count 36 had been preserved.

Code	Description		
8004	D1662 Isambard Kingdom Brunel BRc 2-tone green code 1B28 - 81-00	45	60
-	D1943 Chris Green Virgin red Ltd Edn - 00	70	80
8023	47125 Rft Distribution grey tunnel & Tinsley motifs - 95-00	45	60
8008	47231 The Silcock Express BRe Railfreight Distribution grey Tinsley motif - 88-99	45	60
8008	47378 BRe Railfreight grey (test batch only) - 88?	80	95
8005	47455 BRe blue - 81-99	45	60
8027	47479 Track 29 BRe Parcels red+dark grey - 91-98	45	60
8026	47487 BRe InterCity Exec. grey - 88-92	45	60
8018	47582 County of Norfolk BRe Network SouthEast bright blue - 89-92	45	60
8007	47583 County of Hertfordshire BReLL blue - 82-99	45	60
8025	47594 BRe RES red Crewe Diesel motif - 92-00	45	60
8024	47598 BRe NSE bright blue - 91-99	45	60
80212	47701 Waverley Fragonset - 00	50	65
8001	47708 Waverley BRe ScotRail grey - 88-99	45	60
8022	47710 Lady Godiva Waterman Railways black Sp Edn (silver label) - 96	50	65
8006	47712 Lady Diana Spencer BReLL blue Ltd Edn - 81	55	NA
802C	47744 EWS maroon+yellow Sp Edn (silver label) - 98	50	65
80211	47747 Graham Farish Virgin red Sp Edn - 00	50	65
8002	47813 SS Great Britain First Great Western green - 99-00	45	60
800A	47814 Totnes Castle Virgin red - 99-00	50	65
801A	47817 Porterbrook purple+white Ltd Edn 500 (red label) - 98-99	55	70
8028	47834 Fire Fly ICs grey - 91-00	45	60

L34. Class 50 Co-Co (1983)

The Class 50s were built by English Electric during 1967 and 1968 and were initially hired out to the British Railways Board. Later, all 50 locos were bought by them. Although normally associated with the Western Region, they started life on the LMR on the West Coast Main Line. To this day, the class has had a cult following which may explain why 18 of the locomotives have been preserved.

Code	Description		
8408	50002 Superb NSE blue - 90-00	45	60
8404	50003 Temeraire BReLL blue - 83-88, 00	50	65
8406	50007 Sir Edward Elgar BRe green GWR style - 84-99	45	60
84011	50017 Royal Oak LMS maroon - 00	45	60
8405	50024 Vanguard BReLL blue - 83-99	45	60

L35. Class 52 'Western' (1985)

The 'Westerns' were diesel hydraulics and were designed and constructed at Swindon, while some were built at Crewe. The class of 74 had a very distinctive shape and have attracted a cult interest. They were introduced to the Western Region in 1962 to provide high powered mixed traffic locomotives to the region. They were expensive to maintain and this led to their early replacement by the Class 50s and HSTs. The last was withdrawn in 1978 and seven have been preserved.

Code	Description		
8424	D1002 Western Explorer BRc green - made?	NPG	NPG
8424	D1036 Western Emperor BRc green - 85-88	45	65
8426	D1062 Western Courier BRc maroon - 85-99	45	65
8426	D1065 Western Consort BR maroon - 99-00	45	65
8425	D1070 Western Gauntlet BRe blue - 85-88	45	65

Class 52 diesel hydraulic in BR green livery [L35]

L36. Class 55 'Deltic' Co-Co (1984)

English Electric developed these express passenger locomotives, which were introduced in 1961. 22 were built in 1961 and 1962 for the East Coast Main Line expresses, replacing some of the ex-LNER A4s and other Pacifics that had ruled this route for almost 40 years. The 'Deltics' were built at Vulcan Foundry and performed well, achieving speeds of up to 100mph. Besides pulling crack East Coast expresses, some were later used on Trans-Pennine services. They were ousted from their main function by the introduction of the High Speed Trains. Withdrawals started in 1980 and were completed in 1982. Six of the class have been preserved.

Code	Description		
814A	9016 Gordon Highlander Porterbrook purple+white Ltd Edn 500 (red label) - 00	50	65
8414	D9021 Argyll & Sutherland Highlander BRc 2-tone green - 84-00	45	60
8416	55009 Alcydion BRe blue, white window surrounds - 84-88, 00	45	60
8414	55013 Royal Scots Grey BRe blue -?*	45	60
8415	55013 Black Watch BRe blue - 84-99	45	60

* An example seen has the nameplate printed over a shorter one (perhaps Black Watch). Date unknown.

L37. Class 56 Co-Co (1993)

The Class 56 owes its existence in major part to the oil crisis in the early 1970s and the expected increase in the demand for coal. The first 30 Class 56 locomotives were built by Electroputere at Craiova in Romania but the remaining 105 machines came from BREL at Doncaster and Crewe. They were introduced between 1976 and 1984.

Code	Description		
805D	56055 LoadHaul black+orange Sp Edn (silver label) - 97	50	65

Graham Farish N

805E	**56057** *British Fuels* EW&S maroon Sp Edn (silver label) - 97	50	65
8056	**56059** BRe Raiffreight Construction grey - 93-00	45	60
8055	**56076** BRe blue - 93-00	45	60
8057	**56092** BRe Rft Coal grey Toton motifs - 93-00	45	60

L38. Class 57 Co-Co (1999)

The Class 57 fleet made its debut in 1998. Freightliner had asked Brush Traction to completely rebuild six former Class 47 locomotives and to fit reconditioned General Motors 645-12E3 engines. More were ordered, including 16 by Virgin Trains for hauling its new fleet of 'Pendolinos' when diverted over non-electrified routes. These were also available for rescuing trains in trouble and have become known as 'Thunderbirds', after the cult television series. First Great Western ordered four 57/6 locomotives and these have been named after West Country castles. These are used on the overnight sleepers and on some other services when required.

This was the same model as Class 47 (above).

804A	**57001** *Freightliner Pioneer* green Freightliner Sp Edn (silver label) - 99	45	60
80411	**57011** *Freightliner Challenger* Freightliner green - 00	50	65

Electric Locomotives

L39. Class 87 Bo-Bo (1998)

A total of 36 25kv AC locomotives of the 87 Class were built in 1973 for the West Coast Main Line. They were a development of the Class 86, but powerful enough to easily manage some steep sections of line such as Shap and Beattock. The locomotives had new bogies, which greatly reduced track wear, and Browne Willis pantographs for 110mph running. Many of the class have been exported to Eastern Europe and 3 have been preserved in the UK.

8837	**87001** *Royal Scot* ICs grey - 99-00	50	65
8838	**87009** *City of Birmingham* Virgin red - 98-00	50	65
8835	**87101** *Stephenson* BRe blue - 99-00	50	65

L40. Class 90 Bo-Bo (1995)

Needing some new AC electric locomotives for the West Coast Main Line, British Railways sought funding for a fleet of 50. They were built by BREL Crewe and all were in service in 1990. Driving Van Trailers (DVTs) also had to be built for push-pull operation of passenger trains.

882A	**90013** *The Law Society* Virgin red Sp Edn - 99-00	55	70
8827	**90015** *BBC North West* ICs grey - 95-00	50	65
8825	**90019** *Penny Black* RES red - 95-00	50	65
8828	**90022** *Freightconnection* BRe Raiffreight Distribution grey - 95-00	50	65

L41. Class 91 Bo-Bo Electric (1990)

With the electrification of the East Coast Main Line, locomotives were required to pull the new trains. The result was the IC225, which are designed to run at 140mph with 11 newly designed Mk4 coaches and a Mk4 driving trailer (DVT). Although the locomotives look single ended, they also have a flat fronted cab at the No.2 end. A total of 31 were built by BREL Crewe and introduced between 1988 and 1991. They ran in Intercity Swallow livery in BR ownership and the whole fleet was transferred to GNER on Privatisation.

8807	**91004** ICs grey - 90-00	50	65
8807	**91005** ICs grey - 90-00	50	65
8807	**91007** ICs grey - 90-00	50	65

Diesel Multiple Units & Railcars

L42. AEC Diesel Railcar (1985)

A total of 38 AEC rail cars were built and all those modelled come from the second batch built during the early years of the Second World War. These were built as multiple unit vehicles, fitted with an improved electro-pneumatic control system and buffers, so that they could work in tandem. The last of the AEC railcars were withdrawn in 1962.

Ex-GWR AEC diesel railcar [L42]

8174	**No.19** GWR button brown+cream - 85-00	45	45
8175	**W24W** BRc green - *made?*	NPG	NPG
8176	**W27W** BR red+cream - 85-88	45	45
8175	**W28W** BRc green - 86-88	45	45

L43a. Class 101 DMU (1982)

The Metro-Cammell Class 101 was the most numerous of the first generation diesels. They were introduced between 1956 and 1960 and eventually all regions received an allocation. The combination of the size of the class and the large geographical area of operation made them an obvious subject to model

BR Green

8133	**W50304+W50329** BRc half yellow panel 2-car - 82-00	50	65
8143	**W50304+W59122+W50329** BRc half yellow panel 3-car - 82-00	55	70
8143	**M50313+M59124+M56055** BRc 3-car powered or non-powered - 00?	55	70
8153	BRc half yellow panel driving car only - 85-00	35	50
8133	**M50313+M56055** BRc half yellow panel 2-car - 82-00	50	65
-	**M50331** BRc driving car only - ?	NPG	NPG

BR Blue+Grey

8135	**M50303+M50330** BRe 2-car - 82-00	50	65
8145	**M50303+M59130+M50330** BRe 3-car - 82-00	55	70
8135	**51437+54218** BRe 2-car - 82-00	50	65
?	**53751+59128+51437** BRe 3-car - ?	55	70
8145	**51437+59130+54218** BRe 3-car - ?	50	65
8155	BRe driving car only - 85-00	35	50
-	**59218** BRe driving car only - ?	NPG	NPG

BR Blue

8136	**M50330+M50303** BRe 2-car - 82-00	50	65
8146	**M50330+M59130+M50303** BRe 3-car - 82-00	55	70
?	**M50330+M59130+M50303** BRe 3-car non-powered - ?	40	50
8156	BRe driving car only - 85-00	35	50

BR White+Blue

8137	**E56063+E50202** BRe 2-car - 82-88	50	65
8147	**E56063+E59070+E50202** BRe 3-car - 82-88	55	70
8157	BRe driving car only - 85-00	35	50

Regional Liveries

8148	**L832** (51226+59570+51499) NSE bright blue 3-car - 91-00	55	70
814A	**101304**(51224+59090+53241) Strathclyde PTE orange Ltd Edn 500 (red label) - 92	60	75
8131	**101653**(54358+51426) Regional Railways blue+white 2-car - 91-00	50	65
?	**101653**(54358+51426) Regional Railways blue+white 2-car non-powered - 92-00	50	65

L43b. Class 101 DMC Driving Car (non-powered) (1985)

These are non-powered driving motor cars (DMC) for those who wanted to make up a train of two or more units joined together. They are provided to go with the DTCs in the table below.

0923	**BR** green - 85-?	10	14
0925	**BR** blue+grey - 85-?	10	14
0926	**BR** blue - 85-?	10	14
0927	**BR** white+blue - 85-?	10	14

L43c. Class 101 DTC Driving Car (non-powered) (1985)

These are non-powered driving trailer cars (DTC) for those who wanted to make up a train of two or more units joined together. They are provided to go with the DMCs in the table above.

0903	**BR** ? green - 85-?	10	14
0905	**BR** ? blue+grey - 85-?	10	14
0906	**BR** ? blue - 85-?	10	14
0907	**BR** ? white+blue - 85-?	10	14

L44. Class 158 DMU (1992)

In the late 1980s, British Railway's Provincial Sector needed a large fleet of DMUs for the outer suburban and cross-country trains. The competitive tender was won by BREL who built both 2-car and 3-car formations at BR Derby. In all, 182 sets were built, comprising 381 vehicles and the first were ready for service in 1992. Many variations exist and, since privatisation, the fleet has been owned by Porterbrook and Angel Trains and leased to several TOCs. Rebuilds and refurbishments have also taken place.

8707	**158865** (52860+57860) Regional Railways blue+white - 92-00	55	70

Graham Farish N

0887	as above non-powered - *92-00*	55	70
8707	**158860 (52865+57865)** Regional Railways blue+ white - *92-00*	55	70
8707	as above non-powered - *92-00*	55	70
?	Thai Rail blue+white (export only) - *92-00*	70	100

L45. Class 159 DMU (1994)

Network SouthEast ordered 22 3-car sets in the style of the Class 158, which were then coming into use. Derby started building the Class 159s. After leaving Derby, the units were sent up to Babcock Rail at Rosyth Dockyard where they were rebuilt internally to NSE requirements. The result was some excellent DMUs. They were built in 1992 and 1993 and were finished in NSE livery.

8748	**159007 (52879+58724+57879)** NSE bright blue 3-car - *94-00*	55	70

COACHES

The first coaches were 4-wheeled ones, like those initially released in 1949 for the old 00 gauge system. The first announcement of bogie coaches came early in 1972 and by the end of the year, the full range was available in painted and tampo printed finish as the 'Superstock' range.

The GF Mk1s were originally produced with the windows on a printed strip inserted into the body-side and this allowed virtually any type to be modelled. At some point in the 1980s, they were revised to feature a totally clear body shell with the entire livery printed on.

Cat No.	Company, Number, Colour, Date	£	£

Pre-Grouping Coaches

C1a. 4-Wheeled Coach (Freelance) (1971)
These appear to have been based on a Great Northern Railway design.

NR50T2	light brown 2nd - *71-72*	5	9
NR50T3	light brown 3rd - *71-72*	5	9
NR50M2	maroon 2nd - *71-73*	5	9
NR50M3	maroon 3rd - *71-73*	5	9
NR50G2	green 2nd - *71-73*	5	9

Freelance 4-wheel coach in S&DJR livery [C1a]

NR50G3	green 3rd - *71-73*	5	9
NR50B2	brown 2nd - *71-73*	5	9
NR50B3	brown 3rd - *71-73*	5	9
NR50/3	teak 3rd - *72-73*	5	9
668	**CR** maroon+white 3rd - *81-88*	10	12
667	**S&DJR** 18 dark blue 3rd - *81-88*	10	12
NR66W	**GWR** dark brown+cream 3rd - *78*	7	9
664	**GWR** dark brown+cream 3rd - *78-88*	7	9
NR66M	**LMS** maroon 3rd - *78*	7	9
661	**LMS** maroon 3rd - *78-88*	7	9
NR66N	**LNER** 3567 teak 3rd - *78*	7	9
662	**LNER** 3567 teak 3rd - *78-88*	7	9
NR66S	**SR** 5303 green 3rd - *78*	7	9
663	**SR** 5303 green 3rd - *78-88*	7	9
-	**The Shredded Wheat Co** yellow 3rd * - *89*	5	8
-	**Poole No1** dk.blue, yellow stripe ex set 8350 * - *94-99*	7	9

* These coaches were specially made for train sets (8350) and had a new chassis with non-universal couplings consisting of a hook one end and an oval loop the other. The couplings on the Shredded Wheat coaches had a small circular loop.

C1b. 4-Wheeled Brake (Freelance) (1971)
These appear to have been based on a Great Northern Railway design.

NR51T	light brown - *71-73*	5	9
NR51M	maroon - *71-73*	5	9
NR51G	green - *71-73*	5	9
NR51B	brown - *71-73*	5	9
NR51/1	teak - *72-73*	5	9
678	**CR** dk.red+white - *81-88*	10	12
677	**S&DJR** 14 dark blue - *81-88*	10	12
NR67W	**GWR** 253 dark brown+cream - *78*	7	9
674	**GWR** 253 dark brown+cream - *78-88*	7	9
NR67M	**LMS** 376 maroon - *78*	7	9
671	**LMS** 376 maroon - *78-88*	7	9
NR67N	**LNER** 7894 teak - *78*	7	9
672	**LNER** 7894 teak - *78-88*	7	9
NR67S	**SR** 3725 green - *78*	7	9
673	**SR** 3725 green - *78-88*	7	9
-	**The Shredded Wheat Co** * yellow - *89*	5	8

* These coaches were specially made for train sets and had a new chassis with non-universal couplings consisting of a hook one end and a loop the other.

'Suburban' Coaches

C2a. 57' 'Suburban' Composite (Freelance) (1972)
While popularly called 'Suburban' coaches they were found in many places besides the suburbs. They were used in frequently stopping trains where it was not necessary to have toilets on board and so no side corridor or gangway between coaches. They were divided up into compartments, some of which would be reserved for 1st class passengers.

608	**CR** maroon+white panelled - *81-?*	9	12
NR60W	**GWR** 7053 dark brown+cream - *72-78*	6	8
604	**GWR** 273, 7053 dark brown+cream - *78-80*	6	8
604	**GWR** 269, 270 dark brown+cream lined - *79-00*	6	8
NR60M	**LMS** 7094 maroon - *72-78*	6	8
601	**LMS** 7094 maroon - *78-79*	6	8
606	**LMS** 16093 maroon panelled - *82-00*	6	8
NR60N	**LNER** 52347 teak - *76-78*	6	8
602	**LNER** 52347 teak - *78-00*	6	8
NR60S	**SR** 7253 green - *72-78*	6	8
603	**SR** 7253 green - *78-00*	6	8
NR60BR	**BR** M6743 red - *78*	6	8
605	**BR** M6743 red - *78-00*	6	8

C2b. 57' 'Suburban' Brake 3rd (Freelance) (1972)
This would have been similar to the composite coach above but with 6 third class compartments and a guard's and luggage section at one end.

618	**CR** maroon+white panelled - *81-?*	9	12
NR61W	**GWR** 7294 dark brown+cream - *72-78*	6	8
614	**GWR** 7294 dark brown+cream - *78-80*	6	8
614	**GWR** 849, 854 dark brown+cream lined - *79-00*	6	8
NR61M	**LMS** 3762 maroon - *72-78*	6	8
611	**LMS** 3762 maroon - *78-79?*	6	8
616	**LMS** 20354 red panelled - *82-00*	6	8
NR61N	**LNER** 34789 teak - *76-78*	6	8
612	**LNER** 34789 teak - *78-00*	6	8
NR61S	**SR** 2597 green - *72-78*	6	8
613	**SR** 2597 green - *78-00*	6	8
NR61S	**SR** 2697 green - *72-78*	6	8
NR61BR	**BR** M2570 red - *78*	6	8
615	**BR** M2570 red - *78-00*	6	8

SR 'Surburban' brake 3rd [C2b]

Main Line Coaches

C3a. 57' Main Line Composite (Freelance) (1972)
Like the 'suburban' coaches above, Graham Farish designed these to not appear to be based on those of any one company or region, but to look right in any one of a number of liveries.

NR62W	**GWR** 2387? dark brown+cream - *made?*	NPG	NPG
NR62W	**GWR** 9003 dark brown+cream unlined - *72-78*	6	8
624	**GWR** 2387? dark brown+cream - *78-80*	6	8

Graham Farish N

624	GWR 709 dark brown+cream lined - *79-00*	6	8
NR62M	LMS 9485 maroon - *72-78*	6	8
621	LMS 9485 maroon - *78-81*	6	8
626	LMS 6143? maroon panelled - *82-00*	6	8
NR62N	LNER 75674 teak - *76-78*	6	8
622	LNER 75674 teak - *78-00*	6	8
NR62S	SR 1707? green - *72-78*	6	8
623	SR 1707? green - *78-00*	6	8
NR62BR	BR M5801 red+cream - *76-78*	6	8
625	BR M5801 red+cream - *78-80*	6	8

C3b. 57' Main Line Brake 3rd (Freelance) (1972)

Again, here were have a freelance brake coach which will look right in various liveries.

NR63W	GWR 2778? dark brown+cream - *made?*	NPG	NPG
NR63W	GWR 7094 dark brown+cream unlined - *72-78*	6	8
634	GWR 2778? dark brown+cream - *78-79*	6	8
634	GWR 276 dark brown+cream lined - *79-00*	6	8
NR63M	LMS 9854 maroon - *72-78*	6	8
631	LMS 9854 maroon - *78-81*	6	8
636	LMS 6587 maroon panelled - *82-00*	6	8
NR63N	LNER 45623 teak - *76-78*	6	8
632	LNER 45623 teak - *78-00*	6	8
NR63S	SR 2763 green - *72-78*	6	8
633	SR 2763 green - *78-00*	6	8
NR63BR	BR M5911 red+cream - *76-78*	6	8
635	BR M5911 red+cream - *78-80*	6	8

Pullman Cars

C4a. Pullman 1st Parlour Car (1977)

These were based on Pullman Cars with matchboard sides and were supplied with a choice of transfers for naming them. A version in the blue of Compagnie Internationale des Wagons Lits et des Grands Express Europeens was released in 1980.

NR64	Pullman brown+cream unnamed - *77-78*	7	9
646	Pullman brown+cream unnamed - *78-00*	7	9
646	Pullman Coral brown+cream - *99?*	7	9
646	Pullman Barbara brown+cream- *99-00*	7	9
646	Pullman Agatha brown+cream ex-set - *99*	7	NA
0647	Wagon Lits blue - *80*	50	70

C4b. Pullman 3rd Brake (1977)

Like the model in the table above, this Pullman brake car had matchboard sides and was in Umber and cream livery. It was also supplied with a choice of transfers for names.

Pullman brake coach [C4b]

NR65	Pullman brown+cream unnamed - *77-78*	7	9
656	Pullman brown+cream unnamed - *78-00*	7	9
656	Pullman Irene brown+cream - *99-00*	7	9
656	Pullman Fortune brown+cream ex-set - *99*	7	NA
0657	Wagon Lits blue (labelled 'baggage') - *80*	30	50

BR Mk1 Coaches

C5a. BR Mk1 Corridor 2nd (SK) (1981)

More of these 3rd class corridor coaches were produced than any other design in the history of Britain's railways. The first lot was built in 1952 at Eastleigh and the last in 1963 at the BR coach works at York. The coach had doors both sides at each end and in the centre and the centre vestibule split the compartments into two groups of four. With armrests raised out of the way, 64 passengers could be accommodated. There were two lavatories, one positioned either side of the corridor at one end of the coach.

068B	BR W25238 red+cream - *99-00*	6	8
068C	BR M25168 red+cream Sp Edn - *99-00*	6	8
686	BR W24335, W24753 maroon+cream - *82-00*	6	8
683	BR S24316 green - *81-00*	6	8
068A	BR S24319 green Sp Edn - *99-00*	6	8
684	BR W24167 dark brown+cream - *81-00*	6	8
681	BR M24583, M24824, M25250 maroon - *81-00*	6	8
685	BR E24772 blue+grey - *81-00*	6	8

BR Mk1 all 3rd coach in early livery [C5a]

C5b. BR Mk1 Brake End (BCK) (1981)

The earliest batch came from Derby in 1954 and the final lot, also from Derby, in 1963. There were five compartments, each with six seats with adjustable armrests. Three of the compartments were for 3rd class and two were 1st class. The corridor had a dividing door between them. There was a lavatory and vestibule, with external doors, at either end of the passenger section of the coach. Only a little over a quarter of the coach was left for the guard's compartment and luggage space.

696	BR W24753 red+cream - *made?*	NPG	NPG
069A	BR M21237 red+cream Sp Edn - *99-00*	6	9
069C	BR M25238 red+cream Sp Edn - *99-00*	6	9
696	BR W21021 maroon+cream - *82-00*	6	9
693	BR S21179 green - *81-00*	6	9
694	BR W21023, W21072 dark brown+cream - *81-00*	6	9
691	BR M21033, M21236 maroon - *81-00*	6	9
695	BR E21008 blue+grey - *81-00*	6	9

C5c. BR Mk1 Buffet (RMB) (1983)

A total of 82 of these were built at York and Wolverton between 1957 and 1962. They were provided for shorter distance and cross country routes and had a small buffet counter offering light snacks and drinks. The first 12 vehicles had 48 seats but these were reduced to 44 to allow for additional stock storage. Most had been withdrawn by the time of privatisation. Three survived in service with Anglia Railways until the last was withdrawn in 2001 and many have been preserved.

753	BR S1873, S1849 green - *83-00*	6	9
753	BR W1822 green - *83-00*	6	9
754	BR W1822 dark brown+cream - *83-00*	6	9
751	BR M1825 M1859 maroon - *83-00*	6	9
755	BR E1834 blue+grey - *83-00*	6	9

C6. BR Mk1 Full Brake (BG) (1984)

The full brake had a guard's compartment in the centre and two large areas either side of it for storing luggage. There were four pairs of doors in each side as well as a single door in the centre of each side for the guard. Eight lots of them were built, the first batch at Derby in 1953 and the last lot were built in 1961, by Gloucester Railway Carriage & Wagon Ltd.

775	BR W80657 red+cream - *84-00*	7	9
775	BR W80657 maroon+cream - *84-00*	7	9
773	BR S81542, S81292 green - *84-00*	7	9
771	BR M80723 maroon - *84-00*	7	9
776	BR E81125 blue+grey - *made?*	NPG	NPG
776	BR E81231 blue+grey - *84-00*	7	9
778	BR Express Parcels E81125 blue+grey - *84-00*	7	9
777	BR Newspapers packing van NCV M80826, M80650, E81231 blue - *84-00*	7	9
774	BR I-C Exec 92046, 92075 grey - *88-00*	7	9
772	BR ScotRail 92047, 92086 grey (blue stripe) - *88-00*	7	9
787	Post Office Parcels 92212, 92233 red NEX - *91-00*	7	9

C7. BR Mk1 57ft GUV (1991)

General utility vans have been used for transporting mail and parcels. Several batches were built, the earliest at Doncaster in 1956 and the last ones in 1959 by Pressed Steel Ltd. Built without gangway connections, they had two large end doors and a bottom flap that rested on the buffers when open and thus allowed end-loading with motor vehicles. Some of the GUVs received 'Motorail' branding.

4101	BR M86105 maroon - *93-00*	7	9
4105	BR 93356 blue NKV - *91-00*	7	9
4106	BR RES 93999 red+black NQX - *91-00*	7	9
4107	Post Office 93263 red NJX - *91-00*	7	9

C8. Post Office Sorting (POS) (1991)

This was used in a Travelling Post Office (TPO) and, during the journey, Royal Mail staff sort the mail ready for dropping off at points along the route. 96 of these vehicles were built by British Rail in small batches between 1959 and 1977, all to similar designs and based on the Mk1 coach.

797	Post Office 80387 NSX red - *91-00*	7	9

Graham Farish N

BR Mk2 Coaches

C9a. BR Mk2E 2nd Open (TSO) (1984)
These Mk2 coaches had rounded ends and were of semi-integral construction. The Mk2E design, like that for the Mk2D, was air conditioned and so there were no opening top lights to the windows and the latter were longer and shallower in height than those of the early Mk2 coaches. The Mk2E can be recognised externally by fawn coloured end gangway doors. The 2nd class vehicles had 64 second class seats and 2 toilets.

805	BR I-C M5775 blue+grey - *made?*	NPG	NPG
805	BR I-C M5776 blue+grey - *84-00*	7	9
806	BR I-C 5749 executive grey - *88-89*	9	11
807	BR ICs 5628 executive grey - *90-00*	7	9
807	BR ICs 5756 executive grey - *90-00*	7	9
FA0806	BR ICs 5749 executive grey - *00*	9	12
801	BR ScotRail 5653, 5662 grey (blue stripe) - *88-00*	7	9
808	BR NSE 5523, 5525 bright blue - *88-00*	7	9
802	BRe Reg Rlys 5505, blue+white - *96-00*	9	12
802	BRe Reg Rlys, 5520 blue+white - *made?*	NPG	NPG
804	Virgin 5903 red - *99-00*	9	12

C9b. BR Mk2D 1st Open (FO) (1984)
These were very much like the coach in the above table but had 42 1st class seats and 2 toilets. They were built at BR Derby in 1971-72.

815	BR I-C M3199 blue+grey - *84-00*	10	12
816	BR I-C executive 3191, 3202 grey - *88-89*	8	10
817	BR ICs 3177 grey - *90-00*	10	12
811	BR ScotRail 3248 , 3265 grey (blue stripe) - *88-00*	10	12
818	BR NSE 13443, 13514, 13525 blue - *88-00*	10	12
818	BR NSE 5523 (error) blue - *?*	12	15
818	BR NSE 5525 (error) blue - *?*	12	15
812	BRe Regional Railways blue+white - *not made*	NA	NA
814	Virgin 3278 red - *99-00*	9	12

C9c. BR Mk2F Brake 2nd Open (BSO) (1999)
The running number on this model belonged to a Mk2F BSO which was basically the same in construction as those in the last two tables but half the coach was taken up with a guard's and luggage compartment. The rest of the space contained 32 2nd class seats and one toilet. It was built in 1974 at Derby.

080A	Virgin 9521 red Sp Edn - *99*	9	12

C9d. BR Mk2F Buffet 1st Open (RFB) (1999)
This running number on this model belonged to a Mk2F RFB which is basically the same as those in the last three tables but built as a catering coach. It had a pantry and serving area taking up about 40% of the coach and the rest contained 26 1st class seats at tables and a toilet. It started life as an FO, built at Derby, but was converted sometime from 1988 to an RFB. It was scrapped in 2002.

081A	Virgin 1200 red - *99*	8	10

BR Mk3 Coaches

C10a. BR Mk3 Open Trailer Second (TS) (1981)
Early running numbers suggest that this is a model based on a Mk3 High Speed Train Open Standard car of the type built by BR Derby Carriage and Wagon Works between 1976 and 1985.

705	BR I-C W42023, W42263 blue+grey - *81-00*	6	8
706	BR I-C W42023 grey - *83-89*	6	8
706	BR ICs 42253 grey - *83-89*	6	8
707	BR ICs 42219 grey - *90-00*	6	8
701	BR ScotRail 12023, 12026 grey (blue stripe) - *88-00*	6	8
-	Virgin 42108 red ex-pack - *99-00*	8	NA
708	Virgin 42109 red - *99-00*	8	10
070A	GWT 42079 [b] green+ivory Sp Edn - *00*	8	10
070A	GWT 42079 [c] green+ivory Sp Edn - *99*	8	10
702	GWT 42080 [b] green+ivory - *99-00*	8	10

C10b. BR Mk3 Open Trailer First (TF) (1981)
The model was based on a High Speed Train Open First car of a type being built between 1976 and 1982 by BR Derby Carriage and Wagon Works.

725	BR I-C W41015, W41128 blue+grey - *81-00*	6	8
726	BR I-C W41015, 41121 grey - *83-89*	6	8
726	BR I-C W41025 grey - *89-90*	6	8
727	BR ICs 41108 grey - *90-00*	6	8
728	Virgin 41165 red - *99-00*	8	10
070A	GWT 41007 [h] green - *made?*	NPG	NPG
722	GWT 41007 green - *99-00*	8	10

C10c. BR Mk3 Trailer Guard 2nd (TGS) (1990)
This was HST stock with a guard's compartment in one end of a standard class coach.

767	BR IC 44079 grey+black - *90-00*	6	8
768	Virgin 44076 red - *made?*	NPG	NPG
768	Virgin 44087 red - *99-00*	8	10

C10d. BR Mk3 Trailer Buffet Unclassified (TRUB) (1982)
This model was based on an HST Trailer Buffet Unclassified which was built at Derby during 1978-79.

745	BR I-C W40301, W40325 blue+grey - *82-00*	6	8
746	BR I-C W40301 executive grey - *83-90*	6	8
FA0746	BR I-C W40301 executive grey - *00*	6	8

C10e. BR Mk3 Restaurant Buffet 1st (TRFB) (1990)
This was based on an HST Restaurant Buffet First which was converted from a Trailer Buffet Unclassified (TRUB) in 1985-86.

747	BR ICs 40715 grey+black - *90-00*	6	8

C10f. BR Mk3 Trailer Buffet Standard (TRSB) (1999)
This model was based on an HST Trailer Buffet Standard which was built at Derby in 1976-77. This coach would later be converted to an HST TRBF in 2007.

748	Virgin 40401 red - *99-00*	8	10

C10g. BR Mk3A Sleeper with Pantry (SLEP) (1982)
This model was based on a Sleeper with Pantry which was built at Derby in 1981-83. It later became a departmental staff coach numbered 977989.

765	BR I-C 10536 blue+grey - *82-99*	7	9

BR Mk4 Coaches

GNER Mk4 1st class coach [C11a]

C11a. BR Mk 4 Open First (FO) (1990)
The coach which carries this running number was a Mk4 Open First which was built by Metropolitan-Cammell in Birmingham sometime between 1989 and 1992. It was later converted to an Open First (FO) and renumbered 11412.

827	BR ICs 11209 grey - *90-00*	7	9

C11b. BR Mk 4 Tourist Second Open (TSO) (1990)
This model was based on a Mk4 Open Standard which was built by Metropolitan-Cammell sometime between 1989 and 1992.

837	BR ICs 12406 grey - *90-00*	7	9

C11c. BR Mk 4 Standard Open End (TSEO) (1990)
This number belonged to a Mk4 Open Standard which was built by Metroplitan-Cammell in 1989-91.

857	BR ICs 12203 grey - *90-00*	7	9

C11d. BR Mk 4 Restaurant/Buffet (RFM) (1990)
This model was based on a Mk4 Restaurant First which was built by Metropolitan-Cammell in 1989-91.

847	BR ICs 10300 grey+black - *90-00*	7	9

C12. BR Mk4 Driving Van Trailer (DVT) (1991)
This number was carried by a Mk4 Driving Van Trailer which was built by Metropolitan-Cammell in Birmingham in 1988.

867	BR ICs 82204 grey+black - *91-00*	9	12

Trailer Cars

C13. BR Class 101 Centre Car (TCL) (1985)
The model was based on a Class 101 Trailer Composite Lavatory which was built by Metropolitan-Cammell and contained 12 1st class seats in a separate compartment and 53 second class ones in an open saloon.

0913	BR W59122 green - *85-?*	10	14
0915	BR blue+grey - *85-?*	10	14
0916	BR blue - *85-?*	10	14
0917	BR white+blue - *85-?*	10	14
0918	BR NSE bright blue - *88-?*	10	14

Graham Farish N

WAGONS

The wagons first started to appear at the end of September 1970 and were then added to month by month. Initially, these were non-printed, but a sheet of rub-on transfers, sufficient for 32 wagons, was also available in black or white. From the start, the wagon chassis was also available on its own. It was not long before wagons were leaving the factory in a range of colourful private owner liveries, thanks to the introduction of silicone pad printing. Some of the private owner wagons were initially released only in mixed sets of three but some of these were later available individually.

All wagons with a number prefixed by 'NR' have been found to have blackened wheels and an all plastic coupling. Wagons with a four digit number have all bright metal wheels and sprung couplings.

Like the early coaches produced by Graham Farish, most of their wagons were a little crude by today's standard and they represented a wagon type rather than a specific design. This makes it hard to suggest a prototype for them.

Cat No.	Company, Number, Colour, Date	£	£
W1.	**Double Bolster Wagon (1970)**		

This wagon was illustrated in the first sales leaflet where it was shown with a short wheelbase and two bolsters with pins. The body was brown. It was not shown in later catalogues and may not have been made.

Cat No.	Company, Number, Colour, Date	£	£
NR4	non-printed (transfers) red brown - *not made*	NA	NA
W2.	**Long Flat and Container (1988)**		

This was a long wheelbase flat wagon with a long container which looks as though it is meant to represent a 30ft one. It is probably a freelance design.

Cat No.	Company, Number, Colour, Date	£	£
4005	'OOCL' container - *88-?*	4	6
4005	'Dart' container - *88-?*	4	6
4005	'CP Ships' container - *88-?*	4	6
4005	'Merzario' container - *88-?*	4	6
W3.	**Container (1970)**		

A BD size container was illustrated in the original promotional leaflet and was to be sold with a sheet of transfers. However, the model did not appear after that and it seems unlikely it was made.

Cat No.	Company, Number, Colour, Date	£	£
NR2	non-printed (transfers) brown - *not made*	NA	NA
NR2	non-printed (transfers) grey - *not made*	NA	NA
W4.	**3-plank Wagon (1970)**		

The 3-plank open wagon was shown in the original promotional leaflet but was dropped from other publications. This suggests that it did not reach the production stage.

Cat No.	Company, Number, Colour, Date	£	£
NR17	non-printed (transfers) light grey - *not made*	NA	NA
NR17	non-printed (transfers) maroon - *not made*	NA	NA
W5.	**5-plank wagon (1970)**		

These open wagons were originally sold with no printed detail, but a sheet of black or white transfers was available for the purchaser to provide their own markings. This idea was soon abandoned when a pad-printing machine was installed.

ex3 = from a 3 wagon set

Cat No.	Company, Number, Colour, Date	£	£
NG8	non-printed (transfers) grey - *70-72*	3	5
NG6	non-printed (transfers) brown - *70-72*	3	5
NG6	non-printed (transfers) grey - *70-72*	3	5
NG9	non-printed (transfers) red-brown - *70-72*	3	5
NG10	non-printed (transfers) brown - *70-72*	3	5
NR21/11	'Pitt' 2 grey ex3 - *73-78*	3	NA
2011	'Pitt' 2 grey - *78-00*	3	NA
NR23/1	'Spiers' 513 yellow ex3 - *78*	3	NA
2012	'Spiers' 513 yellow - *78-00*	3	NA
NR21/10	'Snow' black+red ex3 - *78*	3	NA
2013	'Snow' black+red - *78-00*	3	NA
2004	GW 15074 dark grey - *78-00*	3	5
NR20M	LMS 166187 light grey - *72-78*	3	5
2001	LMS 166187 light grey - *78-00*	3	5
NR20M	LMS 165417 light grey - *72-78*	3	5
2001	LMS 165417 light grey - *78-00*	3	5
NR20N	NE 600047 red-brown - *72-78*	3	5
2002	NE 600047 red-brown - *78-00*	3	5
NR20S	SR 5087 dark brown - *72-78*	3	5
2003	SR 5087 dark brown - *78-00*	3	5
2005	BR B475908 dark grey - *87-?*	3	NA
W6.	**Sheet Rail Wagon (1970)**		

This was in the original sales leaflet but not seen after that, which suggests that it was not made. It was to have been issued with a tarpaulin, which would be available in several colours. The tarpaulin also disappeared from following publications.

Cat No.	Company, Number, Colour, Date	£	£
NR9	non-printed (transfers) red-brown - *not made*	NA	NA
W7.	**6-plank wagon (1970)**		

This model was released instead of a 7-plank wagon and was clearly meant to be the coal wagon in the range. These models were originally sold with no printed detail, but a sheet of black or white transfers was available for the purchaser to provide their own markings. However, this idea was dropped when a pad-printing machine was installed.

ex3 = from a 3 wagon set.

Cat No.	Company, Number, Colour, Date	£	£
NR7	non-printed (transfers) brown - *70-72*	3	5
NR7	non-printed (transfers) grey - *70-72*	3	5
NG11	non-printed (transfers) grey - *70-72*	3	5
NG12	non-printed (transfers) red-brown - *70-72*	3	5
NG13	non-printed (transfers) brown - *70-72*	3	5
2128	'Alloa' yellow - *86-?*	3	5
2141	'Barrow Barnsley' 720 cream - *?*	3	5
-	'British Railway Modelling' 2000 - *00-01*	3	5
NR21/3	'Bullcroft' 9471 red * - *75-78*	3	5
2113	'Bullcroft' 9471 red - *78-00*	3	5
NR21/10	'Cam Rys' grey ex3 - *75-78*	3	NA
2120	'Cam Rys' grey - *78-?*	3	NA
2137	'Carlton Main' 5014 red - *99-00*	3	5
2145	'Coalite' 1545 black - *01*	6	10
2132	'Courtaulds' 19 green - *86-?*	3	5
2147	'Dinnington Main' blue - *99-00*	3	5
NR21/10	'Dombey' No.77 green ex3 - *75-78*	3	NA
2121	'Dombey' No.77 green - *78-?*	3	NA
NR21/9	'Dutton Massey' 313 dark grey ex3 - *75-78*	3	NA
2119	'Dutton Massey' 313 dark grey - *78-?*	3	NA
NR21/12	'Earl of Rosslyns' No.353 brown ex3 - *78*	3	5
2127	'Earl of Rosslyns' No.353 brown - *78-?*	3	5
2129	'Ebbw Vale' 6158 black - *86-?*	3	5
2114	'Ellis' - *not released*	NA	NA
NR21/5	'Frost' 31 black * - *75-78*	3	5
2111	'Frost' 31 black - *78-?*	3	5
2138	'Fulton' 795 black - *99-00*	3	5
2131	'General Refractories' 97 yellow - *86-01*	3	5
2139	'Geo. Mills' 15 black - *99-00*	3	5
2140	'Gray Brothers' 52 caramel - *?*	3	5
(7501)	'JK Harrison' 134 red ex-train set - *?*	3	NA
?	'Wm Harrison' 2227 grey - *?*	3	5
2130	'Harrods' 64 brown - *86-?*	3	5
2149	'Ilkeston & Heanor Water Board' 17 blue - *99-00*	3	5
NR21/9	'Lebon' 328 white ex3 - *75-78*	3	NA
2118	'Lebon' 328 white - *78-?*	3	NA
NR23/2	'Ocean' 918 black ex3 - *78*	3	NA
2124	'Ocean' 918 black - *78-00*	3	NA
NR21/12	'Ormiston' 34 navy blue ex3 - *78*	3	NA
2125	'Ormiston' 34 navy blue - *78-?*	3	NA
NR21/2	'Parker & Probert' 80 brown * - *75-78*	3	5
2117	'Parker & Probert' 80 brown - *78-00*	3	5
NR21/11	'Powell Gwinnell' black ex3 - *75-78*	3	NA
2123	'Powell Gwinnell' black - *78-?*	3	NA
2133	'Prince of Wales' 1857 light grey - *?*	3	5
2134	'Princess Royal' 4608 red-brown - *?*	3	5
NR21/4	'Pritchard' 26 black * - *75-78*	3	5
2112	'Pritchard' 26 black - *78-00*	3	5
2146	'Renishaw' 917 brown - *99-00*	3	5

5-plank private owner wagon Snow & Sons [W5] (KJB Models)

Graham Farish N

6-plank private owner wagon S.C. Pritchard & Co. [W7] (KJB Models)

2136	'Richard Thomas' 6871 black - 99-00	3	5
NR21/11	'Sleight' 79 grey ex3 - 75-78	3	NA
2122	'Sleight' 79 grey - 78-?	3	NA
NR21/6	'South Leicester' 373 red brown * - 75-78	3	5
2115	'South Leicester' 373 red brown - 78-?	3	5
NR21/12	'Staveley' black ex3 - 78	3	NA
2126	'Staveley' black - 78-?	3	NA
NR21/1	'JRWood' 1410 yellow * - 75-78	3	5
2116	'JRWood' 1410 yellow - 78-00	3	5
NR21W	GW 102784 dark grey - 72-78	3	5
2104	GW 102784 dark grey - 78-00	3	5
NR21M	LMS 313154 red-brown - 72-78	3	5
2101	LMS 313154 red-brown - 78-00	3	5
NR21N	NE 131457 red-brown - 72-78	3	5
2102	NE 131457 red-brown - 78-00	3	5
NR21S	SR 5079 dark brown - 72-78	3	5
2103	SR 5079 dark brown - 78-00	3	5
2105	BR B785911 brown - 87-?	3	5

* These wagons were also to be found in triple sets.

W8. OAA/OBA Long Open Wagon (1988)

By 1967, British Rail's wagon fleet had fallen in size to about a third of that which it had inherited in 1948. British Rail launched a programme of vigorous marketing in the 1970s and backed this up with a fleet of new air-braked wagons for better bulk handling. For merchandise, BR introduced long wheelbase open wagons and vans with 45 tonnes loading capacity.

3806	BRe 100054 brown Open AB - 88-?	6	8
3805	BR Railfreight 100033 grey+red OAA - 88-?	6	8
3807	EWS 200831 maroon OAB - 98-?	6	8

W9. Steel Mineral Wagon (1970)

An all-welded version was modelled, with doors at sides and ends but no 'London Trader's' flaps. The model had the representation of pressed steel doors.

NR8	non-printed (transfers) light grey - 70-71	3	5
NR8	non-printed (transfers) red-brown - 70-71	3	5
2211	'SC' 07217 dark grey - 79-?	3	5
NR22W	GW 110134 dark grey - 72-78	3	5
2204	GW 110134 dark grey - 78-00	3	5
NR22M	LMS 616014 red-brown - 72-78	3	5
2201	LMS 616014 red-brown - 78-00	3	5
2205	BR B565010 dark grey MCO - 88-?	3	5

W10. Open Hopper Wagons (from 'Presflo') (1982)

This was the lower half of a 'Presflo' wagon.

3411	'BISC' 395 very dark grey - 82-00	3	5
3412	'NCB' 57 dark grey - 82-00	3	5
3413	'Sheepbridge' light brown - 82-00	3	5
3414	'Tarmac' 91 fawn - 82-00	3	5

W11. PGA Aggregate Hopper Wagon (1993)

These small hopper wagons were owned or leased and used by quarry owning companies who were producing limestone and other aggregates.

4411	'ARC' ARC14284 sand - 93-?	5	7
4413	'ECC Quarries' PR14368 blue - 99-00	5	7
4414	'Tilbury' TRL14612 white+brown - 99-00	5	7
4412	'Yeoman' PR14435 grey+blue - 93-?	5	7

PGA aggregate hopper wagon Yeoman [W11]

W12. PGA 38T Covered Hopper Wagon (1993)

These used the body of the PGA in the above table but with the end steps and gantries removed and a top moulding fitted to enclose the hopper. This top moulding also provided end stanchions.

4511	'British Industrial Sand' BIS7842 white PAA – 93-?	5	7
4512	'Tullis Russell' BS7842 blue - not made	NA	NA
4512	'Tullis Russell' TRL12806 blue - 93-?	5	7

W13. MEA, HEA, HSA (2001)

The components for this wagon were made in Poole, but assembled by Bachmann staff at Barwell, following the end of production at the Holton Heath factory on 23 December 2000.

373-502	BR 360075 brown HSA - 01*	NPG	7
373-501	Railfreight Coal 360601 grey+yellow - 01	NPG	7
373-500	EWS 361328 maroon - 01	NPG	7

* Later models from China with this number had different layout of data panels.

W14. CPV 'Presflo' Bulk Powder Wagon (1982)

Dating from 1953, many batches were made for BR between 1955 and 1964 for cement traffic. Some 'Presflos' were later modified for salt traffic and later still for slate powder traffic and eventually they carried fly-ash. Both Associated Portland Cement and Tunnel Cement ordered their own wagons based on the BR design. The 'Presflos' were replaced from 1984 onwards and all had gone by 1991.

3511	'ARC' AR12649 yellow - 82-00	4	6
3512	'Blue Circle Cement' yellow - 82-00	4	6
3513	'Cerebos Salt' red - 82-00	4	6
3514	'Tunnel Bulk Cement' grey - 82-00	4	6
3505	BR brown CSA - 88-?	4	6

W15. PCA 'V Tanker' Bulk Powder Wagon (1993)

This was a cylindrical tank which looked as though it had been cut in half, sunk in the middle and joined together again in that position. They were used in large numbers in the cement industry until replaced by another design. The contents were released under pressure.

4311	'Albright & Wilson' PR10133 blue - 93-00	5	7
4315	'Ketton Cement' PR9466 yellow - 99-00	5	7
4314	'Lever Bros.' TRL10527 purple - 99-00	5	7
4312	'Tiger' TRL9473 yellow - 93-00	5	7
4313	BR 9150 grey - not made	NA	NA
4313	BR 9226 grey - 99-00	5	7
4313	BR APCM9150 grey - 99-00	5	7

W16. PCA 'Presflo' Bulk Powder Wagon (1993)

PCA 'Presflo' bulk powder wagon Castle Cement [W16] (KJB Models)

Graham Farish N

This was a type of 'Presflo' being built between 1975 and 1983 by Standard Wagon and Procor. The odd one out in this bunch was the ICI Mond wagon which was built by Procor as a soda ash bulk powder wagon in the mid-1970s.

4213	'Castle Cement ' RLS10319 grey - 99-00	5	7
4212	'Cerestar' PR10017 white - 93-00	5	7
4214	'ICI' Mond PR10120 white soda ash - 99-00	5	7
4211	'Rugby Cement 'PR10041 grey - 93-00	5	7

W17. Tar Wagon (1970)

These square cornered, flat tank tar wagons were originally sold with no printed detail, but a sheet of black or white transfers was available for the purchaser to provide his own markings.

NR15	non-printed (transfers) black - 70	NPG	NPG
2811	'Burnden' black - 81-?	4	6
2814	'Esso' black - 81-?	4	6
2812	'R S Clare' 19 black - 81-?	4	6
2813	'Shell BP' black - 81-00	4	6

W18. Sand, Salt & Lime Wagon (1980)

This is a single model that was used for both the taller salt wagon and the shorter lime wagon, which is why they are listed in the same table. It was effectively a 5-plank wagon with a two-way pitched roof added as an extra moulding.

?	'Dunlow Lime' brown - 80-?	4	6
2913	'Dunlow Lime' black? - 81-?	4	6
2911	NE Sand grey - 81-?	4	6
2912	'Saxa Salt' yellow - 81-?	4	6
2914	'South Wales Lime' white - 81-?	4	6

W19. Cattle Wagon (1970)

The cattle wagon was another of the original models of 1970 which was sold unprinted but with a sheet of black or white transfers available.

NR13	non-printed (transfers) dark grey - 70-72	4	6
NR26W	GW 106325 dark grey - 72-78	4	6
2604	GW 106325 dark grey - 78-00	4	6
?	GW 10632 dark grey - ?	6	8
NR26M	LMS 22719 green-grey - 72-78	4	6
2601	LMS 22719 green-grey - 78-00	4	6
2601	LMS red-brown - 78-00	4	6
NR26S	SR 53710 dark brown - 72-78	4	6
2603	SR 53710 dark brown - 78-00	4	6

W20. Horsebox (1970)

This model was based on a horsebox on the London, Tilbury & Southend Railway and had a 10' chassis and glazed windows. The chimney on the roof was omitted. Like other models issues at the beginning, it was sold unprinted to start with.

Private owner horsebox [W20]

NR14	non-printed (transfers) pale blue - 70-72	3	5
NG30	non-printed (transfers) red brown - 71-72	3	5
NG30B	non-printed (transfers) pale blue - 71-72	3	5
NG30G	non-printed (transfers) green - 71-72	3	5
NG30F	non-printed (transfers) fawn - 71-72	3	5
2711	'Sir George Widgeon' 2 brown - 78-00	3	5

W21. LNER Fish Van (1970)

Base on an LNER design, this was also initially sold unprinted but with a sheet of black or white transfers available.

NG12	non-printed (transfers) red - 70-72	4	6
NG26	non-printed (transfers) red - 70-72	4	6
NG27	non-printed (transfers) white - 71-72	4	6
NR25N	NE 27456 brown - 72-78	4	6
2502	NE 27456 brown - 78-00	4	6

W22. 12T Single Vent Van (1970)

The model seems to have been based on an LMS design and one which BR continued to build for a while after Nationalisation. It had single sliding doors and corrugated steel end walls. Again this was initially sold unprinted.
ex3 = from a 3 wagon set

NR10	non-printed (transfers) brown - 70-72	4	6
NG10	non-printed (transfers) grey - 70-72	4	6
2318	'Allsops' 4 ivory - 78-00	3	5
2311	'Bass' 14 light grey - 78-00	3	6
2317	'Fremlin Bros.' 1 white - 78-00	3	5
2316	'Fyffes' yellow - 78-00	3	NA
2313	'Knorr' white - 78-00	3	5
?	'Rail Mail' green - ?	4	6
?	'Rail Mail' buff - ?	4	6
2314	'Terrys' brown - 78-?	3	5
2312	'Worthington' 5 dark brown - 78-00	3	5
2315	'Zoflora' green - 78-?	3	5
NR23W	GW 45677 dark grey - 72-78	4	6
2304	GW 45677 dark grey - 78-00	4	6
NR23M	LMS 7701 grey Refrigerator - 72-78	4	6
2301	LMS 7701 grey Refrigerator - 78-00	4	6
2301	LMS red-brown - 78-00	4	6
NR23N	NE 186547 red brown - 72-78	4	6
2302	NE 186547 red brown - 78-00	4	6
NR23S	SR 50567 dark brown - 72-78	4	6
2303	SR 50567 dark brown - 78-00	4	6
2305	BR E568011 brown - 88-?	3	5

W23. 12T Twin Vent Van (1970)

This may have been based on a GWR double vent van design. It also appeared as a private owner van, once a pad printing machine had been acquired by Graham Farish.

NR11	non-printed (transfers) brown - 70-72	3	5
NR11	non-printed (transfers) grey - 70-72	3	5
NR?	non-printed (transfers) black - 70-72	4	6
NG24	non-printed (transfers) grey - 70-72	3	5
NG24	non-printed (transfers) red brn - 70-72	3	5

GWR double vent van [W23] (KJB Models)

2411	'Anglo Sportsman' white - 79-00	3	5
2412	'Gibbs SR' navy - 79-01	3	5
2413	'John West' green+red - 79-00	3	5
NR24W	GW 95253 dark grey - 72-78	3	5
2404	GW 95253 dark grey - 78-00	3	5
NR24M	LMS 7126 dark grey - 72-78	3	5
2401	LMS 7126 dark grey - 78-00	3	5
2401	LMS red-brown - 78-00	3	5
NR24S	SR 52953 dark brown - 72-78	3	5
2403	SR 52953 dark brown - 78-00	3	5

8th Edition

Graham Farish N

W24. VAB/VBA Long Van (1988)
Many of these larger air-braked merchandise vans were built for BR in the '70s and '80s to replace the 10ft wheelbase vans that were being phased out. They had strengthened sliding doors for fork lift working.

3906	**BRe** 200163 brown VAB - *88-?*	6	8
3905	**BR** Rft 200631 red+grey VBA - *88-?*	6	8
3907	**EWS** 200631 maroon VBA - *99-00*	6	8

W25. GWR Brake Van (1971)
Like so much on the Great Western Railway, the 'Toad' brake van changed little in appearance down the years. They had a veranda at only one end and no side duckets. They had mostly restricted and generally carried the name of the yard to which they allocated.

NR16	non-painted (transfers) grey - *71-72*	4	6
NR13DG	non-painted brown - *71-72*	4	6
NR31	**GW** 114926 mid.grey* Plymouth - *72-78*	4	6
3104	**GW** 114926 dark grey* Plymouth - *78-00*	4	6
3105	**BR** 114920, 114926 grey** - *82-00*	4	6

* white and light grey roof variations.   ** with or without handrails painted white.

W26. LBSC Brake Van (1978)
This long wheelbase 20 ton van was the final LBSC wagon design to appear before the Grouping in 1923 and 20 had been built at Lancing Works in 1922 and a further 11 in 1923.

3001	**LMS** red-brown - *79-00*	4	6
3003	**SR** 55657 grey - *79-00*	4	6
3003	**SR** brown - *78-00*	4	6
3106	**BR** M734658 brown - *88-?*	4	6

W27. Freightliner Bogie Flats with Containers (1983)
This was a typical Freightliner bogie flat wagon which was sold with different mixes of colourful containers - both 20ft and 30ft ones.

3605	**'OOCL' + 'OCL' + 'Freightliner'*** - *83-?*	6	8
3616	**'Ford' + 'Danzas'**** - *83-?*	6	8
3609	printed 20' containers - *83-?*	6	8
3619	printed 30' containers - *83-?*	6	8
3639	non-printed 20' containers - *83-?*	6	8
3639	non-printed 30' containers - *83-?*	6	8

* Other container combinations include Dart, Zanussi and Hapag-Lloyd. **Other containers used include ACL, Ford, OOCL and a 30' Freightliner.

W28. Bogie Sulphate Wagon (1978)
The model was based on a 50 ton bogie steel open wagon built by the LNER for the transporting of sulphate of ammonia from the ICI factory at Billingham. 80 of them were built.
  This is an attractive model with a sharply moulded body. It was also non-prototypically used by Graham Farish as a brick wagon.

3211	**GWR** 54004 dark grey Loco Coal - *79-00*	4	6
3212	**NE** 163542 brown Brick - *79-83?*	4	6
NR32N	**NE** red-brown - *78*	4	6
3202	**NE** red-brown - *78*	4	6
NR32BR	**BR** grey - *78*	4	6
3205	**BR** E164857 brown - *79-00*	4	6
3205	**BR** E164857 grey - *79-00*	4	6

W29. TEA Bogie Tank Wagons (1983)
This was a typical 100T bogie tank wagon used for the bulk transportation of oil. It had a gantry along the top and a ladder at one end.

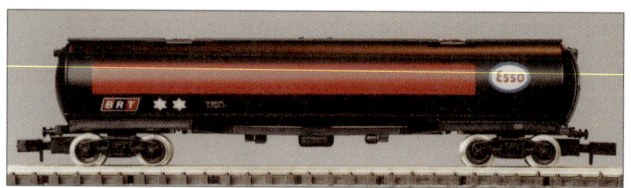

TEA 100T oil tank Esso [W29]

3708	**'BP'** BPO87566 green - *91-?*	8	10
3707	**'BP'** BPO87464 green Sp Edn - *91-?*	8	10
3703	**'Esso'** silver - *83-?*	6	8
3704	**'Esso'** black - *83-?*	6	8
3702	**Shell BP** grey - *83-?*	6	8
3705	**Shell BP** black - *83-?*	6	8
3701	**'Texaco'** red - *83-?*	6	8
3706	**'Total'** red - *83-?*	6	8

W30. LNER Bogie Van (1978)
The model was probably based on a bogie van built for the North Eastern Railway.

3302	**NE** 102496 red-brown York - *78-00*	5	7

W31. Set of Three Wagons (1975)
Some wagons were initially available only in these triple sets.

NR21/7	'Wood', 'Parker & Probert', 'Bullcroft' - *75-?*	NA	20
NR21/8	'Pritchard', 'Frost', 'South Leicester' - *75-?*	NA	20
NR21/9	'Lebon', 'Worthington', 'Dutton Massey' - *75-?*	NA	20
NR21/10	'Dombey', 'Snow', 'Cam Rys' - *75-?*	NA	20
NR21/11	'Sleight', 'Pitt', 'Powell Gwinell' - *75-?*	NA	20
NR21/12	'Ormiston', 'Rosslyn', 'Staveley' - *78-?*	NA	20
NR23/1	'Fyffes', 'Bass', 'Spiers' - *75-?*	NA	20
NR23/2	'Sir G Widgeon', 'Ocean', 'Fremlins' - *78-?*	NA	20
NR23/3	'Knorr', 'Terrys', 'Zoflora' - *78-?*	NA	20
2999	6 PO wagons + vans - *83-?*	NA	30
3799	assorted bogie tankers - *83?*	NA	25

ACCESSORIES
The 'Liveway' track was released at the same time that the first wagons appeared in the autumn of 1970 and the first lineside feature, a pair of tunnel mouths, arrived in May 1971. The Snap power unit was on sale early in 1972.

SETS
The first four train sets arrived in time for Christmas 1971 and consisted of passenger and freight versions with either of the tank engines.

Bachmann WD 2-8-0 (renumbered) with a mineral train - computer aided artwork by Robbie McGavin

Graham Farish
by Bachmann

HISTORY
In the summer of 2000, Peter Graham Farish sold Graham Farish Ltd to Bachmann Industries Europe Ltd. For a while the Holton Heath premises were retained as the Graham Farish headquarters, but production was transferred to China and work started on upgrading the range. It had been planned to carry on making the inherited range, gradually updating it but, as adaptations had to be made before the tooling from Poole could be used on the modern machines in Hong Kong, it was decided that the models should be upgraded individually before any products were released.

LNER Class V2 [L19] (Tony Wright)

Bachmann had announced an extensive range of new versions of existing models at the time of the take-over, but only a few of these materialised at the time, those made in the UK being included in the previous section of this catalogue. Pre-production models of the forthcoming range from China were exhibited at the 2002 British International Toy & Hobby Fair in London. As a result of the transfer of production to China and the need to upgrade tooling, there was a gap in the market as shelves in model shops were emptied of remaining Graham Farish stock. A lot of the original brass tooling was found to be badly worn and a process of replacement with steel tools was begun.

The first models from Hong Kong started to arrive in the second half of 2001, when a few wagons and improved HSTs reached the shops. Early in 2002 we also learnt that work had started on a completely new steam model - an LNER Class V2, for release in 2004.

Retooling of the chassis was the priority in order to improve mechanisms and performance. This involved a reassessment of every model in the range and nothing was reintroduced until it met the standards that Bachmann demanded.

To date, improvements have been made to wheels, motors and valve gear and just about every locomotive has had a new chassis block produced. Initially, the bodies were all original and originated from Poole tooling.

The V2 was the last Poole tooled locomotive. Since then tooling of all new models (and reintroductions) has been carried out by Kader in China.

Some models, such as the 4-4-0s, will not be reintroduced as the tooling is no longer fit for use.

Heritage Range - From 2005, a number of models, based on subjects in the National Collection, were released by Bachmann in a new 'Heritage Range'.

Dates - Wherever possible the year that the model was released is given. In some cases the date quoted is the year that Bachmann planned to release it (i.e. when it appeared in the catalogue), with no confirmation as to whether it was delivered on time. Models were sometimes one or even two years late in arriving. We will correct dates as information becomes available.

Weathering - This is popular with many modellers today, giving models a more realistic appearance. 'Weathered' models have been given a light spay with a thin grey or brown paint to give the appearance of dirt blown up from the track. To save space, weathered models are coded in the text with a 'W' after the colour.

Blue Riband - During 2008, the Blue Riband logo started to appear on some of the new items in the catalogue. This denoted Bachmann's premium range of models. These are designed and manufactured to a higher specification which includes, where appropriate, the use of NEM and DCC standards.

Collectors Club - The Bachmann Collectors Club (BCC) includes Graham Farish in its coverage. Members receive a quarterly magazine and further information about this may be obtained by writing to the Club at Bachmann Europe plc, Moat Way, Barwell, Leicestershire LE9 8EY.

LOCOMOTIVES
DCC - Since 2007, some locomotives have been released ready to receive a DCC chip ('DCC ready'). This means that they have a blanked-off socket into which a standard chip may be plugged.

DCC6 - This indicates that the loco has fitted the standard N gauge 6-pin decoder socket ready to receive a decoder, after removing the blanking-off plate.

DCC/PCB - Some locomotives have provision for fitting decoders by soldering to a factory fitted PCB (printed circuit board). These are identified by the 'DCC/PCB'

Cat No.	Company, Number, Colour, Date	£	£

Tank Engines

0-6-0T

L1.	General Purpose 0-6-0T (Freelance) (2003)		
This was the 'all things to all men' model in the original Graham Farish range and was reintroduced by Bachmann for a cheap train set.			
(370-025A)	**7309** LMS maroon ex-set - *10*	25	NA
(370-025)	**268** Southern green ex-set - *03*	20	NA

L2.	GWR 57xx Class Pannier Tank 0-6-0PT (2002)		

This was a Collett pannier tank design of 1929, but with a Churchward cab. A total of 863 locomotives were built between 1929 and 1950. The last was withdrawn in 1966. 13 had been sold to London Transport between 1957 and 1963 and the last of these worked on the London Transport network until 1971. 16 of the class have been preserved, including 6 of those sold to London Transport.

The original Graham Farish model dates from 1995 and was reintroduced by Bachmann in 2002. This model received a new chassis in 2012.

GWR class 57xx [L2]

371-900	**5710** GWR (button) green -*02*	35	45
371-902	**8700** GWR (button) green - *02*	32	40
371-906	**5786** GWR green - *07*	40	55
371-900	**7702** GWR green - *02*	35	45
371-905	**7713** GWR green - *06*	35	48
371-909	**L97** London Transport maroon - *13*	NPG	NPG
371-901	**8763** BRb lined black - *02*	35	45
371-907	**6724** BRb black - *08*	40	55

Graham Farish by Bachmann

371-903	5796 BRb plain black - 02, 05	32	40
371-904	7739 BRb plain black - 06	35	48
371-908	5757 BRc plain black - 11	NPG	63
371-901	5775 BRc lined black - 02	35	45

L3. GWR 64xx Class Pannier Tank 0-6-0PT (2013)

A total of 40 of these mixed traffic locomotives, designed by Collett, were built between 1932 and 1950. The last was withdrawn in 1964 and 3 have been preserved.

The model has the new coreless motor and is fitted with a 6-pin DCC decoder socket. It is a well detailed model and the tooling allows for two versions of the cab and bunker.

371-985	6407 GWR (button) green - 13	55	70
371-986	6403 BRb black - 13	55	70
371-987	6400 BRc lined green - 13	55	70

L4. GWR 8750 Pannier Tank 0-6-0PT (2002)

The class was designed by C.B.Collett and introduced to the GWR in 1929. It was very similar to the Class 57xx but had a different style of cab. The last one was withdrawn from service in 1966.

The original Graham Farish model dates from 1996 and was reintroduced by Bachmann in 2002. This model received a new chassis in 2012.

371-930	3715 GWR green - 06	35	48
371-931	4612 GWR green - 07	40	55
(370-026)	? GWR green - 13	45	NA
371-931A	4606 GWR green - 11	45	63
371-928	9643 GWR green - 02	32	40
371-925	8763 BR lined black - 02	35	45
371-927	4672 BRc plain black - 02, 05	32	40
371-929	9753 BRc plain black - 06	35	48
371-932	8759 BRc plain black - 08	40	55
371-935	4656 BRc plain black - 12	45	63

L5. GWR 94xx Pannier Tank 0-6-0PT (2002)

This was based on a Hawksworth design. The tanks were built between 1947 and 1956 - most of them by British Railways and so did not run in GWR livery. A total of 210 were constructed and two have been preserved.

The original Graham Farish model dates from 1971 and it was reintroduced by Bachmann in 2002.

371-951	9401 GWR green - 02	35	45
371-954	9402 GWR green - 08	40	55
371-954A	9405 GWR green - 10	40	57
371-953	9409 GWR green - 03, 06	35	48
371-950	8424 BRb plain black - 02	35	45
371-952	9436 BRc plain black - 03	35	48

L6a. LMS 3F Class 'Jinty' 0-6-0T (2004)

The class was designed for the LMS by Henry Fowler, based on an earlier Johnson design. The 'Jinty' became the company's standard 0-6-0 tank shunting engine and 422 were built between 1924 and 1931, much of the work being contracted out. They were highly versatile engines and found themselves on both freight and passenger trains. Seven spent a period on the S&DJR and two went to Northern Ireland in 1944. Some survived to the last days of steam and 10 have been preserved.

The original Graham Farish model dates from 1996 and it was reintroduced by Bachmann in 2004.

(370-025A)	7309 LMS plain maroon ex-set - 10	25	NA
372-205	47332 BRb plain black W - 07	32	50
372-201	47483 BRb plain black - 04	32	40
372-203	47593 BRb plain black W - 05	35	48
(370-076)	47594 BRb plain black ex-set - 05?	35	NA
372-206	47231 BRb plain black W - 09	35	48
372-200	47338 BRc plain black - 04	32	40
372-207	47472 BRc plain black - 11	NPG	64
372-207A	47674 BRc plain black W - 12	NPG	NPG
372-202	47514 BRc plain black - 05	35	46
372-204	47629 BRc plain black - 07	35	48

L6b. LMS 3F Class 'Jinty' 0-6-0T (2013)

This is a completely new model from new tooling, to replace the original Graham Farish model of 1996, and had not been released at the time of writing. The models are 'DCC ready' and are fitted with 6-pin DCC decoder sockets. Bachmann will be making both versions, with or without the sand filler opening ('key-hole') above the footplate in the tank sides.

372-210	7524 LMS plain black - 13	55	70
372-211	47394 BRb plain black - 13	55	70
372-212	47345 BRc plain black - 13	55	70

L7. WD J94 Class 0-6-0ST (2003)

Designed by Riddles, this was based on a Hunslet Class 50550 design and 391 were built for the government during the Second World War, using various locomotive builders. A further 93 were built for other customers. J94 was applied as a class code to the 75 locomotives bought by the LNER after the war and which passed to BR in 1948. Many others were sold to the National Coal Board and to private industry. Their high power and short wheelbase made them versatile machines. Of the 484 built, 70 are still in existence.

BR class J94 Austerity tank [L7]

372-500	8051 LNER black - ?	45	60
372-501	68006 BRb plain black * - 03	35	41
372-501	68079 BRb plain black - 03	35	42
372-501	68006 BRc plain black - not made	NA	NA
372-501	68012 BRc plain black - not made?	NA	NA
372-502	68030 BRc plain black - 06	35	41
(370-050)	68040 BRc plain black ex-set - 03	35	NA
372-503	68071 BRc plain black - 07	35	42
372-504	68059 BRc plain black - 09	40	50

* Has been found in a box numbered for 68012.

2-6-2T

L8. GWR 61xx 'Prairie' Tank 2-6-2T (2003)

Designed by C.B.Collett as a development of the Class 51xx, the Class 61xx tank was introduced to the GWR in 1931. 70 members of the class were built between 1931 and 1935 and allocated to the London area. The last of the class was withdrawn in 1966 and only one example has been preserved at Didcot Railway Centre.

The original Graham Farish model was first released in 1977 and it was re-released by Bachmann in 2003.

371-978	6116 Great Western green W - 03	35	45
371-976	6104 GWR (button) green - 03	40	48
371-981	6110 GWR green - 07	50	67
371-981A	6114 GWR green - 11	50	67
371-979	6169 GWR green - 06	42	57
371-980	6100 BRb plain black - 06	42	57
371-975	6135 BRb lined green - 03	40	48
(370-075)	5136 BRc lined green ex-set - 03	40	NA
371-977	5153 BRc lined green - 03	35	45

L9. BR 3MT Standard Tank 2-6-2T (2010)

BR class 3MT 2-6-2T [L9]

This was the Riddles larger mixed traffic 2-6-2T locomotive of 1952, which was designed and built at Swindon for light passenger work. It was a heavier version of the 2MT, with 10 tons extra weight and larger driving wheels. They were for routes having a 16 ton axle loading but, as these routes were upgraded, larger tank engines took over the work. Only 45 were built and these took the 82xxx number range. They were seen in Wales, the West Country, the northern Pennines and, in later years, they were seen hauling empty stock at Clapham Junction. Withdrawals started in 1964 and all had gone by the end of

1967. Sadly none was preserved, but the Severn Valley Railway has a new one under construction.

The highly detailed model was first released in 2010 and was fitted with a 6-pin DCC decoder socket as standard.

372-325	**82016** BRb lined black - *10*	60	77
372-328	**82026** BRb lined black - *12*	75	91
372-326	**82005** BRc lined green - *10*	60	77
372-331	**82020** BRc plain green - *13*	NPG	NPG
372-330	**82028** BRc lined black weathered - *13*	NPG	NPG
372-327	**82028** BRc lined black - *10*	60	77
372-329	**82041** BRc lined green - *12*	75	91

2-6-4T

L10. LMS Fairburn Tank 2-6-4T (2013)

Designed by Charles Fairburn as a lighter version of the Stanier 2-6-4 passenger tank for use on lighter suburban lines, 277 were built between 1945 and 1951. The last was withdrawn from service in 1967 and two have been preserved.

The model is highly detailed and the chassis incorporates Bachmann's new coreless motor. The tooling allows for two versions of rivet detail on the water tanks and it is fitted with a 6-pin DCC decoder socket.

372-750	**2691** LMS black - *13*	80	100
372-751	**42096** BRb lined black - *13*	80	100
372-752	**42073** BRc lined black (as preserved) - *13*	80	100
372-753	**42267** BRc lined black weathered - *13*	90	110

L11a. BR 4MT Standard Tank 2-6-4T (2004)

Riddles designed this mixed traffic locomotive which first made its appearance in 1951. A total of 155 locomotives were built between 1951 and 1957. They saw service on all regions of British Railways with the exception of the Western Region and were used mainly for branch line and suburban passenger duties. The last of the class was withdrawn in July 1967 and 15 have been preserved for use on heritage railways.

This table shows the models made by Bachmann from the original Graham Farish tooling of 1991. The 4MT tank was completely retooled in 2012 and models from the new tooling will be in the next table.

372-526	**80032** BRb lined black - *04*	45	55
372-528	**80036** BRb lined black - *05*	55	68
372-530	**80048** BRb lined black W - *07*	60	76
372-530	**80136** BRb lined black W - *not made*	NA	NA
372-527	**80038** BRc lined black W - *05*	55	71
372-531	**80086** BRc lined black - *10*	60	76
372-525	**80097** BRc lined black - *04*	45	55
372-529	**80130** BRc lined black - *07*	60	76

L11b. BR 4MT Standard Tank 2-6-4T (2013)

Riddles designed this mixed traffic locomotive which first made its appearance in 1951. A total of 155 locomotives were built between 1951 and 1957. They were used mainly for branch line and suburban passenger duties. The last was withdrawn in 1967 and 15 have been preserved.

This is the super-detailed model from brand new tooling. It has a 6-pin DCC decoder socket fitted.

372-535	**80027** BRb lined black - *13*	NPG	NPG
372-536	**80119** BRc lined black - *13*	NPG	NPG

Tender Engines

4-4-0

L12. LMS Fowler 4P Compound 4-4-0

The LMS adopted the Midland 'Compound' as a standard design and building of them continued from 1924 until 1932. A total of 195 were built and worked throughout the LMS system. Much of their work was later taken over by the 'Jubilee' and 'Black 5' classes. The last 'Compound' was withdrawn in 1961.

The Graham Farish model had been introduced in 1980 but tooling was found by Bachmann to be in a poor state and was abandoned. No doubt this is a subject that Bachmann plan to retool in the future, now that they have done the development work for their 00 scale models

372-100	**41157** BRc lined black - *not made*	NA	NA

0-6-0

L13a. LMS Fowler 4F Class 0-6-0 (2003)

The class was designed by Henry Fowler for the Midland Railway and passed into LMS ownership in 1923. 575 were built for the LMS after 1922 and it was these later ones that were modelled originally by Graham Farish in 1993.

The tooling was taken over by Bachmann in 2000 and reintroduced by them in 2003. In 2013 Bachmann designed a new set of tooling based on the original MR locomotives and these are listed in the next table.

Ex-LMS class 4F [L13a]

372-050	**44018** BRb plain black - *04*	50	65
(370-175)	**44143** BRb black ex-Freight set - *03*	45	NA
372-052	**44027** BRb plain black - *08*	60	75
372-054	**44330** BRc plain black - *11*	NPG	85
372-051	**44388** BRc plain black - *04*	50	65
372-053	**44422** BRc plain black - *08*	60	75

L13b. MR Fowler 4F Class 0-6-0 (2013)

Of a total of 772 of the class built, 192 were built between 1911 and 1922 by the Midland Railway, to a design by Henry Fowler. It became a standard LMS design with improvements and a further 575 were built for the LMS and 5 for the S&DJR. The last 4F was withdrawn from service in 1966 and 4 have been preserved - including one of the original MR locomotives.

The models in this table are from completely new tooling developed in 2013 and with a high level of detail. They depict right-hand drive MR versions and have the new coreless motor in the loco, with an 8-pin DCC decoder socket in the tender. All loco and tender wheels have power contacts and the tooling allows for both Fowler and Johnson tenders to be modelled.

372-061	**3851** LMS plain black, Johnson tender - *13*	80	95
372-062	**43875** BRb plain black, Johnson tender - *13*	80	95
372-060	**43924** BRc plain black (as preserved) Fowler tender - *13*	80	95

L14. LNER J39 Class 0-6-0 (2013)

The Gresley standard 0-6-0 freight locomotive of 1926 replaced many of the 800 plus 0-6-0 locomotives that the LNER inherited in 1923 and which were approaching retirement age They were intended for freight services but were also used on passenger services. 289 of the class were built between 1926 and 1941 and they would have been seen with a wide variety of tenders, which had been handed down as older classes were replaced. This also included the Group Standard 4,200 gallon tenders with either straight sides or with the stepped top. The last of the class was withdrawn in 1962 and none was preserved.

The model has all-wheel pick-up, tender drive, two tender styles, cab interior detail and 6-pin decoder sockets are fitted as standard.

fst = flat-sided tender, sst = step-sided tender.

372-400	**1856** LNER lined black fst - *13*	NPG	83
372-401	**64960** BRb plain black fst - *13*	NPG	83
372-402	**64791** BRc plain black, st - *13*	NPG	83
(370-260)	**64838** BRc plain black ex- Eastern Freight train set - *13*	NPG	NA
372-403	**64841** BRc plain black W, st - *13*	NPG	85

2-6-0

L15. LMS Class 5 'Crab' 2-6-0 (2004)

The 'Crab' Moguls were easily recognisable locos in train-spotting days due to their prominent and steeply angled cylinders, which gave them their nickname. They were the first LMS standard locomotive, being based on a planned Caledonian Railway design. Also called 'Horwich Moguls', they were built at Horwich and arrived in 1926 with a Fowler tender. Building continued until 1932 and the class finally totalled 425. They were a short but powerful design, with large boilers, and were used for both passenger and freight workings, including express work. The last was withdrawn in 1967 and 3 were preserved, including one in the National Collection.

The original Graham Farish model dates from 1993 and it was reintroduced by Bachmann in 2004, The model has a Fowler tender.

372-226	**13098** LMS maroon - *04*	65	80
372-227	**42765** BRb lined black - *09*	70	90
372-225	**42932** BRc lined black - *04*	65	80

L16. LMS Ivatt 2MT 2-6-0 (2013)

This is the Ivatt mixed traffic design of 1946. 128 of the class were built between 1946 and 1952. Construction continued under British Railways after Nationalisation in 1948. Light axle loadings allowed them to be used on branch line passenger and freight duties and their almost enclosed cabs made them ideal for working tender first when no turning facilities existed. The last was withdrawn in 1967 and 7 have survived to work on heritage

Graham Farish by Bachmann

railways.

This is a highly detailed Bachmann designed model and has a 6-pin DCC decoder socket.

372-627	**6404** LMS plain black - *13*	NPG	100
372-626	**46440** BRb lined black - *13*	NPG	100
372-625	**46521** BRc lined green - *13*	NPG	100

L17. BR Riddles 4MT 2-6-0 (2010)

This was Riddles' BR Standard mixed traffic design of 1952 and was based on Ivatt's 'Mucky Duck' LMS 4MT Mogul of 1947. Designed at Doncaster, they were built there and at Horwich and had the standard BR cab and chimney. Members of the class were used on cross-country and secondary routes and were found in all regions except in the West. Those allocated to the Southern Region had high capacity BR1B tenders, whereas elsewhere they were paired with BR2 and BR2A types. The last of the class was withdrawn in 1967 and 4 have been preserved.

This is a well detailed model with a 6-pin DCC decoder socket fitted.

BR class 4MT [L17] (Tony Wright)

372-652	**76020** BRb lined black with a BR2 tender - *10*	75	96
372-650	**76053** BRb lined black with a BR1B tender - *10*	75	96
372-653	**76079** BRb lined black with a BR2 tender - *13*	NPG	NPG
372-654	**76063** BRc lined black with a BR1B tender - *13*	NPG	NPG
372-651	**76069** BRc lined black with a BR1B tender - *10*	75	96

L18. SE&CR N Class 2-6-0 (2013)

Designed by R.E.Maunsell for the South Eastern & Chatham Railway, this class was built between 1917 and 1934 and totalled 80. British Railways rebuilt 25 of the locomotives between 1955 and 1961. The last was withdrawn from service in 1966 and one has been preserved.

The model has the new coreless motor and a tender-mounted 6-pin DCC decoder socket. The loco has all-wheel power contact. The tooling allows for two types of tender (3500 gallon and 4000 gallon) and the option of smoke deflectors.

372-930	**1406** SR olive green slope-sided tender - *13*	110	130
372-931	**31844** BRb lined black straight-sided tender - *13*	110	130
372-932	**31831** BRc lined black slope-sided tender - *13*	110	130

2-6-2

L19. LNER V2 Class 2-6-2 (2004)

This was Gresley's express passenger and freight locomotive of 1936. They were built at Doncaster or Darlington and totalled 184. They did sterling work throughout the Second World War with heavy freight and troop trains to pull, including 700 ton trains of 24 coaches! Three different tenders could be found paired with them and there was much tender swapping over the years. Some were given double chimneys. The last one was withdrawn in 1966 and only one survived into preservation.

The model was the first of a new range of high quality N gauge steam outline models. It has both a single flywheel with damper and a flywheel equivalent Maschima can motor.

372-602	**4844** *Coldstreamer* LNER green - *05*	75	92
372-601	**60807** BRb lined black - *04*	75	92
372-600	**60800** *Green Arrow* BRc green* - *04*	75	92

* Issued as Heritage Range model.

4-6-0

L20. GWR 49xx Class 'Hall' 4-6-0 (2003)

In 1924, Collett modified one of the successful 'Saint' Class locomotives (2925 St Martin) to create the first of the 'Hall' Class. Production started in 1928 when 80 of the new class were built and a further 178 were ordered. The 'Halls' were mixed traffic locomotives and could be found throughout the GWR and BR(WR) network. They sometimes found themselves on express services when larger locomotives were unavailable. They were seen with various tenders including the small 3,500 gallon ones but most had the 'Castle' 4,000 gallon tenders. All but one of the class passed into BR ownership and the last of the 'Halls' was withdrawn in 1966. Ten have been preserved.

The original Graham Farish model dates from 1975, making it one of the oldest Farish N gauge models. It was reintroduced by Bachmann in 2003 and this table contains those versions made since then.

372-001	**4970** *Sketty Hall* Great () Western green - *03*	50	65
372-002	**4965** *Rood Ashton* Hall Great () Western green - *08*	60	80
372-001	**4931** *Banbury Hall* GWR green - *not made*	NA	NA
372-000	**5955** *Garth Hall* BRc green - *03*	50	65
372-003	**4979** *Wootton Hall* BRc green - *08*	60	80

L21a. GWR 'Castle' Class 4-6-0 (2003)

The 'Castles' were a post-Grouping design by Collett and were made over many years (1923-1950) to produce a class of 166 locomotives. The design was a development of Churchward's excellent 'Star' Class of 1907 and 5 members of that earlier class were rebuilt as 'Castles', also *The Great Bear* which had originally been built as the GWR's only 4-6-2.

The original model was released by Graham Farish in 1982 and was not a very accurate model. Bachmann reintroduced the model from the original tooling in 2003 but by 2013 were working on a completely retooled model which is covered in the next table. This table contains Bachmann's models produced from the original tools.

372-025	**7033** *Hartlebury Castle* BRb green single chimney - *03*	55	70
372-026	**4080** *Powderham Castle* BRc green double chimney - *03*	55	70
(370-150)	**7004** *Eastnor Castle* BRc green double chimney ex-Bristolian set - *03*	50	NA

L21b. GWR 'Castle' Class 4-6-0 (2013)

The last of the GWR 'Castle' Class was withdrawn in 1965 but 8 have survived in preservation, thanks largely to the fact that they ended up at Woodham' scrapyard at Barry in South Wales.

Here we have the totally retooled model which replaced the original model of 1982. It has all-wheel power contacts, the new coreless loco-mounted motor and a 6-pin DCC decoder socket in the tender. Both single and double chimney versions can be made and the model is highly detailed, including the cab interior.

sc = single chimney, dc = double chimney.

372-030	**5044** *Earl of Dunraven* GWR green sc - *13*	110	130
372-031	**7004** *Eastnor Castle* BRb green - *13*	110	130
372-032	**5031** *Totnes Castle* BRc green dc - *13*	110	130

L22. GWR 'King' Class 4-6-0 (2003)

This was Collett's 'top of the range' express class and a total of 30 of these locomotives were built at Swindon. The class might not have been built had not the Southern Railway correctly claimed that their new 'Lord Nelson' locomotives were the most powerful locomotives in the country, beating the GWR 'Castles' into second place.

These models are from the original Graham Farish tooling of 2000, the last to be produced by the original company.

372-550	**6021** *King Richard II* BRb blue - *03*	55	70
372-551	**6008** *King James II* BRc green double chimney - *03*	55	70

L23a. LMS 'Black 5' 4-6-0 (2004)

Stanier's Class 5 mixed traffic locomotive of 1934 was one of the most successful and influential designs. The fact that 842 were built between 1934 and 1951 meant that they were a common sight on the LMS. It was to form the basis of the Standard 5 class built by British Railways and 'Black 5s' remained on the network to the very end of steam. 18 have survived in preservation.

These are models produced from the original Graham Farish tooling of 1978 and reintroduced by Bachmann in 2004. They have a Stanier tender.

372-125	**5305** LMS lined black - *04*	65	82
372-126	**44896** BRb lined black - *04*	65	82
(370-102)	**45360** BRb lined black ex-set - *07*	65	NA
372-127	**45231** BRc lined black* - *08*	70	92

* 40 Years of Steam release.

L23b. LMS 'Black 5' 4-6-0 (2010)

This is a highly detailed model from completely new tooling. It replaced the original Graham Farish one of 1978. It has a Stanier tender and a 6-pin DCC decoder socket fitted as standard.

Ex-LMS 'Black 5' [L23b]

372-135	**5020** LMS lined black - *10*	85	105

Graham Farish by Bachmann

372-138	5190 LMS plain black - 13	85	105
372-137	45110 BRb lined black weathered - 10	85	105
372-136	45151 BRb lined black - 10	85	105
372-136	45216 BRb lined black– ?	85	105
372-137	45110 BRc lined black - 10	85	105
372-137K	45157 *The Glasgow Highlander* BRc lined black Sp Edn (BCC) - 10	85	105

L24. LMS 'Jubilee' 4-6-0 (2007)

The class was designed by William Stanier and was introduced to the LMS in 1934. Its duties were express passenger, parcels or fitted freight trains. The class totalled 191 and the last was withdrawn in 1967. Four of the class have been preserved.

This is a highly detailed model and both Fowler and Stanier tenders are available for it. The model has a 6-pin DCC decoder socket fitted as standard.
St = Stanier 4000g tender. Ft = Fowler tender.

372-477	5558 *Kashmir* LMS maroon St - not made	NA	NA
372-477	5563 *Australia* LMS maroon Ft - not made	NA	NA
372-477	5664 *Nelson* LMS maroon St - 13	NPG	NPG
372-477	5682 *Trafalgar* LMS maroon St - 07	75	96
372-476	45568 *Western Australia* BRb green Ft - not made	NA	NA
372-476	45611 *Hong Kong* BRb green St - 07	80	100
372-476A	45643 *Rodney* BRb green St - 07	80	100
372-475	45593 *Kolhapur* BRc green St - not made	NA	NA
372-479	45596 *Bahamas* BRc green St - 11	NPG	116
372-475	45699 *Galatea* BRc green St - 07	75	96
372-478	45698 *Mars* BRc green St - 10	80	102
372-481	45565 BRc green - 13	NPG	NPG

L25. LMS 'Rebuilt Royal Scot' 4-6-0 (2008)

The class was designed by William Stanier for express passenger services and built between 1927 and 1930. All of the class were rebuilt between 1943 and 1955 with tapered boilers and curved smoke deflectors.

This is a highly detailed model and has a 6-pin DCC decoder socket fitted as standard.
St = Stanier 4000g tender. Ft = Fowler tender.

372-578	6100 *Royal Scot* LMS maroon St, as preserved - 13	NPG	NPG
372-577	6115 *Scots Guardsman* LMS black St - 09	80	100
372-576	46106 *Gordon Highlander* BRb green St * - 09	80	100
372-575	46159 *The Royal Air Force* BRc green St - 08	80	100
372-579	46122 *Royal Ulster Rifleman* BRc green W cab-side stripe, shedcode 16D - 13	NPG	NPG

* This has 'Britannia' style smoke deflectors.

L26. LNER Class B1 4-6-0 (2010)

This class was designed by Edward Thompson and arrived in 1942. 410 were built as mixed traffic locomotives - the final batch arriving in 1950. Some of the work was contracted out to the Vulcan Foundry and the North British Locomotive Co. The rest were built at Darlington, except for 10 at Gorton. The last was withdrawn in 1967 and two have been preserved.

The B1 includes the successful Farish tender drive unit and has a 6-pin DCC decoder socket fitted as standard. The model has options for welded or flush riveted smoke box detail as well as variations, including door radius, steps and lamp brackets.

LNER class B1 [L26] (Tony Wright)

372-075	1000 *Springbok* LNER light green - 10	90	110
372-079	1040 *Roedeer* LNER lined black weathered - 13	NPG	NPG
372-076	61139 BRb lined black - 10	90	110
372-080	61045 BRb lined black weathered - 13	NPG	NPG
372-077	61251 *Oliver Bury* BRc lined black - 10	90	110
372-078	61321 BRc lined black W - 10	90	110

L27. BR Riddles 5MT 4-6-0 (2012)

This was a Riddles' mixed traffic design which started to appear on the national network in 1951. Designed at Doncaster, 172 were built at Derby or Doncaster and were a standard equivalent of the LMS 'Black Five'. They were allocated to all the regions and no fewer than six different tender types were used with them. Some of the locomotives allocated to the Southern region adopted names from scrapped 'King Arthur' Class locomotives. The building of them lasted between 1951 and 1957 and the last was withdrawn in 1968. Five of the class have been preserved

This is a highly detailed model. There are three versions of tender body used with the model, which has good cab interior detail and a 6-pin DCC decoder socket fitted as standard.

372-727	73082 *Camelot* BRc lined black - 12	NPG	121
372-728	73014 BRc lined green BR1 tender - 12	NPG	121
372-725	73068 BRc lined green BR1C tender - 12	NPG	121
372-726	73158 BRc lined black BR1B tender - 12	NPG	121

4-6-2

L28a. LMS 'Duchess' Class 4-6-2 (2002)

These are the same class as the 'Coronations' but were either built without streamlined cladding or with the cladding removed. The first batch built without cladding dated from 1938 and the last 'Coronation' to become a 'Duchess', by removal of its cladding, was City of Lancaster in 1949. There were 38 members of the class and the last was withdrawn in 1964. Three of the class have been preserved.

This is the original Graham Farish model of 1982 (with a double chimney), which was reintroduced by Bachmann in 2003.

372-176	6234 *Duchess of Abercorn* LMS maroon, no smoke deflectors - 03	70	80
372-180	6233 *Duchess of Sutherland* LMS maroon - 06	70	86
372-175	46255 *City of Hereford* BRb blue - 03	60	70
(370-100)	46245 *City of London* BRb green ex-Royal Scot set - 03	60	NA
372-179	46248 *City of Leeds* BRb green - 06	70	86
(370-135)	46221 *Queen Elizabeth* BRb green ex-set - 02	70	NA
372-177	46252 *City of Leicester* BRc green - 04	55	70
372-178	46229 *Duchess of Hamilton* BRc maroon - 04	55	75

L28b. LMS 'Duchess' Class 4-6-2 (2013)

This is a highly detailed model from completely new tooling.

372-181	46229 *Duchess of Hamilton* BRb green - 13	NPG	NPG
372-182	46235 *City of Birmingham* BRc green - 13	NPG	NPG
372-183	46255 *City of Coventry* BRc maroon - 13	NPG	NPG
372-184	46245 *City of London* BRc maroon - 13	NPG	NPG

L29. LNER A1 Class 4-6-2 (2011)

To a design by AH Peppercorn, this was a class of express passenger locomotives and 49 were built at Doncaster between 1948 and 1949. They started to arrive in 1948, after Nationalisation of the railways, and, consequently, none appeared in full LNER livery.

This model is highly detailed. The model has powerful 4-axle tender drive mechanism, cab interior detail, a choice of welded or riveted tender sides and disc or spoked tender wheels. A 6-pin DCC decoder socket is fitted as standard..
wt = welded tender, rt = riveted tender

Ex-LNER class A1 [L29]

372-800	60163 *Tornado* BRa light green wt *- 11	120	148
372-800	60163 *Tornado* BRa Express blue wt *- 13	NPG	NPG
372-802	60147 *North Eastern* BRb green wt - 11	115	136
372-800A	60163 *Tornado* BRb green sst *- 13	120	148
372-801	60156 *Great Central* BRc green rt - 11	115	136

* Rimless chimney and roller bearing axlebox detail.

L30. LNER Peppercorn A2 Class 4-6-2 (2014)

Peppercorn's 15 engines were based on Thompson's A2/2 but were almost 2 feet shorter. They started to arrive in 1947 and only two carried LNER livery. A further 20 engines were ordered but subsequently cancelled. Besides being express passenger engines, they were sometimes used for mixed traffic duties. The last of the class was withdrawn in 1966 and one was preserved.

This has powerful 4-axle tender drive mechanism, cab interior detail and disc or spoked tender wheels. It has a 6-pin DCC decoder socket fitted as standard.
sc = single chimney, dc = double chimney.

372-385	525 *A.H.Peppercorn* LNER light green sc - 14	NPG	NPG
372-386	60537 *Batchelors Button* BRb green sc - 14	NPG	NPG
372-387	60533 *Happy Knight* BRc green dc - 14	NPG	NPG
372-388	60532 *Blue Peter* BRc green dc - 14	NPG	NPG

Graham Farish by Bachmann

L31. LNER A3 Class 4-6-2 (2003)

The Class A3s of the LNER were a development of the A1s, which had been designed for the Great Northern Railway by Nigel Gresley in 1922. Almost all existing A1s were rebuilt, while later ones were built as A3s. One of the more visible changes was the new banjo shaped steam dome fitted to the top of the A3's boiler.

The original Graham Farish model of an A3 was released in 1987 and was available with or without German style smoke deflectors. It was reintroduced by Bachmann in 2003, along with double chimney versions and ones with the Great Northern tender.
gsd = German smoke deflectors. GN = GNR type tender. dc = double chimney

372-379	4472 *Flying Scotsman* LNER green gsd dc as preserved* - 05		75	88
372-376	60080 *Dick Turpin* BRb blue - made?		NPG	NPG
372-377	60066 *Merry Hampton* BRb green GN - 03		75	92
372-378	60103 *Flying Scotsman* BRc green gsd corridor tender - 03		55	75
372-375	60051 *Blink Bonny* BRc green dc - made?		NPG	NPG
372-380	60065 *Knight of the Thistle* BRc green dc - 07?		75	89

* Issued as Heritage Range model.

L32. LNER A4 Class 4-6-2 (2003)

Designed by Sir Nigel Gresley, the A4s were largely based on the Gresley A3s and were built in batches at Doncaster. The class eventually totalled 35 in number. The first batch was built for the Silver Jubilee. Most of the rest were initially given the names of birds but later extensive renaming took place to honour individuals and the five British Commonwealth dominions. The last was withdrawn from service in 1966 and six of the class were preserved.

The original Graham Farish model dates from 1999 and so was only a year old when Bachmann took over the company in 2000. The model represents the locomotives after the valancing was removed during the Second World War and so limits the range of liveries that can be used. Only the corridor tender version was tooled.

Ex-LNER class A4 [L32] (David Wild)

372-351A	22 *Mallard* LNER blue with plaque* - 04		65	90
372-354	60033 *Seagull* BRb blue - 06		75	90
372-350	60017 *Silver Fox* BRb blue - made?		NPG	NPG
372-351	60022 *Mallard* BRb express blue - 03		65	80
(370-101)	60017 *Silver Fox* BRc green ex-set - 05		60	NA
372-355	60017 *Silver Fox* BRc green - 07		75	92
372-352	60009 *Union of South Africa* BRc green - 03		60	75
372-353	60027 *Merlin* BRc green - 04		75	90

* Also issued as Heritage Range model.

L33. SR 'Merchant Navy' Class 4-6-2 (2013)

Between 1941 and 1949, 30 of Bulleid's heavy pacific 'Merchant Navy' Class were built at Eastleigh with air-smoothed casing, but all had this removed at Eastleigh between 1956 and 1959, as part of the rebuild. 11 of the class have survived into preservation.

This is a newly tooled super-detail model. It replaces the original Graham Farish model of 1977 which has not been used by Bachmann since taking over the Graham Farish tooling.

372-313	35021 *New Zealand Line* BRa Malachite green - 13		NPG	NPG
372-310	35024 *East Asiatic Company* BRb Express blue - 13		NPG	NPG
372-311	35023 *Holland-Afrika Line* BRb green - 13		NPG	NPG
372-312	35028 *Clan Line* BRc green - 13		NPG	NPG

L34. BR 'Rebuilt MN' Class 4-6-2 (2003)

This is a model of Bulleid's 'Heavy Pacific' design of 1941, as they looked after being rebuilt in BR days. 30 had been built at Eastleigh with air-smoothed casing, like the WC/BB class, but all had this removed at Eastleigh between 1956 and 1959, as part of the rebuild. 11 of the class have survived into preservation.

The original Graham Farish model dates from 1997 and was reintroduced by Bachmann in 2003.

372-301	35024 *East Asiatic Co.* BRb blue - not made		NA	NA
372-301	35005 *Canadian Pacific* * BRb blue - 04		70	87
372-300	35018 *British India Line* BRb green - 04		70	87
(370-225)	35022 *Holland America Line* BRc green ex-'Atlantic Coast Express' set - 03		65	NA
372-302	35028 *Clan Line* BRc green - 09		70	90

*This model carries different colour number plates on each side.

L35. SR 'WC/BB' Class 4-6-2 (2004)

The 'West Country/Battle of Britain' Class (WC/BB) was designed by Oliver Bullied as a smaller and lighter version of the 'Merchant Navy' Class. The first of the class arrived in 1945 and the rebuilding of some of them as more conventional looking locomotives was started by British Railways in 1957. Those for service in the eastern sector had been given 'Battle of Britain' names and the rest, for use further west, were named after places served by the Southern Railway. The last member of the class was withdrawn in 1967, however, 20 of the class have survived in preservation.

The original Graham Farish model dates from 2000 and was reintroduced by Bachmann in 2004.

Ex-SR 'Battle of Britain' class [L33]

372-275	21C101 *Exeter* SR malachite green - 04		70	87
372-277	34051 *Winston Churchill* BRb green - 04		70	87
372-276	34064 *Fighter Command* BRc green rebuilt tender - 04		70	87
372-278	34067 *Tangmere* BRc green - 10		70	93

2-8-0

L36. LMS 8F/06 Class 2-8-0 (2004)

The class was introduced by William Stanier in 1935 to fill a serious gap in the LMS stud. It was based on the highly successful 'Black 5s' and became the standard heavy freight design for the LMS and was adopted by the War Department during the Second World War. In all, 666 locomotives were built, including 331 that the LMS had ordered. The LMS ones were mostly built at Crewe and Horwich but with batches from Vulcan Foundry and North British as well. A batch of the wartime 8Fs was allocated to the LNER for one year (1947) and was known as the Class O6. Others went overseas for war service and some stayed there after the war. The last of the class was not withdrawn from service in Britain until 1968. Nine of the class have been preserved, including three recently repatriated from abroad.

The original Graham Farish model dates from 1986 and was reintroduced by Bachmann in 2004.
Ft = Fowler tender. St = Stanier tender.

372-150	3107 LNER plain black St - 04		65	85
372-152	48709 BRb plain black St - 06		65	84
372-154	48750 BRb plain black St - 11		NPG	108
372-151	48045 BRc plain black Ft - 04		65	84
372-153	48773 BRc plain black* W St - 08		75	94

* 40 Years of Steam release.

L37. WD Austerity Class 2-8-0 (2012)

The class was designed by R.A.Riddles for wartime heavy freight trains. What was needed for the invasion of Europe was an austerity locomotive of equivalent power to the LMS 8F and this was the answer. 935 were built by Vulcan Foundry and North British and the first started to arrive in 1943. After the war, 200 were sold to the LNER and more were sold to overseas railways. BR received 733 of the locos in 1948 and the last was withdrawn in 1967. Despite the large number of them, only one was preserved.

This has loco drive, a diecast body and regional detail variations. It is fitted with a 6-pin DCC decoder socket.

372-425	90732 *Vulcan* BRb plain black - 12		NPG	130
372-427	90201 BRc plain black W - 12		NPG	144
372-426	90566 BRc plain black - 12		NPG	130

2-10-0

L38. BR 9F 2-10-0

This had been planned for 2009, but Dapol introduced their model about this time. In July 2010 it was announced that Bachmann had decided to no proceed with this model for the time being.

372-426	92002 BRb black - not made		NA	NA
372-427	92205 BRc black W - not made		NA	NA
372-425	92220 *Evening Star* BRc green * - not made		NA	NA

* To have been issued as Heritage Range model.

Graham Farish by Bachmann

Diesel Locomotives

L39. Class 03 0-6-0DS (2011)

The class was designed for shunting and pilot duties and building started in 1958. The first locomotive was withdrawn from BR in 1968, although one example (03079) remained in use on the Isle of Wight until 1993. The locomotives became popular with heritage lines and 51 of them have been preserved.

371-060	**D2011** BRc green - *11*	45	63
371-061	**D2388** BRc green, wasp stripes - *11*	45	63
371-062	**03066** BRe blue, wasp stripes, with air tanks - *11*	45	63

L40. Class 04 0-6-0DS (2007)

140 diesel shunters were built by Drewry (but subcontracted to Vulcan Foundry and Robert Stephenson & Hawthorn between 1952 and 1962. The total number of the fleet was 142. Their lightness meant that, the class could be used on lines with severe weight limitations. They were used for general shunting and pilot duties and all were withdrawn from the national network between 1968 and 1972. Many were sold for industrial use and 18 have been preserved as useful shunting engines on heritage lines.

371-052	**11217** BRb black - *09*	40	54
371-050B	**D2228** BRc green, wasp stripes - *11*	45	63
(370-110)	**D2228** BRc green, wasp stripes ex-'Depot Master' train set - *13*	45	NA
371-051A	**D2239** BRe blue, wasp stripes - *10*	40	54
371-050	**D2246** BRc green, wasp stripes - *07*	35	43
371-051	**D2258** BRe blue, wasp stripes - *07*	35	43
371-050A	**D2264** BRc green, wasp stripes - *08*	40	54
371-050	**D2280** BRc green - not made	NA	NA
371-053	**D2290** BRc green - *11*	45	63
371-051B	**D2294** BRe blue, wasp stripes - *11*	45	63

L41a. Class 08 0-6-0DS (2002)

This became the standard BR diesel shunter, dating from 1952, and was based on an LMS design of 1945. 894 were built between 1953 and 1962, for shunting and station pilot duties. For a specific function, they were the most standardized locomotives in Britain. The shunters became the Class 08 and 09 under TOPS and the 08s were found everywhere on the network - and still are. As the fleet was reduced, due to shrinking freight traffic, many found their way into industry and, at the time of writing, at least 60 have found their way onto heritage lines.

These models are from the original Graham Farish tooling of 1979, with inside frames.

371-008	**13029** BRb black - *04*	28	35
371-003	**13365** BRc green - *03*	28	35
(370-051)	**D3032** BRc plain green ex-set * - *05*	28	NA
371-009	**D3336** BRc green with wasp stripes - *06*	28	35
371-001	**D3729** BRc green - *02*	30	38

BR class 08 diesel shunter [L41a] (Tony Wright)

371-003A	**D4192** BRc green W - *04*	28	35
371-006	**08585** Freightliner green - *03*	28	35
371-018	**08585** Freightliner green - *10*	40	59
371-004	**08623** BRe blue - *02*	28	35
371-007	**08645** BRe Departmental grey - not made	NA	NA
371-007	**08648** BRe Departmental grey - *03*	28	35
371-000	**08653** Railfreight Distribution grey - *02*	30	38
371-004A	**08748** BRe blue - *04*	28	35
371-005	**08800** ICs dark grey+white - *03*	28	35
371-002	**08921** EWS maroon - not made	NA	NA
371-002	**08933** EWS maroon - *02*	30	38

* Various other locos have been used in the make up of these sets.

L41b. Class 08 0-6-0DS (2008)

This is a well detailed model and, unlike its predecessor, it has outside frames.

371-018	**08585** Freightliner green - *10*	42	58
371-017	**08653** Rft Distribution triple grey - *08*	42	57
371-015	**08748** BRe blue - *08*	42	57
371-015A	**08763** BRe blue - *10*	42	58
371-015B	**08856** BRe blue - *13*	60	73
371-015K	**08873** BRe(I-C) grey, Stratford logo, Sp Edn 504 (BCC) - *13*	60	73
371-019	**08897** EWS maroon+yellow W - *13*	60	73
371-016	**08921** EWS maroon+yellow - *08*	42	57

L41c. Class 08 (Original Form) 0-6-0DS (2012)

This is a Blue Riband development of the model in the table above. It represents the diesel shunter in an early form with wooden cab doors, footplate mounted left and right battery and exhauster boxes, radiator ladders and bonnet detail.

371-022	**D3729** BRc green W, with wasp stripes - *12*	65	80
371-020	**13029** BRb black - *12*	60	73
371-021	**13365** BRc green - *12*	60	73
371-020Z	**97800 *Ivor*** BRe RTC red+blue, Sp Edn (ModelZone & The Signal Box) - *12*	55	73

L42. Class 14 0-6-0DS (2010)

This was the Swindon 0-6-0 diesel-hydraulic Type 1, later to be classified as the Class 14. It was a 650hp centre cab locomotive for shunting and trip working. 56 of them were built and introduced in 1964 but by the time they arrived, most of the work they were intended for had been lost. Consequently, the first two units were withdrawn only two years after their introduction. The vast majority were sold to industry and at least 17 are now preserved.

This model has no DCC decoder socket.

BR class 14 in National Coal Board livery [L43]

372-951	**D9523** BRc 2-tone green W - *10*	50	65
372-953	**D9526** BRc green W, with wasp stripes - *12*	70	84
372-950	**D9555** BRc 2-tone green, with wasp stripes - *10*	50	65
372-952	**14029** BRe blue as preserved, wasp stripes - *10*	50	65
(370-255)	**7** NCB blue ex-'Colliery Classic Freight' train set - *11*	60	NA

L43a. Class 20 Bo-Bo (2004)

This is an English Electric designed freight loco of 1957, the first of 20 being built at their Vulcan Foundry works. Other batches followed until the final member of the class was delivered in 1968. In all, 228 eventually arrived and were allocated to the Eastern, London Midland and Scottish Regions. It was now the standard BR Type 1 diesel and all the other pilot scheme Type 1s were withdrawn. They were often seen operating in pairs, joined nose to nose so that their cabs were at the outer ends. This allowed them to be driven from either end and thus overcame the visual obstruction created by the long bonnet.

Models have a new crisper finish compared with Graham Farish original model that was introduced in 1982.

371-026	**D8134** BRc green with code boxes - *04*	50	65
371-026	**D8163** BRc green - not made	NA	NA
371-028	**D8307** BRe blue W - *09*	50	65
371-027	**20227** BR Railfreight grey (red stripe) - *04*	50	65
371-025	**20312** DRS blue - not made	NA	NA
371-025	**20906** DRS blue - *04*	50	65

L43b. Class 20 Bo-Bo (2012)

This model has all new tooling for body and chassis and replaces the original Graham Farish model of 1982 in the table above. The model has all-wheel drive, working lights, cab detail with large or standard size windows and separate fan detail below etched metal grilles. It has a 6-pin DCC decoder socket.

371-030	**D8000** BRc green, with disc codes - *12*	80	98
371-032	**20063** BRe blue W, with disc codes - *12*	85	103
371-031	**20192** BRe blue, with codeboxes - *12*	80	98

Graham Farish by Bachmann

L44. Class 24 Bo-Bo (2010)

Built originally at BR Derby Works form 1957, the Class 24 locomotives were for mixed traffic and were introduced to British Railways in 1958. Subsequent orders also involved Crewe and Darlington workshops and 151 were built before the design was modified to produce the Class 25. Withdrawals of the class started in the late 1960s and had been completed by the Autumn of 1980. Four members of the class have been preserved.

This model is fitted with a 6-pin DCC decoder socket. It has working bi-directional lights with working headcode discs. There are two chassis variations with solebar, sandbox and battery box options.

372-976	**D5013** BRc green - *10*	65	80
372-977	**D5038** BRc 2-tone green - *10*	65	80
(370-060)	**D5072** BRc 2-tone green ex-Digital Commuter set - *11*	65	NA
372-979	**D5085** BRc 2-tone green - *12*	NPG	NPG
372-975	**24035** BRe blue - *10*	65	80
(370-065)	**24035** BRe blue ex-'Newspaper Express' train set - *13*	65	NA
372-978	**24081** BRe blue - *12*	NPG	NPG
372-975Z	**97201** RTC Sp Edn 504 (ModelZone & The Signal Box) - *10*	65	80

L45a. Class 25 Bo-Bo (B) (2003)

The Class 25s were introduced to Britain's railways in 1961 as mixed traffic locomotives for the secondary routes. They were a product of the 1955 Modernisation Plan and a development of the Class 24, which they replaced on the production lines. Between 1961 and 1967, a total of 327 were built at Derby, Darlington and by private sector contractor Beyer Peacock in Manchester. There were four subclasses and five slight body differences which affected the appearance of the cab fronts and the ventilation louvres on the sides. A fifth subclass was formed in 1986 by modification of some existing locos. Withdrawals were completed in 1987 and at least 20 have been preserved.

Graham Farish launched their model in 1983 but the current model is from completely new tooling developed during 2002. In 2013 a new body shell was introduced.

BR class 25 [46a]

371-075	**D5237** BRc 2-tone green - *04*	48	63
371-079	**D7638** BRc 2-tone green - *12*	75	94
371-077	**D7646** BRc 2-tone green - *09*	48	63
371-078	**D7649** BRc 2-tone green W 25/3 - *10*	48	63
371-076	**D7667** BRe blue W 25/3 - *04*	55	69
371-080	**25279** BRe blue 25/3 - *12*	75	94
(370-200)	**25322** BRe blue, yellow cabs, silver roof, ex-Diesel Freight set - *03*	55	NA

L45b. Class 25 Bo-Bo (B) (2014)

Graham Farish launched their model in 1983 but the models in this table have a new body shell. The model has all-wheel drive with a flywheel, a 6-pin DCC decoder socket and bi-directional lighting with an illuminated headcode box.

371-085	**D5188** BRc green 25/1 - *14*	80	100
371-086	**D5222** BRc green W 25/1 - *14*	90	110
371-088	**25231** BRe blue W 25/2 - *14*	90	110
371-087	**25234** BRe blue 25/2 - *14*	80	100

L46a. Class 31 Co-Co (2004)

263 members of the class were built between 1957 and 1962 and were intended for mixed traffic duties, originally on the Eastern Region. They were built at the Brush Electrical Engineering Company plant at Loughborough, originally with Mirrlees engines which were later replaced by English Electric ones between 1964 and 1969. A large number of retired members of the class have been preserved, including D5500 by the National Railway Museum..

The model was introduced by Graham Farish in 1995 and reintroduced by Bachmann in 2004. It now has an upgraded mechanism with a twin flywheel 5-pole skew wound motor.

371-?	**5500** BR - *not made*	NA	NA
371-104	**D5672** BRc green - *10*	65	79
(370-202)	**31135** BRe grey+yellow ex-set - *07*	55	NA
371-102	**31285** Railfreight red stripe grey - *06*	55	69
371-101	**31410** BR Regional Railways blue+grey - *04*	55	69
371-101	**31421** BR Regional Railways - *not made*	NA	NA
371-103	**31430** *Sister Dora* BRe blue - *07*	58	72
371-100	**31601** *Bletchley Park* Fragonset black - *04*	55	64
371-105	**31602** *Driver Dave Green* NR yellow - *11*	75	92

L46b. Class 31 Co-Co (2013)

This is a Blue Riband model resulting from the subject being completely retooled and is DCC ready with a 6-pin DCC decoder socket fitted.

371-110	**D5563** BRc green - *13*	NPG	NPG
371-111	**D5596** BRc green with small yellow panels - *13*	NPG	NPG
371-110	**D5826** BRc green - *13*	NPG	NPG
371-112	**31173** BRe blue - *13*	NPG	NPG

L47. Class 33 Bo-Bo (2004)

These were built in 1961 and 1962 by the Birmingham Railway Carriage & Wagon Company. A total of 98 locomotives were built and all were allocated to the Southern Region. They were for mixed traffic duties and the final 12 had narrower bodies for working the Hastings line, which has a restricted loading gauge.

The Graham Farish model dates from 1987 and it was reintroduced by Bachmann in 2004 with an upgraded mechanism and twin flywheel 5-pole skew wound motor.

BR class 33 [L48]

371-128	**D6577** BRc green - *06*	50	65
(370-201)	**33002** *Sea King* BRe Engineers yellow+grey ex-set - *05*	45	NA
371-130	as above - *07*	48	67
371-126	**33021** *Eastleigh* BRe Fragonset red BRe logo + Eastleigh motif - *04*	45	58
371-125K	**33025** DRS Minimodal blue Sp Edn 504 (BCC) - *06*	50	63
371-129	**33028** BRe blue - *06*	50	65
371-127	**33035** *Spitfire* NSE blue Eastleigh motif - *04*	45	58
371-125	**33109** *Captain Bill Smith RNR* BRe blue - *not made*	NA	NA

L48a. Class 37 Co-Co (2003)

The Class 37, as it would become under TOPS, was an English Electric mixed traffic design which entered service in 1960. It became the largest of all the Type 3 classes with 309 built. Construction took place between 1957 and 1962, but, over the following years, modifications and refurbishments created six subclasses. Their original allocation was to the Western, Eastern and Scottish Regions but they were eventually to be found anywhere in mainland Britain.

This is the original Graham Farish model of 1981, which Bachmann reintroduced in 2003 with an upgraded mechanism, which includes a twin flywheel 5-pole skew wound motor.

sh = split headcodes.

371-156	**D6607** *Ben Cruachan* BRc green Eastfield motif - *03*	50	65
371-?	**D6700** (NRM Rail 200) - *not made*	NA	NA
371-159	**37412** *Driver John Elliott* Transrail triple grey 37/4 - *06*	58	74
371-155	**37417** *Highland Region* BReLL blue Inverness motif 37/4 - *03*	58	74
371-153	**37419** EW&S maroon+yellow - *03*	50	65
371-151	**37428** *Loch Long/Loch Awe* EWS Great Scottish dark maroon - *03*	50	65
371-152	BRe Dutch grey+yellow - *not made*	NA	NA
371-154	**37429** *Eisteddfod Genedlaethol* Regional Railways blue+grey - *03*	50	65
371-160	**37431** *Bullidae* InterCity grey+white 37/4 - *07*	60	78
371-150	**37609** DRS blue - *not made*	NA	NA
371-158	**37671** *Tre Pol and Pen* Railfreight Distribution triple grey - *05*	58	74
(370-251)	**37672** *Freight Transport Association* Railfreight Distribution triple grey ex-set - *07*	58	74
371-161	**37672** Transrail triple grey 37/6 - *09*	60	81

Graham Farish by Bachmann

371-157	**37678** BReLL Railfreight red stripe grey - *05*		55	74

L48b. Class 37/0 Co-Co (2008)

This is a model model developed by Bachmann, with better detail and a twin flywheel 5-pole skew wound motor. It has a 6-pin decoder socket fitted as standard. sh = split headcodes.

371-451	**D6707** BRc green sh - *08*	65	80
371-451A	**D6712** BRc green sh - *10*	65	82
371-453	**D6826** BRc green - *08*	65	80
371-454	**D6827** BRc green W - *13*	NPG	NPG
371-450	**37038** BRe blue sh - *08*	65	80
371-456	**37133** BRe (Dutch) grey+yellow - *13*	NPG	NPG
371-452	**37238** BRe blue - *08*	65	80
371-455	**37251** BRe blue W - *13*	NPG	NPG

L48c. Class 37/0 'Cut-nose' Co-Co (2009)

This model has the body cut-away below the cab fronts. It has a twin flywheel 5-pole skew wound motor and a 6-pin CCT decoder socket fitted. sh = split headcodes.

Network Rail class 37/0 [L49c]

371-466Z	**37027** *Loch Eil* BReLL blue Sp Edn 504 (TMC) - *11*	75	99
371-466	**37035** BR Civil Engineers grey+yellow sh - *09*	75	93
371-469	**37174** EWS maroon+yellow - *12*	80	98
371-467	**37239** *The Coal Merchants' Association of Scotland* BR Railfreight Coal grey - *09*	75	93
371-465	**37254** BRe blue - *09*	75	93
371-468	**97302** Network Rail yellow - *12*	80	98

L48d. Class 37/4/5 (Refurbished) Co-Co (2014)

This is a new model developed by Bachmann to represent the 37/4 and 37/5 subclasses. It has a twin flywheel 5-pole skew wound motor and a 6-pin DCC decoder socket.

371-166	**37406** *The Saltire Society* Railfreight Distribution triple grey 37/4 - *14*	NPG	100
371-165	**37407** *Loch Long* BReLL blue 37/4 - *14*	NPG	100
371-169	**37409** DRS (compass) blue 37/4 - *14*	NPG	100
371-165	**37417** *Highland Region* BReLL blue - not made	NA	NA
371-168	**37506** BReLL Railfreight red stripe grey 37/5 - *14*	NPG	100
371-167	**37514** Railfreight Metals triple grey 37/5 - *14*	NPG	100

L49. Class 40 1-Co-Co-1 (2004)

Part of the Modernisation Plan was to build 2,000hp passenger express locomotives and the order was won by English Electric. Construction started in 1956 and the new locomotive was unveiled in the Spring of 1958. They came in several batches which finally made a class of 200 locomotives. Initially they were allocated to the Eastern, London Midland and Scottish Regions. The class was successful and survived until 1985, after which they were considered to be obsolete. The first of the class was the last to go, in 1988. Seven Class 40s have survived in preservation.

The original Graham Farish model of 1986 was given an upgraded mechanism by Bachmann. This has twin flywheel 5-pole skew wound motor.

371-?	**D200** - not made	NA	NA
371-175	**D306** *Atlantic Conveyor* BRc green - *04*	60	70
371-177	**D351** BRc green - *06*	60	75
371-177A	**D382** BRc green - *10*	65	84
371-176	**40051** BRe blue - not made	NA	NA
371-176	**40052** BRe blue - *04*	60	70
371-178A	**40150** BRe blue - *10*	65	84
371-178	**40192** BRe blue - *06*	65	80

L50. Class 42 'Warship' B-B (2008)

The class was entirely built at Swindon and introduced between 1958 and 1961. Based largely on the German V200 Class, a total of 38 were constructed and all were allocated to the Western Region. The first 13 built started life with three figure route indicator frames fitted to the cab fronts. The rest had the four digit code boxes, the original 13 being converted on works visits. Being non-standard, withdrawals started in 1968 and were completed in 1972. Two have been preserved.

This model basically has the same mechanism as the newer Class 37, with a twin flywheel 5-pole skew wound motor, working illuminated headcode boxes, detailed cab interior and vac and air pipes for bufferbeams. The model has a 6-pin DCC decoder socket.

371-601	**D804** *Avenger* BRe blue - made?	NPG	NPG
371-605	**D810** *Cockade* BRe blue W - *13*	NPG	NPG
371-602	**D814** *Dragon* BRe green - *08*	60	79
371-603	**D815** *Druid* BRc maroon yellow front - *08*	70	90
371-600	**D817** *Foxhound* BRc maroon - *08*	60	79
371-602A	**D819*** *Goliath* BRc green small yellow panel - *10*	70	90
371-601	**D822** *Hercules* BRe blue - *08*	60	79
371-600A	**D823** *Hermes* BRc maroon - *10*	70	90
371-601A	**D827** *Kelly* BRe blue yellow front - *10*	70	90
371-603A	**D829** *Magpie* BRc maroon yellow front - *10*	70	90
371-604	**D832** *Onslaught* BRc green - *13*	NPG	NPG

* D814 on the box.

L51. Class 43 'HST 125' (2001)

The Class 43 was the power unit in the InterCity 125 high speed train. The HSTs went into service on the Western Region main line in October 1976 and were still very much in evidence at the turn of the century. They were made up with Mk3 coaches, without buffers, and a Class 43 diesel at each end.

The Graham Farish model first appeared in 1981 and was reintroduced by Bachmann in 2001. Early power bogies were unsatisfactory and a new centrally mounted motor had been introduced in 1984.

371-481	**43006**+**42503**+**43096** Cross Country grey+purple 3-car - not made	NA	NA

Arriva Cross-Country class 43 [L52]

371-475	**43047**+**42157**+**43058** *Midland Pride* MML green+cream 3-car - *01*	70	90
371-475A	*Midland Pride* MML green+cream 3-car - not made	NA	NA
371-476	**43096**+**42064**+**43109** GNER navy blue 3-car - *01*	70	90
371-477	**43004**+**TS**+**43025** FGW purple - not made	NA	NA
371-477	**43029**+**42072**+**43031** FGW purple - *02*	70	90
371-475A	**43056**+**42112**+**43178** Midland Mainline blue+grey - *07*	80	101
371-478	**43089**+**42127**+**43091** Virgin red+black WCML - *02*	70	90
371-478	**43084**+**TS**+**43161** Virgin red+black WCML - not made	NA	NA
371-478	**?**+**?**+**?** GNER navy blue 3-car - not made	NA	NA
371-478A	*Virgin Challenger* silver+red 3-car - not made*	NA	NA
371-480	**43096** *Stirling Castle*+**42058**+**43006** *Kingdom of Fife* GNER Mallard navy blue - *07*	70	90
371-479	**43098**+**42074**+**43107** BR ICs grey 3-car - *03*	80	101
371-475A	**43166** Midland Mainline blue+grey - not made	NA	NA
371-481	**43221**+**42377**+**43378** Cross Country grey+purple 3-car - *09*	80	101

* Virgin Trains did not go ahead with their Challenger refurbished HSTs due to changes made by the SRA. A prototype model was produced but not put into production.

L52. Class 44 'Peak' Co-Co (2006)

The first 10 Type 4 'Peaks' later formed the Class 44 and were required for mixed traffic duties. They were introduced in 1959 and 1960 and further locomotives were subsequently ordered. However, due to technical differences in their construction they became two further classes (45 and 46). All ten locomotives of the Class 44 were allocated to the LMR and later did freight duties in the Nottingham area. Withdrawals were completed in 1980 and two have been preserved.

This is a Blue Riband model with an upgraded mechanism, which includes a twin flywheel 5-pole skew wound motor.

371-201	**D1** *Scafell Pike* BRc green - *06*	65	77
371-202	**D7** *Ingleborough* BRc green - *10*	68	83
371-203	**44001** BRe blue W - *13*	NPG	NPG
371-200	**44008** *Penyghent* BRe blue - *06*	65	80

L53. Class 45 'Peak' Co-Co (2006)

Following the building of the first 10 'Peaks' (Class 44), the British Railways Board decided that it wanted more of these engines but with a slightly more powerful motor installed. 127 were ordered and were built at Crewe and Derby between 1960 and 1963.

Graham Farish by Bachmann

They were allocated to the London Midland and Eastern Regions. Displaced by HSTs, the last member of the class was withdrawn in 1988 and 12 have been preserved.

This model has the upgraded mechanism with twin flywheel 5-pole skew wound motor.

371-575A	D55 **Royal Signals** BRc green - *10*	68	83
371-575	D67 **The Royal Artilleryman** BRc green - *06*	65	80
371-577	45024 BRe blue W - *13*	NPG	NPG
371-576	45114 BRe blue, grey roof - *06*	65	77

L54. Class 46 'Peak' Diesel Co-Co (2006)

These were built between 1961 and 1963 at Derby and totalled 56. Three have been preserved.

This model completes the set of 'Peak' classes, a name they gained because the earlier Class 44 locomotives were named after British mountains. This model has the upgraded mechanism with twin flywheel 5-pole skew wound motor.

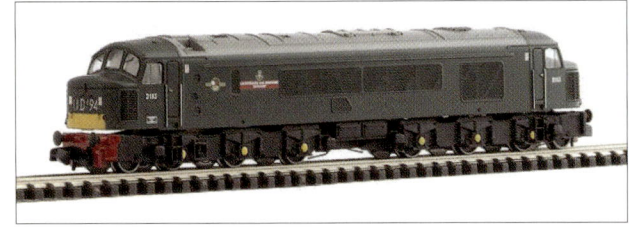

BR class 46 [L55]

371-588	D158 BRc green W - *13*	NPG	NPG
371-585	D163 **Leicestershire** and **Derbyshire Yeomanry** BRc green - *06*	65	80
371-587	D186 BRe blue - *06*	NPG	92
371-586	46053 BRe blue - *06*	65	80

L55a. Class 47 Co-Co (2002)

A total of 512 locomotives were built between 1962 and 1967 by Brush and BR Crewe. They were designed as Type 4 mixed traffic locomotives, in a second phase of diesel locomotive building, and became the British standard Type 4 design. They have had a long life with many variations and subclasses. The first was withdrawn following damage in an accident in 1966 but some remain in traffic today with various operators. At the last count, 36 have been aquired for preservation.

The original Graham Farish model was released in 1981 and many versions were produced before the tooling passed to Bachmann. The model was given an upgraded mechanism by Bachmann before being re-released in 2002. This has a twin flywheel 5-pole skew wound motor.

371-231	D1505 BRc 2-tone green W 47/4 - *04*	58	78
371-229	47150 Freightliner green 47/0 - *02*	55	65
371-232	47237 DRS dark blue 47/0 - *06*	58	75
(370-250)	47306 **The Sapper** Railfreight Distribution triple grey ex-sets (also 370-252) 47/3 - *05, 09*	60	NA
371-233	as above - *07*	60	76
371-230	47635 **The Lass O'Ballochmyle** BReLL blue Highland motif 47/4 - *04*	58	75
371-227	47701 **Waverley** Fragonset black 47/7 - *02*	50	60
(370-125)	47734 **Crewe Diesel Depot** RES red+black 47/7 ex-Royal Mail set - *05*	60	NA
371-225	47747 **Graham Farish** Virgin red 47/7 - not made	NA	NA
371-225K	47805 **Pride of Toton** Virgin red 47/8 Sp Edn 500 (BCC) - *04*	60	74
371-226	47832 **Tamar** FGW green 47/8 - *02*	58	58

L55b. Class 47 Co-Co (2008)

This is a model with an easy to remove body and a 6-pin DCC decoder socket fitted as standard. These models represent original build Class 47s, including some converted to electric train supply (ETS) which were recoded 47/4.

371-825	D1500 BRc 2-tone green small yellow panel - *08*	70	89
371-825A	D1745 BRc 2-tone green small yellow panel - *11*	80	101
371-826	1764 BRc 2-tone green, yellow cab front - *08*	70	89
371-827	47035 BRe blue - *08*	70	89
371-828A	47403 **The Geordie** BRe blue - *11*	80	101
371-828	47404 **Hadrian** BRe blue - *08*	70	89

L55c. Class 47 (Refurbished) Co-Co (2010)

This is a model of the 1980 refurbished 'intermediate' Class 47s. It has an easy to remove body and 6-pin DCC decoder socket fitted as standard.

372-242	47474 **Sir Rowland Hill** BRe Parcels red+very dark grey - *10*	70	95
372-240	47535 **University of Leicester** BReLL blue - *10*	70	95
372-241	47612 **Titan** BRe InterCity grey - *10*	70	95

L55d. Class 47/7 Co-Co (2013)

This is a model of the 1993 conversions of 16 subclass 47/4 locomotives with RCH Time Division Multiplex push-pull equipment for use with trains formed of PCV sets on Royal Mail duties under the Railnet scheme. The model has an easy to remove body and 6-pin DCC decoder socket fitted as standard.

372-243	47701 **Saint Andrew** BRe blue - *13*	90	110
372-245	47710 **Sir Walter Scott** BR ScotRail grey - *13*	90	110
372-244	47711 **Greyfriars Bobby** BReLL blue - *13*	90	110

L56. Class 50 Co-Co (2003)

The Class 50s were built by English Electric during 1967 and 1968 and were initially hired out to the British Railways Board. Later, all 50 locos were bought by them. Although normally associated with the Western Region, they started life on the LMR on the West Coast Main Line. 18 of the locomotives have been preserved.

The Graham Farish model dates from 1983 and was reintroduced by Bachmann in 2003 with an upgraded mechanism which includes a twin flywheel 5-pole skew wound motor.

371-251	50004 **St Vincent** BReLL blue - *03*	55	65
371-250	50017 LMS maroon+gold - *03*	55	65
371-253A	50033 **Glorious** BRe blue - *10*	65	81
371-253	50037 **Illustrious** BRe blue - *06*	65	79
371-252	50149 **Defiance** Rft General triple grey - *05*	58	74

L57. Class 52 'Western' Co-Co (2004)

These were designed at Swindon and were constructed there and at Crewe, eventually totalling 74 in number. The class was introduced to the Western Region in 1962 to provide high powered mixed traffic locomotives to the region. High maintenance costs led to their early replacement by the Class 50s and HSTs. The last was withdrawn in 1978 and seven have been preserved.

The original Graham Farish model was introduced in 1985 and the model was reintroduced by Bachmann in 2004 with a new mechanism and crisper well detailed finish.

371-402	D1013 **Western Ranger** BRe blue - *06*	60	75
371-404	D1015 **Western Champion** BRc maroon - *12*	80	94
371-400	D1023 **Western Fusilier** BRc maroon* - *04*	60	75
371-401	D1030 **Western Musketeer** BRe Swindon chromatic blue - *04*	60	70
371-403	D1035 **Western Yeoman** BRc green - *10*	65	82

* Also issued as Heritage Range model.

L58. DP1 Prototype Deltic Co-Co (2010)

This prototype locomotive, referred to as 'Deltic DP1', was built by English Electric and is now preserved in the National Collection.

This is believed to have been the first time in Britain a laser scan of an actual locomotive was used for an N gauge model. It has a powerful six axle drive chassis with twin flywheels. It also has bi-directional lighting, recessed fan detail with etched grills, wire handrails, detailed cab interiors and a 6-pin decoder socket for DCC users.

Protype'Deltic' [L59a] (Tony Wright)

(370-275)	**Deltic** Nanking blue as first built ex-'The Merseyside Express' set - *10*	80	NA
372-920	**Deltic** Nanking blue as preserved at the NRM - *10*	80	99

59a. Class 55 'Deltic' Co-Co (2003)

In all, 22 of these English Electric locomotives were built at Vulcan Foundry in 1961 and 1962 for the East Coast Main Line expresses, replacing some of the ex-LNER Pacifics that had ruled this route for almost 40 years. They performed well, achieving speeds of up to 100mph. Besides pulling crack East Coast expresses, some were later used on Trans-Pennine services. They were ousted from their main function by the introduction of the High Speed Trains. Withdrawals were completed in 1982 and six of the class were preserved.

The original Graham Farish model was introduced in 1984 and reintroduced by Bachmann in 2003 with an upgraded mechanism which included a twin flywheel 5-pole skew wound motor.

Graham Farish by Bachmann

371-275	D9000 *Royal Scots Grey* BRc 2-tone green - *03*	58	68
371-277	55002 *The King's Own Yorkshire Light Infantry* BRc 2-tone green* - *05*	58	74
371-276	55006 *The Fife & Forfar Yeomanry* BRe blue - *03*	58	68
371-278	55008 *The Green Howards* BRe blue - *09*	65	81

* Issued as Heritage Range model.

L59b.   Class 55 'Deltic' Co-Co (2013)

This is a completely retooled model with a high level of detail. All models fitted with a 6-pin DCC socket.

371-286	D9002 *The Kings Own Yorkshire Light Infantry* BRc 2-tone green, small yellow panels NRM - *13*	NPG	97
371-285	D9007 *Pinza* BRc 2-tone green - *13*	NPG	97
371-287	55005 *The Prince of Wales' Own Regiment of Yorkshire* BRe blue - *13*	NPG	97

L60.   Class 56 Co-Co (2003)

Brush received a contract to build 80 of these locomotives, but, lacking sufficient capacity to build them all themselves, the first 30 of them were built by Electroputere in Romania. As these did not completely meet the required quality standards, the remaining 50 of the original order were built by Brush in Britain. British Rail Engineering were then given an order for a further 55 locomotives which brought the total to 135.. They were introduced between 1976 and 1984.

The Graham Farish model dates from 1993 and was reintroduced by Bachman in 2003 with an upgraded mechanism that included a twin flywheel 5-pole skew wound motor.

371-301	56074 *Kellingley Colliery* LoadHaul black+orange W - *03*	58	77
371-300	56105 EW&S maroon+yellow - *03*	55	65

L61a.   Class 57 Co-Co (2002)

The Class 57 fleet made its debut in 1998 when 6 former Freightliner Class 47 locomotives had reconditioned General Motors 645-12E3 engines fitted. Six more locomotives followed between Autumn 1999 and April 2000, funded by Porterbrook. Virgin Trains ordered 16 Class 57/3 locomotives for hauling its new fleet of 'Pendolinos' when diverted over non-electrified routes. All were subsequently fitted with Dellner couplers for coupling to 'Pendolino' units.

This used the old Graham Farish Class 47 body and one was made in 1999 before the tooling passed to Bachmann.

371-228	57011 *Freightliner Challenger* Freightliner green - *02*	55	65

L61b.   Class 57 Co-Co (2007)

This model is based on the new N gauge Class 47 model tooled by Bachmann with a 6-pin DCC decoder socket ready fitted.

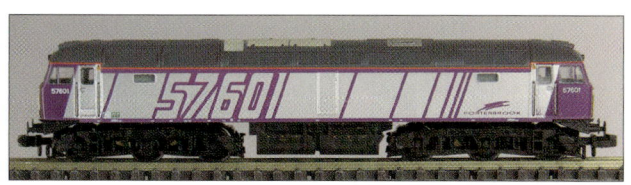

Porterbrook class 57 [L61b]

371-651	57003 *Freightliner Evolution* Freightliner green DCC/PCB - *07*	70	84
371-654	57011 DRS (compass) dark blue - *08*	70	84
371-650	57301 *Scott Tracy* Virgin grey+red - *07*	70	84
371-657	57309 *Pride of Crewe* DRS (compass) blue - *13*	NPG	NPG
371-656	57312 Network Rail yellow - *13*	NPG	NPG
371-653	57601 Porterbrook purple+silver - *07*	60	78
371-652	57602 *Restormel Castle* FGW green - *07*	70	84
371-655	57605 *Totnes Castle* FGW violet blue - *12*	85	108

L62.   Class 60 Co-Co (2007)

The Class 60s were built by Brush Traction in Loughborough between 1989 and 1993, using body shells manufactured by Procor Engineering at Wakefield. They were built as heavy duty freight locomotives and totalled 100. They all went to EWS at Privatisation in the mid 1990s.

This is a model with the upgraded mechanism containing a twin flywheel 5-pole skew wound motor and a 6-pin DCC decoder socket. It is supplied with front end attachments to fit.

371-350K	60006 *Scunthorpe Ironmaster* British Steel light blue Sp Edn 504 (BCC) - *07*	62	78
371-355	60011 DB Schenker bright red - *13*	90	106
371-356	60029 *Ben Nevis* Rft Metals triple grey - *12*	90	106
371-350	60052 *Glofa Twr/Tower Colliery* EWS maroon+yellow DCC/PCB - *07*	70	87
371-354	60054 *Charles Babbage* Railfreight Petroleum triple grey DCC/PCB - *11*	85	100
371-353	60059 *Swinden Dalesman* Loadhaul black+orange DCC/PCB - *09*	70	87
371-350Y	60061 *Alexander Graham Bell* Transrail triple grey Sp Edn 504 (Buffers) - *07*	70	90
371-351	60078 Mainline blue DCC/PCB - *07*	70	87
371-350Z	60081 *Isambard Kingdom Brunel* EWS green Ltd Edn 512 (Kernow MRC) - *07*	70	90
371-352	60084 *Cross Fell* Transrail triple grey DCC/PCB - *08*	70	87

L63a.   Class 66 Co-Co (2005)

This is the General Motors heavy freight design introduced in 1998 and, besides becoming the standard British heavy freight locomotive, it is being adopted further afield in Europe.

250 of an updated Class 59 were ordered by EWS and built in Canada and these became the Class 66. Freightliner, DRS and GB Railfreight all followed suite.

This is a model designed by Bachmann and fitted with the upgraded mechanism with its balanced twin flywheel 5-pole skew wound motor and 6-pin DCC decoder socket..

371-375	66010 EWS maroon+yellow - *not made*	NA	NA
371-380A	66098 EWS maroon+yellow - *09*	68	83
371-375	66135 EWS maroon+yellow - *05*	65	78
371-380	66200 *Railway Heritage Committee* EWS maroon+yellow - *06*	65	78
371-384	66209 EWS maroon+yellow - *13*	NPG	NPG
371-381	66405 *Malcolm Logistics* blue - *08*	68	83
371-376	66502 Freightliner green - *not made*	NA	NA
371-378	66522 Freightliner/Shanks 2 greens - *06*	65	78
371-385	66546 Freightliner green - *13*	NPG	NPG
371-378	66610 Freightliner/Shanks green - *not made*	NA	NA
371-376	66610 Freightliner green - *05*	65	78
371-377	66701 *Whitemoor* GBRailfreight blue+yellow - *05*	68	83
371-379	66709 *Joseph Arnold Davies* GBf/Medite black +yellow - *06*	68	83
371-383	66152 DB Schenker red.- *09*	68	83

L63b.   Class 66/9 Co-Co (2007)

This is a model of the environmentally friendly Class 66. Except for the revised body moulding it is the same as the model in the last table.

Bardon Aggregates class 66 [L63b]

371-393	66301 Fastline grey - *10*	70	86
371-391	66411 *Eddie the Engine* DRS/Stobart dark blue - *07*	68	83
371-382	66412 DRS Malcolm Rail dark blue - *09*	68	83
371-394	66623 Freightliner Bardon Aggregates violet-blue - *10*	70	86
371-392	66725 *Sunderland AFC* First GBRf violet - *08*	68	83
371-396	66731 *InterhubGB* GBRf blue+yellow - *13*	NPG	NPG
371-395	66843 Colas Rail yellow+orange+black - *11*	75	96
371-390	66952 Freightliner green 40th Anniversary - *07*	68	83

L64.   Class 70 'Powerhaul' Co-Co (2013)

This is the 75 mph Co-Co 'PowerHaul' locomotive, built by General Electric in the USA for heavy freight work. It features innovative designs, such as 'Dynamic Braking' and AC traction technology. They are used across all parts of the extensive Freightliner route network.

It is a completely new model designed by Bachmann and based on the 4mm scale model they designed for their Branchline range.

371-636	70003 Freightliner green+yellow - *13*	100	119
371-635	70006 Freightliner green+yellow - *13*	100	119

Graham Farish by Bachmann

Electric Locomotives

These were reissued in 2005 with a brand new chassis with twin flywheels, 5-pole skew wound motors as previously used in the Class 158. The mouldings are crisper and the glazing better fitting than on the old GF models.

L65. Class 87 Bo-Bo (2005)

A total of 36 25kv AC locomotives of the 87 Class were built in 1973 for the West Coast Main Line. They were a development of the Class 86 and were powerful enough for the steep sections of the route. The locomotives had new bogies which greatly reduced track wear and Browne Willis pantographs for 110mph running. When replaced by Pendolinos, many were exported to Eastern Europe. The first of the class is now in the National Collection.

The original Graham Farish model was introduced in 1998 and reintroduced by Bachmann in 2005. It has a unique chassis.

371-750	**87001** *Royal Scot* Virgin red+black - *05*	65	77
371-752	**87002** *Royal Sovereign* BRe blue - *13*	NPG	NPG
371-753	**87005** *City of London* BRe InterCity grey - *13*	NPG	NPG
371-751	**87019** *Sir Winston Churchill* Virgin Trains red+black - *07*	65	82

L66. Class 90 Bo-Bo (2005)

Needing new AC electric locomotives for the West Coast Main Line, 50 of this class were built at BREL Crewe between 1986 and 1990. They are mixed traffic locomotives and were allocated to InterCity and Railfreight Distribution, while later, some were reallocated to postal trains (RES). Displaced by the spread of Virgin multiple units on the West Coast Main Line, 10 of the 50 Class 90s and 120 Mk3 coaches were transferred to the 'One' network in East Anglia.

Virgin Trains class 90 [L66] (Tony Wright)

371-776	**90004** *City of Glasgow* Virgin red+black - *05*	65	77
371-775	**90030** *Crewe Locomotive Works* EWS maroon+yellow - *05*	65	82
371-777	**90046** Freightliner green - *11*	75	94

L67. Class 91 Bo-Bo (2005)

With the electrification of the East Coast Main Line, locomotives were required to pull the trains. The result was the IC225 which are designed to run at 225 kilometers per hour (140mph) for a load of eleven Mk4 coaches and a Mk4 driving trailer. A total of 31 were built by BREL Crewe and introduced between 1988 and 1991.

The model was introduced by Graham Farish in 1990 and reintroduced by Bachmann in 2005.

371-801	**91004** *Grantham* GNER navy + 82212 DVT - *05*	75	92
(371-801)	**91004** *Grantham* on its own - *05*	60	NA
371-802	**91021** *Archbishop Thomas Cranmer* GNER navy blue + 82223 DVT - *11*	NPG	107
(371-802)	**91021** *Archbishop Thomas Cranmer* on its own	80	NA
371-800	**91126** *York Minster* GNER navy + **82226** DVT - *05*	70	87
(371-800)	**91126** *York Minster* on its own - *05*	60	NA

Diesel Multiple Units & Railcars

L68. GWR Railcar (2005)

In all, 38 AEC rail cars were built for the Great Western Railway and all those modelled come from the second batch built during the early years of the Second World War. These were built as multiple unit vehicles, fitted with an improved electro-pneumatic control system, so that they could work in tandem and had buffers.

The Graham Farish model was launched in 1985 and was reintroduced by Bachmann in 2005.

371-626	**19** GWR (shirt button) brown+cream - *05*	55	69
371-626A	**21** GWR brown+cream - *06*	NPG	NPG
371-626B	**22** GWR (button) brown+cream - *07*	60	76
371-625	**W22W** BRc green - *not made*	NA	NA
371-627	**W27W** BR red+cream - *05*	55	69
371-627A	**W20W** BR red+cream - *06*	60	76
371-625A	**W30W** BRc green - *07*	60	76
371-625	**W32W** BRc green - *05*	55	69

L69a. Class 101 2-Car DMU (2011)

The Class 101 is one of the best known of the first generation diesels and it was the most numerous. They were introduced between 1956 and 1960 and eventually all regions received an allocation. The combination of the size of the class and the large geographical area of operation made them an obvious subject to model.

The Graham Farish model was introduced in 1982 and although Bachmann inherited the tooling in 2000, no further models were made. Instead it was decided to completely retool the subject and this table includes those released as 2-car units. It has a 6-pin DCC socket fitted with underfloor micro switches to turn lights on and off. 3 different styles of cab and roof variations have been modelled, as too have passenger and cab interior detail. The models have brass fly-wheels.

BR class 101 DMU [L69a]

371-500	**E56362**+**E51204** BRc green speed whiskers - *11*	90	110
371-502	**M50154**+**M50160** BRe blue - *11*	90	110
371-500	ScotRail - *not made*	NA	NA
371-501	**51533**+**51224** BRe Regional Railways blue - *11*	90	110
371-503	**E53233**+**E53255** BRe blue+grey Express Parcels - *11*	90	110
(370-280)	**?**+**?** BRe Regional Railways blue+grey ex-'Regional Commuter' train set - *13*	90	NA

L69b. Class 101 3-Car DMU (2011)

This table contains the 3-car models and the structural detail is the same as that for the 2-car units in the table above.

371-512	**M50330**+**M59123**+**M50312** BRc green whiskers - *11*	100	120
371-510	**M50325**+**M59118**+**M50307** BRe blue - *11*	100	120
371-511	**SC51227**+**SC59045**+**SC53264** BRe blue+grey - *11*	100	120

L70a. Class 108 2-Car DMU (2008)

These were built by British Railways at its Derby Works. They consisted of 147 2-car, five 3-car and six 4-car units, built between 1958 and 1961. This totalled 210 powered vehicles and 123 trailer cars and they were generically known as 'Derby Lightweights'.

The units have a 6-pin DCC socket fitted and it is the first ready-to-run British N gauge model released that is able to accommodate a LokSound sound decoder and 13mm speaker housing included. The models also have a detailed interior, all wheel power contacts, working lights and a fly-wheel driven motor.

371-875	**M50628**+**M56214** BRc green speed whiskers - *08*	70	89
371-879	**M51563**+**M50926** BRc green with whiskers - *10*	85	103
371-875A	**M56263**+**M50980** BRc green speed whiskers DC6 - *09*	80	100
371-880	**E50622**+ **?** BRc green, small yellow panel - *13*	NPG	NPG
371-876	**M50976**+**M56224** BRe blue - *08*	70	89
371-878	**E53931**+**E51562** BRe blue - *10*	85	103
371-877	**53959**+**54243** BRe blue+grey - *08*	80	100
371-876A	**?**+**?** BRe blue - *09*	80	100

L70b. Class 108 3-Car DMU (2010)

This is a 3-car version of the model in the above table.

371-886	**E50644**+**E59388**+**E50622** BRc green - *10*	90	113
371-885	**E50626**+**E59384**+**E50636** BRe blue - *10*	90	113

L71. Class 150 2-Car 'Sprinter' DMU (2009)

These were the first of the Second Generation DMUs and the contract for them was placed with BREL by BR Provincial Sector in 1983. They were based on the Mk3 coach design and were built at York. The most obvious difference between the two subclasses is the provision of gangway connections on the front ends of the 150/2s. Fifty of the 150/1 sets were built and 85 of the 150/2s.

This is fitted with a 6-pin DCC decoder socket and the upgraded mechanism with its twin flywheel 5-pole skew wound motor. It also has tinted glazing and directional lights.

371-326	**150102** Centro green+blue 150/1 - *not made*	NA	NA

Graham Farish by Bachmann

Arriva Wales class 150 [L71]

371-326	**150125 (57125+52125)** Central Trains green+blue 150/1 - *09*		75	92
371-330	**150128** First Great Western violet blue - *13*		NPG	NPG
371-325	**150144 (57144+ 52144)** First North Western violet 150/1 - *09*		75	92
371-329	**150247** BRe Sprinter W - *13*		NPG	NPG
371-327	**150256 (57256+52256)** Arriva Trains Wales light blue 150/2 - *09*		75	92
371-328	**150270 (57270+52270)** BR Regional Railways violet+pale grey 150/2 - *09*		75	92
(370-105)	**150148 (57148+52148)** BR Provincial original Sprinter livery violet+pale grey 150/1 ex-set - *09*		75	NA

L72a. Class 158 DMU (2002)

In the late 1980s, British Railway's Provincial Sector needed a large fleet of DMUs for the outer suburban and cross-country trains. The competitive tender was won by BREL who built both 2-car and 3-car formations at BR Derby. Due to problems, the programme was not completed until 1992. Many variations exist in the fleet which can be found in many parts of the country.

The Graham Farish model first appeared in 1992 and was reintroduced by Bachmann in 2002. From 2005, it has had the upgraded mechanism developed for the Class 170 with its twin flywheel 5-pole skew wound motor and tinted glazing.

	2-car unit			
371-554	**158726 (57726+52726)** ScotRail Woosh! white+purple - *not made*		NA	NA
371-554	**158741 (57741+52741)** ScotRail Woosh! white+purple - *05*		65	86
371-552	**158745 (57745+52745)** Alphaline Wales & West silver - *02*		55	70
371-553	**158746 (57746+52746)** Wessex Trains Alphaline silver - *05*		65	83
371-551	**158758 (57758+ 52758)** FNW blue - *02*		55	70
371-550	**158783 (57783+52783)** Central green - *02*		65	86
371-557	**158783 (57783+52783)** East Midlands Trains blue +white+red - *10*		80	105
371-556	**158791 (57791+52791)** Northern Rail mauve+violet - *10*		80	105
371-550A	**158797 (57797+52797)** Central green - *05*		65	83
371-554	**158823** Northern Spirit light blue - *not made*		NA	NA
371-555	**158823 (52823+57823)** Arriva lt.blue - *07*		65	86
371-559	**158849 (?+?)** BRe Regional Railways blue+grey W - *13*		NPG	NPG
371-558	**158871 (52871+57871)** ScotRail Saltaire blue - *13*		100	122
	3-car unit			
371-525	**158811 (52811+57811+58811)** Northern Spirit TPE purple - *02*		60	75

L72b. Class 159 3-Car DMU (2005)

With a need to upgrade services on the Waterloo-Salisbury-Exeter line, Network SouthEast ordered 22 3-car sets in the style of the Class 158, then coming into use. Once the Class 158 building programme was complete, Derby started building the Class 159s. They were built in 1992 and 1993 and were finished in NSE livery.

Graham Farish introduced their model in 1994 and Bachmann reintroduced it in 2005 with the upgraded mechanism developed for the Class 170 with its twin flywheel 5-pole skew wound motor and tinted glazing.

371-526	**159019 (52891+58736+57891)** SWT white, blue, red + orange - *05*		72	88

L73. Class 168 'Clubman' 3-Car DMU (2006)

These are the post-Privatisation Adtranz built fast commuter DMUs for the Chiltern Line and were introduced in 2000. Five 3-car sets were ordered by Porterbrook for leasing to Chiltern Railways for the Marylebone - Birmingham service and they were built at Derby.

The model has the upgraded mechanism with its twin flywheel 5-pole skew wound motor.

371-435	**168111 (58161+58461+58261)** Chiltern Railways white+violet 168/1 - *06*		80	99

Chiltern Railways class 168 [L73] (Tony Wright)

L74. Class 170/171 'Turbostar' DMU (2004)

Post-Privatisation, trains were wanted for medium and long distance travel and Adranz had their 'Turbostars' as supplied to Chiltern Railways (Class 168). The design was modified, to produce fast commuter and inter-regional trains and they were given a new cab front. They were built at Derby. Class 170 'Turbostars' supplied to South Central were later provided with Dellner 12 couplers to allow for emergency coupling with its fleet of Class 377 EMUs. These were reclassified as Class 171 but in all other respects they are the same as Class 170 and so are included here.

The model has the upgraded mechanism with its twin flywheel 5-pole skew wound motor. In the case of the 3-car units, the power car is in the centre.

	2-car unit			
371-425	**170105 (50105+79105)** MML teal green 170/1 - *04*		65	84
371-429	**170270 (50270+79270)** Anglia/One blue 170/2 - *07*		70	90
371-427	**170302 (50302+79302)** SWT white+red+ blue 170/3 - *05*		70	88
371-434	**170504 (50504+79504)** Central Trains 170/5 - *13*		NPG	NPG
371-432	**170504 (50504+79504)** London Midland pale grey +green 170/5 - *09*		70	88
371-426	**170514 (50514+79514)** Central green 170/5 - *04*		65	84
371-431	**170519 (50519+79519)** Cross Country silver+purple 170/5 - *10*		80	100
371-430	**171721 (50721+79721)** Southern green+white - *07*		70	90
	3-car unit			
371-428	**170413 (79413+56413+50413)** First ScotRail purple 170/4 - *06*		80	99
371-433	**170434 (50434+56434+79434)** ScotRail Saltire blue - *13*		110	130

L75. Class 220 'Voyager' 4-Car DMU (2008)

A total of 34 non-tilting Class 220 'Voyagers' were built by Bombardier Transportation in 2000 for a fast passenger service. The 5-car trains replaced 8-10 car HSTs and not surprisingly they proved to be inadequate for the amount of passengers they needed to carry. The stock transferred to Arriva when they took over the Cross Country franchise.

This model has a 6-pin DCC decoder socket and a heavy twin fly-wheel chassis with working bi-directional lighting, detailed interiors and optional couplings.

371-675	**220001** *Maiden Voyager* **(60301+60701+ 60201+60401)** Virgin red+silver - *08*		110	132
371-678	**220017 (60317+60717+60217+60417)** Cross Country grey+purple - *08*		110	132
371-679	**220032** *Grampian Voyager* **+?+?+?** Virgin red+silver - *13*		NPG	NPG

L76. Class 222 'Meridian'/'Pioneer' DMU

This had been planned for 2009, but in July 2010 it was announced that Bachmann had decided to no proceed with this model for the time being

371-676	**222011** MML (Meridian) white+blue+grey - *not made*		NA	NA
371-679	**222017** East Midlands (Meridian) white+blue - *not made*		NA	NA
371-677	**222101** Hull Trains dark green+grey (Pioneer) - *not made*		NA	NA

Graham Farish by Bachmann

L77. BR Midland Pullman 6-car (2012)

These units were built in 1960 by Metropolitan Cammell for high speed Pullman train services and operated on the Midland Pullman service between 1961 and 1966. They were then transferred to the Great Western Main Line.

The power cars each have a 3-pole motor and a 6-pin DCC decoder socket. It has directional lights and saloon interior lights. The cars are lettered A to F, making it easy to get them in the right order, and the cars have paired long and short 'Rapido' couplings in NEM pockets, allowing you to alter the gap between cars. Rigid coupling bars are also supplied.

Midland 'Blue Pullman' [L77]

371-740	M60090+M60730+M60740+M60741+M60731+ M60091, Pullman, Nanking Blue+white - 12	220	270
371-741	M60092+M60732+M60742+M60743+M60733+ M60093, Pullman, blue with yellow ends - 12	220	270

Electric Multiple Units

L78. BR Class 350 'Desiro' EMU (2012)

These were built by Siemens AG and introduced 2004/5 for fast passenger services. They started work with the former Central Trains and Silverlink franchises before they were merged in the London Midland City franchise. Five units were loaned to Southern and had the third rail collection shoes attached. A further 37 units were ordered by London Midland and these are now in traffic.

The model has NEM close coupling between cars, running lights set to daytime condition and cab illumination. The PTOSLW unit is with the powered bogie and a 6-pin DCC decoder socket is fitted, plus provision for an ESU sound decoder with speaker housing at the non-powered end. It has an adjustable non-working pantograph and 3rd rail pick-up shoes (350/1) provided.

371-702	350101 London Midland grey+green 350/1 - 12	NPG	150
371-700	350111 *Apollo* (63771+66821+66871+63721) Silverlink (unbranded) grey+blue 350/1 - 12	NPG	150
371-701	350238 (61538+65238+67538+61438) London Midland grey+green 350/2 - 12	NPG	150

L79. BR Class 411 4-CEP EMU (2011)

The units were built in 1956-63 by BR at Eastleigh as express commuter trains. 111 of the 4-car units, were built and were based on the Mk1 coach design. Also based on the 1937 SR built 4-COR units they were mainly built for the Kent Coast electrification scheme. The 4 cars in each unit were a motor brake second open (MBSO), trailer composite corridor (TCK), trailer second corridor (TSK) and another MBSO. All units were refurbished at Swindon Works in 1980-83 and renumbered. Post privatisation, the units saw service with Connex SouthEastern (later South Eastern Trains), Connex South Central and South West Trains. The last unit was withdrawn in 2005 and several vehicles have been preserved.

The models have close coupling mechanisms, a powered MBSO with the drive mechanism, a 6-pin DCC decoder socket with an option for sound, 2 speaker housings and illuminated code boxes.

BR 4-CEP class EMU [L79]

372-675	7105 (S61229+S70229+S70235+S61230) BR green - 11	NPG	151
372-676	7126 (S61553+S70275+S70318+S61334) BR green - 11	NPG	151
372-677	7113 (S61309+S70305+S70262+S61303) BR blue+grey - 11	NPG	151

COACHES

NPCCS - Railway vans that are technically non-passenger carrying coaching stock, in this chapter are listed under wagons.

Cat No.	Company, Number, Colour, Date	£	£

GWR Coaches

C1a. GWR/BR Hawksworth Corridor 3rd (2013)

The side-corridor 3rds had 8 compartments and would seat 64 passengers. They were built by the Gloucester Carriage & Wagon Company in 1948 and had 4 doors to each side, 2 of them within compartments.

The model had not been released at the time of writing.

374-535	BR ? red+cream - 13	17	21

C1b. GWR/BR Hawksworth Composite (2013)

The Hawksworth coaches were built to a new length of 64 feet. The side-corridor composite had four 1st class compartments and three 3rd class ones.

The model had not been released at the time of writing.

374-560	BR ? red+cream - 13	17	21

C1c. GWR/BR Hawksworth Brake 3rd (2013)

The Hawksworth side-corridor brake 3rd coach contained four 3rd class compartments off a side corridor. This left room for the guard's compartment and plenty of space for luggage. They were built between 1949 and 1951.

The model had not been released at the time of writing.

374-510	BR ? red+cream - 13	17	21

C1d. GWR/BR Hawksworth Full Brake (2013)

The Hawksworth full brake was the newest version of a baggage car which could, for example, be added to a boat train in order to handle greater than usual luggage loads.

The model had not been released at the time of writing.

374-585	BR ? red+cream - 13	17	21

C2. BR Auto Trailer (2013)

The BR Auto Trailer is listed here under GWR coaches because they were associated with the Western Region of British Railways and were successors to the GWR auto trailer rather than being Mk1 stock.

The model had not been released at the time of writing.

374-610	BR ? red+cream - 13	NPG	NPG
374-612	BR ? red - 13	NPG	NPG
374-611	BR ? maroon - 13	NPG	NPG

LMS Coaches

These LMS Stanier Period 3 coaches are Blue Riband models.

C3a. LMS Period 3 Corridor 1st (2008)

These 57ft side-corridor coaches were built at Derby or Wolverton from the mid to late 1930s, some surviving until 1965. There were five compartments seating six passengers and one compartment seating three.

374-845	LMS 1062 maroon - *08*	10	15
374-845A	LMS 1066 maroon - *10*	10	16
374-845B	LMS 1080 maroon - *12*	15	19
374-846	BR M1077M red+cream - *08*	10	15
374-846A	BR M1066M red+cream - *10*	12	16
374-846B	BR M1052M red+cream - *12*	15	19
374-847	BR M1062M maroon - *10*	12	16

C3b. LMS Period 3 Corridor 3rd (2008)

EX-LMS Period 3 corridor 2nd [C3b]

These 57ft side-corridor standard TK coaches were built at Derby or Wolverton from the mid to late 1930s, some surviving until 1966. There were seven compartments seating eight passengers and a lavatory at each end of the coach.

374-835	LMS 2040 maroon - *08*	10	15
374-835A	LMS 1674 maroon - *10*	12	16
374-835B	LMS ? maroon - *13*	17	21

Visit the BRM website at: www.model-railways-live.co.uk

374-836	BR M1971M red+cream - 08	10	15
374-836A	BR M1981M red+cream - 10	12	16
374-836B	BR M?M red+cream - 12	12	16
(370-275)	BR M1933M red+cream - ?	12	NA
374-837	BR M1674M maroon - 09	12	16
374-837A	BR M1766M maroon - 12	15	19

C3c. LMS Period 3 Open 3rd (2008)

Open or vestibule coaches in this Period 3 of Stanier's designs were not as common as corridor coaches. They were built at both Derby and Wolverton and building of them went on from 1933 until 1948. Most had 56 seats of which 24 were 'no smoking'.

374-840	LMS 9443 maroon - 08	10	15
374-840A	LMS 4964 maroon - 10	12	16
374-841	BR M9491M red+cream - 08	10	15
374-841A	BR M9502M red+cream - 09	12	16
374-841B	BR M9459M red+cream - 13	15	19
374-842	BR M9443M maroon - 10	12	16
374-842A	BR M9480M maroon - 12	15	19

C3d. LMS Period 3 Open Composite (2008)

Open or vestibule composites were built in smaller numbers, mostly at Derby, but a few at Wolverton. They were built between 1933 and 1939 and seated either 12 or 18 1st class passengers and the rest 3rd class.

374-850	LMS 9755 maroon - 08	10	15
374-850A	LMS 9750 maroon - 10	10	16
374-850B	LMS ? maroon - 13	17	21
374-851	BR M9752M red+cream - 08	10	15
374-851A	BR M9743M red+cream - 10	12	16
374-851B	BR M?M red+cream - 13	17	21
374-852	BR M9755M maroon - 10	12	16
(370-275)	BR M1933M red+cream ex-Deltic set - 10	13	NA

C3e. LMS Period 3 Corridor Brake 1st (2008)

This was the standard Period 3 corridor brake first and 11 were built at Wolverton in 1937-38. This included 3 for the 'Coronation Scot' train. They had 18 first class seats.

374-830	LMS 5062 maroon - 08	10	15
374-830A	LMS 5060 maroon - 10	10	16
374-830B	LMS 5055 maroon - 12	15	19
374-831	BR M5053M red+cream - 08	12	16
374-831A	BR M5055M red+cream - 10	12	16
374-831B	BR M5060M red+cream - 12	15	19
374-832	BR M5062M maroon - 10	12	16

C3f. LMS Period 3 Corridor Brake 3rd (2008)

These 57ft side-corridor coaches were built at Derby or Wolverton from the mid-1930s, some surviving until 1966. There were four compartments seating eight passengers and a lavatory at the end of the passenger section, closest to the guard and luggage area.

374-825	LMS 5789 maroon - 08	10	15
374-825A	LMS 5810 maroon - 10	12	16
374-826	BR M5805M red+cream - 08	10	15
374-826A	BR M5772M red+cream - 11	13	16
374-826B	BR M5777M red+cream - 13	13	19
374-827	BR M5789M maroon - 13	17	21
374-827A	BR M?M maroon - 10	12	16
(370-275)	BR M5775M red+cream ex-Deltic set - 10	13	NA

C4. LMS 50ft Full Brake (2013)

Most of the Stanier Period 3 LMS 50' full brakes were built at Wolverton in the late 1930s and many had been scrapped by 1968. Some were successors to the 'Stove R' and became the most numerous LMS full brakes on the system. Most were rated as having a 12 ton carrying capacity.

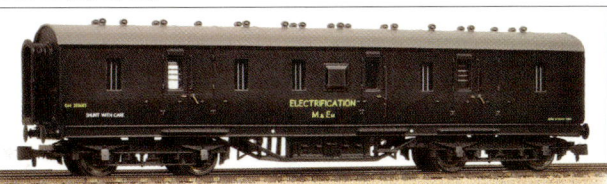

BR Departmental Electrician's coach [C4] (Bachmann)

374-885	LMS ? maroon - 13	15	19
374-887	BR M31413M red W - 13	15	19
374-886	BR M31319M red+cream - 13	15	19
374-888	BR Departmental DM 395663? black 'Electrification' - 13	15	19

C5. LMS Inspection Saloon (2012)

The saloons were built by the LMS in the 1940s to help managers to inspect the line in style. Several have been preserved.

The models have NEM close coupling and detailed interiors. This model is produced exclusively for the N Gauge Society, for sale to its members.

374-875Z	LMS 45021 lined maroon - *not made*	NA	NA
374-875Z	LMS 45036 lined maroon - 12	20	25
374-875U	LMS 45030 lined maroon, yellow ends - 12	20	25
374-875S	LMS 45021 unlined maroon with black ends (war-time livery) - 12	20	25
374-875Y	BR M45026M red+cream - 12	20	25
374-875X	BR M45020M lined maroon with maroon ends - 12	20	25
374-875R	BR M45035M lined maroon - 12	20	25
374-875W	BR M45028M blue+grey - 12	20	25
374-875T	EWS 45029 maroon+yellow - 12	20	25

SR Coaches

The Bulleid SR coaches were designed by the Southern Railway but, by the time they went into production, the railways had been nationalised. They therefore went straight into BR livery. The models had not been released at the time of writing but they will be to Blue Riband standard.

C6a. SR/BR 63ft Bulleid Corridor 3rd (2013)

These are 8-compartment side-corridor 3rd class coaches, which were built at Eastleigh between 1948 and 1950. They were built to diagram 2019.

374-441	BR ? red+cream - 13	17	21
374-440	BR ? green - 13	17	21

C6b. SR/BR 63ft Bulleid Open 3rd (2013)

This time the coaches were 8-bay open 3rds, built to diagram 2017. They were from a very late batch built at Eastleigh in 1950.

374-451	BR ? red+cream - 13	17	21
374-450	BR ? green - 13	17	21

C6c. SR/BR 63ft Bulleid Corridor Composite (2013)

Built at Eastleigh in 1948, these were 7-compartment coaches with side corridors. They were built to diagram 2318 and had four 1st class compartments and three 3rd class ones.

374-461	BR ? red+cream - 13	17	21
374-460	BR ? green - 13	17	21

C6d. SR/BR 63ft Bulleid Semi-Open Brake 3rd (2013)

These were built at Eastleigh in 1949 and each consisted of two compartments and a 32 seat open saloon. The two compartments were at the guard's end of the coach. There were three passenger entrance doors on both sides of the coach.

374-431	BR ? red+cream - 13	17	21
374-430	BR ? green - 13	17	21

C7. SR PL Luggage Van (2013)

This model was still under development at the time of writing. The real vehicle illustrated in the catalogue is of a Parcels & Luggage Van (PLV).

374-415	BR ? red - 13	NPG	NPG
374-416	BR ? green - 13	NPG	NPG

C8. SR 50ft Bogie B Luggage Van (2013)

This highly detailed model is of a 28 ton goods guard's van of which 100 were built at Eastleigh in 1938-39. Some later had a stove fitted in them, after which they were referred to as 'Van B Stoves' and had orange panels painted behind the running number. Some had brackets fitted to take roof destination boards - especially for newspaper trains. Another 30 were built by British Railways at Lancing in 1952-53. They were used for newspapers, mail and parcels. The main cull came in 1980 when BR lost its parcels business.

This model was still under development at the time of writing.

374-461	BR ? red+cream - 13	NPG	NPG
374-460	BR ? green - 13	NPG	NPG

BR Mk1 Non-Gangwayed Coaches

C9a. BR 57' 'Suburban' Coach (2002)

This was the original Graham Farish 'Suburban' coach body of 1972 on a more realistic chassis.

374-277	BR M11497 red all 2nd (also in set 370-075) - 02	8	11
374-278	BR M16751 red - 02	8	11
374-275	BR W6680 maroon lined - 02	8	11

Graham Farish by Bachmann

374-276	BR W5490 maroon lined all 2nd - *02*	8	11

C9b. BR 57' 'Suburban' Brake End (2002)

This was the original Graham Farish 'Suburban' brake end body of 1972 on a more realistic chassis.

374-301	BR M20525 red (also in set 370-075) - *02*	8	11
374-300	BR W4694 maroon lined - *02*	8	11

C10a. BR Mk1 57' 'Suburban' Compartment 3rd (2005)

The 2nd class coaches each had nine compartments and could seats for 108 passengers. With the absence of corridors, compartments were isolated from each other and necessitated nine doors on each side of the coach. The coaches were built at BR Wolverton and Derby in four separate lots during 1954 and 1955.

This is a completely retooled, well detailed, model.

BR Mk1 non-gangwayed 3rd class with compartments [C10a]

374-270	BR W46012 red - *05*	10	14
374-270A	BR M46081 red - *10*	10	16
374-270B	BR E46212 red - *12*	14	17
374-271	BR M46071 maroon lined - *05*	10	13
374-271A	BR M46073 maroon lined - *09*	10	14
374-271B	BR M46067 maroon lined - *13*	10	17

C10b. BR Mk1 57' 'Suburban' Open 3rd (2005)

Two lots of open 3rd class coaches were built at Derby and Doncaster. They were partitioned into two separate uneven sized saloons. There was an off-centre isle with double seats on one side of it and triple seats on the other side. There were long seats across both ends of each of the two saloons, each holding six passengers. The total capacity was 94 and there were ten doors along each side.

374-290	BR W48033 red - *05*	10	14
374-290A	BR W48030 red - *10*	10	16
374-290B	BR E48040 red - *12*	14	17
374-291	BR M48032 maroon lined - *05*	10	13
374-291A	BR W48029 maroon lined - *09*	10	14
374-291B	BR M48040 maroon lined - *13*	10	17
374-292	BR ? blue - *13*	17	21

C10c. BR Mk1 57' 'Suburban' Composite (2005)

These were built at Wolverton in 1954-55 and had 9 compartments with doors on both sides. The middle three compartments were 1st class with a total of 24 seats and the remainder were 3rd class with a total of 72 seats.

374-280	BR W41045 red - *05*	10	14
374-280A	BR M41004 red - *10*	10	16
374-280B	BR E41010 red - *12*	14	17
374-281	BR M41014 maroon lined - *05*	10	13
374-281A	BR W41058 maroon lined - *09*	10	14
374-281B	BR M41008 maroon lined - *13*	10	17
(370-076)	BR M41012 maroon lined ex-set - *05*	8	NA

C10d. BR Mk1 57' 'Suburban' Brake 3rd (2005)

The brake 2nd had 6 compartments, with doors on both sides and the coaches could each accommodate 72 passengers, with 6 people sat on each seat. Four lots were built during 1954 and 1955, the work being divided between BR coach works at York, Derby and Doncaster.

BR Mk1 non-gangwayed brake 3rd [C10d]

374-311	BR W43270 red - *05*	10	14
374-311A	BR W43106 red - *10*	10	14
374-311B	BR E43363 red - *12*	14	17
374-312	BR E43132 red - *11*	14	17
374-312A	BR E43182 red - *12*	14	17
(370-076)	BR M43268 maroon lined ex-set - *05*	8	NA
374-310	BR M43269 maroon lined - *05*	10	14
374-310A	BR W43266 maroon lined - *10*	10	15
374-310B	BR M43233 maroon lined - *13*	10	17
374-311B	BR ? maroon lined - *not made**	NA	NA
374-313	BR ? blue - *13*	17	21

*shown in the 2012 and 2013 catalogues as lined maroon but was released in 2012 as crimson E43363.

BR Mk1 Main Line Coaches

C11a-a. BR Mk1 Corridor 1st (FK) (2005)

These were built in 8 lots, the first in 1952 at Swindon and it was there that the last lot was also built 10 years later. In each coach there were 7 compartments, each with 6 seats, and there was a toilet at each end of the coach. Each end also had a vestibule with external doors and there was an additional door in the centre of the corridor side of the coach.

374-150	BR M13004 red+cream - *05*	11	14
374-150A	BR M13062 red+cream - *08*	11	14
374-150B	BR M13060 red+cream - *11*	12	16
374-151	BR S13143 green - *05*	11	14
374-151A	BR S13003 green - *09*	11	14
374-151B	BR ? green - *?*	NPG	NPG
374-152	BR W13074 brown+cream - *05*	11	14
374-152A	BR W13137 brown+cream - *08*	11	14
374-152B	BR W13185 brown+cream - *11*	12	16
374-153	BR W13030 maroon - *05*	11	14
374-153A	BR E13245 maroon - *07*	11	14
374-153B	BR M13070 maroon - *09*	12	15
374-153C	BR W13127 maroon lined - *11*	12	16
374-156	BR E13107 blue+grey - *08*	11	14
374-156A	BR E13234 blue+grey - *11*	12	16
374-154	BR Intercity M13341 grey+beige - *05*	11	14
374-155	BR Regional Railways 13225 blue+beige - *05*	11	14

C11a-b. BR Mk1 Corridor 1st (FK) New (2012)

This is the Blue Riband replacement model of 2012.

374-160	BR M13060 red+cream - *12*	15	19
374-162	BR S13086 green - *12*	15	19
374-163	BR W13085 dark brown+cream - *12*	15	19
374-161	BR E13333 maroon - *12*	15	19
374-164	BR M13085 blue+grey - *12*	15	19

C11b. BR Mk1 1st Open (FO) New (2012)

Many of the coaches were built at Doncaster and another principal builder was the Birmingham Railway Carriage & Wagon Co. Ltd. In all, 154 were built with 91 of them going to the London Midland Region and the Eastern Region receiving 39. The Western Region received 12, the Southern 8 and the Scottish Region just 4. When first built, the real coaches had only end doors but, to speed up access and egress, a centre door on each side was later added. A 2+1 seating arrangement was used and a two bay non-smoking saloon was provided at one end of the coach. There was also a toilet at each end, on the same side and so externally one side has two frosted windows and the other side has none. Between facing seats there were tables and the FO was sometimes paired with a kitchen car to serve as a restaurant car.

This is a completely new model as there was no FO in the original Graham Farish Mk1 coach range.

374-815	BR M3028 red+cream - *12*	16	20
374-817	BR S3064 green - *12*	16	20
374-818	BR W4085 dark brown+cream - *12*	16	20
374-816	BR M3140 maroon - *12*	16	20
374-819	BR E3080 blue+grey - *12*	16	20

C11c-a. BR Mk1 Corridor 2nd (SK) (2002)

More of these 3rd class corridor coaches were produced than any other design in the history of Britain's railways. The first lot was built in 1952 at Eastleigh and the last in 1963 at the BR coach works at York. The coach had doors both sides at each end and a central vestibule split the compartments into 2 groups of 4. Shared armrests were provided on seats making three positions each side of the compartment and providing space for 48 passengers per coach.

374-050	BR M24446 red+cream - *02*	11	14
374-050A	BR M24813 red+cream - *03*	11	14
374-050B	BR E24807 red+cream - *04*	11	14
374-050C	BR E24783 red+cream - *05*	11	14
374-050D	BR M24159 red+cream - *06*	11	14
374-050E	BR M25889 red+cream - *07*	11	14
374-051	BR S24311 green - *02*	11	14

Graham Farish by Bachmann

374-051A	BR S24324 green * - 04	11	14
374-051B	BR S24309 green - 06	11	14
374-051C	BR S24318 green - 08	11	14
(370-225)	BR S24327 green ex-set - 03	11	NA
(370-225)	BR S24309 green ex-set - 03	11	NA
374-052	BR W24165 brown+cream - 02	11	14
374-052A	BR W25051 brown+cream (also in set 370-150) - 03	11	14
374-052B	BR W25093 brown+cream - 04	11	14
374-052C	BR W26099 brown+cream - 06	11	14
374-052D	BR W26128 brown+cream - 08	11	14
(370-150)	BR W25050 brown+cream ex-set - 03	11	NA
374-053	BR E24538 maroon - 02	11	14
374-053A	BR M25400 maroon - 03	11	14
374-053B	BR M25437 maroon - 04	11	14
374-053C	BR M25409 maroon - 05	11	14
374-053D	BR E24237 maroon - 06	11	14
374-053E	BR E25491 maroon - 07	11	14
374-053F	BR E26057 maroon - 08	11	14
(370-100)	BR M24399 maroon ex-set - 03	11	NA
(370-100)	BR M24823 maroon ex-set - 03	11	NA
(370-101)	BR M24824 maroon ex-sets 370-101 & 370-102 - 05	11	NA
(370-101)	BR M24400 maroon ex-sets 370-101 & 370-102 - 05	11	NA
(370-135)	BR M24567 red+cream ex-set - 02	11	NA
(370-135)	BR M24819 red+cream ex-set - 02	11	NA
374-055	BR E25039 blue+grey - 03	11	14
374-055A	BR E25011 blue+grey - 04	11	14
374-055B	BR E2603 blue+grey - 06	11	14
374-055C	BR M25893 blue+grey - 07	11	14
374-055D	BR E2603 blue+grey - 08	11	14
374-054	BR Intercity M18753 grey+beige - 03	11	14
374-054A	BR E24448 grey+beige - 06	11	14

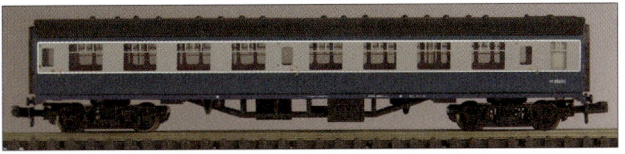

BR Mk1 corridor 2nd (SK) [C11c-a]

* Also shown as 374-051B in the catalogue.

C11c-b. BR Mk1 Corridor 2nd (SK) New (2010)
This is the Blue Riband replacement model of 2010.

374-060	BR M24135 red+cream - 10	14	18
374-060A	BR E24240 red+cream - 11	15	19
374-060B	BR ? red+cream - ?	15	19
374-060C	BR ? red+cream - 13	17	21
374-064	BR W24328 dark brown+cream - 10	14	18
374-064A	BR W25200 dark brown+cream - 11	15	19
374-064B	BR W? dark brown+cream - ?	15	19
374-063	BR S24317 green - 10	14	18
374-063A	BR S24302 green - 11	15	19
374-063B	BR S? green - ?	15	19
374-061	BR M24911 maroon - 10	14	18
374-061A	BR W24165 maroon - 11	15	19
374-061B	BR ? maroon - ?	15	19
374-061C	BR ? maroon W - 13	17	21
(370-060)	BR E24538 maroon - 11	15	NA
374-062	BR Sc18551 blue+grey - 10	14	18
374-062A	BR W18573 blue+grey - 11	15	19
374-062B	BR ? blue+grey - 12	15	19
374-062C	BR ? blue+grey - 13	17	21

C11d-a. BR Mk1 Open 2nd (TSO) (2005)
The external appearance was the same for the SO and TSO. The TSO seated 64 passengers (2+2 abreast). The positions of doors and lavatories were the same as for the SK but, being open plan coaches, the gangway ran down the centre. Again, very large quantities of this type of coach were built between 1953 and 1963, the first ones at Derby and the last batch at York.

374-000	BR E34796 red+cream - not made	NA	NA
374-000	BR E3737 red+cream - 05	11	14
374-000A	BR M4421 red+cream - 07	11	14
374-001	BR S4040 green - 05	11	14
374-002	BR W4739 brown+cream - 05	11	14
374-002A	BR W26093 brown+cream - 07	11	14
374-003	BR M4899 maroon - 05	11	14
374-006	BR E3457 blue+grey - 08	11	14
374-004	InterCity 4909 grey+beige - 05	11	14
374-005	Regional Railways 4873 blue+grey - 05	11	14

C11d-b. BR Mk1 Open 2nd (SO) New (2010)
This is the Blue Riband replacement model of 2010.

BR Mk1 open 3rd (SO) in early livery [C11d-b]

374-010	BR M3741 red+cream - 10	14	18
374-010A	BR W3789 red+cream - 11	15	19
374-010B	BR ? red+cream - ?	15	19
374-010C	BR ? red+cream - 13	17	21
374-011	BR S3824 green - 10	14	18
374-011A	BR S3825 green - 11	15	19
374-011B	BR S? green - ?	15	19
374-014	BR W3821 dark brown+cream - 10	14	18
374-014A	BR W? dark brown+cream - ?	15	19
374-014B	BR W? dark brown+cream - ?	15	19
374-012	BR M4929 maroon - 10	14	18
374-012A	BR ? maroon - ?	15	19
374-012B	BR E3850 maroon - 12	15	19
374-012C	BR ? maroon W - 13	17	21
374-013	BR M4439 blue+grey - 10	14	18
374-013A	BR E4336 blue+grey - 11	15	19
374-013B	BR ? blue+grey - 13	17	21
-	BR RTC Test Coach 5	16	NA
-	BR RTC Laboratory Coach 12	16	NA
374-000Z	above 2 coaches Sp Edn 504 (ModelZone) - 10	NA	40

C11e-a. BR Mk1 Corridor Composite (CK) (2005)
Eleven lots of CKs were built, the first at Derby in 1952 and the last lot, also at Derby, in 1963. There were 3 third class compartments and 4 in the first class end of the coach. They were separated by a door in the corridor, as well as a central vestibule with outside doors. In addition, there were vestibules with external doors at both ends of the coach.

374-250	BR M15019 red+cream - 05	11	14
374-251	BR S15904 green - 05	11	14
374-252	BR W15770 brown+cream - 05	11	14
374-253	BR E15145 maroon - 05	11	14

C11e-b. BR Mk1 Corridor Composite (CK) New (2010)
This is the Blue Riband replacement model of 2010.

374-255	BR M15192 red+cream - 10	14	18
374-255A	BR E15055 red+cream - 11	15	19
374-255B	BR W15059 red+cream - 12	15	19
374-259	BR S15904 green - 10	14	18
374-259A	BR S? green - ?	15	19
374-256	BR W15110 brown+cream - 10	14	18
374-256A	BR W15777 brown+cream - 11	15	19
374-257	BR M15916 maroon - 10	14	18
374-257A	BR ? maroon - ?	15	19
374-257B	BR E15699 maroon - 12	15	19
374-258	BR E15768 blue+grey - 10	14	18
374-258A	BR E16031 blue+grey - 11	15	19
374-258B	BR M15939 blue+grey - 12	15	19

C11f-a. BR Mk1 Corridor Brake 2nd (BSK) (2005)
Over the years 13 lots of these were built, the earliest at Derby in 1952 and the last lot were constructed at Wolverton in 1962. The coach was divided roughly into two, with 4 compartments and a lavatory in one end, followed by the guard's compartment and luggage space at the other end. There were doors both sides, at either end of the passenger section, and two sets of double doors in the luggage compartment. The guard had a private door either side of the coach.

374-175	BR E34226 red+cream - 05	11	14
374-175A	BR red+cream - not made	NA	NA
374-176	BR S35021 green - 05	11	14
374-177	BR W34751 brown+cream - 05	11	14
374-178	BR M35486 maroon - 05	11	14

Graham Farish by Bachmann

374-178A	BR maroon - *not made*	NA	NA
374-181	BR blue+grey - *not made*	NA	NA
374-179	BR Intercity M35465 grey+beige - *05*	11	14
374-180	BR Regional Railways 35452 blue+beige - *05*	11	14
374-190*	NR DB975081 yellow+black gauging main data coach - *12*	15	19

* Despite the catalogue number, the old tooling was used for this model.

C11f-b. BR Mk1 Corridor Brake 2nd (BSK) New (2010)
This is the Blue Riband replacement model of 2010.

374-185	BR M34288 red+cream - *10*	14	18
374-185A	BR W34139 red+cream - *11*	15	19
374-185B	BR ? red+cream - *13*	15	19
374-186	BR S34641 green - *10*	14	18
374-186A	BR S34642 green - *11*	15	19
374-196B	BR S34155 green - *12*	15	19
374-189	BR W34290 brown+cream - *10*	14	18
374-189A	BR W34885 brown+cream - *11*	15	19
374-189B	BR W? dark brown+cream - *?*	15	19
374-187	BR M34140 maroon - *10*	14	18
374-187A	BR W34152 maroon - *11*	15	19
374-187B	BR ? maroon - *13*	15	19
374-187C	BR ? maroon W - *13*	17	21
(370-060)	BR E34168 maroon - *11*	15	NA
374-188	BR M35040 blue+grey - *10*	14	18
374-188A	BR E35119 blue+grey - *11*	15	19
374-188B	BR ? blue+grey - *13*	15	19

BR Mk1 brake 2nd (BSK) [C11f-b]

C11g-a. BR Mk1 Corridor Brake Comp (BCK) (2002)
The earliest batch came from Derby in 1954 and the final lot, also from the same works, in 1963. There were 5 compartments, each with 6 seats with adjustable armrests. 3 of the compartments were for 3rd class and 2 were 1st class. The corridor had a dividing door between the 1st and 2nd class areas. There was a lavatory and vestibule, with external doors, at either end of the passenger section of the coach. Only a little over a quarter of the coach was left for the guard's compartment and luggage space. The latter had one double door each side and the guard also had a single door each side.

374-075	BR M21026 red+cream - *02*	11	14
374-075A	BR E21093 red+cream - *05*	11	14
374-075B	BR W21071 red+cream - *05*	11	14
374-075C	BR E21217 red+cream - *06*	11	14
374-075D	BR E21053 red+cream - *08*	11	14
(370-135)	BR M21030 red+cream ex-set - *02*	11	NA
(370-135)	BR M21238 red+cream ex-set - *02*	11	NA
374-076	BR S21268 green - *02*	11	14
374-076A	BR S21271 green - *04*	11	14
374-076B	BR S21275 green - *08*	11	14
(370-225)	BR S21264 green ex-set - *03*	11	NA
(370-225)	BR S21273 green ex-set - *03*	11	NA
374-077	BR W21067 brown+cream - *02*	11	14
374-077A	BR W21083 brown+cream - *04*	11	14
374-077B	BR W21135 brown+cream - *06*	11	14
374-077C	BR W21192 brown+cream - *08*	11	14
374-078	BR E21202 maroon - *02*	11	14
374-078A	BR M21226 maroon - *03*	11	14
374-078B	BR E21219 maroon - *05*	11	14
374-078C	BR E21259 maroon - *06*	11	14
374-078D	BR E21234 maroon - *08*	11	14
(370-100)	BR M21033 maroon ex-set - *03*	11	NA
(370-100)	BR M21198 maroon ex-set - *03*	11	NA
(370-101)	BR M21199 maroon ex-sets 370-101 & 370-102 - *05*	11	NA
(370-101)	BR M21034 maroon ex-sets 370-101 & 370-102 - *05*	11	NA
374-080	BR M21241 blue+grey - *03*	11	14
374-080A	BR E21037 blue+grey - *06*	11	14
374-080B	BR E21216 blue+grey - *08*	11	14
374-079	BR Intercity 21266 grey+beige - *03*	11	14
374-086*	Network Rail DB975280 yellow gauging generator & staff coach - *12*	15	19

* Despite the catalogue number, the old tooling was used for this model.

C11g-b. BR Mk1 Brake Composite (BCK) New (2011)
This is the Blue Riband replacement model of 2011.

BR Mk1 brake composite (BCK) [C11g-b]

374-081	BR M21029 red+cream - *11*	15	19
374-083	BR S21272 green - *11*	15	19
374-082	BR W21080 dark brown+cream - *11*	15	19
374-084	BR M21026 maroon - *11*	15	19
374-084A	BR ? maroon W - *13*	17	21
374-085	BR E21222 blue+grey - *11*	15	19
374-085A	BR ? blue+grey - *13*	17	21

C11h-a. BR Mk1 Full Brake (BG) (2002)
The full brake had a guard's compartment in the centre and two large areas either side of it for storing luggage. There were 4 pairs of doors in each side as well as a single door in the centre of each side for the guard. The standard Mk1 BG was shorter than other Mk1 coaches, being 57ft (17.37m) long instead of 63ft (19.20m). Eight lots of them were built, the first batch at Derby in 1953 and the last lot was built in 1961, by Gloucester Railway Carriage & Wagon Ltd.

374-026	BR M80541 red+cream - *03*	11	14
374-026A	BR M80549 red+cream - *04*	11	14
374-026B	BR E86308 red+cream - *07*	11	14
374-026C	BR E80623 red+cream - *09*	11	14
374-027	BR E80798 maroon - *02*	11	14
374-027A	BR E80792 maroon - *04*	11	14
374-027B	BR M81299 maroon - *07*	11	14
374-027C	BR M80950 maroon - *09*	11	14
374-028	BR S81510 green - *02*	11	14
374-028A	BR green - *not made*	NA	NA
374-029	BR W81205 brown+cream - *02*	11	14
374-029A	BR W81216 brown+cream - *05*	11	14
374-029B	BR W81019 brown+cream - *07*	11	14
374-029C	BR W80668 brown+cream - *09*	11	14
374-025	BR E80617 blue+grey Newspapers - *02*	11	14
374-025A	BR E80629 blue+grey - *05*	11	14
374-025B	BR M80871 blue+grey - *07*	11	14
374-025C	BR M? blue+grey – *not made*	NA	NA
(370-065)	BR ? blue+grey, ex 'Newspaper Express' train set - *13*	17	NA
(370-065)	BR ? blue, 'Express Parcels', ex 'Newspaper Express' train set - *13*	17	NA
374-030	Inter-City 92151 grey+beige NEA* - *03*	11	14
374-031	Regional Rlys E92058 blue+grey NEA - *03*	11	14
374-032	RES 92322 red+dark grey NEX (also in set 370-125) - *03*	11	14
374-032A	RES 92327 red+dark grey NEX - *08*	11	14
(370-125)	RES 92418 red+dark grey NFA ex-set - *03*	11	NA

* Box marked NHA but model marked NEA.

C11h-b. BR Mk1 Full Brake (BG) New (2012)
This is the Blue Riband replacement model of 2012.

BR Mk1 full brake (BG) [C11h-b]

374-035	BR M80565 red+cream - *12*	15	19
374-037	BR S80893 green - *12*	15	19
374-038	BR W80713 dark brown+cream - *12*	15	19
374-036	BR E80533 maroon - *12*	15	19
374-036A	BR ? maroon W - *13*	17	21
374-039	BR M80906 blue+grey - *12*	15	19
374-039A	BR ? blue+grey - *13*	17	21

374-040	Network Rail ? yellow generator van - *12*	15	19
374-041	BR Departmental 975613 olive green - *12*	15	19

C11i-a. BR Mk1 Mini Buffet (RMB) (2003)

A total of 82 of these were built at York and Wolverton between 1957 and 1962. They were provided for shorter distance and cross country routes and had a small buffet counter offering light snacks and drinks. The first 12 vehicles had 48 seats but these were reduced to 44 to allow for additional stock storage. Numbers 1872 and 1873 were converted for use in Southern Region EMUs around 1975. During the 1980s, the RMBs were refurbished. After sectorisation, they passed to InterCity but most had been withdrawn by the time of Privatisation. Three survived in service with Anglia Railways until the last was withdrawn in 2001 and many have been preserved.

374-100	BR red+cream - *not made*	NA	NA
374-100	BR S1881 green - *03*	11	14
374-100A	BR S1864 green - *05*	11	14
374-100B	BR green – *not made*	NA	NA
374-101	BR green - *not made*	NA	NA
374-101	BR W1814 brown+cream - *03*	11	14
374-101A	BR W1821 brown+cream - *05*	11	14
374-101B	BR W1816 brown+cream - *06*	11	14
374-101C	BR brown+cream – *not made*	NA	NA
374-102	BR brown+cream - *not made*	NA	NA
374-102	BR E1871 maroon - *03*	11	14
374-102A	BR E1879 maroon - *05*	11	14
374-102B	BR M1864 maroon - *06*	11	14
374-102C	BR M1821 maroon - *08*	11	14
374-102D	BR maroon – *not made*	NA	NA
374-103	BR maroon - *not made*	NA	NA
374-104	BR E1871 blue+grey - *03*	11	14
374-104A	BR M1869 blue+grey - *08*	11	14
374-105	BR blue+grey - *not made*	NA	NA
374-103	BR Intercity 1832 grey+beige RBR - *03*	11	14
374-104	BR Intercity grey+beige - *not made*	NA	NA

C11i-b. BR Mk1 Mini Buffet (RMB) New (2011)

This is the Blue Riband replacement model of 2011.

374-108	BR S1849 green - *11*	15	19
374-109	BR W1813 dark brown+cream - *11*	15	19
374-107	BR E1854 maroon - *11*	15	19
374-110	BR M1838 blue+grey - *11*	15	19

C11j-a. BR Mk1 Restaurant Car (RU) (2006)

Two batches of RUs were built in 1957 and 1958. Ashford provided the underframe and Swindon built the body. There was seating for 33 passengers, in each coach, but later a table and 4 seats were removed, reducing the capacity to 29. The rest of the space in the coach was taken up with the pantry and kitchen, staff compartment and staff toilet, as well as corridor links for the public.

374-117	BR W1902 brown+cream - *06*	11	14
374-117A	BR ? brown+cream - *?*	NPG	NPG
374-116	BR E1926 maroon - *06*	11	14
374-116A	BR W1915 maroon - *09*	12	15
374-115	BR E1938 blue+grey - *06*	11	14
374-118	BR Intercity 1981 grey+beige - *06*	11	14

C11j-b. BR Mk1 Restaurant Car (RU) New (2013)

This is the Blue Riband replacement model of 2013.

BR Mk1 unclassified restaurant car (RU) [C11j-b]

374-120	BR W1900 red+cream - *13*	14	18
374-121	BR W1917 maroon - *13*	15	19
374-122	BR M1908 blue+grey - *13*	15	19

C11k-a. BR Mk1 Restaurant Car (RFO) (2005)

These were the very first BR restaurant cars and were built at York in 1951. They were designed to run with kitchen cars. They had 7 first class bays seating 42 diners and only 11 were built.

374-802	BR M4 red+cream - *05*	11	14
374-802A	BR W8 red+cream - *09*	11	14
374-803	BR S9 green - *05*	11	14
374-803A	BR S9 green - *11*	11	15
374-804	BR W7 brown+cream - *05*	11	14
374-804A	BR W8 brown+cream - *11*	11	15
374-801	BR E3 maroon - *05*	11	14
374-801A	BR M6 maroon - *11*	11	15
374-800	BR E3 blue+grey - *05*	11	14

C11k-b BR Mk1 Restaurant Car (RFO) New (2013)

This is the Blue Riband replacement model of 2013.

374-807	BR E10 red+cream - *13*	17	21
374-809	BR S9 green - *13*	17	21
374-804	BR W? brown+cream - *not made*	NA	NA
374-810	BR W7 brown+cream - *13*	17	21
374-801	BR ? maroon - *not made*	NA	NA
374-808	BR M1 maroon - *13*	17	21
374-800	BR E? blue+grey - *not made*	NA	NA
374-811	BR W9 blue+grey - *13*	17	21

C11l. BR Mk1 Sleeping Car (SLF & SLSTP) (2013)

The SLF was a 1st class sleeping car while the SLSTP was a 2nd class sleeping car with a pantry.

As the models are physically the same externally, they share the same table.

374-925	BR ? maroon SLSTP - *13*	16	21
374-926	BR ? maroon SLF - *13*	16	21
374-927	BR Inter-City ? blue+greySLSTP - *13*	16	21
374-928	BR Inter-City? blue+grey SLF - *13*	16	21

C12a. BR Mk1 General Utility Van (GUV) (2003)

General utility vans have been used for transporting mail and parcels. Several batches were built, the earliest at Doncaster in 1956 and the last ones in 1959 by Pressed Steel Ltd. Built without gangway connections, they had 2 large end doors and a bottom flap that rested on the buffers when open and thus allowed end-loading with motor vehicles. Some of the GUVs received 'Motorail' branding. The vans were built with 3 double doors along each side, each with a single window, and there were two intermediate windows between the sets of doors on each side.

374-128	BR green – *not made*	NA	NA
374-129	BR maroon – *not made*	NA	NA
374-125	BRe W86359 blue Express Parcels - *03*	9	12
374-125A	BRe W93180 blue Express Parcels - *05*	10	13
374-125B	BRe 93469 blue - *08*	11	14
374-125C	BRe blue – *not made*	NA	NA
374-126	BR M93337 blue+grey Intercity Motorail - *03*	10	13
374-127	BR RES 95197 red+dark grey - *03*	9	12
374-127A	BR RES 95193 red+dark grey - *05*	11	14
374-127B	BR RES red+dark grey – *not made*	NA	NA
(370-125)	BR RES 95199 red+dark grey NOX ex-set - *03*	10	NA

C12b. BR Mk1 General Utility Van (GUV) New (2012)

This is the Blue Riband replacement model of 2012.

BR Mk1 general utility van (GUV) [C12b]

374-131	BR S86724 green - *12*	15	19
374-130	BR W86148 maroon - *12*	15	19
374-130A	BR M86285 maroon - *12*	15	19
374-130B	BR ? maroon W - *13*	17	21
374-132	BR M86531 blue - *12*	15	19
374-134	BR ? blue Motorail - *13*	17	21
374-133	RES 95199 red+dark grey NOX - *12*	15	19

C13. BR Mk1 Full Brake Super BG (2005)

These are 100mph high security brake vans with air brakes. TOPS coded NBA, they were rebuilt from gangwayed brakes. They have reinforced floors, sealed gangways and roller-shutter doors. They also have built-in tail lamps and are used to convey valuable cargo.

374-775	RES 94451 red+dark grey - *05*	11	14
374-775A	RES 94474 red+dark grey - *12*	14	17
374-776	RES/Royal Mail 94520 red+dark grey - *05*	11	14
374-776A	RES/Royal Mail 94462 red+dark grey - *12*	14	17
374-777	EWS/Royal Mail 94420 red+dark grey - *05*	11	14

Graham Farish by Bachmann

374-777A	EWS/Royal Mail 94433 red+dark grey - *12*	14	17
374-778	Royal Mail 94486 red+dark grey - *05*	11	14
374-778A	Royal Mail 94472 red+dark grey - *12*	14	17
374-035Z	BR RTC RDB975547 'Lab 23' blue+red Sp Edn (ModelZone & The Signal Box) - *11*	15	19

C14.   BR Mk1 CCT Van (2013)
The BR Mk1 4-wheel CCT is a much requested van, which was a common sight on the railway network. Used primarily for parcels traffic, many survived in departmental service long after their parcel carrying days had ended.

374-785	BR ? lined maroon - *13*	NPG	NPG
374-786	Tartan Arrow red+white? - *13*	NPG	NPG
374-787	BR ? blue - *13*	NPG	NPG
374-788	BR ? blue Express Parcels Red Star - *13*	NPG	NPG

C15.   BR Mk1 Travelling Post Office TPO (2010)
This van was used in a Travelling Post Office (TPO) and, during the journey, Royal Mail staff sort the mail ready for dropping off at points along the route. 96 of these vehicles were built by British Rail in small batches between 1959 and 1977, all to similar designs and based on the Mk1 coach. The early batches featured catching nets, which allowed mail bags to be collected from lineside apparatus, while the train was still moving. Bags of sorted mail were also dropped off without a need for the train to stop. From the beginning of 1972, this practice was abandoned and the apparatus removed. However, being able to sorted mail, on the train was a great time saver and gave rail an advantage over road transport. Under the TOPS system the vans were coded 'NS'

BR Mk1 travelling post office sorting van [C15]

374-903	BR/Royal Mail W80300 red - *10*	18	22
374-902	BR Royal Mail M80300 blue+ grey - *10*	18	22
374-901	BR Royal Mail Letters 80300 red NSV - *10*	22	26
374-901A	BR Royal Mail W80301 red NSV with side lights - *13*	23	27
374-900	BR Royal Mail Travelling Post Office 80305 red NSX - *10*	18	22

C16.   BR Mk1 Standard Horse Box (2013)
This model is based on the standard horse boxes built using Mk1 coach principals and with accommodation for the grooms. These were introduced by British Railways in 1957 and made use of coach components. They were also included in the coach numbering system with the prefix letter representing the region to which they were allocated.

373-360	BR E96330 maroon - *13*	15	18
373-361	BR E96346 maroon - *13*	15	18
373-362	BR S96359 green - *13*	15	18

BR Mk1 Pullman Coaches

C17a.   BR Mk1 Pullman Parlour 1st (FP) (2007)
A total of 8 of these were built and given the names of precious and semiprecious stones. As originally built, they had seating for 24 passengers in two banks of single seats facing in pairs across a table. With falling business, this was felt to be a wasteful use of space and the seating was doubled up down one side, bringing the capacity to 29. There was a coupe at one end and a lavatory at both ends of the car.

374-200	Pullman *Emerald* dark brown+cream - *07*	12	15
374-200A	Pullman *Amber* dark brown+cream - *08*	12	16
374-200B	Pullman *Amethyst* dark brown+cream - *09*	15	19
374-200C	Pullman *Garnett* dark brown+cream - *12*	18	23
374-200D	Pullman *Opal* dark brown+cream - *13*	17	21
374-201	Pullman E326E grey+blue - *07*	15	19
374-201A	Pullman E327E grey+blue - *10*	15	19

C17b.   BR Mk1 Pullman Parlour 2nd (SP) (2007)
7 Pullman parlour 2nds were built and had 42 seats in 1+2 (with tables) formation. There was a toilet adjacent to the end vestibule at each end. These later became open first class accommodation.

374-210	Pullman Car 347 dark brown+cream - *07*	12	15
374-210A	Pullman Car 348 dark brown+cream - *08*	12	16
374-210B	Pullman Car 349 dark brown+cream - *09*	15	19
374-210C	Pullman Car 350 dark brown+cream - *12*	19	23
374-210D	Pullman Car 351 dark brown+cream - *13*	17	21
374-211	Pullman E352E grey+blue - *07*	15	19
374-211A	Pullman E347E grey+blue - *10*	15	19

C17c.   BR Mk1 Pullman Kitchen 1st (FK) (2006)
There were 13 of the kitchen first cars built and all were given bird names. They initially seated 20 passengers but, following refurbishment in 1967-68, it was possible to seat 26. Four of the seats were in the traditional Pullman coupe. There was a kitchen and servery at one end and a toilet at the other.

BR Mk1 Pullman kitchen 1st (FK) [C17c]

374-220	Pullman *Eagle* dark brown+cream - *06*	12	15
374-220A	Pullman *Magpie* dark brown+cream - *08*	12	16
374-220B	Pullman *Falcon* dark brown+cream - *09*	15	19
374-220C	Pullman *Hawk* dark brown+cream - *13*	17	21
374-221	Pullman E315E grey+blue - *07*	15	19
374-221A	Pullman E?E grey+blue - *12*	15	19
374-220Z	Pullman RDB975427 *Wren* 'Laboratory 14' red+ blue Sp Edn 504 (ModelZone) - *11*	17	22

C17d.   BR Mk1 Pullman Kitchen 2nd (SK) (2007)
15 Pullman kitchen 2nds were built and these had seating for 30 passengers arranged in 1+2 (with tables) formation. There was a kitchen and servery at one end and a toilet at the other end. There were no coupies in the second class cars.

374-230	Pullman Car 332 dark brown+cream - *07*	12	15
374-230A	Pullman Car 333 dark brown+cream - *07*	12	16
374-230B	Pullman Car 334 dark brown+cream - *09*	15	19
374-230C	Pullman Car 335 dark brown+cream - *13*	17	21
374-231	Pullman E334E grey+blue - *07*	15	19

C17e.   BR Mk1 Pullman Bar Car 2nd (BSP) (2007)
This was a one-off vehicle which, when renumbered as M354E, received the name 'The Nightcap Bar'. It had seating for 24 passengers arranged in 1+2 (with tables) formation. There was also a lavatory at one end of the car.

374-240	Pullman *The Hadrian Bar* dark brown+cream - *07*	15	19
374-241	BR M354E *The Nightcap Bar* blue+grey - *07*	15	19

BR Mk2 Coaches

C18a.   BR Mk2A 1st Corridor (FK) (2013)
Built by BR Derby Carriage & Wagon Works, these were constructed in 1968. Many of them have found their way onto preserved lines. Others were renumbered in the 194xx sequence and some became departmental stock.

374-950	BR E13472 blue+grey - *not made*	NA	NA
374-950	BR E13472 blue+grey - *13*	17	21

C18b.   BR Mk2A Tourist 2nd Open (TSO) (2013)
These were built between 1965 and 1968 at BR Derby Carriage & Wagon Works. A lot of the early members of the class were scrapped but many others have been preserved at heritage sites and a few were transferred to Departmental stock. They provided second class seating for 64 passengers and had two toilets.

374-710	BR E5284 blue+grey - *13*	17	21

C18c.   BR Mk2A Brake 2nd Open (BSO) (2013)
These were built at Derby in 1967-68 and had 31 second class seats and one toilet. The rest of the coach (about 40%) was taken up by a guard's compartment, corridor link and luggage area.

374-680	BR E9430 blue+grey - *13*	17	21
374-681	DRS 9419 dark blue - *13*	17	21

Ex-BR Mk2A brake 2nd DRS courier coach [C18c]

C19a.   BR Mk2D 1st Open (FO) (2004)
The basis of this model was a first open coach built in 1971-72 at Derby. It had 42 first

Graham Farish by Bachmann

class seats, arranged in a 2+1 formation, and two toilets, one at each end. There was an evaporator unit in the roof above one of the toilets.

374-752	BR IC E3186 blue+grey Mk2F - 04	9	12
374-752A	BR IC E3171 blue+grey Mk2F - 06	10	13
374-752B	BR IC M3210 blue+grey Mk2F - 09	11	14
374-750	Virgin 3381 red+black Mk2E - 04	10	13
374-750A	Virgin 3385 red+black Mk2E - 09	11	14
374-751	FGW 3381 green Mk2E - 04	11	14

C19b. BR Mk2D Tourist 2nd Open (TSO) (2004)
The model was based on a tourist open second built at Derby in 1971-72. It had 62 second class seats, arranged in a 2+2 formation, and two toilets. 26 of them were amongst a large number of Mk2 coaches that went to New Zealand, when no longer required on the British network.

374-727	BR IC E5675 blue+grey Mk2D - 04	9	12
374-727A	BR IC E5709 blue+grey Mk2D - 06	10	13
374-727B	BR IC E5681 blue+grey Mk2D - 10	11	14
374-725	Virgin 5966 red+black Mk2E - 04	10	13
374-726	FGW 5657 green Mk2D - 04	9	12
374-726A	FGW 5669 green Mk2D - 06	11	14

C19c. BR Mk2D Brake 2nd Open (BSO) (2004)
The model was based on a Mk2D brake second open coach built at Derby in 1971 which had 31 second class seats and one toilet. Approximately 40% the coach was taken up by the luggage area, corridor link and guard's compartment.

374-677	BR IC E9482 blue+grey Mk2D - 04	9	12
374-677A	BR IC E9491 blue+grey Mk2D - 06	10	13
374-677B	BR IC E9481 blue+grey Mk2D - 09	11	14
374-675	Virgin 9516 red+black Mk2F - 04	11	14
374-676	FGW 9492 green MK2D - 04	11	14

C19d. BR Mk2D Open 2nd Micro Buffet (TSOT) (2004)
This model was based on a coach built at Derby in 1971-72, which had 54 second class seats with tables, a toilet and a small buffet area at one end of the coach. 20 were converted to diagram 107 from TSOs, half for the Eastern Region and the rest for the Western Region, except for two that went to Scotland.

Ex-BR Mk2D micro buffet [C19d]

374-702	BR IC E6614 blue+grey Mk2D TSOT - 04	9	12
374-702A	BR IC E6605 blue+grey Mk2D TSOT - 06	10	13
374-702B	BR IC E6601 blue+grey Mk2D TSOT - 09	11	14
374-700	Virgin 1208 red+black Mk2F RFB - 04	11	14
374-701	FGW 6723 green Mk2D RMBF - 04	11	14

BR Mk2F Coaches

C20a. BR Mk2F 1st Open Coach (FO) (2013)
These were built at Derby in 1973 and contained 42 first class seats and two toilets. The seating was 2+1 with tables and an off-centre isle. Exit doors were at both ends of the coach.

374-760	BR ? blue+grey - 13	17	21
374-762	BR InterCity ? grey - 13	17	21

C20b. BR Mk2F Tourist 2nd Open Coach (TSO) (2013)
These were built at Derby from 1973 and had a central isle with 2+2 seating at tables. Each coach contained 64 second class seats and two toilets, with a vestibule and outside doors at both ends.

374-735	BR ? blue+grey - 13	17	21
374-737	BR InterCity ? grey - 13	17	21

C20c. BR Mk2F 2nd Class Brake Open (BSO) (2013)
These were built at Derby from 1974 and half the coach was taken up with an open seating area with 32 second class seats and a toilet. The seating was in 2+2 formation with tables and the rest of the coach contained the guard's compartment, a corridor and luggage space. There were doors to the outside at both ends of the seating area and double doors both sides of the luggage area.

374-690	BR ? blue+grey - 13	17	21
374-692	BR InterCity ? grey - 13	17	21

C20d. BR Mk2F Buffet 1st Open (RFB) (2013)
Based on a buffet first open, 32 were converted from FOs at Derby to diagram 83 from 1988 onwards. They had 26 first class seats, a toilet and a third of the car was occupied by the pantry and adjoining corridor.

374-660	BR 1215 blue+grey - 13	17	21
347-662	BR InterCity ? grey - 13	17	21

C21. BR Mk2F Driving Brake 2nd (DBSO) (2013)
The driving brake second open was converted from a brake standard open and was for push-pull operation in Scotland. 14 were built at Derby in 1974 of which all have been scrapped except for one that went to Ireland and 5 that passed to Serco. They had 32 second class seats, no toilet and almost half the coach was taken up by the luggage area, guard's compartment and corridor link to a driving cab.

374-650	BR 9707? blue+grey - 13	17	21
374-651	BR ScotRail ? ? - 13	17	21

BR Mk3 Coaches

C22a. BR Mk3 Trailer Open Standard (TS) (2001)
These trailer open standards were built in large quantities at Derby during the period 1976-1982. They were built for use in High Speed Train sets.

374-329	BR ICs 42010 grey+beige - 07	10	13
-	BR ICs 42074 grey+beige ex-pack - 07	10	NA
374-327	GNER 42057 [C] navy blue - 01	9	12
-	GNER 42064 [B] navy blue ex-pack - 01	9	NA
(371-480)	GNER 42058 [B] navy+red ex-pack - 07	10	NA
374-327A	GNER 42235 [G] navy blue, red doors - 08	11	14
374-327B	GNER 42243 [F] navy blue, red doors - 08	11	14
374-327C	GNER 42057 [E] navy blue, red doors - 08	11	14
374-327D	GNER 42219 [C] navy blue, red doors - 08	11	14
374-328	Virgin 42171 [?] red+black - 02	9	12
-	Virgin 42127 [?] red+black ex-pack - 02	9	NA
374-325	MML 42149 [C] teal green+cream - 01	9	12
-	MML 42157 [B] green+cream ex-pack - 01	9	NA
374-325A	MML 42335 [E] white+blue+grey - 07	11	14
(371-475A)	MML 42112 [L] white+blue+grey ex-pack - 07	10	NA
374-326	FGW 42025 [C] purple - 02	9	12
374-326A	FGW [C] purple - *not made*	NA	NA
-	FGW 42072 [D] purple ex-pack - 02	9	NA
374-331	Arriva Cross Country 42378 pale grey - 11	13	16
(371-481)	Arriva Cross Country 42377 pale grey ex-pack - 09	11	NA

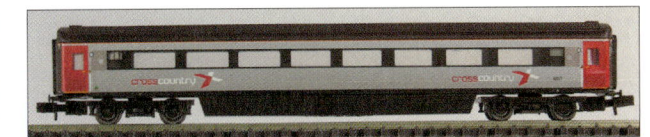

Ex-BR Mk3 standard class (TS) in Arriva Cross-Country livery [C22a]

C22b. BR Mk3 Trailer 1st (TF) (2001)
These trailer open firsts were built at Derby during the period 1976-1982. They were also built for use in High Speed Train sets.

374-354	BR ICs 41036 grey+beige - 07	11	14
374-352	GNER 41091 [G] navy blue - 01	9	12
374-352A	GNER 41100 [L] navy blue, red doors - 08	11	14
374-353	Virgin 41081 [?] red+black - 02	9	12
374-350	MML 41064 [G] teal green+cream - 01	9	12
374-350A	MML 41057 [J] white+blue+grey - 07	11	14
374-351	FGW 41005 [H] purple - 02	9	12
374-355	Arriva Cross Country 41195 pale grey - 11	13	16

C22c. BR Mk3 Restaurant Buffet 1st (TRFB) (2001)
These restaurant buffet firsts were converted from HST unclassified trailer buffet cars (TRUBs) in 1985-86 for use in High Speed Train sets.

374-379	BR ICs 40708 grey+beige - 07	11	14
374-378	GNER 40705 [F] navy blue - 01	10	13
374-378A	GNER 40711 [J] navy blue, red doors - 08	11	14
374-377	Virgin 40732 red+black - 02	9	12
374-375	MML 40729 [F] teal green+cream - 01	9	12
374-375A	MML 40708 [F] white+blue+grey - 07	11	14
374-376	FGW 40707 [F] purple - 02	11	14
374-380	Arriva Cross Country 45003 pale grey - 11	13	16

C22d. BR Mk3 Trailer Guard's Standard (TGS) (2001)
This is HST stock with a guard's compartment in one end of a standard class coach. They were built at Derby between 1980 and 1982.

374-404	BR ICs 44018 grey+beige - 07	11	14
374-403	GNER 44098 [A] navy blue - 01	10	13
374-403A	GNER 44019 [A] navy blue, red doors - 08	11	14
374-402	Virgin 44076 [A] red+black - 02	9	12
374-400	MML 44041 [A] teal green+cream - 01	11	14

Graham Farish by Bachmann

374-400A	MML 44041 [A] white+blue+grey - 07	11	14
374-401	FGW 44023 [A] purple - 02	11	14
374-405	Arriva Cross Country 44052 pale grey - 11	13	16

C22e. BR Mk3 Trailer Buffet Standard (TRSB)
Planned but not made.
374-425	Virgin ? red+black - not made	NA	NA

C22f. BR Mk3 Trailer Buffet 1st (TRB)
Planned but not made.
374-450	FGW ? purple - not made	NA	NA

C22g. BR Mk3 Sleeper Car (SLEP) (2007)
This model is based on Mk3A sleepers with a pantry which were built between 1981 and 1983 by BR Derby Carriage and Wagon Works.

Ex-BR Mk3 sleeper in ScotRail Caledonian livery [C22g]

374-477	BR E10521 blue+grey - 11	13	16
374-475	FGW 10590 green (fag packet) - 07	11	14
374-476	ScotRail Caledonian 10681 purple - 07	12	15
374-476A	ScotRail Caledonian 10688 purple - 12	14	18

C22h. BR Mk3 Restaurant Buffet 1st (RFM) (2007)
Mk3 restaurant buffet firsts were converted from High Speed Train TRFKs, RFBs and FOs during the period 1984-1987.
374-500	Virgin 10202 red+black - 07	11	14

BR Mk4 Coaches

C23a. BR Mk4 Open Standard (TSOD) (2007)
These Mk4 open standards, with provision for disabled passengers, were built in 1989-91 by Metropolitan-Cammell in Birmingham.
374-525	GNER 12313 [F] navy blue - 07	11	14

C23b. BR Mk4 Open Standard (End) (TSOE) (2007)
These Mk4 Open Standards were built in 1989-91 by Metropolitan-Cammell in Birmingham and designed as an end coach.
374-550	GNER 12212 [B] navy blue - 07	11	14

C23c. BR Mk4 Open Standard (TSO) (2007)
These Mk4 open standards were built in 1989-92 by Metropolitan-Cammell in Birmingham.
374-575	GNER 12489 [E] navy blue - 07	11	14

C23d. BR Mk4 Open 1st (TFO) (2007)
These Mk4 open firsts were built in 1989-92 by Metropolitan-Cammell in Birmingham. Many were rebuilt in 2003 by Bombardier in Wakefield, some with provision for disabled passengers.
374-600	GNER 11254 [K] navy blue - 07	11	14

C23e. BR Mk4 Restaurant 1st (RFM) (2007)
These Mk4 restaurant firsts were built in 1989-91 by Metropolitan-Cammell in Birmingham.
374-625	GNER 10323 [H] navy blue - 07	11	14

C24. BR Mk4 Driving Van Trailer (DVT) (2005)
These models are based on Mk4 driving van trailers built in Birmingham in 1988 by Metropolitan Cammell.
374-650	GNER ? navy blue - not made	NA	NA
(371-801)*	GNER 82212 navy blue - 05	10	NA
(371-800)*	GNER 82226 navy blue - 05	10	NA
(371-802)	GNER 82223 navy blue - 11	12	15

* These came in a pack twinned with Class 91 electric locomotives.

Ex-BR Mk4 restaurant 1st (RFM) in GNER livery [C23e]

WAGONS

Most of the wagons have been based on the original Graham Farish range but by 2005, Bachmann were totally retooling some of them, basing the new wagons on their own 00 range. The first samples of a whole new range of open wagons arrived in the summer and, where appropriate, they had separate brakes and V hanger mounted brake handles and there were both spoked and 3-hole disc wheels. They also had turned brass buffers and a choice of timber or steel type floors. The new wagons also had clip plate couplings with an enclosed spring as is common in the USA range of products from Bachmann.

Cat No.	Company, Number, Colour, Date	£	£

Flat Wagons

W1a. 'Conflat A' (2013)
The 'Conflat A' was a post-war Swindon design and the first 400 were built at Swindon and Wolverton. Over the next ten years, 200,000 of them were built, most of them during the BR era. There is little difference between the GWR and BR versions.
Until 2013 the 'Conflat A' had not been sold without a container load.

377-325Z	BR TDB706237 yellow shunter's running wagon Sp Edn 504 (TMC) * - 13	9	11

* Weathered versions have been professionally produced by TMC.

W1b. 'Conflat A' with Type AF Container (2009)
As road transport developed in the 1930s, containers were introduced to the railways in order to compete. Post WW2, there was a big drive to promote container traffic by the four railway companies. Each had a door-to-door service, As delivery had to be made as quickly as possible, the BR 'Conflats' were XP rated. The models in this table have the highly insulated small AF containers which had doors at one end.

377-327	GW 39326 dark grey + AF container AF-2100 white - not made	NA	NA
377-327	GW 39354 dark grey + AF container AF2098 white - 09	5	7
377-327A	GW 39326 dark grey + AF container AF-2100 white - 12	5	7
377-326	BR B709437 brown + AF container AF16392B ice blue - 09	5	7
377-326A	BR B? brown + AF container AF?B ice blue - 11	6	8
377-326B	BR B724734 brown + AF container AF?B ice blue - 12	7	9
377-340	BR B704954 brown + 2 AF containers AF16098B + AF 65098B white - 09	5	7
377-340A	BR B? brown + 2 AF containers AF?B + AF?B white - 12	5	7
-	BR B505501 brown + AF light blue W AF66021B	7	NA
-	BR B505544 brown + AF light blue W AF66066B	7	NA
-	BR B505444 brown + AF light blue W AF66180B	7	NA
377-335	above 3 weathered wagons - 11	NA	26
-	BR B? brown + AF brown AF?B	NPG	NA
-	BR B? brown + AF brown AF?B	NPG	NA
-	BR B? brown + AF brown AF?B	NPG	NA
377-337	above 3 wagons - 13	NA	NPG

W1c. 'Conflat A' with Type AFP Container (2009)

'Conflat A' with 2 Birds Eye AFP containers [W1e]

Graham Farish by Bachmann

The small size container could be fitted two to a 'Conflat' and were known as 'A' type. The 'AF' container, in the above table, was for quick-frozen foods, ice cream etc. and had a rubber-sealed floating door. It could maintain a temperature of -15oF for 24 hours. The models in this table have AFP containers which were highly insulated and for palletised traffic and had doors at one end.

377-341	BR B740503 brown + 2 AFP containers **Birds Eye** AFP66348B + AFP66358B blue+white - *09*	5	7
377-341A	BR B? brown + 2 AFP containers **Birds Eye** AFP?B + AFP?B blue+white - *12*	7	9
377-341B	BR B740736 brown + 2 AFP containers **Birds Eye** AFP66405B + AFP66390B blue+white - *11*	7	9

W1d. 'Conflat A' with Type BD Container (2009)

BDs were general merchandise containers and had side doors as well as doors at one end. They became the most widely used container design of their day and had a capacity of 720 cubic feet.

Models in this table are of a 'Conflat A' with a BD container.

377-325	BR B505569 brown + BD **Speedfreight** BD46491B silver+yellow - *09*	5	7
377-325A	BR B708315 brown + BD **Speedfreight** BD47381B silver+yellow - *13*	7	9
377-328	BR 709708 brown + BD container BD50150B red - *09*	5	7
377-328A	BR B709007 brown + BD container BD50311B red - *11*	6	8
377-328B	BR B? brown + BD container BD?B red - *12*	7	9
-	BR B708778 brown + BD brown W BD48488B	9	NA
-	BR B709179 brown + BD brown W BD40408B	9	NA
-	BR B708313 brown + BD brown W BD46023B	9	NA
377-336	above 3 weathered wagons - *12*	NA	31

Planked Open Wagons

W2. 3-plank Wagon (2007)

The 3-plank wagon was a 'medium' goods wagon, as opposed to a low-sided one. But, despite this, amongst other things, it was used for the transportation of containers. They were particularly found on the LMS and had drop-down sides and fixed ends. New wagons to the LMS design continued to arrive in 1948 and 1949, totalling over 10,000 in all. In 1950 BR changed over to steel construction. 3-plank wagons ended up as ballast carriers in the Engineers Department.

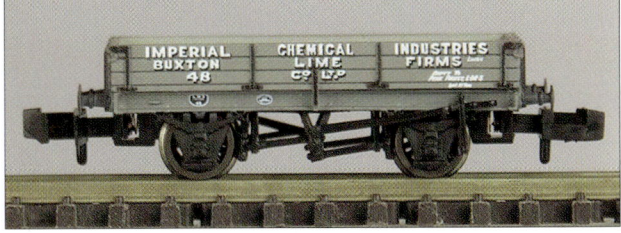

3-plank wagon ICI Buxton Lime Firms [W2]

377-500	'**Imperial Chemical Industries**' 48 grey - *07*	3	4
377-500A	'**Imperial Chemical Industries**' 46 grey - *10*	4	5
377-502	**LMS** 473449 grey - *07*	3	4
377-502A	**LMS** 473215 grey - *10*	4	6
377-501	BR **Medfit** B457203 brown - *07*	3	4
377-501A	BR M470105 brown - *08*	4	5
377-501B	BR M475184 brown - *11*	5	6
377-501C	BR ? brown - *12*	5	6
377-503	BR **Departmental** ? olive green - *12*	5	7

W3a. 5-plank Wagon (2001)

5-plank wagons were considered to be 'high goods wagons' and were referred to as 'Highfits' or 'High NF'. Anything larger was probably specifically for the coal and mineral trade. At one time, 5-plank wagons were highly numerous in Britain and often had their load sheeted over. They were used for the transportation of general merchandise. The British weather and the labour cost of protecting the load made them impractical and some were replaced by vans. However, it seems that many were privately owned and these would be replaced by the railway company's own vans. Private owner vehicles once added to the colourfulness of the railways before they were plunged into standard greys and browns.

Bachmann continued to use the Graham Farish 5-plank tooling until 2005, producing 11 models from it. In 2005 they introduced two new well-detailed 5-planks and these are in the next two tables.

373-150Z	'**Foster Yeoman**' 36 black Sp Edn 500 (Buffers) - *05*	4	5
373-159	'**George Lovegrove**' 215 red sf - *05*	4	5
373-154	'**Harry Whitehouse**' 16 red - *02*	3	4
373-152	'**Hopton-Wood Stone**' 2 grey - *01*	4	5
373-153	'**ICI Lime**' 3034 grey - *01*	4	5
373-155	'**Joshua Grey**' 3 brown - *02*	3	4
373-150	'EA **Stevenson**' 10 blue - *01*	4	5
373-158	'J&R **Stone**' 245 grey - *05*	3	4
373-157	'**Tarslag**' 836 grey - *02*	3	4
373-151	'**Worcester Co-op**' 20 red - *01*	4	5
373-156	BR P143165 grey (also used in sets) - *02*	3	4

W3b. 5-plank Wagon 9ft (steel floor) (2005)

These 5-plank wagons were produced from the new Bachmann tooling and had spoked wheels and separately assembled brake gear. This table contains the models that were produced with a representation of a steel floor.

377-026	'**Arenig Granite**' 207 red - *05*	4	5
377-025B	'John **Arnold & Sons**' 156 red - *11*	5	6
377-026A	'Nath'l. **Atrill**' 6 black - *10*	5	6
377-025A	'**Constable Hart & Co.**' 1004 black - *10*	5	6
377-027	'**George Lovegrove**' 215 red - *05*	4	5
377-025	'**Hopton-Wood Stone**' 2 grey - *05*	4	5
377-028	'**Lilleshall**' 1750 red - *10*	5	6
377-020	'E.B. **Mason**' 26 grey - *13*	NPG	NPG
377-030	'**Roberts Tarmacadam**' 461 black - *12*	6	7
377-029	'**Shap Tarred Granite**' 354 black - *11*	5	6
377-026B	'**Tarbitumac**' 285 black - *11*	5	6
377-027A	BR M318256 grey - *10*	5	6
377-027B	BR M360265 grey - *12*	6	7
377-027B	BR M360583 grey - *13*	NPG	NPG

W3c. 5-plank Wagon 9ft (wood floor) (2005)

These 5-plank wagons were produced from the new Bachmann tooling, with spoked wheels and separately assembled brake gear, and this table contains the models that were produced with a representation of a wood planked floor.

5-plank wagon Edward W. Badland [W3c]

377-057	'Edwin W **Badland** - 50 grey - *12*	6	7
377-050B	'A **Bramley**' 16 dark brown - *11*	5	6
377-053	'R Fred **Cole**' 11 red - *10*	5	6
377-050	'James **Durnford & Son**' 37 black - *05*	4	5
377-050A	'James **Durnford & Son**' 30 black - *10*	5	6
377-058	'**Farndon**' 18 brown - *13*	NPG	NPG
377-056	'Alfred **Jukes**' 10 red-brown - *12*	6	7
377-052	'**Hucknall**' 3422 red - *05*	3	4
377-051	'FH **Silvey**' 191 dark brown - *05*	3	4
377-055	'J **Skinner**' 7 green - *11*	5	6
377-054	BR M354661 grey - *10*	4	5
377-054A	BR M254661 grey - *11*	5	6

W4a. 6-plank Wagon 10ft (2001)

This is the model Bachmann inherited in 2000 from the original Graham Farish company. While it was sold as the 7-plank coal wagon in the catalogues, in reality it was a 6-plank wagon. Bachmann replaced the model with two 7-plank wagon models in 2005 and these will be found in the next two tables, but here we have the models from the original tooling.

373-175U	'**Bradford & Sons**' 1 brown Sp Edn 500 (Buffers) - *05*	4	5
373-175S	'G **Bryer Ash**' 1110 black Sp Edn 500 (Buffers) - *05*	4	5
(370-025)	'**Carlton Main**' 5014 red* ex-set- *03*	3	NA
373-175	'**Charles Roberts**' 70001 black Sp Edn (BCC) - *04*	4	5
373-178	'**Cosy Fires**' 778 grey - *01*	4	5
373-183	'**Douglas Bank Colliery**' 454 brown - *05*	3	4
373-175X	'**Dunkerton Colliery**' 10 blue Sp Edn 500 (Buffers) - *05*	4	5

Graham Farish by Bachmann

373-181	'**Florence** Coal & Iron' 1017 grey - 02	3	4
373-177	'**Flower** & Son' 7 grey-green - 01	4	5
373-182	'**Gellyceidrim**' 719 light grey - 02	3	4
373-183	'The **Great Western Railwaymen's Coal Association**' 1 grey - not made	NA	NA
373-175	'**ICI Salt**' 326 brown (also used in 370-200 set) - 01	4	5
373-2003	'James **Kenworthy**' 47 brown Ltd Edn (BCC) - 03	3	4
373-175T	'**Kilmersdon Colliery**' 25 green Sp Edn 500 (Buffers) - 05	4	5
373-176	'**Kobo**' 15 grey - 01	4	5
373-179	'**Lunt**' 724 grey+black - 02	3	4
373-175R	'The **Mains** Coal & Cannel Co.' 475 light grey Sp Edn 500 (Buffers) - 05	4	5
373-175Z	'**Royal Leamington Spa**' 22 maroon Ltd Edn 500 - 04	3	4
(370-175)	'**South Leicester**' 373 red ex-set - 03	3	NA
373-180	'**Sycobrite**' 650 yellow+black - 02	3	4
373-175N	'**Timsbury Colliery**' 14 red Sp Edn 500 (Buffers) - 05	4	5
373-184	'**Webb**, Hall & Webb' 19 grey - not made	NA	NA
373-184	'WE **Wise**' 18 black - 05	3	4
(370-050)	'JR **Wood** Co.' 346 yellow* ex-set - 03	3	NA
373-175Y	'**Writhlington Colliery**' 160 light blue Sp Edn 500 (Buffers) - 05	4	5
373-175V	'**Yeovil Gas Works**' 24 brown Sp Edn 500 (Buffers) - 05	4	5

* shade variations.

W4b. 7-plank Wagon 9ft (end door) (2005)

The 7-plank wagons in this table are from the new Bachmann tooling, with spoked wheels and separately assembled brake gear. These ones are models of wagons with an end door for mechanical end tipping. The bolts on the end door were released and a ram located the axle at the other end of the wagon and thrust upwards, tipping out the coal into a hopper beneath the track.

7-plank end door wagon Bradleys (Weardale) [W4b]

377-075K2	'**Aberpergwm**' 941 red, Sp Edn 504 (BCC) - 05	7	10
377-080	'**Bradleys (Weardale)**' 246 brown - 06	4	6
377-076	'**Douglas Bank Colliery**' 454 brown - 05	4	6
377-075K3	'**Cains**' 3 black, Sp Edn 504 (BCC) - 05	7	10
377-083	'**Crane & Company**' 107 red - 11	5	7
377-2011K	'W.R.**Davies** & Co.' 701 red-brown, Sp Edn (BCC) - 11	5	7
377-076K	'Edward **Eastwood**' 2 very dark green, Sp Edn (BCC) - 08	6	9
377-075K1	'**Fife Coal**' 1655 brown, Sp Edn 504 (BCC) - 05	7	10
377-079	'**Firestone**' 2004 blue - 06	4	5
377-079A	'**Firestone**' 2005 blue - 10	5	6
377-075	'**Goldendale Iron Co.**' 598 grey - 05	4	6
377-075A	'**Harrisons**' 5038 grey - 10	5	6
377-2009K	'Thomas **Hunter**' brown, Sp Edn (BCC) - 09	6	8
377-082	'**Kobo**' 15 grey - 10	4	6
377-085	'**Park Lane Wigan**' 2060 brown end - 13	NPG	NPG
377-2010K	**Pickering** [R.Y.] & Co. 1002, brown, Sp Edn (BCC) - 10	6	8
377-086	'E&A **Shadrack**' 954 red - 13	NPG	NPG
377-075K	'**Standard Wagon**' ('The Cambrian Wagon Co.') 1923 yellow, Sp Edn (BCC) - 05	7	10
377-084	'**TPP**' Tir Pentwys 29 black - 11	5	7
377-077	'**Wimberry Colliery Co.**' 2 black - 05	4	6
377-078	BR M608163 grey - 08	4	6
377-078A	BR P36147 grey - 10	5	6
377-078B	BR P45129 grey - 13	NPG	NPG

W4c. 7-plank Wagon 9ft (fixed end) (2006)

This is the other version of Bachmann's N gauge 7-plank wagon, which has fixed ends and can be identified from the new end-door wagons in having the four corner plates all the same size. It should not be confused with the original (6-plank) wagon made from the original tooling, which also had fixed ends. This new model has spoked wheels and separately assembled brake gear.

377-081Z	'The **Arley Colliery**' 27 red, Sp Edn 504 (Castle Trains) - 08	4	6
377-075W	'**Cornado E Hijos**' brown, Sp Edn (Britline) ?	NPG	NPG
377-075X	'**Cornado E Hijos**' grey, Sp Edn (Britline) ?	NPG	NPG
377-075B	'**Eales & Roberts**' 6 red - 11	5	7
377-2012K	'**Gloucester** RC&W Co.' brown - 12	7	9
377-081A	'DV **Gostick**' 1 blue - 10	5	6
377-081	'**GWR Railwayman's Coal Assn.**' 1 grey - 06	4	6
377-075Y	'**Leamington Priors Gas Co.**' 10 bright red, Sp Edn - 06	4	5

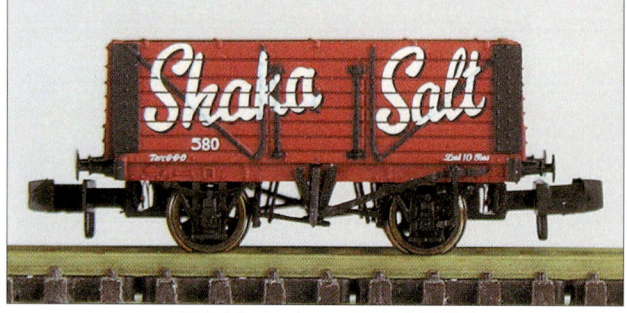

7-plank fixed end wagon Shaka Salt [W4c]

377-076B	'**North Sea Coaling Co.**' 27 red - 13	NPG	NPG
377-076A	'**Shaka Salt**' 580 red-brown - 11	5	7
377-077A	'Thomas **Styles**' 96 maroon - 13	NPG	NPG
377-075U	'**Walker & Rogers**' 3 red, Sp Edn (Castle Trains) - 09	5	6
377-075V	'**Warwick Gas Co.**' 6 grey, Sp Edn (Castle Trains) - 09	5	6

W5. Coal Traders Wagon Sets 9ft (2006)

Some have end doors (end) and some have fixed ends (fix). The sets are normally made up of 7-plank wagons but where there is a mix of wagon types they are described. Many of the sets were produced exclusively for the Bachmann Collectors Club (BCC).

-	'**MA Ray & Sons**' 123 light grey, fix	6	NA
-	'**Fred C Holmes**' 104 red-brown	6	NA
-	'**FW Wacher**' 6 black, fix	6	NA
377-075Z	set of above 3 wagons Kent Coal Traders pack Sp Edn 504 (ModelZone) - 06	NA	24
-	'**Fleetwood Fish**' 2 brown, end	7	NA
-	'**Guard Bridge Paper Co.**' 67 grey, fix	7	NA
-	'**Lewis Merthyr Navigation Colliery**' 674 blk, end	7	NA
377-075K4	set of above 3 Sp Edn (BCC) - 07	NA	25
-	'**St Helens Industrial Coal Department Co-operative Society**' 17 grey, fix 7-plank	6	NA
-	'**Lochgelly**' 1898 red-brown 5-plank	6	NA
-	'**T Jenkerson & Sons**' 277 black, end 7-plank	6	NA
377-075K5	set of above 3 Sp Edn 504 (BCC) - 08	NA	21
-	'**Pilkington Brothers**' 1412, red, fix	6	NA
-	'**Smith Anderson & Co.**' 10, brown, end	6	NA
-	'**David Jones & Sons**' 650, black, end	6	NA
377-077K	above set of 3, Sp Edn 500 (BCC) - 10	NA	21
-	'**Burnley Corporation Gas Dept.**' 17 black, end	6	NA
-	'**Earl of Rosslyn's Collieries**' 4550 red	6	NA
-	'**Crynant Colliery Company**' 330 grey	6	NA
377-075K6	above three wagons Sp Edn 504 (BCC) - 10	NA	21
-	'**Cambrian**' 277 grey	5	NA
-	'**Dutton Massey**' 315 black	5	NA
-	'**Wemyss**' 2866 brown	5	NA
377-075K7	set of above three wagons Sp Edn 504 (BCC) - 11	NA	16

Graham Farish by Bachmann

-	'Balgonie' 1402 brown, fix		6	NA
-	'T&C Scowcroft & Son' 789 red, end		6	NA
-	'The Bwlch Colliery Co.' 131 black, end		6	NA
377-075K8	set of above 3 wagons Sp Edn 504 (BCC) - *12*		NA	22
-	'St Helens Industrial Coal Department Co-operative Society' 17 grey W, fix		7	NA
-	'Burnley Corporation Gas Dept.' 17 black W, end		7	NA
-	'TWW' 2451 brown W, end		7	NA
377-095	above 3 weathered private owner wagons - *13*		NA	24
-	BR P? grey W		7	NA
-	BR P? grey W		7	NA
-	BR P? grey W		7	NA
377-096	set of above 3 ex-private owner wagons - *13*		NA	24

W6. 7-plank with Coke Rail 10ft

Although proposed, they were not put into production before the change to the more appropriate 9ft wheelbase.

373-375	'POP' - *not made*	NA	NA
373-376	'Stringer & Jaggar' - *not made*	NA	NA

W7a. 7-plank with Coke Rail 9ft (end door) (2005)

Coke, being a lot lighter than coal, could be carried in greater volume and so the height of wagons was increased by the addition of extra planks, generally with small gaps between them.

These models were tooled by Bachmann and have spoked wheels and separately assembled brake gear. In this table, all the models have end doors but with extra coke rails moulding loosely attached.

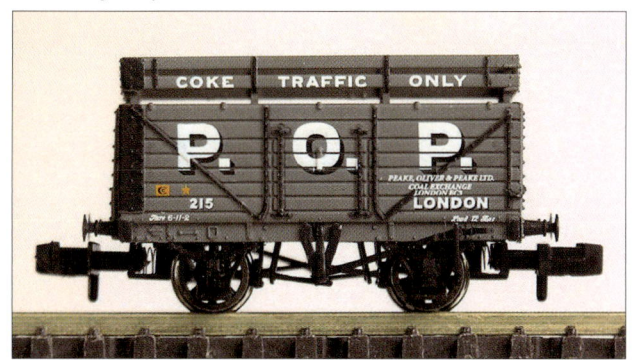

7-plank coke wagon P.O.P [W7a]

377-175B	'Exeter Gas Company' 5 grey - *11*	5	7
377-177	'T.L.**Hale** (Tipton)' 1718 grey - *13*	NPG	NPG
377-175	'New Cransley' 166 red - *05*	4	6
377-175A	'POP' 215 grey - *10*	5	6

W7b. 7-plank with Coke Rail 9ft (fixed end) 2005)

These models are the same as those in the previous table but the fixed end 7-plank wagon has been used.

377-176	**BR** P368515 grey - *05*	3	4
377-176A	**BR** P368502 grey - *08*	4	6
377-176B	**BR** P167248 grey - *10*	5	6
377-176C	**BR** P168259 grey - *13*	NPG	NPG

W8a. 8-plank Wagon 9ft (end door) (2005)

In order to carry greater loads, some companies ordered 8-plank coal wagons but these were far less common.

These models were tooled by Bachmann at the same time as the two new 7-plank wagons and again both end-door and fixed-end models have been made. Consequently they have spoked wheels and separately assembled brake gear. In this table, all the models have end doors.

377-125	'Bagley' 38 red - *05*	4	6
377-126	'The **Boston Deep Sea Fishing**' 86 blue - *05*	4	6
377-128	'G&S **Bull**' ? ? - *13*	NPG	NPG
377-125K	'T **Burnett & Co.**' 1907 red Sp Edn (BCC) - *07*	7	10
377-127A	'Great Mountain' 930 brown - *10*	5	6
377-125B	'James & Emanuel' 451 black - *11*	5	7
377-126A	'Ketton Cement' S89 red+blue - *10*	5	6
377-126B	'Ketton Cement' S88 red+blue W - *11*	5	7
377-125A	'Thorne' (Pease & Partners) 740 red - *10*	5	6
377-127	'JR **Wood & Co.**' 346 orange - *05*	4	6

W8b. 8-plank Wagon 9ft (fixed ends) (2005)

These models are the same as those in the previous table but are the version with fixed ends.

377-152B	'Foster & Co.' 17 red - *11*	5	7
377-153	'R.W.**Hill & Son**' 22 maroon - *13*	NPG	NPG
377-150B	'Isleworth Coal Co.' 10 dark blue - *11*	5	7
377-150K	'Metropolitan' 188 brown Sp Edn (BCC) - *06*	7	10
377-151	'Henry **Musgrave**' 2 grey - *05*	4	6
377-151A	'Henry **Musgrave**' 1 grey - *10*	4	6
377-152A	'Osborne & Son' 10 green - *10*	5	6
377-150	'AJ **Salter**' 202 brown - *05*	4	6
377-150A	'Stewarts and Lloyds' 6301 grey - *10*	5	6
377-152	'Charles **Ward**' 4265 red - *05*	4	6

W9a. 8-plank with Coke Rail 9ft (end door) (2005)

8-plank wagons were also extended in height to carry coke and in this table we have the end-door models with loose-fitted extensions for coke traffic.

8-plank coke wagon Reading [W9a]

377-205	'Bedwas Coke' 621 grey, end - *11*	5	7
377-201	'Modern Transport' 110 black, end - *05*	4	6
377-206	'Suncole' 5061 black, end - *13*	NPG	NPG
377-203	'Reading' 112 black, end - *10*	4	6
377-204	'THos.W. **Ward**' 1644A maroon end - *11*	5	7

W9b. 8-plank with Coke Rail 9ft (fixed end) (2005)

Finally, we have the fixed-end 8-plank wagon with coke rails fitted.

377-200	'Birley' 1605 black, fix - *05*	4	6
377-200A	'Birley' 1610 black, fix - *10*	4	6
377-202	'Stamford' 101 light grey, fix - *05*	3	4

W10. 12T Pipe Wagon (2013)

These wagons were built for transportation of pipes from Stanton Ironworks at Ilkeston in Derbyshire, which was served by both the LNER and LMS. Both companies built wagons for this traffic and BR added further wagons of both designs.

The model was under development at the time of writing but the illustration in the catalogue is of one built in 1957 at BR Wolverton and believed to be based on the LMS design.

377-775	**LMS** ? grey - *13*	NPG	NPG
377-776	**BR** ? brown - *13*	NPG	NPG
377-777	**BR** ? brown - *13*	NPG	NPG

W11. OAA/ZDA 'Squid' 31T 6-plank Open Wagon (2003)

By 1967, the wagon fleet had fallen to about a third the size it had been in 1948. This was partly due to an improved road system and a reduction in demand for coal. British Rail launched a programme of vigorous marketing in the 1970s and backed this up with a fleet of new air-braked vehicles. These were larger and could travel faster than before. For merchandise, long wheelbase open wagons and vans with 45 tonnes loading capacity arrived. The wagons had an 'O' prefix and 'A' suffix (for air-brakes) and the middle letter was used for design variations.

373-400	**BRe** 100013 brown - *03*	4	5
373-402	**BRe** 100078 brown ABN - *05*	5	7
373-401	**Railfreight** 100090 grey+red - *03*	4	5
373-403	**BRe Railfreight** 100005 grey+red - *05*	4	5
373-403A	**BRe Railfreight** 100039 grey+red (also in set 370-252) - *08*	5	7
373-403B	**BRe Railfreight** 100081 grey+red ZDA - *11*	6	8

8th Edition

Graham Farish by Bachmann

373-403C	**BRe** Railfreight 100087 grey+red ZDA - *12*	7	9
373-404	**BR Eng**. DC100031 grey+yellow ZDA - *11*	6	8

W12a.   OBA 31T 5-plank Open (low-end) (2007)
The first OBAs were built at Shildon and Ashford in 1974 and had 5-plank sides with 4 drop-down sections each side, as well as higher ends.

373-626	**BRe** Railfreight 110264 grey+red - *07*	5	7
373-626A	**BRe** Railfreight grey+red - not made	NA	NA
373-626B	**BRe** Railfreight 110583 grey+red (also in set 370-252) - *09*	7	9
373-626C	**BRe** Railfreight 110552 grey+red - *10*	7	9
373-625	**EWS** 110678 maroon+yellow - *07*	5	7
373-625A	**EWS** 110332 maroon+yellow - *08*	6	8
373-625B	**EWS** 110351 maroon+yellow - *09*	7	9
373-625C	**EWS** 110740 maroon+yellow - *09*	7	9

W12b.   OBA 31T 5-plank Open (high-end) (2007)
Some OBAs were built with the ends extended and Bachmann made both versions. This table contains the high-end ones. Plasmore Ltd makes building blocks from pulverised fuel ash at its plant at Heck, near Doncaster. They hired, and later bought, a fleet of OBA wagons.

OBA wagon Plasmor [W12b]

373-627	**Railfreight** '**Plasmor**' 110701 red+green - *07*	5	7
373-627A	**Railfreight** '**Plasmor**' 110662 red+green W - *08*	6	8
373-627B	**Railfreight** '**Plasmor**' 110737 red+green W - *09*	7	9
373-627C	**Railfreight** '**Plasmor**' 110531 grey+red - *10*	7	9
373-628	**EWS** 110636 maroon+yellow - *07*	5	7
373-628A	**EWS** 110639 maroon+yellow - *08*	6	8
373-628B	**EWS** 110545 maroon+yellow - *09*	7	9
373-628C	**EWS** 110636 maroon+yellow - *10*	7	9

Steel Open Wagons

W13.   OCA/ZDA 31t Drop-side Open Wagon (2009)
Here we have the all-steel version of the OBA (above) built in the early 1980s. It was, in fact, a development of the SPA plate wagon and had three drop-down doors on each side and was known as a 'Bass'. They were the last air-braked open wagons built to a new design, as these were no longer required for general merchandise by the end of the decade.

377-550	**BR Departmental** 112115 grey+yellow - *09*	8	11
377-550A	**BR Departmental** 112092 grey+yellow - *10*	8	11
377-550B	**BR Departmental** ? grey+yellow - *13*	8	11
377-551	**BR Railfreight** 112342 red - *09*	8	11
377-551A	**BR Railfreight** 112391 red - *10*	8	11
377-553	**BR ex-Railfreight** ? red+grey - *13*	NPG	NPG
377-552	**EWS** 112256 maroon+yellow - *09*	8	11
377-552A	**EWS** 112173 maroon+yellow - *10*	8	11
377-552B	**EWS** ? maroon+yellow - *13*	NPG	NPG

W14.   SPA/ZAA 13.5t Open Plate Wagon (2011)
The SPA is a 2-axle open steel plate wagon, fitted with bolsters. Similar wagons are the SDAs and SEAs. They were built by BREL at Shildon and Ashford between 1979 and 1981 and used to carry steel coil, rods, plate, tube and wire. Early livery was Railfreight red but later they appeared in EWS maroon. Some became ZAAs and are used by Network Rail for infrastructure work and these are painted yellow. The models are supplied with a coil load (except ZAAs).

377-730	**BR Departmental** DC460323 grey+yell ZAA - *11*	10	13
377-730A	**BR Departmental** DC460264 grey+yell ZAA - *13*	10	13
377-725	**BR Railfreight** 460890 red SPA - *11*	12	15
377-726	**Railfreight Metals** 460433 grey+yellow SPA - *11*	12	15
377-727	**EWS** 460513 maroon+yellow SPA - *11*	12	15

W15a.   LNER 13T High Sided Wagon Type 1 (2012)
In 1945, the LNER had started building open wagons with steel bodies. The side doors were made of either steel or wooden planks. The dimples, seen on the sides and ends of wagons in this table, accommodated rings on the inside of the wagon to which ropes could be tied when securing a load. They became 'Highfit' wagons under BR.

377-950	**BR** B480768 brown (early) - *12*	6	8
377-951	**BR** B480215 brown (late) - *12*	6	8

W15b.   LNER 13T High Sided Wagon Type 2 (2012)
These are the same wagons as in the table above but with smooth sides and so no raised dimples on the outside surface. They also have steel doors.

Ex-LNER 12T high-sided steel wagon [W15b]

377-952	**BR** E281227 brown (early) - *12*	6	8
377-953	**BR** E281604 brown (late) - *12*	6	8
-	**BR** DE281515 brown W	7	NA
-	**BR** E281460 brown W	7	NA
-	**BR** E281394 brown W	7	NA
377-965	set of above 3 weathered wagons - *12*	NA	26

W15c.   LNER 13T High Sided Wagon Type 3 (2012)
Again, these were like the wagons in the last two tables, with smooth sides and so no raised dimples on the outside surface, but this time with wooden doors. These were made up of 6 planks on iron straps.

377-954	**NE** 278785 grey - *12*	6	8

W16a.   BR 16T Steel Mineral Wagon (2002)
British Railways had around a quarter of a million steel mineral wagons. These took over the work of the ageing private owner 7-plank wagons, dominating coal, stone and iron ore transportation in the '50s and '60s. Most common of all was the 16 ton all-steel end door mineral wagon, built for British Railways in their tens of thousands throughout the 1950s. The building of the 16T all-steel mineral wagons carried on unabated until 1959.

This model is of a wagon with pressed steel end and side doors and the tooling is that of the original Graham Farish model inherited by Bachmann in 2000.

373-200	**BR** B38066 grey (also in set 370-175) - *02*	4	5
373-200A	**BR** B38059 grey - *04*	4	5
373-202	**BR** B258683 light grey MCO - *02*	4	5
373-203	**BR** B38066 light grey - not made	NA	NA
373-203	**BR** B38071 light grey - *05*	4	5
(370-201)a	**BR** B68992 brown ex-set* - *05*	5	NA
(370-201)b	**BR** ADB562927 olive ex-set* - *05*	5	NA
(370-201)c	**BR** DB388868 grey+yellow ex-set* - *05*	5	NA
(370-201)d	**BR** DB388869 grey+yellow ex-set* - *05*	5	NA
373-201A	**BR** B68998 brown - *04*	4	5
373-201	**BR** B564872 brown Coal (also in set 370-051) - *02*	4	5

The wagons shown in set 370-201 also appeared in set 370-202.

W16b.   BR 16T Steel Mineral Wagon (top flap) (2006)
One particularly common version of the 16T steel mineral wagon had an opening flap above the side doors, known as a 'London Traders' flap. There are conflicting ideas about its function but it is generally thought to have been provided to make it easier for coal merchants to unload the wagon by hand. The type was built to Diagram 108.

Weathered steel mineral wagon [W16b]

Graham Farish by Bachmann

Cat No	Description		
377-225	BR B80200 grey - *not made*	NA	NA
377-225	BR B100071 grey - *06*	3	4
377-225A	BR B100083 grey - *08*	3	5
377-225B	BR B168553 grey - *09*	4	6
377-225C	BR B591270 grey - *12*	5	7
377-227	BR B106979 grey W - *06*	4	6
377-227B	BR B80285 grey W - *11*	5	7
377-227A	BR B107071 grey W - *10*	4	6
377-227B	BR B80285 grey W - *11*	5	7
377-227C	BR B565332 grey W - *12*	5	7
(370-060)	NCB MCP528 grey ex-Colliery Classic Freight set - *11*	5	NA
(370-060)	as above but numbered MCP95	5	NA
(370-060)	as above but numbered MCP442	5	NA
377-227B	BR B? grey W - *11*	5	7
377-226	BR B68901 brown - *not made*	NA	NA
377-226	BR B68900 brown - *06*	4	6
377-226A	BR B68007 brown - *10*	4	6
377-226B	BR B64026 brown - *13*	4	5
-	BR B150998 grey W	7	NA
-	BR B151226 grey W	7	NA
-	BR B151711 grey W	7	NA
377-235	above set of 3 weathered wagons - *11*	NA	27
(377-225Z)	BR B77701 grey W	4	NA
(377-225Z)	BR 80200 grey W	4	NA
(377-225Z)	BR 168553 grey W	4	NA
(377-225Z)	BR 140952 grey W	4	NA
(377-225Z)	BR 257058 grey W	4	NA
(377-225Z)	BR 82219 grey W	4	NA
377-225Z	above 6 grey wagons Sp Edn 504 (Hattons) - *08*	NA	37

W16c. BR 16T Steel Mineral Wagon (no flap) (2006)

This Blue Riband model is of a 16T steel mineral wagon that has an end door but no 'London Trader' flap above the side doors. These were built to diagram 102.

377-250	BR B227229 grey - *not made*	NA	NA
377-250	BR B38066 grey - *06*	3	4
377-250A	BR B38059 grey - *08*	3	5
377-250B	BR B227229 grey - *09*	4	6
377-250C	BR B37697 grey - *11*	5	7
377-250D	BR B60544 grey - *12*	5	7
377-251	BR B121830 grey MCO - *not made*	NA	NA
377-251	BR B258683 light grey MCO - *06*	3	4
377-251A	BR B? light grey MCO - *09*	4	6
377-251B	BR B121830 light grey MCO - *11*	5	7
377-251C	BR B231349 light grey MCO - *12*	5	7
377-252	BR ADB562927 olive green ZHV - *06*	4	6
377-252A	BR ADB552821 olive green ZHV - *11*	5	7
377-253	BR B654000 brown MXV - *11*	5	7
377-253A	BR B577541 brown MXV - *12*	5	7
377-254	BR B52311 grey - *12*	5	7

W17. BR 16T Slope-Sided Mineral Wagon (2006)

Here we have the Charles Roberts design constructed with rivets rather than welding and with sloping sides. In the early days of steel wagon construction, some contractors did not trust welding and kept to the traditional way of joining steel plates. The Ministry of War Transport (MWT) came into being in 1941.

Ministry of War Transport Slope-sided steel mineral wagon (2nd World War) [W17]

377-450	BR B11532 grey - *not made*	NA	NA
377-450	BR B8128 grey - *06*	4	6
377-450A	BR B11532 grey - *10*	4	6
377-450B	BR B? grey - *13*	NPG	NPG
377-451	MWT 11532 brown - *06*	4	6
377-451A	MWT 9512 brown - *10*	4	6
377-451B	MWT MWT9505 brown - *12*	5	7

W18. BR 27T Steel 'Tippler' Wagon (2006)

Tippler wagons were not fitted with doors as they were emptied by the wagon being turned over in a cradle. Iron ore tippler wagons date back to 1939 when they were first used by Stewarts & Lloyds Ltd at their smelter at Corby. BR developed their own version and these were built in batches between 1951 and 1961. Some were built on 10' wheelbase chassis while most, like those in this table, had a 9' wheelbase. In 1956, BR entered into a contract with the Rugby Portland Cement Co. to transport chalk from a quarry at Totternhoe to the cement works at Rugby and Southby. Former iron ore tipplers were re-branded for this purpose.

377-275	BR B383560 Iron Ore - *not made*	NA	NA
377-275	BR B381550 Iron Ore - *not made*	NA	NA
377-275	BR B381500 Iron Ore - *06*	4	6
377-275A	BR B381934 Iron Ore - *10*	4	6
377-275B	BR B381818 Iron Ore - *11*	5	7
377-276	BR B382888 grey Chalk - *not made*	NA	NA
377-276	BR B381293 grey Chalk - *06*	4	6
377-276A	BR B380510 grey Chalk - *11*	5	7
377-277	BR B380005 grey W Iron Ore - *not made*	NA	NA
377-277	BR B383476 grey W Iron Ore - *06*	3	4
377-277A	BR B380005 grey W Iron Ore - *10*	4	6
377-277B	BR B381900 grey W Iron Ore - *12*	6	8

W19. MFA 24t Open Box Mineral Wagon (2003)

Many HEA coal hopper wagons became surplus to requirements and were stored. Subsequently, a lot of them were re-bodied with high-sided steel box bodies which had strengthening ribs. For carrying heavier loads or for use over lighter tracks, over 600 of the wagons were later cut down to reduce their capacity, They are found in engineers trains and classified as MFA.

373-877	Rft Coal 391070 grey+yellow - *03*	5	5
373-877A	Rft Coal 391078 grey+yellow - *04*	5	7
373-877B	Rft Coal 391075 grey+yellow - *07*	6	8
373-875	EWS 391102 in Mainline blue - *03*	5	6
373-875A	EWS 391146 in Mainline blue - *04*	5	7
373-876	EWS 391572 maroon - *03*	5	6
373-876A	EWS 391575 maroon - *?*	6	8
373-878	EWS 391102 maroon+yellow - *06*	5	7
373-878A	EWS 391257 maroon+yellow - *10*	6	8
373-878B	EWS 391271 maroon+yellow - *12*	8	10

W20. MEA 46t Open Mineral Wagon (2002)

Redundant HEA hopper wagon chassis were used in MEA construction and a steel box body fitted. Early conversions were ordered by Railfreight and these were subsequently divided up equally between Mainline Freight, Loadhaul and Transrail. Mainline and Loadhaul ordered further batches and, after they inherited all three fleets, EWS continued to place orders for them. The most recent were built in 2004.

373-576	Railfreight Coal 391045 grey+yellow - *02*	5	7
373-576a	Railfreight Coal grey+yellow - *not made*	NA	NA
373-577	Mainline M391139 blue - *02*	5	7
373-577A	Mainline blue - *not made*	NA	NA
373-575	EWS 391262 maroon - *02*	5	7
373-575A	EWS 391307 maroon - *04*	5	7
373-575B	EWS 391549 maroon - *07*	5	7
373-575C	EWS 391537 maroon - *08*	5	7
373-575D	EWS 391374 maroon - *10*	5	7
373-575E	EWS 391626 maroon - *12*	7	9

W21. POA/MKA 46t Open Box Mineral Wagon (2007)

These were built by C.C.Crump Ltd of Connahs Quay in 1988, reusing redundant liquid chlorine and caustic soda railtank chassis. Owned by Tiger Rail Leasing, they were mostly used for stone traffic.

POA open box mineral wagon ARC [W21]

Graham Farish by Bachmann

373-976	'ARC'/Tiger TRL5323 yellow PNA - 07	7	9
373-976A	'ARC'/Tiger TRL5321 yellow PNA - 11	8	10
373-975	'Yeoman'/Tiger TRL5352 very pale grey - 07	7	9
373-975A	'Yeoman'/Tiger TRL5377 very pale grey - 11	8	10
373-978	'Yeoman'/Tiger TRL5154 very pale grey - 07	5	7
373-978A	'Yeoman'/Tiger TRL5157 very pale grey - 09	7	9
373-977	Loadhaul 393030 black+orange MKA - 07	7	9
373-979	Tiger TRL5165 very pale grey - 07	5	7
373-979A	Tiger TRL5167 very pale grey - 10	7	9

Open Hopper Wagons

W22. 24T Iron Ore Hopper (2013)

Iron ore is a heavy material and only small hoppers were required for a 24 ton load. Steel iron ore hoppers were used by the LMS and LNER as well as private operators. Those built by BR were similar in design and were built by contractors. Some private owner hoppers passed to the British Iron & Steel Corporation (BISC).

373-217	'Richard Thomas' 9452 red-brown - 13	9	11
373-215	BR B435339L grey 'Iron Ore' - 13	9	11
373-218	BR B? grey W 'Iron Ore' - 13	9	11
373-216	BR B437221 brown 'Sand' - 13	9	11

W23. HEA/HSA 46t Hopper (2002)

These air-braked hoppers were built for coal traffic in their thousands at BREL (Shildon Works) between 1976 and 1979.

See also the HEA listed in the earlier Graham Farish N section.

373-502	BR 360075 brown HSA - 02	5	7
373-502A	BR 360226 brown HSA - 07	5	7
373-502B	BR 360008 brown HSA - 09	5	7
373-509	BR 360008 brown (rusty) W HEA - 13	NPG	NPG
373-503	BRe Railfreight 361862 red+grey - 02	5	7
373-503A	Railfreight red+grey - not made	NA	NA
373-507	BRe Railfreight 360644 red+grey - 06	5	7
373-510	BRe Railfreight 361990 red+grey RNA nuclear barrier wagon - 13	NPG	NPG
373-507A	Railfreight red+grey - not made	NA	NA
373-501	Railfreight Coal 360601 grey+yellow - not made	NA	NA
373-501	Railfreight Coal 361554 grey+yellow - 02	5	7
373-501A	Railfreight Coal grey+yellow - not made	NA	NA
373-506	Rft Coal Load 361579 grey+yellow HEA - 06	5	7
373-506A	Rft Coal Load 361581 grey+yellow HEA - 08	5	7
373-506A	Rft Coal Load ? grey+yellow HEA - 13	NPG	NPG
373-508	Mainline 360643 blue - 07	5	7
373-508A	Mainline ? blue - not made	NA	NA
373-504	ex-Mainline 360940 blue + graffiti - 03	5	7
373-500	EWS 361870 maroon+yellow - 02	5	7
373-505	EWS 361328 maroon+yellow - not made	NA	NA
373-505	EWS 360042 maroon+yellow HEA - 06	5	7
373-505A	EWS maroon+yellow - not made	NA	NA
373-505B	EWS 360059 maroon+yellow HEA - 08	5	7
373-505C	EWS 360677 maroon+yellow HEA - 10?	5	7
373-505D	EWS 361684 maroon+yellow HEA - 12	7	9

W24a. HAA 46t Hopper (2005)

The aluminium bodied air-braked HAA hopper wagons were built at BREL Shildon Wagon Works between the mid 1960s and the end of the 1970s. They had a 32.5 ton capacity and were built for the merry-go-round trains that transferred coal from the mines to the power stations. Nearly 10,000 of this design were built and so intense was their use that the wagon bodies usually wore out after 15 years and had to be replaced.

HAA Merry-Go-Round hopper wagon [W24a] (Tony Wright)

373-900	BR 351540, 352752, 352871, 353269 silver+brown - 05	5	7
373-900A	BR 353687 silver+brown - 07	5	7
373-900B	BR 353855 silver+brown - 08	7	9
373-900C	BR 353269 silver+brown - 11	7	9
373-900D	BR 354317 silver+brown - 11	9	11
373-900E	BR ? silver+brown - 13	NPG	NPG
373-902	Railfreight Coal 356263, 356281, 356297 silver+yellow - 06	7	9
373-902A	Railfreight Coal 358227 silver+yellow - 11	9	11
373-902B	Railfreight Coal ? silver+yellow - 13	NPG	NPG
373-901	EWS 350122, 350357, 350461 silver+maroon - 06	5	7
373-901B	EWS 350357 silver+maroon - 11	9	11
373-901C	EWS ? silver+maroon - 13	NPG	NPG

W24b. HFA Hopper with Dust Cover (2006)

Today, dusty loads are carried in enclosed hoppers to reduce material loss and pollution of the countryside. The air-braked hoppers were built for coal traffic in their thousands at BREL (Shildon Works) between 1976 and 1979.

The type was not represented in the Graham Farish range when it was taken over by Bachmann in 2000, but one was marketed in 2001 having been assembled at Barwell from components made at Poole. The current 46 tonne hopper wagon made in China first appeared in 2002. In this table we have the model introduced in 2006 with a dust cover fitted.

373-950	TransRail 365034 silver+red-brown - 06	5	7
373-950A	TransRail 365908 silver+red-brown - 07	7	9
373-950B	TransRail 351079 silver+red-brown W (HCA) - 12	9	11
373-951	Railfreight red W - not made	NA	NA
373-951	Mainline 355512 silver+yellow - 06	5	7
373-951A	Mainline 355786 silver+yellow W - 08	7	9

W24c. CEA 46t Covered Hopper (2006)

This is a covered coal hopper introduced for dust control. In this case the cover was all-enclosing.

373-475	LoadHaul 361841 black+orange - 06	5	7
373-475A	LoadHaul 361845 black+orange - 10	5	7
373-476	EWS 360726 maroon - 06	5	7
373-476A	EWS 360955 maroon - 10	5	7
373-476B	EWS 360533 maroon - 12	7	9

W25. PGA Bulk Aggregate Hopper (2003)

PGAs were two axle 38 tonne open hoppers built between 1970 and 1988, mostly to a design initiated by Charles Roberts in 1972. The ones modelled were 16ft long and built either by Procor, Standard Wagon or Charles Roberts, for the transportation of aggregates. They were owned or operated by several different companies and so carried various colourful liveries, but never that of British Railways, although some were built at Shildon in the early 1970s.

Graham Farish produced two versions of the PGA in 1993 - an open one and a covered one. Four of the former and three of the latter were released. The models produced by Bachmann started to arrive in 2003. It is impossible to say which prototype they are based on as the running numbers used come from ten different batches and at least three different builders.

373-027	'ARC' AR14245 yellow - 03	4	6
373-037	'ARC'/Caib PR14707 yellow - 04	4	6
373-037A	'ARC'/Procor PR14726 yellow - 06	5	7
373-037B	'ARC'/Procor PR14716 yellow - 08	5	7
373-037C	'ARC'/Procor PR14706 yellow - 11?	5	7
373-037D	'ARC'/Procor PR14256 yellow - 12	8	10
373-030	'British Industrial Sand' BIS7987 white no ladders - 04	5	7
373-030A	'British Industrial Sand' BIS7986 off-white - 08	5	7
373-030B	'British Industrial Sand' BIS7985 off-white - 11?	5	7
373-025	Caib PR14455 grey - 03	4	6
373-031	'ECC Quarries' PR14360 blue - 06	5	7
373-031A	'ECC Quarries' PR14374 blue - 07	5	7
373-031B	'ECC Quarries' PR14268 blue - 11	5	7
373-033	'Lafarge' REDA14783 pale cream - 05	5	7
373-033A	'Lafarge' REDA14796 pale cream - 07	5	7
373-033B	'Lafarge' REDA14815 pale cream – 11?	5	7
373-036	Railease PR14466 white - 03	4	6
373-036A	Railease SRW18506 white - 05?	4	6
373-036B	Railease SRW18511 white - 07	5	7
373-036C	Railease SRW18520 white - 10	5	7
373-035	Railease SRW18506 white - not made	NA	NA
373-035	'Redland' - not made	NA	NA
373-028	'Redland' REDA14792 pale green - 04	4	6
373-028A	'Redland' REDA14506 pale green - 06	5	7
373-028B	'Redland' REDA14514 pale green - 07	5	7

373-028C	'**Redland**' REDA14505 pale green - *11?*		5	7
373-038	'**Tarmac**' TAMC14682 white+brown W - *04*		5	7
373-038A	'**Tarmac**' TAMC14667 white+brown W - *07*		5	7
373-026	'**Tarmac** Quarry Products' TAMC14863 green - *03*		4	6

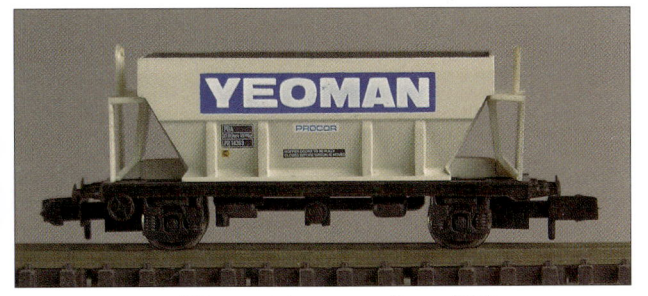

PGA aggregate hopper wagon Yeoman [W25]

373-026A	'**Tarmac** Quarry Products' green - *not made*	NA	NA
373-032	'**VTG**' VTG14372 light grey - *06*	5	7
373-032A	'**VTG**' VTG14348 light grey - *11*	5	7
373-039	'**WBB Minerals**' 30060 grey - *11*	7	9
373-035	'**Yeoman**' PR14466 very pale grey - *03*	5	7
373-035A	'**Yeoman**' PR14333 very pale grey - *05*	5	7
373-035B	'**Yeoman**' PR14363 very pale grey - *07*	5	7
373-035C	'**Yeoman**' PR14180 very pale grey - *11?*	5	7
373-035D	'**Yeoman**' PR14176 very pale grey - *12*	8	10
373-029	'**Yeoman/Caib**' PR14189 blue+grey - *04*	5	7
373-029A	'**Yeoman/Caib**' PR14196 blue+grey W - *07*	5	7
373-029B	'**Yeoman/Caib**' PR14184 blue+grey W - *11*	5	7

Dry Powder Covered Hopper Tanks

W26. 'Covhop' Covered Hopper Wagon (2014)

These were built to diagram 1/210 at BR Ashford in 1963 and their usage spans both the steam and diesel eras. The model had not been released at the time of writing.

377-767	'**BIS Sand for Rockwell Glass**' B870861 red-brown - *14*	NPG	NPG
377-766	**BR** B? light grey 'Soda Ash' - *14*	NPG	NPG
377-765	**BR** B? brown - *14*	NPG	NPG

W27a. 22T 'Presflo' (2005)

Dating from 1953, many batches were made for BR between 1955 and 1964 for cement traffic. Some 'Presflos' were later modified for salt traffic and later still for slate powder traffic and eventually they carried fly-ash. Both Associated Portland Cement and Tunnel Cement ordered their own wagons based on the BR design. The 'Presflos' were replaced from 1984 onwards and all had gone by 1991.

These were a reintroduction of the original Graham Farish model of 1982. Bachmann retooled the model producing a high quality model for release in 2011 and versions of this are listed in the next table.

373-526	'**Blue Circle**' PF20 yellow - *05*	4	5
373-526A	'**Blue Circle**' PF17 yellow W - *07*	4	5
373-526B	'**Blue Circle**' PF14 yellow W - *08*	5	7
373-527	'**Pozzolanic**' B888974 brown - *05*	5	7
373-525	'**Rugby Cement**' B873811 brown - *05*	4	5
373-525A	'**Rugby Cement**' B873814 brown - *08*	5	7

W27b. CPV 20T/22T 'Presflo' (2011)

As with the larger 00 models, both 20T (one cylinder) and 22T (two cylinders) versions have been modelled by Bachmann of these highly detailed wagons. There are also other structural differences to be spotted and they are supplied with vacuum pipes and imitation couplings to be added to the bufferbeams.

377-828	'**Blue Circle**' Snowcem PF100 grey 22T - *12*	7	9
377-828A	'**Blue Circle**' Snowcrete PF? grey 22T - *13*	10	12
377-827	'**Blue Circle**' B873364 brown 22T - *11*	7	9
377-827A	'**Blue Circle**' B888723 brown 22T - *13*	10	12
377-826	**Crown 'Bulk Cement'** B888229 brown 20T - *11*	7	9
377-826A	**Crown 'Bulk Cement'** B888235 brown 20T - *13*	10	12
377-825	'**Bulk Tunnel Cement**' B888113 brown 20T - *12*	7	9
377-825A	'**Bulk Tunnel Cement**' B688112 brown 20T - *13*	10	12
-	**BR** B873295 brown W	8	NA
-	**BR** B873344 brown W	8	NA
-	**BR** B873110 brown W	8	NA
377-840	above 3 weathered 22T wagons - *11*	NA	30

CPV 'Presflo' Blue Circle [W27b]

-	'**Blue Circle**' PF76 yellow W	9	NA
-	'**Blue Circle**' PF109 yellow W	9	NA
-	'**Blue Circle**' PF52 yellow W	9	NA
377-841	above 3 weathered 22T wagons - *13*	NA	33

W28a. PCA Bulk Powder (2003)

PCAs came in a variety of shapes, some with straight tanks, similar to TTA petroleum tank wagons, and some with tanks that dipped in the middle. The straight tank PCA model was introduced by Graham Farish in 1993 and three versions of it were sold before Bachmann sent the tooling to China for production there. The first Kader-made Farish PCA of this type arrived in the shops in 2003.

373-000	'**Alcan**' 55552 silver - *03*	4	6
373-003	'**Alcan**' 55552 silver - *not made*	NA	NA
373-002	'**Blue Circle**' DP102 pale grey - *03*	4	6
373-005	'**Blue Circle**' pale grey - *not made*	NA	NA
373-003	(unbranded) BCC11118 very pale grey - *04*	4	6
373-003A	(unbranded) BCC10994 very pale grey W - *05*	4	6
373-003B	(unbranded) BCC11138 very pale grey W - *06*	5	7
373-003C	(unbranded) BCC11122 very pale grey W - *08*	5	7
373-003D	'**Blue Circle**' BCC11017 very pale grey W - *10*	5	7
373-003E	'**Blue Circle**' BCC11024 very pale grey W - *12*	5	7
373-007	'**Castle Cement**' RLS10319 grey W - *06*	5	7
373-007A	'**Castle Cement**' RLS10327 pale grey W - *08*	5	7
373-007B	'**Castle Cement**' RLS10311 pale grey W - *10*	5	7
373-007C	'**Castle Cement**' RLS10304 pale grey W - *12*	8	10
373-008	'**ICI**' 10120 white - *07*	5	7
373-008A	'**ICI**' 10111 white - *08*	5	7
373-008B	'**ICI**' PR9477 white - *12*	5	7
373-008C	'**ICI**' PR? white - *13*	5	7

PCA bulk powder wagon Blue Circle [W28a]

373-005	'**RMC**' RC10025 orange - *04*	4	6
373-006	'**RMC**' RC10034 orange W - *06*	5	7
373-006A	'**RMC**' RC10041 orange W - *08*	5	7
373-006B	'**RMC**' RC10045 orange W - *10*	5	7
373-002A	'**Rugby Cement**' PR9420 white - *04*	4	6
373-002B	'**Rugby Cement**' PR9409 white - *06*	5	7
373-002C	'**Rugby Cement**' PR9417 white - *08*	5	7
373-002D	'**Rugby Cement**' PR9414 white - *10*	5	7
373-001	'**Tunnel Cement**' RLS10321 very pale grey - *03*	4	6

Graham Farish by Bachmann

373-004	'Tunnel Cement' PL510327 very pale grey W - 04	4	6

W28b. PCA 'Metalair' Bulk Powder (2011)

Powell Duffryn built these in 1984, in association with powder tank specialists Metalair. They had a lightweight tank which allowed for a higher volume of powder, as well as faster discharge. They were built to replace the ageing fleet of 'Presflo' CPV cement wagons.

377-925	'Blue Circle' 10683 pale grey - 11	7	9
377-926	(unbranded) 11137 very pale grey - 11	7	9
377-927	(unbranded) 11138 very pale grey W - 11	7	9
-	(unbranded) 10691 grey W	8	NA
-	(unbranded) 10699 grey W	8	NA
-	(unbranded) 11027 grey W	8	NA
377-935	above 3 weathered wagons - 11	NA	30

W29. PCA Taper Bulk Powder V Tank (2003)

The PCA with a dip in the tank has various names including 'Chevron Tank', 'Depressed Centre Tank' or 'V Tank'. They have the appearance of having been sawn in half and collapsed in the middle. They are a familiar site in the cement industry, although steadily being replaced by other designs. These 'Presflos' owed much to oil tank design of the period. The barrel slopes down, from both directions, to a central discharge point. They were built in batches between 1966 and 1981 for Blue Circle Cement, by various manufacturers. In 1984, the 'Metalair' design started to appear as their replacement.

The model started life in the Graham Farish range in 1993 and six versions were produced prior to Bachmann taking over the company. Bachmann have produced many versions of it, most of them unbranded like many of the real wagons.

373-075	'Blue Circle' 9343 pale grey - 03	4	6
373-076A	(unbranded) BCC10834 very pale grey - 04	5	7
373-076B	(unbranded) BCC10821 very pale grey - 07	5	7
373-076C	(unbranded) BCC10771 very pale grey - 10	5	7
373-076D	(unbranded) BCC10776 very pale grey - 12	7	9
373-077	(unbranded) APCM9138 very pale grey - 04	4	6
373-077A	(unbranded) BCC10809 very pale grey - 06	5	7
373-077B	(unbranded) BCC9171 very pale grey - 07	5	7
373-077D	(unbranded) APCM9278 very pale grey - 10	5	7
373-077E	(unbranded) APCM9296 very pale grey - 12	7	9
373-075A	'Ketton Cement' TLG/PR9468 yellow - 04	4	6
373-075B	'Ketton Cement' TLG/PR9469 yellow - 06	5	7
373-075C	'Ketton Cement' TLG/PR9471 yellow - 07	5	7
373-075D	'Ketton Cement' TLG/PR9464 yellow - 10	5	7
373-075E	'Ketton Cement' TLG9461 yellow - 12	8	10
373-078	'Lever Brothers' TRL10527 purple - 05	5	7
373-078A	'Lever Brothers' TRL10523 purple - 07	5	7
373-078B	'Lever Brothers' TRL10525 purple - 10	5	7
373-076	'Rockware Glass' 10563 blue - 03	4	6

Tank Wagons

W30a. 14T Small Tank Wagon (Type 1) (2005)

Although at Nationalisation of the railways in 1948 most railway wagons became public property, a major exclusion was tank wagons. Their purpose is to carry liquids such as petrol, oil, tar, milk, bitumen, industrial chemicals etc. To avoid the risk of contamination of loads, tank wagons tend to be committed to specified traffic. The specification for Class A (inflammable liquids) came in 1902. In 1907 and 1911, the Railway Clearing House (RCH) establish standards for cylindrical tank wagons of 10T, 12T and 14T sizes. The RCH wagon design on 10ft wheelbase chassis was confirmed in 1917 and remained unchanged until after the Second World War.

This version of the 14 ton tank wagon has a gantry, small flat manhole cover and ladders.

14T tank wagon Bitumuls [W30a]

373-652	'Bitumuls' 12 black - 06	4	5
373-652A	'Bitumuls' ? black - 13	4	5
373-653	'ICI' 159 dark blue-green - 08	5	7
373-653A	'ICI' 743 dark blue-green - 11	5	7
373-653B	'ICI' 741 dark blue-green - 11	6	8
373-655	'Mobil' 1657 black* - 12	7	9
373-650	'National Benzole' 734 silver - 06	5	7
373-650A	'National Benzole' 755 silver - 10	5	7
373-654	'National Fertilizers' 501 brown - 12		
373-679B	'Shell BP' A7287 black - 12	7	9
373-651	'Shell Electrical Oils' SM3102 brown - 05	4	5
373-651A	'Shell Electrical Oils' SM3116 brown - 08	5	7
373-651B	'Shell Electrical Oils' SM2202 brown - 10	5	7
373-651C	'Shell Electrical Oils' SM2443 brown - 11	6	8

* Pictures in the catalogue show this tank wagon with cross stays.

W30b. 14T Small Tank Wagon (Type 2) (2005)

This version of the 14 ton tank wagon had cross stays and large domed manhole cover.

373-677	'Carburine Motor Spirit' 6 yellow - 05	4	5
373-678	'Fina' 136 silver - 08	5	7
373-678A	'Fina' 135 silver - 10	5	7
373-676	'The Kalchester Manufacturing Co.' 101 red - 06	4	5
373-675	'Mobil' 1624 black - 06	5	7
373-675A	'Mobil' 5294 black - 10	5	7
373-675Z	'Power' 115 silver Sp Edn (Osborn's Models) - 11	7	9
373-679	'Shell/BP' A5281 black - 08	5	7
373-679A	'Shell/BP' A7287 black - 10	5	7

W30c. 14T Small Tank Wagon Triple Sets (2007)

These sets consist of three wagons and may be all of the same design or a mixture of types.

-	'Shell BP' 3971 black W type 2	5	NA
-	'Shell BP' 5103 black W type ?	5	NA
-	'Shell BP' A4282 black W type ?	5	NA
373-650Z	above three wagons Sp Edn 504 (Signalbox) - 07	NA	21
-	'Tarmac' 58 black W type 2	8	NA
-	'Tarmac' 60 black W type 2	8	NA
-	'Tarmac' 66 black W type 2	8	NA
373-665	above 3 weathered tank wagons - 12	NA	28
-	'Esso' 1855 black W type 1	8	NA
-	'Esso' 1231 black W type 2	8	NA
-	'Esso' 1869 black W type 1	8	NA
373-666	above 3 weathered tank wagons - 12	NA	28

W31. TTA 45t 'Monobloc' Tank Wagon (2007)

The 'Monobloc' tank wagon appeared on the railways in Britain in 1958 and was based on a French design. By lowering the tank between the solebars the centre of gravity was also lowered, thus allowing the accommodation of a larger tank. Wing plates welded to the solebars hold the tank in place. Following agreements between British Railways and the petroleum industry in 1963, regarding the transportation of petroleum products by rail, there was a massive increase in the building of new tank wagons to form block trains and the 'Monobloc' was the principal design adopted.

The original Graham Farish N gauge range did not include a cylindrical bodied petroleum tank wagon, only the flat tar wagon. The N gauge 'Monobloc' TTA tank wagon was introduced by Bachmann in 2007.

TTA 'Monobloc' tank wagon BP [W31]

373-775	'BP' BPO53774 green - 07	6	8
373-775A	'BP' BPO53779 green - 08	7	9
373-775B	'BP' BPO37086 green - 11	8	10

Graham Farish by Bachmann

Cat No.	Description		
373-775V	'BP' BPO60873 green	7	NA
373-775T	'BP' BPO60880 green	7	NA
373-775U	'BP' BPO60586 green	7	NA
373-775?	above 3 wagons in a set Sp Edn (Model Rail) - 08	NA	24
373-776	'Esso' 57575 light grey - 07	6	8
373-776A	'Esso' 57534 light grey - 08	7	9
373-776B	'Esso' 5961 light grey - 10	7	9
373-776C	'Esso' 5955 light grey - 11	8	10
373-776D	'Esso' 5959 light grey - 12	9	11
373-777	'Shell/BP' 67391 light grey - 07	6	8
373-777A	'Shell/BP' 67389 light grey - 08	7	9
373-777B	'Shell/BP' ? light grey - 11	8	10
373-777C	'Shell/BP' 585 light grey - 12	9	11
373-778	'Shell/BP' 3452 black – 10?	8	10
-	unbranded 65627 black, ex-kit Sp Edn (N Gauge Society) - 11	12	NA
-	'Shell' 65634 black W	9	NA
-	'Shell' 65648 black W	9	NA
-	'Shell' 65701 black W	9	NA
373-785	above 3 weathered tank wagons - 12	NA	32

	Unbranded		
373-775Y	56050 grey W	NA	NA
373-775Z	56039 grey W	NA	NA
373-775X	56177 grey W	NA	NA
373-775W	56103 grey W	NA	NA
373-775T	set of above 4 wagons Sp Edn 500 (Kernow MR Centre) - not made*	NA	NA
373-775W	56103 grey W Ltd Edn 504 - 08	8	10
373-775X	56177 grey W Ltd Edn 504 - 08	8	10
373-775Y	56050 grey W Sp Edn 504 - 08	8	10
373-775Z	56039 grey W Sp Edn 504 - 08	8	10

* This set of four wagons was ordered but later cancelled due to rising prices. As production was already under way, Bachmann decided to release them themselves as limited editions through selected retailers.

Covered Vans

W32.   10T Salt Van
Proposed, but the old tools were unusable and so none were made.

373-350	'Shaka Salt' - not made	NA	NA
373-351	'Stafford Salt Works' - not made	NA	NA

W33a.   12T Cattle Wagon (2003)
The cattle wagon was one of the original models of 1970 and was not particularly good. Although Bachmann continued to use the tooling from 2003, It was only an interim measure while they tooled up a more accurate model. This was released in 2009 and is listed in the next table.

373-250	LMS M14390 light grey - 03	3	4
373-250A	LMS M14393 light grey - 04	3	4
373-252	NE 55787 grey - 03	3	4
373-254	NE 55783 grey - 05	3	4
373-251	BR B891416 brown (also in set) - 03	3	4
373-251A	BR B891419 brown - 04	3	4

W33b.   GWR 8T Cattle Wagon (2009)
Many of the Great Western Railway cattle wagons dated back to the late Victorian period. During the 1930s, there was a decline in livestock traffic on the railways and the GWR rebuilt some of their cattle wagons as fruit vans while others were converted to carry beer barrels. British Railways inherited over 11,000 cattle wagons in 1948 and, despite the continuing decline in traffic, carried on building them up until 1954. 2,300 of these were built at Swindon. There were soon many redundant vans and they were used for other purposes such as the transportation of vegetables. The last two cattle wagons survived until 1975 and are in the National Collection.

373-261	GW 106881 dark grey - 09	5	7
373-261A	GW 106909 dark grey - 11	6	8
373-?	LMS 23717 dark grey - ?	8	NPG
373-260	BR B893343 brown (early) - 09	5	7
373-260A	BR B893111 brown (early) - 11	6	8
373-260B	BR B brown (early) - 12	6	8
373-262	BR B893085 brown (late) - 11	6	8
373-262A	BR B893268 brown (late) - 12	7	9
-	BR B893582 brown W	7	NA
-	BR B893401 brown W	7	NA
-	BR B893177 brown W	7	NA
373-270	above set of 3 weathered wagons - 11	NA	27

GWR 8T cattle wagon [W33b]

W34.   GWR 12T Twin Vent Van (2002)
At Nationalisation, the former GWR had unfulfilled orders of unfitted ventilated vans. They were delivered to British Railways who ordered 330 more of them in 1949.

373-125Z	'Axminster Carpets' B895006 grey Sp Edn 500 (Buffers) - 05	4	6
373-125	GW 139956 dark grey - 02	4	6
373-128	GW 139948 dark grey - 04	4	6
373-130	BR W134035 grey - 04	4	6
373-127	BR W134030 light grey - probably not made	NPG	NPG
373-126	BR W124480 brown (also in sets) - 02	4	6
373-129	BR W124483 brown - 04	4	6

W35.   LMS 12T Single Vent Van (2002)
These had corrugated steel end walls and a single sliding door on both sides. Orders for 1300 plywood-sided and 1000 planked vans were placed immediately after Nationalisation and these carried a B prefix to the number.
  This is the original Graham Farish LMS van from 1970.

(370-025)	'Worthington' 5 brown ex-set - 03	3	NA
373-100	LMS 505969 grey (also in set 370-050) - 02	4	5
373-103	LMS 505953 light grey - 04	3	4
373-101	BR M504891 grey (also in set 370-200) - 02	4	5
373-104	BR M504883 light grey - 04	3	4
373-102	BR ? brown - probably not made	NPG	NPG
373-105	BR E568037 brown - 04	3	4

W36a.   LNER 12T Fruit Van (2012)
For some time, fruit vans on the LNER retained timber ends as it was easier to build in louvres in the lower half of each end to ensure good air circulation. Later LNER fruit vans were built in plywood. In addition to the end louvres, the models have six ventilators in the roof.

LNER fruit van [W36a]

377-985	BR E222599 brown (early) - 12	7	9
377-986	BR E222334 brown (late) - 12	7	9
-	BR E235812 brown W	7	NA
-	BR E236115 brown W	7	NA
-	BR E236396 brown W	7	NA
377-990	above 3 weathered vans - 12	NA	26

8th Edition

Graham Farish by Bachmann

W36b. LNER 12T Vent Van (Planked Ends) (2012)
LNER standard ventilated vans, for general merchandise, were built on both timber and steel underframes, fitted and unfitted, with spoked or disc wheels and with timber or corrugated steel ends. They generally had a single sliding door on each side, similar to LMS ventilated vans.

This model is of an LNER vent van with planked end walls.

377-975	**NE** 236824 brown - *12*	7	9
377-976	**BR** E236698 brown (early) - *12*	7	9

W36c. LNER 12T Vent Van (Corrugated Ends) (2012)
Around 1934, the decision was made to follow LMS practice and build ventilated vans with corrugated steel ends and on steel chassis. Many vans of this type were built and included a number of design variations. Some had a hooded ventilator added in each end and some were built two inches narrower for use in restricted sidings. Some were partitioned inside for specific traffic and some found themselves on fish trains. They became the standard design for LNER ventilated vans from the mid-1930s. By the outbreak of war, almost 3000 had been built and, by Nationalisation, the number had risen to 7700.

377-980	**BR** E211308 brown (early) - *12*	7	9
377-981	**BR** E256948 brown (late) - *12*	7	9

W36d. LNER 12T Fish Van (2005)
In the early days, fish was carried in open trucks with low sides but usually sheeted over. The passing of a fish train on a hot summer's day must have been quite an experience. From around 1900, vans started to be used.

373-225	**NE** 27456 brown - *not made*	NA	NA
373-225	**NE** 414124 brown - *05*	3	4

W37a. SR 12T Vent Van (2013)
Typical Southern Railway vans had a vari-curve roof (inherited from the SE&CR) which had tight curves at the edges but flatter on top. The design later proved to be problematical due to 'racking' which caused the roof boards to move, resulting in leakage.

On this version of the SR ventilated van, the planks used in its construction are all the same width.

377-425	**SR** 48467 dark brown - *13*	NPG	NPG

W37b. SR 12T Vent Van 2+2 Planking (2013)
On this version of the SR ventilated van, two widths of planks have been used in its construction and they were arranged in the order of alternately 2 narrow and 2 wide. Some were built for the LMS and GWR during the Second World War.

377-426	**BR** M523351 grey - *13*	NPG	NPG
377-427	**BR** S59123 brown (early) - *13*	NPG	NPG

W38a. BR 12T Ventilated Van (Planked) (2007)
By the early 1950s, British Railways were looking beyond completing wagon orders inherited from the 'Big Four' and had started to design their own standard wagons which were needed to replace older stock. The series of vans they developed had much in common with former GWR designs but with ideas borrowed from the other three companies. One of these was corrugated end walls which were typical of LMS and LNER vans and the adopting of a single vent at each end for the ventilated vans. The hinged double doors were typical of the GWR and SR designs. The standard ventilated van looked most like the GWR one as it also had the same roof profile, although slightly taller. Most batches were built at Wolverton and some at Darlington and Ashford. Two late batches were contracted out to Charles Roberts Ltd and Press Steel Ltd. Construction continued until 1962, after which the 'Vanwide' design, introduced in 1961, took over.

BR vent van [W38a]

373-700	**BR** B755180 brown - *07*	4	6
373-700A	**BR** B755197 brown - *08*	5	7
373-700B	**BR** B? brown (early) - *12*	5	7
373-701	**BR** B762318 brown Margarine - *07*	4	6
373-701A	**BR** B762324 brown Margarine - *08*	5	7
373-701B	**BR** B762361 brown Margarine - *11*	6	8
373-702	**BR** ADB780575 grey Railstores - *07*	4	6
373-702A	**BR** DB761319 olive green Railstores - *12*	7	9
373-703	**BR** B760289 brown (late) - *11*	6	8
373-703A	**BR** B? brown (late) - *12*	6	8

W38b. BR 12T Ventilated Van (Plywood Doors) (2011)
There were many batches of standard ventilated vans built during the 1950s and this model is based on a batch built at BR Wolverton in 1957-58. The standard vans were either planked or built in plywood or, like these ones, in a combination of both.

These models are of planked vans with plywood doors.

377-627	**BR** B773727 (early) brown - *11*	6	8
377-627A	**BR** B? (early) brown - *13*	NPG	NPG
377-628	**BR** B774238 (late) brown - *11*	6	8
377-628A	**BR** B? (late) brown - *13*	NPG	NPG

W38c. BR 12T Ventilated Van (Plywood) (2007)
Plywood bodywork, compared with the more traditional planked type, simplified van building and probably shortened the building time.

The model represents vans of all plywood construction, built at Wolverton, Darlington and Ashford between 1955 and 1957.

373-750	**BR** grey - *not made*	NA	NA
373-751	**BR** B784873 brown - *07*	4	6
373-751A	**BR** B784887 brown - *08*	4	6
373-751B	**BR** B772139 brown - *11?*	6	8
373-751C	**BR** B? brown - *12*	6	8
373-752	**BR** B775719 brown (late) - *12*	7	9

W38d. BR 12T Fruit Van (Plywood) (2010)
While these were built as fruit vans, they were also used for vegetable traffic and general merchandise. They had a 10ft wheelbase and were vacuum-braked and XP rated.

The model was based on the final version of the standard van, 100 of which were built at Darlington in 1953-54 and of all plywood construction.

BR plywood fruit van [W38d]

377-625	**BR** B875800 (early) brown - *11*	6	8
377-625A	**BR** ? (early) brown - *13*	NPG	NPG
377-626	**BR** B875640 (late) brown - *11*	6	8
377-626A	**BR** B873772 (late) brown - *13*	NPG	NPG
377-625K	**Graham Farish** 40 black * - *10*	7	9
-	**BR** B875702 brown W	7	NA
-	**BR** B875588 brown W	7	NA
-	**BR** B875841 brown W	7	NA
377-635	above 3 weathered fruit vans - *11*	NA	26

* This wagon commemorated the 40th Anniversary of the Graham Farish N gauge range.

W38e. BR 10T Insulated Van (Planked) (2007)
The insulated vans were to the same construction as the standard ventilated van but without the end vents. They had corrugated ends and double hinged doors in each side. There being little use for them, many ended up in ale traffic and some were used for fish - although, with their short wheelbase, they were unsuitable for the fast Blue Spot fish trains. They were gradually absorbed into general traffic and broken up early.

373-725	**BR** B872187 white 'Insulated' - *07*	4	6
373-725A	**BR** B872171 white 'Insulated' - *08*	5	7

Graham Farish by Bachmann

373-725B	BR B972112 white 'Insulated' - 11	6	8
373-725C	BR B? white 'Insulated' - 12	6	8
373-726	BR 041421 brown - 07	4	6
373-726A	BR B872042 brown - 08	5	7
373-726B	BR B872077 brown (late) - 11	6	8
373-726C	BR B? brown (late) - 12	6	8
373-727	BR B872208 pale blue 'Insulated' - 11	6	8
373-727A	BR B? pale blue 'Insulated' - 12	6	8

W38f. BR 10T Quad Vent Meat Van (2011)

The model is based on 100 vans built by British Railways at Wolverton Works in 1952. This was despite there being adequate meat containers already in use. The van was a standard design with planked sides and corrugated steel end walls. The latter each had four large ventilators and there were smaller vents in the sides.

373-740	BR B870006 red - 11	6	8
373-741	BR B870073 brown - 11	6	8
373-742	BR B870032 brown - 11	6	8

W38g. Mixed Box Van Sets (2011)

So far only one of these three van sets has been assembled.

-	BR B755822 brown 'ICI Fertilizer' planked	7	NA
-	BR B7650?? brown 'Blue Circle Portland Cement' planked	7	NA
-	BR B765001 brown 'Carrs Biscuits' plywood	7	NA
373-700Y	above 3 vans with posters on sides Sp Edn 504 ModelZone) - 11	NA	28

W39. VBA 29T Box Van (2003)

By 1967, the wagon fleet had fallen to about a third the size it had been in 1948. British Rail launched a programme of vigorous marketing in the 1970s and backed this up with a fleet of new larger and faster air-braked vehicles. The VBAs were originally coded COV AB. 75 were built at Ashford between November 1970 and August 1971 and a further 100 were constructed at Shildon between December 1974 and April 1975.

Graham Farish introduced a model in 1988 that was passed off as a VAB and a VBA. Three versions were produced before 2000.

373-050	Railfreight 200287 brown VBB - 03	4	5
373-051	Railfreight Dist. 200155 olive green - 03	4	5
373-052	Railfreight 200611 grey+red - 06	4	6
373-052A	Railfreight 200629 grey+red - 08	5	7
373-052B	Railfreight 200602 grey+red - 10	5	7
373-052C	Railfreight 200586 grey+red - 12	5	7
373-053	EWS 200571 maroon - 06	4	6
373-053A	EWS 200557 maroon - 07	5	7
373-053B	EWS 200569 maroon - 10	5	7

W40. VGA 46t Sliding Wall Van (2006)

The VGA began to appear in the early 1980s and showed a similarity with Continental designs. This saw a complete change in design and, instead of sliding doors, it had sliding sides, making access to the interior easier.

Railfreight Speedlink VGA sliding wall van [W40]

373-601	Railfreight Speedlink 210452 silver+red - 06	6	8
(370-252)	Railfreight Speedlink 210452 silver+red ex-set - ?	6	NA
373-601A	Railfreight Speedlink 210646 silver+red W - 08	7	9
373-601B	Railfreight Speedlink 210630 silver+red W - 09	8	10
373-602	Railfreight Distribution 210639 silver+yellow Carlisle Currock motif - 06	6	8
373-602A	Railfreight Distribution 210595 silver+yellow W Carlisle Currock motif - 09	7	9
373-602B	Railfreight Distribution 210493 silver+yellow W Carlisle Currock motif - 09	8	10
373-600	EWS 210444 maroon - 06	6	8
373-600A	EWS 200537 maroon W - 08	7	9
373-600B	EWS 210430 maroon W - 09	8	10

Brake Vans

W41a. GWR 20T 'Toad' Brake Van (2002)

The GWR 'Toad' brake van changed little in appearance over the years. They had a veranda at one end only and no side duckets. Later versions, like this model, had a 16' wheelbase. They were mostly restricted use ('RU') and generally carried the name of the yard to which they were allocated. The vans were painted all-over light grey by BR, but, following the fitting of vacuum brakes and up grading to XP rating, they were painted in BR bauxite brown.

The model was introduced by Graham Farish in 1971 and five versions were made before Bachmann took over the company in 2000. The tooling went out to China and from 2002 a further six versions were made. Bachmann then decided to retool the model and the current model appeared in 2010, as listed in the next table.

373-325	GW 56683 grey Severn Tunnel Junc.- 02	5	7
373-325A	GW 114800 grey Rhymney - 03	5	7
373-325B	GW 68690 grey Dowlais Cae Harris – not made	NA	NA
373-327	BR W35960 grey Shrewsbury (Coton Hill) - 03	5	6
373-326	BR W11496 brown (also in set) - 03?	5	6
373-326A	BR W114961 brown - 03	5	7
373-326B	BR brown – not made	NA	NA
373-328	BR DW17455 brown S&T Department - 05	5	6
373-328A	BR brown S&T Department – not made	NA	NA

W41b GWR 20T 'Toad' Brake Van (2010)

After initially making the original Graham Farish model of 1971, as listed in the table above, Bachmann retooled the model to a high standard for release in 2010.

377-375	GW 68761 grey Birkenhead - 10	5	7
377-375A	GW 17410 grey Birkenhead - 12	7	9
377-375B	GW ? grey S - 13	NPG	NPG
377-376	BR W68834 grey Stourbridge RU - 10	5	7
377-377	BR W114854 brown (early) - 10	5	7
377-378	BR DW68786 brown S&T Department - 10	5	7

W42. MR 20T Brake Van (2013)

Based on Midland Railway design, these brake vans marked the first change from that design by the use of duckets on either side of the van. They had a 12ft wheelbase and were 20ft long over headstocks. 100 were built at Derby during 1926-27.

This model was under development at the time of writing.

377-750	LMS 2045 grey - 13	NA	NA
377-751	BR M295516 grey - 13	NA	NA
377-752	BR M? brown - 13	3	NA

W43. LMS 20T Brake Van (2008)

There were many different variations on the LMS goods brake van and the model is of one built at Derby between 1935 and 1938. There were 670 built at that time, early ones starting life in light grey with large lettering and those built from 1936 onwards were finished in bauxite with small lettering. This was also one of the vans which was 'piped', while later ones built had hand-brakes only. While the van body was planked, the veranda half-height end walls were of steel plate construction.

Ex-LMS brake van [W43]

377-310	LMS 730026 grey - 08	5	7
377-310A	LMS 730081 grey - 11	6	8
377-310B	LMS 730033 grey - 13	7	9
377-311	LMS 730670 brown - 08	5	7
377-301	BR M730836 grey - 08	5	7
377-301A	BR B950197 grey - 10	5	7
377-301B	BR M732484 grey - 11	6	8
377-301C	BR M732264 grey - 13	7	9
377-300	BR M732396 brown - 08	5	7
377-300A	BR M731460 brown - 10	5	7

Graham Farish by Bachmann

377-302	**BR** ? brown (late) - *13*	NPG	NPG

W44. 25T SR 'Pill Box' Brake Van (2012)

The so-called 'Pill Box' brake van was the standard design adopted by the Southern Railway and the original drawing was done at the Lancing Works. Modifications for a later batch were made to the drawings at Eastleigh but the vans were built at Lancing. The main change seen from outside was with regard to the position of the ducket which was in one side only. As one looked at the side of the van containing the ducket, early vans had the ducket on the left but later ones had it on the right. Another change came in BR days when the sand box that had been constructed on the outside of one veranda wall and painted red, was removed. It is interesting to note that this design, which incorporates a small van body placed centrally on a longer chassis, predates the similar LNER design which was later adopted by British Railways to be their standard design.

377-850	**SR** 55995 dark brown with red ends white roof, large letters - *12*	10	13
377-851	**SR** 56365 dark brown with red ends grey roof - *12*	10	13
377-852	**BR** S55642 grey - *12*	10	13
377-853	**BR Departmental** DS65400 olive green - *12*	10	13
377-854	**BR** S55583 brown - *12*	10	13

W45a. 20T Brake Van (2003)

This was the original Graham Farish former LBSC standard brake van of 1978 which Bachmann used only in train sets and did not release as a solo model.

(370-025)	**SR** no number ex-set - *03*	3	NA
373-301	**BR** M732484 grey – *not made*	NA	NA
373-300	**BR** brown – *not made*	NA	NA
(370-050/1)	**NE** 151752 brown ex-set - *03-04*	3	NA
(370-201/2)	**BR** DS62864 grey+yellow ex-set - *05-07*	3	NA

W45b. BR 20T Standard Brake Van (2007)

The BR standardised their brake van design on that developed by the LNER known as a long wheelbase 'Toad E' and, consequently, one normally finds one basic model used for both LNER and BR standard variations, as applies here. The van had a small cabin with a narrow veranda at both ends and, beyond each veranda, there was a platform giving the impression that the chassis was too large for the body. However, the longer chassis ensured a steadier ride and improved visibility. On BR standard brake vans a raised grab-rail was provided along the edges of the two end platforms. Each van also had a ducket on either side to give the guard a view along the train. LNER versions do not have full-length step boards.

LNER brake van [W45b]

377-527	**NE** 260922 brown - *07*	5	7
377-527A	**NE** 234998 brown - *10*	7	9
377-527B	**NE** ? brown - *12*	7	9
377-525	**BR** B954762 brown - *07*	5	7
377-525A	**BR** B951094 brown - *11*	8	10
377-525B	**BR** B953810 brown – *11?*	7	9
377-525C	**BR** B952497 brown - *11*	8	10
377-525D	**BR** B950358 brown W - *13*	9	12
377-526	**BR** B951480 grey - *07*	5	7
377-526A	**BR** B950884 grey - *08*	7	9
377-526B	**BR** B951759 grey - *10*	7	9
377-527	**BR Railfreight** B? grey+red - *not made*	NA	NA

W45c. BR 20T Standard Brake Van (sheeted) (2007)

The final batch of standard brake vans was built in 1963 and had vacuum pipes, roller bearings and hydraulic buffers. Later they were mostly converted to air brakes.

This model represents standard brake vans which had their lives extended by having their veranda walls sheeted over with plywood.

377-535	**Railfreight** B955247 red+grey - *07*	7	9

Bogie Wagons

W46. SR 'Queen Mary' Brake Van (2011)

In 1933, the Southern Railway had used the chassis of redundant AC motor luggage vans to build some bogie brake vans for express freight trains. The success of these prompted the construction of a further 25 vans in 1936, with flat-sided wooden bodies on shortened standard carriage underframes. Not all had plain planked sides as around eight were partially clad in steel sheet from new and a few more gained sheeting later. Nicknamed 'Queen Mary', six received air brakes in 1961. Several remain in service and several more have been preserved.

Both planked and steel plated versions are being developed for the N Gauge Society. The models are exclusively available to the society for the first two years, after which the tooling will be available for general use.

377-875Z	**SR** 56285 dark brown with red ends – *not made*	NA	NA
377-875Z	**SR** 56282 dark brown with red ends - *11*	NPG	NPG
377-875Y	**BR** S56287 brown (early) – *not made*	NA	NA
377-875Y	**BR** S56294 brown (early) - *11*	NPG	NPG
377-876Z	**BR** S56298 brown (later) - *11*	NPG	NPG
377-875X	**BR** ADS56296 olive green, wasp ends - *11*	NPG	NPG
377-876Y	**BR** DS56283 grey+yellow - *11*	NPG	NPG
377-875	**Satlink** red+yellow – *not made*	NA	NA
377-876X	**EWS** ADS56299 maroon – *not made*	NA	NA
377-876X	**EWS** KDS56305 maroon - *11*	NPG	NPG

W47. GWR 30T Macaw B/Bogie Bolster C Wagon (2009)

30 ton bogie bolster wagons were used to carry long loads, such as girders, rails and complete sections of track. The 'Macaw B' was pretty much the GWR's standard bogie bolster wagon and was being built before the First World War, some being converted to tank carriers for use in France. British Railways adopted more than one design from the former railway companies and for its 30 ton 'Bogie C' wagons turned to the GWR 'Macaw B' design which had four moveable bolsters. Between 1949 and 1962, many batches of these were built.

373-927	**LMS** 314000 light grey - *not made*	NA	NA
373-927	**GWR** 84974 dark grey Macaw B - *10*	9	12
373-927A	**GWR** ? dark grey Macaw B + brown girders - *13*	9	12
373-926	**BR** B943405 grey - *09*	9	12
373-926A	**BR** B940050 grey - *11*	11	13
373-926B	**BR** B943405 grey + brown girders - *13*	11	13
373-925	**BR** S&T DB997636 red Prawn - *09*	9	12
373-925A	**BR** S&T DB997653 red Prawn - *11*	11	13
373-925B	**BR** S&T DB? red Prawn+ brown girders - *13*	11	13

W48. BDA/YAA 80T Bogie Bolster Wagon (2010)

British Railways built a large number of bogie bolster wagons between 1949 and 1962. The 52ft long version was originally known as a 'Bogie Bolster D'. Following the move to air braked trains, after 1964, 1,250 of these were rebuilt to become BDA bogie bolster wagons under TOPS, the first vehicle being converted at Swindon in 1975. BDAs were used for the conveyance of mainly metal products such as steel rods but, with the decline of that traffic, those remaining are used in departmental service mainly for carrying rail to and from work sites. 388 BDA wagons remained in service on the national network in 2008.

BR BDA bogie bolster wagon with girder load [W48]

377-600	**Loadhaul** 950414 black+orange with heavy duty bolsters and stanchions - *10*	15	18
377-600A	**Loadhaul** ? black+orange with heavy duty bolsters and stanchions + brown girders - *13*	15	18
377-601	**BR Railfreight** 950954 red with standard bolsters and stanchions - *10*	15	18
377-601A	**BR Railfreight** 951163 red with standard bolsters and stanchions - *11*	17	20
377-601B	**BR Railfreight** ? red with standard bolsters and stanchions + brown girders - *13*	17	20
377-602	**EWS** 950026 maroon with heavy duty bolsters and stanchions - *10*	15	18
377-602A	**EWS** 950049 maroon with heavy duty bolsters and stanchions + brown girders - *11*	17	20
377-603	**BR Departmental** DC950152 yellow YAA - *13*	18	23

Graham Farish by Bachmann

W49. FNA Nuclear Waste Wagon (2012)

This is the DRS 'Flatrol' Atomic Flask Wagon. The first eight were built at Ashford in 1976 and 1978. Two more were built at Shildon in 1982, seven at Swindon in 1986 and the main batch of 34 were built by Procor (UK) Ltd two years later. They are used to carry spent nuclear fuel in flasks from various British Nuclear Fuels Ltd power stations, to the Sellafield reprocessing plant in Cumbria. The flask sits beneath the white hood in the centre of the wagon.

377-800	BR 550014 yellow-brown - 12	23	27
377-801	BR 550023 yellow-brown flat floor - 12	23	27
377-802	BR 550038 yellow-brown sloping floor - 12	23	27
377-803	DRS 550011 dark - 13	NPG	NPG

W50a. 63' Freightliner Flat + 2 x 30ft Containers (2004)

Malcolm McLean started Sea-Land Corp. container service in America around 1960 which was the first major use of containers on ships. However, they were 35 feet long. Like any ISO standard, container sizes would have been arrived at by a mixture of compromise and horse trading. As the USA was involved in the negotiations, the agreed lengths of the ISO containers were 20' and 40', instead of 6m and 12m.

'Freightliner Flats' were built in large numbers from the mid 1960s. Most of them were constructed at Ashford, but some came from Shildon. They were designed to carry three 20ft containers, but could alternatively carry two 30ft ones. They were run in fixed sets but model manufacturers have tended to model them as solo wagons.

In 1983, Graham Farish introduced their first model of a Freightliner flat with containers; they went on to produce six versions. Bachmann started adding to the range in 2004 and these are the ones listed here.

373-450	'Freightliner' 602307 + containers 'Freightliner' white+red 56N08, 56N23 - 04	7	9
373-450A	'Freightliner' B601483 + containers 'Freightliner' white+red 56N05, 56N26 - 05	7	9
373-452	'Freightliner' B602389 + containers 'Freightliner' red 51N37, 60N53 - 05	7	9

W50b. 63' Freightliner Flat + 3 x 20ft Containers (2004)

This version of the model had three 20ft containers instead of two 30ft ones.

373-451	Freightliner 602160 + containers 'Freightliner' grey+ red 08L25, 20L69, 05B04 - 04	7	9
373-451A	Freightliner B6020637 black + containers BRe 'Freightliner' grey+red 08L46, 22L37, 05B17 - 05	7	9
373-453	Freightliner B601237 dark blue + containers 'Freightliner Limited' grey+red 26L24, 24L17, 25L09 - 05	7	9

Freightliner flat with Safmarine containers [W50b]

373-454	Freightliner B602359 black + containers 'P&O Nedlloyd' grey PONU061807[8], PONU093276[7], PONU162677[7] - 08	8	11
373-454A	Freightliner B602305 black + containers 'P&O Nedlloyd' grey PONU162679, PONU093273, PONU061808 - 10	10	13
373-458	Freightliner B601006 + 3 x 20' blue containers 'Safmarine' MSKU 718 755 8 2261, MSKU 777 927 0 2261, MSKU 332 080 5 2261 - ?	12	15
373-455	Freightliner B602291 black + containers 'P&O' blue PONU041942[6], PONU050018[4], PONU032814[1] - 06	7	9
373-455A	Freightliner B602235 black + containers 'P&O' blue POCU032812, POCU050019, POCU041943 - 10	10	13

W50c. 63' Freightliner Flat + 20ft & 40ft Containers (2008)

Here we have a third arrangement of the same wagon. In this case the container flat carries one 20ft container and one of 40ft length.

373-456	Freightliner B602379 + containers 40' 'Hanjin' blue HJCU769573 + 20' 'MSC' yellow MSCU251403 - 08	9	12
373-456A	Freightliner B602351 + containers 40' 'Hanjin' blue HJCU769577[3] + 20' 'MSC' yellow MSCU251404[5] - 10	10	13
373-457	Freightliner B602394 + containers 40' 'Maersk' silver MAEU638436[?]+ 20' 'Cosco' grey CBHU328736[?]- 08	9	12
373-457A	Freightliner B602544 + containers 40' 'Maersk' silver MAEU638434 + 20' 'Cosco' grey CBHU328738 - 10	9	12

W51 'Intermodal' Wagons + 45ft Containers (2008)

Like the real thing, these come as a pair of bogie flat wagons, which usually share the same European style running number. They are intended to be semi-permanently joined and are designed to carry 45ft 'Swap Body' containers. The models' frames are diecast, to lower the centre of gravity.

377-350	EWS (pair) 33 70 4938 713-3 pale green + 2x 'Seawheel' green containers SWLU965245+ SWLU451349 45' - 08	20	28
377-350A	EWS (pair) pale green + 2x 'Seawheel' green 45' containers SWL451345+SWIU965241 - 10	25	30
377-351	EWS (pair) 31 70 4938 002-3 pale green + 2x 'Axis' pale grey 45' containers AXIU716457+ AXIU716309 - 08	20	28
377-351A	Rft Distribution 33 70 4938 004-9 (pair) black + 2x 'Axis' white 45' containers AXIU716451+ AX16370 - 10	25	30
377-352	EWS (pair) 31 70 4938 113-8 pale green + 2x 'Seaco' blue 45' containers SCZU147605+ SCZU146922 - 08	20	28
377-352A	Rft Distribution (pair) pale green + 2x 'Seaco' blue 45' containers SCZU147600+ SCZU146924 - 10	20	30

'Intermodal' pair with Malcolm Logistics containers [W51]

377-353	EWS 33 70 4938716-6 (pair) pale green + 2x 'Malcolm Logistics' dark blue 45' containers WHMU450009+ WHMU450044 - 12	28	34
377-354	EWS 33 70 4938510 -3 (pair) pale green + 2x 'Malcolm' dark blue 45' containers WHMU450015+ WHMU450020 - 10	25	30
377-355	Rft Distribution 33 70 4938535-0 (pair) black + 2x 'DHL' yellow 45' containers DZ7003+DZ5143 - 12	25	30
377-356	EWS 33 70 4938324-9 (pair) pale green + 2x 'Samskip' blue 45' containers SANU 799037-3 + SANU 798868-0 - 12	30	37
377-365	EWS 33 70 4938717-4 (pair) pale green + 2x '2XL' pale purple 45' containers XXLU 1362203+ XXLU 13622734 - 12	28	34
377-366	EWS 33 70 4938130-2 (pair) pale green + 2x 'Geest' blue 45' containers GNSU 597748 4 + GNSU 451546 0 - 11	30	37

W52. Container Packs (2008)

These are packs containing 2 or 4 containers for use with models in the above four tables.

379-350	2x20ft 'China Shipping' CCLU314404 + 2x20ft 'K Line' KKTU740156 - 08	NA	4
379-351	2x20ft 'Maersk Sealand' MSKU206820 + 2x20ft 'OCL' OOLU33664 - 08	NA	4
379-352	2x20ft 'Yang Ming' YMLU317786 + 2x20ft 'Hyundai' HDMU235691 - 08	NA	4
379-353	2x20ft 'Hapag Lloyd' HLXU222317 + 2x20ft 'Hanjin' HJCU810266 - 08	NA	4
379-354	2x20ft 'MSC' MSCU251438 + 2x20ft 'Hamburg Sud' SUDU370512 - 08	NA	4
379-360	40ft 'Hapag' HXLU414034 + 40ft 'China Shipping' CCLU465009 - 08	NA	4
379-361	40ft 'K Line' KKFU150171 + 40ft 'Cosco' CBHU172455 - 08	NA	4
379-362	40ft 'P&O Nedlloydd' PONU1675046 + 40ft 'Yang Ming' YMLU496931 - 08	NA	4
379-370	45ft 'Eucon' EUCU459120 + 45ft 'ECS' ECBU450106 - 08	NA	4
379-371	45ft 'EFS' EFSU452044 + 45ft 'P&O Ferrymaster' FMBU001799 - 08	NA	4

Graham Farish by Bachmann

379-372	45ft '**Powerbox**' PWRU450209 + 45ft '**Consent Leasing**' NEVU220200 - *08*	NA	4	
379-373	45ft '**DHL**' DZ5141 + 45ft '**DHL**' DZ7005 - *08*	NA	4	
379-374	45ft '**Asda**' WHMU450825 + 45ft '**Asda**' WHMU450819 - *08*	NA	4	
379-325	20ft '**K Line**' KXYU740516 + 20ft '**Yang Ming**' YMLU 317786 + 40ft '**Hapag Lloyd**' PONU167504 + 40ft '**P&O Nedlloyd**' HLXU414034 - *08*	NA	4	

W53. 50T Bogie Sulphate Wagon (2004)
The model was based on a 50 ton bogie steel open wagon built by the LNER for the transporting of sulphate of ammonia from the ICI factory at Billingham. 80 of them were built.

373-425	**NE** Sulphate 164852 - *04*	5	6

W54. MBA 'Megabox' (High-sided) (2010)
EWS replaced BR wagons with high volume ones in 1998, when they ordered 300 of these from Thrall Europa at York. They came in two forms as they run in sets of five, made up of 'outers' (with buffers) and 'inners' (without). Within the sets, the wagons are linked with buckeye couplings. They have been used to carry scrap, timber, stone and coal.

EWS MBA 'Megabox' [W54] (Tony Wright)

377-650	**EWS** 500028 maroon with buffers - *10*	16	20
377-651	**EWS** 500178 maroon without buffers - *10*	16	20

W55. MOA 'Megabox' (Low-sided) (2010)
100 of the MBAs (above) were later cut down in height to give easier access and to reduce load capacity by two thirds. They were described as bogie low-sided open box wagons and were built for EWS by Thrall in the Czech Republic in 2003.

377-652	**EWS** 500327 maroon with buffers - *10*	16	20

W56. BAA/BZA Bogie Steel Coil Carriers (2012)
306 of these bogie steel wagons were built between 1972 and 1976 by BREL Ashford and BREL Shildon. They were built for the Railfreight Metals business and were designed to carry steel coils from the steelworks to customers. The coils were very exposed to the elements causing rusting and so the wagons were replaced by the fully enclosed BRA bogie steel carriers.

377-900	**Railfreight** 900047 red+black BAA - *12*	17	21
377-901	**Railfreight Metals** 900205 grey+yellow BAA - *12*	17	21
377-902	**EWS** 900142 maroon BZA - *12*	17	21

W57. BYA/BRA 104t Bogie Steel Carriers (2009)
These are steel coil carriers, each fitted with a cradle and telescopic sliding roof. They were built in York in 1998.

373-825	**EWS** 960015 maroon coil BYA - *09*	15	18
373-826	**EWS** 964014 maroon strip BRA - *09*	15	18
373-826A	**EWS** ? maroon strip BRA - *10*	15	18
373-827	**EWS** ? maroon W strip BRA - *13*	NPG	NPG

W58. JGA 90t Bogie Hopper Wagon (2009)
The JGA TOPS code covers a number of large bogie hopper wagons of different designs. The model is based on wagons built by Tatrastroj Poprad of Slovakia in the mid to late 1990s.

373-802	'**Buxton Lime**' - not made	NA	NA
377-101	'**Buxton Lime Industries**' BLI19206 blue+wht - *09*	15	18
377-101A	'**Buxton Lime Industries**' BLI19218 blue+wht - *10*	15	18
377-101B	'**Buxton Lime Industries**' BLI19211 blue+wht - *13*	17	22
373-801	'**RMC**' - not made	NA	NA
377-100	'**RMC**' RMC19228 orange+white - *09*	15	18
377-100A	'**RMC**' RMC19238 orange+white - *10*	15	19
373-800	'**Tilcon**' - not made	NA	NA
377-102	'**Tarmac'/NACCO** NACCO19177 v.pale grey - *09*	15	18
377-102A	'**Tarmac'/NACCO** NACCO19175 v.pale grey - *10*	15	19

W59. HTA 102t Bulk Coal Hopper (2006)
The HTA was introduced by EWS to use on the coal mine/power station merry-go-round route. They represented the largest order for one specific design of wagon since the mid 1970s. 1162 were built and they have a maximum speed of 75mph.

EWS HTA coal hopper wagon [W59] (Tony Wright)

373-850	**EWS** 310222 maroon+yellow - *06*	14	17
373-850A	**EWS** 310078 maroon+yellow - *08*	14	19
373-850B	**EWS** 310103 maroon+yellow - *10*	17	21
373-850C	**EWS** ? maroon+yellow - *13*	17	21

W60. HHA 100t GLW Bogie Coal Hopper (2007)
This is the Freightliner Heavy Haul bogie coal hopper wagon of which 446 were built by Wagony Swidnica in Poland and introduced in 2000. They have a maximum capacity of 73.6 tonnes and a top speed of 75mph. They were built to transport coal to power stations.

373-800	'**Freightliner Heavy Haul**' 370258 grey - *07*	15	18
373-800A	'**Freightliner Heavy Haul**' 370270 grey - *08*	15	19
373-800B	'**Freightliner Heavy Haul**' 370429 grey - *10*	17	21
373-800C	'**Freightliner Heavy Haul**' 370254 grey - *11*	20	24
373-801	'**Freightliner Heavy Haul**' 370001 grey - *07*	15	18
373-801A	'**Freightliner Heavy Haul**' 370037 grey - *08*	15	19
373-801B	'**Freightliner Heavy Haul**' 370169 grey - *09*	17	21
373-801C	'**Freightliner Heavy Haul**' ? grey - *13*	17	21
373-800Z	'**National Power**' NP?* blue Sp Edn (CJM) - *10*	NPG	NPG
373-802	'**Colas Rail**' (ex-Freightliner) ? grey - *13*	NPG	NPG

Numbered to order with the prefix 'NP', so various numbers will be found.

W61. YGA/B/H 40T 'Sealion'/'Seacow' (2009)
These bogie ballast wagons were a development of the 'Walrus' bogie hopper wagon which originated on the Southern Railway. The model is based on the earlier riveted type of 'Sea Cow'. The 'Sea Lion' and 'Sea Cow' were very similar in appearance but the former had two vacuum cylinders on one end while the latter had only one. The hand wheel below the solebars is a hand-brake while the three hand-wheels on the end platform were for controlling the ballast chutes.

377-000	**BREng** DB982637 olive green YGH - *09*	15	18
377-000A	**BREng** DB982887 olive green YGH - *10*	15	18
377-001	**BR** DB982473 grey+yellow -YGB - *09*	15	18
377-001A	**BR** DB982554 grey+yellow -YGB - *10*	15	18
377-001B	**BR** DB? grey+yellow -YGB - *13*	NPG	NPG
377-002	**EWS** DB982696 maroon - YGA - *09*	15	18
377-002A	**EWS** DB980220 maroon - YGA - *11*	17	21

W62. 'Polybulk' Bulk Grain Hopper Wagon (2014)
The first Traffic Services 'Polybulks' arrived in 1974 and were 80 tonne all-steel bogie vehicles capable of carrying a 58 tonne load. They were built in France with the requirements to also be used in Continental Europe and were initially used for the transportation of china clay as well as grain. A second batch was built in 1981

373-236	'**Polybulk**' ? green+grey? - *14*	20	25
373-235	'**Traffic Services**' ? green+grey W - *14*	22	27
373-237	'**Traffic Services Ltd**' ? green+grey? - *14*	20	25

W63. HYA/IIA 102t GLW Bulk Coal Hopper (2009)
This is the bogie hopper wagon made for GBRf for transporting coal to power stations. They were built by IRS in Romania in 2007.

377-575	**First GBRf** 371054 pale grey - *09*	15	18
377-575A	**First GBRf** VGT 37 70 6791 111-7 pale grey IIA - *10*	16	20
377-575B	**First GBRf** VGT 37 70 6955 207-5 silver IIA - *11*	18	22
377-575C	**First GBRf** VGT 37 70 6955 ? silver IIA - *12*	18	22
377-576	**Fastline** 37 70 6791 087-9 pale grey IIA - *09*	16	20
377-576A	**Fastline** 37 70 6791 034-1 pale grey IIA - *11*	18	22
377-577	**First GBRf** 371051 pale grey HYA - *11*	18	22
377-577A	**First GBRf** ? pale grey HYA - *13*	18	22

W64. JPA 100t Cement Tank Wagon (2010)
These are a new design of 100 tonne tank for the transportation of cement. They were built in 2007 by VTG Feldbinder in Germany. Their introduction has seen a reduction of the use of the two-axle cement wagons that have been familiar on Britain's railways for so many years.

Graham Farish by Bachmann

Bachmann introduced both 00 and N gauge versions in 2010

JPA cement tank wagon Lafarge Cement [W64]

377-675	**VTG** 'Lafarge Cement' VTG12434 silver - *10*		15	18
377-675A	**VTG** 'Lafarge Cement' VTG12405 silver - *12*		15	18
377-676	**VTG** 'Castle Cement' VTG12461 pale grey - *10*		15	18
377-676A	**VTG** 'Castle Cement' VTG12459 pale grey - *12*		15	18

W65. TEA 100T Bogie Tank Wagon (2004)

Where large quantities needed to be carried by rail, bogie tank wagons of 100 ton capacity could be used. These started to appear in 1966 when Shell-Mex, BP and Esso were forming block trains of them. They also rode better than the four-wheeled tank wagons. With the arrival of the new 100T bogie tank wagons, the small 2-axle tankers quickly disappeared from trains carrying petroleum products.

Graham Farish introduced a 100T bogie tank wagon in 1983 and released eight versions of it. Since reintroducing it in 2004, the following N gauge models were made by Bachmann.

373-552	'**BP**' BPO83786 black - *05*	7	9
373-553	'**BP**' BPO87467 grey - *05*	7	9
373-554	'**BP**' BPO83681 black W - *06*	7	10
373-554A	'**BP**' BPO83693 black W - *08*	10	13
373-554B	'**BP**' BPO83588 black W - *10*	10	13
373-558	'**BP**' BPO? green - *13*	NPG	NPG
373-551	'**Fina**' 508 grey - *04*	7	9
373-551A	'**Fina**' 503 grey - *05*	7	9
373-556	'**Fina**' FINA85519 grey - *06*	7	10
373-556A	'**Fina**' FINA85527 grey W - *06*	10	13
373-556B	'**Fina**' FINA85522 grey W - *10*	10	13
373-556C	'**Fina**' FINA85525 grey W - *12*	12	15
(370-250)	'**Fina**' 504 grey - *06*	7	NA
(370-250)	'**Fina**' 505 grey - *06*	7	NA
373-557	'**Gulf**' 85021 grey W - *11*	12	15
373-550	'**Shell BP**' 4001 grey - *04*	7	9
373-550A	'**Shell BP**' 4007 grey - *05*	7	9
(370-250)	'**Shell BP**' 4008 grey - *06*	7	NA
(370-250)	'**Shell BP**' 4009 grey - *06*	7	NA
373-555	'**Shell**' 87317 grey - *06*	7	10
373-555A	'**Shell**' SHELL87324 grey W - *08*	10	13
373-555B	'**Shell**' SHELL87321 grey W - *10*	10	13
373-555C	'**Shell**' SHELL87313 grey W - *12*	12	15

Those in set 370-250 are also in set 370-251.

Track Maintenance

T1. JJA Railtrack 'Auto-Ballaster' Mk2 (2012)

These were conversions of Tiphook Rail 90 tonne aggregate wagons which had originally been built by AFR. Some had their height reduced so that they would safely pass under the loading hopper at Buxton Lime, which explains why some have flat tops and some have curved ones. At first they were in Tiphook blue and 10 of these were built as the Mark 1 type. The Mark 2 followed in RailTrack livery and 104 were built.

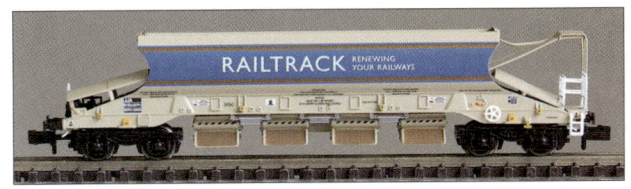

Railtrack JJA 'Auto-Ballaster' [T1]

377-700	**Railtrack** GERS12976 blue+buff (outer) with generator - *12*		22	28
377-701	**Railtrack** GERS13005 blue+buff (flat top) - *12*		22	28
377-702	**Railtrack** GERS12967 blue+buff (curved top) - *12*		22	28

Bachmann 'Jubilee' Class Baroda coming off-shed, computer enhanced photograph by Robbie McGavin.

8th Edition

Visit the BRM website at: www.model-railways-live.co.uk

GRAHAM FARISH by BACHMANN
BR Blue Locomotives
N Scale Model Locomotives

371-511 Class 101 3-Car DMU
Livery: BR Blue & Grey **Finish:** Pristine **Features:** DCC Speaker Housing

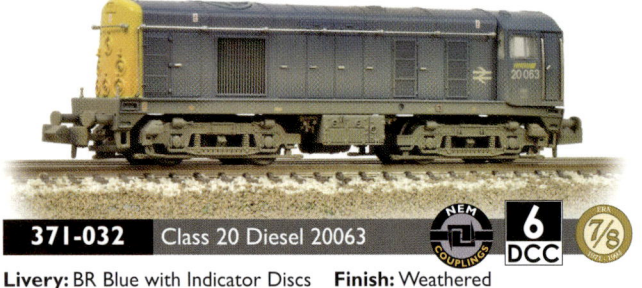

371-032 Class 20 Diesel 20063
Livery: BR Blue with Indicator Discs **Finish:** Weathered

371-051B Class 04 Diesel Shunter D2294
Livery: BR Blue with Wasp Stripes **Finish:** Pristine

371-080 Class 25/3 Diesel 25279
Livery: BR Blue **Finish:** Pristine

371-587 Class 46 D186
Livery: BR Blue **Finish:** Pristine

371-828A Class 47 Diesel 47403
Livery: BR Blue Full Yellow Ends **Finish:** Pristine

372-677 Class 411/4CEP
Livery: BR Blue & Grey **Finish:** Pristine

Era ⑥ locos suitable for period 1967 - 1971 British Railways Blue Pre-TOPs
Era ⑦ locos suitable for period 1971 - 1982 British Railways Blue TOPs
Era ⑧ locos suitable for period 1982 - 1994 British Railways Sectorisation

DCC Indicates that the locomotives have a NMRA/NEM 651 6 pin decoder socket.

Indicates that the locomotive or rolling stock features NEM couplings

N Scale Bachmann Europe Plc. Moat Way, Barwell, Leicestershire. LE9 8EY
www.bachmann.co.uk

BACHMANN EUROPE Plc
A Bachmann Product

Notes

Notes